BEST PRACTICES
IN SCHOOL PSYCHOLOGY

FOUNDATIONS

NASP

EDITED BY
PATTI L. HARRISON & ALEX THOMAS

From the NASP Publications Board Operations Manual

The content of this document reflects the ideas and positions of the authors. The responsibility lies solely with the authors and editors and does not necessarily reflect the position or ideas of the National Association of School Psychologists.

Published by the National Association of School Psychologists

Copyright © 2014 by the National Association of School Psychologists.

Copies may be ordered from:
NASP Publications
4340 East West Highway, Suite 402
Bethesda, MD 20814
301-657-0270
301-657-3127, fax
866-331-NASP, Toll Free
e-mail: *publications@naspweb.org*
www.nasponline.org/publications

Best Practices in School Psychology: Foundations
ISBN: 978 0932955-56-2 (print);

Best Practices in School Psychology (4-book series)
ISBN: 978-0-932955-52-4 (print), ISBN: 978-0-932955-51-7 (electronic)

Printed in the United States of America

16 17 10 9 8 7 6 5 4 3

Table of Contents

Research and Program Evaluation

Legal, Ethical, and Professional Practice

Introduction

BEST PRACTICES IN SCHOOL PSYCHOLOGY: OVERVIEW OF THE SERIES

Best Practices in School Psychology is the sixth iteration of an intraprofessional collaborative effort to provide a single source for contemporary knowledge about many valued topics within school psychology. It has been more than 30 years since the first edition of *Best Practices in School Psychology* was published. In those 30 years and six editions, there have been substantial changes in the quantity of chapters, range of topics, and intended outcomes of school psychology services. However, the purpose of all editions of *Best Practices in School Psychology*, including the current edition, has remained constant over the years: to provide the current, relevant, and valued information necessary for competent delivery of school psychological services. Thus, chapters across editions have focused on *practices* by school psychology practitioners. Although chapters are not intended to be detailed reviews of research, research documentation is included in the chapters to provide an evidence-based foundation for recommended best practices.

This edition of *Best Practices in School Psychology* is designed to be a comprehensive resource, allowing readers to refer to chapters in the process of gaining information about specific, important professional practice topics and updating readers about contemporary techniques and methods. The primary target audience is school psychology practitioners who provide services in school settings, as was the case for previous editions. Similarly, the chapters may provide useful resources for other school-based professionals, as well as those who provide services to children in other settings. *Best Practices* also may serve as a helpful supplement for graduate courses when used in conjunction with primary course textbooks. As a compilation of best practices on major topics, *Best Practices in School Psychology* will assist school psychology practitioners, graduate students, interns, faculty, and others by providing readings on many specific areas of interest.

The content in this edition of *Best Practices in School Psychology* is expanded from earlier editions to include a broader range of topics, with considerable attention to multitiered, problem-solving, and evidence-based approaches for the delivery of effective school psychology services. The school psychology services outlined in this edition focus on improving student outcomes through data-based and collaborative activities in schools. Chapters emphasize prevention and intervention efforts for both student-level and systems-level services that recognize the importance of culture and individual differences across students, families, schools, and communities.

This edition of *Best Practices* was developed over 5 years, with multiple focus groups consisting of practitioner school psychologists, as well as graduate students and faculty, assisting the editors with organization and new topics for chapters to represent current and future needs. In addition, chapter authors and reviewers identified additional chapter topics.

The result is that this edition is organized a bit differently than previous editions. This edition is a four book series, with each book corresponding to one of the four interrelated components of the broad framework of the 2010 National Association of School Psychologists (NASP) *Model for Comprehensive and Integrated School Psychological Services* (i.e., the NASP Practice Model; see http://www.nasponline.org/standards/2010standards/2_PracticeModel.pdf): (a) *practices that permeate all aspects of service delivery*, including data-based and collaborative decision making; (b) *student-level services*, including instructional and academic supports and social and mental health services; (c) *systems-level services*, including school-wide learning practices, preventive and response services, and family–school collaboration; and (d) *foundations* of school psychological services, including diversity, research and program evaluation, and legal/ethical/professional practices.

About half of the chapters in this edition are updates of chapters included in earlier editions, and the other half focus on new and topical issues of importance in contemporary school psychology. Although it is impossible to include chapters for *all* areas of relevance to school psychology, it is hoped that the resulting 150 chapters provide a good representation of major services and issues in the field.

Organizational Framework of the Series

Each of the four books in the series has two or three separate sections corresponding to the specific domains of school psychology established in the 2010 NASP Practice Model. The titles of the four books and of the sections within each are outlined below:

1. *Best Practices in School Psychology: Data-Based and Collaborative Decision Making*

   Introduction and Framework
   Data-Based Decision Making and Accountability
   Consultation and Collaboration

2. *Best Practices in School Psychology: Student-Level Services*

   Interventions and Instructional Support to Develop Academic Skills
   Interventions and Mental Health Services to Develop Social and Life Skills

3. *Best Practices in School Psychology: Systems-Level Services*

   School-Wide Practices to Promote Learning
   Preventive and Responsive Services
   Family–School Collaboration Services

4. *Best Practices in School Psychology: Foundations*

   Diversity in Development and Learning
   Research and Program Evaluation
   Legal, Ethical, and Professional Practice

Chapter Structure

Typically, chapters include the following components, which provide readers with a predictable chapter structure:

Overview. Includes a definition and history of the topic and may provide situations for which a practicing school psychologist may wish to consult the chapter. This section orients the reader to the major issues, characteristics, and needs related to a chapter topic. It is introductory and establishes the context for the information presented.

Basic Considerations. Provides background information, research, training, experience, equipment, and other basics that school psychologists should know to effectively deal with the topic.

Best Practices. The heart and most extensive part of a chapter. Authors were asked to provide best practices and to include options and perspectives so that school psychologists can mesh their professional orientation with other successful possibilities.

Summary. A synopsis of the topic, which includes a brief review and discussion of the best practices.

References. Publications and resources that support the chapter authors' information. Authors were asked to not make exhaustive lists, because chapters are intended to focus on evidence-based practices and not simply present a compilation of research.

Unlike previous editions of *Best Practices*, the current edition does not include Annotated Bibliographies at the end of each chapter. Instead, readers have online access to each chapter's Annotated Bibliography on the NASP website (http://www.nasponline.org/publications). Annotated Bibliographies include articles, books, Web-based information, and other resources suggested by authors of each chapter for follow-up reading to gain a more detailed view of best practices for the topic discussed in a chapter.

It is our hope that this edition of *Best Practices in School Psychology* will support current and future school psychologists in their ongoing quest for improved procedures and practices and the acquisition of professional skills needed to enhance students' success in their schools, homes, and communities.

INTRODUCTION TO THE BOOK: BEST PRACTICES IN SCHOOL PSYCHOLOGY: SYSTEMS-LEVEL SERVICES

This book includes three sections of chapters about foundations of school psychology services, including diversity, research and program evaluation, and legal/ethical/professional practices.

Diversity in Development and Learning

Chapters in this section focus on the Diversity in Development and Learning domain of the 2010 NASP *Model for Comprehensive and Integrated School Psychological Services*. The domain represents foundations of all service delivery by school psychologists (see http://www.nasponline.org/standards/2010standards/2_PracticeModel.pdf, pp. 7–8):

School psychologists have knowledge of individual differences, abilities, disabilities, and other diverse characteristics; principles and research related to diversity factors for children, families, and schools, including factors related to culture, context, and individual and role differences; and evidence-based strategies to enhance services and address potential influences related to diversity. School psychologists demonstrate skills to provide effective professional services that promote effective functioning for individuals, families, and schools with diverse characteristics, cultures, and backgrounds and across multiple contexts, with recognition that an understanding and respect for diversity in development and learning and advocacy for social justice are foundations for all aspects of service delivery. Examples of professional practices that promote and respect diversity include:

- School psychologists apply their understanding of the influence of culture, background, and individual learning characteristics (e.g., age, gender or gender identity, cognitive capabilities, social–emotional skills, developmental level, race, ethnicity, national origin, religion, sexual and gender orientation, disability, chronic illness, language, socioeconomic status) when designing and implementing interventions to achieve learning and behavioral outcomes.
- School psychologists, in collaboration with others, address individual differences, strengths, backgrounds, talents, and needs in the design, implementation, and evaluation of services in order to improve learning and mental health outcomes for all children in family, school, and community contexts.
- School psychologists provide culturally competent and effective practices in all areas of school psychology service delivery and in the contexts of diverse individual, family, school, and community characteristics.
- School psychologists work collaboratively with cultural brokers or community liaisons to understand and address the needs of diverse learners.
- School psychologists utilize a problem solving framework for addressing the needs of English language learners.

- School psychologists recognize in themselves and others the subtle racial, class, gender, cultural and other biases they may bring to their work and the way these biases influence decision-making, instruction, behavior, and long-term outcomes for students.
- School psychologists promote fairness and social justice in educational programs and services.

Research and Program Evaluation

Chapters in this section focus on the Research and Program Evaluation domain of the 2010 NASP *Model for Comprehensive and Integrated School Psychological Services*. The domain represents foundations of all service delivery by school psychologists (see http://www.nasponline.org/standards/2010standards/2_PracticeModel.pdf, p. 8):

School psychologists have knowledge of research design, statistics, measurement, varied data collection and analysis techniques, and program evaluation sufficient for under- standing research and interpreting data in applied settings. School psychologists demonstrate skills to evaluate and apply research as a foundation for service delivery and, in collaboration with others, use various techniques and technology resources for data collection, measurement, and analysis to support effective practices at the individual, group, and/or systems levels. Examples of professional practices associated with research and program evaluation include the following:

- School psychologists evaluate and synthesize a cumulative body of research findings as a foundation for effective service delivery.
- School psychologists incorporate techniques for data collection, analyses, and accountability in evaluation of services at the individual, group, and system levels.
- School psychologists, in collaboration with others, collect, analyze, and interpret program evaluation data in applied settings.
- School psychologists provide support for classroom teachers in collecting and analyzing progress monitoring data.
- School psychologists apply knowledge of evidence-based interventions and programs in designing, implementing, and evaluating the fidelity and effectiveness of school-based intervention plans.
- School psychologists provide assistance in schools and other settings for analyzing, interpreting, and using empirical foundations for effective practices at the individual, group, and/or systems levels.
- School psychologists incorporate various techniques for data collection, measurement, analysis, accountability, and use of technology resources in evaluation of services at the individual, group, and/or systems levels.

Legal, Ethical, and Professional Practice

Chapters in this section focus on the Legal, Ethical, and Professional Practice domain of the 2010 NASP *Model for Comprehensive and Integrated School Psychological Services*. The domain represents foundations of all service delivery by school psychologists (see http://www.nasponline.org/standards/2010standards/2_PracticeModel.pdf, pp. 8–9):

School psychologists have knowledge of the history and foundations of school psychology; multiple service models and methods; ethical, legal, and professional standards; and other factors related to professional identity and effective practice as school psychologists. School psychologists demonstrate skills to provide services consistent with ethical, legal, and professional standards; engage in responsive ethical and professional decision-making; collaborate with other professionals; and apply professional work characteristics needed for effective practice as school psychologists, including respect for human diversity and social justice, communication skills, effective interpersonal skills, responsibility, adaptability, initiative, dependability, and technology skills. Examples of legal, ethical, and professional practice include the following:

- School psychologists practice in ways that are consistent with ethical, professional, and legal standards and regulations.
- School psychologists engage in effective, collaborative, and ethical professional relationships.
- School psychologists use supervision and mentoring for effective practice.
- School psychologists access, evaluate, and utilize information sources and technology in ways that safeguard and enhance the quality of services and responsible record keeping.
- School psychologists assist administrators, teachers, other school personnel, and parents in understanding and adhering to legislation and regulations relevant to regular education and special education.
- School psychologists advocate for professional roles as providers of effective services that enhance the learning and mental health of all children and youth.
- School psychologists engage in lifelong learning and formulate personal plans for ongoing professional growth.
- School psychologists participate in continuing education activities at a level consistent with maintenance of the NCSP credential (i.e., a minimum of 25 hours of professional development per year).

ACKNOWLEDGMENTS

It is fascinating to compare the assembling and publication of this sixth edition of *Best Practices in School Psychology* with the circumstances surrounding the first edition. The comparison highlights the growth and diversity of the profession, the organizational vitality and commitment of NASP, and the increasing influence and importance of school psychologists during the intervening 30+ years.

In 1982, when work began on the first edition, NASP had 7,500 members (2014 membership exceeds 25,000), and training, field placement, practice, and credentialing standards for school psychology were at a much earlier stage of development. For the first edition of *Best Practices*, the acknowledgments section thanked six individuals who assisted in reviewing the 39 chapters and in typesetting—yes, literally setting type of the text. Selection of font style and size, space between lines, paper stock, cover art, selection of the printer, obtaining copyright, design of shipping cartons, method of shipping, cost, and the like were made by the coeditors, and communications with authors and reviewers were primarily by U.S. mail along with occasional phone calls. Three thousand copies of the first edition of *Best Practices* were printed and then trucked to, stored at, and eventually distributed from a school psychologist's garage in Connecticut. The introductory price to members, including shipping, was $22. Times change.

For this sixth edition of *Best Practices*, there are hundreds of people to thank and acknowledge. First, the approximately 300 authors of our 150 chapters spread across four books deserve our gratitude. We appreciate the dedication, enthusiasm, and efforts of this highly talented group.

In addition to our editorial review, an earnest effort was made to have each chapter peer-reviewed by at least three school psychologists (two current practitioners and a university- or other non-school-based school psychologist). We must heartily thank the reviewers who read first drafts, provided important feedback to authors, and shared their suggestions for improvement of the chapters. Once these reviews were received, the reviewed chapters were forwarded to the author along with copies of comprehensive reviewer notations and editor comments. It was a time-consuming process for the reviewers, and our authors' final manuscripts substantially benefited from these extensive reviewer efforts. Reviewers who contributed to this edition, and who receive our appreciation, are:

Melinda Adkins	Bryn Harris	Karen O'Brien
Elsa Arroyos	Denise Hildebrand	Rivka I. Olley
Barry Barbarasch	Daniel Hyson	Ronald S. Palomares
Brian J. Bartels	Jessica (Dempsey) Johnston	Anna M. Peña
John Biltz	Cathy Kennedy-Paine	Madi Phillips
Alan Brue	Laurie McGarry Klose	Pamela M. Radford
Elliot J. Davis	Brian Leung	Alecia Rahn-Blakeslee
Bill Donelson	Jane Lineman-Coffman	Tracy Schatzberg
Amy N. Esler	Courtney L. McLaughlin	Nicole Skaar
René Fetchkan	Dawn Miller	Marlene Sotelo-Dynega
Beth Glew	Karin Mussman	Vicki Stumme

Jackie Ternus	Julie Hanson	Leslie Z. Paige
Lori Unruh	Jasolyn Henderson	Shamim S. Patwa
Ellie L. Young	Candis Hogan	Debbie Phares
Ashley Arnold	Susan Jarmuz-Smith	E. Jeanne Pound
Michelle S. Athanasiou	Rita Lynne Jones	Stephanie Rahill
Susan Bartels	Regina K. Kimbrel	Nancy Peña Razo
Jill Berger	Misty Lay	Margaret Sedor
Brandee Boothe	Mary Levinsohn-Klyap	Carole A. Sorrenti
Kelly R. Swanson Dalrymple	Monica McKevitt	Patricia Steinert-Otto
Emma Dickinson	Katherine Mezher	James M. Stumme
Katie Eklund	Sara Moses	Lynne Ostroff Thies
Pam Fenning	Mary Alice Myers	Nate von der Embse
Marika Ginsburg-Block	Ed O'Connor	

This sixth edition of *Best Practices* is the first edition that does not include Jeff Grimes as coeditor. Jeff worked with Alex Thomas as coeditor of all previous editions and made many contributions to the framework and content of *Best Practices* editions over the years. Further, Jeff has been a long-time leader in school psychology, and our field has benefitted greatly from his commitment, wisdom, and vision. We thank Jeff for all he has done for *Best Practices* and school psychology.

The efforts of Mike Schwartz have proved invaluable to the completion of this edition. Mike Schwartz has been the copyeditor for every chapter in this and in the last two editions of *Best Practices*. He read and reread each of the chapters and contributed substantive comments and perspectives in addition to making sure that references were properly cited, tenses agreed, tables aligned, verbs and nouns were compatible, and ideas remained focused. We thank him for his talent and good humor.

The look and feel of this edition, and the consistency and ease of reference, is due to the metadiligent efforts of Linda Morgan, NASP Director of Production. She actively participated in the myriad details associated with this work and took the lead in the design and presentation. Additionally, she fact checked and triple fact checked every reference and citation. NASP is fortunate to have her talents, and this edition of *Best Practices* is richer due to her involvement.

There are other people at the NASP national office who quietly and competently worked to enhance this edition of *Best Practices*. We thank Brieann Kinsey, Manager of Editorial Production, for her time fact checking, proofreading, and ensuring that what was printed was accurate and consistent with the overall "feel" of the publication. We also thank Denise Ferrenz, Director of Publications, for dealing with the multitude of planning, publication, and marketing considerations associated with a project of this magnitude.

Alex Thomas
Patti Harrison

EDITOR NOTE

Authors were invited to write chapters for this edition of *Best Practices* because of their expertise and experience in a specific topic. In a number of cases, these authors have written other publications or developed resources on the same topic and reference these materials in their *Best Practices* chapters. Therefore, authors were instructed to include a disclosure statement at the end of their *Best Practices* chapters, in line with the 2010 NASP *Principles for Professional Ethics*, Standard III.V.6 (see http://www.nasponline.org/standards/2010standards/1_%20Ethical%20Principles. pdf), which requires school psychologists to disclose financial interests in resources or services they discuss in presentations or writings.

Disclosure. Alex Thomas and Patti Harrison have financial interests in publications they coauthored or coedited and that are referenced by authors of several chapters in this edition of *Best Practices in School Psychology*. These include, for Alex Thomas, previous editions of *Best Practices in School Psychology* and, for Patti Harrison, *Contemporary Intellectual Assessment: Theories, Tests, and Issues; Adaptive Behavior Assessment System;* and *ABAS-II: Clinical Use and Interpretation.*

Section 1
Diversity in Development and Learning

1

Best Practices in Increasing Cross-Cultural Competency

Antoinette Halsell Miranda
The Ohio State University

OVERVIEW

At the Olympia Conference in 1982, the profession of school psychology recognized that there would be a significant increase in minority students in public schools in the future that would most likely have an effect on practice and services provided. Education, also recognizing this, began to push for multicultural education as efforts were made to prepare educators to work with a population of children that many teachers previously had little to no experience teaching. This movement was in large part due to an acknowledgement that many culturally different children and their families had values, beliefs, and norms that differed from the majority culture and in some instances had a negative impact on academic achievement.

This increasing diversity in the United States has outpaced what had been previously projected. According to the 2010 census, minorities account for 36.6% of the total population (U.S. Census Bureau, 2010). It is projected that non-Hispanic Whites will become a minority by 2042. Previously, it was projected that this would not occur until 2050. In 1980, non-Hispanic Whites were 74.6% of the children in the age range of 5 and 17. In contrast, they accounted for only 54.7% of that population in 2010, a 20% decrease. Whites were almost half of the school age population in the 21st century. In 1980, African Americans, Latinos, Asians, and Native Americans accounted for 14.5%, 8.5%, 1.7%, 0.8%, respectively. In 2010, African Americans, Latinos, Asians, and Native Americans were 14.2%, 22.4%, 4.4%, and 0.9% of the school age population (5–17 years of age). Children with two or more races were 3.3% of that population as well. For the first time, in 2011, racial and ethnic minorities made up more than half of all children born in the United States, 50.4% (U.S. Census Bureau, 2012).

Unfortunately, this diversity is not reflected in the school psychology profession, which continues to be predominately Caucasian. The latest demographics of the profession indicate that approximately 10% of the profession is racially/ethnically diverse. Given that there has been very little increase in diversity in the profession since the 1980s (Castillo, Curtis, Chappel, & Cunningham, 2011), it is expected that there will continue to be underrepresented groups in the field of school psychology. Thus, it is imperative that future practitioners as well as current practitioners have the skills to work effectively with diverse populations.

The National Association of School Psychologists (NASP) and American Psychological Association (APA) have both addressed this increasing diversity through guidelines, position papers, standards, and competencies. These tools provide guidance to the profession in terms of best practice when working with populations that are culturally, ethnically, racially, and socioeconomically diverse. APA (2003) has articulated six guidelines that are founded on six principles. These guidelines reflect the knowledge and skills needed for psychologists to effectively practice in an increasingly diverse U.S. society.

NASP has also provided a number of resources related to multicultural issues. As described by Harrison (2010), "virtually every NASP activity reflects our emphasis on diversity and multicultural competence" (para. 2). In 2009–2010, NASP had a priority initiative to increase cultural competence and cultural and linguistic diversity of school psychology. In 2009, NASP published *The Psychology of Multiculturalism in the Schools: A Primer for Practice, Training, and Research* (Jones,

2009). It was only the second diversity book published by NASP, with the first one published in 1990. NASP's website has a link (http://www.nasponline.org/resources/culturalcompetence/cultcomppractice.aspx) devoted to multicultural resources and publications, with many of the resources and publications describing culturally competent practices (e.g., culturally competent assessment and consultation). Position statements have been developed that demonstrate the commitment of the organization to multicultural competence across a variety of areas. The NASP (2010b) Standards emphasize the development of multicultural competence as part of the practice of school psychology. NASP has also successfully provided scholarships for minority students for the past decade. Thus, the organizations that represent school psychology have made valiant efforts to promote and validate the importance of the profession to develop cultural competencies that inform practice.

More recently, the term *social justice* has become part of the vernacular in school psychology. In 2008, *School Psychology Review* had a special issue entitled "Promoting Social Justice." In the introduction to the issue, Power (2008) suggests that school psychology's advocacy on behalf of disabled children and more recently to marginalized youth demonstrates the profession's commitment to a social justice agenda. Often, multiculturalism and social justice are used as interchangeable terms. While they do indeed overlap, social justice is generally more narrowly defined than multiculturalism (Pieterse, Evans, Risner-Butner, Collins, & Mason, 2009). Increasingly, psychology and counseling disciplines view multiculturalism and social justice as fundamental elements of the curriculum and training of future professionals. Thus, issues of justice and fairness are the backdrop and foundation to much of the work in multiculturalism, equity, and diversity (Hage 2005). While much of school psychologists' work in advocacy has been at the individual level, there is an increasing recognition that school psychologists need to intervene at a systems level.

Research in school psychology addressing issues of diversity has not increased much since the 1990s. Rogers Wiese (1992) was the first to examine diversity literature in major school psychology journals, in which she found that only 9% of the total articles in the three major journals (*Psychology in the Schools, Journal of School Psychology*, and *School Psychology Review*) reflected multicultural content. A second study by Miranda and Gutter (2002) found that multicultural content in four major school psychology journals had increased slightly from 9 to 10.8%. Brown, Shriberg, and Wang (2007) reviewed five major school psychology journals and found that 16.9% of the total articles were diversity related. Grunewald et al. (in press) found that 15.5% of the total articles in seven major school psychology journals were diversity related. It should be noted that in every study conducted after the Rogers Wiese study, additional categories of diversity were added as well as more journals that were considered focused on school psychology. Thus, there has been a modest increase of about 7% since the 1990s of diversity-related articles.

As the field continues to examine best practice in working with culturally and linguistically diverse children, research with these populations is critical. Culture should be studied as a process that is ever changing rather than as an index or variable. Cultural considerations should be a part of school psychology research to determine the validity of theories, measures, and interventions beyond just being studied with one population. Research that looks at school psychology practices through multiple lenses will improve school psychologists' practice with diverse populations. This is an area that the field of school psychology needs to continue to improve upon.

Diversity training continues to be an area of focus as it is perceived to be an essential element in preparing future professionals to work with populations that are culturally and linguistically diverse. It would seem that infusing such training in graduate programs would be ideal as it provides students with the tools before they enter the field. There are a number of training models on how best to incorporate diversity into the curriculum. Unfortunately, what most training programs do is require one single diversity course. Ideally, there would also be infusion of diversity content throughout the program and where possible field-based experiences in culturally diverse settings. NASP (2010b) as well as APA (2003) attempt to provide guidance on incorporating diversity into graduate programs and set standards for the importance of diversity.

The purpose of this chapter is to provide school psychologists with knowledge, guidance, and practical suggestions on how to effectively work with populations that are culturally, linguistically, and economically diverse. An overview of some of the most salient issues school psychologists will encounter with diverse populations will be highlighted as they may potentially have an impact on practice. Strategies and suggestions will be provided that will enhance school psychologists' cultural competencies in working effectively with diverse populations The chapter addresses the NASP domain of Diversity in Development and Learning in the *Model for*

Comprehensive and Integrated School Psychological Services (NASP, 2010a).

BASIC CONSIDERATIONS

In working with culturally diverse populations, it is important for school psychologists to understand the complexity of the diverse student population and to view students from a multidimensional rather than a one-dimensional perspective. It is difficult to thoroughly explore the multifaceted dimensions of diversity in this chapter. Therefore, selected issues will be highlighted.

Diversity Is Reality

In education it has been known for many years that schools will experience a vastly changing population that will have significant impact on what happens in schools and ultimately how school psychologists are prepared to provide services. The initial response in teacher education to these changing demographics was multi-cultural education. At the same time, psychology and counseling began to address this demographic shift, most often through guidelines, standards, and the development of multicultural competencies. Initially, the increasing diversity was viewed as regionally bound or only existing in urban environments. But since 2000 there has been increasing movement of culturally diverse populations into new cities and states and from urban schools to suburban and rural. It is no longer a regional issue but an issue nationwide.

The increase in childhood poverty also has had a significant impact on educational attainment that disproportionately effects ethnic minority populations. Socioeconomic status is strongly associated with achievement, literacy, and grade retention. There is growing disparity between poor children and their middle class peers in almost all aspects of educational attainment. Thus, it is equally as important to understand the impact that poverty has on school-age children as it may be of more significance than race or ethnicity.

There is increased urgency for education professionals to demonstrate cultural responsiveness and sensitivity to diverse populations as the focus on the achievement gap continues to dominate education policy and programs. No Child Left Behind (NCLB) had as one of its major goals the reduction of the achievement gap. While NCLB was often viewed as punitive, it also highlighted the plight of many marginalized students in public schools through their failure to academically achieve. As a result, increasing attention and funding has been focused on how to reduce the achievement gap. Schools actually know what poor children lack and what they need, but education has been stymied with how to deliver the necessary interventions to all poor children (e.g., early reading intervention). It is also clear that there is no silver bullet to closing the achievement gap. It takes effort from multiple sources to affect change in schools that is meaningful. Increasing focus is on how education professionals can be a part of change through a better understanding of the populations with which they work. Cross-cultural competency is a major attribute for practitioners to have in their repertoire of skills.

Diversity's Impact on Education

The achievement gap in the education community is not a new phenomenon. It has been evident for decades that achievement is most closely linked to poverty. Unfortunately, because ethnic minorities are disproportionately in the lowest socioeconomic rungs of the ladder, they experience the greatest disparities when it comes to academic achievement. Family income and parent's educational level have been shown to be the strongest predictor of student success (Reardon, 2011). For years many theories have attempted to explain this lack of educational attainment including poverty theories. But no single theory adequately explains this discrepancy as there are always students who defy the odds. So instead of focusing on one single theory to explain the achievement gap, it may be more productive to understand that the achievement gap is an artifact that is a result of a multitude of factors that combine to be detrimental to poor ethnic minority students. It should be noted that poor White students also experience an achievement gap as well when compared to their more financially well off peers. In sum, this is a sociocultural issue. The reality is that there is a need for systemic change that goes beyond what happens in schools.

One example of systemic change is the Harlem Children's Zone, which wraps health, social, and other services all embedded in a community. While the charter school in the zone appears to be successful, the data are unclear about the other aspects of the project. In addition, it is quite expensive. But the premise of the project is noteworthy in that there is a recognition that the whole community has be to transformed in order to more broadly affect change in the educational attainment of poor children. With that said, it is important to understand the broader systemic issues that affect children, but also be cognizant of the fact that change can happen in schools despite what occurs outside of the schools' walls.

Understanding the Gaps

In understanding the achievement gap, it is important to understand that it is not simply a single gap but multiple gaps that contribute to its existence in racial/ethnic and social class groups. As practitioners work to understand the issues, this knowledge will help them as they develop interventions that take these gaps into consideration.

Preparation Gap

Poor children, from the time they are born, enter the world with many things stacked against them. As a result, poor children lack many of the essentials that prepare them for the educational environment they will enter. In addition, culturally and linguistically diverse children who are poor may also have cultural issues that have an impact on educational attainment. Hart and Risley (1995) found in their study of professional, working class, and welfare families stark differences in the language skills of the children. They estimated that in a year children in professional families heard an average of 11 million words, working class families heard an average of 6 million words, and children in welfare families heard an average of 3 million words. Thus by age 4, welfare children will have heard more than 30 million fewer words than their middle class peers. Not only are poor children less prepared in the area of literacy, they are also less prepared when it comes to school experience. The vast majority of poor and ethnic minority children have less access to high quality preschools with most not attending preschool at all. Many of these children entering kindergarten must first learn to "play school," but curriculum's today are designed with the expectation that students in kindergarten come to school already knowing how to write their name, recite the alphabet, and count to 10. These poor children are already behind and the achievement gap grows.

Opportunity Gap

The most marginalized students often lack experiences and background information that help them to be successful academically. Students most often gain these experiences through exposure in their families and later in schools. This is also called culture capital, a sociological concept. For example, having two parents who are college educated provides a student with cultural

capital as he or she has parents who can successfully navigate the educational system. These students also come to school ready to learn as they have the requisite skills necessary to start kindergarten. The opportunity gap potentially grows wider with marginalized students because the schools they attend may lack gifted and talented services, honors classes, Advanced Placement classes, technology, and highly qualified teachers.

Environmental Gap

This gap incorporates such things as adequate nutrition, medical care, and stable living situations, which tend to be lacking or problematic in low income families. Because many culturally and linguistically diverse students live in poverty, these areas are particularly salient in their lives. These are considered out-of-school factors that correspond to gaps in academic outcome. To address the environmental gap, school-based health centers are being proposed and would be located within schools. These centers would provide a range of services that address both the physical and mental health needs of children in the surrounding community (O'Brien, 2011) and thus improve the academic outcomes of children.

BEST PRACTICES IN INCREASING CROSS-CULTURAL COMPETENCY

Generally, school psychologists who are not experts in issues of diversity may become overwhelmed with how to provide culturally relevant practice to such diverse populations. A framework for moving forward will be shared that can start the journey to cross-cultural competence. This section will highlight the process of cross-cultural competence as well as several concepts that may help a practitioner understand the culturally diverse population that is part of his or her everyday practice. These ideas and practices are not confined to a specific diversity group but are general and broad enough to be effective with all culturally and linguistically diverse groups. These practices are appropriate for K–12 schools.

Cross-Cultural Competence

As school psychologists search for best practice in working with diverse populations, the tripartite model of cross-cultural competence is often suggested as one such model. Cross-cultural competency has been written about extensively and represents a vital conceptual framework (Worthington, Soth-McNutt, & Moreno,

2007). This model has three aspects: awareness, knowledge, and skills. Cross-cultural competence is the ability to work effectively with people from a variety of cultural, ethnic, economic, and religious backgrounds often different from themselves. All three aspects of the model are important to acquire.

Developing a Personal Awareness

The awareness stage is mostly about self-awareness and requires self-reflection. In order to understand another culture, a professional must first understand his or her own culture and how it has influenced how he or she views the world. In many respects, it is about how a person was socialized to view majority and minority cultures in the United States. How people view the world is influenced by experiences, family, friends, and community. This stage requires individuals to examine their personal assumptions, values, beliefs, and biases with respect to ethnic minorities. For Caucasians, part of the awareness stage is also about understanding White privilege. An excellent article that explores this idea but can also create cognitive dissonance is McIntosh (1990). While it might appear dated, it still resonates today and is very much applicable as it was in 1990. School psychologists can specifically review the daily effects of White privilege in the article to see if those conditions exist in their lives. It would also be an excellent piece to use as part of an "article talk" with a school staff or school psychology staff. This activity could be incorporated as part of professional development around cultural diversity. Another resource to compliment McIntosh (1990) is Levine (2008).

There are at least five steps to developing cross-cultural awareness. First, there is an acknowledgement of one's own personal prejudices and biases. Often, individuals are not even aware that they have these prejudices and biases until they are brought to their attention or through self-reflection. But it is important for people to recognize prejudices and biases in order to prevent inequitable treatment or faulty assumptions related to racial and ethnic stereotyping. Second, a person must be aware that there are cultural standards, attitudes, and beliefs that might be different than his or hers. As a person becomes more aware, he or she often begins to realize that he or she sees the world through a filtered lens, which is from his or her own cultural perspective. That said, recognizing that cultural groups may have different perspectives that guide and influence their behaviors allows practitioners to better understand why behavior occurs. The third step is valuing cultural diversity that exists. The fourth step is a willingness to

reach out to the community or the society. And the fifth step is developing a comfort level in a variety of novel situations that involve ethnic minority populations. The author's experience is that awareness is probably the most difficult stage but one that is critical and necessary.

Developing Knowledge of Other Cultures

This stage is probably the one most practitioners are familiar with and have engaged in because courses on diversity most often provide information about ethnic minority groups. While the information gained through courses and readings is important, there must also be a resistance from stereotyping groups based on the information. Stereotypes are generalizations about a group of people in which characteristics are ascribed to that group. These characteristics can be either negative or positive. What school psychologists have to remember is that there are often more differences within groups than between groups. For example, an upper middle class African American probably has more in common with an upper middle class Caucasian than a working class African American. While they are both of the same race, their socioeconomic class provides differential experiences that will influence their opportunities as well as their outlook on life. While they may have some culture-bound beliefs and values, social class will probably be more of a defining characteristic.

Information about cultural groups provides clues based on these characteristics with the idea that it will help school psychologists work with culturally diverse individuals more effectively, but with a caution that school psychologists do not engage in stereotyping. Culture is a continuum and the reality is that people from a certain cultural group do not always embrace all aspects of the culture in the same way. School psychologists must also consider other issues such as socioeconomic class, region of the country they reside in, and gender.

Surface culture is generally those things that are associated with groups such as foods, traditions, and celebrations. Deep culture, on the other hand, is often associated with the thoughts, beliefs, and values of a group. It is much harder to see deep culture. Focusing simply on surface culture, unfortunately, does not allow a school psychologist to really know and understand groups he or she is working with. Thus, biographies, fiction, nonfiction, and movies provide school psychologists with a broader perspective of cultures while helping them see the continuum of culture. Another way to build knowledge about groups is through a cultural immersion experience or participating in the daily life of another culture. In fact, cultural immersion experiences are wonderful ways to learn about the deep culture of a group.

The use of cultural mediators is another excellent way to learn about different cultural groups. A cultural mediator is simply someone from the cultural group the school psychologist is interested in learning about. These mediators are an excellent source to validate what has been learned with respect to different cultures and provide an opportunity to ask questions about particular cultural groups. Generally, people are open and willing to share their culture, especially if they believe someone is genuinely interested. The important point to remember is that a cultural mediator sharing his or her culture is doing so through his or her own lens and may not be representative of others in the group.

Applying the Knowledge

To effectively practice school psychology in a culturally relevant manner, it is a prerequisite to have the first two parts of the tripartite model: personal awareness and a knowledge base about cultures. These two aspects contribute to culturally responsive practice by using this knowledge to provide direct and indirect services that enhances a student's educational experiences. If the first two pieces are sufficiently developed and embraced it becomes easier to practice in a culturally relevant manner. Understanding the student's cultural background allows the practitioner to engage in an analysis of ways in which learning and performance are conceptualized for that student that may be different than what is typically conceptualized in mainstream culture (Sullivan, 2010).

School psychologists are practicing in an unprecedented time in which there has been a tremendous focus on the disproportionality in academic achievement and behavior between Caucasians and many marginalized students (e.g. African Americans, Latinos, Native Americans). More so than ever before, there is an increasing recognition that culture counts when developing and implementing prevention and intervention programs with culturally different populations. There is a great deal of literature on characteristics of effective schools as well as high poverty, high performing schools. While there is good knowledge on what characteristics are necessary, there is less consensus on how to get there. In other words, there are no magic bullets, and change still requires professionals to practice and advocate for students of color in a manner that promotes academic and behavioral success. Ultimately, cross-cultural competence leads to practice that is culturally responsive to the needs of diverse populations.

The journey to developing cross-cultural competence is not necessarily smooth or easy. It requires school psychologists to be self-reflective, open-minded, patient, and open to new knowledge. How do school psychologists know when they get there? There is not necessarily an endpoint; it is a journey. The increasing presence of culturally and linguistically diverse students in the United States will require a professional commitment to address the challenges that these students may encounter in school systems through the implementation of culturally responsive intervention skills.

Identity Development

Cross (1971) has studied racial identity since the early 1970s. Most of his work has focused on the process of becoming an African American. He has developed a theory and a model that has been modified over the years that examines the progression of identification of individuals as they move toward a healthy African American identity. (For more detailed information on the model see Cross and Fhagen-Smith 2001.) Atkinson, Morten, and Sue (1977) and Helms (1995) have also developed theories and models that examine the identity development of other ethnic groups including Caucasians. Identity development is particularly important in the adolescent years when the search for personal identity involves several dimensions, including religious beliefs, values, gender roles, career goals, and ethnic identities. Charmaraman and Grossman (2010) found that adolescents from different cultural backgrounds view their racial–ethnic backgrounds as important aspects of their identities.

One aspect of this identity development in adolescents (as well as adults) is that people tend to congregate with people they feel they have something in common. This is particularly true in middle and high school when students often take cues from their peers in terms of socialization and fitting in with a group. The best example of this is a phenomenon often seen in racially mixed schools where students segregate in the cafeteria down racial or ethnic lines. What is interesting is that people will often ask the question, "Why do all the Black kids sit together?" but rarely ask, "Why do all the White kids sit together?" Students associate with those whom they feel most comfortable being around and they often tend to be from the same racial group. As suburban schools deal with increasing diversity, they often grapple with the issue of segregated groups as if the phenomena were negative or bad. Especially when ethnic minorities are few in number, there is an even greater tendency for them to associate with each other.

Identify development of minority adolescents, particularly African Americans, has been researched in terms of its connection to or influence on academic achievement. This has become particularly important in research that is examining the achievement gap of African American students in predominately Caucasian schools where even middle class African Americans have an achievement gap (Ferguson, 2007; Ogbu, 2003). Since the 1980s, one of the most popular explanations for African American underachievement has been that African American students choose an oppositional identity (acting-White hypothesis) which is detrimental to academic achievement. Much of the research studying oppositional identity over the years has produced conflicting results. Tyson, Darity, & Castellino (2005) in one of the more extensive studies on African Americans and identity development in schools, state that the "inconsistencies in research findings related to an oppositional peer culture among Black students become more understandable once the importance of context is recognized" (p. 600). Essentially, by studying multiple schools with different demographics, they found that oppositional identity depended on the socioeconomic and racial make up of the school and that while it was present, it was not as prevalent as many researchers and popular media would have believed.

Dual Socialization

One of the challenges for culturally and linguistically diverse people in the United States is that their cultural norms, values, and beliefs are, at times, inconsistent with mainstream culture. In order to be successful academically and professionally, it often requires acculturation into mainstream culture. Individuals who are able to negotiate two cultures successfully are said to be bicultural. Dual socialization is "the process of bicultural socialization through which minority parents teach their children how to function in two distinct sociocultural environments" (DeAnda, 1984, cited in Gibbs and Huang, 1998, p.12). This important concept helps explain some of the variability within cultural groups. DeAnda believes six factors influence the outcome of the process of dual socialization:

… the degree of overlap or commonality between the two cultures with regard to norms, values,

perceptions, and beliefs; the availability of cultural translators, mediators, and models; the amount and type of corrective feedback provided by each culture regarding a person's behaviors in the specific culture; the congruence of conceptual and problem-solving styles of the minority individual with those of the mainstream culture; the individual's degree of bilingualism; and the degree of similarity in physical appearance to the mainstream culture. (p. 12)

Sue and Sue (1977) identified three variables to assess minority students in determining the impact or influence of culture: culture bound, language bound, and class bound. These also influence the socialization process and can affect the continuum of biculturalism. Culture-bound variables include knowledge of cultural background, attitudes, and norms. Language-bound variables are knowledge of the family's first language, immigration history, and acculturation level of the family. Class-bound variables include the family's socioeconomic status and its impact, community experiences, and the family's aspirations. Many marginalized students do not have parents who can guide them through this process because the parents themselves are not bicultural. Thus, schools become even more important in providing access and knowledge to those variables that enable individuals to be successful in mainstream America.

At the same time, school psychologists also need to be aware that many middle class people of color are no longer bicultural. There is a significant number of students of color that are second generation middle class. Owing to integration, many of these students reside in predominately White neighborhoods, go to predominately White schools, and socialize with Whites. As a Latino shared with the author in a workshop: "I look Mexican American, have a very Latina name, but I grew up in small town America that was White. I grew up in a home that didn't transmit ethnic culture to us children and as a result I would feel completely out of place in a barrio of Mexican Americans." Thus, for many of these students, their culture is mainstream middle class. They have not experienced dual socialization that would enable them to be bicultural.

Professional Relationships

Research that has examined the characteristics of successful schools with culturally and linguistically diverse students consistently found that positive relationships are an essential key. A commitment to working cross culturally requires effectively building relationships with students and their parents. Researchers such as Ferguson (2007) have found that students who have positive relationships with educators tend to be more responsive to high expectations. In addition, he found that African American and Latino students were more motivated to try hard and pay attention in class and tended to earn higher grades when they had positive relationships with teachers. Another study found that African American youth were more engaged and cooperative in classrooms where teachers focused on building trusting relationships (Bergin & Bergin, 2009). As school psychologists consult with teachers on how to improve the academic achievement of students of color, these will be important concepts to incorporate into their intervention programs.

As with students, building relationships with culturally different parents is important. Many parents of marginalized students did not have positive school experiences themselves. Thus, school may be a place where the parents feel uncomfortable and uncertain. The parents generally do not have a sense of empowerment when it comes to schools and often do not know how to effectively advocate for their child. Often there is an assumption that families are unwilling to be active partners with schools. Rather than operating from that assumption, school psychologists may want to identify barriers that produce low levels of parent involvement. For example, in one elementary urban school, many students were not evaluated for special education services because the parent would not return the permission slip. The following year a new principal arrived and questioned the process for securing permission. The principal instituted a practice of visiting the child's home with the school psychologist, discussing with the parent the reason for the referral, and what the process would entail. As a result, the principal was able to secure parent permission for every student referred.

Building positive relationships with parents requires effective communication between the parties. A school psychologist's interactions with parents should demonstrate that he or she cares and has respect for the family. It is important to resist stereotyping parents and treat them as individuals. Be open and honest with parents and view them as equal partners in the education of their children as most parents know their child best.

Ecological Perspective

The use of an ecological perspective as proposed by Bronfenbrenner (1979) is an ideal way of viewing a child in a cultural context. An ecological perspective views the child as an active participant in a system that is connected at all levels. Deficits are not seen as existing within the child, which has been the traditional way of looking at children's problems, but instead aspects of the child's environment, ranging from the family and the school systems to the community and even the larger society, and are evaluated for their potential impact on the child. Many ethnic minority families, particularly those who live in poverty, experience a number of ecological stressors that have a negative impact on their children's lives. Since most school psychologists do not live in the community in which they work, they should consider doing a trajectory of the community as well as a community mapping. Often, this information is readily available and can be done through interviews with community leaders or parents who have been long time residents of the community. This information not only assists school psychologists in understanding the stressors of the community (e.g., crime, unemployment) but also resources that may be beneficial to the school. In addition, it allows school psychologists to develop better connections with parents when they understand the community in which they live.

An ecological perspective is particularly useful when developing interventions in a multitiered support system. For example, in high poverty schools it is important to understand the needs of the population entering the school as it will determine the type and intensity of interventions that are needed. School psychologists know that, in most instances, poverty populations enter school lagging behind their middle class peers in literacy development, which has a negative effect on academic achievement. Thus, school psychologists should take into consideration how poverty has an impact on literacy and develop an intervention program that not only builds literacy skills but addresses issues that occur as a result of poverty. For example, school psychologists can have a book drive or seek out organizations willing to donate books. These books can then be given free to parents who attend school functions such as open houses, parent–teacher conferences, or PTA or PTO meetings. In addition, a bookshelf can be placed at the entry to the school with free books encouraging parents to take one with a commitment to read to their child.

Support and Resources

To assist school psychologists in becoming cross-culturally competent, attention should be given to the APA multicultural guidelines as well as NASP's

Table 1.1. Cross Cultural Strategies for School Psychologists

Individual–Personal

- Instead of always seeing through a cultural lens, try on the cultural lens of students and families in the school. McIntosh (1990) is a good beginning to understanding the world through a different lens.
- Be mindful and listen to what and how information and issues are being communicated by others. These websites on cross-cultural communication provide useful tips: http://www.mindtools.com/CommSkll/Cross-Cultural-communication.htm; http://education-portal.com/academy/lesson/cross-cultural-communication-definition-strategies-examples.html
- Be educated by getting out of a comfort zone and interacting with people who do not look like you. Learn about the community in which the school resides and consider attending a community activity.
- Be flexible in thinking and behavior. Be willing to think outside of the box.
- Be familiar with the values, beliefs, and behaviors of the population served.
- Find cultural mediators that can help in understanding and navigating the diverse cultures in the building and district.

Working With Students

- Learn the correct pronunciation of parents' and student's names. Do not give children nicknames because the pronunciation is difficult. While some names may be hard to pronounce, it is important to learn the correct pronunciation. Their names are their identity.
- Be involved in school activities to increase visibility to students and parents. Become a part of the school rather than the person who stays in his or her room and tests.
- Acknowledge students in the hallway and learn about something personal. For example, if they play in the band or a sport, let them know that they did a great job. This is a great relationship builder in high schools.
- Spend time learning about the students in the school. Interview them by engaging in a conversation to learn from and about them. The interview could provide information about the student that could be beneficial in building a relationship.
- Learn about the lives of the students in the school. For example, in one elementary school, fifth-grade boys were starting to be initiated in gangs in the neighborhood. School psychologists can counter this activity by developing support groups and activities specifically for boys that provide them a different outlet. One program paired a high school football team with an elementary school in which the football players served as mentors for the fourth- and fifth-grade boys. In addition, the senior football players did their 1 day internship/volunteer hours at the elementary school and worked with the fourth- and fifth-grade boys in their classroom. In turn, the elementary school boys attended the football games on Friday night if they had good behavior for the week. The school psychologist assisted in developing the behavior program that tracked the behavior of the boys.
- In meetings with parents, spend time getting to know the parents and what concerns they have regarding their child. Ask parents how the school can be of assistance to them. While this seems simple, it is not something poor ethnic minority parents hear often.
- Be willing to meet parents at a time convenient for them and possibly in the community. Oftentimes parents work hourly jobs and cannot take the time off of work. Take a coworker or principal if the neighborhood is considered dangerous.
- Treat parents with respect. Ask the question, "Would I want to be treated in this way?"
- Try to understand the parent's perspective and determine if there are cultural issues that may be affecting the situation. Ask parents what their goals are for their child. For example, if they are recent immigrants or second generation, it will be important to have an understanding of how they view schooling and their role as a participant in the education process.
- In meetings, greet the parents warmly and have coffee, tea, or water available. It is a welcoming gesture.

Working With the School

- Determine if the school is inviting. This is applicable to all levels of schools. What is the culture and climate of the school? Find ways to make the school inviting by suggesting signs, artwork, greeters, and children's pictures on the wall.
- Learn about the trajectory of the school and the community. What positives are there in the community and figure out ways to tap into that as a resource.
- Find ways to connect with the school and to provide needed resources that will address the many gaps that lead to the achievement gap. For example, spearhead a book drive in which free books are handed out to parents at different meetings.
- Develop short handouts for parents that assist them in helping their children at home with academics. For example, a hand-out on reading with their child that could accompany the free book. Make sure it is not wordy. Keep it simple.
- At open houses and parent–teacher conferences, set up a table that has information about a variety of topics that will help parents assist their child academically and become positive advocates for their child educationally. This will encourage parents to talk with school psychologists and other educators and, it is hoped, view them as resources.

resources on cultural competence. Since the 1970s, APA attended to multicultural issues in a number of applied psychology subfields. The development of the guidelines is a result of several iterations of the tripartite model of multicultural counseling competencies and the dedicated efforts of several leaders in the field of psychology who have been committed to recognizing and integrating issues of diversity within the psychology community. The guidelines were scheduled to expire in 2009 but were extended until 2012 and are currently under review. However, APA is in the process of reviewing the guidelines and investigating "the differential impact of historical, economic, and sociopolitical forces on individuals' behavior and perceptions" (APA, 2003. p. 61).

While these principles were designed to influence the planning and actualization of education, research, practice, and organizational change informed by diversity, the APA multicultural guidelines encourage psychologists to be leaders in social justice in their practice of psychology and active advocates of equity and diversity (Constantine & Sue, 2005). The recent writings in school psychology around social justice are excellent resources for supporting cross-cultural competency. Shiberg, Song, Miranda, and Radliff (2012) provide practical advice for practitioners working with diverse individuals, groups, and communities. NASP has excellent resources on its website that can be of assistance to school psychologists on a variety of topics. The resources can assist in the development of self-awareness, building a knowledge base with respect to culturally diverse populations, and cross-cultural skills in school psychology service delivery.

Table 1.1 presents a number of cross-cultural strategies and considerations that can be incorporated in school psychology practice. While by no means exhaustive, it is a starting place for culturally responsive practices. These strategies incorporate the tripartite model of awareness, knowledge, and skills.

SUMMARY

As the population of the United States continues to be increasingly diverse, school psychology faces the challenge of preparing future school psychologists to practice in a culturally competent manner. This is especially important given the urgency to close the achievement gap for the most marginalized students in school systems. It is essential that school psychologists learn to view each child in a cultural context with the goal of providing optimal services. In order to do this, school psychologists will need to practice in a culturally

responsive fashion. This involves developing a personal awareness, acquiring knowledge of other cultures, and applying the knowledge in skill-based practice. As school psychologists understand diverse cultures they must also take into account the impact of poverty on those cultures and how it contributes to the lack of academic achievement.

Effective cross-cultural practice relies on the practitioner being able to both accept and respect human differences as well as the similarities. Knowledge that is gained helps practitioners understand how cultural factors may affect students in school settings whether it is related to academics or behavior. Professional organizations have provided guidance and resources to move practitioners through their journey to become cross-culturally competent. It is a process that will present some challenges but many more rewards. It is a journey worth taking because culturally competent practice is simply best practice.

AUTHOR NOTE

Disclosure. Antoinette Halsell Miranda has a financial interest in books she edited or coedited referenced in this chapter.

REFERENCES

American Psychological Association. (2003). Guidelines on multicultural education, training, research, practice, and organizational change for psychologists. *American Psychologists, 58*, 377–402.

Atkinson, D. R., Morten, G., & Sue, D. W. (1979). *Counseling American minorities.* New York, NY: McGraw-Hill.

Bergin, C., & Bergin, D. (2009). Attachment in the classroom. *Educational Psychology Review, 21*, 141–170.

Bronfenbrenner, U. (1979). *The ecology of human development: Experiments by nature and design.* Cambridge, MA: Harvard University Press.

Brown, S. L., Shriberg, D., & Wang, A. (2007). Diversity research literature on the rise? A review of school psychology journals from 2000 to 2003. *Psychology in the Schools, 44*, 639–650.

Castillo, J. M., Curtis, M. J., Chappel, A., & Cunningham, J. (2011, February). *School psychology 2010: Results of the national membership study.* Special session at the annual meeting of the National Association of School Psychologists, San Francisco, CA

Charmaraman, L., & Grossman, J. M. (2010). Importance of race-ethnicity: An exploration of Asian, Black, Latino, and multiracial adolescent identity. *Cultural Diversity & Ethnic Minority Psychology, 16*, 144–151.

Constantine, M. G., & Sue, D. W. (2005). The American Psychological Association's guidelines on multicultural education, training, research, practice, and organizational psychology: Initial development and summary. In M. G. Constantine & D. W. Sue (Eds.), *Strategies for building multicultural competence in mental health and educational settings* (pp. 3–18). Hoboken, NJ: Wiley.

Cross, W. E. (1971). *Shades of Black*. Philadelphia, PA: Temple University Press.

Cross, W. E., & Fhagen-Smith, P. (2001). A life-span developmental model of racial identity. In C. J. Wijeyesinghe & B. W. Jackson (Eds.), *Reflections on racial identity development: Essays on theory, practice and discourse*. New York, NY: New York University Press.

Ferguson, R. F. (2007). *Toward excellence in the equity: An emerging vision for closing the achievement gap*. Cambridge, MA: Harvard Education Press.

Gibbs, J. T., & Huang, L. H. (Eds.). (1998). *Children of color: Psychological interventions with culturally diverse youth*. San Francisco, CA: Jossey-Bass.

Grunewald, S., Wheeler, A., O'Bryon, E., Shriberg, D., Miranda, A. H., & Rogers, M. (in press). Examining diversity research literature in school psychology from 2004 to 2010. *Psychology in the Schools*

Hage, S. M. (2005). Future considerations for fostering multicultural competence in mental health and educational settings: Social justice implications. In M. G. Constantine & D. W. Sue (Eds.), *Strategies for building multicultural competence in mental health and educational settings* (pp. 285–303). Hoboken, NJ: Wiley.

Harrison, P. L. (2010). Multicultral competence of school psychologists. *Communiqué, 38*(7), Retrieved from http://www.nasponline.org/publications/cq/mocq387PresidentsMessage.aspx

Hart, B., & Risley, T. R. (1995). *Meaningful differences in the everyday experience of young American children*. Baltimore, MD: Brookes.

Helms, J. E. (1995). An update of Helm's white and people of color racial identity models. In J. M. Casas, L. A. Suzuki, & C. M. Alexander (Eds.), *Handbook of multicultural counseling* (pp. 181–198). Thousand Oaks, CA: SAGE.

Jones, J. (Ed.). (2009). *The psychology of multiculturalism in the schools: A primer for practice, training, and research*. Bethesda, MD: National Association of School Psychologists.

Levine, M. (2008). *The price of privilege*. New York, NY: Harper.

McIntosh, P. (1990). White privilege: Unpacking the invisible knapsack. *Independent School, 49*, 31–36.

Miranda, A. H., & Gutter, P. (2002). Diversity and equity research in school psychology: 1990–1999. *Psychology in the Schools, 39*, 597–604.

National Association of School Psychologists. (2010a). *Model for comprehensive and integrated school psychological services*. Bethesda, MD: Author. Retrieved from http://www.nasponline.org/standards/2010standards/2_PracticeModel.pdf

National Association of School Psychologists. (2010b). *Standards for graduate preparation of school psychologists*. Bethesda, MD: Author. Retrieved from http://www.nasponline.org/standards/2010standards/1_Graduate_Preparation.pdf

O'Brien, A. (2011). *How school-based health care can contribute to closing the achievement gap*. San Rafael, CA: Edutopia. Retrieved from http://www.edutopia.org/blog/school-based-health-care-closing-gap-obrien

Ogbu, J. U. (2003). *Black American students in an affluent suburb: A study of academic disengagement*. Mahwah, NJ: Erlbaum.

Pieterse, A. L., Evans, S. A., Risner-Butner, A., Collins, N. M., & Mason, L. B. (2009). Multicultural competence and social justice training in counseling psychology and counselor education. *The Counseling Psychologist, 37*, 93–115.

Power, T. (2008). Editorial note: Promoting social justice. *School Psychology Review, 37*, 451–452.

Reardon, S. F. (2011). The widening academic achievement gap between the rich and the poor: New evidence and possible explanations. In R. Murnane & G. Duncan (Eds.), *Whither opportunity: Rising inequality, schools, and children's life chances* (pp. 91–116). New York, NY: Russell Sage Foundation.

Rogers Wiese, M. R. (1992). Racial/ethnic minority research in school psychology. *Psychology in the Schools, 29*, 267–272.

Shriberg, D., Song, S. Y., Miranda, A. H., & Radliff, K. M. (2012). *School psychology and social justice: Conceptual foundations and tools for practice*. New York, NY: Routledge.

Sue, D. W., & Sue, E. (1977). Barriers to effective cross-cultural counseling. *Journal of Counseling Psychology, 24*, 420–429.

Sullivan, A. (2010). Preventing disproportionality: A framework for culturally responsive assessment. *Communiqué, 39*(3), Retrieved from http://www.nasponline.org/publications/cq/mocq393PreventingDisproportionality.aspx

Tyson, K., Darity, W., & Castellino, D. (2005). It's not "a Black thing": Understanding the burden of acting White and other dilemmas of high achievement. *American Sociological Review, 70*, 582–605.

U.S. Census Bureau. (2010). *National resident population estimates by race, Hispanic origin, and age: 2000 and 2009*. Washington, DC: Author. Retrieved from http://www.census.gov/compendia/statab/2012/tables/12s0010.pdf

U.S. Census Bureau. (2012). *Most children younger than age 1 are minorities*. Washington, DC: Author. Retrieved from http://www.census.gov/newsroom/releases/archives/population/cb12-90.html

Worthington, R. L., Soth-McNett, A. M., & Moreno, M. V. (2007). Multicultural counseling competencies research: A 20-year content analysis. *Journal of Counseling Psychology, 54*, 351–361.

2

Best Practices in School Psychologists Acting as Agents of Social Justice

David Shriberg
Gregory Moy
Loyola University Chicago (IL)

OVERVIEW

Although the term *social justice* has roots over many centuries across many disciplines, this concept has recently begun to be more prominent in school psychology, to the point where social justice is referenced several times in the most recent National Association of School Psychologists (NASP) *Model for Comprehensive and Integrated School Psychological Services* (NASP, 2010a) and *Principles for Professional Ethics* (NASP, 2010b). As an overarching framework for practice, social justice touches upon all 10 domains covered in the NASP Practice Model (NASP, 2010a) to a significant degree. In particular, there is a direct linkage between the Diversity in Development and Learning foundational domain and the application of social justice principles and strategies. As quoted in this domain:

> School psychologists demonstrate skills to provide effective professional services that promote effective functioning for individuals, families, and schools with diverse characteristics, cultures, and backgrounds and across multiple contexts, with recognition that an understanding and respect for diversity in development and learning and advocacy for social justice are foundations for all aspects of service delivery. (NASP, 2010a, p. 7)

As an aspirational goal, social justice is likely to be a concept that most—if not all—school psychologists embrace (who is for social *injustice*?). However, the focus is not only with the broad aspiration, but in translating this aspiration to practice is quite challenging.

Accordingly, this chapter first provides an overview of social justice, including the results of research done with NASP members as to how this social justice concept might be best defined and applied. It will be argued that social justice can be viewed not only as an aspirational goal, but also as a verb, as something school psychologists *do*. Social justice will be presented as the latest evolution of multicultural school psychology, with a commitment both to multiculturalism and to ethics at the core of this emerging framework. Ways in which applied social justice both reflects and expands upon the application of a multitiered system of support (MTSS) framework will be discussed. Ongoing reflection, collaboration, and advocacy will be presented as the primary mechanisms from which school psychologists "do" social justice, with several practice examples highlighted.

BASIC CONSIDERATIONS

School psychology practice does not occur in a vacuum, but rather within a social, political, cultural, and educational context. Whereas persons from all walks of life are drawn to the field, it is reasonable to deduce that the profession is particularly attractive to individuals who share in the belief that, through working with students in schools, they can make a positive impact on society. However, the provision of educational and psychological services in schools is confronted by major social challenges. A rising child poverty rate; extensive segregation along racial and social class divisions; inadequate instruction for poor and minority students;

and the perpetration of violence in schools, homes, and communities are all identifiable problems that underscore the importance of attending to the societal factors that have an impact on the educational aspirations of this nation's youth. Inasmuch as the problems of society encroach on the fulfillment of educational goals, the solutions to these problems may also lie in the manner in which educators—specifically school psychologists—approach their work with students, families, and communities. Our position is that the intentional practice of school psychology through a social justice lens enacts the potential of school psychologists who aim to serve as agents of positive change.

Defining Social Justice

Social justice is not easily defined. According to North (2008), common terminology related to social justice is that the concept reflects the dual pillars of recognition (the right to be treated with respect and dignity) and redistribution (equitable sharing of wealth and power). The goal of social justice can be understood as:

> ... full and equal participation of all groups in a society that is mutually shaped to meet their needs. Social justice includes a vision of society in which the distribution of resources is equitable and all members are physically and psychologically safe and secure. (Bell, 2013, p. 21)

Over the past several decades, many professions have worked to create definitions and models of social justice that relate directly to their work, and school psychology is no different. To date, there have been two studies seeking to define social justice from a school psychology perspective, both of which support a definition of social justice that reflects equitable distribution of resources and respectful, culturally responsive practice. First, Shriberg et al. (2008) conducted a Delphi study (this is a technique in which selected experts work in a series of rounds to bring greater clarity a to challenging topic) with 17 multicultural experts in school psychology. The participants in this study most strongly endorsed a definition of social justice centered on the idea of "protecting the rights and opportunities for all." Shriberg, Wynne, Briggs, Bartucci, and Lombardo (2011) surveyed 1,000 randomly selected NASP members regarding their opinions related to social justice. As with the multicultural experts, respondents rated "ensuring the protection of educational rights and opportunities" and "promoting nondiscriminatory practice" as significantly more critical to the definition than all other items, except each other.

Ethics and Law

Translating social justice aspirations to practice involves a strong grounding in ethics and the law (Shriberg et al., 2011). Accordingly, in both language and function, NASP's *Principles of Professional Ethics* (NASP, 2010b) and the American Psychological Association's (APA) *Ethical Principles for Psychologists and Code of Conduct* (APA, 2010) overlap significantly with social justice frameworks. For example, Principle 1 of the NASP ethics principles (NASP, 2010b) is titled, "Respecting the Dignity and Rights of All Persons." This principle is elaborated through the assertion:

> In their words and actions, school psychologists promote fairness and justice. They use their expertise to cultivate school climates that are safe and welcoming to all persons regardless of actual or perceived characteristics, including race, ethnicity, color, religion, ancestry, national origin, immigration status, socioeconomic status, primary language, gender, sexual orientation, gender identity, gender expression, disability, or any other distinguishing characteristics. (NASP, 2010b, p. 5)

This principle is further elaborated through statements in the NASP ethics code that oppose engaging in discriminatory actions and policies (Standard I.3.1). In addition, school psychologists are ethically bound to "correct school practices that are unjustly discriminatory" (I.3.3).

The ethical principles of fairness and justice also course through federal legislation on education. Whereas ethical guidelines lay out broad and global aspirations of fairness and justice, they do not prescribe actions that school psychologists should take in order to achieve these goals. However, federal legislation on education has contributed to the profession some additional avenues for achieving social justice through education. The first authorization of the Elementary and Secondary Education Act of 1965 (ESEA), and the Individuals with Disabilities Education Improvement Act of 2004 have targeted two historic obstacles to the attainment of social justice through education: poverty and disability, respectively.

The passage of ESEA marked the recognition that public education was at the crux of the nation's War on

Poverty. According to the first authorization of ESEA, Congress made the declaration:

> In recognition of the special educational needs of children of low-income families and the impact that concentrations of low income families have on the ability of local educational agencies to support adequate educational programs, the Congress hereby declares it to be the policy of the United States to provide financial assistance ... to local educational agencies serving areas with concentrations of children from low-income families to expand and improve their educational programs by various means ... which contribute particularly to meeting the special educational needs of educationally deprived children. (Sec. 201)

Through their elected representatives in Congress, the American people recognized the impact the concentration of poverty had on schools in those areas, and moved to take steps to ameliorate the negative impact poverty had on students' access to adequate educational opportunities. That this legislation was ratified a year after the passage of the Civil Rights Act of 1964 during the apex of the U.S. civil rights movement is no mere coincidence. Access to adequate education, it would seem, has since been viewed as a necessary condition to the formation of a more just and fair society, and a potential remedy for economically impoverished communities. When Congress enacted the Education of All Handicapped Children Act in 1975, millions of children with disabilities were either excluded from school or not receiving an appropriate education. Recognizing the need to create legal protections for the rights of students with disabilities to attain free and appropriate public education was a significant step toward attaining social justice. To the extent that these laws delineate school practices, they also provide legal foundations for the advancement of social justice through school psychology.

BEST PRACTICES FOR SCHOOL PSYCHOLOGISTS ACTING AS AGENTS OF SOCIAL JUSTICE

The remainder of this chapter will be devoted to offering suggested action strategies in order to help the reader to think through what applied social justice looks like in practice. However, it should be noted that the very idea of best practices when it comes to social justice is quite controversial. It is not controversial regarding the notion of bringing the current best existing evidence to practice—this is simply common sense—but rather with the idea of labeling specific actions as best practice. This is likely due to at least two primary factors. First, there is the reality that every individual school psychologist practices within a unique context where specific action steps related to advocacy, or questioning the status quo, may be more or less possible. Thus, a person might be able to adopt a social justice orientation wherever he or she works, but the ability to act effectively and expansively on this orientation varies widely from setting to setting. Second, and relatedly, while numerical targets can be set (e.g., the goal of students from all backgrounds achieving above benchmark in a desired area), applying social justice invariably involves being comfortable with the idea that not every important action can or should be measured easily. For example, how does one measure with precision whether students and families who have been marginalized view an individual school psychologist as someone they can trust? That said, increasing consensus has emerged in recent years that the most effective social justice practices are rooted in multiculturalism (e.g., Ratts, 2011; Shriberg, Song, Miranda, & Radliff, 2012) and that collaboration and advocacy are core social justice actions (Briggs, 2012). These core components will be described in this section.

Understanding of and Commitment to Multiculturalism

As noted by several authors, social justice can be seen as the latest development in the evolution of multicultural psychology (Ratts, 2011; Vera & Speight, 2003). This evolution has been marked by three primary stages. In the first stage, the struggle centered around the acceptance of topics that can be broadly labeled as *cultural diversity topics* that are germane to scholarship and practice. For example, might the way that children typically experience the world be affected by factors such as race/ethnicity, nationality, gender, socioeconomic status, sexual orientation, and/or religion? Rogers (2005) documents many major milestones (e.g., the first specifications for curriculum content in culture, position statements on LGBTQ youth) related to training standards and organizational positions articulated by APA and NASP that reflect a growing awareness of cultural differences. Summarizing trends in counseling psychology that could also apply to school psychology—certainly this trend is evident by this volume—Vera and Speight (2003) noted:

> It is a sure sign of progress that we are no longer reading articles that argue whether diversity is important, but instead have a developing body of literature that allows for scholarly debate regarding how to integrate multiculturalism into our research, training, and practice. (p. 253)

As multiculturalism has gained acceptance in all areas of psychology, there has been a need for scholarship and training standards that describe what culturally responsive research and practice might look like. These models typically emphasize how mental health professionals can develop appropriate levels of self-awareness, knowledge, and skills as they relate to working with individuals from diverse backgrounds (Constantine, Hage, Kindaichi, & Bryant, 2007). Within school psychology, there have been numerous efforts toward providing models of culturally competent practice and training (e.g., Rogers & Lopez, 2002). Additionally, culturally responsive practice is both a stated and an implied goal in the most recent version of NASP's Practice Model (NASP, 2010a) and APA's Multicultural Guidelines (APA, 2003).

Although defining and working toward cultural competence are important goals, critics (e.g., Prilleltensky & Nelson, 2002; Shriberg, 2009; Vera & Speight, 2003) argue that separating multicultural competencies from a commitment to social justice results in psychologists maintaining the status quo rather than working toward social change. This is an important distinction. For example, suppose that in a given school 90% of English language learners are referred for special education evaluation. A school psychologist may conduct these evaluations in a manner consistent with culturally responsive practice, but if this school psychologist is not on some level working to question why such a large proportion of English language learners are being referred for special education, then this school psychologist is likely falling short of his or her potential as an agent of social justice. School psychologists who adopt a social justice orientation acknowledge the interplay of the social dynamics of privilege and marginalization associated with the various social identities of students (Miranda, Boland, & Hemmeler, 2009) and take affirmative steps to address these injustices at individual and systemic levels.

A central theme of social justice multicultural models is the importance of self-awareness (Constantine et al., 2007). Awareness requires a degree of reflection, and taking the time to reflect—both on one's own practices and on what one observes in others—can be a powerful tool. Thus, before acting, school psychologists are encouraged to analyze critically the situation around them as it relates to social justice. Questions school psychologists might ask are: (a) What are the conditions that have led to the unjust situation? (b) Whose voices are being heard and whose are not being heard in this situation? (c) What action steps have the greatest potential for positive systemic change? (d) Who potentially stands to gain and who might be harmed by a movement toward change? (e) Am I the best person to lead this change effort, or should my role be more of a facilitator? Essentially, this step involves merging the traditional problem-solving steps of identifying the problem, analyzing the problem, creating a plan, and monitoring effectiveness and making adjustments with a critical consciousness that includes evaluating one's own role as an agent in this process and ways in which institutional structures may provide obstacles to and opportunities in support of justice.

In a commentary on school psychology and social justice, Speight and Vera (2009) challenge school psychologists to engage in critical self-reflection not only at the individual and school level, but also at the level of the field as a whole. They argue that a field that embraces social justice is not afraid to question its own history and priorities from the lens of how the profession can best support justice and wellness and work to understand and then seek to mitigate or eliminate practices that do not support justice.

As such, a social justice framework rooted in multiculturalism can be seen as a form of goggles worn by school psychology practitioners, students, supervisors, and professors. These goggles serve as a precondition to action. One exemplar of this precursor to action is Sofia (name changed to protect anonymity), a bilingual school psychologist in a major metropolitan area. To Sofia, social justice is not just a set of practices, but a value system and a mind-set. She states:

> It is hard to describe why people should care about social justice because it just seems like the natural and humane thing to do. Any argument that what is afforded to one child but not to another because of language, immigration status, race, or socioeconomic status is simply hurtful and disheartening.

Social justice is a philosophy in how you choose to live your life.

Collaboration and Advocacy

If an understanding of multicultural school psychology, including looking for and critically examining indicators of privilege and oppression, is a precursor to action, how can a person desiring to be an agent of social justice utilize his or her talents most effectively? To date there are two empirical studies that have studied school psychologists' perception of the relevance and applicability of social justice ideas to practice. In both studies, participants were asked to identify priority social justice topics. In the first study, multicultural experts in school psychology nearly universally spoke to the importance of challenging institutional power structures (Shriberg et al., 2008). Based on these participants' responses, "institutional power" was defined as "the exertion of control on individuals or groups by society's primary institutions (e.g., schools, local agencies, and government)." In a follow-up study of randomly selected NASP members, participants were asked if institutional power was a topic that was salient to the discussion of social justice in school psychology. Given answer options of *agree* or *disagree*, 94% of respondents agreed that consideration of institutional power is salient to the discussion of social justice within school psychology (Shriberg et al., 2011). As one participant wrote in a representative comment:

> I believe that the institutional power of schools has not been given the attention it deserves. On a very basic level, I think that we have all run into numerous decisions made about students because "this school or district doesn't do it that way." An in-depth study of how and where power is held in schools and districts would be very valuable to those of us in the field. I feel that sometimes we are asked to function under the assumption that all is fair and transparent even though all evidence is to the contrary. (p. 43)

Participants in both studies identified advocacy—particularly advocacy that is directly related to elements of cultural diversity—as the key activity for school psychologists to support social justice. Within this broad category of advocacy, a number of strategies were offered, coalescing around the importance of knowledge (e.g., knowledge of best practices and the law) and action (e.g., advocacy to support children and families). When asked how realistic it is for school psychologists to engage in a variety of actions to support social justice, "promoting best practices in school psychology," "conducting culturally fair assessments," and "advocating for the rights of children and families" were rated significantly higher by randomly selected NASP members than all other items except for each other (Shriberg et al., 2011).

Speaking to the concept of social justice advocacy, NASP's (2010b) *Principles for Professional Ethics* states:

> School psychologists consider the interests and rights of children and youth to be their highest priority in decision making, and act as advocates for all students. These assumptions necessitate that school psychologists speak up for the needs and rights of students even when it may be difficult to do so. (p. 2)

How then might school psychologists speak up? The most extensive advocacy strategies geared toward individual practitioners has been developed by the American Counseling Association (ACA). Defining advocacy competency as "the ability, understanding, and knowledge to carry about advocacy ethically and effectively" (Toporek, Lewis, & Crethar, 2009, p. 262), in 2003 the ACA endorsed 48 competencies. These competencies are based on six dimensions organized into three distinct categories. The first category refers to whether the advocacy strategy is *acting with* or *acting on behalf of* clients. The second category relates to whether the advocacy strategy is primarily targeted at micro- or macrolevel change. The third category relates to whether the intended impact is at the client/student, school/community, or public arena level. Figure 2.1 depicts the dimensions and categories of the advocacy framework visually, and Table 2.1 provides a listing of all 48 advocacy competencies.

Collaboration and Advocacy Within a Multitiered Systems of Support Model

School psychology has reached a point where a problem-solving model based on MTSS principles is considered the standard of practice. This raises questions of how social justice frameworks and the MTSS framework may coincide. While more extensive research is needed, the existing evidence suggests that these two frameworks for school psychology can be

Figure 2.1. American Counseling Association Advocacy Competencies

	Individual/Client	School/Community	Public Arena
Acting with	Client/student empowerment	Community collaboration	Public information
Acting on behalf of	Client/student advocacy	Systems advocacy	Social/political advocacy

Microlevel ←————————→ Macrolevel

applied in concert, yet considerations for the broad societal implications of tiered service delivery must be taken.

As noted by Artiles, Bal, and King Thorius (2010) in their analysis of social justice and response to intervention (RTI), the assumptions underlying each framework overlap in some ways but differ in others. In terms of similarities, both approaches seek to address gross inequities. Additionally, consistent with the "redistribution" social justice pillar (North, 2008), both frameworks are highly concerned with the distribution of resources as it relates to educational opportunities. Both frameworks place a premium on prevention and both advocate for changes in educational structures toward the goal of all students receiving a high-quality education regardless of what school they attend, their family's background, or any other cultural or educational determinant. Similarly, both frameworks support data-based decision making and bringing evidence-based techniques and interventions to practice.

According to Artiles et al. (2010), where these frameworks differ relates to the "recognition" social justice pillar. This is not to say that RTI researchers and policy makers actively seek to promote discriminatory practices, but rather that how to adjust for and combat societal oppression that has an impact on student performance is not well articulated in the RTI research. Relatedly, social justice advocates tend to think ecologically, while the suggested remedies within an RTI or MTSS framework tend to focus either on instructional changes or within-child factors, both individualistic considerations. Contextual variables that do not reside either within the child or within the domain of instructional techniques are not well explained. For example, if a child is being harassed in the hallways based on race, gender, sexual orientation, class, religion, or any other dimension, it is less likely

that child will reach his or her academic potential in the classroom. While advocates of RTI and MTSS clearly do not support harassment, ecological considerations generally and ways to respond to oppressive conditions specifically are not a major focus of MTSS research and practice guidelines.

How then might MTSS and social justice frameworks be combined in practice? Briggs (2012) synthesizes social justice research and prevention frameworks to develop a list of potential social justice advocacy steps and guiding questions at each tier. Consistent with the ACA standards and common social justice guidelines, particular emphasis is given to distinguishing between actions done *with* and *on behalf of* others, the key distinction being that it is important to consider if and when school psychologists should speak on behalf of others as opposed to working in collaboration to help to create and support a platform for others to speak for themselves more effectively. These suggested advocacy steps and guiding questions are provided in Table 2.2.

Concrete Social Justice Action Steps

The ACA Advocacy Frameworks and the suggested action steps and guiding questions provided by Briggs (2012) provide a starting point for listing out concrete steps that practitioners can take that reflect applied social justice within an MTSS framework. To further demonstrate the application of these steps, this section closes with three scenarios. The first two are based in part on experiences of real school psychology practitioners (names changed to protect anonymity) who have sought to bring social justice principles to bear in their practice. The third scenario is based loosely on work conducted by the first author and another school psychologist.

Table 2.1. American Counseling Association Advocacy Competency Domains

Empowerment Counselor Competencies: In direct interventions, the counselor is able to:
- Identify strengths and resources of clients and students
- Identify the social, political, economic, and cultural factors that affect the client/student
- Recognize the signs indicating that an individual's behaviors and concerns reflect responses to systemic or internalized oppression
- At an appropriate development level, help the individual identify the external barriers that affect his or her development
- Train students and clients in self-advocacy skills
- Help students and clients develop self-advocacy action plans
- Assist students and clients in carrying out action plans

Client/Student Advocacy Counselor Competencies: In environmental interventions on behalf of clients and students, the counselor is able to:
- Negotiate relevant services and education systems on behalf of clients and students
- Help clients and students gain access to needed resources
- Identify barriers to the well-being of individuals and vulnerable groups
- Develop an initial plan of action for confronting these barriers
- Identify potential allies for confronting the barriers
- Carry out the plan of action

Community Collaboration Counselor Competencies
- Identify environmental factors that impinge upon students' and clients' development
- Alert community or school groups with common concerns related to the issue
- Develop alliances with groups working for change
- Use effective listening skills to gain understanding of the group's goals
- Identify the strengths and resources that the group members bring to the process of systemic change
- Communicate recognition of and respect for these strengths and resources
- Identify and offer the skills that the counselor can bring to the collaboration
- Assess the effect of the counselor's interaction with the community

Systems Advocacy Counselor Competencies: In exerting systems-change leadership at the school or community level, the advocacy-oriented counselor is able to:
- Identify environmental factors impinging on the students' or clients' development
- Provide and interpret data to show the urgency for change
- In collaboration with other stakeholders, develop a vision to guide change
- Analyze the sources of political power and social influence within the system
- Develop a step-by-step plan for implementing the change process
- Develop a plan for dealing with probable responses to change
- Recognize and deal with resistance
- Assess the effect of the counselor's advocacy efforts on the system and constituents

Public Information Counselor Competencies: In informing the public about the role of environmental factors in human development, the advocacy-oriented counselor is able to:
- Recognize the impact of oppression and other barriers to healthy development
- Identify environmental factors that are protective of healthy development
- Prepare written and multimedia materials that provide clear explanations of the role of specific environmental factors in human development
- Communicate information in ways that are ethical and appropriate for the target population
- Disseminate information through a variety of media
- Identify and collaborate with other professionals who are involved in disseminating public information
- Assess the influence of public information efforts undertaken by the counselor

Social/Political Advocacy Counselor Competencies: In influencing public policy in a large, public arena, the advocacy-oriented counselor is able to:
- Distinguish those problems that can best be resolved through social/political action
- Identify the appropriate mechanisms and avenues for addressing these problems
- Seek out and join with potential allies
- Support existing alliances for change
- With allies, prepare convincing data and rationales for change
- With allies, lobby legislators and other policy makers
- Maintain an open dialogue with communities and clients to ensure that the social/political advocacy is consistent with the initial goals

Note. From *Advocacy Competencies*, 2003, by the American Counseling Association, Alexandria, VA: American Counseling Association. Copyright 2003 by the American Counseling Association. Adapted with permission.

Table 2.2. Social Justice Advocacy Steps and Guiding Questions

Level	Type	Steps	Guiding Questions
Zero	Overall	• Critically evaluate laws and policies for their ability to promote social justice	• What laws and policies affect educational practice in my community? • Do these laws and policies promote equity, access, and respect? What evidence do I have to support my conclusions?
	With	• Call stakeholders to action in a contextually appropriate manner	• How can I call stakeholders to action in a manner that will be heard?
	On behalf	• Gather evidence • Present concerns and evidence to legislators and/or policy makers • Work with legislators to affect change	• Do I feel that action on my part is critical to affecting change? • Who are my legislators and/or policy makers and how can I get them on board?
Tier 1	Overall	• Critically evaluate school-wide systems and practices • Identify needs and priorities for change • Assemble or identify a team representative of the school • Develop an action plan • Communicate regularly	• Do school curricula align with the diverse needs and lives of students? • Do data highlight discrepancies in access and achievement? • What are the perspectives of school stakeholders regarding how the school as a whole is supporting the healthy development of children? What do they identify as needs and priorities? • What systems and/or practices need to be developed or modified? Who needs to be involved in this process? What steps need to be taken? • How can communication be facilitated in order to ensure the action plan is acted upon?
	With	• Identify allies who have common concerns • Meet with allies and discuss common concerns and goals • Identify strengths and resources all allies have to offer • Develop an action plan • Monitor progress and problem solve along the way	• Who in the school is working toward similar goals? • How can we work together? • What is our time line? • How are we progressing? Does our action plan need revision?
	On behalf	• Synthesize and share data; call others to action • Gather a team of school stakeholders and develop a mission • Develop an action plan • Communicate regularly about progress and problem solve when needed	• What data highlight priorities for change and how can I share this so that others will be inspired to act? • Who needs to be at the table in order for change to occur? • Are action items being completed on time, and if not, why not? What can be done to help move the process forward?
Tiers 2 and 3	Overall	• Identify groups and individuals who may experience oppression or who may need extra support	• Is there a group of students who is experiencing bullying or discrimination or students who specific types of support?
	With	• Support children in identifying their strengths and resources • Support children in identifying barriers to their well-being • Create an action plan with children that will support them in using their strengths and resources to address and be resilient in the face of barriers to their well-being	• What are the sources of resilience in this child? • What societal, cultural, political, and/or economic factors are preventing this child from developing? • How does the child respond to barriers to his or her progress? • What can the child do in order to advocate for his or her development? • How can I support the child without taking over the process?

Continued

Table 2.2. Continued

Level	Type	Steps	Guiding Questions
	On behalf	• Identify or develop intervention(s) • Implement intervention(s) • Monitor progress and modify or change intervention(s) as necessary	• Do research-based interventions exist for the issue of concern? If not, what research can I draw from in developing an intervention? • Are the interventions respectful of the context of the child and do the interventions support the child in making decisions for himself or herself and/or advocating for himself or herself?

Note. From "The School Psychologist as Social Justice Advocate," by A. Briggs, in *School Psychology and Social Justice: Conceptual Foundations and Implications for Practice* (pp. 294–310), edited by D. Shriberg, S. Y. Song, A. H. Miranda, and K. M. Radliff, 2012, New York, NY: Routledge. Copyright 2012 by Routledge. Reprinted with permission.

Case Study 1: Social Justice Within the School Walls

Gina is a school psychologist who works full-time at a high school in a rural area that has very high levels of poverty. Soon after her arrival, it became apparent that many unjust practices have occurred. For example, she found many examples of students who had been labeled as having a cognitive impairment when assessment results and even a cursory review of the students' daily living skills showed this not to be the case. As a result, she set about conducting many reevaluations, including students who were not yet up for review, and ended up successfully advocating for many classification changes as a result. Similarly, over the past several years she has worked to change the classification for several students with undiagnosed or misdiagnosed mental health impairments. Finally, she has challenged the school's unjust discipline policies and has worked to bring positive behavioral interventions and supports principles and strategies to her school. Likely due to her visibility and reputation for supporting students, she recently was approached by students to help to form an LGBTQ support group. While she takes great satisfaction in the children she has helped, she worries about burnout.

Viewed from the perspective of the ACA advocacy frameworks, Gina is engaging in advocacy strategies at multiple levels. At the individual/client level, she is both acting with and acting on behalf of others in terms working both to overturn inappropriate diagnoses and to help the students have the most appropriate education experience. Similarly, at the school/community level, she is both acting directly with students to help promote a safe and respectful climate, as well as working with school leadership to remediate outdated practices. Her work has the potential to have an impact on social justice at all tiers, both in terms of supporting students who are already in the special education system and working preventively to reduce the likelihood that future students will reach the special education evaluation stage in the first place and/or be in a position where the school is tolerating harassment based on actual or perceived sexual orientation.

As school psychologists, a basic step one might take in this kind of situation would be, similar to any type of systems change effort, to first get the lay of the land and assess what the problems are and what might be contributing to these problems. A person with a social justice orientation might ask questions such as: What power dynamics are at play? What are the personal skills that I bring to the table as a potential agent of social justice? Who are my allies in this work? How do I make sure that all voices, especially those with less power and influence, are heard in working to solve these challenges (Shriberg, 2009)?

Case Study 2: School Psychologist as Advocate Outside the School Walls

Just as schools do not exist in a bubble, neither does the capacity of a school psychologist to be an effective agent of social justice reside solely within the walls of a school. Kristen is a school psychologist in an urban school district. She provides a great model of seeing an injustice that has the potential to negatively affect practice and taking it upon herself to challenge this injustice. After becoming aware that a group that engages in homosexual conversion therapy was on the list of approved providers of continuing education hours in her state, she wrote to the appropriate board in her state indicating her concerns. When this letter was ignored, she enlisted the support of numerous LGBTQ bloggers. Word spread around the Internet and in the LGBTQ community, ultimately resulting in a successful online petition to have this group removed as a continuing education provider.

Kristen's story is an excellent example of advocacy in the political arena, both through public information and social–political advocacy. Her successful effort involved gathering and sharing information, building networks, and displaying the courage to get involved in the political arena in a visible way. Whether working individually or in partnership with large organizations such as NASP, there are many ways in which school psychologists can make their voices heard in the public arena. The Advocacy/Public Policy page on NASP's website offers a wealth of information and suggested action steps on a variety of topics germane to school psychology advocacy.

Case Study 3: Combating Bullying Through a Social Justice Framework

John is a school psychologist who has been asked to lead his middle school's antibullying efforts. The school, which is located in a suburb that is multiethnic and predominantly lower middle class, has attempted many antibullying initiatives over the past few years, ranging from a daylong event to the students creating a motto about eliminating bullying that is posted throughout the school. Prior to John's leadership, these ad hoc initiatives had been implemented by the antibullying committee in a piecemeal fashion. Although the principal publicly acknowledged this committee's activities as a high priority for the school, the principal states that she is under considerable pressure to get more bang for the buck in terms of providing the school with tangible deliverables while conserving staff time and energy.

At the outset of John's involvement, no data have been collected on the effectiveness of the initiatives, nor has the committee given much consideration to how the initiatives could relate to and complement one another. Equipped with his training in MTSS and his adoption of a social justice orientation to his work, John identified how he could organize existing initiatives and weave in new practices to more effectively combat bullying at his school.

John's first thought was to urge his fellow committee members to view school bullying as an issue of power, rights, and justice. He wanted to the committee to focus on why combating bullying was important in addition to the ongoing discussion of how to combat bullying. The committee reached a consensus based on literature that bullying was a fundamental abuse of power (Pepler et al., 2006) to create an unsafe and unjust climate for one or more persons. This definition provided stakeholders with a basis for understanding the functions of students' bullying behavior, and the committee's agreement on this definition had an immediate organizing impact on how the committee would provide the school with a multitiered system of antibullying efforts.

The inefficiencies of problem admiration, incessant and unproductive debates about the behaviors of specific children and adults in particular situations, and repetitive debates on the merits of particular antibullying interventions were reduced. Whereas these types of debates previously consumed much of the time and energy of the committee with little fruition, committee members could now use these scenarios to constructively evaluate and shape their coordinated and multitiered plan to reduce the occurrences of bullying and related abuses of power. Instead of relying solely on anecdotes provided by the most vocal members of the committee, they agreed to initiate fair and representative data collection procedures focused on the frequency, type, intensity, and location of bullying behaviors throughout the school, with additional input from stakeholders who shared information on the power dynamics of certain types of bullying. This information could be used to shape the type and intensity of the different services planned out by the committee.

The motto and daylong antibullying event were preserved as part of the universal primary prevention efforts, but the daylong event was modified to include presentations and skits explaining the committee's new perspective on bullying. There were also meetings to talk about shared power in problem solving, empathy, respect for the rights of others, and restoring peace and power after injustices occur. The committee was open and explicit about how students could access a range of tiered resources and assistance when the students witnessed or experienced bullying. As a result, students received the message that bullying was something that affected the entire school community and that adults were committed to sharing power with students in the interest of protecting student rights. Students understood that the school was committed to providing more than a broad antibullying motto and punishment for offenders. It became clear that a wide range of assistance was available to students inclusive of all levels of involvement in bullying, and that simultaneous commitment to fairness and care for others underscored this range of services.

SUMMARY

Social justice has emerged in school psychology as a focus of inquiry and a stated practice guideline. This chapter provides an overview of common definitions of social justice, with the common finding that applied social justice involves attention both to distribution (Are resources distributed equitably? Do all students have a fair opportunity to learn and grow?) and recognition (Are students being treated respectfully and in a nondiscriminatory manner?).

Both an aspiration and a set of actions, social justice is challenging to distill into universal best practices due to the contextual nature of school psychology work and the challenge of directly mapping social justice actions with specific outcomes. However, several core elements have emerged. First, applied social justice is rooted in ethics and the law. Second, applied social justice is rooted in multiculturalism, with a commitment to culturally responsive practice and ongoing reflection as core considerations.

Finally, applied social justice is characterized by a commitment to collaboration and advocacy. Applied social justice is both complementary to MTSS and also different in that social justice frameworks tend to provide stronger consideration to the cultural and ecological context in which education takes place.

Moving forward, the future of social justice as a vibrant framework to guide school psychology practice is unknown. School psychology has fought long and hard to achieve the strong heartbeat it has as a respected and valued profession. A more overt and nuanced commitment to social justice has the potential to nurture the field's soul. Will the field of school psychology have the foresight and the courage to go there when it comes to social justice? We humbly hope that this chapter represents a further step in this direction.

AUTHOR NOTE

Disclosure. David Shriberg has a financial interest in books he authored or coauthored that are referenced in this chapter.

REFERENCES

American Counseling Association. (2003). *Advocacy competencies.* Alexandria, VA: Author. Retrieved from http://www.counseling.org/docs/competencies/advocacy_competencies.pdf?sfvrsn=3

American Psychological Association. (2003). Guidelines on multicultural education, training, Artiles research, practice, and organizational change for school psychologists. *American Psychologist, 58,* 377–402. doi:10.1037/0003-066X.58.5.377

American Psychological Association. (2010). *Ethical principles of psychologists and code of conduct.* Washington, DC: Author. Retrieved from http://www.apa.org/ethics/code/index.aspx

Artiles, A. J., Bal, A., & King Thorius, K. A. (2010). Back to the future: A critique of response to intervention's social justice views. *Theory Into Practice, 49,* 250–257. doi:10.1080/00405841.2010.510447

Bell, L. A. (2013). Theoretical foundations. In M. Adams, W. J. Blumenfeld, C. Castañeda, H. W. Hackman, M. L. Peters, & X. Zúñiga (Eds.), *Readings for diversity and social justice.* (3rd ed., pp. 21–26). New York, NY: Routledge.

Briggs, A. (2012). The school psychologist as social justice advocate. In D. Shriberg, S. Y. Song, A. H. Miranda, & K. M. Radliff (Eds.), *School psychology and social justice: Conceptual foundations and tools for practice.* (pp. 294–310) New York, NY: Routledge.

Constantine, M. G., Hage, S. M., Kindaichi, M. M., & Bryant, R. M. (2007). Social justice and multicultural issues: Implications for the practice and training of counselors and counseling psychologists. *Journal of Counseling & Development, 85,* 24–29. doi:10.1002/j.1556-6678.2007.tb00440.x

Miranda, A. H., Boland, A., & Hemmeler, M. (2009). Understanding privilege in America. In J. M. Jones (Ed.), *The psychology of multiculturalism in schools: A primer for practice, training, and research.* (pp. 67–82). Bethesda, MD: National Association of School Psychologists.

National Association of School Psychologists. (2010a). *Model for comprehensive and integrated school psychological services.* Bethesda, MD: Author. Retrieved from http://www.nasponline.org/standards/2010standards/2_PracticeModel.pdf

National Association of School Psychologists. (2010b). *Principles for professional ethics.* Bethesda, MD: Author. Retrieved from http://www.nasponline.org/standards/2010standards/1_%20Ethical%20Principles.pdf

North, C. E. (2008). What is all this talk about "social justice"? Mapping the terrain of education's latest catchphrase. *Teacher's College Record, 110,* 1182–1206.

Pepler, D. J., Craig, W. M., Connolly, J. A., Yuile, A., McMaster, L., & Jiang, D. (2006). A developmental perspective on bullying. *Aggressive Behaviour, 32,* 376–384. doi:10.1002/ab.20136

Prilleltensky, I., & Nelson, G. (2002). *Doing psychology critically: Making a difference in diverse settings.* New York, NY: Palgrave Macmillan.

Ratts, M. V. (2011). Multiculturalism and social justice: Two sides of the same coin. *Journal of Multicultural Counseling and Development, 39,* 24–37. doi:10.1002/j.2161-1912.2011.tb00137.x

Rogers, M. R. (2005). Multicultural training in school psychology. In C. L. Frisby & C. R. Reynolds (Eds.), *Comprehensive handbook of multicultural school psychology.* (pp. 993–1022). New York, NY: Wiley.

Rogers, M. R., & Lopez, E. C. (2002). Identifying critical cross-cultural school psychology competencies. *Journal of School Psychology, 40,* 115–141. doi:10.1016/S0022-4405(02)00093-6

Shriberg, D. (2009). Social justice and school mental health: Evolution and implications for practice. In J. M. Jones (Ed.), *The psychology of multiculturalism in schools: A primer for practice, training, and research.* (pp. 49–66). Bethesda, MD: National Association of School Psychologists.

Shriberg, D., Bonner, M., Sarr, B. J., Walker, A. M., Hyland, M., & Chester, C. (2008). Social justice through a school psychology lens: Definition and applications. *School Psychology Review, 37,* 453–468.

Shriberg, D., Song, S. Y., Miranda, A. H., & Radliff, K. M. (2012). *School psychology and social justice: Conceptual foundations and tools for practice.* New York, NY: Routledge.

Shriberg, D., Wynne, M. E., Bartucci, G., Briggs, A., & Lombardo, A. (2011). School psychologists' perspectives on social justice. *School Psychology Forum: Research in Practice, 5*(2), 37–53.

Speight, S. L., & Vera, E. M. (2009). The challenge of social justice for school psychology. *Journal of Educational and Psychological Consultation, 19,* 82–92. doi:10.1080/10474410802463338

Toporek, R. L., Lewis, J. A., & Crethar, H. C. (2009). Promoting system change through the ACA Advocacy Competencies. *Journal of Counseling & Development, 87*, 260–268. doi:10.1002/j.1556-6678.2009.tb00105.x

Vera, E. M., & Speight, S. L. (2003). Multicultural competence, social justice, and counseling psychology: Expanding our roles. *The Counseling Psychologist, 31*, 253–272. doi:10.1177/0011000003031003001

3

Best Practices in Primary Prevention in Diverse Schools and Communities

Sherrie L. Proctor
Queens College, City University of New York
Joel Meyers
Georgia State University

OVERVIEW

The U.S. population is rapidly becoming more diverse in race, ethnicity, nationality, sexual orientation, religions, and other dimensions of human diversity. The impact of diversity is present not only in larger society, but also in the pre-K–12 student population. While increasing diversity offers educators the opportunity to teach students important lessons about how to live in a pluralistic American society and an increasingly global world, there are challenges regarding how to provide culturally responsive and competent academic, behavioral, and mental health services in diverse schools and communities. From both a theoretical and practical perspective, primary prevention provides an organizing framework for school psychologists to deliver culturally responsive services to students and other stakeholders within diverse schools and communities.

The primary prevention framework presented in this chapter is based on an adaptation of Gerald Caplan's original discussion of prevention that differentiated between primary, secondary, and tertiary prevention (Meyers & Meyers, 2003; Meyers & Nastasi, 1999). The adapted framework includes four categories of prevention designed to clarify primary prevention and distinguish it from secondary prevention: primary prevention, risk reduction, early intervention, and treatment. Primary prevention and risk reduction are relevant to the definition of primary prevention presented in this chapter. Primary prevention is designed to prevent the population of the school, school district, or community as a whole from developing a learning or adjustment problem (Meyers & Nastasi, 1999). Risk reduction is designed to prevent learning and adjustment problems for all members of a particular subgroup who are placed at risk for academic and social–emotional challenges (Meyers & Nastasi, 1999). In this chapter, primary prevention and risk reduction are discussed together and referred to under the heading *primary prevention*.

Primary prevention is an essential component of multitiered systems of support (MTSS) where the first tier aims to reach everyone in the setting and additional tiers target those with increasingly more severe learning, behavioral, or social–emotional problems. The initial focus of MTSS on all students, regardless of symptoms, indicates that school psychologists must understand primary prevention from a multicultural perspective. According to the National Association of School Psychologists (NASP) *Model for Comprehensive and Integrated School Psychological Services* (NASP, 2010a), the domain of Diversity in Development and Learning is foundational to service delivery. This is evidenced when school psychologists demonstrate knowledge of the diversity represented by those in the schools and communities they serve, understand research about diverse populations, and possess knowledge of evidence-based prevention and intervention strategies to enhance services to diverse populations. Integration of knowledge and skills related to diverse populations coupled with skills regarding MTSS will position school psychologists to provide culturally relevant and competent primary prevention to diverse populations.

School psychologists who work in racially, ethnically, and linguistically diverse, and/or economically disadvantaged schools and communities may find the information within this chapter particularly salient given evidence that these dimensions of diversity can contribute to differential outcomes in academic achievement, special education placement, and school-based discipline practices (Proctor, Graves, & Esch, 2012; Skiba et al., 2011). For instance, school psychologists working in settings with racial and/or economic disparities in educational practices may reference this chapter for help designing and implementing primary prevention that accounts for ecological and systemic influences, including those related to diversity and culture, that affect individuals. Similarly, the chapter's content provides school psychologists with guidance regarding primary prevention in relation to the full range of diverse populations (e.g., sexual minorities, students of different religious backgrounds and genders), as well as the full range of problems that occur within schools (e.g., bullying of sexual minority students, unequal use of discipline strategies with students based on race or gender, failure of specific instructional strategies to work effectively with certain minority groups).

The overall purpose of the chapter is to provide school psychologists with relevant and salient issues to consider when working with others to plan and implement primary prevention for diverse student populations, their schools, and their communities. To provide context for the need to understand issues related to diversity and primary prevention, the chapter first discusses demographics of the current school-age population along with some important issues in relation to diverse student populations. Then, the chapter explores the training and experience school psychologists need to implement primary prevention for diverse students and communities. Finally, the chapter presents a discussion of best practices for school psychologists regarding primary prevention for diverse students and communities.

BASIC CONSIDERATIONS

Shifts in U.S. population demographics require school psychologists to develop knowledge related to diverse populations and to obtain appropriate professional training to develop competencies to serve such populations. In particular, school psychologists must understand issues relevant to diverse student populations and those within their communities. The discussion below addresses diversity within the current school-age population and

provides school psychologists with fundamental considerations regarding the multicultural competencies they need to facilitate the development of primary prevention programs for diverse populations.

Diversity and School-Age Population

Similar to the NASP Practice Model (NASP, 2010a), the chapter defines diversity in terms of age, chronic illness, gender or gender identity, race, ethnicity, national origin, religion, sexual and gender orientation, disability, language, and socioeconomic status. This conceptualization of diversity is important because all individuals possess dimensions of individual identity that represent diversity. The importance of understanding how diversity-related factors affect students and their communities is emphasized in documents that guide school psychologists' professional practices. For instance, NASP's *Principles for Professional Ethics* (NASP, 2010b) dictates that school psychologists use their knowledge and skills to create school climates that are safe and welcoming to everyone regardless of background. Additionally, *School Psychology: A Blueprint for Training and Practice III* directs school psychologists to "use their knowledge and skills to help schools embrace and address diversity issues effectively at all levels" (Ysseldyke et al., 2006, p. 16).

Consequently, school psychologists must have the dispositions, knowledge, and skills to work with individuals who represent a variety of backgrounds, since increased diversity is present in U.S. schools and communities. In 2011, for example, Caucasian students represented 52% of the pre-K–12 enrollment, while Hispanic/Latino students accounted for 23%; African Americans 16%; and Asian/Pacific Islander, Native American/Alaska Native, Native Hawaiian, and students of two or more races accounted for 9% (National Center for Education Statistics [NCES], 2013). Increased linguistic diversity is also evident, with more than 400 languages spoken in U.S. public schools, Spanish being the most prevalent non-English language (Russakoff, 2011). Approximately 4.7 million students, or 10% of the total public school population, are English language learners (ELLs; NCES, 2013). The number of ELLs is due, in part, to the increased presence of children of immigrants who embody a range of linguistic, cultural, and ethnic backgrounds (Batalova & Lee, 2012).

Students in U.S. public schools are also diverse in terms of family structure, socioeconomic status, religion, and sexual orientation (Lopez & Bursztyn, 2013). For example, in 2011 among children living in poverty, those who resided in mother-only households had the highest rate of poverty (NCES, 2013). Additionally, compared to Caucasian children, higher percentages of African American, Hispanic/Latino, American Indian/Alaska Native, Native Hawaiian/Pacific Islander children, and children of two or more races, live in families below the poverty line (NCES, 2013). Regarding religion, Lopez and Bursztyn (2013) indicated that 78% of Americans identify as Christian, but the influence of immigrant populations who are Buddhist, Catholic, Hindu, and Islamic is expanding the range of religions and beliefs represented in the public school student population. Finally, lesbian, gay, bisexual, and/or transgender (LGBT) youth make up approximately 4–5% of the student population. These findings underscore the need for school psychologists to be prepared to work with a wide range of students, families, and communities.

Salient Issues in Student Diversity

Research documents that students can have differential school experiences and educational outcomes due, in part, to their status as members of racial, ethnic, linguistic, economic, and other (e.g., disability status, religious, sexual orientation) diverse subgroups. For example, 86% of African American and 82% of Hispanic/Latino eighth graders read below grade level compared to 59% of their Caucasian peers, with similar outcomes for math (U.S. Department of Education, 2012). Additionally, ELLs consistently perform below English-proficient students on reading and writing assessments, and it is estimated that fewer than one in five students identified as ELLs meet state standards in reading (Thorius & Sullivan, 2013). Both ELLs and African Americans are also overrepresented in grade retentions (U.S. Department of Education, 2012). Less than two thirds of African American and Hispanic/Latino students graduate from high school on time (Children's Defense Fund, 2012). Importantly, there is evidence that independent of race and ethnicity, socioeconomic status affects academic outcomes. School psychologists should be aware that often students from low socioeconomic backgrounds begin school behind their middle- and upper-class peers, and research has shown that achievement gaps based on socioeconomic group membership persist throughout schooling.

Currently, African American students are 1.5 times more likely than students of other races and ethnicities to receive special education services under the Learning Disability category (U.S. Department of Education,

2011). Data from states in the southwestern United States suggest that ELLs are increasingly overrepresented in special education, possibly due to inappropriate identification practices (Thorius & Sullivan, 2013). These findings are concerning, given evidence that some students who receive special education experience high dropout rates, limited preparation for college admissions and employment, as well as an increased chance of incarceration (Proctor et al., 2012). In contrast, African American and Hispanic/Latino are underrepresented in programs for the gifted and talented, with Caucasian students making up 62% and Asian/Pacific Islanders constituting 10% of those enrolled in such programs (U.S. Department of Education, 2012).

Issues related to school climate are also important to understand in relation to diverse student populations. For instance, there is ample research documenting the detrimental effects of school-based victimization for sexual minority students, as well as the impact of school climate on academic achievement and sense of belonging for LGBT students (Russell, Ryan, Toomey, Diaz, & Sanchez, 2011). Youth who identify as lesbian, gay, or bisexual experience increased levels of depression, suicidal ideation, substance abuse, and school avoidance as well as lower grades, less postsecondary educational aspirations, and higher dropout rates when compared with students who do not identify as lesbian, gay, or bisexual (Russell et al., 2011). School psychologists must be knowledgeable about these findings, given evidence that the average age individuals come out is 16 (Lopez & Bursztyn, 2013).

Finally, research also reveals disparate school-based discipline practices (e.g., office disciplinary referrals, corporal punishment, and school expulsion) at the national, state, and building level for African American and Hispanic/Latino students (Skiba et al., 2011). This means that African American and Hispanic/Latino students are likely to receive more severe school-based discipline consequences for the same or similar behavior exhibited by their Caucasian peers. These consequences are evidenced regardless of students' socioeconomic status, indicating that race contributes significantly to students' disciplinary experiences in school (Skiba et al., 2011). Disparate school-based disciplinary practices also result in African American and Hispanic/Latino students being more likely than their Caucasian peers to be referred to law enforcement and experience school-related arrests (Children's Defense Fund, 2012; U.S. Department of Education, 2012). The impact of disparate disciplinary practices is particularly important information for school psychologists since such practices have negative effects on individual students (e.g., loss of academic instruction, academic failure, school dropout, involvement with the juvenile justice system) and overall school climates (e.g., student and teacher perceptions of a less inviting school climate, less favorable racial climate in schools, and students alienated from school environment; Skiba et al., 2011).

The discussion above represents just a sample of issues relevant to diverse student subgroups, their schools, and their communities. It is important to note that one complexity inherent in human diversity is that all individuals belong to multiple, and often intersecting, cultural groups. School psychologists must acknowledge and be able to identify the various dimensions of diversity that individual students possess so as not to oversimplify the human experience or miss important student characteristics that might affect understanding of students' needs for primary prevention. It is also crucial for school psychologists to recognize the strengths that diverse students and those within their communities possess, because school psychologists can use such strengths to assist schools and communities in creating culturally responsive primary prevention programs.

Training and Experience

School psychologists must attend to all 10 domains of professional practice in the NASP Practice Model (NASP, 2010a) to implement primary prevention in schools serving diverse students and communities. Because the NASP Practice Model is designed for use with the NASP *Standards for Graduate Preparation of School Psychologists* (http://www.nasponline.org/standards/2010standards/1_Graduate_Preparation.pdf), ideally graduates of NASP-approved school psychology programs have obtained basic competencies in each of the 10 domains of school psychology service delivery discussed in the Practice Model. However, to successfully implement primary prevention with diverse populations, school psychologists need to develop these competencies within a multicultural framework. Table 3.1 lists the 10 NASP Practice Model domains, with corresponding examples of cultural competencies (Rogers & Lopez, 2002) that are needed to implement effective primary prevention programs.

To facilitate competency in primary prevention with diverse populations, school psychologists should connect with colleagues who are engaged in work (both practice and research) on key issues relevant to diverse students

Table 3.1. Examples of Cultural Competencies Applied to Primary Prevention in Diverse Schools and Communities

NASP Practice Model Service Delivery Domain	Example of Cultural Competency
Diversity in Development and Learning	Knowledge about the strengths and weaknesses of the major theoretical paradigms in school psychology and the appropriateness of their application for diverse populations
Research and Program Evaluation	Knowledge about sociocultural variables and perspectives that have an impact on data analysis and interpretation
Legal, Ethical, and Professional Practice	Skills in applying laws and regulations to protect diverse populations from sources of bias and discrimination
Data-Based Decision Making and Accountability	Skills in using a variety of data collection techniques for problem identification and clarification, and planning and implementing programs that are sensitive to diverse populations
Consultation and Collaboration	Skills in working with diverse parents, children, and school staff
Interventions and Instructional Support to Develop Academic Skills	Knowledge about the most successful (evidence-based) instructional strategies for diverse populations
Interventions and Mental Health Services to Develop Social and Life Skills	Knowledge about the culture, cultural context, values, world view, and social norms of the populations served
School-Wide Practices to Promote Learning	Skills in making curriculum and behavior management recommendations that are culturally relevant
Preventive and Responsive Services	Knowledge about the attitudes of culturally diverse parents toward different forms of prevention and intervention programs
Family–School Collaboration Services	Skills in implementing home–school collaboration programs

Note. Some of the contents in this table were based on Rogers and Lopez (2002).

and their communities. School psychologists might join NASP communities or interest groups focused on specific populations or topics (e.g., bilingual, LGBT, social justice, Native American). While dialogue regarding salient issues related to diverse populations is essential at local school and community levels, these NASP groups allow school psychologists access to nationwide networks that offer resources, outside perspectives, and professional support. School psychologists should be cognizant that ongoing professional development (e.g., sessions at the annual NASP conference designated in the convention program as covering diversity-related issues, diversity workshops conducted by national experts, webinars and inservices on prevention and tiered service delivery), coupled with firsthand experience working in diverse schools and communities, will enhance their knowledge and skill development in primary prevention for diverse populations.

BEST PRACTICES FOR IMPLEMENTING PRIMARY PREVENTION FOR DIVERSE STUDENTS AND COMMUNITIES

This section details best practices for school psychologists' implementation of primary prevention with diverse students, schools, and communities. This section begins with a discussion of the multicultural competency areas school psychologists must develop to deliver effective primary prevention to diverse populations. This is followed by description of a model of primary prevention that school psychologists can use as a decision-making framework for developing and implementing preventive programs in schools with diverse populations. This model includes discussions of key ideas needed to implement primary prevention successfully, with a focus on cultural issues that influence effective practice. The chapter concludes with a case example that illustrates the practical application of best practices in primary prevention with diverse student populations.

Develop Multicultural Competency

Newell et al. (2010) defined multicultural competence as the ability to consider differences in behavior, beliefs, and perspectives while providing services to students of diverse backgrounds. The development of multicultural competence requires awareness, knowledge, and skills application. For effective implementation of primary prevention with diverse students and communities, school psychologists must develop competency in these three areas, as discussed below.

Awareness

Awareness is a necessary precursor to school psychologists' development of multicultural competency (Carroll, 2009). School psychologists must be aware of the various dimensions of human diversity they represent. This may be a challenge for some school psychologists who may not view themselves through a diversity lens. Yet, it is important for school psychologists of all backgrounds to acknowledge and understand their dimensions of diversity, since group membership influences school psychologists' life experiences and their construction of knowledge and biases toward, for example, certain groups, religions, and customs. For instance, an African American school psychologist from a middle-class background may hold biases and stereotypical beliefs that can negatively affect his or her service delivery to students from lower income families, including African American students. Similarly, a heterosexual school psychologist may have preconceived notions about and biases regarding students, school staff, and community members who identify as sexual minorities. These biases have the potential to impede the development of culturally relevant primary prevention programs for specific groups. From a systemic perspective, Carroll (2009) noted that awareness involves school psychologists' recognition of various forms of cultural bias as well as understanding of the impact that such biases can have on students, especially students who have been placed at risk for developmental problems within their schools and communities.

Knowledge

School psychologists must gain knowledge about diverse students and their needs, in particular the specific populations they serve. Newell et al. (2010) noted that learning about the histories, beliefs, traditions, and practices of diverse children and their families is a foundation of multicultural competency. In relation to primary prevention, it is essential that school psychologists develop both content knowledge of the diverse populations served, including knowledge of the cultural subgroups within each diverse population, and knowledge of research that supports effective instructional, behavioral, and mental health preventive strategies for diverse students and those within their communities. While it is important for school psychologists to learn about between-group cultural differences, it is equally important to gain knowledge of within-group cultural differences. This can be accomplished through immersion in research, but also through engagement in meaningful interactions (e.g., attendance at school and community events like cultural festivals, celebrations of ethnic or religious holidays) and discussions (e.g., conversations with students, teachers, and parents that include inquiry into their culture, values, and expectations) with those in the local school and community. Table 3.2 provides resources school psychologists can access to increase their knowledge of educational and social issues relevant to diverse populations.

Skills Application

School psychologists must transform knowledge related to diverse populations they serve into school psychological skills in the major domains of service delivery, including primary prevention. Rogers and Lopez (2002) defined skills as the behaviors required of school psychologists in relation to multiculturally competent practice. Carroll (2009) discussed skills application in terms of action or the act of doing something in a proactive way that promotes multiculturalism. For example, a school psychologist engaged in primary prevention efforts might apply his or her skills to help school staff develop culturally responsive primary prevention models that create safe school and community environments for students who identify as LGBT. School psychologists can conduct a self-assessment of the frequency with which they engage in behaviors that promote culturally diverse and competent service delivery (see the NASP checklist: http://www.nasponline.org/resources/culturalcompetence/checklist.aspx).

Use a Primary Prevention Framework That Facilitates Program Planning

Best practices in primary prevention require a multicomponent approach that addresses multiple factors simultaneously. Based on prior work on primary prevention, Meyers and Meyers (2003) developed a framework to guide development of primary prevention programs. This framework can be used to conceptualize the school psychologist's role in implementing primary prevention in diverse settings. The prevention framework simultaneously addresses problems requiring prevention and factors facilitating prevention that promote positive life outcomes like learning, adjustment, and wellness.

Problems requiring prevention in schools include stress, exploitation, and individual predisposition to learning and adjustment problems. Examples of individual predispositions are anxiety, depression, and low motivation. Stressors can include death, divorce, or mobility. Exploitation can include societal variables that result in unfair treatment of children from certain groups based on their socioeconomic status, gender, race, sexual identity, and so forth.

Factors facilitating prevention include subjective well-being, competence, and supports. Subjective well-being is a construct from positive psychology that reflects general good feelings related to social–emotional functioning that can include a positive self-concept and feelings of self-efficacy. Competence refers to the student's skills for solving social problems and includes

Table 3.2. Resources to Build Multicultural Awareness and Knowledge

Name of Resource	Source	Content
Civil Rights Project at UCLA	http://Civilrightsproject.ucla.edu	Effective educational practices for ELLs, long-term implications of U.S. demographic shifts, racial disparities in school discipline and special education
EdChange	http://www.edchange.org	Diversity awareness activities; diversity climate assessments for schools and organizations; journal articles, books, and essays on multicultural education and social justice
Gay, Lesbian, & Straight Education Network (GLSEN)	http://www.glsen.org	Research and evaluation on LGBT issues in K–12 education
National Center for Cultural Competence	http://nccc.georgetown.edu	Cultural competence checklists, cultural competence curricula for mental health providers, content related to specific subgroups
Southern Poverty Law Center	http://www.splcenter.org	Information on children at risk, immigrant justice, LGBT rights, and teaching tolerance
National Multicultural Conference and Summit	http://www.apadivisions.org/multicultural-summit.aspx	Biannual conference for researchers, practitioners, and graduate students designed to explore multicultural theory, research, and practice

individual coping skills. Supports refer to the perception that people in the environment provide important supports that help to facilitate students' social–emotional growth and development.

School psychologists can use this framework to create primary prevention programs by simultaneously seeking to reduce problems requiring prevention while enhancing factors facilitating prevention. School psychologists can implement this prevention framework by applying a systematic problem-solving process that accounts for the unique cultural context of each school or community setting.

A key principle of this framework is that effective prevention in diverse settings requires school psychologists to work with school and community members to establish programs that take advantage of interactions between the child and relevant environmental contexts. This is well illustrated in research on the efficacy of social competence curricula. When these curricula are implemented with the goal of changing children by building their social skills and competencies (referred to as person-centered approaches; Meyers & Nastasi, 1999)

without using the environmental supports needed to reinforce the use of these new skills, there has been a failure to achieve consistently positive results.

Yet, when curricula that teach social skills have been used in conjunction with key environmental supports (e.g., having teachers and parents reinforce children's use of social skills learned in these curricula), positive results are more likely. In schools characterized by diversity that have substantial environmental stress, preventive strategies can be used to promote coping skills and reduce the negative effects of stress. Such school settings might have stressors that are associated with exploitation in which differential treatment of students can result from community environments and negative school climates supporting aggression and bullying of students from various groups (e.g., LGBT students, students from low socioeconomic households, students who identify as Goth). Prevention programs addressing such problems would be strengthened by school-wide policies that encourage intervention from teachers and bystanders to reduce aggression, bullying, and their resultant stress (see Figure 3.1).

Figure 3.1. The Recursive Process of Primary Prevention

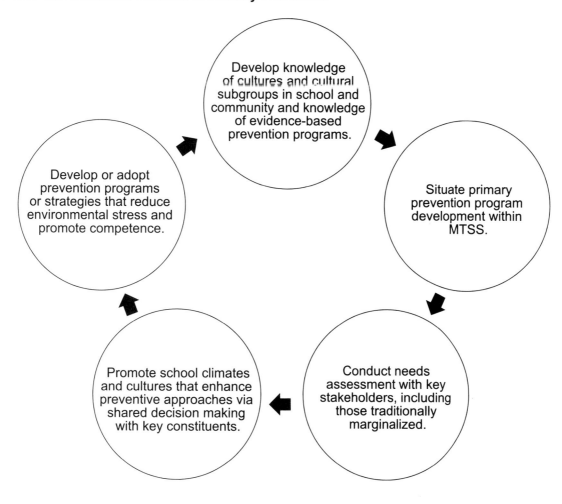

Reduce Environmental Stress and Promote Competence

The literature on primary prevention has typically included two approaches that are consistent with the prevention framework in this chapter. The first approach is to modify educational environments in ways that reduce stress and its negative effects on social–emotional development and academic performance. In particular, the goal is to reduce unnecessary stressors that have been found to result in negative outcomes for children and youth.

One example would be related to recent efforts to pressure students to perform well on high-stakes academic tests that are used to evaluate schools and teachers. Specifically, schools deemed "low performing" located in lower income communities and serving diverse student populations are often under intense pressure to increase students' performance on such tests. One way to reduce stress in this scenario would be to focus on a wide range of educational outcomes rather than basing such evaluations on one annual test. Stress can also be reduced in schools by working to enhance collaborative school climates where students, parents, and teachers work together to support students' development and performance. Strategies like cooperative learning and peer tutoring can encourage students to work together, and these strategies have been found to be effective for students across cultural groups (Johnson & Johnson, 2009). Also, approaches to shared government where students and parents have a voice in setting the structure and rules followed by schools can enhance school climate and reduce stress. Any of these prevention approaches that are based on modifying the school environment to produce a positive school climate must be conceptualized in relation to the ecological structures characterizing the school and community settings as well as the cultural values of relevant groups (i.e., students, parents, teachers, administrators, and community).

A second major approach that has received substantial attention regarding prevention programming is to modify the individual to promote competence. These programs typically seek to promote social skills, decision-making skills, and coping skills that all help to enhance social competence (Varjas et al., 2009). These kinds of programs have been used to develop competence in children and youth participating in programs designed to prevent substance abuse, bullying, and externalizing and internalizing emotional symptoms (Varjas et al., 2009). Social competence is also a focus in programs designed to promote healthy social, emotional, and sexual development of children and youth. While there has been some support for this approach to prevention, there has been some evidence that efforts to promote competence in individuals are most likely to be effective when efforts to change the individual are reinforced by complementary environmental changes that are developed by conceptualizing interactions between the person and the environment. In addition, it is important to use these strategies with a focus on culture and diversity.

An example of the interaction between environmental and person-centered interventions is presented below to illustrate the use of the prevention framework as a decision-making tool for school psychologists. This example illustrates an effort to address diversity factors by seeking to use schools to prevent commercial sexual exploitation. In this example the focus is on middle school African American girls placed at risk for commercial sexual exploitation because they live in communities with high rates of sexual exploitation (Kruger et al., 2013). Following a needs assessment based on interviews of key service providers, a curriculum was developed in an effort to be sensitive to the cultural experiences of the African American girls. The curriculum focused on healthy sexual and social development. In addition, the curriculum addressed social problem-solving skills that the girls could use to avoid dangerous and unhealthy social situations. This was done to enhance the probability of healthy social and sexual development as well as decreasing the likelihood of their involvement in commercial sexual exploitation. This curriculum was developed using the Participatory Culture–Specific Intervention Model (see Nastasi, Moore, & Varjas, 2004) so that the curriculum was congruent with the cultural background of the girls. Based on input from the girls and their teachers, the curriculum covered aggression; the media's portrayal of women, particularly African American women; and the relevance of hair to African American women. Environmental supports for the curriculum were facilitated by having school staff sit in when the curriculum was presented. As a result, the teachers learned what was being taught and were able to reinforce the girls' use of these skills at other times throughout the school day. For example, the staff observed the girls using the problem-solving skills from the curriculum and provided reinforcement for the use of these skills. This environmental support was made feasible by encouraging the active involvement of staff members during implementation of the curriculum.

Promote School Climates and Cultures That Enhance Preventive Approaches

School climate includes relationships among the key participants in schools such as students, educators, administrators, staff, and parents. It also includes key elements of schools such as physical characteristics, policies, and procedures (Meyers, Meyers, Graybill, Proctor, & Huddleston, 2012). Another key factor that is intricately related to school climate is culture, including variables like the cultural backgrounds of students and educators, the cultural values of families with children in the school, and the cultural factors in the community that influence relationships in schools. All of these factors can influence the experiences that students have in schools as well as their perceptions of the school climate. Researchers have found that perceptions of school climate have been related to academic achievement, school violence, treatment implementation, and teacher empowerment (Meyers et al., 2012).

There are several approaches to promoting positive school climate that can support the effective and sustained implementation of primary prevention programs. These include approaches to school reform that enhance the active participation of students, parents, and educators in decision making that affects their experiences with schools. One example of this approach is Comer's School Development Program that assigns formal roles (i.e., classroom aide) to a number of parents in low socio-economic schools to enhance the parents' active involvement in the school. One additional part of the role of these parents is to attend meetings that parents are invited to in order to increase parental involvement. Parents are also encouraged to bring other parents to these school meetings to further strengthen parent involvement. Another approach to promoting school climate is work on positive behavioral interventions and supports (PBIS), which has been demonstrated to have a positive impact on school climate (Meyers et al., 2012).

In another example of an approach to strengthening school climate, a school district worked to implement systematic shared decision making throughout the school district. This effort paid attention to school culture by including teachers and parents on the shared decision-making teams as well as administrators and various specialists. The overall approach was to change school climate by creating systems in which teachers and parents became actively involved in decision making. However, observations of the behaviors of leaders throughout the school reform process suggested that school climate was not changing because administrators and shared decision-making team leaders dominated the discussion and the decision making. Only by sharing data about these observations with the administrators who played this dominating role was it possible to begin making some of the desired changes in school climate that were designed to support preventive strategies like implementing school-wide cooperative learning in the middle school and alcohol abuse prevention in the high school.

Use MTSS as a Vehicle for Primary Prevention

MTSS mandates a preventive framework where students in Tier 1 receive academic or behavioral instruction and intervention that target all students using primary prevention strategies. Those at Tier 2 receive intervention because they exhibit signs of a learning or behavioral problem (secondary prevention) and those at Tier 3 receive intense individually oriented intervention because of their serious problems and high needs. Tier 1 is the component of MTSS that is relevant to this chapter. Although traditionally school psychologists have been involved in more direct service delivery at Tiers 2 and 3, school psychologists can become involved at Tier 1 by participating on MTSS teams, literacy teams that examine school achievement, and positive behavior support teams.

School psychologists' involvement at Tier 1 is particularly relevant given Proctor et al.'s (2012) indication that Tier 1 holds several important implications for prevention. First, school-wide prevention strategies implemented at Tier 1 can help to prevent the development of students' deficits within the general education setting. Second, universal screening used as part of Tier 1 allows school personnel to continuously monitor the entire student population's response to primary prevention programs that are designed to decrease the percentage of students in need of more intense services. Third, there is potential to decrease the overrepresentation for minority students in special education by providing primary prevention strategies that help to eliminate unnecessary referrals. Procter et al. (2012) also suggest that considerations for diversity within MTSS are important because prevention program relevance is a direct function of the extent to which a community's norms, cultural beliefs, and practices have been integrated into content, delivery, and evaluation.

Universal Screening

Universal screening is the systemic assessment of all children within a given class, grade, school building, or school district on academic and/or social–emotional indicators that the school personnel and community have agreed are important. School staff and other stakeholders must agree that the school needs to examine academic and/or behavioral health. School staff must be committed to studying, understanding, and having an impact on social–emotional health of the entire student body, as well as subgroups of students as indicated by screening results (e.g., social–emotional screening data that suggest LGBT students are at risk for social–emotional difficulty).

Importantly, universal screeners should be validated on the populations in which the screeners will be used. When interpreting data from universal screeners, school psychologists should guide school staff to ask the following questions: (a) Do data suggest a problem with the entire student population? (b) Do data suggest a problem with a targeted group of the population? (c) Do data indicate an intense problem with individual students? Screening data that indicate a problem with the entire student population suggest that existing primary prevention approaches may be ineffective and school personnel should attend to the development of programs that address the specific needs of its population, taking into account diversity factors.

Data-Based Decision Making

An important component of MTSS is data-based decision making. It is important because it helps to define the focus of primary prevention efforts and it enables systematic monitoring to examine the impact of prevention programs. This aspect of MTSS has implications for diversity since school psychologists and other educators can use data to examine achievement by group (i.e., differences by gender, ethnicity, socioeconomic status) to see if there are trends in underachievement or behavior problems. Similar analyses can be conducted for routinely collected data concerning social–behavioral variables such as office referrals, suspensions, behavior grades, and measures of student perceptions of school climate. In this way, MTSS can be used to put into place culturally responsive school-wide academic and behavioral approaches such as particular approaches to instruction and positive behavioral support systems (Proctor et al., 2012).

Evidence-Based Interventions

A basic principle underlying MTSS is the notion that evidence-based interventions are used to help reach goals. This is true at each tier of the model. Relevant to Tier 1, one example of an evidence-based primary prevention program focused on behavior is the Stop & Think Social Skills Program. This program focuses on teaching students interpersonal conflict resolution and problem-solving skills in a developmentally appropriate manner (Knoff, 2012). (Other examples of evidence-based social skills programs can be found at http://www.nasponline.org/resources/factsheets/socialskills_fs.aspx.)

A key aspect of evidence-based interventions is that the interventions should be implemented with fidelity to maximize effectiveness (Meyers et al., 2012). This is critically important because the student's degree of responsiveness to an intervention or prevention program is used to assess the student's needs. If a program is not implemented with fidelity, or if there is not information about how the program has been modified to meet the needs of the student, then it is not possible to use a student's response to the program as a diagnostic indicator (Meyers et al., 2012). By keeping track of how a prevention program has been modified to meet a student's needs, rather than expecting only one way to implement a program, it is possible to enhance the use of culturally appropriate programs that are targeted to the unique cultural background of the student.

Use Systematic Problem Solving

A critically important component for effective implementation of primary prevention is to use a systematic set of problem-solving stages. Consistent with the literature on consultation (Meyers et al., 2012) and MTSS (Proctor et al., 2012), problem-solving stages are key aspects of school psychologists' roles. There are many descriptions of problem-solving stages, such as problem identification/definition, data collection, intervention development, implementation, and evaluation.

It is important to use problem-solving stages in a manner that accounts for diversity and cultural issues. Two factors are needed to ensure this outcome. One factor is to actively involve participants in the development of prevention programs. This includes active participation of all stakeholder groups across the stages of program development, implementation, and evaluation. This includes participation in defining the problem or goals of the prevention program, developing ideas about the evidence-based practices that may be effective in the local setting, implementing the program and evaluating and interpreting evaluation data.

Active involvement of all constituent groups is a critically important component of effective implementation of primary prevention in diverse communities and settings. It is important to seek involvement from all constituent groups including those traditionally excluded from decision making in schools. This is congruent with the construct of strong objectivity, suggesting that the most accurate ideas about intervention and research result from input obtained from marginalized group members (Meyers, Truscott, Meyers, Varjas, & Kim, in press). This aspect of active involvement is important to implement prevention programs in ways that show respect for the multiple constituents present in diverse schools and communities.

A key component of prevention programming is to conduct program evaluation to examine fidelity, acceptability, and efficacy of the program. School psychologists and other educators can evaluate efficacy using the screening and data-based decision-making techniques discussed earlier in relation to MTSS. The measures used to assess primary prevention can include content tests assessing the knowledge that is taught to students receiving the prevention program, questionnaires that examine the attitudes and feelings of students related to the programs used, and rating scales or observation strategies to measure key behaviors connected to the program (Meyers et al., 2012).

Treatment acceptability can be assessed through surveys, interviews, or observations of students who participate in the prevention program. By learning about students' and educators' views of prevention programming, it is possible for school psychologists to understand why there may be relatively high or low levels of treatment fidelity since programs with low acceptability may have poor fidelity. Therefore, information about acceptability has important implications for shaping the most effective approaches to implementation.

The evaluation of acceptability also has important implications for culturally relevant approaches to prevention. By obtaining information about the perceived acceptability of a prevention program from the perspective of diverse groups of participants, it is possible to maximize program efficacy in various cultural circumstances (Meyers et al., 2012). Finally, it is also important to examine the integrity (fidelity) of program implementation. Given our focus on diversity, it is important to examine fidelity by determining the modifications that are needed to meet the needs of diverse populations and to use these data to ensure that key modifications are enhanced.

A last point about the problem-solving stages in primary prevention that is important for the focus on diversity and the implementation of primary prevention programs is the use of recursive methods wherein

educators' and stakeholders' views of the goals of prevention and program implementation are consistently modified by the data collected throughout the stages of implementation (Meyers et al., 2012). This may result in multiple definitions of goals and multiple revisions to the prevention program throughout the process of implementation, and this is a key factor to ensure that prevention meets the needs of the participating students from a range of diverse cultural contexts. This requires that data be continuously collected and that school psychologists and other educators have a willingness to modify aspects of preventive programs to meet needs that are determined based on the data that are collected. These modifications would help to ensure attention to diversity.

Case Example

New American Middle School is located in a large urban city and serves a racially, ethnically, and socioeconomically diverse population of sixth through eighth graders. Sally Windrom, the school psychologist, plays a key role in the school's MTSS process wherein universal screening focuses on both academic and behavioral outcomes. Each year, the state's education department requests that a school climate survey be conducted. The MTSS team uses data from the annual school climate survey as a part of behavioral screening. This year, the results indicated that students at New American Middle School held negative perceptions of the school's climate and reported high levels of school-based bullying. The MTSS team viewed these survey results as an indication of safety concerns that might interfere with learning. As a result, the MTSS team met several times early during the fall semester and decided that a school-wide intervention might be helpful. The MTSS team was prepared to report its recommendations to the school's administration when two students were referred to the MTSS team.

Joelle, a Caucasian student, had been a victim of bullying due to others perceptions that she might identify as a lesbian. Joelle showed signs of depression and was experiencing a decline in academic performance. The second student, Brian, an African American student, was referred because of problems associated with aggression. Brian had bullied other students and was viewed by the teachers as a major disruption in class. The MTSS team reviewed these two cases in the context of the screening data that had been collected about school climate, and as a result the team decided to recommend an approach that addressed multiple tiers simultaneously.

Ms. Windrom recommended that Joelle's and Brian's cases be addressed at Tier 3 with intense individual interventions. Brian's aggressive and bullying behaviors were the focus of individual counseling and conjoint behavioral consultation that involved the teacher and parent in a cross-cultural effort to use the home and school environments to reinforce prosocial behaviors instead of bullying. Joelle also received individual counseling to help her learn to avoid bullying and to cope with bullying more effectively when it occurred. Joelle also participated in a group intervention, as described later, that was directed to students who were at risk of being victimized by bullying (Tier 2 of MTSS). Finally, both Brian and Joelle participated in school-wide primary prevention (see discussion of Tier 1) designed to modify the school climate to enhance positive intervention from bystanders and to reduce the overall occurrence of bullying throughout the school. Ms. Windrom recognized that the implementation of Tier 2 and Tier 1 would require additional support to conduct school-wide data collection, consultations, and interventions. To increase the potential to accomplish the goals associated with primary prevention and risk reduction at these levels, Ms. Windrom enlisted support from researchers at a local university to help with data collection and initial planning.

Needs Assessment

The first problem-solving step to address the primary prevention and risk reduction goals was to gather data to add to the universal screening that had been collected as a routine component of the school's MTSS process. Ms. Windrom suggested using the Participatory Culture-Specific Intervention Model, a model that takes into account cultural issues in intervention development (Nastasi et al., 2004). Ms. Windrom and her colleagues used systematic steps to obtain active involvement of all relevant stakeholders so that the views of multiple relevant cultural groups, including those who had historically been marginalized in school-based decision making (i.e., parents and students and to a lesser extent teachers), were represented in developing intervention plans. Ms. Windrom and other members of the MTSS team accomplished this by interviewing administrators, teachers, parents, and students to obtain their perceptions of bullying within the particular culture of their school. This resulted in information about the local definition of bullying as well as the intervention and coping strategies that were viewed as potentially helpful in efforts to prevent bullying. Following the needs assessment, Ms. Windrom and other members of

the MTSS team developed plans for both Tier 2 and Tier 1.

Tier 2: Risk Reduction Intervention for Students at Risk of Victimization

A curriculum was developed for students at risk of being victimized by bullying (Varjas et al., 2009). This curriculum focused simultaneously on stress, person-centered interventions, and environmental interventions. Person-centered interventions included an evidence-based problem-solving model that school counselors and students could use to address bullying along with coping skills that derived from the needs assessment. An additional person-centered focus was an exercise designed to help students identify their own personal strengths, as an alternative to their tendency to focus on weaknesses.

In addition to these person-centered interventions, the curriculum sought to reduce stress by enhancing environmental supports for students at risk of bullying. This was done by presenting the curriculum to small groups of students who could become social supports for one another. In addition, stress was reduced by teaching students to examine New American Middle School's environment to determine places in the school where there was high risk for bullying as well as places in the school that were relatively safe. By analyzing these issues in the group, students were able to develop culture-specific strategies that they could use to enhance their safety while in school.

The Tier 2 intervention sought to maximize effects by using interventions based on an interaction between person-centered strategies and environmental support. For example, when students were asked to examine school safety by creating maps of the school environment and identifying safe and unsafe places, they analyzed these data to benefit the overall school environment by reducing bullying throughout the school. Based on the students' analysis, they created a report for New American Middle School's administration to convey information about factors contributing to safe and unsafe places in the school. As a result of this report, New American Middle School reduced stress and enhanced safety by ensuring a greater presence of educators in hallways and certain stairwells during transition times.

Tier 1: Primary Prevention of School-Based Bullying

Primary prevention was used to reduce bullying and aggression at New American Middle School.

Ms. Windrom recommended that school staff, bystanders, and parents could help to change the school climate by seeking to eliminate the existing environmental factors that promoted bullying and enhancing environmental factors that contribute to a climate that reduces bullying. This was done using five primary components. First, the MTSS team created a School Climate Committee to oversee efforts to reduce bullying and promote a positive school climate. This committee included teachers, parents, and students. Since findings in the needs assessment suggested that cross-racial bullying and bullying directed to LGBT students were particular problems, this committee was charged with ensuring that prevention efforts addressed these findings. Second, teachers and parents each received training about bullying so that they could learn to identify bullying. This training also helped teachers and parents develop strategies that could be used to respond when bullying occurred and to support efforts by students to prevent bullying. Third, students were taught lessons about bullying and the role of bystanders to prevent bullying. These lessons addressed cross-racial bullying and bullying of LGBT students. In addition, the lessons promoting the roles of bystanders in preventing bullying were taught by teachers, with support from the university researchers, during homeroom periods. Fourth, the School Climate Committee held meetings with the MTSS team and with school administration, and the result was a decision to implement PBIS to improve the school-wide approach to discipline and to enhance data-based decision making about the school's efforts to enhance school climate and reduce bullying. Fifth, scales were developed to assess teacher, student, and parental perceptions of school climate and bullying. Ms. Windrom led the efforts to administer these scales on a pre–post basis each year.

Evaluation Outcomes

After the second year of intervention there was a significant increase in positive perceptions of school climate for New American Middle School reflected in the survey data collected from teachers, students, and parents. These scales were used to ensure that any results from the prevention programs applied equally to the school's at-risk groups that reported the most involvement with bullying (i.e., cross-racial bullying and bullying directed at those who were viewed as LGBT). Results indicated that the positive results obtained for climate and bullying were consistent across these subgroups.

SUMMARY

The U.S. population's demographic shifts present challenges for school psychologists regarding culturally responsive and competent primary prevention of academic, behavior, and mental health problems. These challenges exist not because diversity is problematic, but because increased diversity requires school psychologists to develop awareness, knowledge, and skills regarding the continuously evolving populations they serve. This is particularly important within the context of school psychologists' role in facilitating primary prevention with diverse populations.

All school psychologists should exhibit basic competencies in each of the 10 domains represented in the NASP Practice Model (NASP, 2010a). However, these competencies must be developed within a multicultural framework when considering how to implement primary prevention programs with diverse populations. Initially, school psychologists must become aware of the dimensions of individual diversity they represent, acknowledge their own preconceived notions and biases regarding certain groups, and work to understand how such biases can have an impact on their service delivery to diverse populations.

School psychologists must also develop knowledge of the diversity represented by those they serve, understand research about diverse populations, and possess knowledge of evidence-based prevention strategies to enhance services to diverse populations. Multicultural knowledge can be fostered by joining NASP online communities or interest groups focused on specific populations or topics related to diversity and by attending sessions at the annual NASP meeting designated as addressing diversity content. Such professional development combined with webinars and inservices focused on prevention and tiered service delivery can be used as a foundation for school psychologists' primary prevention work with diverse populations.

When school psychologists implement primary prevention for diverse populations, a primary prevention framework should be used that simultaneously addresses problems requiring prevention and factors facilitating prevention that promote positive life outcomes such as learning, adjustment, and wellness should. This primary prevention framework used within MTSS offers school psychologists the opportunity to work with school and community members to establish programs that take advantage of the interactions between the child and relevant environmental contexts. Developing primary prevention programs within MTSS also provides an existing structure for program development that includes such things as universal screening, data-based decision making, and a systematic problem-solving process.

School psychologists' awareness and knowledge regarding multicultural issues will facilitate cultural relevance when developing and implementing primary prevention with diverse populations. Cultural considerations in primary prevention include gathering input regarding program development and implementation from those who are traditionally marginalized, using interventions that are culturally relevant and created with input from key stakeholders, and using a recursive process in which data from relevant constituents are used to modify programs to ensure cultural relevance. Given the multicultural awareness, knowledge, and skill development, school psychologists are in a prime position to lead efforts to implement primary prevention programs with those within diverse schools and communities.

AUTHOR NOTE

The authors would like to acknowledge Laura Hackimer and Jacqueline Levin of the Graduate Center, City University of New York, for their research contributions to this chapter.

REFERENCES

Batalova, J., & Lee, A. (2012). *US in focus: Frequently requested statistics on immigrants and immigration in the United States*. Washington, DC: Migration Policy Institute. Retrieved from http://www.migrationinformation.org/usfocus/display.cfm?ID=886

Carroll, D. W. (2009). Toward multicultural competence: A practical model for implementation in the schools. In J. M. Jones (Ed.), *The psychology of multiculturalism in schools* (pp. 1–16). Bethesda, MD: National Association of School Psychologists.

Children's Defense Fund. (2012). *The state of America's children handbook*. Washington, DC: Author. Retrieved from http://www.childrensdefense.org/child-research-data-publications/data/soac-2012-handbook.html

Husser, W. J., & Bailey, T. M. (2011). *Projections of education statistics to 2020* (NCES 2011-026). Washington, DC: National Center for Education Statistics.

Johnson, D. W., & Johnson, R. T. (2009). An educational psychology success story: Social interdependence and cooperative learning. *Educational Researcher, 38*, 365–379. doi:10.3102/0013189X09339057

Knoff, K. M. (2012). *School discipline, classroom management, and student self-management: A PBS implementation guide*. Thousand Oaks, CA: Corwin Press.

Kruger, A. C., Harper, E., Harris, P., Sanders, D., Levin, K., & Meyers, J. (2013). Sexualized and dangerous relationships: The voices of low-income African American girls placed at risk for sexual exploitation. *Western Journal of Emergency Medicine, 14*, 370–376. doi:10.5811/westjem.2013.2.16195

Lopez, E. C., & Bursztyn, A. M. (2013). Future challenges and opportunities: Toward culturally responsive training in school psychology. *Psychology in the Schools, 50*, 212–228. doi:10.1002/pits.21674

Meyers, A. B., Meyers, J., Graybill, E. C., Proctor, S. L., & Huddleston, L. (2012). Ecological approaches to organizational consultation and systems change in educational settings. *Journal of Educational and Psychological Consultation, 22*, 106–124. doi:10.1080/10474412.2011.649649

Meyers, J., & Meyers, A. B. (2003). Bi-directional influences between positive psychology and primary prevention. *School Psychology Quarterly, 18*, 222–229.

Meyers, J., & Nastasi, B. (1999). Primary prevention as a framework for the delivery of psychological services in the schools. In T. Gutkin & C. Reynolds (Eds.), *Handbook of school psychology* (pp. 764–799). Hoboken, NJ: Wiley.

Meyers, J., Truscott, S. D., Meyers, A. B., Varjas, K., & Kim, S. (in press). Qualitative and mixed methods designs in consultation research. In W. P. Erchul & S. M. Sheridan (Eds.), *Handbook of research in school consultation: Empirical foundations for the field* (2nd ed.). Mahwah, NJ: Erlbaum.

Nastasi, B. K., Moore, R., & Varjas, K. (2004). *School-based mental health services: Creating comprehensive and culturally specific programs*. Washington, DC: American Psychological Association.

National Association of School Psychologists. (2010a). *Model for comprehensive and integrated school psychological services*. Bethesda, MD: Author. Retrieved from http://www.nasponline.org/standards/2010standards/2_PracticeModel.pdf

National Association of School Psychologists. (2010b). *Principles for professional ethics*. Bethesda, MD: Author. Retrieved from http://www.nasponline.org/standards/2010standards/1_%20Ethical%20Principles.pdf

National Center for Education Statistics. (2013). *Condition of education 2013*. Washington, DC: Author.

Newell, M. L., Nastasi, B. K., Hatzichristou, C., Jones, J. M., Schanding, G. T., Jr., & Yetter, G. (2010). Evidence on multicultural training in school psychology: Recommendations for future directions. *School Psychology Quarterly, 25*, 249–278. doi:10.1037/a002154

Proctor, S. L., Graves, S. L., & Esch, R. (2012). Assessing African American students for specific learning disabilities: The promises and perils of response to intervention. *Journal of Negro Education, 81*, 268–282.

Rogers, M. R., & Lopez, E. C. (2002). Identifying critical cross-cultural school psychology competencies. *Journal of School Psychology, 40*, 129–131.

Russakoff, D. (2011). *Pre-K–3rd: Raising the educational performance of English language learners (ELLs)* (Report No. 6). New York, NY: Foundation for Child Development.

Russell, S. T., Ryan, C., Toomey, R. B., Diaz, R. M., & Sanchez, J. (2011). Lesbian, gay, bisexual, and transgender adolescent school victimization: Implications for young adult health and adjustment. *Journal of School Health, 81*, 223–230. doi:10.1111/j.1746-1561.2011.00583.x

Skiba, R. J., Horner, R. H., Chung, C.-G., Rausch, M. K., May, S. L., & Tobin, T. (2011). Race is not neutral: A national investigation of African American and Latino disproportionality in school discipline. *School Psychology Review, 40,* 85–107.

Thorius, K. K., & Sullivan, A. L. (2013). Interrogating instruction and intervention in RTI research with students identified as English language learners. *Reading & Writing Quarterly: Overcoming Learning Difficulties, 29,* 64–88. doi:10.1080/10573569.2013.741953

U.S. Department of Education. (2011). *Thirtieth annual report to Congress on the implementation of the Individuals with Disabilities Education Act, Parts B and C.* Washington, DC: Author.

U.S. Department of Education. (2012). *The transformed civil rights data collection.* Washington, DC: Author. Retrieved from http://ocrdata.ed.gov/

Varjas, K., Meyers, J., Meyers, B., Kim, S., Henrich, C., & Subbiah, L. (2009). Positive psychology and the prevention of school-based victimization. In S. Huebner & R. Gillman (Eds.), *Handbook of positive psychology* (pp. 323–338). New York, NY: Routledge.

Ysseldyke, J. E., Burns, M., Dawson, P., Kelley, B., Morrison, D., Ortiz, S., … Telzrow, C. (2006). *School psychology: A blueprint for training and practice III.* Bethesda, MD: National Association of School Psychologists.

Best Practices in Providing Culturally Responsive Interventions

4

Janine Jones
University of Washington

OVERVIEW

The ultimate goal of a school psychologist is to provide comprehensive services to children and families. As part of this goal, school psychologists have accepted the responsibility of offering services to children and adolescents that will help them succeed in academic, social, emotional, and behavioral contexts. Thus, school psychologists must perform competently not only as assessment and intervention specialists, but also as mental health service providers. In these capacities, school psychologists are expected to serve all children, including those children who come from a range of cultural and ethnic backgrounds.

The demographics of the United States have been changing each year, with increased proportions of people of color. For example, the 2010 U.S. Census showed an increase in the overall representation of ethnic minorities in the population, up to 36.6%. Much of this growth is attributable to live births in the United States, where in 2011, 50.4% of children born were from ethnic minority backgrounds. Compared to 37% of live births back in 1990, the trend is dramatically apparent. As the U.S. demographics have changed, the demographics of school psychologists, unfortunately, has not adapted to follow this trend. According to the 2009–2010 National Association of School Psychologists (NASP) membership survey, 90.7% of school psychologists are White/Caucasian, 3.4% are Hispanic/Latino, 3% are Black/African American, 1.3% are Asian American/Pacific Islander, and fewer than than 1% are American Indian/Alaskan Native (Curtis, Castillo, & Gelley, 2012). This pattern has existed for some time and has been represented in previous studies of NASP

membership (Curtis, Lopez, Batsche, & Smith, 2006). Loe and Miranda (2005) addressed the ethnic incongruence between school psychologists and the student population as well. They acknowledged the ethnic incongruence as an impetus for ensuring high-quality multicultural preparation in school psychology graduate programs.

For mental health professionals in schools, one of the most challenging aspects of the job is to provide direct intervention services to children who are experiencing intrapersonal distress, interpersonal conflict, or situational crises. These stressors can be complex, with many layers of both positive and negative factors. Also known as risk and protective factors, risk (negative) factors may exacerbate the problems and disrupt the probability of adaptive responses, while protective (positive) factors facilitate adaptive behavior and healing. Since these factors are usually culturally formed, this chapter offers guidelines for school psychologists to recognize and use the risk and protective factors to provide culturally responsive services for children and adolescents in schools.

Standards of Practice: NASP Practice Model

NASP has consistently endorsed standards of practice to assist practitioners in providing the highest quality of services in schools. The importance of recognizing diverse perspectives continues to be demonstrated in the NASP *Model for Comprehensive and Integrated School Psychological Services* (NASP, 2010). One of the foundations of school psychological service delivery is the domain of Diversity in Development and Learning. According to the NASP Practice Model (NASP, 2010), effective intervention results when the needs of multicultural populations are considered. For example, multicultural competence provides a solid base for practice where a school psychologist's beliefs, commitments, and behaviors are explored with diverse experiences in mind. If a school psychologist truly applies diversity in development and learning as a foundational principal of practice, then all decisions and actions by the school psychologist will address the multicultural needs of the changing population.

While NASP does not have specific guidelines for the provision of multicultural counseling in schools, another organization, the Association for Multicultural Counseling and Development, developed a basic set of multicultural competencies (Sue, Arredondo, & McDavis, 1992) that are directly applicable to school psychologists. The goals of the competencies are to address three areas: cultural self-awareness, awareness of the world view of the client, and culturally appropriate intervention strategies. These competencies are echoed and applied to the work of school psychologists by Jones (2009) as *multicultural intentionality*, that is, an approach to providing culturally responsive interventions in schools.

All of these standards are designed to cover the breadth of services provided by school psychologists. To assist with the implementation of the standards of practice, NASP has a wide range of resources to assist practicing school psychologists in moving toward culturally competent practice. There are a variety of downloadable papers and presentations on NASP's website (http://www.nasponline.org) that cover topics such as cultural competence in crisis response, trauma, consultation, and assessment.

The focus of this chapter addresses providing culturally responsive services to children and adolescents in schools, with special emphasis on integrating cultural factors in all interventions. Although the implied emphasis of the chapter is on service delivery to multicultural populations, school psychologists will find that having the skills necessary for success with multicultural groups will also enhance their ability to serve all children. Thus, this chapter has relevance to the everyday professional lives of school psychologists.

BASIC CONSIDERATIONS

According to Banks and McGee Banks (2004), culture includes shared ideas, symbols, values, and beliefs between members of a group. It can encompass any of the following categories: race, socioeconomic status, language, ethnicity, disability, sexual orientation, and religious/spiritual identity. Culture affects everything people think, do, and feel in a given day. Therefore, culture is the lens through which people view the world. *Cultural world view* is a term to describe expressions of commonality among a group of individuals who share a common concept of reality (Jenkins, 2006).

As school psychologists fulfill roles including evaluator, consultant to educational staff and parents, and provider of mental health interventions for students in need, they must be open and prepared for differences in world view from their own. School psychologists are faced with the challenge of not only understanding their own cultural world view (self-awareness) as it affects professional relationships and decisions, but also how the cultural world view of the child and family influences coping with stress. School psychologists must understand that the cultural world view of children and adolescents is formative and heavily influenced by the socialization provided by parents. Consequently, school psychologists cannot serve children and adolescents in isolation, nor can they use a color-blind approach (Bonilla-Silva, 2010) and view all children and adolescents as the same.

The term *multicultural* applies to "a confluence of three or more coexisting and unintegrated cultures (e.g., those that differ by age, gender, race, ethnicity, social class, or sexual orientation) each of which displays patterns of human behavior" (Oakland, 2005, p. 6). Behavior is guided by thinking and feeling, and the intergenerational transmission of the cultural world view sustains it. Sue and Sue (2007) affirmed that in multiculturalism, behavior can only be understood within the context that the behaviors exist. It honors human variation that occurs between and within groups. The term multicultural shall be used throughout this chapter to represent the potential incongruence between the multidimensional cultures of the student and the school psychologist as well as the interaction of the cultures in the intervention process.

Acculturation

Acculturation is a concept that is related to a person's individual cultural perspective. It is the process by which a person changes when he or she is influenced by contact with a different culture. Berry (2005) described four acculturation styles that can be applied to cross-cultural situations: assimilation, separation, integration, and marginalization. Assimilation is the response style where the person chooses to adopt the values and characteristics of the dominant or majority culture. The separation style is an approach where the person wishes to maintain his or her native cultural identity and rejects the values and norms of the majority culture. The integration acculturation style is the approach where a person adopts characteristics of the majority culture while also maintaining the values and norms of his or her native cultural identity. Finally, the marginalization style involves the person dissociating from both the majority culture as well as the native culture. The person prefers to identify himself or herself as unique and not connected with any particular group. Although it is beyond the scope of this chapter, it is notable that research studies have identified the marginalization style as the one associated with the highest levels of acculturative stress (Berry, 2005; Berry & Kim, 1988). Understanding acculturation styles provides school psychologists a window into the cultural adaptation of students of color in schools.

Preparation for School Psychologists

School psychologists' expertise begins with graduate-level preparation in psychological and educational assessment, consultation to staff and families, as well as interventions for children. In a more traditional model of school psychology practice, there has historically been heavier emphasis on psychological assessment as the primary mode of service delivery. Given this history, the research literature for school psychologists has focused more on assessment and less on interventions. Regardless, providing direct and indirect interventions for students is an important part of the profession that warrants attention.

Intervention Competence

School psychology graduate programs typically include coursework that covers child psychopathology, child development, emotional and behavioral assessment and intervention, multicultural issues, and formal practicum experiences in interventions for children. Microskills such as reflection and summarization as well as techniques for demonstrating empathy through problem solving are included in the practicum courses. Through these experiences, graduate students develop a professional interpersonal awareness that is grounded in theory. Graduate students learn empirically supported intervention approaches in the context of psychopathology and disorders and how to manage behaviors through communication and behavior modification techniques. Typically, in separate or more specialized coursework, graduate students begin to learn about cultural competence and are expected to integrate issues

of culture into their current level of understanding of interventions.

Cultural Competence

Cultural competence, on the other hand, is formed through specific experiences that emphasize cultural self-awareness as well as multicultural experiences with students and peers. According to Lynch and Hanson (2004), cultural competence is a process and includes the ability to "think, feel, and act in ways that acknowledge, respect, and build on ethnic, sociocultural, and linguistic diversity" (p. 43). Cultural competence includes intra-personal awareness, or understanding one's own personal world view, as well as awareness and sensitivity to the world view of others. Graduate programs must provide experiences for candidates to evaluate themselves, develop an understanding of their own cultural lens, learn more about the world views of others, and develop an ability to integrate individual differences into their cultural world view (Constantine, 2002; Pedersen & Carey, 2003; Reynolds, 1999; Sue & Sue, 2007). Both intervention skills and cultural competence are the foundational skills for providing culturally responsive services in schools.

BEST PRACTICES IN PROVIDING CULTURALLY RESPONSIVE INTERVENTIONS IN SCHOOLS

The school psychologist with skills in providing culturally responsive interventions has the ability to work with students through a cultural frame of reference, to recognize the complexity of culture, and to incorporate individual differences during intervention planning. Ivey, D'Andrea, and Ivey's (2012) theory of multicultural counseling and therapy includes an integrative perspective of theoretical orientations where the focus is on the individual in the context of family as well as culture. This theory is easily applied to the school setting since students can be viewed in the context of the family culture as well as the school culture. This approach requires the school psychologist to assess the combined influences of society, social justice, race, ethnicity, gender, and other cultural factors on the development of the child or adolescent.

School psychologists who use this culturally responsive approach develop their skills by having a strong sense of cultural self-awareness, an acute understanding of other cultures, and the tenacity to adapt interventions to the individual needs of the student. The combined forces of cultural self-awareness, cultural literacy, and individualized adaptations ultimately lead to multicultural interventions that are provided with multicultural intentionality (Jones, 2009).

Build Cultural Self-Awareness

Self-awareness is one of the initial components of developing cross-cultural competence. This self-awareness influences the school psychologist's ability to work with all children. Monitoring intrapersonal cultural awareness is an ongoing process and requires intentional thinking (Reynolds, 1999). Sue and Sue (2007) indicate the importance of being aware of assumptions, values, and biases toward others. These biases can be related to race, ethnicity, socioeconomic status, family status, sexual orientation, or any other human-related context. The NASP Practice Model (NASP, 2010) echoes the necessity of self-evaluation. "School psychologists recognize in themselves and others the subtle racial, class, gender, cultural, and other biases they may bring to their work and the way these biases influence decision-making, instruction, behavior, and long-term outcomes for students" (p. 8).

Every individual has some form of bias, and those who are aware of their biases are the most skilled at serving the public. School psychologists may develop in this area by using journaling as a technique for self-reflection. The journal might include personal reactions toward others that may affect interventions. Another approach is to form multicultural consulting groups (e.g., workgroups, consultation meetings, or even ongoing dialogue through Listserv communication) with colleagues to engage in regular dialogue about multicultural factors. At a minimum, school psychologists should develop a list of professionals they may contact for consultation on multicultural issues. These consultations can include discussion about cultural factors that may influence an intervention, and based on the consultation, revisions to an intervention plan may occur.

Other structured approaches to self-awareness analysis are also available. Several other scales were developed to assist school psychologists in evaluating their level of self-awareness. For example, Rogers and Ponterotto (1997) developed a scale for school psychologist graduate programs to evaluate competence of candidates. This scale, the Multicultural School Psychology Counseling Competency Scale, consists of 11 items with broad questions to assess various levels of proficiency in self-awareness, other awareness, comfort with racial differences, understanding of the sociopolitical

consequences of minority status, and communication styles. Although the scale was designed for use by graduate programs, school psychologists may also review the questions and rate themselves on the same domains.

Even more pertinent to school psychology practitioners is the self-assessment checklist adopted by NASP. The Self-Assessment Checklist for Personnel Providing Services and Supports to Children and Their Families (Goode, 2002) includes 33 questions that provoke cognitive awareness of the values and practices that foster an environment for culturally competent practice. The checklist includes items in the following domains: physical environment, materials, and resources; communication styles; and values and attitudes. This checklist is particularly unique because it also includes attention to the nonverbal and environmental cues that school psychologists convey in their office. For example, a statement on the checklist might encourage a school psychologist to consider whether his or her office environment is reflective of different cultures, particularly those members of cultures who attend the school. Similarly, items remind the school psychologists to consider whether the materials used (e.g., storybooks, games, puppets, dolls) are reflective of the ethnic background of the children and families served.

Strengthen Cultural Literacy

Sue and Sue (2007) stress the importance of increasing cultural literacy. This includes learning more about specific norms within a culture so that school psychologists may develop a better understanding of the world view of culturally diverse clients. The process of strengthening cultural literacy occurs simultaneously with increasing cultural self-awareness. For example, the psychologist might ask, "How are my beliefs affecting my relationship with _____?" while also asking, "I have never known anyone of _____ ethnicity (the ethnicity of a new referral). How will I address my lack of cultural literacy about this group?" Sue and Sue (2007) and Paniagua (2005) both provide chapters to assist readers in increasing cultural literacy for African Americans, Native Americans, Asian Americans, and Hispanic/Latino Americans.

Communication style is a form of cultural literacy. School psychologists should be aware of the communication style of the student and family as well as the potential of a mismatch with their own communication style. Cultural literacy also includes staying current in the literature so that the political and social dynamics that affect the cultural norms within a particular group can be understood (Canino & Spurlock, 2000). School psychologists should have a strong awareness of appropriate language to use when referencing a group (e.g., African American versus Negro or colored). Similarly, identifying a person by referencing his or her skin color (e.g., Black or White) may be offensive to some, but preferred by another. To know what is most appropriate, a school psychologist should listen for cultural cues and have open dialogue with the school community about cultural factors and preferences.

Cultural literacy also includes developing understanding of the historical experiences that affect the world view of the client's group. Greater awareness of the social, political, and historical challenges that fall in line with group membership increases the school psychologist's ability to understand the cultural world view of the child and the family. Similarly, gaining understanding about the child's cultural literacy (e.g., the connection between cultural identity development and the child's awareness of how multicultural issues affect his or her life) is also essential. Younger children may not be able to articulate cultural values and the impact on their behavior and emotions without direct prompting. Thus, for example, a school psychologist may state, "Cultural issues are really not an issue for this child. The child said she doesn't think it makes a difference." However, this conclusion may better reflect the school psychologist's desire to avoid discussing issues of oppression and racism. Historically, media (e.g., fashion magazines, television commercials, toys) have primarily included imagery that implied that the norms of dominant society are desirable and differences are not necessarily celebrated. Children with these exposures and those who are "one of few" in a school setting may adopt a preferred orientation of sameness in order to fit in. Therefore, they would be less likely to describe cultural values that differ from the dominant culture unless prompted to do so. Without direct inquiry or prompting, the impact of culture will be unrecognized by the novice school psychologist.

By increasing cultural literacy about a particular cultural group, school psychologists may gain insight into the child and family views toward mental health supports and interventions. They will also learn about common approaches to healing that are considered the first stop for getting help within the cultural group. Gaining an understanding about culturally acceptable forms of assistance, the school psychologist can also learn the expectations of the child and family. Further, increasing cultural literacy enables the school

psychologist to recognize that some common theories of psychotherapy have historically reflected a host of biased values and beliefs that are not universal. For example, there were culture-bound syndromes identified in the Appendix of the *Diagnostic and Statistical Manual of Mental Disorders* (4th ed., text rev.; American Psychiatric Association, 2000) that should be considered as differential diagnoses. For example, *amok* is a dissociative episode common to Malaysia while *ataque de nervios* is an idiom of distress that is recognized by Latin Americans. By overlooking the fact that culture-bound syndromes exist, the school psychologist is less likely to develop a strong working rapport with the child and family because the school psychologist is unable to understand the family's interpretation of the symptoms. In the newest edition of the *Diagnostic and Statistical Manual of Mental Disorders*, cultural literacy is not just an add-on consideration. In fact, the Cultural Formulation Interview has been added to guide mental health providers in making diagnostic decisions in the context of culture (American Psychiatric Association, 2013). Thus, increasing cultural literacy is now formally recognized as a key component of providing mental health services to all populations.

Practice With Multicultural Intentionality

School psychologists with multicultural intentionality have the ability to generate culturally responsive solutions to problems using different points of view. They are also able to communicate by looking at the child through a cultural lens and taking into account a variety of diverse groups as well as the complex interaction of the child's culture and their own. Both the child and the school psychologist must have the opportunity to communicate within their own culture and learn how to understand other cultures (Ivey et al., 2012). School psychologists with multicultural intentionality can also formulate intervention plans that consider a range of options that exist within a culture and act upon those options. For example, when a child or adolescent becomes stuck in a pattern of the same behavior and responses to situations, the school psychologist with multicultural intentionality is able to consider the cultural world view of the child (or adolescent) that influences the behavior and then develop plans that may be effective within the context of the cultural world view. School psychologists with multicultural intentionality will be aware of the trends and have the ability to explore these issues in an intentional clinical interview (Ivey et al., 2012).

Apply Culturally Responsive Microskills

Basic counseling skills, also referred to as microskills (Ivey, Pedersen, & Ivey, 2001), are the foundation for mental health interventions. Microskills include the use of attending skills and influencing skills as well as the integration of the microskills into a particular theoretical orientation. Attending skills involve the use of open-ended questions, paraphrasing, encouraging, reflection of feeling, and summarization. These skills facilitate the development of a positive rapport (or relationship) between the school psychologist and the student. Influencing skills involve more advanced listening techniques including reframing, being directive, giving feedback, applying logical consequences, and knowing when to therapeutically use self-disclosure.

While microskills are developed with practice, it is essential that school psychologists adjust the use of microskills to complement the cultural experience of the student and family. Graduate programs often teach school psychologists to use attending skills such as paraphrasing and reflection of feeling as a way of building rapport. However, without an understanding of cultural norms, the school psychologist may apply the skill in a way that exacerbates a cultural mismatch with the student and/or his or her family. For example, the help-seeking behavior of some ethnic minority cultures includes a desire for direction and advice, even before a solid relationship is established (Paniagua, 2005). If the school psychologist applies microskills that emphasize reflection of feeling and paraphrasing, then the student or family may interpret that the school psychologist cannot help them because the school psychologist did not tell them what to do. Rather, a collaborative communication style using questions like "How can 'we' work together to solve the difficulties you are experiencing?" or "Who else in your community would you like to have support you in solving this problem?" are much more culturally responsive than reflecting back a problem or concern. Thus, subtle, yet nuanced adaptations in microskills are necessary when working with multicultural populations.

Intentional Multicultural Interviews

While there are numerous options available for school psychologists to use for collecting background information on students, very few guide in collecting information within the context of cultural mores and values. As a result, some techniques have been developed that are designed to assist school psychologists in altering their clinical interviews to be culturally responsive.

Hardy and Laszloffy (1995) originally developed the concept of creating a "cultural genogram." They enhanced the method for constructing traditional genograms (McGoldrick, Gerson, & Petry, 2008) by adding interview questions to assist the school psychologist in gathering information about cultural issues. For example, "Under what conditions did your family/ancestors enter the United States?" and "What has been your experience with racism and oppression and how does your family respond to it?" Similarly, Ivey et al. (2012) use a technique of completing a "community genogram" as a strengths-oriented approach to viewing the self within the context of the community. This genogram can assist the school psychologist in identifying the important groups that influence the everyday lives of the child and family. The goal of the community genogram is similar to the traditional genogram in that it provides a visual image of the child within the family system. However, the community genogram adds the dimension of community relationships (church, school, neighborhood) and encourages the discussion of how the community influences the everyday decisions of the child and family. Drawing the symbols in the genogram is a useful technique for generating perceptions from the child or family and encouraging either the child or family to organize relationships in ways that are familiar. The goal is for cultural context to emerge in the visual representation and in the verbal communication, setting the stage for open discussion about multicultural issues.

Another approach to conducting intentional interviews is using the RESPECTFUL model (Ivey et al., 2012). RESPECTFUL is an acronym for the dimensions that may relate to issues presented in multicultural treatment. The multicultural issues represented in the acronym are: religion/spirituality, economic class, sexual identity, psychological maturity, ethnic/racial identity, chronological challenges, trauma, family history, unique physical characteristics, and language and location of residence. This model encourages the exploration of these potential multicultural issues in the context of locus of control and level of cultural identity development. Similarly, ADDRESSING (Hays, 2006) is another framework to guide mental health professionals in learning the complex cultural factors that govern the behavior of an individual. Much like the RESPECTFUL model, ADDRESSING is an acronym for the following variables: age/generational, developmental, disability, religion/spirituality, ethnic/racial identity, socioeconomic status, sexual orientation, indigenous heritage, national origin, gender. They apply all of these variables to minority groups and relationships with people.

Assessing Acculturation Through the Multicultural Interview

The aforementioned approaches all provide an infrastructure for conducting culturally responsive interviews, but they do not help guide school psychologists in *how* to collect the information needed as they relate to cultural norms. Too often, mental health professionals jump directly into problem solving instead of examining family history and learning more about the underlying perspectives of the child or adolescent and the family. The Jones Intentional Multicultural Interview Schedule was developed to help prepare school psychologists to complete multicultural interviews (Jones, 2009). This interview method includes questions that facilitate discussion of cultural issues as they relate to stress and coping with children and adolescents. By asking multicultural questions while also completing a community genogram and/or cultural genogram, the school psychologist will collect relevant cultural information about the family within the cultural context. Table 4.1 shows the application of the Jones Intentional Multicultural Interview Schedule within the domains of Hays' (2006) ADDRESSING framework. School psychologists can use this method to begin the process of assessing acculturation.

Assessing acculturation is a nuanced process that involves recognizing the aspects of culture that may be risk or protective factors. The multicultural interview questions are designed to target those variables in an open-ended fashion that is nonthreatening while also showing the student that the school psychologist understands the importance of these cultural factors in their everyday life experience.

Case Example: Amina

Amina is a 9-year-old girl in the fourth grade at an elementary school in a large urban area. Amina's teacher approached the school psychologist and expressed concerns about Amina's frequent mood swings. Some days Amina is gregarious and an active participant in lessons at school. Other days she is withdrawn, irritable, and annoyed when she does not get what she wants. The teacher hopes that the school psychologist can determine what causes Amina to have mood swings and also give recommendations on how to keep her engaged in the classroom.

Preparing for the Interview

Prior to making contact with Amina's family, the school psychologist spent time organizing the information gathered about Amina's community. The school psychologist is aware that Amina's family emigrated from Eritrea when Amina was in the first grade. Amina has two brothers who attend the school, one in the sixth grade and the other in kindergarten. Based on the school psychologist's experiences with Eritrean families, the school psychologist was aware that many Eritrean families speak Tigrinya while others may speak Arabic, Amharic, or Italian in addition to English. To gain additional insight into the cultural values of the family, the school psychologist researched the meaning of Amina's name and learned that Amina means "trustful" and Medhane means "medicine." The school psychologist reviewed Amina's student record and learned that her family speaks Tigrinya, Amharic, and English. The school psychologist sought the names of two interpreters (one male, one female) who speak Tigrinya in case they are needed for the consultation meeting. When the school psychologist selected one interpreter from each gender, the school psychologist was using a background knowledge of Eritrean culture that indicates a preference for the same-gender provider when working with interpreters and other health professionals.

Multicultural Interview

The school psychologist completed the interview without the use of an interpreter since Amina's mother told the school psychologist by phone that she, Amina's mother, and her husband would attend the meeting together and are comfortable communicating fully in English. To accommodate both parents, the consultation occurred at Amina's home after school. This opportunity was advantageous as the school psychologist not only was able to ask about cultural factors and beliefs, but also was able to observe the interactions among the family members. The school psychologist organized the multicultural interview schedule questions by the ADDRESSING framework (see Table 4.1) and adapted the items to generate responses from the adult perspective.

Summary of Cultural Factors Learned

Amina lives in a household with three generations of immediate family as well as extended family. She not only has the two siblings that attend the school, but she also has twin brothers who are 2 years old. Amina is the only female child in the household with four siblings and two cousins. They are active members of the Eritrean

Table 4.1. ADDRESSING Framework and the Jones Intentional Multicultural Interview Schedule

ADDRESSING Framework Cultural Influences	Application to Minority Groups	Sample Questions From the Jones Intentional Multicultural Interview Schedule
Age/generational	Children, adolescents, elders	How do you define family? Who is in your family? Who lives in your home? What do your family members call you? Where were you born? Where does most of your family live now? Who makes the decisions about your daily care (e.g., transportation, food, discipline)?
Developmental disabilities Disabilities acquired	Developmental disabilities or acquired disabilities	What are some challenges that you or your family members have to deal with? Tell me what you think about school. What emotions come to mind when you think about your schoolwork?
Religion and spirituality	Religious minority cultures	How does your family deal with feelings? What are some coping strategies that they use? How do religion and spirituality affect your family? Who do you turn to when you are sad, scared, or worried about something?
Ethnic and racial identity	Ethnic and racial minority cultures	What does your family think about counseling? What do you think about it? What are some things about your family that few people know? How do you describe yourself in terms of your race? How does your race affect your relationships with other people? What issues to you have with hair and/or skin color? What experiences do you have with racial conflict? Who supports you the most at school? At home?
Socioeconomic status	Class status (education, income, rural)	If you were to choose a job today, what would it be? Would your family approve of this job? What would your family prefer for you to do when you grow up? What is a job you would like to do but would never choose it?
Sexual orientation	Gay, lesbian, bisexual people	What are some characteristics about you that make you similar or different from people in your peer group? Is there a label that your peers use to describe groups of kids at your school? Which label best identifies your group?
Indigenous heritage	Indigenous/aboriginal/native people	What are some rituals/routines that your family does daily? Which are used to cope with stress? What situations are most stressful for you?
National origin	Refugees, immigrants, international	How and when did your family arrive in the United States? What were the circumstances of your family's arrival?
Gender	Women, transgender people	When there is conflict with peers at school, what is the usual cause? What are some characteristics about you that make you different from people in your peer group? What do you believe are the responsibilities of women or men?

Note. From "Counseling With Multicultural Intentionality: The Process of Counseling and Integrating Client Cultural Variables," by J. M. Jones, in *The Psychology of Multiculturalism in the Schools: A Primer for Practice, Training, and Research* (pp. 191–213), edited by J. M. Jones, 2009, Bethesda, MD: National Association of School Psychologists. Copyright 2009 by National Association of School Psychologists. Adapted with permission. See Hays (2006) for a more comprehensive description of the ADDRESSING framework.

community and her father is an elder in the Coptic Christian Church. The family believes that Amina should be fluent in Tigrinya and use the language in as many situations as possible. Amina is from an educated family. Her father is an international trade dealer and travels to the Horn of Africa at least once per month. Members of Amina's family place a high value on developing and maintaining Eritrean culture in their children. When Amina's father is at home, Amina is expected to actively engage in traditional Eritrean gender roles (household tasks), but when her father is out of the country, her mother, grandmother, and aunt take responsibility for all household duties. Amina wishes to speak English at all times and will respond to her parents using English rather than Tigrinya. This is a source of tension in the home. At school, Amina has a large group of friends, and she complained that she rarely socializes with friends outside of school. Her parents confirmed this and said, "There is only time to study and pray." The value of an education was reinforced numerous times during the interview.

Analysis of Acculturation

Amina's family interview highlights a common situation for multigenerational immigrant families: The younger generation adopts an assimilation style of acculturation while the elders are applying a separation style of acculturation. At school, Amina interacts in a way that is more consistent with American culture (e.g., speaking English even at home, resisting traditional gender roles). She may be experiencing a lot of pressure from home to adhere to cultural practices and participate in Eritrean traditions, particularly when her father is at home. In meetings with Amina, the school psychologist will need to complete the multicultural interview and cultural genogram with Amina to determine if these are the salient issues for Amina. Once the school psychologist gains insight from Amina, a plan for intervention can be developed.

By using multicultural interviewing techniques to assess acculturation, school psychologists set the tone for open discussions on sensitive cultural variables such as ethnicity, race, and the dynamics associated with cross-cultural conflict. Simultaneously, school psychologists will gather insight into the values and norms of the child's home culture. This provides a more complete picture of the socioemotional factors that may hinder a

student's educational progress. Thus, this comprehensive approach facilitates the development of interventions that are most appropriate for the student and the cultural context.

Forming Interventions Based on Acculturation Style

Once the school psychologist has a sense of acculturation style, interventions can be shaped to address the needs of the student within the context of his or her cultural experience. Interventions need to be adapted to match the acculturation style so that outcomes are more likely to be successful. Figure 4.1 includes the four acculturation styles and potential foci of intervention based on the challenges that each style presents. Students operating under the integration style may have a complex set of issues that they are dealing with, including challenging family values, navigating multiple types of peer relationships, and cultural collisions, situations where they do not know how to act because multiple cultures are interacting simultaneously. Students applying the separation style may need interventions to focus solely on cultural factors. They may need to address cultural conflicts in peer relationships because their way of interaction may not be socially acceptable within the dominant culture. With the assimilation style, students may strive for matching the dominant cultural norms and behave in a way that causes them to experience rejection from racially similar peers. On the other hand, the isolation associated with the marginalization style may be the factor that draws students to seek support from the school psychologist.

Figure 4.1. Acculturation Style and Potential Intervention Foci

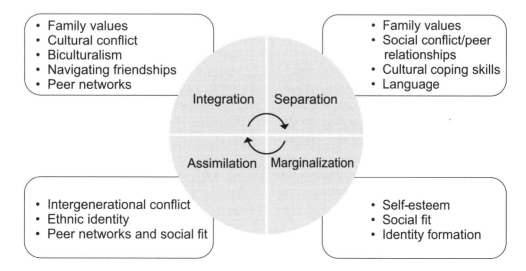

Interventions may need to focus on the emotions associated with feeling different, feeling socially isolated, and searching for identity. Thus, acculturation style can be used to guide school psychologists in intervention planning and implementation (Canino & Spurlock, 2000; Jones, 2009).

There are two factors that have risen in the literature as crucial to culturally responsive care: integrating family into interventions and applying a strengths-based approach to interventions. The amount of integration is directly related to acculturation style. Styles that have a higher emphasis on native cultural values (e.g., separation and integration) require higher levels of family involvement and analysis of cultural strengths.

Involving Families

Involving the family in the intervention process is often difficult when providing services in the school setting. If family members are not easily accessible, school psychologists are forced to collect information from the student's file and directly from the student once parental consent is obtained. Because services are provided in the school setting, it is not uncommon for school psychologists to offer direct interventions (such as counseling) to students and to have little or no involvement of the parents. This is *not* the best practice when providing culturally responsive services.

Integrating the family into the intervention process is necessary to foster systemic change in the child or adolescent. At least one family member should be active in the process of determining needs, developing an intervention plan, and implementing interventions at home. If family members are perceived as necessary collaborators in the process, then significant efforts are more likely to be made to foster involvement in the intervention process. School psychologists need to have a broad perspective and use creativity to make intervention planning accessible to the family. Creative approaches to involving the family include being open to home visits, evening phone calls, e-mail, and lunch meetings. When the family is a partner in the intervention process, the school psychologist will also have an enhanced ability to support specific family needs rather than taking a general approach to intervention.

The questions from the intentional multicultural interview may be adapted to suit the adult members of the family as well. For example, What is the best way to communicate with your family? How does your child communicate needs and feelings at home? What is the best way to make your child feel comfortable? What are your child's strengths? What are your concerns for your child? What are some of the factors that affect your child's learning and/or ability to get along with peers? How do issues of race affect your family? Following this line of questioning will foster a relationship with the parent that reflects recognition that the family's culture and immediate environment are important variables for the intervention.

Strengths-Based Care

School psychologists with multicultural intentionality think from a strengths perspective rather than solely based on diagnosis. Traditionally, they use problem-solving techniques to find the problem, diagnose the problem, and treat the problem. Interventions often fall short when a Eurocentric paradigm is used to develop and implement solutions. For example, some school psychologists rigidly adhere to separating church and state when serving children in schools. When serving families of color, the school psychologist may overlook the fact that spirituality and faith may be a primary source of support for that family and child. By learning about and exploring the strengths within a given culture, school psychologists are more prepared to serve children and families within the cultural framework. By using intentional multicultural interviews and other multicultural techniques, the school psychologist learns what supports are currently working, who is involved with providing support, and how to facilitate growth within the culture and the support network.

SUMMARY

This chapter presents best practices in providing culturally responsive interventions for children and adolescents in schools. Statistically, school psychologists are overwhelmingly from Eurocentric backgrounds while the demographics of the United States are changing to be increasingly diverse. Multiculturalism reflects the current and future status of schools, and school psychologists must serve all children appropriately. NASP and other mental health organizations have developed standards of practice to assist school psychologists in understanding the factors that go into providing multicultural services, but very little structure is given to the process of engaging in such a relationship.

By engaging in the techniques described in this chapter, school psychologists will have greater self-awareness, a better understanding of the cultural characteristics of groups, and an increased likelihood of successful interventions and support in the context of

Table 4.2. Best Practice Tips for School Psychologists Providing Culturally Responsive Interventions

- Continue exploring your own culture, beliefs, and values.
- Believe that you can serve individuals of a different race or ethnicity.
- Develop a list of professionals for consultation on multicultural issues.
- Engage in dialogue with colleagues and continue to increase cultural literacy.
- Complete intentional multicultural interviews.
- Always work with the child or adolescent systemically.
- Learn more about the culture of the child through the child and family.
- Alter your microskills based on the cultural norms and behaviors of the child and family.
- Assume that there is heterogeneity within an ethnic group but that the foundation of cultural values is likely to be homogenous.
- Have awareness of culture-bound syndromes and of the meaning of the behaviors or symptoms to the student and the family.
- Keep the family active in the intervention planning and progress monitoring.
- Work from a strengths-based perspective.
- Continue exploring multicultural issues throughout the intervention process.
- Assess acculturation and focus interventions around the student's acculturation style.

Note. From "Best Practices in Multicultural Counseling," by J. M. Jones, in *Best Practices in School Psychology V* (pp. 1771–1783), edited by A. Thomas and J. Grimes, 2008, Bethesda, MD: National Association of School Psychologists. Copyright 2008 by National Association of School Psychologists. Adapted with permission.

the student's culture. This chapter offers techniques for developing multicultural intentionality, including assessing acculturation and incorporating family, culture, and values into strengths-based interventions. School psychologists can use these methods to develop better self-awareness, increase cultural literacy, and practice multicultural intentionality in all aspects of their work in schools. Table 4.2 summarizes some of the best practices presented in this chapter.

School psychologists must recognize that increasing competence in multicultural service delivery is a process. The process occurs along with experience and does not end with preparation in a graduate program. School psychologists should have a strong multicultural emphasis in all services and should focus on the ability to integrate individual cultural differences into interventions with multicultural populations. This skill is best formulated through experiences with children from a range of cultures and ethnicities. The more exposure school psychologists have to other cultures, the more culturally savvy they will be.

AUTHOR NOTE

Disclosure. Janine Jones has a financial interest in books she authored or coauthored referenced in this chapter.

REFERENCES

American Psychiatric Association. (2000). *Diagnostic and statistical manual of mental disorders* (4th ed., text rev.). Washington, DC: Author.

American Psychiatric Association. (2013). *Diagnostic and statistical manual of mental disorders* (5th ed.). Washington, DC: Author.

Banks, J. A., & McGee Banks, C. A. (Eds.). (2004). *Multicultural education: Issues and perspectives* (5th ed.). Hoboken, NJ: Wiley.

Berry, J. W. (2005). Acculturation: Living successfully in two cultures. *International Journal of Intercultural Relations, 29,* 697–712.

Berry, J. W., & Kim, L. (1988). Acculturation and mental health. In P. R. Dasen, J. W. Berry, & N. Sartorius (Eds.), *Health and cross-cultural psychology: Towards applications.* (pp. 207–238). Newbury Park, CA: SAGE.

Bonilla-Silva, E. (2010). *Racism without racists: Color-blind racism and the persistence of racial inequality in the United States* (3rd ed.). Lanham, MD: Rowman & Littlefield.

Canino, I. A., & Spurlock, J. (2000). *Culturally diverse children and adolescents* (2nd ed.). New York, NY: Guilford Press.

Constantine, M. G. (2002). Racism attitudes, White racial identity attitudes, and multicultural counseling competence in school counselor trainees. *Counselor Education and Supervision, 41,* 162–174.

Curtis, M. J., Castillo, J. M., & Gelley, C. (2012). School psychology 2010: Demographics, employment, and the context for professional practices—Part I. *Communiqué, 40*(7), 1, 28–30.

Curtis, M. J., Lopez, A. D., Batsche, G. M., & Smith, J. C. (2006, March). *School psychology 2005: A national perspective.* Paper presented at the annual meeting of the National Association of School Psychologists, Anaheim, CA

Goode, T. D. (2002). *Promoting cultural diversity and cultural competency: Self-assessment checklist for personnel providing services and supports to children and their families.* Bethesda, MD: National Association of School Psychologists. Retrieved from http://www.nasponline.org/resources/culturalcompetence/checklist.aspx

Hardy, K., & Laszloffy, T. (1995). The cultural genogram: Key to training culturally competent family therapists. *Journal of Marital and Family Therapy, 21,* 227–237.

Hays, P. A. (2006). Introduction: Developing culturally responsive cognitive-behavioral therapies. In P. A. Hays & G. Y. Iwamasa (Eds.), *Culturally responsive cognitive-behavioral therapy: Assessment, practice, and supervision.* (pp. 3–19). Washington, DC: American Psychological Association.

Ivey, A. E., D'Andrea, M. J., & Ivey, M. B. (2012). *Theories of counseling and psychotherapy: A multicultural perspective* (7th ed.). Thousand Oaks, CA: SAGE.

Ivey, A. E., Pedersen, P. B., & Ivey, M. B. (2001). *Intentional group counseling: A microskills approach.* Belmont, CA: Brooks/Cole.

Jenkins, O. B. (2006). *What is world view?* Retrieved from http://orvillejenkins.com/world view/worldvwhat.html

Jones, J. M. (2008). Best practices in multicultural counseling. In A. Thomas & J. Grimes (Eds.), *Best practices in school psychology V.* (pp. 1771–1783). Bethesda, MD: National Association of School Psychologists.

Jones, J. M. (2009). Counseling with multicultural intentionality: The process of counseling and integrating client cultural variables. In J. M. Jones (Ed.), *The psychology of multiculturalism in the schools: A primer for practice, training, and research.* (pp. 191–213). Bethesda, MD: National Association of School Psychologists.

Loe, S. A., & Miranda, M. H. (2005). An examination of ethnic incongruence in school-based psychological services and diversity training experiences among school psychologists. *Psychology in the Schools, 42,* 419–432.

Lynch, E. W., & Hanson, M. J. (2004). *Developing cross-cultural competence: A guide for working with children and their families* (3rd ed.). Baltimore, MD: Brookes.

McGoldrick, M., Gerson, R., & Petry, S. (2008). *Genograms: Assessment and intervention* (3rd ed.). New York, NY: Norton.

National Association of School Psychologists. (2010). *Model for comprehensive and integrated school psychological services.* Bethesda, MD: Author. Retrieved from http://www.nasponline.org/standards/2010standards/2_PracticeModel.pdf

Oakland, T. (2005). Commentary 1: What is multicultural school psychology? In C. L. Frisby & C. R. Reynolds (Eds.), *Comprehensive handbook of multicultural school psychology.* (pp. 3–13). Hoboken, NJ: Wiley.

Paniagua, F. A. (2005). *Assessing and treating culturally diverse clients: A practical guide* (3rd ed.). Thousand Oaks, CA: SAGE.

Pedersen, P. B., & Carey, J. C. (2003). *Multicultural counseling in the schools: A practical handbook.* Boston, MA: Pearson.

Reynolds, A. L. (1999). Working with children and adolescents in the schools: Multicultural counseling implications. In R. H. Sheets & E. R. Hollins (Eds.), *Racial and ethnic identity in school practices: Aspects of human development.* Mahwah, NJ: Erlbaum.

Rogers, M. R., & Ponterotto, J. G. (1997). Development of the multicultural school psychology counseling competency scale. *Psychology in the Schools, 34,* 211–217.

Sue, D., Arredondo, P., & McDavis, R. (1992). Multicultural counseling competencies and standards: A call to the profession. *Journal of Multicultural Counseling and Development, 20,* 64–88.

Sue, D. W., & Sue, D. (2007). *Counseling the culturally diverse: Theory and practice* (5th ed.). Hoboken, NJ: Wiley.

5

Best Practices in Nondiscriminatory Assessment

Samuel O. Ortiz
St. John's University (NY)

OVERVIEW

Nondiscriminatory assessment is an aspirational goal in evaluation that seeks to generate reliable and valid data that support conclusions that are as unbiased, equitable, and fair as possible. So defined, nondiscriminatory assessment applies to all individuals and in all cases where evaluation is conducted, irrespective of the characteristics of the examinee, particularly those most often associated with diversity (e.g., race, ethnicity). There remains a natural tendency in the evaluation process to view nondiscriminatory assessment as a concern that arises only when the examinee displays some form of diversity that merits special attention. For example, when it becomes known that an individual hails from a culture outside the United States or speaks a language other than English, evaluators must attend to the potential impact such factors may have on data collection efforts and the meaning that may be assigned to information gathered in the course of the assessment.

While it may be true to some extent that characteristics of diversity are clear indicators that the process of evaluation must now consider factors that are not ordinarily considered, what constitutes diversity and the variables that have the potential to affect data collection and interpretation efforts extend well beyond those related to skin color or country of origin. Rather, diversity should rightly be viewed as encompassing any individual for whom differences in general life and developmental experiences are sufficiently different from the individuals against whom comparisons are to be made.

In short, nondiscriminatory assessment is simply fair and equitable assessment, irrespective of the individual being evaluated, which adopts a process that dutifully considers all factors that may influence the meaning assigned to any collected data. The only difference between what might be called "typical" assessment practices and those that constitute "nondiscriminatory" assessment practices is that in some cases there are simply more relevant variables at play that thereby merit increased and deliberate attention on the part of the evaluator as compared to what might be needed in cases where few such variables are present.

When defined in this manner, nondiscriminatory assessment becomes a set of skills that should be contained in the repertoire of all school psychologists, not merely those who might characterize themselves as diverse or bilingual. This notion is reinforced in the National Association of School Psychologists (NASP) *Model for Comprehensive and Integrated School Psychological Services* (NASP, 2010), where knowledge regarding diversity in development and learning forms one of the three main foundational domains upon which all aspects of service delivery are built, including both direct and indirect services across all levels or tiers of service, such as individual students, groups of children, their families, and even their schools and communities. This chapter focuses on school psychologists' effective and competent management of any issue of diversity within the context of assessment and application of a systematic, comprehensive nondiscriminatory framework that is integrated within any of the general problem-solving activities of school psychology practice.

At its core, nondiscriminatory assessment is about reducing potential bias, ensuring equity in the evaluation process, and establishing fairness that extends across the evaluation to include outcomes. Although these terms are often used interchangeably, they are not synonymous and speak to various aspects of evaluation and refer to specific issues.

Equity is a general term applied in assessment that refers to efforts designed to ensure that all individuals are treated in an equivalent manner throughout the course of an evaluation. For example, all things being equal, tests that are used for a specific purpose with members of one group should be used for that same purpose with members of other groups. Likewise, unless other factors warrant it, the amount of time spent on the evaluation should not differ as a function of the individual's race or ethnicity. Equity thus refers primarily to the way individuals are treated as well as the nature of the interactions these individuals encounter in the evaluation process.

Although it is often applied in much the same way as equity, fairness extends further in the assessment framework and is most often related to the decisions and outcomes that emanate from evaluation. In particular, whenever evaluations for one group lead to decisions or outcomes that are different from those made for other groups, solely on the basis of irrelevant differences (e.g., appearance, parental socioeconomic status), fairness becomes a central issue. If such outcomes prove to be more detrimental for one group than the other, then the negative consequences are seen as a lack of fairness in the broader assessment process. Whereas it is recognized that outcomes may vary and that individuals with different types of issues evaluated for different purposes should not lead to similar outcomes, the variation in outcome cannot adversely affect one group versus another on the basis of factors irrelevant to the decision. Otherwise it is not fair.

Equity and fairness are issues that relate primarily to the ethical responsibilities of evaluators. Although these issues are not fully within the control of all evaluators, since it must be recognized that decisions that may lead to unfair outcomes are not always at the discretion of the evaluator, they are nevertheless expected goals within the scope of practice, and all efforts to ensure both remain incumbent upon all school psychologists in the process of assessment. However, the most significant source of difficulty in nondiscriminatory assessment is likely to rise from the use of tests and other measurement techniques within the assessment process.

Unlike equity and fairness, bias is generally a term reserved for examination of the psychometric properties of tests and the degree to which those properties may be altered systematically when used with one group versus another group that differs on some specific characteristic. Examinations of bias typically look at such things as item content. For example, do certain items result in a significant change in the reliability of a scale as a function of their being more familiar to members of one race versus another? Similarly, the question may be asked again relative to the sequence of the items; that is, does the order of difficulty of items on a test change when administered to one population versus another? Most often, however, investigations of bias have tended to center on whether the factorial structure of the test remains invariant across groups and whether the test's predictive power (e.g., predicting academic achievement) changes as a function of group membership.

Despite a history of fierce debate on such issues, and the prevailing belief in the field and public perception, there has been surprisingly little evidence that, when defined in this manner, tests demonstrate bias (Reynolds & Carson, 2005). This does not, however, mean that tests are not biased toward some individuals or groups. Rather, it suggests that bias cannot be understood by elements related solely or primarily to reliability but must be extended to better include the concept of validity. A test that is reliable is not automatically valid, and high reliability is not a guarantee of validity. A test may yield very accurate and consistent measurements, predict without fail, and result in equivalent associations and correlations between its subcomponents for all groups, but whether the test actually measures what it is intended to measure is a question not answerable via examination of bias as related to reliability, but only as related to validity.

Over the course of the last few decades, studies regarding bias have tended to remain wedded to explanations of Black–White differences, and test developers have relied on technical improvements and advanced methodology in test construction (e.g., item response theory) that have rendered bias an extremely rare occurrence, which inadvertently might have reduced efforts to understand it better (Reynolds & Carson, 2005). What has emerged since the advent of the new millennium is a renewed understanding of bias comes from the aspect of validity and from a recognition of two particular variables strongly related to test performance, including opportunity for acculturative knowledge acquisition and developmental language proficiency (Ortiz, Ochoa, & Dynda, 2012).

Test developers and researchers alike have become more cognizant that attributes such as race and ethnicity are at best indirect correlates of more fundamental variables that create developmentally based differences that are reflected with great precision in test performance. An individual may be racially different but be fully acculturated to the U.S. mainstream and be a native English speaker. In a similar vein, a child who comes to the mainland United States from Puerto Rico at the age of 14 has a substantially different experiential background and pattern of linguistic and acculturative knowledge development than a 14-year-old child from Puerto Rican parents who was born and raised in the United States. It is only the degree to which an individual possesses both age- or grade-related proficiency in the language in which the test is being administered, as well as the child's equivalent levels of opportunity for acquiring the culture-specific knowledge contained or expected by the test (as compared with individuals on whom the test was normed), that directly and profoundly affect test performance (Ortiz et al., 2012; Rhodes, Ochoa, & Ortiz, 2005).

BASIC CONSIDERATIONS

Best practice in conducting nondiscriminatory assessment is predicated on four basic areas of competency and knowledge, including use of a comprehensive and systematic framework, adoption of a hypothesis-driven approach, recognition of the extent of one's own cultural and linguistic competence, and knowledge regarding how characteristics of diversity operate in the assessment process to influence measured performance, particularly in the use of standardized tests and measures. These components are described in the following sections.

Comprehensive Framework

The majority of attempts to develop procedures for nondiscriminatory assessment tend to revolve more around the use of tests than around the process as a whole. The focus on reducing or avoiding bias related to the use of standardized, norm-referenced instruments is not surprising, given that tests are ubiquitous in psychoeducational assessment and often carry significant implications with respect to questions regarding diagnosis and intervention (e.g., special education eligibility). But even if efforts to control bias in testing situations were sufficient to conduct nondiscriminatory assessment, the training of school psychologists often fails to provide opportunity for the necessary level of competence (Ochoa, 2003; Reynolds & Carson, 2005).

This chapter emphasizes the need to engage in a wide variety of procedures that are designed to increase fairness and equity in as many areas of practice as possible, as well as to reduce bias, specifically in testing, in a systematic manner and in accordance with both legal requirements (e.g., Individuals with Disabilities Education Act [IDEA]) and professional standards.

Assessment activities that reflect fairness and equity must be undertaken within a broad framework built upon the use and application of a systematic and informed procedure that ultimately permits formation of a valid context for unbiased data interpretation.

Hypothesis Testing

Critical to nondiscriminatory assessment is the process of hypothesis generation and testing. No information or data used in any evaluation provide meaning in isolation and independent of the judgment of the evaluator who collected it. Although psychometric data in particular are often viewed as representing objective measurement, data have no inherent meaning and derive significance only from interpretation within the broader, ecological context of the examinee. Without such context, personal beliefs, preconceptions, or expectations of performance may result in unfair and inequitable interpretation of data, a process that, whether it be conscious or unconscious, represents confirmatory bias (not in the psychometric sense, of course). The chances of making incorrect inferences about data on the basis of preconceived ideas can be reduced through an approach that utilizes hypothesis generation and testing and the individual's entire learning and educational ecology.

Although it is difficult to refrain from preconceived notions regarding the reasons for an individual's learning difficulties, particularly if efforts at intervention and treatment have already failed to ameliorate them, evaluation of data must remain squarely focused on whether hypotheses, not opinions, attitudes, or beliefs, are, or are not, supported. Such support comes primarily from a convergence of data and multiple sources of information that show agreement and create manifold evidence in support of a particular hypothesis. It is largely the presence of convergent data that strengthens and substantiates one or more of the hypotheses developed in the course of evaluation.

Thus, evaluators must adhere to the principle that until the collected data suggest strongly to the contrary, the null hypothesis, that an individual's learning problems are related to extrinsic or situational, not intrinsic, variables, cannot be rejected. Such a stance remains applicable irrespective of the assessment domain and can be readily employed with individuals from diverse backgrounds who might encompass a variety of domains. In any such instance or application, the alternative hypothesis should not be considered as providing de facto support for any preconception. The reasons why an individual may be having true problems learning in the classroom or why performance on any given test might fall outside of the normal range are numerous.

Nondiscriminatory assessment seeks to ensure that the array of potential causes for learning difficulties, behavior problems, or low performance (e.g., low motivation, physical illness, anxiety, cultural or linguistic difference) have been ruled out as primary causes for any observed learning problems or patterns of deficit in the collected data. The act of developing and using hypotheses that affirm normality to guide the collection and interpretation of data remains central to reducing confirmatory bias and establishing defensible practices in nondiscriminatory (i.e., less discriminatory) assessment.

Cultural and Linguistic Competence

Cultural and linguistic competence is necessary across all aspects of nondiscriminatory assessment. Cultural competence reflects a knowledge base of, or direct experience with, the values, attitudes, beliefs, and customs of a particular culture, which can be used as both guide and context for collecting, evaluating, and assigning meaning to any and all assessment data (Lopez, 2006; Mpofu & Ortiz, 2009; Okazaki & Tanaka-Matsumi, 2006). School psychologists need not be raised natively in a particular culture in order to derive such competence, but the necessary skills will not develop by simply reading a book or taking a trip. Those not fortunate enough to receive direct experience and education toward development of cultural competence from their training programs will need to embark on a focused process that includes a variety of professional development activities. In general, this process includes development of proficiency in three broad domains: knowledge, communication, and skills (Rhodes et al., 2005). In some cases, cultural advocates from the community can assist in providing consultation regarding the particular aspects of culture that may be relevant to the evaluation.

Linguistic competence is reflected in two distinct ways: the ability to communicate effectively in an individual's native language (eliminating the need for an interpreter) and possession of a knowledge base related to first and second language development and instructional methodology and pedagogy. Possession of the ability to communicate effectively in an individual's native language does not automatically imply competency in first and second language development, instructional methodology, and pedagogy. As noted previously, research has demonstrated that both cultural

(not race, but the opportunity for acculturative learning) and linguistic (i.e., proficiency in English) differences are significant factors that can significantly attenuate an individual's performance on psychological, neuropsychological, language, and academic achievement tests (Figueroa & Newsome, 2006; Ortiz & Dynda, 2005). Irrespective of the evaluator's bilingual capabilities, the entire process of assessment is subject to bias whenever there is a failure to account for developmentally based influences that arise from differences in culturally and linguistically bound experiences, including cultural artifacts, communicative patterns, worldviews, patterns of acculturative learning, normative behaviors, beliefs, values, attitudes, and expectations (Ortiz et al., 2012).

Understanding and Addressing Bias in Testing and Assessment

Part of the identity of school psychologists is rooted in the use of psychometric instruments in the course of carrying out assessment and evaluation activities. Of course, not all evaluations require the use of standardized tests, but even when a school psychologist elects not to use any tests, all other components of nondiscriminatory assessment remain fully applicable. Thus, any debate regarding the value of tests and testing aside, standardized measures continue to be a common and sometimes necessary component of evaluations that school psychologists are frequently called upon to perform. In this regard, it is crucial that school psychologists gain and exercise competence in their use of those measures in such situations.

The educational and training experiences of school psychologists continue to lag behind the rapid increase in the diversity of the school-age population to be served as student trainees graduate from preservice to inservice practice. Whether because of a lack of instructors with suitable expertise in the area or the equally limited opportunities for practice and supervision in working with diverse populations, school psychologists often find themselves at a loss regarding nondiscriminatory assessment and may resort to utilizing unproven clinical methods or misguided procedures that are not suitable or appropriate for measuring cognitive abilities or intellectual functioning in any way that could be construed as valid, let alone equitable (Sotelo-Dynega, Cuskley, Geddes, McSwiggan, & Soldano, 2011; Vazquez-Nuttall et al., 2007). School psychologists by and large seem to believe that the maintenance or establishment of validity in testing and test results stems simply from selection of the "right" test. Apart from simply switching to the native language, there is little evidence that anything else is considered or done in evaluations where standardized tests in the native language are utilized (Ochoa, Riccio, Jimenez, Garcia de Alba, & Sines, 2004). On the whole, it appears that school psychologists have very little idea regarding what might render test scores invalid or even how to gauge the impact of relevant variables on the validity of measured performance and subsequent interpretation of test scores, information that is indispensable to the process of nondiscriminatory assessment.

BEST PRACTICES IN NONDISCRIMINATORY ASSESSMENT

The considerations outlined in the previous section are fundamental to any attempt at drawing valid and defensible inferences from assessment data. Nondiscriminatory assessment practices of school psychologists must necessarily be multifaceted and couched within a comprehensive framework that integrates efforts to maintain fairness, ensure equity, and, where tests are used, reduce bias in a cohesive and systematic manner to the maximum extent possible. The various steps that constitute the framework are summarized in Table 5.1. The framework coalesces the more salient and promising procedures and recommendations for nondiscriminatory assessment offered by both researchers and practitioners in school psychology and related fields. The framework is both linear and recursive in that a return to already completed steps in the process may well be necessary as new data are uncovered and new hypotheses formed, evaluated, and reevaluated. The framework accommodates both individual and assessment team activities. Collaborative assessment, where members of an assessment team (including

Table 5.1. A Comprehensive Framework for Nondiscriminatory Assessment

- Assess for the purpose of intervention
- Assess initially with authentic and alternative procedures
- Assess and evaluate the learning ecology
- Assess and evaluate developmental language proficiency
- Assess and evaluate opportunity for learning
- Assess and evaluate relevant acculturative and developmental language factors
- Evaluate, revise, and retest hypotheses
- Determine the need for and language(s) of formal assessment
- Reduce bias in testing practices
- Support conclusions through data convergence and multiple indicators

parents) work together and where information is shared and decisions rendered jointly, significantly improves the likelihood of success of any and all nondiscriminatory efforts.

Assess for the Purpose of Intervention

Assessment is of little value unless it can be extended to incorporate appropriate interventions and treatment options irrespective of the identification of a disorder or disability. In school-based evaluations, modifications to the instructional program and the provision of specific remedial strategies are necessary whether or not the individual qualifies for special education services. Because a process of nondiscriminatory assessment will generate information regarding both relative performance as well as causal and contributory factors, it has considerable value in guiding the development of appropriate interventions and treatment strategies. As with use of the hypothesis-driven approach, awareness of the need to link assessment to intervention significantly affects the manner in which activities are conducted and the type of data that are collected. It is for this reason that intervention-driven evaluation must necessarily be the first step in nondiscriminatory assessment. Failure to engage in a process that will generate data for the purpose of intervention can be construed as the most discriminatory aspect of assessment as it will bias all subsequent activities.

Assess Initially With Authentic and Alternative Assessment Procedures

Whereas standardized, norm-referenced tests are driven mainly by questions and needs related to classification, diagnosis, and legal eligibility, authentic assessment is geared more toward answering questions regarding instructional needs and interventions, something that standardized tests do not address well. The emergence of response to intervention (RTI) in school psychology attests to the value of intervention-based assessment and its potential value in reducing some of the discriminatory aspects of evaluation, particularly those procedures that do not focus on the appropriateness or adequacy of classroom instruction (Kovaleski & Prasse, 2004). Implementation of a proper three- or four-tier RTI framework is an example of a rigorous approach to utilizing authentic methods at this step. Likewise, in addition to the activities that constitute RIOT procedures (record review, interviews, observation, informal testing), other examples of authentic or informal procedures include informal analysis of work samples, curriculum- or criterion-based assessment, performance-based assessment, portfolio assessment, and various test–teach–test frameworks, such as dynamic assessment, all of which are designed to generate data relevant to intervention purposes.

When properly applied, authentic and alternative assessment strategies can provide valuable information, especially in school-based and subsequent special education evaluations. In educational settings, authentic assessment often utilizes material that is being provided through direct classroom instruction. Evaluation of learning and performance through use of the curriculum-based materials and content reflects an authentic nondiscriminatory approach because it seeks to measure that which the student has actually been taught. Accordingly, comprehensive nondiscriminatory assessment should include information and data obtained through such methods. As noted, examples include curriculum-based assessment or authentic measures of academic achievement and skill development but could also include performance-based assessment that evaluates more by task completion within context than by answering of factual questions out of context,

criterion-referenced assessment using minimum levels or standards of performance, portfolio assessment that documents development of skills learning and academic progress, informal analysis of actual work completed in the classroom setting, symbolic dynamic assessment of learning propensity using abstract stimuli, and authentic dynamic assessment of learning propensity using actual materials from the curriculum.

As illustrated in Figure 5.1, evaluation of data from these methods may be dependent on additional procedures, including analysis of differences in learning; examination of expectations for rates of progress; improvement in learning, or growth rates; and evaluation of educational needs or requirements. The major difficulty lies in establishing the appropriate basis for comparison. In Figure 5.1, the top line represents an aimline that might have been established on the basis of one classroom, a whole school, or an entire district and is designed to assess reading skills, specifically, words read correctly per minute.

The second line represents the starting point for a fictional English language learner (ELL), Egberto, whose reading level is below that of native English-speaking peers, as is often the case, but who still manages to make

Figure 5.1. Nondiscriminatory Evaluation of Rates of Progress for an English Language Learner, Egberto

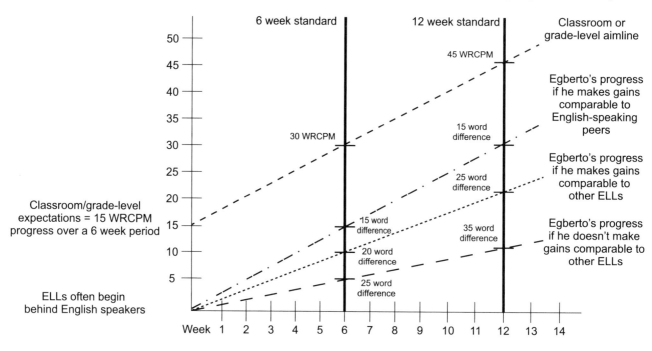

Example Second Grade Progress Monitoring Chart

Note. ELLs = English language learners; WRCPM = words read correctly per minute. The name "Egberto" is based on "Egbert," borrowed with permission from Dan Reschley.

the same rate of progress relative to the aimline. In this case Egberto will never actually reach the aimline, but he cannot rightfully be said to be failing either. He is benefiting every bit as much as his grade-level peers, but because he started behind, he could only catch up if he actually made progress at a rate faster than his peers, certainly an unreasonable expectation.

The third line down is perhaps a more realistic rate for children like Egberto, if he is compared to other ELLs. If he is instead held to the standard depicted by the original top aimline, then his progress seems dire in that he not only starts behind but is unable to make as much progress in reading as his peers. This lack of similar progress may occur for reasons other than lack of ability and is commonly rooted in the fact that Egberto's developmental experiences in English are simply less than those of his native English-speaking peers. Consequently, he is unlikely to benefit as readily from the same level of instruction (Vanderwood & Nam, 2007). Therefore, he actually begins to look as if he is falling farther and farther behind, when the reality is that he is making progress that is reasonable and expected, given his background and when compared to other ELLs, not native speakers.

The last line at the bottom of the figure is similar, but in this case Egberto does not make as much progress as his English-speaking or his ELL peers. He is clearly quite behind native English peers but only somewhat behind what would be considered his true peer group. Therefore, whether such progress indicates a failure to respond to intervention is not entirely clear just yet. Conversely, were Egberto compared to the original top aimline, it is very likely that major concerns about his ability would have been raised. Thus, the degree to which any decision regarding rate of progress, expected levels of achievement, and so forth may prove to be discriminatory will emanate from the standard chosen as the basis of comparison. Much as with testing, the more such standards are based on individuals with backgrounds and developmental experiences that differ from those on whom the standards were derived, the more likely any conclusions drawn regarding their meaning will be biased.

In short, use of curriculum-based methods in evaluation will not automatically result in unbiased data, and subsequent decisions may be far from fair or equitable. The formation of any particular standard for comparison of academic progress must be based on students who possess developmental experiences that are as comparable as possible to those for whom the standard will be applied.

Assess and Evaluate the Learning Ecology

School psychologists should recognize that there exists an infinite number of reasons why any given student is having learning difficulties and that intrinsic factors form only a small fraction of these possibilities. Nondiscriminatory evaluation begins with directing initial assessment efforts toward exploration of the extrinsic causes that might be related to any observed learning difficulties. Hypotheses should be developed that revolve around the student's unique experiential background within the context of the learning environment. When assessment is conducted on culturally and linguistically diverse students, in particular, there are many reasons related to these experiential factors that can adversely affect classroom performance or behavior.

Very often it is the systemic interaction between these factors and those that exist in the learning environment that simply do not or are not able to accommodate them that creates a mismatch between instruction delivered and instruction needed. Although cultural or linguistic differences are probably two of the most common factors that are evaluated relative to the learning ecology, they are by no means the only ones. For example, others might include health, family situations, socioeconomic issues, teacher biases, and ineffective instruction. Therefore, the learning ecology should not be ignored simply because a student's background is not characterized by diversity on these two dimensions. In addition, a student's learning ecology should not be thought of as being restricted solely to the classroom environment. Although focus on the classroom environment is central to the evaluation of learning problems, students learn a great many things in contexts other than the classroom. Comparison of behavior, performance, or functioning between these contexts (e.g., physical education, nonacademic instruction, recess, home, community) is crucial in conducting nondiscriminatory assessment.

Data that inform evaluation of hypotheses related to ecological and systemic factors may be obtained through a variety of methods, including review of educational records; direct observation of instruction and teaching; review of the content, level, relevancy, and appropriateness of the curriculum; analysis of the match between the curriculum and the student's needs; interview with parents, teachers, or the individual; and medical records. Often culture and its concomitant experiences dictate most strongly the unique history of a student, but the student should not be equated to or measured simply by skin color or ethnic heritage. Evaluation of cultural difference should be viewed as examination of unique circumstances or learning experiences that cannot be considered comparable to the experiences of students raised in the U.S. mainstream. Some examples that may be consistent with this definition include poverty, deafness or other disability, bicultural students, students with childhood trauma or abuse, and students from dysfunctional families. Although culture tends to be the major factor that influences a student's development, it need not be thought of as being neatly circumscribed. Evaluation of the extent to which a student's experiences differ from those of mainstream students may not even be a function of culture but simply the result of unusual or highly idiosyncratic experience. Specification of hypotheses should be null based (i.e., performance, behavior, or learning problems are due to extrinsic factors such as differences in experience, not intrinsic factors like ability) in order to prevent bias in the collection and interpretation of data.

Assess and Evaluate Developmental Language Proficiency

Fair and equitable assessment often has a tendency to go astray in cases where the student's native or heritage language is not English. Part of the problem seems to revolve around the use and misconception of the meaning of language dominance. Driven in part by wording in both IDEA and the Standards for Educational and Psychological Testing (American Educational Research Association, American Psychological Association, & National Council on Measurement in Education, 2014), school psychologists have adopted a simplistic notion that validity in testing is ensured when it is conducted in the native or preferred language. In actuality, dominance only means that one language is better developed than another language, not that the student is proficient in the dominant language. A student may well be dominant in one language and yet lack any degree of fluency in both. Dominance does relate to expectations regarding performance in that testing conducted in the dominant language should produce results that are less affected by a developmental language difference. But *less affected* is not the same as *not affected*, and merely because it might be less subject to attenuation does not mean it automatically becomes valid.

Therefore, dominance has very little utility in terms of understanding potential bias as related to validity and should not be viewed as a guide for generating acceptable test results. Rather, what does assist school psychologists

in understanding the influence on test scores is the degree of difference between the developmental language proficiency of the student with two languages and the language proficiency of the students on whom a given test has been normed. This consideration applies regardless of the language of administration and irrespective of any determination regarding dominance.

Determination of developmental language proficiency in one or both languages spoken by a student is critical because students who are not native English speakers begin learning English at a later point in their lives and because they will necessarily have far less experience with and exposure to it compared with native English speakers. Gauging their developmental proficiency will require evaluation of a variety of experiential factors, including such things as amount of experience with and opportunity to learn the language, time spent in and use of the language in any formal instruction, parental fluency, literacy, education, socioeconomic status, and any educational experiences outside of the school system. It may also require standardized language proficiency testing. Ultimately, this information will assist school psychologists in determining the degree to which a student is linguistically "different" from the students against whom his or her performance is to be compared. No matter how the information is generated, it should be recent (no older than 6 months) and not only will serve to guide interpretation of performance on other tests, but also will form the basis for the development of instructional interventions that are linguistically and pedagogically appropriate.

Assess and Evaluate Opportunity for Learning

The school setting provides perhaps the most significant context for learning. However, it is by no means the only one, and it is not always successful in engendering academic success. It is not uncommon for diverse students to become casualties of the educational system's failure to provide an effective or appropriate instructional program. The school itself, including the curriculum, personnel, policies, and even the instructional setting, must be carefully evaluated to determine whether the student has been provided with adequate opportunity to learn, particularly in the case where significant differences in English or acculturative learning exist.

Usual methods for collecting such data include evaluation of classroom environment and teaching methods; direct observation of academic performance;

review of the content, level, relevancy, and appropriateness of the curriculum; analysis of the match between the curriculum and the student's needs; interviews with parents and current and previous teachers; interview with the student; and review of existing educational records and progress reports. Specific factors that should be examined include regularity of school attendance; experience with the school environment and setting; match between the student's native language and the language of instruction; parent's ability to support language of instruction; years (duration) of instruction in the native language and English; quality of instruction in the native language and English as a second language, or bilingual programs; cultural relevance of the curriculum; frequency of changes in schools; relative consistency in and across curricula; teaching strategies, styles, attitudes, and expectations; the system's attitude regarding dual language learners; and socialization with peers versus isolation from peers.

Students whose experiences are more limited in terms of what they have been exposed to (culturally and linguistically, compared with same-age peers who have vastly more such experiences with the culture and language, must be seen as likely "different" rather than "disabled." Because the very processes that educators and evaluators seek to evaluate and assess in students are often rooted in development, falling behind in any area of development even to a small degree because of circumstance may prove too difficult for a student of average ability to overcome. Fairness in assessment requires that students not be penalized for not having acquired knowledge or developed skills in areas where they have not had comparable opportunity for learning.

Assess and Evaluate Relevant Acculturative and Developmental Language Factors

Formal learning experiences take place primarily in school, but incidental learning occurs in virtually all areas of a student's life both in and out of school. There exist many factors as well that may originate outside the educational setting but that still significantly affect the formal learning process. Careful evaluation of the extent to which such factors might be present and whether the factors might be affecting learning in the school is necessary in order to evaluate data from a nondiscriminatory standpoint. In cases where the student is culturally or linguistically diverse, it will be necessary to assess and evaluate the experiential aspects of these particular variables and their relative influence on school-based learning, language development, and

educational progress. The effect of small amounts of exposure to two or more cultures or languages during early childhood development may create circumstances that cause the student to have experiences that differ markedly from those of other students within the U.S. mainstream and that can negatively affect school performance.

In short, the ability to draw valid conclusions regarding school dysfunction from the whole of assessment data rests squarely on proper identification and understanding of the student's total linguistic history as well as other factors that may have influenced the development of both languages. This information is most commonly collected via observations across multiple settings; interviews with parents, teachers, and the student; and review of existing educational records. Additionally, home visits are particularly effective for gathering this type of data. Factors that should specifically be examined include current languages of the home, the student's initial or primary language, the student's total informal experience with the native language and English, the student's birth order and the relative impact of siblings on his or her language development, the student's fluency in the native language and English, the student's and parent's level of acculturation, the parent's fluency in the native language and English, the parent's level of literacy in the native language and English, the parent's level of education, and the parent's socioeconomic status.

Evaluate, Revise, and Retest Hypotheses

When a school psychologist or other evaluator conducts an assessment with preconceived notions regarding what the data will show (e.g., expected level of performance on a test), confirmatory bias can occur both in the manner and type of data that are collected and the way in which the data are interpreted. For example, learning problems in the classroom may be erroneously ascribed to attention difficulties, and thus subsequent data-gathering efforts will tend to focus only on examining issues related to attention at the expense of other potential factors, such as limited English language comprehension, that may be related to the learning problem.

Conversely, attributions of behavior that are made on the basis of stereotyped or preconceived notions can often steer assessment away from the real cause of many school-related problems. Indeed, if there exists a belief that a student's learning problems or behavior are attributable to personality, environmental, cultural, or linguistic differences, then no assessment may even be undertaken in cases where the learning difficulties may in fact be related to factors that can be readily ameliorated (e.g., instructional mismatch, health problems, sensory dysfunction). These preconceptions can be particularly unfair and discriminatory whenever standardized tests are used. Believing that a student is in some way disabled or deficient in a given domain of knowledge or functioning can directly affect the manner in which the test is administered and scored and the manner in which data are interpreted. Without conscious awareness of the process, the benefit of the doubt will lean toward evidence as suggesting dysfunction or disability and not the other way around. This is because evaluators tend to look for patterns and results in the data that support their preconceptions and are thereby predisposed to perceiving only those patterns consistent with the a priori beliefs. Moreover, there is a tendency to ignore, minimize, or reject data that run counter to the a priori assumption (Ortiz et al., 2012; Rhodes et al., 2005).

Confirmatory bias related to preconceived notions of dysfunction or discriminatory misattributions of performance or behavior tends to influence the very nature and range of data that will be collected. Consider, for example, the use of techniques such as records review, interviews, observation, and informal testing (i.e., RIOT), which are important components of any assessment and often taken as intrinsically valid. Yet, the very questions asked during interviews, the behaviors observed in the classroom, the work samples chosen for analysis and selected in support of presuppositions, and expectations of performance on various tasks will all be influenced by the evaluator's preconceptions. Asking parents when their child first learned to walk is qualitatively different than asking if their child was a late walker.

School psychologists may reduce this form of inequity by avoiding attempts to confirm presumptions of preexisting deficits and testing hypotheses instead. The process of assessment should begin with the hypothesis that the student's difficulties are not intrinsic in nature, but rather, that the difficulties are more likely attributable to external or environmental problems. When standardized tests are used, the same assumption of normality should be used. In other words, evaluators must enter the testing situation with a mindset rooted in fairness, that is, that the student being tested is not impaired, possesses average or better general ability, and is able to perform or function in any specific domain in a manner that will be within normal limits. This assumption forms, in essence, a null hypothesis that can be evaluated with both quantitative and qualitative data to determine if it should be retained or rejected in favor of an alternative hypothesis (i.e., that performance is not average or within normal limits). When the process of evaluation is initiated with a presumption of normality, it reduces the tendency to search for data or to see patterns of dysfunction where none may exist. Unless and until the data suggest otherwise, nondiscriminatory assessment requires an a priori belief that there is very likely nothing at all unusual about the student or his or her abilities.

Another benefit of testing hypotheses that are not based on preconceptions involving deficiency is achieved by using the process for intervention in a proactive rather than reactive manner. For example, evaluation that seeks to determine the particular conditions under which a student's learning may be improved or accelerated leads to the collection of data that are directly tied to intervention. The very purpose of the evaluation in such cases is to enhance learning rather than simply diagnose the causes of poor performance. Even when there may be a diagnostic component to evaluation, assessment should always be linked to intervention, and the potential discriminatory influence of confirmatory bias can be reduced significantly when the focus is on identifying ways to improve school performance and learning rather than merely attempting to pinpoint the underlying cause of observed problems. Only when difficulties learning in the classroom setting or behavioral problems cannot be reasonably ascribed to the primary influence of any such extrinsic factors can assessment proceed appropriately to explore potential intrinsic factors with confidence that the process is operating in a fair and equitable manner.

Determine the Need for and Language of Assessment

In cases where the student is not a native English speaker or uses an alternative mode of communication, questions arise regarding the language of assessment. Although this chapter pointed out that IDEA 2004 contains legacy wording that appears to mandate testing in the student's primary language (or other mode of communication), the act now provides a clearer intent regarding testing in that it must be "provided and administered in the language and form most likely to yield accurate information on what the child knows and can do academically, developmentally, and functionally, unless it is not feasible to so provide" (20 USC 1414, Sec. 614(b)(3)(A)(ii)). The implicit intent of the law appears to relate to validity, that is, by ensuring that results are actually valid reflections of the abilities that they are intended to reflect.

Thus, if it cannot be demonstrated that testing in the native language or other mode of communication yields results that are valid, there is no reason to believe that doing so complies with the objective of the statute. It has been argued that testing in English may well be the only current approach in the use of tests that can be evaluated for validity, meaning it is likely to be the only method that could meet a strict interpretation of this legislative standard (Ortiz et al., 2012). What is important to recognize here is that testing need not be conducted solely in the primary language or solely in English. Nothing in IDEA 2004 or any other regulatory guideline mandates parallel testing in both languages. Rather, the language in which testing is conducted will likely depend on the questions that need to be answered. Exactly what should be assessed and in what language it will be assessed are decisions that rest with the assessor or assessment team.

Factors that affect the selection of linguistically appropriate tools and techniques come from examination and review of existing prereferral data, the unique background variables of the student, and relevant referral concerns. Because each case is unique, and because the foundation of IDEA 2004 rests on the notion of individualization in both evaluation and instruction, it is inappropriate to make specific guidelines or rules with respect to decisions about the most appropriate language or combination of languages for testing. Within the framework of nondiscriminatory assessment, these decisions may be guided by the following general statements that represent only the most basic of guidelines: (a) students who are not proficient in English should be assessed in their primary language or native mode of communication in addition to any English language testing that may be appropriate; (b) students who are proficient in English may be assessed in their primary language or native mode of communication in addition to any English language testing that may be appropriate; and (c) all students, whether proficient in English or not, should always be treated and evaluated as bilingual, irrespective of which language may be dominant.

Reduce Bias in Testing Practices

Use of standardized tests within the context of nondiscriminatory assessment requires knowledge of (a) the adequacy of representation of each norm or comparison group, (b) the full range of abilities that are being measured and those that are not, (c) research regarding the manner in which diverse students perform on any given test, and (d) the degree to which test score validity has or has not been compromised by extraneous variables such as linguistic and cultural differences (Figueroa & Newsome, 2006; Flanagan, Ortiz, & Alfonso, 2013). For school psychologists, information regarding the two former criteria is readily available, whereas the two latter are underresearched and more difficult to apply in practice. Whenever tests are selected, administered, and interpreted in a manner that is not systematic or guided by research, decisions and conclusions based on resulting data may be invalid or largely indefensible.

In general, use of well-constructed, technically sound native language tests (for students who are evaluated in a language other than, or in addition to, English), where available, is preferable to use of tests with limited, poor, or unknown technical properties, even if available in the native language (Reynolds & Carson, 2005). To reduce the potentially biased aspects of testing that may arise from the use of standardized tests, knowledge regarding the ways in which students of average ability from diverse experiential backgrounds perform on tests administered to them in English or their native language, as well as the manner in which and the extent to which these variables attenuate performance, must become routine tools within every school psychologist's repertoire (Ortiz et al., 2012).

A full and detailed discussion of the advantages and disadvantages of various approaches in the use of tests is beyond the scope of this chapter. More utility is likely derived from broader guidance related to a formalized approach using tests that may begin in English but ultimately rely on the native language. In consideration of all methods for generating test results and the need to evaluate validity, an evidence-based approach that may permit reduction of potential bias as related to validity can be described as a two-step process, particularly for linguistically diverse students: (a) establish the validity of test scores in English, and (b) establish the validity of suspected disorders in the native language. The entire two-step approach to testing and evaluating test score validity is summarized in Table 5.2, and readers may wish to refer to it for a concise outline of the various steps.

Support Conclusions Through Data Convergence and Multiple Indicators

All data collected in the course of nondiscriminatory assessment should be evaluated in an integrated manner utilizing the information obtained regarding the student's unique experience and background as the appropriate context. Knowledge of factors that may have played a part in creating significant differences between the experiences of the student in terms of acculturation or language development provides the least discriminatory framework with which to evaluate and assign meaning to the patterns seen in the data. Although less obvious and more difficult to judge, information related to differences in acculturation are every bit as important as the more overt differences seen in language and should not be minimized or ignored. Very often the meaning of the data will depend in large part on an understanding of the environmental influences (most data are associated with cultural and linguistic differences) that have transpired to shape the student in unique ways and set the stage for observed and measured performance. In the final analysis, successful nondiscriminatory assessment is contingent upon application of this information.

A necessary method for ensuring fairness and equity in this process is based on the notion of convergence. The data collected in the course of assessment should cut across procedure or method and come together in a cohesive and convincing manner that supports the plausibility of final conclusions. In some cases, it may be difficult to find convergence (e.g., in cases where data are based on third-party ratings of behavior). Whereas data from standardized tests are expected to converge, for various reasons data from independent ratings of psychopathology may not, leaving the school psychologist to decide which data should be ascribed the most credibility. In practice, a preponderance of evidence is sufficient to provide validity to conclusions, but care should be taken not to assign unwarranted importance or significance to any single piece of information or data. Using single scores or combinations or products of scores, and unduly favoring certain data over other data, will lead to discriminatory inferences and outcomes. In the final analysis, nondiscriminatory assessment holds that equivocal data support the null hypothesis, that functioning is within normal limits, and that any observed difficulties are the result of factors other than internal disability.

SUMMARY

The framework outlined in this chapter is intended to promote fairness, ensure equity, and, where tests are employed, reduce bias in as many aspects of assessment as possible. These aspects include activities inherent in evaluation, such as evaluating the validity of data, interpreting data fairly, making nondiscriminatory decisions, and engendering equitable outcomes. Nondiscriminatory assessment is not a single tool or procedure. It includes a variety of data generated from a review of records, interviews, observations, standardized tests, and authentic methods, and it recognizes that bias,

Table 5.2. A Two-Step Approach to Reducing Bias in Testing

Step 1. Establish the validity of test scores in English:
- Select or create an appropriate battery that is comprehensive and responds to the needs of the referral concerns, irrespective of language differences.
- Administer all tests in a standardized manner in English only, with no modifications.
- Score tests and plot them for analysis via the Culture–Language Interpretive Matrix.
- If analysis indicates that performance is within the expected range and shows a pattern of decline, the evaluation ends, and no disability is likely.
- If analysis does not indicate that performance is within the expected range or shows a pattern of decline, apply the Cross-Battery Assessment (or other) interpretive methods to determine specific areas of weakness and difficulty and continue to Step 2.

Step 2. Establish the validity of suspected disorders in the native language:
- Review prior results and create a select set of tests related to the areas where the suspected weaknesses or difficulties were noted.
- Select tests that are as parallel as possible to the original tests using one of two methods: (a) native language test administered in the native language (e.g., WJ III/Batería III or WISC-IV/WISC-IV Spanish) or (b) native language test administered via assistance of a trained interpreter.
- Administer all tests in standardized manner *and* then employ any modifications or alterations necessary to ensure full comprehension and reduce barriers to performance.
- Observe and document your approach to tasks, errors in responding, and behavior during testing.
- Analyze data both quantitatively and qualitatively to evaluate areas of weakness or difficulty.
- If areas of weakness do not match areas of weakness from Step 1 analyses, disability is *not* likely.
- If areas of weakness match areas of weakness from Step 1 analyses, disability is likely.

as traditionally defined, is not a function of technical or psychometric deficiencies in testing but rather is manifested as potential problems in validity related to differences in developmentally based experiences between a student taking the test and the students on whom the test was normed. Differences in race, ethnicity, or culture do not by themselves always reflect significant experiential differences. Differences in English language proficiency and relative opportunity for acculturative learning often do.

Nondiscriminatory assessment is a process that unites a variety of activities and procedures designed to assist in generating valid results that lead to fairness in interpretation, decision making, and equivalent outcomes. It begins at any point at which a student begins to evidence learning or behavioral problems in school learning, and 8 of the 10 components of the model can be implemented as part of the general education and prereferral activities in which school psychologists typically engage. It is an integrative problem-solving activity that cuts across every level or tier of evaluation and provides guidance for gathering relevant data useful in informing the development of appropriate instructional interventions and for guiding subsequent assessment activities. It can be managed within current school psychology service delivery and requires no additional effort to implement. Application of a nondiscriminatory assessment framework assists school psychologists in making decisions that are more likely to have fair, positive, and equitable outcomes based on evaluation of behavior, learning issues, academic attainment, socioemotional functioning, and cognitive development and on their use in developing appropriate interventions for all children.

AUTHOR NOTE

Disclosure. Samuel O. Ortiz has a financial interest in books he authored or coauthored referenced in this chapter.

REFERENCES

American Educational Research Association, American Psychological Association, & National Council on Measurement in Education. (2014). *The standards for educational and psychological testing.* Washington, DC: Author.

Figueroa, R. A., & Newsome, P. (2006). The diagnosis of LD in English learners: Is it nondiscriminatory? *Journal of Learning Disabilities, 39,* 206–214.

Flanagan, D. P., Ortiz, S. O., & Alfonso, V. C. (2013). *Essentials of Cross-Battery Assessment* (3rd ed.). Hoboken, NJ: Wiley.

Kovaleski, J. F., & Prasse, D. P. (2004). Response to instruction in the identification of learning disabilities: A guide for school teams. In A. Canter, L. Z. Paige, M. D. Roth, I. Romero, & S. A. Carroll (Eds.), *Helping children at home and school II: Handouts for families and educators* (S8–S159). Bethesda, MD: National Association of School Psychologists.

Lopez, E. C. (2006). English language learners. In G. G. Bear & K. M. Minke (Eds.), *Children's needs III: Development, prevention, and intervention* (pp. 647–659). Bethesda, MD: National Association of School Psychologists.

Mpofu, E., & Ortiz, S. O. (2009). Equitable assessment practices in diverse contexts. In E. L. Grigorenko (Ed.), *Multicultural psychoeducational assessment* (pp. 41–76). New York, NY: Springer.

National Association of School Psychologists. (2010). *Model for comprehensive and integrated school psychological services.* Bethesda, MD: Author. Retrieved from http://www.nasponline.org/standards/2010standards/2_PracticeModel.pdf

Ochoa, S. H. (2003). Assessment of culturally and linguistically diverse children. In C. R. Reynolds & R. W. Kamphaus (Eds.), *Handbook of psychological and educational assessment of children: Intelligence, aptitude, and achievement* (2nd ed., pp. 563–583). New York, NY: Guilford Press.

Ochoa, S. H., Riccio, C. A., Jimenez, S., Garcia de Alba, R., & Sines, M. (2004). Psychological assessment of limited English proficient and/or bilingual students: An investigation of school psychologists' current practices. *Journal of Psychoeducational Assessment, 22,* 93–105.

Okazaki, S., & Tanaka-Matsumi, J. (2006). Cultural considerations in cognitive-behavioral assessment. In P. A. Hays & G. Y. Iwamasa (Eds.), *Culturally responsive cognitive-behavioral therapy: Assessment, practice, and supervision* (pp. 247–266). Washington, DC: American Psychological Association.

Ortiz, S. O., & Dynda, A. M. (2005). The use of intelligence tests with culturally and linguistically diverse populations. In D. P. Flanagan & P. L. Harrison (Eds.), *Contemporary intellectual assessment* (2nd ed., pp. 545–556). New York, NY: Guilford Press.

Ortiz, S. O., Ochoa, H. S., & Dynda, A. M. (2012). Testing with culturally and linguistically diverse populations: Moving beyond the verbal-performance dichotomy into evidence-based practice. In D. P. Flanagan & P. L. Harrison (Eds.), *Contemporary intellectual assessment* (3rd ed., pp. 526–552). New York, NY: Guilford Press.

Reynolds, C. R., & Carson, A. D. (2005). Methods for assessing cultural bias in tests. In C. Frisby & C. R. Reynolds (Eds.), *Comprehensive handbook of multicultural school psychology* (pp. 795–823). Hoboken, NJ: Wiley.

Rhodes, R., Ochoa, S. H., & Ortiz, S. O. (2005). *Assessment of culturally and linguistically diverse students: A practical guide.* New York, NY: Guilford Press.

Sotelo-Dynega, M., Cuskley, T., Geddes, L. McSwiggan, K., & Soldano, A. (2011, February). *Cognitive assessment: A survey of current school psychologists' practices.* Poster session presented at the annual conference of the National Association of School Psychologists, San Francisco, CA

Vanderwood, M. L., & Nam, J. E. (2007). Response to intervention for English language learners: Current developments and future directions. In S. R. Jimerson, M. K. Burns, & A. M. VanDerHeyden (Eds.), *Handbook of response to intervention: The science and practice of assessment and intervention* (pp. 408–417). New York, NY: Springer.

Vazquez-Nuttall, E., Li, C., Dynda, A. M., Ortiz, S. O., Armengol, C., Walton, J., & Phoenix, K. (2007). Cognitive assessment of culturally and linguistically diverse students. In G. Esquivel, E. Lopez, & S. Nahari (Eds.), *Handbook of multicultural school psychology.* Mahwah, NJ: Erlbaum.

6

Best Practices in the Assessment of English Language Learners

Catharina Carvalho
Andrea Dennison
Ivonne Estrella
Texas A&M University

OVERVIEW

This chapter will address the specific issues, practices, and considerations related to the assessment of students who are English language learners (ELLs). It addresses the National Association of School Psychologists (NASP) *Model for Comprehensive and Integrated School Psychological Services* (NASP, 2010) domain of Diversity in Development and Learning, particularly working with children of diverse backgrounds. The chapter is structured to help the reader design and implement an effective and meaningful assessment when working with students who speak a language other than English natively. This chapter should be helpful to school psychologists working with ELLs, regardless of whether the school psychologist is bilingual or speaks only English.

Assessment of ELLs

As students, ELLs have more similarities to the majority of students than differences. One important difference, however, lies in the presence of a language other than English as their native language and as an integral part of their learning processes. It is important to consider that these students are acquiring English at the same time as they are acquiring academic knowledge, when evaluating their academic progress and their overall performance. Therefore, a psychoeducational assessment designed to explore the strengths and areas of need of ELLs has to provide due consideration to language development, language acquisition, and language dominance as possible explanatory factors for the results.

In addition to specific issues regarding the acquisition of two or more languages, this type of assessment demands an understanding of how multicultural factors may affect or interact with the academic performance of ELLs. The school psychologist must then determine whether the difficulties the student is having are due to the normative process of second language acquisition, are due to multicultural differences, or are in fact due to an identifiable disability.

Assessment of ELLs is often referred to as *bilingual assessment* (or multilingual assessment if more than two languages are included). Although the term bilingual assessment may suggest that the student has mastered both languages and is, in fact, bilingual, in practice the term generally refers to a student who speaks a native language other than English, and this language may have a significant impact on the academic and social performance of the student in school. Therefore, throughout this chapter the term bilingual assessment will be used to describe the process of evaluating students for special education by considering the role that the home language and culture play in an ELL's linguistic, cognitive, and academic development.

Brief Background

The demand for bilingual or multilingual assessment has its roots in case law that established the rights of bilinguals and ELLs to nondiscriminatory evaluations in order to determine the need for special education. Two seminal cases specifically related to Spanish-speaking students are *Diana v. State Board of Education* (1970) and

Guadalupe Organization v. Temple Elementary School District No. 3 (1972). These cases, together with other case law, specifically related to the assessment of culturally and linguistically diverse students (see *Brown v. Board of Education* [1954] and *PARC v. Commonwealth of Pennsylvania* [1972]) and set the stage for the practice of bilingual or multilingual assessment by outlining minimal expectations for legally defensible evaluations. Finally, three class action suits in the early 1980s (*Jose P. v. Ambach, 557 F. Supp. 11230* [EDNY, 1983]; *United Cerebral Palsy (UCP) of New York v. Board of Education of the City of New York, 79 C. 560* [EDNY, 1979]; and *Dyrcia S. v. Board of Education, 79 C. 2562* [EDNY, 1979]) were together responsible for establishing that ELLs, requiring special education, had to be identified using bilingual materials and resources, had to be assessed in two languages with nondiscriminatory procedures, and had to be offered bilingual alternatives at each stage of the assessment process. Finally, schools had to protect the rights of the parents by informing them in their native language about the content of all documents and by facilitating their involvement in the development of educational plans for their children (Baca & Baca, 2004).

Through these cases and federal legislation, the practice of assessment of ELLs for special education has become better defined and more culturally and linguistically attuned. Today, school psychologists continue to struggle while designing and implementing nondiscriminatory assessment procedures for ELLs, who collectively speak more than 315 languages (U.S. Census, 2010).

When to Use Bilingual Assessment

A bilingual or multilingual assessment is necessary when the referred student's native language is different from English, which means that another language is spoken within the student's family or community. The student may still be acquiring English while appearing to be fluent in English. Additionally, it is critical to consider a bilingual evaluation when the student to be assessed has received academic instruction in a language other than English or is in an academic program that facilitates learning through the use of two or more languages. This mode of instruction is often called bilingual or dual language education and has different modalities depending on the program, school district, or state in which it is implemented.

BASIC CONSIDERATIONS

A school psychologist who conducts assessments of children who are ELLs must possess three areas of competence, according to Alvarado and the Bilingual Special Education Network of Texas (2011). The school psychologist must be "fluent and literate in the languages spoken by the student, knowledgeable of the student's culture, and trained on evaluation materials and practices appropriate for students from diverse backgrounds" (p. 17). However, this gold standard may be difficult or impossible to uphold in culturally homogeneous communities, in school districts with only monolingual English-speaking assessment staff, or in assessment of students from language backgrounds not often encountered in U.S. schools. While the first two characteristics are desirable, the only essential criterion for conducting an assessment of ELLs that adheres to professional and ethical standards is the third; that is, the examiner must have been trained in the processes and materials necessary for the assessment of students from culturally and linguistically diverse backgrounds.

The term *bilingual school psychologist* is one of the more commonly chosen expressions to refer to someone who conducts assessments of ELLs. However, this term can be misleading. Bilingual school psychologists may be assumed to all possess a specific skill set. However, they do not all have the same level of proficiency in the target language, they may have oral but no written proficiency, and in most cases they have never had their language skills formally assessed. Very few individuals, including bilingual school psychologists, are what is referred to as *balanced bilinguals*, who are equally skilled in oral and written communication in both languages. Even a balanced bilingual may possess certain gaps in knowledge owing to his or her unique experiences, history of instruction, and patterns of abilities and interests.

Considering the array of skillsets that a bilingual school psychologist may possess, it is important to acknowledge that although it is undoubtedly advantageous to possess second (or third or fourth) language skills in addition to the ability to conduct psychoeducational assessments, these are not sufficient qualities on their own to conduct a bilingual assessment. In fact, Rhodes, Ochoa, and Ortiz (2005) have emphasized the difference between bilingual assessment and the assessment of bilingual individuals. Bilingual assessment, as they have defined it, involves the "evaluation of a bilingual individual, by a bilingual examiner, in a bilingual manner" (p. 161). However, the assessment of bilingual students or ELLs does not have to be conducted by a bilingual examiner as long as the appropriate process is used. Nor does a bilingual examiner have to be bilingual in the same languages as the student in order to conduct a well-planned, valid assessment.

Credentialing and Specialization

There is currently no nationally recognized certification or credentialing program to govern universal competence standards for those who conduct assessments of ELLs. Only New York, Illinois, and California have state-level credentials or certificates to certify that minimal standards of language proficiency have been met for persons conducting such assessments (Sotelo-Dynega, Geddes, Luhrs, & Teague, 2009). New York and Illinois require that bilingual assessment professionals obtain a state-issued credential in order to conduct bilingual assessments.

Several practitioner training programs in the United States offer course content related to issues of linguistic and cultural diversity, and some offer the opportunity to specialize in bilingual and multicultural issues. Refer to the NASP website for the most current information regarding training programs and the ways that these programs integrate multilingual and multicultural issues.

Team Approach to Assessing ELLs

The school psychologist who does not possess second language skills may nevertheless be called upon to assess an ELL to determine special education eligibility. This might provoke feelings of insecurity along with the question of where to begin. As in other situations in which a school psychologist does not possess the experience necessary, there are options for seeking out support and resources to develop this competence. This is where a team approach to the assessment can be advantageous. The first course of action is to seek out the services of a school psychologist trained in the process of bilingual assessment. Even if this person is not able to complete the entire evaluation, he or she may agree, for example, to assess the oral language skills of the referred student in the home language. The information obtained from these data, when compared to the oral language testing completed in English by the monolingual school psychologist, will be instrumental for planning the remainder of the evaluation.

While a school psychologist fluent in the student's home language may be contracted to do the testing in that language, the monolingual school psychologist can conduct the English testing components and then rely upon the expertise and recommendations from the bilingual school psychologist to guide the process of assessment. Especially if the student is believed to be eligible to receive special education services, a school psychologist trained in bilingual assessment should review the report before it is complete in order to check that the necessary information is included and that valid conclusions and recommendations are given. If such a school psychologist is not available locally, consultation with members of the NASP bilingual school psychology interest group is advised before embarking upon the assessment.

When a Bilingual School Psychologist Is Not Available

It is important to remember that while school psychologists are often the ones who assemble the components of the evaluation and contribute much of the written report, there are other members of the school and community who may be able to provide input into the assessment. If the school district employs or contracts a bilingual speech–language pathologist, then this person is a valuable member to include on the assessment team or as a consultant. Other personnel fluent in the student's home language may also be able to provide valuable input. These persons could serve as ancillary examiners or interpreters during the assessment. If no such person is available, then the next step would be to seek out a professional interpreter who is fluent in English as well as the student's home language. A necessary step when using an interpreter's services is to ensure that he or she is familiar with the basic tenets of psychological/psychoeducational assessment (e.g., confidentiality, standardized procedures). It is important to remember that the use of an interpreter is not part of a standardized test administration and therefore must be documented in the evaluation procedures section of the report.

The school psychologist may seek the input of members of the student's family and community during the assessment, but should not generally rely upon such individuals to provide interpretive services. When the school psychologist is unfamiliar with the culture or language of the student, one option is to interview a cultural agent, a person who is familiar with the student's native language and is often a member of the student's culture. This person may be a layperson, sometimes the child's parents or relatives, who, although unfamiliar with psychoeducational assessment, can provide information about cultural norms and practices. When speaking with a cultural agent, the school psychologist should ask questions that target the referral concern and the appropriateness of school-based expectations for members of the cultural group to which the student belongs. Including the input of these persons in the assessment process is a way to increase the likelihood of conducting a culturally sensitive assessment.

When it is not possible to assess the student's oral language abilities in the home language, caution must be used if conducting an English-only cognitive assessment for the purposes of special education eligibility. Given that most test instructions are heavily language loaded, and often contain academic language, using an English-language cognitive battery is not appropriate as a stand-alone measure unless the student has had ample exposure to academic English. Doing so may yield results that reflect the student's limited English language abilities and not the student's actual cognitive functioning. Incorrect conclusions about the student's abilities may furthermore lead to an inappropriate placement. Using a nonverbal cognitive battery, paired with a test of verbal ability in the native language and English (such as the Bilingual Verbal Ability Test–NU) would be an alternate method of assessment.

Cultural Competence

Assessment of ELLs requires a familiarity with psychosocial and sociocultural concepts that are relevant to the child's or adolescent's life. Although these facets are important to consider during any psychological or psychoeducational assessment, deliberately considering their impact on the student's language, behaviors, and adaptive and academic skills in addition to cognitive ability is of paramount importance when planning, conducting, and interpreting the assessment of ELLs.

Additionally, the lens through which a school psychologist is most inclined to peer is the one that comes from his or her own cultural heritage. The student who is being assessed is often involuntarily subject to the pressures of attempting to navigate two or more cultures successfully while trying to attain all the desirable milestones of academic achievement. By contrast, the school psychologist who has been raised in the dominant culture of the United States often has not been forced to inspect his or her own cultural perspective, which necessarily includes certain preferences or biases. The responsibility for developing multicultural competence then falls upon the school psychologist. To develop cultural competence, the school psychologist must be willing to undertake the (often uncomfortable) journey of examining the origins of his or her own values, beliefs, behaviors, and emotions.

Enculturation and Acculturation

The ELL who is the focus of an evaluation is often in the process of developing an awareness of his or her home culture. This process is referred to as *enculturation*. By virtue of living in the United States, ELLs are also learning to navigate the culture of the society in which they are growing up. *Acculturation* is the process of becoming aware of and adapting to a culture distinct from the home culture. One cultural milieu that is not often given due consideration is the culture of the school. The school culture more often represents the norms, values, and rules associated with the society at large than the diverse cultures of ELLs.

Depending on the experiences that a student has inside and outside of school, the student may find that he or she is drawn to identify with the home culture, the mainstream culture, both, or neither, with psychological and sociocultural implications associated with each of these identity profiles (Sam & Berry, 2010). Acculturative stress may occur as part of the normative process of adapting to two or more cultures and must be taken into consideration when interpreting assessment results, given its significant negative impact on mental health. Acculturation and acculturative stress should be considered at all levels to ensure that the assessment is nondiscriminatory and valid.

Limitations

Several practical limitations exist that affect the assessment of ELLs. The most salient to the decision of whether a student has a disability or is in the normative process of second language acquisition is associated with the fact that many of the characteristics of a language-based disability are similar to those found in a typically developing ELL. Difficulty with word recall, low English vocabulary and verbal comprehension, or underdeveloped syntax can all be mistaken for signs of impairment when none exists.

In addition, there is no single profile of a so-called typical bilingual student, given individual differences. Owing in part to this variability, there are currently no tests that use bilingual students as the normative group, although undoubtedly bilinguals constitute a small, if unidentified, portion of the students in some norm samples (Rhodes et al., 2005). Furthermore, owing to the absence of official national standards for the practice of bilingual assessment, practitioners possess disparate knowledge and skills, which has an impact on the quality of their assessments.

The presiding paradigm in assessment has come from a deficit perspective. The student is tested with a focus on which abilities fail to reach a certain level of expected performance within certain domains. Those unfamiliar with second language acquisition processes may overlook the many strengths that ELLs possess, namely the cognitive and social flexibility that is required to successfully navigate two worlds.

Issues in Language Acquisition

When working with ELLs it is important for school psychologists to understand the development both of a student's native language and of English as a second language to make adequate assessment decisions (de Valenzuela & Niccolai, 2004).

Monolingual Versus Bilingual Language Acquisition

Most of the focus on language acquisition or psycholinguistics has been on monolingual speakers. However, in recent years attention to the effects of a second language on language development has begun to increase. In fact, probably the most important overall finding in the study of bilingualism is the critical interaction of the native language with the one being learned (de Groot, 2011).

Various theories of language development exist. Nativists argue that all children are born with innate knowledge that guides their language acquisition. Noam Chomsky (1965) proposed that brains are hardwired to acquire language through the language acquisition device. However, researchers have acknowledged that although in language development some processes are innate, environmental systems such as social contexts contribute to the process of language growth. Although various theories of language development exist, most coincide in a general sequence of developmental milestones in language acquisition consistent across languages. A child's primary language development takes approximately 4–5 years. Most of the growth in the area of phonological, semantic, and grammatical knowledge occurs between the ages of birth and 6 years (Byrnes & Wasik, 2009). After that time, growth in vocabulary (semantics) and pragmatics continues across childhood and into adulthood through contextual use. Understanding monolingual language acquisition will

help school psychologists develop a framework for second language acquisition.

Language Development of ELLs

Children who are exposed to English after having acquired proficiency in their native language show some similar characteristics that are important to consider when conducting an assessment. First, receptive language develops initially at a higher rate than expressive language. This suggests that, regardless of the method of instruction, children will understand language before they can speak it (Griffin & Hartley, 1996). Most second language learners pass through five stages of language production: preproduction, early production, speech emergence, intermediate fluency, and advanced fluency. The first two stages focus on receptive language development in which English is stored and compared to the vocabulary, syntax, and grammatical structure of the native language, while the next two stages represent the initial meaningful expression or production of language as well as more complex comprehension. The final stage represents a bilingual use of language. When engaging in a bilingual assessment, considering what language development stage the child is traversing assists the school psychologist in determining the types of instruments and the process appropriate to complete a valid and nondiscriminatory assessment.

Second, Cummins (1984, 1999) proposed that there are two types of language proficiencies that are essential in all language acquisition: basic interpersonal communication skills and cognitive–academic language proficiency. Basic interpersonal communication skills, or social language, refers to the initial stage of language acquisition developed through social and informal settings. This level of proficiency in language is generally acquired in a period of 2 or 3 years. On the other hand, cognitive–academic language proficiency, or academic language, involves a more profound understanding and utilization of language. This is the language necessary for academic and cognitively challenging activities and is associated with literacy and vocabulary knowledge. Attaining academic language requires a longer process that typically takes between 5 and 7 years (Cummins, 1984). Furthermore, learning a second language does not occur in a vacuum. As words or phrases in English are acquired, they are associated with knowledge of the native language already stored. This interaction between a student's native language and English Cummins (1984) named *common underlying proficiency*. The development of this underlying proficiency is based on students' opportunities to master their native language to a minimum threshold so that they can build upon that foundation and acquire the second language. Thus, testing a student's language proficiency is critical to planning an effective assessment.

It is important to consider the instructional placement of ELLs when looking at second language acquisition. Depending on the state and district characteristics, ELLs can receive instruction in three possible language placements: all English classes without language support, English as a second language instruction, or bilingual classes (Rhodes et al., 2005). There are variations to these placements depending on the amount of English instruction and native language support during instruction.

Second Language Acquisition

When considering a child's second language acquisition, research suggests that meeting milestones in a first language facilitates acquisition of a second language. Also, the age of exposure of the first and second language has an impact on a child's language development. So, if a child is exposed to two languages from a young age (before age 3), then the child's process of second language acquisition may be more similar to his or her first language development (de Valenzuela & Niccolai, 2004) and the child will likely be bilingual. Bilingual children have been exposed to both languages, understand their use in different situations or circumstances, and show relative proficiency in both languages (Bedore et al., 2012; Jorshchick, Quick, Glässer, Lieven, & Tomasello, 2011). Often bilingual students do not have language dominance, since they are proficient in both and are exposed to the use of both. Proficiency is defined as the language skills relative to a monolingual speaker's vocabulary, while language dominance is related to both proficiency and exposure to the language.

On the other hand, children may initially acquire one language for the first few years and later be exposed to a second language. Second language exposure typically occurs after age 3 and is labeled sequential language development (de Valenzuela & Niccolai, 2004; Hoff, 2009).

When considering the language acquisition of ELLs it is important to consider three factors: instructional placement, formal and informal access to native language and English during instructional time, and the length of time the ELL has been exposed to English. This knowledge will be critical in the selection and use of formal and informal assessment measures and should be also considered when analyzing the results of all measures.

BEST PRACTICES IN ASSESSMENT OF ELLS

Being aware of the implications of standardized assessment becomes a pressing concern when the goal is to conduct nondiscriminatory evaluations of ELLs. ELLs have many levels of language proficiency, creating a spectrum of linguistic and acculturation levels that directly relate to their achievement and cognitive assessment. These areas need to be considered when developing an assessment plan as described in the case study that follows.

Case Study

Adela is 8 years old and is just completing the third grade. Her parents emigrated from Uruguay when she was 3 years old for her father to attend graduate school in the United States. Her mother has a master's degree and is a homemaker at this time. When not at school, Adela spends most of her time with her parents. Currently, they speak only Spanish at home. She is an only child and her mother reported that she is gregarious, well behaved, and happy.

Adela has attended the same school since prekindergarten. Her formal education has been in an all-English classroom with English as a second language pullout support twice per week for 1 hour. For the past 2 years she has not attained benchmark minimum performance in reading and writing, but has performed above expectations in math. Small group interventions were offered with moderate success. Her parents have requested testing based upon their impression that she is struggling with reading.

After interviewing Adela's parents, the school psychologist decided on an assessment plan that began with formal and informal evaluation of her language proficiency. The school psychologist interviewed Adela about her language preferences and utilized a formal measure to determine her academic language proficiency in listening, speaking, reading, and writing in English and Spanish. The results indicated that in Spanish, Adela has conversational language abilities in listening and speaking but limited academic skills in reading and writing. In English, her skills are limited in reading and writing, and she is academically proficient in listening and speaking.

These language proficiency results indicated that Adela has language dominance in English and is proficient in spoken English, and she has conversational abilities in Spanish. Therefore, the school psychologist decided to utilize a norm-referenced measure to evaluate her cognitive functioning in English. In addition, the school psychologist administered a subtest that allowed Adela to demonstrate the additional gains in knowledge and understanding based on her bilingual abilities. Results of the cognitive measure indicated that most areas of functioning were in the average range, although her crystallized intelligence (based upon a bilingual ability measure) and short-term memory were slightly below the average range.

Regarding the academic dimension of the assessment, the school psychologist considered the type of setting that Adela had attended and noted that her formal education had been all in English and that she had not received instruction in Spanish. However, Adela's mother reported that she reads to Adela in Spanish every night. So, the school psychologist decided to evaluate Adela's academic performance in English and Spanish utilizing both norm-referenced and curriculum-based measures. Results indicated that in both English and Spanish, Adela had average basic reading and decoding skills but showed below average reading comprehension skills as well as limited writing skills. Her performance in math was above average. Curriculum-based measures indicated that Adela is able to complete grade-level work in areas of phonemic awareness, decoding, basic dictation, and reading fluency, but she struggles with comprehension of even second-grade-level passages.

As the school psychologist integrated the information, it became evident that Adela has the cognitive ability to complete grade-level work in some subject areas, but reading comprehension is difficult for her. She has had adequate exposure to English (5 consecutive years of formal instruction) to develop academic skills in English, but is falling behind her classmates. Despite growing up in a language-rich household with parents who value education, she has not developed sufficient cognitive and academic language proficiency in her native language in any of the language domains. She has acquired the skills to decode using phonological rules but has not mechanized this skill to be able to focus on comprehension. The school psychologist considers all factors and recommends that Adela be eligible to receive special education as a child with a learning disability in reading comprehension and written expression.

Standardized Measures

Most assessments of ELLs include standardized tests. Standardized measures have specific limitations when they are used with ELLs. One major limitation of standardized tests is that they may not be representative of the student being assessed. Conducting an evaluation that is defensible is critical. Therefore, utilizing valid instruments is of the utmost importance. Valid and nondiscriminatory assessments measure constructs such as achievement, ability, adaptive, or social–emotional functioning and not merely the student's ability to understand the English language and U.S. culture (Flanagan, McGrew, & Ortiz, 2000). Although standardized tests are the gold standard for formal cognitive and achievement testing, these tests derive their utility from their norming sample. However, norming standards are not able to cover all of the variations in cultural differences present among ELLs. Therefore, the cultural competence of the school psychologist is best put to the test when the evaluator has to attend to the possible cultural and dialectical differences that the student is displaying during the assessments. It is incumbent upon the school psychologist to keep in mind that "these differences in experience represent a variable that is not stratified in any norm sample available today" (Flanagan, Ortiz, & Alfonso, 2007, p. 160).

Despite the nuances characteristic of the assessment of ELLs, for high-incidence languages such as Spanish, standardized assessments are available and allow for the completion of comprehensive bilingual assessments. Some of these measures are described in Table 6.1. For low-incidence languages, however, the availability of standardized instruments is sparse. For these evaluations, standardized nonverbal measures in addition to nonstandardized assessment techniques tend to be the most useful. By including nonstandardized assessment methods within the scope of bilingual evaluations, the school psychologist enhances the breadth of information that is available about the student.

Steps of a Bilingual Evaluation

Whether the school psychologist is conducting the assessment with a high- or low- incidence native language will directly influence the number of standardized versus nonstandardized measures that will constitute the assessment. Regardless, the school psychologist should attend to specific steps when assessing ELLs. These steps are summarized in the flowchart described in Figure 6.1. Along the way it is imperative that the school psychologist and the evaluation team take into consideration the cultural background of the student when interpreting the data.

Table 6.1. Standardized Assessment Instruments for ELLs

Area	Test Name	Published	Languages
Language	Woodcock-Muñoz Language Survey–Revised Normative Update	2010	English and Spanish
Acculturation	Receptive and Expressive One-Word Picture Vocabulary Tests, Fourth Edition	Spanish 2000; English 2010	English and Spanish
	Acculturation Rating Scale for Mexican Americans-II	1995	English and Spanish
	Acculturation Scale for Vietnamese Adolescents	1999	English and Vietnamese
Achievement	Aprenda: La prueba de logros en español, Tercera edición	2009	English and Spanish
	Batería III Woodcock-Muñoz: Pruebas de aprovechamiento	2007	Spanish
	Prueba de Habilidades Académicas Iniciales	2006	Spanish
Cognitive	Batería III Woodcock-Muñoz: Pruebas de habilidades cognitivas	2007	Spanish
	The Bilingual Verbal Ability Tests	2005	Arabic, Chinese (two forms), English, French, German, Haitian Creole, Hindi, Hmong, Italian, Japanese, Korean, Navajo, Polish, Portuguese, Russian, Spanish, Turkish, and Vietnamese
	Developmental Profile 3	2007	English, Spanish
	Wechsler Intelligence Scale for Children, Fourth Edition–Spanish	2004	Spanish
	Test of Phonological Awareness	2004	Spanish
Nonverbal	Test of Nonverbal Intelligence, Fourth Edition	2010	Nonverbal
	Comprehensive Test of Nonverbal Intelligence	2009	Nonverbal
	Naglieri Nonverbal Ability Test, Second Edition	2007; new norms 2011	Nonverbal
	Differential Ability Scales, Second Edition–Nonverbal Scale	2007	English, Spanish, Nonverbal
	Wechsler Nonverbal Scale of Ability	2006	Nonverbal
	Kaufman Assessment Battery for Children, Second Edition–Nonverbal Scale	2004	English, Nonverbal
	Universal Nonverbal Intelligence Test	1997	Nonverbal
	Leiter International Performance Scale, Revised	1997	Nonverbal
Adaptive	Vineland Adaptive Behavior Scales, Second Edition	2005	English and Spanish (interview only)
	Adaptive Behavior Assessment System, Second Edition	2003	English and Spanish

Language Proficiency

The first element of an assessment designed for ELLs is establishing the language proficiency of the student. The purpose of determining the language proficiency of the student is to identify in which of two languages the student is dominant, and to compare the level of language proficiency in each language (de Valenzuela & Baca, 2004a). Although it is most common to focus mainly on oral language to obtain an accurate picture of an ELL's language proficiency, all four major domains of language (listening, speaking, reading, and writing) should be explored (Vazquez-Nuttall et al., 2007). Information about the student's language abilities in the student's native language and English will guide the school psychologist in selecting instruments in the language that more closely matches the student's language profile. Determining if a student's proficiency is minimal, emergent, fluent, or advanced for each language will provide the school psychologist information about how to assess cognitive and academic abilities

Figure 6.1. The Sequence of Steps to Take When Assessing ELLs

Language and Culture
- First, the child's language proficiency is assessed in order to establish which language is dominant (if there is dominance), and to determine the appropriate language(s) and method of assessment.
- This is done using formal and informal assessment data (bilingual oral language measures, asking the student about language use and preferences, interviewing the parent regarding current and past language exposure, home language survey).
- Acculturation data is gathered through interviews with the student and parents. If needed, the school psychologist consults with cultural agents familiar with the student's home culture.

Achievement
- Second, the student's achievement is assessed in each language to which he or she has been exposed or had formal instruction. This will help to determine current academic functioning as well as cognitive academic language proficiency levels.
- This is done using formal and informal assessment data (achievement tests, school records, prior assessments, teacher input, classroom observations, history of instruction, language(s) of instruction and intervention).
- If a learning disability is suspected, the academic weakness must be present in both languages to be considered evidence of a true disability.

Cognitive Abilities
- Third, the appropriate language and method of cognitive assessment is determined. More than one battery may be used.
- If the student has adequate verbal skills, and an appropriate language battery is available, a verbal IQ measure may be given in the dominant or native language (the Bilingual Verbal Ability Tests can help establish bilingual verbal ability and is available in many languages).
- If the student has no language, very low oral language skills or there is no battery available to give in the dominant language, a nonverbal measure may be more appropriate.

Adaptive Behavior
- Finally, as appropriate to the referral question, or if intellectual disability is suspected, assess adaptive behvior at home and in school.
- Adaptive behavior scales should be given to persons familiar with the student's daily functioning. If the student's home language is Spanish, the Adaptive Behavior Assessment System, Second Edition or the Vineland Adaptive Behavior Scales, Second Edition can be used. If the home language is not English or Spanish, conduct a parent interview.
- Adaptive behavior, cognitive ability (and any problem behaviors) must be interpreted in light of the student's cultural experiences.

through a nondiscriminatory inclusion of the student's dominant language. Language dominance can be determined using formal and informal methods.

Formal methods. Standardized language proficiency tests generally constitute the most frequently used formal methods of assessing oral language ability. Although different instruments exist, choosing one can be a challenge. There are several factors that can assist the school psychologist when selecting an instrument. Rhodes et al. (2005) recommended that school psychologists consider the instrument's norming practices, psychometric characteristics, and measured skills.

However, several limitations exist when using formal language proficiency tests, including weak psychometric properties, nonrepresentative norms, and poor test translations. Additionally, language tests are available only in a limited number of languages, and very few account for dialectical variations or cultural differences in language. Therefore, the appropriate use of formal measures is limited to high-incidence languages such as Spanish. See Table 6.1 for a list of examples of formal language proficiency measures.

The school psychologist should find out information about the student's language proficiency in both the student's native language and English, that is, the student's basic and academic language levels. In the case of Spanish, school psychologists can use the oral expression and listening comprehension clusters in standardized tests of achievement. Based on these findings, the school psychologist should be able to determine if the student shows no dominant language or language dominance in the native language or English. It is important to note that if a learning disability is suspected, the academic weakness must be present in both languages to be considered evidence of a true disability.

Informal methods. For languages in which no formal measures exist, the use of informal methods is recommended. Informal methods can include observations or interviews focused on the complexity and quality of the language the student uses in different contexts, such as classroom, playground, and home (Gottlieb, 2006). The languages the student uses are also described on the Home Language Survey. These informal methods also include language samples for high versus low context situations as well as the use of abstract versus concrete information. Also, parent and teacher rating scales are utilized to obtain information useful to establishing proficiency in both the native language and English. In an instructional context, performance tasks scored with rubrics can provide information on reading and writing. Specific resources such as Gottlieb (2006) can assist school psychologists and teachers in developing these performance tasks. Since informal methods can provide a wide range of information regarding proficiency, it is important that, unless the student has absolutely no proficiency in one of the two languages, proficiency be assessed in both languages (Gottlieb & Sanchez-Lopez, 2008). See Table 6.2 for a list of methods of nonstandardized assessments for ELLs.

Acculturation

Consideration of the level of acculturation to the mainstream culture as well as maintenance of ties to the home country/culture should be an integral part of every bilingual assessment. Although formal instruments are available to measure acculturation, these may not be standardized for use with all cultural groups. In this area, informal assessment is advised and should be integrated into the initial data-gathering phase of each assessment. The school psychologist should ask parents questions about their child's age at immigration (if applicable), length of time in the United States, ongoing contact with family and friends in the country of origin

including frequency of visits to that country, and previous and current educational experiences in the home language. The school psychologist should also inquire about acculturation with the student being assessed by asking about the student's preferred language for reading, listening to music, watching TV, and talking with friends at school and friends and family. By gathering these data, the school psychologist can gain a more nuanced picture of the student's cultural experiences and may develop hypotheses about the impact of biculturalism/bilingualism on the student's current functioning.

Academic Achievement

The second step in the process of assessing ELLs includes evaluating the academic achievement of the student. Regarding the measure of achievement or academic skills of ELLs, the educational background of the student must be carefully taken into consideration. Evaluation of academic achievement in the native language is not required if the student has never received formal instruction in that language. Therefore, academic performance should be assessed in the languages in which instruction has been received. This is particularly important for ELLs who receive bilingual instruction in which the native language is used to deliver content material.

For Spanish speakers, standardized measures can be used to establish the academic functioning and the cognitive–academic language proficiency levels. It is not uncommon to find ELLs who present with very distinct proficiency and achievement levels in each of the languages being assessed depending on their level of exposure to formal instruction. In the case of a native language that is not Spanish, school psychologists can use non norm-referenced approaches to gather information on the student's academic achievement. These include standardized curriculum-based measurements and teacher-made curriculum-based assessments. These measures help inform school psychologists about discrepancies that ELLs demonstrate when compared to other students in their classroom or school. Criterion-referenced testing for specific topics is another approach that allows student performance to be compared to predetermined criteria rather than to a norming population that may not be representative of the student's characteristics. Although criterion-referenced measures can be very helpful in identifying specific knowledge obtained and areas of growth, extreme caution must be taken when using these tests because these tests may not be based on valid universal criteria

Table 6.2. Nonstandardized Assessment for ELLs

	Method	Purpose
Language	• Observations/interviews	Identify language preferences and complexity/quality of the language use in different contexts (home, classroom, and playground)
Achievement	• Curriculum-based measurements	Normed and standardized curriculum-based measurements compare the student with school, district, state, or national norms
	• Curriculum-based assessments	Teacher-made tests based on the curriculum being used in the classroom serve as a thermometer of student's academic performance
	• Criterion-referenced tests	Topic-specific testing of what the student is expected to know at a given time
	• Portfolio assessment	Work samples and activities completed by the student
	• Supplemental	Teacher ratings/checklists, student self-ratings, work progress records, dialogue journals, role-plays, story retelling, semantic maps, dictations, and writing samples
Cognitive	• Observations	Structured observations of the student in action show the student's ability to navigate cognitive challenges in the environment
	• Culturally sensitive interviews	Parents, teachers, and the students can offer information on how the student handles cognitive challenges and how the student uses specific strategies to complete tasks
	• Testing the limits	Specific tasks within standardized and normed tests can inform about the student's performance under specific conditions and challenges
	• Dynamic assessment (test-teach-test)	Given an established baseline, teaching specific, relevant skills and then retesting informs learning potential of the student
	• Supplemental	Teacher ratings/checklists, student self-ratings, work progress records, dialogue journals, role plays, story retelling, semantic maps, dictations, and writing samples
Adaptive	• Observations/interviews	Parents, teachers, and caregivers can provide information about functioning levels of the student in daily living activities

and do not allow for cross-subject comparisons (de Valenzuela & Baca, 2004b).

Cognitive Ability

The next step in the process of assessing ELLs includes determining the method of assessing the student's cognitive ability (verbal and nonverbal). If the student is a Spanish speaker, then verbal measures are readily available for use. The initial assessment of language dominance aids in the determination of the languages to be used for the rest of the assessment process. In that sense, it is important to keep in mind that the 2004 Individuals with Disabilities Education Act calls for the use of a measure in a language that allows for the student to demonstrate most accurately his or her potential to perform cognitively, academically, developmentally, and functionally.

If the student is dominant in a language for which standardized cognitive measures are not available, or if the student does not present with adequate verbal skills,

then the school psychologist can use a nonverbal measure. This would also be appropriate for a student with severe oral language delays or a speech–language impairment.

When nonverbal cognitive measures are used, it is important to keep in mind three areas of concern. First, nonverbal batteries are not primarily normed on bilingual individuals. Second, nonverbal measures are not entirely nonverbal, as some communication has to occur between the examiner and the examinee (Ortiz, 2001). Third, nonverbal measures focus on the assessment of the student's performance on nonverbal abilities, but not the student's verbal ability. Areas of cognitive ability such as comprehension knowledge, auditory processing, and long-term memory are not measured by most nonverbal test batteries.

Given the numerous languages being spoken in U.S. schools, multiple nonverbal measures of cognitive ability are available for use. Some of these measures are listed in Table 6.1. When using nonverbal measures, school psychologists should carefully document the need for their use and pursue alternative methods to gather information that will lead to a comprehensive understanding of the student's cognitive ability. Some of these alternative methods fall into the nonstandardized portion of the information gathering process.

A proxy for cognitive ability can be assessed through structured observations where the school psychologist can see the student handling the challenges in the student's environment. In addition, interviews that are culturally sensitive serve to collect information from parents, teachers, and the student regarding strategies used to solve specific problems and achieve goals. There are two additional objective, nonstandardized methods to assess cognitive functioning in ELLs: testing the limits, where the school psychologist observes the student performance within specific conditions or parameters; and dynamic assessment or test-teach-test, where given a measured baseline the student is taught specific, relevant skills and then is retested on these skills.

Adaptive Skills

Depending on the referral question posed at the beginning of the evaluation and the student's level of cognitive functioning, data are necessary regarding adaptive skills levels. For assessment with Spanish speakers, school psychologists can use standardized measures. For speakers of other languages, nonstandardized assessment of adaptive skills can be completed through observations and interviews. Observations of the daily living, communicative, or social activities that the student can handle independently can be very informative in regard to the student's cognitive functioning and his or her abilities to navigate everyday living. Finally, the school psychologist should conduct interviews with the parents, caregivers, and teachers to compile information about the student's daily functioning.

Final Considerations

When conducting the assessment of ELLs, test bias should always be a consideration. Test bias can occur through multiple ways, given that no measure, instrument, or technique is culture free. Test bias can be introduced by the underrepresentation of ELLs in the normative sample and by the cultural and linguistic demands of the instrument. However, most well-respected standardized instruments have strong psychometric properties such that the bias is not inherent to the instrument but is introduced by its use with ELLs. Therefore, in order to conduct a nondiscriminatory

assessment, school psychologists must be aware of utilizing standardized measures with good psychometric properties and also be aware of limitations of their use (Rhodes et al., 2005).

Given the significant impact a psychoeducational assessment can have in the educational trajectory of an individual, it is essential for school psychologists to be knowledgeable about the fundamental skills needed to assess ELLs. Gaining cultural competence, proficiency in the use of assessment instruments, and sensitivity to the unique characteristics of ELLs empowers school psychologists to conduct nondiscriminatory evaluations. The significant role school psychologists have in the assessment of diverse individuals is not a novel concept. Cummins (2001) wrote that "the influence of the societal power structure is mediated by the way educators define their roles in relation to students' language and culture, community participation, pedagogy and assessment" (p. 652).

SUMMARY

The comprehensive assessment of ELLs includes many of the same areas (e.g., cognition and achievement) and procedures as the assessment of their monolingual peers. However, in this type of assessment the role of the child's native language plays a critical part. Throughout this chapter, school psychologists who are called upon to conduct assessments of ELLs are alerted to the legal and professional expectations placed on them in order to conduct a meaningful assessment. Working in assessment teams is suggested as a procedure for addressing the potential cultural and linguistic biases in the assessment. This chapter also summarizes the critical nature of the cultural and linguistic dimensions that must be considered when conducting a bilingual assessment, and school psychologists are alerted to become aware of and sensitive to the personal cultural perspective that they bring to the process. Additionally, there are alternate choices in measures and methods available to complete a legally defensible bilingual assessment. The assessment of ELLs will be an ever increasing demand placed on school psychologists regardless of whether they speak a language other than English, given that ELLs are a continually increasing segment of the public school population.

AUTHOR NOTE

The authors wish to acknowledge the generous participation of Anita Sohn McCormick for her coordination of this joint project. Without her, this chapter would not have been completed.

REFERENCES

Alvarado, C. G., & the Bilingual Special Education Network of Texas. (2011). *Best practices in the special education evaluation of students who are culturally and linguistically diverse.* Retrieved from http://www.educationeval.com

Baca, L., & Baca, E. (2004). Bilingual special education: A judicial perspective. In L. Baca & H. Cervantes (Eds.), *The bilingual special education interface* (pp. 76–99). Upper Saddle River, NJ: Merrill.

Bedore, L., Peña, E., Summers, C., Boerger, K., Resendiz, M., Greene, K., ... Gillam, R. (2012). The measure matters: Language dominance profiles across measures in Spanish–English bilingual children. *Bilingualism: Language and Cognition, 15,* 616–629.

Byrnes, J. P., & Wasik, B. A. (2009). *Language and literacy development.* New York, NY: Guilford Press.

Chomsky, N. (1965). *Aspects of the theory of syntax.* Cambridge, MA: MIT Press.

Cummins, J. (1984). *Bilingualism and special education: Issues in assessment and pedagogy.* San Diego, CA: College Hill.

Cummins, J. (1999). *BICS and CALP: Clarifying the distinction.* Retrieved from ERIC database. (ED438 551).

Cummins, J. (2001). Empowering minority students: A framework for introduction. *Harvard Educational Review, 71,* 649–655.

de Groot, A. M. B. (2011). *Language and cognition in bilinguals and multilinguals: An introduction.* New York, NY: Psychology Press.

de Valenzuela, S., & Baca, L. M. (2004a). Issues and theoretical considerations in the assessment of bilingual children. In L. Baca & H. Cervantes (Eds.), *The bilingual special education interface* (pp. 162–183). Upper Saddle River, NJ: Merrill.

de Valenzuela, S., & Baca, L. M. (2004b). Procedures and techniques for assessing the bilingual exceptional child. In L. Baca & H. Cervantes (Eds.), *The bilingual special education interface* (pp. 184–203). Upper Saddle River, NJ: Merrill.

de Valenzuela, J. S., & Niccolai, S. L. (2004). Language development in culturally and linguistically diverse students with special education needs. In L. Baca & H. Cervantes (Eds.), *The bilingual special education interface* (pp. 125–161). Upper Saddle River, NJ: Merrill.

Flanagan, D. P., McGrew, K. S., & Ortiz, S. O. (2000). *The Wechsler intelligence scales and Gf-Gc theory: A contemporary approach to interpretation.* Boston, MA: Allyn & Bacon.

Flanagan, D. P., Ortiz, S. O., & Alfonso, V. C. (2007). *Essentials of cross-battery assessment* (2nd ed.). New York, NY: Wiley.

Gottlieb, M. H. (2006). *Assessing English language learners: Bridges from language proficiency to academic achievement.* Thousand Oaks, CA: Corwin.

Gottlieb, M., & Sanchez-Lopez, C. (2008). Assessing English language learners: A perplexing puzzle. *Perspectives on School-Based Issues, 9,* 45–51.

Griffin, G., & Hartley, T. A. (1996). List learning of second language vocabulary: The effect of the direction of learning on comprehension and generation. *Applied Psycholinguistics, 17,* 443–460.

Hoff, E. (2009). *Language development.* Belmont, CA: Wadsworth.

Jorshchick, L., Quick, A., Glässer, D., Lieven, E., & Tomasello, M. (2011). German-English–speaking children's mixed NPs with "correct" agreement. *Bilingualism: Language and Cognition, 14,* 173–183.

National Association of School Psychologists. (2010). *Model for comprehensive and integrated school psychological services.* Bethesda, MD: Author. Retrieved from http://www.nasponline.org/standards/2010standards/2_PracticeModel.pdf

Ortiz, S. O. (2001). Assessment of cognitive abilities in Hispanic children. *Seminars in Speech and Language, 22,* 17–37.

Rhodes, R. L., Ochoa, S. H., & Ortiz, S. O. (2005). *Assessing culturally and linguistically diverse students.* New York, NY: Guilford Press.

Sam, D. L., & Berry, J. W. (2010). Acculturation: When individuals and groups of different cultural backgrounds meet. *Perspectives on Psychological Science, 5,* 472–481.

Sotelo-Dynega, M., Geddes, L., Luhrs, A., & Teague, J. (2009). *Frequently asked questions: Bilingual school psychology certification.* Bethesda, MD: National Association of School Psychologists. Retrieved from http://www.nasponline.org/resources/culturalcompetence/faq_bilingualcertif.aspx

U.S. Census Bureau. (2010). *Language use.* Washington, DC: Author. Retrieved from http://www.census.gov/hhes/socdemo/language/index.html

Vazquez-Nuttall, E., Li, C., Dynda, A. M., Ortiz, S. O., Armengol, C., Walton, J., & Phoenix, K. (2007). Cognitive assessment of culturally and linguistically diverse students. In G. Esquivel, E. Lopez, & S. Nahari (Eds.), *Handbook of multicultural school psychology* (pp. 269–288). New York, NY: Erlbaum.

7

Best Practices in Assessing and Improving English Language Learners' Literacy Performance

Michael L. Vanderwood
Diana Socie
University of California, Riverside

OVERVIEW

As the demographics of the United States continue to rapidly shift, it will become increasingly rare for school psychologists to work in districts where there are no language minority students. Recent data suggest that there are approximately 11 million English language learners (ELLs) in grades K–12 in the United States, which accounts for about 12% of the total number of students enrolled in school (Aud et al., 2011). Further, by 2015, it is projected that 30% of the school-age population in the United States will be ELLs (Francis, Rivera, Lesaux, Kieffer, & Rivera, 2006). Although initially these numbers may not present as cause for concern, longitudinal data suggest that ELLs consistently perform well below their native English speaking peers in reading (Francis et al., 2006).

Fortunately, school psychologists are in a unique position in schools and have a distinct skill set to help inform practices related to ELLs. The National Association of School Psychologists (NASP) states in their *Model for Comprehensive and Integrated School Psychological Services* that school psychologists should "apply their knowledge and skills by creating and maintaining safe, supportive, fair, and effective learning environments and enhancing family–school collaboration for all students" (NASP, 2010). This chapter will address the NASP practice domain of Diversity in Development and Learning by providing the background knowledge and recommended practices school psychologists should employ when supporting students with reading concerns who are ELLs. Although special education eligibility will

be addressed, the primary focus of this chapter is on the knowledge and skills necessary to implement a multitiered system of support focused on reading for ELLs. To support a multitiered system, school psychologists need to know about issues related to Tier 1 instruction and Tier 2 intervention, screening, and progress monitoring.

ELL Growth

In the past 2 decades, the population of ELLs has grown 169%, whereas in this same time period the general school-age population has only grown 12% (Francis et al., 2006). The largest percentage of ELL students are in Arizona, California, Florida, Illinois, New York, and Texas. However, the vast majority of states have experienced more than 100% growth of their ELL population over the past 20 years (National Clearinghouse for English Language Acquisition, 2011). ELLs in the United States speak more than 400 different languages, with Spanish being spoken by the overwhelming majority, representing between 75 and 89% of ELLs (Aud et al., 2011; Office of English Language Acquisition, Language Enhancement, and Academic Achievement for Limited English Proficient Students, 2012). While Spanish is the most common language spoken by ELLs, states vary in terms of the linguistic diversity of their populations. In the 2006–2007 school year, Spanish was listed as the "most frequently spoken language" among ELL students in 43 states and the District of Columbia. Additionally, there were 19 states in which 80% or more of the ELL population were Spanish speakers.

In addition to difficulties with language that may have an impact on reading development, there is also research that suggests income level may be a mediating factor in educational achievement. It is important to note that longitudinal data suggest that first and second generation ELLs tend to come from households in low socio-economic status neighborhoods. Further, recent statistics from the U.S. Department of Education indicate that in 2008–2009 there was an overwhelming overrepresentation of ELLs in high poverty schools (Aud et al., 2011). During this school year, although more than half of public school students were Caucasian, only 14% of Caucasian children attended high poverty schools (Aud et al., 2011). In contrast, in the same year (2008–2009), ELLs made up 21% of students in public school and 45% of students in high poverty schools (Aud et al., 2011).

Not only are ELLs more likely to attend low performing, high poverty schools, they are also more likely than their native English speaking peers to struggle to meet grade-level standards in all academic areas (Francis et al., 2006). This is true especially in the area of reading, where recent data continue to highlight the achievement gap between Spanish-speaking Latino and Caucasian students (Aud et al., 2011). (Note: This chapter focuses exclusively on research related to teaching ELLs how to read in English, yet there are many ELLs who are taught how to read in their home/first language. The conclusions from this chapter should not be applied to ELLs who are not learning to read in English.)

BASIC CONSIDERATIONS

It is hard to argue that there is any more important academic skill than reading, and reading deficits make up the bulk of referrals for special education evaluations for both native English speakers and ELLs. To be able to properly understand how to best support ELLs who struggle in reading, school psychologists need to know the foundations of reading and language development and how those concepts are intertwined. Additionally, knowledge about standards to help guide the selection of assessment and intervention tools is essential to ensure the best and most appropriate decisions are made for ELLs at all levels of English proficiency. There are many opinions and beliefs about the best way to provide literacy instruction for ELLs, but very few of these ideas actually meet recommended standards for assessments or interventions. Most of what is known about intervention and assessment for ELLs has been conducted with Spanish-speaking students because of the sheer number of Spanish-speaking ELLs in comparison to

other groups of ELLs. School psychologists are in a strong position to help inform and relay information to school teams regarding the limitations of some of these findings to other groups of ELL students. In fact, school psychologists who consult with general education teachers and administrators can guide teams to implement the most appropriate research-based practices, even if the school psychologist is not actually the person who implements the programs or procedures.

Foundations of Reading Skills

Literacy theorists conceptualize reading as a language process that is initially heavily dependent on the early oral language experiences of children to build basic reading skills. There is a clear and obvious link between the number of words students are exposed to before school and both their initial reading level and their reading growth during the first few years of schooling. Fortunately, our understanding of how reading skills develop has improved dramatically over the last 2 decades, and strides have been made in producing instructional procedures and interventions to remediate the differences caused by diversity in language experiences (Gersten et al., 2007).

In 2000, the National Reading Panel (NRP) identified that reading programs that facilitated mastery of the big five skills (phonemic awareness, phonics, vocabulary, fluency, and comprehension) were the most likely to produce successful outcomes (National Institute of Child Health and Human Development, 2000; NRP, 2000). Although the NRP findings served to advance the field of education as related to teaching reading, these findings were limited to studies of reading outcomes for native English speakers. As a result, in 2002 a separate panel was charged with the task of specifically studying how these big five ideas contributed to the development of reading in language minority children (August & Shanahan, 2008).

The findings from the National Literacy Panel on Language-Minority Children and Youth indicate that the recommendations from the NRP are also appropriate for ELLs who are learning how to read. Along with the big five ideas, August and Shanahan (2008) also recommend that in order for ELLs to become successful readers they must be given access to separate English language development instruction to help them build academic language capacity in English. August and Shanahan (2008) emphasize that while ELLs typically develop appropriate word-level skills (i.e., phonemic awareness and phonics), the breakdown for ELLs usually occurs in the acquisition of comprehension-related skills. In fact, they report that "second language readers are more likely to achieve adequate performance on measures of word recognition and spelling than on measure of reading vocabulary, comprehension, and writing" (August & Shanahan, 2008, p. 277). When trying to identify the cause of a reading deficit, school psychologists must consider the level of English language development for ELLs in addition to reading skills.

Language Development

English language development for ELLs typically occurs in the general education classroom through explicit language instruction. School psychologists can be important consultants to teachers and school teams regarding the importance of good Tier 1 instruction in English language development as a means to support the development of reading skills. ELLs who enter kindergarten with little to no English skills are fundamentally at a disadvantage when compared to their native English speaking peers. In English immersion programs (which constitute the majority of English language development programs in the United States), ELLs are required to simultaneously develop their English and academic skills in an environment where all of the instruction is delivered in English. In order to develop the English language skills necessary to become successful readers, ELLs must receive specific and explicit instruction in English language development with a focus on the skills and words necessary to access the general education curriculum (i.e., academic English).

In terms of second language development, it is important for school psychologists to have familiarity with Cummins' (1984) seminal work in language acquisition. This understanding will help guide both intervention and assessment practices. Cummins' (1984) linguistic interdependence hypothesis suggests the acquisition of a second language (e.g., Spanish) in part depends on the adequate development of a student's native language (e.g., English). In other words, the more developed the primary language is, the quicker the student will pick up the second language.

School psychologists must understand the difference between social and/or interpersonal English language use and academic language. A teacher may infer a student's problem is not due to English language development because the student appears to use English quite well with peers. This type of English language use is typically referred to as basic interpersonal communication skills.

Students who develop the English language skills necessary to access all aspects of the curriculum possess cognitive academic language proficiency skills (Cummins, 1984). When attempting to understand the cause of a reading problem, school psychologists should examine assessment data that are designed to clarify whether students have basic interpersonal communication skills or cognitive academic language proficiency skills. As the next section indicates, students who are at the basic interpersonal communication skills stage need a different intervention focus than those at the cognitive academic language proficiency skills stage.

BEST PRACTICES IN ASSESSING AND IMPROVING ELL'S LITERACY PERFORMANCE

School psychologists are in a unique position to help teachers understand the best way to provide support for ELLs before and after a problem arises. Although there is still a need for more research, recommendations can be produced for practice based on the success of the use of multitier models to prevent and remediate reading problems for ELLs. For example, most of the reading assessments used in multitier systems (e.g., screening and progress monitoring tools) are appropriate for ELLs, but how to determine who is at risk of developing a reading deficit may need to be adjusted. Understanding how to modify or differentiate instruction within a multitiered model is inarguably as essential, if not more so, for ELLs as for native English speakers (Gersten et al., 2007). School psychologists need to emphasize the importance of providing high quality core instruction for ELLs before more intensive efforts are considered. Obviously, this same approach is used with native English speakers, but the difference when consulting about students who are ELLs is that instruction should incorporate evidence-based teaching strategies for both reading and English language development.

In the following sections we address best practices for assessment and intervention in a multitiered framework with the goal of providing school psychologists information they can use to improve outcomes for ELLs. This knowledge can serve school psychologists who act as interventionists, consultants, and members of school-based prereferral and/or problem-solving teams. As previously mentioned, many current practices used with ELLs are not supported by empirical research, and there is therefore a need for school psychologists to bring a scientific perspective to ELL student support.

Assessment

Multitiered system assessments are used for screening, progress monitoring, and diagnostic/analytic purposes. Yet, regardless of the purpose and the population, all assessments must meet specific standards. When searching for norms regarding professional practice for assessment and psychological testing, school psychologists can turn to the *Standards for Educational and Psychological Testing* (American Educational Research Association, American Psychological Association, & National Council on Measurement in Education [AERA, APA, & NCME], 1999). With respect to ELLs, the authors of the Standards give various recommendations to help school psychologists evaluate assessment tools. They point out that one of the biggest concerns for assessment of ELL students has to do with issues regarding development, validation, and norming. If test developers do not include ELL students in the standardization sample, it may call into question the validity of the test for these students. This is especially true for high-stakes decisions, such as eligibility for special education.

It is important to understand treating ELLs as one homogenous group when evaluating validity evidence for assessments may be inappropriate. The Standards (AERA, APA, & NCME, 1999) suggest psychometric information should be provided for any "linguistic" group that represents a student that may be tested with a measure. It is clear a student who is close to being considered English proficient has quite different linguistic skills than a student who is classified at the beginning level of English language proficiency. As we recommend in Table 7.1, school psychologists must emphasize the need to use measures that meet the Standards guidelines for students who have limited English proficiency. For example, school psychologists should look for information that states whether a measure is appropriate for a student who has intermediate English language proficiency and Spanish is his or her first language versus just providing information about ELLs as a group. School psychologists can help educators understand the limitations of test results for ELLs, especially when interpreting scores that are based on measures with limited validity evidence for a specific ELL subgroup.

Screening and Progress Monitoring

Phonological awareness, alphabetic principle, fluency, and comprehension are the typical skills assessed by screening and progress-monitoring measures in multitiered systems. As previously mentioned, these same constructs should be assessed for ELLs and used to help determine who needs additional help and whether the additional support is working (August & Shanahan, 2008; Brown & Sanford, 2011). The challenge for school psychologists who work with ELLs is to interpret the screening and progress-monitoring results within a context that is quite different than for native English speakers. For example, it is expected that an ELL will grow at a slower rate than a native English speaker if the ELL's English language proficiency is in the beginning stage. Conversely, if a student is an ELL and has language proficiency close to the established range, then it is expected that the student will grow at a rate very similar to native English speakers. A recent study completed with second grade ELLs who were being taught to read in English supported the conclusion that level of English proficiency affects a student's initial reading level and growth throughout an academic year (Gutierrez & Vanderwood, 2013).

Besides English language proficiency, Cummins' (1984) linguistic interdependence hypothesis suggests a student who has strong home language skills will acquire English faster than a student who does not. These two concepts are critical for school psychologists who help

---

Table 7.1. Reading Assessment Recommendations for ELLs

- When possible, use tests that included ELLs who are representative of the target student's home language and level of English language proficiency in the test development and validation process.
- Conduct screening for phonological awareness, alphabetic principle, fluency, and comprehension in the language of instruction.
- Complete an educational history to determine the extent to identify factors that may influence a student's response to instruction and intervention and can be used to create solutions to reading problems.
- Use screening and progress-monitoring tools that provide separate cut scores and rate of improvement goal setting guidelines for ELLs based on the level of English proficiency.
- Ensure language proficiency is assessed with reliable and valid measures.
- Conduct systematic observations of ELL students during core instruction when attempting to diagnose the cause of a reading problem.

teachers and teams determine the cause of a student's lack of response to an intervention or determine the primary focus of instruction/intervention. As indicated in Table 7.1, we recommend completing an educational history for any ELL when attempting to identify possible interventions or instructional modifications. The impact of home language on second language acquisition should be discussed and possibly examined when school psychologists are trying to help teams problem solve inadequate growth in reading skills. This statement is not to suggest that teams should intervene in the home language, but instead to suggest that teams consider this hypothesis before changing reading interventions for a student who is struggling.

Because of the differences between ELLs and native English speakers just highlighted, there are efforts underway to determine if the commonly used measures for reading screening and progress monitoring (e.g., AIMSweb and DIBELS) have similar psychometric properties for ELLs as they do for native English speakers. As part of this process, several authors have conducted studies to determine if these reading measures predict differently for ELLs than for native English speakers (e.g., Johnson, Jenkins, Petscher, & Catts, 2009; Gutierrez & Vanderwood, 2013). This concept is typically called predictive bias, and is examined by determining whether a measure predicts more accurately for one group than another. When looking at skill-based measures of reading (e.g., curriculum-based measures), the literature examining the predictive bias by ELL status has yielded conflicting results. Some authors provided evidence of predictive bias while others did not. At this point it is difficult to make conclusive statements about the effect of ELL status on the predictive validity of curriculum-based measures of reading performance. One challenge that prevents making strong conclusions is that studies have typically characterized ELLs as a homogeneous group or, at best, as separated by native language. However, it is clear ELLs come to school with a wide range of English language proficiency.

Another aspect of a test's predictive bias is the use of cut scores to determine a student's level of risk for reading problems. Initial research in this area suggests there may be a need for separate at-risk cut scores for ELLs and for subgroups with ELLs (Johnson et al., 2009). To address these concerns, test developers (e.g., AIMSweb) are starting to develop separate norms and cut scores for ELLs, but at this point these approaches should be considered with caution given the lack of substantial validity evidence for the decisions made with the new norms. Yet, as recommended in Table 7.1, school psychologists should compare ELL students' performance to cut scores and rates of improvement that were developed specifically for ELLs who have a similar level of English language proficiency to the target student or students.

English Language Proficiency Assessments

Determining how to appropriately evaluate a student's language proficiency in his or her native language and in English can be a significant challenge owing to the lack of agreement about the nature of the construct. As previously mentioned, Cummins (1984) suggests language proficiency is the ability to use language for both academic purposes and basic communicative tasks. Most language proficiency measures will provide some type of score about academic skills and communication. Given the contrasting theories about the nature of language proficiency, language proficiency test results may differ substantially from one another (Del Vecchio & Guerrero, 1995; Schrank, Fletcher, & Alvarado, 1996).

The data about current language proficiency measures suggest prior to using a test the measure should be carefully examined to determine what components of language proficiency are being addressed. Tests that measure basic interpersonal communication skills may mistakenly lead educators to assume that a student possesses cognitive academic language proficiency skills. Language proficiency tests are often used to make high-stakes decisions about the program of instruction in which a student is best suited to learn. For example, results may be used to determine whether a student is able to meet the academic demands of English-only instruction or whether the student would be better suited in a bilingual or English as a second language instructional program (Schrank et al., 1996). In these situations, school psychologists can help educators interpret test scores to help school teams determine appropriate placement, as incorrect placement decisions or denial of services may result from misinterpretations of the tests. As recommended in Table 7.1, school psychologists should ensure measures used to assess English proficiency are considered reliable and valid and have recent norms. Unfortunately, it is common practice to use English proficiency measures with limited reliability and validity data.

Diagnostic Assessment

School psychologists who use a multitiered approach to address reading problems will have opportunities to provide diagnostic support for ELLs at multiple levels.

At Tiers 1 and 2, the primary focus will be determining whether a reading problem is primarily caused by deficits in the big five reading skills, oral language, or behavioral concerns that are negatively affecting student engagement. As already mentioned in this chapter, an understanding of a student's educational history will be critical for identifying the cause of reading problems for ELLs. In addition, as we recommend in Table 7.1, when a reading concern exists for ELLs, school psychologists should conduct systematic direct observations in the student's classroom. Unfortunately, many ELLs struggle staying engaged in classroom settings unless teachers use instructional techniques we describe later in this chapter that accommodate the oral and written language differences that characterize ELLs (Gersten et al., 2007).

School psychologists also play a key role diagnosing whether a student who is an ELL has a learning disability. Multiple factors must be addressed when teams are attempting to determine if a student should be classified as having a learning disability. For students who are ELLs, the exclusionary factors are often challenging to eliminate as causes for a student's low performance. In addition, there are clear and well-documented challenges to assessing the cognitive ability of ELLs (Wagner, Francis, & Morris, 2005).

An alternative or possible supplemental approach to focusing on norm-referenced cognitive and achievement measures is to identify academic skills deficits (e.g., reading skills) and provide intervention with progress monitoring (Klingner, Artiles, & Barletta, 2006). These data can be used to help address exclusionary factors and help support the decision about the need for special education. Although this process is typically used in a response to intervention for eligibility model, we suggest these data are critical regardless of the learning disability eligibility model used. In fact, we suggest an assessment for determining an ELL student's learning disability eligibility would not be comprehensive unless response data are included in the process and report.

By identifying a student's reading skill deficit, providing intervention, and then monitoring growth, school psychologists will be able to reduce the impact of prior learning experiences on the data that are used for the decision-making process. For example, if 10 ELLs with similar language backgrounds and levels of English proficiency receive an intervention focused on phonological awareness, and the target student is 1 of only 2 of the students who did not grow at the desired rate, the team will be able to be more convinced that language and culture are not the primary causes of a student's low performance. Obviously, if this approach is used, it is

absolutely essential teams select interventions and progress-monitoring tools that are validated to work with ELLs, and measures of interrater reliability and treatment fidelity are collected.

Instruction and Intervention

Although assessment practices are often the primary focus of school psychologists, there is a growing consensus for the need for school psychologists to be able to examine and understand instruction and intervention as part of their role in the problem-solving process. In fact, as addressed in the previous section, to be able to address all the exclusionary factors that are part of a learning disability diagnosis, school psychologists must have at least a basic understanding of instruction and intervention. As mentioned throughout this chapter, when attempting to address reading concerns for ELLs, it is critical to understand the student's background related to previous exposure to oral language and reading experiences. In this section we highlight the importance of using research-based reading interventions, and we point out the critical components of instruction and intervention that should be part of problem-solving conversations. We finish this section by providing a quick overview of the components of effective oral language programs. We do not expect school psychologists to be experts about reading instruction or oral language, but it is important to emphasize the impact of these components on reading skill development and to be able to generate informed options for instructional modifications and interventions.

Research Standards

In addition to standards about how to best select assessments for ELLs, school psychologists must also know how to select reading interventions and instructional procedures that have established research support. Although there is not a consensus about what constitutes a validated intervention, in the last decade significant progress was provided through the leadership of the Institute of Education Science's (IES) What Works Clearinghouse. The IES's commitment to use randomized controlled trials as the gold standard for intervention research has not been without criticism, but other types of designs including regression discontinuity and single case are considered as part of the process to evaluate research-evaluating interventions.

Owing to the differences in language experiences between native English speakers and ELLs, the IES created a process to evaluate interventions separately for ELLs. For the IES to consider an intervention to meet research standards for ELLs, a study must clearly identify the ELL population and describe characteristics of the sample in a manner that will allow users to know to whom the results can be generalized. As we recommend in Table 7.2, school psychologists who work with ELLs should routinely refer to this database to identify interventions that can be considered empirically supported and meeting research standards. In most cases, reading interventions that work with native English speakers appear to also work with ELLs, but our knowledge in this area needs further development (Linan-Thompson, Cirino, & Vaughn, 2007). As previously mentioned, there is an abundance of options available to use with ELLs that are not research supported. School psychologists are in a unique role that allows for integration of science and practice and could possibly discourage educators from using techniques and procedures that lack a strong empirical evidence base.

Reading Instruction and Intervention

It is clear ELLs develop English reading skills in a manner that is very similar to native English speaking students (August & Shanahan, 2008), and that the use of a multitiered framework is the most appropriate way to deliver and manage reading support (Gersten et al., 2007). As previously mentioned, the five constructs of phonological awareness, alphabetic principle, fluency, vocabulary, and comprehension are the appropriate reading skill targets for reading assessment and intervention for ELLs. In fact, there is some evidence that suggests ELLs can benefit even more than native English speaking students from a prevention and skill-focused model of service delivery that focuses on the big five (August & Shanahan, 2008). Yet, there are a few slight differences in the application of these ideas that warrant further discussion and elaboration.

There are some aspects of Tier 1 instruction that should be highlighted and examined with scrutiny when attempting to address the cause of an ELL student's reading problems. As we point out in Table 7.2, ELLs learn best when instruction is explicit and systematic (Gersten et al., 2007). Yet, because of ELLs' lack of experience with the English language, there is an increased need for interaction and discussion for ELLs who are learning to read. School psychologists should encourage teachers to use strategies that create opportunities for students to talk about and to learn to gain meaning from the passages that were just read. In addition to providing more opportunities to use the information gained from reading, school psychologists should also encourage teachers to more explicitly focus on vocabulary and systematically identify and teach words that have the most effect on passage meaning (Manyak, 2012).

As we recommend in Table 7.2, peer-assisted learning strategies are gaining research support as a means to enhance differentiation for ELLs during core instruction and provide opportunities to develop vocabulary and comprehension skills (Gersten et al., 2007). Peer tutoring gives ELLs an opportunity to use language and get immediate feedback about their reading skills using material that is at their instructional level. Peer tutoring is especially useful when Tier 1 screening data indicate a high percentage (i.e., more than 20%) of students needs supplemental reading support, yet resources are not available to provide pull-out reading interventions for all students.

An important consideration when delivering reading interventions is whether the reading intervention groups should be heterogeneous or homogenous in relation to English language proficiency. Unfortunately, there are very few studies that examine the differences between providing reading intervention with ELLs who are all at

Table 7.2. Reading Intervention Recommendations

- Whenever possible, use rigorous research standards (e.g., What Works Clearinghouse) to guide selection of interventions for ELLs.
- Use instruction and intervention materials that are systematic and explicit, match the language of instruction, and provide strategies for addressing language diversity.
- Provide opportunities for ELLs to use new vocabulary and comprehension strategies during core instruction.
- Use peer-assisted learning strategies during core reading instruction to enhance instructional differentiation and student engagement.
- Provide core reading instruction to ELLs in heterogeneous language groups to provide exposure to typically developing peers.
- Provide, to the greatest extent possible, reading interventions in homogenous language groups to enhance differentiation and targeted support.
- Evaluate interventions routinely and use evaluation data to improve the intervention.

a similar level versus a diverse group that might also contain native English speaking students who have reading challenges. Yet, from a practical standpoint, intervention with a homogenous group should allow interventionists to more appropriately target support for the group and identify strategies that can be used for multiple students. It is important to note there is no evidence or theoretical support for providing Tier 1 instruction to ELLs in a homogeneous group. As we recommend in Table 7.2, to the greatest extent possible ELLs should receive core instruction in heterogeneous language groups (i.e., all levels of language proficiency) so that the students will have access to typically developing peers and should receive intervention in homogenous groups to allow appropriate differentiation and targeted support.

While students are receiving intervention, it is essential that progress monitoring of reading skills occur to evaluate the impact of the intervention. As with native English speakers, in most cases for students in elementary settings, oral reading fluency is the most appropriate measure to use to identify the impact of the intervention. Some educators may be concerned the students are decoding without comprehension, but at this point research has not identified a large percentage of students who read more fluently than would be predicted by their comprehension skills (i.e., word callers). As students progress into middle and high school, more direct measures of comprehension (e.g., maze) may be necessary to supplement the information obtain from oral reading fluency measures. Regardless of the measure used, as previously mentioned, school psychologists need to identify whether unique progress-monitoring goals are available for ELLs at different levels of English proficiency.

Research-Based English Language Development Instruction

Table 7.3 provides several research-based recommendations for the provision of English language development instruction that will support the development of readings skills for ELLs. First, there is fairly strong evidence that targeted English language development instruction leads to improved language skills at a faster rate than providing typical instruction. As a result, it is important to stress that time should be specifically carved out of the instructional day to teach these skills in addition to the core English language arts curriculum. The content of English language development instruction should include a combination of activities that place a focus on developing language skills in a broad sense versus specifically targeting reading or writing skills. This is not to suggest that reading and writing instruction cannot be part of an English language development program, but the content should not be limited to these two areas (Saunders & Goldenberg, 2010).

It is clear academic English is best acquired through explicit instruction in English that gives students opportunities to use the language in appropriate contexts with a goal of helping the students acquire meaning and use language to communicate. The use of language should include listening and speaking activities related to academic tasks as well as social conversation topics. As part of the focus on general language development, it is important to ensure grammar, syntax, and vocabulary are explicitly taught and students are given opportunities to practice the use of these components in both oral and written language. While students are using language, they should be given corrective feedback designed to strengthen their understanding of the underlying form of English. Although

Table 7.3. Tier 1 English Language Development Recommendations

English language development instruction should be:	*English language development should not be:*
<ul><li>Delivered via a research-based curriculum and supported by research-based strategies of English language development delivery</li><li>Distinct instruction in systematic English language development</li><li>An instructional time in which students are grouped by language proficiency levels (students groupings should be fairly homogenous for English language development instruction)</li><li>Assessed using the statewide measures at least one time per year</li><li>A scope and sequence of vocabulary, language functions, and grammatical forms</li><li>Delivered on a regular basis</li></ul>	<ul><li>Extra reading instruction</li><li>An extra adult to help in the classroom/teacher assistant</li><li>Tutoring time, academic support, independent work time</li><li>Just vocabulary development</li><li>A strategy for delivering English language development instruction, such as the Sheltered Instruction Observation Protocol or Specially Designate Academic Instruction in English (although these strategies can be used in an English language development class)</li></ul>

more research is needed to better understand the degree to which English language development instruction should be homogenous, when possible students receiving English language development instruction should be grouped according to English language proficiency (Saunders & Goldenberg, 2010).

Several structured programs are available for educators to use to support the provision of English language development instruction. As mentioned earlier, the What Works Clearinghouse (http://ies.ed.gov/ncee/wwc/) provides rigorous reviews of programs that have external research to support their impact on student outcomes. English language development programs are one of the many content areas reviewed by the website and the content is specifically provided for educators who need to determine whether a program should be used with their students. It is important to understand the reviews are regularly updated and it is quite common for interventions that previously lacked support to have evidence of effectiveness a few months later. A common characteristic of many of the currently supported programs is the use of peer-assisted learning strategies that give students many opportunities to use language and receive immediate feedback.

In addition to the structured programs that focus specifically on developing English language proficiency, there are also programs designed to enhance the delivery of content area instruction to make it more appropriate for ELLs. The Sheltered Instruction Observation Protocol (Echevarria, Short, & Powers, 2006) incorporates specialized strategies and techniques to increase ELLs access to subject matter concepts and support language development with a specific focus on enhancing academic language (Echevarria et al., 2006). The best way to perceive the Sheltered Instruction Observation Protocol model is as a Tier 1 lesson planning and delivery approach that prompts teachers to use strategies that are designed to increase an ELL student's ability to access the content.

SUMMARY

ELLs are one of the fastest growing student populations in U.S. public schools and are expected to increase in every state over the next decade. Given the short supply of bilingual psychologists and the diversity of languages in U.S. schools, many school psychologists will find themselves in the role of evaluating students whose first language is not English. Given that reading problems are the most common academic skill deficit for ELLs who are referred for a comprehensive evaluation for special education eligibility, school psychologists should be aware of the most validated reading assessment and intervention strategies available to use with ELLs. A critical aspect of this knowledge is understanding that language plays a significant and substantial role in reading development, and students who have a diverse language background may have challenges acquiring the oral language that is essential to developing reading skills. As part of understanding the cause of an ELL's reading struggles, it is important to determine whether the student was provided a research-based English language development program, in addition to high quality Tier 1 reading instruction and Tier 2 reading intervention.

This chapter focused on the knowledge necessary to understand an ELL student's reading performance when he or she is being taught to read in English. Although a detailed discussion of language transfer is beyond the scope of this chapter, it is important to keep in mind the acquisition of English is going to be affected by how well the first language is developed (Cummins, 1984). Arguments can be made that ELLs may benefit more from being taught reading skills in their first language until those skills have reached a proficient level, and then are taught how to read in English. Unfortunately, there is not a consensus in this area, and these decisions are affected more by community expectations and politics than scientifically supported policy. To the greatest extent possible, school psychologists should endeavor to bring the strongest science to address the question of how to best provide reading support to ELLs and help them achieve desired outcomes.

REFERENCES

American Educational Research Association, American Psychological Association, & National Council on Measurement in Education. (1999). Testing individuals of diverse linguistic backgrounds. In *Standards for educational and psychological testing* (pp. 91–97). Washington, DC: American Educational Research Association.

Aud, S., Hussar, W., Kena, G., Bianco, K., Frohlich, L., Kemp, J., & Tahan, K. (2011). *The condition of education 2011* (NCES 2011-033). Washington, DC: U.S. Department of Education, National Center for Education Statistics.

August, D., & Shanahan, T. (2008). *Developing literacy in second-language learners: Report of the National Literacy Panel on language-minority children and youth.* Mahwah, NJ: Erlbaum.

Brown, J. E., & Sanford, A. (2011). *RTI for English language learners: Appropriately using screening and progress monitoring tools to improve instructional outcomes.* Washington, DC: National Center on Response to Intervention. Retrieved from http://www.rti4success.org/pdf/rtiforells.pdf

Cummins, J. C. (1984). *Bilingual and special education: Issues in assessment and pedagogy.* Austin, TX: PRO-ED.

Del Vecchio, A., & Guerrero, M. (1995). *Handbook of English language proficiency tests*. Albuquerque, NM: Evaluation Assistance Center-West, New Mexico Highlands University. Retrieved from http://www.ncela.gwu.edu/files/rcd/BE020503/Handbook_of_English.pdf

Echevarria, J., Short, D., & Powers, K. (2006). School reform and standards-based education: A model for English-language learners. *The Journal of Educational Research, 99*, 195–210, Retrieved from http://edfs200ell.pbworks.com/w/file/fetch/54561001/EchevarriaShort-SchRefSBEELLs.pdf

Francis, D., Rivera, M., Lesaux, N., Kieffer, M., & Rivera, H. (2006). *Practical guidelines for the education of English language learners: Research-based recommendations for instruction and academic interventions*. Portsmouth, NH: RMC Research. Retrieved from http://www.centeroninstruction.org/files/ELL1-Interventions.pdf

Gersten, R., Baker, S. K., Shanahan, T., Linan-Thompson, S., Collins, P., & Scarcella, R. (2007). *Effective literacy and English language instruction for English learners in the elementary grades*. Washington, DC: U.S. Department of Education. Retrieved from http://ies.ed.gov/ncee/wwc/pdf/practice_guides/20074011.pdf

Gutierrez, G., & Vanderwood, M. L. (2013). A growth curve analysis of literacy performance among second-grade, Spanish-speaking, English-language learners. *School Psychology Review, 42*, 3–21.

Johnson, E., Jenkins, J., Petscher, Y., & Catts, H. (2009). How can we improve the accuracy of screening instruments? *Learning Disabilities Research & Practice, 24*, 174–185.

Klingner, J. K., Artiles, A. J., & Barletta, L. M. (2006). English language learners who struggle with reading: Language acquisition or LD? *Journal of Learning Disabilities, 39*, 108–128.

Linan-Thompson, S., Cirino, P. T., & Vaughn, S. (2007). Determining English language learners' response to intervention: Questions and some answers. *Learning Disability Quarterly, 30*, 185–195.

Manyak, P. C. (2012). Powerful vocabulary instruction for English learners. In E. J. Kame'enui & J. F. Baumann (Eds.), *Vocabulary instruction: Research to practice* (2nd ed., pp. 280–302). New York, NY: Guilford Press.

National Association of School Psychologists. (2010). *Model for comprehensive and integrated school psychological services*. Bethesda, MD: Author. Retrieved from http://www.nasponline.org/standards/2010standards/2_PracticeModel.pdf

National Clearinghouse for English Language Acquisition. (2011). *What language instruction educational programs do states use to serve English learners?* Washington, DC: Author. Retrieved from http://www.ncela.gwu.edu/files/uploads/5/LIEPs0406BR.pdf

National Institute of Child Health and Human Development. (2000). *Report of the National Reading Panel: Teaching children to read: An evidence-based assessment of the scientific research literature on reading and its implications for reading instruction: Reports of the subgroups* (NIH Publication No. 00-4754). Washington, DC: Author.

National Reading Panel. (2000). *Teaching children to read: An evidence-based assessment of the scientific research literature on reading and its implications for reading instruction*. Washington, DC: Author. Retrieved from http://www.nichd.nih.gov/publications/pubs/nrp/pages/smallbook.aspx

Office of English Language Acquisition, Language Enhancement, and Academic Achievement for Limited English Proficient Students. (2012). *Biennial report to Congress on the implementation of the Title III State Formula Grant program, school years 2006–07 and 2007–08*. Washington, DC: Author.

Saunders, W., & Goldenberg, C. (2010). Research to guide English language development instruction. In California Department of Education (Eds.), *Improving education for English learners* (pp. 21–81). Sacramento, CA: California Department of Education.

Schrank, F. A., Fletcher, T. V., & Alvarado, C. G. (1996). Comparative validity of three English oral language proficiency tests. *The Bilingual Research Journal, 20*, 55–68.

Wagner, R. K., Francis, D. J., & Morris, R. D. (2005). Identifying English language learners with learning disabilities: Key challenges and possible approaches. *Learning Disabilities Research & Practice, 20*, 6–15.

8

Best Practices in School-Based Services for Immigrant Children and Families

Graciela Elizalde-Utnick
Brooklyn College, City University of New York
Carlos Guerrero
Los Angeles (CA) Unified School District, Loyola Marymount University

OVERVIEW

The United States in the 21st century continues to undergo great waves of immigration (U.S. Department of Homeland Security, 2012). Current immigrants represent Europe, Latin America, the Caribbean, Africa, and Asia. As the immigrant population steadily increases, there is the concomitant need for schools to provide support to immigrant students and their families. Children and their parents face a number of challenges, and providing support serves the dual purpose of addressing their unique needs as well as fostering a collaborative, home–school relationship that benefits the child being raised in these families. This chapter is intended to assist school psychologists in building capacity in direct and indirect service provision to provide safe and effective learning environments for immigrant students and to foster partnerships with their families.

A wide variety of competencies outlined in the National Association of School Psychologists (NASP) *Model for Comprehensive and Integrated School Psychological Services* (NASP, 2010) are utilized when working effectively with immigrant families and addressing issues associated with acculturation. For example, consultation and collaboration skills are necessary components embedded within direct and indirect service provision to immigrant students and parents. By providing academic interventions and mental health services for students to develop social and life skills, and family–school collaboration services for parents, the domain of Diversity in Development and Learning is firmly

supported. As such, school psychologists are uniquely positioned to advocate for social justice and the recognition that cultural and linguistic diversity produces different strengths and needs. Providing culturally competent services and effective practices in all areas of school psychology service delivery improves academic, learning, social, and mental health outcomes for all students, especially those from immigrant families.

BASIC CONSIDERATIONS

Immigrant students and their families are a diverse population. Beyond differences in culture and language, immigrant students and families vary significantly in their experiences as immigrants, depending on how and under what circumstances they arrive in the United States. Some families come voluntarily to seek new opportunities or join other family members, while others may be forced to leave their native countries as refugees to escape economic stress or political or religious harassment (Gonzales, Suárez-Orozco, & Dedios-Sanguineti, 2013). Thus, some families arrive in the United States with substantial resources, while others arrive with very little social or economic support. Some arrive with advanced degrees, while others arrive with minimal levels of education. Some come to this country already fluent in English, while many are learning a new language while also adapting to a new culture. Regardless of difference, immigrant families share common values with each other and with native families. Most notably, many immigrant parents share a desire for a better life for themselves and their children rooted in the perception that hard work, dedication, and education can produce the American dream of upward mobility and all the benefits that come with it (Motti-Stefanidi, Berry, Chryssochoou, Sam, & Phinney, 2012). To this end, immigrant families may view the United States through the prism of opportunity based on its ideals of fairness, equality, and respect. Schools are a primary extension of these ideals and have a responsibility to serve all students, especially those from immigrant families, and to help them achieve success.

Social, linguistic, and economic barriers are common challenges to immigrant students and can have a significant impact on adjustment at school. Such challenges often include the process of acculturation, racism and discrimination, difficulties related to immigration status, the need to learn English as a second language, and financial resources and school accessibility. Even the most affluent and educated immigrant students will likely face some degree of stress due to differences between their native cultures and the new communities to which they have moved. Adolescents have the added social pressures of trying to fit in to the complex social systems in middle and high school (Katsiaficas, Suárez-Orozco, Sirin, & Gupta, 2013).

Acculturation

Acculturation is a developmental process of change in which individuals adjust to a new culture, usually by merging their native traditions with those of the new culture (Motti-Stefanidi et al., 2012). While interacting with an established immigrant population of a similar background can ease the process of settling into a new community, migration is still stressful (Schwartz, Unger, Zamboanga, & Szapocznik, 2010).

Possible Acculturation Strategies

This process of change yields a number of possible strategies, including (to varying degrees) assimilation, integration, separation, and marginalization (Motti-Stefanidi et al., 2012). When individuals *assimilate* to a new culture, they give up their original cultural identity and take on the beliefs, attitudes, and behaviors of the majority culture. With *integration*, individuals continue to hold on to their cultural identity but also become integral members of the majority culture. With *separation*, the individual withdraws from the majority culture. When the individual is not interested in holding on to the native culture (or there is little opportunity to maintain the culture) *and* the individual withdraws from

the majority culture, often due to discrimination, then there is *marginalization*. For most immigrants, their acculturation will fall along a continuum from assimilation to separation, with many preferring to integrate.

Acculturative Stress

Immigrants can experience acculturative stress, which can last as long as 3–4 years and may include issues such as anxiety and depression, feelings of marginality and isolation, elevated psychosomatic symptoms (i.e., body and/or health concerns without a medical basis), identity confusion, difficulty in school performance, and family stress (Gonzales et al., 2013; Motti-Stefanidi et al., 2012). Several variables affect acculturative stress: reason for immigration (e.g., fleeing oppression versus seeking educational opportunities), premigration and postmigration trauma, socioeconomic status (e.g., poverty), acceptance or prestige of one's cultural/ethnic group, opportunity for contact with other cultural groups, prior knowledge of the new culture, and attitudes about acculturation. Schwartz et al. (2010) describe acculturative stress as resulting from "perceptions that either (a) receiving-culture individuals may scorn the person for not being sufficiently oriented toward the receiving culture and/or (b) the heritage-culture community may be displeased with the person for abandoning the heritage culture" (p. 248). In other words, immigrants may feel pressured to assimilate and/or maintain their culture of origin. Schwartz and Zamboanga (2008) suggest that acculturative stress can be alleviated by becoming *bicultural*, which refers to both adopting the new culture and holding on to the original culture and is consistent with integration. In fact, becoming bicultural has been found to be associated with a better adjustment to school (Motti-Stefanidi et al., 2012). Yet, as Motti-Stefanidi and colleagues (2012) note, immigrant youth do not always develop a bicultural identity:

> Some youth retain a separated ethnic identity, often as a result of obstacles or rejection that prevents them from identifying with the larger society. Other youth may strive for an assimilated national identity. These differing identity patterns are formed as young people wrestle with the demands of the environment and make decisions across the diverse contexts of their lives, including family, peers, school, and community. (p. 33)

Regardless of the acculturation strategy utilized, the process is ongoing as the individuals attempt to establish a sense of belonging.

Individual members of a family acculturate at different rates, and children and adolescents often acculturate faster than adults (Yoon, Langrehr, & Ong, 2010). For adolescents, in particular, this can cause family dissension if the parents feel their child is engaging in activities, dressing, or behaving in a manner that is not in keeping with their cultural and/or family values. This can result in intergenerational conflict between adolescents and older family members. Hwang (2006) describes *acculturative family distancing,* which increases the risk for intergenerational conflict. Acculturative family distancing can result when there is a breakdown in communication and/or incongruent cultural values. As immigrant students become increasingly proficient in English, a language shift may occur, with the students preferring to speak English. If the parents have little to no ability in English, then a linguistic barrier may occur, particularly if a student becomes English dominant over time. Similarly, language differences with school psychologists and other school personnel can create communication difficulties that can impede parental engagement and understanding of issues pertinent to their children (Elizalde-Utnick, 2010). In terms of cultural values, unless the parents come from higher socioeconomic or educational backgrounds, they are likely to acculturate more slowly than their children. Furthermore, continued exposure to mainstream American values can lead to ethnic identity changes that distance parents from their culture of origin. And for some adolescents, acculturation is situational. Their behavior at school might reflect assimilation (i.e., behavior consistent with mainstream U.S. values), while their behavior at home reflects the traditions of the family's culture.

Not only can delayed parental acculturation affect acculturative family distancing, it can also negatively affect the home–school relationship if the school is not aware of and responsive to culturally bound expectations and behaviors still held by immigrant parents. Differences in cultural values between parents and school staff can also negatively affect communication and problem-solving efforts.

Age of arrival makes a difference when it comes to immigrant children's and youth's adjustment and performance at school. First-generation students who arrive at the age of 5 or younger typically perform better than those who arrive at the age of 12 or older (Cortina, 2013). The process of acculturation and adaptation at school is easier for the younger students. Cortina (2013) notes that interventions that incorporate the family have better outcomes for the students. Such interventions will be discussed later in this chapter.

Racism and Discrimination

Immigrants often encounter social barriers, and those who experience discrimination are less likely to become bicultural (Motti-Stefanidi et al., 2012). Moreover, immigrants of color often undergo additional stressors in acculturation due to racism. For adolescent immigrants of color, in particular, who are undergoing their own identity development, the experience of racism at school interferes with maintaining a sense of pride in their culture of origin and may be deleterious to their achievement and vocational aspirations. While Caucasian immigrants can experience discrimination at school due to cultural and linguistic differences, immigrants of color have the added burden of racism (Sue, 2010).

Types of Racism

Racism occurs at the institutional, cultural, and individual levels (Sue, 2010). At the institutional level, racism can occur when laws and policies oppress minority groups. For example, if educational policies focus on assimilating immigrant children into the dominant culture, it would reflect racial discrimination at the institutional level, since it goes against freedom of expression. Cultural racism occurs when a cultural group is devalued, and individual racism occurs when a person displays racist acts and discrimination against another person.

Perceived Racism

In addition to overt racism, immigrant students who lack skills for interacting with other cultural groups (perhaps because they have not had experience or opportunities to interact with individuals from other cultures) may experience increased levels of perceived discrimination, which is often associated with higher rates of depression and anxiety (Fuertes, Alfonso, & Schultz, 2007). Such experience with discrimination often leads to an internalization of negative stereotypes, especially negative stereotypes reflected by teachers, counselors, parents, peers, and siblings. Immigrants of color, including the second generation, who are visibly different are often treated in ways that are perceived as discriminatory (Devos, Gavin, & Quintana, 2010). For example, being asked where one is from or where one was born is a constant reminder of being "different." Sue (2010) describes such statements as *microaggressions,* or "brief and commonplace daily verbal, behavioral, and environmental indignities, whether intentional or unintentional, that communicate hostile, derogatory, or negative racial, gender, sexual orientation, and religious slights and insults to the target person or group" (p. 5). Statements related to one's place of birth or one's English language fluency can make the individual feel like an alien in one's own land, with the implicit message being that he or she is a foreigner and not an American. Rumbaut (2008) notes that when immigrant youth experience discrimination, they undergo a process of forming a *reactive ethnicity*. This refers to the immigrants holding on tightly to their ethnic heritage and resisting the majority culture, thereby avoiding integration and maintaining separation.

Immigration Status

The legal status of immigration can further compound stress levels. While many immigrants have come legally to the United States, there has been a surge of undocumented immigrants in recent years, with approximately 2.1 million undocumented immigrants who migrate as children (Gonzales et al., 2013). Undocumented immigrants might be fearful of becoming involved with mainstream institutions, such as schools, due to fears that information will be given to the U.S. Citizenship and Immigration Services and thus strain family–school relationships as well as risk deportation. Other immigrants who are in the United States legally may experience stress related to the status of relatives or difficulties arranging immigration for other family members.

Undocumented immigrant youth face numerous barriers growing up (Gonzales et al., 2013). They often live in poverty with limited access to resources. Their status excludes them from activities that their documented peers are engaging in, such as driving and receiving financial aid for college. They often keep their undocumented status a secret, which compounds their acculturative stress.

Second Language Acquisition

Depending on country of origin, many immigrants might be unfamiliar with the English language. As a result, immigrant children and children of immigrants (as well as their parents) undergo second language acquisition and are designated English language learners (ELLs). Level of proficiency attained in the first language at the time the second language is introduced may directly affect how easily and efficiently the second language will

be learned (Shin, 2013). In addition, a number of other variables influence second language acquisition, including quality of instruction, the type of bilingual education that might be provided, support outside of schools, practice opportunities with students who are proficient in the second language, level of acculturation, sociocultural background, history of education in the first language, age, and motivation (Rhodes, Ochoa, & Ortiz, 2005). It takes about 7–10 years of learning English for ELLs to be able to perform cognitively demanding tasks on par with their monolingual-English peers. In practice, however, ELLs typically exit English as a second language (ESL) programs after 3 years (Shin, 2013). Such practice places ELLs at risk for not having the sufficient proficiency level in English to succeed in general education classrooms, thereby increasing the risk of an inappropriate special education referral. For example, an ELL may present with conversational ability in English, and the teacher may assume that the student should be able to perform cognitively demanding academic tasks, based on the student's English proficiency level. However, it is critical to distinguish between conversational language ability (known as basic interpersonal communication skills) and the much deeper level of proficiency that is required to perform demanding cognitive tasks (known as cognitive academic language proficiency). Thus, a student with only a superficial level of language proficiency (i.e., basic interpersonal communication skills or conversational ability) will not be successful with academic activities that are cognitively demanding because a cognitive academic language proficiency would be required to succeed at such tasks (Rhodes et al., 2005; Shin, 2013).

Immigrant students can experience additional social–emotional difficulties as the result of the process of second language acquisition. While basic interpersonal communication skills are developing, peer relations can be adversely affected due to limited verbal communication. This may have an impact on a student's ability to initiate friendships or play, build sustaining relationships, and verbally problem solve. Similarly, a student's ability to advocate for himself or herself may be compromised if it must be done in a second language that is still developing. For example, if students find themselves needing to explain why they do not understand material or why they are being unfairly implicated in a dispute, deficiencies in verbal expression will impede their ability to articulate important information. By advocating for themselves, students are able to have their perspectives heard and validated by teachers and administrators.

Financial Resources and School Accessibility

Many immigrants have to deal with poverty and related stressful life conditions. Child-care issues, difficulty finding transportation and housing, and dealing with government agencies are some of the factors that can make it difficult for immigrant parents to play an active role in their children's education (Elizalde-Utnick, 2007a). Employment status can present additional challenges, since work schedules and physically exhausting hours can impede attendance at school functions and other opportunities for school involvement. Yet, even families with adequate financial support may encounter some initial difficulties dealing with cultural differences in the expectations for and nature of parent involvement with children's schooling.

BEST PRACTICES IN SERVICES FOR IMMIGRANT FAMILIES

In addition to the everyday challenges of immigration, schools provide another arena of challenge. School psychologists are often not knowledgeable about the immigration process, and immigrant students and their families can feel out of place in this unfamiliar setting (Fuertes et al., 2007). Since the school may be the first contact immigrants have with social services in the United States, it is critical that educators and support personnel provide assistance to immigrant families in need and encourage them to take on meaningful roles in the school. School psychologists can help immigrant families find services in the school and community.

As a result, it is critical to respond to these families in a culturally competent manner. Cultural competence refers to the ability to engage in behaviors that are consistent with a culture's values, beliefs, and customs (Sue & Torino, 2005). Cultural competence entails a three-pronged approach: self-awareness, knowledge of other cultures, and skill (culturally responsive intervention strategies).

Self-Awareness

In order to work effectively with immigrants from other cultures, school psychologists first need to develop personal self-awareness. This entails understanding one's cultural heritage, including values and immigration history. This process also involves understanding what cultural values are embedded in one's professional practices. For example, individuality and independence are mainstream U.S. values that might be held by a school psychologist, both personally and professionally. Other cultures may not necessarily place as much importance on independence (e.g., children's autonomy and independent thinking). Instead, priority may be given to the group's (e.g., family's) needs rather than that of the individual. The focus on the group's needs is known as collectivism or interdependence, which is valued by approximately 70% of the world's population (including Latin America, Asia, Africa, and Eastern Europe). The process of developing self-awareness is not always easy, as it might entail confronting potential biases that have been a part of one's socialization process (Sue & Torino, 2005). Engaging in a process of self-reflection increases attention to how one's experiences and exposures influence the assumptions made about other groups, cultures, and subsequent behaviors.

Knowledge of Other Cultures

Knowledge refers to understanding the values, beliefs, customs, mannerisms, and language of different groups of people (Sue & Torino, 2005). This includes understanding the experience of marginalized, disempowered groups in U.S. society. School psychologists can learn about other cultures using a variety of strategies. These include reading books about other cultures, watching films that depict the immigrant experiences or life in another culture, speaking and interacting with individuals from other cultures, attending cultural events, and learning the language of the families with whom one works (Elizalde-Utnick, 2007a; see Hays & Erford, 2014, for further strategies and reflection activities to develop multicultural awareness and knowledge). Building a knowledge base of common cultural traits, practices, and beliefs supports a school psychologist's ability to be prepared, sensitive, and understanding of differences when interacting with immigrant parents.

School psychologists should also understand parents' cultural belief systems as these systems relate to parenting and educational practices and expectations, which may differ significantly from those of mainstream American families. Some immigrants may believe that the teacher is the ultimate authority for educating children and, therefore, may have learned to not interfere in their children's education. For example, among Latino cultures it is generally believed that, while the family is responsible for socializing the child (e.g., teaching socially appropriate behavior), the school is responsible for providing formal knowledge (Elizalde-Utnick, 2007a). Furthermore, close-knit families that prefer to resolve difficulties within the confines of the family might view professionals as outsiders. As with other competencies, focusing attention on the positive or adaptive strategies (such as collective problem solving or respect for elders) that are expressed within cultures fortifies communication and acknowledges strengths.

Skill: Culturally Responsive Support Strategies

School psychologists are in an excellent position to provide support to immigrant families. In fact, making connections between immigrant students and caring teachers and other school personnel helps foster resilience in immigrant youth (Green, Rhodes, Hirsch, Suárez-Orozco, & Camic, 2007). Such relationships increase students' motivation and engagement, as well as facilitate academic adjustment. Figure 8.1 shows the types of support that can be provided to immigrant students and their families. As the figure illustrates, home–school collaboration is at the core of effective, culturally competent provision of services. A critical component of home–school collaboration is effective communication. Once this is established, then the other supports can be put in place, with the school psychologist and the family working together for positive school outcomes for immigrant students. The other services include providing support to families, implementing a tiered system of support for ELL students, and providing multicultural counseling and other emotional support services for students. Many of these

support services and strategies work in tandem and complement each other by taking into account the unique circumstances affecting the lives of these students to address issues of academic achievement, school engagement, and social–emotional well-being for immigrant students.

Establish Collaborative Relationships

There is extensive literature supporting the benefits of home–school collaboration (NASP, 2012). Though it can be challenging for school psychologists to collaborate with members of immigrant families who do not necessarily share a philosophy of active participation in schools, opportunities persist if school psychologists expand their practice to be responsive to this population. For example, immigrant parents might not consider approaching an outsider (i.e., someone not sharing their cultural or ethnic background) for help. Take the example of Maria. Maria is a 15-year-old student who immigrated to the United States from rural Ecuador 7 years ago with her parents and younger brother. Neither of her parents possess more than a middle school education and came to this country in search of vocational and educational opportunities. Maria's father recently returned to Ecuador, leaving behind his family with limited resources. Maria's mother has taken a second job in order to support the family. Maria's teacher has become increasingly concerned in recent months due to her drop in grades and apparent depression. The school psychologist met with Maria,

Figure 8.1. Culturally Responsive Support Services

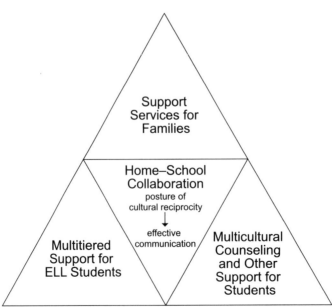

who reported that she is not allowed to socialize with her school peers after school hours. She must go home every day after school to take care of her brother, help him with his homework, and prepare dinner. Maria misses her father and is very angry at her mother's restrictions. The school psychologist has tried to set up a meeting with Maria and her mother, but her mother seems hesitant to come to the school.

In this case, Maria's mother may be apprehensive to ask school personnel about the increasing difficulties that she is having with her daughter, because in rural Ecuador, schools may not have the resources to help in these types of situations and problem solving of this sort typically occurs within the family or through a cultural means of support, like a church. In this scenario, the school psychologist may reach out and attempt to establish a collaborative relationship as he or she becomes aware of the difficulties that Maria is experiencing and tailor the outreach to the family with information that the school psychologist is able to gather.

Finding methods of facilitating home–school collaboration is a key ingredient in the communication process, particularly with immigrant families that may lack exposure and familiarity with the U.S. educational system. Families may even lack significant experience with secondary education in their native country, as in Maria's mother's case. As such, the school psychologist needs to be mindful of the fact that immigrant families might not share a philosophy of active participation in schools (Elizalde-Utnick, 2010). Not only is this understanding important when working directly with immigrant families, but it is crucial that other school personnel be mindful of these differences as well. School psychologists can consult with other school staff members to help them understand cultural differences as well as economic realities that many immigrant parents face. As in Maria's mother's situation, school staff may benefit from an explanation that many immigrant parents have to work multiple low-paying jobs in order to support their families and that a lack of parental involvement might be inevitable and/or even a choice.

Furthermore, immigrant families in need or in crisis may not consider approaching an outsider for help, as many cultures believe that family problems are private and should be dealt with only by members of the family (Sue & Zane, 2009). Understanding that there may be limits to the extent that school psychologists can reach out to immigrant families can also be beneficial and protect the integrity of the relationship by respecting culturally accepted boundaries. In addition, the provision of mental health services often holds a stigma in many cultures and needed referrals may take additional time and care to complete (Sue & Zane, 2009).

In Maria's mother's case, additional explanation and patient listening may be required for her to become comfortable with an idea so foreign to her upbringing as outside counseling services. Not only do these resources not exist in her village, but outside agencies offering support of any kind are typically viewed with suspicion. Once a fair amount of time and space is given to allow Maria's mother to understand fully how this type of support is a socially acceptable means of addressing the difficulties her daughter is experiencing, she is more likely to agree to complete the referral and actively participate in the intake process. Therefore, regardless of difficulty, the benefits of home–school collaboration are well established, and the culturally competent school psychologist can help bridge the differences between the home and school cultures.

Effective two-way communication is at the core of partnerships between families and schools (Guerrero & Leung, 2008). In this manner, school psychologists seek information from families as well as provide it to them. Communication can take the form of telephone calls, visits to the classroom, or visits to the school psychologist. It is important to communicate when good things are happening, and not just during crises, so that parents feel that educators are just as concerned with facilitating success as addressing problem situations. Similarly, parents are much more willing to be receptive and contribute to problem solving when they feel that members of the school staff know their child and are vested in progress and achievement, and not just making their own lives easier. While two-way communication is preferable, schools can provide information through one-way communication vehicles: newsletters, notes, suggestion boxes, and handbooks. It is important to remember that families have different needs. For example, some parents might only need information (e.g., a newsletter), while others might need information as well as consultation. And yet other families might need ongoing outreach and support (Elizalde-Utnick, 2010).

Families often prefer informal communication to formal communication (Elizalde-Utnick, 2010). A more personal approach not only facilitates communication with many families, but also helps diminish the sense of alienation that some parents might be experiencing. A school-wide strategy such as this might be necessary in order to change the dynamic negatively affecting different groups of parents. School psychologists trained in assessing and improving school climate can make positive contributions by consulting administrators on the linkages between parental involvement, school culture, and student outcomes (i.e., academic achievement, reduction in behavior referrals). In addition, effective communication also entails accounting for linguistic diversity and families' preferred language. School psychologists who do not speak the parents' language can help address this preference by utilizing interpreters, parent volunteers, and community members who speak the parents' primary language. Furthermore, face-to-face meetings may be more effective than providing information solely in writing. The authors have worked with many illiterate parents for whom letters and other printed material are meaningless. Therefore, oral presentation of material is not only more personal but also more comprehensible and effective for those parents with limited education (Elizalde-Utnick, 2007a).

Regardless of origin or upbringing, all parents want the best for their children. Unfortunately, navigating the educational system to get them the help they need can be a daunting task for parents who do not share mainstream values and cultural expectations. At its most basic level, communicating effectively with immigrant parents is predicated on the same principles used in effective communication with any parent: respect, clarity, and care (Guerrero & Leung, 2008). School psychologists should remember that time invested in getting to know immigrant families and in earning their trust in a meaningful way can make a huge difference in fashioning a home–school collaboration that works best to meet the educational needs of immigrant students.

School psychologists can engage in respectful, clear, and caring communication by incorporating the *posture of cultural reciprocity*, a model of reciprocal perspective taking originally proposed by Kalyanpur and Harry (1999). This approach entails families and school psychologists engaging in a multistep sharing of perspectives, a process that includes listening to and respecting multiple perspectives. This process is helpful because it avoids stereotyping, goes beyond awareness of differences to self-awareness, and ensures that both families and the school psychologist are empowered. A posture of cultural reciprocity develops as follows:

School psychologists identify the cultural values embedded in their professional practices. A school psychologist can ask: What cultural values are embedded in my interpretations of a child's difficulties or in the development of an intervention? For

example, in the case of Maria and her mother, the school psychologist might value common "American" traits such as independence and individuality, both personally and professionally. As such, the school psychologist might think that Maria should be allowed to individuate and socialize with her peers after school.

The school psychologist finds out if the family recognizes and values these assumptions and, if not, how their view differs from that of the school psychologist. In the case of Maria, the school psychologist meets with Maria and her mother to discuss the difficulties that Maria is experiencing. When Maria tells her mother to "back off" and leave her alone, her mother declares that Maria has become "too Americanized," is only interested in herself, and shows very little interest in her family. Here we see how Maria has assimilated the mainstream U.S. values of autonomy and individual needs. Yet, conversely, her mother is traditionally Ecuadorian and believes in the Latino values of *familismo* (i.e., the importance of family) and *respeto* (i.e., respect). Acculturative family distancing can occur as a result of these differences which must be addressed and worked through.

School psychologists recognize and respect any cultural differences identified, and fully explain the cultural basis of their assumptions. For instance, though the school psychologist believes in the same cultural values that Maria now holds, the school psychologist must be aware of this potential bias when providing recommendations to the family, since suggestions may be offered from the school psychologist's perspective solely or from only one member of the family. By asking the family for its perspective and delving into alternative value systems (like Maria's mother) and problem-solving styles, school psychologists are demonstrating an understanding that their own cultural beliefs are not the only way to view the world and that multiple possibilities for resolution are available.

School psychologists, through two-way communication and collaboration, determine the most effective way to adapt their professional interpretation or recommendations to the family's cultural value system. By looking at each person's cultural perspective, each value is understood to be adaptive within its social context. What about the school psychologist's perspective? Would it make a difference? Yes. The school psychologist might believe that Maria is asserting her sense of autonomy. But does this not reflect the American value of individualism? It is critical that school psychologists and other school professionals be sensitive to different worldviews and understand behaviors within their cultural context. It would be helpful, in this case, for the school psychologist to discuss each individual's perspective in terms of cultural values. In other words, Maria's mother's concerns and parenting style can be validated within the context of her culture. Maria's mother can also come to understand that Maria is acculturating to U.S. mainstream values as she attends school and develops her identity as she progresses through adolescence. Once this is understood, then the school psychologist, together with Maria and her mother, can develop a plan that reflects a compromise, a plan that makes sense to all parties involved.

As illustrated in Figure 8.1, home–school collaboration and the posture of cultural reciprocity are at the core of culturally responsive support services. They form the basis for appropriate interventions at other levels, such as specific services for immigrant families, multitiered support for ELLs, and multicultural counseling and other emotional support services.

Provide Support Services for Immigrant Families

School psychologists, with the help of social workers, counselors, and family liaisons, can help immigrant families find services in the school and community such as orientation programs for new immigrants, free and reduced breakfast and lunch programs, free transportation for parents to attend school meetings and events, after-school child-care programs that provide homework support, family involvement programs that support the development of reading and mathematical reasoning, parenting workshops and parent-support groups, ESL classes for parents, school interpreters to facilitate two-way communication between parents and school professionals, and community-based and culturally based social service agencies. By providing support to immigrant families, schools can help improve the lives of these families and foster safe learning environments for students. The strategies and services described in this section can help empower families who often feel alienated from the school and mainstream society in general. School psychologists can improve their ability to function as conduits to school and community support services by creating (or updating) a compilation of assets and resources that exist within a given school's area at the start of each school year for easy access when helping families.

Provide Multitiered Systems of Support for ELLs

School psychologists are in the position to serve as consultants to parents and school personnel regarding an ELL's learning and development. Educators often fail to recognize the impact of sociocultural and linguistic variables on learning, as well as acculturation processes affecting the social–emotional development of immigrant students (Rhodes et al., 2005). Through consultation and collaboration at the staff level, school psychologists can influence pedagogical approaches and strategies that are research based and culturally appropriate. For example, by participating in grade-level meetings or presenting the merits of culturally sensitive instructional interventions at school- or district-level professional development, the school psychologist can support the socialization and academic achievement of immigrant students.

School psychologists working with ELLs need to be familiar with the process of second language acquisition, including normal processes and errors. Furthermore, it is critical to understand the relationship between a child's oral language proficiency and literacy acquisition in the second language. School psychologists and educators should also familiarize themselves with an ELL's cultural background, as well as acculturation processes, as such background knowledge has implications for the identification and interpretation of problem behaviors. Interventions should be evidence based and tailored to the culture of the student in question. Furthermore, in an effort to gather accurate data as well as develop appropriate interventions that promote an ELL's academic and social–emotional development, school psychologists should involve families in this process.

The basis for learning in school is quality general education, and multiple tiers of support can be helpful in promoting an ELL's success at school (Baker, Gersten, & Linan-Thompson, 2010). As such, school psychologists can assist in the development of optimal learning environments for ELLs, which include strategies consistent with the Center for Research on Education, Diversity & Excellence (CREDE) standards, differentiated instruction strategies and other Tier 1 interventions, as well as Tier 2 interventions. Classroom instruction should focus on social communication as well as academic language proficiency in English.

CREDE's Five Standards for Effective Pedagogy. CREDE established standards to improve all students' learning outcomes, particularly those students considered at risk for educational difficulty due to cultural, linguistic, or economic factors (Tharpe, 2008). The Five Standards for Effective Pedagogy are joint productive activity, language and literacy development, contextualization, challenging activities, and instructional conversation.

Joint productive activity: This standard entails a teacher and a small group of five to seven students working collaboratively in a productive activity that results in tangible or intangible products. Tangible products include reports, debates, concept maps, math problems, games, or plays. Intangible products are more conceptual in nature and include elaborated understandings, procedures, and other ideas. While it is important for the teacher and students to work together, it is critical that the teacher not dominate participation in classroom activities and conversations. Nevertheless, the teacher needs to elicit higher-level thinking on the part of the students.

Language and literacy development: This standard supports students' language development across the curriculum through activities that promote extensive speaking and writing. To meet this standard, the teacher needs to implement activities that generate language expression, develop content vocabulary, as well as assist students' language and literacy development through questioning, rephrasing, and/or modeling.

Contextualization: This standard entails making connections with what students already know by contextualizing new information in terms of the students' home and community. Students' cultural preferences (e.g., cooperative versus competitive, conarration versus call-and-response versus choral) are considered when designing instructional activities.

Challenging activities: The teacher fosters higher, more complex thinking by designing and implementing challenging activities. Students are provided with clear standards upon which their performance will be judged as well as feedback on their performance.

Instructional conversation: The teacher designs and implements an instructional conversation with a clear instructional goal, listens to students carefully to assess and foster student understanding, and questions students on their reasoning and views. It is critical that the "student talk" occurs at a greater frequency than the "teacher talk."

Tier 1 interventions. In addition to classroom instruction that conforms to CREDE's standards, ELLs would benefit from differentiated instructional strategies. Differentiation of instruction requires teachers to adapt instruction according to student differences, such as

readiness levels, learning style preferences, and interests. Instruction is modified in several ways: (a) content (what the teacher wants students to learn), (b) process (activities designed to ensure that students use key skills to make sense of essential ideas and information), and (c) product (student outcomes, or types of assignments and measures). These modifications are accomplished through a range of instructional and management strategies. Elizalde-Utnick (2007a) describes several strategies to differentiate instruction for ELLs: (a) previewing key academic vocabulary before each lesson, (b) scaffolding critical lesson concepts, (c) contextualizing vocabulary, (d) providing photo illustrations and manipulatives, (e) providing support or scaffolding materials in the first language, (f) teaching concepts and vocabulary in the first language through a community volunteer or a proficient bilingual peer, and (g) providing ELLs with translated key concepts to preview at home prior to the lesson in English.

To make significant gains in literacy acquisition in their second language, ELLs need teachers who are using effective instructional techniques. Such teachers adjust their instruction when students experience difficulty, engage their students in interactive activities, foster vocabulary and comprehension development, and provide high-quality explicit instruction in phonemic awareness and decoding (Baker et al., 2010). Furthermore, Lesaux and Geva (2006) note that it is not enough to teach literacy skills to ELLs. It is critical to continue working on these students' oral language development in English (i.e., receptive and expressive language, phonemic awareness, vocabulary, syntax, and pragmatics). While most ELLs eventually perform age-appropriately on measures of word reading accuracy and spelling, reading comprehension is often compromised when oral language skills and pertinent prior knowledge are insufficient to support understanding of the text (Lesaux & Geva, 2006).

In addition to differentiated instruction, class-wide peer tutoring has been used to promote learning at the Tier 1 level (Greenwood, Seals, & Kamps, 2010). Peer-Assisted Learning Strategies (PALS) is a commonly used evidence-based practice that targets literacy acquisition for ELLs. PALS provides small-group, structured, and reciprocal learning opportunities with a heterogeneous mix of peers, where ELLs read and discuss text in a manner that allows for immediate feedback and contextual cues as well as the active integration of new subject matter into higher order language skills necessary for cognitive academic language proficiency. Positive effects on literacy performance, especially reading comprehension, have been observed with ELLs with learning disabilities as well as with their low-, medium-, and high-achieving ELL counterparts (Sáenz, Fuchs, & Fuchs, 2005).

Tier 2 interventions. When ELLs continue to struggle, despite differentiated instruction and other Tier 1 interventions, Tier 2 interventions can be very effective. Baker et al. (2010) note that:

> … small group instruction is one of the most powerful, instructionally intense, and efficient ways of providing the instruction English learners need to reach grade-level goals. Putting English learners in small group formats with well-trained personnel and quality curriculum gives them frequent opportunities to use academic language—to explain content, provide answers, and build on the responses of their peers and teacher. (pp. 516–517)

School psychologists with a firm understanding of multitiered systems of instructional support and their relation to second language acquisition will be a valuable asset to teachers and administrators alike. This information will allow them to be active collaborators at child study team meetings when crafting targeted interventions or culturally responsive pedagogical approaches geared toward improving learning for immigrant students.

Provide Multicultural Counseling and Other Social–Emotional Support

Counseling services can be helpful to immigrant students and children of immigrants suffering from acculturative stress. Students who have gone through the process of immigration may have experienced traumatic events and/or loss due to separation from loved ones. Adolescents might be at greater risk, particularly if they arrive at the age of 12 or older due to the greater difficulty of adjusting at school (Cortina, 2013) compared with younger immigrants. Gonzales and colleagues (2013) note that:

> … adolescence is also a period of particular psychological vulnerability; three-quarters of lifetime psychiatric disorders emerge in adolescence and early adulthood…. Studies focusing on Hispanic immigrants in the U.S. have demonstrated that depressive and anxiety symptoms, along with substance abuse disorders, are the most prevalent among this specific group. (p. 6)

Counseling interventions, including individual and group counseling, should be formulated within the context of the student's culture and needs (Fuertes et al., 2007) and provided in the dominant language when feasible (Elizalde-Utnick, 2007b). Furthermore, since these students are often vigilant as to how they are being perceived and accepted by others, teachers' and counselors' verbal and nonverbal responses need to be sensitive to this (Fuertes et al., 2007). Interventions should be aimed at fostering a sense of belonging, acceptance, and respect.

With younger students, multicultural play therapy is often the counseling intervention of choice (Gil & Drewes, 2005). It is important to provide appropriate counseling toys that take into account the age, gender, and culture of the child. It is equally critical to be mindful of acculturation levels and to not stereotype a child, as well as be mindful that there is diversity within groups (e.g., among Latinos and Asians, each broad culture constitutes many ethnic groups with differing cultural practices).

Immigrant students' ability to regulate their emotions is often severely strained during migration and acculturation (Fuertes et al., 2007). Self-regulation is needed to complete tasks, achieve goals, or control behavior. The ability to self-regulate is also critical when immigrant youth negotiate both the demands of their families and those of society (e.g., peers, teachers, community; Motti-Stefanidi et al., 2012). Furthermore, chronic exposure to stress, particularly during childhood and adolescence, hinders individuals' ability to manage stress and regulate their emotions (Gonzales et al, 2013). Therefore, immigrant students often benefit from self-regulation training aimed at helping them develop goal-setting and problem-solving strategies, as well as helping to increase self-efficacy beliefs and self-monitoring. School psychologists can be directly involved in this process through individual and group counseling that explicitly models and allows role-playing scenarios. Indirectly, they can consult with teachers regarding the importance of using self-regulation strategies for immigrant students and developing activities that strengthen self-regulation in their classrooms. For those students with more severe difficulties who require a higher level of care, school psychologists can help facilitate and link families to outside mental health support services.

Cultural competence development is also something that can be addressed in counseling (Motti-Stefanidi et al., 2012). Counseling in the form of socialization groups can assist immigrant youth in developing skills in interacting with individuals from the majority culture as they undergo the process of acculturation. As noted previously, perceived racism could result in an avoidance of contact with members of the majority culture (Fuertes et al., 2007). Furthermore, consistent with children and youth in general, immigrant youth tend to associate themselves with peers from their own ethnic group. Motti-Stefanidi and colleagues (2012) note that:

> ... length of residence in the new country and ethnic composition of the neighborhood are related to immigrant youth choices regarding their friends. Longer residence in the society of settlement and living in more ethnically diverse neighborhoods are related to more contact with national peers than with peers from their own ethnic group. (pp. 28–29)

Socialization groups can assist with the process of interacting with peers from other groups, including the majority culture.

Counseling can provide students with the opportunity to explore their identities. With the process of acculturation come possible changes in ethnic identity. Furthermore, racial/ethnic identity exploration seems to peak during middle adolescence, and youth of color's experience with discrimination and racism trigger such a process of exploration (Quintana, 2007). Quintana suggests that counselors should integrate identity exploration in their work with youth regarding discrimination and racism. For undocumented youth, their status interferes with their identity development, as they often experience anxiety, confusion, and uncertainty about their future as they come of age (Gonzales et al., 2013). As described previously in this chapter, as their documented peers go through several rites of passage (i.e., obtaining a driver's license, applying to college, obtaining a job with working papers), undocumented youth hit a legal wall. Furthermore, negative feelings about their status often become integrated into their sense of self. As a result, it is critical to promote resilience and a sense of belonging in these youth.

SUMMARY

Immigrant students and families face a number of challenges, ranging from the unique circumstances associated with their journey to the United States to everyday stresses related to learning English, surviving economically in a competitive job market, and acculturating into the broader mainstream culture. Entering the public school system and successfully navigating it can be a daunting task as well. When difficulties at school arise and additional support is needed, school psychologists are in the position to provide direct and indirect assistance to these students and parents in need. Through ongoing training and professional practice, school psychologists can build cultural competencies that improve their ability to help implement interventions in a culturally responsive manner.

In order to best provide school-based services to immigrant students and families, effective communication serves as the foundation for forging strong home–school collaborations. By doing so, school psychologists can then be proactive in the integration of various support services needed to help immigrant students succeed. Through consultation and collaboration with school staff and parents, multiple aspects of student functioning can be addressed. Culturally responsive pedagogy and multitiered systems of support for ELLs provide specialized academic instruction. Similarly, counseling with a multicultural focus and ongoing parental consultation target social–emotional needs. Further, school psychologists can be vital partners in helping immigrant families access community and district-wide resources. By providing support to immigrant students and their families, schools ensure that these students not only develop a sense of belonging but also learn in an environment that fosters success and achievement for all.

REFERENCES

Baker, S. K., Gersten, R., & Linan-Thompson, S. (2010). Early reading instruction and intervention with English learners: Key considerations in a multitiered approach. In M. R. Shinn & H. M. Walker (Eds.), *Interventions for achievement and behavior problems in a three-tiered model including RTI* (pp. 501–526). Bethesda, MD: National Association of School Psychologists.

Cortina, J. (2013) Children, education and migration: Win-win policy responses for co-development. *QScience Proceedings 2013.* Retrieved from http://www.qscience.com/doi/pdf/10.5339/qproc.2013.fmd.3

Devos, T., Gavin, K., & Quintana, F. J. (2010). Say "Adios" to the American dream? The interplay between ethnic and national identity among Latino and Caucasian Americans. *Cultural Diversity & Ethnic Minority Psychology, 16,* 37–49.

Elizalde-Utnick, G. (2007a). Culturally and linguistically diverse preschoolers. In G. B. Esquivel, E. C. Lopez, & S. Nahari (Eds.), *Handbook of multicultural school psychology: An interdisciplinary perspective* (pp. 497–525). Mahwah, NJ: Erlbaum.

Elizalde-Utnick, G. (2007b). Young selectively mute English language learners: School-based intervention strategies. *Journal of Early Childhood and Infant Psychology, 3,* 141–161.

Elizalde-Utnick, G. (2010). Immigrant families: Strategies for school support. *Principal Leadership, 10,* 12–16.

Fuertes, J. N., Alfonso, V. C., & Schultz, J. T. (2007). Counseling culturally and linguistically diverse children and youth: A self-regulatory approach. In G. B. Esquivel, E. C. Lopez, & S. Nahari (Eds.), *Handbook of multicultural school psychology: An interdisciplinary perspective* (pp. 409–427). Mahwah, NJ: Erlbaum.

Gil, E., & Drewes, A. A. (Eds.). (2005). *Cultural issues in play therapy.* New York, NY: Guilford Press.

Gonzales, R. G., Suárez-Orozco, C., & Dedios-Sanguineti, M. C. (2013). No place to belong: Contextualizing concepts of mental health among undocumented immigrant youth in the United States. *American Behavioral Scientist, 20,* 1–26.

Green, G., Rhodes, J., Hirsch, A. H., Suárez-Orozco, C., & Camic, P. M. (2007). Supportive adult relationships and the academic engagement of Latin American immigrant youth. *Journal of School Psychology, 46,* 393–412.

Greenwood, C. R., Seals, K., & Kamps, D. (2010). Peer teaching interventions for multiple levels of support. In M. R. Shinn & H. M. Walker (Eds.), *Interventions for achievement and behavior problems in a three-tiered model including RTI* (pp. 501–526). Bethesda, MD: National Association of School Psychologists.

Guerrero, C., & Leung, B. (2008). Communicating effectively with culturally and linguistically diverse (CLD) families. *Communiqué, 36*(8), 19. Retrieved from http://www.nasponline.org/publications/cq/mocq368commmatters.aspx

Hays, D. G., & Erford, B. T. (2014). *Developing multicultural counseling competence: A systems approach* (2nd ed.). Upper Saddle River, NJ: Pearson.

Hwang, W.-C. (2006). Acculturative family distancing: Theory, research, and clinical practice. *Psychotherapy: Theory, Research, Practice, Training, 43,* 397–409.

Kalyanpur, M., & Harry, B. (1999). *Culture in special education: Building reciprocal family-professional relationships.* Baltimore, MD: Brookes.

Katsiaficas, D., Suárez-Orozco, C., Sirin, S. R., & Gupta, T. (2013). Mediators of the relationship between acculturative stress and internalization symptoms for immigrant origin youth. *Cultural Diversity & Ethnic Minority Psychology, 19,* 27–37.

Lesaux, N. K., & Geva, E. (2006). Synthesis: Development of literacy in language-minority students. In D. August & T. Shanahan (Eds.), *Developing literacy in second-language learners: Report of the National Literacy Panel on Language: Minority children and youth* (pp. 53–74). Mahwah, NJ: Erlbaum.

Motti-Stefanidi, F., Berry, J. W., Chryssochoou, X., Sam, D. L., & Phinney, J. (2012). Positive immigrant youth adaptation in context: Developmental, acculturation, and social psychological perspectives. In A. S. Masten, K. Liebkind, & D. J. Hernandez (Eds.), *Realizing the potential of immigrant youth* (pp. 117–158). New York, NY: Cambridge University Press.

National Association of School Psychologists. (2010). *Model for comprehensive and integrated school psychological services.* Bethesda, MD: Author. Retrieved from http://www.nasponline.org/standards/2010standards/2_PracticeModel.pdf

National Association of School Psychologists. (2012). *School–family partnering to enhance learning: Essential elements and responsibilities* [Position statement]. Bethesda, MD: Author. Retrieved from http://www.nasponline.org/about_nasp/positionpapers/Home-SchoolCollaboration.pdf

Quintana, S. M. (2007). Racial and ethnic identity: Developmental perspectives and research. *Journal of Counseling Psychology, 54,* 259–270.

Rhodes, R. L., Ochoa, S. H., & Ortiz, S. O. (2005). *Assessing culturally and linguistically diverse students: A practical guide.* New York, NY: Guilford Press.

Rumbaut, R. G. (2008). Reaping what you sow: Immigration, youth, and reactive ethnicity. *Applied Development Science, 12,* 108–111.

Sáenz, L. M., Fuchs, L. S., & Fuchs, D. (2005). Peer-Assisted Learning Strategies for English language learners with learning disabilities. *Exceptional Children, 71,* 231–247.

Schwartz, S. J., Unger, J. B., Zamboanga, B. L., & Szapocznik, J. (2010). Rethinking the concept of acculturation: Implications for theory and research. *American Psychologist, 65,* 237–251.

Schwartz, S. J., & Zamboanga, B. L. (2008). Testing Berry's model of acculturation: A confirmatory latent class approach. *Cultural Diversity & Ethnic Minority Psychology, 14,* 275–285.

Shin, S. J. (2013). *Bilingualism in schools and society: Language, identity, and policy.* New York, NY: Routledge.

Sue, D. W. (2010). *Microaggressions in everyday life: Race, gender, and sexual orientation.* Hoboken, NJ: Wiley.

Sue, D. W., & Torino, G. C. (2005). Racial-cultural competence: Awareness, knowledge and skills. In R. T. Carter (Ed.), *Handbook of racial-cultural psychology and counseling* (pp. 3–18). Hoboken, NJ: Wiley.

Sue, S., & Zane, N. (2009). The role of culture and cultural techniques in psychotherapy: A critique and reformulation. *Asian American Journal of Psychology, 1,* 3–14.

Tharpe, R. G. (2008). *Effective teaching: How the standards come to be.* Berkeley, CA: Center for Research on Education, Diversity, and Excellence. Retrieved from http://crede.berkeley.edu/research/crede/tharp_development.html

U.S. Department of Homeland Security. (2012). *Yearbook of immigration statistics: 2011.* Washington, DC: Author.

Yoon, E., Langrehr, K., & Ong, L. Z. (2011). Content analysis of acculturation research in counseling and counseling psychology: A 22-year review. *Journal of Counseling Psychology, 58,* 83–96. doi:10.1037/a0021128

9 Best Practices in Conducting Assessments via School Interpreters

Emilia C. Lopez

Queens College, City University of New York

OVERVIEW

Significant numbers of English language learners (ELLs) and children who speak languages other than English have created an increasing demand for bilingual school psychological services. At the current time, more than 4.7 million students in U.S. school systems are ELLs (i.e., students who demonstrate limited English proficiency), and the number of students ranging from 5 to 17 years old who speak languages other than English at home increased from 10% to 21% from 1980 to 2009 (National Center for Education Statistics, 2012). According to the U.S. Department of Education (2008), 63 languages were reported as frequently spoken by ELLs between 2007 and 2008. Although the majority of ELLs in pre-K–12 speak Spanish as their primary language, the other most common languages are Arabic, Chinese, French, Haitian Creole, German, Hmong/Miao, Korean, Russian, and Tagalog/Filipino.

Increases in the number of ELLs from diverse language backgrounds have created greater need for bilingual school psychologists who are able to provide these students and their families with education and psychological supports in general and special education settings. The National Association of School Psychologists (NASP) *Model for Comprehensive and Integrated School Psychological Services* (NASP, 2010a) emphasizes providing students and their families with multitiered supports while engaging in culturally competent practices in all areas of school psychology service delivery under the Diversity in Development and Learning domain. The multitiered supports needed by ELLs may include student-directed services such as instructional, behavioral, and mental health

interventions; indirect services such as parent and teacher consultation; and systems-level services such as crisis intervention and family–school collaboration strategies.

As school psychologists work with ELLs, teachers, and parents, data gathering and assessment are pivotal in order to use the information gathered for decision making (e.g., identifying ELLs who need educational and psychological supports, providing appropriate interventions and programs, evaluating intervention outcomes) at various tiers of service delivery. Bilingual school psychologists have important roles in gathering assessment data using nonbiased approaches. However, significant shortages of bilingual school psychologists proficient in the many languages other than English represented in students' diverse language backgrounds have led to the use of interpreters in schools to gather educational and psychological data for ELLs (Lopez, Irigoyen, Romero, & Birch, 2013). The purposes of this chapter are to discuss facilitators, barriers, and best practices when school psychologists conduct assessments of ELLs via interpreters.

BASIC CONSIDERATIONS

The assessment of ELLs should be conducted by bilingual school psychologists who have the language and professional competencies to engage in culturally responsive assessment practices. Interpreters should only be used after all means have been exhausted to locate bilingual school psychologists who have the language, cultural, and assessment competencies to evaluate ELLs in their native languages (Lopez & Rogers, 2007).

In this chapter, the term *interpreters* refers to professionals who demonstrate expertise in translating the spoken language, whereas translators are professionals who engage in the process of translating written language (e.g., translating letters and legal documents; Tribe & Raval, 2003). The term *translation* refers to the process of changing messages produced in one language to another language. The translated language is referred to as the *source language* whereas the language into which the translation is made is the *target language*.

Two styles of translations are prevalent: consecutive and simultaneous (Tribe & Raval, 2003). In consecutive translation, speakers deliver their messages in the source language and stop to allow interpreters to deliver the translations in the target language. The interpreters translate short (i.e., individual sentence) or long messages (i.e., longer streams of communication). In simultaneous translation, interpreters translate while the speakers are delivering their messages.

Interpreters as Facilitators in the Assessment Process

A primary benefit of working with interpreters is facilitating communicative interactions between individuals who speak different languages or dialects. In a recent survey investigation of bilingual school psychologists, O'Bryon and Rogers (2010) reported that bilingual school psychologists used interpreters for 14% of their assessment cases to assess students across 58 different languages. The contexts in which interpreters are used in the assessment process vary. Interpreters work with school psychologists during parent interviews to collect assessment data and during parent conferences to provide feedback based on assessment results. Interpreters are also used to conduct student interviews and student assessments (Lopez et al., 2013). O'Bryon and Rogers (2010) found that bilingual school psychologists work with interpreters during assessment activities to communicate with parents, translate permission forms for testing, and conduct assessments in the areas of language proficiency, intelligence, adaptive behaviors, and academic achievement.

Challenges in Conducting Assessments via Interpreters

Conducting assessments via interpreters is a complex procedure that requires school psychologists to carefully examine processes and outcomes in order to ultimately evaluate the validity of the results and the implications for decision making. Among the challenges that school psychologists find when conducting assessments via interpreters are establishing rapport and trust with interpreters and students, and gathering, interpreting, and reporting assessment results obtained via interpreters.

Establishing Rapport and Trust

Establishing rapport with students is a critical component of the assessment process. Communicating via interpreters to collect problem identification data from ELLs and their parents may hinder rapport and communication between school psychologists and students. For example, a student can feel uncomfortable communicating through an interpreter who is part of his or her community and may fear that confidentiality will not be maintained, which will have an impact on the student's comfort level with the school psychologist (Lopez, 2000). The presence of an interpreter may inhibit a student's engagement and responses during assessments. In addition, a school psychologist may experience difficulty establishing rapport because a student may more easily engage with an interpreter as a result of sharing similar languages and cultures.

School psychologists and interpreters must establish rapport in order to collaborate and work effectively to assess ELLs. Establishing rapport with interpreters may be difficult because school psychologists do not often have the opportunity to work with the same interpreter for assessment purposes. Interpreters are sometimes hired as outside consultants through agencies for itinerant work, and these arrangements do not facilitate the establishing of ongoing collaborative relationships with school psychologists and other school personnel. Clinicians in mental health settings report experiencing difficulties in establishing coworker alliances with interpreters because of power differentials (i.e., the nature of the unequal relationship between the interpreter and clinician) and issues of trust (e.g., a clinician's lack of trust in the interpreter's translations; see Tribe & Lane, 2009). A lack of rapport and collaborative relationship between school psychologists and the interpreters may hinder the establishment of rapport with students during the assessment process. School psychologists must be attentive to these issues during the administration and interpretation phases in terms of how those dynamics have an impact on assessment outcomes.

Gathering, Interpreting, and Reporting Results

Assessment involves administering formal as well as informal tools and procedures in order to gather data.

Perhaps one of the most challenging and controversial issues is the use of interpreters in the practice of test administration. School psychologists engage in several practices that include (a) using tests that have been translated and validated in languages other than English via interpreters, (b) providing interpreters with testing manuals prior to the assessment so that the interpreters prepare by translating the test items, and (c) asking interpreters to translate test items on the spot (Lopez et al., 2013).

Several assessment instruments have been pilot tested and normed in languages other than English. The availability of translated and validated versions of cognitive, achievement, and other tests certainly provides school psychologists with a more viable way to assess via interpreters as it will reduce potential problems with translations that significantly alter the validity of the tests and findings. However, most of the few tools available are in Spanish, which accentuates the lack of validated tools to assess ELLs from other language backgrounds.

Given the lack of translated tests that have been validated in different languages, a practice used by school psychologists is to provide the interpreters with the testing manuals prior to the assessment session to prepare for the translation (Lopez et al., 2013). The assumption made is that if the translation is conducted prior to the assessment session, the quality of the translation will be better because the interpreters have more time to work on more accurate translations.

School psychologists are also engaging interpreters in on-the-spot translations (Lopez et al., 2013). On-the-spot translations involve the school psychologist reading testing questions to the interpreter and the interpreter translating the questions during the testing session for the student being assessed. The interpreter then translates the student's responses to the school psychologist.

Bracken and Barona (1991) contend that translating test items is problematic because test directions are frequently too "psychotechnical" or difficult to allow for easy translation and that versions of translated tests produced by practitioners and interpreters are rarely "sufficiently perfected" to provide equivalent meanings across languages (pp. 119–120). In addition, many words and concepts cannot be directly translated from one language to another, and the content of the test items may be substantially altered. The developmental level of items or questions may also change when the items are translated into the target language. Neither the school psychologist nor the interpreters will be able to

accurately judge the developmental level of the items simply based on their practical experiences. Variations in vocabulary due to regional differences also render translations difficult because interpreters must have knowledge of the lexical variations used in specific regions or geographical areas (e.g., many Puerto Ricans call kites *cometas* whereas many Cubans call kites *papalotes*).

The practices of translating tests prior to the assessment session and on the spot are clearly problematic. The *Standards for Educational and Psychological Testing* (American Educational Research Association [AERA], American Psychological Association, & National Council on Measurement in Education, 1999) state that when a test is translated from one language or dialect to another, its reliability and validity should be established for the uses intended with the linguistic groups to be tested. The standards also indicate that assessment results are not valid when tests are used to assess students that are not represented in the tests' norming samples.

Hambleton and Li (2005) discuss myths about translations that include "[j]ust about anyone with the language skills can produce an acceptable test translation and adaptation" (p. 82), and "[a] good literal translation is what is needed" (p. 83). They cite research showing that informal translations result in poorly constructed tests with literal translations that are "problematic because they [do] not represent the original meaning [of the items] or [are] difficult to understand" (p. 883). Hambleton and Li outline recommended steps in adapting and translating tests that include (a) reviewing the constructs measured in the test in the context of the language and culture that the test is being translated for, (b) selecting interpreters who are qualified to engage in test translation (i.e., they are familiar with both languages and cultures, have knowledge of constructs being assessed, and have knowledge of test construction), (c) translating and adapting the test using multiple translation methods (e.g., one group of interpreters translate from language 1 to language 2, and a second group translates backward from language 2 to language 1 to double check for equivalence), (d) reviewing and revising the translated test, (e) pilot testing the translated test, (f) conducting validation investigations, (g) placing test scores from the different versions of the test on a common reporting scale, and (h) developing a technical manual with standardization and norming data.

The availability of translated and validated versions of tests and the practice of training interpreters facilitate the assessment of ELLs when bilingual school psychologists are not available. However, the complexity of the process is not diminished because school psychologists must rely on interpreters to translate during informal and less structured assessment procedures such as interviews, curriculum-based assessments, and testing of the limits. Interpreters must also translate all responses provided by students and others involved in the assessment process (i.e., parents). Since school psychologists rely on the interpreters' rendition of the speakers' messages, interpreters must demonstrate highly proficient translation skills in order to communicate, for example, emotional content during behavioral and mental health evaluations. Interpreters must also avoid delivering literal translations and must filter messages so that the translation conveys the original intent of the senders.

An exchange during assessment sessions illustrates the importance of obtaining meaningful translations: During an assessment interview, a Spanish-speaking adolescent shared with the school psychologist, via the interpreter, that he was very much like his father in the way that he behaved by using the proverb "*De tal palo, tal astilla.*" If translated literally, the translation would be "From such a stick, such a splinter," which would not be very meaningful to the English-speaking school psychologist. The interpreter translated the proverb literally, but also explained to the school psychologist that the proverb meant that the child's behavior was a reflection of the parent's behavior, and that it was similar to the proverb "The apple does not fall far from the tree." The school psychologist then proceeded to explore with the child, via the interpreter, in what ways the child viewed himself as similar to his father. In this example, the interpreter provided the translation and the context to help the school psychologist to understand the child's intent and opened the way for the school psychologist to probe farther.

The translation process also introduces a number of potential serious risks to the assessment process, including translation errors. For example, Flores et al. (2003) found that interpreters made an average of 31 errors per patient encounter in pediatric emergency hospital visits, and 63% of those errors had serious potential impacts on rendered diagnoses. Although trained interpreters made fewer errors, their errors included significant instances of miscommunications. In assessment sessions, Spanish-speaking interpreters with little or no training in translation omitted, added, and substituted words and phrases that significantly changed the content and the meaning of test questions and directions in a cognitive assessment tool (Lopez, 1994). In some instances, the interpreters were unable to translate specific assessment items because they did not have the appropriate vocabulary in Spanish.

Ultimately, the school psychologist is dependent on the interpreters' translations to conduct the assessment and establish clear lines of communication. Major translation errors that alter meaning result in significant changes in the assessment questions and student's responses, which subsequently lead to inaccurate interpretations of the information or data gathered. For example, when a school psychologist interviewed a Spanish-speaking student via an interpreter and asked how the student felt about being teased by classmates, the student shared with the school psychologist that she felt "*avergonzada*" or embarrassed. When translating the word "embarrassed" to Spanish, instead of translating it to "*avergonzada,*" the interpreter translated it as "*embarazada,*" which means pregnant. Gathering assessment data and information via interpreters obviously demands translations that facilitate communication between school psychologists, students, and interpreters.

BEST PRACTICES IN CONDUCTING ASSESSMENTS VIA SCHOOL INTERPRETERS

The significant numbers of students who are unable to communicate effectively in English and the pronounced shortages of bilingual school personnel mean that school psychologists engage interpreters in assessing students who demonstrate low proficiency in English. The complexity and limitations of the process call for school psychologists to carefully plan for assessment sessions and cautiously evaluate outcomes in order to establish their utility for decision making.

Engaging in Ethical Practices

Ethical guidelines are available to guide both school psychologists' and interpreters' professional conduct, competencies, and training when working together in the context of assessments. Table 9.1 summarizes ethical guidelines relevant to the assessment process for school psychologists and interpreters. NASP's *Principles for Professional Ethics* (NASP, 2010b) Standard III.3.6 states that "[w]hen interpreters are used to facilitate the provision of assessment and intervention services, school psychologists take steps to ensure that the interpreters are appropriately trained and are acceptable to the clients" (p. 7). The *Standards for*

Table 9.1. Ethical Guidelines Relevant to Assessment for School Psychologists and Interpreters

Guidelines for School Psychologists Conducting Assessments Through Interpreters[a]
- Work with qualified interpreters
- Refrain from promoting the use of psychological assessment tools and techniques by unqualified persons, except when conducted for training purposes and with appropriate supervision
- Provide interpreters with training to translate during assessment sessions
- Obtain informed consent from parents or legal guardians as to the use of interpreters during assessment
- Inform the interpreter of the requirements to maintain confidentiality and test security
- Recognize the limitations of the interpreter's training as examiners
- Obtain supervision and professional development to deliver assessment services via interpreters
- Report results indicating that an interpreter was used during the assessment and describe the procedures used
- Evaluate the utility of the results obtained via interpreters, taking into consideration that translating test and assessment procedures compromises the validity of the findings
- Communicate the limitations and validity of the results obtained via interpreters

Guidelines for Interpreters Working With School Psychologists[b]
- Accept work assignments that are within the range of the interpreter's skills and abilities (e.g., language fluency, level of training)
- Seek supervision when appropriate
- Receive training and demonstrate knowledge and skills in the process of educational and psychological assessment
- Engage in professional behaviors (e.g., refrain from translating for family or friends to avoid dual relationships that may interfere with objectivity)
- Engage with colleagues and clients in respectful ways
- Maintain confidentiality in regard to all information and data collected in the process of assessment
- Maintain test security
- Translate information with accuracy while also conveying the communicative intent of the speakers
- Maintain a neutral and professional attitude that entails refraining from interjecting personal opinions or influencing the student's performance
- Refrain from translating information that is beyond the boundaries of assessment or clinical services without the direction of the qualified examiner
- Engage in student advocacy and in the role of cultural broker with clinicians and clients when appropriate (e.g., sharing culturally relevant information with the student or parents under the direction of the examiner, and sharing information before or after an evaluation with examiners)
- Request fees for services in a professional manner
- Seek opportunities to engage in ongoing professional development

Guidelines for School Psychologists and Interpreters[c]
- Use the standard wording provided in the test
- When required, select the language and mode of interpretation that most accurately conveys the content and spirit of the messages of the student
- Identify skillful and unobtrusive interactions to communicate during the assessment that will not interfere with the flow of communication (e.g., a signal that means that the interpreter wants to speak to the school psychologist about a student's behaviors or communication)
- Become familiar with each other's style of communication and work speed prior to the assessment session
- Review assessment results after the assessment session.

Note. [a]Based on information from AERA (1999) and NASP (2010b); [b]based on information from Elliott (2012) and Rhodes, Ochoa, and Ortiz (2005); [c]based on information from Elliott (2012).

Educational and Psychological Testing (AERA, 1999) provide the most comprehensive guidelines pertaining to psychologists delivering assessment services via interpreters through Standard 9: Testing Individuals of Diverse Linguistic Backgrounds.

Ethical standards are not available for interpreters engaged in translating during assessment sessions within educational settings. However, standards are available to guide their professional conduct. Elliott (2012) refers to ethical standards for interpreters in the medical field,

whereas Rhodes, Ochoa, and Ortiz (2005) draw from standards for interpreters for the deaf. Both Elliott (2012) and Rhodes et al. (2005) have used available ethical standards in these fields and have applied them to interpreters providing their services during assessment sessions. School psychologists have the responsibility of engaging in ethical practices when assessing via interpreters, and they are also responsible for discussing and reviewing ethical and professional practices with interpreters, such as maintaining confidentiality and test security (i.e., interpreters should not share information gathered about students and families during the assessment session or the contents of test items).

Identifying Interpreters

O'Bryon and Rogers (2010) found that school psychologists located interpreters through lists provided by districts, school staff, or hospitals (71.9%); outside agencies (18.4%); family or religious groups (5.3%); and colleagues or university contacts (4.9%). The survey participants noted that it was difficult to locate interpreters, and that is particularly the case when trying to identify interpreters who had training and expertise in the process of assessment. Trained interpreters can also be located by contacting local interpreter training institutions and universities' programs and agencies that provide trained itinerant interpreters. State and district directories outlining the interpreters' qualifications, training, experiences, and areas of expertise to guide school psychologists in contacting interpreters with assessment competencies are also helpful.

School psychologists and other school personnel need to advocate for ELL students and families within school districts to ensure that administrators allocate funding to hire trained interpreters. When professionally trained interpreters cannot be located, school psychologists may find themselves in the position of having to use bilingual school personnel with educational expertise to provide translation services (Rhodes et al., 2005). Among the bilingual school personnel who may provide assistance are teachers, social workers, counselors, teachers' aides, and trained paraprofessionals. However, interpreters translating during assessment sessions should be trained in a number of important areas.

Providing Training for Interpreters and School Psychologists

A number of pivotal competencies for interpreters and school psychologists collaborating during the assessment process are outlined in Table 9.2. Ideally, interpreters should have training in the translation process and high levels of language proficiency in both the source and the target languages. They should also have training in how to translate for assessment sessions and in how to work collaboratively with school psychologists. Since trained interpreters may have little or no background working in school settings, school psychologists may need to provide

interpreters with specific training pertinent to conducting assessments in schools (e.g., knowledge of validity and reliability, administration procedures, process of assessing students at various developmental stages and with a range of disabilities, establishing of rapport with students under the direction of the school psychologist).

When school psychologists do not have access to trained interpreters, they work with school personnel and individuals from the community who demonstrate bilingual proficiency and who are familiar with the cultural backgrounds of the students (Lopez et al., 2013). School personnel and community members serving as interpreters will require extensive training if they are unfamiliar with the educational and psychological assessment issues that they will encounter in their roles as interpreters.

The availability of translated tests that have been validated with different language groups provides school psychologists with opportunities to train interpreters in the process of test administration. For example, the Woodcock-Johnson Bateria III Test of Cognitive Abilities is available in Spanish (Schrank, Mather, McGrew, & Woodcock, 2007). The Bilingual Verbal Ability Tests is also available in Spanish and 16 other languages (Muñoz-Sandoval, Cummins, Alvarado, & Ruet, 1998). These tests provide models for examiners to partner with interpreters as assistant examiners.

In the Woodcock-Johnson Bateria III Test of Cognitive Abilities and the Bilingual Verbal Ability Tests, Schrank et al. (2005) recommend the use of a primary and ancillary team approach. In this approach, the primary examiner (i.e., school psychologist) is always present and leads the test administration, while the ancillary examiner administers the test items while using the testing manual in Spanish. A translation of the Differential Ability Scales II Early Years is also available in Spanish and includes an interpreter's handbook (Elliott, 2012).

The manuals for these tools stress the importance of training of interpreters as assistant examiners. Shrank et al. (2005) recommend training the ancillary examiner on test administration, then requiring the ancillary examiner to conduct three practice tests with practice subjects, and finally having the ancillary examiner conduct two more practice tests while being observed by the primary examiner. Feedback should be provided to the assistant examiner based on the observations of the practice test administrations.

School psychologists also need to demonstrate a number of pivotal competencies in assessing via interpreters. However, training for school psychologists

Table 9.2. Assessment Competencies for School Interpreters and School Psychologists

	Knowledge of:	Skills in:
School interpreters	• The process of translation • Their roles as interpreters in the assessment process • Educational contexts (e.g., education system, district policies, school policies, referral process, special education assessment policies and terminology) • Psychological issues relevant to providing translation services during assessment sessions • Professional behavior in maintaining test security • Assessment process, tools, and procedures used in the assessment of ELLs, including administration procedures	• High levels of proficiency in the source and target languages • Translating information accurately • Working with children and adolescents • Following standardized assessment procedures and following school psychologists' directions (e.g., when testing limits) • Interacting appropriately with school psychologists and students during assessment sessions (e.g., remaining neutral and objective, refraining from interjecting personal opinions, approaching the school psychologist professionally to discuss observations about cultural or language issues) • Communicating effectively with the school psychologist to review assessment results • Working with school psychologists to provide parents and students with feedback based on assessment results
School psychologists	• Facilitators, barriers, and challenges of working with interpreters during the assessment process • Issues related to validity of tests and procedures when assessing via interpreters • Nonbiased assessment	• Assessing and obtaining problem identification data via interpreters • Interpreting and reporting assessment data (formal and informal) collected via interpreters • Training interpreters to translate during educational and psychological assessments • Evaluating the validity of the information/data obtained via interpreters and the utility of the outcomes for decision making • Communicating assessment results obtained via interpreters in psychoeducational reports, and during meetings with parents and colleagues (e.g., special education committee meetings to discuss assessment outcomes)
Shared competencies	• The problems inherent in the translation process within the context of educational and psychological assessment • Ethical standards relevant to assessments • Students' linguistic, cultural, and educational backgrounds, including knowledge of cultural beliefs, values, and practices to help interpreters and school psychologists to understand the populations they are assessing • Language development, second language acquisition and acculturation • Cultural differences in regard to views of exceptionality, cross-cultural communication, child rearing, educational practices, and other issues relevant to working with ELLs and their families • Cross-cultural communication	• Collaborating to establish rapport with students and optimal assessment conditions • Working together to provide educational and psychological assessment services (e.g., briefing, debriefing) to students and families

in working with interpreters is scarce. O'Bryon and Rogers (2010) found that only 5% of the bilingual school psychologists in their survey had learned how to use interpreters during their graduate preparation programs, and the implication is that preparation programs need to provide more coursework and fieldwork experiences in this area. School psychologists are encouraged to attend workshops and to engage in self-study focused on assessing via interpreters.

Given the collaborative nature of delivering assessment services via interpreters, workshops that jointly prepare school psychologists and interpreters are helpful to practice required skills while receiving performance feedback. Courses and workshops incorporating didactic experiences (e.g., presentations), observations of scripted scenarios in which interpreters were used (e.g., videos or vignettes), and group discussions based on actual experiences in the field are potential options (Marion, Hildebrandt, Davis, Marin, & Crandall 2008). Sessions for school psychologists and interpreters should include preparation for test administration (i.e., practicing translations and administrations of specific tools). Other topics that can be explored in joint sessions include communication and rapport-building strategies that are relevant to the assessment process (e.g., discussing topics that the interpreter may be uncomfortable with, building rapport with the student or parents).

Supervision should be available to interpreters in order to help them improve their skills. Supervisors of interpreters should have extensive experience with translations in the context of assessment situations in order to discuss and explore relevant topics. Although school psychologists have the skills to provide training and supervision to interpreters in areas specific to educational and psychological assessments, training pertinent to the process of translation and language skills should be conducted by professionals with expertise in training interpreters (e.g., skills in simultaneous and consecutive translation; Tribe & Raval, 2003).

Joint supervision is also recommended for both school psychologists and interpreters in order to gain basic to advanced skills. For example, when attending a supervision session led by a school psychologist with expertise in working with interpreters, a school psychologist from the district and a Korean interpreter shared that they had recently worked together during a session in which the student was an adolescent who demonstrated disorganized language and thinking that were symptoms of mental health problems. As the interpreter proceeded to translate the content of the communication, the school psychologist felt confused during the assessment session and asked herself why she was having difficulty understanding what was being communicated. Was the communication unclear because the translation was not adequate? Or, was the translation a function of a student communicating in such a confusing and disorganized manner? The interpreter also felt frustrated and worried that the school psychologist would think that the translation was inadequate. The interpreter felt confused about how to communicate with the school psychologist that the student was having significant problems expressing himself clearly and that the student's thought process was disorganized. The supervisor helped the school psychologist and interpreter explore how the scenario led to miscommunication and confusion. With the help of the supervisor, both the school psychologist and the interpreter agreed that this was a situation that called for some form of communication between them during the assessment session to clarify context. The school psychologist and the interpreter came up with a signal that they would use whenever they needed to find the time to communicate with each other outside of the testing situation. The signal was that either the school psychologist or the interpreter could pull on an earlobe to communicate to the other that there was a need to take a break and talk in private. The supervisor encouraged the examiner and the school psychologist to incorporate that practice into their professional repertoire. The school psychologist decided that she would use this strategy with any interpreter she worked with in the future, and incorporated it as a routine practice when assessing via interpreters. In subsequent supervision sessions, the school psychologist reported that the strategy had been useful in another situation in which the interpreter had conveyed to her that the student had a significant speech impairment in Russian. The interpreter she had worked with had signaled her as agreed, and they stepped out of the assessment room to share the information, which helped the school psychologist to understand that the student's responses were difficult to translate because the interpreter was having a difficult time understanding the student. They agreed that the interpreter should continue to translate in ways that reflected the student's language difficulties and that they would discuss the specifics after the assessment session so that the interpreter could describe and elaborate as to the student's language deficits in Russian.

Ongoing individual and group supervision experiences are ideal opportunities for school psychologists and interpreters to explore the challenges and barriers found when working together to conduct assessments while also exploring potential strategies to overcome barriers. Issues related to collaboration, the establishment of rapport and trust, and assessment procedures can also be discussed in order to use supervision as a supportive and continuing education experience.

Defining Roles and Functions in the Assessment Process

Interpreters play important roles in school psychologists' efforts to deliver educational and psychological assessment services to ELLs and families. Interpreters' roles and functions must be clearly defined within the context of their skills and the assessment process. On the one hand, an interpreter's role may be defined as that of language translator or language conduit who merely translates language. Contemporary models of mental health translation propose that the conduit model is too simplistic because it does not recognize that interpreters are an integral part of working with clients and their presence adds a new dimension to the traditional clinician–client interaction (Tribe & Lane, 2009). Interpreters may also have valuable information to offer as cultural brokers pertaining to cultural issues and differences. For example, interpreters who are knowledgeable about clients' cultural backgrounds and communication styles are helpful to school psychologists when interpreting results that suggest that the clients' responses are based on knowledge, attitudes, beliefs, or values connected to their cultural backgrounds.

The culturally interactive model proposes that interpreters can adopt more active roles as cultural brokers (i.e., by helping school personnel to bridge cultural differences with students), cultural consultants (i.e., by helping school psychologists and other professionals to solve problems focused on cultural and linguistic differences), and even advocates (i.e., by advocating for the culturally and linguistically diverse clients that they work with as interpreters; Tribe & Lane, 2009). Avery (2001) argues that the roles of interpreters should be defined along a continuum that ranges from linguistic conversion to "actively assisting, when necessary, to overcome barriers to communication embedded in cultural, class, religious, and other social differences" (p. 7). Avery also clearly draws boundaries along this continuum of roles by arguing that "the interpreter is responsible for clear communication" and the clinician is responsible for the ultimate outcome (p. 10). Similar boundaries are applicable to interpreters assisting school psychologists in the assessment process.

Adopting a more culturally interactive model during the assessment process does imply that interpreters must receive training in areas relevant to cultural and language issues. It also implies that school psychologists

must be open to engaging interpreters as cultural brokers in examining cultural issues while also remaining vigilant that the interpreters' own values and beliefs are not biasing the way in which they are describing students' performances. As such, school psychologists working with interpreters should consider the extent of the interpreters' training and background experiences to fulfill the roles of cultural brokers so that interpreters are not asked to assume roles that they are unprepared to perform during the assessment process (Tribe & Lane, 2009).

Trained interpreters, school personnel, and community members who have dual relationships with specific students should not be placed in the position of providing translation services for those students and families. Schoolchildren and family members should also not be placed in the role of translating during assessment sessions or during meetings to discuss assessment results (Tribe & Raval, 2003). Students and family members who are placed in the roles of interpreters may have difficulty delivering accurate translations because they may lack the language skills needed for the task. In addition, their personal involvement with the student and family may interfere with their ability to remain objective during the translation process. As such, they may refrain from translating everything that is said because they do not agree with the content of the discussion or because they may wish to protect the student or family member they are helping. The confidential nature of the assessment process and ethical guidelines referring to the importance of maintaining test security also provide strong rationale for not using students and family members as interpreters.

Allocating Time

Providing school psychological services through interpreters is very time consuming (Lopez, 2000). The challenges are inherent in the process of translation because all communication is filtered through the interpreter and thus demands more time. The use of consecutive translation also adds considerable time to assessment sessions. Young children and students with disabilities (e.g., students with attention deficit disorder) may find working via interpreters particularly demanding because the exposure to two languages during the assessment process feels overwhelming.

School psychologists should acknowledge and expect that assessments conducted through interpreters will take additional time. School administrators overseeing assessment cases need to be aware of this factor so that time constraints are acknowledged early on during the process and steps are taken to prevent the violation of any explicit or implicit deadlines. A final note on the issue of needed time is that planning for the assessment session (i.e., briefing), and taking the time to discuss the assessment process and results after the assessment session (i.e., debriefing), also require time for the school psychologist and interpreter to collaborate.

Identifying Tools and Procedures to Gather Assessment Data

The assessment of ELLs calls for the use of multiple sources and methods of assessment that include informal tools such as interviews, observations, language samples, teach–test–teach approaches, and curriculum-based assessment. Assessment tools should focus on identifying the students' strengths and weaknesses as well as examining the learning environment (e.g., instruction, classroom management; Lopez, 2006; Rhodes et al., 2005). These are basic building blocks that also apply to assessing ELLs.

The decision to translate a test is a major modification that, as previously discussed, has an impact on the test's validity and places limitations on the interpretation of assessment results. The quantitative data obtained will not be informative given the questionable validity of the results. Modifications and testing of the limits, such as extending or eliminating time limits, using and adding queries to explore questionable or incorrect responses, providing additional directions and sample items, and accepting responses that are more culturally congruent with the student's background, will provide useful qualitative data for school psychologists when working with competent interpreters.

Fernandez, Boccaccini, and Noland (2007) provide guidelines as to judicious test selection for Spanish-speaking clients. However, these guidelines are applicable when assessing ELLs from other language groups. Fernandez et al. (2007) recommend that school psychologists identify the available tests in the primary language of the student (i.e., language other than English), examine the available literature and empirical support related to the norming of the assessment instrument and translation procedures (i.e., validity for the tool, taking into consideration the characteristics of the student, process of translation, and validation for the test), and establish the level of research support for using the translated test with each student. In essence, the procedures point to best practices that call for school

psychologists to carefully examine the validity of any translated test for ELLs and to choose tools that have been validated with samples similar to the students being assessed.

Using Assessment Phases When Working With Interpreters

Three phases are recommended when working with interpreters (Langdon, 1994). The first phase is referred to as briefing and entails devoting time to meet with interpreters prior to the translation session to prepare and set clear goals for the session. The second phase is the active phase and refers to the actual time during which school psychologists are working with interpreters to provide services to ELL students and families. The third phase is the debriefing phase and involves school psychologists and interpreters meeting to discuss and review the translation session. Table 9.3 provides an outline of the practices relevant to the three phases of working with interpreters during the assessment process. The practices recommended during these three phases assume that the interpreters have adequate competencies in the process of translation, training in providing translations during assessment sessions, and high levels of language proficiency in English and the second language.

Briefing Phase

Prior to assessment sessions, school psychologists should conduct briefing sessions with interpreters. Briefing sessions provide school psychologists and interpreters with opportunities to develop rapport and a professional relationship. During this phase school psychologists should take the time to become acquainted with the interpreters' training and background experiences in the area of assessment. It is also the time when issues of confidentiality and test security should be discussed. Interpreters should also be provided with the background information needed to prepare for the translation session such as procedures that will be used (e.g., interviews, meetings, assessment) and pertinent information regarding students (e.g., if the student has language deficits in the primary language or a thought disorder, the issue of translating information accurately to reflect the student's communication style should be discussed). The briefing sessions are useful when school psychologists want to explore the cultural issues that they need to be aware of when working with ELLs from diverse cultural backgrounds. Seating arrangements should be established, and Elliott (2012) recommends placing the

Table 9.3. Recommended Practices for School Psychologists to Conduct Assessments via Interpreters

General Recommendations
- Engage in ethical practices when working with interpreters
- Identify interpreters who have the required competencies to translate during assessment sessions
- Provide training and supervisor for interpreters In the context of assessment
- Seek training and supervision as a school psychologist to acquire and enhance assessment skills needed to work with interpreters
- Define the roles and functions of interpreters, taking into consideration their competencies in the context of assessment and working with ELLs from diverse cultural backgrounds
- Allocate sufficient time to assess via interpreters
- Use a multimethod approach to gather data when assessing ELLs via interpreters, and choose procedures/tools that will provide meaningful and useful information for decision making
- Carefully evaluate the validity of the assessment procedures and tools used when assessing ELLs via interpreters, and interpret results cautiously while taking into consideration the ELL's language and cultural background

During Briefing Sessions
- Establish rapport with the interpreter
- Establish seating arrangements
- Provide the interpreter with any information that the interpreter needs to understand the context of the assessment process (e.g., procedures, student background)
- Review issues relevant to confidentiality and test security
- Discuss and make decisions about styles of translation (e.g., consecutive or simultaneous translation), but remain flexible to make needed modifications depending on the student's responses and communication style
- Discuss technical terms or vocabulary that may need to be translated
- Discuss cross-cultural issues and differences that may be relevant to behavioral or communicative interactions
- Review all assessment materials and discuss relevant questions with the interpreter
- Review concepts related to standardization, validity, reliability, and conduct during assessment sessions (e.g., do not coax students)

During Assessment Sessions
- Collaborate with the interpreter to establish rapport with the student, and introduce the school psychologist and the interpreter to the student
- Speak directly to the student using the first person
- If engaging in consecutive translation, speak in short sentences and allow time for the interpreter to translate everything said during the session
- Mediate communication patterns (e.g., speed, timing, how much is translated) with the interpreter and the student (e.g., ask the student to slow down, ask the interpreter to translate all that is said) as necessary
- Along with the interpreter, write the student's responses down, and take notes relevant to the student's verbal and nonverbal communication and behaviors
- Check for clarification whenever it is felt that communication is not clear
- Establish a predetermined signal that communicates the need for the school psychologist and the interpreter to share information about the student's performance or behavior, and make time to communicate to each other outside of the assessment room as appropriate and necessary by taking periodic breaks
- Take the lead in the administration of the questions and test items
- If the test is available in the student's language other than English, the interpreter can follow the manual during the administration
- Observe the student's and interpreter's verbal and nonverbal communication during the assessment session to note patterns of communication and interactions

During Debriefing Sessions
- Discuss responses to items and difficulties translating vocabulary or concepts
- Discuss cross-cultural issues relevant to the student's responses and nonverbal behaviors
- Identify and discuss ways in which the assessment session could have been improved or changed within the contexts of cultural responsiveness and translation of communication

Evaluating Process and Outcomes
- Evaluate the data that were obtained via interpreters by taking into consideration the quality of the translation, relational and social aspects, cultural responsiveness, language differences, professional interactions, and adherence to best practices
- Consider a variety of options in decision making if the data gathered are not useful, such as working with a different interpreter during future assessments, obtaining additional data via response-to-intervention practices, and finding different means by which to obtain information (e.g., bilingual school psychologist)
- Report results indicating that an interpreter was used and clearly discussing the validity and limitations of the assessment data

interpreter between the school psychologist and the student.

School psychologists should also discuss with the interpreters the type of translation that will be used, consecutive or simultaneous translation. The numbers of translation errors made by interpreters increase as speakers increase their speech rates, and interpreters tend to omit more information if the message givers speak for a long period of time and do not allow interpreters to translate messages periodically (Barik, 1973). Thus, school psychologists should avoid speaking at a fast rate and should pause frequently to allow interpreters to translate messages when communicating via the consecutive translation style. Simultaneous translation is difficult and should not be attempted unless interpreters have substantial training and experience in this area.

School psychologists and interpreters should be flexible in their attempts to use either translation style. Some students and parents find simultaneous translation to be demanding and even distracting because they are listening to both languages simultaneously. However, in some scenarios, simultaneous translation is very helpful in encouraging uninterrupted communication (e.g., situations in which the student is relating very emotional or traumatic experiences that the school psychologist may not want to constantly interrupt via the consecutive translation medium). Although school psychologists and interpreters may decide on a translation style during the briefing stage, a flexible approach should be maintained to allow modifications during the assessment as necessary and appropriate. Collaboration and flexibility is further facilitated when school psychologists and interpreters plan as to how to communicate with each other during the assessment active stage to address questions, concerns, or changes in strategies (e.g., using a signal to communicate a change in translation style, taking short breaks to discuss interpreters' and school psychologists' questions or concerns).

Interpreters and school psychologists should also review all assessment materials and allow the interpreter to ask relevant questions during the briefing stage. Concepts related to standardization, validity, and assessment procedures (e.g., do not coax students' responses) are reviewed during the briefing stage. Decisions should be made as to how a student's responses will be recorded (e.g., the interpreter writing down the student's responses in the protocol and taking notes during the session while the school psychologist also notes responses as the interpreter translates them).

Active Phase

This is the phase during which school psychologists and interpreters actively work together to assess students. Practices recommended include school psychologists making time to establish rapport with students and families (e.g., during parent interviews) via the interpreters, and using effective communication skills (e.g., avoiding the use of long chunks of communication and technical language, summarizing and reviewing information discussed to check for clarity of information). Procedures discussed during the briefing phase should be followed, such as following standardized procedures.

The school psychologist should be responsible for leading the test administration. Elliott (2012) suggests that the interpreter handle the timer and the manipulatives during the test administration. However, this should also be the case when interpreters have been extensively trained in test administration with each specific test used during the assessment session. If the manual is available in English and the student's language is other than English, then the school psychologist is able to follow the English manual while the interpreter follows the manual in the language the student is using.

Both the school psychologist and the interpreter should note the student's responses (i.e., the interpreter writes responses in the language other than English, translates the responses to English, and the school psychologist records the responses in English). Recording the student's responses in both languages has two purposes: one is to have data available in both languages for accountability purposes, and the other is to provide the school psychologist and interpreters with opportunities to review the responses after the assessment session for interpretation purposes.

On-the-spot translations do not result in valid translations of testing tools, and school psychologists should not engage in this practice. The first choice should be using assessment tools that have been validated for the population being tested after providing interpreters with the appropriate training. If validated versions of translated tests are not available that are appropriate for the student being assessed, then data should only be gathered informally and for explorative purposes. Nonverbal assessment tools such as the Universal Nonverbal Intelligence Test (McCallum & Bracken, 2005), which entails administering testing items without the use of verbal communication, should be incorporated into the assessment battery to avoid having to translate directions for nonverbal tests, which also violate standardization.

Rousseau, Measham, and Moro (2010) recommend that clinicians carefully observe clients' nonverbal communication, and this recommendation is certainly applicable during assessments as it will inform the school psychologist about the student's comfort level in the context of working via interpreters. Searight and Searight (2009) also recommend careful observation of interpreters that may provide school psychologists with cues about the interpreters' level of comfort and skill during the process. For example, the interpreter may be embarrassed about the student's behavior and may correct the student because the interpreter may feel that the student's behavior is inappropriate in front of an authority figure such as a school psychologist. Interpreters may avoid translating certain issues or topics because they feel that they may reflect poorly on the students or on their shared community.

Interpreters may also not translate all communication and may summarize the content of the message, which results in the student delivering a long response but the interpreter delivering a short translation that leaves the school psychologist perplexed and wondering what was lost in communication. School psychologists should recommend observing the student's and interpreter's nonverbal communication and note persistent patterns of vague and tangential responses that may be the result of the interpreters not translating accurately (Searight & Searight, 2009). This dynamic must be carefully taken into consideration in terms of interpretations of findings and evaluations of assessment outcomes, and all observations must be interpreted in the context of the students' and interpreters' cultural backgrounds and the contextual experience of conducting assessments via interpreters (e.g., the student does not establish eye contact with the interpreter or assessor because the interpreter or assessor is an adult, and this may be appropriate in the student's culture; the student may feel uncomfortable sharing information about his or her family with an interpreter who is from the same background because the student may fear that the interpreter will violate confidentiality within their shared community). These issues, as previously discussed, can also be addressed during training and supervision experiences to help school psychologists and interpreters enhance their competencies when assessing ELLs.

Debriefing Phase
Debriefing sessions are held after translation sessions for school psychologists and interpreters to discuss out-comes, questions, and problems that surfaced during the translation process. This is the time when school psychologists and interpreters discuss concepts that were difficult to translate during the assessment session, cross-cultural differences that may have influenced the translation session (e.g., differences in communication styles or challenges encountered using different styles of translation), patterns of responses to questions or assessment items, or observations relevant to the student's behaviors and nonverbal communication. During debriefing, school psychologists and interpreters should triangulate their findings by examining the student's responses in the context of their observations and notes. (For example, administering item x, the interpreter may state that the student said y. What does that response mean? Does it have a different meaning in English?) Responses to assessment items are also reviewed with the interpreter for the purposes of clarification and interpretation.

Reporting Results of Assessments Conducted via Interpreters

Psychoeducational reports generated for the purposes of describing assessment data obtained through interpreters should include a number of points. In addition to any language and cultural data pertinent to the student's background, the report should clearly indicate that an interpreter was used. A clear description should also be included of the extent to which the interpreter was needed. The report should indicate the style of translation that was used (e.g., simultaneous, consecutive, or combined styles) and a clear description of any assessment procedures that involved the use of interpreters. Assessment procedures and adaptations should be clearly described in the test administration section of the report. A description should also be included of how the presence of the interpreters influenced the assessment sessions (e.g., establishment of rapport, comfort level of the student) and outcomes.

Reports discussing evaluation data collected through interpreters should address the validity and reliability of the findings, taking into consideration the interpreter's training, the validity of the assessment tools and procedures used, and the availability of norms that are representative of the student being assessed. When assessing with highly trained interpreters acting as ancillary or assistant examiners, school psychologists must carefully evaluate the validity of the data that they have obtained in order to decide if they will report scores. This is especially the case because the use of interpreters as ancillary or assistant examiners lacks empirical support at this time (see Noland, 2009). Although the interpreter may be highly trained, issues related to adequate norming must be considered. Examiners must also evaluate if they have the required competencies to interpret the results obtained in the context of the student's languages and cultural backgrounds. Using an interpreter does not eliminate discriminatory practices in the assessment process and does not provide a pass for reporting results. If the validity of the results is questionable when assessing via interpreters, testing results should be presented in a qualitative format.

Best practices in assessment also call for the school psychologist to triangulate results from multiple data sources using culturally responsive interpretation practices. All assessment data should be interpreted within the context of the student's cultural background. If the findings are questionable because the process of working with the interpreter did not yield useful assessment data, then the assessment report should clearly state so, and the recommendations should address the need for a bilingual evaluation by a qualified school psychologist or the collection of additional data using alternative assessment procedures such as test–teach–test methods over time or response to intervention (RTI).

Evaluating the Process and the Information Obtained via Interpreters

When working via interpreters, schools psychologists must be careful to evaluate the process and the information and data obtained. The questions below will guide school psychologists in evaluating the utility of the assessment outcomes:

- *Quality of the translation:* Were there problems with translating specific terms, concepts, or vocabulary during the assessment? Does the interpreter possess high levels of language proficiency in English and in the other language? Does the interpreter have formal training in the process of translation during assessment sessions? How did those translation problems or barriers have an impact on the validity of the findings obtained?
- *Relational and social aspects:* Was rapport easily established during the assessment session? Was communication effective and conducive to positive interactions and relationship building? How did the process of working via an interpreter influence the establishment of rapport with the student? Did social

differences in gender, religion, sexual orientation, and socioeconomic or educational factors influence the interactions between the school psychologist, interpreter, and student? How did those factors have an impact on assessment outcomes?
- *Cultural responsiveness:* Were cultural differences acknowledged and addressed? Was there a match between the cultural background of the student and the interpreter that led to effective communication and well-established rapport? Were the interpreter and school psychologist familiar with the cultural background of the student and with the culturally diverse issues relevant to the assessment session? Was the information obtained helpful in pinpointing cultural differences and providing culturally responsive interventions?
- *Language differences:* Was there a match between the languages/dialects and the communication styles (e.g., differences based on educational backgrounds) of the student and that of the interpreter? Did language differences have an impact on assessment results?
- *Professional context:* Was the interpreter trained in assessment issues? Was the school psychologist trained to work with language interpreters during assessment sessions? Does the interpreter have sufficient expertise to function as a cultural broker, cultural consultant, and/or advocate? Did the status of the interpreter influence the translation outcomes (e.g., family member or student translating, community member who may not be trusted by the student because of confidentiality concerns) during the assessment?
- *Best practice context:* Were best practices followed in working with interpreters? What factors interfered with best practices and how did they have an impact on assessment findings?

The responses to these questions should be helpful to school psychologists in terms of decision making and exploring successful outcomes for students. For example, if the match between the interpreter and the student was poor because they were from different educational or socioeconomic backgrounds, if rapport was not well established, or if the interpreter did not have the required competencies in assessment, then the school psychologist should consider and determine if a different interpreter should be used for further assessment. Assessment data collected via interpreters that are invalid and questionable may not be helpful in the process of data-based decision making and may require additional evaluations by a qualified bilingual school psychologist. If interpreters must be used, then the data collected are applied to plan and implement interventions that are evaluated periodically to examine outcomes and make appropriate recommendations in the future (e.g., change in instruction or program). The use of RTI is also helpful as additional data are collected to explore how students respond to interventions that are monitored closely and periodically.

Providing Feedback to Parents and Students Based on Assessment Results

When providing feedback to parents and students based on assessment results, Elliott (2012) suggests deciding on (a) the method of translation that will be used (i.e., consecutive versus simultaneous), (b) the information that will be shared during the feedback sessions to ensure that it is accurate and appropriate, and (c) the professional or clinical terminology that will be used to share findings and achieve clarity. The recommendations provided in Table 9.3 are also applicable when providing feedback to parents and students based on assessment results. An additional recommendation is to ask the student and parents clarifying questions to ascertain that they have understood the feedback provided.

SUMMARY

ELLs should be assessed by bilingual school psychologists with the language and cultural competencies to conduct nonbiased assessments. When bilingual school psychologists are not available, interpreters facilitate the process of gathering assessment data. Interpreters are defined as professionals who provide translation services in the context of spoken communication. School psychologists' processes in conducting assessments via interpreters is complex and difficult. Among the challenges that school psychologists will encounter are problems inherent in the process of translation (e.g., some concepts cannot be translated), and difficulties establishing rapport with students and interpreters. Translating tests prior to assessment sessions or on the spot leads to significant changes in the items and the psychological constructs measured by the tests, which directly have an impact on the validity of assessment results.

Recommendations include using ethical principles to guide practices, identifying interpreters with the required competencies, providing training for interpreters and

school psychologists in the area of assessment of ELLs, defining the roles and functions of interpreters taking into consideration their competencies, and allocating sufficient time to assess via interpreters. School psychologists must also identify procedures and tools that will facilitate gathering meaningful and useful data for this student population. Best practices entail school psychologists' briefing and debriefing with interpreters in order to prepare for assessment sessions and to review issues encountered during the assessment sessions. Results reported should communicate the validity of the findings and should facilitate decision making for ELLs in school settings. Overall, conducting assessments via interpreters requires numerous competencies from school psychologists that are pivotal in order to provide quality services to ELLs in general and special education settings.

AUTHOR NOTE

Disclosure. Emilia C. Lopez has a financial interest in books she authored or coauthored that are referenced in this chapter.

REFERENCES

American Educational Research Association, American Psychological Association, & National Council on Measurement in Education. (1999). *Standards for educational and psychological testing*. Washington, DC: Author.

Avery, M. B. (2001). *The role of the health care interpreter: An evolving dialogue*. Albany, NY: National Council on Interpreting in Health Care.

Barik, H. C. (1973). Simultaneous interpretation: Temporal and quantitative data. *Language and Speech, 16*, 237–270.

Bracken, B. A., & Barona, A. (1991). State of the art procedures for translating, validating, and using psychoeducational tests in cross-cultural assessment. *School Psychology International, 12*, 119–132. doi: 10.1177/0143034391121010

Elliott, C. D. (2012). *Differential Ability Scales-Second edition: Early years Spanish supplement: Interpreter's handbook*. Bloomington, MN: Pearson.

Fernandez, K., Boccaccini, M. T., & Noland, R. M. (2007). Professionally responsible test selection for Spanish-speaking clients: A four-step approach for identifying and selecting translated tests. *Professional Psychology: Research and Practice, 38*, 363–374. doi:10.1037/00735-7028.38.4.363

Flores, G. F., Laws, M. B., Mayo, S. J., Zuckerman, B., Abreu, M., Medina, L., & Hardt, E. J. (2003). Errors in medical interpretation and their potential clinical consequences in pediatric encounters. *Pediatrics, 111*, 6–14. doi:10.1542/peds.111.1.6.

Hambleton, R. K., & Li, S. (2005). Translation and adaptation issues and methods for educational and psychological tests. In C. L. Frisby & C. R. Reynolds (Eds.), *Comprehensive handbook of multicultural school psychology* (pp. 881–993). Hoboken, NJ: Wiley.

Langdon, H. W. (1994, May). *Working with interpreters and translators in a school setting*. Paper presented at the Fordham University Bilingual Conference, New York, NY.

Lopez, E. C. (1994, March). *Errors made by interpreters during on the spot translation of WISC-R questions*. Paper presented at the annual meeting of the National Association of School Psychologists, Seattle, WA.

Lopez, E. C. (2000). Conducting instructional consultation through interpreters. *School Psychology Review, 29*, 378–388.

Lopez, E. C. (2006). Targeting English language learners, tasks, and treatments in instructional consultation. *Journal of Applied School Psychology, 22*, 59–79.

Lopez, E. C., Irigoyen, M. A., Romero, P., & Birch, S. (2013). *School psychologists working via interpreters: Practices and recommendations*. Manuscript in preparation.

Lopez, E. C., & Rogers, M. R. (2007). Multicultural competencies for school psychologists. In G. Esquivel, E. C. Lopez, & S. Nahari (Eds.), *Handbook of multicultural school psychology: A multidisciplinary perspective* (pp. 47–70). Mahwah, NJ: Erlbaum.

Marion, G. S., Hildebrandt, C. A., Davis, S. W., Marin, A. J., & Crandall, S. J. (2008). Working effectively with interpreters: A model curriculum for physician assistant students. *Medical Teacher, 30*, 612–617. doi:10.1080/01421590801986539

McCallum, R. S., & Bracken, B. A. (2005). The Universal Nonverbal Intelligence Test. In D. P. Flanagan, J. L. Genshaft, & P. L. Harrison (Eds.), *Contemporary intellectual assessment: Theories, tests, and issues* (3rd ed., pp. 425–440). New York, NY: Guilford Press.

Muñoz-Sandoval, A. F., Cummins, J., Alvarado, G. G., & Ruet, M. L. (1998). *The Bilingual Verbal Ability Tests*. Chicago, IL: Riverside.

National Association of School Psychologists. (2010a). *Model for comprehensive and integrated school psychological services*. Bethesda, MD: Author. Retrieved from http://www.nasponline.org/standards/2010standards/2_PracticeModel.pdf

National Association of School Psychologists. (2010b). *Principles for professional ethics*. Bethesda, MD: Author. Retrieved from http://www.nasponline.org/standards/2010standards/1_%20Ethical%20Principles.pdf

National Center for Education Statistics. (2012). *The condition of education 2012*. Washington, DC: Author. Retrieved from http://nces.ed.gov/pubsearch/pubsinfo.asp?pubid=2012045

Noland, R. M. (2009). When no bilingual examiner is available: Exploring the use of ancillary examiners as a viable testing solution. *Journal of Psychoeducational Assessment, 27*, 29–45. doi:10.1177/0734282908319666

O'Bryon, E. C., & Rogers, M. R. (2010). Bilingual school psychologists' assessment practices with English language learners. *Psychology in the Schools, 47*, 1018–1034. doi:10.1002/pits.20521

Rhodes, R. L., Ochoa, S. H., & Ortiz, S. O. (2005). *Assessing culturally and linguistically diverse students: A practical guide*. New York, NY: Guilford Press.

Rousseau, C., Measham, T., & Moro, M. (2010). Working with interpreters in child mental health. *Child and Adolescent Mental Health, 16*, 55–59. doi:10.1111/j.1475-3588.2010.00589.x

Schrank, F. A., Mather, N., McGrew, K. S., & Woodcock, R. W. (2007). *Woodcock-Johnson III/Batería III Diagnostic Supplement to the Tests of Cognitive Abilities: Manual*. Rolling Meadows, IL: Riverside.

Searight, H. R., & Searight, B. K. (2009). Working with foreign language interpreters: Recommendations for psychological practice. *Professional Psychology: Research and Practice, 40*, 444–451. doi:10.1037/a0016788

Tribe, R., & Lane, P. (2009). Working with interpreters across language and culture in mental health. *Journal of Mental Health, 18*, 233–241. doi:10.1080/09638230701879102

Tribe, R., & Raval, H. (Eds.). (2003). *Working with interpreters in mental health*. New York, NY: Brunner-Routledge.

U.S. Department of Education. (2008). *Biennial report to Congress on the implementation of the Title III state formula grant program school years 2006–2008*. Washington, DC: Author. Retrieved from http://www.ncela.gwu.edu/files/uploads/3/Biennial_Report_0608.pdf

10

Best Practices in Working With Children From Economically Disadvantaged Backgrounds

Christina Mulé
Northeastern University (MA) Tufts Medical Center, Center for Children with Special Needs
Alissa Briggs
Lincoln County (KY) Schools
Samuel Song
Seattle University (WA)

OVERVIEW

According to the National Association of School Psychologists (NASP) *Model for Comprehensive and Integrated School Psychological Services* (NASP, 2010), a foundation of school psychology is the domain of Diversity in Development and Learning, where school psychologists are charged with providing "culturally competent and effective practices in all areas of school psychology" (NASP, 2010, p. 8). However, providing culturally competent services has become increasingly challenging as demographics in the United States have become progressively more diverse. Most often school psychology literature has cited rapid changes in racial and ethnic demographics as the cause of struggle in providing culturally competent services. However, as a result of the 2008 economic crises, the number of children and families living in poverty has increased dramatically and may be the most rapidly changing demographic instead (U.S. Census Bureau, 2011).

Poverty has been defined in several ways with distinctions that highlight different facets of being poor. One of the most common definitions used is a "lack of means of providing material needs or comforts" (Yoshikawa, Aber, & Beardslee, 2012, p. 272). The U.S. federal government uses an official definition of poverty to determine eligibility for government assistance: living in a household with a gross income under the official poverty line (i.e., a predetermined income for a family of four; in

2009 the official poverty line was set at $22,000 for a family of four; Yoshikawa et al., 2012). Other definitions range from *absolute poverty* (defined as falling below an objective external standard of the cost of meeting the most basic needs) to *relative poverty* (defined as falling below 50% or 60% of the national median household income) to *subjective poverty* (defined as falling below a subjective perception of the amount of income it takes to get by; Yoshikawa et al., 2012). In this chapter, poverty is referred to as *economic disadvantage*, due to its less pejorative nature, and is defined as family, school, and community resources that are insufficient in ensuring the material, medical, psychological, and educational needs of a child.

The rise in economic disadvantage is a serious problem, as children from economically disadvantaged backgrounds are disproportionately affected by physical health; mental, emotional, and behavioral health; and educational problems. These problems often are exacerbated by difficulties accessing treatment (Richardson, 2008) and equal educational opportunities. Together, these problems are an issue of *social justice*, an advocacy-related construct that includes three specific ecological system qualities that promote educational and psychological well-being: (a) access to necessary and appropriate resources, (b) experiences of being treated with respect, and (c) experiences of being treated with fairness (Sander et al., 2011).

The disparity between the need for and receipt of services and educational opportunities highlights the importance of service delivery in the schools, as well as the need for school psychologists to act as agents of social change and justice. A challenge to this work is that, like families, many schools have also been faced with budgetary shortfalls that have resulted in the elimination of jobs and resources and a reduction in the schools' ability to adequately serve children and families who are economically disadvantaged. A further persisting challenge is the potential discrepancy in economic class between some school psychologists and families experiencing economic disadvantage. While some school psychologists may have had experience with economic disadvantage in the past, some may not. Even still, school psychologists are operating with more privilege in schools relative to many families due to their education, training, and role. It is therefore critical that school psychologists and other school staff understand economic disadvantage and how to support families experiencing it and its associated challenges (Williams & Crockett, 2013).

BASIC CONSIDERATIONS

One of the greatest challenges facing schools and school psychologists who work with children and families from economically disadvantaged backgrounds is understanding the unique needs of the individual, the family, and the community. Yet, an understanding of economic disadvantage is critical to being an effective school psychologist who is able to promote social justice in educational programs and services. Also critical to being an effective school psychologist is acknowledging the vast diversity among children and families that are economically disadvantaged, as it cuts across culture, race and ethnicity, gender, and sex.

Population Trends

In the United States approximately 14 million children, or one in five children, are economically disadvantaged (Yoshikawa et al., 2012). Although economic disadvantage cuts across racial and ethnic groups, culturally, ethnically, and linguistically diverse families are over-represented among the poor (Jensen, 2009; Thomas-Presswood & Presswood, 2008; Williams & Crockett, 2013). Whereas 38.2% of African American and 35% of Hispanic children are living in economic disadvantage, only 12.4% of Caucasian children are, despite their being 72% of the population (U.S. Census Bureau, 2011). These racial and ethnic disparities have been linked to historical marginalization of ethnic minority groups and entrenched barriers to education and

employment (Hummer & Hamilton, 2010). Finally, economic disadvantage disproportionately affects children and families living in the southern region of the country (U.S. Department of Agriculture Economic Research Service, 2005).

Effects of Economic Disadvantage on Children

Several researchers have demonstrated the profound impact that economic disadvantages can have on a child's physical health; mental, emotional, and behavioral health; and educational attainment (Jensen, 2009; Rothstein, 2008). With respect to physical health, due to a variety of environmental risk factors (e.g., inadequate prenatal care, environmental toxins, poor nutrition, and exposure to drugs and alcohol), children from economically disadvantaged backgrounds are disproportionately prone to, for example, low birth weight, malnutrition, stunted growth, lead poisoning, asthma, and iron-deficiency anemia (Rothstein, 2008). Because many children from economically disadvantaged backgrounds often do not have private health insurance coverage, they receive limited access to preventive medical care, timely healthcare services, the latest medications, and follow-up medical programs (Rothstein, 2008). How this will change under the Affordable Care Act is yet to be seen.

In addition to physical health challenges, children from economically disadvantaged backgrounds are at risk for developing social–emotional and behavioral health problems at a much higher rate than their more advantaged counterparts (Jensen, 2009; Wadsworth & Achenbach, 2005). Parent report data from the National Survey of America's Families, a nationwide household interview survey, suggests that approximately 21% of children ages 6–17 from economically disadvantaged backgrounds have had an emotional or behavioral problem. Approximately half of these children are uninsured and experience difficulty accessing mental health services (Howell, 2004). An analysis of three national databases indicated that nearly 80% of economically disadvantaged youth in need of mental health services did not receive services within the preceding 12 months, with rates approaching 90% for uninsured youth (Atkins et al., 2006). Conversely, only 6% of children from economically more advantaged backgrounds experience mental health problems, and well more than half obtain comprehensive mental health services (Howell, 2004).

Given the strong relationship between economic disadvantage and physical and mental health, it is not surprising that data indicate that it also may have a negative impact on educational attainment and achievement (Jensen, 2009; Richardson, 2008). Research has demonstrated that children from economically disadvantaged backgrounds are more likely to attend under-resourced public schools and are academically behind their more advantaged peers, starting as early as preschool and kindergarten (e.g., they do not possess the pre-K readiness literacy and math skills that their more affluent peers possess; Richardson, 2008). Furthermore, research has documented strong correlations between economic disadvantage and several other academic variables, such as poor school attendance, grade retention, learning disabilities, school dropout, and suspension or expulsion from school (Jensen, 2009). Children who are economically disadvantaged, and who may also experience periods of homelessness, are at an even greater disadvantage educationally, as they may move several times throughout the academic year, resulting in frequent school transfers and excessive absences. These children may have difficulty mastering the curriculum (as there may be serious gaps in their education), becoming part of a class, and/or forming social relationships with peers and teachers (Jensen, 2009).

Effects of Economic Disadvantage on Families

Family well-being is intricately tied to the functioning of every child. Yet, family ecology of economically disadvantaged children seems to be changing over time (Centers for Disease Control and Prevention, 2011). In the mid-1960s approximately two-thirds of all economically disadvantaged children lived with intact families (i.e., families with two primary caregivers). Today, more than half of these children live in single-parent households (which is more prevalent among African American and Hispanic families), many of which are led by teenage mothers who have customarily earned less than their male counterparts (Hummer & Hamilton, 2010; U.S. Census Bureau, 2011; Williams & Crockett, 2013). This shift to single-parent families reduces the financial resources available to children but can also have an impact on the availability of social resources (i.e., children from intact families have access to more than one adult who can assist them with daily needs) if these single-parent families are not blended with other family members (e.g., grandparents, aunts, uncles).

As more families from economically disadvantaged backgrounds struggle to meet their daily needs (i.e., food, clothing, and shelter) and face more chronic stress,

parental mental health problems become more prevalent (Thomas-Presswood & Presswood, 2008). In fact, there is evidence that rates of psychopathology, including substance abuse, are greater among individuals from economically disadvantaged backgrounds than those from more economically advantaged backgrounds (Wadsworth & Achenbach, 2005). These statistics are alarming as parental psychopathology, coupled with an economically stressful environment, can lead to ineffective parenting strategies (Williams & Crockett, 2013). For example, research has demonstrated that parents from economically disadvantaged backgrounds with mental illness and/or substance abuse problems may often be less responsive to and supportive of their children. Additionally, children of parents living in depressed environments with chronic stressors are at higher risk for physical abuse and/or neglect because of low parental frustration tolerance (Williams & Crockett, 2013).

Finally, economically disadvantaged families today are arguably more likely than in the past to be socially and spatially isolated from more affluent communities (Hopson & Lee, 2011; Williams & Crockett, 2013). Many economically disadvantaged families reside in communities characterized by social disorganization (e.g., crime, violence, unemployment, failure to monitor residents' behavior) and fewer resources for child development (e.g., adequate housing options, high quality child-care centers, healthcare centers, healthy recreational activities, role models in the community; Thomas-Presswood & Presswood, 2008). Families with economic concerns may experience periods of homelessness and thus will have access to even fewer opportunities to advance their livelihood. Finally, within their home environments, relative to families with higher income levels, some economically disadvantaged families may provide less cognitive stimulation (e.g., reading materials and toys) for their children (Klein & Knitzer, 2007). This is particularly true of families experiencing homelessness who are only able to travel with limited material goods.

Effects of Economic Disadvantage on Schools

Schools that predominantly serve children from economically disadvantaged backgrounds often are inadequately funded and equipped, spending less per capita for materials, supplies, and books than better resourced schools (Jensen, 2009). As a consequence of these budgetary constraints, school facilities often appear to be ill-maintained, ill-functioning, and unsafe (Kozol,

2005). Some teachers working in these school districts may be underpaid, frustrated by the lack of resources in their schools, and encumbered by the academic and social–emotional needs of the children they serve (Jensen, 2009). Often, teacher preparation programs do not adequately prepare teachers to work with economically disadvantaged children and families, adversely affecting the teachers' competence to work in low-socioeconomic communities (Jensen, 2009). As a consequence, many high-performing teachers abandon the profession (Rothstein, 2008) and economically disadvantaged children may be left with less experienced teachers who provide substandard instruction and have lower expectations of their students (Jensen, 2009; Thomas-Presswood & Presswood, 2008). For example, core academic classes in economically disadvantaged schools are twice as likely to be taught by a teacher with neither a major degree nor certification in his or her assigned subject (Jerald, Haycock, & Wilkins, 2009).

Unfortunately, the school climate in underresourced areas has not improved over the years. As a consequence of the 2008 economic crisis, underresourced schools have had to increase budget cuts, with more than half of the states having educational budget cuts on top of severe cuts made in previous years (Oliff, Mai, & Leachman, 2012). Federal data suggest that school funding remains well below prerecession levels, with 35 states providing less funding per student than they did 5 years earlier. These cuts counteract, and in many cases undermine, education reform initiatives (e.g., lengthening the school day; expanding early childhood education programs; recruiting, developing, and retaining high-quality teachers) aimed at better preparing children for the future (Oliff et al., 2012). Additionally, more than 300,000 school district jobs were lost between 2008 and 2012 (Oliff et al., 2012).

In summary, research has documented the profound impact that economic disadvantage can have on developing children, families, and schools. Nevertheless, the data presented above are not intended to imply that the trajectory for children from economically disadvantaged backgrounds cannot be changed, nor that economic disadvantage is a sentence for a substandard life (Jensen, 2009). It is true that children from economically disadvantaged backgrounds are susceptible to adverse effects of risk factors, but it is also true that many children are equally susceptible to the positive effects of protective factors (i.e., experiences that minimize the effects of negative events in a child's life by enhancing the child's coping strategies and feelings of self-efficacy; Hopson & Lee, 2011), which can lead to the child's resilience (i.e., the ability to overcome adversarial factors that would typically predict failure; Jensen, 2009; Richardson, 2008).

BEST PRACTICES IN WORKING WITH CHILDREN FROM ECONOMICALLY DISADVANTAGED BACKGROUNDS

Before reviewing best practice recommendations, it is perhaps more important to address the practical problem of how one school psychologist might accomplish all of these interventions. To help address this concern, a framework is provided for prioritizing areas of concern based on recent social justice and school psychology work termed *loving justice* (Song & Marth, 2013). Loving justice is a vision for social justice practice in school psychology that provides anchors from which to act. The first anchor is *outwardness*, which reminds school psychologists to focus on other students who do not represent the majority group or culture (e.g., economically disadvantaged; racial, ethnic, or cultural minorities). Outwardness also directs school psychologists to focus on environmental factors and interventions first before internal change efforts. The second anchor is *transformation*, which reminds school psychologists to meet the needs of students in the short term (e.g., providing immediate resources) as well as the long term (i.e., systemic change). For example, a school psychologist faced with a problem of school bullying, with 30% of the population receiving free or reduced lunch, might proceed practically in these ways:

- The anchor of outwardness suggests (a) that those 30% of the population receiving free/reduced lunch would be a focal priority of school-wide services (i.e., other students who do not represent the majority group or culture) and (b) that environmental factors should be targeted by services (e.g., improving home–school partnerships and school climate).
- The anchor of transformation suggests that (a) a short-term change strategy should be implemented as soon as possible (e.g., providing necessary material goods to students) and (b) the long-term change strategy focused on improving home–school partnerships and school climate should be implemented.

By employing the two anchors of loving justice, school psychologists can have more confidence that their practice is aligned to a social justice vision as they attempt interventions from a multitiered service approach (see Figure 10.1).

Figure 10.1. Economic Disadvantage: From Risk to Resilience

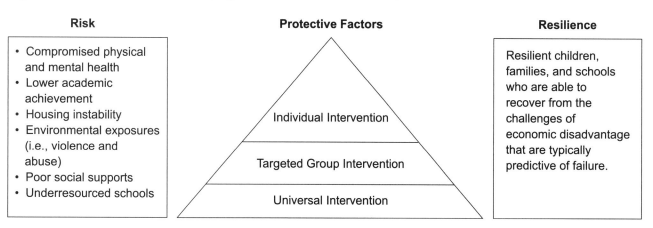

Risk	**Protective Factors**	**Resilience**
• Compromised physical and mental health • Lower academic achievement • Housing instability • Environmental exposures (i.e., violence and abuse) • Poor social supports • Underresourced schools	Individual Intervention Targeted Group Intervention Universal Intervention	Resilient children, families, and schools who are able to recover from the challenges of economic disadvantage that are typically predictive of failure.

Tier 1: Universal Intervention

Universal approaches can be employed to advance social justice for children from economically disadvantaged backgrounds. In this stage of primary prevention, school psychologists seek to reduce the incidence of new referrals for mental, emotional, and behavioral problems, as well as academic concerns. Universal interventions in the area of economic disadvantage should, at a minimum, include (a) comprehensive staff training regarding economic disadvantage and its impact on the students, families, schools, and community; (b) family–school partnerships; (c) community partnerships; and (d) effective policy reform.

Comprehensive Staff Training

As mentioned above, many teacher preparation programs have not adequately prepared teachers to educate and serve children from economically disadvantaged backgrounds. Consequently, an economical and primary-level intervention that school psychologists could support is providing advanced training, education, and professional development around issues of economic disadvantage to teachers and other school personnel. Once school psychologists have examined their own understanding and assumptions around economic disadvantage and educated themselves (via readings, trainings, and professional development), they are ideal candidates to take on an active role in training other educators, given their understanding and background in development, cognition, learning, psychological processes, and issues of diversity. Trainings ideally are developed and implemented in collaboration with other school

personnel and community partners so as to be sensitive to the community context.

A general goal of the training should be to increase staff awareness and knowledge of issues related to economic disadvantage (e.g., providing statistics on increased prevalence of physical, mental, and educational problems). But more importantly, training should support, challenge, and nurture staff so that the staff feels equipped to effect change in students' lives. From here school psychologists can encourage staff to share success stories or ways to overcome frustrations and guide staff toward developing a solution-focused action plan that capitalizes on protective factors and student, school, and community strengths.

Family–School Partnerships

Developing family–school partnerships that are collaborative in nature is critical to ameliorating the effects of economic disadvantage on children and families. However, this can be particularly challenging for families who may mistrust school personnel because of prior negative experiences (e.g., families who may have been involved in child welfare due to a school filing; Leff, 2007) or for families who may not feel comfortable collaborating because of class differences (e.g., some families with lower educational attainment may feel incompetent or ill-prepared to provide opinions with school personnel). To overcome the barriers to forming collaborative relationships, school psychologists and other school personnel can work in partnership in order to reach these families. For example, school psychologists and other school personnel can call the students' homes regularly to discuss the strengths and needs of the students and attend community events and talk with families in attendance. In doing so, school psychologists and other school personnel may become familiar with families' fears and misperceptions, and can work toward dispelling those beliefs and better serve their students. Further, school psychologists are encouraged to orient families toward a solution-focused approach, whereby all parties engage in shared communication and mutual respect, responsibility, and ownership of the issues at hand.

Once school psychologists and other school personnel and families have established a collaborative partnership, school psychologists and other school personnel can begin to better understand each individual family's needs. For example, some families living in temporary shelters may not have access to a stove and so may be in most need of nutritious foods that can be made with little preparation as opposed to assistance obtaining additional clothing. In better understanding what families need, school psychologists and other school personnel can help point families toward relevant local resources available to the families (e.g., child-care facilities, food pantries).

Community Partnerships

An important primary-level intervention for children and families from economically disadvantaged backgrounds relates to strategic partnerships and program collaboration with other community health and mental health centers or organizations. These collaborations are often sorely lacking as many programs function in disciplinary silos (Richardson, 2008). However, these collaborations are critical and necessary as many schools are limited in what services they can provide because of breaks in the academic year (i.e., weekends, holiday breaks, and summer vacations), as well as because of shortages in trained professionals in the school setting (e.g., some children may require medical attention beyond what a school nurse can provide, and other children may necessitate more extensive therapeutic services beyond what a school psychologist, social worker, or guidance counselor can provide in the school setting; Richardson, 2008).

In order to establish collaborations with community health and mental health centers, school psychologists might invite a representative from the center to attend a team meeting. At the meeting, the representative might share information about what services the center offers and how referrals can be made. At this stage it is critical for the school psychologist or other school personnel to log information about the center's services so that it is accessible when referrals need to be made, as well as to

avoid any duplication of existing services. Beyond these logistical steps, community health and mental health centers can be a great resource to schools, as many of these centers will offer consultation services and will provide ongoing treatment in collaboration with schools.

Community-based organizations. Along with building partnerships with community health and mental health centers, schools can also form strong collaborations with community-based organizations (e.g., religious institutions, YMCA, Boys & Girls Clubs) to build a wider support network for children and families who are economically disadvantaged. Fostering relationships with community-based organizations has the ability to change the climate of economically depressed neighborhoods, potentially making the neighborhood a safer and more caring environment. Joint projects between schools and community-based organizations (e.g., community gardens) can serve multiple beneficial purposes. For example, joint projects can serve to strengthen relationships (between organizations and individuals) or provide children and families with safe and enriching activities outside of school. School psychologists can help support relationship building with community organizations by enlisting the community to help support school activities. School psychologists might first start by reaching out to a community-based organization by attending the organization's events (e.g., attending a community organization's meeting and getting to know the membership), then they might offer to give a talk about community needs, and thereafter they might solicit the community organization to assist with school-based projects (e.g., schools have called upon retired community members to provide academic interventions to students).

Universities and academic medical centers. A final primary-level intervention relating to partnership and collaboration is participatory action research, that is, a framework to form partnerships between researchers, educators, students, school staff, and community members to enhance a school's prevention and intervention capacity (Leff, 2007). Participatory action research approaches merge scientific methods and extant research with feedback from key school and community stakeholders to ensure that the resulting prevention and intervention methods are empirically grounded, based on scientific information, and meet the needs of the community. Additionally, it is cited as a culturally sensitive and respectful approach to address some of the most pressing issues facing today's school systems (Leff, 2007), including economic hardship.

For example, utilizing a participatory action research approach, underresourced schools in the Philadelphia area have engaged in numerous prevention and intervention projects with the faculty at the University of Pennsylvania's Children's Hospital of Philadelphia. Faculty at the Children's Hospital of Philadelphia has helped schools develop school-wide positive behavior support programming for children who are at risk for mental health problems and underutilization of mental health services (Eiraldi, Mazzuca, Clarke, & Power, 2006). Additionally, they have several ongoing projects in underresourced schools and communities that proactively address relational, physical, and cyber aggression and bullying (Leff, Lefler, Khera, Paskewich, & Jawad, 2012).

These examples are just some of the many participatory action research projects taking place nationwide, but they demonstrate how building relationships with community partners can be possible and beneficial for students, schools, and communities. To initiate partnerships with universities and academic medical centers, school psychologists are encouraged to follow steps similar to those recommended above for forming relationships with community health centers, community mental health centers, and community organizations. Additionally, school psychologists might consider attending local conferences and national conventions to network with other professionals in psychology and education, as well as researchers interested in forming similar partnerships.

Policy Reform

In addition to providing staff training and forming community partnerships as primary-level interventions, school psychologists are also encouraged to critically examine the policies and practices that guide their schools, as many schools may inadvertently perpetuate injustice for economically disadvantaged children and families (Briggs, 2013). For example, as mentioned above, students who are economically disadvantaged are often denied access to the most qualified teachers and the best curriculum (Jerald et al., 2009; Rothstein, 2008). As a consequence, these students may academically underperform and suffer educationally compared to their more economically advantaged peers, but schools could begin to close the achievement gap by providing vulnerable children access to strong teachers rather than disproportionately assigning the most vulnerable students to the least able teachers (Jerald et

al., 2009). However, in order for this change to be realized, advocacy and policy reform are necessary.

To start, school psychologists should critically evaluate school policies, with the two following guiding questions in mind (Briggs, 2013): (a) What policies affect educational practice in my school? (b) Do these policies promote equity, access, and respect? If there is evidence to suggest that policies shape practice and service delivery in a manner that does not respect diversity or promote equity and access, then school psychologists can assemble or identify a team that is representative of the school community (e.g., involving students, parents, teachers, administrators, community members) and that can identify needs and priorities for change, and subsequently develop an action plan for change (Briggs, 2013).

Tier 2: Targeted Group Intervention

The second tier of the multilevel prevention system includes interventions for targeted groups of at-risk children and families known or suspected to be economically disadvantaged. At this level, interventions are typically provided in group formats and are targeted at known problems before these problems become more significant and require more individualized attention. Interventions at this level, that are relevant for this specific population, include (a) access to resources, (b) small group support networks, (c) after-school enrichment programs, and (d) parent or guardian supports.

Access to Resources

As mentioned above, children and families from economically disadvantaged backgrounds often have difficulty accessing basic material goods. In many schools, social workers have assumed the responsibility of collecting goods for redistribution and directing children and families to community resources where they can obtain access to food, clothes, and school supplies free of charge. However, not all schools have the luxury of having social workers in their building. Consequently, school psychologists need to be prepared to undertake this necessary responsibility. School psychologists are encouraged to consider ways to develop sustainable programs that can provide material assistance to children and families, as research has demonstrated that an increase in material services has led to reduction in child maltreatment for economically disadvantaged families (Loman & Siegel, 2012). Funding for these projects may be obtained through various means (e.g., grant money), but many are sustained by donations from community-based organizations. Additionally, community food, clothing (including prom dresses), and school supply drives have been a major supplier of goods. If drives in a school district's local communities do not yield enough resources for all of the children and families in need, school psychologists might consider setting up drives in more resourced communities where community members may be more able to contribute. A final consideration for school psychologists is how to work in partnership with other school personnel and community members on these initiatives, given the time-intensive nature of holding such drives (e.g., advertising the drive, setting up the location for the dropping off of goods, organizing the goods, and fairly distributing the goods to children and families).

Small Group Support Networks

An additional targeted group intervention relates to small group support networks. As described above, economic disadvantage has alienating effects on children and families. To help buffer these effects, school psychologists along with other school personnel can help develop small group social support networks for children and families. In addition to supporting children and families, these social support networks can help build family–school–community partnerships as well as trust and respect between families and school personnel. Support networks can serve multiple purposes: (a) a place for families to share experiences navigating various social programs (e.g., food assistance and public housing programs), (b) a place for families to coordinate child care among other families, (c) a place where families can come together for fun social activities (e.g., introduce family nights out, where school staff can assist in organizing and managing activities), and (d) a place where families can learn about or engage in low-cost activities that can help them increase self-care and decrease distress associated with economic hardship (e.g., gardening, practicing yoga, going to the library, planning self-improvement).

After-School Enrichment Programming

Although after-school programs are not a novel idea, they are an invaluable targeted group intervention for children from economically disadvantaged backgrounds. As was mentioned above, some of these children may not have a space in their home environment conducive to homework and studying or they may not have access to an adult who is able to assist them with academic challenges, all things that an after-school enrichment program can offer. When after-school enrichment programs embrace family-centered priorities (e.g., location of the program, transportation, low cost, curricular goals), students from economically disadvantaged backgrounds improve their overall school performance, demonstrate stronger interest in class material, and increase their school attendance (Jensen, 2009). School psychologists can be integral in establishing such a program with the support of other school personnel, and can play an important role in the progress monitoring of students who participate.

Parent or Guardian Supports

Finally, after or while school psychologists and other school personnel help to meet the immediate needs of students and families, and after they work to develop collaborative relationships with families, they can provide supports for those parents or guardians who may benefit from coaching on positive parenting practices (e.g., providing consistent expectations, allocating time for affection, recognizing children when they are engaging in prosocial behavior) and parent or guardian management training (Eamon & Venkataraman, 2003). For example, school personnel can highlight the importance of parent/guardian involvement in education and the importance of structuring the home environment in a way that promotes self-regulation and prepares the child to become actively engaged in academic work (e.g., provide relevant antecedent and consequent procedures to gain child compliance).

Unquestionably, these are challenging requests to make of families who are economically disadvantaged, given how many burdens they face and their limited resources (e.g., parents/guardians may have limited time to participate in school activities because of work responsibilities, or they may have transportation constraints that make it difficult for them to be in attendance). School psychologists can work with their school to survey families to determine how best to meet the families' needs. If time or transportation are concerns, school psychologists can work with their school and community centers to bring services to parents/guardians (e.g., provide workshops at local religious institutions at a time when most parents/guardians are available).

Furthermore, school psychologists can acknowledge the difficulty that some parents/guardians may have in engaging in suggested behaviors, such as reinforcement and meeting attendance, and offer suggestions of ways to improve the current situation. For example, some parents/guardians might indicate that it is difficult for them to purchase reinforcers for good behavior. Here a school psychologist might remind families that non-tangible reinforcers (e.g., special time with a family member) can be just as effective as tangible reinforcers. Some families might also indicate difficulty attending school meetings (e.g., parent–teacher conferences or Individualized Education Program [IEP] meetings). In these instances, school psychologists can encourage family involvement by offering a flexible schedule or phone conference option for families working through economic hardships.

Tier 3: Individual Intervention

Finally, at the third tier, individuals with specific or intensive challenges are provided with assessments and interventions that are customized to meet their needs. Therefore, third-tier intervention services for children from economically disadvantaged backgrounds should appropriately address assessment and intervention needs.

Individualized Assessment

Individualized assessments (including cognitive, behavioral, social–emotional, and academic assessments) are possible third tier interventions that can contribute significantly to evaluating the needs of children from economically disadvantaged backgrounds and contribute to plans for services and interventions. Specifically, assessment information can lead to the most effective intervention strategies, if school psychologists are able to take into account their knowledge of economic disadvantage and are sensitive to the differences in children's lives that are produced by economic hardship.

To accomplish this, comprehensive evaluations are recommended that emphasize multiple sources of information (e.g., child, parents/guardians, teachers, and community members), multiple methods of data collection (e.g., direct and indirect assessments such as school, home, and community observations and rating scales), and methods for analyzing and interpreting data on multiple levels and from a variety of perspectives. Furthermore, when utilizing standardized assessments, it is imperative to ascertain if, and to what degree, these assessments are appropriate for children and families who experience economic disadvantage. For example, several intelligence tests assess a child's understanding of vocabulary and general knowledge. If a child has not received instruction targeted to his or her needs, these tests may underestimate the child's ability. In addition, rating scales may be written in a language foreign to

parents/guardians who have not had access to more than a few years of high school. Thus, the school psychologist may need to explain these scales and then discuss responses and questions with the parents/guardians to address any confusion or misunderstandings.

Many will argue that the above recommendations are simply based on best practice in assessment for all children. However, because of increasingly heavy case-loads in school settings, especially many settings affected by economic disadvantage, school psychologists often limit their assessments to focus only on the individual child, only in the context of the school, and have access to and/or use only one to a few tools for data collection (Thomas-Presswood & Presswood, 2008). While this approach is undesirable for all children, it is a particularly detrimental approach for vulnerable populations of children who require more in-depth assessments. Consequently, school psychologists are encouraged to problem solve how they can improve systems-level issues within their school that can later allow them to engage in more comprehensive assessment batteries. While school psychologists address transformation via systems-level issues, they could also practice outwardness and prioritize their most thorough assessments for children whose civil rights are being violated via misdiagnosis or exclusion and/or whose educational outcomes have the greatest potential for improvement as a result of assessment. For example, the school psychologist may prioritize an initial evaluation of a child who is frequently suspended over the reevaluation of a child who has had two prior, consistent, and thorough evaluations.

Individualized Interventions

Once a comprehensive assessment is complete, school psychologists should have the necessary data to inform functionally relevant intervention procedures. Intervention procedures might involve some of the more standard interventions provided in the school setting (e.g., counseling for internalizing disorders, individualized behavior support plan for externalizing disorders, academic remediation strategies for achievement deficits), but may also involve collaboration with outside agencies (e.g., there may be unresolved questions postassessment that school psychologists might want to collaborate with primary care physicians about, or assessment data might warrant a referral to therapeutic mentoring services).

Whatever the area of intervention may be, school psychologists are encouraged to spend ample time with their case conceptualizations, allowing themselves to recognize the challenges that children from economically disadvantaged backgrounds face that may impede the children's wellness and personal development. For example, a child who might have stolen from the school cafeteria may not be engaging in problem behavior out of ill will but because of limited resources in his or her home. In this case, school psychologists can work to identify interventions that can help to address the child's basic needs instead of focusing on the externalizing psychological processes that may not be functionally relevant.

Individualizing Practice and Developmental Difference

Evidence-based interventions are essential to improving student outcomes. However, it is critical to point out that these interventions need to address the ecological realities of families and schools experiencing economic disadvantage. While many are actively researching interventions with these populations, the data are still emerging. For example, a recent independent review of the positive behavior interventions and supports (PBIS) literature acknowledged that despite the popularity of PBIS, the peer-reviewed effectiveness research within an economically disadvantaged ecology is preliminary (Noltemeyer & Fenning, 2013). In light of this, school psychologists need to feel comfortable adapting an intervention appropriately for the ecological realities of students, families, and schools, while relying on evidence-based practice guidelines.

In addition to being sensitive to cultural factors that relate to economic disadvantage, intervention adaptation also needs to be sensitive to developmental differences. Notably, however, not all interventions will require significant tailoring. For example, systems interventions at Tier 1 may require less individualizing for developmental differences, while Tier 3 interventions will require the most. However, because school psychologists typically have more extensive experience tailoring Tier 3 assessments and interventions, this section will focus the discussion on the Tier 2 interventions described above.

Related to access to resources, while all students experiencing economic disadvantage will need increased access to resources, the types of resources or material goods will vary depending on student development. Food, clothing, and school supplies are likely to be easier to obtain for younger children and their families, simply because these children eat less, clothes are less expensive, and school supplies are less expensive and

common (e.g., crayons and pencils). However, as children grow into adolescence and reach high school, these supplies grow more expensive (e.g., clothes, scientific calculators, computers, and other technology such as tablets to run educational applications). Small group support networks may also need to be adjusted for developmental needs of children and families. For example, child care is likely to be important for parents/guardians with younger children, especially so that the parents/guardians may participate more with the schools. Small group support networks will also be less effective if older children and adolescents do not perceive them as being "cool," to accommodate their growing concern with peer relationships.

Third, after-school enrichment programs are likely to be most important for elementary to early middle school students, as these children are too young to be home alone. These programs might incorporate peer collaborative tutoring strategies to help keep the cost of these programs low, but also for the benefits to both tutor and pupil. Still, after-school enrichment programs may be equally important for adolescents, especially when they offer positive and attractive alternatives (e.g., basketball and dance) to being on the streets. Finally, parent/guardian supports in regard to education needs are also different for younger children compared to adolescents. Parents/guardians of younger children, for example, may need basic training in behavioral management, support for their children's academic and social development, and nutrition. In contrast, parents/guardians of older children and adolescents will require education regarding puberty, identity development, combatting of cyberbullying, and preparation of their children for postsecondary schooling (e.g., college, vocational training, trade programs) or career.

Effectiveness and Outcome Evaluation

When serving children and families experiencing economic disadvantage via the aforementioned interventions, the school psychologist must evaluate and understand his or her own biases, the needs of children and families he or she serves, and the needs of those with whom he or she collaborates. Then, the school psychologist must ensure needs are aligned with interventions grounded in research. Finally, the school psychologist must examine data to determine if interventions are relating to positive outcomes and unintended, negative outcomes.

In order to serve children and families currently experiencing economic disadvantage, the school psychologist and those with whom he or she collaborates need to understand the unique positions and needs of these children and families. Biases, assumptions, and lack of knowledge can interfere with this understanding and build barriers between families and the school rather than avenues for support. Therefore, the school psychologist should identify his or her assumptions and knowledge about people experiencing economic disadvantage and actively evaluate these assumptions by listening to the stories of families experiencing economic disadvantage, reviewing the literature, examining publicly available community statistics, and engaging in professional development. The school psychologist should also engage colleagues in critical self-reflection regarding biases and assumptions about families experiencing economic disadvantage. The school psychologist must be a critical consumer of information and recognize that one family does not speak for all families experiencing economic disadvantage.

After self-evaluation, the school psychologist must evaluate his or her efforts to support children and families who are experiencing economic disadvantage. Prilleltensky and Nelson's (2002) cycle of praxis (process of change) in critical psychology outlines four interacting and reciprocal domains for understanding the need for and effecting change. First, the school psychologist should evaluate his or her vision for change by asking what the ideal state of affairs is. Then, the school psychologist could evaluate where gaps between the ideal and the actual state of affairs may exist. Because it is unlikely that the school psychologist will be able to address all needs simultaneously, he or she should continue to prioritize interventions by investigating how the current state of affairs is perceived by school stakeholders, especially for children and families experiencing economic disadvantage (i.e., through surveys, interviews, and focus groups). But most importantly, the approach to data collection must enable those with the least advantage to participate. Once needs are identified and prioritized, the school psychologist can then investigate interventions. With his or her colleagues, the school psychologist might also assess pooled areas of strength and weakness in implementing interventions, so the school psychologist might identify professional development needs and guide colleagues toward interventions aligned with his or her colleagues' strengths.

Finally, the school psychologist must evaluate multiple sources of data to determine if interventions are having their intended effect, and if interventions are socially valid (i.e., if the recipients of the interventions feel helped). What data the school psychologist examines

may depend upon the targets of intervention. That being said, the major indicators of school and student well-being upon which schools are frequently evaluated—attendance rates, graduate rates, dropout rates, academic achievement, discipline referrals, suspension, and expulsion—should be continuously evaluated by subgroup (e.g., free/reduced lunch status, IEP status, racial/ethnic minority group). The degree to which these groups differ and overlap should be of concern. Last, brief surveys could be utilized to determine the social validity of interventions.

Case Example

The following case example demonstrates the transformation of a fictional rural high school, where the majority of students experience economic disadvantage, through the implementation of universal, targeted, and individual interventions. The high school serves a large rural community where almost 25% live below the poverty level. Approximately 1,000 students attend the school and almost 70% of the students receive free or reduced lunch.

Intervention or Protective Factors

In order to address the needs of the students and families experiencing economic disadvantage, the school has several community partners. There is a center, funded through grants and donations, located in the high school that offers a variety of supports to students and their families. For students who receive free/reduced lunch who may go the weekend without access to regular meals, the center provides a backpack of nonperishable food on Fridays. The center also provides students with school supplies, toiletries, and clothes on an as-needed basis. When a family is without utilities or is in danger of having them turned off, the center coordinates fundraising to help the family pay the bills. Another significant partner for the middle and high school is the local university's adolescent clinic, which provides free biweekly medical and psychiatric care to middle and high school students who have no health insurance. The district provides some reimbursement for these services through Medicaid funds. The school psychologist collaborates with these community partners in identifying students in need of support and monitoring students who are receiving support to ensure their needs are being met.

In addition to community partners, parents/guardians need to be a significant partner in serving students. This is an area of growth for the school district identified through community-wide surveys. To address the need to better connect with families, the high school administration started reaching out to families at places they frequent, such as high school sporting events and religious activities. To support collaboration with families, the school principal recently required teachers to call the parents/guardians of students who are in their first period class once a week to discuss students' strengths and needs. The school psychologist spends time talking with parents/guardians of all the students she works with in order to build the respect and trust that is critical for a collaborative relationship.

Participatory action research. Another unique resource at the high school is a state-designated (and funded) turnaround team of several experts in school reform. These experts currently work at the school full-time and will do so for 3 years in order to support school improvement. The turnaround team was placed at the high school because it was consistently designated a low-achieving school and thus targeted for transformation. Given a complex formula that considers schools' standardized test scores, graduate rate, dropout rate, achievement gap, and college and career readiness, the high school was below the 15th percentile in the state when the turnaround team arrived.

The school administration, school psychologist, school counselors, representative group of teachers, and turnaround team all worked together to revamp school systems to support universal and targeted academic interventions. Teachers aligned their curricula with the Common Core State Standards and tracked students' mastery of standards. All students kept and reviewed data notebooks on their progress on benchmark assessments in English and math. Based on benchmark data, some students participated in reading and math intervention classes that utilized evidence-based interventions. One year later, the school was above the 65th percentile in the state according to the aforementioned combination of academic indicators. To support further transformation, there will be a systems change team to guide overall systems change, a response-to-intervention team, and a school-wide positive behavior supports team. The principal, turnaround team, and school psychologist serve on all these teams.

Assessment. During the previous school year, the school psychologist was responsible for more than 60 evaluations. The assessment load is high due to historical overidentification of students for special education in the district, relatively high rates of teacher

referrals for evaluation for a high school of its size, and several ninth graders with diagnoses of intellectual disabilities (many of whom were thought to have been misdiagnosed during elementary school). Ideally, a thorough evaluation would be conducted for all of these students. Given that one school psychologist is responsible for all of these evaluations in addition to consultation and intervention, the school psychologist must practice outwardness (i.e., focus attention on those experiencing the greatest threats to social justice). Instances where a misdiagnosis of intellectual disability was suspected received the greatest priority because students with this diagnosis were often in self-contained classes and placed on a track where they would receive a certificate of attendance instead of a diploma, further perpetuating the cycle of economic disadvantage. Children with two consistent and relatively thorough prior evaluations received the least priority.

In all cases, parent/guardian involvement was a priority. The school psychologist contacted the students' parents/guardians and sought input, questions, and concerns. The school psychologist explained the assessment process and its purpose prior to conducting the evaluation. If a parent/guardian rating scale was necessary, the school psychologist discussed the scale in person or on the phone, sometimes reading and explaining each question. Once the assessment was completed, the school psychologist discussed the results and potential implications with the parents/guardians. Sometimes the need for further access to community resources was evident through involving the parents/guardians in the assessment process, and the school psychologist worked to connect the student and his or her family to these resources. Given the relationship and trust built through this process, parents/guardians were more likely to attend IEP meetings that involved eligibility determinations.

Conclusion

The case example described above indicates that the needs of economically disadvantaged students can be addressed by a school. Parents/guardians experiencing financial hardship can be involved in and contribute to the education of the children. These children can achieve academic success. However, these "can dos" require partnering of the school and school psychologist with the community and parents/guardians and the development of systems within the school to support academic goals and well-being of students. The school psychologist must be strategic in tackling evaluations, prioritizing the ones that relate to the greatest change in students' well-being, so that there is time to engage in the important systems work and family–school–community partnerships. Finally, if anything, the above case example indicates that all of this is a constant work in progress. In the case example, academic interventions are not yet happening at Tier 3. Staff members have not received comprehensive training. No support groups exist for parents/guardians. It would be quite challenging for a single school to illustrate all of the best practices outlined in this chapter, but a school psychologist can constantly aspire to improve his or her practice and his or her school.

SUMMARY

Indeed, economic disadvantage for students and their families may be one of the most pernicious social justice issues facing school psychology in the 21st century, as children from economically disadvantaged backgrounds face numerous ecological adversities: disproportionately affected by developmental, mental health, and academic problems; having difficulty accessing treatment; and attending schools that may be underresourced and ill-equipped to serve them well. While evidence has documented the profound impact that poverty has on developing children, the trajectory for students living in these conditions *can* be changed through experiences with protective factors that can lead these students toward resilience.

AUTHOR NOTE

Disclosure. Samuel Song has a financial interest in books he authored or coauthored referenced in this chapter.

REFERENCES

Atkins, M. S., Frazier, S. L., Birman, D., Ail, J. A., Jackson, M., Graczyk, P. A., … McKay, M. M. (2006). School-based mental health services for children living in high poverty urban communities. *Administration and Policy in Mental Health and Mental Health Services Research, 33*, 146–159. doi:10.1007/s10488-006-0031-9

Briggs, A. (2013). The school psychologist as social justice advocate. In D. Shriberg, S. Song, A. Miranda, & K. Radliff (Eds.), *School psychology and social justice: Conceptual foundations and tools for practice* (pp. 295–310). New York, NY: Routledge.

Centers for Disease Control and Prevention. (2011). *National marriage and divorce rate trends.* Atlanta, GA: Author. Retrieved from http://www.cdc.gov/nchs/nvss/marriage_divorce_tables.htm

Eamon, M. K., & Venkataraman, M. (2003). Implementing parent management training in the context of poverty. *American Journal of Family Therapy, 31*, 281–293.

Eiraldi, R. B., Mazzuca, L. B., Clarke, A. T., & Power, T. J. (2006). Service utilization among ethnic minority children with ADHD: A model of help-seeking behavior. *Administration and Policy in Mental Health and Mental Health Service Research, 33*, 607–622.

Hopson, L. M., & Lee, E. (2011). Mitigating the effect of family poverty on academic and behavioral outcomes: The role of school climate in middle and high school. *Children and Youth Services Review, 33*, 2221–2229.

Howell, E. (2004). *Access to children's mental health services under Medicaid and SCHIP.* Washington, DC: Urban Institute.

Hummer, R. A., & Hamilton, E. R. (2010). Race and ethnicity in fragile families. *Future of Children, 20*, 113–117.

Jensen, E. (2009). *Teaching with poverty in mind: What being poor does to kids' brains and what schools can do about it.* Alexandra, VA: ASCD.

Jerald, C. D., Haycock, K., & Wilkins, A. (2009). *Fighting for quality and equality, too: How state policymakers can ensure the drive to improve teacher quality doesn't just trickle down to poor and minority children.* Washington, DC: Education Trust. Retrieved from http://myboe.org/cognoti/content/file/resources/documents/b0/b0155517/b01555172962e8ce0a1309b192133343d9a87dfa/QualityEquity_09.pdf

Klein, L. G., & Knitzer, J. (2007). *Promoting effective early learning: What every policymaker and educator should know.* New York, NY: National Center for Children in Poverty. Retrieved from http://www.nccp.org/publications/pdf/text_695.pdf

Kozol, J. (2005). *The shame of the nation: The restoration of apartheid schooling in America.* New York, NY: Three Rivers Press.

Leff, S. S. (2007). Bullying and peer victimization at school: Considerations and future directions. *School Psychology Review, 36*, 406–412.

Leff, S. S., Lefler, E. K., Khera, G. S., Paskewich, B., & Jawad, A. F. (2012). Preliminary examination of a cartoon-based hostile attributional bias measure for African American boys. *American Journal of Community Psychology, 49*, 332–346.

Loman, L. A., & Siegel, G. L. (2012). Effects of anti-poverty services under the differential response approach to child welfare. *Children and Youth Services Review, 34*, 1659–1666.

National Association of School Psychologists. (2010). *Model for comprehensive and integrated school psychological services.* Bethesda, MD: Author. Retrieved from http://www.nasponline.org/standards/2010standards/2_PracticeModel.pdf

Noltemeyer, A., & Fenning, P. (2013). Systemic school discipline: Issues of equity from a social justice perspective. In D. Shriberg, S. Song, A. Miranda, & K. Radliff (Eds.), *School psychology and social justice: Conceptual foundations and tools for practice* (pp. 91–117). New York, NY: Routledge.

Oliff, P., Mai, C., & Leachman, M. (2012). *New school year brings more cuts in state funding for schools.* Washington, DC: Center on Budget and Policy Priorities. Retrieved from http://www.cbpp.org/files/9-4-12sfp.pdf

Prilleltensky, I., & Nelson, G. (2002). *Doing psychology critically: Making a difference in diverse settings.* New York, NY: Palgrave Macmillan.

Richardson, J. W. (2008). From risk to resilience: Promoting school–health partnerships for children. *International Journal of Educational Reform, 17*, 19–36.

Rothstein, R. (2008). Whose problem is poverty? *Educational Leadership, 68*(7), 8–13.

Sander, J. B., Sharkey, J. D., Groomes, A. N., Krumholz, L., Walker, K., & Hsu, J. Y. (2011). Social justice and juvenile offenders: Examples of fairness, access, and respect in educational settings. *Journal of Educational and Psychological Consultation, 21*, 309–337.

Song, S. Y., & Marth, K. (2013). Social justice in the air: School culture and climate. In D. Shriberg, S. Song, A. Miranda, & K. Radliff (Eds.), *School psychology and social justice: Conceptual foundations and tools for practice* (pp. 155–170). New York, NY: Routledge.

Thomas-Presswood, T. N., & Presswood, D. (2008). *Meeting the needs of students and families from poverty: A handbook for school and mental health professionals.* Baltimore, MD: Brookes.

U.S. Census Bureau. (2011). *Child poverty in the United States 2009 and 2010: Selected race groups and Hispanic origin.* Washington, DC: Author. Retrieved from http://www.census.gov/prod/2011pubs/acsbr10-05.pdf

U.S. Department of Agriculture Economic Research Service. (2005). *Rural children at a glance* (Economic Information Bulletin No. 1). Washington, DC: Author. Retrieved from http://www.ers.usda.gov/publications/eib-economic-information-bulletin/eib1.aspx#.UnZ8Jt4o7b0

Wadsworth, M. E., & Achenbach, T. M. (2005). Explaining the link between socioeconomic status and psychopathology: Testing two mechanisms of the social causation hypothesis. *Journal of Consulting and Clinical Psychology, 73*, 1146–1153.

Williams, S. A. S., & Crockett, D. P. (2013). Institutional barriers: Poverty and education. In D. Shriberg, S. Song, A. Miranda, & K. Radliff (Eds.), *School psychology and social justice: Conceptual foundations and tools for practice* (pp. 137–154). New York, NY: Routledge.

Yoshikawa, H., Aber, J. L., & Beardslee, W. R. (2012). The effects of poverty on the mental, emotional, and behavioral health of children and youth. *American Psychologist, 67*, 272–284.

Best Practices in Providing School Psychological Services in Rural Settings

11

Margaret Beebe-Frankenberger
Anisa N. Goforth
The University of Montana

OVERVIEW

In 1990, Reschly and Connolly (1990) asked this question: "Is there a 'rural' school psychology?" Their study compared the practices of school psychologists in urban, suburban, and rural settings and found no significant differences in the practice of school psychology and concluded "school psychology appears to be far more the same than different in the city and the country" (p. 548). What makes the difference, however, is the experience of working in the rural culture. Context is the difference; that is, the rural setting offers divergent experiences from urban and suburban settings. For example, it is unlikely in an urban or suburban context that one school psychologist would be the only school psychologist in a 500 square mile area, or as one rural school psychologist wrote: "I have, at one time or another in the past 12 years, been the only school psychologist for 14 school districts.... None of the districts can be reached by road" (Goforth & Beebe-Frankenberger, 2012). We contend that the practice of school psychology in a rural or frontier context brings similar, yet qualitatively different, advantages and challenges than in urban or suburban areas. Therefore, this chapter is offered as one facet of the domain of Diversity in Development and Learning in the National Association of School Psychologists (NASP) *Model for Comprehensive and Integrated School Psychological Services* (NASP, 2010).

The intent of this chapter is twofold: to inform those who wish to consider working in a rural context and to promote best practice and support for rural school psychologists. Preliminary information from a study we conducted in fall of 2012 (Goforth & Beebe-Frankenberger, 2012) about the diverse experiences of rural psychologists will be referenced in the chapter, and we have inserted direct quotes of rural school psychologists as a way to more deeply characterize the rural context. The chapter begins by setting the framework with a brief demographic and historical overview about rural areas and present-day challenges faced by rural communities in general. The next section describes rural schools, the practice of school psychology in rural America, and provides best practice suggestions for specific professional responsibilities and topics relevant to rural school psychologists that were identified through our study and earlier studies (e.g., Clopton & Knesting, 2006).

BASIC CONSIDERATIONS

The definition of a rural area is open country and settlements of fewer than 2,500 residents (U.S. Census Bureau, 2010). The 2010 census indicates that 19.3% of the U.S. population lives in rural areas, although populations vary by state, ranging from 5 to 61%. Similarly, population densities vary, with average population densities in rural areas being 38 persons per square mile compared to 2,301 in urban areas (U.S. Census Bureau, 2010). These statistics highlight the large differences in context in which school psychologists work. The number of people per square mile, the scope of geographic area, and the resources available in that area greatly affect the ability to provide services.

Further, the proximity of rural areas to urbanized areas highly influences access to resources. For instance, Vermont has a high percentage of people living in rural areas, but given the state's proximity to the large metropolitan areas of the east coast, it is likely Vermont's rural populations have greater access to resources than rural populations in Alaska. Similarly, a suburban school psychologist may serve two schools consisting of 800 students with a distance of 5 miles between schools, while a rural school psychologist may serve six schools consisting of 400 students, with a 300 mile scope of service.

Historical Overview

A stereotype about all rural communities is that they are simple and static. Yet history supports a different view of rural communities. Rural communities are dynamically complex with great diversity.

There have been large shifts in rural industry since the 1950s. Historically, rural communities with generational roots supplied the bulk of food and building materials for America with agriculture, ranching, mining, timber management, and fishing. Then a so-called rural renaissance began in the early 1970s with a shift from primarily farming to an economy based upon small business, manufacturing, and recreational activities (Helge, 1985). But since 2005, with the advent of the U.S. recession, rural areas experienced real loss in manufacturing, educational and health services, and leisure/hospitality industries, with a slight corresponding employment increase in agriculture and mining. For instance, because of the boom in oil/gas extraction technology, there was an 11% increase in mining employment (Economic Research Services, 2012).

There have also been shifts in population. Beginning in the 1950s there was an out-migration as young residents left rural areas for urban job opportunities. The population decline resulted in lower tax revenues, a decline in property values, lower enrollment in schools, and fewer employment opportunities that, in turn, resulted in even more people leaving rural areas. Rural communities made fiscal decisions to close some schools and consolidate into one school within a geographical region, sometimes very distant from students' homes. Although necessary fiscally, school consolidation weakened the sense of community that characterized rural communities. But by the 1980s the out-migration eased as migration of people of all ages from suburban and urban regions settled in rural areas. A study of migration patterns to rural areas found that many migrants were young and highly educated professionals who chose to reduce income in favor of outdoor recreation, slower pace, scenic beauty, and climate (Rudzitis, 2001).

Rural communities also experienced an increase in immigrants from other countries. These immigrants introduced a new challenge to rural schools as children enrolled were sometimes English language learners. Families displaced by war, turmoil, and poverty in foreign countries during the 1990s also immigrated, and, consequently, children from these families now pose perhaps a greater challenge beyond English language learners because of the emotional trauma many have experienced. However, beginning in 2006, migration rates from foreign countries, especially from Mexico, declined dramatically likely due to the U.S. economic recession (Economic Research Service, 2012).

The substantial changes in the population since the 1950s have resulted in greater complexity because of an increase in ethnic/cultural diversity, which in turn has diffused long-standing social networks.

Rural Community Challenges

There are several challenges that affect rural communities and have a direct impact on the provision of school psychological services in rural schools. These challenges include poverty, unemployment, access to mental health and services, and substance abuse.

Poverty and Unemployment

Poverty and unemployment are significant issues in rural areas. Rural areas have had a higher rate of poverty than urban areas since the 1960s. In 2010, nearly 8 million people living in rural areas met the poverty threshold, which is approximately $17,268 for a family of two adults and one child (Economic Research Service, 2012). Persistent poverty, or poverty rates more than 20% for a period of 30 years, is of even greater concern. Nearly 88% of those U.S. counties identified with persistent poverty are rural (Economic Research Service, 2012). There is a clear and important link between unemployment, poverty persistence, and degree of rurality. In early 2011, rates of rural unemployment of working adults rose to 27%, the highest since 1983, primarily because of the loss of jobs in the manufacturing, educational and health services, and leisure/hospitality industries (Economic Research Service, 2012).

About one fifth of children in poverty live in rural areas and are more likely to live in extreme poverty (i.e., less than half of the poverty threshold). These children experience greater challenges than urban children because they are more isolated and have limited access to quality health services and resources for public schools. Moreover, rural parents tend to have less education and are more likely to be underemployed, increasing the risk for extreme poverty. As one rural school psychologists told us: "I remember talking to a kid who had no water. That was off the charts for me. To see how little people have can be stunning" (Goforth & Beebe-Frankenberger, 2012).

There is also an important cultural worldview characterizing rural communities with high poverty. O'Hare (2009) noted that "rural poverty can be especially persistent because, in addition to a scarcity of jobs and physical and social isolation in rural areas, many rural residents shun government assistance out of a high value placed on self-reliance and the stigma that often goes with welfare." In sum, a significant concern in rural areas is the high percentage of children and families living in extreme poverty and the lack of resources available in these rural communities.

Mental Health and Services

As a result of extreme poverty, high unemployment rates, low educational opportunities, and a sense of isolation, people living in rural communities are more likely to experience significant stress. There are higher rates of major depression and teen and older adult suicide in rural areas than in nonrural areas (Gustafson, Preston, & Hudson, 2009). Similarly, rural children are also at greater risk for mental health problems. The rates and chronicity of mental disorders are likely related to lack of availability and access to mental health providers (Moore et al., 2005). Importantly, there is a great deal of social stigma about seeking care for mental health problems because of the lack of anonymity in rural communities (Gustafson et al., 2009).

Substance Use and Abuse

Rural Americans are at a higher risk for substance use than urban Americans (Van Gundy, 2006). Rural youth are more likely to engage in underage drinking. Among rural youth aged 16–17, three out of five report alcohol consumption. Illicit drug use in rural areas is on the rise with 17% of rural youth reporting use of illicit drugs. In particular, use of methamphetamine stimulants is seven times more likely among rural than urban unemployed, and rural adults living in households with children are more likely to use methamphetamine stimulants than their urban counterparts (Van Gundy, 2006). Generally, in rural and small towns, alcohol and illicit drug abuse

are more likely to occur if young adults are male, less educated, unemployed, and unmarried. Alcohol abuse generally exceeds illicit drug abuse, but is equally and consistently high for Native American youth (Van Gundy, 2006).

Summary

It is important for current and future practitioners to appreciate the shifts in rural populations over time and to recognize that change in rural community life does indeed occur, albeit at a slower pace than in urban areas. It is even more critical for school psychologists to recognize the particular challenges of the rural communities they serve and to suggest ways to incorporate prevention and intervention activities in the schools that create positive change in the community.

BEST PRACTICES IN RURAL SCHOOL PSYCHOLOGY

The way that rural school psychology differs from urban and suburban school psychology is primarily by the context. That context is based upon the basic nature of rural schools and a relatively short history of school psychology in rural areas.

Rural Schools

Today, 20% percent of American students attend rural schools, comprising 33% of public school buildings across America; that is, one third of public school buildings are located in rural areas, yet only one fifth of students attend rural schools. Rural communities have to maintain a higher number of school buildings relative to their enrollments, a fiscal challenge that competes with other community-funded expenditures.

From 1999 to 2009, rural schools experienced an increase in student enrollment, Hispanic student enrollment, and students eligible for free and reduced price meals. Rural schools also increased the percentage of students who graduated from high school as well as National Assessment of Education Progress reading and math scores for fourth- and eighth-grade students (Rural School and Community Trust, 2012). Rural school demographics from 2008 to 2009 are summarized in Table 11.1.

Rural School Strengths

Rural schools are embedded in small communities, are often the center of community activity, and can be

Table 11.1. Rural School Demographics for 2008–2009, National Center for Education Statistics

Demographic	U.S. Rural *M* %	Highest *M* %	State	Lowest *M* %	State
Percent rural schools	33.0	78.6	SD	6.6	MA
Percent rural students	20.2	54.7	MS	4.3	MA
Percent minority students	25.8	82.5	NM	3.2	RI
Percent English language learners	3.7	18.1	CA	0.4	NH
Percent students with an Individualized Education Program	12.1	17.6	KY	8.7	CA
Percent students eligible for free and reduced meals (poverty)	41.0	80.0	NM	7.2	CT
Percent student mobility in 1 year	12.7	17.6	KY	8.7	CA
Rural high school graduation rate	77.5	96.2	NJ	60.0	LA
Percent change in rural school enrollment 1999–2009	22.2	228.9	AZ	−64.3	MA
Percent change in rural school Hispanic enrollment 1999–2009	150.9	578.4	WV	1.8	CT
Percent change in rural students eligible for free and reduced meals 1999–2009	5.9	28.7	AZ	−6.0	NC

Note. From *Why Rural Matters 2011–2012: The Condition of Rural Education in the 50 States* by Rural School and Community Trust, 2012, Washington, DC: Author. Copyright 2012 by Rural School and Community Trust. Adapted with permission.

described as a microcosm of the local culture. The strong sense of connectedness translates into a sense of responsibility for each other person. Rural schools often serve as the community meeting place, with some schools serving as a place for community health and mental health services.

Rural schools are characterized by a number of factors such as a sense of belonging, small class sizes, wide grade spans, safety, and high teacher job satisfaction (Jimerson, 2006). First, the sense of belonging that often characterizes small communities naturally flows into the school. This belongingness creates a connected school climate that fosters respect and reduces school dropout and substance abuse. Second, rural schools typically have small class size, which gives students more time with a teacher and more individualized instruction. Smaller enrollments in rural schools also lead to multiage and mixed-ability classes. When mixed classes are combined with high academic expectations and challenging curriculum, students are even more likely to be successful and competitive at the national level. Third, rural schools often serve more grades. For example, schools may include grades K–8 or K–12. This wide grade span in one school building alleviates problems related to student adjustment associated with transitioning to new schools (Jimerson, 2006). Fourth, rural schools offer safety, satisfied teachers, and less district bureaucracy. Rural schools have been shown to have fewer violent incidents, less vandalism, theft, truancy, and gang participation than

urban schools. Strong relationships between and among students and teachers likely fosters feelings of trust and safety. Moreover, rural school teachers tend to be more satisfied, take greater responsibility for student learning, are more likely to initiate innovative changes in teaching, and have less absenteeism and turnover than their urban counterparts.

There is also much less bureaucracy in small rural schools. Indeed, the school is often also the school district and a school teacher may be the school principal or even superintendent. As a result, there are fewer people and more direct policies to negotiate when making changes.

Rural School Challenges
Ironically, the biggest challenges for rural schools emanate from their biggest strength: being small. The small number of school staff, lack of internal and external resources, and status quo policies present the biggest obstacles to expanding into school-wide processes such as response to intervention and positive behavioral interventions and supports. School staff frequently serve in multiple roles. Curriculum is often taught to several grade levels. There are still single-room schoolhouses where a teacher is required to teach curriculum for whatever grade of children are enrolled.

Members of the school staff who serve in multiple capacities may have less time to be engaged in professional development workshops or continued education classes. Rural school psychologists often assist by presenting seminars that bring new ideas in education, evidenced-based curriculum, assessment, and teaching innovations.

Outside referrals. A challenge that makes outside referrals difficult for students in need of more intensive services than the school can provide is meager access to external resources such as mental health providers, medical specialists, homeless shelters, and poverty assistance programs. Scarcity of public transportation, fuel costs for private transportation, and time away from home and school make outside referrals even more problematic and less likely to be followed. As one school psychologist told us: "The most challenging aspect of working in a rural community is the lack of community services and resources, such as medical specialty practices, counselor/therapists, and after-school programs" (Goforth & Beebe-Frankenberger, 2012).

The shortage of community services and resources is being addressed somewhat now through the advent of such programs as Telehealth, which provides medical and mental health practitioner services via computer in regions of the United States. Rural school psychologists should continue to seek innovative ways to link students and their families to programs such as Telehealth that eliminate distance as a barrier.

Educational cooperatives. Internal resources are also a challenge in rural schools. Factors such as low enrollment and a reduced tax base for educational costs contribute to the challenge. To combat this, rural schools access specialists such as school psychologists and speech/language therapists through educational cooperatives that contract to many rural schools in an area. Rural schools rarely have access to full-time school counselors, behavioral specialists, and specialized interventionists. As a result, rural school psychologists may feel compelled to take on additional roles and responsibilities to meet the needs of the school. However, great caution should be taken not to exceed competency limits in any given area. School psychologists typically are in the school on a regular basis, but only for a limited amount of time.

Best practice is to maintain as consistent a schedule as possible for each rural school. The school psychologist should notify staff and parents of ways to contact him or her if circumstances arise for which the school psychologist is needed but is not onsite. Dependability and communication are fundamental to establishing trust with school staff and parents.

Combating entrenched beliefs. Although one of the strengths of rural schools is lack of bureaucracy, the infrastructure, policies, and procedures in place may be too narrow and outdated to meet the changing dynamics in rural schools. The autonomy of the rural school is prized, but may also promote a status quo perspective; that is, an attitude of "we've always done it this way and it works." Autonomy and status quo both make it less likely that school administrators and teachers are aware that the curriculum, teaching practices, and programs may be outdated. Without an awareness of updates in educational practices or the current needs of the community, rural schools may be slow to recognize the need for change.

Best practice for the school psychologist to facilitate change begins with familiarizing school administrators and teachers with innovative methods. Facilitating discussion about change takes a great deal of time, patience, and strong consultation skills. Resistance to change because of status quo can be interpreted as a need to avoid risk or a fear that the school staff does not have the knowledge or skill necessary for the change. Best practice for a school psychologist to overcome such resistance include strategies such as (a) providing support and praise for the school staff's accomplishments, (b) frequently expressing respect for school staff knowledge, (c) using programs or interventions similar to what school staff already does in the school or classroom (as much as possible), and (d) making a connection between proposed change and the school mission or the staff's professional values. A completely different approach to change can be successful if the school feels that it is being selected to participate in an innovative program/intervention. Once successful in recognizing the need for change, rural schools are quicker to implement changes because of the lack of bureaucracy and the inherent cooperation among rural educators.

Rural School Psychology

Rural school psychologists typically travel a lot in a week, mostly by car, but it is not unknown for school psychologists to travel by airplane, seaplane, snowmobile, hiking, and just about any means of transportation available. One rural school psychologist said to us: "Nobody could prepare someone for my first few years on the job…. I drove 110 miles to my first school of the day and served in many truly one-room school houses. I can change a flat tire in 15 minutes by the side of the road because of those early years (Goforth & Beebe-Frankenberger, 2012).

Background

Until the early 1980s, rural school psychological services developed very slowly and were based almost entirely upon the numbers of students with disabilities. School psychologists became more common in rural areas after national legislation (i.e., the 1975 Education of All Handicapped Children Act that has been codified as the 2004 Individuals with Disabilities Education Act [IDEA]) mandated public schools serve all children, including those with disabilities. This legislation was responsible for school psychologists practicing in rural settings on a widespread and permanent basis, but also narrowed the scope of practice to primarily the role of assessment. Fagan and Hughes (1985) commented that "had school psychology developed along lines of prevention, regular school programs, curriculum, and ability (as contrasted with disability), the situation in urban and rural areas may have been much different" (p. 444).

Every rural school required the services of a school psychologist to fulfill the federal mandate, but most rural schools could not afford to employ or even contract with a single school psychologist. As a result, privately owned regional agencies emerged and employed school psychologists to ensure provision of services to students with disabilities. This model of service delivery enabled small rural districts to pool resources and provide levels of service that otherwise would be unavailable, insufficient, too expensive, or inefficient for one district. Thus, today rural school psychologists are often employed by independent agencies and not districts.

These independent educational cooperatives provide increased opportunity for professional development, specialized practice, and increased professional and administrative supervision. The collaborative nature of regional agencies has helped alleviate many former negative features of rural school psychology such as inadequate supervision and professional isolation (Reschly & Connolly, 1990).

The reauthorization of IDEA in 2007 provided the potential to expand the role of the school psychologist beyond the role of test-and-place with the change in learning disability identification that allows a response-to-intervention method. Although tiered systems of support may still be less common in rural areas, rural school psychologists are expanding their roles as academic and social–behavioral interventionists, system consultants, and mental health providers. Interestingly, in our study (Goforth & Beebe-Frankenberger, 2012), rural school psychologists reported that they have either a narrow assessment role or a diverse role that includes counseling, group work, and consultation with administrators, teachers, and parents. As school psychologists become better known for their array of skills, it is expected their roles will expand to the benefit of the rural community.

Demographics

Nearly 24% of U.S. school psychologists work in rural settings (Curtis, Castillo, & Gelley, 2012). A rural school psychologist expressed how working in rural areas is similar and different to working in urban or suburban areas: "Rural is same and different. In the urban poor [ethnic] minority area I was closer to more resources and experts in many areas. In the rural White community there are fewer resources and the community seems isolated in education and culture. I learned the ways of my new area and worked with what I had available" (Goforth & Beebe-Frankenberger, 2012).

Thus, the nature of a school psychologist's work across settings is more similar than different; however, the context in which practice occurs differs. In our study (Goforth & Beebe-Frankenberger, 2012), the sample (N = 231) composed of rural, suburban, and urban school psychologists had similar salaries, degree of job satisfaction, number of students served, availability of updated and appropriate assessments, and access to parents of children.

However, there were some key differences between settings that emphasize the importance of the unique overall context of rural school psychological practice. Rural school psychologists in our study (Goforth & Beebe-Frankenberger, 2012) serve fewer ethnic minority students than their colleagues in urban and suburban areas. Rural school psychologists, however, serve more schools than their urban or suburban counterparts, while still serving similar numbers of students and traveling a great deal more every week. In fact, 74% of rural school psychologists serve three or more schools and 32% traveled more than 250 miles per week (Goforth & Beebe-Frankenberger, 2012).

Rural school psychologists also shared their perspectives on how they would change their role in schools. Generally, they indicated they would like to reduce paperwork and report writing, reduce the number of schools served, reduce the student-to-school psychologist ratio, and have more direct time in intervention with students. Suburban and urban school psychologists shared similar responses but with less frequency, while they indicated they wished to expand their role and reduce time in disability assessment for eligibility with more frequency than their rural counterparts (Goforth, Beebe-Frankenberger, & Yosai, 2013).

Benefits and Challenges

The benefits of working in rural settings may also be the challenges. Rural school psychologists who live in the same small community where they work have the advantage of developing deepened relationships through actively engaging in community activities outside of school. However, this puts the school psychologist in the position of being in multiple roles, requiring skillful balance to fulfill each role. One rural school psychologist said to us: "It takes skill to work with people, keep them happy, please the parents, deliver potentially bad news, watch out for the child, and live around these people while trying to be a part of the community and find an identity for your family" (Goforth & Beebe-Frankenberger, 2012).

An initial challenge might be adapting to each school's culture and identifying the unique needs of each school. This can be difficult and take a great deal of time and patience because it requires establishing trust within a close-knit community that may be suspicious of outsiders. Developing a trusting relationship with school administrators is especially important for future prospects of influencing change.

In addition to developing close relationships, the rural school psychologist can play a variety of roles that include not only assessment and Individualized Education Program (IEP) eligibility, but also assisting with intervention, serving as a trainer to school staff and community, group and individual counseling, connecting staff and parents to distant resources, and consulting with administrators about policy/procedural changes. Rural school psychologists are often the most informed person in the school about special education law and thus are often consulted about procedures. When necessary, they also protect their schools by interceding when compliance issues are threatened. Being knowledgeable and staying current on special education laws and procedures is especially critical to serving rural schools.

Once established in a rural school and viewed as a resource on multiple topics, rural school psychologists are often invited to present local staff and parent trainings. By providing staff professional development, the obstacle for rural school personnel to obtain professional development is alleviated. School psychologists can also direct administrators and teachers to online webinars that provide professional development.

Cultural Competence

School psychologists working in rural communities are likely to work with children and families from culturally and linguistically diverse backgrounds. While many of the children in rural schools may be Caucasian, the cultural values, beliefs, and norms within rural communities are unique and should be recognized. One rural school psychologist said to us:

> The biggest difficulty I had was the sheer culture shock. I didn't and still don't have much in common with the majority of the population here as far as religious or political beliefs and I tend to enjoy a different variety of activities than many of them. However ..., I want to be clear that I am now a trusted and respected member of this community and many of these differences are things that I keep private. (Goforth & Beebe-Frankenberger, 2012)

Indeed, school psychologists who have been raised or trained in programs located in nonrural settings and who then obtain positions in rural schools recognize the saliency of rural culture in these communities.

Current national census data show an increase in Hispanic and English language learner students in rural areas and reflect what we heard from rural school psychologists participating in our study (Goforth & Beebe-Frankenberger, 2012). Many rural school psychologists indicated a need for additional training in cultural competence and assessment of English language learners because of Hispanic and foreign refugee immigrants in their schools. While most school psychologists obtain graduate and follow-up training in cultural competence, many in our study expressed that the deepest and richest training comes from applying and extending theory learned from texts to their actual experience. One rural psychologist said to us:

> Cultural competence is a large scope. Yes, I received training [in school]. We have a large Hispanic population in my communities. One of my communities has a large religious population that does not believe in the use of doctors. A class can give you the beginnings of understanding, but living with it daily is a bigger understanding. (Goforth & Beebe-Frankenberger, 2012)

Many rural communities include children and families from ethnic minority groups such as Hispanic and Native Americans. Consequently, developing strong cultural competence with diverse populations is an essential aspect of rural school psychological practice.

A cultural competence framework that may be helpful for rural school psychologists includes three major components: (a) developing awareness of personal values and biases, (b) accumulating skills for working with specific populations, and (c) acquiring knowledge of the cultural issues relevant to that population (Sue, 2001). Guiding questions for this cultural competence framework are available in Table 11.2.

Developing awareness. Rural school psychologists should work toward developing awareness of their own personal values, beliefs, and biases that may influence interactions with others. Some rural school psychologists may have been raised in rural communities, and therefore have similar belief systems and values of others in the community. Other school psychologists, however, may have different values and beliefs. For example, many rural communities maintain strong religious traditions and conservative sociopolitical beliefs. Some school psychologists who work in rural schools may have more liberal sociopolitical beliefs and, consequently, may not share similar cultural values. An important first step in developing cultural competence,

therefore, is to be aware of and acknowledge similarities and differences in these values and belief systems.

Acquiring skills. Acquiring additional skills can be accomplished by obtaining additional training in working with specific populations, being engaged with the community through attendance in activities or events, or being able to use nonverbal styles of communication (Sue, 2001). Some school psychologists, for example, may be skilled at conducting interviews with parents; however, these skills may need to be more culturally relevant when interviewing a Native American parent. Instead of an interview method involving a question-and-answer session, for example, a school psychologist may need to be aware of Native American communication styles that may be more "circular" rather than "linear." Similarly, rural school psychologists should consider engaging with Native American communities and learning about traditional healing practices to address mental health issues. By taking steps toward developing their collaboration and consultation skills, rural school psychologists will improve their ability to integrate school psychological services within that community. The knowledge to develop culturally specific skills can be learned through

Table 11.2. Guiding Questions in Developing Cultural Competence in Rural Communities

Awareness	Skills	Knowledge
• How do I identify myself? What is my cultural group? • What are my own biases or stereotypes? • How do my biases affect my practice? • What are my religious and sociopolitical beliefs that may influence my practice? • What is my communication style? How does it differ compared to this group? • What is the power basis in the school district or cooperative where I work? Who has the power? Why? • What are the perceptions of ethnic minority children in the school and community where I work? • How do I fit in within this rural community? Am I part of this community? How do I know?	• What additional training could I obtain to better serve this rural community? • In what ways can I get engaged with the community? • If I work with a Native American family, how can I modify my communication style to facilitate this relationship? • When interviewing a rural family, how do I take into account the stigma often associated with mental health? • In what ways can I use nondiscriminatory assessment for rural English language learners? • How I can implement best practices in assessment and intervention with children of migrant workers? • How can I obtain professional development to further my skills? Are there inexpensive and efficient ways to obtain professional development, such as NASP webinars? • With whom can I consult to improve my cultural competency skills?	• What information do I need to know to better serve this group? Is a book sufficient or is there someone I can speak to? • Do the norms in a standardized test include members of the group that I serve? • In what ways can I implement culturally appropriate response to intervention in this rural school? • If I work with Native American families, is there a cultural broker from whom I can learn? • For agricultural communities, how can I take into account the planting or harvest time when scheduling meetings with parents? • How can I provide consultation with teachers about Native American traditions and culture? • Is the rural community in which I work religious? What are the religious practices and traditions?

formalized training opportunities as well as informal means, such as working with a tribal elder or other community member.

Rural school psychologists should also consider developing culturally relevant skills in working with English language learners. In many agricultural communities across the United States, there are a significant number of Hispanic Americans, many of whom live in these communities temporarily during harvest season. Children of migrant or seasonal workers may work alongside their parents or attend public schools in these communities. Given that English language learners and ethnic minority students are disproportionally referred for special education (Sullivan, 2011), rural school psychologists should enhance their skills in conducting nondiscriminatory assessments that take into account the English ability of these children.

Additionally, rural school psychologists may want to consider further refining their consultation and collaboration skills to better serve children from diverse backgrounds in schools. Misunderstandings about cultural values may have a significant impact on children's learning. For example, for some Native American communities, a death of someone from the community requires specific traditions and rituals and involves all members of that community. Native American children may attend these funerals, which may last more than a week, and therefore these children must be absent from school. Teachers may be concerned that these children are missing important academic content. Therefore, school psychologists have an important role to play in collaborating and consulting with teachers in ensuring that children from diverse backgrounds are able to adhere to their cultural practices and have opportunities to make up assignments and learn the content. Rural school psychologists may also want to consider developing a form of communication with parents about how to notify the school prior to the student's absence. The school psychologist can play an important role in connecting the home and school, developing mutual trust, and further supporting the student's academic success.

Acquiring knowledge. Rural school psychologists should have an understanding of the traditions and history of the community they serve. For example, rural school psychologists may serve Hutterite or Mennonite communities where ranching and farming have been a long-standing tradition. Understanding the specific gender roles and expectations within that community, the minimal or no use of technology, or the community's

time line for planting or harvesting crops would help the school psychologist develop culturally appropriate IEP goals or schedule parent meetings. Moreover, if a rural school psychologist serves a large population of Native American children, he or she should understand the history of that community, including the historical genocide and discrimination that continues to influence these communities. Acquiring knowledge of the history, beliefs, and traditions improves relationships with the youth and families.

Students Living in Poverty

As noted earlier, poverty is a significant concern in many rural communities. The percentage of rural students eligible for free and reduced price meals increased from 31% in 1999 to 41% in 2009; that is, two out of five rural students are eligible for free and reduced price meals. Poverty is highly correlated with child abuse and neglect, substance abuse, lower academic achievement, and a host of serious outcomes that can be mediated by schools with proactive prevention and intervention. Experiencing the influence of extreme and persistent poverty on students can be overwhelming. As one rural school psychologist said to us: "We don't send school books home over winter break because families have used them for fuel in their fireplaces to warm their homes" (Goforth & Beebe-Frankenberger, 2012).

Best practices in serving children living in poverty should involve understanding the various ecological contexts that affect child academic and social–emotional outcomes. The so-called culture of poverty is one that is less likely discussed during training, yet absolutely essential for working in schools today. Factors such as family poverty and parent or youth substance abuse can influence early school dropout and level of academic achievement. Rural school psychologists who have a clear understanding of these factors can better provide academic and social–emotional support. For example, the Backpack Program is a program supported by donations from the rural community in which students known to live in poverty are sent home on Fridays with a backpack of food for the weekend. By collaborating with the community and other agencies, school psychologists can be part of the solution. Thus, school psychologists play a meaningful role in establishing and institutionalizing academic and social–behavioral prevention programs that support resiliency and student success. By acknowledging and addressing the culture of poverty, school psychologists deepen their understanding and adopt expanded worldviews that enrich work with families.

Students With Disabilities

School psychologists should consider a number of factors when providing services to rural students, including higher rates of disability identification in rural areas. In 2008–2009, 12% of rural students had IEPs (see Table 11.1). One possible reason for this high rate is the strong association between poverty and disability identification in rural children compared to urban, suburban, and nonpoverty children (Rural School and Community Trust, 2012). However, data presented in the Rural School and Community Trust report contradicts the correlation with poverty since three of the five rural states with the highest percentage of IEPs were characterized as having low rates of poverty. The report concludes there is a higher willingness to provide special services in these states. We speculate, however, that higher identification rates in rural areas are an artifact of few options for intervention beyond the general classroom. In other words, rural schools may be identifying children with disabilities to a greater extent knowing that there are few, if any, resources outside of the school.

Given the high numbers of children with disabilities, rural school psychologists must consider best practices in supporting these children's academic and social–emotional needs. School psychologists can encourage and help design a continuum of academic, behavioral, and social–emotional learning programs and interventions to promote academic success. These programs in turn will reduce referrals for eligibility and avoid unnecessary labels of "disability." Rural school psychologists should use various multitiered systems of support and should work collaboratively with the school multidisciplinary team to support all children.

Students With Mental Health Issues

Children living in rural areas, and particularly those who live in poverty, are at higher risk for mental health issues (Yoshikawa, Aber, & Beardslee, 2012). Consequently, rural school psychologists should use multitiered systems of support and universal screening of behavioral issues to ensure that these children receive appropriate support services. Developing strategic and individualized social–emotional interventions in a school-based setting would allow for these children to get support they may not otherwise access. Frequently, community mental health services are not readily available in rural communities and there is often stigma associated with seeking mental health care. Rural residents are less likely to seek mental health care, often because they fear prejudice, discrimination, or rejection from the wider community (Murimi & Harpel, 2010).

Rural parents report their concern about how community members will perceive their family if their child receives mental health services (Starr, Campbell, & Herrick, 2002).

Consequently, rural school psychologists should consider using multitiered systems of support in school to screen and implement interventions for children living in poverty. For example, one school-based intervention that does not require special materials or specialist personnel is the Check-in/Check-out system (Everett, Sugai, Fallon, Simonsen, & O'Keeffe, 2011). Students who need extra support for either behavioral or emotional difficulties are anchored by an adult in the school who fosters positive adjustment on a daily basis. A Check-in/Check-out intervention (a) prevents children from developing more serious problems, (b) does not stigmatize a child with labels, and (c) fosters resiliency in children to overcome the effects of external factors not within their control. For rural schools that have minimal available resources, Check-in/Check-out may be a relevant and useful tool for supporting children. In addition to using such interventions, schools can play an important role in providing a variety of services to these children by collaborating with community mental health agencies in the region. When available, community social workers, psychiatrists, and medical practitioners can work alongside the school psychologist in the school itself to find children at risk for a variety of mental health issues.

In addition to the significant risk of mental health among rural children, there is also a significant risk of substance use. Substance abuse treatment centers in rural areas are more likely to have younger clients and more likely to be referred by the criminal justice system (Substance Abuse and Mental Health Services Administration, 2012). Often, rural youth are likely to abuse or misuse substances such as alcohol, prescription drugs, and methamphetamine. As a result, school-wide prevention program in collaboration with other mental health agencies in the communities may be useful in not only reducing the stigma associated with discussing mental health issues, but also providing evidence-based prevention programs to reduce substance use among rural youth. Conducting a thorough needs assessment, choosing an evidence-based program that meets those needs, and determining at what grade children should receive the program may reduce the likelihood that rural children and adolescents use drugs.

School psychologists working in communities with little or no immediate access to mental health and substance abuse treatment may consider fostering development of a regional school-based health center

(Brown & Bolen, 2003) to provide treatment services closer to isolated rural communities than currently available. School-based health centers exist in most states and provide immediate access to healthcare services by rural residents who may otherwise go unserved owing to barriers of distance, transportation costs, and expense of time away from work for parents. The essential elements include (a) a continuum of health and mental health prevention and intervention services, (b) services offered all students (general and special education), (c) services augmenting the work of school-hired mental health professionals, and (d) are developed through partnerships between schools and community agencies and programs (Weist, Goldstein, Morris, & Bryant, 2003). The positive effects for students who use school-based health center services include a decrease in student absences, an increase in graduation rates, a decrease in disciplinary referrals, and a decrease in failing grades (Brown & Bolen, 2003).

Ethical and Legal Issues

One of the defining characteristics of rural culture is the small population and close sense of community. A sense of community may be an advantage because children and families know each other well and school psychologists who live and work within a community have a clearer understanding of the problems and concerns specific to the community. On the other hand, this sense of community may be problematic for rural school psychologists. School psychologists in small towns and rural areas are more likely to encounter multiple relationship behaviors and situations compared to school psychologists in urban and suburban areas (Helbok, Marinelli, & Walls, 2006). One rural school psychologist reported to us:

> My biggest worry is keeping community know-ledge separate from school-based knowledge. I can keep my dealings with students confidential. However, I struggle with keeping quiet [during meetings] about things I've learned on the soccer field. When I worked in a large city, I lived in a nearby city and never crossed paths with families from my work community. Living and working in a small town, where my children go to school, entwines all aspects of my life and means I never do anything that people would gossip about. (Goforth & Beebe-Frankenberger, 2012)

School psychologists, therefore, must take into consideration the variety of ethical and legal issues and implement best practice in resolving any ethical dilemmas.

Multiple relationships are a common ethical concern for rural school psychologists. For example, a school psychologist may be providing counseling services to a child of a family with whom they socialize. This multiple relationship with the child is an ethical concern. However, there is a significant lack of mental health services in many rural communities and, consequently, without the school psychologist's expertise as a mental health service provider and his or her knowledge about psychological and academic outcomes, that child may not receive necessary services within that community.

Rural school psychologists may also be actively involved in their community and socialize with community members through religious groups or community events. As a result, rural school psychologists may encounter students from their schools or be involved in business with families.

Another common issue is the use of out-of-date tests for comprehensive assessments. The lack of funding and lower student enrollment of many rural public schools often means that new tests are not purchased when they become available. Yet without comprehensive psychological evaluations based upon psychometrically reliable assessments, children in rural schools are at greater risk for not receiving special education services.

While these ethical issues permeate all aspects of school psychological services whether the school is located in an urban, suburban, or rural area, there are specific considerations for rural school psychologists. Jacob, Decker, and Hartshorne (2010) provide a multi-step problem-solving model that is useful for addressing any ethical and legal challenges that arise in professional rural practice.

When a rural school psychologist encounters an ethical dilemma, he or she will want to consider the situations and potential ethical–legal issues. Consulting with a colleague or supervisor may also be beneficial in determining which parties would be affected. Prior to making any final decision, the rural school psychologist will want to consider the various consequences of each decision, remembering that ethical dilemmas are often neither black nor white. By taking a systematic approach to each ethical dilemma, the rural school psychologist will have a clearer understanding of the short- and long-term consequences of a decision.

In addition to the ethical issues, school psychologists may also come across legal issues that affect their practice. In some rural public schools, the school psychologist may be the only professional with comprehensive knowledge about special education law. School administrators may rely on this knowledge to ensure that the school is in compliance with a child's IEP. However, many rural school psychologists work across several schools and are not often physically present at any one school. They may learn that some school personnel are not adhering to the IEP or, worse, use practices such as seclusion and isolation of children with severe disabilities. As a result, school psychologists have an important role in disseminating information about special education law and compliance with IEP goals to school personnel. Discussing updates to special education law, describing the importance of adhering to IEP goals, and providing information about best practices in addressing disruptive behavior that does not include seclusion of a child may be a critical aspect of the rural school psychologist's role in the school. It is incumbent upon rural school psychologists to keep abreast of changes in federal and state special education law, regulations, and procedures. A good source for specific information is Wrightslaw (http://www.wrightslaw.com).

Professional Development

Given the context, it may not be surprising that many rural school psychologists may experience a sense of professional isolation (Clopton & Knesting, 2006). Rural school psychologists may travel hundreds of miles between schools, and consequently have little access to their colleagues or supervisors. Nonetheless, consultation from colleagues is important for developing more thorough case conceptualizations, brainstorming academic interventions, addressing ethical concerns, as well as having an opportunity to process and vent about work.

There are a number of ways to improve the likelihood that a rural school psychologist can obtain consultation from colleagues. First, the Internet can be a valuable way to communicate and interact with other school psychologists. Free Web conference tools such as Google Hangouts or Skype can be useful in meeting virtually to discuss cases. Second, monthly consultation meetings that are scheduled throughout the year in different locations can also be a useful way to ensure that rural school psychologists meet frequently. These meetings could include school psychologists from the local educational cooperative as well as school psychologists from the surrounding region. It may be beneficial to expand the school psychologist's professional circle and seek a supportive group from outside his or her immediate work so that discussions of ethical or legal issues are less likely to affect professional relationships.

Ongoing professional supervision is also a critical component of rural school psychological practice, even for school psychologists who have been working for a number of years. Obtaining supervision from an experienced school psychologist, however, can be difficult because the school psychologist's immediate supervisor may be a special educator or other professional who provides administrative supervision rather than professional or case supervision. Rural school psychologists, therefore, may want to contact senior school psychologists within their region to obtain professional supervision. The school psychologist may want to contact the state association of school psychologists or a university that houses a school psychology program to find senior-level school psychologists interested in providing supervision. This supervision could occur face to face or through Web conferencing. While obtaining supervision may be challenging, it is essential that school psychologists continue to expand their competencies and skills.

Resources

A major concern by rural school psychologists is the lack of resources, something that is not as easily addressed through a school psychologist's training or practice. Lack of resources, especially in isolated rural schools, includes, for example, up-to-date curriculum materials, standardized testing materials, targeted academic intervention materials, specialized programs for students with unique needs, access to specialists, and professional development. One rural school psychologist said to us:

> Small/remote schools don't have as many resources [e.g., counselors, full-time administrators, interventionists, community resources], so I get creative with recommendations and often feel obligated to pick up slack by providing more direct service. I've learned to plan ahead since it is inconvenient to get materials on short notice. (Goforth & Beebe-Frankenberger, 2012)

Because of the Internet, information can more easily be accessed once educators are aware of what is needed. For instance, the U.S. Department of Education report on distance education in public high schools states that in 2009–2010, 53% of U.S. high school districts had students enrolled in distance education courses, and rural schools reported that 61% of distance courses were delivered by postsecondary sources (National Center for Educational Statistics, 2010). Rural schools are finding ways to fill in some of the gaps but continue to need support. Keeping abreast of new innovations and staying informed is incumbent upon the rural school psychologist as a way to provide this support.

Some of the websites we feel are particularly helpful to stay abreast of professional issues and materials include the NASP Online Rural School Psychology Interest Group (http://www.nasponline.org/about_nasp/interestgroups.aspx); NASP resources (http://www.nasponline.org/resources); School Psychology Resources Online (http://www.schoolpsychology.net); School Psychologist Files (http://www.schoolpsychologistfiles.com); School Psychologist Resources for Parents, Teachers, and Psychologists (http://school-psychology.org); the National Center on Response to Intervention (http://www.rti4success.org); and the Center for Effective Collaboration and Practice (http://cecp.air.org). Academic, behavioral, and social–emotional related websites of importance include Literacy Resources for School Psychologists (http://www.readingrockets.org/audience/professionals/schoolpsychologists); Intervention Central (http://www.interventioncentral.org); the American Foundation for Suicide Prevention (http://www.afsp.org); the Center for the Study and Prevention of Violence (http://www.colorado.edu/cspv); UCLA School Mental Health Project (http://smhp.psych.ucla.edu); and Collaborative for Academic, Social, and Emotional Learning (http://casel.org). Similarly, technological tools that are helpful to school psychologists for implementing best practice in rural schools include iPad/iPhone applications such as School Psychology Tools, Behavioral Assessment Application, PAR Assessment Toolkit, Behavior Tracker Pro, and EverNote Organizational Tool. Finally, skills-based training and informative seminars are available through webinars, podcasts, and audio articles sponsored by NASP, while targeted training is offered by several universities through on demand Web-based video and PowerPoint, such as the Iris Peabody College of Education at Vanderbilt University (http://iris.peabody.vanderbilt.edu). Training podcasts are also available through the PsychFiles (http://www.thepsychfiles.com) and ShrinkRap Radio (http://shrinkrapradio.com), to name just a few.

SUMMARY

There is a scarcity of recent literature that describes the delivery of school psychological services in rural settings. We contend that school psychologists who practice in rural areas are more similar to urban and suburban school psychologists in respect to professional skills and the use of these skills in practice. It is the context that differentiates the professional roles, benefits, and challenges of being a school psychologist in a rural setting. Our intent with this chapter was to inform those who wish to consider working in a rural context and to promote best practice and support for our rural school psychologists. We hope the information we provided, along with the words and wisdom of practicing rural school psychologists, have achieved our purpose. We conclude here with a comment from a rural school psychologist who participated in a focus group we headed. We prompted the group with "Share with us one humorous or joyful experience you've had as a school psychologist." A rural school psychologist said: "I knew I was truly a rural school psychologist on my first day in the field when I saw a man and woman chasing a cow down the street."

REFERENCES

Brown, M. B., & Bolen, L. M. (2003). School-based health centers: Strategies for meeting the physical and mental health needs of children and families. *Psychology in the Schools, 40*, 279–287. doi:10.1002/pits.10084

Clopton, K. L., & Knesting, K. (2006). Rural school psychology: Re-opening the discussion. *Journal of Research in Rural Education, 21*(5), 1–11, Retrieved from http://www.jrre.psu.edu/articles/21-5.pdf

Curtis, M. J., Castillo, J. M., & Gelley, C. (2012). School psychology 2010: Demographics, employment, and the context for professional practices—Part 1. *Communiqué, 40*(7), 28–30.

Economic Research Service. (2012). *Rural America at a glance: 2012 edition.* Washington, DC: Author. Retrieved from http://www.ers.usda.gov/publications/eb-economic-brief/cb21.aspx

Everett, S., Sugai, G., Fallon, L., Simonsen, B., & O'Keeffe, B. (2011). *School-wide Tier 2 interventions: Check-in/Check-out getting started workbook.* Retrieved from http://www.pbis.org/common/pbisresources/presentations/8APBS_Tier2_GettingStartedWorkbook.pdf

Fagan, T. K., & Hughes, J. (1985). Rural school psychology: perspectives on lessons learned and future directions. *School Psychology Review, 14*, 444–451.

Goforth, A. N., & Beebe-Frankenberger, M. (2012). *Roles and responsibilities of urban, suburban, and rural school psychologists: Preliminary study data.* Unpublished manuscript.

Goforth, A. N., Beebe-Frankenberger, M., & Yosai, E. (2013, February). *Roles and responsibilities of rural school psychologists.* Poster presented at the national conference of the National Association of School Psychologists, Seattle, WA.

Gustafson, D. T., Preston, K., & Hudson, J. (2009). *Mental health: Overlooked and disregarded in rural America.* Lyon, NE: Center for Rural Affairs. Retrieved from http://www.cfra.org

Helbok, C. M., Marinelli, R. P., & Walls, R. T. (2006). National survey of ethical practices across rural and urban communities. *Professional Psychology: Research and Practice, 37*, 36–44. doi:10.1037/0003-066x.47.12.1597

Helge, D. (1985). The school psychologist in the rural education context. *School Psychology Review, 14*, 402–420.

Jacob, S., Decker, D. M., & Hartshorne, T. S. (2010). *Ethics and law for school psychologists*. (6th ed.). Hoboken, NJ: Wiley.

Jimerson, L. (2006). *The Hobbit effect: Why small works in public schools*. Washington, DC: Rural School and Community Trust. Retrieved from http://www.ruraledu.org

Moore, C. G., Mink, M., Probst, J. C., Tompkins, M., Johnson, A., & Hughley, S. (2005). *Mental health risk factors, unmet needs and provider availability for rural children*. Columbia, SC: South Carolina Rural Health. Retrieved from http://rhr.sph.sc.edu/report/scrhrc_mh_risk_children_exec_sum.pdf

Murimi, M. W., & Harpel, T. (2010). Practicing preventive health: The underlying culture among low income rural populations. *Journal of Rural Health, 26*, 273–282.

National Association of School Psychologists. (2010). *Model for comprehensive and integrated school psychological services*. Bethesda, MD: Author. Retrieved from http://www.nasponline.org/standards/2010standards/2_PracticeModel.pdf

National Center for Education Statistics. (2012). *The condition of education*. (NCES 2012-045). Washington, DC: U.S. Department of Education. Retrieved from http://nces.ed.gov/fastfacts/display.asp?id=79

O'Hare, W. (2009). Poverty is persistent reality for many rural children in U.S. Washington, DC: Population Reference Bureau. Retrieved from http://www.prb.org/Publications/Articles/2009/ruralchildpoverty.aspx

Reschley, D. J., & Connolly, L. M. (1990). Comparisons of school psychologists in the city and country: Is there a "rural" school psychology? *School Psychology Review, 19*, 534–549.

Rudzitis, G. (2001). Amenities increasingly draw people to the rural west. *Rural Development Perspectives, 14*, 9–13, Retrieved from http://www.colorado.edu/AmStudies/lewis/west/amenities.pdf

Rural School and Community Trust. (2012). *Why rural matters 2011–2012: The condition of rural education in the 50 states*. Washington, DC: Author. Retrieved from http://www.ruraledu.org/articles.php?id=2820

Starr, S., Campbell, L. R., & Herrick, C. A. (2002). Factors affecting use of the mental health system by rural children. *Issues in Mental Health Nursing, 23*, 291–304. doi:10.1080/016128402753543027

Substance Abuse and Mental Health Services Administration Center. (2012). *A comparison of rural and urban substance abuse treatment admissions*. Rockville, MD: Author.

Sue, D. W. (2001). Multidimensional facets of cultural competence. *The Counseling Psychologist, 29*, 790–821. doi:10.1177/0011000001296002

Sullivan, A. L. (2011). Disproportionality in special education identification and placement of English language learners. *Exceptional Children, 77*, 317–334.

U.S. Census Bureau. (2010). *Census 2010 urban and rural classification*. Washington, DC: Author. Retrieved from http://www.census.gov/geo/reference/ua/urban-rural-2010.html

Van Gundy, K. (2006). *Substance abuse in rural and small town America*. Durham, NH: The Carsey Institute. Retrieved from http://carseyinstitute.unh.edu/publication/substance-abuse-rural-and-small-town-america

Weist, M. D., Goldstein, A., Morris, L., & Bryant, T. (2003). Integrating expanded school mental health programs and school-based health centers. *Psychology in the Schools, 40*, 297–308. doi:10.1002/pits.10089

Yoshikawa, H., Aber, J. L., & Beardslee, W. R. (2012). The effects of poverty on the mental, emotional, and behavioral health of children and youth: Implications for prevention. *American Psychologist, 67*, 272–284. doi:10.1037/a0028015

12 Best Practices in Working With Homeless Students in Schools

Brenda Kabler
Immaculata University (PA)
Elana Weinstein
Interboro (PA) School District
Philadelphia College of Osteopathic Medicine
Ruth T. Joffe
Upper Darby (PA) School District

OVERVIEW

More than 1.6 million children (1 in 45) are homeless in America. Families that are homeless are found throughout the United States in both urban and rural areas. Children who are homeless have been described as having lost privacy, safety, the comforts of home and friends, regular routines, possessions, pets, and communities. Not surprisingly, these children have disproportionately high rates of chronic health conditions, asthma, traumatic stress, and emotional problems when compared to their housed counterparts (National Center on Family Homelessness, 2011).

This chapter will help school psychologists to develop a better understanding of the unique needs of homeless children using the guiding principles of the domain of Diversity in Development and Learning in the National Association of School Psychologist (NASP) *Model for Comprehensive and Integrated School Psychological Services* (NASP, 2010).

Public schools are the only institutions that are legally responsible for identifying and serving children who are homeless. The McKinney-Vento Homeless Assistance Act, Subtitle VII-B, passed in 1987 and reauthorized as part of the No Child Left Behind Act (NCLB) in 2001, is designed to increase the school enrollment, attendance, and success of children and youth experiencing homelessness. It establishes educational rights for students who are homeless. This chapter will outline provisions of

this law and practices for implementation in the school setting, with the focus on the school psychologist's role. Given the overlap between homelessness and other challenges, including poverty, foster care placement, and migrant and immigrant status, much of the information in this chapter may apply to school psychologists working with those populations as well. Schools may be the one place where youth who are homeless have consistency and continuity (Miller, 2009).

Definition of Homelessness

The McKinney-Vento Act and NCLB (Title X, Part C) consider homeless children and youth as "individuals who lack a fixed, regular, and adequate nighttime residence." This includes children and youth who are (a) sharing the housing of other persons due to the loss of housing, economic hardship, or a similar reason (sometimes referred to as "doubled-up"); (b) living in motels, hotels, trailer parks, or campgrounds due to lack of alternative accommodations; (c) living in emergency or transitional shelters; (d) living or abandoned in hospitals; (e) awaiting foster care placement; (f) using a primary nighttime residence that is a public or private place not designated for, or ordinarily used as, a regular sleeping accommodation for human beings; and (g) living in cars, parks, public spaces, abandoned buildings, substandard housing, bus or train stations, or similar settings.

Provisions of the Federal Law

The McKinney-Vento Act contains many provisions designed to support the education of children and youth experiencing homelessness. The law specifically mandates provision of services to preschool- and school-age children as well as unaccompanied youth. Listed below are key provisions of the law:

- Students who are homeless can remain in one school if that is in their best interest, even if their living situation is located in another district or attendance area.
- School districts must provide transportation to school.
- Children and youth who are homeless can enroll in school and begin attending within 48 hours of registration, even if they are unable to produce normally required documents, such as birth certificates, proof of guardianship, immunization records, or proof of residency.
- Every Local Education Agency (LEA, more commonly referred to as a school district) must designate a homeless liaison to ensure that the McKinney-Vento Act is implemented in the school district. Homeless liaisons must conduct outreach efforts to identify homeless youth, assist them with school enrollment, and refer them to health and other community services. Liaisons must also report the number of students who are identified as homeless to state coordinators.
- Every state must designate a coordinator to ensure the McKinney-Vento Act is implemented and that mandated reporting procedures are followed.
- State coordinators and homeless liaisons must collaborate with other agencies serving homeless youth and families to enhance educational attendance and success.
- State and local agencies must review and revise their policies and practices to eliminate barriers to the school enrollment and attendance of homeless children and youth.

Implementation

The responsibility for implementing the McKinney-Vento Act lies with school districts. However, there is no designated funding source to facilitate implementation. The law stipulates that every LEA must appoint a homeless liaison to ensure that homeless students have access to school and that the numbers of homeless students are reported to state coordinators. However, no formalized training has been developed for this position. Thus, inconsistencies in role performance exist across districts. The McKinney-Vento Act requirements are unlike the Child Find provisions of the Individuals with Disabilities in Education Improvement Act in that implementation relies on self-disclosure on the part of homeless families and youth. Persistent stigma about homelessness is a deterrent to self-disclosure, causing members of this population to "hide" from those individuals who would help them. School psychologists can assume the role of homeless liaison or they can work collaboratively with other professionals appointed to fill this role. The goal is to expedite appropriate identification and enrollment as well as to ensure that homeless students receive the supports they need to be successful in school.

Access to School

According to the provisions of the McKinney-Vento Act, students may stay in their school of origin during their entire period of homelessness even if they move to permanent housing in another location. Students also have the option of transferring to the school district in which they are currently living without required documents, such as school records, medical records, or proof of residency. It is appropriate for school personnel to make continued efforts to access student information from previous schools without disrupting the attendance of the student. Under the McKinney-Vento Act, a student is considered enrolled if the student is attending classes and participating in school activities. Transportation is one of the school services the McKinney-Vento Act guarantees to homeless students. A lack of transportation can be a significant impediment to school attendance.

Mandated Reporting

The first step in helping homeless students is to identify these students (Saxberg, 2011). The McKinney-Vento Act requires that all state education agencies and LEAs collect and submit information to the U.S. Department of Education about the numbers of identified homeless students enrolled in all local school districts in the state during the academic year (National Center for Homeless Education, 2008). The McKinney-Vento Act requirement for data collection represents the only comprehensive census of homeless students attending public schools.

The National Center for Homeless Education (2008) identifies several reporting problems with the national homelessness database. The main problem is that the database does not include all homeless students. It includes only students enrolled in public school and identified by school personnel as homeless (National Center on Family Homelessness, 2011). It does not include students enrolled in school who are unknown to be homeless because of issues of self-disclosure, lack of awareness of homelessness among school staff, or unfamiliarity with the U.S. Department of Education data collection requirements, which are relatively new. Reporting problems can also be accounted for by an inadequate number of liaisons and funding in large, urban districts, which have an impact on outreach and identification efforts. Participation in the data submission process is inconsistent, and in 2008 only 87% of LEAs across the United States submitted data on student homelessness (National Center for Homeless Education, 2008). These issues likely result in an underrepresentation of the numbers of homeless students in the national homeless database (National Center for Homeless Education, 2008). Given these problematic reporting issues, the best estimate of the number of homeless children in the United States is 933,572 school-age children and 676,035 preschool age children (National Center on Family Homelessness, 2011). The high number of homeless children and families likely results from the most recent economic crisis, home foreclosures, and natural disasters across the United States.

BASIC CONSIDERATIONS

Recent statistics reveal that 43% of homeless families are African American, 38% are White/non-Hispanic, 15% are Hispanic, and 3% are Native American (Bassuk, 2010; Bassuk, Volk, & Olivet, 2010; National Center on Family Homelessness, 2011). Homeless families are located throughout the United States. According to the U.S. Conference of Mayors (2009) the four main reasons reported in 2009 for family homelessness were lack of affordable housing (74%), poverty (52%), unemployment (44%), and domestic violence (44%). States with the highest percentage of homeless children are generally located in the south and southwest, reflecting the higher level of poverty in these regions. States with the lowest percentage of homeless children are generally located in the north and northeast, where there is less poverty and stronger social supports for children (National Center for Homeless Education, 2011). Fifty percent of children without homes are under the age of 5 (U.S. Conference of Mayors, 2009).

Factors Leading to Homelessness

"The path that leads to homelessness is traumatic" (Bassuk, 2010). Homelessness is associated with numerous, intertwining, and stressful circumstances. Extreme poverty, lack of affordable housing, lack of social supports, domestic violence or other kinds of trauma, mental illness, and foster care placement are the main factors that contribute to homelessness. These issues are interrelated and are discussed below in more detail.

Poverty

Homeless young people are a subpopulation of the more than 12.3 million children living in poverty in the United States (Eckholm, 2007). Single parent families are among the poorest in the country and are therefore more vulnerable to homelessness. Homeless mothers frequently have limited education, are unemployed, and have been the victims of severe physical or sexual abuse. These women often have childhood histories of having lived outside their own homes in foster care placement and may have experienced physical and mental health problems (Bassuk, 2010; Bassuk et al., 2010; Julianelle, 2007; National Center on Family Homelessness, 2011).

Housing Insecurity

Housing insecurity is associated with high rates of mobility and homelessness; 97% of homeless children move up to three times within a single year (National Center on Family Homelessness, 2011). Before turning to shelters, most families double-up in overcrowded apartments with relatives or friends (Bassuk, 2010). According to the National Center on Family Homelessness (2011), the U.S. Census counted more than 6 million doubled-up households nationwide in 2009, a 12% increase above 2008 levels. In the course of a year, 1 of every 10 of those doubled-up households can be expected to experience homelessness. Other families may stay in motel rooms or campgrounds or sleep in cars (National Center on Family Homelessness, 2011). Homeless families are often forced to split up, placing children with family members, friends, or in foster care (Barrow & Lawinski, 2009).

Foster Care Placement

Foster care placement is strongly associated with homelessness. Across the country, 26% of homeless adults, 34% of homeless young people ages 20–24, and 61% of homeless youth 18–19 years of age have spent time in foster care. In contrast, only 3% of the overall population have lived in foster care (Juliannelle, 2007). Mothers with histories of foster care placement are more likely to become homeless and tend to become homeless at earlier ages than those who do not have a history of foster care placement (Bassuk et al., 2010; National Center on Family Homelessness, 2011). Some studies indicate that one in five youth in foster care at age 16 run away from their placements and become homeless (Juliannelle, 2007).

Unaccompanied Youth

Unaccompanied youth, or minors who live on their own, are differentiated from homeless children living with their parents (Aratani, 2009; Julianelle, 2007). Unaccompanied youth may live on their own for a variety of reasons. Runaways may leave home of their own accord without permission, as they are often the victims of physical or sexual abuse and choose to run away from unsafe situations. Throwaways, or rejected youth, may be encouraged to leave home or are actively prevented from returning home. Parental rejection often stems from disapproval of teen pregnancy or sexual orientation. In one study, 20–40% of homeless youth identified themselves as LGBTQ (Lesbian, Gay, Bisexual, Transgender and Questioning) in contrast to 3–5% of the general population (Julianelle, 2007). Among all unaccompanied youth, African American and Native American youth are represented in higher than expected numbers. Females are less likely to be rejected, but are more likely to run away (Aratani, 2009).

Impact of Homelessness

In order to address the needs of homeless students, school psychologists must consider the underlying physical and psychosocial factors specific to this population.

Physical Health Challenges

Compared with low-income children who have homes, homeless children often exhibit higher rates of acute and chronic health problems. These problems can include increased rates of respiratory, infectious, and gastro-intestinal diseases. These children may also suffer from increased incidence of otitis media (inflammation of the inner ear), diarrhea, bronchitis, and dental cavities. Dermatologic concerns include scabies and lice. Another common problem is food insecurity, which leads to malnutrition, stunting, and obesity (Briggs,

2013). In addition to these problems, unaccompanied youth often are at risk for sexually transmitted infections, teen pregnancy, substance abuse, depression, and suicide (Aratani, 2009; Juliannelle, 2007).

Academic and Social–Emotional–Behavioral Issues

Compared with students in stable housing, homeless students exhibit four times the rate of delays in social–emotional and academic functioning (Wynne et al., 2013). Compared with their peers, they score 16% lower on tests of reading and math (National Center on Family Homelessness, 2011). These issues are especially problematic for children who have moved more than three times. Each housing change potentially sets a student back 4–6 months academically (Wynne et al., 2013). In one study, 60% of children who fell behind in school experienced extended periods of homelessness with multiple housing moves and irregular school attendance (McAuley, 2011). These children may be English language learners, have parents with mental health issues, or may have been exposed to violence (Aratani, 2009; Bassuk, 2010; Bassuk et al., 2010; National Center on Family Homelessness, 2011). These factors can compound the negative impact of homelessness on school performance.

Homeless children are frequently the victims of inadequate parenting, as their mothers, who are often single without social supports, frequently suffer from a host of physical and emotional problems, including high rates of posttraumatic stress disorder, drug and alcohol dependence, and medical problems (Aratani, 2009; Bassuk, 2010; Bassuk et al., 2010; National Center on Family Homelessness, 2011). These issues may make it difficult for homeless parents to provide their children with the basic necessities of food, clothing, and shelter. These issues also make it challenging for parents to interact appropriately with their children, to respond sensitively to their children's emotional needs, and to foster feelings of safety and security. Compounding these problems is the public nature of parenting in shelters, where the lack of privacy can undermine a parent's confidence in his or her parenting (Swick, 2009). In turn, poor parenting has deleterious effects on a child's ability to form supportive and trusting relationships with others (Bassuk, 2010). Parents with limited education often have difficulty supporting their children academically, thus further disadvantaging them (Moore & McArthur, 2011).

The experience of many homeless youth and their parents fits the definition of complex trauma or repetitive, prolonged exposure to stress that occurs at vulnerable periods of development (Bassuk, 2010; Bassuk et al., 2010; Ford & Courtois, 2009). In response to this type of trauma, many children exhibit hyperarousal and hypervigilance in an attempt to avoid additional trauma. They also develop a distrust of and detachment from relationships, display emotional dysregulation, and demonstrate aggressive, antisocial, and fearful behavior. Consequences of complex trauma include problems with executive function, including difficulties with attention, short- and long-term memory for events, anticipatory planning, and follow through (Bassuk et al., 2010; Ford & Courtois, 2009). These problems may interfere with the ability of these children to learn and ultimately with their chances for success in life (National Center on Family Homelessness, 2011).

Developmental Considerations

Once reaching elementary school age, the task for most children is skill mastery and the development of a sense of competence (Erikson, 1968). The loss of possessions and disrupted relationships resulting from homelessness, in addition to transiency and housing instability, can interfere with skill acquisition and leave children feeling inadequate. Poor executive functioning and the developmental regression associated with complex trauma may also disrupt development of skill mastery (Ford & Courtois, 2009).

Normal adolescent social development involves the formation of identity and individuation from authority (Erikson, 1968). In order to survive, homeless youth must attach to new caregivers and forge new adult and peer relationships when they otherwise would be securing separation from parents or caregivers in their progression to adulthood. Thus, development is stunted and the experience of homelessness is exacerbated (Chittooran & Chittooran, 2010).

Protective Factors

Factors that may protect children from the adverse impact of homelessness often have to do with the functioning of their parents and guardians. Fewer housing moves, shorter periods of homelessness, and absence of exposure to physical and sexual violence are important factors for academic, social, emotional, and behavioral functioning. Characteristics of resilience also play an important role in determining successful long-term outcomes for homeless students (Bassuk, 2010; McAuley, 2011).

Parents and guardians with good mental health and good coping skills may be in a better position to provide effective parenting in spite of housing circumstances. The ability of a parent or caregiver to inspire feelings of safety and security is significant in a child's ability to recover from the trauma often attendant to homelessness. In one study, homeless children who experienced fewer housing moves, whose parents accessed crisis or transitional accommodations quickly and avoided school disruption, met with academic success. Children who were younger and received appropriate support coped better in terms of their emotional adjustment and adaptation to new school environments than those who were older at the time of homelessness (McAuley, 2011).

Protective factors for homeless children also include the structure and stability of the school system (Chittooran & Chittooran, 2010; Moore & McArthur, 2011). With positive relationships and a strong connection to a school system, students can develop characteristics of resilience that can enable them to negotiate periods of homelessness successfully (Bassuk, 2010).

BEST PRACTICES IN WORKING WITH HOMELESS STUDENTS IN SCHOOLS

Best practices for school psychologists working with the homeless student population primarily involve advocacy and support that can be implemented using a multi-tiered model. Empirically based research on the effectiveness of these practices is sparse, due to problems with identification and reporting, discussed above, the high rates of mobility in this population, as well as the need to maintain confidentiality. Universal interventions include the promotion of systems that ensure adherence to the McKinney-Vento Act. They also include the creation of environments that are accepting, rather than stigmatizing, and the establishment of relationships between schools, agencies, and parents that result in proactive collaboration (Murphy & Tobin, 2011). Universal supports and interventions can be provided to district and school personnel as well as parents and students.

Targeted interventions focus on delivery of services and support to homeless students and their families. Intensive interventions are individualized based on student need, including basic health and physical services and academic and social–emotional–behavioral supports. Monitoring of the effectiveness of these interventions is likely to be best accomplished through curriculum-based assessments or other brief, frequent, and specific measures, given issues of transiency and mobility.

Universal Interventions

At the universal level, the legal requirements of the McKinney-Vento Act must be implemented school-wide. School psychologists can conduct training sessions to educate administrators and professional and non-professional staff in these requirements. Aspects of the McKinney-Vento Act that should be highlighted for school personnel include enrollment and identification of homeless students, district transportation requirements, and school choice opportunities. School psychologists can help create culturally sensitive environments that are supportive. These environments can be created through diversity training, advocacy, referral systems to outside agencies, confidentiality safeguards, sensitivity awareness, and procedures for stigma reduction. Wynne et al. (2013) at Loyola University of Chicago's School of Education have developed a PowerPoint presentation that can be used at the universal level for staff training in the issues of homelessness in schools. This group has also created screening tools that can be used at the universal level for identification and enrollment purposes. Once homeless students are identified and their needs clarified, staff can implement interventions at the targeted and intensive levels.

Parents

Parents of homeless students need to be apprised of their rights under the McKinney-Vento Act. Owing to the stigma around their living situation and many other obstacles to self-identification, efforts to educate parents about their rights should be made in as confidential and nonthreatening a manner as possible. Wynne et al. (2013) have also developed resources for parents (http://www.schoolresourcesforhomelessfamilies.org) that can be distributed along with other registration materials at the time of enrollment to inform parents of their rights in as comfortable a way as possible. To address the problem of students who become homeless after they have enrolled in school, school psychologists can conduct workshops to disseminate information to parents, such as homeless identification criteria as well as rights to school choice, transportation, and access to education support services (Kabler & Weinstein, 2009; Murphy & Tobin, 2011). Parents may also benefit from information about where to obtain skill training and

continuing education for themselves and other children in the family. Resources can be provided to parents to help them access community services and resources, such as medical care, food, and shelter (Chittooran & Chittooran, 2010; Gibson & Morphett, 2011). School psychologists may find the need to refer parents to the National Center for Homeless Education toll-free help line: (800) 308-2145 (http://center.serve.org/nche or e-mail homeless@serve.org).

Students

The identification of homeless students requires sensitivity on the part of all school personnel, due to associated insecurity and shame around nighttime residence and lack of basic needs. Students can play a role in identifying themselves as homeless when approached in a discreet manner.

Identification of homeless status. Wynne et al. (2013) offer a questionnaire for students, similar to the one mentioned above for parents, that aims at homeless identification in a sensitive manner, asking, for example, if the student lives with family members other than his or her parents rather than inquiring specifically if he or she is homeless. For those who disclose that they are unaccompanied youth, referrals to the child welfare system through appropriate channels must be made immediately.

School access. Once students have been identified as homeless, universal interventions include compliance with the McKinney-Vento Act requirements for access to school and a Free and Appropriate Public Education, either in the district of previous enrollment or in the district of current residence. Transportation must be provided, even across districts to and from shelters. In urban districts where vouchers are provided for public transportation, safety issues must be considered.

Promotion of resilience. Participation in extra-curricular and after school programs is important for homeless students in maintaining peer relationships and social supports. These factors are critical for the development of resilience, which contributes to academic and personal success. School psychologists can implement programs on district- and school-wide levels to promote resilience as well as other aspects of positive psychology. Types of programs include those originating from the University of Pennsylvania's Positive Psychology Center (http://www.ppc.sas.upenn.edu), which provides information about resilience training for schools. An example of this type of program is Fishful Thinking (http://www.goldfishsmiles.com), which teaches positive thinking and optimism.

Targeted Interventions

As compared with universal interventions, which are broad based and primarily informational in nature, targeted interventions promote effective service provision. School psychologists can hold intake meetings upon enrollment of homeless students in order to gather basic information, such as educational history, the necessary supports for basic needs, and classroom accommodations (MacGillivray, Ardell, & Curwen, 2010). School psychologists should monitor the progress of these students closely in order to quickly implement supports for attendance, lateness, and falling grades. School psychologists can work collaboratively with administrators, teachers, and other school professionals to secure free and reduced breakfast and lunch programs and school uniforms. They can work to eliminate additional fees, such as those typically charged for calculators, laboratory use, and school trips. School psychologists should be aware of the federally funded programs for health and dental care and vision services, such as Medicaid, the American Dental Association, and the Lion's Club that offer free services for homeless students. School psychologists may also want to work with school staff to arrange for older students to have access to school showers, lockers, and laundry facilities.

Parents

Parents of homeless students may need to be empowered so they can advocate for their own needs as well as those of their children. The transitory nature of their life circumstances makes it difficult for homeless families to establish ways for schools and other agencies to contact them. Schools can provide the use of a mailbox, telephones, and the Internet for the purpose of communication. School psychologists can assess the need for parent support groups and counseling services to address the many issues of homeless students. They can advocate for child-care programs before school and after school, which can ensure safe and secure environments for homeless children. Providing access to transportation for parents to school for meetings, conferences, and various functions serves to establish important connections and build trusting relationships with parents.

Students

School psychologists can assist school personnel in understanding the academic and behavioral needs that arise when children suffer housing instability. In order to create an atmosphere of sensitivity, teachers can be encouraged to protect the physical space of homeless students in the classroom. A desk or cubby becomes a "home" for a homeless student who lacks personal space outside of the school setting (Gargiulo, 2006). For this population, cooperative and hands-on learning activities, active involvement, and group work are effective, as are peer buddies or tutors (Chittooran & Chittooran, 2010).

Lacking a consistent and quiet place to work after school hours, homeless students are frequently unprepared for class and are unable to complete homework assignments. To address this problem, school psychologists may want to develop plans for teachers to shorten assignments or to identify alternatives for completing homework. One approach is to provide homeless students with access to computers and the Internet before or after school hours. Flexibility with regard to due dates and format requirements may maximize the chances that these students complete their work. For example, permitting students to hand-write papers rather than insisting on the use of a computer is a reasonable accommodation, as is shortening the amount of homework, perhaps by assigning only even-numbered problems (MacGillivray et al., 2010). Providing shorter, focused learning experiences, chunking assignments into smaller units that can be completed expediently, and allowing students to start and complete homework during the school day are individualized approaches that work well for this population (Murphy & Tobin, 2011). In addition to completing homework, it is often difficult for homeless children to obtain parent signatures on assignments and tests. Teachers may want the school psychologist to assume responsibility for signatures and for communicating with parents about results. Flexibility for grading purposes is critical at all school levels for homeless students. Providing students with choices for projects and multiple methods for credit are examples of this kind of flexibility (Chittooran & Chittooran, 2010).

Intensive Interventions

The skill set of school psychologists places them in a unique position to help homeless students within a school system. School psychologists can communicate effectively and collaboratively with parents, staff, and outside agencies, and they can respond immediately to academic and social–emotional–behavioral problems in a sensitive and confidential manner.

In most school settings, child study teams, student support teams, and student assistance teams make referrals to the school psychologist when students are at risk for academic and social–emotional–behavioral problems. Given the negative impact of high rates of mobility, transiency, and trauma on the successful functioning of homeless students (Aratani, 2009; Bassuk, 2010; Bassuk et al., 2010; McAuley, 2011; National Center on Family Homelessness, 2011), it is necessary for these teams to collaborate to support these students. The role of the school psychologist is essential to identify specific types of programming, based on need.

Parents

School psychologists should connect with parents of homeless students to establish relationships in order to better support homeless students in schools. If parents cannot travel to school because of a lack of transportation, school psychologists may offer to visit the shelter in order to meet with parents. It is vital that parents know that their opinions about their children are valued.

Students

School psychologists can provide academic support by assisting school personnel in obtaining records promptly. Review of these records, along with academic screening and possible evaluations, are important to determine student needs, which then lead to provision of appropriate services and placements. Possible services include Title I supports, gifted education, special education, 504 Service Agreement Plans, and response to intervention. Working with administrators, school psychologists can create academic supports and interventions that will help reduce the dropout rate and decrease grade retention.

Owing to frequent moves and other risk factors associated with being homeless, it is common for this population of students to be absent from school frequently. School psychologists can help develop incentive systems to encourage regular attendance. In addition, they can help contact families to explore reasons for school absences and identify supports that would ameliorate this problem. At the high school level, school psychologists can advocate for flexible polices, such as provision of academic credit for partially completed course work and credit recovery. For example, homeless students attending the Fresno Unified School District are granted one course credit for 15 hours of on-the-job work (Julianelle, 2007). Homeless students may need to access alternative education programs, such as evening high school and work-study experiences.

School psychologists can ensure that programs are implemented to address the social and emotional needs of homeless students to combat a feeling of isolation common in this population (Gibson & Morphett, 2011; Shinn et al., 2008). They can encourage students to participate in school clubs and events, as well as neighborhood activities. As mentioned above, involvement in extracurricular activities can build a connectedness to the school and positive relationships with other students and staff that can lead to continued enrollment in school.

Homeless students need time to talk about their feelings and concerns. Some may need school-based counseling services while others may need more involved mental health services, such as cognitive behavior therapy, provided through community mental health agencies (Markos & Lima, 2003). At the school level, topics for counseling sessions with this student population include ways to cope with stress, anxiety, and trauma; development of trust; self-esteem; internal locus of control; and continuity of relationships (Moore & McArthur, 2011). Counseling sessions can be provided individually or in small groups.

Homeless Case Study

This hypothetical case study presents the details of a family experiencing homelessness and the efforts of school psychologists to provide support to the children and the family.

A mother and her four children fled from the home of her abusive partner in the middle of the night without clothing, basic necessities, and the children's school materials. The family became temporary residents at a shelter for abused women. After 3 months, the family moved to a shelter in a nearby city where they remained for a period of 1 year. Their housing situation improved as the family was able to move to a transitional home.

During their period of homelessness, which extended for 15 months, the children remained in their original schools within their home school district. Their mother felt that the stability of remaining in the same schools with the same routine and the same friendships was critical for her children during this stressful period.

Transportation to school from the shelters continued to be provided during these 15 months.

The two oldest children were in high school when the family became homeless. Since that time, the oldest child graduated from high school and attended college. The younger of the high school-age children experienced behavior problems in school. According to his mother, he felt embarrassed about being homeless and isolated himself in the large high school setting. His behavior problems necessitated placement in an alternative school program. He struggled to stay focused in school and to attend class regularly, even with a truncated school day and the limited assignments and schedule created by the school psychologist in this alternative placement. Eventually he dropped out of school and began attending evening classes to obtain his GED.

The two youngest children were enrolled in elementary school. The youngest child was successful in general education in second grade, maintaining appropriate friendships. The fourth-grade child was evaluated for special education services and was eligible for an Individualized Education Program under the educational classification of Emotional Disturbance. Concerns about frequent class disruptions required the school psychologist and teacher to implement an individual classroom behavior plan. A referral was made to the student assistance program (prevention and support services), and mental health supports were secured. With the advocacy of the school psychologist, a psychiatric evaluation was conducted and medication was prescribed. The school psychologist, in collaboration with the school social worker, promoted family therapy with an outside provider. This child's academic performance improved with small group instruction and behavior goals. The child succeeded socially, participated in classroom activities, and had a productive school year.

As illustrated in this case study, interventions implemented by school psychologists in collaboration with school staff can be transformative for a family during a period of homelessness. Changes in a student's program, goals, assignments, and supports can give homeless students opportunities for success. Establishing relationships with students and parents is critical in facilitating this process.

Open dialogue with the parent led to the following recommendations: Be discreet in working with homeless children. The children are embarrassed and upset with their situation and do not want other students to know what they are experiencing. Be sensitive and aware that the lack of housing may result in frustrations expressed in acting-out behaviors. Allow students time to talk about their feelings and concerns. In contacting parents, be aware that frequent calls from school regarding rule violations, lateness, and missing homework assignments are often ignored because homeless parents are overwhelmed with their situations. When school personnel call these parents, they should offer suggestions for help rather than listing a series of complaints.

Program Example for Homeless Student Populations

The Homeless Student Initiative Program (Pennsylvania Department of Education, 2009) was initially established by the Pennsylvania Department of Education following the enactment of the McKinney-Vento Act. The goal of the program was to keep the lives of homeless students as stable as possible, monitor the numbers of homeless students in the state of Pennsylvania, and provide resources and support to these students and their families. In 2009, an urban school district and local shelters collaborated to support this initiative. The program assisted with school registration and location of records, collaborative referrals to agencies, purchase of school supplies, tutoring, and provision of transportation, including bus tickets for students to attend schools of origin. Preschool and afterschool programming was available. Workshops, newsletters, and parent outreach were also important aspects of this program. The program aimed to increase self-esteem, student motivation, and responsibility (Pennsylvania Department of Education, 2009).

SUMMARY

The state of child homelessness creates life-altering experiences with profound effects. Homeless children face substantial challenges from conception. These children often suffer from multiple health problems, poor nutrition, and educational and social–emotional–behavioral problems. Poverty, lack of affordable housing, and domestic violence can be counterbalanced by protective factors, such as minimized school disruption and positive parenting. As illustrated in this chapter's case study, the school psychologists played a role in supporting the needs of each of the school-age children in the family.

School psychologists working with homeless students have a framework to develop a multitiered system of supports in order to implement the McKinney-Vento Act.

At the universal level, school psychologists should become familiar with the legal requirements of the McKinney-Vento Act and work to implement the requirements at both the district and individual school levels. At the targeted level, general education supports can be provided for school personnel, parents, and students to ensure academic success. At the intensive level of support, school psychologists should intervene on a case-by-case basis to evaluate the need for specific services to reduce the risk of student failure and improve the probability of successful outcomes. Often, these supports require collaboration between school personnel, parents, and outside agencies.

The school psychologist plays a critical role in ensuring that academic, social, emotional, and behavioral supports are provided to homeless students in the school setting. The NASP Practice Model (NASP, 2010), which includes a multitiered system of support services, based on a foundation of sensitivity to diversity in development and learning is best practice for school psychologists working with homeless students in schools.

REFERENCES

Aratani, Y. (2009). *Homeless children and youth: Causes and consequences.* New York, NY: National Center for Children in Poverty. Retrieved from http://homeless.samhsa.gov/ResourceFiles/vthrrc0x.pdf

Barrow, S. M., & Lawinski, T. (2009). Contexts of mother-child separations in homeless families. *Analyses of Social Issues and Public Policy, 9,* 157–176. doi:10.1111/j.1530-2415.2009.01171.x

Bassuk, E. L. (2010). Ending child homelessness in America. *American Journal of Orthopsychiatry, 80,* 496–504. doi:10.1111/j.1939-0025.2010.01052.x

Bassuk, E. L., Volk, K. T., & Olivet, J. (2010). A framework for developing supports and services for families experiencing homelessness. *The Open Health Services and Policy Journal, 3,* 34–40, Retrieved from http://homeless.samhsa.gov/ResourceFiles/eyn4xm01.pdf

Briggs, M. A. (2013). Providing care for children and adolescents facing homelessness and housing insecurity. *Pediatrics, 131,* 1206–1210. doi:10.1542/peds.2013-0645

Chittooran, M. M., & Chittooran, J. T. (2010). Homeless children in the schools. In A. S. Canter, L. Z. Paige, & S. Shaw (Eds.), *Helping children at home and school III.* (S8H19). Bethesda, MD: National Association of School Psychologists.

Eckholm, E. (2007, January 25) Childhood poverty is found to portend high adult costs. *The New York Times,* p. 19A. Retrieved from http://www.nytimes.com/2007/01/25/us/25poverty.html

Erikson, E. H. (1968). *Identity, youth and crisis.* New York, NY: Norton.

Ford, J. D., & Courtois, C. A. (2009). Defining and understanding complex trauma and complex traumatic stress disorders. In C. A. Courtois & J. D. Ford (Eds.), *Treating complex traumatic stress disorders.* New York, NY: Guilford Press.

Gargiulo, R. M. (2006). Homeless and disabled: Rights, responsibilities, and recommendations for serving young children with special needs. *Early Childhood Education Journal, 33,* 357–362. doi:10.1007/s10643-006-0067-1

Gibson, C., & Morphett, K. (2011). Creative responses to the needs of homeless children: Promising practice. *Developing Practice, 28,* 23–31.

Julianelle, P. F. (2007). *The educational success of homeless youth in California: Challenge and solutions.* Sacramento, CA: California Research Bureau, California State Library.

Kabler, B., & Weinstein, E. (2009). The state of homeless children in the United States. *Communiqué, 38*(4), 1, 28–29. Retrieved from http://www.nasponline.org/publications/cq/mocq384homeless.aspx

MacGillivray, L., Ardell, A. L., & Curwen, M. S. (2010). Supporting the literacy development of children living in homeless shelters. *The Reading Teacher, 63,* 384–392. doi:10.1598/RT.63.5.4

Markos, P. A., & Lima, N. R. (2003). Homelessness in the United States and its effect on children. *Guidance Counseling, 18,* 118–124.

McAuley, K. (2011). Joining the dots: Homeless children's experience of education. *Parity, 24,* 19–22.

Miller, P. M. (2009). An examination of the McKinney-Vento Act and its influence on the homeless education situation. *Educational Policy, 25,* 424–450.

Moore, T., & McArthur, M. (2011). "Good for kids": Children who have been homeless talk about school. *Australian Journal of Education, 44,* 147–160.

Murphy, J. F., & Tobin, K. J. (2011). Homelessness comes to school: How homeless children can succeed. *Poverty and Learning, 93,* 32–37.

National Association of School Psychologists. (2010). *Model for comprehensive and integrated school psychological services.* Bethesda, MD: Author. Retrieved from http://www.nasponline.org/standards/2010standards/2_PracticeModel.pdf

National Center for Homeless Education. (2008). *Education for homeless children and youth programs data collection summary.* Greensboro, NC: Author.

National Center on Family Homelessness. (2011). *America's youngest outcasts: 2010: State report card on child homelessness.* Waltham, MA: Author.

Pennsylvania Department of Education. (2009). *Pennsylvania Homeless Student Initiative.* Harrisburg, PA: Author. Retrieved from http://homeless.center-school.org/providers/290/blue_book_final.pdf

Saxberg, D. (2011). No homeless child left behind. *Principal, 90,* 30–33.

Shinn, M., Schteingart, J., Williams, N. C., Carlin-Mathis, J., Bialo-Karagis, N., Becker-Klein, R., & Weitzman, B. C. (2008). Long-term associations of homelessness with children's well-being. *American Behavioral Scientist, 51,* 789–809. doi:10.1177/0002764207311988

Swick, K. J. (2009). Strengthening homeless parents with young children through meaningful parent education and support. *Early Childhood Education, 36,* 327–332. doi:10.1007/s10643-008-0274-z

U.S. Conference of Mayors. (2009). *Hunger and homelessness survey: A status report on hunger and homelessness in America's cities.* Washington, DC: Author. Retrieved from http://usmayors.org/pressreleases/uploads/2012/1219-report-HH.pdf

Wynne, M. E., Ausikaitis, A. E., Loyola University Home–School–Community Research Team. (2013). Addressing the educational needs of homeless students. *Communiqué, 42*(2), 4–6. Retrieved from http://www.nasponline.org/publications/cq/42/2/advocacy.aspx

13 Best Practices in Working With Children Living in Foster Care

Tracey G. Scherr
University of Wisconsin–Whitewater

OVERVIEW

More than 400,000 children reside in foster care in the United States (U.S. Department of Health and Human Services, 2012a). This number has declined consistently (29%) since reaching a peak of 567,000 in 1999 (U.S. Department of Health and Human Services, 2006, 2012b). The reasons for the decrease of children in out-of-home placements are multifaceted and include social work practices and state and federal legislation focused on prevention of maltreatment and placement and improved permanency planning for youth in care. More commonly now than in previous years, courts facilitate goals to reunify children with their families of origin when possible, to terminate parental rights and secure adoptive families if necessary, and to create stable trajectories for children rather than allowing them to linger in more temporary foster homes for countless years.

Although children move from foster care into more permanent arrangements more quickly in recent years, the 400,000 plus children living in foster care still present a unique group of young people. They face particular challenges and could benefit from services of school psychologists. In order to maximize the effectiveness of school psychology services, school psychologists must understand who these students are and why they require comprehensive, consistent assistance at all problem-solving tiers plus additional systemic supports.

The median age of these youth is 8.8 years. There are slightly more males than females living in foster care. Although Caucasian children comprise the largest ethnoracial group in foster care, ethnoracial minorities, primarily African American and Hispanic youth, represent the rest (U.S. Department of Health and Human Services, 2012a).

Most children remain in care a median of 13.5 months. However, a mean stay of 23.9 months indicates some children do remain in foster care for longer periods. Most live in nonrelative or relative family foster homes and other settings such as residential treatment facilities, group homes, and preadoptive homes (U.S. Department of Health and Human Services, 2012a).

Reunification with their parents or other relatives is the permanency goal for most children in foster care, followed by adoption and guardianship. Long-term foster care has been reserved for a small proportion of youth for whom more desirable goals have been deemed implausible. The smallest numbers of children have no goal yet established or else will emancipate (5%) from the foster care system when they "age out" between the ages of 18 and 21 (U.S. Department of Health and Human Services, 2012a). In sum, most children in foster care are elementary age, have ethnoracial minority backgrounds, live in nonrelative or relative family foster homes, remain in care for a year or two, and appear to return to their original homes or are adopted following their foster care experiences.

Working with students living in foster care coincides with the multicultural competencies inherent in the National Association of School Psychologists (NASP) *Model for Comprehensive and Integrated School Psychological Services* (NASP, 2010) domain of Diversity in Development and Learning. Hence, the primary aims of this chapter will be to describe the challenges and outcomes characteristic of youth living in foster care at various developmental points and to identify best practices for school psychologists to maximize the likelihood of more successful futures for these young people. A problem-solving approach that implements multiple tiers of interventions will best meet the unique needs of this population of students.

BASIC CONSIDERATIONS

In addition to understanding demographic characteristics of students in foster care, school psychologists need to consider the educational, behavioral, and mental health challenges and outcomes commonly experienced by these students as well as contributors to risk and resilience. Successful intervention relies on accurate problem identification. Further, legislation influences how schools and social welfare agencies interact with each other, and school psychologists' awareness of legislative requirements will help them better serve students living in foster care.

Education, Behavior, and Mental Health

Researchers in social work, education, and psychology have identified a variety of academic and social–emotional challenges faced by these youth. The psychoeducational difficulties youth in foster care encounter tend to begin early and last long. For example, early literacy delays, especially in phonological awareness, have been found in young children living in foster care (Pears, Heywood, Kim, & Fisher, 2011). Yet, young children in foster care are not guaranteed early childhood intervention or preventive educational programming. They have a greater likelihood of receiving early childhood services if identified with a disability. Availability of prekindergarten education in the school district where they reside and financial status of their biological parents (i.e., subsidized care for impoverished families or ability to pay for wealthier families) and foster parents also influence the likelihood of receipt of early childhood programming (Meloy & Phillips, 2012). Young children in foster care have qualified for Head Start independent of household income.

Specific academic indicators such as special education proportions, grade retention, and disciplinary rates have been reported with some frequency in the corresponding literature. In a meta-analysis of these studies, Scherr (2007) determined 31% of students in foster care qualified for and/or used special education services. This rate compares to a current national average of 13% of children from birth to 21 years of age qualifying for and receiving special education services (Aud et al., 2012). Students living in foster care have been disproportionately represented in special education, especially considering gaps in education are an exclusionary factor for educational disability identification.

Relatively poor psychoeducational outcomes have been demonstrated for students in special education as well as for students in foster care. Additive risk must be considered for students who share both experiences. Maltreatment risk increases for students with disabilities, with greatest risk for children with emotional–behavioral disabilities and with cognitive disabilities. However, there is a lack of consistent data regarding proportions of children in foster care who also have disabilities due to inconsistent reporting (Lightfoot, Hill, & LaLiberte, 2011). Some research has determined that youth with disabilities tend to remain in foster care for longer periods of time and experience more transiency in placements than their peers living in foster care without disabilities (Hill, 2012).

Owing to mobility, including days, weeks, or months away from school during placement changes, and lack of identified educational advocates across child welfare agencies and local education agencies, students in foster care with Individualized Education Programs (IEP) frequently suffer from discontinuity in and lacking coordination of services across child protection and school domains. Students may move in the middle of an assessment process, and records may not accompany them. Time gets wasted, and redundant assessments occur. If the student's special education status is unknown, current IEPs are not implemented at all or implementation is delayed until an IEP surfaces, a new evaluation is completed, or a student is referred for evaluation due to their challenges at the receiving school. In districts where response to intervention has been implemented, prereferral interventions are interrupted, and documentation rarely follows children to their receiving school.

Concurrently, there may be a lack of understanding about who to involve in the child's educational decision making from the school's perspective, and child welfare agents and foster parents may lack knowledge of school systems and special educations processes, might feel unwelcome in schools, and often need to prioritize more immediate child safety and permanency planning over educational and mental health concerns. Regardless of special educational needs, school moves interrupt curriculum and sever attachments to educators and peers. For older students, school changes can result in lost credits toward graduation for youth who already encounter multiple hurdles to completion of secondary education.

In addition to disproportionate representation in special education, it is estimated that approximately 33% of fostered children have been retained at least once during their academic careers (Scherr, 2007). Estimates of grade retention rates in the broader population of students have varied significantly over the years, depending on the source of the data. Current estimates reflect that 10% of older high school age students have been retained at some point during their academic careers (NASP, 2011). Based on data available at the time, Scherr (2007) concluded children living in foster care appeared to be retained at rates comparable to their peers. That assertion should be reevaluated using more recent estimates of grade retention overall and with youth in foster care in particular. Given the clearly established limited effectiveness of retention as an academic "intervention," the relationship between retention and such deleterious outcomes as increased high school dropout (NASP, 2011), and the probable overlap between special education service provision and retention among fostered children, there is reason for concern about such outcomes.

Further, children who live in foster care seem to be disciplined more frequently in the academic setting than their peers. Approximately 24% of children living in foster care have been suspended or expelled at least once (Scherr, 2007). This proportion compares to a current national figure of 7% annually (Planty et al., 2009). Annual comparison statistics specific to children in foster care are not available, yet the negative effects of suspension and expulsion on academic achievement have been delineated in the literature. The apparent inequality between groups may be due to negative assumptions being made when foster children enter school. However, children living in foster care face numerous social–emotional difficulties that may manifest themselves in challenging behaviors.

These myriad obstacles affect receipt of education and result in the majority of students emancipating from foster care without a high school diploma or GED, and the effects of educational underachievement reverberate for years. The Midwest Evaluation of the Adult Functioning of Former Foster Youth is one of the most recent, comprehensive longitudinal studies of outcomes for young adults who emancipated from the foster care system in three midwestern states. Outcome data for hundreds of young people have been collected from participants from ages 17 to 26. Prior to emancipation, only 15% of participants had earned a high school diploma or GED, with a substantial increase to 66% at age 19. By age 26, 83% of participants had earned a high school diploma or GED. In sum, later high school completion rates for youth who lived in foster care eventually reach similar levels as the overall population's high school completion proportion (83% versus 85%), but college completion for young adults who had lived in foster care is much lower than for those in the general population (11% versus 28%; Courtney et al., 2011;

Ryan & Siebens, 2012). Ongoing problems for many young adults who emancipated from foster care include poverty and homelessness, physical and mental health problems, criminal involvement as perpetrators and victims, young parenthood, and intergenerational child welfare system involvement (Courtney et al., 2011).

Not always, but most often, children enter out-of-home placement due to maltreatment or abuse or neglect inflicted by their biological parents. Even if placement comes as a relief on some level, loss accompanies removal from one's home. This loss involves altered relationships with the child's family of origin; change in communities; and loss of pets, belongings, familiarity, and sometimes culture. Grief responses to these losses are common. Traumatic responses and internalizing or externalizing behaviors can be normal reactions to the abnormal experiences of maltreatment and removal. Future attachments to others may be problematic. Further, the well documented transiency in foster placements presents additional hurdles to healthy development.

Resilience

Statistics alone paint a bleak picture of overall quality of life for youth in foster care. But numbers overshadow the survival instincts and resilience that characterize these youth and the incredible strengths that have allowed a consequential number to transcend the odds. Although researchers have attempted to develop typologies of risk and resilience considering dispositional factors and contextual models, no consistent magic formula for success has resulted. This phenomenon may be due to the heterogeneous personalities and experiences of young people who have lived in foster care and to fluctuations in the balance of risk and protective factors over time. Youth who are goal oriented, persistent, and who possess strong social skills may be best poised for success. Across contextual risk typologies, researchers have identified early arrests, school enrollment, and placement instability as among the most powerful risk predictors, at least for males (Ryan, Hernandez, & Herz, 2007). The school psychologists' task is to focus intervention efforts on those influential variables and outcomes they have the greatest power and likelihood to affect.

Legislation

Comprehending educational, behavioral, and mental health challenges and outcomes for children in foster care contributes to the development of best practices for serving these students. Knowledge of current legislation regarding education of students living in foster care also influences practices. The 2008 Fostering Connections to Success and Increasing Adoptions Act specified that states must provide children in their care with educational stability plans. In particular, placement decisions are to be made with consideration of proximity to the child's current school of enrollment. Further, children are to remain in their original schools, if the schools are meeting their educational needs, even if placed in foster homes out of district. If a school move is deemed necessary following consideration of these factors, it must occur promptly, and records should accompany the student from the previous school to the new school (Flango & Sydow, 2011).

The Act also allowed states to extend foster care to age 21 for those young people who maintain employment, vocational training, or other postsecondary education unless a medical condition prevents them from so doing. Further, the Act specified that youth must work with a caseworker to develop a transition plan approximately 90 days prior to reaching 18 years of age (Henig, 2009). The Act requires child welfare agencies to collaborate with Medicaid programs and local education agencies to meet these goals (Meloy & Phillips, 2012).

For secondary age students in particular, the 1999 John H. Chafee Foster Care Independence Act further amended Title IV-E of the Social Security Act to provide states flexible funding on a voluntary basis to improve transition services for youth before, during, and after aging out of care up to the age of 21 years. In particular, the Chafee Act specified funds could be used to offer young people independent living skills and mentors to provide practical and emotional support. Funds can also be used for vocational training, employment services, and preparation for postsecondary education. Substantial vouchers are to be used to further support postsecondary education on an annual basis. The Act allowed Medicaid to be extended for these young people until 21 years of age and for money to be applied toward room and board as well (Atkinson, 2008; Hill, 2009).

Although not focused on children aging out of foster care exclusively, the 2001 McKinney-Vento Homeless Education Assistance Improvements Act has the potential to positively influence students living in foster care. It was designed to offer more stable education for children who are homeless. Schools must allow children to remain in their original school or enroll in an expedited

manner in a new school, even without complete documentation, if desired by the student or guardian and despite homelessness or "awaiting a foster care placement," a situation that has been interpreted to mean placement in emergency or otherwise short-term care. Additionally, the school must provide transportation to facilitate the student's attendance (Atkinson, 2008).

Similarly, the 2004 reauthorization of the Individuals with Disabilities Education Act (IDEA) indirectly relates to meeting the needs of many children in foster care. Exact numbers of children in foster care who also have educational or other disabilities are difficult to determine due to inconsistent data tracking. However, considerable overlap between residing in foster care and qualifying for/receiving special education services has been established. Whether due to early maltreatment or the confluence of multiple risk factors, children who live in foster care often experience developmental challenges early in life. IDEA Part C has addressed the need for early intervention for infants and toddlers with delayed development. IDEA Part B requires local education agencies to provide students aged 3–21 years with educational disabilities with a free appropriate public education in the local education agency's least restrictive environment. This includes the requirement that the IEP team begins planning for a student's transition from high school so that a transition plan is established and in force by the time the student is 16 years old (Hill, 2009).

BEST PRACTICES IN WORKING WITH CHILDREN LIVING IN FOSTER CARE

School psychologists' services with youth living in foster care will vary depending on a variety of factors, including a particular student's developmental level. For preschool children, the focus is necessarily more preventive and is geared toward ensuring children are enrolled in early childhood programming and receive other relevant early interventions. For elementary school students, academic and behavioral interventions within a problem-solving and multitiered framework that minimize risk and maximize resiliency may be helpful. For secondary students, targeted planning for emancipation from foster care must begin. Systemic practices that improve work with students in foster care should be implemented, too, especially those that improve home–school communication and interagency collaboration.

Practices need to be implemented within a problem-solving, multitiered model. Most of the research regarding children living in foster care has focused on child welfare practices rather than on school-based interventions. Where possible, progress monitoring of movement toward both short- and long-term goals for individual students and for systems can make valuable contributions to a more solid evidence base for work specific to these students in schools. In addition, school psychologists should consider student needs holistically, not just as separate academic, behavioral, or mental health needs. With purposeful planning, problem solving, communication, consultation, and collaboration, risk factors can be minimized and resilience promoted thereby improving the likelihood of successful outcomes for students living in foster care.

Case Study: Jayden and Izzie

The case study of Jayden and Izzie will help to illustrate best practices for school psychologists to implement in their work with children living in foster care. Jayden was an 8-year-old, second grade student, when he arrived at McClelland Elementary School in November. Jayden and his 3-year-old sister, Izzie, were both removed from their mother's custody and placed in a receiving foster home in October. Apparently Izzie's father, who lived with the family, had grabbed Jayden's arm and thrown him across the room. Jayden's face hit the wall, and the impact left a substantial bruise near his eye. An unknown caller reported the abuse allegation to the county child welfare office.

The child welfare investigation resulted in substantiation, or verification, of the abuse allegation. Child abuse charges were filed. The children's mother had been suffering from methamphetamine addiction, and did not follow through with child welfare requirements that she not allow Izzie's father in the home anymore and that she seek drug treatment. Jayden's biological father was incarcerated for burglary at the time, and no relatives who lived locally were willing or able to take the children. The permanency plan was to reunify the children with their mother if she completed inpatient drug treatment and lived separately from Izzie's father.

After a few weeks, during which Jayden did not attend school, a more permanent foster home that had room for both siblings was secured. This foster home was in a different school district than the one Jayden had previously attended. When Jayden arrived at McClelland, his new teacher noticed he was struggling with reading and that he seemed to have difficulty following directions.

Early Childhood Education and Intervention

For children who experience maltreatment and/or who enter foster care at younger ages, early childhood education and intervention are essential to offset psychoeducational challenges. Strong early childhood educational programming can help to meet the needs of both young students and their foster caregivers. When children experience deprived environments, they can benefit from more frequent, higher quality cognitive stimulation and healthier social–emotional experiences with peers and adults. Early childhood education can provide the necessary enrichment and educators may recognize signs of special educational needs that require additional early intervention. In environments with consistent, caring staff, students may be able to experience positive attachment with caregivers.

Early childhood programs can provide foster parents with much needed respite from the demands of caring for the children in their charge. This relief can increase retention of foster parents, prevent movement of children between multiple placements, and give foster parents the opportunity to seek additional employment and income to help with household management. These programs can provide additional parenting and child development education to foster parents as well. The potential for stronger attachment between children and foster parents may increase in response to contributions from early childhood education centers (Meloy & Phillips, 2012). Also, school readiness preparation can give young children in foster care a much needed jump start to prepare for their elementary school years.

Case Study Part 2

Jayden did not receive any universal prevention in the form of early childhood education. Thus, he did not receive any targeted interventions within the context of an early childhood classroom. When the school psychologist in Jayden's new school becomes aware of him and his family, it is important that the school psychologist inform the foster parent of early childhood educational resources within the district for Izzie if the foster parent is not aware of the options for her. School psychologists may be involved in screening Izzie and in assessing her further and consulting with the foster parent about more targeted interventions if needed. School psychologists may also provide the foster parent with referrals to other community-based services for Izzie as necessary. Typically, children in state custody have health insurance coverage, so providers who accept government insurance may be accessed.

Elementary Education and Intervention

For elementary school students, interventions ought to relate to maximizing the effectiveness of the time educators have to assist children living in foster care. Academic and behavioral interventions within a problem-solving and multitiered framework that minimize the likelihood of special education identification, grade retention, and suspension and expulsion may be helpful. Specifically, interventions that help alleviate grief, trauma, and other internalizing and externalizing behaviors as they are expressed can be useful. Students may benefit from social skills, problem solving, conflict resolution, and anger management interventions. More problematic behaviors lead to greater likelihood of placement disruption. School psychologists could support foster parents by involving them in school-based behavioral consultation teams to facilitate generalization of learned skills across environments.

Connecting students with extracurricular activities, including after school and summer programs, can promote positive social interactions, engagement in school and the surrounding community, and decrease time and motivation for delinquent behaviors. The respite time extracurriculars offer foster parents presents a secondary benefit. Help with arranging carpools may be necessary if the timing of activities and transportation needs would prevent a child's involvement. If cost is prohibitive, schools may opt to waive participation fees or subsidize with any school fund for disadvantaged students. In addition to considering NASP Tiny Grants for help meeting basic clothing and supply needs, readers should consider those resources listed in the Annotated Bibliography (available at http://www.nasponline.org/publications) for meeting additional individual needs, such as sports equipment and team uniforms.

Case Study Part 3

As a second-grade student, Jayden may benefit from some of the aforementioned assistance from a school psychologist. Jayden's new teacher noticed he was struggling with reading. Universal screening would likely catch his challenges with reading, too. It would be important to give him a little time to adjust to his new school but, if the next benchmarking was scheduled to take place in spring, Jayden should be screened much sooner. Because of the relatively high rates of special education and grade retention among children living in foster care and the potential for transiency, Jayden needs to get help as soon as possible.

Following screening, small group or targeted reading intervention may be implemented and progress monitored. Documentation of efforts is essential so that information could follow Jayden if a move occurs. Further, with the provisions of the Fostering Connections to Success and Increasing Adoptions Act, documentation of progress could help guarantee that Jayden stay at his new school even if an out-of-district foster home move took place. Depending on established procedures for screening, intervention, and progress monitoring, the school psychologist could be involved at all phases of this process.

Similarly, Jayden's difficulty following directions should be assessed and monitored following some adjustment time. Jayden has suffered trauma and loss. His difficulty following directions could be a manifestation of his recent experiences. Conversely, they could be related to his difficulty with reading. The school psychologist might interview Jayden and his teacher and observe Jayden across settings to help better identify the problem. From there, interventions and progress monitoring could be implemented if needed. In the interim, the school psychologist could check in with Jayden daily at first, then less frequently, to build his connection to his new school and a positive adult and to ascertain how he is responding to all the changes in his life.

The school psychologist might assist the classroom teacher in keeping Jayden's foster parent, mother, and child welfare caseworker apprised of his progress. Discussions with the foster parent could include topics such as extracurricular options for Jayden and meeting any of his basic needs (e.g., school supplies). Ongoing consultation with the teacher could be helpful for addressing specific problems (i.e., reading and following directions) and more general issues. For example, the school psychologist might work with the teacher on adapting assignments to be as sensitive as possible to diverse family structures and might discuss the effects of trauma and how behavioral changes might be observed around times when Jayden visits with his mother.

Secondary Education and Intervention

At the secondary level, school psychologists should continue to focus services for youth living in foster care on identifying, intervening with, and progress monitoring academic, behavioral, and mental health concerns. School psychologists should also assist with coordination and provision of life skills training. This is imperative because these youth will face emancipation from care or from their original homes in just a short time.

Independent Living Services

Although states can receive funding to support independent living services through the Chafee Act, not all opt to do so. The way programs are administered differs between states and counties, so it cannot be assumed that students are receiving any independent living services at all, much less comprehensively or in specific areas. Job search, housekeeping, and educational planning of some sort seem to be the more commonly handled topics (Shin, 2009).

Among the most alarming findings in light of the amount of former foster youth who experience homelessness, significant portions of young people have not received training in how to locate and secure a place to live. In addition, many have not been taught how to keep a job, how to budget and manage their finances, or parenting skills (Shin, 2009). Given the economic challenges and heightened risk of young parenthood among this group, these topics seem overdue.

Young adults leaving foster homes have to learn how to monitor their physical and mental health and seek corresponding care. Arrangements for health insurance must be made, and sometimes government assistance with this is available for a short time following the child's emancipation, making coordination with the child protection agency involved imperative. Students need to develop financial knowledge and skills such as budgeting, opening and balancing checking and savings accounts, and establishment and responsible use of credit. Additional topics for transition planning include shopping and food preparation, use of public transportation, and securing a driver's license.

Scant research has been conducted regarding the effectiveness of independent living training techniques. However, most children learn skills to become independent over time and through hands-on real-world experiences, not by a condensed classroom curriculum. In addition to school psychologists, other pupil service professionals and mentors may be able to impart independent living lessons and assist with corresponding exercises.

Transition Planning

As previously noted, students living in foster care are identified with educational disabilities more frequently than their nonfostered peers. IDEA requires that students with IEPs have active transition plans that they participate in developing by the age of 16 years. These plans delineate postsecondary goals to include education/training, employment, and independent living as appropriate. IEP goals should help students achieve postsecondary goals, and specific transition services needed are identified to achieve the goals. Transition services can include instruction, related services, community experiences, development of employment and other adult living objectives, daily living skills development, and functional vocational assessment (National Dissemination Center for Children with Disabilities, 2012).

Of utmost importance, both child welfare agencies and schools must give fostered youth a voice in planning their futures. School psychologists can help with this by ensuring children in foster care are active participants in their transition planning. In fact, IDEA requires student input into transition planning. Beyond IDEA regulations, youth need to be empowered to chart their courses. This can be a dramatic change for students who have had many circumstances beyond their control dictating twists and turns in their lives to being expected to steer their own lives at an autonomous level beyond what is expected of most other young people of the same ages. Empowerment is essential for students to make life-altering decisions about postsecondary pursuits.

College and Vocational Preparation

The difficulties students emancipating from foster care encounter are many, but the challenges can be offset by school psychologists who advocate for them. Indeed, involvement in job shadowing, school-to-work programs, and vocational training may benefit workforce-bound students. Assistance with creating a résumé, conducting a job search, and interviewing techniques may be beneficial. Federal programs that assist with vocational development and postsecondary education might be appropriate for some students following careful consideration of the costs and benefits of each. For example, Workforce Investment Act centers, Job Corps, Conservation Corps, the Peace Corps, the AmeriCorps National Civilian Community Corps, and the military are all possibilities (Allen, 2005). School guidance counselors and social workers can assist with making these arrangements.

School psychologists can advocate for students to earn sufficient high school credits to graduate, to take high school courses that will prevent the need for remedial college coursework, and to take Advanced Placement classes and classes for college credit while still in high school when appropriate. Additional interventions to enhance time management and study skills might be helpful also.

College awareness programs can help students better comprehend their options. Talent Search, Upward Bound, and Educational Opportunity Centers, among others in the Federal TRIO Programs, help low-income students, first generation college students, and students with disabilities access higher education. Youth from foster care are supposed to be granted priority consideration for these programs through the 2008 Higher Education Opportunities Act (Hernandez & Naccarato, 2010). In the absence of formal programs at the secondary level, school psychologists can collaborate with guidance counselors, social workers, and regional colleges and universities to provide campus tours and assistance with admissions and financial aid applications.

Financing a college education is worrisome for many, and may seem especially daunting to a young adult leaving foster care with few resources. When students in foster care are dependents of the state and apply for federal financial aid using the Free Application for Federal Student Aid, their financial need is considered independent of any parents. The aforementioned Education and Training Vouchers associated with the Chafee Act provide up to $5,000 per student annually for costs such as tuition and room and board (Atkinson, 2008). Some states provide scholarships and tuition waivers for formerly fostered youth. Some private and nonprofit organizations provide scholarship support to foster alumni also (e.g., Foster Care to Success). In addition to tuition, expenses for textbooks, computer access, housing, food, clothing and personal hygiene, and medical insurance need to be considered. Avenues for securing medical coverage include campus-based insurance programs and government assistance such as Medicaid.

Once students get to college, their challenges continue. So, it is important that helping fostered students prepare for college does not stop with application for admissions and financial aid. As students select colleges, and following their acceptances, pupil service professionals ought to help them identify those supports that will improve the likelihood of remaining in college and earning a degree. If they have been previously identified with a disability that affects their learning, students should be connected with campus disability services for support and provided the required disability documentation to help them access education more equitably on campus (Hernandez & Naccarato, 2010).

Mentoring and Social Networks

Across elementary and secondary levels, school psychologists recognize that mentoring can benefit at-risk students by offering protective support. Research on the effectiveness of mentorship with fostered youth has uncovered similar results (e.g., Collins, Spencer, & Ward, 2010; Johnson, Pryce, & Martinovich, 2011). Of paramount importance, though, are the quality and length of the mentoring relationship.

When mentors provide developmentally appropriate activities to their mentees and receive regular supervision themselves, they tend to be more successful. Frequent and consistent contact (i.e., weekly) seems to be best for most students. In fact, receiving less frequent, inconsistent, or shorter term (i.e., 6 months or less) mentoring may actually be detrimental to youth who have experienced trauma and broken relationships. Those who are engaged in more intensive and longer term mentoring relationships (e.g., 12–18 months and longer), conversely, show improvements in family and social relationships, behavior at school, academic achievement, school attendance, involvement in recreational activities, and trauma symptoms (Johnson et al., 2010). Formal and informal mentor relationships have been related to increased high school completion rates and decreased homelessness as well. In particular, youth report that strong relationships with mentors provide them with acceptance, encouragement, reliability, and help when needed (Collins et al., 2010).

In part, mentoring is helpful to students in foster care because placement threatens the development of social networks necessary for healthy functioning. When removal and placement occur, ties to biological family members can be further weakened, and changes in residence mean that connections with community members, including educators and peers, may be severed. Although children in stable foster placements can potentially build stronger social networks than if they had remained in their original homes, stability is not the norm in foster care. It may be helpful to identify sources of support with students living in foster care, so they know where to turn for emotional and practical help in times of crisis or even on a more regular basis. A physical list to be referenced in times of need could be developed along with current contact information. See Figure 13.1 for suggested personal and community resources to consider.

Case Study Part 4

After initial work has been done to begin to address concerns about Jayden's reading and following directions, the school psychologist could ask the foster parent whether Jayden is connected with a mentor. If not, then

Figure 13.1. Social Network: Personal and Community Resources for Children in Foster Care

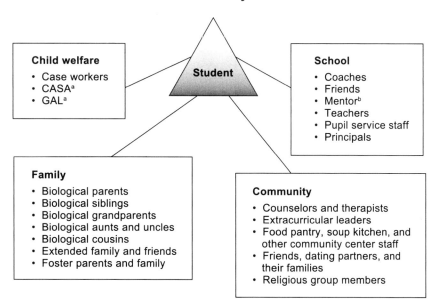

Note. [a]Court-appointed special advocate; court-appointed special advocates are appointed by the court as advocates for children. Guardians ad litem; Guardians ad litem are appointed by the court to represent the child's interests in legal actions. States specify qualifications and roles, and both court-appointed special advocates and guardians ad litem usually gather information and make recommendations to the court. [b]Mentors may be provided in child welfare and community contexts alternatively.

the school psychologist might contact the child welfare case worker to determine if a mentor has been planned for Jayden and if there are mentoring resources available through the social service agency. If not, then the school psychologist can arrange for mentoring for Jayden through school or community resources. For example, a mentoring program involving high school or college student volunteers could be implemented or established mentoring programs in the community could be accessed. Other pupil service staff might assist with these arrangements as well.

The school psychologist may want to work with Jayden, his foster parent, and perhaps his child welfare caseworker to develop a network map, similar to that in Figure 13.1. The map could be used in individual meetings with Jayden to help him understand the many people now involved in his life and their roles. The network may also be used to help Jayden identify his feelings about his situation, people he finds safe and reliable, and to help him feel connected and supported.

Systemic Change

Efforts to advocate for social justice for youth in foster care occur on an individual basis, and the most far reaching effects happen when changes occur within and between the systems that serve youth, especially child welfare and education. These broader efforts can be considered secondary, or targeted, interventions in a tiered system. Lack of understanding of how each other's system operates seems pervasive, and youth suffer as a result. For example, schools tend to lack background information and educational history for students living in foster care, rarely know in a timely manner when a child has entered or changed foster homes, and are frequently unsure who is legally responsible for educational decision making for their students living in foster care. Similarly, child welfare workers and foster parents may not be familiar with school procedures, particularly special education processes and rights, and may not know how much schools would like them to be involved.

Further, systems' goals differ. Child welfare takes responsibility for safety of youth in their custody and for family reunification whenever possible. Schools educate students while also promoting mental health. An overlapping, but unstated, goal across systems ought to be nurturing the holistic well-being of young people.

Educational liaisons can help bridge this gap. Whether employed by one system or both, they possess knowledge and experience across the child welfare and educational systems so they can facilitate communication between both systems to help ensure educational needs for students in foster care are planned for and met while safety and placement decisions are made. Despite initial performance lower than a control group, students in foster care who were served by educational liaisons demonstrated improved math and reading from pretests to posttests when compared to controls (Zetlin, Weinberg, & Shea, 2006).

If formal liaisons are not established, then school psychologists and other pupil services staff can assume leadership for improved interagency collaboration. In addition to advocacy for individual students, child welfare agencies and local education agencies have created memoranda of understanding (MOU) to facilitate timely information sharing in legally approved ways that do not violate confidentiality dictates of the Family Educational Rights and Privacy Act. Some MOUs have also clarified agreements about financial responsibilities for transportation in placement change situations in order to decrease school transiency. Cross-agency trainings could be beneficial for information sharing, and joint workgroups or summits would allow for interagency problem solving. Although school psychologists can promote establishing MOUs and educational liaisons where they are lacking and facilitate cross-agency trainings and meetings, these methods require administrative support to optimize success (Weinberg, Zetlin, & Shea, 2009).

Case Study Part 5

If McClelland Elementary School and the local child welfare system have established strong communication with each other, the child welfare authorities or educational liaison would inform the school that Jayden lived in foster care. They would share all educational records and pertinent information about his living and family situations, identify the person legally able to make educational decisions for him, and provide contact information for his child welfare case worker.

In the absence of systematized information sharing, the school psychologist can seek out this information. A mid-semester enrollment may prompt staff to review the parent/guardian contact information provided at registration and make contact with the adults listed on relevant forms. If foster care placement is suspected, but cannot be verified this way or by asking Jayden about with whom he lives, an inquiry about Jayden's living arrangements could be made to the local child welfare agency.

Legal responsibility for educational decision making for Jayden should be established by obtaining a copy of the most recent court order from the child welfare caseworker. The caseworker should be asked questions about family dynamics and preferred involvement of foster and biological parents. Because reunification with Jayden's mother is the ultimate case goal, all parties would need to be involved in decision-making processes if possible. Yet, Jayden's mother's substance abuse and need for treatment may prohibit her active involvement, at least temporarily.

Further, the school psychologist should request educational records from the child welfare worker. If these are not available, the names of his most recent schools would provide a starting point for tracking down any existing records. In Jayden's case, it would be helpful to know whether concerns about reading and following directions have been noted previously and whether particular interventions have been implemented successfully or not in the past.

Communication between the school psychologist at McClelland Elementary and Jayden's child welfare worker will allow the greatest chance of comprehensive service coordination and success for Jayden. Patience in this process is essential as child welfare workers must prioritize child safety and family preservation while managing hefty caseloads. If Jayden's caseworker and the school psychologist establish communication, perhaps the caseworker will inform the school psychologist of any placement changes prior to or just after their occurrence. Then, the school psychologist could help prepare Jayden for changes in his living conditions, assist him with processing them after they happen, and send his records along to another school if a school change is unavoidable. Of course, the school psychologist could share some of this work with other pupil service professionals, such as school social workers or counselors.

SUMMARY

School psychologists can advocate for improved outcomes for children living in foster care from preschool years into early adulthood. First, school psychologists must be familiar with and keep current on legislation that affects students in foster care. School psychologists can work to ensure that children in foster care receive quality early childhood education for prevention and intervention. At the elementary level, school psychologists can address special education disproportionality, grade retention, excessive suspension and expulsion, and other academic and mental health challenges by intervening within a multitiered model that includes screening and monitoring progress. Social skills training, extracurricular activities, and mentoring relationships can all be established as indicated. At the secondary level, similar work needs to continue, independent living skills have to be enhanced, and transition plans for students with disabilities must be carried out simultaneously for students preparing to emancipate from foster care. School psychologists can collaborate with other professionals to ensure students graduate from high school and are ready for postsecondary endeavors.

Individual work with students living in foster care is necessary, and targeted systemic changes must occur to assist larger numbers of students more efficiently. Establishing educational liaisons, information sharing mechanisms, and interagency trainings and workgroups are suggested for making systemic improvements. Systemic changes and student-specific interventions share the goals of raising expectations for children who have lived in foster care. Following best practices will not be sufficient, though. School psychologists must lead efforts to ensure all essential supports are provided, planning is comprehensive, and communication and collaboration are targeted. This advocacy will make it possible for students in foster care to meet higher expectations by leveling the playing field and giving a voice to those like Jayden and Izzie who have suffered in relative silence for far too long.

REFERENCES

Allen, M. (2005). *Teens aging out of foster care in Oregon: A guide to transition planning for caseworkers, judges, and advocates.* Portland, OR: Juvenile Rights Project. Retrieved from http://www.youthrightsjustice.org/Documents%20Teens%20Aging%20Out%20of%20Foster%20Care%20in%20Oregon.pdf

Atkinson, M. (2008). Aging out of foster care: Towards a universal safety net for former foster care youth. *Harvard Civil Rights-Civil Liberties Law Review, 43*, 183–212.

Aud, S., Hussar, W., Johnson, F., Kena, G., Roth, E., Manning, E., … Zhang, J. (2012). *The condition of education 2012* (NCES 2012-045). Washington, DC: National Center for Education Statistics. Retrieved from http://nces.ed.gov/pubsearch/pubsinfo.asp?pubid=2012045

Collins, M. E., Spencer, R., & Ward, R. (2010). Supporting youth in the transition from foster care: Formal and informal connections. *Child Welfare, 89*(1), 125–143.

Courtney, M., Dworsky, A., Brown, A., Cary, C., Love, K., & Vorhies, V. (2011). *Midwest evaluation of the adult functioning of former foster youth: Outcomes at age 26.* Chicago, IL: Chapin Hall at the University of Chicago. Retrieved from http://www.chapinhall.org/sites/default/files/Midwest%20Evaluation_Report_4_10_12.pdf

Flango, V. E., & Sydow, N. (2011). Educational well-being: Court outcome measures for children in foster care. *Future Trends in State Courts 2011*, 123–128. Williamsburg, VA: National Center for State Courts. Retrieved from http://ncsc.contentdm.oclc.org/cdm/ref/collection/famct/id/379

Henig, A. (2009). Employment aid for youth aging out of foster care: Extending one-stop career centers to include a division for foster care youth. *Family Court Review, 47*, 570–585. doi:10.1111/j.1744-1617.2009.01274.x

Hernandez, L., & Naccarato, T. (2010). Scholarships and supports available to foster care alumni: A study of 12 programs across the US. *Children and Youth Services Review, 32*, 758–766. doi:10.1016/j.childyouth.2010.01.014

Hill, K. (2009). Individuals with Disabilities Act of 2004 and the John H. Chafee Foster Care Independence Act of 1999: What are the policy implications of youth with disabilities transitioning from foster care? *Child Welfare, 86*(2), 5–23.

Hill, K. (2012). Permanency and placement planning for older youth with disabilities in out-of-home placement. *Children and Youth Services Review, 34*, 1418–1424. doi:10.1016/j.childyouth.2012.03.012

Johnson, S. B., Pryce, J. M., & Martinovich, Z. (2011). The role of therapeutic mentoring in enhancing outcomes for youth in foster care. *Child Welfare, 90*(5), 51–69.

Lightfoot, E., Hill, K., & LaLiberte, T. (2011). Prevalence of children with disabilities in the child welfare system and out of home placement: An examination of administrative records. *Children and Youth Services Review, 33*, 2069–2075. doi:10.1016/j.childyouth.2011.02.019

Meloy, M. E., & Phillips, D. A. (2012). Rethinking the role of early care and education in foster care. *Children and Youth Services Review, 34*, 882–890. doi:10.1016/j.childyouth.2012.01.012

National Association of School Psychologists. (2010). *Model for comprehensive and integrated school psychological services.* Bethesda, MD: Author. Retrieved from http://www.nasponline.org/standards/2010standards/2_PracticeModel.pdf

National Association of School Psychologists. (2011). *Grade retention and social promotion.* (White Paper). Bethesda, MD: Author. Retrieved from http://www.nasponline.org/about_nasp/positionpapers/WhitePaper_GradeRetentionandSocialPromotion.pdf

National Dissemination Center for Children with Disabilities. (2012). *Transition goals in the IEP.* Washington, DC: Author. Retrieved from http://nichcy.org/schoolage/transitionadult/goals#first

Pears, K. C., Heywood, C. V., Kim, H. K., & Fisher, P. A. (2011). Prereading deficits in children in foster care. *School Psychology Review, 40*, 140–148.

Planty, M., Hussar, W., Snyder, T., Kena, G., KewalRamani, A., Kemp, J., … Dinkes, R. (2009). *The condition of education 2009* (NCES 2009-081). Washington, DC: National Center for Education Statistics. Retrieved from http://nces.ed.gov/pubs2009/2009081.pdf

Ryan, J. P., Hernandez, P. M., & Herz, D. (2007). Developmental trajectories of offending for male adolescents leaving foster care. *Social Work Research, 31*, 83–93. doi:10.1093/swr/31.2.83

Ryan, C. L., & Siebens, J. (2012). *Educational attainment in the United States: 2009.* Washington, DC: U.S. Census Bureau. Retrieved from http://www.census.gov/prod/2012pubs/p20-566.pdf

Scherr, T. G. (2007). Educational experiences of children in foster care: Meta-analyses of special education, retention, and discipline rates. *School Psychology International, 28*, 419–436. doi:10.1177/0143034307084133

Shin, S. H. (2009). Improving social work practice with foster adolescents: Examining readiness for independence. *Journal of Public Child Welfare, 3*, 354–371. doi:10.1080/15548730903347820

U.S. Department of Health and Human Services. (2006). *The AFCARS report: Final estimates for FY 1998 through FY 2002.* Washington, DC: Author. Retrieved from http://archive.acf.hhs.gov/programs/cb/stats_research/afcars/tar/report12.pdf

U.S. Department of Health and Human Services. (2012a). *The AFCARS report: Preliminary estimates for FY 2011 as of July 2012.* Washington, DC: Author. Retrieved from http://www.acf.hhs.gov/sites/default/files/cb/afcarsreport19.pdf

U.S. Department of Health and Human Services. (2012b). *Trends in foster care and adoption- FY 2002–FY 2011.* Washington, DC: Author. Retrieved from http://www.acf.hhs.gov/sites/default/files/cb/trends_fostercare_adoption.pdf

Weinberg, L. A., Zetlin, A., & Shea, N. M. (2009). Removing barriers to educating children in foster care through interagency collaboration: A seven county multiple-case study. *Child Welfare, 88*(4), 77–111.

Zetlin, A. G., Weinberg, L. A., & Shea, N. M. (2006). Improving educational prospects for youth in foster care: The education liaison model. *Intervention in School and Clinic, 41*, 267–262. doi:10.1177/10534512060410050301

14

Best Practices in Service to Children in Military Families

Mark C. Pisano
U.S. Department of Defense

OVERVIEW

No military in the history of the world has been more widely deployed than the U.S. military. Since October 2001, multiple deployments as well as extended deployments have been a routine part of life for many military families. Many of these troops experience trauma while deployed and return home with mental health conditions (Jenkins et al., 2011). In 2009, approximately 1.98 million children had one or both parents in the military; that is, 1.25 million had parents in the active component and 728,000 had parents in the reserve components (U.S. Department of Defense, 2010b). While the Department of Defense still maintains 190 schools across the world for military dependents living on bases, the majority of military dependent children are educated in public schools.

Given their expertise in counseling, consultation, and collaboration, school psychologists are in a unique position to provide various forms of support to military children and their families such as small and large deployment support groups, faculty and staff inservices explaining the deployment stages, and military family support activities (bulletin boards, morning announcements, flag raising ceremonies).

Family members of those who are civilian federal employees as well as National Guard and Reserve are affected as well. There are many National Guard and Reserve units located in every state in United States. These families experience unique issues. Families that are associated with the National Guard and Reserve branches or are civilian employees do not typically live on military bases. Active duty families that live on military installations can easily access organizations for support such as Military One Source and Army Community Services. Also, active duty families live in a neighborhood with other active duty families that are experiencing the same lifestyle, that of a family managing the deployment cycle. Families of National Guard and Reserve members do not have such easy access to support and often note feeling isolated during their family members' military service because friends and neighbors may not understand the impact the deployment cycle has on families.

This chapter reflects important school psychological services related to the foundational domain of diversity in development and learning in the National Association of School Psychologists (NASP) *Model for Comprehensive and Integrated School Psychological Services* (NASP, 2010). Knowledge about the deployment cycle is essential for school psychologists working with military children, and typical deployment stages are presented in the chapter. This chapter will review the stressors of deployment on children and military families and offer suggestions on what school psychologists can do to provide much needed support to these children and their families. Distinctions between how children of different ages typically react to the various stages of deployment will be described.

BASIC CONSIDERATIONS

As a result of multiple and extended deployments, more than 2 million youth from military families have experienced significant periods of parental absence (U.S. Department of Defense, 2010b). While there are positive aspects of deployment, including a sense of pride, increased camaraderie, and financial benefits, deployments can take a heavy toll on families concerned for the safety of their loved ones (Tanielian & Jaycox, 2008). Evidence suggests that children in military families, especially those who have experienced longer periods of time away from a deployed parent, have significantly higher rates of problems, especially emotional and behavioral difficulties, than nonmilitary children. The Chandra, Larea-Cinisomo, et al. (2010) study shows that children of currently deployed parents have higher rates of anxiety symptoms than a comparable national sample of same-aged children (by roughly 4%). Gorman et al. (2010) tracked health claim records during 2006 and 2007 of nearly 650,000 children ages 3–8 and found that those with a parent deployed within those 2 years had an 11% higher rate of clinic visits because of mental health or behavioral issues than military children whose parents were not deployed.

An important predictor of how well a child will cope with a parent's deployment is the health and well-being of the child's nondeployed parent. (Throughout this chapter we will use the word *parent* to refer to the *caregiver*. Of course, many homes only have one parent, so the child is often left in the hands of a caregiver related to the child or a close friend.) Research suggests that longer deployments lead to increased need for psychiatric treatment for the remaining parent (Mansfield, Kaufman, Engel, & Gaynes, 2011). Given that the mental health of the remaining parent strongly influences adjustment in the home during deployment (Huebner & Mancini, 2005), the home may potentially become an insecure and volatile place. The school potentially becomes a safe haven and source of security and support for many children.

Several studies have found academic performance to be affected for children of deployed parents. A study of children of fathers deployed for 8 months or longer found that father absence was negatively related to academic performance based on the Classroom Adjustment Rating Scale (Hiew, 1992). Pisano (1996) found that daughters of deployed 82nd Airborne Army fathers demonstrated a significant decrease in reading comprehension scores during Operation Desert Storm. Another study found that children's academic performance tends to be lower during parental deployment (Engel, Gallagher, & Lyle, 2010). A U.S. Department of Defense (2009) report indicates that on average a child of a military family may change schools six to nine times throughout his or her academic career. The impact of deployment on children's academic performance is fully reviewed in a U.S. Department of Defense (2011) report, which notes that long and frequent deployments have placed stress on Army children and families already challenged by frequent moves and parental absences. Findings indicate that the longer parental deployments were, the larger the impact on child academic achievement. Children who participated in the study were found to have lower achievement scores when their parents had been deployed 19 months or more since 2001, across all academic subjects.

There are some unique educational challenges that children in military families may experience:

- High mobility rates; that is, active duty families move every 2 or 3 years, which is approximately three times more often than the civilian population (Collins, 2009; children often experience six to nine moves during their pre-K–12 school education)
- Separations from a parent owing to deployments
- Difficulties qualifying for, receiving, or continuing special needs services in new school districts owing to differences in regulation interpretation, testing required to enroll in or receive special needs services, and resource availability
- Academic or social changes attributed to frequent school changes, deployment of a parent, return of a deployed parent, or injury to or death of a parent
- Understanding and interpreting new school regulations and policies
- Elevated stress; that is making new friends and finding a new peer group in a new school, adjustment to a new school, community, and home
- At risk for depression and anxiety due to relocation, as well as deployment of a parent
- Adjusting to curriculum and instructional methods or school climate/culture that may differ from school to school.

Resilience

A parent's deployment does not necessarily translate into behavioral or academic problems for a child. While children (and to some degree parents) in military families experience a decline in well-being, particularly during parental absence due to a deployment, most families find ways to cope. Along certain measures of functioning and well-being, children from military families are no different from other children. Children from military families, during peacetime, show the same frequency of mental health and behavioral outcomes as their nonmilitary peers. In some instances, the military children fare better on these outcomes (Meadows, 2012).

Chandra, Martin, Hawkins, and Richardson (2010) conducted a series of focus groups and semistructured interviews with teachers, the school counselor, and administrative staff at schools servicing children from

U.S. Army families. Staff members shared that although there might have been a decline in academic performance when the parent was initially deployed, many of these children were able to organize themselves to perform well in the future. For instance, some students learned skills from the first deployment that have strengthened their abilities to cope and function well for the subsequent deployments. One teacher, from the same study, reported seeing children transition from being totally disconnected with the routines of school after the first round of deployments to picking themselves up and living day to day, which becomes the new normal for these families. However, Chandra, Martin, et al. (2010) found that school staff reported that some children who were able to handle a parent's first deployment fairly well became less engaged in school work and more interested in avoidant behaviors, including risk-taking behaviors, after a parent's second deployment.

Stress in Military Families

The stress of deployments, promotions, job transitions, child birth, or needs of an aging parent may occur in proximity or even coincide at a single point in time for military families. In fact, research is pinpointing adverse effects of stress on three specific subpopulations: spouses, children, and caregivers (those extended family members who are primarily responsible for the child during the parents' deployment) in military families. These subpopulations are under increased pressure owing to a variety of factors, such as deployments and subsequent lengthy separations, anxiety or concern for the safety and well-being of loved ones serving in combat environments, and the increased demands of temporary single parenthood (U.S. Army, 2012).

The U.S. Army (2012) reports that children of military families experience high levels of stress owing to routinely enduring unique challenges: repeated moves, parental separation, and in some instances the trauma of a parent's death or return from deployment with a combat injury or illness. Stress levels may be especially high during periods of deployment for several reasons including concern for the deployed parent's safety and high stress levels in the nondeployed parent. A longitudinal study conducted by Flake, Davis, Johnson, and Middleton (2009) noted that the mental state of the nondeployed parent was the single most influential factor in determining how well a child adjusts. The nondeployed parent's mental state is considered more of an influence on the child than multiple deployments or the threat of injury or death to the deployed parent (U.S. Army, 2012). The added stress on children and teenagers often manifests in increased incidence of emotional and behavioral problems (Mansfield et al., 2011). In an effort to mitigate, it is important that parents, teachers, and medical providers recognize symptoms of stress in children and teenagers (i.e., anger, acting withdrawn, sleep difficulties, low self-esteem).

Military families often experience multiple deployments throughout a typical military career. However, military families experiencing multiple deployments may not find future deployments easier to manage. Another dynamic of the deployment that often leads to worry and concern is the realistic possibility of the family member engaging in dangerous activities that could cause significant injury (mental or physical) or even death. As school psychologists conduct parent support groups or small group sessions with children of deployed parents, having knowledge about typical military family functioning during deployment will be critical. When a school psychologist understands the stressors experienced by the military family, then he or she can provide targeted mental health services with heightened effectiveness.

Deployment Cycles

To best understand what military families endure during deployment, school psychologists will need to be familiar with the deployment cycle. The five stages of the deployment cycle present various challenges for the military family. Familiarity with these major stages of deployment will afford the school psychologist the knowledge needed to not only prepare interventions for the child and the family but to also intervene with confidence knowing what the child may be experiencing. This section will detail typical characteristics of the five major stages of deployment: predeployment, deployment, rest and relaxation (R&R), reunion, and reintegration.

Predeployment

- Typically about a month advanced notice when to be deployed
- High family stress levels as the service member attends to both his or her family and job
- Family members feel anger, sadness, fear, confusion, and nervousness, as well as pride
- The service member is often already mentally deployed and can appear disconnected with the family
- Some deployments occur before reintegration is complete from the previous deployment

Deployment

- Deployment can last from a few weeks to more than a year
- Children often report mixed emotional feelings, security issues, and difficulty sleeping, particularly during the first month of deployment (Fitzsimons & Krause-Parello, 2009)
- Routine change in the home with the service member no longer actively engaged with familial issues
- School-related issues with children may arise (poor attention, grades drop, withdrawal)
- Family activities center around an expectant phone call or some other contact with the deployed parent
- School administrators and teachers report that children may assume responsibilities typically expected of a parent: additional chores, child care for a younger sibling, or even the emotional care of the nondeployed parent (Chandra, Martin et al., 2010).

Rest and Relaxation

- This is typically a 10 day to 3 week "vacation" midway through the deployment period that allows the deployed parent to come home and be with his or her family
- The family routine is disrupted by the returning parent
- Can be a stressful time (An adolescent female upon learning of her father's homecoming made the decision to simply not be home when he arrived. She chose to live with her grandparents so she did not have to see her father at all during the 10 days he was home because it would be too hard to say goodbye to him again.)

Reunion

- The return of the parent at the end of the deployment is generally a happy and hectic time

- Possibly the most important priority for both spouses is to be ready to be understanding and patient with each other
- New routine to begin at home that will now include the previously deployed parent

Reintegration

- The reintegration of the parent back into his or her family and society reportedly can take upward of 7 months (Pisano, 2010).
- A rise in posttraumatic stress disorder and brain injury for the parent may also have an impact on the reintegration process (Sayer et al., 2010).

BEST PRACTICES IN SERVICE TO CHILDREN IN MILITARY FAMILIES

Children of a military family may have a number of challenges that school psychologists are in a position to address and support. The following information will assist school psychologists in their efforts to meet the needs of these children and their families.

Factors That Help Children Cope

Table 14.1 lists the top five factors for helping children cope with parental deployment. Family separation because of deployment is a major stressor for military children. Parental absence or loss prompts emotional uncertainty and ambiguity in the family. School psychologists, in their role as educators, can facilitate military family resilience by sharing these top five factors.

Children's Responses During Stages of Deployment

Many children of deployed parents may not be able to manage problems they have easily handled before or

Table 14.1. Factors That Help Children Cope With Parental Deployment

Parents on Active Duty	Parents in Reserve
Nondeployed spouse's ability to maintain a stable household routine	Nondeployed spouse's ability to maintain a stable household routine
Communication with deployed parent	Communication with deployed parent
Temporary reunions with deployed parent	Nondeployed spouse's support for the deployment
Geographic stability during deployment	Family members support for the deployment
Nondeployed spouse's support for the deployment	Parent and teacher reaction to the deployment

Note. Based on information from U.S. Department of Defense (2010b).

they may have emotional meltdowns. Younger children may simply not have the vocabulary to express themselves. Table 14.2 lists possible responses often experienced by children during the various stages of parental deployment. As school psychologists become familiar with children's potential reactions during the deployment cycle, they will be to provide children and parents full support as well as a commitment toward understanding what these families are experiencing.

Various strategies can be implemented to address children's emotional stressors in each of the deployment stages. Some strategies that may be implemented by school psychologists and other school staff for children and families managing deployment stress are summarized in Table 14.3.

Small group deployment support sessions should target addressing the range of emotions often experienced by children of military families. These emotions include sadness, anger, loneliness, panic, concern, guilt, fear, pride, depression, frustration, hopelessness, and uncertainty. Some children may actually show relief that the parent has deployed since the time leading up to the actual departure often is extremely stressful and can prompt family discord.

Collaborating With Teachers/Administrators

School psychologists are in a position to lead and guide preventive and responsive services for military children across various aspects of the educational setting. School psychologists may collaborate with administrators, teachers, and parents in implementing universal school-wide and classroom strategies, as well as working with teachers to identify children who may be at greater risk following deployment of a parent.

School-Wide Strategies

Providing a warm and supportive environment for children of a military family can be achieved through connecting the child and his or her family with the school. Once familiar with the deployment cycle, the school psychologist can review the cycle with the staff members and emphasize the emotional stressors children face. Training opportunities can be found at websites such as www.militarychild.org and www.militarykidsconnect.org. School psychologists should consult with their building administrator and lead the coordination of the following five initiatives offered by Collins (2009) to support military children and their families:

- *Develop a welcome packet for military children.* Include information about the mission of the school district, graduation requirements, curriculum requirements, attendance requirements, dress code requirements, immunizations, and school calendar, as well as school-specific information about clubs and organizations, a map of the school, and bell schedule. Also include information about resources for military families, including special workshops, orientations, and transition activities.
- *Establish a buddy program for military children at each school.* The buddy is a friendly face, a key source of

Table 14.2. Deployment Stages and Children's Possible Responses

Stages	Responses
Predeployment	
Infants	Fussy, changes in eating habits
Preschoolers	Confused, sad
School-age	Sad, angry or anxious, moody
Adolescents	Withdrawn, deny feelings about pending separation
Deployment (and R&R)	
Infants	Fussy, poor eating habits
Preschoolers	Sad, tantrums, changes in eating/elimination habits, symptoms of separation anxiety, feelings of guilt that it was their fault the parent has left
School-age	Increased somatic complaints, mood changes, decline in school performance, aggressive
Adolescents	Angry, aloof, apathetic, acting out behaviors may increase, loss of interest in normal activities, decline in school performance
Postdeployment (and reunion/reintegration)	
Infants	May not recognize returning service member and be fearful of him or her
Preschoolers	Happy and excited, but also experience anger at separation
School-age	Happy and angry, often leading to acting-out behaviors
Adolescents	Defiant, disappointed if their contributions at home are not acknowledged

Table 14.3. Strategies During Deployment

Deployment Stage	Strategies
Predeployment	• Conduct support groups and encourage the deploying parent to take time to be with each child individually. Exchange items to keep while separated during deployment. For example, a child reported that her father kept a marble that she gave him in his pocket at all times. This was a reassuring feeling for the child to know her father always had her marble. • In counseling sessions, educate the child about where the deploying parent is going. • During support groups, encourage the deploying parent to make a video or an audio recording reading a children's book or of a loving dialogue between the deploying parent and child. • Assure the child that the child's home will still be safe even though the deploying parent is leaving. • During support groups, encourage both parents to establish a plan for future communication (e-mail, Skype). • Alert the teacher of the deployment so the teacher can monitor the child's behavior throughout all deployment stages.
Deployment	• In individual sessions, assist the child in helping to create a journal/book to log daily/weekly events to share with the deployed parent upon return. Include photos and other ways to document events. • For young children having nightmares, encourage the family to put a pair of the deployed parent's combat boots under the bed for "protection." • Create a deployment support group to meet weekly. • During support groups, suggest the family keep a calendar or some other means (paper clip chain, remove one clip per week; jelly beans in a jar, eat one jelly bean per week) to count down the weeks until the deployed parent comes home. • Be sure to encourage the child to talk openly in counseling sessions about the deployment. • During support groups, encourage families to maintain a normal routine at home as much as possible. • In group or individual sessions, address potential feelings of guilt in young children who may feel it is their fault their parent had to deploy. • Have children create posters for bulletin boards honoring military families.
R&R	• Explain in counseling the importance of allowing the parent time to adjust to being home. • In counseling, the school psychologist should talk to the child about the anticipated changes in family roles while the deployed parent is home. • During support groups, stress the need to remain patient with the changes in routine the family will have. • In support sessions, remind the child to be prepared for another "goodbye" within about a week and to rehearse what to do and say.
Reunion	• In counseling, prepare the child for another change in routine and a renegotiation of roles and responsibilities in the family. • Just like with R&R, remind the child that the returning parent may need time to adjust and get comfortable with being home again. • Encourage the family to hang flags and banners and make signs for the returning parent. • During support groups, emphasize the importance of patience while the deployed parent adjusts to being home.
Reintegration	• In counseling, explain how the deployed parent sometimes changes following a deployment. • In support sessions, explain how typically it can take 6–8 months for full reintegration. • If the deployed parent returns with a mental or physical injury, explain to the child how this complicates the reintegration process.

information about the school, its programs, extracurricular activities, sports, expectations, and traditions, and someone to sit with at lunch and at athletic events.

• *Encourage parents to be active in the school.* The parents' presence in the school may provide a sense of comfort to ease their child's transition. Encourage their involvement in the PTA, on committees, and on school and district planning teams. In addition, parents may be able to share some insights into how the school can make their child feel more connected.

• *Promote student participation in extracurricular activities.* Extracurricular activities are an excellent way for children to meet classmates and quickly feel a part of the school, so help them explore all the options. Children of military families may come to the school after the deadline for signing up for activities, auditioning for drama productions, or trying out for sports, so encourage teachers and coaches to find a place for the child anyway.

- *Encourage parents and their children to become involved with organizations.* Involvement in organizations such as Boy Scouts, Girl Scouts, and 4H or local groups will help families connect to the community. Association with organizations that have groups across the country also will pave the way for continued connections when the families move to a different community, where the organization can provide a sense of continuity.

Classroom Strategies

School psychologists may collaborate with teachers to implement a number of classroom activities for children of military families. One of the most reassuring things a child can hear from a teacher is: "I know what you are going through." Children from military families often feel very alone during military deployment. School psychologists can assist classroom teachers by teaching the teachers about the intricacies of the deployment cycle. Once a teacher understands the typical stressors faced by military families, the teacher can better understand what could be affecting the child's behavior. That is, if there is an observed increase in such things as the child's activity level, unwillingness to comply, mood shifts, poor attention, and impulsiveness, then the teacher will know that what he or she is observing is *not* a child who suddenly has developed a learning or behavioral challenge but rather a child who is suddenly thrust into a parent's military deployment. There are classroom activities that integrate deployment themes into subject areas (math, reading, art, social studies, history, technology; Harrison & Vannest, 2008).

Teachers can assist students with writing a journal, with the student highlighting daily and weekly activities the child would want to share with the deployed parent. The school psychologist could meet weekly with the child and allow the child to dictate events of the week (books read, movies seen, sporting events, activities with family, pet stories) that would be fun or important to share with the deployed parent upon his or her return. Explain that the journal is a gift the child can give to the parent that they both can read together. In the beginning, the child may be hesitant to share so the school psychologist should prompt the conversation with questions: What did you do last weekend? What book are you reading now? Who are your friends and what do you like to do? What did you think about the last movie you watched? How have you

helped around the house lately? Has your pet done anything funny or silly lately?

Writing e-mails or letters can also be beneficial for children with deployed parents, as well as with other children. Operation Military Pride is a website (www. operationmilitarypride.org) that can assist in setting up connections for pen pal activities and other supportive efforts for the soldiers. Addition activities could include sending care packages to soldiers or even adopting a soldier.

At-Risk Students

When consulting and collaborating with teachers regarding children demonstrating emotional or behavioral concerns following parental deployment, school psychologists should encourage teachers to follow the *Educator's Guide to the Military Children During Deployment* (U.S. Department of Defense, 2010a). A prompt referral to the school psychologist could be considered for those students who experience the following after 3–4 weeks of parental deployment:

- Has not been able to resume normal classroom assignments and activities
- Continues to have high levels of emotional responses such as continued crying and intense sadness
- Continues to appear depressed, withdrawn, or noncommunicative
- Continues to have difficulty concentrating in school
- Expresses violent or depressed feelings in dark drawings or writings
- Intentionally hurts or cuts himself or herself or is at risk for hurting others
- Gains or loses a significant amount of weight in a period of weeks
- Discontinues taking care of his or her personal appearance
- Exhibits a possible drug or alcohol abuse problem

Supporting Military Families

Resilience specialist Froma Walsh (2006) identified nine characteristics that resilient families share. These characteristics reveal the family belief systems, organizational patterns, and communication/problem-solving skills that can foster resilience in all adults and children. These areas could be the focus of support from the school psychologist in working with military families.

- *Finding meaning in adversity:* Resilient families view crises as shared challenges that together they can understand, manage, and make meaningful in some way. They see their emotions as human and understandable under the circumstances and believe in their ability to learn from their experiences and move forward.

- *Positive outlook:* Resilient families have an optimistic rather than pessimistic view of life. They see each other's strengths and offer encouragement to overcome difficulties or accept what cannot be changed.
- *Transcendence and spirituality:* Resilient families have beliefs and values that offer meaning, purpose, and connection beyond personal lives and troubles. They find strength and comfort in their cultural traditions and experience spiritual inspiration in a variety of ways, including nature, the arts, and service to others.
- *Flexibility:* Resilient families adapt to change. They are able to adjust their family roles and rules to fit new life challenges while maintaining the rituals and traditions that provide stability in their relationships. Their flexibility depends on strong yet nurturing leadership, guidance, protection of children, and mutual respect in the marital relationship.
- *Connectedness:* Resilient families pull together during times of crisis. They are able to function as a team and support each other while respecting individual needs, differences, and boundaries.
- *Social and economic resources:* Resilient families reach out for help when they cannot solve problems on their own by turning to extended family, friends, neighbors, community services, and/or counseling.
- *Open emotional sharing:* Resilient families accept and encourage a wide range of emotional expression (joy, sadness, fear, silliness) in adults and children. They take responsibility for their own feelings and accept others who have different feelings. They value positive interactions and appreciate humor, even as they cope with difficult circumstances.
- *Clarity:* Resilient families practice clear, consistent, and honest communication. They say what they mean and thus they avoid sending vague, confusing, or mixed messages to each other.
- *Collaborative problem solving:* Resilient families manage difficulties by working together to understand a problem and identify ways to solve it. They make decisions together in ways that allow members to disagree openly, then resolve those disagreements through negotiation, compromise, and give and take. They seek to repair the hurts and misunderstandings that go along with conflicts and act proactively to solve current problems and prevent future ones. They also learn from their mistakes.

Mental Health Support for Military Families

School psychologists should become familiar with the deployment cycle and its potential emotional impact on children and the military family. School psychologists should identify the child's needs as well as relate to the stressors of the military family. The predominant goal with all interventions is to emphasize and strengthen that feeling of connectedness the family has with the deployed family member. Conducting small group as well as individual counseling is a standard practice school psychologists use to address children's needs.

Two programs aid in addressing the social/emotional needs of children of a military family: the Kimochis Educator Kit for all children and the Kimochis Military Family Kit, specifically for military children (www. kimochis.com). Both kits provide a social/emotional learning curriculum with activities on self-awareness, self-management, social awareness, relationship skills, and responsible decision making. The Kimochis Military Family Kit specifically provides social/emotional interventions to use with children throughout each stage of deployment.

There may also be community resources available to military families such as Military One Source (www. militaryonesource.com) and Strategic Outreach to Families of All Reservists (www.sofarusa.org). Both of these programs offer mental health sessions for military families free of charge. Some of these programs are also seeking professionals to donate their time and become part of their endeavor. Another critical part will be to connect with the local military base and as well as the veterans clinic to explore available resources for military families.

Support for Nondeployed Spouses

School psychologists also are in a position to use their skills to conduct deployment support groups with the nondeployed spouses. The following suggestions could be topics for discussion and sharing of ideas with nondeployed spouses:

- Discuss the easiest part of deployment versus the hardest part of deployment.
- Encourage parents to talk with their children about the deployment. (Parents talking with school-age children is important; that is, giving the child no news is worse than giving the child bad news. Many parents would like to ignore the situation because it makes them feel vulnerable and powerless to protect their children. Children will think and imagine the

worst if told nothing. When talking with children, be honest yet gentle.)

- Encourage parents to limit the child's exposure to news, especially violent news.
- Encourage parents to be a role model by demonstrating good coping techniques to their children, and suggest positive and creative ways of coping for older children (create scrapbooks and videos, write letters, take photos).
- Discuss how to handle sadness.
- Establish family rules and limits before deployment by addressing chores and responsibilities, consequences for disobeying rules, and avoiding saying "Wait until your [other parent] gets home!" and being flexible to adjust rules and limits as necessary.
- Discuss how to spend time together as a family, with each child and as a couple.
- Discuss techniques for communication: video and audio, letters, e-mail, journals, pictures, phone, Skype.
- Emphasize the importance of school and share updates with the deployed parent.
- Encourage allowing children to help with preparation during predeployment: pack, how to assist at home, family plans.
- Explore available support services.
- Establish "rules of communication" with the deployed spouse, such as agreeing to minimize arguments, not texting too much, not sharing all the negative things, and end all communications on a positive note.
- Discuss strategies with the parents if their children are having nightmares.

Death of a Deployed Parent

When a tragedy occurs, and a military parent does not return home, the thought of consoling a grieving child can be daunting. There are some services, however, that a school psychologist can provide to assist surviving parents and others in helping children cope with loss.

As military families react to the death of a loved one, there can be a sense that nothing can be done to make the child feel better. Research suggests, however, that parents and caring adults have a great natural ability to soothe even if they are sad themselves (Goodman, Cohen, & Cozza, 2010). Here are some suggestions the school psychologist can share with grieving families:

- Be clear and make sure to use the word "death" when talking with children. Referring to death using phrases such as "going to sleep" can be confusing.

- Children will need to talk about loss more than once. Encourage parents to follow their child's lead and stay open to talking as needed over time. It helps just to be ready and accessible, rather than pushing their child to talk.
- Encourage parents to take care of themselves by eating well, getting plenty of rest, and exercising. This will help them build resilience, tackle stress, and have the strength to be there for their family.
- Encourage parents to try to get back to normal routines and schedules at home. Bedtime rituals and keeping up with school activities can help their child feel secure.
- Encourage parents to take note of their child's behavior to get a sense of how their child is feeling. If the child acts out, remind them that it may be because of anger. Have them explain to their child how to express that anger in other ways, such as through drawing or writing.
- Encourage parents they should let their child know that any feelings the child may have are okay. Sadness, anger, guilt, and even happiness, as their lives keep moving, are all normal.

Sesame Street (2010) has produced an exceptional program for helping military families manage their grief of losing a loved one. *Talk, Listen, Connect: When Families Grieve* is designed for military families and provides a curriculum to address the grief feelings. Although designed for families, this remains a useful tool for school psychologists to use and follow in their administration of mental health services to grieving families.

SUMMARY

School psychologists are in a unique position to provide support to military families and children. The great majority of school psychologists are working with National Guard and Reserve families in public schools as opposed to Department of Defense schools. The impact deployment has on children can be profound and it is the responsibility of the school psychologist to become familiar with the deployment cycle and the struggles children can face. Research has found that during a parental deployment, some children experience positive effects (with feelings of increased pride and increased camaraderie) while others experience significantly higher rates of academic, emotional, and behavioral problems. There are other unique educational challenges faced by these children such as high mobility rates, elevated stress, and differing curriculum from school to school and differences in special education guidelines from school to school.

The school psychologist is also in a position to lead in educating faculty and staff about military deployment and service to the children. An essential part of this service would be to provide inservice training to staff members as well as consult with school administrators on how to support the child and his or her family. More research continues to be needed on specifically designed programs and social emotional curricula for children of military families.

REFERENCES

Chandra, A., Larea-Cinisomo, S., Jaycox, L., Tanielian Bing Han, T., Burns, R., & Ruder, T. (2010). Children on the home front: The experiences of children from military families. *Journal of American Academy of Pediatrics, 125*, 16–25. doi:10.1542/Peds.2009-1180

Chandra, A., Martin, L., Hawkins, S., & Richardson, A. (2010). The impact of parental deployment on child social and emotional functioning: Perspective of school staff. *Journal of Adolescent Health, 46*, 218–223.

Collins, R. (2009). *Five things school leaders can do to build connections.* Alexandria, VA: American Association of School Administrators. Retrieved from http://www.aasa.org/content.aspx?id=8996

Engel, R. C., Gallagher, L. B., & Lyle, D. S. (2010). Military deployment and children's academic achievement: Evidence from Department of Defense Education Activity schools. *Economics of Education Review, 29*, 73–82.

Fitzsimons, V. M., & Krause-Parello, C. A. (2009). Military children when parents are deployed overseas. *Journal of School Nursing, 25*, 40–47.

Flake, E., Davis, B., Johnson, P., & Middleton, L. (2009). The psychosocial effects of deployment on military children. *Journal of Developmental and Behavioral Pediatrics, 30*, 271–278.

Goodman, R., Cohen, J., & Cozza, S. (2010). *Helping bereaved military children.* Arlington, VA: Defense Centers of Excellence for Psychological Health and Traumatic Brain Injury. Retrieved from http://www.dcoe.health.mil/blog/10-04-01/Helping_Bereaved_Military_Children.aspx

Gorman, G., Eide, M., & Hisle-Gorman, E. (2010). Wartime military deployment and increased mental and behavioral health complaints. *Pediatrics, 126*, 1058. Retrieved from http://pediatrics.aappublications.org/content/126/6/1058.full.html

Harrison, J., & Vannest, K. (2008). Educators supporting families in times of crisis: Military reserve deployments. *Preventing School Failure, 52*(4), 17–23.

Hiew, C. C. (1992). Separated by their work: Families with fathers living apart. *Environment and Behavior, 24*, 206–225.

Huebner, A. J., & Mancini, J. A. (2005). *Adjustment among adolescents in military families when a parent is deployed: A final report submitted to the Military Family Research Institute and the Department of Defense Quality of Life Office.* Falls Church, VA: Department of Human Development, Virginia Tech. Retrieved from http://www.ausa.org/resources/familyprograms/update/Documents/Huebner.pdf

Jenkins, B., Godges, J., Munoz, A., Larson, E., Riley, K., Dixon, L., ...Wiseman, S. (2011). Beyond the shadow of 9/11. *Rand Review, 35*(2), Retrieved from http://www.rand.org/content/dam/rand/pubs/corporate_pubs/2011/RAND_CP22-2011-09.pdf

Mansfield, A., Kaufman, J., Engel, C., & Gaynes, B. (2011). Deployment and mental health diagnoses among children of US Army personnel. *Archives of Pediatric and Adolescent Medicine, 165*, 999–1005.

Meadows, S. (2012). *Military families: What we know and what we don't know.* Santa Monica, CA: RAND Corporation. Retrieved from http://rand.org/blog/2012/03/military-families-what-we-know-and-what-we-dont-know.html

National Association of School Psychologists. (2010). *Model for comprehensive and integrated school psychological services.* Bethesda, MD: Author. Retrieved from http://www.nasponline.org/standards/2010standards/2_PracticeModel.pdf

Pisano, M. C. (1996, March). *Implications of deployed and nondeployed fathers on seventh graders' California Achievement Test Scores during a military crisis.* Paper presented at the annual meeting of the National Association of School Psychologists, Atlanta, GA

Pisano, M. (2010). Military deployment and family reintegration. In A. Canter, L. Z. Paige, & S. Shaw (Eds.), *Helping children at home and school III: Handouts for families and educators* (S9H13). Bethesda, MD: National Association of School Psychologists.

Richardson, A., Chandra, A., Martin, L., Setodji, C., Hallmark, B., Campbell, N., ...Grady, P. (2011). *The effects of soldiers' deployment on children's academic performance and behavioral health.* Santa Monica, CA: RAND Corporation.

Sayer, N., Noorbaloochi, S., Frazier, P., Carlson, K., Gravely, A., & Murdoch, M. (2010). Reintegration problems and treatment interests among Iraq and Afghanistan combat veterans receiving VA medical care. *Psychiatric Services, 61*, 589–597.

Sesame Street. (2010). *Talk, listen, connect: When families grieve.* New York, NY: Author. Retrieved from http://www.sesamestreet.org/parents/topicsandactivities/toolkits/grief

Stafford, E. M., & Grady, B. A. (2003). Military family support. *Pediatric Annals, 32*, 110–115.

Tanielian, T. L., & Jaycox, L. H. (Eds.). (2008). *Invisible wounds of war: Psychological and cognitive injuries, their consequences, and services to assist recovery.* Santa Monica, CA: RAND Corporation.

U.S. Army. (2012). *Army 2020: Generating health and discipline in the force: Ahead of the strategic reset.* Washington, DC: U.S. Department of Defense. Retrieved from http://usarmy.vo.llnwd.net/e2/c/downloads/235822.pdf

U.S. Department of Defense. (2009). *DODEA partnership.* Washington, DC: Author. Retrieved from http://www.militaryk12partners.dodea.edu/studentsAtTheCenter/about/about-dofdea.html

U.S. Department of Defense. (2010a). *Educator's guide to the military child during deployment.* Washington, DC: Author. Retrieved from http://www.ed.gov/about/offices/list/os/homefront/homefront.pdf

U.S. Department of Defense. (2010b). *Report on the impact of deployment of members of the armed forces on their dependent children.* Washington, DC: Author. Retrieved from http://www.militaryonesource.mil/12038/MOS/Reports/Report_to_Congress_on_Impact_of_Deployment_on_Military_Children.pdf

Walsh, F. (2006). *Strengthening family resilience* (2nd ed.). New York, NY: Guilford Press.

Best Practices in Supporting Students Who Are Lesbian, Gay, Bisexual, Transgender, and Questioning

15

Emily S. Fisher
Loyola Marymount University (CA)

OVERVIEW

The school experiences of students who identify as lesbian, gay, bisexual, transgender, and questioning (LGBTQ) have gained increased attention over the last few years. This greater awareness has been fueled, in part, by highly publicized cases of anti-LGBTQ bullying and large monetary awards for bullied students, ongoing national debates about gay rights issues such as marriage, and overall increased visibility of LGBTQ people in the media (Fisher & Kennedy, 2012). Though research has consistently found that LGBTQ students are at risk for a number of negative academic, social, and emotional outcomes, such as lower grade point average and higher levels of depression (e.g., Varjas et al., 2008), it is critical to keep in mind that identifying as LGBTQ does not automatically put a student at risk. Rather, identifying as LGBTQ within hostile, homophobic, and heterosexist environments exacerbates risk (Fisher & Kennedy, 2012). Thus, efforts to improve school climate can serve to ameliorate these risks and support healthy development for all students (Kosciw, Greytak, Bartkiewicz, Boesen, & Palmer, 2012).

School psychologists have a moral, ethical, and legal obligation to ensure they have the awareness, knowledge, and skills to serve LGBTQ students as part of the National Association of School Psychologists (NASP) *Model for Comprehensive and Integrated School Psychological Services* (NASP, 2010a) domain of Diversity in Development and Learning. At the core of school psychologists' work is the fair, just, respectful, and dignified treatment of all students; the duty to seek training and supervision to ensure the provision of culturally competent services; and the responsibility to promote practices that support healthy development and safety for all students (NASP, 2010b).

This chapter provides school psychologists with the background information necessary to work effectively with LGBTQ students. Further, keeping with the idea that LGBTQ students may experience negative outcomes primarily due to environmental factors, this chapter focuses on universal prevention and intervention strategies to improve the school climate for LGBTQ students, targeted supports to help promote resilience and ameliorate risk for LGBTQ students, and LGBTQ-affirmative intensive interventions for students needing greater individualized support. This chapter also addresses how school psychologists can use a problem-solving approach to collect data about the school climate specific to LGBTQ students, identify areas for intervention, and monitor school-wide changes. Finally, this chapter offers resources for school psychologists who may need more detailed information about providing a broad range of culturally competent and affirmative direct and indirect services for this population.

BASIC CONSIDERATIONS

To work most effectively with LGBTQ students, school psychologists need to be aware of developmental issues; students' experiences of bullying and harassment in the schools; within group differences; and ethical, professional, and legal obligations.

Sexual and Gender Identity Development

Sexuality is a natural part of childhood and adolescence (DeLamater & Friedrich, 2002). For heterosexual individuals, *sexual identity* development, or how one defines his or her physical and emotional attractions, occurs without much consideration (Wolfe & Mash, 2006). However, for individuals who ultimately identify as gay, lesbian, bisexual, or some other variation of nonheterosexual sexual identity, feelings of differentness often occur during childhood that later may be recognized as early indicators of sexual identity (Savin-Williams, 2005). *Sexual orientation* is closely related to sexual identity and is typically defined by an individual's attractions, with those experiencing same-sex attractions having a gay, lesbian, or bisexual sexual orientation. School psychologists might think of sexual orientation more as socially defined labels (e.g., heterosexual, lesbian, gay, or bisexual) and sexual identity as self-defined labels. More and more, students are using a wide array of terms to define their sexual identity, such as "bi-queer" or "polysexual," and they may experience sexuality as more fluid and flexible than previous generations (Savin-Williams, 2005).

Gender identity, or one's internal feeling of maleness or femaleness, typically develops within the first 3 years of life, and for most individuals aligns with their biological sex (DeLamater & Friedrich, 2002). Some individuals experience *gender dysphoria*, or a discomfort with their assigned gender, and feel strongly that they are the wrong gender and want to change their gender. These individuals may identify or be identified by others as transgender (Zucker, 2006). The best practices described in this chapter broadly address LGBTQ students, and transgender students also may have needs that are distinct from lesbian, gay, and bisexual (LGB) students. A fuller examination of this topic can be found in Singh (2013).

In schools, and in society in general, labels are used to help us more quickly understand people, yet sexual and gender identity are complex and interrelated constructs that can seem to defy these labels. Take, for example, a student who was born male (i.e., with male sex organs) but who strongly feels like a girl and has a female gender identity. This student is attracted to boys, and because this student's gender identity is that of a girl, the student identifies as straight (sexual identity). What is most important for school psychologists is to respect the individual's identity, ask questions to understand how he or she is using terms, and allow for natural exploration to occur.

Experiences of LGBTQ Students

Since 1999, the Gay, Lesbian, and Straight Education Network (GLSEN) has been conducting national school climate surveys with lesbian, gay, bisexual, and transgender (LGBT) students (Kosciw et al., 2012). Key findings from the 2011 survey reveal that, overall, LGBT students experienced high levels of harassment and victimization at school based on sexual orientation and gender expression, with 81.9% reporting verbal harassment due to sexual orientation and 63.9% due to gender expression; 38.3% reporting physical harassment due to sexual orientation and 27.1% due to gender expression; and 56.9% reporting that teachers and other school staff made homophobic remarks and negative remarks about gender expression (Kosciw et al., 2012). Furthermore, when students experienced victimization, more than half (60.4%) did not report the incident, believing school staff members were unlikely to respond appropriately or that the situation could be exacerbated by reporting (Kosciw et al., 2012). Greater victimization at school was associated with higher levels of depression, poorer attendance, lower grade point average, and fewer intentions to attend college (Kosciw et al., 2012). Higher levels of victimization have also been associated with greater health and mental health problems, including anxiety, alcohol and drug use, sexual risk behaviors, and suicidality (Espelage, Aragon, Birkett, & Koenig, 2008; Varjas et al., 2008).

Diversity Among LGBTQ Students

There is a wide range of diversity among LGBTQ students. LGBTQ students are not only diverse in terms of race, ethnicity, socioeconomic status, religion, and urban density, but there is diversity among the subgroups of gay, lesbian, bisexual, transgender, and questioning that can have an impact on their experiences at school. Some examples of this diversity include students who are uncertain about their sexual identity, or those referred to as questioning, may be at greater risk for victimization at school and the related academic and mental health outcomes (Espelage et al., 2008), and students who identify as bisexual may experience greater marginalization and discrimination at school due to misconceptions and stereotypes about bisexuality (Kennedy & Fisher, 2010). Similarly, as described in the previous subsection, sexual orientation (LGB) and gender identity (transgender) are distinct, yet interrelated, constructs, and transgender students have experiences and needs that may differ from their LGB peers (Singh, 2013). Despite this wide diversity, the supports and interventions discussed in this chapter may serve all groups if school psychologists pay attention to learning about students as individuals, with sexual and gender identity as just one aspect of their identity. Further, school psychologists can help ensure that each group is explicitly included in efforts to create safer school climates. For example, Gay-Straight Alliances, discussed later in this chapter, can be more "trans-inclusive" by specifically addressing gender identity and expression in their promotional materials and as topics in meetings.

Ethical and Professional Obligations

School psychologists are ethically bound to respect the rights and dignity of all students, to take steps to change discriminatory practices, and to educate themselves about aspects of diversity that impact student well-being and service delivery (NASP, 2010b). Ethical principles mandate that school psychologists practice only within the scope of their competence and make referrals as necessary. However, the same principles mandate that school psychologists seek supervision, consultation, training, and assistance with personal problems to ensure effective practice (NASP, 2010b). This means that school psychologists who lack knowledge about LGBTQ issues, feel unprepared to work with LGBTQ students, or have personal beliefs that have an impact on their ability to provide affirmative services for LGBTQ students must seek information, training, supervision, and counseling rather than simply referring LGBTQ students to other practitioners (Fisher & Kennedy, 2012).

In order to ensure multicultural competence in working with LGBTQ students, it is important for school psychologists to examine their own beliefs and values related to sexuality and gender identity, understand the concepts of heterosexual privilege and heterosexism, and develop an awareness of the lived experiences of LGBTQ individuals (Garner & Emano, 2013). School psychologists can start the process of developing competence in working with LGBTQ students by reflecting on these questions (Garner & Emano, 2013; Whitman, 2013):

- When did I first become aware of my own sexual orientation and gender identity? Was there a time that I questioned these aspects of myself?
- Were sexual orientation and gender identity talked about in my family? What overt and covert messages did I receive about LGBTQ people growing up? What factors influenced these messages (culture, religion)?

- What stereotypes do I hold about LGBTQ people? How might these stereotypes shape my interactions with LGBTQ individuals?
- When I first meet someone, do I assume he or she is heterosexual and cisgender?
- Have I ever had to worry about negative consequences (such as losing friends, getting fired, being physically harassed) because of someone discovering my sexual orientation or gender identity?
- What steps have I taken to educate myself about LGBTQ students and their experiences at school? Do I believe that LGBTQ students have the right to be out and open at school? In what ways do I think that they bring harassment and bullying on themselves?
- What concerns do I have about being able to provide affirmative services for LGBTQ students?

It is through self-reflection activities such as these that school psychologists can help uncover their own biases and seek appropriate training and support to ensure they can provide ethical and affirmative services for LGBTQ students.

NASP has taken a clear position that school psychologists have a duty to ensure that LGBTQ students "have equal opportunities to participate in and benefit from educational and mental health services … in a school climate that is safe, accepting, and respectful of all persons and free from discrimination, harassment, violence, and abuse" (NASP, 2011, p. 1). School psychologists can do this by modeling ethical practices, ensuring their visibility as a resource for LGBTQ students, providing trainings for school staff on LGBTQ issues, addressing discriminatory practices, providing appropriate counseling services, and advocating for LGBTQ students (NASP, 2011).

Legal Considerations

In the ideal world, all educators would be inclusive of and support LGBTQ students because it is the moral, ethical, and just thing to do. In reality, it often takes legal action or threats of lawsuits for some school personnel to make changes in their practices. School psychologists should take both stances: encouraging school personnel to examine their ethical duty to care for all students and ensuring that school personnel understand their legal obligations to equally educate and protect all students and the potential consequences if they do not. This may be particularly helpful in schools and communities that are more resistant to efforts to be inclusive of LGBTQ students.

Although there currently are no federal laws that specifically protect against LGBTQ-related bullying, harassment, or discrimination, federal laws do provide LGBTQ students with legal recourse when their rights are violated. Fisher and Kennedy (2012) outlined the most relevant federal laws:

- The Equal Protection Clause of the Fourteenth Amendment to the U.S. Constitution (§ 1983) holds that if a school district protects any student from bullying, harassment, or discrimination, it must equally protect all students. Thus, LGBTQ students have successfully sued districts and school personnel when their complaints of harassment and discrimination were not treated the same as non-LGBTQ students' complaints.
- Title IX of the Educational Amendments of 1972 (20 U.S.C. §1681) protects students from sexual harassment. Under Title IX, courts have found that LGBTQ students' rights were violated when they were harassed for failing to conform to sex or gender stereotypes or when harassment included sexually explicit messages.
- The First Amendment to the U.S. Constitution protects freedom of speech. For LGBTQ students, this protection extends to their right to be out at school, to express their gender identity, and to have access to supportive LGBTQ materials and websites.
- The Equal Access Act (U.S.C. § 4071) applies to schools that receive any federal funding. Related to LGBTQ students, it requires that if a school allows any noncurricular group or club to meet on campus, it also must allow a Gay-Straight Alliance or similar club to meet on campus.

At the state level, laws related to LGBTQ individuals vary widely and seem to be in constant flux. School psychologists are encouraged to keep abreast of the latest developments in the states in which they work. One excellent resource for this is the Human Rights Campaign (http://www.hrc.org), which provides up-to-date information on all state laws that have an impact on LGBTQ individuals (e.g., marriage, adoption), as well as specific information about each state's school antibullying and antidiscrimination laws and policies.

BEST PRACTICES IN SUPPORTING STUDENTS WHO ARE LGBTQ

Holding with the view that the risks LGBTQ students face in large part are due to environmental factors, it stands that school-wide interventions focusing on improving school climate will have the greatest impact on students' school experiences. Further, because these environmental risk factors exist in home, school, and community domains, some universal supports aimed at affecting all students may also serve as targeted interventions for LGBTQ students needing additional support (e.g., a Gay-Straight Alliance has an impact on school climate and also may provide targeted support for LGBTQ students). Thus, school psychologists can feel assured that if the following best practices are implemented with integrity and consistency, LGBTQ students likely will experience improved academic and social–emotional outcomes. Though one person certainly can make a difference in the lives of LGBTQ students, school-wide and long-term success will not come from school psychologists working in isolation. School psychologists should seek other individuals within the school, district, and community to support these change efforts. For example, school psychologists may discover willing collaborators among teachers, administrators, parents, or community members in their efforts to make schools safer for LGBTQ students, and this team approach can help positive changes endure even if one person leaves the school.

The best practices outlined in this chapter primarily target students in middle and high school, as adolescence is the time in which sexual identity usually emerges (DeLamater & Friedrich, 2002). Practices that promote LGBTQ inclusiveness in elementary school typically focus on recognizing family diversity and creating a positive foundation for students' sexual and gender identity development (Fisher & Kennedy, 2012).

Universal Support

There are a number of universal supports that can have a positive impact on school climate for LGBTQ students. These include school policies that explicitly protect students on the basis of sexuality and gender identity, staff development activities surrounding LGBTQ issues, school-wide bullying prevention efforts, and LGBTQ-inclusive curriculum.

School Policy

The development of a comprehensive and inclusive policy that protects students on the basis of actual or perceived sexual orientation and gender identity is arguably the single most important action a school can take in creating safe and supportive climates for LGBTQ students (Fisher & Kennedy, 2012; Kosciw et al., 2012). This policy sets the stage for all other efforts to change school climate. Some states have clear antidiscrimination, antiharassment, and/or antibullying laws that provide explicit protections based on sexual orientation and gender identity. Other states offer no such guidance, forcing district and school administrators to develop their own policies. School psychologists can play an important role in helping administrators develop policies that provide protections for LGBTQ students by providing relevant information about legal issues, bullying, and harassment, such as the information provided in the Basic Considerations section of this chapter. School psychologists should promote policies that "explicitly state protection based on personal characteristics, such as sexual orientation and gender identity/expression, among others" (Kosciw et al., 2012, p. 53).

With a comprehensive policy in place, school psychologists can work with school administrative teams to ensure teachers and other school staff know the policy, recognize behaviors that violate the policy, and understand how they are expected to respond when they witness anti-LGBTQ bullying or harassment (Fisher & Kennedy, 2012). These topics may be covered through professional development activities with school staff which will be discussed in the next section of this chapter. Similarly, students and parents need to be educated about the policy, unacceptable behaviors, and consequences for policy violations, which can be done through publications, such as student handbooks, or through school-wide assemblies (Fisher & Kennedy, 2012).

Along with the creation of comprehensive policies and educating everyone in the school community about policies, consistent enforcement is critical for policies to have a positive impact on school climate for LGBTQ students (Fisher & Kennedy, 2012). School psychologists may head or be members of a school team that develops protocols to ensure that all types of bullying and harassment are handled in a similar manner and that consequences are applied equitably (Fisher & Kennedy, 2012). These protocols can highlight a zero-tolerance stance in that school personnel are expected to respond to any and all instances of discrimination, harassment, and bullying in a consistent manner (Fisher et al., 2008). Additionally, as part of these protocols, school psychologists can lead the efforts to outline appropriate disciplinary actions, supports for students who are targeted, and skills training or counseling for students who continually violate other students' rights (Young & Mendez, 2003).

Staff Development

Along with ensuring that school personnel understand school policy, it is recommended that teachers, administrators, and mental health professionals in the schools receive training around LGBTQ issues (Fisher et al., 2008). In reviewing the research on training on LGBTQ issues, Whitman (2013) concluded that school personnel, across disciplines and including school psychologists, have not been adequately trained in LGBTQ issues in their preparation programs. Thus, inservice professional development is necessary (Whitman, 2013).

Whitman (2013) summarizes the research as to what these inservice trainings should entail, focusing on three areas: knowledge, awareness, and skill. In the area of knowledge, it is important for school personnel to understand (a) language and terminology related to LGBTQ individuals, (b) sexual and gender identity development and resources to support healthy development, and (c) the school experiences of LGBTQ students and the corresponding academic and social–emotional outcomes. In the area of awareness, school personnel should be encouraged to explore their own sexual and gender identity development and their "biases, assumptions, stereotypes, and attitudes" (Whitman, 2013, p. 130) about LGBTQ students in a manner that encourages open discussion and facilitates questioning these beliefs. School personnel also need the skill to provide support for LGBTQ students, including (a) being visible within the school as a support person, (b) responding appropriately to harassment and bullying, (c) integrating LGBTQ topics into classroom curriculum, and (d) providing affirmative counseling services. Further, Whitman (2013) suggests that inservice professional development include the use of handouts, activities, directed readings, videos, and guest speakers to engage adult learners in the material.

Ideally, school psychologists would be able to offer this kind of professional development, and they should strive to develop the expertise in LGBTQ issues to be able to do so. This may be done through reading, attending sessions on LGBTQ issues at professional conferences, seeking information through credible online sources, and, when available, collaborating with experts from local community agencies. If school psychologists are still developing their expertise in LGBTQ issues, it is recommended that they help identify individuals and agencies that can provide professional development for their school communities. More information on agencies that offer support for professional development in schools can be found in Fisher and Kennedy (2012).

Bullying Intervention and Prevention

School psychologists have long been involved with bullying prevention and intervention. Unfortunately, research on bullying intervention programs has demonstrated modest results overall and little to no impact on actual bullying behaviors (Merrell, Gueldner, Ross, & Isava, 2008), and there is no systematic research on the effects of these programs on bullying directed toward LGBTQ students (Espelage & Rao, 2013). Given the impact bullying has on school-age youth and the resources schools devote to intervention and prevention efforts, Espelage and Rao (2013) suggest that future research in bullying prevention and intervention must examine "contextual variables that are promoting bullying within schools" (p. 148) and should include information from across diverse disciplines to understand the larger "historical and sociological nature of bullying" (p. 148).

An area of bullying research receiving greater attention is the role of bystanders and bystander intervention in bullying incidents (Espelage & Rao, 2013). Espelage and Rao suggest that schools need to explicate expectations for bystander behavior and teach bystanders how to respond when they witness acts of bullying. This research is not specific to LGBTQ students, but it suggests the need for the development of effective programming to build students' empathy and teach strategies to intervene when bullying occurs. This may be especially true related to LGBTQ issues, as research suggests that even heterosexual students who do not actively engage in bullying their LGBTQ classmates still engage in more subtle forms of prejudice and discrimination (Poteat, Espelage, & Koenig, 2009).

School psychologists are uniquely trained to support the aforementioned shift in bullying prevention efforts by promoting school-wide social–emotional learning activities. Additionally, perhaps as part of a larger commitment to diversity, school-wide awareness activities around LGBTQ issues may serve to promote greater empathy and understanding (Espelage & Rao, 2013). These activities may also be promoted by the Gay-Straight Alliance or similar club at school. Two nationwide awareness activities that school psychologists can help promote, both sponsored by GLSEN, are The Day of Silence (http://www.dayofsilence.org) to bring attention to the silencing effects of anti-LGBTQ bullying and No Name-Calling Week (http://www.nonamecallingweek.org), which provides a week-long program of educational activities to promote dialogue and end name calling, harassment, and bullying at school. Using these activities to engage all students in discussions about LGBTQ issues, including bullying and expected bystander behavior, may help to improve school climate for LGBTQ youth.

Inclusive Curriculum

Curriculum can be viewed as a way to validate students and their experiences, increase visibility of underrepresented and marginalized groups, and teach students about other people and the world around them (Greytak & Kosciw, 2013). Given the ever-increasing diversity in our schools, there has been a push to make curricula more representative of students and more relevant to their lives, but these efforts primarily have focused on racial, ethnic, cultural, and linguistic diversity (Fisher & Kennedy, 2012). Through professional development activities and consultation, school psychologists can help teachers integrate LGBTQ topics into curriculum so that all students feel valued and validated. Engaging in discussions with teachers about LGBTQ inclusive curriculum may be easier after other staff development activities around LGBTQ issues have been completed, such as those previously discussed in this chapter.

School psychologists can help teachers see that it is possible to integrate LGBTQ topics into any subject (e.g., English, history, civics, science, math, sexuality education, health, music, art; Fisher & Kennedy, 2012; Greytak & Kosciw, 2013). School psychologists can bring ideas of how others have created inclusive curricula in these different areas and encourage teachers to engage in discussions with their teams about different ways they can include LGBTQ topics. Some examples include discussions of the civil rights movement in the United States and current experiences of social and institutionalized racism (e.g., overrepresentation of African American men in the prison system) lend to exploration of other civil rights movements and marginalized groups, such as LGBTQ individuals; lessons in art class about artists and artistic periods can include biographical information about artists and how personal characteristics influenced their art and acceptance in the art world; and a unit in science can examine the nature/nurture debate and include activities of how this debate plays out in current society (including sexual and gender identity development). It is recommended that school psychologists seek administrative support before engaging teachers in these kinds of discussions and activities.

At the secondary level, a responsive and inclusive curriculum often involves discussions of racism, sexism, heterosexism, oppression, and discrimination, along with historical and social contexts. When teachers are comfortable talking about these topics and create a climate where students can engage in respectful discussions of these topics, students can begin to relate their experiences of discrimination and prejudice to those of other students. By using questions similar to those school psychologists might use to increase their own self-awareness, they can help teachers examine their own feelings about these topics and their comfort in discussing these topics with students, ultimately encouraging teachers to try one lesson or activity that is inclusive of LGBTQ individuals (Fisher & Kennedy, 2012).

Targeted Support

School psychologists can provide additional support for LGBTQ students by helping them build community connections. At school, this might be done through supporting a Gay-Straight Alliance. Outside of school, school psychologists can help students connect to appropriate local and Internet resources and services.

Gay-Straight Alliances

Gay-Straight Alliances and similar clubs are nonacademic, student-led school groups that support LGBTQ students and their heterosexual peers (Kennedy, 2013). The simple presence of a Gay-Straight Alliance on campus can have an impact on the wider school climate, and it has been consistently demonstrated that LGBTQ students who attended schools with Gay-Straight Alliances reported less victimization and greater school connectedness (Kosciw et al., 2012). As previously mentioned, the Equal Access Act protects students' right to form a Gay-Straight Alliance if the school allows other nonacademic student clubs to meet on campus.

Gay-Straight Alliances can provide targeted support for members. Research has shown that Gay-Straight Alliances can help students by increasing their comfort with their sexual orientation, by helping them develop strategies to address harassment, by providing increased social support and a sense of belonging, and by helping them feel empowered to have a voice and contribute to society (Lee, 2002; Russell, Muraco, Subramanaim, & Laub, 2009).

Most often, schools require student clubs to have a faculty advisor, and this is a major role school psychologists can play related to Gay-Straight Alliances. As advisors, school psychologists can support Gay-Straight Alliances in many ways, including sharing legal information about students' rights with school administrators, supporting the development of a club if one does not yet exist on campus, helping students access information about Gay-Straight Alliance development and activities online (such as from the Gay-Straight Alliance network; http://www.gsanetwork.org), and managing resistance from others in the school community (Fisher & Kennedy, 2012). In this role, school psychologists will be more visible around school as a resource for students, teachers, administrators, and parents seeking information or support around LGBTQ issues (Kennedy, 2013).

Community Resources

Community connections are critical for providing a full range of services for students across the levels of support, and school psychologists can access community resources to supplement school-based services for LGBTQ students. In many areas, there are local agencies that can provide an array of services for LGBTQ students, and in areas without such agencies, the Internet may provide information and community access (Kennedy, 2013). One way school psychologists can provide targeted support for LGBTQ students is to help them find a community with which they can connect. Similar to the benefits of Gay-Straight Alliances, this connection can help normalize students' experiences and create a sense of belonging and hope. School psychologists can create a list of local and Internet resources and services to provide to students (Kennedy, 2013). It is important to help students recognize legitimate youth-based Internet support sites, such as The Trevor Project (http://www.thetrevorproject.org), so as to ensure safe Internet use and avoid potentially harmful sites. School psychologists can also help LGBTQ students connect with community resources to provide a certain type of service not available at school, such as a doctor who is sensitive to LGBTQ health issues or a homeless shelter that caters to LGBTQ youth (Kennedy, 2013).

Intensive Support: Counseling

LGBTQ students may seek or be referred for counseling for a variety of reasons, such as issues related to their sexual orientation or gender identity, issues exacerbated by their sexual orientation or gender identity, or issues unrelated to their sexual orientation or gender identity (Fisher & Kennedy, 2012). As school psychologists begin the counseling process, they should be open to discussing sexual orientation and gender identity, but not assume that it is at the heart of the student's problems. Further, students may choose not to disclose their sexual orientation or gender identity at the beginning of counseling, so it is important to always create an environment that facilitates trust and openness regardless of the presenting problem. Early in the counseling process, school psychologists should strive to gather information about different aspects of students' lives by asking open-ended and gender-neutral questions. For example, school psychologists might ask, "Do you have any romantic interests?" to avoid the assumption of heterosexuality.

The information that follows in this chapter is specific to students whose presenting problems are due to or exacerbated by their sexual orientation or gender identity, but taking an affirmative approach regardless of students' presenting problem can help create a safe space in which students may feel more comfortable to disclose their identity at some later point.

Affirmative Approach

Good basic counseling skills that build a positive therapeutic relationship are at the heart of counseling LGBTQ students. These include listening, validating and affirming, displaying understanding and empathy, and taking a nonjudgmental stance (Israel, Gorcheva, Burnes, & Walther, 2008; Malley & Tasker, 2007). It is also important that school psychologists display positive attitudes about all sexual orientations and gender identities, are knowledgeable about LGBTQ issues, focus on sexual orientation or gender identity only when appropriate, and avoid misattributing problems to sexual orientation or gender identity (Israel et al., 2008; Malley & Tasker, 2007). It is recommended that school psychologists bring up sexual orientation and gender identity during their introduction to counseling, as two of the many issues that students talk about in counseling, and address any limits to confidentiality around these topics (Fisher & Kennedy, 2012).

Supporting Identity Development and Coming Out

Identity exploration can be a major theme in counseling LGBTQ students. If students are earlier in the process of identity development, school psychologists can provide a safe place where students feel comfortable to explore their feelings, thoughts, and desires without pressure to "choose" an identity (Hunter, 2007). School psychologists can also help students explore images of LGBTQ people and their reactions to these images to better understand and challenge students' internalized homophobia or heterosexism (Hunter, 2007). Students who are later in the process of identity development may benefit from discussing their experiences connecting with members of the LGBTQ community, either in person or online, as well as their thoughts and feelings about engaging in romantic and sexual relationships (Hunter, 2007). Overall, school psychologists want to be open to discussing any topics students bring up. School psychologists should ask questions or seek information if students raise topics that are unfamiliar to them.

Typically, disclosure of sexual or gender identity (i.e., coming out) is part of the developmental process for students. It used to be thought that disclosure was a mark of identity achievement for LGBT individuals, but this might not be true for students who may experience family rejection or abuse as a result of their disclosure. School psychologists can help students explore their thoughts and feelings about disclosing their identity to others in their lives and help them weigh the pros and cons of disclosure (Hunter, 2007). If students decide to disclose, it can be helpful for them to develop a disclosure script in counseling, and it has been suggested that youth make positive statements, such as "I am a lesbian and I am happy" when they disclose to avoid ambiguity (Heatherington & Lavner, 2008). Further, school psychologists can help the student understand that, just as it took the student time to come to understand his or her identity, it may take others time to come to terms with the student's disclosure (Mosher, 2001).

Suicide Prevention and Intervention

Researchers have consistently found that LGBTQ youth are at increased risk for suicide (Haas et al., 2011). Once again, it is critical to point out that sexual orientation and gender identity status do not place an individual at increased risk for suicide. Rather, increased risk factors (e.g., victimization at school) and lack of protective factors (e.g., family connectedness) contribute to this increased suicide risk (Eisenberg & Resnick, 2006; Haas et al., 2011). In fact, as a result of their study of gay, lesbian, and bisexual (GLB) youth, Eisenberg and Resnick (2006) concluded that "if all GLB youth reported protective factors at the level of non-GLB youth, suicidal ideation and attempts are expected to be considerably lower" (p. 666). Thus, effective suicide prevention and intervention strategies will need to focus on reducing risks and increasing protections, which may be done by implementing the other best practices described in this chapter such as inclusive school policies and Gay-Straight Alliances. One important issue to consider when addressing suicidality among LGBTQ students is to avoid unnecessary disclosure of a student's sexual or gender identity if school psychologists must break confidentiality to ensure a student's safety (Garner & Emano, 2013).

Reparative Therapy: A Denounced Practice

Reparative therapy, also called conversion therapy, is aimed at changing an individual's sexual orientation from LGB to heterosexual. This practice has been denounced by every major mainstream mental health organization (e.g., NASP, American Psychological Association, American School Counseling Association) as unethical and potentially damaging to students (Just the Facts Coalition, 2008). Not only must school psychologists avoid engaging in these unethical and harmful practices, but also they can strive to educate others in the school community about healthy sexual identity development and ethical and affirmative counseling approaches.

Case Example

John is a high achieving 13 year old, eighth-grade general education student. He began weekly counseling with the school psychologist primarily to address social anxiety and test anxiety. At times, John's anxiety has made it difficult for him to attend school, and when he does attend, he is sometimes unable to fully participate in class. John speaks easily with the school psychologist, seeking insight about his anxiety and practicing anxiety management techniques. As John has grown more comfortable in counseling, he has also started to talk more about body image issues and about his peer relationships and feelings of differentness. He has often commented that he does not feel that he "fits in" with other eighth graders, and that while he "has friends," he does not think that any of them truly "get him." The school psychologist finds John to be bright, engaged, thoughtful, and self-reflective, and given John's maturity, she can understand why John might find it difficult to feel connected with his peers.

In counseling, John has not expressed having any romantic interests, but he has talked about some of his peers' romances. One day, seemingly out of the blue, John asks the school psychologist, "Do you think I'm gay?" The school psychologist responds, "Huh, that's something we haven't really talked about before so I would like to know more about what you've been

thinking." John tells the school psychologist that he has been wondering about being gay because he hasn't been feeling a desire to date girls like his guy friends have. The school psychologist asks if John has been having any feelings about boys. John replies, "Not sexual feelings, but, well, I'm kind of embarrassed to tell you." The school psychologist assures John that students talk about all kinds of issues in counseling, and that many students this age are thinking more about sex and sexuality. John goes on to share that he has found himself looking at other boys' bodies during physical education classes. The school psychologist gently questions John, asking what thoughts and feelings he experiences when he looks at boys' bodies. John replies, "Well, I don't want to touch them or anything. Mostly, I just look at how muscular they are, and I wish that I was like that." The conversation turns more to John's ideas about body image. Near the end of the session, the school psychologist brings the conversation back to sexuality saying, "It sounds like you're exploring the 'what ifs' of sexuality. As you have more thoughts and feelings, let's explore them together."

Identify Needs and Evaluating Impact

School psychologists can learn a great deal about the needs of LGBTQ students and the impact of interventions by assessing school climate and the effectiveness of staff development activities.

School Climate

Given the influence that school climate has on the experiences of LGBTQ students, assessing school climate is a logical place for school psychologists to begin in understanding the current state of their school or district, targeting areas for intervention, and monitoring progress. Fisher and Kennedy (2012) created a Safe School Climate Checklist to help school psychologist quickly identify whether or not key indicators of safe school climates for LGBTQ students are present across four areas. First, school psychologists assess their own knowledge and skills related to law and policy, ability and willingness to intervene when hearing anti-LGBTQ comments, and comfort level using LGBTQ-inclusive language and responding to student questions. Next, school psychologists assess school-level variables related to policies, curriculum, libraries and resources, Gay-Straight Alliances or similar clubs, and school-wide awareness activities. School psychologists then assess their colleagues' knowledge and skills related to responding to student questions, intervening when anti-LGBTQ comments are made, and using inclusive language. Finally, school psychologists assess LGBTQ and heterosexual students' experiences related to asking for help, witnessing school staff intervening when harassment occurs, knowing how to respond as bystanders, and being familiar with school policies. School psychologists may have to do some investigation to be able to answer these questions, and the information gathered from this informal assessment can help school psychologists identify areas for intervention.

Another way school psychologists can collect data and assess school climate is through the use of school climate surveys that explicitly ask students about experiences of LGBTQ-related harassment and bullying. In many schools, school climate surveys may already exist, and school psychologists can help develop LGBTQ-specific items to add to these surveys. In other schools, school psychologists might consider administering a school-wide school climate survey specific to LGBTQ issues or with a specific section on LGBTQ issues. One example that can be obtained online from GLSEN (2006) is the Local School Climate Survey. By analyzing the survey responses, school psychologists can work with their school teams to prioritize areas of need and plan for interventions.

School climate surveys can also be an excellent way to monitor progress and document changes over time. For example, GLSEN administers their national school climate survey every 2 years, and their data have highlighted some positive changes in LGBTQ students' experiences over the past 12 years (Kosciw et al., 2012). School psychologists might consider setting some measurable short-term and long-term goals related to changes in school climate. These goals will differ greatly for each school psychologist depending on myriad factors, such as the school community's openness to LGBTQ issues. For school psychologists in schools that are considering LGBTQ issues for the first time, a short-term goal might be to find an ally in the school community or convene a team of three teachers and/or administrators to plan the administration of the first school climate survey. For school psychologists in schools more open to LGBTQ issues, a long-term goal might be to see positive trends in students' reports of anti-LGBTQ harassment across two years on the annual school climate survey.

Staff Development

Teachers and other school staff play a large role in the overall school climate and in the experiences of LGBTQ students, and it is important for school psychologists to develop tools to assess teachers' needs related to LGBTQ issues and assess the impact of professional development activities on teachers' attitudes, knowledge, and behaviors. Before beginning any kind of inservice or professional development program for school staff, school psychologists should conduct a needs assessment to understand what issues are most salient for the particular audience (Fisher & Kennedy, 2012). This needs assessment also may serve as a pretest to help evaluate the impact of the training, and should assess knowledge of risks faced by LGBTQ students, understanding of laws and school or district policies related to protection for LGBTQ students, and comfort level intervening when witnessing anti-LGBTQ bullying (Fisher & Kennedy, 2012). After the training, a post-training survey using the same items as the needs assessment can help determine the impact of the training and areas of need for further development. Further, school psychologists are in the unique position to be able provide ongoing support for teachers related to changes in their practices to be more inclusive of LGBTQ students after professional development activities through consultation and collaboration. Given this expanded role, school psychologists should consider assessing the impact of the initial inservice training and follow up activities by administering the survey again several months after the posttraining survey.

School Psychologist as Ally and Advocate

Across the tiers of support, school psychologists have immensely important roles to play as allies and advocates for LGBTQ students. Allies are those who speak out and stand up for LGBTQ students, work to end oppression of LGBTQ students, and advocate for LGBTQ students in the school system (McGarry, 2013). In support of this role, the NASP *Principles for Professional Ethics* (2010b) state:

> School psychologists use their professional expertise to promote changes in schools and community service systems that will benefit children and other clients. They advocate for school policies and practices that are in the best interests of children and that respect and protect the legal rights of students and parents. (p. 14)

Becoming an ally and advocate is a process, not an event. This process occurs through honest self-reflection; the development of an awareness of overt and subtle forms of homophobia and heterosexist privilege; and the decision to take action in the face of prejudice, discrimination, and injustice (McGarry, 2013). There are many ways for school psychologists to engage in this process, and their development as allies and advocates will occur as they learn more about LGBTQ issues, take notice of more subtle forms of LGBTQ discrimination, risk speaking out when anti-LGBTQ language is used, engage school personnel in discussions about LGBTQ issues, and takes steps to make schools more inclusive for LGBTQ students. What is most critical is that school psychologists begin this process and continue to strive to ensure LGBTQ students are served in a safe, supportive, and equitable manner. School psychologists may consider engaging in some or all of the following activities in their development toward being allies and advocates (Fisher & Kennedy, 2012; McGarry, 2013):

- Exploring their personal values, biases, beliefs, and behaviors related to sexual orientation and gender identity
- Committing to ongoing professional development related to LGBTQ issues, such as that offered at professional conferences
- Reflecting on situations in which subtle and overt anti-LGBTQ biases are present and considering how they responded in the moment and how they might like to respond differently in the future
- Practicing using affirmative language to avoid assumptions of heterosexuality, such as using "partner" or "romantic interest" instead of "boyfriend" or "girlfriend"
- Displaying affirmative posters or stickers around the office to develop visibility as an ally
- Seeking consultation, supervision, and/or counseling to address any anti-LGBTQ personal beliefs that affect work with students
- Organizing and/or conducting inservice trainings on LGBTQ topics, including addressing bullying and harassment and developing inclusive curriculum
- Serving as a Gay-Straight Alliance advisor
- Educating others about sexual and gender identity development and the dangers of practices such as reparative therapy
- Mentoring and supervising other school psychologists in LGBTQ-affirmative practices

SUMMARY

Students who are LGBTQ face increased risks for academic, social, emotional, and health problems related to the marginalization, discrimination, and victimization they experience at school and in other environments. From hearing peers and teachers make negative remarks about students' sexual orientation and gender expression, to being subjected to inequitable disciplinary practices, to being invisible in the curriculum, LGBTQ students often experience the school climate as hostile, homophobic, and heterosexist. Ethically, school psychologists cannot stand by while such practices exist, and they must take actions to advocate for policies and practices that promote healthy development and allow all students to learn in a safe school environment.

Universal supports are particularly important for changing the school climate for LGBTQ students. School psychologists, working with a team of administrators and teachers, can lead the charge in ensuring that school antidiscrimination policies are specific and inclusive of actual or perceived sexual orientation or gender identity, all school staff are adequately trained in LGBTQ issues and know how they are expected to respond to anti-LGBTQ harassment and bullying, bullying prevention programming addresses expectations for bystanders and includes information and activities specific to LGBTQ students, and curriculum provides visibility and validation of LGBTQ individuals. With these school-wide efforts in place, school psychologists can assist LGBTQ students experiencing greater need by connecting them with a supportive community, whether through a Gay-Straight Alliance at school, a local community organization, or a reputable online community, to increase their social support, feelings of belonging, and sense of empowerment. School psychologists can also provide affirmative counseling for students most at risk to ensure their healthy development and personal safety.

Across the levels of support, school psychologists must work to ensure they are developing the knowledge and skills to advocate for LGBTQ students. This process of becoming an ally and advocate can start by taking one small step, such as making a conscious effort to use nonbiased language when talking with students, and can lead to greater action, such as conducting a series of professional development activities on LGBTQ issues. As school psychologists find their voice in speaking up for LGBTQ students, they will empower students to find their voices to stand up in the face of injustice.

AUTHOR NOTE

Disclosure. Emily S. Fisher has a financial interest in books she authored or coauthored referenced in this chapter.

REFERENCES

DeLamater, J., & Friedrich, W. N. (2002). Human sexual development. *The Journal of Sex Research, 39,* 10–14.

Eisenberg, M. E., & Resnick, M. D. (2006). Suicidality among gay, lesbian and bisexual youth: The role of protective factors. *Journal of Adolescent Health, 39,* 662–228. doi:10.1016/j.jadohealth.2006.04.024

Espelage, D. L., Aragon, S. R., Birkett, M., & Koenig, B. W. (2008). Homophobic teasing, psychological outcomes, and sexual orientation among high school students: What influence do parents and schools have? *School Psychology Review, 37,* 202–216.

Espelage, D. L., & Rao, M. A. (2013). Safe schools: Prevention and intervention for bullying and harassment. In E. S. Fisher & K. Komosa-Hawkins (Eds.), *Creating safe and supportive learning environments: A guide for working with lesbian, gay, bisexual, transgender, and questioning youth and families.* (pp. 140–155). New York, NY: Routledge.

Fisher, E. S., & Kennedy, K. S. (2012). *Responsive school practices to support lesbian, gay, bisexual, transgender, and questioning students and families.* New York, NY: Routledge.

Fisher, E. S., Komosa-Hawkins, K., Saldaña, E., Thomas, G. M., Hsiao, C., Rauld, M., & Miller, D. (2006). Promoting school success for lesbian, gay, bisexual, and questioning students: Primary, secondary, and tertiary prevention and intervention strategies. *The California School Psychologist, 13,* 79–91, Retrieved from http://www.caspsurveys.org/NEW/pdfs/journal08.pdf#page=79

Garner, G. L., & Emano, D. M. (2013). Counseling lesbian, gay, bisexual, transgender, and questioning students. In E. S. Fisher & K. Komosa-Hawkins (Eds.), *Creating safe and supportive learning environments: A guide for working with lesbian, gay, bisexual, transgender, and questioning youth and families.* (pp. 189–208). New York, NY: Routledge.

Gay, Lesbian, and Straight Education Network. (2006). *Local School Climate Survey.* New York, NY: Author. Retrieved from http://glsen.org/lscs

Greytak, E. A., & Kosciw, J. G. (2013). Responsive classroom curriculum for lesbian, gay, bisexual, transgender, and questioning students. In E. S. Fisher & K. Komosa-Hawkins (Eds.), *Creating safe and supportive learning environments: A guide for working with lesbian, gay, bisexual, transgender, and questioning youth and families.* (pp. 156–174). New York, NY: Routledge.

Haas, A. P., Eliason, M., Mays, V. M., Mathy, R. M., Cochran, S. D., D'Augelli, A. R., ... Clayton, P. J. (2011). Suicide and suicide risk in lesbian, gay, bisexual, and transgender populations: Review and recommendations. *Journal of Homosexuality, 58,* 10–51. doi:10.1080/00918369.2011.534038

Heatherington, L., & Lavner, J. A. (2008). Coming to terms with coming out: Review and recommendations for family systems-focused research. *Journal of Family Psychology, 22,* 329–343. doi:10.1037/0893-3200.22.3.329

Hunter, S. (2007). *Coming out and disclosures: LGBT persons across the life span.* Binghamton, NY: Haworth Press.

Israel, T., Gorcheva, R., Burnes, T. R., & Walther, W. A. (2008). Helpful and unhelpful therapy experiences of LGBT clients. *Psychotherapy Research, 18,* 294–305. doi:10.1080/10503300701506920

Just the Facts Coalition. (2008). *Just the facts about sexual orientation and youth: A primer for principals, educators, and school personnel.* Washington, DC: American Psychological Association. Retrieved from http://www.apa.org/pi/lgbc/publications/justthefacts.html

Kennedy, K. G., & Fisher, E. S. (2010). Bisexual students in secondary schools: Understanding unique experiences and developing responsive practices. *Journal of Bisexuality, 10,* 427–485. doi:10.1080/15299716.2010.521061

Kennedy, K. S. (2013). Accessing community resources: Providing support for all. In E. S. Fisher & K. Komosa-Hawkins (Eds.), *Creating safe and supportive learning environments: A guide for working with lesbian, gay, bisexual, transgender, and questioning youth and families.* (pp. 243–255). New York, NY: Routledge.

Kosciw, J. G., Greytak, E. A., Bartkiewicz, M. J., Boesen, M. J., & Palmer, N. A. (2012). *The 2011 National School Climate Survey: The experiences of lesbian, gay, bisexual and transgender youth in our nation's schools.* New York, NY: GLSEN.

Lee, C. (2002). The impact of belonging to a high school gay/straight alliance. *The High School Journal, 85*(3), 13–26. doi:10.1353/hsj.2002.0005

Malley, M., & Tasker, F. (2007). "The difference that makes a difference": What matters to lesbians and gay men in psychotherapy. *Journal of Gay & Lesbian Psychotherapy, 11,* 93–109. doi:10.1300/J236v11n01_07

McGarry, R. A. (2013). Educators as allies in support of lesbian, gay, bisexual, transgender, and questioning students and parents. In E. S. Fisher & K. Komosa-Hawkins (Eds.), *Creating safe and supportive learning environments: A guide for working with lesbian, gay, bisexual, transgender, and questioning youth and families.* (pp. 230–242). New York, NY: Routledge.

Merrell, K. W., Gueldner, B. A., Ross, S. W., & Isava, D. M. (2008). How effective are school bullying intervention programs: A meta-analysis of intervention research. *School Psychology Quarterly, 23,* 26–42. doi:10.1037/1045-3830.23.1.26

Mosher, C. M. (2001). The social implications of sexual identity formation and the coming-out process: A review of the theoretical and empirical literature. *The Family Journal: Counseling and Therapy for Couples and Families, 9,* 164–173. doi:10.1177/1066480701092011

National Association of School Psychologists. (2010a). *Model for comprehensive and integrated school psychological services.* Bethesda, MD: Author. Retrieved from http://www.nasponline.org/standards/2010standards/2_PracticeModel.pdf

National Association of School Psychologists. (2010b). *Principles for professional ethics.* Bethesda, MD: Author. Retrieved from http://www.nasponline.org/standards/2010standards.aspx

National Association of School Psychologists. (2011). *Lesbian, gay, bisexual, transgender, and questioning (LGBTQ) youth* [Position Statement]. Bethesda, MD: Author. Retrieved from http://www.nasponline.org/about_nasp/positionpapers/LGBTQ_Youth.pdf

Poteat, V. P., Espelage, D. L., & Koenig, B. W. (2009). Willingness to remain friends and attend school with lesbian and gay peers: Relational expressions of prejudice among heterosexual youth. *Journal of Youth Adolescence, 38,* 952–962. doi:10.1007/s10964-009-9416-x

Russell, S. T., Muraco, A., Subramaniam, A., & Laub, C. (2009). Youth empowerment and high school gay-straight alliances. *Journal of Youth Adolescence, 38,* 891–903. doi:10.1007/s10964-9382-8

Savin-Williams, R. C. (2005). *The new gay teenager.* Cambridge, MA: Harvard University Press.

Singh, A. A. (2013). Transgender and intersex students: Supporting resilience and empowerment. In E. S. Fisher & K. Komosa-Hawkins (Eds.), *Creating safe and supportive learning environments: A guide for working with lesbian, gay, bisexual, transgender, and questioning youth and families.* (pp. 57–72). New York, NY: Routledge.

Varjas, K., Dew, B., Marshall, M., Graybill, E., Singh, A., Meyers, J., & Birckbichler, L. (2008). Bullying in schools toward sexual minority youth. *Journal of School Violence, 7,* 59–86. doi:10.1300/J202v07n02_05

Whitman, J. S. (2013). Training school professionals to work with lesbian, gay, bisexual, transgender, and questioning students and parents. In E. S. Fisher & K. Komosa-Hawkins (Eds.), *Creating safe and supportive learning environments: A guide for working with lesbian, gay,* bisexual, transgender, and questioning youth and families. (pp. 123–139). New York, NY: Routledge.

Wolfe, D. A., & Mash, E. J. (2006). Behavioral and emotional problems in adolescents: Overview and issues. In D. A. Wolfe & E. J. Mash (Eds.), *Behavioral and emotional disorders in adolescents: Nature, assessment, and treatment.* (pp. 3–20). New York, NY: Guilford Press.

Young, E. L., & Mendez, L. M. R. (2003). The mental health professional's role in understanding, preventing, and responding to student sexual harassment. *Journal of Applied School Psychology, 19*(2), 7–23. doi:10.1300/J008v19n02_02

Zucker, K. J. (2006). Gender identity disorder. In D. A. Wolfe & E. J. Mash (Eds.), *Behavioral and emotional disorders in adolescents: Nature, assessment, and treatment.* (pp. 535–562). New York, NY: Guildford Press.

16

Best Practices in Working With LGBT Parents and Their Families

Julie C. Herbstrith
Western Illinois University

OVERVIEW

It is estimated that 7 million students are being raised by parents who are lesbian, gay, bisexual, or transgender (LGBT; Kosciw, Greytak, Bartkiewicz, Boesen, & Palmer, 2012). There is considerable evidence that these children and adolescents do not differ from their peers who are raised by heterosexual parents on outcomes such as mental health and well-being, academic achievement, their own sexual orientation, or other factors (for a comprehensive review see Wainright, Russell, & Patterson, 2004). These students and families, however, still face a number of obstacles, including marriage laws, custody issues, and social problems (e.g., bullying, ostracism) in their schools and communities. Although there is a trend of increased focus on issues of diversity and multiculturalism in public schools, it remains unclear whether school personnel are adequately prepared to work with families whose heads of household are gay or lesbian. Given the established importance of positive home–school relations (Fedewa & Clark, 2009), addressing issues relevant to these families becomes vital.

School psychologists are perhaps in the best position to work with LGBT-parent families because they are trained to provide a broad range of services to teachers, students and their families, and school systems. As examples, school psychologists can provide consultation with teachers who have students with LGBT parents. School psychologists can also provide inservice training sessions that serve to educate school personnel on issues relevant to parent sexual orientation and disseminate findings on the positive outcomes of children raised by LGBT parents. In addition, school psychologists can work at the systems level to help incorporate such issues into their schools' plan for creating a positive school climate for all students. Including children and families with LGBT parents in these initiatives may enhance relations between LGBT parents and the schools attended by their children.

The focus of this chapter is multifaceted. First, it will inform school psychologists on the issues relevant to LGBT parents and their children. Specifically, the chapter will provide a brief review of the factors related to sexual prejudice, the term that refers to negative attitudes based on sexual orientation. Then the chapter will present the concerns of LGBT parents as they navigate the school system. In addition, it will discuss the concerns of students who face many challenges, from curricula that may exclude discussions of sexual orientation to social issues related to coming out about their families. Finally, this chapter will provide school psychologists with tools to help them support LGBT parents and their children.

According to the domain of Diversity and Development and Learning of the National Association of School Psychologists (NASP) *Model for Comprehensive and Integrated School Psychological Services* (NASP, 2010), school psychologists are trained to understand how diversity factors influence learning. This chapter provides school psychologists with a comprehensive overview of issues faced by a unique subset of students and families that until now have not been widely recognized in school psychology or other school-based professions.

BASIC CONSIDERATIONS

There are many terms that capture how people self-identify in terms of sexual orientation (e.g., gay, lesbian, bisexual, transgendered, queer, questioning), and it is important to understand the importance of these identities to each individual. For brevity's sake, however, and because of the limited literature base in this area, this chapter will use the acronym LGBT to refer to nonheterosexual parents. That said, it is important for school psychologists to approach sexual orientation as they would any other diversity issue, recognizing that there is never a one-size-fits-all label for people who identify in ways that are different from the majority culture, regardless of how they are different.

Prevalence Rate

Estimates indicate that between one fifth and one third of gay men and lesbians are raising children (U.S. Census Bureau, 2010). Changes in adoption laws and advances in medicine (e.g., surrogacy, artificial insemination) have likely increased these numbers, making gay- and lesbian-headed households more common in society. In addition to being more common, gay men and lesbians are choosing to come out, or disclose their sexual orientation, more than ever before (Kosciw et al., 2012). This increased visibility may have mental health benefits for those who come out, but it also often leads to criticism and hostile debates, given that homosexuality remains a highly sensitive topic in the United States.

Prejudice

A negative attitude toward a group of people that is based purely on group membership is termed prejudice (Allport, 1954). There are many theories of prejudice. To be brief, one theory is that everyone is exposed to biased, stereotypical information, and therefore everyone experiences prejudicial thoughts when this stereotypical information is activated. Once activated, people must determine how to manage their thoughts. A simple example would be students from a neighborhood school who have learned over time to dislike students from their rival school in another neighborhood. When a student sees someone with the school's colors or mascot on his or her shirt, the stereotype about people from that school is activated. Then, the student must determine whether or not to act on the prejudicial thought (i.e., engage in discriminatory behavior).

Another theory is that prejudicial attitudes develop according to social norms. That is, people tend to adopt the attitudes that are acceptable to their social reference groups. An example would be a student who identifies with a particular social group in school and subsequently adopts the beliefs and attitudes that are displayed by members of that social group.

Sexual prejudice is the term that is used to refer to negative attitudes toward people who are not heterosexual (Herek, 2007). Compared to what is known about the mechanisms of other kinds of prejudice (e.g., racial), little is known about sexual prejudice. Generally, research suggests that heterosexual people hold more negative attitudes toward gay men than lesbians (Herek, 2007). Also, there seems to be consensus that sexual prejudice is related to personality traits such as right-wing authoritarianism, or the tendency to hold and work to maintain highly rigid, traditional ideas about gender roles.

Finally, research shows that people who are higher in the trait of religious fundamentalism tend to hold more negative attitudes toward gay men and lesbians than do people who are lower (Poteat, DiGiovanni, & Scheer, 2013). It has been suggested that the United States is unique in the degree of polarization that exists on the issue of homosexuality, with the historical chasm between the right-wing fundamentalist movement and the gay rights movement being so large that it has created an illusion that most people fall into one extreme or the other, thus fueling a considerable amount of controversy.

Coming Out

This controversy has regularly been brought to the forefront in the United States due to recent elections, legislation, and legal rulings. Public discourse about marriage equality has become commonplace in the news, and public polls show increasing levels of support for it among U.S. citizens. It is important to understand, however, that LGBT people still experience prejudice and discrimination, albeit in more subtle ways (e.g., microaggressions). Also, historically, LGBT families have lived in secrecy (Fedewa & Clark, 2009) and, although there are pockets of the country where they are more readily accepted than others, many LGBT families still struggle with prejudice and discrimination when they choose to disclose their sexual orientation.

School Experiences

Schools play a central role in the lives of children and families. The following section provides an overview of the school experiences reported by LGBT parents and their children. It also provides information about teacher attitudes toward LGBT parents and their children.

Parents' Perspective

LGBT parents report feeling that school personnel are misinformed (Gay, Lesbian, and Straight Education Network [GLSEN], 2012). Further, they report a belief that school officials do not see sexual orientation as an issue in their buildings. These beliefs, coupled with fear that their children might be asked difficult questions about their families, are reasons that LGBT parents often feel that coming out to their children's schools is too risky. This decision may have negative consequences, however, including higher levels of anxiety for their children (Goldberg & Kuvalanka, 2012) and a lack of a positive, communicative relationship with the school.

Another concern of LGBT parents is that discussions of families like theirs and other issues related to sexual orientation are excluded from school curricula. Fedewa and Clark (2009) found that LGBT parents often perceive schools as an institution that reinforces traditional family structures, thereby excluding families similar to their own. These parents report that the curricula used by their children's teachers do not represent them in any way, which serves to delegitimize their families. Relatedly, although some teachers report a willingness to include gay and lesbian themes into their instruction, they report hesitation to do so because of "parental surveillance" (Martino & Cumming-Potvin, 2011). That is, they fear that introducing this type of content will incite anger on the part of other parents and the community.

Children's Perspective

Many children and adolescents consider whether or not to come out about their families very carefully. Bullying that is based on sexual orientation is a common occurrence in schools (Poteat et al., 2013). It is estimated that up to half of students with LGBT parents have been bullied or harassed for this reason (Kosciw et al., 2012). These estimates may be low, however, as incidents may be underreported for multiple reasons. First, students may be less likely to report bullying related to parent sexual orientation because no action was taken when similar incidents were reported previously (Kosciw et al., 2012). Second, because some students choose not to come out about their families, these incidents may not happen as frequently as they might otherwise occur. Some students, especially those whose parents modeled—either overtly or covertly—extreme caution about

disclosure, engaged in "information management" wherein they made very careful judgments about who they felt they could trust and confide in (Lindsay et al., 2006).

The research in this area indicates that, like many other children's issues, there are developmental differences to consider in terms of how and when children decide to disclose parent sexual orientation. Gianino, Goldberg, and Lewis (2009) found that the major factors that children and adolescents consider when making this decision are the perceived trustworthiness of a person, the extent to which the person may be homophobic, and the extent to which that person himself or herself may be perceived as gay or lesbian.

Early adolescence was perceived by children as the most difficult time to come out about their parents. During middle school, children reported being vigilant about guarding their secret about their families. In contrast, older adolescents seemed to be more adept at finding language to use to explain their family structure. They felt better able to screen potential friends and to assess their trustworthiness. Older adolescents also reported a sense of control about ending the friendships with those who rejected their families.

Those children who have disclosed to others about their families report being harassed and bullied at school. Additionally, they report that teachers and administrators are largely unresponsive to these incidents (GLSEN, 2012). Approximately 69% of teachers report willingness to intervene when they witness teasing and homophobic remarks (Harris Interactive & GLSEN, 2005). Of those who reported not intervening, common reasons included an inability to determine who made the remark or the belief that the remark was made in jest and not intended to hurt anyone.

Teachers' Perspective

Teachers play a major role in the lives of the children they educate. In addition to teaching academic knowledge and skills, teachers influence the social world of the children in their classrooms. Therefore, LGBT parents often have concerns about how their children will be treated by their teachers.

Similar to school psychology training programs, teacher education programs have attempted to prepare teachers to work in multiculturally competent ways. Preservice teachers typically must enroll in diversity courses to learn skills that will help them interact effectively with students and parents from an array of backgrounds. Unfortunately, it is unclear whether or not these courses are effective when it comes to issues of sexual orientation.

The research that has examined teacher attitudes toward homosexuality is largely outdated and limited in that it relies almost exclusively on self-report and interview data. Mudrey and Medina-Adams (2006) found that, although teachers understood the importance of supporting LGBT youth in schools, their attitudes toward homosexuality remained mostly negative. Further, many teachers may be misinformed, uninformed, or unsure of how to respond to the needs of LGBT youth (GLSEN, 2012).

Recently, more rigorous methods to measure teacher attitudes toward LGBT parents have been used. Herbstrith, Tobin, Hesson-McInnis, and Schneider (2013) measured teacher attitudes using a well-established priming technique and confirmed findings from earlier work that prejudice toward gay men and lesbians exists. Further, they found that women held more negative attitudes toward lesbian parents than they held toward gay parents. This finding is particularly interesting given that about 76% of teachers in the United States are women (National Center for Education Statistics, 2012).

BEST PRACTICES IN WORKING WITH LGBT PARENTS AND THEIR FAMILIES

The previous section provided an overview of issues related to LGBT-parent families as they navigate the school system. The following section provides suggestions for practitioners to address those challenges in ways that are consistent with best practices in school psychology. The approach is in line with the NASP multitiered model of service delivery in which services fall under universal, targeted, or intensive levels. In addition, this section focuses on describing how consultation can be used to serve LGBT parents, their children, teachers and other school staff, and the school system. To illustrate the ways that school psychologists can support LGBT-parent families, a case study will be used throughout this section.

Prior to a discussion of services that can be provided by school psychologists, it may be useful to consider the issues that are often faced by LGBT-parent families in a way that is consistent with the social–psychological literature that suggests that these issues stem largely from societal attitudes. Many of the issues can be conceptualized as microaggressions, which are brief, everyday assaults on minority groups that communicate hostility or exclude, ignore, or minimize their

experiences (Shelton & Delgado-Romero, 2011). Examples of microaggressions that exist at the systems level in many public schools are an unwelcoming school climate, exclusion from policy and curriculum, and a lack of representation in the school building (e.g., no posters or literature that depict a diverse array of family configurations).

Microaggressions can be quite subtle and often go unrecognized, even by those who are targeted. Research suggests, however, that they have significant detrimental effects on minority groups who are the targets of these assaults because they send messages such as "You don't belong here," "You won't succeed here," or "You need to change or conform" (Shelton & Delgado-Romero, 2011). The following section outlines three areas that school psychologists can target to reduce or eliminate prejudice and discrimination by initiating or bolstering Tier 1 services. General recommendations are provided within each area. Specific recommendations for addressing these issues can be aimed at more than one of these areas. Therefore, a comprehensive list is presented at the end of this section.

Universal Services

School psychologists can provide an array of universal services to help eliminate the kinds of microaggressions that are present in school climate, policy, and curricula. Many examples of these services fall under the umbrella of positive behavioral intervention and supports (PBIS) services (Sugai, O'Keeffe, & Fallon, 2012) and school-wide violence prevention programs. School psychologists can also provide a wide range of training to teachers and administrators, including psychoeducation on issues relevant to sexual orientation, curriculum workshops for teachers and librarians that familiarize them with literature that represents gay- and lesbian-led families, and examples of lesson plans that teachers can incorporate into their classroom curricula.

School Climate

It is important to understand the significance of a positive school climate for LGBT-parent families. Many of the concerns raised are related to victimization, harassment, and feeling unsafe at school. Consider the case of 11-year-old Anthony and his parents, Karla and Kim. Like most parents, Karla and Kim want their child's school to have a safe, welcoming atmosphere. They are concerned about coming out to Anthony's teachers because their disclosure has been met with negative reactions in the past.

These concerns are warranted (Fedewa & Clark, 2009). School psychologists have the knowledge and skills to address them, however. Creating schools that are safe and welcoming for all students is possible with universal services such as PBIS, which is used successfully in many schools throughout the United States (Sugai et al., 2012). As consultants, school psychologists can help administrators develop a comprehensive safe-schools policy that reflects a strong element of zero tolerance for harassment or discrimination based on actual or perceived sexual orientation and gender expression.

There are some unique factors to consider when setting the stage for a positive, inclusive school climate for LGBT-parent families. Often, public schools are the first system that these families encounter that tends to reinforce traditional models of family structure (Fedewa & Clark, 2009). Schools are often structured in a way that is geared toward traditional families, an example of what is referred to as heteronormative (Herek, 2007). That is, schools are often set up to run in a way that reflects the societal norm of heterosexuality and leaves little flexibility for people who fall outside of that norm.

Anthony and his parents may find that families like theirs are not represented in a number of ways that influence school climate. For example, PBIS messages typically contain broad themes of respect and dignity for all and they reinforce positive behavior while providing clear consequences for misbehavior. But Anthony may find that posters and other PBIS materials that are often displayed throughout schools do not include any messages about respecting people of diverse sexual orientations. Or he may notice that none of the rules that are posted in the hallways are related to antigay slurs or other offensive language. Although these kinds of exclusions may be unintended, the message they send to students and families can be strong. School psychologists can help ensure that these issues are not overlooked in their systems' PBIS plans.

School Policy

Some schools' mission statements do not include language about respect for diversity. Moreover, mission statements that do include this language sometimes exclude sexual orientation as a kind of diversity, a problem that is not unique to public schools (Herek, 2007). Using our example, Anthony's parents, Karla and Kim, may notice that the antiharassment, antibullying policies enforced at Anthony's school exclude harassment or bullying based on actual or perceived orientation or gender expression. Although it may seem like this problem relates more to students who are, or are perceived to be, nonheterosexual themselves, research shows that some children are assumed to be gay or lesbian simply because they have a gay or lesbian parent (Goldberg & Kuvalanka, 2012).

LGBT parents whose children's school had an antiharassment policy that specifically included bullying based on actual or perceived sexual orientation reported fewer incidents of harassment than parents whose children's school did not include this kind of protection (Kosciw et al., 2012). School psychologists can use systems-level consultation to work with their districts on this policy issue.

Another policy issue relates to something mundane but important: paperwork. Imagine that Anthony's school registration forms have blank spaces labeled "Mother" and "Father" and do not provide an alternative way to provide accurate information about his parents. Often, schools do not have forms that are designed to reflect diverse households (Fox, 2007). LGBT parents report that it is difficult or impossible to complete many forms that come from their children's schools because their family composition does not align with them, a microaggression that leads to a sense of delegitimization (Fedewa & Clark, 2009).

This problem has also been cited by teachers and other school personnel who reported that their schools' policies and forms limited their ability to include LGBT parents (Fox, 2007). In addition to providing valuable input at the systems level to incorporate the needs of LGBT-parent families, school psychologists can support individual personnel who want to be more inclusive. Referring again to our example, the school nurse, upon learning that Anthony will attend school in the building, may wish to revise the forms that are sent home with students to better reflect diverse families. The school psychologist can help by consulting resources such as the ones provided in this chapter to advise the nurse on how to create forms that are inclusive of all families.

School Curriculum

An additional concern raised by LGBT parents was that their families would not be represented in the school curriculum (Patterson, 2013). When children see only heterosexual relationships acknowledged, they often conclude that their parents' relationship is not legitimate or healthy (Fedewa & Clark, 2009). The School Climate Survey conducted by GLSEN (Kosciw et al., 2012) found several positive outcomes for students in schools with an inclusive curriculum. Some of these outcomes include fewer homophobic remarks, fewer school absences, a higher sense of connectedness to the school than other students, and higher levels of reported acceptance of LGBT people.

Creating an inclusive curriculum can be a difficult task, however, even for administrators and teachers who are willing to introduce LGBT themes. Martino and Cumming-Potvin (2011) found that teachers are hesitant to do so because they fear backlash from the community. Moreover, they reported a need to take a subtle approach to the inclusion of issues that many parents might find contentious.

Consider the case of Anthony and his new social studies teacher, who recognizes the importance of an inclusive curriculum but is not sure how to proceed. The school psychologist can help this teacher by providing consultation services within a multicultural framework (see Ingraham, 2000). As an example, the school psychologist might begin the consultation process by engaging the teacher in a discussion about LGBT culture and related issues.

In line with Ingraham's (2000) framework, this can be approached in a way that models two key points for the teacher. The first point is that it is okay to not know everything about everyone when it comes to diversity issues. The second point is related to continuing education about novel issues. School psychologists, as consumers of research, can help teachers locate information when they encounter new situations. In the example of Anthony, the school psychologist can consult the diversity literature and the extant resources on LGBT-inclusive curricula, and work with the social studies teacher to incorporate appropriate, inclusive materials into the curriculum.

As mentioned previously, LGBT issues remain sensitive even today. When thinking about how schools might address these issues, it is important to consider the school system within the context of the broader community. School systems tend to reflect the belief systems of the broader society in which they are rooted and it is likely that prejudicial attitudes found in the community have influenced schools at the systems level (Jeltova & Fish, 2005). Therefore, when considering changes that may be considered significant, it is beneficial to reach out to parents and other community members in addition to school personnel.

As an example, school psychologists can engage the community by offering workshops on LGBT issues, which may be a positive step toward attitude change and decrease resistance to initiatives that would make schools more welcoming to all families.

There are numerous educational resources and tools that can be used for such workshops and seminars. Also, schools can arrange to have outside speakers who are sponsored by various organizations across the country that are interested in social justice issues, safe learning environments for all students, and family equality.

Jeltova and Fish (2005) recommend that school psychologists use their systems-level consultation skills to help ensure that (a) the concerns of each entity are communicated, (b) misconceptions are reduced or eliminated through education, and (c) sufficient resources are provided for initiating and maintaining change. Providing consultation at the ecological level helps to create a positive microclimate within the school system, even if negative attitudes prevail in the community.

Specific Recommendations
The following list of suggestions serves as a guide to school psychologists who want to create an inclusive, welcoming school climate for all families.

- Start a Gay–Straight Alliance in middle or high schools.
- Educate teachers, staff, and students on the offensive use of language such as "That's so gay," which are often perceived as acceptable; show no tolerance for this language or name calling related to sexual orientation or gender.
- Modify existing policy and procedures, including those for problem-solving and Individualized Education Program meetings, to make them inclusive of diverse family compositions, including changes in language (e.g., substitute the word "parent" for the words "mother" and "father").
- Use an inclusive definition of "family" in school handbooks.
- Provide training to teachers and administrators on protocol for working with gay and lesbian parents.
- Address home–school communications to "Dear Families" rather than "Dear Mom and Dad."
- Help librarians develop a collection of books that are representative of a diverse array of families.
- Help librarians include literature by LGBT authors and literature that contains LGBT themes.
- Consult with teachers to help them include positive representation of LGBT figures and events in history in their curricula.
- Allow students to have Internet access to information about LGBT issues.

- Plan activities and events centered around the theme of family diversity to help students, teachers, and community members understand the array of different family configurations.
- Invite students, families, and school personnel to view one of the variety of documentary films that portray a diverse array of families, including those with parents of different races or religions, divorced or single parents, gay and lesbian parents, and adoptive parents.
- Display posters that depict a diverse array of family configurations, including same-gender parents.
- Display symbols or icons (e.g., upside-down pink triangles, rainbows) that indicate that the school is a safe space for LGBT people.

Targeted Services

In contrast to universal services that are designed to help all students, services that fall into the second tier of the three-tiered model address the needs of a select group of students whose needs go beyond what Tier 1 services can address. Students who are identified for targeted services receive low-intensity interventions at the individual or small group level. Often, students are grouped together based on common needs or issues. There are many ways to address the needs of gay- and lesbian-led families using Tier 2 services. This section addresses some of these common needs.

Perhaps the most effective Tier 2 intervention for children of LGBT parents is group counseling, a mode of service delivery that has been shown to have many advantages for children. The most central advantages are the therapeutic factors called universality and group cohesiveness (Yalom & Leszcz, 2005). Universality refers to the realization that one is not alone in his or her experience. Rather, other people face similar problems to one's own.

Group cohesiveness refers to the development of a supportive environment among group members, which ultimately allows and encourages self-disclosure. Once group cohesiveness develops, group members feel safe and comfortable talking about issues related to their families. In addition, the group process gives students a safe space to talk about struggles they face. Finally, group counseling provides students with a safe space to practice talking about their families to others. As noted earlier in the chapter, one of the key struggles for many students is to find the language to explain their families

to others. Groups provide an ideal environment to try out different ways to do so.

Although the number of children being raised by LGBT parents is on the rise, it is still unique. Group counseling can help connect students via shared experiences and provide them with a sense that they are not the only ones dealing with these sometimes complex issues. It must be noted, however, that many schools may not have enough students with LGBT parents to form a group.

One solution is to broaden the theme of the group to one of family diversity. This theme could include a wide range of family configurations. Referring back to the case study example, Anthony could participate in a group designed for students of diverse families that includes children whose families are biracial, single parent, multigenerational, grandparent-as-parent, and adoptive. Group facilitators can develop activities that help students understand that families come in many different configurations, but that all families operate in ways that are more similar rather than different.

One important note on group counseling for students with LGBT parents is that many curricula geared toward this topic already exist. As just one example, the Family Diversity Project developed a curriculum guide titled *Love Makes a Family: Portraits of Lesbian, Gay, Bisexual, and Transgender Parents and Their Families* (Gillespie & Kaeser, 1999) that could be adapted into group lessons.

It is important to recognize that some children and adolescents with LGBT parents may need individual, albeit low-intensity, direct services that fall under the domain of Tier 2 interventions. Students may benefit from simple check-in, check-out interventions or occasional drop-in sessions with the school psychologist. Such sessions might be used to monitor students' general well-being or to provide a sense of ongoing support as they navigate common, everyday obstacles. They could also be used to help students with occasional stressful incidents, such as making decisions about coming out to new friends about their families, or to bolster coping skills related to issues such as peers who question their sexual orientation.

One more consideration for school psychologists is related to the type of school district in which they provide services. Students who attend school in smaller, rural areas report less support related to LGBT issues than students who attend school in larger suburban areas (Kosciw et al., 2012). Similarly, students in rural areas report higher frequencies of slurs about sexual orientation (including slurs from other parents in the school community), more victimization based on sexual orientation, and less positive school climates than students in suburban areas. Therefore, school psychologists who work in more rural areas may need to be especially aware of these environmental factors and the potential negative influence they may have on children of gay and lesbian parents.

Intensive Services

As discussed earlier, children raised by LGBT parents do not systematically differ from their peers who are raised by a heterosexual parent on several outcomes, including attachment, mental health issues, academic achievement, or their own sexual orientation (Wainright et al., 2004). There may be several unique factors, however, that influence these outcomes for this group of children.

As with any presenting problem, some students will struggle more than others will, and approximately 5% of children require specialized, intensive interventions (Stormont & Reinke, 2013). Referring to our example, if Anthony is already predisposed to anxiety and attends a school that does not have a positive, inclusive school climate for LGBT students and families, he may experience symptoms of anxiety. In contrast, if Anthony's school takes a positive, proactive, and visible stance on LGBT issues, he may not experience anxiety or may experience it to a lesser degree. The following section addresses some specific issues that students with LGBT parents may have and outlines considerations for best practices.

Stigma

Sexual orientation is stigmatized in the United States, and this stigma has historically reinforced the notion that heterosexual orientation is the norm and that nonheterosexual orientation is abnormal, unnatural, and inferior to heterosexual orientation (Herek, 2007). Thus, gay men and lesbians are frequently confronted with decisions on whether to disclose their sexual orientation to others.

Children of LGBT parents may share this stigma and struggle with the same decisions about coming out about their families to peers and teachers. In fact, children of LGBT parents reported the fear of outing their families as one of their primary concerns (Telingator, 2013). It is important to understand that coming out is not a singular event. That is, LGBT parents and their children are faced with the decision about coming out

frequently, potentially every time they are introduced to someone new. Therefore, they often develop a strategy for determining whether or not to come out.

Coming Out Strategies

Coming out strategies vary from family to family and often depend on factors such as the early experiences of parents with prejudice and discrimination. Some parents unwittingly teach their children to be hypervigilant, or to make a series of assessments about how safe it is to disclose sexual orientation. Children may become preoccupied with scanning their environments for cues about who is trustworthy, who may be homophobic, or who may think they are gay or lesbian (Telingator, 2013). This hypervigilance can lead to distraction and anxiety, among other negative outcomes.

Other parents explicitly coach their children not to come out because of the risks of bullying, exclusion, and the possibility of their children being forced to answer difficult questions about their families. In an effort to foresee struggles and protect their children from harm, some parents may inadvertently send the message that they should not trust anyone with their "secret." This may lead children to engage in information management strategies that employ extreme caution with regard to disclosing any information about their families (Lindsay et al., 2006).

Developmental Differences

The grade school and middle school years may be more difficult than later years for children of LGBT parents (Goldberg, 2010). Young children often do not have a firm grasp on the language used to talk about sexual orientation. Not only do they have difficulty explaining their family configuration to others, but their peers may struggle to understand what they mean. This lack of clear communication compounds with another problem in the earlier school years, which is that sexual orientation is not a topic that is broached often (if at all) by peers or adults. It is easy to understand the confusion that may result from miscommunication.

Also, young children may receive the message that they are different from their peers because they come from different family structures, yet they are too young to comprehend what is different, thus leaving them confused as to why the issue continues to surface (Telingator, 2013).

Gianino et al. (2009) found that middle school students had the most difficult time coming out about their families. This time period was when students reported being the most scared and the least likely to come out. In terms of peer relations, Gianino et al. (2009) reported that adolescents in middle school and high school found that it was easier at this age to have friends who were accepting of their families simply because they had more control over who their friends were and they could stop being friends with those who expressed negative attitudes about their families.

Transracial Adoption

Many LGBT parents adopt children. Some adoptions are transracial, meaning that the child's race or ethnicity is different from the race or ethnicity of the parents. Gianino et al. (2009) found that children in multiracial families with LGBT parents struggle more than children in monoracial families with LGBT parents. Aside from identity formation related to race and ethnicity, these children report feeling that they are automatically outed when they are in public with their families. They report that, first, people notice racial differences within the family, which leads to further attention. Then, people notice other things about the family, such as two adults of the same gender. Taken together, this information often leads people to conclude that the adults are gay men or lesbians who have adopted children. Although this conclusion is not always associated with negative outcomes, LGBT parents and their children may feel a loss of control over a sensitive piece of information.

Social Isolation

School psychologists understand that all families have distinctive characteristics, including unique relationships with their children's schools and communities, and they take these characteristics into consideration when providing direct services to children and families. There are, however, some specific considerations to make when working with LGBT-parent families. First, despite statistics that show that they are more involved in their children's education than non-LGBT parents, it is not unusual for LGBT parents to report being excluded from their school communities or prevented from full participation in their children's school activities (Kosciw et al., 2012).

Second, a common assumption about LGBT people is that they have close ties with an LGBT community in their area (Oswald & Holman, 2013). In fact, however, LGBT-parent families are more likely to live in areas that have low concentrations of other LGBT people, often in rural rather than suburban areas. Thus, LGBT parents and their children may feel isolated from their schools and communities.

Services

The types of intensive services for students with LGBT parents do not vary systematically from the types of intensive services that any student might receive in the schools and typically revolve around individualized interventions such as counseling. The concerns discussed throughout this chapter, however, must be taken into consideration during treatment planning. In particular, school psychologists can focus on the primary concerns of both LGBT parents and their children, which revolve around physical and emotional safety issues.

One key theme that underlies the aforementioned issues is the decision about whether or not to come out. As parents and their children see it, there are risks and benefits to coming out. This ambivalence may serve as a treatment barrier for children of LGBT parents who could benefit from services. There is evidence that, compared to other students, children of LGBT parents tend to utilize school-based services less frequently (Rivers, Poteat, & Noret, 2008). Therefore, it might be helpful for school psychologists to make concerted efforts to convey acceptance of all children and families and to reach out to those who may want help but fear the ramifications of receiving it.

Another issue related to intensive services is related to microaggressions. School psychologists can ensure that their multicultural competencies include knowledge of common microaggressions related to sexual orientation (for a comprehensive review see Shelton & Delgado-Romero, 2011). For example, many LGBT people who receive counseling report a number of microaggressions committed by counselors. One common microaggression is the assumption that sexual orientation issues are the cause of the presenting issues in counseling (Shelton & Delgado-Romero, 2011). Children of LGBT parents may present with the same wide range of concerns as other students, and it is important for school psychologists to focus on the concerns raised by the student and to avoid assumptions that the treatment issues are related to parent sexual orientation.

Making Referrals

The ethical guidelines put forth by NASP dictate that school psychologists recognize the limits of their competencies and understand that under certain situations they are ethically bound to refer students and/or families to other school personnel with training in mental health services or to agencies outside of the school system. There are many local and national resources available to school psychologists who are in a position to refer students and families, including professional networks of therapists connected on Listservs such as the NASP GLBTQ community and the American Psychological Association's AFFIRM Listerv.

SUMMARY

The number of children being raised by LGBT parents exceeds 7 million, and these families are increasingly visible in schools and communities. Homosexuality still carries a stigma in the United States, and events such as legislation and prominent court cases on adoption rights and marriage equality for LGBT people have sharpened the focus on these families. To date, the research literature suggests that school systems are not as prepared as necessary to work with LGBT parents and their children. Attitudes toward homosexuality remain negative, teachers report little to no training on sexual orientation issues, and LGBT parents and their children report bullying and harassment that goes unreported or unpunished and exclusion from school activities and curricula.

This chapter provides school psychologists with information about the concerns of LGBT parents and their children. It also presents ways that school psychologists can address the needs of LGBT-parent families within the school system. The types of services that can be utilized include systems-level consultation, individual and conjoint consultation, inservice training, and individual and group counseling.

REFERENCES

Allport, G. W. (1954). *The nature of prejudice.* New York, NY: Doubleday.

Fedewa, A. L., & Clark, T. P. (2009). Parent practices and home–school partnerships: A differential effect for children with same-sex coupled parents? *Journal of GLBT Family Studies, 5*, 312–339.

Fox, R. K. (2007). One of the hidden diversities in schools: Families with parents who are lesbian or gay. *Childhood Education, 83*, 277–281. doi:10.1080/00094056.2007.10522932

Gay, Lesbian, and Straight Education Network. (2012). *Playgrounds and prejudice: Elementary school climate in the United States: A survey of students and teachers.* New York, NY: Author. Retrieved from http://glsen.org/learn/research/national/playgrounds-and-prejudice

Gianino, M., Goldberg, A., & Lewis, T. (2009). Family outings: Disclosure and practices among adopted youth with gay and lesbian parents. *Adoption Quarterly, 12*, 205–228.

Gillespie, P., & Kaeser, G. (1999). *Love makes a family: Portraits of lesbian, gay, bisexual, and transgender parents and their families.* Amherst, MA: University of Massachusetts Press.

Goldberg, A. E. (2010). *Lesbian and gay parents and their children: Research on the family life cycle.* Washington, DC: American Psychological Association.

Goldberg, A. E., & Kuvalanka, K. A. (2012). Marriage (in)equality: The perspectives of adolescents and emerging adults with lesbian, gay, and bisexual parents. *Journal of Marriage and Family, 74*, 34–52. doi:10.1111/j.1741-3737.2011.00876.x

Harris Interactive & GLSEN. (2005). *From teasing to torment: School climate in America. A survey of students and teachers.* New York, NY: Author.

Herbstrith, J. C., Tobin, R. M., Hesson-McInnis, M. S., & Schneider, W. J. (2013). Preservice teacher attitudes toward gay and lesbian parents. *School Psychology Quarterly, 28*, 183–194. doi:10.1037/spq0000022

Herek, G. M. (2007). Confronting sexual stigma and prejudice: Theory and practice. *Journal of Social Issues, 63*, 905–925.

Ingraham, C. L. (2000). Consultation through a multicultural lens: Multicultural and cross-cultural consultation in schools. *School Psychology Review, 29*, 320–343.

Jeltova, I., & Fish, M. C. (2005). Creating school environments responsive to gay, lesbian, bisexual, and transgender families: Traditional and systemic approaches for consultation. *Journal of Educational and Psychological Consultation, 16*, 17–33.

Kosciw, J. G., Greytak, E. A., Bartkiewicz, M. J., Boesen, M. J., & Palmer, N. A. (2012). *The 2011 National School Climate Survey: The experiences of lesbian, gay, bisexual and transgender youth in our nation's schools.* New York, NY: GLSEN.

Lindsay, J., Perlesz, A., Brown, R., McNair, R., de Vaus, D., & Pitts, M. (2006). Stigma or respect: Lesbian-parented families negotiating school settings. *Sociology, 40*, 1059–1077.

Martino, W., & Cumming-Potvin, W. (2011). They didn't have out there gay parents—They just looked like normal regular parents: Investigating teachers' approaches to addressing same-sex parenting and non-normative sexuality in the elementary school classroom. *Curriculum Inquiry, 41*, 480–501.

Mudrey, R., & Medina-Adams, A. (2006). Attitudes, perceptions, and knowledge of preservice teachers regarding the educational isolation of sexual minority youth. *Journal of Homosexuality, 51*(4), 63–90.

National Association of School Psychologists. (2010). *Model for comprehensive and integrated school psychological services.* Bethesda, MD: Author. Retrieved from http://www.nasponline.org/standards/2010standards/2_PracticeModel.pdf

National Center for Education Statistics. (2012). *Schools and staffing survey.* Washington, DC: Author. Retrieved from http://www.nces.ed.gov/surveys/sass/

Oswald, R. F., & Holman, E. G. (2013). Place matters: LGB families in community context. In A. E. Goldberg & K. R. Allen (Eds.), *LGBT-parent families: Innovations in research and implications for practice* (pp. 193–208). New York, NY: Springer. doi:10.1007/978-1-4614-4556-2_17

Patterson, C. J. (2013). Schooling, sexual orientation, law, and policy: Making schools safe for all students. *Theory Into Practice, 52*, 190–195. doi:10.1080/00405841.2013.804312

Poteat, V., DiGiovanni, C., & Scheer, J. (2013). Predicting homophobic behavior among heterosexual youth: Domain general and sexual orientation-specific factors at the individual and contextual level. *Journal of Youth and Adolescence, 42*, 351–362. doi:10.1007/s10964-012-9813-4

Rivers, I., Poteat, V., & Noret, N. (2008). Victimization, social support, and psychosocial functioning among children of same-sex and opposite-sex couples in the United Kingdom. *Developmental Psychology, 44*, 127–134. doi:10.1037/0012-1649.44.1.127

Shelton, K., & Delgado-Romero, E. A. (2011). Sexual orientation microaggressions: The experience of lesbian, gay, bisexual, and queer clients in psychotherapy. *Journal of Counseling Psychology, 58*, 210–221. doi:10.1037/a0022251

Stormont, M., & Reinke, W. M. (2013). Implementing Tier 2 social behavioral interventions: Current issues, challenges, and promising approaches. *Journal of Applied School Psychology, 29*, 121–125. doi:10.1080/15377903.2013.778769

Sugai, G., O'Keeffe, B., & Fallon, L. (2012). A contextual consideration of culture and school-wide positive behavior support. *Journal of Positive Behavior Interventions, 14*, 197–208. doi:10.1177/1098300711426334

Telingator, C. J. (2013). Clinical work with children and adolescents growing up with lesbian, gay, and bisexual parents. In A. E. Goldberg & K. R. Allen (Eds.), *LGBT-parent families: Innovations in research and implications for practice* (pp. 261–274). New York, NY: Springer. doi:10.1007/978-1-4614-4556-2_17

U.S. Census Bureau. (2010). *Census Bureau releases estimates of same-sex married couples*. Washington, DC: Author. Retrieved from http://www.census.gov/newsroom/releases/archives/2010_census/cb11-cn181.html

Wainright, J. L., Russell, S. T., & Patterson, C. J. (2004). Psychosocial adjustment, school outcomes, and romantic relationships of adolescents with same-sex parents. *Child Development, 75*, 1886–1898.

Yalom, I. D., & Leszcz, M. (2005). *Theory and practice of group counseling* (5th ed.). New York, NY: Basic Books.

17 Best Practices in School Psychologists' Services for Juvenile Offenders

Janay B. Sander
Ball State University (IN)
Alexandra L. Fisher
The University of Texas at Austin

OVERVIEW

The focus of this chapter is on how school psychologists can best serve students who are involved in juvenile justice systems, or juvenile offenders. This chapter is intended to address the practice area from the domain of Diversity in Development in Learning in the National Association of School Psychologists (NASP) *Model for Comprehensive and Integrated School Psychological Services* (NASP, 2010). Diversity among students who are juvenile offenders may include the following areas: academic skill weaknesses, specific or general cognitive weaknesses, gaps or inconsistencies in educational history, exposure to traumatic events, inadequate financial resources, family and community stress, individual ethnic or cultural practices and experiences, mental health concerns, and sexual orientation– or gender identity–related stress or adjustment. School psychologists can consider the individual student's diversity within the context of academic and mental health needs, and then address those needs using best practices from this chapter.

It should be a top priority for school psychologists to identify juvenile offenders as students potentially in need of academic and behavioral interventions. These students are the most likely to be disciplined, expelled, or suspended and to drop out of school (Council of State Governments Justice Center, 2011). Regardless of the criminal offense, the key idea is for school psychologists to serve juvenile offenders as students within the context of individual diversity. It is also important for school psychologists to remember that this group of students is diverse; that is, there is no single best practice owing to

that variation. A system to identify the diverse needs is useful to consider how to serve juvenile offenders well and will be discussed below.

Another starting point to keep in mind is that juvenile offending is a complex social, educational, and community challenge. This is not an area where a person, even someone as talented as a school psychologist, can provide best practices as an individual. This is a group effort, and it will require a team of some type to help juvenile offenders. School psychologists will use administrative, organizational, and individual teacher consultation approaches in addition to individual student services to provide best practices for this group of students.

School interactions with juvenile justice–involved youth appear to be on the rise, so it is important for school psychologists to be ready to serve this population. In part, the increase in school–juvenile justice interactions may be due to zero-tolerance discipline policies. Some discretionary misbehaviors are becoming criminalized rather than being addressed within school disciplinary channels (Krezmien, Leone, Zablocki, & Wells, 2010). Juvenile offenders often exhibit a host of educational disabilities, mental health diagnoses, trauma histories, and complex social/environmental challenges. School psychologists are an important, but likely underutilized, resource for these students. School psychologists are already trained to address concurrent mental health, behavioral, and learning concerns in students. With this set of skills, school psychologists are well suited for helping this population.

In many ways, serving juvenile justice–involved youth simply requires school psychologists to routinely address all components of the NASP Practice Model (NASP, 2010) and not just the domain of Diversity in Learning and Development, including cultural sensitivity as a key feature of all service delivery. Abiding by these professional standards, school psychologists are ideal members of an interdisciplinary or, better yet, interagency team to serve these youth.

Education for juvenile offenders takes place in traditional and nontraditional school settings, in detention and residential facilities, and through probation programs. Therefore, the information included in this chapter is intended to provide a targeted introduction to the most important aspects of school psychology practice with these youth, including prevention, with emphasis on traditional school settings where most school psychologists work.

BASIC CONSIDERATIONS

There is background information about juvenile offending that would be useful to school psychologists. In addition, there are some important similarities and differences between traditional schools and juvenile justice systems that would be helpful for school psychologists to recognize in order to collaborate across systems.

Juvenile Justice System Overview

In order for school psychologists to work effectively with juvenile offenders and an interagency team, an overview of the juvenile justice system and its terminology is helpful. First, the primary goal of juvenile justice is to keep the public safe. This includes promoting policies and interventions to reduce likelihood of future juvenile crime victims (Kinscherff, 2012). In most states, the juvenile justice system will usually handle the case if a person under 17 years of age has been arrested for a crime, but the exact age that juveniles are handled in juvenile or adult court varies by state and can be between 15 and 17 years (Office of Juvenile Justice and Delinquency Prevention, 2012). When a juvenile commits a more serious crime or shows a pattern of serious criminal behavior, that person may be handled through the adult criminal justice system. School psychologists are more likely to encounter youth served in the juvenile system compared to adult systems.

Juvenile justice has its own set of procedures and terms. Juvenile court does not involve a jury, only a judge. If the youth is found guilty, then the term is *adjudicated* (versus *convicted*) in juvenile systems. At that point the court makes a decision about placement and programs, such as placement in a secure juvenile facility or less secure probation setting, along with what type of treatment program, or restitution. The court may also request a psychological evaluation to inform the court decisions on placement or programs. Rehabilitation is an important element. This can include education and vocation programs, psychotherapy, family services, or public service.

Another topic for background is that the juvenile justice system is not a single system. It refers to a network of legal entities to address juvenile crime and delinquency. This system is most often within the jurisdiction of a county or other local government administrative body. A county system, for example, may include a specific juvenile court and judge, juvenile probation services and staff, juvenile detention facilities and staff, and an array of youth and family services intended to help reduce juvenile crime. Programs and components offered by any specific juvenile system can vary considerably from year to year and between systems.

Typically, there is a chief juvenile justice officer who would oversee various aspects within the juvenile services system. Detention may have two components: county and state. The state level may include higher security detention facilities, including more serious offenses but also detention facilities designed to handle emotionally disturbed youth offenders. For more information, school psychologists can refer to the Office of Juvenile Justice and Delinquency Prevention, a branch of the federal government, that maintains a website about juvenile justice topics across the United States (http://www.ojjdp.gov/index.html). Probation departments sometimes provide community outreach programs, or have probation officers housed within schools to allow easier communication and monitoring for juvenile offenders. These officers can be a bridge for interagency collaboration with school psychologists.

Approximately 1.6 million juveniles are arrested each year (Puzzanchera & Kang, 2013), 1.3 million formally processed in a court (Sickmund, Sladky, & Kang, 2013). Authorities attempt to divert youth from formally entering the juvenile justice system whenever possible. Law enforcement is usually the agency to process a youth in the justice system, but schools also refer up to 20% of all juvenile cases.

Schools Versus Juvenile Justice Settings

There are some important similarities and differences between schools and juvenile justice systems in general.

First, one of the primary differences in juvenile justice settings relative to school settings is the priority of the administration. Juvenile justice's primary goal is to reduce the likelihood of future juvenile crime and delinquency, lower recidivism rates, and enhance public safety, as well as the secondary goal of rehabilitation for the youth.

Juvenile justice systems, like public schools, are often subject to funding fluctuations, including budget cuts that can put strain on staff and compromise the quality and breadth of services offered. Schools located on juvenile justice sites are subject to all federal and state education laws. They are public schools. These alternative education placements are highly variable in terms of teacher quality and administrative support. There are teachers in juvenile justice settings who use exceptional instructional strategies and show a deep commitment for working with troubled youth. There are also teachers who are assigned to disciplinary schools as a result of poor performance on accountability measures in other schools.

Most juvenile justice setting schools pose unique challenges in terms of education. Student enrollment is often temporary. Students come and go throughout the school year based on legal considerations. Those students may be in the juvenile justice school for 2 weeks, 2 months, or an entire school year, depending on court decisions.

Another challenge for juvenile justice setting teachers, which school psychologists should be aware of, is the huge variability in student academic skills within this population. Some are on grade level, but most are not. They also come from different schools and different school districts or school corporations, since the facility serves a county, geographic region, or state. The curriculum that each student has had is often different. It is also difficult to provide evidence-based educational interventions due to training of staff as well as the variability in length of time in the juvenile justice school for the student (Cruise, Evans, & Pickens, 2011; Katsiyannis, Ryan, Zhang, & Spann, 2008). For a number of reasons, providing education or school psychological services in juvenile justice settings is a challenge. Knowing about these challenges can help a school psychologist work effectively and also be realistic in goal setting.

After the juvenile offender has encountered the court and been placed, that youth is most likely to return to a public education setting at some point. Getting involved with juvenile offending, and its consequences, is stressful. The reentry to school after juvenile justice placement comes with its own challenges. The reentry process for a juvenile offender returning to school is also stressful, and a smoother transition is associated with higher success of the student. National rates of reoffending, or recidivism, vary from about 40 to 60%, but some geographic areas are even higher, for juvenile offenders 1 year after release (Snyder & Sickmund, 2006). Juvenile offenders who reengage in school, including vocationally focused programs that have been shown to be successful in several studies, have a much higher success rate than youth who drop out of school. The first year after release is the critical window for success. Once a juvenile offender has reentered the community without reoffending for 12 months, the chances of recidivism decrease dramatically after that point (Matvya, Lever, & Boyle, 2006). If prevention and early intervention or intensive intervention at school has not been successful, there is one more opportunity. Reentry to school is a key transition point that school psychologists need to consider as a specific component in best practices with juvenile offenders.

Overview of Juvenile Offender Population

The population of students who are juvenile offenders is diverse. An overview of the general statistics will show how diverse the population is. The majority (around 70–80%) is in a juvenile probation setting and enrolled in a public school in the community (Office of Juvenile Justice and Delinquency Prevention, 2012). Most (78%) juvenile offenders are 16 years or younger, and still within the age of compulsory school attendance for all states (Sickmund et al., 2013).

A disproportionate percentage of minority youth, particularly African American youth, are arrested compared to other population categories. The arrest rates for African American youth in general were twice the rate of Caucasian youth (Office of Juvenile Justice and Delinquency Prevention, 2012). Arrests for violent crimes, such as murder, non-negligent manslaughter, forcible rape, robbery, and aggravated assault, reveal an even larger disproportionality. African American youth arrest rates were 5 times higher than Caucasian youth, 6 times higher than American Indian juveniles, and nearly 15 times higher than Asian youth (Office of Juvenile Justice and Delinquency Prevention, 2012).

The most common crimes committed by juveniles vary somewhat by gender. The most common crimes male juveniles are arrested for are larceny-theft, drug violations, simple assault (involving no serious injury or weapon), and disorderly conduct. Females are most commonly arrested for property crimes, larceny-theft, and disorderly conduct (Office of Juvenile Justice and Delinquency Prevention, 2012). For status offenses, the majority are truancy, alcohol-related crimes, and running away (Snyder & Sickmund, 2006).

School psychologists might be curious about arrest trends, but it is not necessary to inquire about the specific offenses of individual students who are juvenile offenders. Juveniles are often advised by legal representatives to not discuss their crimes with anyone other than their attorney or probation officer, particularly if they are still serving probation or are not yet adjudicated. It is helpful to know that if the youth is considered a high risk, then the youth would likely still be under juvenile court supervision, but juvenile court records and specifics may not be available due to confidentiality in the juvenile system.

Mental Health

Of notable concern is the level of mental illness that juvenile offenders are likely experiencing, including co-occurring diagnoses. In studies about mental health needs in juvenile justice settings, roughly 70% of juvenile offenders met the criteria for at least one mental health disorder (Sedlak & McPherson, 2010). Substance abuse is a big concern in this population (Kinscherff, 2012), but even when conduct disorder and substance abuse are omitted, more than 45% of youth offenders meet criteria for a mental illness (Shufelt & Cocozza, 2006).

Trauma symptoms, in particular, are a pervasive concern for juvenile offenders (Abram et al., 2013). Trauma symptoms are a nebulous symptom cluster, and they often relate to a host of problematic behaviors due to emotion dysregulation, hyperarousal, neurologic and learning challenges, and reactivity (Kinscherff, 2012). School psychologists need to be aware of the possibility of underlying trauma and related symptoms when serving juvenile offenders.

The presence of mental health needs within juvenile offender populations is well documented. Unfortunately, there is also an alarming paucity of available, evidence-based, accessible mental health intervention for these youth (Cocozza, Skowyra, & Shufelt, 2010; Kinscherff, 2012). There is also more specific concern about the availability of appropriate mental health intervention for females in juvenile justice systems. Girls show higher rates of mental illness in general within the juvenile offender population, as well as more frequent trauma histories, compared to boys in the same settings. In addition, the historical structure of juvenile justice

systems is oriented toward providing services for boys, rather than girls, and evidence-based mental health interventions are less well defined in their applications with girls (Veysey, 2003).

The lack of mental health services is a wide spread concern for this population. At times, families are unable to access necessary mental health services, and the juvenile justice system is simply the last resort once their child escalates problem behaviors related to a mental health concern (Cocozza et al., 2010; Sander, Sharkey, Olivarri, Tanigawa, & Mauseth, 2010). The Office of Juvenile Justice and Delinquency Prevention has been advocating for a decade for juvenile justice systems to routinely screen youth for mental health needs, including suicide risk factors. Even when mental health needs are identified, in most facilities the need for treatment far exceeds the available resources for delivering treatment. The recommended mechanism for providing treatment rests with a partnership approach; that is, the juvenile justice system partnering with community care options (Kinscherff, 2012), including schools, school psychologists, and mental health clinics.

In summary, juvenile offenders frequently face a cumulative effect from a host of mental health concerns: developmental psychopathology, multiple areas of functional impairment, complex and sometimes unclear developmental history, considerable trauma, and challenge of clearly identifying the link between emotional impairment and aggression or other behavior problems (Kinscherff, 2012).

Special Education Eligibility and Disproportionality

In addition to the mental health concerns, juvenile offenders frequently have academic needs. An additional consideration is the trend of disproportionality and overrepresentation of youth with educational disabilities in juvenile justice. Furthermore, there is a lack of evidence-based instructional interventions to address the combined needs of juvenile offenders (Cruise et al., 2011; Katsiyannis et al., 2008; Sander, Patall, Amoscato, Fisher, & Funk, 2012; Skiba et al., 2011). There is overlap in findings about disproportionate suspension rates for students with emotional and behavior disorders and the juvenile offender population. Juvenile offenders participate in special education at four times the rate of the general population (Katsiyannis et al., 2008; Quinn, Rutherford, Leone, Osher, & Poirier, 2005). A U.S. Department of

Education (2007) report indicates that 38% of youth in correctional settings receiving Individuals with Disabilities Education Act services are classified as eligible for special education for an emotional disturbance. Compare this to the national percentage of all students in the United States who are eligible for services under the category of Serious Emotional Disturbance, which is only 2% (U.S. Department of Education, 2007). The disproportionality of specific groups, including special education classifications as well as ethnic/racial groups, in juvenile justice settings is astounding (Skiba et al., 2011). Best practices for addressing the overrepresentation of ethnic minority groups as well as students who are receiving special education services for emotional disabilities are similar and will be discussed below.

Given the prevalence of juvenile offending in general, as well as the high incidence of educational disabilities in this population, it is likely that school psychologists already serve juvenile offenders, particularly school psychologists who work in secondary education settings that are within high-crime communities. At the same time, school psychologists may or may not be aware of exactly which students, or under what circumstances, the juvenile justice system is involved. The juvenile justice system and its records are separate from public education records. Juvenile records are confidential. What school psychologists also may not realize is that all federal and state education laws apply to the juvenile justice system. Juvenile justice facilities are required to provide education to juveniles in their care, and are supposed to follow the student's current Individualized Education Program (IEP) when one is in place (Snyder & Sickmund, 2006). Given how many juvenile offenders are enrolled in special education, particularly for emotional disturbance eligibility, it is very important for school psychologists to recognize and take action to address the likely educational challenges they face.

BEST PRACTICES IN SCHOOL PSYCHOLOGISTS' SERVICES FOR JUVENILE OFFENDERS

The most important challenge for school psychologists is to keep in mind that this population typically has a host of overlapping mental health and educational challenges. With all the background presented above, we can proceed with the core challenges of working with this population, along with best practices to address them. School psychologists can also be involved in providing early intervention for students with known

risks for later delinquency and criminal involvement before the behavior occurs. There are empirically based interventions that can improve outcomes and behaviors for these youth, including systemic-, individual-, and school-based programs. School engagement and higher academic achievement are clearly linked with better outcomes for these youth (Skiba et al., 2011), so school psychologists are especially important as part of the team who can help these youth be successful and further criminal activity. The main points and considerations to help school psychologists serve these students are summarized below, organized along a continuum of services from prevention to reentry in traditional school after juvenile justice placement.

Prevention and Early Intervention: Positive Practices Are Key

There are several options for school psychologists to consider in terms of positive options for preventing involvement in juvenile justice. First, there is clear evidence that positive school-wide behavior programs are effective in reducing delinquency (Wilson & Lipsey, 2007; Wilson, Lipsey, & Derzon, 2003). School experiences that are positive, such as involvement in extracurricular activities, positive feelings toward school in general, and academic achievement are associated with lower disciplinary action rates (Lösel & Farrington, 2012). It is also important to note that punitive discipline strategies are not effective in reducing delinquency or juvenile crime. Furthermore, those punitive practices ultimately might escalate the problem of school dropout and ongoing delinquency and criminal activity (Skiba et al., 2011). School psychologists can play a key role in prevention by facilitating positive approaches that will not alienate struggling students from these important school-based activities and programs. Informally, when working with a juvenile offender, it is important to consider the ways that school could be positive, and make sure the youth has access, in some form, to that at school.

More formally, school-wide programs that use positive approaches for all students to correct behaviors, including positive behavior support and social emotional learning components, are recommended best practice (Skiba et al., 2011; Wilson & Lipsey, 2007). School psychologists can regularly provide consultation to instill a school culture of teaching positive behaviors, rather than relying on harsh, exclusionary policies and practices. An important message for school psychologists to convey to teachers and administrators about implementation of positive disciplinary situations is that the *behavior* should change. It is important to impart the message within the general school culture that while a specific behavior is not acceptable, the student is worthy of education, respect as a human being, and fair treatment (Sander et al., 2010). This should be the message for all student disciplinary behaviors, especially students who have frequent disciplinary concerns.

Universal, school-wide social emotional learning programs are also empirically supported for reducing and preventing many problem behaviors associated with juvenile offending (Durlak, Weissberg, Dymnicki, Taylor, & Schellinger, 2011). Social–emotional programs address emotional awareness, problem-solving skills, empathy, and stress management. There are several programs with research support. Importantly, these are also helpful in raising academic achievement at the school level. The effectiveness of these programs is in part due to teachers infusing the skills into classrooms. School engagement is one of the protective factors associated with lower delinquency rates (Lösel & Farrington, 2012; Skiba et al., 2011), and it is an important area to consider in order to prevent juvenile offending. Social–emotional learning programs offer activities that encourage student belongingness, a key ingredient for student engagement in school. School psychologists can encourage and support the use of these programs within classrooms, at the school level, or at the district as a policy.

The positive school-wide practices and social–emotional learning programs are most effective when they are universal (Wilson & Lipsey, 2007). School psychologists are not supposed to be the only school personnel implementing these programs in order to prevent problem behaviors related to juvenile offending. School psychologists, in the prevention aspect of address juvenile offending, would be in the role of administrative consultant to facilitate and enhance these universal positive programs in schools. It is important for school psychologists to look for opportunities to move toward adopting positive school-wide programs over time, even if the current school administration still believes that exclusionary policies are preferable.

School psychologists, to act on behalf of best practices for preventing juvenile offending, will incorporate formal and informal consultation and systems change approaches. The administration must support and adopt this positive philosophy for it to be effective in a meaningful way, and the data support the academic gains in addition to behavioral benefits. Adopting positive strategies to reduce juvenile offending can be an unwelcome message to an administration that believes in a punitive approach. The facts are clear: Punitive, harsh, exclusionary school discipline does not deter juvenile offending, and could possibly make it more likely. Positive approaches that teach new behaviors in respectful ways to all students as part of the school culture are the recommended best prevention practices. School psychologists can continue to get that message out to their schools and be a voice for change during informal opportunities as well as during formal presentations.

Response-to-Intervention Model

For youth at risk of involvement in juvenile offending, there are more warning signs than surprises. School psychologists can identify these students and potentially influence intervention and school success, rather than detention, dropout, or incarceration. Repeated suspensions and expulsions from school is one of the strongest predictors of juvenile offending. It seems the tenth suspension is the tipping point for a path out of school and deeper into juvenile justice (Council of State Governments Justice Center, 2011). Academic failure, or low achievement in general, is another strong predictor of juvenile justice involvement. These struggling students are most likely already on the radar and are cause for concern in schools before they end up involved in juvenile crime. Many of them are already enrolled in special education services, which warrants a reconsideration of their IEP if they are still struggling.

Monitoring and providing targeted intervention for these students who are at highest risk for school failure, dropout, and juvenile justice involvement is necessary. School psychologists can work with school administrators to build in mechanisms for progress monitoring students with the triangle of risks: history of behavior challenges, low academic achievement, and suspensions (Council of State Governments Justice Center, 2011). These students need intervention, and school psychologists can use data-based methods to identify them, advocate for services, and monitor their progress.

Intervention in Schools

School psychologists would ideally serve juvenile offenders in schools as part of a team, an interagency and collaborative team that includes mental health professionals, behavioral interventionists, and juvenile justice staff, for example. The recommended approach for intervention is one that includes multiple agencies, including school and community-based service providers, and evidence-based approaches (Cocozza et al., 2010). As part of an interagency approach, interventions to improve behavior and mental health are obviously important. In order to address the range of individualized needs that present themselves in juvenile offender groups, levels of intervention, from school-wide prevention, to early intervention to targeted symptom interventions are discussed below.

Evidence-Based Interventions

Although schools vary in the level and range of mental health interventions delivered in a school setting, it is important for school psychologists to be aware of the interventions with the most empirical support. It is hoped that school psychologists are providing these evidence-based interventions in schools or are collaborating with other mental health professionals to offer them.

The most effective interventions targeted for juvenile offenders, particularly to address conduct and affective disorders, are cognitive–behavioral approaches implemented with high integrity (Landenberger & Lipsey, 2005). Providing cognitive–behavioral approaches is highly recommended. Many of these techniques could be delivered in a school context if the school psychologist has received training in this approach and the array of techniques. It is very important to first consider the student's needs and create a case conceptualization in order to select the best cognitive–behavioral approach. Using a functional behavioral analysis approach, even as part of a formal behavioral assessment plan or in an IEP, as part of this conceptualization is also recommended.

For example, a student may act disruptively for different reasons. One student may talk disrespectfully to the teacher in order to escape academic demands due to low academic skills. That would be a very different case conceptualization from a student who acts disruptively or uses foul language due to unexpected trauma triggers and emotional flooding. For these cases, the cognitive–behavioral techniques to improve those behaviors would be quite different. The academic skill disruptive scenario, for instance, should include emotional coping skills in conjunction with academic interventions to improve academic weaknesses. The emotional trauma trigger response would include some trauma-focused cognitive–behavioral approaches, as well as specific alternative methods to get to a location where the student feels safe, and skills for self-soothing in the school setting that would not be disruptive to other students. Cognitive–behavioral therapy can also address the concurrent depression, anxiety, or other disruptive behaviors that may impair academic engagement.

Multisystemic Family Therapy has also been effective in improving outcomes for juvenile offenders, even in long-term follow up studies (Sawyer & Borduin, 2011). This model includes a multidisciplinary team and family involvement. Nevertheless, it is recommended that school psychologists in districts with high juvenile justice involvement consider becoming involved formally in this treatment approach.

After the Fact: Transition and School Reentry

The transition from juvenile justice systems back to community and school settings is one of the most important components of rehabilitation for juvenile offenders. School psychologists are strongly encouraged to participate in this process and to advocate for creating a system to address school reentry if there is no such plan in place. Table 17.1 outlines the main components of a reentry system. Best practices for reentry include

Table 17.1. Recommended Actions for School Psychologists to Facilitate School Reentry of Juvenile Offenders

- Establish and ensure a clear system of communication among the school, related agencies, and the family.
- Designate specific individuals, including their roles, to participate in a reentry-planning team.
- Provide training to the school-based professionals to work with juvenile justice systems in order to address the differences in educational systems and maintain confidentiality and dignity for the student and the family.
- Begin the planning and information sharing process well before the youth arrives back at school.
- Identify the appropriate educational placement, and avoid an automatic disciplinary setting placement for school reentry. Appropriate placement includes, but is not limited to, special education and related services.
- Consider both academic and vocational programs as placement options.
- Place the youth as quickly as possible, preferably on the first day of school reenrollment.
- Follow up with monitoring and communication with involved systems to facilitate stability and success for the youth and the family.

having a plan and procedure in place to determine the appropriate student placement ahead of time and not after a student is reenrolling.

Ideally, a reentry team would look much like a case study team, prereferral team, or problem-solving team that many school psychologists would already be familiar with. This is a team composed of a few core members on a consistent basis, and individual students and teachers rotate into the agenda based on the specific student needs and concerns. In the case of a juvenile offender reentry plan, it is best if the consistent core members have training in juvenile justice considerations and information about the complexity of educational and mental health needs for this group of students. It is not always possible to have notice, such as when a juvenile offender arrives in the district due to a foster placement, for example.

The reentry components are most applicable when a student resides within district, leaves to attend a juvenile justice placement, and the school would anticipate a possible reentry in the future. Even with no notice, the team approach is recommended in order to serve that student as quickly as possible to facilitate student success.

With a juvenile justice–involved student, there is frequently social stigma along with a challenging set of emotional and behavioral concerns, making it very important to infuse positive approaches to assist that student and the family. School discipline policies that rely on zero tolerance and punitive discipline may further alienate these students who are already at risk for school dropout and future criminal activity (Skiba et al., 2011). For example, some schools have an automatic disciplinary location for students returning from other alternative education disciplinary settings. This does not support successful reentry, and prolongs exclusionary practices for that student. If a reentry committee considers a disciplinary setting appropriate, then that could indeed be best. The main point in terms of best practices is that disciplinary placement should not be automatic for reentry with all juvenile offending students due to diversity considerations and individual needs and circumstances. School psychologists should consider what the juvenile offender needs in order to be included and successful at school, rather than automatically assign another form of exclusionary setting.

Planning ahead, when it is possible, is very useful to assist juvenile offenders who are transitioning from probation settings and alternative schools back to a traditional school placement (Gies, 2003). There is not a unified evidence-based model for transition and school reentry, and national juvenile justice agencies are actively seeking research-based programs specifically about this phase of services and outcomes. Even so, there are some promising programs and consensus recommendations in the literature. Within these programs the transition and reentry plan includes school success and reentry as a key component.

Several research and policy groups have summarized the available information about school reentry programs. School reentry recommendations across different summaries include several common components (JustChildren, 2004; Matvya et al., 2006; Bilchik, 2011), listed in Table 17.2. Two particularly comprehensive summaries are from the Center for School

Table 17.2. Ten Key Points of Best Practices for School Psychologists Serving Juvenile Offenders

- Foster a school-wide community that is welcoming and safe for all students, including emphasis on student success, universal positive behavior intervention, and social–emotional skill development.
- Implement and facilitate data-based procedures to identify students with low academic performance and disciplinary referrals as important early warning signs for juvenile offending risk.
- Provide consultation to interdisciplinary teams and administrators that will facilitate appropriate educational, emotional, and behavioral intervention for juvenile offenders.
- Interact with the leadership teams in juvenile justice systems, community agencies, and schools to foster interagency collaboration.
- Adopt a social justice orientation to facilitate access to education, respect, and fair treatment of the juvenile offender based on his or her diverse needs and circumstances.
- Keep current on applicable federal and state education laws as well as local school discipline policies and procedures in order to provide services, advise, and advocate from an informed perspective.
- Provide comprehensive school psychological services to address combined problem behaviors, mental health concerns, and academic weaknesses for juvenile offenders.
- Implement consistent progress monitoring and response to academic and mental health interventions for youth identified as juvenile offenders.
- Consider suspension or juvenile justice involvement a red flag for increasing monitoring and intervention.
- Create and/or facilitate coordinated transition and school reentry services between systems when juvenile offenders move from one educational setting to another (see Table 17.1).

Mental Health Analysis and Action (Matvya et al., 2006) and JustChildren, a legal aid justice center located in Charlottesville, Virginia. The National Reentry Resource Center's Advisory Committee on juvenile justice issues strongly encourages systems to prioritize emphasis on education and employment connections, along with clear attention to the youth's strengths and weaknesses as part of a transition/reentry plan (Bilchik, 2011). The idea is to facilitate positive connections, thereby weakening socially undesirable and criminally influential connection in the community.

In summary, school psychologists could be especially helpful as part of a transition planning team at any school location where a youth is reentering school from a juvenile justice setting of any type. If a case worker or other representative or advocate contacts the school about a reentry plan, school psychologists are well suited to collaborate with an interdisciplinary team, including necessary interagency communication during the reentry planning process. School psychologists are well suited to facilitate that interagency collaboration process and to implement effective reentry planning practices in schools.

Integrating the Big Picture

For school psychologists to provide the best practices to work with juvenile offenders, including preventing offending when possible, there are several systemic components to address. Table 17.2 provides a summary of the components of big picture best practices. Working effectively to serve juvenile offenders requires an interdisciplinary and multisystemic approach.

Best practice includes facilitating an organized set of procedures to identify youth at risk for juvenile offending through the three hallmark warning signs: low achievement, high disciplinary referrals, and expulsion. The school psychologist should consider these youth in need of academic and behavioral progress monitoring as would be the case in response-to-intervention approaches. This student, when flagged for monitoring, could possibly receive appropriate intensive classroom interventions to address academic skills or classroom behaviors at the time it would be most helpful to foster school success rather than after problem behaviors increase.

The school psychologist's goal is not to prevent juvenile justice involvement, per se, but to consider these particular students as educationally at risk and in need of ongoing monitoring and possibly interventions at school to meet their educational needs. This is largely a

regular education area, but school psychologists are a valuable source of input about the overlap in academic, behavioral, and emotional risks, and school psychologists can share their perspective with administrators to inform helpful prevention and early intervention policies. Even though there are many considerations in working with juvenile offenders, school psychologists can be instrumental in facilitating success in several ways.

Case Example

Danny was a 14-year-old Hispanic male, attending school in a disciplinary alternative education placement. The school psychologist was a member of a case study team as part of the alternative disciplinary enrollment process in the school district. Danny had recently been suspended from his middle school due to sexual misconduct, which was also related to his adjudication. Child welfare services had recently placed him, his younger sister, and younger brother in the custody of their paternal grandmother. Danny's mother was struggling with drug use and was unable to care for them. A paternal aunt lived nearby and was also involved in their care. Danny was not allowed any contact with his mother per court instructions. Child welfare agencies in the other state had conducted investigations about reports of neglect and physical abuse. There had not been enough evidence for child welfare to conclude the reports were substantiated, but the concerns had been present for several years prior to removing the children.

There was little educational information available about Danny since his transfer to the new city and state. The children had been living out of state for the past 5 years. Danny was having conflicts at home and school. His probation stipulations included receiving individual counseling. He had been diagnosed with attention deficit hyperactivity disorder while living out of state but it was unclear if he had been receiving services at school. The school psychologist obtained consent to exchange information with the probation officer about Danny to assist in coordinated efforts across systems and get his educational records in order. The school psychologist was concerned that Danny was in need of, and possibly qualified already for, special education and related services. School psychology services addressed several areas of concern. The school psychologist obtained all necessary informed consent and services were not offered as part of an IEP but as standard services that were routine at the alternative disciplinary placement. The school psychologist's work with Danny included the following goals: (a) provide cognitive–behavioral counseling to address emotional coping skills, anger control, conflict management; (b) provide general support in the form of teacher consultation at school to help with classroom behavior success; (c) coordinate with probation and school to ensure appropriate supervision; (d) provide information, consistent communication, and general support to the guardians as needed, and this would be in coordination with a school social worker; and (e) pursue educational records to determine if Danny might be in need of identification for special education and related services.

First, connecting with probation (after obtaining necessary consents to exchange education-related information) provided the school psychologist with helpful information. For example, probation had given Danny a curfew and his probation officer did not want Danny to travel by city bus on his own to school. The probation officer specifically wanted Danny to take the school bus to ensure he did not become truant. This was an issue as the alternative education placement was unable to pick him up near his house and he had to walk approximately 1 mile to the school bus stop. There were resources to give him a free city bus pass, but probation did not want him to have an open access to the whole city. Coordination among systems was critical in this situation to resolve the transportation concerns.

Within a few weeks, as part of a regular check-in with the family, Danny's aunt informed the alternative disciplinary school social worker that Danny had been caught trying to get back in touch with his mother and was possibly helping her get access to drugs. He had stolen money from his grandmother. The guardian family was having difficulty monitoring him and providing consistent consequences. The grandmother was aging, in poor health, and easily gave in to Danny's requests. The aunt, even though she was willing and involved in their care, was not approved to have the children in her home because her partner was on parole for endangering the welfare of a child. The school psychologist communicated these challenges to the probation officer, and also facilitated enrolling the family in a family therapy program offered through a nearby university at no cost to the family.

Regarding Danny's educational needs, the middle school that was the home campus for a few weeks prior to the disciplinary placement had conducted an assessment with him. The final report was ready, but no case conference had convened to discuss the findings or create an IEP. The school psychologist scheduled an interdisciplinary case conference committee for the earliest possible date to determine eligibility based on available information and the recent assessment.

The focus of individual therapy included practical cognitive and behavioral skills, such as "taking responsibility" and considering "short-term versus long-term gains." Individual work also included anger control, emotion regulation, and emotion education activities in sessions. Sessions were brief, around 20 minutes twice per week.

Working with Danny individually was a challenge at times, as he gave different information to different people; that is, he would give false information with sometimes no clear gain or motive. Ensuring all the adults had the same information became a priority for the school psychologist. In addition, while the family had initially expressed willingness to start in family therapy, they missed three intake appointments without offering an explanation and were dropped from the program. During this period, family conflicts were increasing, leading to a physical incident between Danny and his grandmother.

After the school psychologist worked with Danny for 8 weeks, Danny suddenly stopped attending the alternative disciplinary school where the school psychologist worked. His aunt informed the school after a few days that child welfare services had come in the middle of the night and taken Danny away. They had placed him in an emergency shelter in another town, in a different school district, and were now looking for a new suitable foster home.

At this point the focus shifted, but the school psychologist did not simply close the file. To ensure Danny received appropriate educational services that met both his educational and behavioral needs, there was still a need to have his full evaluation follow him to his new school, new probation officer, and new foster family. Educational information, as well as emotional assessment data, would be helpful to planning his future interventions and success. The school psychologist contacted the middle school that conducted the evaluation. The family had to submit a request to the district's main special education department to have Danny's records transferred over to the new school system, but the family had not done this. The school psychologist called the family to inform them of the importance of this paperwork to get Danny's school services in place, but the school psychologist never heard back.

The school psychologist contacted the probation officer and requested if the probation officer could assist, as the family had given probation an official copy of the evaluation. The probation officer was initially unsure why this was important. The school psychologist used the opportunity to explain the potential setback this had on Danny, that he was in need of services in school but now had to wait for the new school to get to know him and then conduct a new evaluation from scratch. They discussed how behind he was already and how much this might delay his school progress in general. While the probation officer could not give the education records to the school, but was able to send it to Danny's new probation officer in the new town and inform the new probation officer of the importance of coordinating with the school to get Danny appropriate education services.

While there was no clear resolution to this case with the abrupt change in placement, the value of working across systems was evident. Most importantly, this case highlights a typical juvenile offender scenario, if there is one, including trauma history, disruptions in education, and family crises. It also highlights the importance of someone, in this case a school psychologist, taking the time to facilitate the process of the student receiving appropriate educational services and to coordinate with juvenile probation to identify and then obtain services. The school psychologists in this case was taking clear action consistent with the best practices offered in Table 17.2 to assist this one juvenile offender. Owing to the change in placement, it is unclear how these steps may have benefitted Danny, but in other situations there could easily be data to show improvement over time. In this case, the recent assessment included good baseline data that another professional could use to guide services, which is a great start.

SUMMARY

Juvenile offenders often have multiple emotional and behavioral challenges. These youth often have educational difficulties as well. Juvenile offenders are commonly served in special education and related services, but many may be unidentified. The juvenile justice system refers to a decentralized system of services intended to rehabilitate and reduce juvenile crime. Juvenile justice systems include educational placement and are considered public schools, but meeting the educational needs of juvenile offenders poses a host of challenges within the juvenile justice system. School psychologists can be particularly important as part of an interdisciplinary team serving these students and in addressing the array of challenges. School psychologists are the likely best single resource as part of an

interagency and interdisciplinary team. School psychologists can provide or facilitate necessary individual and systemic interventions, educational and behavioral recommendations, and psychological services to address the complex educational needs these youth often face.

Juvenile offenders typically have a combination of behavioral, academic, emotional, and community/family challenges. Trauma is also a very common mental health concern for this population, and trauma reactions should be a highlighted consideration when dealing with challenging behaviors. School psychologists will need to employ a full range of mental health and academic intervention skills, knowledge of special education eligibility, procedures and services, cultural sensitivity, consultation and systems collaboration, as well as advocacy to provide best practices in this high needs population. In particular, school psychologists can facilitate transition and school reentry planning for these students.

REFERENCES

Abram, K. M., Telpin, L. A., King, D. C., Longworth, S. L., Emanuel, K. M., Romero, … Olson, N. D. (2013, June). PTSD, trauma and comorbid psychiatric disorder in detained youth. *Juvenile Justice Bulletin.* Retrieved from http://www.ojjdp.gov/pubs/239603.pdf

Bilchik, S. C. (2011). *Addressing the needs of youth known to both the child welfare and juvenile justice systems.* Williamsburg, VA: National Center for State Courts. Retrieved from http://cdm16501.contentdm.oclc.org/cdm/ref/collection/famct/id/305

Cocozza, J. J., Skowyra, K. R., & Shufelt, J. L. (2010). *Addressing the mental health needs of youth in contact with the juvenile justice system in system of care communities: An overview and summary of key issues.* Washington, DC: Technical Assistance Partnership for Child and Family Mental Health.

Council of State Governments Justice Center. (2011). *Breaking schools' rules: A statewide study of how school discipline relates to students' success and juvenile justice involvement.* New York, NY: Author.

Cruise, K. R., Evans, L. J., & Pickens, I. B. (2011). Integrating mental health and special education needs into comprehensive service planning for juvenile offenders in long-term custody settings. *Learning and Individual Differences, 21,* 30–40. doi:10.1016/j.lindif.2010.11.004

Durlak, J. A., Weissberg, R. P., Dymnicki, A. B., Taylor, R. D., & Schellinger, K. B. (2011). The impact of enhancing students' social and emotional learning: A meta-analysis of school-based universal interventions. *Child Development, 82,* 405–432. doi:10.1111/j.1467-8624.2010.01564.x

Gies, S. V. (2003, September). Aftercare services. *Juvenile Justice Bulletin.* Retrieved from http://www.ncjrs.gov/pdffiles1/ojjdp/201800.pdf

JustChildren. (2004). *A summary of best practice in school reentry for incarcerated youth returning home.* Charlottesville, VA: Legal Aid Justice Center.

Katsiyannis, A., Ryan, J. B., Zhang, D., & Spann, A. (2008). Juvenile delinquency and recidivism: The impact of academic achievement. *Reading & Writing Quarterly: Overcoming Learning Difficulties, 24,* 177–196. doi:10.1080/10573560701808460

Kinscherff, R. (2012). *A primer for mental health practitioners working with youth involved in the juvenile justice system.* Washington, DC: Technical Assistance Partnership for Child and Family Mental Health.

Krezmien, M. P., Leone, P. E., Zablocki, M. S., & Wells, C. S. (2010). Juvenile court referrals and the public schools: Nature and extent of the practice in five states. *Journal of Contemporary Criminal Justice, 26,* 273–293. doi:10.1177/1043986210368642

Landenberger, N. A., & Lipsey, M. W. (2005). The positive effects of cognitive-behavioral programs for offenders: A meta-analysis of factors associated with effective treatment. *Journal of Experimental Criminology, 1,* 451–476. doi:10.1007/s11292-005-3541-7

Lösel, F., & Farrington, D. P. (2012). Direct protective and buffering protective factors in the development of youth violence. *American Journal of Preventive Medicine, 43,* S8–S23. doi:10.1016/j.amepre.2012.04.029

Matvya, J., Lever, N. A., & Boyle, R. (2006). *School reentry of juvenile offenders.* Baltimore, MD: Center for School Mental Health Analysis and Action, Department of Psychiatry, University of Maryland School of Medicine. Retrieved from http://www.nationalreentryresourcecenter.org/publications/school-reentry-of-juvenile-offenders

National Association of School Psychologists. (2010). *Model for comprehensive and integrated school psychological services.* Bethesda, MD: Author. Retrieved from http://www.nasponline.org/standards/2010standards/2_PracticeModel.pdf

Office of Juvenile Justice and Delinquency Prevention. (2012). *Statistical briefing book.* Washington, DC: Author. Retrieved from http://www.ojjdp.gov/ojstatbb/crime/qa05102.asp?qaDate=2010

Puzzanchera, C., & Kang, W. (2013). *Easy access to FBI arrest statistics 1994–2010.* Washington, DC: Office of Juvenile Justice and Delinquency Prevention. Retrieved from http://www.ojjdp.gov/ojstatbb/ezaucr/

Quinn, M., Rutherford, R. B., Leone, P. E., Osher, D. M., & Poirier, J. M. (2005). Youth with disabilities in juvenile corrections: A national survey. *Exceptional Children, 71,* 339–345.

Sander, J. B., Patall, E. A., Amoscato, L. A., Fisher, A. L., & Funk, C. (2012). A meta-analysis of the effect of juvenile delinquency interventions on academic outcomes. *Children and Youth Services Review, 34,* 1695–1708. doi:10.1016/j.childyouth.2012.04.005

Sander, J. B., Sharkey, J. D., Olivarri, R., Tanigawa, D. A., & Mauseth, T. (2010). A qualitative study of juvenile offenders, student engagement, and interpersonal relationships: Implications for research directions and preventionist approaches. *Journal of Educational and Psychological Consultation, 20,* 288–315. doi:10.1080/10474412.2010.522878

Sawyer, A. M., & Borduin, C. M. (2011). Effects of multisystemic therapy through midlife: A 21.9-year follow-up to a randomized clinical trial with serious and violent juvenile offenders. *Journal of Consulting and Clinical Psychology, 79,* 643–652. doi:10.1037/a0024862

Sedlak, A. J., & McPherson, K. (2010). *Survey of youth in residential placement: Youth's needs and services.* Rockville, MD: Westat. Retrieved from http://www.ncjrs.gov/pdffiles1/ojjdp/grants/227660.pdf

Shufelt, J., & Cocozza, J. J. (2006). *Youth with mental health disorders in the juvenile justice system: Results from a multi-state prevalence study.* Delmar, NY: National Center for Mental Health and Juvenile Justice. Retrieved from http://www.ncmhjj.com/pdfs/publications/PrevalenceRPB.pdf

Sickmund, M., Sladky, A., & Kang, W. (2013). *Easy access to juvenile court statistics: 1985–2010.* Washington, DC: Office of Juvenile Justice and Delinquency Prevention. Retrieved from http://www.ojjdp.gov/ojstatbb/ezajcs/

Skiba, R. J., Horner, R. H., Chung, C., Rausch, M., May, S. L., & Tobin, T. (2011). Race is not neutral: A national investigation of African American and Latino disproportionality in school discipline. *School Psychology Review, 40,* 85–107.

Snyder, H. N., & Sickmund, M. (2006). *Juvenile offenders and victims: 2006 national report.* Washington, DC: Office of Juvenile Justice and Delinquency Prevention.

U.S. Department of Education. (2007). *Twenty-ninth annual report to Congress on the implementation of the Individuals with Disabilities Education Act, 2007, Vol. 2.* Washington, DC: Author. Retrieved from http://www2.ed.gov/about/reports/annual/osep/index.html

Veysey, B. M. (2003). *Adolescent girls with mental health disorders involved with the juvenile justice system.* Delmar, NY: National Center for Mental Health and Juvenile Justice. Retrieved from http://www.ncmhjj.com/pdfs/publications/Adol_girls.pdf

Wilson, S., & Lipsey, M. W. (2007). School-based interventions for aggressive and disruptive behavior: Update of a meta-analysis. *American Journal of Preventive Medicine, 33,* S130–S143. doi:10.1016/j.amepre.2007.04.011

Wilson, S., Lipsey, M. W., & Derzon, J. H. (2003). The effects of school-based intervention programs on aggressive behavior: A meta-analysis. *Journal of Consulting and Clinical Psychology, 71,* 136–149. doi:10.1037/0022-006X.71.1.136

18 Best Practices in Planning Effective Instruction for Children Who Are Deaf or Hard of Hearing

Jennifer Lukomski
Rochester Institute of Technology (NY)

OVERVIEW

Students who are deaf or hard of hearing offer school psychologists an opportunity to apply their understanding of diversity in development and learning. The deaf or hard of hearing population is as heterogeneous as the hearing population with regard to religion, gender identity, cognitive capabilities, social–emotional skills, race, ethnicity, national origin, language, and socioeconomic status. The heterogeneous nature of the deaf population is magnified, however, by a constellation of variables such as type of hearing loss, home language environment, early intervention services, and use of residual hearing. These additional variables make generalizations about a typical deaf learner difficult. A diversity feature that is unique to deafness is that a hearing loss qualifies that person to become a member of a strong cultural minority group. Accordingly, the school psychologist must navigate the two worlds of the deaf, the disability world and the deaf culture world.

School psychologists may want to consult this chapter to gain an overview of the complexities and intricacies of working with children who are deaf or hard of hearing. The focus is on developmental approaches to providing effective learning environments. The intention is to provide practical information to help with developing effective learning environments for the deaf child. The intent is to help school psychology practitioners to patiently practice problem-solving strategies as they collaborate with parents, the deaf or hard of hearing child, teachers, other related service providers (e.g., teachers of the deaf, interpreters, audiologists), and community members (e.g., deaf role models, vocational rehabilitation specialists).

Research regarding deaf or hard of hearing children's learning and social–emotional functioning has been refined in recent years. One of the biggest advances is an understanding of how much we do not know and the understanding that one intervention or approach not only will not fit all deaf or hard of hearing students, but that an approach that is beneficial for one student with a hearing loss may be not beneficial for another student (Marschark & Knorrs, 2012). An individualized response to intervention approach is mandatory.

This chapter is closely linked to the National Association of School Psychologists (NASP) *Model for Comprehensive and Integrated School Psychological Services* (NASP, 2010). Although all 10 domains are inherent in any school psychological services, this chapter focuses on the foundational domain of Diversity in Development and Learning in relation to academic, social, and life skills interventions. The multitiered themes will focus on the level of providing preventive and responsive service. Of course, data-based decision making, collaboration, and consultation are guiding processes that apply to the implementation of the practical information provided.

Student Demographics/Delineations

Deafness is considered a low incidence disability with less than 1% of children identified at birth as deaf. The current estimates are that within the first couple of years, 2–3 out of 1,000 children are identified as having a hearing loss (National Institute on Deafness and Other Communication Disorders, n.d.). This number does not include all children who have mild to moderate hearing losses who may not be identified with a hearing loss in the first years of life. Furthermore, the cause of the hearing loss (e.g., high fevers, infections, prematurity, head injuries) frequently has an impact on other areas of the brain leading to co-occurring disabilities or multiple disabilities.

Students who have a hearing loss may be eligible for special education services under 1 of 4 of the 13 Individuals with Disabilities Education Act of 2004 classifications: Deafness, Hearing-Impairment, Deaf-Blindness, and Multiple Disabilities. The classification term Hearing-Impairment is considered offensive to most deaf individuals and professionals who specialize in the area of deafness. When possible, avoid using hearing impairment when referring to a deaf or hard of hearing student. In comparison, person-first language that is required and considered respectful and inclusive for any other disability does not apply to most deaf or hard of hearing individuals.

The distinction between *deaf* and *hard of hearing* is not always clear and not necessarily delineated by an individual's level of hearing loss. From an audition point of view, a person who is deaf typically has a severe to profound hearing loss, whereas a person who is hard of hearing has a mild to moderate hearing loss. The hearing loss, per se, does not necessarily dictate the person's speech awareness and communication skills. A person with a severe hearing loss may communicate both receptively and expressively with intelligible speech, whereas a person with a moderate hearing loss may require interpreters in all communication environments where there are non-signers. In contrast, a student with a moderate to mild hearing loss who has good speech and communication skills may identify with the deaf community strongly and label himself or herself as deaf.

Most frequently when a child who has a hearing loss speaks for himself or herself, has intelligible speech, and whose respective language skills are within the speech threshold for a mild to moderate range of hearing loss, the child is considered hard of hearing. The deaf child, in comparison, is the child who requires an interpreter for receptive and expressive language communication, whereas the hard of hearing child may not need an interpreter in one-on-one quiet settings, or may rely on an interpreter for receptive language but not for expressive language. That said, the lines between the two are much more nuanced, especially when factoring in the identification and affiliation with the deaf culture. In most cases, a deaf child receives services with the Deafness classification whereas a hard of hearing child receives services with a Hearing Impairment classification. In general more research has been conducted with deaf children than with hard of hearing children and/or deaf children with multiple disabilities (Marschark & Knorrs, 2012).

Cochlear Implants

Deaf children who have cochlear implants make up another subgroup of deaf children. A cochlear implant is a powerful hearing aid that is surgically implanted into the child's head. The surgeon places the internal stimulating electrode array inside the cochlea and also attaches a magnet under the skin to maintain contact between the externally worn components and implanted electrode components. The external components consist of a microphone, sound processor, transmitter, transmitting cable, and battery. Sound is transmitted via the speech processor, which converts the sounds to electrical impulses in the cochlea. The speech processor requires individual programming called *mapping* before use and may require remapping periodically. This first mapping typically occurs a month after the internal components have been inserted. Once the speech processor has been mapped, the work begins for the child to learn how to perceive and produce speech. An essential component for the success and effectiveness of the cochlear implant is the parents' and child's involvement and motivation in early auditory simulation and sound comprehension therapy such as Auditory-Verbal Therapy. Auditory-Verbal Therapy uses a systematic family intensive approach to teach deaf children how to use their residual hearing to listen and to speak.

Four main points about cochlear implants to remember are that (a) children who use cochlear implants are not hearing children; (b) not all deaf children are viable candidates for cochlear implants; (c) not all children with cochlear implants are able to benefit from the cochlear implant; and (d) when the cochlear implant is detached (e.g., for swimming and for sleeping) or when the speech processor battery dies, the child does not have the benefit of auditory input and becomes deaf. Furthermore, the early hopes that spoken language, literacy, and social development would be significantly enhanced for the child who has a cochlear implant has not been supported (Marschark & Spencer, 2010). Most importantly, children who have a cochlear implant do not have the same hearing capabilities and communication advantages as do hearing children (Spencer & Marschark, 2010).

Deaf and Co-Occurring Disability

The current estimates are that 40–60% of children who have a hearing loss have a secondary or co-occurring condition in addition to deafness (van Dijk, Nelson, Postman, & van Dikj, 2010). Fewer studies have been conducted and less is known about best practices and effective interventions for deaf children with multiple disabilities (van Dijk, et al., 2010). What is known is that interventions for children with a hearing loss and additional severe disabilities need to incorporate empirically based strategies that have been developed for the specific type of disability and at the same time are sensitive to the accommodations needed for the hearing loss.

For the child who is deaf and blind, deaf with autism, or deaf with an intellectual disability, there are specialized curricula that have been developed (van Dijk et al., 2010). Two key components that need to be part of any intervention for a child who is deaf and has a co-occurring severe disability are high quality communication and development of healthy attachments. For all deaf children who have a co-occurring multiple disability the use of manual communication is important. In addition, the school professionals who work with deaf children who have additional disabilities must have excellent communication skills and a good understanding of the high-tech alternative and augmentative communication aids.

Deaf Culture

Another aspect of being deaf relates to the richness and specialness of deaf culture (Padden, 1980). Even though approximately 95% of deaf children are born to hearing parents who may not have much awareness of deaf culture at the time of the child's birth, there is a large proportion of deaf or hard of hearing individuals who identify and belong to the deaf culture. The degree of participating in the deaf community varies. The outstanding feature of the deaf community and belonging to the deaf culture is a shared language (for U.S. deaf children that would be American sign language [ASL] and the communication customs that come with this language). Most hearing children of deaf parents are also members of the deaf culture. Hearing professionals, friends, and family may also have some form of membership to the deaf community depending on the degree of affiliation and immersion.

Historically, for many deaf or hard of hearing children, the residential schools for the deaf were a focal place where deaf cultural awareness was developed. Owing to a drop in the enrollment in these state schools, this identity exploration may not be fully initiated until adolescence when children participate in summer camps for deaf youth and or when they are even older and attend colleges such as Gallaudet

University and the National Technical Institute of the Deaf.

From the cultural perspective, deaf individuals view themselves as different rather than defective. In addition, the hearing loss for many deaf individuals is itself less of an obstacle than are society attitudes and the inability to provide full communication access. School psychologists need to be sensitive to the cultural aspects and differences in behavior related to being deaf. First, it is important to realize there is a difference in how deaf individuals communicate and to ask the child's extended family members about the child's cultural background and hearing status. This is true for children who are hearing and who have deaf parents. Recognize that the child's first language may not be English. A language assessment in the child's primary language (i.e., ASL) may be necessary. Be aware of cultural behaviors that are not standard hearing cultural behaviors, such as vigorous waving of a hand to get a person's attention, physical touch to get a person's attention, visual scanning, and pronounced facial expressions.

Another aspect related to deaf culture is to realize that there is a rich tradition not only of language but of history and heritage. Teaching the child and others about deaf culture and history is something that a school psychologist can make happen.

BASIC CONSIDERATIONS

Specialized training in the area of school psychology and deafness is highly recommended to accurately assess, diagnose, and treat deaf or hard of hearing learners (NASP, 2012). Owing to the limitations of most of the current test instruments for use with deaf or hard of hearing children, the school psychologist needs to be sensitive and knowledgeable about the interpretation and integration of both the quantitative and qualitative information the child provides. Even when speech is the native language of the child, the communication patterns and needs of the child need to be thoroughly understood before assessing, diagnosing, and developing interventions. The availability of norm-referenced tests for deaf or hard of hearing children is limited. Furthermore, the interactions of etiology of deafness, degree of hearing loss, age when hearing loss was identified, early language and intervention experiences, family's hearing status and communication modes, cultural variables, and the child's language development are a few variables that the school psychologist who is trained in working with deaf or hard of hearing youth will need to weigh and consider in conjunction with the normative and informal assessment behaviors gathered.

The background information and observations are perhaps the most important parts of the assessment. The hypotheses gathered during the collection of the deaf or hard of hearing child's developmental and social educational history guide the selection, scoring, and test interpretation. This is where the core hypotheses are formed, including the possible diagnoses and recommendations. For example, two 8-year-old deaf children are referred for an assessment because they are not reading at a first grade level. Child 1 is genetically deaf, has two deaf professional parents, is fluent in ASL, and is socially well adjusted. Child 2 has hearing parents, the child's hearing loss was identified when the child was 4, and the child received no early intervention services. A hypothesis for Child 1 is that perhaps the child has a specific learning disability in reading whereas a hypothesis for Child 2 is that the child's reading difficulties perhaps are due to the lack of adequate instruction.

Additionally, during the collection of the background information the interview with the parents and teachers is important as part of the assessment and as part of the intervention. One purpose of the interview is to indirectly assess the influential individuals who interact with the child. For example, involving the parents is critical since the family sets the learning environment for the child and the parents are powerful decision makers in this process. The family environment and parent–child relationship are critical factors to address not only for early intervention but as the child develops. Parents can influence identity exploration, perception, and interpretation of the various life activities (Leigh & Stinson, 1991; Lukomski, 2007).

Using the hearing populations' experience as a benchmark to assess a deaf person's experience may lead to misinterpretations. Test items sometimes mean different things to deaf individuals. For example, "hears sounds that are not there" and "makes loud noises when playing" may not be atypical occurrences for deaf children. For deaf or hard of hearing students who are not in contact with other children who are deaf or hard of hearing, behaviors such as "readily starts up conversations with new people" and "says nobody understands me" may also not be rare behaviors. A deaf person's endorsement of items regarding "having few friends," "being without company," and "feeling cut off from others" may be a confirmation of part of the deaf experience, especially when interacting with the hearing world. Similarly, hearing individuals who are unfamiliar

with ASL tend to initially stare at ASL users. Accordingly, deaf individuals who endorse an item such as "people frequently stare at me" confirms an actual life experience and is not an indication of paranoia. Again, these comments and endorsements must be placed in context in order to make correct conclusions about what they mean.

BEST PRACTICES FOR CHILDREN WHO ARE DEAF OR HARD OF HEARING

Thoroughly understanding the transactional aspect of a deaf or hard of hearing child's development is desired when providing best practices. Examining the child's social contexts and how the social contexts do or do not provide learning experiences within the child's zone of proximal development is important. School psychologists are in an excellent position to provide parents with the information, assess the learning environments of deaf or hard of hearing children, and collaborate with the teachers on interventions that can be effective. For example, school psychologists can emphasize to parents and teachers to not underestimate the deaf child's language and cognitive and academic potential and thus create lower performance expectations. Parents and teachers must not overestimate the child's hearing capabilities and assume comprehension of dialogue, vocabulary, and interactions in group settings and noisy environments based on the child's performance in quiet and slower paced face-to-face interactions.

In the hearing world, the amount of language development and communication that occurs incidentally is significant. A hearing person learns about communication, language, human interactions, family dynamics, cultural mores, and world affairs by overhearing conversations at home, school, and the community and listening to radio and television. Frequently, these incidental auditory input experiences lead to follow-up discussions or questions related to what was heard. Deaf or hard of hearing children, in comparison, frequently miss out on these influential learning opportunities unless these situations are made accessible.

This section is organized according to three amorphous developmental groups: (a) early childhood, (b) middle childhood, and (c) adolescence. For school psychologists working with students in the older age range it is recommended to read through each section to understand the foundational aspects that need to be considered when evaluating the current context. Tables 18.1, 18.2, and 18.3 summarize the key points for each developmental group.

Table 18.1. Development Considerations for Early Childhood

- Hearing parents need to learn how their baby/toddler orients by sight, not sound.
- Parents need to be sensitive to their child's processing of verbal and visual information consecutively rather than simultaneously.
- Parents should be taught how to incorporate natural opportunities to teach listening skills and how to make listening and communication fun and playful.
- Parents can increase early literacy development by providing interactive storybook reading, sign-print exposure, extensive reading, and social interactions around literacy activities.
- Parents need unbiased information regarding hearing loss, assistive listening devices, communication and language development, and special education practices.

Preschool
- Mild to moderate hearing losses are typically identified.
- Parents should be provided with information about their child's developmental needs.
- Communication issues should be addressed before assuming defiant behavior.
- Play situations and language opportunities need to be structured.
- Children should be provided many language opportunities.
- Children should be provided sequential visual cues and sequential visual presentation of instructions.
- Incidental learning experiences should be recognized and explicitly explained to children.

Table 18.2. Educational/Social/Emotional Considerations for Middle Childhood

Characteristics
- Deaf students show better detection skills of objects in the periphery.
- Deaf student's visual spatial memory is better developed than their sequential memory.
- Serial order information tasks are more challenging for deaf children.
- Deaf children have lesser automaticity in activating prior knowledge during reading and problem solving.
- Generalizing previously learned knowledge and making connections to use all their resources is more challenging.
- Reliance on the visual field dictates that for instructional purposes, lighting and seating arrangements are of paramount importance.

Conditions
- Be sensitive to interpreter lag.
- Supplement instruction with visual aids (i.e., notes, captioning, overheads, charts).
- Encourage dyad activities.
- Increase sustained peer interactions.
- Be sensitive to communication difficulties in large groups.
- Plan for communication needs in the cafeteria, on the bus, and during recreational activities (i.e., playground, gym, swimming pool).
- Invite deaf or hard of hearing speakers to the classroom to act as role models.
- Limit simultaneous presentation of material, allow for pauses in presentation of activities, identify speakers, and monitor turn taking.
- Assess the child's language in all languages.
- Direct context-based instruction and timely feedback.
- Increase opportunities to make connections with regard to social discourse.
- Direct context-based problem solving with regard to interactions.

Table 18.3. Educational/Social/Emotional Considerations for Adolescence

- Educate the adolescent about his or her hearing loss through discussions about IEPs, individual strengths, and communication needs.
- Identity issues as a deaf or hard of hearing person become salient.
- Important topics include self-advocacy and normalizing feelings.
- Teach appropriate problem-solving strategies.
- Continue to be aware of the lack of incidental learning.
- Middle school and high school can be socially isolating.
- Educate about health, healthy relationships, and sexuality.
- Address communication access and social interactions.
- Teach about deaf culture, history, and language.
- Involve the student in the discussion regarding transition planning to vocational and postsecondary options.

Early Childhood

Universal newborn hearing screenings have greatly increased the early identification and intervention efforts for children who are born deaf, especially children who have a severe to profound hearing loss at birth. Early detection followed by early intervention can provide parents with effective strategies and support to face the communication challenges and differences between deaf and hearing children. When early intervention occurs before 6 months of age, deaf children can have age-appropriate language skills, whereas children who receive early intervention after age 6 months can still make significant language progress (Meinzen-Derr, Wiley, & Choo, 2011). Early childhood hearing loss identification, early amplification (when born to hearing parents), and early intensive language intervention make a difference in a child's early language development (Marschark & Spencer, 2010).

The school psychologist can lead the multidisciplinary team in the assessment of the child's early intervention experiences. For example, one effective component of early intervention programs is to teach and model for parent's preverbal communication strategies, such as gaining attention and turn taking. Since communication patterns are different for deaf children, most hearing parents will not intuitively know how to communicate with their deaf infant (Traci & Koester, 2011). Explicit and modeled instruction needs to be provided to parents regarding how deaf children orient by sight and not by sound. Parents need to be taught visual and manual cues to gain their child's attention prior to initiating communication. For example, parents need to be taught how to use their eyes to visually orient their infant to participate in a communication interaction. The school psychologist can assess and recommend that these components are included in the early interventions that the deaf child receives or received.

An effective early intervention plan includes frequent assessments, modeling, and ongoing instruction of families in how to make communication and language accessible. School psychologists can help with the progress monitoring of parents' sensitivity to their child's processing of verbal and visual information consecutively rather than simultaneously. In addition, for children who have cochlear implants, parents should be taught how to incorporate natural opportunities to teach listening skills and how to make listening and communication fun and playful. The consensus is that to improve the child's language development there needs to be an increased number of interactions as well as an increase in the length of interactions (Traci & Koester, 2011). Language, language, and more language!

School psychologists can assess whether parents need to be taught how to increase early literacy development. For example, by providing interactive storybook reading, sign-print exposure, extensive reading, and social interactions around literacy activities, parents can facilitate language development and literacy (Schirmer & Williams, 2011). In addition, the parent–child attachment benefits from the structured interaction.

School psychologist collaboration with parents at the time of identification and early intervention is a crucial one. Most hearing parents when told they have a deaf child are not prepared and lack the knowledge necessary for fully understanding the issues related to having a child with a hearing loss. Parents can be overwhelmed when professionals provide conflicting opinions about the most appropriate and effective communication and educational methods. A generalized approach is difficult to provide because of the heterogeneous and diverse experiential context for each deaf child. The different options are not necessarily mutually exclusive. Whether the child should have a cochlear implant, be taught in an oral setting education, use cued speech or use sign language, should be a child and family-based decision. The school psychologist can provide parents with unbiased information regarding the program options, communication and language development, and special education practices (Marschark & Spencer, 2003). The current research finds that whether the child is mainstreamed or in a special class is not significantly going to make a difference in the child's language comprehension levels, nor is there an educational advantage if the child uses spoken or sign language. Additionally, there is no evidence that the use of sign language sabotages a child's speech and language learning (Marschark & Knoors, 2012).

Preschool

Preschool is frequently the time when a child who has a mild to moderate hearing loss, or a child who has a unilateral hearing loss, is identified. In contrast to the toddler, this is an age when school psychologists are more involved in the evaluation and intervention planning. Perhaps, surprisingly, a child identified with a mild to moderate hearing loss can be identified later than the child with the severe to profound hearing loss. Possible reasons for this later identification is that home environment acoustics tend be better than school acoustics, parents are better able to orient a hard of hearing child in a less noisy environment, and hard of hearing children develop spoken language in a similar, but delayed, pattern to hearing children (Jamieson, 2010). Parents may not become concerned or recognize delays until their child is compared to children without language delays. Sometimes, the parents are concerned that something is wrong but the pediatrician dismisses the concern.

When a mild to moderate hearing loss is identified when the child is in the preschool years, the school psychologist can inform parents about their child's developmental needs and teach parents methods to solve common problems (Caldroon & Greenberg, 2011). In order to gain this information, mothers of deaf children typically benefit best from strong support networks whereas fathers benefit from specialized interventions (Caldron & Greenberg, 2011). Sometimes parents have a difficult time differentiating whether the child's hearing loss is contributing to disobedient behavior or whether the child's attention and willfulness is creating communication difficulties. In collaboration with the school psychologist the function of the child's behaviors can be thoroughly assessed. In most cases, the child's communication issues should be addressed before assuming defiant behavior. For example, when a hearing parent picks up his or her child from a noisy daycare, the parent must make eye contact and greet the child, instead of talking to the child from a location where the child does not see the parent. If the parent tells the child to clean up prior to making eye contact, the child may not implement the desired behavior, which in turn may make the parent irritated and make the interaction a negative one.

Preschool is one setting where many children practice socializing with peers. Play situations and language opportunities need to be systematically structured for the deaf or hard of hearing child. One way children learn theory of mind and perspective taking is through language; that is, overhearing people's conversations and being explicitly told what other people may be thinking. This access can be limited, so the school psychologist can ensure that explicit instruction regarding play dynamics is provided and language modeling occurs. In addition, when observing a classroom setting, it is recommended that school psychologists critically examine that the instruction is delivered in sequential visual cues and sequential visual presentation of interactions, rather than in a simultaneous auditory and visual presentation. For example, when instructing children to line up to go outside for recess the teacher needs to make eye contact with the deaf child and face the children when

giving a direction rather than having his or her back to the children while making an announcement.

Few longitudinal studies exist that capture whether the gains made with early childhood interventions continue into school age, nor is there data to support that early intervention brings the child closer to functioning at the level of a typical hearing child (Spencer & Marschark, 2010). However, good quality early childhood intervention continues to be the best practice recommendation.

Elementary Age

From an Erikson developmental framework, middle childhood is the time when a child focuses on the task of industry versus inferiority (Erikson, 1959). Middle childhood is a time of building friendship skills, learning basic academic skills, and cementing the foundations for higher order reasoning skills. When these tasks of middle childhood are not mastered, the child's self-esteem and a sense of accomplishment are diminished (Erikson, 1959). For the school-age deaf or hard of hearing child, differences in cognitive processes, learning, communication, and socialization become more noticeable (Marschark & Knoors, 2012). These differences, if not appropriately addressed with effective accommodations and interventions, may discourage deaf or hard of hearing children and make them less confident in their learning and social interactions.

Cognitive Processing Differences

In general, deaf children of deaf parents and hearing children are not significantly different when it comes to intelligence scores (Marschark, Lang, & Albertini, 2002). However, examination of specific cognitive processes and executive functioning suggest that a hearing loss changes how one cognitively processes information, how one learns, and how one interacts with others. Even though there are more similarities than differences between deaf and hearing children's cognitive processing there are significant differences in deaf students' visual spatial abilities, memory, and executive functioning (Marschark & Knoors, 2012).

Visual Spatial Abilities

Deaf students have been found to have better periphery abilities (Bavelier et al., 2000). Specifically, deaf individuals are better at detecting distracted moving stimuli in their peripheral vision, whereas hearing individuals are better at detecting moving stimuli in the central field. How this difference in visual spatial ability influences academic learning, especially in the area of reading, is yet to be completely understood.

Memory

Deaf students' visual spatial memory has been found to be better developed than their sequential memory. Conway, Pisoni, and Kronenberger (2009) proposed that in the absence of sound, a sequential signal changes how one acquires cognitive sequencing skills, making serial order information tasks more challenging for deaf children.

Executive Functions

Deaf children have been found to have lesser automaticity in activating prior knowledge during reading and problem solving (Borgna, Convertino, Marschark, Morrison, & Rizzolo, 2011). They have difficulty generalizing previously learned knowledge and making connections to use all of their resources. Even when reading strategies, problem-solving aids, and scaffolding are offered, deaf students are less likely to know when to apply these resources when encountering reading blocks (Spencer & Marschark, 2010). To help deaf students learn to read and to use context cues and reading strategies, school psychologists can support teachers in carefully progress monitoring what conceptual knowledge students have, and then explicitly connecting new information to the learned information. Additionally, with respect to executive functions, deaf students often have a more difficult time than hearing students with self-monitoring. In comparison to hearing students, deaf students overestimate how they do on tasks and are less likely to know when they have made a mistake (Borgna et al., 2011).

Instructional Tips

Despite all we do know about deaf children's performance and abilities, the present field continues to lack validated instructional methods for deaf or hard of hearing children (Marschark and Knorrs, 2012). For example, even though deaf students are relatively more dependent than hearing peers on vision for language (sign language, speech reading print) and have a preference for visual presentation of information, there is no research supporting the claim that deaf students are any more visual learners than hearing individuals (Marschark, Morrison, Lukomski, Borgna, & Convertino, 2013). In other words, research does not support the claim that deaf students have a preference for a visual learning style; that is, receiving instruction through diagrams or pictures (static or animated) (Marschark et al., 2013). Nonetheless, owing to the

visual mode being the primary mode of accessing instruction for most deaf and hard of hearing children, the visual field is the child's primary sense used to orient to the environment.

Visual attention and visual orientation to the world have ramifications. Reliance on the visual field influences the way deaf or hard of hearing individuals experience the world. Dependence on visual information can also make deaf or hard of hearing children more prone to visual distraction than their hearing peers. When the school psychologist performs classroom observations, the classroom lighting and seating arrangements are important elements to note. The classroom needs to be well lit, and glare on the windows and the positioning of the teacher in relation to the lighting needs to be examined. The child needs to be seated close to the teacher, so that the child can visually track the teacher without any visual obstructions. One of the best seating arrangements for the classroom is placing tables or seats in a horseshoe shape. When the seating arrangement is in a horseshoe, the deaf or hard of hearing child can visually locate other children who are participating in class discussion as well as track class activity.

The teacher must attend carefully to communication and instruction because the deaf or hard of hearing child's attention is divided among the various tasks presented in the classroom. To begin communication, the teacher first needs to gain the child's visual attention either by a tap on the child's shoulder, a hand movement in the child's visual field, or a flick of the overhead lights. Then, the teacher needs to allow the child to orient visually to the teacher or object of discussion. The child has to shift visual attention from the environment to the communicator in order to receive a person's message. Often teachers present material and talk about the material at the same time. For example, frequently teachers lecture while writing on the blackboard or explain points during a movie. For a deaf or hard of hearing child, this simultaneous presentation, rather than complementing the material presented, may compete with the salient information to be learned. Instead, the teacher should point to the visual material, pause, allow the child to scan the visual material, and then the teacher can discuss the material. In addition, taking lecture notes is another activity that can become a competing rather than a supplementing task for deaf or hard of hearing children.

Daily interactions in the classroom, such as rapid rate of discussion, rapid turn taking, rapid change of topics, and more than one child talking at a time are also difficult for the deaf or hard of hearing child to follow (Stinson, Liu, Saur, & Long 1996). To facilitate communication, classroom activities need to be structured in a manner that allows the child to fully participate. The school psychologist can observe whether the teacher is limiting simultaneous presentation of material, allowing for pauses in presentation of activities, identifying speakers, and monitoring turn taking. In addition depending on the child's age, some form of note taker may also be necessary.

The school psychologist when doing classroom observations should note whether these instructional tips are implemented and consider modeling for the teacher more adaptive and effective teaching methods for the deaf and hard of hearing student.

Interpreters in the Classroom

Many deaf or hard of hearing children, with and without cochlear implants, require interpreting services for access to formal and informal learning experiences. The multiple visual stimuli, distractions, and variety of speakers in a classroom make it difficult for even a child with good speech reading skills and one-on-one conversational abilities to effectively participate in group situations. For deaf children whose preferred mode of communication is sign language, an educational interpreter, according to IDEA, must be provided to facilitate communication. Often, the function of the educational interpreter in the public school system is not clearly defined, and school personnel tend to misunderstand the role of the interpreter. The primary function of the interpreter is to be the voice and ears for the student and to be the voice of the teacher. Knowing sign language does not qualify someone to be an interpreter. Especially in a formal setting, the interpreter must have specialized training and be certified by the state or the national Registry of Interpreters for the Deaf. In addition, the interpreter must not only be a certified interpreter, but also must be qualified to interpret in the communication form (e.g., ASL, Pidgin Signed English, Signed Exact English, Cued Speech). Research has shown that even skilled interpreters capture less than 50% of what is said in the classroom (Schick, 2008).

When a classroom uses an interpreter, a few communication dynamics occur. First, the lag time between the spoken and signed message can affect the deaf or hard of hearing child's ability to fully participate in classroom discussion. In addition, the interpreter may need to further explain or define terms. However, it is important that the interpreter maintain the integrity of the communication between the teacher and the student. Teachers, therefore, need to build in pauses, especially before calling on students, to allow for the deaf or hard of hearing child to catch up and be included in the discussion.

Reading

To conduct a thorough reading assessment of the deaf or hard of hearing student, the student's background knowledge and language background need to be assessed. Many of the academic lags that deaf or hard of hearing children experience are due to their poorly developed language skills from an early age (Marschark & Spencer, 2003). The language background of the child as a toddler and preschooler sets the stage for the child as he or she enters into kindergarten and beyond. Assessing the child's language, in both English and in ASL or all other languages, is important. Deaf or hard of hearing students enter classrooms behind hearing students in vocabulary and content knowledge. In turn, adults' lack of sign language skills, communication limitations, and poor understanding of hearing loss ramification and implications can handicap the deaf or hard of hearing child (Marschark, Spencer, Adams, & Sapere, 2011).

Reading achievement is an area that students continue to lag behind hearing students (Marschark & Knoors, 2012). Explicit, directed, and ongoing instruction in reading is required. For some deaf students that may mean they need a form of visual phonics, which is a tool to help with phoneme and word production. Visual phonics incorporates a one-to-one correspondence between hand cues and sounds. The visual, tactile, kinesthetic feedback helps students relate mouth movements to different sounds and facilitates recognition of sound/symbol relationships. Although there is no conclusive evidence that for all deaf students' phonological awareness there is a strong relationship between reading skills and phonological awareness for children who use cochlear implants (Marschark & Spencer, 2010).

Overall, deaf or hard of hearing children must have direct context-based instruction that includes timely feedback. Instruction that focuses on basic skills such as using worksheets, answering teachers' questions, or memorizing vocabulary words is not as effective as instruction that focuses on metacognitive skills and reading for meaning.

Social–Emotional Arena

For the most part, deaf children are more similar to hearing children when it comes to social–emotional functioning. However, there are differences related to assertiveness, loneliness, theory of mind, and making friends. Owing to the limited incidental learning experiences when around hearing individuals, deaf children frequently lack making connections with regard to social discourse. Not overhearing their peers' informal conversations creates social barriers and social isolation. Sadly, too often in peer interactions they do not even know the questions to be asking (Calderon & Greenberg, 2011). Elementary-age deaf students continue to need more adult structured peer interaction. Direct context-based problem solving with regard to interactions and to daily life experiences needs to be in place. The Promoting Alternative Thinking Strategies curriculum has been shown to be effective in teaching deaf children conflict resolution, self-control, and problem-solving skills (Calderon & Greenberg, 2011). School psychologists can ensure that evidence-based programs such as the Promoting Alternative Thinking Strategies curriculum is implemented at a universal level.

Additional Accessibility Considerations

Children's functional communication is dynamic and context dependent (Jamieson, 2010). Hard of hearing children (including children who have cochlear implants) may appear successful in one-on-one interactions without interpreters, but can become socially isolated when there are multiple conversations or simultaneous conversations. Most school social environments (i.e., cafeteria, hallways, playground, or buses) have poor acoustics and high decibel levels thereby creating more barriers for deaf or hard of hearing students (Martin, Bat-Chava, Lalwani, & Waltzman, 2010). The school psychologist needs to be aware of the various environments that a child must function in, and systematically observe the child, the environment, and the interactions of others with the child in the different settings. The child's communication plan should include strategies for handling communication breakdowns, handling the child's fatigue, training school personnel and classmates in communication strategies, and parent training in communication modes (e.g., ASL).

In general, most elementary school classrooms are not good listening environments. That is, the signal to noise ratio, the relationship between the intensity of the signal and the intensity of the background noise, is not favorable in classroom settings (Jamieson, 2010). Playgrounds, cafeterias, and buses have even less favorable signal to noise ratio, increasing the likelihood that hard of hearing students become followers and loners. To encourage a more inclusive learning setting,

interactive whiteboards such as the SMART Board and ActivBoard as well as captioned media should be utilized by teachers. Captioned Media Program provides free lending services to schools to help provide students with access to closed captioning for television, for the Web, and for classroom videos. Other technologies that might be helpful include Web-based sign language instruction, signing science dictionary for teaching vocabulary, portable hand-held technologies, and smartphones (Stinson, 2010). As with all media and written communication, ongoing assessment of student understanding determines the effectiveness of captioning and written information.

Middle School/High School/Adolescents

Deaf or hard of hearing adolescents' learning and interactions continue to build on the foundations set at younger ages. The aware school psychologist should assess the adolescent's early intervention services and early school experiences when developing an understanding of the deaf adolescent. Unique developmental considerations become more apparent and need to be addressed in adolescence. Erikson proposed that adolescence is the time of identity exploration versus identity diffusion (Erikson, 1959). Providing deaf or hard of hearing deaf students with as many opportunities to explore and learn about themselves and prepare them for the postsecondary school should be a focus for the school psychologist.

Friendships

For the deaf adolescent, middle school and high school can become more socially isolating than elementary school. During adolescence, friendships take on a different meaning and depth. Adolescent friendships become a place where students begin to explore their identity, who they are, and who they want to become. Developing intimate safe friendships is difficult when there are few other adolescents who have a hearing loss or, depending on the school culture, few hearing students who are interested in individuals who appear different in any way.

For the deaf student who uses an interpreter, the interpreter typically provides communication access. However, the use of an interpreter may inadvertently isolate the student from accessing informal social interactions. For example, sometimes the deaf student is more engaged with the interpreter in conversations than with peers. Other times, having an adult interpreter to be the voice and ears for the deaf adolescent is uncomfortable for the hearing adolescents and therefore the hearing adolescents do not include the deaf adolescent in social interactions. A more time-consuming but viable communication method for deaf and hearing students is the use of their palm devices or computers for conversations.

To encourage socialization between deaf and hearing students, school personnel can emphasize the value of diversity. The more students learn about deaf culture and deaf students' communication needs, the more comfortable hearing students may become with communicating with a deaf student. In turn, deaf students will be encouraged to share their uniqueness with others. When the differences are not acknowledged and the communication needs are not discussed, misunderstandings can occur that hearing students may label as weird or strange. For example, when deaf or hard of hearing students talk too loud, do not follow the conversation thread, make odd comments, or answer a question that has already been answered, hearing adolescents may avoid and not include the student in social interactions.

The school psychologist can normalize the deaf or hard of hearing child's perceptions of feeling different, and teach the deaf or hard of hearing adolescent how to become a self-advocate. The school psychologist may find it helpful to coordinate activities with the other deaf or hard of hearing adolescents in the district. Having a shared hearing loss, however, does not equate nor guarantee that a friendship will be made. A better strategy is for school psychologists to encourage teachers to structure dyad work, small group discussions, and implement diversity awareness.

Dating and sexual development is an area that needs to be more explicitly addressed with deaf or hard of hearing adolescents. A significantly higher number of deaf college students compared to hearing respondents have reported experiencing inappropriate sexual contact (Schenkel, Rothman-Marshall, & Burnash, 2012). Educating deaf or hard of hearing students about their bodies and feelings that correspond with sexual development is not the solution to others' inappropriately touching deaf students. However, the more students are informed about their bodies the better they can articulate their rights and alleviate their anxieties about their bodies. For example, a 12-year-old boy who was in therapy for anxiety issues one evening ran to his parent's bedroom shouting that his penis had exploded. He was terrified and no one had informed him about wet dreams in a way that he understood. Skills in developing and maintaining healthy romantic relationships must also be explicitly discussed and role-played.

Although there is limited empirical research regarding the substance abuse rates in deaf or hard of hearing adolescents, school professionals must consider how to create positive social environments for deaf or hard of hearing students. Not caving into peer pressure can be more difficult for an outsider who wants to be included in social events. Good problem-solving skills and healthy coping skills can give deaf adolescents the necessary tools to circumvent experimentation with negative substances.

Deaf Identity
Educating others about what it is to be deaf or have a hearing loss is an important method to address communication access and social interactions. Teaching the deaf adolescent about deaf culture, history, and language can also benefit the student's sense of identity. It is helpful for the school psychologist to model for the student, in context, how to educate others on what it means to have a hearing loss. Additionally, connecting with community resources is important. Inviting in deaf speakers and role models can give the deaf or hard of hearing adolescent courage and hope.

One way that deaf or hard of hearing students establish and socialize with other deaf or hard of hearing children is by forming relationships during weekends or school breaks. Attending college exploration programs or workshops geared for deaf or hard of hearing adolescents can be inspirational. Gallaudet University in Washington, DC, and the National Institute of the Deaf in Rochester, New York, host such events and welcome deaf or hard of hearing adolescents from around the nation and the world. Frequently, these special camps and exploration programs have a family component that helps parents learn about and understand the needs of their deaf or hard of hearing adolescent. The deaf or hard of hearing student can have an extensive social network of friends that are maintained by the social media.

Ramifications of Lack of Incidental Learning
The scope of not having access to incidental learning experiences is hard to comprehend. In the health field, researchers have found that limited incidental learning experiences can have negative ramifications (Hauser, O'Hearn, McKee, Steider, & Thew, 2010). With health issues, when the adolescent has limited family communication, deaf or hard of hearing students do not know about family medical history and other health related issues. Furthermore, they may not have accurate information about sexual development and sexuality.

In general, deaf individuals have been shown to have limited health literacy, because they had limited access to elaborations about their family history and health habits (Hauser et al., 2010). Students who do not have health information and education can become deaf adults who lack the skills to make appropriate health decisions.

Executive Functions

For many hearing children, middle school is an important time to begin to strengthen and practice executive functions. Changing classrooms, doing more homework, organizing a locker and book bag, and adapting to a variety of teaching styles and teacher's expectations challenges and develops a student's behavior regulation and metacognitive skills. For deaf or hard of hearing children, the transition to middle school can be more overwhelming than it is for hearing students. Deaf or hard of hearing students who may have a team of service providers (i.e., interpreters, teacher of the deaf) may receive too much help with initiating, planning, studying, and organizing school classes and work. Parents and school service providers may inadvertently provide too much support, which can hinder the student from practicing and learning important life skills. A lack of opportunities to try out skills, such as managing time and money and organizing and planning homework, can backfire. Students learn valuable problem-solving skills from assessing problem-solving strategies that were implemented and were found to not be effective. When too much support is provided, students do not learn how to solve problems, learn from their mistakes, or make better choices. The school psychologist can encourage the deaf or hard of hearing adolescent's primary service providers to calibrate the amount of scaffolding the student needs. Teaching and practicing problem-solving steps may help deaf adolescents become better at self-assessment of their performance. The student is enabled to then practice problem solving in real life contexts, with natural and logical consequences in place.

Individual Education Planning/Transitional Planning

Another way to encourage self-awareness is by including deaf or hard of hearing adolescents in the process of developing their educational plan. Invite the adolescent to participate in their Individualized Education Program (IEP) team. Deaf or hard of hearing adolescents should be informed about their present levels of performance, their areas of need, and their learning goals.

Understanding how they are performing is beneficial, and creates self-knowledge, especially when the information provided is valid and reliable. The school psychologist can explain to the IEP team how student self-knowledge of strengths and needs can help with the development of the student's identity and of self-advocacy skills.

When the deaf or hard of hearing adolescent is 14, if not sooner, he or she should be involved in the discussions regarding transition planning to vocational options. The more the student is provided with opportunities to explore job options, informed about educational and skill requirements of various careers, job shadows, and has co-op experiences, the more relevant schoolwork becomes. The student and family need to be made aware of vocational rehabilitation services and other community agencies that will be a resource post high school. The earlier these discussions take place, the more prepared the student and family will be for this critical transition from high school.

Most deaf or hard of hearing adolescents want to fit in and not be different. They may assert their independence by acting out when being pulled out of their regular education class to attend resource room services, or they may assert their need to be more like hearing students by refusing to wear their hearing aids. Also, using an interpreter makes them feel different from hearing peers. In situations where the deaf or hard of hearing adolescent is asserting his or her independence, the adults need to listen, and within a reasonable limit, allow the adolescent to experience the natural and logical consequences of his or her choices. In many situations, once the adolescent feels heard and understood, it may be possible to negotiate with the adolescent regarding options. Sometimes adults can be more flexible regarding what the required behavior is. Perhaps the student who does not want to be pulled from the regular education classes may be willing to attend his or her support services at times that are less disruptive (i.e., at lunch, study hall, after school). For the student who does not want to wear hearing aids, perhaps the student can be given the option to not wear hearing aids all the time, or perhaps by making the hearing aid more colorful and attractive, the student will want to wear the hearing aids. Listen to the student and negotiate reasonable accommodations that create a happier learner.

SUMMARY

Deaf or hard of hearing students offer school psychologists an opportunity to apply their understanding of diversity in development and learning. Generalizations about the typical deaf or hard of hearing student are difficult. For most deaf or hard of hearing students, the crucial incidental learning experiences that are naturally accessible to most hearing students are foreign when navigating in a hearing world. Hearing caregivers and school professionals need to provide as much access to context-based problem solving learning experiences starting with the young toddler. Formal and informal learning needs to be as much about teaching the deaf or hard of hearing student to listen and think as it is for adults to listen and engage deaf or hard of hearing students in conversations.

REFERENCES

Bavelier, D., Tomann, A., Hutton, C., Mitchell, T., Liu, G., Corina, D., & Neville, H. (2000). Visual attention to the periphery is enhanced in congenitally deaf individuals. *Journal of Neuroscience*, *20*(17)(RC 93), 1–6.

Borgna, G., Convertino, C., Marschark, M., Morrison, C., & Rizzolo, K. (2011). Enhancing deaf students learning from sign language and text: Metacognitive, modality, and the effectiveness of content scaffolding. *Journal of Deaf Studies and Deaf Education, 16*, 79–100.

Calderon, R., & Greenberg, M. (2011). Social and emotional development of deaf children: Family, school, and program effects. In M. Marschark & P. E. Spencer (Eds.), *The Oxford handbook of deaf studies, language, and education* (Vol. 1, pp. 188–199). New York, NY: Oxford University Press

Conway, C. M., Pisoni, D. B., & Kronenberger, W. G. (2009). The importance of sound for cognitive sequencing abilities. *Current Directions in Psychological Science, 18*, 275–279. doi:10.1111/j.1467-8721.2009.01651.x

Erikson, E. (1959). *Identity and the life cycle.* New York, NY: International Universities Press.

Hauser, P. C., O'Hearn, A., McKee, M., Steider, A., & Thew, D. (2010). Deaf epistemology: Deafhood and deafness. *American Annals of the Deaf, 154*, 486–496.

Jamieson, J. R. (2010). Children and youth who are hard of hearing: Hearing accessibility, acoustical context, and development. In M. Marschark & P. E. Spencer (Eds.), *The Oxford handbook of deaf studies, language, and education* (Vol. 2, pp. 376–389). New York, NY: Oxford University Press.

Leigh, I. W., & Stinson, M. S. (1991). Social environments, self-perceptions, and identity of hearing-impaired adolescents. *Volta Review, 93*(5), 7–22.

Lukomski, J. (2007). Deaf college students' perceptions of their social emotional adjustment. *Journal of Deaf Studies and Deaf Education, 12*, 472–485.

Marschark, M., & Knoors, H. (2012). Educating deaf children: Language, cognition, and learning. *Deafness & Education International, 14*, 136–160.

Marschark, M., Lang, H. C., & Albertini, J. A. (2002). *Educating deaf students: From research to practice.* New York, NY: Oxford University Press.

Marschark, M., Morrison, C., Lukomski, J., Borgna, G., & Convertino, C. (2013). Are deaf students visual learners? *Learning and Individual Differences, 25*, 156–162.

Marschark, M., & Spencer, P. E. (Eds.). (2003). *Oxford handbook of deaf studies, language, and education.* New York, NY: Oxford University Press.

Marschark, M., & Spencer, P. E. (2010). Promises of deaf education: From research to practice and back again. In M. Marschark & P. E. Spencer (Eds.), *The Oxford handbook of deaf studies, language, and education* (Vol. 2, pp. 1–14). New York, NY: Oxford University Press.

Marschark, M., Spencer, P. E., Adams, J., & Sapere, P. (2011). Teaching to the strengths and needs of deaf and hard-of-hearing children. *European Journal of Special Needs Education, 26*, 17–23.

Martin, D., Bat-Chava, Y., Lalwani, A., & Waltzman, S. B. (2010). Peer relationships of deaf children with cochlear implants: Predictors of peer entry and peer interaction success. *Journal of Deaf Studies and Deaf Education, 16*, 108–120. doi:10.1093/deafed/enq037

Meinzen-Derr, J., Wiley, S., & Choo, D. I. (2011). Impact of early intervention on expressive and receptive language development among young children with permanent hearing loss. *American Annals of the Deaf, 155*, 580–591.

National Institute on Deafness and Other Communication Disorders. (n.d.). *Statistical report: Prevalence of hearing loss in U.S. children, 2005* Retrieved from http://www.nidcd.nih.gov/funding/programs/hb/outcomes/Pages/report.aspx

National Association of School Psychologists. (2010). *Model for comprehensive and integrated school psychological services.* Bethesda, MD: Author. Retrieved from http://www.nasponline.org/standards/2010standards/2_PracticeModel.pdf

National Association of School Psychologists. (2012). *Students who are deaf or hard of hearing and their families* [Position statement]. Bethesda, MD: Author. http://www.nasponline.org/about_nasp/positionpapers/ServingStudentsWhoAreDeaf.pdf

Padden, C. (1980). The deaf community and the culture of deaf people. In C. Baker & R. Battison (Eds.), *Sign language in the deaf community: Essays in honor of William C. Stokoe* (pp. 89–103). Silver Spring, MD: National Association of the Deaf.

Schenkel, L., Rothman-Marshall, G., & Burnash, D. (2010, November). *Abuse rates higher among deaf and hard-of-hearing children compared with hearing youth.* Poster presented at the Association of Behavioral and Cognitive Therapies, San Francisco

Schick, B. (2008). The development of American sign language and manually coded English systems. In M. Marschark & P. E. Spencer (Eds.), *The Oxford handbook of deaf studies, language, and education* (Vol. 1, pp. 229–240). New York, NY: Oxford University Press.

Schirmer, B. R., & Williams, S. (2011). Approaches to reading instruction. In M. Marschark & P. E. Spencer (Eds.), *The Oxford handbook of deaf studies, language, and education* (Vol. 1, pp. 115–129). New York, NY: Oxford University Press.

Spencer, P. E., & Marschark, M. (Eds.). (2010). *Evidence-based practice in educating deaf and hard-of-hearing students.* New York, NY: Oxford University Press.

Stinson, M. S. (2010). Current and future technologies in the education of deaf students. In M. Marschark & P. E. Spencer (Eds.), *The Oxford handbook of deaf studies, language, and education* (Vol. 2, pp. 93–110). New York, NY: Oxford University Press.

Stinson, M. S., Liu, Y., Saur, R., & Long, G. (1996). Deaf college students' perceptions of communication in mainstreamed classes. *Journal of Deaf Studies and Deaf Education, 1*, 140–151.

Thagard, E. K., Hilsmer, A. S., & Eastbrooks, S. R. (2011). Pragmatic language in deaf and hard of hearing students: Correlation with success in general education. *American Annals of the Deaf, 155*, 526–534.

Traci, M., & Koester, L. S. (2011). Parent-infant interactions: A transactional approach to understanding the development of deaf infants. In M. Marschark & P. E. Spencer (Eds.), *The Oxford handbook of deaf studies, language, and education* (Vol. 1, pp. 200–213). New York, NY: Oxford University Press.

van Dijk, R., Nelson, C., Postma, A., & van Dikj, J. (2010). Deaf children with severe multiple disabilities: Etiologies, intervention, and assessment. In M. Marschark & P. E. Spencer (Eds.), *The Oxford handbook of deaf studies, language, and education* (Vol. 2, pp. 93–110). New York, NY: Oxford University Press.

19 Best Practices in School-Based Services for Students With Visual Impairments

Sharon Bradley-Johnson
Andrew Cook
Central Michigan University

OVERVIEW

This chapter will familiarize school psychologists with background issues on visual impairment relevant to assessment and instruction of students with a visual impairment and provide background information to facilitate a multidisciplinary approach to intervention. Research-based issues and methods for instruction are presented for early intervention as well as for classroom behavior, social skills, achievement, and physical exercise for school-age students. This information can aid school psychologists in working with other team members to meet the individual needs of these students. The approaches described are consistent with the National Association of School Psychologists (NASP) *Model for Comprehensive and Integrated School Psychological Services* (NASP, 2010) Diversity in Development and Learning domain and can be applied at all levels of a multitiered problem-solving approach.

Background on Visual Impairment

Because numerous variables affect visual functioning, students classified with a visual impairment comprise a heterogeneous group. Such variables include the etiology, type, and severity of vision loss; age of the student at the time of onset of the loss of vision; and whether or not a student has additional disabilities. Even students with the same etiology may function quite differently depending upon whether they have additional disabilities and the type of experiences they have had. Approximately 90% of students with a visual

impairment have some degree of vision (Kelley, Sanspree, & Davidson, 2000). Even those with severe losses can employ this residual vision to help them with adaptive behaviors.

Some terms that describe severity of vision loss can be confusing. The term *legally blind* is used to determine eligibility for government benefits. Criteria for this classification are a visual acuity of less than 20/200 in the better eye with corrected distance vision or a restricted visual field of 20 degrees or less (approximately 180 degrees is normal). Visual acuity describes clarity of vision measured with a standard eye chart. The 20 indicates the distance in feet at which an individual can identify a letter on the chart, and 200 indicates the distance at which someone with normal vision can identify the same letter on the chart. These students are eligible for special education services under the classification of *visual impairment*, because their visual loss, even when corrected (e.g., with glasses), interferes with their educational performance. *Blindness* refers to those who have a complete loss of vision or those whose loss is so severe they mainly depend upon their other senses for learning, conducting daily activities, and traveling. These students typically use braille for reading along with auditory input (e.g., use of a reader or recorded information) and may need a long cane or guide dog for travel. Also eligible for special education services are students with *low vision*. Even with correction their vision loss interferes with their educational performance, but they are not blind. These students require adaptations that may include low-vision equipment and environmental changes to enable them to function adequately in the classroom. Examples of low vision equipment include book stands, magnifiers, and a large-print calculator. Some may need large print, whereas others may be able to read standard-size print. Some students may read print, but require tactile and auditory material for instruction. Thus, because of the heterogeneity of students with visual impairments, a variety of adaptations and specialized instruction are necessary to meet their needs in school.

Incidence

Of students from 3 to 21 years of age who receive special education services, .4% are classified as having a visual impairment (U.S. Department of Education, 2011). About 63% of these students are taught in general education classrooms for 80% or more of their school day (U.S. Department of Education, 2012).

Etiology

Approximately half of vision losses are a result of congenital factors, and the remainder are adventitious (i.e., a result of illness or injury). Congenital vision losses can result from prenatal damage, a genetic malformation, or an inherited condition. Examples of inherited conditions include albinism and retinitis pigmentosa. Albinism involves abnormal pigment production in the eye resulting in poor visual acuity and extreme sensitivity to light. Classroom adaptations might include sunglasses for light sensitivity, magnification, holding objects and materials close, and special lighting. Retinitis pigmentosa is an inherited condition involving degeneration mainly of light-sensitive cells in the retina, resulting in a profound visual impairment for some students. The symptoms are rarely evident to a large extent until at least late childhood. Adaptations may include use of closed-circuit television, special lighting, and avoidance of glare.

Adventitious losses occur because of diseases or accidents including head injury, anoxia at birth, infection of the central nervous system (e.g., meningitis), or a reaction to medications. An example is cortical visual impairment, which can result from insufficient oxygen during birth, prematurity, infections, or traumatic brain injury that damages the visual cortex or pathways to the brain. These students have poor visual acuity and can display various types of unique visual responses including light gazing, looking away when reaching for objects, and poor visual attending. Cortical visual impairment is a complicated condition and

adaptations are based on the idiosyncratic needs of the student. Examples of adaptations include orientation and mobility training, braille instruction, a sighted guide, an uncluttered work space, and lighting accommodations.

BASIC CONSIDERATIONS

Most students with visual impairments have one or more additional impairments. Not only is consultation with a student's caregivers, medical specialist, and classroom teacher necessary, but other consultants will be required to address the unique needs of these students.

To be effective, assessment and instruction for students with visual impairments must be based on a multidisciplinary approach. In addition to caregivers and teachers, specialists such as certified teachers for students with visual impairments, medical specialists, and orientation and mobility instructors may be needed.

Certified teachers of students with visual impairments may conduct a functional vision assessment and a media assessment that can provide important recommendations for working with these students. These teachers assess how a student uses his or her vision when performing academic and daily living tasks in his or her natural environment, and they can recommend positioning and environmental modifications to enhance a student's visual efficiency. For example, their reports might include recommendations for intensity of illumination, position of a light source, and low-vision equipment. Media assessment results suggest whether a child should be a print or braille reader, or both. However, this decision often cannot be made until preschool or later because vision conditions change and observations of the effects of instruction over time are needed to obtain sufficient information to reach this conclusion. Functional vision assessments and media assessments can be carried out with students from infancy through adolescence. School psychologists need the information from these assessments prior to planning a psychoeducational assessment and when planning instruction and supports in collaboration with caregivers, teachers, and specialists.

Medical reports also provide important information regarding a vision loss. Ophthalmologists' and optometrists' reports include a description of medical interventions needed, prescriptions, prognosis, and any restrictions on eye use. To clarify information in these reports, commonly used abbreviations and their meaning are presented in Table 19.1.

A medical report describes visual acuity measured separately for each eye. Acuity is measured with and

Table 19.1. Commonly Used Medical Abbreviations

Abbreviation	Definition
C.C	With correction
C.F.	Counts fingers; vision may be measured by the ability to count fingers held up at varying distances
H.M.	Hand movement; vision may be measured by the ability to see hand movement at varying distances
L.P.	Light perception
N.L.P.	No light perception (totally blind)
O.D.	Ocular dexter (right eye)
O.S.	Ocular sinister (left eye)
O.U.	Oculi unitis (both eyes)
P.P.	Near point
P.R.	Far point
S., S.S., or S.C.	Without correction
V.A.	Visual acuity
V.F.	Visual field
W.N.L.	Within normal limits

without correction (i.e., with and without glasses). Usually such information is provided for both near vision and distance viewing.

Because vision conditions change frequently, vision assessments should be no more than a year old. Hearing assessments also should be current because students with visual impairments rely heavily on what they hear and maximizing this ability is critical. Recommendations from a medical report, however, may not apply to the classroom. Anxiety and the unfamiliar environment of a medical office may affect a student's use of vision during a medical examination. Thus, recommendations from a functional vision assessment conducted within the school also are important for planning instruction.

An orientation and mobility instructor has specialized training for teaching safe, independent travel for students with a visual impairment. These skills provide access to opportunities in various settings. An untrained observer may think a student moves about quite well considering the student's vision loss, whereas an orientation and mobility specialist might suggest several options that would increase independent functioning substantially. Training in orientation and mobility skills often begins in infancy. An orientation and mobility assessment will include evaluation of a student's skills for moving about safely such as balance, posture, and gait. An orientation and mobility instructor may teach a student directly, including indoor and outdoor travel, travel in urban and rural areas, concept development, as well as use of a cane, low-vision equipment, electronic travel devices, and public transportation. This specialist

also may work with teachers, family members, and others who can help students practice these skills.

Thus, to develop comprehensive, effective educational programs that maximize the benefit of services and ensure continuity for students with visual impairments, school psychologists must work collaboratively with other professionals. Understanding the importance of what these specialists can contribute to assessment and intervention is important for effective teaming.

BEST PRACTICES IN SCHOOL-BASED SERVICES FOR STUDENTS WITH VISUAL IMPAIRMENTS

The cultural diversity of the population of students with visual impairments is similar to the makeup of the population of sighted students in education in general. The majority are White non-Hispanics, followed by Hispanics, then Black non-Hispanics, next Asians or Pacific Islanders, and then American Indians or Alaskan Natives (Correa-Torres & Durando, 2011). Thus, as the population of the United States continues to become more and more diverse in terms of both culture and language, school psychologists are very likely to work with students and their families from diverse backgrounds.

School psychologists can consult and collaborate with teachers and administrators to support their efforts to provide schools that are culturally responsive environments. Also, school psychologists should ensure that assessment measures they use and recommendations they make are culturally sensitive. For example, when working with a student from a diverse background it is important to consider whether students from his or her cultural group were included in the test norms and whether data are provided on the validity of the test for this group of students.

To ensure educational environments that value diversity, school psychologists themselves need to understand various cultures and their associated traditions. To better serve students from diverse backgrounds and their families, NASP encourages school psychologists to use cultural brokers. A cultural broker may be from the student's culture and would be able to provide cross-cultural information relevant to the student's needs. Such information could have important implications for recommendations for working with the student as well as for communicating with the student's family. An understanding of how to work with interpreters also is important for effective communication with some of these students and their families. To enable collaboration with some families, use of both cultural brokers and interpreters may be necessary. Unfortunately, there is a paucity of information regarding how various cultures perceive visual impairments. Thus, this is an area where school psychologists might provide needed research for the field.

Assessment

Because of their unique needs, carrying out an instructionally useful and comprehensive psychoeducational assessment for students with a visual impairment requires consideration of a number of factors that are not a concern, or are of less concern, with sighted students. This is true before, during, and following an assessment of a student with a visual impairment. Fortunately, there are various assessment options (e.g., norm referenced, criterion referenced, curriculum based, and informal procedures) that can provide school psychologists with useful information. To thoroughly describe the process of assessment of these students is beyond the scope of this chapter, but Bradley-Johnson and Morgan (2008) address these issues and assessment options in detail.

Infants, Toddlers, and Preschoolers

There are various ways in which school psychologists can help caregivers enhance their interactions and instruction with the youngest children with a severe vision loss. Table 19.2 presents common concerns encountered when working with caregivers of these children followed by recommendations.

School-Age Students

It is not uncommon for teachers to feel overwhelmed by the prospect of having a student with a vision loss in the classroom. However, by understanding common concerns that arise in the classroom with these students, school psychologists can help teachers cope effectively with these events and implement interventions when necessary.

Caregivers also can assist their child and the teacher. If school psychologists encourage family members to observe their child in the classroom this can help them understand how their child functions in this setting. This information should help family members determine how they can provide assistance.

Because of their vision loss these students often require more teacher support than their classmates. In other settings these students may need assistance from others. Thus, to ensure that others are willing to provide this assistance, it is important that these students request, accept, and refuse help appropriately. If this is not the case, school psychologists can use role-playing and coaching to teach these skills to the students.

To function efficiently and avoid wasting time and frustrating searches for materials, students with a visual impairment will benefit from being well organized. Teaching students to organize their desks, to return items to their designated spots, and praising them for doing so will be beneficial. These skills promote independence, an area with which teachers report these students have difficulty (Agran, Hong, & Blankenship, 2007). School psychologists will be able to determine whether or not organization skills need to be addressed by observing the student's functioning in the classroom and talking with the teacher.

Students with visual impairments typically require more time to complete assignments than their classmates. Braille and enlarged print both take longer to read than regular print and are more tiring. Thus, school psychologists can ensure that teachers consider the constraints for these students and set realistic time expectations for assignment completion. Setting realistic expectations will avoid frustration for both the student and teacher.

Teachers also need to be vigilant about ensuring that students with a visual impairment understand instructions and are academically engaged. Teachers' instructions are partially conveyed via eye contact, gestures, and other nonvocal behavior that is likely to be missed by these students. School psychologists can remind teachers to praise these students when they demonstrate that they listened carefully. Also, before beginning an assignment, teachers can ask students to repeat directions to ensure that they heard them.

Difficulty with attending may give way to poor academic engagement. Bardin and Lewis (2011) examined the level of academic engagement of students with visual impairments relative to sighted peers who were average or low academic achievers. Although the students with a vision loss were braille readers achieving at grade level, the authors' found their levels of inattention, effort, and self-determination were similar to those of low-achieving sighted students. Thus, consistent with the authors' recommendations, teachers and school psychologists can help these students increase their engagement by holding them accountable for their work, encouraging their creativity, and promoting their independence.

Table 19.2. Concerns and Recommendations for Infants, Toddlers, and Preschoolers

Concern	Recommendation
Caregivers of children with visual impairments often have difficulty recognizing and understanding their children's signals. For example, because of their vision loss these children may not make eye contact or direct their gaze toward someone speaking to them. The communicative behaviors used by children whose vision is compromised can be subtle, unique, and difficult to interpret.	Any fairly consistent change in behavior (e.g., quieting, squirming, changing facial expression, and other increases or decreases in activity level) can indicate attempts by these children to initiate or respond to others. They may inhibit activity to help focus on what they hear, and some caregivers may interpret this as a lack of interest. School psychologists can help caregivers identify the positive responses these children make, and then model back-and-forth interaction with the children to facilitate productive caregiver–child interactions.
Smiles are often difficult to evoke from children with visual impairments. Without visual feedback, children's smiling behavior may decline.	Frequently vigorous physical play is required to evoke a smile from these children. Encouraging caregivers to provide verbal feedback and physical contact to reinforce smiles will be helpful.
Reaching for objects by children who are congenitally blind tends to be delayed compared with sighted children, which reduces early opportunities for exploration of their environment.	To enhance reaching and searching for objects, school psychologists can encourage caregivers to frequently present toys that make noise at distances the children can easily reach. Change the position at which they are presented, for example, from midline, to right side, to left. Large toys are easier for children to locate.
Some children will be startled or frightened when someone approaches because they were unable to see when the person was approaching.	School psychologists can remind caregivers to talk as they approach the child to avoid this problem.
Crawling and walking tend to be delayed in children who are blind. Crawling on hands and knees appears in 55% of children who are blind at a mean age of 15 months, whereas this ability appears in 75–82% of sighted children at a mean age of 13 months, 2 weeks. Independent walking appears for children who are blind at a mean age of 19 months, 3 weeks compared with sighted children for whom the ability appears with a mean age of 12 months (Elisa, MacLillan, Tucker, & Bennett, 2002).	If school psychologists inform caregivers of these delays prior to the time their child reaches the age when sighted children usually attain these milestones, this may alleviate caregivers' fears regarding additional disabilities. This information can assist them in keeping any delay in crawling or walking in perspective considering their child's vision loss. Also, it is helpful to encourage caregivers to provide physical guidance to increase their child's use of these muscles because this can decrease or even eliminate such delays.
Children with a severe vision loss need to be taught the importance of organization as early as possible. Learning this skill will be beneficial when they are young and it is critical once they attend school.	School psychologists can emphasize to caregivers the importance of having a designated place for storing a child's favorite toys and belongings (e.g., coat and shoes). The children will need to be taught to get desired objects from their places and return objects to their designated places when finished with them. Doing so can help teach object permanence, facilitate walking, and encourage a child to move about to get his or her toys. Keeping things in predictable places also gives a child a feeling of control and enables independent functioning.
Children with a severe vision loss need to explore their environment more than their sighted peers to compensate for what they are unable to see. However, because of a child's vision loss, some caregivers may be overprotective to the point of interfering with the child's learning and social development.	Teaching these children to avoid hazards and respond appropriately to "no" is important for their safety. However, school psychologists may need to assist some caregivers in finding a balance between ensuring their child's safety and encouraging their child to explore the environment and interact with others.

Continued

Table 19.2. Continued

Concern	Recommendation
Language development may be slower in some areas than it is for sighted children.	To facilitate language development, school psychologists can recommend that caregivers name objects and describe their own actions even with infants. Comprehensive, detailed verbal descriptions of the environment are helpful. Encouraging caregivers to develop a habit of saying the child's name before speaking to him or her is beneficial. This indicates that the caregiver is speaking directly to the child and helps the child with name recognition (a skill often delayed for these children).
Children with a severe vision loss frequently have sleep problems. Although sleep problems are common in sighted children, those with visual impairments have more difficulty falling asleep, have longer night awakenings, awaken more frequently per night, and awaken more nights per week (Fazzi et al., 2008). Early intervention is important because sleep problems tend to continue without treatment.	Behavioral interventions used with sighted children may help children with a severe vision loss. Establishing consistent bedtime routines helps cue the body that it is time to sleep (Ferber, 2006). Other effective strategies include progressive delayed responding from caregivers (Ferber, 2006), crying it out, and scheduled awakenings (Rickert & Johnson, 1988). We do not recommend crying it out because caregivers frequently have difficulty consistently implementing the procedure and most child abuse occurs during prolonged crying. Use of oral melatonin improves the sleep of children with visual impairments (Stores & Ramchandani, 1999). School psychologists can help caregivers select a research-based intervention, and in doing so may lessen the impact of sleep problems on the family.

Social Skills

As with any student with a disability, consideration of the quality and frequency of use of their social skills is important when planning instruction for a student with a visual loss. Vision is a major component in communicating with others, particularly in terms of facial expressions and gestures. The fact that some students whose vision is compromised benefit from instruction in initiating and responding to others is not surprising.

Acquisition of effective social skills plays a major role in later successful performance for students with visual impairments. If social skills for these students are inadequate, the students may be isolated, and if unable to obtain employment, they will have considerable difficulty in functioning independently.

If students with a visual impairment are able to appropriately address others' questions about their vision loss, this can reduce others' fears and concerns and aid in social interaction. If these students try to hide their disability, others may think they are unusual or even incompetent. This is especially the case for students with low vision who appear as if they are sighted. Hence, school psychologists can assist these students through counseling, role-playing, and coaching to enable them to develop ways they are comfortable with to explain their visual disability to others. When appropriate, school psychologists might work with a student's family members to help them explain the student's disability to others as well.

School psychologists also might arrange for adult or college-age mentors with a visual impairment to work with students with a visual loss. These role models can assist students in accepting their disability, address questions about various social situations, and perhaps offer suggestions to them on how to handle difficult social interactions.

A complicating factor in terms of social interaction for adolescents with a visual impairment is being unable to drive. School psychologists can help adolescents prepare to deal with this issue. Discussing various options such as traveling with friends and using different types of public transportation can be beneficial, including consideration of the expense of various public transportation options.

Several factors specific to students with a severe visual loss can contribute to social interaction difficulties. For example, these students may need to be taught to face someone who is speaking to them. Without this skill, interactions will be awkward. School psychologists can teach this skill to these students using prompting and coaching, and teachers can help by prompting students to use this skill in the classroom. Orienting to a speaker can be particularly difficult when several people speak at the same time.

Although to some extent everyone engages in self-stimulation when bored or stressed, students with a visual impairment may self-stimulate at a higher frequency or engage in unusual behaviors. Eye pressing and body rocking are the most frequent forms of self-stimulation for young children who are blind, and these behaviors tend to be rather stable without intervention. Such behaviors interfere with learning, may be perceived negatively by peers, and can interfere with social interaction. Thus, school psychologists should complete a functional analysis for such behaviors and help to design an intervention as early as possible.

Social skill training programs designed for sighted students can be used with students with visual impairments as well, such as the Social Skills Improvement System (Gresham & Elliott, 2008).

The participation of adolescents with visual impairments in extracurricular activities and paid work experiences is significantly related to their composite ratings on scales measuring social skills (Smith & Zebehazy, 2011). Whether good social skills facilitated involvement in these activities or involvement in these activities aided the development of good social skills is unclear. However, school psychologists should encourage students' participation in clubs, recreational activities, sporting events, and after-school activities. Such experiences can enhance the social confidence of students with a disability.

Reading

Prior to and during formal reading instruction, all children benefit from exposure to books and reading with adults. These experiences are particularly important for children with visual impairments to enhance their language, listening, and early reading skills. Books written in print and braille allow sighted family members to read to the child, and the braille enables the child to tactilely experience the text. Real objects can be substituted for pictures. These objects can be placed with the book in a box or bag so that when the book is to be read, the child or adult can select the book box (or bag) and have the relevant objects available. Numerous print/braille books should be available so children can choose those they enjoy for repeated reading. Several programs designed for young children as well as older children with a developmental delay can help caregivers support early literacy development. The Perkins Panda Early Literacy Program (www.perkinspublications.org) for children from birth to age 8 includes storybooks in large print and braille with high-contrast illustrations, activity guides, recordings, a toy panda, and a bag to hold objects for the story. A

video from the American Printing House for the Blind (www.aph.org), *Discovering the Magic of Reading*, is for caregivers and teachers of children from birth to age 5, and presents methods for involving children in a story and choosing books of interest to children with a vision loss. Seedlings Braille Books (www.seedlings.org) also has many low-cost print/braille books. Braille books should be stored upright and loosely stacked. Too much pressure on the book will cause the braille to press flat and become unreadable.

Phonological awareness skills are important for sighted students, potential braille readers, and low-vision children. Beginning braille readers develop phonological awareness skills in the same way print readers do (Monson & Bowen, 2008), and thus many instructional approaches used with sighted students can be recommended for students with a vision loss.

For children who will become braille readers, school psychologists can encourage family members to learn the basic braille components, including the alphabet and primary punctuation marks. Some family members may be willing to learn additional braille skills, which would provide good models for children.

Both braille and sighted readers must learn sound–symbol relationships to decode words, but braille readers must learn considerably more symbols. Many contractions are used to increase reading speed and decrease the bulk of braille material. Braille characters are used for frequently occurring letter combinations such as *er*, contractions for frequently appearing whole words such as *the*, and single letter contractions are used for words, such as *c* for *can*. The complete braille code includes the alphabet and 189 contractions and short-form words. The three grades of braille vary in the number of contractions used. Grade 1 has no contractions for beginning readers, Grade 2 is most commonly used and involves many contractions, and Grade 3 is used mainly by scientists and engineers and has the most contractions.

Whether it is more effective to teach uncontracted braille first and then introduce contractions, or teach contractions earlier in instruction, is unclear from current studies. Braille contraction cards for practicing these contractions can be ordered from the American Printing House for the Blind.

Learning to read braille is difficult because of braille's complexity, and there are few studies that have systematically evaluated the effectiveness of different methods for teaching braille (Troussaint & Tiger, 2010). Patterns (Caton, Pester, & Bradley, 1980) is the only basal braille program that begins with prebraille skills and progresses through the third-level reader. Despite braille's complexity, once braille readers become fluent in decoding, those with sufficient life experiences to aid comprehension are unlikely to perform any differently than sighted readers (Steinman, LeJeune, & Kimbrough, 2006).

For students with degenerative visual impairments, school psychologists should encourage teachers to begin teaching braille to these students while they still have some vision. Their remaining vision will facilitate learning. Troussaint and Tiger (2010) evaluated a procedure for teaching early braille-letter identification to students with degenerative visual impairments who had some sight remaining at the time of instruction. They were taught to match a braille symbol and a printed letter using a motor response. Thus, correct responses could be prompted when necessary to aid acquisition. Prior studies first taught braille letter naming by requiring a vocal response, which could not be physically prompted. In the Troussaint and Tiger (2010) study, not only were students successful in learning braille-to-printed-letter relationships, but they learned to correctly match printed letters to their braille symbols, the names of letters to their braille symbols, and braille symbols to their letter names. These latter three skills were learned incidentally through the procedure (i.e., not directly taught). Thus, this procedure would be an efficient instruction method for school psychologists to recommend for teaching students to match braille symbols and printed letters, matching printed letters and braille symbols, matching letter names and braille symbols, and braille symbols and letter names.

To monitor progress in braille reading (NASP Practice Model domain of Data-Based Decision Making and Accountability), a modified version of curriculum-based measurement (CBM) can be informative. School psychologists who do not read braille can follow along on a printed copy to score performance. Morgan and Bradley-Johnson (1995) found that a modified CBM procedure with braille probes was as reliable and valid as the standardized CBM method is for sighted students. The modification involves use of a 2-minute rather than 1-minute probe, and use of 6 seconds rather than 3 seconds to prompt unknown words on probes.

Speed is a concern with braille reading. Trent and Truan (1997) found that the factor most related to reading speed is age at onset of blindness; that is, the later the onset, the slower the speed. They suggested that to develop speed, students need to read braille on a daily basis for a considerable amount of time, and that braille instruction should begin early, especially for students whose vision is degenerative. The sooner students begin braille, the more time they have to practice. Those who begin braille in third grade or later usually do not catch up to those who began braille reading upon school entry. Because braille typically takes considerably longer to read than regular print, even the fastest braille reader will not read at a rate commensurate with that of print readers. Because of the amount of required reading in regular classrooms, students with low reading rates will need orally read material, recorded material, or both, as well as access to braille.

Students with low vision can be taught with regular basal readers using magnifiers or enlarged print. The appropriate size print for a student must be determined on an individual basis. Farmer and Morse (2007) noted limitations of using enlarged type including access only to those materials that have been enlarged, difficulty trying to read non-enlarged print encountered daily such as menus and bills, and the high costs of enlarging printed materials. Their study compared the performance of large-print readers with readers who only used magnifiers. Over an academic year, those using magnifiers not only gained more in reading speed but also in comprehension.

Gompel, Janssen, van Bon, and Schreuder (2003) found children with low vision were as accurate in decoding as their sighted peers, but they read slower. Further, the students' slower reading was a result of reduced visual input, not a lack of orthographic knowledge. Thus, consistent with Gompel et al.'s (2003) suggestions, school psychologists should recommend that efforts to increase reading speed for these students focus on adapting visual input (e.g., print size, font, contrast) to better meet each student's individual needs. As with sighted students, having students with low vision repeatedly read a short paragraph until they meet a fluency standard can increase their oral reading fluency. To ensure that these students are exposed to similar amounts of material as their sighted peers, adequate fluency is important. Students with low vision appear to comprehend material they read as well as their sighted peers.

Assistive Technology

The development of assistive technology devices provides individuals with visual impairments enhanced ability to access materials important for learning.

Examples of assistive technology include software that magnifies and reads contents on a computer screen, braille note-takers with speech synthesizers, and refreshable braille (hardware that produces and allows for modification of braille). The number of students using braille through computers with adapted software and braille note-takers rather than paper braille is increasing. This technology provides numerous resources including access to e-mail, calendars, and the Web.

D'Andrea (2012) interviewed 12 high school and college student braille readers regarding their practices and preferences. All students used computers and portable braille-compatible devices. Most high school students used embossed braille for textbooks, whereas college students used electronic textbooks. However, both groups clearly preferred paper braille for mathematics, science, and foreign languages. Regarding the need to learn braille, the students indicated that braille was beneficial in learning written language skills such as spelling, sentence structure, and punctuation, skills that are not so obvious when speech access alone is used. Advantages noted for technology were that it is faster (especially with speech access), more easily portable than bulky paper braille materials, and provides increased access to information. Disadvantages included the expense (e.g., $5,000–$6,000 for a portable note-taker), cost of maintenance of the equipment, and the inconvenience of being without it when the device is being repaired. These students clearly felt it important that young children learn to read braille. They also felt knowledge of technology is important so that students can make choices to fit their individual needs in various academic areas. Thus, school psychologists should ensure that Individualized Education Programs (IEP) for students with visual impairments allow use of multiple methods (e.g., print braille, speech readers, refreshable braille) to improve students' access to curricula.

Despite widespread availability of technology for students with visual impairments, data from longitudinal studies indicate that less than half of elementary, middle, and high school students who use large print or braille media, and who are close to or at grade level, actually use the devices (Kelly, 2011). Research suggests that children who use assistive technology while learning braille have greater knowledge of the braille code and improved reading and writing skills (Cooper & Nichols, 2007). Thus, school psychologists should help and encourage teachers to use assistive devices to teach early literacy skills to young children, because this is not often done. Regular online communication for older students with visual impairments is associated with a

higher likelihood of employment, education, and community engagement after high school. Unfortunately, fewer than half of these students used the Internet for such purposes consistently compared to more than 90% of their nondisabled peers (Kelly & Wolffe, 2012). Thus, encouraging use of online communication for older students is important as well.

The amount of support students receive from their caregivers is an important factor in students' use of technology. School psychologists can encourage caregivers of students with visual impairments to learn at least some braille skills as well as how to use assistive devices. Students are more likely to use braille during independent study periods when their caregivers know braille (Argyropoulos, Sideridis, & Katsoulis, 2008) and are more likely to use assistive technology if their caregivers attend training sessions and meetings for families of students with disabilities (Kelly, 2011).

Mathematics

Few studies have examined the development of arithmetic skills in children with a severe vision loss. Young children who are blind may be somewhat behind their sighted peers in arithmetical ability, but this difference seems to disappear by about ages 8–11 (Warren, 1994). Ahlberg and Csocsan (1999) found that children who were congenitally blind do not spontaneously use their fingers to solve arithmetic problems and have trouble showing a given number of fingers. They hypothesized that lack of finger counting occurs because children who are blind only perceive by touch the finger most recently counted.

Thus, rather than finger counting for these students, school psychologists can recommend that students group elements to be counted with both hands so that they can experience the elements as units to compose and decompose. Large Lego blocks work well for this purpose. Because the blocks fit together, students can experience the individual blocks as well as the total quantity. Also, use of the blocks may decrease losing track of and dropping the items to be counted.

To write out mathematical operations, braille readers need to learn the Nemeth Code, which is rather complicated. This is the standard code used to represent numbers and math symbols within the six-dot braille cell. The code can be used to write all arithmetic operations including decimals and fractions, as well as algebra, geometry, trigonometry, and calculus.

When planning an assessment or developing recommendations in mathematics, school psychologists will need to work closely with a certified teacher consultant for visual impairment who will have considerable knowledge regarding the types of adaptive equipment that may be appropriate for a student. If a student uses an abacus in the classroom, during testing the student should be allowed to use the abacus on test items for which sighted students are allowed to use paper and pencil. Examples of other adaptive equipment include braille versions of rulers, compasses, clocks, and protractors. A talking calculator also might be used. For students learning about graphing, a rubber graph board enables a teacher to draw graphs with raised lines for instruction.

Written Language

Students who lose their vision after learning to write may be able to use script writing on raised-lined paper, such as that available from American Printing House for the Blind. Students who cannot use script writing may use a computer with speech, print, or braille output, an electronic note-taker, a brailler (similar to a typewriter, but for braille), or a slate and stylus.

Spelling skills of students who are blind appear well developed. For example, Grenier and Giroux (1997) found that spelling skills of students in ninth to eleventh grades who were Grade 2 braille readers were superior to those of their sighted peers. Although further studies are needed, it appears that spelling skills of braille readers typically are well developed. Few studies have examined spelling skills for students with low vision. However, Gompel et al. (2002) found that spelling skills of students with low vision and no additional learning problems were as strong as those of their sighted peers.

Physical Exercise

Students with visual impairments tend to be less physically fit than their sighted peers, especially in terms of cardiovascular endurance and upper body strength (Lieberman, Byrne, Mattern, Watt, & Fernandez-Vivo, 2010). These students sometimes may feel excluded in physical education classes. To enhance their physical fitness they need opportunities equal to those of their sighted peers.

School psychologists can assist physical education teachers in working with these students. For example, they might help train peer tutors to provide appropriate instruction, use physical guidance techniques, and provide positive corrective feedback and tactile modeling

for students with visual impairments. Wiskochil, Lieberman, Houston-Wilson, and Petersen (2007) found that with these procedures students with visual impairments spend more time engaged in appropriate motor activity during physical education. With some initial instruction, activities such as jumping rope, using a tread mill, riding a stationary bike, and carrying a talking pedometer while walking are activities these students can carry out independently. School psychologists can ensure that such easily implemented accommodations are incorporated in students' IEPs.

Besides considering the academic areas discussed above, school psychologists should ensure that services for school-age students with a vision loss also include transition planning whenever these students are faced with a change in programs. Assistance in preparing for college or vocational pursuits also must be incorporated into their educational plans.

SUMMARY

Students with visual impairments are a diverse, low-incidence group. School psychologists are encouraged to take a developmental and culturally sensitive approach in working with these students and their families. To plan effective interventions for these students, school psychologists must collaborate with individuals from various disciplines, all of which can make unique contributions to an instructional plan. Understanding the contributions of certified teachers for students with visual impairments, orientation and mobility instructors, and medical personnel can facilitate collaboration.

School psychologists can help caregivers meet challenges the youngest children with vision impairment present, particularly with social interaction and exploration of the environment. Ensuring the provision of an organized environment, and teaching children how to function within that environment, will enhance several skills including independence.

Teachers of school-age students with visual impairments often feel overwhelmed when they have a student with a visual impairment in their classroom. Fortunately there are many research-based procedures that school psychologists, other consultants, and caregivers can use to assist these students and their teachers. Areas of particular concern include classroom behavior, social skills, braille or enlarged print reading, assistive technology, arithmetic, and physical education. A modified version of CBM works well for monitoring progress in braille reading.

AUTHOR NOTE

Disclosure. Sharon Bradley-Johnson has a financial interest in books she authored or coauthored referenced in this chapter.

REFERENCES

Agran, M., Hong, S., & Blankenship, K. (2007). Promoting the self-determination of students with visual impairments: Reducing the gap between knowledge and practice. *Journal of Visual Impairment & Blindness, 101,* 452–464.

Ahlberg, A., & Csocsan, E. (1999). How children who are blind experience numbers. *Journal of Visual Impairment & Blindness, 93,* 549–560.

Argyropoulos, V. S., Sideridis, G. D., & Katsoulis, P. (2008). The impact of the perspectives of teachers and parents on the literacy media selections for independent study of students who are visually impaired. *Journal of Visual Impairment & Blindness, 102,* 221–231.

Bardin, J. A., & Lewis, S. (2011). General education teachers' ratings of the academic engagement level of students who read braille: A comparison with sighted peers. *Journal of Visual Impairment & Blindness, 105,* 479–492.

Bradley-Johnson, S., & Morgan, S. K. (2008). *Psychological assessment of students who are visually impaired or blind: Infancy through high school* (3rd ed.). Houston, TX: Region 4 Education Service Center.

Caton, H., Pester, H., & Bradley, W. J. (1980). *Patterns: The primary braille reading program.* Louisville, KY: American Printing House for the Blind

Cooper, H. L., & Nichols, S. K. (2007). Technology and early braille literacy: Using the Mountbatten Pro Brailler in primary-grade classrooms. *Journal of Visual Impairment & Blindness, 101,* 22–31.

Correa-Torres, S. M., & Durando, J. (2011). Perceived training needs of teachers of students with visual impairments who work with student from culturally and linguistically diverse backgrounds. *Journal of Visual Impairment & Blindness, 105,* 521–532.

D'Andrea, M. F. (2012). Preferences and practices among students who read braille and use assistive technology. *Journal of Visual Impairment & Blindness, 106,* 585–596.

Elisa, F., MacLillan, M., Tucker, A., & Bennett, S. (2002). Gross motor development and reach on sound as critical tools for the development of the blind child. *Brain & Development, 24,* 269–275. doi:10.1016/S0387-7604(02)00021-9

Farmer, J., & Morse, S. E. (2007). Project magnify: Increasing reading skills in students with low vision. *Journal of Visual Impairment & Blindness, 101,* 763–768.

Fazzi, E., Zaccagnino, M., Gahagan, S., Capsoni, C., Signorini, S., Ariaudo, G., ... Orcesi, S. (2008). Sleep disturbances in visually impaired toddlers. *Brain & Development, 30,* 572–578. doi:10.1016/j.braindev.2008.01.008

Ferber, R. (2006). *Solve your child's sleep problems.* New York, NY: Simon & Schuster.

Gompel, M., Janssen, N. M., van Bon, W. H. J., & Schreuder, R. (2003). Visual input and orthographic knowledge in word reading of children with low vision. *Journal of Visual Impairment & Blindness, 97,* 273–284.

Gompel, M., van Bon, W. H. J., Schreuder, R., & Adriaansen, J. J. M. (2002). Reading and spelling competence of Dutch children with low vision. *Journal of Visual Impairment & Blindness, 96,* 435–447.

Gresham, F., & Elliott, S. (2008). *Social Skills Improvement System.* Upper Saddle River, NJ: Pearson.

Grenier, D., & Giroux, N. (1997). A comparative study of spelling performance of sighted and blind students in senior high school. *Journal of Visual Impairment & Blindness, 91,* 393–400.

Kelley, P., Sanspree, M. J., & Davidson, R. (2000). Vision impairment in children and youth. In B. Silverstone, M. A. Lang, B. Rosenthal, & E. Faye (Eds.), *The Lighthouse handbook on vision impairment and vision rehabilitation* (vol. 2, pp. 1137–1141). New York, NY: Oxford University Press.

Kelly, S. M. (2011). The use of assistive technology by high school students with visual impairments: A second look at the current problem. *Journal of Visual Impairment & Blindness, 105,* 235–239.

Kelly, S. M., & Wolffe, K. F. (2012). Internet use by transition-aged youths with visual impairments in the united states: Assessing the impact of postsecondary predictors. *Journal of Visual Impairment & Blindness, 106,* 597–608.

Lieberman, L. J., Byrne, H., Mattern, C. O., Watt, C. A., & Fernandez-Vivo, M. (2010). Health-related fitness of youths with visual impairments. *Journal of Visual Impairment & Blindness, 104,* 349–358.

Monson, M. R., & Bowen, S. K. (2008). The development of phonological awareness by braille users: A review of the research. *Journal of Visual Impairment & Blindness, 102,* 210–220.

Morgan, S., & Bradley-Johnson, S. (1995). Technical adequacy of curriculum-based measures for braille readers. *School Psychology Review, 24,* 94–103.

Rickert, V. I., & Johnson, C. M. (1988). Reducing nocturnal awakening and crying episodes in infants and young children: A comparison between scheduled awakenings and systematic ignoring. *Pediatrics, 81,* 203–212.

Smith, T. J., & Zebehazy, K. T. (2011). An examination of characteristics related to the social skills of youths with visual impairments. *Journal of Visual Impairment & Blindness, 105,* 84–95.

Steinman, B., LeJeune, B., & Kimbrough, R. (2006). Developmental stages of reading processes in children who are blind and sighted. *Journal of Visual Impairment & Blindness, 100,* 36–46.

Stores, G., & Ramchandani, P. (1999). Sleep disorders in visually impaired children. *Developmental Medicine & Child Neurology, 41,* 348–352. doi:10.1017/S0012162299000766

Trent, S. D., & Truan, M. B. (1997). Speed, accuracy, and comprehension of adolescent Braille readers in a specialized school. *Journal of Visual Impairment & Blindness, 91,* 494–500.

Troussaint, K. A., & Tiger, J. H. (2010). Teaching early braille literacy skills within a stimulus equivalence paradigm to children with degenerative visual impairment. *Journal of Applied Behavior Analysis, 43,* 181–194. doi:10.1901/jaba.2010.43-181

U.S. Department of Education. (2011). 30th annual report to Congress on the implementation of the Individuals with

Disabilities Education Act, 2008 [Table 12]. Washington, DC: Author. Retrieved from http://www2.ed.gov/about/reports/annual/osep/2008/parts-b-c/30th-idea-arc.pdf

U.S. Department of Education. (2012). *The digest of education statistics, 2011* (NCES 2012-001), Table 47. Washington, DC: Author. Retrieved from http://nces.ed.gov/programs/digest/d11/tables/dt11_047.asp

Warren, D. (1994). *Blindness and children: An individual differences approach.* New York, NY: Cambridge University Press. doi:10.1017/CBO9780511582288

Wiskochil, B., Lieberman, L. J., Houston-Wilson, C., & Petersen, S. (2007). The effects of trained peer tutors on the physical education of children who are visually impaired. *Journal of Visual Impairment & Blindness, 101,* 339–350.

Section 2
Research and Program Evaluation

20 Best Practices in Conducting School-Based Action Research

Samuel Song
Jeffrey Anderson
Seattle University
Annie Kuvinka
Edmonds (WA) School District

OVERVIEW

The scope of professional school psychology practice is vast, ranging from direct services with students to indirect services with school personnel and the wider school community. School psychologists must make numerous decisions regarding their practice, such as which intervention might be most effective for a particular student, classroom, or school. These practice decisions can be conceptualized as problems (or questions) of practice. Some practice problems and questions may require a systematic plan of investigation that is led *by* a school psychologist *for* that school psychologist's practice in the schools. Because school psychologists are experts in their local school practice, this type of school psychologist-led inquiry is always relevant to schools. Imagine for example being asked by the school administrator to solve a recurrent bullying problem. A number of practical questions arise, such as whether to continue to use the existing bullying program, address the problem at a class or school level, or involve student and family input. Action research is a tool to help answer these questions faced by school psychologists in their daily practice.

Action research has two characteristics distinguishing it from other forms of systematic inquiry: (a) it is conducted by and for the ones taking the action (i.e., school psychologists) and (b) the local researcher (i.e., school psychologist) is in a position of power and authority to implement the recommendations that come from the research (i.e., leading to change and action). Therefore, while a school psychologist may be involved in research at the school, it does not constitute action research unless the school psychologist is able to make the changes or actions that are developed from the action research process. A definition then is that action research is a form of systematic inquiry that primarily aims to solve a practice problem leading to change in school psychology practice with the goal of improving it (and their school clients) by implementing actions (Sagor, 2012; Stringer, 2007).

Action research is different from traditional research (i.e., group experimental or quasi-experimental designs). Action research is conducted by school psychologists rather than researchers from outside the school setting, such as university professors or community partners. In addition, traditional group research typically seeks to develop new knowledge and advance theory (e.g., discover generalizable findings), while action research seeks to improve local practice by solving practical problems. Action research values the complexities of local practice that are situated in a particular context by discovering solutions that work *for that particular situation* of local practice (Pine, 2009; Reason & Bradbury, 2008). One size fits all would not be a core assumption of action research (Clauset, Lick, & Murphy, 2008). Therefore, the standard for high-quality action research is whether the research results in desired local change. Therefore, the primary audience for action research is members of the school psychology and school communities instead of other researchers or government agencies. In sum, the ultimate goal of action research is to improve professional practice by generating solutions for action that are based in localized systematic inquiry.

A final advantage of action research in comparison to other types of research is that it can be a gratifying professional experience. Empirical work on action research in schools has found that it is an effective approach to improving teachers' academic strategies and improving the work climate (Brown & Macatangay, 2002; Nir & Bogler, 2008). Action research may be enjoyable for professionals because of its direct relevance to local practice compared to other forms of research. Indeed, there are numerous occasions in which a school psychologist may decide to engage in action research. Practice problems that would be appropriate for action research could include questions related to whether Individualized Education Program (IEP) goals are enhanced by a certain written report format or whether the school psychologist leads the IEP meetings. Action research might focus on whether abbreviated functional behavior assessments lead to effective behavioral interventions (i.e., actually implemented by teachers). At a broader level, action research could focus on the practice of giving discipline referrals at recess and whether that affects student engagement during recess.

Due to its focus on improving local school practice, action research is a very important tool for school psychologists (Leff, 2007; Power, Eiraldi, Clarke, Mazzuca, & Krain, 2005). Action research can help school psychologists provide "culturally competent and effective practices in all areas of school psychology service delivery" (National Association of School Psychologists [NASP], 2010). For example, as evidence-based interventions are not equally applicable to all cultural groups and local school contexts, action research can be used to systematically modify and evaluate evidence-based interventions for a particular group and school context. Moreover, action research follows a systematic problem-solving procedure that promotes the type of professional reflection on a school psychologist's practice that is needed to enhance culturally competent practice (i.e., the domain of Data-Based Decision Making and Accountability in the NASP *Model for Comprehensive and Integrated School Psychological Services* [NASP, 2010, p. 8]). For example, action research findings can be used to identify cultural factors within the school that create barriers for certain diverse student groups (e.g., English language learners; gay, lesbian, bisexual, transgender, and questioning). Action research falls within a foundation area of service delivery, Research and Program Evaluation, according to the NASP Practice Model (NASP, 2010), and can be used across a multitiered approach. This chapter aims to explain action research, provide a protocol to conduct it, and provide resources

for school psychologists to further build their action research skills.

BASIC CONSIDERATIONS

The beginnings of action research in education can be traced back to Dewey's (1938) work on improving teaching practice through collaborative research relationships. However, the phrase *action research* was not coined until 1944 by Lewin, who emphasized the need to bring about social change and action from systematic inquiry (Lewin, 1946). In the decades since that time, various types of action research have been described in the literature that is reflective of different disciplines: participatory action research, collaborative inquiry, emancipatory research, action learning, and contextual action research. In contrast, community-based research models consist of two or more community partners such as a university and public school collaboratively researching the needs of the public school. This is not considered action research because the public school is not necessarily empowered to make practice changes based on the research, nor does the school own the entire research process, but rather the researcher is typically conducting much of the research for the school. While little peer-reviewed action research has been published in school psychology in comparison to, for example, teacher education, much of what has been published in school psychology appears to focus on participatory action research models or community-based research (Hughes, 2003; Nastasi et al., 2000).

Unfortunately, basic action research or school-based action research is not discussed as much in the school psychology literature. For this reason, this chapter seeks to fill this void in the school psychology literature by describing action research that is conducted by a school psychologist. Although these two characteristics that distinguish action research were mentioned above, further discussion of them is needed (Sagor, 2012; Stringer, 2007).

Action research is focused on the practitioner's professional action: Rather than esoteric theories or highly controlled intervention research, action research is primarily about studying a school psychologist's action at work. It may be a past action (e.g., evaluation study), present action (e.g., monitoring current intervention), or future action (e.g., appropriateness of a program for adoption), as detailed by Kemmis and McTaggart (1988).

Change in practice is possible based on the action research findings: Action research focuses on questions and problems that are realistic targets for change and improvement. School psychologists will want to ensure to the extent possible that they can help produce change in their practice (i.e., empowered) and that the setting is likely to support improvement (e.g., Is improvement possible in the area? Is the school psychologist able to promote change in this area? Are there sufficient resources available to produce change?). For example, although many local districts have guidelines and policies for school psychologists to follow in their work (e.g., assessments), school psychologists' use of professional judgment is often required to provide ethical and culturally competent services for all children, youth, and their families. School psychologists also have much decision-making autonomy in their choice of intervention strategies to recommend, how and when to consult with teachers, and who to include at meetings for students and school issues. If the school psychologist has serious doubts that change will occur after the action research project is completed, then it may be wise to determine a more realistic focus for action research. However, a more important option might be to advocate for change in the area of concern by using the findings from the action research, which is more consistent with a social justice vision of school psychology practice.

Action research is often collaborative. If it is not, then it should be collaborative. Often, the practical problem is shared among other school professionals. At a minimum, the problem is best addressed by including the opinions of other stakeholders during the action research process. To illustrate, a school psychologist could collaborate with other school-based mental health personnel (e.g., school counselor, social worker, nurse, behavioral specialist) to address a common problem of practice such as bullying. They might all complete the action research together by sharing tasks, making the work more manageable, and finally completing the tasks together. Another way of collaboration might be for each individual to examine the bullying problem from his or her own vantage point, share the findings, and integrate the findings to understand the problem more fully than he or she could have done alone. Still another way might be for the school psychologist to initially complete one cycle of action research primarily alone, and then based on the results, use the action research findings to inform a larger whole-school action research cycle that includes various other school personnel. This approach may be prudent to demonstrate to unwilling or busy stakeholders that positive change is possible in the school with a systematic process of inquiry.

As might be inferred from the above discussion, action research can have varying purposes. First, action research can be engaged in by an individual school psychologist to build skills in professional reflection and improve professional practice. Action research can also be accomplished by a collaborative group of colleagues (e.g., school psychologists, teachers) sharing a common concern to make progress on school-wide priorities such as bullying. Finally, an entire school can engage in action research to build a collaborative school culture and make school-wide changes (e.g., improving home–school partnerships and connectedness).

BEST PRACTICES IN CONDUCTING SCHOOL-BASED ACTION RESEARCH

Conducting action research is straightforward, but it requires some forethought and planning. While there is consensus on the general process involved in action research, the specific steps involved vary widely (Reason & Bradbury, 2008; Stringer, 2007). From examining the current literature, a general protocol has been developed that fits well with what school psychologists already know and their role in schools. It has seven steps and they are described below. The steps are generally written for individual action research with the school psychologist as the researcher because school psychologists are typically the only psychologists in a school; this type of action research and its benefits have been neglected in the literature (discussed above). Still, the seven steps would be the same for individual, small group, or school-wide action research. The only differences would be that for groups and school-level action research more time is needed to meet and gather relevant stakeholders' input into the process, and evaluation may need to be resourced out due to its complexity and time limitations of the school psychologist.

Step 1: Prioritize a Practice Problem and Outcome

A school psychologist's time is limited and a priority problem is needed to begin the action research. Taking time to reflect on one's school practice is essential. Often, the business of practice does not give school psychologists much time to reflect on what is really happening. It might be helpful for school psychologists to use a journal for observations and thoughts about their practice and/or have open discussions with other colleagues or relevant stakeholders. Often it is helpful to think about common problems in practice (real) compared to what it would be like if the problems were solved (ideal). For example, the reality may be that teachers are not implementing interventions with fidelity and that teachers need much more support in this area, while the ideal would be that teachers are implementing interventions with fidelity and supporting one another to do so. The end product of this thinking is a vision of school practice.

Once a general vision of school practice has been reflected upon and written down, a priority outcome for the action research may be identified. While this may seem premature for some, the reason is that thinking of outcomes now will help focus the rest of the process and make it more efficient. To help with this process, there are two different types of action research outcomes that should be decided upon as a focus (based on Sagor, 2012).

Performance outcomes: Change in student outcomes is a priority either at the individual or systems level. Other recipient outcomes, such as teacher or parent, may also be considered. For example, a school psychologist may want to focus on students' behavior at recess or teachers' use of consultation. Linking performance outcomes to the idealistic reflection activity above, school psychologists should reflect on what students, teachers, and parents would be doing if their problems in practice were solved.

Service delivery outcomes: Change in how the school psychologist delivers services may also be the focus of action research. One may want to improve certain professional skills in assessment, report writing, consultation, counseling, social justice, diversity, or systems interventions. Again, linking performance outcomes to the idealistic reflection activity above, school psychologists should reflect on what they would be doing if their problems in practice were solved.

Finally, after reflecting on the vision of practice and selecting outcomes, it would also be helpful to examine any existing data that are readily available to help prioritize the focus of the action research. For example, data on attendance, suspensions, curriculum-based measures, or mental health screeners would be helpful in determining priorities.

Step 2: Explore the Practice Problem

Having prioritized a practice problem, it is important for school psychologists to explore the area of focus until a rich picture emerges. A rich picture is one that is defined and described well with much complexity, or multiple ecological factors are considered that may influence the practice problem. This is accomplished by looking at data. One way to look at data is to examine the existing literature on the topic. While this can be done by searching journal databases, many school psychologists do not have free access to these resources. Still, school psychologists can examine reputable Internet resources. When consulting these resources, one would be looking at effective solutions to the practice problem, listing them, and making notes about any relevant information regarding why the solutions worked and what pitfalls to avoid.

In addition to the literature review, school psychologists can interview other professionals, colleagues, and stakeholders who have been effective at addressing the prioritized practice problem. The school psychologist would want to interview as many individuals as feasible and ask similar questions that were asked as part of the literature review: effective solutions to the practice problem, any relevant information regarding why the solutions worked, and pitfalls to avoid.

Interviewing experienced practitioners and conducting a literature review are critical for high quality action research. However, some suggest that it may sometimes be reasonable to skip the literature review due to resource and time limitations in practice, in which case only the interviews would occur (Sagor, 2012). While it is important to highlight the tension between best practice and real-world concerns, school psychologists should strive for best practice whenever possible.

Step 3: Define the Prioritized Practice Problem Outcome

At this point, the school psychologist has given much thoughtful and intelligent consideration to the focus of the action research and its outcomes. Defining the prioritized outcome of the action research will come naturally. This step is essentially a process of operationalizing the outcome, in which school psychologists are well trained. Nevertheless, the process of problem definition is somewhat unique in action research and is detailed here (Pine, 2009; Stringer, 2007).

Operationalize what the prioritized outcome looks like: Likely, the outcome will contain a variety of indicators for each outcome and they all should be listed. For example, a teacher outcome related to implementing interventions with fidelity might include teacher implementation checklists and observations of teacher implementation by the school psychologist.

Create a performance rating scale for each indicator: A rubric is developed to help assess progress. Sagor (2012) recommends using odd scaling anchors because the midpoint is considered to be "meeting expectations" or "good performance," which is useful to know in action research. Each indicator is operationalized on a scale, and descriptions are carefully constructed to answer the question "What does it look like?" for each anchor, beginning with the middle anchor. The middle anchor is considered typical performance for the indicator by asking what average looks like. Next, the lowest anchor is described by asking what the minimum performance would look like. Finally, the opposite extreme is created by considering what exceptional and outstanding performance would look like. For example, a performance rating scale could include these anchors: emerging (<50%), developing (50%), typical (60%), proficient (80%), and fluent (90%).

Step 4: Develop a Theory of Action

This step involves the school psychologist reflecting in a more creative yet systematic way on the work that has been done thus far. The primary result is developing a theory of action and research questions to guide the action in the next step. The understanding gained in the previous three steps is foundational for effective work at this step. For example, bullying may be occurring for numerous reasons that may include individual factors (social and emotional skills), environmental factors (disorganized recess time, hostile school climate), and an interaction between them. This step of reflection will help build a sophisticated understanding of why bullying occurs and, most important, a practical understanding.

The school psychologist will think creatively about how to change the prioritized problem outcome identified in the last step. A process of brainstorming occurs in which all relevant actions that should lead to change in the prioritized outcomes are listed (Sagor, 2012). Then, to prioritize the most important actions, it is helpful to think about how important each action is to achieving change in the problem outcome, given the limited time that one has in practice to implement them. Other considerations to help prioritize actions are to cross-reference each one with the data that have been accumulated in the first stage (i.e., successful experiences of colleagues, literature review). Finally, it is important to articulate the theory of action in writing and perhaps visually (see Sagor, 2012, for a detailed discussion of this process). At the minimum, it is important to develop action hypotheses that can be evaluated (Clauset et al., 2012). The task here is to write out if–then statements summarizing the work completed in this stage that

identifies what actions, if taken, will lead to the desired outcomes.

Research questions should be developed to guide implementation and evaluation in the final steps. The school psychologist action researcher may ask any research question that comes to mind. However, Sagor (2012) recommends these three: What actions were actually completed? What changes were observed in the prioritized outcomes? Were any relations observed between the actions taken and changes observed?

Step 5: Develop an Action Plan

This step represents the core of action research and asks what action will take place A plan is developed detailing all relevant actions to be implemented, by whom, and by what dates. Time for training and resources should also be included, as well as any communication to students, teachers, staff, and parents (e.g., securing parental consent and child assent, if applicable).

Step 6: Implement and Evaluate the Action Plan

In this step, the school psychologist implements and evaluates the action plan. Before implementing the action plan, it is important to collect pre-action plan data to help evaluate whether change occurred from implementing the actions. Measurement and evaluation involves data collection and analysis from any relevant research tradition (e.g., quantitative and qualitative approaches). Fortunately, school psychologists have a well-developed skill set regarding evaluation procedures. Still it is important to note that multiple informants should be considered, such as the school psychologist, teachers, students, and parents. Multiple methods of data collection should also be considered, including observational techniques, goal attainment scoring scales, permanent products (attendance, office discipline referrals), curriculum-based measures, and norm-referenced scales and instruments. The action plan will help guide decisions about which informants and methods make most sense. Feasibility of data collection in practice should also be considered when choosing a method.

Data analysis and evaluation of the action research most commonly takes a qualitative case study approach to data analysis related to the three research questions listed previously. Because of the focus on changing professional practice, often rigorous experimental research is not feasible for school psychologists. School psychologists have pressing needs to know sooner rather than later whether practice should be changed or action research is efficient for this practical need in the schools. One recommended strategy is to develop a chart that lists three independent data sources for each research question, or a multimethod approach (Sagor, 2012). Doing so would result in a rigorous triangulation of data from which to evaluate the research questions and preliminary evidence in support of the action plan that is still very useful. Eventually, the school psychologist can work with a larger team to do more rigorous evaluation of an action plan. Additionally, action research evaluation should follow best practice guidelines for research and evaluation more generally.

Step 7: Refine the Theory of Action and Plan

In this step, the school psychologist reflects on the evaluation and refines the action plan by cycling through the process again. Once evaluation has occurred, the school psychologist should go back to the fourth step where the theory of action was developed. Then, the theory of action should be revised in light of the action research findings. A process of critically evaluating the theory in light of the findings should take place. With a revised theory of action, a new action plan can be developed and evaluated. Finally, instead of returning to the fourth step, the school psychologist may also return to the first step to prioritize another related, or new, practice problem to act upon.

Case Example

A school psychologist is assigned to an elementary school in an urban and diverse neighborhood. A fifth-grade teacher tells the school psychologist that there are bullying concerns again in her classroom (e.g., teasing). Because this is a repeated concern and because of the principal's recent school-wide efforts to reduce bullying, the school psychologist decides that action research seems appropriate because a serious look into this practice problem is needed.

The first step is to prioritize a practice problem. The school psychologist begins to reflect on his school practice related to bullying. His vision of school practice is that students will get along better, not bully one another, and that teachers will implement the school bullying curriculum. A priority outcome is that students in the fifth grade will get along better and that bullying will decrease.

The second step consists of exploring the practice problem to develop a rich picture. From conducting a

literature review and interviewing a school social worker with much experience with bullying, the school psychologist discovered the many factors influencing this practice problem. For example, the most relevant facts were that, developmentally, bullying in elementary school is more common in the upper grades; a focus on building strengths and resilience in peer relationships is critical (e.g., getting along and friendships); recess interventions have been successfully used because bullying often begins there and comes into the classroom; and the teacher reported that students rush out to recess before they have been dismissed to get the ball first, which creates recess conflicts from the beginning.

In the third step the school psychologist defined the prioritized practice problem outcome: Students in the fifth grade will get along better, and bullying will decrease. First, the school psychologist operationalized what the prioritized outcomes look like. Student outcomes related to bullying might include these indicators: there are fewer student reports of bullying, more students go out to recess when dismissed by the teacher, students have someone to play with at recess, and students report that recess was fun. Next, a performance rating scale was created for each indicator: "Students go out to recess when dismissed by teacher" was rated on a scale from emerging (<50%), developing (50%), typical (60%), proficient (80%), and fluent (90%). "Students have someone to play with at recess" and "Students report that recess was fun" were also rated similarly.

The fourth step consists of developing a theory of action. The school psychologist reflected more deeply on the work accomplished so far in the previous steps. While school bullying is multifaceted and ecological, the school psychologist believed that focusing on the recess setting was critical for this particular grade and teacher, which was also supported theoretically from the research literature and consistent with what the school psychologist had time to do given competing responsibilities. Next, the school psychologist reflected specifically on how to change the prioritized outcome and developed these if–then statements: (a) If recess monitors are motivated and trained better, then students will report that recess was fun and bullying will decrease. (b) If students go out to recess when dismissed, then students will report that recess was fun and bullying will decrease. (c) If organized games are introduced at recess, then students will have someone to play with at recess, students will report that recess was fun, and bullying will decrease. The school psychologist also decided to use these research questions to help guide the implementation and evaluation process: What actions were actually completed? What changes were observed in the prioritized outcomes? Were any relations observed between the actions taken and changes observed?

In the fifth step the school psychologist developed the action plan based on all of the previous steps' findings. See the Appendix for an example.

For the sixth step, the school psychologist implemented the action plan. Next, the evaluation process began as well. For evaluation, the school psychologist used the multimethod triangulation method for data analysis (see the Appendix for an example). To measure decreases in bullying, the school psychologist trained recess monitors in data observation techniques and collected those summaries daily. In addition, the school psychologist collected student reports of bullying using a standardized rating scale and analyzed office referrals related to recess both before and after the plan. To measure enjoyment of recess, the school psychologist used a class survey designed to assess this variable along with teacher reports of how students behaved and what they reported in this regard after returning from recess. Examining the findings as a whole on a line graph, the school psychologist was able to support the conclusions that implementing the action plan seemed to be related to decreases in bullying and enjoyment of recess. The teacher, recess monitors, and students all expressed that they saw improvements at recess and generally had positive feelings about the action plan.

For the seventh step the school psychologist reflected on the evaluation findings and the action plan. Because of the positive conclusions that were made during the evaluation, the school psychologist decided to implement this action plan across the whole school with the principal's support. However, because of the limitations on the school psychologist's time and competency for such a large-scale project, the principal agreed to support the school psychologist by assembling an action research team at school and securing the district evaluation expert to help support the complex evaluation needs of this project. The school psychologist was appointed to be the leader of this school action research team and began the first meeting by asking how to broaden the fifth-grade action plan after examining the data together, which meets the criterion that successful action research practice involves continued change and actions.

Concluding Thoughts

While the benefits of action research have been discussed previously, there are some challenges of which

to be aware. As in any type of research, ethical issues around confidentiality of data and ownership of data arise. Moreover, conducting research on one's own practice has been critiqued based on objectivity. In response to these concerns, school psychologists should consult colleagues and ethical guidelines before conducting action research. For example, as discussed previously, parent consent and child assent will likely be necessary, especially when evaluation becomes more rigorous, although the action research is part of a school psychologist's regular professional practice in schools. Conducting action research collaboratively with others rather than in isolation is also highly recommended. Collaborative projects address time and resource limitations in practice, especially if partnering with an outside member such as a community agency or research consultant.

SUMMARY

Action research is a form of systematic inquiry that is conducted, by practitioners, to solve a practice problem that leads to change in their practice with the goal of improving it and their clients. The ultimate goal of action research is to improve practice by generating solutions that are based in localized systematic inquiry. Therefore, action research will serve school psychologists well in critically reflecting on their own practice to enhance it for the benefit of children, youth, and families, which is a hallmark of ethical and culturally competent professional practice.

REFERENCES

Brown, M., & Macatangay, A. (2002). The impact of action research for professional development: Case studies in two Manchester schools. *Westminster Studies in Education, 25*, 35–45.

Clauset, K., Lick, D., & Murphy, C. (2008). *School-wide action research for professional learning communities.* Thousand Oaks, CA: Corwin Press.

Dewey, J. (1938). *Experience and education.* New York, NY: Macmillan.

Hughes, J. N. (2003). Commentary: Participatory action research leads to sustainable school and community improvement. *School Psychology Review, 32*, 38–43.

Kemmis, S., & McTaggart, R. (1988). *The action research planner.* Victoria, BC, Canada: Deakin University Press.

Leff, S. S. (2007). Bullying and peer victimization at school: Considerations and future directions. *School Psychology Review, 36*, 406–412.

Lewin, K. (1946). Action research and minority problems. *Journal of Social Issues, 2*, 34–46.

Nastasi, B. K., Varjas, K., Schensul, S. L., Silva, K. T., Schensul, J. J., & Ratnayake, P. (2000). The participatory intervention model: A framework for conceptualizing and promoting intervention acceptability. *School Psychology Quarterly, 15*, 207–232.

National Association of School Psychologists. (2010). *Model for comprehensive and integrated school psychological services.* Bethesda, MD: Author. Retrieved from http://www.nasponline.org/standards/2010standards/2_PracticeModel.pdf

Nir, A. E., & Bogler, R. (2008). The antecedents of teacher satisfaction with professional development programs. *Teaching and Teacher Education: An International Journal of Research and Studies, 24,* 377–386.

Pine, G. (2009). *Teacher action research: Building knowledge democracies.* Thousand Oaks, CA: Corwin Press.

Power, T. J., Eiraldi, R. B., Clarke, A. T., Mazzuca, L. B., & Krain, A. L. (2005). Improving mental health service utilization for children and adolescents. *School Psychology Quarterly, 20,* 187–205.

Reason, P., & Bradbury, H. (2008). *The SAGE handbook of action research: Participative inquiry and practice.* Thousand Oaks, CA: SAGE.

Sagor, R. (2012). *The action research guidebook: A four-stage process for educators and school teams.* Thousand Oaks, CA: Corwin Press.

Stringer, E. (2007). *Action research* (3rd ed.). Thousand Oaks, CA: Corwin Press.

APPENDIX. EXAMPLE ACTION PLANNING SHEET FOR BULLYING

Action Step	Who?	Start Date	End Date	Training and Materials
Recess monitors are motivated and trained better.	School psychologist	Jan 7	Jan 30	Create training materials; provide a room and computer screen.
Organized games are introduced at recess.	Recess teacher	Feb 10	March 10	PE teacher will teach games in PE class, communicate with the playground teacher, and provide required equipment.
Individual activities (e.g., jump ropes) are introduced at recess.	Recess teacher	Feb 10	March 10	Principal will purchase the equipment.

Example of a Multimethod Evaluation Chart for Research Questions (partially filled out)			
Research Question	Data 1	Data 2	Data 3
What actions were actually completed?	School psychologist action checklist	Teacher action checklist	Notes from implementation meetings.
What changes were observed in the prioritized outcomes?			
Were any relations observed between the actions taken and changes observed?			

21

Best Practices in Identifying, Evaluating, and Communicating Research Evidence

Randy G. Floyd
Philip A. Norfolk
The University of Memphis (TN)

OVERVIEW

School psychologists are often called on to be the research experts in school settings, and their doing so makes sense because they serve at the interface of psychological science and education science. Based on school psychologists' expertise in these areas of science and as articulated in the domain of Research and Program Evaluation of the National Association of School Psychologists (NASP) *Model for Comprehensive and Integrated School Psychological Services* (NASP, 2010), school psychologists should "evaluate and synthesize a cumulative body of research findings as a foundation for effective service delivery" (p. 9) and, in particular, "apply knowledge of evidence-based interventions and programs in designing, implementing, and evaluating the fidelity and effectiveness of school-based intervention plans" (p. 9). As part of school psychologists' provision of comprehensive and integrated services, they may be asked to review the research literature and interpret research findings to aid in decision making at multiple levels. They may be asked to advise other professionals in making policy decisions at the state, district, and school levels and evaluate how research supports existing policies. They may be asked to provide evidence-based recommendations at the level of the individual child, adolescent, or teacher in their roles as consultants and collaborators. Furthermore, they themselves may be asked to develop empirically supported interventions and supports to enhance academic skills and promote healthy lifestyles.

To actualize their role as research experts in school settings, school psychologists must be able to identify and evaluate research evidence and communicate this evidence in a meaningful way to school audiences. Although positive outcomes for students are not guaranteed through school psychologists' identifying, evaluating, and communicating research evidence, the probability of achieving these positive outcomes is greatly increased if practices are based on the best available research.

The purpose of this chapter is to provide support to school psychologists as the research experts in school settings. First, the chapter reviews the key features of evidence-based practice. Second, the chapter presents best practices in (a) finding and evaluating high-quality research-based information, (b) communicating research-based findings to school audiences, and (c) responding to misunderstandings about or resistance to the conclusions drawn from these findings. It concludes with a case study in which best practices in identifying, evaluating, and communicating research evidence to school audiences is modeled.

BASIC CONSIDERATIONS

The movement to promote the application of a science-based approach to psychology and education is best described by the term *evidence-based practice*. The American Psychological Association (APA) Presidential Task Force on Evidence-Based Practice (2006) has defined evidence-based practice as "the integration of the best available research with clinical expertise in the context of patient characteristics, culture, and preferences" (p. 273). Although the scientific research base assumes priority in this definition (Norcross, Hogan, & Koocher, 2008), it is not solely considered. The training, knowledge, and experience of the clinicians charged with implementing evidence-base practices must be taken into consideration. Furthermore, the age, gender, race/ethnicity, and background of those targeted by the interventions, the larger context of the interventions (e.g., resources available in the school or community), and the preferences and commitment of major stakeholders must also be considered. It is important to note that this chapter focuses primarily on the research-based component of evidence-based practices. Other resources are available that present integrative decision-making frameworks underlying evidence-based practice (see Spencer, Detrich, & Slocum, 2012).

Reference to evidence-based practice is now prominent in the school psychology literature. For example, the NASP Practice Model (NASP, 2010) refers to evidence-based curricula, services, and strategies 13 times across the 12 pages of this document. Due to their comprehensive graduate preparation, school psychologists are poised to actualize evidence-based practices in schools.

School psychologists must confront at least three types of challenges in order to best promote evidence-based practice: (a) training and access to information, (b) decision making, and (c) communication. First, school psychologists must face their own limitations in training and knowledge. Even with the field of school psychology as a whole and graduate programs in particular increasingly focusing on the standards of science and evidence-based practices, some studies have suggested that school psychologists are not being offered sufficient training in identifying and applying evidence-based practices (e.g., Shernoff, Kratochwill, & Stoiber, 2003). Even if training includes instruction that emphasizes evidence-based practices, school psychologists may struggle to keep up with the newest research findings that could inform practice. Furthermore, even if they realize that they do not have knowledge of evidence-based practices in a particular area (see Nelson & Machek, 2007), they may be unable to locate appropriate resources to overcome their knowledge deficits.

Second, when school psychologists have been trained to seek out evidence-based practices and critically evaluate the claims of researchers, prominent leaders in the field, other educators, and parents, they may still struggle to evaluate competing claims regarding what is best practice.

Third, even when school psychologists have identified the best evidence to inform practice and have committed to a course of action, they may be unable to effectively promote evidence-based change. This difficult position may be due, in part, to struggles with appropriately communicating their knowledge to their audiences. Subtle skill deficits may leave them unable to clearly explain the complexities of the research in a manner that engages audiences, or they may face outright resistance to evidence-based practices and be unable to directly counter false and pseudoscientific claims made by others.

BEST PRACTICES IN IDENTIFYING, EVALUATING, AND COMMUNICATING RESEARCH EVIDENCE

The following sections address specific practices in identifying, evaluating, and communicating research evidence that could be employed by school psychologists.

Finding the Best Information and Evaluating It

Because of both the breadth of school psychologists' skills and their expanded roles in school settings, they are no longer able to turn to a few seminal texts to guide the vast majority of their practices. Fortunately, school psychologists no longer need to rely primarily on memories from their graduate preparation and their personal library for professional guidance regarding evidence-based practices. They now have the equivalent of national libraries full of information at their fingertips via the Internet; hundreds of books that can be purchased; numerous peer-reviewed journals in school psychology, special education, and clinical psychology to consult; and two prominent school psychology newsletters to reference.

In this section, sources of information that are most likely to inform evidence-based practice are reviewed. Most of these information sources are available free of charge on the Internet so that school psychologists without full library access in a university setting (e.g., access to PsycInfo, ERIC, and MEDLINE) will be able to retain ties to the empirical literature. In addition, this section addresses sources providing background information, filtered information, and unfiltered information (based on Norcross et al., 2008) and follows with an overview of information sources targeting psychological tests. This section will end with a description of methods for evaluating the research information located during literature searches.

Background Information

School psychologists often need background information—an overview of the literature in a specific area—and need to locate this information rapidly. For example, they may need information about a psychological intervention provided by a therapist outside the school setting (e.g., equine therapy and visual perceptual therapy), a prescription medication (Abilify or aripiprazole), or a medical condition (Kawasaki disease or Hashimoto's disease). As evident in Table 21.1, numerous websites are available to provide such information.

Although some commercial websites barrage their visitors with ads, and the influences of website sponsors on website content cannot easily be evaluated, such commercial websites can provide useful background information to school psychologists (see Table 21.1). For example, a school psychologist can visit WebMD for background information about medical conditions and pharmacological interventions. In the same vein, Drugs.com provides not only information about pharmacological interventions but links to audio files, including the pronunciation of trade names and generic names of the medications. Access to full content from other commercial websites targeting physicians and other medical professionals is restricted to members or subscribers only. Three examples described in Table 21.1 include the Micromedex 2.0 (offered by Truven Health Analytics), the Physician's Information and Education Resource (offered by the American College of Physicians), and UpToDate. School psychologists employed by universities or medical facilities may have access to these information sources.

Other sources of background information include the American Psychological Association's Division 53 (Society of Clinical Child and Adolescent Psychology) Effective Child Therapy website, which provides information about evidence-based interventions for a variety of childhood disorders and problems. Some content is devoted to parents and the public in general, but other content is devoted to professionals and educators. For school psychologists, the brief lists of evidence-based interventions for specific disorders and related problems (based on summaries of review articles) and the free videos of presentations by experts addressing interventions for aggression, anxiety,

attention deficit hyperactivity disorder (ADHD), depression, learning problems, autism spectrum disorders, tic disorders, and substance abuse should be welcomed.

School psychologists may also benefit from accessing federally sponsored websites that provide overviews and evaluations of interventions. For example, the National Registry of Evidence-Based Programs and Practices (offered by the Substance Abuse and Mental Health Services) offers a searchable database of summaries of more than 300 interventions targeting mental health and substance abuse problems. About one half of these interventions are appropriate for implementation in schools. All interventions were nominated by their developers, and these interventions and the research evaluating their effects have been independently reviewed and rated by the National Registry of Evidence-Based Programs and Practices reviewers. The database can be searched by keyword and selection of optional search categories including age, gender, and race/ethnicity of the client; the area of interest for intervention; and the intervention setting. Each summary includes extensive citations of research examining the interventions; costs of the intervention and materials; ratings of the quality of research supporting it, its replications, and its readiness for dissemination; and contact information of the developer who posted the intervention. In much the same way, the Intervention Central website provides resources to support academic and behavioral interventions, and interventions are supported by a summary of their key components and at least one reference.

Filtered Information

Filtered information refers to "sources . . . designed to save busy practitioners time and effort by providing expert analysis, removing the burden of reading and synthesizing dozens, if not hundreds, of individual studies" (Norcross et al., 2008, p. 31). This filtered information typically appears in two forms: narrative reviews and meta-analysis. In addition, practice guidelines fall into this class of information.

Narrative reviews. Narrative reviews are scholarly summaries of research findings integrated with the logic and clinical insights of their authors. In them, the authors strive to identify common themes across findings from disparate studies and frequently offer recommendations for practice and future research. Many books and book chapters are composed of narrative reviews of the literature. For example, Shinn and Walker (2010) and Steele, Elkin, and Roberts (2008) include numerous

Table 21.1. Websites Informing Evidence-Based Practice for School Psychologists

Source and Website Link	Free or Cost for Full Access	Key Features
WebMD: http://www.webmd.com/	Free	Offers information about an array of health problems: symptoms, diagnosis, intervention, medications, side effects, developmental information, parenting information, updated news or research, and other related issues and problems. Provides information about pharmacological interventions: warnings, uses, side effects, interactions, overdose potential, and conditions and interventions related to medications.
Drugs.com: http://www.drugs.com/	Free	Provides easy access to information about pharmacological interventions. Includes audio files for pronunciation of drug names.
Truven Health Analytics Micromedex 2.0: http://www.micromedex.com/index.html	Cost	Requires registration and membership for full access. Provides searchable database. Devoted to evidence-based pharmacological interventions, drug interactions, toxins, and medical interventions. Available on smartphone and tablets for mobile viewing.
American College of Physicians: Physician's Information and Education Resource: http://pier.acponline.org/index.html or http://www.acponline.org/clinical_information/pier/	Cost	Requires membership for access. Provides educational modules targeting medical problems. Addresses screening and diagnosis, interventions, drug prescription, and patient education. Extensive links to research literature.
UpToDate: http://www.uptodate.com/home	Free, Cost	Requires subscription for full access. Provides practice guideline updates, one-paragraph reviews of recent publications, information for patients written in plain language, and drug information distilled through peer review. Available on smartphone and tablets for mobile viewing.
American Psychological Association's Division 53 Effective Child Therapy: http://www.effectivechildtherapy.com/	Free	Offers evidence-based mental health intervention for children and adolescents. Search unavailable, but has easy-to-access interventions. Parent resources available.
Substance Abuse and Mental Health Services Administration National Registry of Evidence-Based Programs and Practices: http://www.nrepp.samhsa.gov/	Free	Identifies interventions to fit presenting problems in school, community, and other settings. Provides search options by keyword and categories like age, race/ethnicity, and gender of client; area of interest for intervention; and intervention setting. Provides intervention costs; ratings of the quality of research, replications, and readiness for dissemination; and developer contact information. Includes summaries and links to systematic reviews of interventions.
Intervention Central: http://www.Interventioncentral.org/	Free	Provides information regarding how to develop and implement academic and behavior interventions. All interventions are supported by at least one research article. Offers downloadables and distributable resources.
NASP Research Center: http://www.nasponline.org/advocacy/researchmain.aspx	Free	Provides narrative research summaries, reports, and fact sheets.
National Guideline Clearinghouse: http://guideline.gov/	Free	Provides guidelines and recommendations for assessment and intervention practices focused primarily on medical conditions. Includes searchable database. Offers rich summary of sources of evidence supporting guidelines.
American Academy of Pediatrics: http://pediatrics.aappublications.org/search?flag=practice_guidelines&submit=yes&x=18&y=8&format=standard&hits=30&sortspec=date&submit=Go		Provides full-text clinical practice guidelines for several developmental and school-related disorders and medical conditions. Finding practice guidelines requires electronic search.

Continued

Table 21.1. Continued

Source and Website Link	Free or Cost for Full Access	Key Features
Medscape Reference: http://emedicine.medscape.com/	Free, Cost	Some information modules freely accessible. Can browse by specialty. Modules address developmental and behavioral issues, genetic and metabolic diseases, and general medicine. Each module supported by references. Updated frequently.
Cochrane Database of Systematic Reviews: http://www.cochrane.org/cochrane-reviews	Free, Cost	Provides systematic reviews of evidence-based healthcare. Includes searchable database. Updated regularly. Free access to abstracts. Fee for full review (e.g., through Wiley Online Library).
Campbell Collaboration Library of Systematic Reviews http://www.campbellcollaboration.org/lib/?go=monograph	Free	Offers systematic reviews of interventions in education, crime and justice, social welfare, and international development. Provides searchable database.
What Works Clearinghouse: http://ies.ed.gov/ncee/wwc/	Free	Provides systematic reviews of educational interventions. Includes searchable database. Updated regularly.
National Center on Response to Intervention: http://www.rti4success.org/instructionTools	Free	Reports evaluation of study quality and effect size estimates for about 65 individual studies examining the effects of instructional interventions targeting reading, math, spelling, and written expression. Summarizes descriptive information, usage, acquisition and cost information, and training requirements for targeted instructional interventions. Updated regularly.
National Center on Intensive Interventions: http://www.intensiveintervention.org/chart/instructional-intervention-tools	Free	Reports evaluation of study quality and effect size estimates for more than 50 individual studies examining the effects of academic interventions targeting reading, math, spelling, and written expression. Evaluation also includes consideration of intervention group size, duration, and interventionist requirements. Provides links across studies examining the same academic intervention and links to reviews by What Works Clearinghouse. Summarizes descriptive information, usage, acquisition and cost information, and training requirements for targeted instructional interventions.
Best Evidence Encyclopedia: http://www.bestevidence.org/	Free	Provides about 10 full-text, systematic reviews regarding the strength of evidence for a variety of instructional programs targeting mathematics, reading, and science education for use with students in Grades K–12. Offers about five reviews of programs addressing school reform and early childhood education. Applies quantitative evaluation methods to effect sizes that are unique among systematic review clearinghouses. Some reviews are somewhat dated (from 2008 and 2009).
Evidence-Based Intervention Network: http://ebi.missouri.edu/	Free	Provides guidance for selecting and implementing evidence-based interventions. Offers a how-to guide for selecting an evidence-based intervention. Links to resources to develop problem-solving teams and track effectiveness using a response-to-intervention model. Shares resources for use with English language learners.

chapters that provide narrative reviews of interventions as well as evaluative commentary from the chapter authors. Furthermore, the NASP Research Committee periodically prepares research summaries for the NASP newsletter, *Communiqué*, and many of these research summaries are posted online at the NASP Research Center (see Table 21.1). One limitation of books, book chapters, and these other sources of information is that they are not updated frequently (e.g., in comparison to websites), and thus they may not reflect the latest, state-of-the-art evidence-based practice.

Meta-analysis. Like narrative reviews, a meta-analysis produces a summary of the research, but the summary is, at its heart, quantitative in nature. Thus, a meta-analysis is a quantitative summary of the many studies targeted in the analysis. Its two key features are (a) that it stems from a systematic search and review of the research articles and (b) that it employs statistics (usually in the form of effect size estimates) to produce the quantitative summary and to control for the most prominent confounds in the research. Whereas narrative reviews are likely to omit key studies due to the somewhat unsystematic manner in which many are conducted and to be highly influenced by the experiences and perspective of their authors, meta-analyses tend to be much more comprehensive and objective. For this reason, meta-analyses have become the benchmark for filtered information reviews (Norcross et al., 2008).

Practice guidelines. Practice guidelines are typically extensions of narrative reviews of the literature. These guidelines offer evidence-based recommendations for addressing common academic, behavioral, and medical conditions (Norcross et al., 2008). One example of a website devoted to practice guidelines is the U.S. Department of Health and Human Services National Guideline Clearinghouse (see Table 21.1). Although the National Guideline Clearinghouse targets physicians and others in the healthcare field, its searchable database of guidelines is relevant to school psychologists. In particular, guidelines targeting children and adolescents with psychiatric disorders, such as ADHD, obsessive compulsive disorder, schizophrenia, and autism spectrum disorders, as well as medical conditions, such as febrile seizures and diabetes, seem relevant. Other relevant guidelines address sexual orientation as well as gender nonconformity and discordance, psychodynamic psychotherapy, child safety issues, and communicating of stressful information to children. All guidelines include a thorough review of the research

evidence supporting them and culminate in "Major Recommendations." For example, the practice guidelines for addressing schizophrenia include information about performing assessments: delivering, monitoring, and reviewing psychological interventions; and using medication (among other recommendations).

In addition to the National Guideline Clearinghouse, several other groups and websites provide practice guidelines. For example, NASP publishes position statements and white papers that include recommendations for practice supported by research citations. The American Academy of Pediatrics (see Table 21.1) offers several clinical practice guidelines, made available in full text online, that may be of use to school psychologists. Medscape Reference (see Table 21.1) provides modules that include recommendations for diagnosis, laboratory workup, treatment, medication, and follow-up.

Accessing the best filtered information. A variety of information clearinghouses are available to school psychologists who are seeking filtered information generated by experts in the field. Four are highlighted here (and in Table 21.1), but other organizations, such as the National Center on Response to Intervention and National Center on Intensive Interventions, and other resources, such as the Best Evidence Encyclopedia, also provide recent filtered information (see Table 21.1).

The Cochrane Database of Systematic Reviews provides systematic reviews of evidence-based healthcare that are updated regularly. Its site includes a searchable database of reviews, a "Top 50" list of most-accessed reviews, and free access to study abstracts. Full-text reviews must be accessed through another service (e.g., Wiley Online Library) for a fee. For school psychologists, Cochrane reviews focusing on child health and developmental, psychosocial, and learning problems are the most relevant. For example, entering *ADHD* as a keyword into the search bar yielded 55 reviews, *autism* yielded 36 reviews, and both *learning disability* and *intellectual disability* yielded 10 reviews apiece. Most reviews returned from these search terms focused on medications or psychological interventions.

Campbell Collaboration Library of Systematic Reviews also provides systematic reviews, and the reviews focus on interventions in education, crime and justice, social welfare, and international development. There are far fewer reviews available for the Campbell Collaboration than the Cochrane Database, and the Campbell Collaboration reviews are not updated like those in the Cochrane Database. Campbell Collaboration reviews, however, seem to be much more applicable to interventions addressing school-related problems. For example, of the 10 most frequently downloaded Campbell Collaboration reviews, 7 focus on children and adolescents and seem highly relevant to school-based practitioners. Examples include *School-Based Programs to Reduce Bullying and Victimization* and *Approaches to Parent Involvement for Improving the Academic Performance of Elementary School Age Children: A Systematic Review*. School psychologists should definitely be aware of these comprehensive reviews.

The What Works Clearinghouse was established by the U.S. Department of Education's Institute of Education Sciences to provide educators, policy makers, and the public with a central, independent, and trusted source of scientific evidence regarding what works in education. The website includes links to a variety of "Topics in Education" (including early childhood education, English language learners, school choice, and teacher and leader effectiveness) and a keyword search to access intervention reports, practice guides, single-study reviews, and quick reviews. According to its website, its intervention reports summarize the results of the "highest-quality research on a given program, practice, or policy in education." Intervention reports target many commercial curricula (e.g., Scott Foresman-Addison Wesley Elementary Mathematics) and intervention programs (e.g., Fast ForWord) and provide systematic reviews and effectiveness ratings, percentile gains for the average student, and categories representing the extent of evidence (e.g., small, medium, and large). These interventions can be filtered by topic/outcome domains (e.g., early reading/writing, oral language, and print knowledge), grade, effectiveness rating, extent of evidence, and delivery method (individual, small group, whole class, and whole school) and then compared using the "Find What Works" option. Its practice guides offer "recommendations for educators to address challenges in their classrooms and schools." Its single-study reviews evaluate the results of a study using rigorous standards, whereas quick reviews evaluate a recently published study that may have immediate relevance. Top downloads include the practice guides *Assisting Students Struggling With Mathematics: Response to Intervention for Elementary and Middle Schools* and *Improving Reading Comprehension in Kindergarten Through 3rd Grade*.

Finally, the National Registry of Evidence-Based Programs and Practices website, described previously, also includes a summary of systematic reviews for eight topic areas, including early childhood programs, parenting programs, and school-based violence prevention programs. These summaries include links to the National Library of Medicine's PubMed website, to provide free access to abstracts and articles.

Unfiltered Information

Most school psychologists frequently use Web-based search engines and are familiar with bibliographic databases, such as PsycInfo, ERIC, and MEDLINE, that catalog journal articles, books, and book chapters associated with specific disciplines. These sources provide unfiltered information because this information likely needs to be evaluated and integrated in order to draw firm conclusions about the evidence base (Norcross et al., 2008). It is important that school psychologists are able to access and understand the original research studies as published in major research journals. Such studies are the foundations of both the background information and the filtered information described in this section of the chapter. There is the potential, however, to place too much weight on the results of a single study or a few studies when forming conclusions, rather than relying on the body of evidence (across researchers, research sites, and years of study) to guide evidence-based practices.

This chapter highlights two Web-based search engines that are freely accessible and may provide full-text access to some journal articles. Google Scholar (http://scholar.google.com) performs many of the same functions as the traditional bibliographic databases along with other functions. It identifies "articles, theses, books, abstracts and court opinions, from academic publishers, professional societies, online repositories, universities and other websites" across all disciplines. Users can sort results by year or select the most recent references, select other references that have cited the references identified in the search, find related references, sign up for updates and alerts when new references are published or cited, and locate full-text copies of select articles (see Google Scholar Search Tips: http://www.google.com/intl/en/scholar/help.html).

PubMed (http://www.ncbi.nlm.nih.gov/pubmed) is maintained by the U.S. National Library of Medicine at the National Institutes of Health. PubMed provides access to biomedical journal articles through the bibliographic database MEDLINE (http://www.nlm.nih.gov/bsd/pmresources.html). Abstracts are available for all articles included in PubMed, and PubMed Central (http://www.ncbi.nlm.nih.gov/pmc/) provides access to full-text documents for select articles. Both

PubMed and PubMed Central allow users to select article filters based on type (e.g., clinical trial), publication date, and age (including birth to 18 years). Google Scholar and PubMed can enhance school psychologists' knowledge of evidence-based practices.

Test Reviews

School psychologists should seek out published reviews of the assessment instruments and tests they use to ensure that they are engaging in evidence-based assessment practices (Hunsley & Mash, 2007). These instruments include not only standardized norm-referenced intelligence and achievement tests but also self-report rating scales, caregiver rating scales, structured observation systems, and academic screening and progress monitoring tools. There are numerous texts that provide descriptions of the development and norming of tests as well as the reliability and validity evidence supporting interpretation of the scores from such instruments. Some peer-reviewed journals publish test reviews: *Assessment for Effective Intervention, Canadian Journal of School Psychology,* and *Journal of Psychoeducational Assessment.*

One long-standing source for test reviews is the Buros Institute for Mental Measurements (http://buros.org) and its *Mental Measurement Yearbooks.* The *Mental Measurement Yearbooks* include independently completed pairs of reviews for every assessment instrument targeted, and they are published about every other year in hardcopy form. These reviews are regularly updated on the institute's website and can be downloaded for a fee.

There are some limitations associated with test reviews published in journals and in the *Mental Measurement Yearbooks.* First, they are not always subjected to rigorous peer review and cross-checking. Second, they typically summarize and evaluate information included in the test manuals and do not incorporate research articles and other sources of information published since release of the tests. As a result of these limitations, school psychologists should steadfastly evaluate the evidence supporting the use and interpretation of the instruments they employ based on their own reviews and consideration of student characteristics (e.g., age, gender, and race/ethnicity) as well as the intended uses of the instrument.

In addition to these more traditional sources for test reviews, there are two external review organizations employing committees of national experts using standard review protocols to evaluate the technical adequacy of commercially available screening and progress monitoring tools. They include the National Center on Response to Intervention (http://www.rti4success.org) and the National Center on Intensive Intervention (http://www.intensiveintervention.org), which are both under the aegis of the American Institutes for Research. The National Center on Response to Intervention provides reviews of approximately 50 group-administered and individually administered screening tools targeting early literacy, early numeracy, oral reading, reading comprehension, vocabulary and English language arts, and mathematics. Technical adequacy reviews focus on data supporting classification accuracy, generalizability, reliability, validity, and efficiency. In the same vein, the National Center on Response to Intervention provides reviews of more than 50 progress-monitoring general outcome measures and 5 mastery measures targeting most of the same academic areas covered in the screening measures. For general outcome measures, technical adequacy reviews focus on data supporting reliability and validity of performance level and slope values, alternate form reliability, sensitivity to and rates of student improvement, and end-of-year benchmarks. For mastery measures, reviews focus on skill sequences, sensitivity to student improvement, and reliability and validity evidence. Tool charts summarize the cost, required training and resources, support services, implementation information, and reporting information associated with each screening or progress monitoring tool. Systematic reviews supporting these tool charts are conducted periodically (approximately every year), so it is likely that they remain reasonably up to date.

The National Center on Intensive Interventions also offers tool charts focusing on academic progress monitoring across the same academic domains as the National Center on Response to Intervention, and their technical review criteria are also similar. Only a set of data-based individualization standards appears to have been added to these criteria. In addition, the National Center on Intensive Interventions offers technical reviews of seven behavioral progress-monitoring tools targeting constructs such as attention, negative affect, social skills, engagement, and disruptiveness. Technical reviews of the behavior progress monitoring tools generally match those of the academic progress monitoring tools, but usability is also explicitly addressed. It is not clear how often these technical reviews are conducted, but they likely are approximately as frequent as those from the National Center on Response to Intervention.

Evaluating the Best Available Research Evidence

School psychologists must equip themselves with the skills that enable them to distinguish evidence-based from non-evidence-based practices. First, they should ground themselves in the central tenets of evidence-based practice by reviewing some of the most powerful and clearly written guidelines on this topic. These guidelines include *Identifying and Selecting Evidence-Based Programs and Practices: Questions To Consider* (National Registry of Evidence-Based Programs and Practices, n.d.). It addresses ways to identify evidence-based practices, determine their effectiveness, weigh their organizational and community fit as well as an organization's capacity to implement them, and monitor and sustain such practices. In addition to reviewing the first article from the APA's Presidential Task Force on Evidence-Based Practice (2006), and the APA Council of Representatives' policy statement on Evidence-Based Practive in Psychology (APA, 2013), school psychologists should review the *Disseminating Evidence-Based Practice for Children and Adolescents: A Systems Approach to Enhancing Care* (APA Task Force on Evidence-Based Practice for Children and Adolescents, 2008). These resources should provide a detailed overview of the evidence-based practice movement for school psychologists.

Next, school psychologists should review the research-based underpinnings of evidence-based practice. *Identifying and Implementing Educational Practices Supported by Rigorous Evidence: A User Friendly Guide* (Whitehurst, 2003) offers rich yet clear discussions of the methods used to identify interventions supported by evidence of effectiveness. This guide focuses primarily on the randomized controlled trial as the gold standard in making this distinction and offers a checklist that could be used by school psychologists to evaluate interventions they encounter. Furthermore, the guide defines randomized controlled trials as "studies that randomly assign individuals to an intervention group or to a control group, in order to measure the effects of the intervention" (Whitehurst, 2003, p. 1) and continues by highlighting the importance of random assignment of participants to conditions, its superiority to more basic designs (e.g., a pretest–posttest study design), how such trials (and their results) should be described in publications, and the importance of quality outcome measures and design elements that control for confounds. This document is a useful introduction to the research standards that should be applied when evaluating evidence-based interventions, but it is not comprehensive in its coverage of varying research methods, statistics, and interpretation of results.

Busy school psychologists (seeking a research overview) or those in graduate preparation (seeking an introduction to research design and statistics) should consider reading Norcross et al. (2008) because of its comprehensive yet crystal-clear coverage of research methods, statistics, and their interpretation. For example, it addresses research hypotheses, statistical hypotheses, and statistical significance testing; a variety of research designs, such as randomized controlled trials, time series designs, survey designs, observational studies, and case studies; random assignment versus random sampling; and multivariate statistical techniques. In general, Norcross et al. (2008) empower readers to evaluate at least five features of research: the research participants, the independent variable (e.g., the intervention elements), the dependent variable (e.g., the outcomes that might reflect intervention effects), the comparison groups (e.g., those not receiving the intervention), and the relation of conclusions to actual results. School psychologists should ensure that they are well equipped to evaluate these features.

Sharing the Best Available Research Evidence

Once school psychologists have accessed the best available and most complete evidence, they must be able to share it effectively with others. They must be armed with both strong general communication skills and specific scripts that address the features of scientific evidence.

Communicate Effectively
Gastel (1983) outlined numerous key components of effective science communication. These components are grouped into three categories in this chapter.

Pay attention to the audience before sharing and while sharing information. According to Gastel (1983), school psychologists must carefully consider their audience—their experiences, beliefs, and positions—before they begin presenting their information. A bit of mindreading is needed here. School psychologists should put themselves in the figurative shoes of a passionate parent or a frustrated teacher and strive to see the situation as others might. It is wise for school psychologists to ask questions such as, "What are this parent's goals?" and "What might this teacher be most fearful that I will recommend?" as they prepare for their interactions with parents and teachers.

School psychologists should ground their communications in what they anticipate that their audiences already know; that is, building on the background knowledge that their audience most likely has. Analogies and metaphors can be useful. For example, a school psychologist could use the analogy of learning to ride a bike when discussing the topic of learning to read in an effort to promote the idea that practice makes perfect or the analogy of holding in mind phone numbers through verbal rehearsal when introducing interventions employing mnemonic strategies.

Throughout conversation, school psychologists should not forget to check in with their audience using questions such as "So, what do you think so far?" and "Sometimes, I don't explain things very well. What can I explain better for you?" and statements such as "Please stop me if there is something I have said that is not clear." Periodically touching base with the audience may prevent limited understanding from spiraling into utter confusion.

Keep communication simple. School psychologists should strive to speak using language that is intended to be maximally clear, even if it sounds like they are not as smart or as educated as they actually are. According to Gastel (1983) and the Plain Language Action and Information Network (2011), school psychologists should simplify the words, sentences, and paragraphs they write and utter, and they should keep them simple and concrete. They should also avoid jargon, especially avoiding technical psychology or psychiatric terms (e.g., etiology and prognosis) and educational and psychiatric acronyms (e.g., RTI, SED, FBA, and PBIS). School psychologists should introduce new terms and technical terms with great care, and after introducing technical terms they should use the same term repeatedly rather than substituting alternatives along the way to promote clarity in understanding.

Support key points with concrete details and repetition. When presenting information, school psychologists should always start by describing a concept in general before providing details (Gastel, 1983). Thus, it is important to ground the audience in understanding before expanding. School psychologists should also consider how numbers might improve the clarity and meaning of their utterances. Gastel (1983) conveyed that clear communication can include numbers, but not too many. When presenting information, school psychologists should consider providing simple illustrations (e.g., graphs and figures) as adjuncts to their oral presentation.

For example, some school psychologists present images of the normal curve to parents to support their oral presentation of norm-referenced scores from achievement tests. Finally, school psychologists should repeat their main points—promoting what text researchers call *argument overlap*—throughout presentation of information. For example, in a team meeting, a school psychologist might convey repeatedly that his or her role on the team is to compare the child's progress in learning reading skills to other children the child's age to determine if the child is in need of additional support by teachers trained to assist children who have fallen behind their peers.

Communicating the Key Features of Science

The general communication strategies already reviewed are necessary for school psychologists to communicate clearly, but it is also important that school psychologists focus on the most central tenets of science and evidence-based practice during their communication. In doing so, school psychologists should not only maintain an attitude of skepticism and engage in critical thinking but also demonstrate a self-critical attitude (Lilienfeld, Ammirati, & David, 2012). What follows are some examples of scripts that school psychologists can apply when presenting results to audiences in school settings:

- "I care about children, and it is my job to draw on what has been shown to work best for children who experience X problems when making recommendations."
- "When I looked at all the past projects that have studied the kinds of challenges that Gabrielle faces, it seems to me that X is the best option for her."
- "I selected some of the best tests to measure Jacob's reading skills and was careful to study only those test results that we can trust."
- "From my reviewing the books and journal articles focusing on X, it seems to me that the risk of future problems associated with Y action is far too high for us. I think, in this case, that we should avoid that risk of Y yet keep track of Jake's progress throughout the year."
- "Many studies have shown that X leads to improved Y behaviors in children just like Ronald."
- "When we compare groups of kids who engaged in the X program and other kids who did what was typical after school, those children who engaged in X program almost always performed better than the others."

- "We know from watching children that they tend to follow certain pathways at school as they get older. We want to make sure that Ximena is on the right path."
- "When we try X intervention, we will be sure to look carefully at how it affects Julia's Y behaviors."
- "It is possible that another intervention option will work for Malik or that he will get better on his own with time, but I think that the best option is for us to try Y based on my understanding of the research on this topic."

Responding to Resistance

School psychologists may be faced with vigorous challenges to their conclusions drawn from review of the literature and evidence-based practices. They must decide when it is appropriate to exercise patience and grin and bear it when faced with false or pseudoscientific claims as well as thinking errors that frequently enter into individual and group decision making (see Table 21.2 for examples of thinking errors that are linked to the scripts listed in the sections to follow). For example, when a parent says that fish oil helps her son to read better or when a teacher implies that food coloring and sugar are the root causes of ADHD, school psychologists may be wise to ignore these statements and move on about their business. School psychologists must also be prepared to respond with great civility and strong reason. The following scripts should prepare school psychologists to face false or pseudoscientific claims and thinking errors in a scientific manner.

Table 21.2. Thinking Errors That May Interfere With Evidence-Based Practice in School Psychology and Their Descriptions

Thinking Error	Description
Heeding word-of-mouth	Basing beliefs on catchy phrases, urban legends, and testimonials from parents, teachers, or relatives
Believing everything you see on TV or read on the Internet	Basing beliefs on inaccurate (but often vivid) portrayals of events in movies, television, books, or other media outlets; due in part to the availability heuristic: judging the probability of an event by the ease with which it comes to mind
Looking for the easy answer	Believing that simple remedies solve complex problems
Falling prey to selective memory and selective perception	Drawing incorrect conclusions about the world because of errors in how we understand and remember events; due in part to the following: naive realism (believing precisely what we see and experience), illusory correlations (perceiving patterns between events that are objectively absent), confirmation bias (seeking out evidence consistent with our beliefs, and denying, dismissing, or distorting evidence that is not), and belief perseverance (clinging to beliefs despite repeated contradictory evidence)
Identifying cause-and-effect relations when events co-occur	Believing that one event caused another because they happened about the same time without considering how other events may be the actual cause
Identifying cause-and-effect relations when one follows the other	Believing that one event causes another because of the order in which they occur (e.g., B came after A, so A must have caused B) without considering how other events may be the actual cause
Concluding that because two things can go together, they actually do	Believing that surface-level similarities between two phenomena (i.e., representativeness) reveals a meaningful connection between them
Not being able to see the big picture due to our own limited experiences	Believing that something is true based on our own selective experiences (i.e., a biased sample)
Making a mountain out of a molehill	Tending to see mental disorders and educational handicapping conditions in relatively normative behavior (pathology bias)
Feeling "I am a special case" or "This child or adolescent is a special case"	Believing that group-based research is irrelevant to ourselves, or any other individual child, adolescent, or adult (aggregate bias)

Note. The terms for the first eight thinking errors were modified from the sources of error described in Lilienfeld, Lynn, Ruscio, and Beyerstein (2010, pp. 9–17). The terms for the final two thinking errors were modified from Lilienfeld et al. (2012, Table 21.1, p. 15). Descriptions of the availability heuristic, naive realism, the illusory correlation, confirmation bias, belief perseverance, pathology bias, and aggregate bias were from Lilienfeld et al. (2012, Table 21.1, p. 15).

Use these scripts in response to a mention of word of mouth or a reference to prominent media stars advocating psychological or educational interventions:

- "I know that some parents find X intervention helps their children, but I worry both about the cost of X intervention and that there isn't much information from doctors and psychologists saying that it helps children any more than letting the child outgrow the problems."
- "It seems to me, based on all that I have read, that X intervention is not likely to help, but I could be wrong. If Christine were my daughter, I think that I would rather go with something that has a greater chance of turning things around more quickly."
- "There will always be experts out there who disagree about what is best, but it seems to me that hundreds of studies of thousands of kids show that Y is probably the best option."
- "When we try to figure out what is the best path for children, we don't want to rely on gossip, hearsay, or ideas coming from one doctor, one psychologist, or one talk show host. I know that they can be very persuasive. We want our decisions to be based on careful, hard work across years and hundreds of caring people trying to figure out what is the best path. I have looked for that information, and I want to share it with you."

Use these scripts in response to looking for the easy answer:

- "Evan is struggling with quite a few problems at school right now. Although X intervention alone may help, I think that we should tackle these problems using several strategies that are likely to head them off before they get worse. We can improve his situation at school this way."

Use these scripts in response to selective memory and selective perception (i.e., naive realism, illusory correlations, confirmation bias, and belief perseverance) as well as incorrect inferences about cause-and-effect relations:

- "It is easy for all of us to see patterns between things that aren't actually there. Think about seeing the man in the moon and how optical illusions trick our eyes. The same thing can sometimes happen when we look at children's patterns in behavior."
- "Although you could be right and I could be wrong, based on everything I have read on this topic, I don't think that X causes Y."

- "It is my understanding that very smart people from across the globe have studied this issue and decided that X and Y are not related."

Use these scripts in response to references to similarities between things that indicate a relation when there is none (i.e., the representativeness heuristic):

- "Although X behavior can sometimes signal Y disorder, just because Mollie does it, doesn't mean that Mollie has Y disorder. We have to look for a lot of other problem behaviors to come to the conclusion that a child has Y disorder."
- "Some people say that X in a child's drawing signals that the child feels down about himself, but I like to base my decisions on what Barbara says and how she acts rather than on drawings."

Use these scripts in response to being unable to see the big picture due to limited experiences (i.e., biased sampling) and making a mountain out of a molehill (i.e., pathology bias):

- "It is so hard to say whether X is a problem or not when we have not seen Merritt interact with other children. We need to conduct more assessment before we jump to any conclusions."
- "Sometimes children do some odd things, like X, but what's often surprising to learn is that most all children at this age do these odd things, too. What's important to us is (a) they not harm themselves when they do it and (b) we use other children as a comparison before we determine that it's a serious problem."
- "The power that my tests have is that they allow me to compare Ivy's reading, writing, and math skills to other children her age. Sometimes, it's hard to tell when a child is on track and when a child is off track. My tests allow me to understand that better."

Use these scripts in response to interactions indicating perceptions that "I am a special case" or "This child or adolescent is a special case" (i.e., aggregate bias):

- "I know that X strategy has not worked for you in the past, but let's give it some close scrutiny and figure out why it might not have worked for you. Are you willing to give it a shot again with my help?"
- "I do not know what is best, but I think that, based on study of thousands of children with X condition, Sue

will improve her Y behavior most effectively if we try Z intervention."

- "Although X strategies do not work with every child who has problems in class like Samuel has, these strategies work for most children like him. I am confident that starting with these strategies is the best option."

It is our hope that these scripts will enable school psychologists to more effectively promote adoption of evidence-based practices in school settings.

Case Example

Paul, a school psychologist at Shady Creek Elementary, was recently approached by the principal and asked to consider some of the problems that Emily, a new second-grade student at the school, has been having. Paul first met with Emily's homeroom teacher. During their meeting, the teacher described Emily as being a "bright student" who always completes her assignments and does well on them. He added, however, that Emily does not talk in class. The teacher said that when he asks Emily direct questions, she always gestures or writes her answers in response. The teacher also told Paul that he has not seen Emily talk to any of her classmates.

Paul met with Emily's mother, who provided a different view of Emily than the teacher did. Emily's mother agreed that Emily can be shy, but she told Paul that Emily is often quite noisy at home, talking, laughing, and screaming at her siblings. She described Emily's speech and language as having developed normally but mentioned that Emily continues to refuse to go to bed unless she has five nightlights on in her room and nearby hallway and that Emily also "freaks out" when she does not know where both of her parents and her siblings are. Concerned about this discrepancy between Emily's communication skills displayed at home and school, Paul planned to conduct classroom observations to figure out what may be causing Emily to avoid speaking at school.

After conducting his observations and referencing the fifth edition of the *Diagnostic and Statistical Manual of Mental Disorders* (DSM-5; American Psychiatric Association, 2013), Paul hypothesized that Emily has selective mutism. From the DSM-5, Paul learned that selective mutism can be considered one part anxiety disorder and one part communication disorder. Paul had no previous experience with children with selective mutism, so he enlisted the help of his school's speech–language pathologist, and the two agreed that they

would collaborate to help Emily. In the meantime, Paul continued to conduct literature searches to learn more about the disorder and locate evidence-based interventions to assist Emily and her teachers.

First, Paul conducted a general Internet search to locate background information about selective mutism. Paul visited the NASP website and completed a search using the term *selective mutism*. He found a primer for parents and educators by Kehle, Bray, and Theodore (2004) that provided him with an overview of the characteristics of selective mutism, how it develops, and possible interventions for treating it. Paul also searched through the online archives of *School Psychology Forum* to find an article he remembered seeing about evidence-based interventions for selective mutism implemented in school settings (i.e., Hagermoser Sanetti & Luiselli, 2009). Paul considered the interventions suggested in these references and attempted to find systematic reviews and practice guidelines for selective mutism.

Paul located a systematic review of the literature on interventions for selective mutism by Cohan, Chavira, and Stein (2006). Although Paul recognized that the article noted that most of the studies reviewed possessed weak research methodology, Paul began to feel more comfortable with the idea of using behavioral or cognitive–behavioral therapy to help improve Emily's communication at school. He carefully studied the cognitive–behavioral intervention package suggested at the end of Cohan et al. (2006) and searched for other programs and guidelines.

During this search, Paul located a randomized controlled pilot study on integrated behavior therapy for selective mutism conducted by Bergman, Gonzalez, Piacentini, and Keller (2013) that appeared to demonstrate promise as an efficacious intervention. Paul considered buying Bergman's (2013) manualized intervention program and using it with Emily. This intervention program consists of 20 sessions employing a mixture of traditional behavioral techniques used alongside exposure-based interventions.

Although Paul liked what he had found, he was not sure whether therapy sessions with Emily lasting only an hour a week will be enough to help her overcome her selective mutism at school. Paul was also concerned about some of the other anxious symptoms described by Emily's mother (e.g., showing significant distress when unsure about the location of her parents and siblings). Even though Paul had considerable experience providing group-based interventions for anxiety management, he completed the same process of searching through databases for systematic reviews and program guidelines for the most current and efficacious interventions in this area to be sure that he is still employing best practices. Paul wanted to provide Emily's mother with the necessary resources to help her locate and establish services with a cognitive–behavioral therapist in the community that Emily and her family can utilize outside of school.

While Paul planned to use Bergman's (2013) program guidelines during therapy sessions with Emily, he also wanted to provide the teacher with some interventions that could be used in the classroom. Paul compiled a list of possible interventions (including stimulus fading, shaping, and social skills training) that can be used to help students overcome selective mutism and read through the referenced articles so that he would be able to share the purpose and reasoning behind their use. Armed with handouts, lists of referrals, behavior tracking tools, as well as a confidence that comes with following best practices, Paul was ready. During individual and group consultation with the teacher, the principal, and Emily's parents, Paul was able to effectively communicate why Emily needed assistance at school and to answer questions regarding how to implement the interventions he recommended.

SUMMARY

Evidence-based practice is defined as "the integration of the best available research with clinical expertise in the context of patient characteristics, culture, and preferences" (APA Presidential Task Force on Evidence-Based Practice, 2006, p. 273). In order to promote evidence-based practice, enact NASP's Practice Model (NASP, 2010), and facilitate positive outcomes for those they serve, school psychologists must be able to identify and evaluate research evidence and communicate this evidence in a meaningful way to school audiences. To reach these goals, school psychologists must access top-quality sources of information. Sources providing background and unfiltered and filtered information as well as those reviewing the evidence supporting educational and psychological interventions and assessment instruments should be consulted. Accessing information from the Internet through use of Web-based search engines, such as Google Scholar, and websites serving as information clearinghouses has never been easier. In particular, websites such as the Cochrane Database of Systematic Reviews, the Campbell Collaboration Library of Systematic Reviews, the What Works Clearinghouse, the National Center on Response to Intervention, and the National Center on Intensive Interventions provide up-to-date, peer-reviewed, and synthesized research evidence to empower school psychologists involved in intervention selection and implementation. In addition, the Buros Institute for Mental Measurements and the National Center on Response to Intervention offer test reviews to promote evidence-based assessment practices.

Despite the availability of these rich sources of information, school psychologists must distinguish evidence-based practices from non-evidence-based practices. Resources such as *Disseminating Evidence-Based Practice for Children and Adolescents: A Systems Approach to Enhancing Care* (APA Task Force on Evidence-Based Practice for Children and Adolescents, 2008), *Identifying and Implementing Educational Practices Supported by Rigorous Evidence: A User Friendly Guide* (Whitehurst, 2003), and the *Clinician's Guide to Evidence-Based Practices: Mental Health and the Addictions* (Norcross et al., 2008) summarize the central tenets of evidence-based practice and offer guidelines for evaluating the quality of research evidence informing educational and psychological practices. After accessing and identifying the best available research, school psychologists must communicate the key features of evidence-based practice, advocate for practices that are consistent with the preponderance of scientific evidence, and counter resistance from their audiences that might stem from common thinking errors. Equipped with these skills, school psychologists serving as research experts in school settings will be better able to promote evidence-based practices for the students, teachers, parents, and others they serve.

AUTHOR NOTE

The authors are appreciative of Isaac Wood's contributions to literature searches and construction of Table 21.1 as well as Leah Singh's assistance in reviewing page proofs of this chapter.

REFERENCES

American Academy of Pediatrics. (2013). Search results for "evidence-based decision-making tools for managing common pediatric conditions" in AAP Practice Guidelines online database. Retrieved from http://pediatrics.aappublications.org/search?flag=practice_guidelines&submit=yes&x=18&y=8&format=standard&hits=30&sortspec=date&submit=Go

American Psychiatric Association. (2013). *Diagnostic and statistical manual of mental disorders* (5th ed.). Arlington, VA: Author.

American Psychological Association. (2013). *Evidence-based practice in psychology*. Washington, DC: Author. Retrieved from http://www.apa.org/practice/resources/evidence/index.aspx

American Psychological Association Presidential Task Force on Evidence-Based Practice. (2006). Evidence-based practice in psychology. *American Psychologist, 61*, 271–285.

American Psychological Association Task Force on Evidence-Based Practice for Children and Adolescents. (2008). *Disseminating evidence-based practice for children and adolescents: A systems approach to enhancing care.* Washington, DC: American Psychological Association. Retrieved from http://www.apa.org/practice/resources/evidence/children-report.pdf

Bergman, R. L. (2013). *Treatment for children with selective mutism: An integrative behavioral approach.* New York, NY: Oxford University Press.

Bergman, R. L., Gonzalez, A., Piacentini, J., & Keller, M. L. (2013). Integrated behavior therapy for selective mutism: A randomized controlled pilot study. *Behaviour Research and Therapy, 51*, 680–689. doi:10.1016/j.brat.2013.07.003

Cohan, S. L., Chavira, D. A., & Stein, M. B. (2006). Practitioner review: Psychosocial interventions for children with selective mutism: A critical evaluation of the literature from 1990-2005. *Journal of Child Psychology and Psychiatry, 47*, 1085–1097. doi:10.1111/j.1469-7610.2006.01662.x

Gastel, B. (1983). *Presenting science to the public.* Philadelphia, PA: ISI Press.

Hagermoser Sanetti, L. M., & Luiselli, J. K. (2009). Evidence-based practices for selective mutism: Implementation by a school team. *School Psychology Forum, 3*(1), 27–42.

Hunsley, J., & Mash, E. J. (2007). Evidence-based assessment. *Annual Review of Clinical Psychology, 3*, 29–51.

Kehle, T. J., Bray, M. A., & Theodore, L. A. (2004). Selective mutism: A primer for parents and educators. In A. S. Canter, L. Z. Paige, M. D. Roth, I. Romero, & S. A. Carroll (Eds.), *Helping children at home and school II. Handouts for families and educators* (S8-167–170). Bethesda, MD: National Association of School Psychologists.

Lilienfeld, S. O., Ammirati, R., & David, M. (2012). Distinguishing science from pseudoscience in school psychology: Science and scientific thinking as safeguards against human error. *Journal of School Psychology, 50*, 7–36.

Lilienfeld, S. O., Lynn, S. J., Ruscio, J., & Beyerstein, B. L. (2010). *50 great myths of popular psychology: Shattering widespread misconceptions about human behavior.* Hoboken, NJ: Wiley-Blackwell.

National Association of School Psychologists. (2010). *Model for comprehensive and integrated school psychological services.* Bethesda, MD: Author. Retrieved from http://www.nasponline.org/standards/2010standards/2_PracticeModel.pdf

National Registry of Evidence-Based Programs and Practices. (n.d.). *Identifying and selecting evidence-based programs and practices: Questions to consider.* Washington, DC: Author. Retrieved from http://www.nrepp.samhsa.gov/pdfs/identifyingandselecting.pdf

Nelson, J. M., & Machek, G. R. (2007). A survey of training, practice, and competence in reading assessment and intervention. *School Psychology Review, 36*, 311–327.

Norcross, J. C., Hogan, T. P., & Koocher, G. P. (2008). *Clinician's guide to evidence-based practices: Mental health and the addictions.* New York, NY: Oxford University Press.

Plain Language Action and Information Network. (2011). *Federal plain language guidelines* (rev. 1). Retrieved from http://www.plainlanguage.gov/howto/guidelines/FederalPLGuidelines/FederalPLGuidelines.pdf

Shernoff, E. S., Kratochwill, T. R., & Stoiber, K. C. (2003). Training in evidence-based interventions: What are school psychology programs teaching? *Journal of School Psychology, 41*, 467–483.

Shinn, M. R., & Walker, H. M. (2010). *Interventions for achievement and behavior problems in a three-tier model including RTI.* Bethesda, MD: National Association of School Psychologists.

Spencer, T. D., Detrich, R., & Slocum, T. A. (2012). Evidence-based practice: A framework for making effective decisions. *Education and Treatment of Children, 35*, 127–151.

Steele, R. G., Elkin, T. D., & Roberts, M. C. (Eds.). (2008). *Handbook of evidence-based therapies for children and adolescents: Bridging science and practice.* New York, NY: Springer.

Whitehurst, G. J. (2003). *Identifying and implementing educational practices supported by rigorous evidence: A user friendly guide.* Washington, DC: U.S. Department of Education, Institute of Education Sciences, National Center for Education Evaluation and Regional Assistance. Retrieved from http://www2.ed.gov/rschstat/research/pubs/rigorousevid/rigorousevid.pdf

22

A Psychometric Primer for School Psychologists

Cecil R. Reynolds
Texas A&M University
Ronald B. Livingston
The University of Texas at Tyler

OVERVIEW

This chapter is a psychometric primer and as such the overriding goal is to cover the basic concepts and principles of the field that are most relevant to school psychologists. School psychologists are often the most sophisticated users of assessment data in the public schools, and thus they should be well versed in psychometric theories and applications. Most (if not all) school psychologists have had graduate training in psychometrics, and as a result this chapter may serve largely as a refresher or reference. The discipline is continuously evolving so this chapter will also serve to update school psychologists on recent developments (e.g., that using terms such as *content validity* is outdated and no longer technically accurate). We do, however, want to emphasize that as a primer this chapter does not provide comprehensive coverage of the growing discipline of psychometrics. At numerous points in this chapter we will note that certain topics are beyond the scope of this chapter (e.g., detailed and/or technical explanations of measurement theories).

In this context, we hope this chapter will encourage readers to delve farther into the study of psychometrics. We do provide suggestions on where interested readers can find additional information, and the Annotated Bibliography (available at http://www.nasponline.org/publications) should serve as a good resource for those interested in learning more about psychometric theories and applications.

THE LANGUAGE OF ASSESSMENT

Psychometrics is the science of psychological measurement, and a psychometrician is a psychological or educational professional who specializes in psychological tests and measurement. When people refer to the psychometric properties of a test they typically mean the measurement or statistical characteristics of a test.

Before proceeding, some key words and concepts that are used in this chapter need to be defined.

- *Test:* A test is a device or procedure in which a sample of an individual's behavior is obtained, evaluated, and scored using standardized procedures (American Educational Research Association [AERA], American Psychological Association, & National Council on Measurement in Education, 1999). One aspect of the definition of a test is that a test is a sample of behavior. Because a test is only a sample of behavior, it is important that tests obtain a representative sample of the behavior or characteristic one is interested in measuring.

- *Standardized test:* A standardized test is a test that is administered, scored, and interpreted in a standard manner. The goal of standardization is to ensure that the testing conditions are as close to identical as possible for all examinees. This way, no student will have an advantage or disadvantage relative to another due to differences in administration or scoring procedures, and assessment results will be comparable.

- *Measurement:* Measurement is a set of rules for assigning numbers to represent objects, traits, attributes, or behaviors. A psychological test is a measuring device, and therefore involves rules (e.g., administration, scoring, and interpretive guidelines) for assigning numbers that reflect each individual's performance.

- *Assessment:* Assessment is defined as a systematic process for collecting information that can be used to make inferences about the characteristics of people or objects (AERA et al., 1999). Tests are one systematic procedure for collecting information and therefore fall under the broad rubric of assessment. Reviewing medical, legal, and educational records, interviews, and observations are also legitimate and important assessment procedures, and they are most useful when they are integrated systematically. In fact, assessment typically refers to a process that involves the integration of information obtained from multiple sources using multiple methods to arrive at conclusions (i.e., interpretations) about the person or variable in question.

We are advocates of a philosophy or model of assessment that incorporates psychometric sophistication, clinical insight, knowledge of psychological theory, and thoughtful reasoning grounded in the psychological and educational sciences of school psychology. With this model, assessment involves a synthesis of information that is obtained in a technically rigorous manner from multiple sources using multiple procedures. Kaufman (1994) suggests that a school psychologist conducting an assessment should assume the role of a detective who collects, evaluates, and synthesizes information and integrates that information with a thorough understanding of human development, psychopathology, and individual differences. When performed appropriately, psychological and educational assessment is a demanding and sophisticated process. For more detailed information on these and related concepts, see Reynolds and Livingston (2012).

WHY USE TESTS

Since psychological assessments can incorporate a number of procedures in addition to tests (e.g., interviews, observations), it is reasonable to ask why do school psychologists so often use tests in their professional practice. The answer is simple: People are not good at judging other people in an objective and unbiased manner, and most "nontest" procedures involve subjective judgment. Subjective judgments are notably unreliable, and one of the principles of psychometrics is that the lower the reliability of a method, the more likely it is to be systematically biased. It is well documented that people are all susceptible to a multitude of biases that undermine the accuracy of their judgment.

For example, if someone is seen initially as outstanding on one trait (or extremely negative on one trait), then that single evaluation colors one's overall impression of that person. As a result, a person who is viewed as physically attractive might also be considered smart, trustworthy, and personable. In contrast, someone who is seen as physically unattractive might also be considered uneducated, lazy, and boring. This is a well-documented cognitive bias that is referred to as the *halo effect*. It is by no means the only bias that impairs an ability to judge other people accurately. Because of this and a host of other biases, subjective judgment is fallible and subject to error (e.g., Dahlstrom, 1993; Reynolds & Livingston, 2012).

Tests are used to overcome the fallibility of human judgment. The benefits of tests are numerous:

- Tests provide objective data that can reduce uncertainty. Tests can allow prediction and allow us to control events with less error. Predictions will never be perfect and uncertainty never goes to zero. But to the extent that by using tests, predictions can be enhanced and uncertainty can be reduced, then tests are useful.

- As much as possible, characteristics of tests can be measured, and therefore the results can be used with confidence. For example, it can be estimated how reliable or stable scores are and how accurate those scores are at predicting specific outcomes.

- Tests quantify behavior. This means that behavior can be subjected to more detailed and sophisticated observation and a deeper and more complex understanding of behavior can be developed than is possible through other means. For example, many psychological tests are interpreted in such a way that each client is compared to a group of his or her peers. This allows school psychologists to determine if a student's responses or performance is within normal limits. For example, based on clinical interviews and observations a skilled clinician might conclude that a client has a deficit in short-term memory. However, the use of a memory test might indicate that the client's performance is 2 standard deviations below the mean (i.e., below that of 98% of his or her peers).

In this case the use of the test confirms the clinician's impression and documents the severity of the deficit.

- Many psychological tests are designed to assess a large number of characteristics, behaviors, or traits, and as a result these tests may help ensure that important behavioral and clinical concerns are not overlooked. For example, a pediatric behavior rating scale may cover such rare behaviors as "fire-setting" and "cruelty to animals," topics that might be overlooked in a clinical interview or observation.
- The use of tests, in addition to interviews and observations, helps ensure that multiple sources of data are included.
- Tests allow useful inferences to be drawn in a far shorter period of time than would be required if there were no standardized samples of behavior and reference groups to compare with.

In summary, tests are valuable because they provide objective sources of information and allow the clinician or school psychologist to act efficaciously with less error than would be possible without the information provided by the tests (e.g., Dahlstrom, 1993; McFall & Trent, 1999; Reynolds & Livingston, 2012). This does not mean that school psychologists should eschew the use of clinical interviews and observations. It means that they should use multiple sources of information whenever making professional decisions. When there is consistency in the information obtained by using multiple sources of information (e.g., interviews, observations, tests), then there can be an increased confidence in the findings. When different assessment procedures produce inconsistent results, different hypotheses systematically should be generated and tested until the most accurate explanation can be ascertained. This process is often complex, requires extensive professional skill, and is the hallmark of psychological assessment when done in a competent, professional manner. Indeed, it is largely the reason school psychologists need to use and interpret tests appropriately as opposed to being stimulus-bound technicians.

UNDERSTANDING TEST SCORES

Test scores are mathematical representations of the performance or ratings of an examinee completing a test. Since test scores are the keys to understanding an examinee's performance, their meaning and interpretation are extremely important. There is a wide assortment of scores available, and each format has its own unique characteristics and applications.

Scales of Measurement

When something is measured, the units of measurement (e.g., scores) have a mathematical property referred to as the scale of measurement. A scale is a system or scheme for assigning values or scores to the characteristic being measured. Stevens (1946) originally proposed a taxonomy that specified four scales of measurement that have distinct properties and convey different types of information. The four scales of measurement are nominal, ordinal, interval, and ratio. These scales form a hierarchy, and as nominal scales progress to ratio scales, increasingly precise measurements can be performed that capture more detailed information.

Nominal Scales

Nominal scales are the simplest of the four scales. Nominal scales provide a qualitative system for categorizing people or objects into categories, classes, or sets. For example, assigning college students to categories based on their academic major (e.g., biology, chemistry, psychology) results in a nominal scale. In this example numbers were not assigned to the categories, just the name of the majors was used. In some situations numbers are used in nominal scales to identify or label the categories (e. g., male = 1, female = 2), but the numbers simply serve as names for the categories and do not convey quantitative information. As a result, numbers assigned to nominal scales should not be added, subtracted, ranked, or otherwise manipulated. Accordingly, most common statistical procedures cannot be used with nominal scales, and their usefulness is limited.

Ordinal Scales

Using ordinal scale measurement allows a ranking (or ordering) of people or objects according to the amount or quantity of a characteristic the people or objects possess. Ordinal scales quantify the variable under examination and therefore provide more information than nominal scales. Ranking people according to height from the tallest to the shortest is an example of ordinal measurement. Traditionally the ranking is ordered from the "most" to the "least." For example, the tallest person in the class would receive the rank of 1, the next tallest a rank of 2, and so on. Although ordinal scale measurement provides quantitative information, it does not ensure that the intervals between the ranks are consistent. That is, the difference in height between the individuals ranked 1 and 2 might be 3 inches while the difference between those ranked 3 and 4 might be 1 inch.

Ordinal scales indicate the rank-order position among individuals or objects, but ordinal scales do not indicate the extent by which they differ. As a result, these scales are somewhat limited in both the measurement information they provide and the statistical procedures that can be applied.

While it can be done, it rarely makes sense to add, subtract, multiply, or divide ordinal scores or to find their mean. Nevertheless, ordinal level scores are useful and commonly used by school psychologists.

Interval Scales

Using an interval scale measurement allows a ranking of people or objects like an ordinal scale but on a scale with equal units. That is, the difference between adjacent units on the scale is equivalent. Many psychological tests are designed to produce interval level scores (e.g., IQs are interval level scores). Interval level data can be manipulated using common mathematical operations (e.g., addition, subtraction, multiplication, and division) whereas lesser scales (i.e., nominal and ordinal) cannot. Another advantage is that most statistical procedures can be used with interval scale data. While interval scales represent a substantial improvement over ordinal scales and provide considerable information, interval scales do not have a true zero point. In other words, on interval scales a score of zero does not reflect the total absence of the attribute. In fact, zero cannot be located accurately on an interval scale. The origin of an interval scale then is at the mean of the score distribution (and then scores move outward in both directions) as opposed to a zero point of origin. As a result, ratios are not meaningful with interval scales. For example, even though an IQ of 120 is twice as large as an IQ of 60, it does not mean that the person with a score of 120 is twice as intelligent as the person with a score of 60. For such a statement to be accurate there needs to be a true zero point.

Ratio Scales

Ratio scales have the properties of interval scales plus a true zero point that reflects the complete absence of the characteristic being measured. Miles per hour, length, and weight are all examples of ratio scales. As the name suggests, with ratio scales ratios between scores can be interpreted. For example, 120 miles per hour is twice as fast as 60 miles per hour, 6 feet is twice as long as 3 feet, and 200 pounds is four times as much as 50 pounds. With the exception of the percent of items correct and the measurement of some behavioral responses (e.g., reaction time), there are relatively few ratio scales in

Table 22.1. Scales of Measurement

Scale	Example	Sample
Nominal	Gender	Female = 1 Male = 2
Ordinal	Graduation rank	Valedictorian = 1 Salutatorian = 2 Third rank = 3
Interval	Intelligence scores Personality test score	IQ = 100 Anxiety *T*-score = 75
Ratio	Weight in pounds Percent correct on a test	100 pounds 80%

psychological measurement. Fortunately, most of the measurement issues in psychology can be adequately addressed by using interval scales.

Norm-Referenced and Criterion-Referenced Scores

Test scores are mathematical representations of the performance or ratings of an examinee completing a test, and there are a number of score formats available. Possibly the simplest type of score is a raw score. A raw score is simply the number of items scored or coded in a specific manner such as correct/incorrect, true/false, and so on. While the calculation of raw scores is typically straightforward, they usually provide little useful information. A frame of reference is needed to interpret and understand test results. That is, the examinee's performance to "something" must be compared (or referenced). Most score interpretations can be classified as either *norm referenced* or *criterion referenced*, and this distinction refers to the "something" to which the examinee's performance is compared. There is another score format available based on item response theory, but we will wait until the end of this section to discuss it.

Norm-Referenced Score Interpretations

With norm-referenced score interpretations, the examinee's performance is compared to the performance of some other group (a reference or standardization group). For example, scores on tests of intelligence are norm-referenced. If a student has an IQ of 100, this indicates that he or she scored at the mean of the standardization or reference sample. This is a norm-referenced interpretation, and the examinee's performance is being compared to that of other test takers. Personality tests arc also usually reported as norm-referenced scores. For example, it might be reported that an examinee scored higher than 98% of the standardization sample on some trait such as introversion or aggressiveness. With all norm-referenced interpretations, the examinee's performance is compared to that of others. To accomplish this, raw scores are typically converted to derived scores based on information about the performance of a specific reference group.

For norm-referenced interpretations to be meaningful, the examinee's performance needs to be compared to that of a relevant reference or standardization group or sample. The reference group most often used to derive scores is called a national standardization sample. Most test publishers and developers select a national standardization sample using a procedure known as population proportionate stratified random sampling. This means that samples of people are selected in such a way as to ensure that the national population as a whole is proportionately represented on important variables (e.g., gender, ethnicity). Once the reference or standardization sample has been selected and tested, tables of derived scores are developed. These tables are based on the performance of the standardization sample and are typically referred to as normative tables or *norms*.

While a nationally representative sample is the most common type of reference group used by developers of major standardized tests, other reference groups are sometimes selected. For example, the standardized achievement tests used in many school districts provide local normative data that are based on students in individual school districts. This allows school officials and parents to be sure that their students are being compared with students that are comparable on many important variables. Other types of reference data are provided with some tests. For example, the Behavioral Assessment System for Children-Second Edition (Reynolds & Kamphaus, 2004) includes normative data based on clinical samples as well as general population norms. These clinical norms may be helpful in refining or narrowing in on a diagnostic impression or in a process of triage when, in a finite environment, making decisions about the most important area of intervention when a student has multiple problems.

Whenever special normative group data are provided, the publisher should describe the normative group thoroughly in the test manual so school psychologists can make informed decisions about how appropriate these data are for a given examinee and for a given purpose. Different normative or reference samples answer different questions (see Reynolds & Livingston, 2012, for more information on this topic), and it is crucial the proper reference group be applied when test scores are interpreted.

With norm-referenced score interpretations, *standard scores* (sometimes called scaled scores) are the most common type of derived score. Transforming raw scores into standard scores involves creating a set of scores with a predetermined mean and standard deviation that remains constant across some preselected variable such as age (termed *scaling* because the underlying metric is changed or the scores are rescaled). All standard scores use standard deviation units to indicate where an examinee's score is located relative to the mean of the distribution obtained with the standardization sample. Different standard score formats differ in their means and standard deviations. Here are brief descriptions of some of the more common standard score formats.

- *z-scores:* z-scores are the simplest of the standard score formats and have a mean of 0 and a standard deviation of 1. As a result, all scores above the mean will be positive and all scores below the mean will be negative. Since many find z-scores difficult to use and interpret since they involve negative numbers and decimals, few test publishers routinely report z-scores for their tests. However, researchers commonly use z-scores because scores with a mean of 0 and a standard deviation of 1 make statistical formulas easier to calculate.

- *T-scores:* T-scores have a mean of 50 and a standard deviation of 10. Relative to z-scores they have the advantage of all scores being positive and avoid decimals.

- *IQs:* Most intelligence scales in use today employ a standard score format with a mean of 100 and a standard deviation of 15. Like T-scores, the IQ format avoids decimals and negative values. It should be noted that many modern intelligence tests do not produce a score specifically labeled as an IQ. For example, the Reynolds Intellectual Assessment Scales (Reynolds & Kamphaus, 2003) produces the Composite Intelligence Index that represents general intelligence. Like the IQ, these alternatives typically retain a mean of 100 and a standard deviation of 15.

- *CEEB scores:* This format was developed by the College Entrance Examination Board and has been used with tests such as the SAT as well as the CEEB achievement tests and many other college admissions tests. CEEB scores have a mean of 500 and standard deviation of 100 and avoid decimals and negative values.

As we noted, standard scores can be set to essentially any desired mean and standard deviation. Fortunately, the few standard score formats just summarized account for the majority of standardized tests in education and psychology.

Our discussion of standard scores so far applies to scores from distributions that are normal (or that at least approximate normality) and were computed using a linear transformation. While many variables of interest to school psychologists are approximately normally distributed, not all are. As a result it is not unusual for test developers to end up with distributions that deviate from normality enough to cause concern. In these situations, test developers may elect to develop normalized standard scores. Normalized standard scores are standard scores based on underlying distributions that were not originally normal but were transformed into normal distributions. The transformations applied in these situations are often nonlinear transformations. Whereas standard scores calculated with linear transformations retain a direct relationship with the original raw scores and the distribution retains its original shape, this is not necessarily so with normalized standard scores based on nonlinear transformations.

This does not mean that normalized standard scores are undesirable. In situations in which the obtained distribution is not normal because the variable is not normally distributed, normalization is not generally useful and indeed may be misleading. However, in situations in which the obtained distribution is not normal because of sampling error or choice of subjects, normalization can enhance the usefulness and interpretability of the scores.

In most situations, normalized standard scores are interpreted in a manner similar to other standard scores and often appear strikingly similar to linear standard scores. For example, normalized standard scores may be reported as normalized *z*-scores or normalized *T*-scores and often reported without the prefix "normalized" at all. In this context they will have the same mean and standard deviation as their counterparts derived with linear transformations. Many school psychologists are familiar with Wechsler scaled scores, which are normalized standard scores with a mean of 10 and a standard deviation of 3. These scores were transformed so the Wechsler subtest scores would be comparable, even though their underlying distributions may have deviated from the normal curve and each other to some degree.

Unfortunately, some believe that all scores referred to as scaled scores have a mean of 10 and standard deviation of 3. This is a gross misapplication of the term,

since any transformed score, regardless of the underlying metric of the transformation, is a scaled score. For clarification, we recommend the use of the designation *S*-score to refer to scores scaled to a mean of 10 and a standard deviation of 3, just as other scores have been given names (e.g., *T*-scores [mean of 50 and a standard deviation of 10] and *z*-scores [mean of 0 and a standard deviation of 1]).

One of the most popular and easily understood ways to interpret and report a test score is the percentile rank. Like all norm-referenced scores, the percentile rank simply reflects the examinee's performance relative to a specific group. Although there are subtle differences in the ways percentile ranks are calculated and interpreted, the typical way of interpreting them is as reflecting the percentage of individuals scoring below a given point in a distribution. For example, a percentile rank of 60 indicates that 60% of the individuals in the standardization sample scored below this score. A percentile rank of 30 indicates that only 30% of the individuals in the standardization sample scored below this score. Percentile ranks range from 1 to 99, and a rank of 50 indicates the median performance.

Percentile ranks can be explained easily to and understood by individuals without formal training in psychometrics, and are often useful when explaining test results to students and/or parents.

Although percentile ranks can be interpreted easily, they do not represent interval level measurement. That is, percentile ranks are not equal across all parts of a distribution. Percentile ranks are compressed near the middle of the distribution, where there are large numbers of scores, and spread out near the tails, where there are relatively few scores. This implies that small differences in percentile ranks near the middle of the distribution might be of little importance, whereas the same difference at the extreme might be substantial. Therefore, it is often noted that use of percentile ranks will exaggerate small differences near the mean and obscure large differences near the tails of the distribution. However, because the pattern of inequality is predictable, this can be taken into consideration when interpreting scores and it is not particularly problematic so long as the user is aware of this particularity of percentile ranks.

Grade equivalents are norm-referenced derived scores that are often misinterpreted as identifying the academic grade level achieved by the student. Although grade equivalents are popular in some settings (especially schools) and appear to be easy to interpret, they actually need to be interpreted with considerable caution. Much has been written about the limitations of grade equivalents, and while we will not go into great detail, we will highlight some of their major limitations:

- The calculation of grade equivalents assumes that academic skills are achieved at a constant rate over the 10-month academic year and that there is no gain or loss during the summer vacation. This assumption is probably not accurate in many (if not most) situations.

- There is no predictable relationship between grade equivalents and percentile ranks. For example, a student in grade 8.0 may have a grade equivalent of 6.0 on a reading test and 6.0 on a math test, but the percentile rank for the reading score could easily be 30 and for the math score 5, indicating considerably different levels of potential academic problems in these content areas.

- A common misperception is that children should receive instruction at the level suggested by their grade equivalents. A parent may ask, "Juan is only in the fourth grade but has a grade equivalent of 6.5 in math. Doesn't that mean he is ready for sixth grade math instruction?" The answer is clearly no. Although Juan correctly answered the same number of items as an average sixth grader on the specific test in question, this does not indicate that he has mastered the necessary prerequisites to succeed in math in the sixth-grade standard curriculum.

- Unfortunately, grade equivalents tend to become standards of performance. For example, lawmakers might decide that all students entering the sixth grade should achieve grade equivalents of 6.0 or better on a standardized reading test. Because the mean raw score at each grade level is designated the grade equivalent, 50% of the standardization sample scored below the grade equivalent. As a result, it would be expected that a large number of students with average reading skills would enter the sixth grade with grade equivalents below 6.0. It is a law of mathematics that not everyone can score above the average.

As the result of these and other limitations, we recommend that using grade equivalents should be avoided.

Age equivalents are another derived score format that indicates the age, typically in years and months, at which a raw score is the mean or median. Age equivalents have the same limitations as grade equivalents, and should also be avoided. Many test publishers report grade and age equivalents and occasionally a testing expert will favor them (at least at the lower grade levels). Nevertheless, grade and age equivalents are subject to misinterpretation and should be avoided when possible. If it is required to use grade and age equivalents, then standard scores and percentile ranks should also be reported and emphasized when explaining test results.

Criterion-Referenced Score Interpretations

With criterion-referenced score interpretations, the examinee's performance is not compared to that of other people; instead it is compared to a specified level of performance (i.e., a criterion). With criterion-referenced interpretations, the emphasis is on what an examinee knows or what he or she can do and not his or her standing relative to other test takers. Possibly the most common example of a criterion-referenced score is the percentage of correct responses on a classroom examination. If it is reported that a student correctly answered 85% of the items on a classroom test, then this is a criterion-referenced interpretation. Notice the student's performance is not being compared to that of other examinees; it is being compared to a standard or criterion, in this case a perfect performance on the test.

In addition to percent correct, another type of criterion-referenced interpretation is referred to as *mastery testing*. Mastery testing involves determining whether the examinee has achieved a specific level of mastery of the knowledge or skills domain and is usually reported in an all-or-none score such as a pass/fail designation (AERA et al., 1999). Most of us have had experience with mastery testing in obtaining a driver's license. The written exam required to obtain a driver's license is designed to determine whether the applicant has acquired the basic knowledge necessary to operate a motor vehicle successfully and safely (e.g., state motoring laws and standards). A *cut score* had been previously established, and all scores equal to or above this score are reported as "pass" whereas scores below it are reported as "fail."

Another common criterion-referenced interpretative approach is referred to as *standards-based interpretations*. Whereas mastery testing typically results in an all-or-none interpretation (i.e., the student either passes or fails), standards-based interpretations usually involve three to five performance categories. For example, the results of an achievement test might be reported as basic, proficient, or advanced. An old variant of this approach is the assignment of letter grades to reflect performance on classroom achievement tests. For example, many teachers assign letter grades based on the percentage of items correct on a test, which is another type of criterion-referenced interpretation. For example, an A might be assigned for percentage correct scores between 90 and 100%, a B for scores between 80 and 89%, a C for scores between 70 and 79%, a D for scores between 60 and 69%, and an F for scores below 60%. Note that with this system a student with a score of 95% receives an A regardless of how other students scored. If all of the students in the class correctly answered 90% or more of the items correctly, they would all receive an A on the test.

As noted previously, with norm-referenced interpretations the most important consideration is the relevance of the group with which the examinee's performance is compared. However, with criterion-referenced interpretations, there is no comparison group and the most important consideration is how clearly the knowledge or skill domain being assessed is specified or defined (e.g., Popham, 2000). For criterion-referenced interpretations to provide useful information about what an examinee knows or what skills he or she possesses, it is important that the knowledge or skill domain assessed by the test be clearly defined. To facilitate this it is common for tests specifically designed to produce criterion-referenced interpretations to assess more limited or narrowly focused content domains than those designed to produce norm-referenced interpretations.

Scores Based on Item Response Theory

To this point we have focused on norm-referenced and criterion-referenced score interpretations. In recent years, theoretical and technical advances have ushered in new types of scores that are based on item response theory. Item response theory is a modern test theory that has had a great impact on test development. A formal introduction of item response theory is beyond the scope of this chapter, so we will simply define item response theory as a theory or model of mental measurement that holds that the responses to test items are accounted for by latent traits (see Reynolds & Livingston, 2012, for a general introduction). In item response theory it is assumed that each examinee possesses a certain amount of any given latent trait and the goal is to estimate the examinee's ability level on the latent trait. The specific ability level of an examinee is defined as the level on a scale where the examinee can get half of the items correct. In item response theory terminology, an examinee's ability level is designated by the Greek letter theta (θ).

The scores assigned to reflect an individual's ability level in item response theory models are similar to the raw scores on tests developed using traditional models (i.e., classical test theory). For example, these scores can be transformed into either norm or criterion-referenced scores. However, these scores have a distinct advantage in that, unlike traditional raw scores, they are equal interval level scores (i.e., having equal intervals between values) and have stable standard deviations across age groups. These item response theory scores go by different names, including W-scores, growth scores, and change sensitive scores. Some refer to item response theory scores generically as Rasch or Rasch-type scores after the originator of the mathematical models. W-scores are used on the Woodcock-Johnson III (Woodcock, McGrew, & Mather, 2001) and are set so a score of 500 reflects cognitive performance at the beginning fifth-grade ability level. W-scores have proven to be particularly useful in measuring changes in cognitive abilities. For example, W-scores can help measure gains in achievement due to learning or declines in cognitive abilities due to dementia. In terms of measuring gains, if over time an examinee's W-score increases by 10 units (e.g., from 500 to 510), he or she can now complete tasks with 75% probability of success that he or she originally could only complete with a 50% probability of success. Conversely, if an examinee's W-score decreases by 10 units (e.g., 500 to 490), he or she can now complete tasks with only 25% probability of success that he or she originally could complete with 50% probability of success (Woodcock, 1978, 1999).

What Scores Should Be Used

Just as different reference groups or standardization samples provide different kinds of information and answers different questions, different types of test scores answer different questions. In order to answer the question of which scores to use, we need to consider what information different test scores provide.

- *Raw scores:* The number of points accumulated by a person on a measure and that person's relative rank among test takers (assuming everyone's raw score is known). Raw scores typically provide only ordinal scale measurement.
- *Traditional norm-referenced standard scores:* Address the general question of how does this person's performance compare to the performance of some specified reference group and typically reflect interval scale measurement.

- *Criterion-referenced scores*: Indicate to what extent a person's performance has or has not approached a desired level of proficiency.
- *Rasch (or item response theory) based scores:* Equal interval scales that reflect position on some underlying or latent trait. These scores are particularly useful in evaluating the degree of change in scores over time and in comparing scores across tests of a common latent trait.

Thus, each type of score provides a different type of information. Which score should be used is dependent upon the type of information desired.

RELIABILITY AND MEASUREMENT ERROR

In the context of measurement, reliability refers to the stability, accuracy, or consistency of scores produced by a measurement. As has been emphasized, tests and other assessments are useful to the degree that they provide information that helps school psychologists make better professional decisions. However, the reliability of that information is of paramount importance: Reliability is a precursor to validity. For school psychologists to make good decisions, reliable information is needed. Estimating the reliability of assessment results gives an indication of how much confidence can be place in them. If there is highly reliable and valid information (validity will be discussed in the next section), it is likely that information can be used to make better decisions. If the results are unreliable, they are of little value. This has even been recognized by the U.S. Supreme Court in a decision popularly known simply as the *Daubert* decision (Daubert v. Merrell, 509 U.S. 579, 113 S. Ct. 2786, 125 L. Ed. 2d 469, 1993), in which the Court ruled that if an expert's methods of gathering data or otherwise arriving at an opinion were not reliable, then those methods were "no evidence" and could not be presented in the federal court system. Most but not all states have adopted similar rules.

Measurement Error

Errors of measurement undermine the reliability of measurement and therefore reduce the utility of the measurement. Measurement error reduces the usefulness of measurement, the ability to generalize test results, and the confidence in those results (AERA et al., 1999). Measurement error is not unique to psychological and educational tests. In fact, Nunnally and Bernstein (1994) point out that measurement in other scientific disciplines has as much, if not more, error than that in psychology and education. They give the example of physiological blood pressure measurement, which is considerably less reliable than many psychological and educational tests. Even in situations in which measurement is believed to be precise, some error is present. For example, if there were a dozen people and a measuring tape graduated in millimeters, and if each person were asked to measure independently the length of a 50-foot strip of land, it is unlikely all of them would report the same answer to the nearest millimeter. In the physical sciences the introduction of more technologically sophisticated measurement devices has reduced, but not eliminated, measurement error.

To have an adequate understanding of measurement error it is helpful to be familiar with classical test theory (also referred to as true score theory), which provides the foundation for most contemporary approaches to estimating reliability. According to classical test theory, every obtained or observed score on a test is composed of two components: the *true score* (i.e., the score that would be obtained if there were no errors of measurement), and the *error score*. Therefore an obtained score = true score + error score. This can be represented in a very simple equation:

$$X_i = T + E$$

Here X_i is used to represent the observed score of an individual. In other words, X_i is the score the student received on a test. T represents the student's true skills, knowledge, feelings, attitudes, or whatever the test measures, assuming the absence of measurement error. E represents measurement error. An individual has only one true score, but he or she may receive different obtained scores on different administrations of a test due to different amounts of measurement error.

Consider these examples. On a 100 item multiple-choice test Shelly actually knows the answer to 80 items (i.e., her true score) and makes lucky guesses on 3 and gets them correct (i.e., errors of measurement). Her observed score is 83. Here $X_i = 83$, $T = 80$, and $E = 3$ ($83 = 80 + 3$). In this situation, measurement error resulted in an increase in her observed score. This is not always the case, and measurement errors can also reduce an individual's observed score. For example, if Shelly knew the answer to 80 items (i.e., true score) but incorrectly marked the answer sheet on 3 items, her observed scores would now be 77. Here $X_i = 73$, $T = 80$, and $E = -3$ ($77 = 80 - 3$).

In actual practice there are a multitude of factors that can introduce error into a test score, some raising the score and some lowering the score. These errors of measurement have a cumulative or additive effect. For example, if Shelly knew the answer to 80 items, correctly guessed the answer on 4, and incorrectly marked the answer sheet on 2 items, her observed scores would be 82. The error score component is now 2 (i.e., $4 - 2$). Here $X_i = 82$, $T = 80$, and $E = 2$ (i.e., $82 = 80 + 2$).

This has been only a cursory introduction to classical test theory and a comprehensive discussion of this theory is beyond the scope of this chapter. Readers interested in developing a better understanding of classical test theory and measurement error should review a quality psychometric text that provides a more thorough presentation of classical test theory (e.g., for a user-friendly introduction, see Reynolds & Livingston, 2012).

At this point it is most important to be familiar with the concept of measurement error and be aware that there are multiple sources of measurement error. The two major sources of measurement error are *content sampling errors* and *time sampling errors*.

Content Sampling Error

Content sampling errors are the result of less-than-perfect sampling of the content domain. In the context of content sampling, tests rarely, if ever, could include every possible question or evaluate every possible behavior that is relevant to the construct being measured.

For example, consider a teacher who administers a math test designed to assess students' skill in adding three-digit numbers with a 30-item test. There are literally hundreds of three-digit addition problems and it would be impractical (and unnecessary) for the teacher to develop and administer a test that includes all possible items. Instead, a universe or domain of test items is defined based on the content of the material to be covered, and from this domain a sample of test questions is taken. In this example, the teacher decided to select 30 items to measure students' ability. These 30 items are simply a sample of the item domain and, as with any sampling procedure, may or may not be representative of the domain from which the items are drawn. The error that results from differences between the sample of items (i.e., the test) and the domain of items (i.e., all the possible items) is referred to as content sampling error.

If the items on a test are a good sample of the domain, then the amount of measurement error due to content sampling will be relatively small. If the items on a test are a poor sample of the domain, then the amount of measurement error due to content sampling will be relatively large.

Content sampling error is typically considered the largest source of error in test scores and therefore is the source that concerns us most. Fortunately, content sampling error is also the easiest and most accurately estimated source of measurement error. We will discuss a variety of methods for estimating measurement errors due to content sampling later in this section.

Time Sampling Error

Measurement error can also be introduced by the choice of a particular time to administer the test. Going back to the example of the teacher giving a 30-item math test, if a student did not have breakfast and the math test was just before lunch, the student might be hungry and distracted and not perform as well as if he or she took the test after lunch. If during an afternoon testing session a neighboring class was being disruptive, then the class might have performed better in the morning when the neighboring class was relatively quiet. These are just two examples of situations in which random changes in test takers (e.g., hunger) or the testing environment (e.g., distractions) may have an impact on performance on the test.

Obviously there are a multitude of environmental and personal factors that can have an impact on test performance. This type of measurement error is referred to as time sampling error and reflects random fluctuations in performance from one situation or time to another and limits the ability to generalize test results across different situations (some assessment experts refer to this type of error as temporal instability). Testing experts have developed methods of estimating error due to time sampling.

Other Sources of Error

Although errors due to content sampling and time sampling typically account for the largest proportion of random error in testing, administrative and scoring errors that do not affect all test takers equally will also contribute to the random error observed in scores. Clerical errors committed while adding up a student's score or an administrative error on an individually administered test are common examples. When the scoring of a test relies heavily on the subjective judgment of the person grading the test it is important to consider differences in graders, usually referred to as *interrater* or *interscorer differences*. That is, would the test taker receive the same score if different individuals graded the test? These are just a few examples of sources of error that do not fit neatly into the broad categories of content or time sampling errors.

Types of Reliability Coefficients

Psychometricians have developed methods of estimating errors due to these and other sources. All of these methods result in reliability coefficients that are generically designated with r_{xx}. Reliability coefficients are interpreted in terms of the proportion of observed variance attributable to true variance as opposed to error variance. For example, a reliability coefficient of .90 indicates that 90% of the observed variance in a set of scores reflects true score variance (i.e., variance due to stable differences between examinees) and 10% reflects error variance (i.e., variance due to random errors of measurement). Reliability coefficients can be classified into three broad categories (AERA et al., 1999). These include (a) coefficients derived from the administration of the same test on different occasions (i.e., test–retest reliability), (b) coefficients based on the administration of parallel forms of a test (i.e., alternate-form reliability), and (c) coefficients derived from a single administration of a test (internal consistency coefficients). A fourth type, interrater reliability, is indicated when scoring involves a significant degree of subjective judgment. We will now consider each of these methods of estimating reliability.

Test–Retest Reliability

Probably the most straightforward way to estimate the reliability of a test score is to administer the same test to the same group of individuals on two different occasions. With this approach, the reliability coefficient is obtained by simply calculating the correlation between the scores on the two administrations. For example, in our scenario we used previously, the teacher could administer the 30-item math test a week after the initial administration and then correlate the scores obtained on the two administrations. This estimate of reliability is referred to as *test–retest reliability* and is primarily sensitive to measurement error due to time sampling. It is an index of the stability of test scores over time, and some authors refer to coefficients obtained with this approach as stability coefficients.

The test–retest approach does have some limitations, the most prominent being the influence of carryover effects from the first to second testing. Practice and memory effects may result in different amounts of improvement in retest scores for different test takers. These carryover effects prevent the two administrations from being independent and as a result the reliability coefficients may be artificially inflated. Thus, only tests that are not significantly influenced by carryover effects are suitable for this method of estimating reliability.

Research suggests that nonverbal and novel tests tend to be most susceptible to carryover effects (e. g., Reynolds & Kamphaus, 2003). This method of reliability determination also is unsuitable for use when measuring variables (e.g., state anxiety) that are expected to change over the interval between the two measurements.

Alternate Form Reliability

Another approach to estimating reliability involves the development of two equivalent or parallel forms of the test. The development of these alternate forms requires a detailed test plan and considerable effort since the tests must be truly parallel in terms of content, difficulty, and other salient measurement characteristics. The two forms of the test are then administered to the same group of individuals and the correlation is calculated between the scores on the two assessments. In our example of the 30-item math test, the teacher could develop a parallel test containing 30 different problems involving the addition of triple digits (i.e., from the same item domain).

Two fairly common procedures are used to establish *alternate form reliability*. One is based on simultaneous administrations and is obtained when the two forms of the test are administered on the same occasion (i.e., back to back). The other is obtained when the two forms of the test are administered on two different occasions. Alternate form reliability based on simultaneous administration is primarily sensitive to measurement error related to content sampling. Alternate form reliability with delayed administration is sensitive to measurement error due to both content sampling and time sampling.

Alternate form reliability has the advantage of reducing the carryover effects that are a prominent concern with test–retest reliability. However, although practice and memory effects may be reduced using the alternate form approach, typically they are often not fully eliminated. Simply exposing examinees to the common format required for parallel tests often results in some carryover effects even if the content of the two tests is different. For example, an examinee given a test measuring verbal memory may develop strategies during the administration of the first form that alter his or her approach to the second form, even if the specific content of the items is different.

Another limitation of the alternate form approach to estimating reliability is that relatively few tests, standardized or teacher made, have alternate forms. At times it is desirable to have more than one form of a test, and when multiple forms exist, alternate form reliability is an important consideration.

Internal Consistency Reliability

Internal consistency reliability estimates primarily reflect errors due to content sampling. These estimates are based on the relationship between items within a test and are derived from a single administration of the test.

Split-half reliability.

Estimating split-half reliability involves administering a test and then dividing the test into two equivalent halves that are scored independently. The results on half the test are then correlated with results on the other half. While there are many ways a test can be divided in half, the most common approach is to use an odd–even split. Here, all odd-numbered items go into one half and all even-numbered items go into the other half. A correlation is then calculated between scores on the odd-numbered and even-numbered items.

Before this correlation coefficient can be used as an estimate of reliability, there is one more task to perform. Since two halves of the test are actually being correlated, the reliability coefficient does not take into account the reliability of the test scores when the two halves are combined. To address this, a correction formula is used. This is commonly referred to as the Spearman-Brown formula and it provides an estimate of the reliability of the full or whole test.

An advantage of the split-half approach to reliability is that it can be calculated from a single administration of a test. However, because only one testing session is involved, this approach primarily reflects errors due to content sampling.

Coefficient alpha and Kuder-Richardson reliability.

Other approaches to estimating reliability from a single administration of a test are based on formulas developed by Kuder and Richardson (1937) and Cronbach (1951). Instead of comparing responses on two halves of the test as in split-half reliability, this approach examines the consistency of responding to all the individual items on the test. Reliability estimates produced with these formulas can be thought of as the average of all possible split-half coefficients and are properly corrected for the length of the whole test. Like split-half reliability, these estimates are primarily sensitive to measurement error introduced by content sampling. Additionally, they are also sensitive to the heterogeneity of the test content; that is, the degree to which the test items measure related characteristics. For example, our 30-item math test involving adding three-digit numbers would probably be more homogeneous than a test designed to measure both multiplication and division. An even more heterogeneous test would be one

Table 22.2. Types of Reliability Estimates

Reliability Estimate	Major Source of Measurement Error	Number of Forms	Number of Sessions	Testing Procedures
Test–retest	Time sampling	One form	Two sessions	Administer the same test to the same group at two different sessions
Alternate forms Simultaneous administration	Content sampling	Two forms	One session	Administer two forms of the test to the same group in the same session
Delayed administration	Content and time sampling	Two forms	Two sessions	Administer two forms of the test to the same group at two different sessions
Split-half	Content sampling	One form	One session	Administer the test to a group one time; split the test into two equivalent halves
Coefficient alpha or KR-20	Content sampling	One form	One session	Administer the test to a group one time; apply appropriate procedures
Interrater	Error due to raters/scorers	One form	One session	Administer the test to a group one time; two or more raters score the test independently

Note. KR-20 = Kuder-Richardson formula 20.

that involves multiplication and reading comprehension, two fairly dissimilar content domains.

While Kuder and Richardson's formulas and coefficient alpha both reflect item heterogeneity and errors due to content sampling, there is a significant difference in terms of their application. Kuder and Richardson (1937) presented numerous formulas for estimating reliability. The most commonly used formula is known as the Kuder-Richardson formula 20. This formula is applicable when test items are scored dichotomously; that is, simply right or wrong, scored 0 or 1. Coefficient alpha (Cronbach, 1951) is a more general form of the Kuder-Richardson formula that also deals with test items that produce scores with multiple values (e.g., 0, 1, or 2). Because coefficient alpha is more broadly applicable, it has become the preferred statistic for estimating internal consistency.

Interrater Reliability

If the scoring of a test relies on subjective judgment, it is important to evaluate the degree of agreement between different individuals scoring the test. This is referred to as interscorer or interrater reliability. To estimate interrater reliability the test is administered one time and two individuals independently score each test. A correlation is then calculated between the scores obtained by the two scorers. This estimate of reliability primarily reflects differences due to the individuals scoring the test and largely ignores error due to content or time sampling. In addition to the correlational approach, interrater agreement can also be evaluated by calculating the percentage of times that two individuals assign the same scores to the performances of students. This approach is typically referred to as *interrater agreement* or *percent agreement*. Many authors prefer Cohen's kappa over the standard percent of agreement when analyzing categorical data because kappa is a more robust measure of agreement and because it takes into consideration the degree of agreement expected by chance (Hays, 1994).

Evaluating Reliability Coefficients

It is reasonable to ask how large do reliability coefficients need to be for the scores to be useful. There is not a single, simple answer. What constitutes acceptable reliability depends on numerous factors, including the construct being measured, the amount of time available for testing, the way the scores will be used, and the method of estimating reliability. Nevertheless, we will offer some general guidelines.

- If test results are being used to make important decisions that will significantly have an impact on individuals, it is reasonable to expect reliability coefficients of 0.90 or even 0.95. This standard is regularly obtained with contemporary individually administered tests of intelligence.

- Reliability estimates of 0.80 or more are considered acceptable in many testing situations and are commonly reported for group and individually administered achievement and personality tests.

- For teacher-made classroom tests and tests used for screening, reliability estimates of at least 0.70 for scores are generally expected. For example, reliability coefficients in the 0.70s might be acceptable when more thorough assessment procedures are available to address concerns about individual cases (e.g., when a school psychologist is screening a large number of individuals in a school sample).

Some authors suggest that reliability coefficients as low as 0.60 are acceptable in limited situations (e.g., group research, projective measures), but we are reluctant to endorse the use of any assessment that produces scores with reliability estimates below 0.70. A reliability coefficient of 0.70 indicates that 30% of the observed variance may be due to random error. There cannot be much confidence in assessment results when more than 30% of the observed variance is due to random measurement error.

Reliability: Concluding Comments

Each of these methods of estimating reliability will produce different numbers because they are looking at different sources of error. They are not independent, however. Some have tried to add together the error components detected by each procedure and then argue that most test scores are far less reliable than one might think from looking at a single method of estimating reliability. However, the error components cannot simply be added together. Take, for example, this simple limitation on reliability in a retest format: The limit of the test–retest correlation between two administrations of a test is equal to the square root of the internal consistency reliability coefficient, which is itself lowered by the presence of any scoring errors across examiners. It is easily proven then that errors of measurement under each condition of reliability are not independent and cannot simply be added together. In general, internal consistency reliability coefficients then are considered the best estimates of the accuracy of a test score.

This has been a very brief introduction to reliability and there are many topics that have not been addressed. For example, in this section we have focused on the different types of reliability coefficients available and their interpretation. While reliability coefficients are useful when comparing the reliability of different tests, the *standard error of measurement* is more useful when interpreting scores. The standard error of measurement is an index of the amount of error in test scores and is used in calculating confidence intervals within which it is expected an examinee's true score to fall. An advantage of the standard error of measurement and the use of confidence intervals is that both serve to remind us that measurement error is present in all scores and that caution should be used when interpreting scores.

Additionally, in this chapter we focused on classical test theory due to its prominent role in the current conceptualization of reliability. However, there are two newer test theories that were developed in the latter part of the 20th century. These are generalizability theory and item response theory. It is recommend that readers research these models so they understand how both complement and extend classical test theory in terms of reliability information (for a gentle introduction, see Reynolds & Livingston, 2012).

VALIDITY

The Standards for Educational and Psychological Testing (AERA et al., 1999) defined validity as "... the degree to which evidence and theory support the interpretations of test scores entailed by proposed uses of the tests" (p. 9). In essence, the validity question is: Are the intended interpretations of test scores appropriate and accurate? Validity is illustrated in the following series of questions:

- If test scores are interpreted as reflecting intelligence, then do the scores actually reflect intellectual ability?
- If test scores are interpreted as reflecting anxiety, then do the scores actually reflect a client's level of anxiety?
- If test scores are intended to predict success in college, then can the scores accurately predict who will succeed in college?

Naturally, the validity of the interpretations of test scores is directly tied to the usefulness of the interpretations. Valid interpretations help school psychologists make better decisions. Invalid interpretations do not.

Numerous factors can limit the validity of score interpretations. The two major internal threats to validity are construct underrepresentation (i.e., the test is not a comprehensive measure of the construct it is supposed to measure) and construct-irrelevant variance (i.e., the test measures abilities, content, or skills unrelated to the construct). There is also a close relationship between validity and reliability. For a test score to be interpreted validly it must be reliable. Yet test score reliability does not ensure validity of interpretations of the score. Put another way, reliability is a necessary but insufficient condition for validity.

As a psychometric concept, validity has evolved and changed. Until the 1970s validity was generally divided into three distinct types: content validity, criterion-related validity, and construct validity. This terminology was widely accepted and is still referred to as the traditional nomenclature. However, in the 1970s and 1980s, measurement professionals started conceptualizing validity as a unitary construct. That is, although there are different ways of collecting validity evidence, there are no distinct types of validity. To get away from the perception of distinct types of validity, the contemporary conceptualization of validity recognizes different types of validity evidence, but not different types of validity. The Standards (AERA et al., 1999) identify the following five categories of evidence that are related to the validity of test score interpretations: evidence based on test content, evidence based on relations to other variables, evidence based on internal structure, evidence based on response processes, and evidence based on consequences of testing.

Evidence Based on Test Content

The Standards (AERA et al., 1999) note that important validity evidence can be gained by examining the relationship between the content of the test and the construct or domain the test is designed to measure. In this context, test content includes the "themes, wording, and format of the items, tasks, or questions on a test, as well as the guidelines ... regarding administration and scoring" (p. 11). Popham (2000) succinctly frames it as: "Does the test cover the content it's supposed to cover?" (p. 96).

Collecting content-based validity evidence is often based on the evaluation of expert judges about the correspondence between the test's content and the construct it is designed to measure. The key issues addressed by these expert judges are whether the test items assess relevant content (i.e., item relevance) and the degree to which the construct is assessed in a comprehensive manner (i.e., content coverage). As a result, the collection of content-based validity evidence is usually qualitative in nature. While test developers might rely extensively on these traditional qualitative approaches, they often take steps to report their results in a more quantitative manner. For example, they might report the number and qualifications of the experts, the number of chances the experts had to review and comment on the assessment, and the experts' degree of agreement on content-related issues.

Before leaving our discussion of content-based validity evidence, the distinction between content-based evidence and face validity must be highlighted. Face validity is not technically a form of validity, but refers to a test "appearing" to measure what it is interpreted to measure. That is, does the test score interpretation appear valid to untrained individuals who take, administer, or examine the test. Face validity really has nothing to do with what a test actually measures, just what it appears to measure. For example, does a test of intelligence look like an intelligence test to untrained individuals. Face validity involves only the superficial appearance of a test to lay individuals while content-based evidence of validity is acquired through a systematic and technical analysis of the test content. A test can appear face valid to the general public, but not hold up under the systematic scrutiny involved in a technical analysis of the test content. This does not mean that face validity is an undesirable or even irrelevant characteristic. A test that has good face validity is likely to be better received by both examinees and the general public. If a test has poor face validity, the general public is likely to see it as less meaningful or useful.

Evidence Based on Relations to Other Variables

Validity evidence can also be garnered by examining the relationship of test scores to other variables (AERA et al., 1999). In describing this type of validity evidence, the Standards recognize several related but distinct applications. One involves the examination of test-criterion evidence, one on convergent and discriminant evidence, and one based on group differences. Below are brief descriptions of these applications.

Test-Criterion Evidence

Many tests are designed to predict performance on some variable that is typically referred to as a criterion. The criterion can be academic performance as reflected by the grade point average, job performance as measured by a supervisor's ratings, or anything else that is of importance to the test user. There are two different types of validity studies used to collect test-criterion evidence: predictive studies and concurrent studies. In a predictive study, the test is administered, there is an intervening time interval, and then the criterion is measured. In a concurrent study, the test is administered and the criterion is measured at about the same time.

If prediction of future performance or status is important, then predictive studies maintain the temporal relationship and other potentially important characteristics of the real-life situation and are preferable. However, when the goal of the test is to measure the current level of performance or status of the examinee, concurrent studies are appropriate (AERA et al., 1999). For example, in selecting students at high risk of developing a psychological disorder in the future (e.g., for participation in a prevention program), a predictive study would be appropriate. The assessment question in this context is how well or accurately the test score predicts who will develop the disorder at some future time.

However, if a test is to provide an accurate assessment of the individual's current condition, then concurrent studies are most applicable. For example, a brief screening test might be evaluated to determine whether it can serve as an adequate substitute for a more extensive psychological assessment process.

Validity evidence from predictive and concurrent studies is often reported in terms of a validity coefficient. But how large should validity coefficients be? There is no simple answer, but validity coefficients should be sufficient to suggest that test results will help in predicting how examinees will perform (or do perform) on the criterion measure. If a test provides information that helps predict criterion performance better than any other existing predictor, then the test may be useful even if its validity coefficients are relatively small. As a result, testing experts avoid specifying a minimum coefficient size that is acceptable. In the prediction of classroom achievement, tests should have coefficients in the mid to high .50s and above before they can be considered useful. However, much smaller coefficients can have an enormous impact on the ability to improve certain outcomes.

For example, Hunter, Schmidt, and Rauschenberger (1984) have demonstrated the far-reaching implications on productivity of workers and subsequently the gross domestic product of the United States (reaching into the hundreds of billions of dollars) if employers used employment tests to place workers in the best jobs, even if the employment tests had validity coefficients only in the .20s–.30s. This is another reason the Standards recommend that statistical significance of correlations between a test score and some criterion be deemphasized or even disregarded in favor of looking at the actual magnitude of the correlation.

Convergent and Discriminant Evidence

Convergent evidence of validity is obtained when a test is correlated with existing tests that measure the same or similar constructs. For example, if we are developing a new intelligence test we might elect to correlate scores on our new test with scores on the Wechsler Intelligence Scale for Children-Fourth Edition (WISC-IV; Wechsler, 2003). Because the WISC-IV is a respected test of intelligence with considerable validity evidence, a strong correlation between the WISC-IV and our new intelligence test could provide evidence that our test is actually measuring the construct of intelligence. Discriminant evidence of validity is obtained when a test is correlated with existing tests that measure dissimilar constructs. For example, if we were validating a test designed to measure anxiety, we might correlate the anxiety scores with a measure of sensation seeking. Because anxious individuals do not typically engage in high levels of sensation-seeking behaviors, a negative correlation between the measures would be expected. If the analyses produce the expected negative correlations, this would support our hypothesis.

Contrasted Group Studies

Validity evidence can also be garnered by examining different groups, which are expected, based on theory, to differ on the construct the test is designed to measure. This is referred to as a contrasted group study. For example, if we are attempting to validate a new measure of depression, we might form two groups: individuals with severe depression and normal control participants. In this type of study, the diagnoses or group assignment would have been made using assessment procedures that do not involve the test under consideration. Each group would then be administered the new test, and its validity as a measure of depression would be supported if the predefined groups differed in performance in the predicted manner.

While the preceding example is rather simplistic, it illustrates a general approach that has numerous applications. For example, many constructs in psychology and education have a developmental component.

That is, younger participants are expected to perform differently than older participants. Tests designed to measure these constructs can be examined to determine if they demonstrate the expected developmental changes by looking at the performance of groups reflecting different ages and/or education.

Evidence Based on Internal Structure

By examining the internal structure of a test (or battery of tests) it can be determined whether the relationships among test items (or, in the case of test batteries, component tests) are consistent with the construct the test is designed to measure (AERA et al., 1999). For example, one test might be designed to measure a construct that is hypothesized to involve a single dimension, whereas another test might measure a construct thought to involve multiple dimensions. By examining the internal structure of the test, it can be determined whether its actual structure is consistent with the hypothesized structure of the construct it measures. Factor analysis is a fairly sophisticated statistical procedure used to determine the number of conceptually distinct factors or dimensions underlying a test or battery of tests.

Factor analysis is not the only approach researchers use to examine the internal structure of a test. Any technique that allows researchers to examine the relationships between test components can be used in this context. For example, if the items on a test are assumed to reflect a continuum from very easy to very difficult, empirical evidence of a pattern of increasing difficulty can be used as validity evidence. If a test is thought to measure a one-dimensional construct, a measure of item homogeneity might be useful (e.g., coefficient alpha). The essential feature of this type of validity evidence is that researchers empirically examine the internal structure of the test and compare it to the structure of the construct of interest.

Evidence Based on Response Processes

Validity evidence based on the response processes invoked by a test involves an analysis of the fit between the performance and actions the examinees engage in and the construct being assessed. While this type of validity evidence has not received as much attention as the approaches discussed to this point, it has considerable potential. For example, consider a test designed to measure mathematical reasoning ability. In this situation it would be important to investigate the examinees' response processes to verify that they are actually engaging in analysis and reasoning as opposed to applying rote mathematical calculations (AERA et al., 1999). There are numerous ways of collecting this type of validity evidence, including interviewing examinees about their response processes and strategies, recording behavioral indicators such as response times and eye movements, or even analyzing the types of errors committed (AERA et al., 1999; Messick, 1989).

Evidence Based on Consequences of Testing

In recent years, researchers have started examining the consequences of test use, both intended and unintended, as an aspect of validity. In many situations the use of tests is based largely on the assumption that their use will result in some specific benefit (AERA et al., 1999; also see McFall & Trent, 1999). For example, if a test is used to help select students for admission to a college program, it is assumed that the use of the test will result in better admissions decisions (e.g., greater student success and higher retention). This line of validity evidence simply asks if these benefits are being achieved. This type of validity evidence, sometimes referred to as consequential validity evidence, is most applicable to tests designed for selection and promotion.

Some authors have advocated a broader conception of validity, one that incorporates social issues and values. For example, Messick (1989) suggested that the conception of validity should be expanded so that it "... formally brings consideration of value implications and social consequences into the validity framework"

(p. 20). Other testing experts have criticized this position and the Standards (AERA et al., 1999) largely avoid this broader conceptualization of validity. The Standards distinguish between consequential evidence that is directly tied to the concept of validity and evidence that is related to social policy. This is an important but potentially difficult distinction to make at times.

Another component to this process is to consider the consequences of not using tests. Even though the consequences of testing may produce some adverse effects, these consequences must be contrasted with the positive and negative effects of alternatives to using psychological tests. For example, if more subjective approaches to decision making are employed, then the likelihood of cultural, ethnic, and gender biases in the decision-making process will likely increase (see Reynolds & Livingston, 2012, for more information on bias in testing).

Validity: Concluding Comments

The Standards (AERA et al., 1999) note that "[v]alidation can be viewed as developing a scientifically sound validity argument to support the intended interpretation of test scores and their relevance to the proposed use" (p. 9). The integration of multiple lines of research or types of evidence results in a more compelling validity argument. While we have emphasized a number of distinct approaches to collecting evidence to support the validity of score interpretations, validity evidence is actually broader then the strategies described in this chapter. The Standards (AERA et al., 1999) state:

Table 22.3. Sources of Validity Evidence

Source	Example	Major Applications
Evidence based on test content	Quantitative analysis of item relevance and content coverage	Achievement tests; tests used in the employee selection
Evidence based on relations to other variables	Test-criterion studies; convergent and discriminant evidence; contrasted groups studies	Wide variety of tests, but test-criterion evidence particularly important on tests used in selection (e.g., SAT, ACT)
Evidence based on internal structure	Factor analysis; analysis of test homogeneity	Wide variety of tests, but especially applicable with tests of constructs like intelligence or personality
Evidence based on response processes	Analysis of the processes engaged in by the examinee or examiner	Any test that requires test takers to engage in a cognitive or behavioral activity
Evidence based on consequences of testing structure	Analysis of the intended and unintended consequences of testing	Most applicable to tests designed for selection and promotion, but useful on a wide range of tests

Ultimately, the validity of an intended interpretation of test scores relies on all the evidence relevant to the technical quality of a testing system. This includes evidence of careful test construction; adequate score **reliability**; appropriate test administration and scoring; accurate score scaling; equating, and standard setting; and careful attention to fairness for all examinees. (p. 17)

In other words, when considering the validity of score interpretations, the evidence of the technical quality of the test should be considered in totality. Obviously, the five sources of validity evidence described in this chapter are central to building a validity argument, but other information should be carefully considered. Does the test produce reliable scores? Is the standardization sample representative and of sufficient size to serve as a proper reference group for the interpretations to be made? Is there adequate standardization of both administration and scoring? In sum, is the test a well-developed and technically sound instrument? The development of a validity argument is an ongoing process. It takes into consideration existing research and incorporates new scientific findings as they emerge.

While test developers are obligated to provide initial evidence of the validity of the score interpretations they are proposing, research from independent researchers after the release of the test is also important. A number of excellent professional journals (e.g., *Psychological Assessment, School Psychology Review*) routinely publish research articles addressing the psychometric properties of tests. Additionally, those using tests are expected to weigh the validity evidence and make their own judgments about the appropriateness of the interpretations they make of the test scores obtained in their own situations and settings. This places the school psychologists who use tests in the final and ultimately responsible role in the validation process.

BEST PRACTICES IN APPLYING PSYCHOMETRIC PRINCIPLES WHEN SELECTING AND USING ASSESSMENT INSTRUMENTS

While this is not actually a chapter on best practices, it seems appropriate to offer some guidelines for applying the principles presented in this chapter. To that end, here are 10 best practice guidelines for selecting and using assessments:

- When using assessments that produce norm-referenced scores, ensure that the reference data are representative, technically adequate, and best address the referral questions: When selecting tests that produce norm-referenced scores, it is important to ensure that the reference group or standardization sample is appropriate for the type of students to be tested and the questions needed to be answered. Different reference groups (standardization samples) provide different types of information.

- Use a score format that provides the information that best addresses the referral/clinical questions: Just as different standardization samples provide different information, different types of scores also provide different types of information. Carefully consider the questions needed to be answered and select the scores that provide information that will best address these questions.

- Select and use assessment instruments that have adequate reliability for the specific application: Tests and others assessments are useful to the degree that they provide information that helps school psychologists make better professional decisions. For a test to provide useful information, the test must produce information that is reliable. When selecting assessments, carefully evaluate the reliability of the available assessments and select those that produce scores with sufficient reliability for the specific application.

- Select and use assessment instruments that have been validated for the intended applications: Validity refers to the appropriateness or accuracy of the interpretations of test scores. Carefully evaluate the information supporting the validity of score interpretations and select the instruments with the most compelling validity arguments for the specific application (i.e., those that provide the most persuasive empirical validity evidence). When test scores are interpreted in multiple ways, the validity evidence for each interpretation needs to be considered and evaluated.

- School psychologists should only use instruments they are qualified through training and experience to use: An ethical principle that applies in all disciplines is to practice within an area of competence. In the context of assessment this requires school psychologists to only administer and interpret tests that they are trained to use. It is important to note that areas of competence are not static, and school psychologists should always be growing as professionals and expanding their area of competence. In other words, it is important to stay current with new developments in the field and pursue training that expands the assessment repertoire.

- Carefully follow standardized administration and scoring procedures: It is of paramount importance to adhere strictly to standardized procedures when administering and scoring tests and other assessments. This is necessary to maintain the reliability of test scores and the validity of score interpretations. Even if a specific test has been administered and scored hundreds of times it is important to keep the manual handy and avoid adlibbing.

- Be sensitive to the special needs of individuals with disabilities or diverse linguistic/cultural backgrounds: There are times when assessment accommodations are appropriate. Standard assessment procedures may not be appropriate for an examinee with a disability if the assessment requires him or her to use some ability (e.g., sensory, motor, language) that is affected by the disability but is irrelevant to the construct being measured. The Standards (AREA et al., 1999) note that the goal of accommodations is to provide the most valid and accurate measurement of the construct of interest for each examinee. Many contemporary tests publishers provide guidelines regarding what accommodations are appropriate for their tests, and when these are available they should be followed strictly.

- Do not let personal preferences and biases have an impact on the scoring and interpretations of assessments. As was noted earlier, people are not good at judging other people in an objective and unbiased manner, and most nontest procedures involve subjective judgment. One of the primary reasons to use tests is provide objective information, and every effort should be made to avoid allowing personal preferences and biases to influence the scoring and interpretation of assessment results.

- Do not base high-stake decisions on a single assessment: There are different approaches to measuring any given construct, and each approach has its own strengths and weaknesses. As a result, it follows that psychological assessments should incorporate information from multiple sources using multiple methods. Important decisions should never be based on the results of a single test or other assessment procedure.

- Practice intelligent testing: As noted, we are advocates of a model of assessment that incorporates psychometric sophistication, actuarial data, clinical insight, knowledge of psychological theory, and thoughtful reasoning grounded in the psychological and educational sciences of our discipline. Assessment should involve a synthesis of information that is obtained in a technically rigorous manner from multiple sources using multiple procedures. When conducting an assessment, school psychologists should assume the role of a detective and collect, evaluate, and synthesize information (idiopathic and actuarial), and integrate that information with a comprehensive understanding of human development, psychopathology, and individual differences. Assessment is not a rote process, but should nevertheless be directed by real data and actuarial findings, incorporate theory to broaden understanding of the test results and what they mean, and acknowledge that when performed correctly, psychological assessment is a challenging and sophisticated process.

SUMMARY

This chapter has been a very brief review of major psychometric concepts. However, it is important to note that, as stated in the title, this is simply a primer for school psychologists. School psychologists are often the most sophisticated users of assessment data in the public schools, and as such they should be well versed in psychometric theories and applications. There were many important concepts that were only alluded to in the chapter (e.g., item response theory, bias in testing), and we hope this brief primer might spark an interest and encourage readers to seek out additional analyses in psychometrics.

AUTHOR NOTE

Disclosure. Cecil R. Reynolds and Ronald B. Livingston have a financial interest in books they authored or coauthored referenced in this chapter.

REFERENCES

American Educational Research Association, American Psychological Association, & National Council on Measurement in Education. (1999). *Standards for educational and psychological testing*. Washington, DC: American Educational Research Association.

Cronbach, L. J. (1951). Coefficient alpha and the internal structure of tests. *Psychometrika, 16,* 297–334.

Dahlstrom, W. G. (1993). Tests: Small samples, large consequences. *American Psychologist, 48,* 393–399.

Hays, W. (1994). *Statistics* (5th ed.). New York, NY: Harcourt Brace.

Hunter, J. E., Schmidt, F. L., & Rauschenberger, L. (1984). Methodological, statistical, and ethical issues in the study of bias in psychological tests. In C. R. Reynolds & R. T. Brown (Eds.), *Perspectives on bias in mental testing* (pp. 41–100). New York, NY: Plenum Press.

Kaufman, A. S. (1994). *Intelligent testing with the WISC-III*. New York, NY: Wiley.

Kuder, G. F., & Richardson, M. W. (1937). The theory of the estimation of reliability. *Psychometrika, 2*, 151–160.

McFall, R. M., & Trent, T. T. (1999). Quantifying the information value of clinical assessment with signal detection theory. *Annual Review of Psychology, 50*, 215–241. doi:10.1146/annurev.psych.50.1.215

Messick, S. (1989). Validity. In R. L. Linn (Ed.), *Educational measurement* (3rd ed., pp. 13–103). Upper Saddle River, NJ: Merrill/Prentice Hall.

Nunnally, J., & Bernstein, I. (1994). *Psychometric theory* (3rd. ed.). New York, NY: McGraw-Hill.

Popham, W. J. (2000). *Modern educational measurement: Practical guidelines for educational leaders*. Boston, MA: Allyn & Bacon.

Reynolds, C. R., & Kamphaus, R. W. (2003). *Reynolds Intellectual Assessment Scales: Professional manual*. Luntz, FL: Psychological Assessment Resources.

Reynolds, C. R., & Kamphaus, R. W. (2004). *Behavior Assessment System for Children* (2nd ed.). Circle Pine, MN: American Guidance Service.

Reynolds, C. R., & Livingston, R. B. (2012). *Mastering modern psychological testing: Theory and methods*. Boston, MA: Pearson.

Stevens, S. S. (1946). On the theory of scales of measurement. *Science, 103*, 677–680.

Wechsler, D. W. (2003). *Wechsler Intelligence Scale for Children-Fourth edition: Technical and interpretive manual*. San Antonio, TX: The Psychological Corporation.

Woodcock, R. W. (1978). *Development and standardization of the Woodcock-Johnson Psycho-Educational Battery*. Rolling Meadows, IL: Riverside.

Woodcock, R. W. (1999). What can Rasch-based scores convey about a person's test performance? In S. E. Embretson & S. L. Hershberger (Eds.), *The new rules of measurement: What every psychologist and educator should know* (pp. 105–127). Mahwah, NJ: Erlbaum.

Woodcock, R. W., McGrew, K. S., & Mather, N. (2001). *Woodcock-Johnson III Tests of Achievement*. Itasca, IL: Riverside.

23 Best Practices in Developing Academic Local Norms

Lisa Habedank Stewart
Minnesota State University Moorhead

OVERVIEW

Local norms are a critical component of effective early intervention and data-based decision making. Informally, teachers are constantly comparing student skill levels, behavior, and response to instruction. Well-constructed local norms provide an intentionally focused, less biased, and more easily communicated representation of classroom, grade-level, school, and district comparisons. School psychologists bring the measurement and consultation skills needed to ensure that local norms are well constructed and interpreted correctly. The National Association of School Psychologists (NASP) *Model for Comprehensive and Integrated School Psychological Services* (NASP, 2010) and competencies in the domain of Research and Program Evaluation make school psychologists uniquely prepared to take on a leadership role in local norm development. This chapter will provide the background and specific information on what, when, and how to create local norms and examples of how to use academic local norms in data-based problem solving.

Schools using a problem-solving multitiered system of supports framework can use local norms at the student and systems levels to make better decisions about students, curriculum, instruction, and resource allocation. Knowing a fourth grader, Sara, reads 89 words correctly per minute aloud from grade-level text is informative, but knowing that Sara's classmates read 126 words correctly per minute on average and that Sara is at the 8th percentile compared to grade-level norms provides even more information for problem solving. Local norms help determine the severity and uniqueness of Sara's reading problems and can be used to develop goals and allocate resources efficiently.

If norms are collected at different times during the school year (e.g., three times per year) and across grade levels, then local norms also provide a basis for determining, at a systems level, how students are progressing over time. This type of normative data is relevant to decisions about the effectiveness of the current curriculum, instructional routines, and schedules. Furthermore, local norms allow schools to look at how certain groups of students are performing compared to others (e.g., how the skill level and rate of progress of English language learners compares to students whose first language is English, or how Sara's reading level compares to other students in intensive Tier 3 reading interventions).

Although it is possible to collect local norms on just about any test or rating scale, local norm development became commonplace when schools started developing curriculum-based measurement (CBM) norms, particularly in the area of reading (Deno, 2003). CBM local norms were used to identify whether a student had an academic problem and how big that problem was. Initially, local norms were collected every few years or when there was a population or curriculum change. Over time, schools began collecting norms more frequently as they began using local norms collected on all students as screening tools to identify students in need of additional instruction. This rise in local norming was influenced by the development of school-wide data-based problem-solving models and laws such as the No Child Left Behind legislation and the 2004 reauthorization of the Individuals with Disabilities Education Act. These innovative practices and laws focused on prevention, earlier identification and remediation of academic difficulties, research-based interventions, and accountability.

Developments in testing and technology also have made local norms easier to develop and use. Reports showing system-wide trends are now readily available through online data management services or data warehouses. Computer adaptive tests are starting to allow for more detailed analysis of local norm data (Shapiro, 2012; Shapiro, Christ, & Alonzo, 2013). The use of local norms has also evolved as schools have learned how to interpret and use local norm data to make individual and system-wide decisions. For example, local norms play an important role in making special education eligibility decisions using a response-to-intervention (RTI) framework (Burns & Gibbons, 2012; Koehler-Hak & Snyder, 2012).

The focus of this chapter is on academic local norms, that is, normative data collected on specific academic skills and tasks. The nuts and bolts of the development of academic local norms will be covered, as well as the use of academic local norms at both the individual and systems levels. The level of local norms discussed in this chapter will typically be aimed at norms collected at the school building level. These norms could then be disaggregated to look at a particular grade or even classroom in the school or combined with other school norms to create district or cooperative level norms.

BASIC CONSIDERATIONS

School psychologists often provide leadership in the development of academic local norms. Some basic considerations for school psychologists developing local norms include the specific measurement knowledge most relevant for developing local norms and the utilization of effective consultation skills, particularly in the areas of academic and system or program evaluation. It is also important for school psychologists to be clear about the terminology used to talk about local norming and to develop effective ways to explain those terms to others.

Measurement Knowledge

Background knowledge in selecting the correct tests to use for local norming requires an understanding of the technical properties and intended uses of the tests. It would be inappropriate for a school to develop local norms using teacher-made common core assessments, for example, unless there were some way to show those tests were reliable and valid. School psychologists understand that the validity of the test involves more than just face validity or content validity. For use in local

norms, a test needs to have treatment validity for the types of decisions that will be made with the data. If the local norm data will be used for screening purposes, as is typically the case, an understanding of test specificity and sensitivity is important (VanDerHeyden, 2011). Likewise, school psychologists can explain why a test may be a good fit for screening, but may not be the best tool to use for individual progress monitoring. While some tests may be able to serve multiple purposes, it is important not to assume that is the case.

Another aspect of measurement expertise needed in local norm data collection is an appreciation for standardized data collection. School psychologists may need to explain to staff why it is important to collect data in a standardized way and why training and integrity checks are important in maintaining the validity of the information collected.

Interpreting local norm data provides school psychologists the chance to hone their measurement skills. Understanding the impact of a skewed distribution on local norm percentiles, or explaining how a child could be at the 50th percentile on local norms but at the 10th percentile on a nationally normed test, requires an understanding of the tests themselves, sampling distributions, and the characteristics of a national versus local sample. Explaining computer adaptive testing or Rausch Unit scores to staff or establishing cut scores or growth rates require a deep understanding of measurement principles and techniques.

Consultation and Collaboration Skills

Even if a school psychologist has the measurement background to understand the proper development of local norms, without good consultation skills the data are unlikely to be used to improve outcomes for children. Promoting a climate of data-based decision making with teams, modeling and affirming the appropriate use of local norm data, listening to teacher or administrative concerns about the tests or data collection process, and communicating effectively about local norm data with parents or the community are all examples of the opportunities for consultation and collaboration around local norms.

Indeed, academic local norms may provide ways for school psychologists to expand their role. For example, local norms can be used as a catalyst to expand roles in the areas of consultation (Gansle & Noell, 2008) and program evaluation. School psychologists without a strong background in state or district academic standards, curriculum, and instruction can use this as an opportunity for collaboration and professional development. Looking at school or district-wide data with administrators and teachers typically sparks discussion about patterns of achievement and possible reasons for those patterns. If fifth-grade math scores remain flat across the year, then discussion about the math tests, math curriculum and instruction, the schedule, or other systems variables will take place. School psychologists can seize this opportunity to consult and collaborate with team members to identify potential solutions. Local norm data can then be used to evaluate the system changes.

BEST PRACTICES IN DEVELOPING ACADEMIC LOCAL NORMS

Local norms provide school psychologists with timely data representing the student's particular educational context. The norms also represent important academic outcomes tied to school curriculum scope and sequence and state standards. Because of this, the data produced have direct relevance for practical educational decision making at many levels. Local norms have utility for (a) identifying and validating problems and focusing future assessment; (b) creating ideas for instructional grouping, focus, or intensity; (c) calculating goals based on predictions to criteria such as high-stakes tests; (d) moving students to different levels or tiers of intervention; and (e) systems-level resource allocation and evaluation.

Reducing Bias

With local norms it is possible to have a depth of knowledge about the normative students' cultures, language backgrounds, socioeconomic status, community, and even curriculum and instructional opportunities. Because of this, local norms may be less biased and more meaningful than national or even state or regional norms. Also, because teachers often use comparisons between the students in their classrooms to determine their level of concern about students and whether to refer a student for additional intervention or assessment, local norms help quantify and make those types of decisions more objective and consistent (Shinn, Tindal, & Spira, 1997; VanDerHeyden & Witt, 2005).

Local norms are less biased than informal perceptions of skills in part because norms use standardized tests collected by trained personnel during a known point in time. School psychologists can easily describe what the students were asked to do, quantify the results, and

provide a graph or table representing the range and variability of scores. Although it is always possible for bias to enter into decision making, the transparency and immediacy of local norms reduce the chance for bias.

Systems-Level Feedback

Local norm data provide an overall look at the instructional and systems-level resource needs in a school and allow schools to make important decisions about how to allocate limited resources. For example, students who fall below the 25th percentile on the local norm in grade-level math computation could be targeted for additional assessment and intervention. Combining local norms with benchmark criteria can be even more useful. A school with 80% of its students below the criteria on a phonics measure may make a different decision about core curriculum, instructional grouping, professional development, and other resources than a school with 20% of its students below criteria.

Local norms collected over time and across grades provide opportunities for checking on the overall health of the school system. Areas of strength and weakness in student outcomes can be identified. If reading scores are strong but math outcomes are consistently stagnant in second grade, then the school will want to find out why this is happening and consider what can be done to boost second-grade math skills. The norms then can provide feedback to the school psychologist and teams regarding systems-level changes.

Developing Academic Local Norms

Several considerations and skills are needed to create high-quality local norms, such as understanding the purpose of the norms, what to norm, when and how to collect the norm data, and how to interpret local norm results.

Determining the Purpose of the Norms

Inherent in the decision to develop local norms is some idea of why the norm is being developed in the first place. Will the normative data be used primarily as a comparison group for teacher-referred students or will it also be used for screening, allocation of resources, and systems-level feedback? If the norms are to be used only as a comparison for referred students, then norms could be developed every 5–7 years, barring drastic population or curriculum changes, and on all students or a random sample of students. However, if the local norms are to be used within an RTI multitiered system of support, then model local norms would be collected multiple times per year on all students every year in core academic areas.

Local norms collected at the beginning, middle, and end of the school year are often referred to as benchmarks or screeners. This can lead to some confusion. Benchmarking implies the use of benchmark criteria or target scores to divide and describe the data. Likewise, calling local norming screening implies the use of a cut score for determining groups of students who are at risk for failure and may need further assessment or remediation. This chapter will use the term *local norm* to describe the process of collecting data on students in a local population at specified points in the school year regardless of whether benchmark criteria are used.

As the use of local norms in multitiered systems of support has grown, a body of research and practice has evolved around the technical adequacy of tests used for screening purposes and around the development of normative or criterion-referenced cut points or targets, often referred to as benchmark criteria, for use in decision making (e.g., Nese, Park, Alonzo, & Tindal, 2011; VanDerHeyden, 2011). In fact, the terms local norming, universal screening, and benchmarking are often used interchangeably.

Even if the intended uses of local norms are similar in different schools, the process of developing local norms will not look the same in every school. Local resources for data collection and the instructional support accompanying the use of the data need to be taken into account. Some schools may utilize technology more than others in collecting the data. For a school just starting the process of developing local norms, it may take professional development and time to implement a local norming plan. For example, a school may choose to begin to develop reading norms first and then add math and writing the following school year or phase in norming for different grade levels across time.

What to Norm

Academic local norms need to provide information linked to important academic outcomes for students. Academic local norms should be developed using assessment tools with the technical adequacy needed given the intended use of the norms. If the norm will be used as a screener to identify students at risk of academic difficulty, then the measures chosen should have the sensitivity and specificity needed to make good screening decisions and cut scores that maximize good decision making for the local population (VanDerHeyden, 2011). If the school wants to use the norms to link more directly

to curriculum or instructional decisions at the student or systems level, then tools more closely linked to relevant academic standards or research-based core subskills would be helpful.

It is important to know if adding additional tests really gives enough of an increase in practical decision making to justify the time spent testing, scoring, and reporting those results. It is best not to collect data that will not be used. In a school district where 90% of the first-grade students are consistently above the fall target on a phonological awareness measure and the curriculum and population are stable, yearly updating of local norms in the fall on that measure may not be needed. There are more efficient ways to identify the subset of students with phonemic awareness problems. School psychologists can help determine the briefest and easiest ways to administer measures and ensure that multiple measures are collected only if their use is justified. If a school collects CBM oral reading fluency data three times per year and collects Measures of Academic Progress reading data on all students two times a year, what decision making is improved because of having both? Is collecting both CBM oral reading fluency measures and CBM reading maze on all students in eighth grade necessary? The answers may be yes, but it will depend on the technical adequacy of the tests themselves for the grade level being tested, the characteristics of the population being tested, and how the school intends to use the information.

Academic local norming in high school is a particularly thorny question. Because there should already be a wealth of academic data available on high school students, it may be possible to use existing data to identify at-risk students and then screen only those students rather than collecting a school-wide local norm (Windram, Bollman, & Johnson, 2012). On the other hand, collecting local norm data on key skills, particularly in ninth grade, can provide data for having conversations about the range of student skills in high school and differentiating instruction.

The process of going through each grade level and academic area and deciding what assessments will be used is referred to as a local norm measurement net. A sample measurement net in reading grades K–6 is provided in Table 23.1. However, the measurement net for each school should be determined by the curriculum standards, population, and needs of the school.

Because CBMs were developed as brief general outcome measures in the core academic areas, typically have good technical adequacy for both local norming and progress monitoring, and are brief and easy to

Table 23.1. Example Local Norm Measurement Net for Reading Grades K–3

	Beginning of the Year	Middle of the Year	End of the Year
K	Letter names	Letter sounds	Letter sounds
	Letter sounds	Phoneme segmentation	Phoneme segmentation
		Nonsense words	Nonsense words
1	Letter sounds	Nonsense words	Nonsense words
	Nonsense words	Word use	Word use
	Word use	Oral reading fluency	Oral reading fluency
2	Word use	Word use	Word use
	Oral reading fluency	Oral reading fluency	Oral reading fluency
3	Oral reading fluency	Oral reading fluency	Oral reading fluency

Note. All measures are CBM fluency measures using standardized administration and scoring.

administer, many schools choose to use CBMs of reading, writing, and math in their measurement net (Jenkins, Schiller, Blackorby, Thayer, & Tilly, 2013). There are multiple ways to access CBM measures. For example, there are online services such as AIMSweb (http://www.aimsweb.com), DIBELS (https://dibels.uoregon.edu), EasyCBM (http://www.easycbm.com), FAST (https://www.faip.umn.edu/faip/login.do), and iSTEEP (http://www.isteep.com/login.aspx). The Individual Growth and Development Indicators (Roseth, Missall, & McConnell, 2012) may be used to measure key outcomes in children ages 3–5. The Test of Early Numeracy (Clarke & Shinn, 2004) or the Preschool Numeracy Indicators (Hojnoski, Silberglitt, & Floyd, 2009) can be used to assess early math skills.

Other types of tests can be used for local norming. Some computer adaptive tests such as the Measures of Academic Progress (http://www.nwea.org) or the STAR Enterprise (http://www.renlearn.com) tests also provide local norm data at the district, school, grade, and classroom levels, including information about instructional strands or standards. Many other tests also could be used to create a local normative comparison. Furthermore, although it is not the focus of this chapter, local norm data can be collected on important behavioral outcomes through measures such as standardized behavior reports, office referrals, and attendance. Regardless of the choice of what specific areas to norm, data have to be linked to important outcomes and have demonstrated validity and utility for the kinds of decisions that need to be made.

Another consideration when deciding what to norm is the local population. For example, if a school has a student population extremely at risk for academic difficulty, then it may need to include measures that reach into the domain of skills typically mastered at earlier ages. Likewise, unique characteristics about the language backgrounds of students in the school may

have an impact on the measurement net. If a school has an English as a second language Spanish population that is large and the curriculum includes instruction in Spanish literacy, then it is possible to include Spanish literacy measures for that subset of students in addition to measuring the English literacy skills of all students.

A final word of advice for deciding what to norm: Keep an eye on the literature and the data for ways to improve the measurement net. Advances in testing tools and technology will improve schools' measurement options. Also, schools learn a lot by collecting the norm data and using it. It is fine to adjust the measurement net to meet the needs of the school.

Whom to Norm

A multitiered model implies norming on all students so data can be used to make decisions about each student in the school on an ongoing basis. The scores of different subgroups can certainly be disaggregated from that larger norm sample. However, in certain cases, such as the example earlier about the school with the Spanish curriculum, it may make sense to also create a local norm using a different assessment tool on just a subset of the population. Also, if the norm is not being used for screening purposes, then it may be possible to create a norm based on a random sample of students that provides representative data on the local level and variability of scores. Many online tools now are available for determining the sample size needed based on the tools being used.

Even when norming all students in a building or district, however, there are some things to keep in mind regarding the sample. First, if the norm is to present the whole population, then it is important that all students, including special education students, are represented in the local norm. Most tests have discontinuation rules to prevent undue stress on students. If accommodations are needed, then those students with accommodations should be well documented, and a determination should be made regarding how the data should be included in reports. Some test manuals provide guidelines for accommodations, or the district can develop guidelines for accommodations.

Second, if there are fewer than 100 students per grade level, then percentile rank tables cannot be calculated reliably. While it is possible to calculate a percentile rank on just a few students, those percentiles may not be stable across time, are more skewed by cohort effects, and are easily misinterpreted. Be aware that some of the Web-based data management systems may automatically provide a percentile rank even if the number of students in the sample is very low.

Combining data across years for some reports, such as percentile tables, and using a great deal of caution in comparing performance across years, can address some of these problems. Having the local norm data each year will allow the school psychologist to see and understand those cohort effects and document them. For example, if a teacher is asking for additional support because she has never had a kindergarten class with this wide of a range of academic needs before, then the norm data can demonstrate how students' skills this year compare to previous years.

Some online systems may also provide a percentile rank table not based on the local norm but on all the students in their entire system. These are sometimes referred to as user norms or aggregated norms. While this can provide a point of comparison for how students perform compared to this larger pool of students, it is important to know the demographics of the aggregated online group of students before making comparisons.

When to Norm

The precise timing of data collection will be influenced by when the data are needed and when the scheduling works best. Care should be taken to avoid setting norm data collection too close to school breaks or other large group testing. Having a date in mind for when data reports are needed (e.g., for parent–teacher conferences or monthly collaborative planning meetings) also may have an impact on scheduling. Time should be built in for administration and scoring training and updates. A schedule and plan for following up with missing students should be in place. Scheduling also needs to take into account data entry and report turnaround time.

How to Norm

The logistics of local norming vary widely by school and include the need to gather materials or schedule

computer access if using a computerized test, selecting and training data collectors, and communicating with all staff about the timing and purpose of the local norming. A variety of sources for materials are available through publishers and online. In some cases, downloaded or purchased printed student booklets are used that contain all the materials for a particular norming period or contain three sets of materials for an entire year of norming. Some local norming has gone paperless by using either handheld devices or computers to provide the stimulus materials for the students, and then the students record answers directly on the device or the administrator scores on their own digital device as a student takes the test.

Having materials accessible, well organized, and affordable has made it easier to prepare for local norming. However, sometimes the prepackaged booklets or computer tests include tests not included in the measurement net or have a level of difficulty or weighting of items that does not match the district standards. Wise consumers will look for a description of how the materials were developed and make their own choices about what tests to include.

Who collects the data and how data are collected are interrelated. Many people in the school can be trained to reliably collect local norm data: classroom teachers, administrators, paraprofessionals, related services staff, volunteers, and even school board members. School psychologists are often involved in organizing data collection and being a part of the data collection team. There are several approaches to local norm data collection: the classroom approach, the whole school centralized approach, and the whole school decentralized approach. The classroom approach involves the classroom teacher and some assistants collecting the data within a short 2- to 5-day period. In a centralized approach a team of data collectors uses a large space such as the media center or cafeteria and sets up several testing stations. A whole classroom of students comes at one time and students wait in line to be assessed at one of the stations. If the testing takes 7 minutes per child and there are eight stations, then it would take 21 minutes to gather data on a class of 24 students. The decentralized approach also uses a team of data collectors, but the team may be smaller and the stations spread out throughout the school (e.g., near different grade-level classrooms).

An ongoing aspect of local norm development is ensuring the integrity of the data collected. If administration or scoring will involve digital devices or computers, then it is critical that data collectors know how to use the devices quickly and accurately and know how to correct scoring mistakes. However, after tests are administered, initial training must be followed up with ongoing reliability checks and training updates. At least once per year all data collectors can conduct an assessment fidelity check with another person or based on video examples. Without reliable data collection, reports will be meaningless and teachers will not have faith in the data.

Managing and Reporting Local Norm Data

Once data are collected, entry and reporting are the next steps. If data were collected digitally, then the data can be immediately uploaded electronically. If data were collected using paper and pencil, then data entry does involve clerical time, but Web-based data management systems greatly facilitate the data entry process and make generating reports almost instantaneous. Some districts or states have developed their own Web-based data management systems or participate in cooperatives that provide these systems, while others utilize university systems or for-profit services. In online data management systems, users are assigned passwords and different levels of access to the data and reports (e.g., classroom grade level, building, district) as needed. Educators have access to reports and graphs immediately after data are entered into the system. Schools also can use spreadsheets and statistical programs such as Excel, Google Docs, Access, or SPSS to enter data or to generate graphs and reports for measures not supported by an online data management system or to generate graphs and reports not provided by the system.

Local norm reports can be generated at many different levels: by student, classroom, and grade, and across grade, across buildings, and across years. In fact, the number and kinds of reports available can be overwhelming, and school psychologists can help teams determine the most appropriate reports. Data can be sorted by, for example, grade level, ethnicity, socio-economic status, or level of academic support. The types of data reports and formats also have a large range: class ranking lists, instructional recommendation charts based on benchmark criteria, boxplots, histograms, norm tables with percentile, rate-of-growth charts, line graphs showing progress over time, and effectiveness of curriculum reports.

Interpreting Local Norm Results

School psychologists play a key role in understanding different reporting formats and providing consultation about how to select and interpret the tables and graphs

generated. Interpreting different types of reports and graphs, validating data through looking at other data sources or collecting additional information, and making decisions based on the data are not skills that can be assumed. At a systems level, a culture of data-based decision making should be fostered by having training and prompts for using data. Regular grade-level, problem-solving, and RTI leadership team meetings with agenda items for looking at local norm data provide the context for using the data. School administrators or curriculum and instruction staff may need training regarding how to look at school- or system-wide reports and results. Providing guidelines and opportunities for parents to learn how to read and interpret local norm results through newsletters and parent–teacher conferences are yet other aspects of teaching others how to interpret local norm results.

One aspect of local norm interpretation that needs to be considered is the careful use of percentile ranks. If the local norm scores are not normally distributed, then it can be misleading to use percentile ranks. For example, if the norm is heavily positively skewed (e.g., letter sound fluency data in fall or even winter of kindergarten in some schools), then scores on the low end, for example, between the 5th and 40th percentile, could be just a few data points different. It would be easy to think that a student at the 5th percentile needed more or different instruction than the student at the 40th percentile when in fact because of the skewed distribution the students may have pretty similar skills. Using a research-based or high-stakes benchmark criterion score to categorize the risk level of students would decrease the likelihood of overinterpretation of the percentile rank differences, but this is an area where the school psychologist's measurement knowledge can help teams look at the data more critically.

It is also important to understand the measurement error typically associated with the assessment tools being used. School psychologists are especially well prepared to be a building leader in this effort. Christ and Silberglitt (2007) provide an example of developing local estimates of the standard error of measurement of building- or district-wide assessments. In recent years comparisons of different assessment probes and assessment tools have provided information on the standard errors of measurement schools might expect when norming (e.g., Christ & Ardoin, 2009).

Another aspect of interpreting some local norm reports is an understanding of the benchmark criteria used to determine students' level of instructional support needed and overall level of risk. Criteria may be based on cut scores related to skill proficiency. Criteria also may be based on the probability of meeting future goals such as meeting the next benchmark goal, meeting a set percentile or criterion on another norm-referenced test (e.g., DIBELS Next Benchmark Goals), or passing high-stakes state tests (Hintze & Silberglitt, 2005). Teachers, administrators, and parents given reports based on criterion-referenced interpretation of local norm data need to know what the criterion cut off scores are based on and implications these scores may have for instruction or other educational decisions.

Understanding Local Norm Growth

Another related way of using local norms is to look at the typical slope or rate of improvement of local students over time and use these to generate growth standards that can be used to set goals and evaluate progress (Fuchs, 1986). However, five significant concerns emerge when using local norms to create growth norms or standards that are then used as a comparison for determining if students are responding to interventions. First, these local slope norms are typically based on data gathered three times per year, while students in Tier 2 and Tier 3 interventions are typically being monitored more frequently. Second is the concern about error in establishing a student's slope of progress. Christ (2006) and Christ and Ardoin (2009) have reported differences in the degree of the standard error of the slope, depending on characteristics of the assessments and the frequency of measurement. Third, local norms for slope can only be gathered post hoc. For example, in a school that measures all students three times per year, it would not be possible to know how the growth of a student being monitored weekly compared to peers until after January, when at least two data points (beginning and middle of the year) have been gathered on all students. An alternative would be to use the growth rates of prior cohorts, but the applicability of these data, given possible changes in curriculum and instruction, may be questionable. Fourth, using the growth rate of the average (or 50th percentile) student as a benchmark may not be appropriate. Silberglitt and Hintze (2007) found growth rates in one large norm sample were significantly lower for both very low and very high performing students, and the range of low-performing students who demonstrated lower growth rates was much wider, and differences much more pronounced, in the early grades. Fifth, typically local norm growth rates have been calculated by taking the growth of the average student across the year and dividing that number by the number of school weeks. However, individual student growth

rates across a school year are not unchanging and linear, as this way of calculating local norm growth rates might suggest. Christ, Silberglitt, Yeo, and Cormier (2010) found growth rates in the fall were generally steeper than spring growth rates. This has implications for goal setting goals and making decisions based on expected progress.

An alternative to using normative slope criteria is to use the rate of increase of the criterion-based target scores on three-times-per-year benchmark assessments. These criterion-based slope criteria have been successfully used within a multitiered framework (Burns & Gibbons, 2012). While the target scores provide an indication of performance that is on track to meet success on some outcome measure (such as a statewide assessment), the rate of growth of the targets provides an indication of the improvement necessary to keep pace with these targets. However, it is still important to address the issue of nonlinear growth curves, and more research is needed on the best way to determine target growth rates.

Avoiding Common Mistakes When Developing Local Norms

Local norms provide valuable information, but there are mistakes schools need to avoid when developing norms. This section and Table 23.2 provide topics to consider so mistakes are avoided and norms are developed using best practice.

Typical Is Not Always the Same as Good

While local norms can reduce bias in decision making, it is also important to remember to keep an eye on how local students are faring compared to research-based benchmark criteria and regional or national norms. If Adam is an eighth grader scoring at the 50th percentile in Prairie Middle School in the fall, then he may be in the average range for that school, but that does not tell us whether Adam is a proficient reader or is on track to pass high-stakes tests in reading in the spring. If the local norm is quite a bit higher or lower than the national average, then schools need to take this into account. For example, in a low-achieving school it would be important to strive for improvements in curriculum and instruction for all students, not just those at the lower end of the local norm.

Local Norms Often Are Not Diagnostic

Local norm data are not typically diagnostic. Although advances in measurement and technology have made

Table 23.2. How to Avoid Common Norming Mistakes

Developing Norms	Reporting and Using Norms
• Provide professional development on rationale for norming and foundations of the measures. • Collect only data that will be used. • Use measures with appropriate technical adequacy. • Ensure administration and scoring integrity. • Be efficient: minimize data collection time and the use of instructional spaces such as classrooms, computer labs, and media centers. • Collect data on all students if the norm is to represent the whole local population. • Collect and organize qualitative data and information on any test accommodations. • Do not use test materials in teaching.	• Provide professional development on the measures, scores, criteria, and reports. • Document who is in the norm and when and how data are collected. • Ensure data are available when needed. • Train staff in data privacy and how to appropriately share and store data. • Build time into staff and team schedules to look at and use the data. • Provide access to reports at multiple levels of analysis (individual, class, grade, building) as needed. • Interpret norms with small Ns or use subgroup analysis with caution. • Develop data warehouses where local norm data can be compared with other student data. • Lead by example: administrators, school psychologists, and others model local norm use and data-based decision making at all levels of analysis.

curriculum strand analysis or error analysis more feasible, the measures used for local norms for a particular time period are often brief in nature and are collected on a student in one session. Additional academic assessment or a convergence of data from other sources is needed to validate and pinpoint a student's instructional needs.

Local norms also do not require that a particular curriculum, instructional strategy, or teaching method be used. School psychologists can help teams understand the tests used for local norming and implications of the scores. For example, CBM oral reading fluency, often expressed as an oral reading rate or words read correctly per minute, is commonly used for creating reading local norms, but a low score on CBM oral reading fluency just indicates the student may be at risk in the area of reading. Further information is needed to determine if the student has problems with decoding, fluency, vocabulary, or comprehension. It would be a mistake to automatically put all students with low scores on an oral reading fluency measure into a reading fluency intervention.

Some schools using local norms in a multitiered system of support have taken this idea a step further by using the local norm data as just a first step in the process of problem identification. Local norm data are collected on all students as a screener to identify who may be at risk and who is likely not at risk of reading difficulty. Those students identified as at risk go through a second assessment to help verify students' levels of risk and provide additional information. This process is referred to as a multigated screening process (Compton, Fuchs, Fuchs, & Bryant, 2006).

Using Academic Local Norms Within a Multitiered Problem-Solving System

Table 23.3 outlines how local norms can be used at the individual and systems level across different problem-solving decisions. Different types of information and reports based on the local norms might be used to answer different questions. The following sections provide examples of how to use local norms across different types of problems and at both the individual and system levels.

Identifying the Problem

At the individual student level, local norm data have long been used to determine whether a student is similar to or different from peers (Deno, 2003). For example, Keenan (student in Figure 23.1) is a third-grade student at Riverside Elementary. Local norm data have great utility for understanding the severity of Keenan's academic needs. Keenan's oral reading fluency score was lower than most of the other third graders in his building in the fall of third grade. Norm data in other academic areas indicated his math and writing scores were well within the average range of his classmates. Keenan appears to have a problem in the area of reading. If local norms have been collected on all students across years, then it may also be possible to go back and see how Keenan's scores have

Table 23.3. Using Local Norms in Problem Solving

Question	Local Norm Use	
	Individual Student Level	Systems Level
What is the problem?	• Are student scores discrepant from same-grade peers? From benchmark criteria? From students at lower grade levels? • What is the pattern of student scores across local norm measures? • How long has the student struggled?	• How many students need support? • How much support do they need?
Why is it happening?	• What are the implications for further assessment based on, for example, the student's pattern of results, errors, accuracy, rate, and qualitative information on local norm tests?	• Are there any clear weaknesses in the pattern of results for all students across years or grades? • Are students in Tier 1, Tier 2, and Tier 3 all making progress over time?
What should be done about it?	• How severe is the problem? • What level of support is indicated by benchmark criteria? • Are the student's level of skill and instructional needs similar to others'? • What is the long-term goal for this student? (Use local norms to create a local criterion-based growth norm.)	• What implications do systems-level data have for instructional grouping, professional development, scheduling, curriculum decisions, and resource allocation? • What systems-level goals would show adequate improvement in areas of weakness?
Did it work?	• Is the discrepancy between the student and peers decreasing? • How does the student's rate of progress compare to the progress of peers? • Does the student continue to maintain skills over time on subsequent local norms?	• What was the impact of a systems-level change across time? Was the goal reached? • Are there any ripple effects of systems-level changes in other skills or grades?

progressed over time, both individually and in comparison to peers.

In a school with a multitiered system of support, local norms would be used not only as a comparison group for students referred by teachers or parents, but also as a mechanism for universal screening to determine the pattern and level of need of students in the building and start proactively identifying the students in the building who might benefit from Tier 2 or Tier 3 supports. For this purpose, local norms may be presented as a simple class list of students by name and by performance on the measures normed. It may be possible to sort this list by highest to lowest performance or to color code students' names, according to what tier of services their score indicates. Table 23.4 is an example of a simple, abbreviated class list displaying three different types of reading data. Lists can be generated by grade and by classroom.

Local norms also provide information to determine whether there are more widespread or systemic problems in the school. School psychologists can work with administrators, curriculum and instruction staff, and school-level teams to analyze local norm data at the systems level for curricular and instructional implications. Figure 23.2 illustrates CBM reading data for spring of second grade. Using the school's benchmark criteria, these data indicate 22% of the students may need intensive instructional support, an additional 40% may need Tier 2 support, and only 38% appear to be on track for reading success with only core instructional support needed. These data indicate a level of overall student need that requires changes to Tier 1 curriculum and instruction so all students get more practice and support and not just more Tier 2 and Tier 3 small group or individual interventions.

Local norm information about the level and intensity of student needs have implications for curriculum review, resource allocation, professional development, and instructional grouping. What the local norm data look like at other grade levels and across years also will help identify potential problems at the systems level. If the second-grade local norm data discussed earlier have shown a pattern like this across the year, or have shown a substantial drop in the spring of second grade each year, there likely is some larger issue with the Tier 1 curriculum and instruction that needs to be addressed.

Figure 23.1. Grade 3 Reading Local Norm Boxplot and Individual Student Data for Keenan

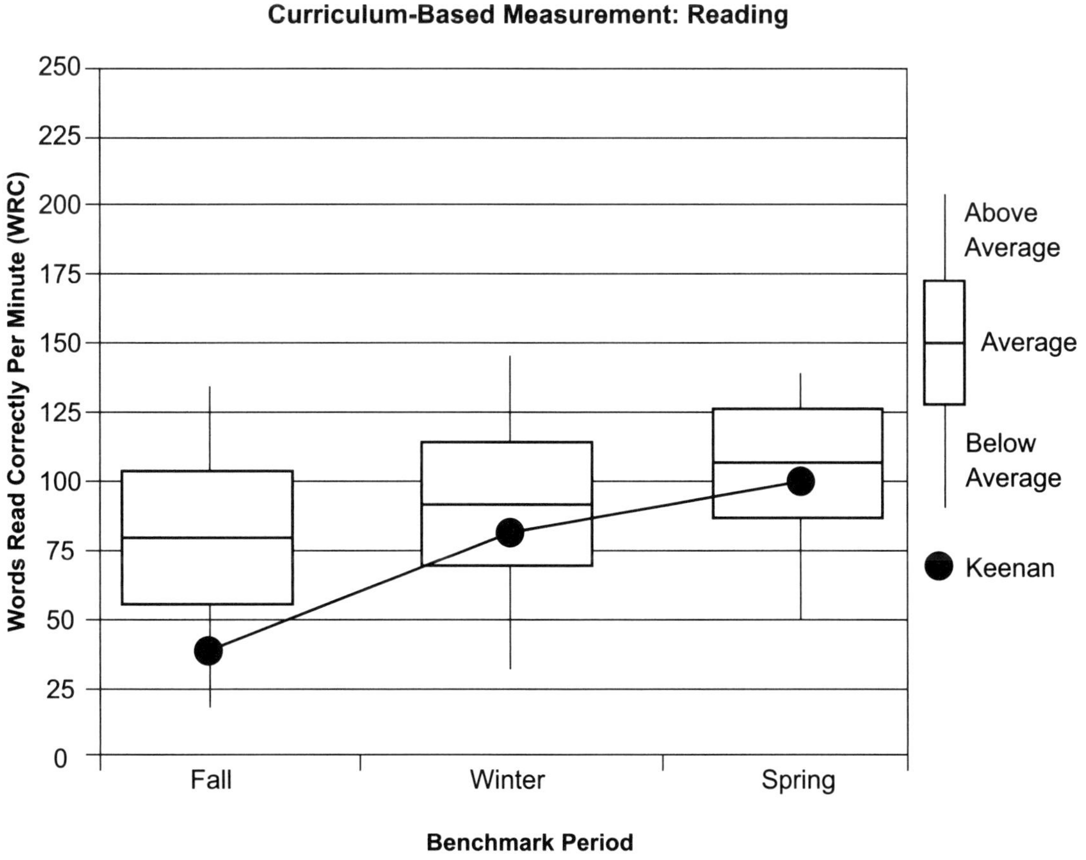

Curriculum-Based Measurement: Reading

Why Is There a Problem?

At the individual student level, local norm data are just the first step toward determining why a student may be experiencing academic difficulty. Because local norms are typically collected on brief indicators of core academic skills, other sources of information and additional testing using the local norm measures or other tests are needed to validate the problem and determine why the student is having difficulty. However, local norm data can help guide further assessment. Percentage correct and rate information provide clues regarding automaticity and accuracy of skills. Error types, error patterns, and qualitative data provide clues about how a student approached the task. Patterns of strengths and weaknesses on different measures being normed, or strand, or problem-type analysis, can also provide guidance at the student or group level about what skills students may be missing or need more practice on. While collecting and analyzing additional data on all students in the building may be a

monumental task, testing and technological advances, particularly with the computer adaptive tests, make this type of analysis more feasible. Also, additional data would only need to be collected for those students whose initial data presents a concern.

As mentioned above, at the systems level patterns of strength and weakness can provide clues about the effectiveness of curriculum and instruction. If the assessment tools used are linked to state standards, then local norms can provide information about how the curriculum is meeting the instructional standards outlined by the state. For example, if local norm data indicate a consistent problem with fractions in Grade 4, then it would make sense to look at how and when fractions are taught in the school.

Local norm reports can also be generated, for example, for different ethnic groups, levels of academic support (e.g., general education, Title I, special education, talented and gifted), and socioeconomic status, to get a picture of how particular programs or

Table 23.4. Example (Abbreviated) Class List: Grade 1 Spring Reading Data

Student	PSF			NWF			ORF		
	Score	Percentile	Status	Score	Percentile	Status	Score	Percentile	Status
Isaac	2	<1	Deficit	3	<1	Deficit	3	<1	At risk
Andrea	37	20	Established	33	44	Emerging	10	5	At risk
Connor	34	15	Emerging	27	35	Deficit	32	48	Some risk
Maria	41	34	Established	50	69	Established	36	57	Some risk
Mia	35	17	Established	64	78	Established	60	72	Low risk
Finn	40	28	Established	92	93	Established	72	87	Low risk

Note. PSF = phoneme segmentation fluency; NWF = nonsense word fluency; ORF = oral reading fluency.

groups are doing. Care needs to be taken that sample sizes are adequate for evaluating and reporting data for these subgroups, however, and that students are accurately coded in the data set. These types of subgroup analyses are more compelling if data are collected across years and the pattern is consistent.

Breaking the local norm data into Tier 1, Tier 2, and Tier 3 instructional support recommendations based on some research-based criteria and then looking at the progress of each of these groups across time is another way to report and use local norm data. Likewise, students getting Tier 3 intensive support should make gains over time and may move into other categories of support. If large numbers of students seem stuck in a particular level of support, if students make gains only to lose them again when the support is removed, or if many students are needing more support over time instead of less, the system is not meeting students' needs.

If local norms are used for systems-level evaluation, many aspects of the whole system need to be taken into account. It may be tempting to conclude that the curriculum and instruction at a particular level (e.g., Tier 2 in the Riverside example) needs to be changed. While the data do point to potential problems in the intervention curriculum and instruction in that area, before changing curriculum or programs it is also important to ask if the Tier 2 students actually received the interventions and if the interventions were done with integrity. The dynamics of the whole system need to be taken into account when interpreting these data. Additional systems-level data, including input from parents, teachers, and students, may be needed to more fully understand the problem and potential solutions.

What Should Be Done About the Problem?

Local norm data are not designed to be prescriptive about what particular curriculum or strategies should be

Figure 23.2. Example CBM Reading Local Norm Histogram: Spring Grade 2

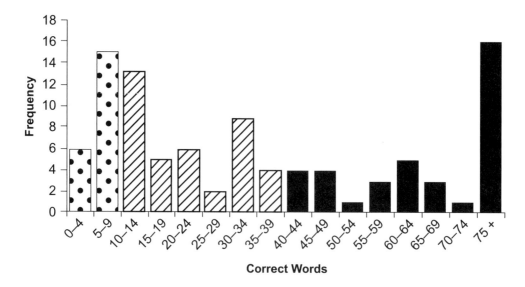

used. That said, some Web-based data management systems are moving toward providing suggested links to particular products or programs to, for example, the instructional recommendations on the class list. Specific teaching recommendations need to be taken with a healthy amount of skepticism because the data may be too limited or there may be a bias toward particular programs.

At the individual level, knowing the severity of a student's needs and how that student compares to others has implications about what should be done about the problem. For example, from Figure 23.1, Keenan's instructional needs appear to warrant some type of research-based intervention. He is discrepant from peers and is in need of instructional support to read future benchmark goals and pass state tests. Although Keenan is discrepant from most of his peers, he has several classmates whose scores fall in a similar range. Instead of just creating a separate instructional intervention for Keenan, it may be possible to create an instructional group that meets many students' needs.

At the systems level, knowing how many students need support and how much support they need in what academic areas has implications for efficient allocation of resources or professional development. For example, a school with a large percentage of students in need of intensive support may choose to utilize a more explicit core curriculum, provide related professional development to teachers, keep class sizes and instructional groups smaller, or put into place scheduling that allows for flexibility and more time allocated to prioritized core academic needs. Local norm data may also point out gaps in curriculum and instruction, such as a lack of computation skill building.

When monitoring student progress, local norms are sometimes used as a means for determining the long-term goal for a student. The local norm provides a rich database that allows a school or district to determine its own criterion-based growth norms, such as growth norms reflecting the progress needed to pass the state high-stakes test. In some cases if there are no other clear research-based standards for growth or proficiency on the specific academic measure being used, local norms can at least provide some context for setting goals and evaluating progress. However, that expectation may be too low if the overall norm growth rate is based on ineffective Tier 1 instruction. As discussed earlier, setting goals based on local norms should be done with extreme caution.

Did the intervention Work?

At the individual student level, local norm data provide a clear graphic comparison for a student's academic progress over time compared to peers. Keenan made strong gains compared to his peers and scored near the average for his grade by the spring of third grade (Figure 23.1). Local norms collected in fourth grade would be able to document whether Keenan maintained his skills over the summer and if he built on those skills throughout the year.

At the systems level, changes put in place to strengthen overall academic achievement or more specific changes put in place to shore up a weak spot in student scores can be evaluated using local norm data across time. For example, local norms could be used to document the impact of a change in curriculum and instruction on the phonemic awareness skills of kindergarteners over a several-year period. Local norms could also be used in this case to look at subsequent increases in literacy skills linked to phonemic awareness. Also, local norms provide the data needed to document the effectiveness of the different tiers of instruction and evaluate systems-level changes put in place to improve outcomes for a particular level of intervention.

SUMMARY

Local norms provide an important tool for describing the educational context for a student. This educational context is important and relevant for decision making. In addition to being useful at many levels of decision making about students, norms also provide data for systems-level evaluation. Advances in assessment and technology have made developing local norms a regular part of monitoring student performance in many schools.

School psychologists have the skills to promote best practices in the development of local norms. School psychologists should be involved in selecting measurement tools; collecting, analyzing, and reporting data; and working with teachers, administrators, and teams to use the data. Finally, school psychologists' knowledge of school systems and ability to link assessment to intervention provides the background for using local norms to promote well-matched, evidence-based programs and interventions. By ensuring that common mistakes are avoided, school psychologists can maximize the validity and utility of information for the students in their schools. Local norming can help school psychologists expand their role in the schools in the areas of academic assessment and intervention across the different tiers of service delivery and system-level evaluation. School psychologists have a key role to play in making sure the school system does not just collect data, but actually uses the local norm data to make better decisions about children and their instruction.

REFERENCES

Burns, M., & Gibbons, K. (2012). *Implementing response to intervention in elementary and secondary schools: Procedures to assure scientific-based practices* (2nd ed.). New York, NY: Routledge.

Christ, T. J. (2006). Short-term estimates of growth using curriculum-based measurement of oral reading fluency: Estimates of standard error of the slope to construct confidence intervals. *School Psychology Review, 35,* 128–133.

Christ, T. J., & Ardoin, S. P. (2009). Curriculum-based measurement of oral reading: Passage equivalence and probe-set development. *Journal of School Psychology, 47,* 55–75.

Christ, T. J., & Silberglitt, B. (2007). Estimates of the standard error of measurement for curriculum-based measures of oral reading fluency. *School Psychology Review, 36,* 130–146.

Christ, T. J., Silberglitt, B., Yeo, S., & Cormier, D. (2010). Curriculum-based measurement of oral reading fluency: Evaluation of growth rates and seasonal effects among students served in general and special education. *School Psychology Review, 39,* 447–462.

Clarke, B., & Shinn, M. R. (2004). A preliminary investigation in the identification and development of early mathematics curriculum-based measurement. *School Psychology Review, 33,* 234–248.

Compton, D. L., Fuchs, D., Fuchs, L. S., & Bryant, J. D. (2006). Selecting at-risk readers in first grade for early intervention: A two-year longitudinal study of decision rules and procedures. *Journal of Educational Psychology, 98,* 394–409.

Deno, S. L. (2003). Developments in curriculum-based measurement. *Journal of Special Education, 37,* 184–192.

Fuchs, L. S. (1986). Monitoring progress among mildly handicapped pupils: Review of current practice and research. *Remedial and Special Education, 7,* 5–12.

Gansle, K. A., & Noell, G. H. (2008). Consulting with teachers regarding academic skills: Problem solving for basic skills. *International Journal of Behavioral Consultation and Therapy, 4,* 199–212.

Hintze, J. M., & Silberglitt, B. (2005). A longitudinal examination of the diagnostic accuracy and predictive validity of R-CBM and high-stakes testing. *School Psychology Review, 34,* 372–386.

Hojnoski, R. L., Silberglitt, B., & Floyd, R. G. (2009). Sensitivity to growth over time of the Preschool Numeracy Indicators with a sample of preschoolers in Head Start. *School Psychology Review, 38,* 402–418.

Jenkins, J., Schiller, E., Blackorby, J., Thayer, S. K., & Tilly, W. D., III. (2013). Responsiveness to intervention in reading: Architecture and practices. *Learning Disability Quarterly, 36,* 36–46.

Koehler-Hak, K., & Snyder, J. (2012). Local norms within a model of response to intervention: Implications for practice. *School Psychologist, 66,* 7–11.

National Association of School Psychologists. (2010). *Model for comprehensive and integrated school psychological services.* Bethesda, MD: Author. Retrieved from http://www.nasponline.org/standards/2010standards/2_PracticeModel.pdf

Nese, J. F., Park, B. J., Alonzo, J., & Tindal, G. (2011). Applied curriculum-based measurement as a predictor of high-stakes assessment: Implications for researchers and teachers. *Elementary School Journal, 111,* 604–624.

Roseth, C. J., Missall, K. N., & McConnell, S. R. (2012). Early literacy individual growth and development indicators: Growth trajectories using a large, Internet-based sample. *Journal of School Psychology, 50,* 483–501.

Shapiro, E. (2012). *New thinking in response to intervention: A comparison of computer adaptive tests and curriculum-based measurement within RTI.* Wisconsin Rapids, WI: Renaissance Learning. Retrieved from http://doc.renlearn.com/KMNet/R00547943CE5AC66.pdf

Shapiro, E., Christ, T., & Alonzo, J. (2013, February). New developments in technology enhanced assessment methods for RTI models. Paper presented at the annual meeting of the National Association of School Psychologists, Seattle, WA.

Shinn, M. R., Tindal, G., & Spira, D. (1997). Special education referrals as an index of teacher tolerance: Are teachers imperfect tests? *Exceptional Children, 54,* 32–40.

Silberglitt, B., & Hintze, J. M. (2007). How much growth can we expect? A conditional analysis of R-CBM growth rates by level of performance. *Exceptional Children, 74,* 71–84.

VanDerHeyden, A. (2011). Technical adequacy of response to intervention decisions. *Exceptional Children, 77,* 335–350.

VanDerHeyden, A., & Witt, J. (2005). Quantifying context in assessment: Capturing the effect of base rates on teacher referral and a problem-solving model of identification. *School Psychology Review, 34,* 161–183.

Windram, H., Bollman, K., & Johnson, S. (2012). *How RTI works in secondary schools: Building a framework for success.* Bloomington, IN: Solution Tree Press.

24 Best Practices in Designing and Conducting Needs Assessment

Richard J. Nagle
University of South Carolina
Sandra Glover Gagnon
Appalachian State University (NC)

OVERVIEW

School psychologists are charged with positively contributing to students' development and supporting the learning environment. This task is accomplished not only through the provision of direct services to individual children and teachers, but also through systems-level approaches that focus on issues such as school improvement and the development of new programs. School psychologists regularly engage in data-driven practice when working with individual students and teachers but have fewer opportunities for involvement in programmatic, systems-level efforts.

However, economic and social policy shifts are forcing many school psychologists to meet the needs of more students with fewer resources (Merrill, Ervin, & Peacock, 2012). This situation requires an expansion of roles such that school psychologists in the 21st century will influence not only individual students, but also entire schools and systems. Needs assessment is one method that allows school psychologists to influence a larger number of constituents on a broader systems level. The aim of the present chapter is to provide school psychologists with information to guide their participation in comprehensive needs assessments and encourage them to engage in these activities.

Needs assessments are an integral component of Organizational Principle 1 of the National Association of School Psychologists (NASP) *Model for Comprehensive and Integrated School Psychological Services* (NASP, 2010), which makes reference to "a systematic assessment of the educational and psychological needs of students and families in the local community" that is "based on the

needs of the school system and community" (p. 9). The placement of this chapter in the context of the NASP Practice Model (NASP, 2010) domain of Research and Program Evaluation is appropriate, yet may provide a somewhat limited context, as needs assessments require knowledge and skills comprising all domains of school psychology practice.

BASIC CONSIDERATIONS

Needs assessments can serve many purposes for school psychologists, such as providing the foundation for program planning, development, and modification. The scope of a needs assessment can be broad based, such as at the school district or community level, or much narrower, such as at the school, grade, or department level. The literature is replete with examples of how needs assessments can be conducted in the schools.

Rationale for Conducting Needs Assessments

Many school psychologists may ask why they may want to conduct needs assessments. There are many reasons for doing so. School psychologists' training and understanding of research design and methodology, consultation and collaboration, and systems-level change are necessary to initiate and carry out needs assessments. Needs assessments allow school psychologists to be agents of change in the schools.

A second question school psychologists might ask is how can they can make this a priority when they have so many other competing demands. The field of school psychology is experiencing a change in identity that includes a move toward a more contemporary conceptualization that reflects the extent of training and encompasses the many functions provided by school psychologists. Despite ongoing attempts to expand services, school psychologists' daily activities are driven by district-level policies and limited perceptions of appropriate roles. Needs assessments can be used to examine current and desired practice and identify gaps to be addressed in promoting systems change so that schools can benefit from the diverse services school psychologists can offer.

Additionally, needs assessments offer valuable opportunities to increase parent and teacher involvement in school-related programs and activities by incorporating their perceptions and needs. This practice enhances the quality of decision making and communicates appreciation for their contributions and involvement. Decision makers often consider the opinions of upper-level or external professionals as superior to the ideas and perceptions of parents and teachers, which can lead parents and teachers to feel marginalized and devalued. In contrast, using parents' and teachers' input to help guide program development and other related activities can lead to feelings of being valued and respected. It is, however, important to recognize that parents' ideas and experiences may be quite different from those of teachers, and that those differences may serve as obstacles to successful program implementation or modification. For example, Voyles (2012) found differences between teachers' beliefs about how much parents valued education and parents' self-reported values, and these differences could have affected the school districts' programming efforts and outcomes and parents' feelings of connectedness to the school.

Needs assessments can also be useful in promoting the professional development of school personnel. Training needs may be established and needs assessment information can aid in the design of staff development activities that are both relevant and appropriate to improving job functioning among school personnel. Needs assessments may assist with resource issues, in that they can provide information to decision-making bodies, such as a school board, to justify budgeting priorities. When a strong correspondence between allocation of money and other resources and needed services is observed, decision makers demonstrate strong accountability for their actions. Last, dissemination of needs assessment data may serve an important informative function within the schools and community. This practice can serve as the basis for school and community awareness of what the needs are and which courses of action decision makers are considering to address those needs. Disseminating results is particularly helpful if carried out within the context of promoting "solution-oriented activity among providers" (Finifter, Jensen, Wilson, & Koenig, 2005, p. 302).

Defining Needs

Clearly, there are numerous benefits for school psychologists who conduct needs assessments. A need has been defined as a "value judgment that some group has a problem that can be solved" (McKillip, 1998, p. 10). By defining need in this manner, McKillip underscores several important considerations for those who conduct needs assessments. First, since needs involve values, it must be recognized that different people may perceive different needs for the same situation. It also is quite possible that those observing needs may differ from the individuals experiencing the needs. Second, the fact that needs may emerge for a particular group implies an environmental context that will require careful description to facilitate needs analysis. This is particularly important in identifying groups that may be at risk for poor outcomes. Caution is urged when assessing the needs of groups considered at risk, as the label may promote negative feelings and impressions (Voyles, 2012). Third, the definitional component of problems reflects an inadequate outcome that falls short of expectations. Fourth, recognition of a need implies a judgment that problems that are detected can be solved. Since problems may be created by multiple causes or factors, potential solutions must be judged by their probable efficacy in alleviating the problem, the general cost of the solution, and the feasibility and ease of implementation of the solution.

BEST PRACTICES IN DESIGNING AND CONDUCTING NEEDS ASSESSMENT

Needs assessments vary in terms of nature and scope. They can be conducted proactively, with the goal of identifying prospects for improvements; continuously, for progress monitoring; and reactively, when effectiveness is determined to be lacking (Watkins, Meiers, & Visser, 2012). Regardless of nature and scope, needs assessments should be guided by the decisions to be made with the data that are collected. Small-scale needs assessments, such as those conducted at the individual school level, may be accomplished by three steps: (a) identify the data to be collected, who will collect it, and by what methods; (b) analyze the data gathered and prioritize identified needs; and (c) decide what to do with the results (see Watkins et al., 2012). More extensive needs assessments, such as those carried out at the district level, typically require a similar, yet more extensive approach that is broadly divided into three distinct phases: preassessment, assessment, and postassessment (Altschuld & White, 2010). Figure 24.1 provides an overview of this process.

The following sections provide steps for school psychologists to follow when conducting needs assessments. School psychologists are well positioned to oversee these projects, as they are among the few professionals in the schools with measurement expertise and training in statistical and research methodology and evaluation (Romualdi & Sandoval, 1995). School psychologists' training in collaboration and consultation will allow them to oversee management of the project.

Preassessment Phase

The preassessment phase is a time for planning and determining the nature and scope of the needs assessment. The goal of this phase is to provide "systematic information to place the problem(s) in context and to assure that appropriate planning occurs based on a clear understanding of service needs" (Illback, Zins, Maher, & Greenberg, 1990, p. 807). To establish need and clarify the problem from different perspectives, school psychologists should review school documents, reports, and files and conduct direct observations and brief interviews with involved persons (Illback et al., 1990), including program planners and a

diverse sample of school personnel. These methods are used to determine what is already known about the needs of the system and to identify issues and major areas of concern (Altschuld & Witkin, 2000). Another important dimension of the problem clarification phase is that it provides an estimate how receptive the school and community will be to change, as commitment to program planning by key stakeholders is critical. Before new information is gathered, schools must carefully consider the changes they are willing and able to make based on the information obtained (Soriano, 2012).

Establishing a Needs Assessment Team

The school psychologist should establish a team that is responsible for planning, monitoring, and executing the needs assessment process. Typically, a team of six is manageable, but team size should be based upon the nature and scope of the needs assessment. Team members should be selected based on their familiarity with the target population and with school and community resources.

Other members selected for the team should be individuals who work cooperatively in a group, are task oriented, are capable of making fair and objective decisions, and are committed to program planning in the area of demonstrated need (National Urban League, 1983). The team should include individuals from a variety of school and community institutions, such as students, teachers, principals, parents, members of the PTA and school advisory council, community leaders and decision makers, representatives from appropriate community agencies, school board members, and school

Figure 24.1. Outline of the Process for Conducting Needs Assessments

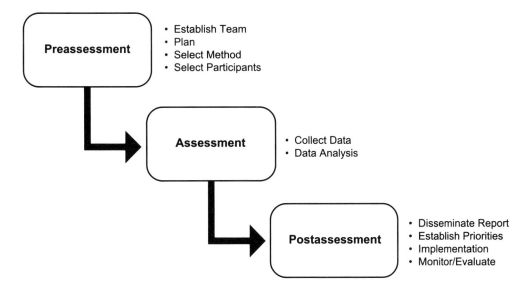

administrative level personnel. The inclusion of members who are decision makers (i.e., have authority), such as principals or school administrators/board members, is necessary to build in commitment and political influence for program development recommendations based on the final needs assessment report.

Interest in and commitment to the needs assessment may be high, but existing resources may be limited. Practical considerations of budget and human resources will influence the method and level of information that can be gathered. The team should determine any type of technical expertise it requires that is not possessed by any of the members, as it may be necessary to hire external consultants or recruit volunteers.

Identifying Information to Collect

After the initial planning activities are completed, the assessment team must determine the critical issues to be studied and the necessary information to collect. The information should specify the extent of the problems, influences on the problems, community resources available to deal with the problems, and hypotheses about potential solutions. If the assessment process becomes too burdensome in terms of time and energy, then it may delay or detract from program development and implementation activities.

Establishing Time Lines

Once the plan has been formulated, the team should establish a time line for completion of the needs assessment (Carter, 1996). It may take anywhere from a week to several months to complete the process (Watkins et al., 2012), though the process likely will take less time when team members have experience with needs assessments. A good plan should consider how to cope with barriers that may emerge during the assessment process (Carter, 1996). When unexpected or difficult circumstances arise, the team should be flexible and creative. Although plans should be closely adhered to, needs assessors may have to modify them as necessary. A well-conceived plan maximizes the probability of obtaining quality information to be used in program planning.

Assessment Phase

Once the preassessment activities are completed, the needs assessment process moves to the assessment phase, which involves data collection and analysis. School psychologists should use an empirically based, multifaceted approach that includes multiple measures from multiple informants (Finifter et al., 2005). There are a number of commonly used methods to assess needs, each with its own set of advantages and disadvantages. This information is provided in Table 24.1. Each method can be easily modified relative to the scope of the needs assessment.

Selection of Methods

Needs assessment methods vary considerably in terms of their comprehensiveness, cost, and required time to complete. Some believe that cost and time should be held to a minimum so as not to interfere with other goals in the program planning process (Hobbs, 1987). In performing needs assessments, no component is more important than the clear specification of the purpose and desired accomplishments. The purpose and individuals to be influenced are the most central criteria in choosing methods (Hobbs, 1987). Additional criteria include the appropriateness of the method for the purpose of the assessment and type of data desired, the required and available resources (e.g., cost benefit), the practicality of the method, skills of the needs assessment team members and experience with the particular method, characteristics of the client system, decision makers' preferences, acceptability by the team members, and allowable time frame for the needs assessment project (Watkins et al., 2012). It has been recommended that needs assessors rely as much as possible on existing information, with less emphasis on the collection of new data (Watkins et al., 2012).

All needs assessment methods have inherent strengths and limitations and, therefore, the use of multiple methods is recommended. This strategy helps assure that the potential limitations of one approach can be minimized by the use of additional, complementary methods. Multiple activities also help estimate the reliability and validity of the results and subsequently increase accuracy and decrease bias in the final results (Jeffery, Hache, & Lehr, 1995).

Resource (Program) Inventory

A resource inventory is a compilation of services available to the target group in a specific service area (McKillip, 1998) that is gathered by surveying service providers in the local community and school district. The central aim of a resource inventory is to describe available services, with particular emphasis placed upon identifying who is providing services, the characteristics and eligibility criteria of clients receiving services, and the service capacity of the program. Programs also are

Table 24.1. Needs Assessment Methods, Advantages, and Disadvantages

Method	Advantages	Disadvantages
Informational Methods		
Resource Inventory	• Quick and inexpensive • Identifies gaps in services • Identifies underutilized services	• Gaps may not reflect program needs • May not be helpful in prevention planning
Social Indicators	• Information readily available • Inexpensive • Limited expertise/technical skills	• Inferential approach • Data format may not conform to informational requirements
Survey Methods		
Interviews	• Provide in-depth information • Cover broad range of topics • Serve as starting point for questionnaires	• Time consuming • Cost • Not suited for large samples
Questionnaires	• Suitable for large samples • Can be cost-effective • Various formats can be used	• Response rates • Skill required to construct valid questionnaire
Structured Groups		
Focus Groups	• Group synergy • Can assist with questionnaire construction	• Requires well-trained facilitator • Data analysis
Nominal Group	• Facilitates contributions by all members • Structured approach • Establishes priorities	• May be viewed as too structured by some participants
Delphi Technique	• Avoids confrontation among experts • Cost effective when using Web-based questionnaires and electronic voting	• Completion time • Sustaining motivation
Community Forum	• Easy to conduct • Cost effective • Allows input from many segments of school community	• Representativeness of attendees • Requires skilled leader

characterized based on their geographical location and organizational setting.

Programs also can be described in terms of the utilization patterns of services offered. The underlying assumption of this approach is that program participants are those in the population who need services. Since utilization rates represent manifestations of problems that have already developed, they are not helpful in prevention planning (Rhodes & Jason, 1991). Resource inventories detail programs that previously have been implemented and, therefore, conclusions based on data drawn from this method may provide a status quo orientation to program planning (McKillip, 1998).

An important outcome of a resource or program inventory is that it may reveal significant gaps in services and identify underutilized services and services that were previously unknown to the needs assessment team (McKillip, 1998). Furthermore, results may indicate that different agencies provide overlapping services. In times of limited resources and budgets within the schools, the reduction in overlap of services may result in the allocation of resources into other areas of need.

Resource inventories are commonly used in the initial steps of a needs assessment. When considered alone, a resource inventory does not indicate need, as gaps in programming may reflect services that are not needed. For this reason, resource inventories should be supplemented with measures of the extent of the problem and potential demand for services (McKillip, 1998).

Social Indicators

The social indicators approach presumes that need estimates can be inferred by selected social and demographic statistics that have been found to correlate highly with service utilization (Lewis & Lewis, 1983). These statistics are presumed to be indicators of need. In other words, it is assumed that the number of resources allocated to address a particular problem serves as an indicator of the extent of the problem. Because many federal, state, and local agencies, including schools, are required to maintain statistical information (Illback et al., 1990), social indicator data are readily available through government publications. Social indicator data can be accessed through various websites, such as the U.S.

Census Bureau (http://www.census.gov), the U.S. Department of Education (http://www2.ed.gov/rschstat/landing.jhtml), and the Annie E. Casey Foundation (http://datacenter.kidscount.org). These websites provide county, state, and national statistics on topics such as school dropout, graduation rates, public education expenditures, and child poverty. Additionally, state departments of public instruction, health organizations, social services agencies, and law enforcement may provide important sources of indicator information. With social indicator analysis, information is readily accessible and generally can be gathered inexpensively by those who have limited research expertise or technical skills (Warheit, Bell, & Schwab, 1977).

Social indicator analyses are inferential in nature and make the assumption that certain social indicators predict service needs. In order to validate this assumption, substantial evidence based on the research literature and previous needs assessment results is essential. Data from large geographic areas may not pertain or generalize to smaller communities or rural areas of interest (Rhodes & Jason, 1991). Before rates can be compared, differences in population characteristics need to be carefully considered. Although extensive indicator data are available, they may not conform to the assessment team's informational requirements.

School psychologists who use the social indicator approach to needs assessment must be vigilant to population shifts that may occur in their schools. Social indicator information is reported over a long time interval and it is possible that communities undergo rapid changes. For this reason, social indicator analyses can provide baseline data on school or district demographics that allow school officials to monitor change and help guide future needs assessment programs.

Survey Methods

Surveys are the most commonly used needs assessment methods as they are flexible in format and can be conducted with a range of respondents. Surveys can be conducted face to face or by phone or questionnaires. The selection of methodology generally is based on the intended scope of the needs assessment, the technical expertise available to conduct the survey, and the time and resources needed to complete the project.

Interviews. If the number to be surveyed is relatively small, such as at the school level, then interviews probably are the most efficient means of gathering information. The success of interviews is largely a function of the skillfulness of the interviewer, who must be able to establish trust and convey empathy for the respondent to answer questions without feeling self-conscious or suspicious.

Interviews provide in-depth information about demographic characteristics, needs, feelings, desires, and solutions to the problems the respondent is experiencing. Interviews also allow for follow-up questions to explicate ambiguous responses, elicit more information than would be attained through group methods, and are particularly well suited to surveying the needs of marginalized individuals (McKillip, 1998). The team may also consider conducting phone interviews, which may better accommodate the schedules of parents.

Questionnaires. Questionnaires are generally the preferred survey method when large numbers of respondents are required. The development of an effective questionnaire requires a certain degree of technical expertise that school psychologists possess. Central concerns in questionnaire construction are that items should be understandable, elicit the desired information, and motivate respondents to participate. Additional considerations include controlling for social desirability of responding, selection of open- versus closed-ended questions, and the use of ranking versus rating questions (McKillip, 1998). The dual-response format presents a statement or question (e.g., "The counseling services available at my high school are satisfactory.") and directs respondents to provide ratings on two different Likert scales, one that captures the current status ("Things are okay.") and another that reflects the way the respondent would like things to be ("Things could be better."), thus making it particularly well suited for needs assessments (Watkins et al., 2012).

Since it is beyond the scope of this chapter to provide an in-depth description of questionnaire construction, the reader is referred to several sources: Centers for Disease Control and Prevention (http://www.cdc.gov), McKillip (1998), Soriano (2012), and Watkins et al. (2012).

Once items have been written, the questionnaire should be piloted with a representative group that should complete it and also critique the items and wording to determine whether the desired information was elicited. Failure to undertake item piloting may result in wasted time and resources. Poorly written and designed questions may also result in decreased response rates.

Questionnaires can be designed in either paper-and-pencil or Web-based formats. When deciding on the most appropriate format, needs assessors should consider which is most likely to provide the highest response rate (Watkins et al., 2012). This consideration is directly related to the target audience, as some respondents will not have access to or feel comfortable using technology while others may need help reading items and completing the questionnaire, regardless of format.

The team should consider strategies to adopt if it encounters low response rates. The Centers for Disease Control and Prevention (http://www.cdc.gov), which heavily relies upon questionnaire data, offers many tips for increasing response rates, such as sending a prenotification letter, provide a limited number of clearly written questions with easy instructions, and personalizing mailings.

Structured Groups

Structured groups provide a supplemental and alternative methodology to other needs assessment approaches already reviewed in this chapter. Structured groups can be the most active and informative approaches to needs assessment since structured groups involve people in systematic problem analysis and discussion (Illback et al., 1990).

Focus groups. A focus group is a guided discussion intended to yield information about a specific group's feelings and beliefs about a particular topic (Sussman, Barton, Dent, Stacy, & Flay, 1991). Focus groups are commonly used for exploratory purposes, hypothesis generation, or confirmation of results from other needs assessment approaches. The interactive nature of focus groups provides the opportunity to gain rich, valuable information about needs. However, focus groups can be difficult to conduct and they require sufficient planning, clearly formulated and specific questions, an effective facilitator, and systematic data analysis to be successful (Krueger, 2005). Focus groups should be led by a well-trained facilitator who is knowledgeable about the problem under study. The facilitator should be someone who is able to keep the discussion focused, as the conversations generated often make it easy for individuals to veer from the topic of interest (Watkins et al., 2012). The facilitator also should be skilled at eliciting responses from reluctant participants and reigning in the comments of those who tend to take over the discussion.

To begin, the facilitator presents the group with broad, open-ended questions about the problem, followed by more specific questions. The facilitator may also employ techniques such as brainstorming, critical incidents (reports of previous experiences), round-robin, or straw polls (Watkins et al., 2012). The size of focus groups is usually 6–10. Homogeneous

grouping is essential to allow free interaction among group members (McKillip, 1998); however, comparisons of several groups with varied characteristics may provide useful information about subgroup needs.

Focus groups may be viewed as similar to open-ended interviews, but are considered superior to individual interviews because of the so-called synergistic group effect that results in more identified needs and solutions (Sussman et al., 1991). It is strongly recommended that focus groups be recorded by audio or video (with consent from the participants), as the data that emerge tend to be rich and copious and difficult to capture by hand. Facilitators should, however, record in writing observations during the discussions. Focus groups are useful in helping explicate differences between professional (key informant) and target audiences (clients/community members). They also may aid in the construction of questionnaires by identifying issues to be addressed in the survey and terminology and phrases used by the target population. Finally, focus groups can be used to gather reactions to findings generated from other needs assessment methodologies, which may subsequently lead to solutions to the identified areas of need.

Nominal group technique. The nominal group technique (NGT) was developed to overcome the common problems of group dynamics, including domination of talking high status group members, noninvolvement of reticent members, evaluation of ideas impeding idea generation, and group tendencies to get off task from the agenda (McKillip, 1998; Watkins et al., 2012). The NGT was designed to give individuals with disparate interests, capabilities, information, or influence more equity in the decision-making and priority-setting process (Lauffer, 1982). The term nominal describes the process of bringing groups together but minimizing verbal communication (Miller & Hustedde, 1987). The NGT is unique in that it combines both qualitative (discussions) and quantitative (voting) data.

The NGT requires a well-trained group leader or facilitator. The group can be composed of key informants, clients, teachers, students, or service providers (McKillip, 1998). Although there are a number of variants in the NGT, most involve the following steps (Watkins et al., 2012):

- Facilitator of group presents a problem or question that is clearly defined (e.g., How can we prevent school violence?).
- Each group member is asked to write down independently and silently as many solutions as

possible on paper or index cards. At this point no discussion is permitted.

- Each group member presents one solution or idea, one at a time, round-robin. The facilitator records each idea on a flip chart until all are recorded.
- Solutions are then clarified and evaluated through discussion.
- Group members are asked to either secretly rate each proposed solution or to rank order their top five choices.
- Ratings are tabulated and a summary of the results is presented.
- If clear choices or priorities result from the vote, then the NGT is complete. In the event of no clear choices, additional clarification, discussion, and voting are undertaken until a clear choice is obtained.
- The cycle is repeated for each problem or solution area.

The priorities established by the group may not be accepted by others in the school or community. To minimize this possibility, the needs assessment team should develop a plan that has adequate representation among subgroups in the school or community.

Delphi technique. The Delphi technique is used to obtain group opinion from experts or individuals with exceptional knowledge about a particular subject area and is a structured process for identifying needs or desired outcomes, recommending solutions, or predicting events when inadequate information exists (Watkins et al., 2012). This technique is an iterative process in that it involves the administration of successive questionnaires that are based on the domains of interest and administered to a selected panel of experts, with feedback and summarization provided between administrations (Lauffer, 1982). The Delphi technique has been used successfully in school program planning activities (Altschuld & White, 2010).

Miller and Hustedde (1987) have outlined the basic steps for panelists completing the series of questionnaires. For the first questionnaire, respondents are asked to answer questions regarding a problem situation. The questionnaire is returned to the needs assessment team, which then summarizes the distribution of responses. This summary then serves as the basis for the second questionnaire. The second questionnaire is sent to the panelists, and they are asked to rank their concerns, agree or disagree with the group's central tendencies, and clarify their judgments. A third questionnaire is mailed and respondents are asked to reassess prior

answers, clarify their ratings relative to the group, and again vote by ranking the items listed on the questionnaire. This process is considered complete when there is general agreement among panelists. For most school applications, a series of three questionnaires is probably adequate if using a panel of 8–12 experts. In the event of substantial differences among panelists, the questionnaire refinement-feedback cycle is continued. The central aim of the Delphi technique is to clarify problems and needs, not reach group consensus. However, consensus does provide justification for goal setting (Watkins et al., 2012). Once the process is complete, respondents should be provided with a final report.

One challenge in using Delphi technique is that respondents must have well-developed writing skills and a high level of motivation because no facilitator is present to help stimulate responses (Miller & Hustedde, 1987). Although the length of time to conduct a Delphi panel will vary as a function of the number of questionnaire mailings, it typically takes about 2 months to complete the process. The use of Web-based questionnaires and electronic voting can increase efficiency.

Community forum. The community forum is similar to a town meeting in which community members' views and opinions about their needs and problems are gathered. The community forum is appealing because it is generally easy to arrange and can be conducted inexpensively. The community forum can be easily adapted to the scope of needs assessments in the schools and is commonly used in conjunction with questionnaires to assess the needs of the community. If the scope of the assessment is at the school level, then the forum can be held at an individual school, whereas a district-wide needs assessment may involve a sample of schools or all schools within a given district.

To enhance the effectiveness of a community forum, a certain degree of planning is required. First, the needs assessment planning team should prepare questions designed to structure the meeting around the issues and, at the same time, provide sufficient flexibility to allow for spontaneous comments and candor among the participants (Warheit et al., 1977). The meeting should be highly publicized through advertising and the media and held at a convenient time and accessible location, because it is essential that a representative sample of the community attend. Early evening meetings at the local school in the community member's attendance area fit these criteria.

A leader for the forum should have sufficient skills to keep the audience discussion on track. The leader must clearly state the purpose of the forum and explain any ground rules that will be used, such as time limits on talking by participants. In the event of large turnouts for the forum, it may be necessary to divide the groups into smaller sections to facilitate discussion. Obviously, in these instances, several group leaders will be necessary. A member of the needs assessment team should also be present to record the proceedings of the meeting. The group leader also may wish to take a vote on priorities and concerns. A sign-up sheet for all participants should be used so that follow-up mailings can be sent to those attending the meeting.

The community forum builds rapport and trust with the community and can enhance community members' commitment to program planning. Garcia and Hasson (2004) commented that going out into the community increases program planners' understanding of specific groups' situations that, in turn, can help service providers match programs to the target groups' specific needs. It also identifies citizens who may be valuable resources for the future implementation of programs.

The validity of data gathered from a community forum will largely be a function of the representativeness of the group. Only a partial view of the community's needs or problems will be portrayed if the group is not representative of the general community. It is important to keep in mind that the community forum approach is impressionistic and assumes that citizens are aware of and knowledgeable about their own problems and needs. The forum leader must keep participants focused on the agenda, or else the meeting will degenerate into a gripe and grievance session. The forum leader also must prevent special interest groups that wish to express their viewpoints at the expense of others' opposing or different perspectives from controlling the meeting. Similar to other needs assessment methods, the community forum raises expectations that something will be done to solve problems or to satisfy unmet needs. An excellent example of a school district community forum on issues related to bullying is provided in the Community Toolbox (2013).

Selection of Respondents

Once the methods have been selected, the team should determine whether or not it requires information from the general school population or from specific subgroups. Finifter et al. (2005) suggest a multitiered approach in which data are gathered from multiple groups, thus addressing the potential problem of sample bias and avoiding the common problem of missing crucial subgroups of the population of interest. When the objective is to estimate the frequency of need in the general population, a representative sample of that population is required. In instances where information about a specific subgroup is required, purposive sampling is the methodology of choice (McKillip, 1998).

Key Informants

Key informants are individuals presumed to have knowledge about the problem under consideration and a good understanding of the needs of the target population because of the nature of their work or position in the school or community. Depending on the informational requirements of the needs assessment, the team should select relevant school personnel and community professionals. If this approach is well planned and a diverse sample of key informants is used, the needs assessment can result in a comprehensive impression of the needs of the school or community. Additionally, because many school personnel and community agencies are involved, these interactions can serve as the groundwork for cooperation and the development of coalitions between these agencies or groups.

The assessment team should keep in mind that key informants may be biased since their views are impressionistic and they tend to see needs through their organizational perspectives. Additionally, key informants may not fully comprehend the potential needs of those they are responsible to serve. For this reason, the team should evaluate the adequacy of the number and type of informants used. The key informant approach can be a valuable first step in the needs assessment process as it helps narrow the focus by assuring the appropriate design of other methods and identifying potential misconceptions on the part of upper-level decision makers that may ultimately lead to problems.

Client and Community Respondents

Client and community respondents may include parents, students, and teachers, as well as others drawn from the general community. As suggested by Finifter et al. (2005), inclusion of these types of respondents provides a comprehensive viewpoint of the problem and needed services as well as the acceptability of potential solutions. The most important advantage of this approach is that it directly assesses the problems and needs of the sample.

Students' and parents' expressed needs may be different than those of educators and policy makers, who ultimately determine how to best serve those students. The importance of considering parent and student perspectives is critical in school-based needs assessments. If service providers are to successfully meet the needs of their clients, they should include data collected directly from those clients in their needs assessments.

Involving clients and community members in needs assessments can lead to increased expectations that schools will address the problem areas. However, inclusion also may result in marshaling support for program initiatives, increasing commitment to the needs assessment process, and promoting resulting outcomes (Garcia & Hasson, 2004).

Data Analysis and Prioritization

Once the process of data collection is complete, the challenge of analyzing the data presents itself. There are many different types of analyses that can be conducted, depending on the method used. Based on the scope of the assessment and the amount of information gathered, this process can either be easily accomplished or quite laborious. If the needs assessment included only one type of method, analyzing the data should be relatively straightforward. However, if the recommended multimethod approach is followed, the resulting combination of different types of data complicates the analysis, as it is necessary to integrate and synthesize both quantitative and qualitative data (Altschuld & White, 2010). The use of multiple methods and informants makes it difficult to adhere to a standardized approach and presents a challenge for the assessment team. For example, differences in the wording of parent and teacher questionnaires may affect comparisons of group responses. The differences between the measurement tools may affect comparisons between the measures for the different groups (Altschuld & White, 2010). Nonetheless, a multifaceted approach to assessment in any context is considered best practice.

Once the team has completed data analysis, the identified needs must be prioritized. Prioritization is a critical, yet often neglected, unplanned, and unstructured aspect of the needs assessment process (Altschuld & White, 2010). When needs are simple and relatively straightforward, the process of prioritization can run smoothly. Prioritization can be challenging when the data reveal a multitude of needs experienced by different parties that exceed the organization's ability to address. Teams can use various methods to prioritize needs, including group discussions and rank ordering

(Altschuld & White, 2010), and the team should be prepared to manage conflicting interests, lack of consensus, and reluctance to compromise (Watkins et al., 2012). Whatever the method used, the team should consider the importance of the needs, the short- and long-term risk of not attending to identified needs, the feasibility of addressing the needs, and the impact of responding to the needs of some but not all constituents.

The involvement of stakeholders in the process of interpreting results and developing recommendations is strongly encouraged (Carter, 1996), as they likely have greater insight into the practicality of implementing recommendations within their organizations. The involvement of stakeholders also promotes a sense of ownership and commitment to carrying out recommended plans.

Postassessment Phase

Once the data are collected, analyzed, and prioritized, the team must communicate the findings to be used for program planning, development, and modification (Aponte, 1983). Carter (1996) notes that teams tend to focus most of their attention on the evaluative process and much less on dissemination. Decision makers will act upon needs assessment information only when they can understand the findings and see a clear connection between the results and program planning. The team must devise a plan for communicating the findings to various audiences and making the results as meaningful as possible (Carter, 1996). It is important to consider characteristics of the audience, such as its need for the information, the audience's level of education and ability to make sense of the information, and the ways in which the audience obtains information.

Communication of Needs Assessment Findings

The scope and framework of the final report depends on the audience to be addressed. The communication must fit audience interests, keeping in mind that the audience is busy and often unsophisticated about research methodology (McKillip, 1998). In instances where the school psychologist will report the findings to several audiences with divergent interests, modifications in the report may be necessary. The findings should be reported to correspond to the questions raised by the decision makers who most likely initiated the needs assessment. Equally important is the timely presentation of the results. If too much time has elapsed in the process of conducting the assessment, then the final report may include outdated information or issues that no longer are priorities for decision makers.

The findings can be presented written or orally and should provide information about the study from its inception to completion (Carter, 1996). According to Carter (1996), the most common and effective means of communicating findings is the written final report, which should include the following sections: (a) Executive Summary, (b) Statement of Problem, (c) Historical Background, (d) Methods, (e) Findings, and (f) Recommendations. Written reports should be as concise as possible, free of jargon or technical terms, and only provide information that is necessary to facilitate decision making. Poor grammar and typographical errors should be avoided because these will detract from the credibility of the report. The visual display of the findings also tends to facilitate clarity and understanding.

If an oral presentation is used, the needs assessment team must be sure that the presenter will be articulate, knowledgeable, and enthusiastic about the findings. A distinct advantage of the oral presentation is that it allows for face-to-face contact and provides the opportunity for the exchange of information. Oral presentations should be supplemented with handouts and/or audiovisual materials of the major findings to structure the presentation and avoid information overload. Written and oral briefings are typically combined when communicating needs assessment findings.

Finifter et al. (2005) describe a number of alternative dissemination methods. These include community forums for service providers, state professional meetings, school advisory committees, and electronic versions of the final needs assessment report on appropriate websites.

Many needs assessment efforts fail to plan adequately for the postassessment phase. Amodeo and Gal (1997) lamented the failure of their organization to utilize their findings in program implementation, attributing their lack of success to a variety of factors that could have been avoided. First, they felt that too much time was spent in data collection and, consequently, decision makers felt a sense of urgency to implement programs without waiting for the needs assessment findings. Second, insufficient time was provided to decision makers to reflect upon the findings of the final report before its oral presentation. These results underscore the importance of keeping the decision makers apprised of the progress of the needs assessment through the use of interim reports from the planning team. Communication with administrators also informs the team about organizational changes within the school or agency that may affect the focus of the needs assessment.

The likelihood that the school or organization accepts the recommendations generated by the report will be enhanced if the proposed changes are based on factual data from the needs assessment, rank ordered by time–cost benefits, achievable, reflective of the best interests of the school, and have the highest potential for resolving the need (Warheit et al., 1977). Once priorities are established by the team and/or decision makers, action plans should be developed that require commitment from leaders within the organization (Altschuld & Witkin, 2000). Thus, the responsibilities for planning activities are shifted to stakeholders within the organization. In describing the development of their Safe Schools Plan, Armstrong, Massey, and Boroughs (2006) noted the benefits derived from existing long-term cooperative relationships between the schools and community service providers in terms of increased levels of acceptance and commitment by the schools.

Implementation and Evaluation

A major problem involved in the needs assessment process is the failure to implement proposed solutions (Finifter et al., 2005). Carter (1996) describes implementation as the "culmination of the needs assessment process" (p. 199) and notes that the success of a needs assessment is evidenced by the development of new or modified policies, programs, and/or service delivery. If the needs assessment is to achieve its goal of improving some perceived problem and helping an organization achieve some desired state, implementation of proposed solutions is essential. A plan for implementation should be embedded within the needs assessment process to ease the transition into program planning and to ensure that the resources expended to conduct the assessment were well spent. In order to ensure commitment to the program and subsequent implementation, ongoing collaboration between stakeholders and service providers is essential (Armstrong et al., 2006). To guide this effort, Armstrong et al. (2006) emphasized the importance of developing a steering committee, whose ultimate responsibility involved ongoing management and maintenance of the program. The outcomes of needs assessments can lead to "rippling effects" (Watkins et al., 2012, p. 25) that can extend beyond the system of focus to other systems and subsystems.

Once implemented, programs need to be continuously monitored and evaluated, and these procedures should be integrated into the implementation plan (Watkins et al., 2012). Needs assessment data should be used as part of the evaluative process, informing the team about accomplishments and emerging needs

(Smith & Freeman, 2002). The Community Toolbox (2013) suggests that evaluations should focus on answering three simple questions: What happened? So what? Now what? To address these questions, implementation and evaluation teams should gather both process and outcome data from key stakeholders using various methods, such as satisfaction surveys, observations, and behavioral ratings. The team should use the results to determine how to proceed with the new program or intervention. Readers are referred to the Community Toolbox (2013) for detailed guidelines for evaluating programs.

SUMMARY

Needs assessment activities pervade all domains of the NASP Practice Model (NASP, 2010). As schools become increasingly involved in reform and restructuring activities, school psychologists will require system-based skills. Data derived from needs assessments should form the foundation upon which programs in the schools are designed. In addition to providing valuable information for program planning, the process of conducting needs assessments can strengthen relationships between schools, families, and the community. Needs assessments also provide opportunities for school psychologists to use their many skills and to expand their roles and influence at a broader level. Depending on the resources available in the school districts in which they work, school psychologists can play an active role in contributing their unique skills to needs assessment activities. Such participation will increase the visibility of the school psychologist at all levels of the school district and the community.

REFERENCES

Altschuld, J. W., & White, J. L. (2010). *Needs assessment: Analysis and prioritization.* Thousand Oaks, CA: SAGE. doi:10.4135/9781452230542

Altschuld, J., & Witkin, R. (2000). *From needs assessment to action: Transforming needs into solution strategies.* Thousand Oaks, CA: SAGE.

Amodeo, M., & Gal, C. (1997). Strategies for ensuring use of needs assessment findings: Experiences of a community substance abuse prevention program. *The Journal of Primary Prevention, 18,* 227–242. doi:10.1023/A:102469452556310.1023/A:1024694525563

Aponte, J. (1983). Need assessment: The state of the art and future directions. In R. A. Bell, M. Sandel, J. F. Aponte, S. A. Murrell, & L. Lin (Eds.), *Assessing health and human service needs: Concepts, methods, and applications.* (pp. 285–301). New York, NY: Human Sciences Press.

Armstrong, K. H., Massey, O. T., & Boroughs, M. (2006). Implementing comprehensive safe school plans in Pinellas county schools, Florida: Planning, implementation, operation,

sustainability, and lessons learned. In S. R. Jimerson & M. Furlong (Eds.), *Handbook of school violence and school safety: From research to practice.* (pp. 525–536). Mahwah, NJ: Erlbaum.

Carter, C. (1996). Using and communicating findings. In R. Reviere, S. Berkowitz, C. Carter, & C. Ferguson (Eds.), *Needs assessment: A creative and practical guide for social scientists.* (pp. 185–202). Washington, DC: Taylor & Francis.

Community Toolbox. (2013). *Assessing community needs and resources.* Lawrence, KS: Author. Retrieved from http://ctb.ku.edu/en/dothework/tools_tk_2.aspx

Finifter, D. H., Jensen, C. J., Wilson, C. E., & Koenig, B. L. (2005). A comprehensive, multitiered, targeted community needs assessment model: Methodology, dissemination, and implementation. *Family Community Health, 28,* 293–306. doi:10.1023/A:1024694525563

Garcia, D. C., & Hasson, D. J. (2004). Implementing family literacy programs for linguistically and culturally diverse populations: Key elements to consider. *The School Community Journal, 14,* 113–137, (ERIC Document Reproduction Service No. ED EJ794831)

Hobbs, D. (1987). Strategy for needs assessments. In D. E. Johnson, L. R. Meiller, L. C. Miller, & G. R. Summers (Eds.), *Needs assessment: Theory and methods.* (pp. 20–34). Ames, IA: Iowa State University Press.

Illback, R. J., Zins, J. F., Maher, C. A., & Greenberg, R. (1990). An overview of principles and procedures of program planning and evaluation. In C. Reynolds & T. Gutkin (Eds.), *Handbook of school psychology.* (2nd ed., pp. 799–820). New York, NY: Wiley.

Jeffery, G. H., Hache, G., & Lehr, R. (1995). A group-based Delphi application: Defining rural career counseling needs. *Measurement and Evaluation in Counseling and Development, 28,* 45–60. (ERIC Document Reproduction Service No. EJ507898)

Krueger, R. A. (2005). Focus groups. In S. Mathison (Ed.), *Encyclopedia of evaluation.* (pp. 159–161). Thousand Oaks, CA: SAGE.

Lauffer, A. (1982). *Assessment tools for practitioners, managers, and trainers.* Beverly Hills, CA: SAGE.

Lewis, J. A., & Lewis, M. D. (1983). *Management of human service programs.* Monterey, CA: Brooks/Cole.

McKillip, J. (1998). Needs analysis: Process and techniques. In L. Bickman & D. Rog (Eds.), *Handbook of applied social research methods.* (pp. 261–284). Thousand Oaks, CA: SAGE.

Merrill, K. W., Ervin, R. A., & Peacock, G. G. (2012). *School psychology for the 21st century: Foundations and practices.* New York, NY: Guilford Press.

Miller, L. C., & Hustedde, R. J. (1987). Group approaches. In D. Johnson, L. Meiller, C. Miller, & G. R. Summers (Eds.), *Needs assessment: Theory and methods.* (pp. 91–125). Ames, IA: Iowa State University Press.

National Association of School Psychologists. (2010). *Model for comprehensive and integrated school psychological services.* Bethesda, MD: Author. Retrieved from http://www.nasponline.org/standards/2010standards/2_PracticeModel.pdf

National Urban League. (1983). *A guide for developing non-instructional programs.* New York, NY: Author.

Rhodes, J. E., & Jason, L. A. (1991). Community needs assessment. In E. Schroeder (Ed.), *New directions in health psychology assessment.* (pp. 159–173). New York, NY: Hemisphere.

Romualdi, V., & Sandoval, J. (1995). Comprehensive school-linked services: Implications for school psychologists. *Psychology in the Schools, 32,* 306–317. doi:10.1002/1520-6807(199510)32:4<306::AID-PITS2310320409>3.0.CO;2-K

Smith, C. L., & Freeman, R. L. (2002). Using continuous system level assessment to build school capacity. *American Journal of Evaluation*, *23*, 307–319. doi:10.1016/S1098-2140(02)00208-4

Soriano, F. (2012). *Conducting needs assessments: A multidisciplinary approach*. (2nd ed.). Thousand Oaks, CA: SAGE.

Sussman, S., Barton, D., Dent, C. W., Stacy, A. W., & Flay, B. (1991). Use of focus groups in developing an adolescent tobacco use cessation program: Collective norm effects. *Journal of Applied Social Psychology*, *21*, 1772–1782. doi:10.1111/j.1559-1816.1991.tb00503.x

Voyles, M. M. (2012). Perceived needs of at-risk families in a small town: Implications for full-service community schools. *School Community Journal*, *22*, 31–63, Retrieved from http://www.adi.org/journal/2012fw/VoylesFall2012.pdf

Warheit, G. J., Bell, R. A., & Schwab, J. J. (1977). *Needs assessment approaches: Concepts and methods*. (Publication No. ADM-77-472). Washington, DC: Department of Health, Education, and Welfare.

Watkins, R., Meiers, M. W., & Visser, Y. (2012). *A guide to assessing needs: Essential tools for collecting information, making decisions, and achieving development results*. Washington, DC: World Bank.

25

Best Practices in Program Evaluation in a Model of Response to Intervention/Multitiered System of Supports

Jose M. Castillo
University of South Florida

OVERVIEW

Many school psychologists' introduction to response to intervention (RTI) was likely a result of the reauthorization of the 2004 Individuals with Disabilities Education Act, which included provisions allowing districts to examine students' response to scientifically based interventions as part of a comprehensive evaluation to determine eligibility for special education services. Although eligibility determination remains a central issue in the implementation of RTI, researchers, policy makers, and educators have been advocating for a broader vision of RTI. In fact, RTI is frequently discussed as a multitiered system of supports (MTSS) for matching instruction and intervention to student need (e.g., Batsche et al., 2005).

Conceptualizing RTI as an MTSS, rather than a set of procedures designed to identify students who are eligible for special education services, shifts the focus of assessment from identifying students who may be eligible for special education programs to using data to inform prevention and early intervention activities. Calls for public health approaches like MTSS have been emanating from school psychology (e.g., Dawson et al., 2004) and other disciplines (e.g., Sugai & Horner, 2009). Furthermore, the critical elements of an MTSS (e.g., data-based problem solving, evidence-based instruction, and interventions across multiple tiers) are supported by research and are becoming increasingly evident in legislation, policy proposals, and recent initiatives at the federal and state levels (Castillo & Batsche, 2012).

Data from a nationwide survey on RTI implementation provide evidence that educators are responding to the research, policy, and other forces exerting pressure to implement an MTSS. Results from the survey indicated that the vast majority of districts that responded are at some stage of implementation of the model (Spectrum K–12 School Solutions, 2011). In 2011, 62% of districts reported implementing RTI for the purpose of personalizing instruction for all students (previously 49% in 2010), and 88% of districts reported implementing RTI to provide early intervening services and supports to students identified as at risk. The emphasis on prevention and intervention services suggests that many districts are conceptualizing RTI as an MTSS.

Educators' conceptualization of RTI as an MTSS is critical for school psychologists to understand and embrace. MTSS appears to be increasingly viewed as a school reform effort rather than procedures required for special education eligibility determination. Given that special education-related activities continue to dominate the professional lives of many school psychologists despite reported desires to engage in more comprehensive service delivery (Castillo, Curtis, & Gelley, 2012), school psychologists can view this shifting emphasis as an opportunity to deliver a broader array of services that support students and the goals of educational stakeholders.

The National Association of School Psychologists (NASP) *Model for Comprehensive and Integrated School Psychological Services* (NASP, 2010) emphasizes practices that place school psychologists in a position to be leaders in the implementation of an MTSS. This chapter focuses on knowledge, skills, and practices that are reflected in the Research and Program Evaluation domain. Specifically, the application of program evaluation principles and practices in an MTSS is discussed. School psychologists' role in facilitating systematic program evaluation is highlighted.

The role school psychologists can play in facilitating program evaluation in an MTSS is evident when examining current implementation efforts. Data from the nationwide survey of districts referenced above (Spectrum K-12 School Solutions, 2011) indicate that only 26% of districts evaluate the critical elements of implementing an MTSS. Researchers suggest that many school initiatives do not result in meaningful changes in educators' practices and that data-based decision making increases the probability that new practices will be implemented (e.g., Fullan, 2010; Sharratt & Fullan, 2009). School psychologists' knowledge and skills in research and program evaluation make them ideal candidates to both advocate for and support efforts to engage in program evaluation.

The purpose of this chapter is to increase school psychologists' understanding of the knowledge, skills, and practices needed to facilitate program evaluation in an MTSS. The information provided in this chapter is intended to help school psychologists engage in ongoing evaluation activities to inform efforts to increase the fidelity of MTSS implementation. After reading this chapter, school psychologists will understand basic principles of program evaluation, understand critical elements of implementing an MTSS that should be evaluated, and be familiar with program evaluation approaches and strategies in an MTSS.

BASIC CONSIDERATIONS

School psychologists facilitating program evaluation in an MTSS should consider basic principles of program evaluation. Comprehensive discussions of program evaluation principles and processes are beyond the scope of this chapter (see Stufflebeam & Shinkfield, 2007, and Yarbrough, Shulha, Hopson, & Caruthers, 2011, for more information). However, a summary of critical issues as they relate to MTSS implementation is provided. It is critical that school psychologists understand the relationship between program evaluation and MTSS implementation. MTSS implementation represents a fundamental change in the way schools educate students and requires a data-based approach to implementation.

Fundamental Program Evaluation Principles to Consider

School psychologists facilitating program evaluation in an MTSS must take into account the constant changes that occur in schools. Research designs that assume that practices will be implemented uniformly across settings are useful for determining what works (i.e., efficacy), but they are typically less useful for determining effectiveness in an applied setting. Uniform implementation of the critical elements of an MTSS from classroom to classroom and from school to school is unrealistic. Program evaluation designs that take this variability (e.g., student needs and characteristics; educator beliefs, values, knowledge, and skills; available resources; current implementation levels) into account are needed. Program evaluation designs typically emphasize collecting data on a number of factors thought to have an impact on implementation and outcomes. The information derived is used to improve service delivery and make decisions regarding the benefits of the services (see Kratochwill & Shernoff, 2004, for a discussion of research-to-practice issues).

Many program evaluation approaches exist. Each approach has strengths and weaknesses and decisions regarding which approach to adopt should be based on the circumstances under which program evaluation will occur (Stufflebeam & Shinkfield, 2007). Whenever possible, school psychologists should collaborate with stakeholders to design evaluation processes and procedures prior to implementing MTSS to ensure adequate data are available for decision making. Implementation of an MTSS will require adjustments over time, and data should be used to inform those decisions. Flexible designs that allow for adjustments to program evaluation processes and procedures also should be considered, as stakeholders often find that additional information is required or that information previously collected is no longer useful for informing decisions.

Formative Versus Summative Decision Making

Program evaluation efforts should result in data that allow opportunities for both formative and summative decision making (Stufflebeam & Shinkfield, 2007). Formative decisions are those that are intended to result in continuous improvement. Data must not only be available not only on students' academic, behavioral, and/or social–emotional outcomes, but also on the implementation of the critical elements of an MTSS. In this way, formative evaluation of a school's or district's progress in implementing an MTSS is no different than ongoing progress monitoring of a student's response to an intervention.

Summative decisions are those that are intended to result in a judgment of the benefit of continuing implementation of an MTSS. Summative decision making regarding the elements of an MTSS should occur periodically as school systems possess finite resources (e.g., time, money, staff allocations, materials) and cannot afford to dedicate these resources to practices that do not positively contribute to the student outcomes for which they are being held accountable. However, summative judgments cannot occur prematurely. Making a decision about the effectiveness of an MTSS in the absence of data suggesting that the critical elements were implemented with fidelity can lead to inaccurate decisions. The assessment, curricular, and instructional practices that must be implemented represent massive systems change efforts in and of themselves. However, when the need to align and integrate practices across tiers (Tiers 1, 2, and 3), content areas (e.g., reading, math, behavior), and grade levels is considered, years, if not decades, will be required before the effects of the change can truly be realized. For this reason, it is critical that formative decisions are made that maximize implementation fidelity prior to summative decisions regarding the benefit of an MTSS. Given the current accountability climate that places pressure on educators to produce immediate increases in student outcomes, school psychologists will likely need to advocate for the time necessary to improve implementation fidelity through formative decision making.

Multiple Method, Multiple Informant Assessment

The accuracy of formative and summative decisions can be improved when multiple data sources and multiple informants are included in program evaluation designs. Data sources and informants will vary somewhat given the local context. However, some general guidelines will likely apply (see Stufflebeam & Shinkfield, 2007, for a detailed discussion of these issues). A combination of quantitative (e.g., surveys using rating scales, fidelity checklists, student performance data) and qualitative (e.g., focus groups, open-ended questions on surveys) methods provides the most complete picture of the status of MTSS implementation.

Quantitative data can provide a snapshot of how the system is progressing on a strategic goal (e.g., increasing the percentage of students meeting educational standards) as well as how much variability exists. Quantitative data also can help identify issues that may need to be targeted for systemic intervention (e.g., insufficient implementation levels of the critical elements of an MTSS). Qualitative data provide valuable information on the perspectives of teachers and other stakeholders who are actually implementing the practices. Useful information regarding what is occurring, barriers to implementation, and the value stakeholders place on implementing the practices (i.e., acceptability) can be derived from analyzing stakeholder perspectives.

In addition to the use of multiple methods, representatives from key stakeholder groups should be included to achieve a more complete understanding of what is occurring. Varying roles and responsibilities of stakeholders typically result in different perspectives regarding how the system functions. Differing viewpoints can be a source of tension among educators, but also can be a source of rich information. For example, in the case of data suggesting teachers are not implementing interventions with fidelity during a district-mandated intervention time block, district administrators and principals may view a lack of fidelity as noncompliance or teacher resistance. However, teachers and support staff may view the same data as an indication of a lack of time to plan for interventions. Consideration of the data provided by both informant groups increases the probability that actions will be taken that appropriately balance accountability and support.

Assessment Functions

Assessments that serve many functions are necessary when facilitating program evaluation in an MTSS. However, the concepts of needs assessment, resource mapping, and measuring of fidelity of implementation warrant particular attention. *Needs assessment* involves collecting data to identify both strengths and targets for improvement in the implementation of an MTSS. *Resource mapping* includes identifying the time, personnel, material, and other resources available to support implementation (needs assessment and resource mapping are described in more detail below). *Fidelity* assessment involves examination of the extent to which the critical elements of an MTSS are being implemented as intended.

Noell and Gansle (2006) describe three ways to examine fidelity: self-report, permanent product review, and observations. (Although Noell and Gansle's primary focus is on implementation of student-focused interventions, the concepts described are applicable to other components of implementing an MTSS, such as fidelity of core instruction and fidelity of data-based problem-solving.) *Self-report* methods ask educators to provide data on the extent to which they are implementing the critical elements of an MTSS. Self-report is the most efficient but least reliable form of fidelity assessment as it tends to be upwardly biased. *Observation* methods, on the other hand, are the most reliable but least efficient. Direct observation of educators' implementation of the critical elements of an MTSS can lead to the most accurate information. However, logistical requirements (e.g., time, personnel, funding) can make this method impractical. *Permanent product reviews* strike a balance between reliability and efficiency. Permanent product reviews typically involve gathering notes, graphs and charts, forms, worksheets, or any other product that would be generated as a result of implementation and systematically reviewing them for the critical elements. This method is less reliable than observation because the absence of a permanent product does not always mean that a particular element was not implemented, but it is more efficient because trained reviewers can access the documentation at any time. Noell and Gansle (2006) suggest that an approach that includes both observation and permanent product review may be the best method to evaluate implementation fidelity. The inclusion of self-report data also can be beneficial. However, consumers of the information should interpret the data cautiously. See Castillo, Hines, Batsche, and Curtis (2011) for an example of how these three methods were applied to evaluating implementation fidelity in an MTSS.

Program Evaluation and Systems Change

School psychologists often encounter barriers to supporting program evaluation in an MTSS such as a lack of time available, stakeholders' traditional views of what school psychologists do, key stakeholders' support for MTSS, and the infrastructure available to support program evaluation efforts. As a result, school psychologists' opportunities to engage in program evaluation and their contributions to increases in MTSS implementation are to a great extent dependent on their skills in facilitating systems change.

Systems perspective. Prior to facilitating program evaluation in an MTSS, school psychologists should consider the context within which the model is being implemented. Although schools and districts share many attributes, program evaluation processes must be designed to fit the unique circumstances of each school and district. Schools often have some flexibility to engage in program evaluation practices that are unique to their context. However, state and district policies, procedures, and infrastructure (e.g., data systems available) typically exert pressure on schools to engage in certain evaluation processes and procedures. The conceptualization of an MTSS, strategic planning to guide resource implementation efforts, mandates for the use of data and the development of structures to collect the data, and mandates for reporting data often occur at the district level. As a result, this chapter discusses evaluation at both the school and district levels. In the instances in which only school- or district-level evaluation is discussed, school psychologists are encouraged to consider issues related to the other unit of analysis. Schools should design evaluation procedures that are consistent with district expectations, and districts must include school-level stakeholders in the development of evaluation processes and procedures.

The critical elements of an MTSS (i.e., multiple tiers of instruction and intervention, data-based problem solving) should remain consistent, but the implementation of these elements will vary based on factors such as student needs, resources available (e.g., data systems, personnel), and how stakeholders view MTSS (e.g., one more requirement versus a way of work that matches instruction and intervention to student needs).

Key stakeholder involvement. Involving key stakeholders throughout the process facilitates the identification of critical issues that should be evaluated. District- and school-level administrators, general and special education teachers, content specialists, student support services personnel, teachers union representatives, school board members, and family and community representatives can provide valuable information about the current functioning of the system as well as factors to be considered when engaging in program evaluation. Furthermore, the support of formal leaders within the system (e.g., school board members, superintendents, principals) will undoubtedly have an impact on the priority for, and resources dedicated to, MTSS program evaluation efforts. School psychologists cannot underestimate the importance of systematic involvement of key stakeholders if program evaluation in an MTSS is to be prioritized.

Involvement of key stakeholders also increases the chances that the data will be used to inform important decisions. Increasingly, educators are being asked to collect data on student outcomes and the implementation of evidence-based practices. However, failure to involve important stakeholders (e.g., teachers) in these decisions contributes to situations in which rich sources of data may exist (e.g., curriculum-based measures of student performance), but little data are used to actually inform important educational decisions (e.g., the identification of students at risk for reading failure). School psychologists can prevent this common problem by involving key stakeholders in the process from the beginning so that a shared understanding of the data to be collected and how the data should inform decisions can be reached. Surveys, focus groups, the use of already scheduled meeting times, and having representatives of key stakeholder groups on teams that make decisions are a few of the ways to facilitate input and feedback.

Accountability versus data-based decision making. Accountability is an important aspect of implementing change. However, the overreliance on policy and procedure to facilitate change is a problem that has plagued educational reform efforts. Fullan (2010) argues that an intelligent accountability system emphasizes internal accountability based on the collective ownership and responsibility of educators. Data are collected on practices and student performance and are used transparently by all key stakeholders to improve the effectiveness of services across the system. Mandates that establish policies and procedures for implementation and evaluation still play a role. However, they are not the primary mechanism for change. Thus, data collection activities designed to determine compliance with implementation procedures and to penalize schools that are out of compliance are not aligned with the purpose of program evaluation. Rather, data are collected and communicated in ways that support educators to collectively improve their practices and student outcomes. School psychologists can contribute to this culture change by collaborating with school- and district-level leaders to design data meetings in which planning and problem-solving procedures are used to empower educators.

Structured Planning and Problem Solving

Access to data does not guarantee that educators will make data-based decisions. Many school psychologists have participated in meetings in which the data needed to inform decisions were present. However, the discussions lacked focus and direction. Using a structured planning and problem-solving process, on the other hand, provides a mechanism for key stakeholders (a) to identify strategic goals or problems, (b) to determine systemic barriers to sustainable improvement, (c) to design strategies to address identified barriers, and (d) to formatively evaluate progress. School psychologists can

use their problem-solving skills to empower educators to use data to improve their practices.

BEST PRACTICES IN PROGRAM EVALUATION IN AN MTSS

Literature on program evaluation can be a useful resource for school psychologists. However, the number of different approaches can make designing evaluation processes and procedures challenging. Therefore, the remainder of this chapter will focus on strategies for program evaluation in an MTSS that have been used by school psychologists facilitating implementation of the model. The specific components of the evaluation design would need to be adapted based on local conditions (e.g., resources, local priorities, district and state policies). Furthermore, it is assumed that school psychologists attempting to facilitate the evaluation processes and procedures would have addressed the basic considerations described above. The steps are presented in the general order in which they occur. However, like planning and problem-solving, evaluation processes are iterative. Previously completed steps may need to be revisited as new information is obtained.

Step 1: Define MTSS and Identify Implementation Targets

Widespread adoption of the Common Core State Standards likely will result in common curriculum standards for the majority of states and more uniformity in the assessments used to measure student progress. However, schools, districts, and states will define the other critical elements of an MTSS model differently (e.g., number of tiers included, standard protocol interventions versus interventions developed based on problem analysis). The capacity of the system to support implementation (e.g., data sources available, personnel and instructional resources) and the extent to which educational stakeholders understand the need for and commit to MTSS implementation will vary across settings. For these reasons, it is important that school psychologists collaborate with key stakeholders to define the critical elements of an MTSS and identify variables that will likely have an impact on implementation in their local context. Logic modeling is one approach that can be used to accomplish this aim.

Logic models are typically visual representations of the implementation of a program or initiative (Rodriguez-Campos & Ricones-Gomez, 2013). Most logic models include inputs, processes, and outcomes. In the context of MTSS implementation, *inputs* are the resources (e.g., community organizations) and characteristics (e.g., student socioeconomic status, current achievement levels) of students, schools, and districts. *Processes* are the activities engaged in to implement the critical elements of an MTSS (e.g., delivery of evidence-based instruction and intervention across multiple tiers). *Outcomes* are the changes that would be expected as a result of implementation. Common outcomes associated with implementing an MTSS include increases in achievement scores, decreases in office discipline referrals, and decreases in referrals for and placements in special education programs (e.g., Burns, Appleton, & Stehouwer, 2005; Burns, Griffiths, Parson, Tilly, & VanDerHeyden, 2007). Because the implementation of an MTSS typically requires a systems change effort, it can be useful to include a second level of inputs (e.g., time, personnel), processes (e.g., professional development, scheduling), and outcomes (e.g., educator beliefs and skills) focused on issues related to building capacity to implement the model.

Logic models also can include contextual factors, external factors, and the goals of stakeholders. *Contextual factors* involve issues that are not directly related to the implementation of an MTSS, but typically influence any services delivered and the associated outcomes (e.g., school climate, leadership). *External factors* are variables that exert pressure on educators to engage in certain behaviors (e.g., mandates to implement an MTSS, budget cuts at the state and district levels). Finally, the *goals* of schools and districts implementing an MTSS should be considered because they influence the extent to which educators will prioritize activities. The existence of a policy or mandate does not ensure that a critical mass of educators will embrace the new practices as a priority.

Figure 25.1 illustrates a logic model depicting MTSS implementation at the school level. In the logic model, issues related to building capacity to implement an MTSS (represented by the first level of blocks and arrows), implementation of an MTSS (represented by the second level of blocks and arrows), and factors likely

Figure 25.1. Logic Model Depicting Implementation of an MTSS at the School Level

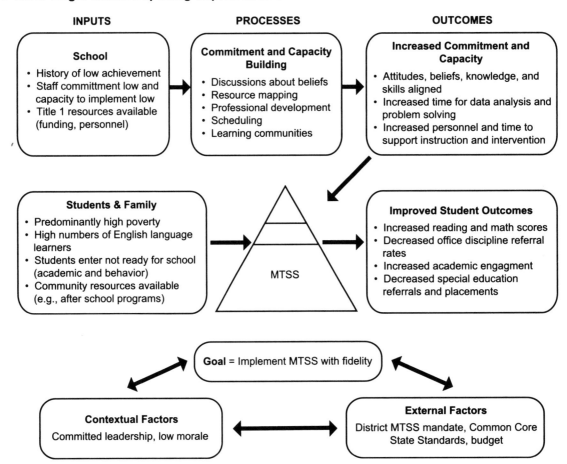

to have an impact on implementation (represented by the three boxes below the MTSS triangle) are delineated.

Step 2: Identify and Develop a Strategic Plan

Logic models can help facilitate a shared understanding of factors to be addressed. However, strategic planning is required for MTSS implementation and program evaluation to occur. Strategic planning is most effective when completed in accordance with systems change principles. Resources have been developed that provide guidance on implementation of an MTSS (e.g., Kurns & Tilly, 2008; Sugai et al., 2010). Whether these resources or another systematic approach to implementation are used, the specific components of the logic model should be incorporated into a plan that specifies the goals of implementing an MTSS as well as the actions that will be taken to achieve the goals. Given the number of potential issues to be addressed, conducting thorough needs and resource assessments (i.e., resource mapping) to inform strategic planning is recommended.

Needs assessments should address the extent to which (a) students are meeting expected outcomes, (b) the critical elements of an MTSS are currently being implemented, and (c) critical processes and procedures required to implement an MTSS are occurring. Resource assessments should focus on the time, personnel, materials, and funding available to support MTSS implementation. Tools can be helpful in facilitating the completion of needs and resource assessments. However, tools are only useful to the extent that the tools yield meaningful information that can inform strategic planning efforts. This last statement may seem obvious. However, generic tools created to examine MTSS implementation are most useful when stakeholders make connections between the content of instruments and relevant language, structures, processes, and procedures used in the stakeholders' local context. School psychologists can compare available tools to the components of a logic model developed in Step 1 to determine which tools will provide the most relevant information for their school and/or district planning efforts. See Elliott and Morrison (2008) and Kurns and Tilly (2008) for examples of tools that may be useful at this step.

Step 3: Develop an Evaluation Plan

An evaluation plan serves as the blueprint that drives program evaluation activities in an MTSS. Similar to the development of a strategic plan for implementation, the greater the specificity in an evaluation plan, the greater the likelihood that the plan will be carried out with fidelity. What follows is an explanation of critical components to consider when developing an evaluation plan. For each component, important information to include and an illustration are provided. The illustrations are based on the experiences of schools and districts that participated in a statewide pilot project to evaluate implementation of an MTSS (see Castillo et al., 2011, for more information). School psychologists will need to collaborate with key stakeholders to adapt the elements of their evaluation plan to fit their local context. Table 25.1 includes the illustration of each of the components discussed below.

Use Evaluation Questions Drive Data Collection

Evaluation questions are critical questions that stakeholders will need to answer to understand the status of MTSS implementation. Questions are the most useful when aligned with the goals and activities outlined in a strategic plan. Aligning questions with the language used in a strategic plan helps facilitate connections between the data being collected and the decisions the data should inform. Questions should be specific enough to provide information that can be used to inform decisions, but not so numerous that the proverbial forest is lost through the trees. The development of evaluation questions is an iterative process. Data collected may result in additional or more specific questions that need to be answered to inform implementation. Table 25.1 includes questions that are based on the strategic approach to implementation described by Elliott and Morrison (2008) and Kurns and Tilly (2008). The change model used in the blueprints includes three major stages: consensus development (i.e., securing commitment for implementation from key stakeholders), infrastructure development (i.e., building capacity to support implementation), and implementation of the critical elements of an MTSS.

Identify Data Sources to Answer Evaluation Questions

Educators already collect data on students' demographics, academic performance, disciplinary infractions, and attendance, among other variables. Educators also may collect data on instruction and intervention fidelity, the outcomes of professional development activities, school climate, or other data that may be relevant to evaluation in an MTSS. Whenever possible, data that are already being collected should be

Table 25.1. Example Evaluation Plan Designed to Inform MTSS Implementation

Evaluation Questions	Data Sources	Data Collection Procedures			Data Analysis
		Person Responsible	Steps Required	Time Line	
To what extent are our students meeting expectations for learning proficiency and growth?	Statewide assessment scores[a]	Principal	Send data file to school psychologist to analyze	When file received at the end of the year	Percent of students proficient; percent of students who made annual growth target
	Districts' universal screener for reading and math[a]	Classroom teachers	Administer assessments and upload data using an electronic scoring tool	See district assessment calendar	Percent of students on track; percent of students at risk
	Office discipline referral rates[a]	Assistant principal	Provide copies of office discipline referrals to school psychologist to analyze	End of each month	Monthly rate of referrals per 100 students
To what extent are we implementing with fidelity the critical elements of an MTSS?[b]	Districts' personnel evaluation system[a]	Principal and assistant principal	Complete district observation protocol	See district required time lines	See district provided report
	MTSS Implementation Inventory[c]	School psychologist	Facilitate completion by the school leadership team using district-specified administration procedures	By 10/15 for beginning of the year and 6/15 for end of the year	Implementation level for each critical element
	Staff focus groups[d]	Guidance counselor	Facilitate interviews with lead teacher from each grade (use four evaluation questions)	By 10/15 for beginning of the year and 6/15 for end of the year	Derive themes from responses to questions
What is our capacity to implement the critical elements of an MTSS?	MTSS Implementation Inventory[c]	School psychologist	Facilitate completion by the school leadership team using district-specified administration procedures	By 10/15 for beginning of the year and 6/15 for end of the year	Implementation level for each critical element
	Staff focus groups[d]	Guidance counselor	Facilitate interviews with lead teacher from each grade (use four evaluation questions)	By 10/15 for beginning of the year and 6/15 for end of the year	Derive themes from responses to questions
What is our understanding of and commitment to the critical elements of an MTSS?	MTSS Implementation Inventory[c]	School psychologist	Facilitate completion by the school leadership team using district-specified administration procedures	By 10/15 for beginning of the year and 6/15 for end of the year	Implementation level for each critical element
	Staff focus groups[d]	Guidance counselor	Facilitate interviews with lead teacher from each grade (use four evaluation questions)	By 10/15 for beginning of the year and 6/15 for end of the year	Derive themes from responses to questions

Note. This plan does not reflect all elements of program evaluation that will occur. Adjustments will need to be made as information needs evolve. [a]Already existing data element. [b]The district intends to add a product review protocol the following year. [c]The MTSS Implementation Inventory contains questions that can be used to answer multiple evaluation questions. [d]Questions are asked in one session that address multiple evaluation questions.

incorporated into an evaluation plan. Many of the data elements collected by educators are mandated by district, state, and federal policy. Although mandates to collect data do not guarantee the data will be used to inform decisions, these data are often used for accountability purposes, thereby elevating their importance to administrators. Additionally, data collection requirements cannot be too cumbersome. Reliable data collection is less likely when too many new or unfamiliar procedures are introduced.

Another consideration when selecting data sources involves concepts that school psychologists are ideally suited to address: reliability and validity. Educators will sometimes use existing data for a purpose for which it was not intended. Although maximizing the use of existing data is an important consideration when developing an evaluation plan, any data used to answer an evaluation question must be a valid source of information *for that question*. Furthermore, the data must be collected reliably to inform decisions. Administrators can mandate that data be collected and train personnel to collect the data. However, these steps do not guarantee accurate information.

School psychologists' understanding of reliability and validity concepts also should be applied when decisions are made to develop or adopt additional data sources. Tools designed to examine the fidelity of MTSS implementation and the capacity-building activities that facilitate implementation are available from a number of resources. Decisions regarding which tools and methods to use must be made based on reliability and validity concepts as well as local circumstances. In particular, balancing the benefit of information that would be derived from administering a given tool and the costs associated with its use (e.g., direct expenditures, personnel time, instructional time lost) is an important consideration. Selecting a tool without considering how it helps answer evaluation questions or how feasible the data are to be collected may result in the tool being used for purposes for which it was not intended and thus unreliable data.

Finally, educators should not overemphasize the use of tools to answer evaluation questions. Qualitative information derived from stakeholder interviews, focus groups, and informal conversations can provide valuable information regarding stakeholder perceptions and contextual factors. Qualitative methods include mechanisms to collect, organize, and understand information so that themes or patterns can be derived. Mixed-methods analysis can provide a framework for triangulating quantitative and qualitative data so that

decisions can be made that are consistent with a multimethod, multiple informant approach to program evaluation (Stufflebeam & Shinkfield, 2007). See Table 25.1 for examples of data sources that can be used to answer evaluation questions.

Specify Data Collection, Management, and Reporting Procedures

Procedures should be developed that specify who will collect the identified data sources and when the data will be collected. When data elements are already available, it is a matter of determining when the data are collected, who manages the data, and how to gain access. The involvement of school- and district-level administrators at this point is often necessary as school psychologists typically need permissions to access data for which other stakeholders are responsible. When new data sources are selected, how frequently to collect the data, when to collect the data, and who will be responsible must be specified. Any professional development that will be necessary to collect the data should be specified. Procedures should be developed indicating how data will be entered into a database and who will be responsible for managing it. Specifying these procedures increases the probability that data needed to inform MTSS implementation will be readily available.

Procedures for analyzing and communicating data also should be specified to the greatest extent possible. Decisions regarding how to analyze data and communicate information to stakeholders should be made purposefully. Guidelines exist for analyzing and reporting data to inform decision making (Stufflebeam & Shinkfield, 2007). Frequently, simple descriptive statistics (e.g., means, medians, frequency counts, and percentages) provide a wealth of information. Presentation of these descriptive data using simple graphs and charts can help stakeholders visualize patterns and trends in the data. Although sophisticated analyses that examine relationships between variables such as implementation fidelity and student outcomes are important for more summative decisions regarding the value of MTSS, simple is often better when it comes to reporting data to stakeholders. See Table 25.1 for examples of data collection and analysis procedures.

Report Data to Key Stakeholders

Data needed to inform implementation of MTSS will vary as a function of stakeholder roles and responsibilities within the system. Administrators (e.g., superintendent, superintendent's cabinet, principals) will need data that inform strategic priorities for implementation of an MTSS, policy development, resource allocation, and the removal or reduction of barriers to implementation. School board members also will need access to data to inform policy development and resource allocation given their oversight roles and responsibilities. District and school personnel charged with supporting implementation will require data to inform training and coaching activities as well as information on barriers to implementation. The specific data needed will depend on the decisions to be made at a given time. However, data on student outcomes, school-level implementation fidelity, the capacity of educators to implement the practices, and commitment from school staff should be made available.

Teachers and other support staff (e.g., curriculum specialists, reading coaches, behavior specialists) should have access to data that can help them match instruction and intervention to student needs. Data on student outcomes and implementation of the evidence-based assessment, instruction, and intervention practices that compose an MTSS can help educators select instructional targets, identify practices that need to be implemented or improved upon, and evaluate the effectiveness of instruction and intervention strategies. Periodically, data gathered on teacher and support staff commitment and capacity to implement an MTSS should be provided to facilitate discussions regarding issues such as the value of engaging in certain practices and what supports are needed for implementation to be successful.

Family and community stakeholders should be provided with basic information on the status of MTSS implementation and how it is having an impact on student outcomes. The purpose of this information is to keep families and community members informed and to gather or maintain support for the initiative. Families of students who are receiving more intensive services (e.g., Tier 2 or Tier 3 interventions) will require additional information to help the families understand what is being implemented and the impact on their child's outcomes.

Determining when and where to provide data to stakeholders is another component of reporting data. Once again, relying on the natural ecology of the system as much as possible increases the probability that stakeholders will use the data being generated. At the district level, district leadership team meetings, school board meetings, and committee or department meetings are common examples of naturally occurring opportunities to present data and discuss the implications for ongoing efforts to implement an MTSS. At the school level, school leadership team meetings, professional learning community meetings, grade-level or department meetings, PTA/PTO meetings, and School Advisory Council meetings are common examples of venues to engage various stakeholders.

Data also can be communicated through reports, newsletters, presentations, and e-mail. These methods can be valuable in disseminating information. However, these methods cannot supplant meaningful data-based discussion and collaborative decision making. Schools and districts vary in how well they communicate within and across organizational structures (e.g., grade levels, departments, general and special education) and in how well they use information that is shared to inform decision making. In this regard, the concept of educator professional learning communities is critical. A professional learning community consists of a group of educators who work together to improve student outcomes by improving their practices (Hall & Hord, 2011). Professional learning communities use data to identify practices that are contributing to positive student outcomes as well as practices that need to be improved upon. Professional learning communities also can involve the examination of the beliefs, attitudes, knowledge, and skills of educators that relate to the delivery of evidence-based practices. Thus, school psychologists can increase the likelihood that educators will use program evaluation data by capitalizing on existing professional learning community structures or collaborating with stakeholders to build professional learning communities that value using data to inform implementation of an MTSS.

Illustration of Program Evaluation

The following example illustrates program evaluation in an MTSS at the school level. The case example is based on the experiences of school psychologists working with schools to use data to inform implementation. The example builds upon the logic model represented in Figure 25.1 and the evaluation plan represented in Table 25.1.

Background Information

Bukowski Elementary School is located within the Coppertop School District. Coppertop School District is committed to the implementation of an MTSS and is requiring that all schools implement the model. The district's expectation in recent years has been that teachers will use data during regularly scheduled professional learning community meetings to examine student outcomes and adjust instructional practices. More recently, all schools in the district have begun implementing the Common Core State Standards and collecting data on instructional practices in response to district- and state-level requirements. As a result of these efforts and other existing requirements, schools collect and submit a number of data elements to the district office. Some of the data elements already existed (e.g., statewide assessment scores, universal screening data, office discipline referrals, attendance data) while other data elements have been added (e.g., tools and strategies for gathering data on MTSS implementation). Schools are instructed to use data to inform MTSS implementation and have been told that district personnel will provide ongoing professional development and support. Included in the information principals have received from the district office is a logic model depicting MTSS implementation at the school level (see Figure 25.1) and the district's framework for schools to engage in program evaluation (see Table 25.1).

The principal at Bukowski Elementary has been at the school less than a year and has identified some academic and behavioral needs at the school. Scores on the statewide assessment have been stagnant, with fewer than 60% of students performing at the proficient level each of the last 5 years. Rates of referrals to the office for disciplinary infractions are well above the district average and are costing the principal, the teachers, and the students valuable time. While attending the district's monthly principal meetings, the principal received information regarding MTSS and the district's rationale for implementing the model and believes MTSS can help address the needs of the school. The principal has had conversations with the school leadership team to build consensus regarding the district's plan for implementation and evaluation of an MTSS. The school psychologist for the school is a member of the school's leadership team and was assigned the responsibility of helping the team analyze and use the data to inform decisions. The school psychologist is familiar with MTSS and program evaluation and has embraced the leadership role.

Fall, First Year of Implementation

Team members met to review data on student performance and MTSS implementation activities following the administration of the district's universal screener and completion of the MTSS Implementation Inventory. (The MTSS Implementation Inventory is a fictitious instrument created for this example. The instrument was used in this example to simplify the illustration of using data to inform MTSS implementation. The items parallel those found on a number of available instruments used to monitor MTSS implementation efforts.)

The MTSS Implementation Inventory is a self-report survey completed by school leadership team members that the district adapted from existing tools. The instrument provides data on implementation of the critical elements of an MTSS as well as data on activities that reflect educator capacity and commitment to implementation. Prior to the meeting, the school psychologist accessed and analyzed relevant data and presented information to the team using the four evaluation questions included in Table 25.1.

Findings from the data. Discussions regarding the data resulted in a few themes emerging. Data from the district's universal screener suggested that large percentages of students are entering the school at risk for reading failure and that the percentage of students identified as at risk tends to be greater in subsequent grade levels. Office discipline referral numbers continue to be high, and a substantial proportion of the referrals are a result of incidents occurring during instructional time.

Themes also emerged when the team began to examine data from the MTSS Implementation Inventory (see year 1, fall data in Figure 25.2). First, effective Tier 1 curricular, assessment, and instructional practices were not being implemented consistently (item number 10 was rated as *not started*). Team members believed that implementation of the Common Core State Standards represented a fundamental shift in what was taught and how performance was being assessed. Second, although data existed on academic and behavior outcomes as well as time for teachers to meet to collaboratively plan for instruction (regular professional learning community meetings), teachers were not consistently using the time to engage in data-based planning and problem solving (item number 9 was rated as *not started*).

Next, the team reviewed data from sections of the MTSS Implementation Inventory that address capacity and commitment issues. The team agreed that many teachers did not have the knowledge and skills (item number 5 was rated as *not started*) nor were they receiving sufficient support to engage in data-based planning and problem solving (item number 6 was rated as *not started*). The data suggested that many staff were not committed to implementing the critical elements of an MTSS (item number 3 was rated as *not started*). In fact, the teacher

Figure 25.2. Data Displaying Bukowski Elementary's Implementation of an MTSS

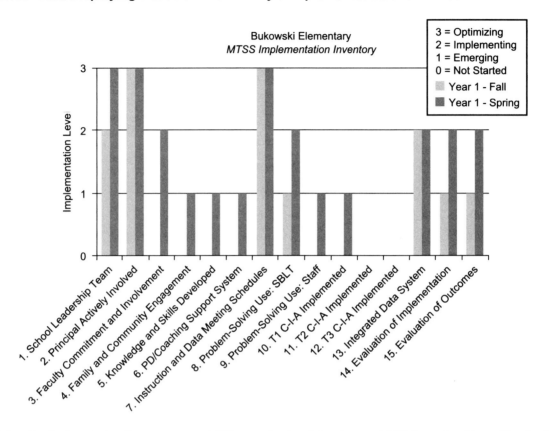

Note. C-I-A = Curriculum–instruction–assessment; PD = professional development; SBLT = school-based leadership team; T1 = Tier 1; T2 = Tier 2; T3 = Tier 3.

representatives on the team expressed their perspective that many teachers were overwhelmed with the number of changes in the district in recent years and that they have heard many teachers say that "MTSS is one more thing that will soon pass." The guidance counselor, who was responsible for facilitating focus groups at the school, indicated that the teachers interviewed also indicated a frustration with the amount of change.

Actions taken based on findings. Team members discussed how to best proceed given the needs they had identified from the data. The team agreed that it could not address every need at once and that it needed to be strategic to be successful. The district's strategic plan included goals to increase the commitment of school staff to implement an MTSS and increase educator capacity to use data to inform instruction. These issues were viewed as two critical components of establishing the conditions under which MTSS was likely to be implemented with fidelity. Given this emphasis, the team agreed that although teachers' frustrations were understandable, teachers' commitment

to implementing an MTSS was critical if meaningful changes in practice were to occur.

The team identified increasing teacher commitment to implementing an MTSS as a goal for the team to start addressing immediately. Team members engaged in a structured planning process and identified several strategies they would use. These strategies included the principal presenting aggregated student outcome data at the next staff meeting and discussing why the leadership team believes that MTSS can meet student needs. The staff would be provided anonymous surveys regarding perspectives on implementing an MTSS and the information would be used to inform discussions with teachers during their regularly scheduled professional learning community times.

The principal indicated a desire to increase the support available to teachers when using data to inform their instruction. After some discussion regarding what resources were available to support teachers, a decision was made to begin with kindergarten and first-grade teachers this year. The principal worked with the reading coach and school psychologist to establish a schedule specifying when the two would attend professional learning community meetings to support teachers. The school psychologist was to provide training in using data to inform instruction and the reading coach was to provide training in the delivery of evidence-based instruction matched to identified needs. The team decided to revisit this plan throughout the year to improve supports to teachers.

Spring, End of First Year of Implementation

The team met again at the end of the school year to examine progress in MTSS implementation and student outcomes. The team members also discussed the extent to which the action steps agreed to following the meeting at the beginning of the year contributed to improvements in MTSS implementation. A summary of the meeting follows.

Findings from the data. Data on student outcomes suggested that progress had been made by kindergarten and first-grade students. The end-of-the year universal screener suggested that fewer students were at risk for reading failure than at the end of previous school years. Data from the MTSS Implementation Inventory (see year 1, spring data included in Figure 25.2) suggested increases in the fidelity of data-based problem solving that occurred during professional learning community meetings (item number 9 was now rated as *emerging*), which the team attributed to the support provided to the teachers. The data also suggested that teachers' commitment to implementation had increased (item number 3 was now rated as *implementing*). Data from the MTSS Implementation Inventory, informal surveys collected from the staff, and focus groups conducted at the end of the year suggested that teachers tended to better understand why they were implementing an MTSS and that opportunities to discuss issues related to implementation should continue.

Actions taken based on the findings. Following the evaluation of progress on the previously identified goal, the team discussed what its next steps should be. A plan for supporting teachers in grades 2–5 did not exist although it had been identified as an important need. To address this goal, the team engaged in a structured planning process. The principal agreed to work on scheduling, material, and personnel issues to support the initiative during the summer and to support the team reconvening to plan for the final details when it reported in August. Members of the team indicated that

they would be willing to support the principal in planning during the summer.

Rates of referrals to the office for disciplinary infractions remained high with 36% of students receiving two or more referrals to the office for disciplinary reasons (the national criterion for effective core instruction for behavior is 20% of students). The principal and members of the leadership team had attempted to address student behavior through a few discussions with teachers at staff meetings, professional learning communities, and other venues. However, these attempts had not resulted in any marked change in student behavior. After some discussion, the team agreed that it needed to improve its core behavior instruction and that training in positive behavior supports should be pursued. The principal committed to pursuing this training prior to the next school year.

Multicultural Competence and Program Evaluation

Data can be both valued and interpreted very differently by stakeholders, and one of the factors that often plays a role in this variability is cultural differences. Cultural differences are not defined solely by factors at the individual level (e.g., race, ethnicity, socioeconomic status, geographic region), but also factors at the organizational (e.g., school beliefs and values regarding data and student learning) and societal levels. In fact, federal policy has pushed issues related to culture to the forefront by requiring schools to disaggregate outcomes by variables such as race, socioeconomic status, English language learner status, and disability status. However, schools and districts vary tremendously in the extent to which they value examining disaggregated student data as well as the extent to which they use data collected to target improved outcomes for groups of students who are struggling.

School psychologists can work with key stakeholders to understand the perspectives of educators, students, families, and communities regarding data by involving them in program evaluation design and implementation. Ongoing communication, incorporation of data important to key stakeholder groups, and input from stakeholders during decision making do not guarantee positive outcomes, but they should increase the probability that stakeholders both value and use the information. Improvement in the outcomes of all students, including students from traditionally underperforming and disenfranchised groups, requires the meaningful involvement of all stakeholders in the design of program evaluation processes and procedures, in discussions regarding the data, and in decisions that are made.

Evaluation of Efforts in Facilitating Change

School psychologists' role in program evaluation in an MTSS has been addressed throughout this chapter. During the accountability era, school psychologists should pay particular attention to communicating the outcomes of implementing an MTSS. Ultimately, the success of any initiative will be judged by whether it improves student outcomes. However, factors such as the extent to which essential practices were implemented with fidelity, educators' knowledge and skill levels, and commitment to implementing new practices also should be evaluated. School psychologists have knowledge and skills that lend themselves to contributing to ongoing program evaluation efforts. Contributing to the provision of information that can inform implementation of an MTSS and its relationship to student outcomes is a role that school psychologists can fulfill in a system increasingly focused on accountability.

SUMMARY

The NASP Practice Model (NASP, 2010) indicates that school psychologists possess the foundational research and evaluation skills required to facilitate program evaluation in an MTSS. These skills can be capitalized on to support schools and districts implementing an MTSS to improve the outcomes of students. School psychologists' contribution and commitment to program evaluation can help schools avoid the predictable failure of other large-scale initiatives that have preceded it. Formative decisions, based on data sources derived as part of a systematic program evaluation effort, can help increase and sustain MTSS implementation levels by proactively responding to the unique needs of schools and the students they serve.

REFERENCES

Batsche, G. M., Elliot, J., Graden, J. L., Grimes, J., Kovaleski, J. F., Prasse, D., … Tilly, W. D., III. (2005). *Response to intervention: Policy considerations and implementation.* Alexandria, VA: National Association of State Directors of Special Education.

Burns, M., Appleton, J. J., & Stehouwer, J. D. (2005). Meta-analytic review of responsiveness-to-intervention research: Examining field-based and research-implemented models. *Journal of Psychoeducational Assessment, 23,* 381–394. doi:10.1177/073428290502300406

Burns, M. K., Griffiths, A., Parson, L. B., Tilly, W. D., III, & VanDerHeyden, A. (2007). *Response to intervention: Research to practice.* Alexandria, VA: National Association of State Directors of Special Education.

Castillo, J. M., & Batsche, G. M. (2012). Scaling up response to intervention: The influence of policy and research and the role of program evaluation. *Communiqué, 40*(8), 14–16.

Castillo, J. M., Curtis, M. J., & Gelley, C. D. (2012). School psychology 2010–Part 2: School psychologists' professional practices and implications for the field. *Communiqué, 40*(8), 4–6.

Castillo, J. M., Hines, C. M., Batsche, G. M., & Curtis, M. J. (2011). *Problem Solving and Response to Intervention Project: Year 3 evaluation report.* Tampa, FL: Problem Solving and Response to Intervention Project. Retrieved from http://floridarti.usf.edu/resources/program_evaluation/index.html

Dawson, M., Cummings, J. A., Harrison, P. L., Short, R. J., Gorin, S., & Palomares, R. (2004). The 2002 multisite conference on the future of school psychology: Next steps. *School Psychology Review, 33,* 115–125.

Elliott, J., & Morrison, D. (2008). *Response to intervention blueprints: District-level edition.* Alexandria, VA: National Association of State Directors of Special Education.

Fullan, M. (2010). *All systems go: The change imperative for whole system reform.* Thousand Oaks, CA: Corwin.

Hall, G. E., & Hord, S. M. (2011). *Implementing change: Patterns, principles and potholes.* (3rd ed.). Boston, MA: Allyn & Bacon.

Kratochwill, T. R., & Shernoff, E. S. (2004). Evidence-based practice: Promoting evidence-based interventions in school psychology. *School Psychology Review, 33,* 34–48.

Kurns, S., & Tilly, W. D., III. (2008). *Response to intervention blueprints for implementation: School-level edition.* Alexandria, VA: National Association of State Directors of Special Education.

National Association of School Psychologists. (2010). *Model for comprehensive and integrated school psychological services.* Bethesda, MD: Author. Retrieved from http://www.nasponline.org/standards/2010standards/2_PracticeModel.pdf

Noell, G. H., & Gansle, K. A. (2006). Assuring the form has substance: Treatment plan implementation as the foundation of assessing response to intervention. *Assessment for Effective Intervention, 32,* 32–39. doi:10.1177/15345084060320010501

Rodriguez-Campos, L., & Ricones-Gomez, R. (2013). *Collaborative evaluations: A step-by-step model for the evaluator.* (2nd ed.). Stanford, CA: Stanford University Press.

Sharratt, L., & Fullan, M. (2009). *Realization: The change imperative for deepening district-wide reform.* Thousand Oaks, CA: Corwin.

Spectrum K12 School Solutions. (2011). *Response to Intervention Adoption Survey 2011.* Bellevue, WA: Global Scholar.

Stufflebeam, D. L., & Shinkfield, A. J. (2007). *Evaluation theory, models, and applications.* San Francisco, CA: Jossey-Bass.

Sugai, G., & Horner, R. H. (2009). Responsiveness-to-intervention and school-wide positive behavior supports: Integration of multi-tiered system approaches. *Exceptionality, 17,* 223–237.

Sugai, G., Horner, R. H., Algozzine, R., Barrett, S., Lewis, T., Anderson, C., … Simonsen, B. (2010). *School-wide positive behavior support: Implementers' blueprint and self-assessment.* Eugene, OR: University of Oregon.

Yarbrough, D. B., Shulha, L. M., Hopson, R. K., & Caruthers, F. A. (2011). *The program evaluation standards: A guide for evaluators and evaluation users* (3rd ed.). Thousand Oaks, CA: SAGE.

26

Best Practices in the Analysis of Progress Monitoring Data and Decision Making

Michael D. Hixson
Central Michigan University
Theodore J. Christ
University of Minnesota
Teryn Bruni
Central Michigan University

OVERVIEW

Progress monitoring is one of the most important tools used by school psychologists to evaluate student response to both academic and behavioral interventions. It is the basis for data-based decision making within a multitiered problem-solving model and it solidifies the linkage between assessment and intervention. Research and program evaluation is a foundation of service delivery in the National Association of School Psychologists (NASP) *Model for Comprehensive and Integrated Psychological Services* (NASP, 2010). Progress monitoring is essential in ensuring that student outcomes are tightly linked with services and programs provided within schools. By providing a real-time account of how interventions are effectively (or not effectively) moving students toward predetermined goals, it helps to ensure accountability for school personnel and adds a self-correcting feature to intervention efforts. Within a multitiered system, evaluation of student progress within tiers and movement between tiers highly depends on careful and accurate evaluation of student performance over time.

This chapter provides general guidelines for school psychologists for selecting and measuring student behavior, displaying and analyzing ongoing data, and making decisions based on progress monitoring data. After reading this chapter, school psychologists will be aware of issues related to selecting valid and reliable measures of student behavior, they will be able to analyze characteristics of graphic displays, and they will be able to apply decision guidelines to determine the effectiveness of interventions.

BASIC CONSIDERATIONS

In the 1920s and 1930s, B. F. Skinner took repeated measures of individual rats to determine the effects of various environmental manipulations on the frequency of lever pressing. His simple experimental arrangement uncovered the basic principles of behavior and learning. The methods he used were adapted in the 1950s and 1960s to study human behavior. It is a version of those methods of single-case design that are used for progress monitoring in schools. The term, but not the concept, of *progress monitoring* emerged alongside curriculum-based measurement (CBM) and problem solving, but it is used today in school psychology to reference practices with a variety of measurement methods and domains of behavior.

Progress monitoring is a hallmark feature of problem solving within a multitiered service delivery model. By measuring behavior over time and observing how changes in the environment have an impact on that behavior, school psychologists can make more informed instructional decisions to improve student outcomes. Instructional time is not wasted on ineffective interventions and specific variables affecting behavior can be systematically tested and monitored (e.g., Batsche et al., 2005; Stecker, Fuchs, & Fuchs, 2005). One of the most commonly used systems to measure academic progress is curriculum-based measurement (CBM). Although progress monitoring using CBM is recommended in the professional literature, the research basis of CBM for progress monitoring is limited, as demonstrated in four publications. First, the report on multitiered services in reading, which was developed by an expert panel convened by the Institute for Educational Sciences in the U.S. Department of Education, found that CBM reading progress monitoring does not result in improved student outcomes. Specifically, the expert panel stated:

> Of the 11 randomized controlled trials and quasi-experimental design studies that evaluated effects of Tier 2 interventions and that met WWC [What Works Clearinghouse] standards or that met WWC standards with reservations, only 3 reported using mastery checks or progress monitoring in instructional decision making. None of the studies demonstrate[s] that progress monitoring is essential in Tier 2 instruction. However, in the opinion of the panel, awareness of Tier 2 student progress is essential for understanding whether Tier 2 is helping the students and whether modifications are needed. (Gersten, 2009, p. 24)

Second, in their review of the literature, Stecker et al. (2005) concluded that CBM was often ineffective because educators do not implement the procedures with fidelity and they often fail to respond to the data. Third, in another review of the literature, Ardoin, Christ, Morena, Cormier, and Klingbeil (2013) concluded that there was poor to moderate support for the frequently reported guidelines associated with progress monitoring using CBM. Neither the guidelines for progress monitoring duration, such as the number of baseline data points to collect, nor the corresponding decision rules were well supported in the literature. Finally, a number of published studies refute the notion that CBM oral reading fluency progress monitoring is reliable, valid, and accurate when the duration of monitoring is short, procedures are poorly standardized, or instrumentation is of poor quality (Christ, 2006; Christ, Zopluoglu, Long, & Monaghen, 2012; Christ, Zopluoglu, Monaghen, & Van Norman, 2013).

Although the research literature on using CBM for progress monitoring is limited, there has been a large body of basic and applied research using direct measures of behavior for progress monitoring. School psychologists need to carefully consider a number of variables when designing progress monitoring measures.

BEST PRACTICES IN THE ANALYSIS OF PROGRESS MONITORING DATA AND DECISION MAKING

The following sections describe best practices for school psychologists for collecting and graphically displaying progress monitoring data, for analyzing data, and for making decisions based on progress monitoring data. These activities fall within the area of formative evaluation, which is a key component of the problem-solving model. Formative evaluation of progress monitoring data most commonly occurs within Tiers 2 and 3 of a multitiered system of service delivery. Although there is a large research literature in behavior analysis that has used what could be reasonably referred to as progress-monitoring data as the primary dependent variable, the research on certain types of data for progress monitoring is still evolving. Therefore, specific best practice guidelines are not always possible. Rather, school psychologists need to be aware of the issues related to interpreting and analyzing progress monitoring data.

Best Practices in Data Collection and Data Display

Identifying a valid and reliable behavior for progress monitoring is challenging. This section presents a summary of best practices for school psychologists for data collection and data display and discusses issues related to selecting valid and reliable progress monitoring measures.

Validity and Reliability of Progress Monitoring Data

School psychologists must use valid measures of behavior. Validity refers to whether the assessment instrument measures what it purports to measure. The first step in developing a valid progress monitoring measure is to define the behavior in observable terms. It is often quite difficult to turn teacher and parent concerns into objective definitions of behavior. In order to have a direct measure of the behavior, the behavior should have a clear beginning and end and the conditions under which the behavior occur should be identified. The behavior measured should be the same as the one in which conclusions will be drawn (Johnston & Pennypacker, 2009). For example, if the student frequently does not follow teacher directions, then this behavior can be directly measured by recording the number of instances of noncompliance and dividing it by the number of teacher directions. An indirect measure of the behavior would be the completion of a behavior rating scale by the teacher that measured student compliance. This is indirect because teacher behavior is measured, but school psychologists are interested in student behavior. When the appropriate dimension of the behavior of concern is directly measured, then the measure is a valid one. As another example, if the concern is accuracy in solving addition problems, then the number of correct and incorrect problems can be recorded from the student's independent practice worksheets. If accuracy with solving math problems was the concern but duration of solving the math worksheets was recorded, then the measure would be indirect and invalid.

In addition to directly measuring the appropriate dimension of behavior, the measurement should take place at the appropriate time and place. Student performance can only be understood within a given environmental context. If a student's noncompliance occurs in academic subjects but not during other activities, such as gym class and recess, then the behavior should be measured during the academic subjects. Ideally, all instances of the target behavior are recorded (this is called continuous recording), but if the behavior is only sampled then the issue of whether a representative or valid sample was obtained becomes a concern.

Direct measures of specific behaviors provide valid and accurate accounts of behavior and are preferred over indirect measures, particularly when providing more targeted or intensive interventions. Indirect measures are often convenient to obtain, but school psychologists should always be concerned with validity. The validity of indirect measures may be obtained by correlating scores on the indirect measures with scores on a direct measure.

Measuring behavior using curriculum materials for progress monitoring can be considered direct or indirect measures of behavior depending on how precisely they correspond with the behavior of interest. For example, if the behavior of interest is reading rate and CBM reading is derived from curriculum materials or closely related materials, then there is a direct measure of the target behavior, which is reading rate. But if the same CBM passages are used as a general outcome measure of reading (i.e., to assess the broader skill of reading or general reading achievement), then the broad behavior of reading is being indirectly measured. CBM reading

and reading rate are only *indicators* of reading, which is composed of many behaviors. Because general outcome measures are used as indicators of a broader skill set, validity and reliability must first be demonstrated to support their use as formative measures of student progress. Fortunately, a large amount of reliability and validity research supports the use of CBM reading for screening. However, data collected from broad measures that sample skills, such as CBM reading, tend to be highly variable when used for progress monitoring.

A reliable measure is one in which the same value is obtained under similar conditions. With indirect measures, traditional psychometric reliability procedures are used to determine the reliability of the measure, such as administering the test two times under the same conditions and correlating the scores in test–retest reliability. Because progress monitoring measures are often direct measures of behavior or behavior products, the most relevant type of reliability measure is interrater reliability or interobserver agreement. School psychologists should collect interobserver agreement data when there is concern about the reliability of the data or when the data are used to make important decisions. Interobserver agreement is calculated from the data from two observers who have measured the same behavior at the same time. There are various methods to collect interobserver agreement data, some of which depend on the type of data that have been collected. If the data recorded were the number of call-outs in class, one observer might have recorded 8 instances of the behavior and the other 10 instances. With this type of frequency data, interobserver agreement is typically calculated by dividing the smaller number by the larger and multiplying by 100%, in this case yielding 80% interobserver agreement. The same calculation is used with duration data; that is, the smaller duration is divided by the larger duration. This calculation is sometimes referred to as overall agreement or total percent agreement. With interval data, trial data, or permanent product data, the calculation can be based on each instance of agreement or disagreement. This type of interobserver agreement is sometimes called point-by-point agreement. If interval data were collected, then the data from each interval are compared across observers and the number of intervals in which there were agreements is divided by the number of agreements plus disagreements. The results are multiplied by 100% to yield the percentage of intervals in which the observers agreed. The same approach to calculating interobserver agreement can be used with trial-by-trial data by substituting intervals with trials.

Parallel Measurements and Variability

Progress monitoring requires measurements that are approximately parallel across time. That is, the measurement conditions must be consistent so that data are comparable. Thus, school psychologists should conduct observations of classroom behavior while controlling for time of day, activity, educators, and other potentially influential factors. Ensuring parallel measurement conditions allows us to maximize the potential to observe true intervention effects.

Christ et al. (2013) engaged in extensive and systematic research to evaluate the effects of assessment conditions on CBM reading progress monitoring outcomes, and these general findings may apply to some other progress monitoring measures. In the case of academic assessment and CBM, alternate forms must be approximately parallel, which means that content and difficulty of alternate forms should be very similar. As with any progress monitoring measure, the other conditions of assessment must also be standardized, such as time of day, administrator, and setting.

Display of Progress Monitoring Data

Once the relevant dimension of behavior is identified and accurate, reliable, parallel, and valid measures of performance are selected, school psychologists must decide how to present data so that changes in performance over time can be effectively interpreted and evaluated. Progress monitoring data are displayed graphically and interpreted through methods of visual analysis. Graphic displays of data are useful because they provide a clear presentation of behavior change over time and allow for quick and easy interpretation of many different sources of information. Accurate interpretation and analysis of data depends highly on how it is displayed and organized.

There are many formats that school psychologists can use to display data including bar graphs, scatterplots, and tables. The most common progress monitoring format is the line graph. Line graphs are useful because they facilitate visual analysis with or without supplemental graphic or statistical aides. Graphical aides include goal lines, trendlines, level lines, and envelopes of variability. Statistical aides include estimates of the average level or slope of the trendline of behavior across observations.

Graphs typically include data points, data paths, phase changes (i.e., alternate conditions), and axes. Figure 26.1 presents each component using hypothetical data. The lower horizontal axis corresponds with the

Figure 26.1. Basic Components of a Line Graph

Student: Tina Smith   School: Pretend Elementary   Teacher: Mrs. S   Year/Sem.: Spring 2012

Measurement Strategy: DIBELS Oral Reading Fluency Probe Score for Accuracy
Intervention: Individual intervention using *Reading for Phonics* direct instruction program
Objective: In 16 weeks, when presented with DIBELS ORF probes, Tina will read words at 98% accuracy.

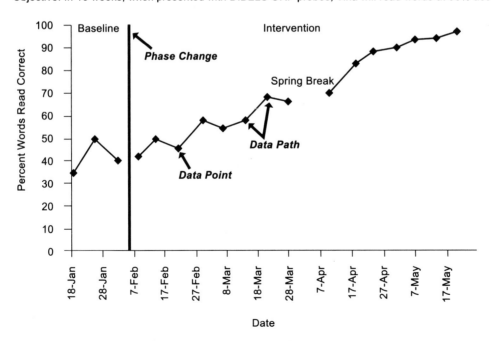

time variable, which is often measured in days or weeks. The units along the horizontal axis should be depicted in a manner that preserves that unit of time, rather than a scale that indicates session numbers or observation intervals that do not indicate how much time passed between measurements. The time metric is required to accurately represent changes in student performance and to calculate trend. The vertical axis corresponds with the measurement variable (i.e., the outcome) being measured, such as the number of words read correctly per minute. The scale used for the dependent variable will depend on the student's current level of performance, expected gains over time, and the overall goal of the intervention. Performance is then measured repeatedly over time within the different conditions or phases.

Data points are typically represented by small symbols such as open circles, triangles, or squares. Each symbol depicts a data series or outcome measure. The symbols are placed on the graph to represent performance at specific points in time. The lines that connect each data point are called the data path. Data paths connect data points within a condition. New conditions are depicted by solid vertical lines that correspond to a point in time. As shown on the sample graph in Figure 26.1, it is also useful to insert a text box above the graph that defines relevant information about the student (e.g., name, teacher, grade, year), specific measurement procedures, intervention conditions, and a clearly stated measurable objective or goal for the student. Milestones that define intermediate goals (e.g., monthly, quarterly) are often helpful. Such information communicates the purpose, features, goals, and subject of the graphic display, which is useful as an archival record and for purposes of sharing the data with others who might be less familiar with the case.

Specific best practices and conventions to construct line graphs exist within the single-case design literature to facilitate interpretation and analysis that can help guide school psychologists in constructing clear and useful graphs to monitor student progress (Cooper, Heron, & Heward, 2007; Gast, 2010; Riley-Tillman & Burns, 2009). First, clarity can be impeded by including more than three behaviors on a single graph (Gast, 2010). If multiple behaviors are represented on the same graphic display, then each behavior should be related to one another to provide meaningful comparisons between the data series (e.g., behavior to decrease presented with the corresponding replacement behavior). Also, trendlines and data paths are disconnected between phase changes, extended gaps in data collection, and follow-up data collections. Finally, school

psychologists should ensure that the scales used accurately represent the outcome being measured, including the maximum and minimum values that could be obtained. Each axis should be clearly labeled to indicate the variable of interest, dimension measured (in the case of the vertical axis) and the scale of measurement used (e.g., *percent correct* on the vertical axis with *days* on the horizontal axis).

Frequency data on the vertical axis are usually displayed with equal intervals; that is, the distance between any two points is always the same. For example, the distance between 3 and 4 words read correctly is the same as between 20 and 21 words on a particular graph. On equal interval graphs, change from one unit to the next across all values of a particular scale is represented by the same distance between each unit. Rather than looking at these absolute changes, school psychologists may also find it useful to look at relative changes in performance. Relative changes can be visually analyzed by using a logarithmic or ratio scaled vertical axis. Although it requires some training and practice initially, it helps to visually analyze the *proportional change* in behavior. For example, a change from 10 to 20 words read correctly would appear as the same degree of change as from 40 to 80 words because the proportional change is the same; that is, both are doubling over time. Equal interval graphs by necessity use different scales to measure behaviors that differ greatly in their frequency. It is difficult to use a standard nonlogarithmic graph to depict behaviors with very different frequencies, such as one that occurs a few times per day and another that occurs hundreds of times per day. In contrast, it is easy to accomplish this with a logarithmic graph. Figure 26.2 illustrates the difference between equal interval and logarithmically scaled data when two behaviors of very different frequencies are plotted on the same graph. The graph on the top shows relatively stable correct and incorrect responses, but it is more evident on bottom graph that errors are increasing.

A particular semilogarithmic graph called the Standard Celeration Chart (Graf & Lindsley, 2002; Pennypacker, Gutierrez & Lindsley, 2003) can display behaviors that occur as infrequently as once per day to as often as 1,000 times per minute. Being able to graph almost any human behavior on the same chart is not only convenient but also makes it easy to compare behaviors across charts. Also, it is often the case that school psychologists are interested in relative/proportional change. A change from talking with peers 20 times per day to 21 times may not be very important, but a change from 0 to 1 could very well be. While a full

Figure 26.2. Hypothetical Student Data Using an Equal Interval Scale Compared to a Semilogarithmic Scale

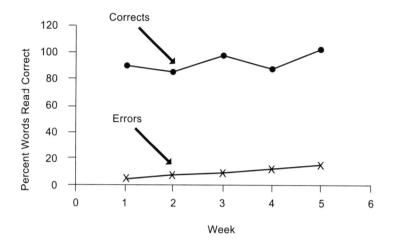

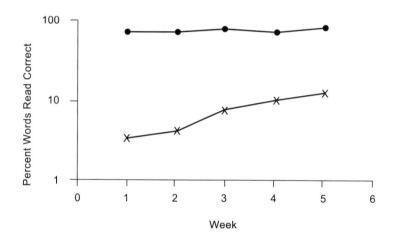

discussion of the differences between equal interval line graphs and the Standard Celeration Chart falls beyond the scope of this chapter, analysis, interpretation, and communication of student outcomes can be enhanced with the Standard Celeration Chart (Kubina & Yurich, 2012).

Best Practices in Analysis and Decision Making

This section presents a summary of best practices in the analysis of progress monitoring data to guide educational decisions. In order to make important decisions regarding student progress, school psychologists must engage in careful analysis of student data. Accurate analysis of progress monitoring data involves evaluating data within and across conditions, setting goals, and analyzing intervention effects and variability in the data to guide decision making.

Analysis of Progress Monitoring Data in Baseline

Progress monitoring data are repeatedly collected across time before an intervention is implemented. This preintervention condition is called the baseline condition, and the data in this condition are collected to permit a comparison to the intervention data. Baseline data can also help school psychologists determine whether or not the reported problem is a real concern. If the baseline data indicate that the student's performance is not significantly discrepant from peers, then no intervention is warranted. Baseline data should be collected and charted until a stable pattern of behavior emerges. The characteristics of the data that are considered in determining whether there is a stable pattern of behavior are level, trend, and variability.

Level refers to the average performance within a condition. Level is often the characteristic school psychologists are most concerned with; that is, the student may be doing something too often or not enough. To estimate a student's level of behavior, the mean or median can be calculated and illustrated by a horizontal line on the graph. School psychologists should exercise caution when interpreting level if there is a trend in the data or the data are highly variable because level might not be substantially representative of the behavior.

Trend refers to systematic increases or decreases in behavior over time. It is often estimated with a trendline, which is a graphical aide, or slope, which is a statistical aide. It may take many data points to get an accurate measure of trend. The addition of a trendline may aid in the analysis of trend.

Variability refers to how much a student's data deviate from the level or trendline. It is often estimated with the standard deviation, range, or the standard error of the estimate (Christ, 2006; Christ et al., 2013). There are many influences of behavior that are beyond the school psychologist's control that can produce highly variable performance. The academic tasks and other classroom factors vary from day to day as do many factors outside of school. Highly variable data obscure trends and levels and, therefore, hinder interpretation of progress monitoring data. The sources of variability should be identified and controlled, if possible.

The collection of additional baseline data is particularly helpful when the data are variable. There are many kinds of extraneous variables that could be responsible for variable performance, including the measurement system itself. The variability of CBM oral reading fluency tends to be relatively high, as might other measures of very broad skills. School psychologists should ensure a relatively stable baseline is obtained so

that effects of the intervention can be accurately interpreted. What is considered stable depends on many factors, such as the type of measure being taken and the extent to which clear experimental control is needed. In most cases, school psychologists should consider the data stable if 80% of the data points fall within 20% of the median line (Gast, 2010). The median rather than the mean is used because the mean is more sensitive to extreme scores. If there is an increasing or decreasing trend in the data, then it is helpful to determine the stability of the data around the trendline using the same criterion: If 80% of the data fall within 20% of the trendline, then the trend may be considered stable. See Figure 26.3.

For the data in Figure 26.3 a mean line has been drawn that equals 4.9 responses. The mean or level of these data is not their most important characteristic, however, because of the increasing trend in performance which is summarized by the trendline. A stability envelope (Gast, 2010) has been drawn around the data to determine if the data meet the 80–20% criterion for stability around a trendline. In this case, 77% of the data points fall within 20% of the trendline, which is close to the stability criterion. Attending to the most prominent characteristic of the data—level, trend, or variability—is important for understanding the target behavior and for comparing performance across baseline and intervention conditions. After sufficient and relatively stable baseline data have been gathered, the intervention can be introduced.

Analysis of Data Across Conditions

Collecting progress monitoring data and thereby obtaining information on the level, trend, and variability of the

Figure 26.3. Illustration of the 80–20% Stability Rule

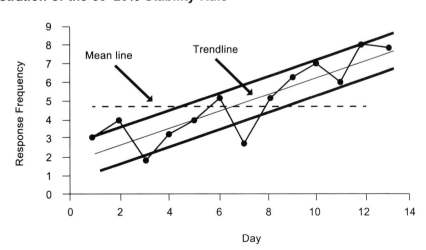

target behavior before an intervention is implemented is useful in helping to understand the target behavior and the extent to which the behavior is a problem. If the progress monitoring data are collected from direct observations, then the observer may also identify environmental events that trigger or consequate the behavior, which is helpful for intervention planning because it may give clues to the function of the behavior, as is often done as part of a functional assessment or functional analysis. In addition to these benefits, collecting progress monitoring data in baseline allows an objective evaluation of the effects of interventions.

If sufficient baseline data have been collected to determine the level, trend, and variability of behavior, then this information can be used to predict what is likely to happen if conditions stay the same. If the intervention data are very different from this predicted pattern, then it is possible that the change is due to the intervention. Any three of the data characteristics— level, trend, or variability—may change because of the intervention. School psychologists should consider the following factors when trying to determine if any of the three characteristics changed because of the intervention. First, consider whether there were a sufficient number of data points in each condition to obtain a predictable pattern of behavior under both the baseline and intervention conditions. Second, consider the immediacy of effect or how closely the change in behavior corresponds with the introduction of the intervention. According to Kratochwill et al. (2010), the last three data points from the baseline condition should be compared to the first three data points of the intervention condition to evaluate immediacy. Third,

consider the degree of overlap of data points across conditions. If few data points overlap, then the results are more likely the result of the intervention. High variability increases the probability of overlapping data points across conditions, which can obscure the effects of the intervention. The percentage of nonoverlapping data points across conditions may be calculated as a summary statistic of overlap. To help determine the degree of overlapping data points across conditions, an envelope can be drawn around the data in baseline and projected into the intervention condition. In Figure 26.4 there is no overlap in data across conditions with the target behavior rapidly decreasing during the intervention and leveling off at around four responses. The envelope encompasses all of the data in the baseline condition and the lines are drawn horizontally. If there is a clear trend in the data, as in Figure 26.5, then the envelope can be drawn by using the slope obtained from the trendline. The data in Figure 26.5 also show a clear change in trend across conditions and no overlapping data points using the slope of the trendline to extend the data envelope.

More advanced statistical procedures may be used to analyze trends and changes in data with certain types of progress monitoring data. For example, in the case of CBM reading progress monitoring data, Christ (2006) and Christ et al. (2013) have advocated for the use of confidence intervals to help guide interpretation, especially if it is used for high-stakes diagnostic and eligibility decisions. CBM progress monitoring measures have published estimates of the standard error of measurement (e.g., median standard error of measurement for CBM reading is 10; Christ & Silberglitt, 2007). Moreover, regression-based estimates of trend have standard errors

Figure 26.4. Illustration of Data Envelope Showing No Overlap Across Conditions

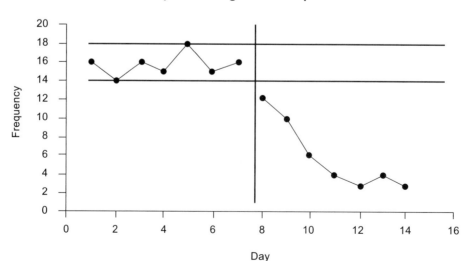

Figure 26.5. Illustration of Data Envelope Defining a Clear Change in Trend Across Conditions

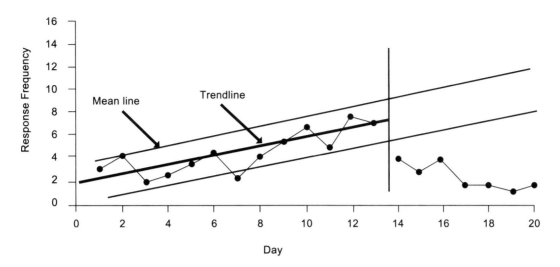

that are easily derived with spreadsheet software. The function for MS Excel is "=STEYX(*y*-values, *x*-values)." The standard error of the slope (SEb) can be applied in a manner similar to the standard error of measurement. That is, the 68% confidence interval is $\pm$ SEb and the 95% confidence interval is $\pm$ 1.96 × SEb (see Christ & Coolong-Chaffin, 2007, for a more detailed description).

The final factor to consider when trying to determine whether or not an intervention was effective is replication of effect. Replication is one of the most powerful ways to show a functional relationship between an intervention and a target behavior. There are various single-case experimental designs that handle replication differently. The two designs most relevant for the progress monitoring of individual students are the withdrawal and alternating treatments designs. In the most common version of a withdrawal design, a no-intervention (i.e., baseline) condition is alternated with an intervention condition. The target behavior is measured repeatedly within each condition. In the alternating treatments design, two conditions, which could be no-intervention and intervention conditions, are rapidly alternated. In a withdrawal design the same condition should have a similar effect across phases. For example, if the behavior were low in the first baseline, then it should also be low when the baseline condition is repeated, and if it were high in the first intervention condition, then it should be high in subsequent intervention conditions. For research purposes, a single-case design should have at least three replications of an effect or, in the case of the alternating treatments design, at least five repetitions of the alternating sequence (e.g., BCBCBCBCBC; Kratochwill et al., 2010). We believe these criteria are also useful for

school psychologists when high-stakes decisions need to be made with progress monitoring data, as is discussed in the next section.

Best Practices in Data-Based Decision Making

Progress monitoring alone does not produce meaningful gains in student performance. Decisions must also be made based on careful analysis of student data (Stecker et al., 2005). Although there has been research on the use of decision rules, few studies have investigated the effects of specific rules. However research in the areas of single-case designs, CBM, and response to intervention outline important considerations to help guide school psychologists in making decisions based on student data.

Student performance data should be evaluated in relation to a specific goal. Goals can be based on local norms, benchmark data, classroom norms, or peer comparisons. Goals are set over a specified amount of time, allowing for short-term objectives to be set regarding the student's rate of progress (e.g., acquire two letter sounds per week). A student's expected rate of progress can be represented by an aimline, which is a line drawn from the last or median baseline point to the expected goal (see Figure 26.6). The aimline is used as a guide for determining whether or not the student is making sufficient progress toward the goal. Progress should be evaluated in a manner that takes into consideration all elements related to the students' environment and should be applied flexibly. The following considerations provide some general rules or guidelines for decision making that have been used in research on progress monitoring or have been recommended by experts.

Figure 26.6. Expected Rate of Progress Represented by Aimline and Illustration of Trendline Based on Hypothetical Student Data

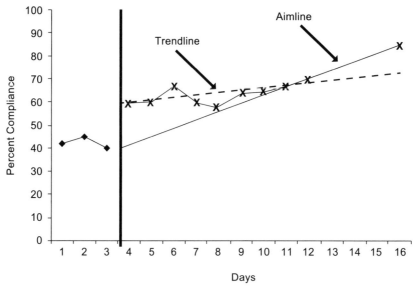

Interpreting Changes in Performance

In many cases it may not be vital to determine if it was the intervention or some other factor that improved student performance. But as students move through Tiers 2 and 3 and they are given more intensive instruction, it becomes increasingly important to correctly identify controlling variables. If progress-monitoring data are being used to help determine eligibility for special education, then it is of primary importance that an effective intervention is identified (Riley-Tillman & Burns, 2009). If the effective intervention is highly intensive, then it may require special education placement. Knowing that the intervention is in fact responsible for the improvement is necessary because student eligibility for special education is one of the most important decisions school psychologists make. Using an experimental design that involves replication such as a reversal, multiple-baseline, or alternating treatment design provides a powerful demonstration for the necessity of that intervention for student success and greatly increases the reliability of the school psychologist's decision. Because the use of a rigorous experimental design takes time to implement, it should ideally be done before a request for a special education evaluation because of the evaluation time lines that begin once a referral is made.

Variability in data and/or the occasional extreme value can be the result of many factors, as previously discussed. Parallelism should be considered if progress-monitoring data are highly variable. Measurement factors are important to evaluate, such as standardization of conditions, instrumentation, and reliability of scoring. In addition, a possible problem with CBM is nonequivalent probes, which could be evaluated by administering different probes under the same conditions (time, assessor) and calculating differences in scores. Variability may also be due to instructional factors, which include the fidelity of implementation and instructor characteristics (e.g., how fluently the intervention is implemented). Student factors should be examined carefully. These could include biological variables (e.g., student illness), interfering behavior (e.g., noncompliance, failure to scan/attend), or lack of motivation to comply with instructional demands (e.g., insufficient reinforcement for correct responding). If the sources of variability are identified, then they can be controlled to improve the potential for effective, efficient, and accurate decisions.

Using Decision Rules

There are 40 or more years of recommendations to apply a variety of specific decision rules to progress monitoring data, which are intended to improve decision accuracy. Student outcomes tend to improve as a function of progress monitoring only if decision rules are explicit and implemented with integrity (Stecker et al., 2005). Two commonly used decision rules are data point rules and trendline rules and neither is supported by substantial evidence (Ardoin et al., 2013). The accuracy of decisions using data point rules has not been researched, but there has been some research on the trendline rule. The data point rule uses a graphically depicted goal line, which displays the expected growth in performance. If three consecutive points are distributed above and below the goal line, then the intervention is continued, presumably because there is evidence of sufficient progress toward the goal. If three consecutive points are all below the goal line, then the intervention is changed because there is evidence of insufficient progress. Finally, if three consecutive points are all above the goal line, then the goal is increased because there is evidence of an insufficiently ambitious goal.

The trendline rule compares an estimate of trend to the intended goal. Prior to the proliferation of computers, the trendline rule was guided by visual analysis or one of a variety of techniques to estimate trend, such as the split-middle technique. These estimates of trend should be replaced with statistical methods such as regression (i.e., ordinary least-squares regression). A regression line is the line of best fit to progress monitoring data, such that it establishes the minimal distance between all points on the trendline and all data points (see Figure 26.6). Regression-based estimates of trend are readily available in spreadsheet software and by vendors of many progress-monitoring assessment systems (e.g., Formative Assessment System for Teachers, http://fast.cehd.umn.edu). This method is likely to result in the best estimates of growth and predictions of future performance. However, regression is highly sensitive to extreme values. Visual analysis should be used to identify extreme values. Such values should be judiciously removed from the calculation of the trendline lest they have undue influence on regression-based estimates of trend. That being said, extreme scores may be highly informative if the variables responsible for the extreme score are identified.

Overall, decision rules provide school psychologists with a general guide to help evaluate student progress toward a predetermined goal. Accurate and valid measures of behavior, parallel conditions, identifying and controlling for sources of variability, and skills in visual analysis allow school psychologists to make more accurate decisions based on student data.

SUMMARY

What are the possible consequences of providing an evidence-based treatment in the absence of monitoring the effects of that treatment? Ideally, the treatment would be effective at ameliorating the problem. Unfortunately, school psychologists do not have at their disposal treatments that are 100% effective. Another possibility is that the treatment is ineffective, resulting in wasted time and resources. Finally, the treatment could further impair performance (i.e., have a teratogenic effect). Because of the risk of the second two outcomes, school psychologists are ethically obligated to monitor intervention effects and terminate or change the intervention when appropriate (see Standard II.2.2 of the NASP *Principles for Professional Ethics*, http://www.nasponline.org/standards/2010standards/1_%20Ethical%20Principles.pdf).

Ongoing progress monitoring is an essential component of data-based decision making within a problem-solving model. School psychologists must first select measures that are reliable, accurate, valid, and sensitive to change. Progress monitoring data are collected repeatedly over time and plotted graphically to allow for systematic interpretation of results. Level, trend, and variability are three characteristics of progress monitoring data. Prior to intervention, school psychologists should collect baseline data until sufficient data points permit prediction of the student's future performance without an intervention. When analyzing data across phases of intervention, school psychologists should carefully inspect the overlap of data points between conditions, the immediacy of change from one condition to the next, and the results from replication of the intervention. Reversal designs, multiple baselines, and alternating treatment designs allow systematic replication and control of independent variables. How systematic school psychologists are in their analysis depends on the types of decisions to be made and the potential impact that decision would have on a particular student. A careful analysis of controlling variables related to instruction, consistency of implementation, setting, and other extraneous variables are necessary when evaluating student progress.

REFERENCES

Ardoin, S. P., Christ, T. J., Morena, L. S., Cormier, D. C., & Klingbeil, D. A. (2013). A systematic review and summarization of the recommendations and research surrounding curriculum-based measurement of oral reading fluency (CBM-R) decision rules. *Journal of School Psychology, 51*, 1–18. doi:10.1016/j.jsp.2012.09.004

Batsche, G., Elliott, J., Graden, J. L., Grimes, J., Kovaleski, J. F., Prasse, D., ... Tilly, W. D., III. (2005). *Response to intervention*. Alexandria, VA: National Association of State Directors of Special Education.

Christ, T. J. (2006). Short-term estimates of growth using curriculum-based measurement of oral reading fluency: Estimating standard error of the slope to construct confidence intervals. *School Psychology Review, 35*, 128–133.

Christ, T., & Coolong-Chaffin, M. (2007). Interpretations of curriculum-based measurement outcomes: Standard error and confidence intervals. *School Psychology Forum, 1*(2), 75–86.

Christ, T. J., & Silberglitt, B. (2007). Estimates of the standard error of measurement for curriculum-based measures of oral reading fluency. *School Psychology Review, 36,* 130–146.

Christ, T. J., Zopluoglu, C., Long, J. D., & Monaghen, B. D. (2012). Curriculum-based measurement of oral reading: Quality of progress monitoring outcomes. *Exceptional Children, 78,* 356–373.

Christ, T. J., Zopluoglu, C., Monaghen, B. D., & Van Norman, E. R. (2013). Curriculum-based measurement of oral reading: Multistudy evaluation of schedule, duration, and dataset quality on progress monitoring outcomes. *Journal of School Psychology, 51,* 19–57.

Cooper, J. O., Heron, T. E., & Heward, W. L. (2007). *Applied behavior analysis* (2nd ed.). Upper Saddle River, NJ: Pearson.

Gast, D. L. (2010). *Single subject research methodology in behavioral sciences.* New York, NY: Routledge.

Gersten, R. M. (2009). *Assisting students struggling with reading: Response to intervention and multitier intervention in the primary grades.* Washington, DC: U.S. Department of Education, National Center for Education Evaluation and Regional Assistance.

Graf, S., & Lindsley, O. (2002). *Standard Celeration Charting 2002.* Youngstown, OH: Graf Implements.

Johnston, J. M., & Pennypacker, H. S. (2009). *Strategies and tactics of behavioral research.* New York, NY: Routledge.

Kratochwill, T. R., Hitchcock, J., Horner, R. H., Levin, J. R., Odom, S. L., Rindskopf, D. M., & Shadish, W. R. (2010). *Single-case designs technical documentation.* Washington, DC: Institute of Education Science. Retrieved from http://ies.ed.gov/ncee/wwc/pdf/wwc_scd.pdf

Kubina, R. M., Jr., & Yurich, K. K. (2012). *The precision teaching book.* Lemont, PA: Greatness Achieved.

National Association of School Psychologists. (2010). *Model for comprehensive and integrated school psychological services.* Bethesda, MD: Author. Retrieved from http://www.nasponline.org/standards/2010standards/2_PracticeModel.pdf

Pennypacker, H. S., Gutierrez, A., & Lindsley, O. R. (2003). *Handbook of the Standard Celeration Chart.* Cambridge, MA: Cambridge Center for Behavioral Studies.

Riley-Tillman, T. C., & Burns, M. K. (2009). *Evaluating educational interventions: Single-case design for measuring response to intervention.* New York, NY: Guilford Press.

Stecker, P. M., Fuchs, L. S., & Fuchs, D. (2005). Using curriculum-based measurement to improve student achievement: Review of research. *Psychology in the Schools, 42,* 795–819.

27

Best Practices in Evaluating Psychoeducational Services Based on Student Outcome Data

Kim Gibbons
St. Croix River (MN) Education District
Sarah Brown
Iowa Department of Education

OVERVIEW

School psychologists currently practice in an era when the demands for accountability have never been so strong (Kane, Taylor, Tyler, & Wooten, 2011). Districts are now held accountable for the progress of all students, and a series of negative consequences are implemented when progress is insufficient (2002 No Child Left Behind Act [NCLB]). Federal initiatives such as the Race to the Top (2009 American Recovery and Reinvestment Act) grant competition have intensified accountability and prompted new attention to the processes used for the evaluation of teachers and school administrators (Kane et al., 2011). Race to the Top has provided competitive grants to states to reward the states for designing and implementing comprehensive educational reform through adopting teacher evaluation systems that incorporate student growth. Thus, many states now require that student outcome data be included as part of teacher and administrator evaluations. For example, Minnesota requires that data regarding student achievement must comprise 35% of administrator evaluations in 2013–2014 and teacher evaluations the following school year (Minn. Stat. 122A.40 Subd.8(8)).

Educational experts argue that collaboration among staff will increase by holding all instructional personnel responsible for student achievement, resulting in better student outcomes (Steele, Hamilton, & Steecher, 2010). However, these types of evaluation systems create an intriguing dilemma when applied to school psychologists and other related-service providers who do not directly

work with an entire class of students (Minke, 2011). Although related service providers may serve as a small part of a student's time, usually on a short-term basis, they are not typically involved in daily classroom instruction.

A wide variety of professionals other than teachers and administrators contractually fall under the classification of "instructional personnel." Subsequently, when designing evaluation systems that include student achievement as a factor, local educational agencies are in the position of addressing evaluation practices of these groups as well. Central to these conversations is the relevance of developing evaluation tools that capture student and professional growth accurately and fairly, are sufficient in scope to evaluate the broad-based services of the professional, utilize proven evaluation methods, and provide a uniform system common to all professionals (National Association of School Psychologists [NASP], 2012).

In order to keep pace with demands for accountability, school psychologists must demonstrate skills to address complex student needs, and they must provide comprehensive services that have a direct and measurable impact. A literature review of just the past decade will produce countless documents calling for and describing changes in the services provided by the school psychologist. Going back to the 1990s, there have been demands for school psychologists to evaluate the effectiveness of their services, including documentation of improved student outcomes as the criterion for success. The NASP *Model for Comprehensive and Integrated School*

Psychological Services (NASP, 2010) describes 10 domains of practice under which school psychologists practice. Many of these standards focus on accountability for improved student outcomes, including Data-Based Decision Making and Accountability, Consultation and Collaboration, Effective Instruction and Development of Cognitive/Academic Skills, and Research and Program Evaluation.

However, even with a continued and almost relentless emphasis on accountability in education, there is limited information about the use of student outcome data to evaluate the effectiveness of the services provided by school psychologists. In fact, of the current methods being used to evaluate effectiveness of services provided, outcome data are among the least often utilized (Harvey & Pearrow, 2010).

Traditionally, performance appraisal rubrics and rating scales have been the most widely used methods to evaluate the effectiveness of psychoeducational services (Morrison, 2013). Surveys or rating scales commonly are used by school psychologists to collect information about the perceived effectiveness of their services, personal characteristics, effectiveness of recommendations provided to teachers, and professional skills. Surveys typically include a series of questions, either open ended or with a rating scale, and are completed by teachers, students, administrators, and parents. There are many advantages to rating scales and surveys. They tend to be well aligned with professional training skills, and they are generally accepted and considered to be fair. However, these measures are often criticized owing to their subjective nature and the fact that direct observation of skills included on rating scales may be difficult to assess in some situations (Prus & Waldron, 2008).

Other methods involve having a school psychologist keep a log describing the types of services provided and the amount of time spent in certain activities (Fairchild & Zins, 1992). This type of time analysis allows school psychologists to monitor the amount of time they spend by activity and examine any changes in service delivery that occur either as a result of personal goals or departmental goals.

Beyond time analyses and surveys, school psychologists also evaluate the effectiveness of their services by collecting outcome data. The most common outcome is that of student improvement over time as the result of involvement by a school psychologist. Although the school psychologist often is not the academic or behavior interventionist, he or she is an integral part of the process in designing and evaluating academic and behavioral interventions through consultation with individual teachers and as a member of school-level

problem-solving teams (Morrision, 2013). The most common method for evaluating intervention effectiveness and linking school psychologist efforts to student growth over time is the use of single-case design (Riley-Tillman, Burns, & Gibbons, 2013). The basic single-case design compares a student's initial level of performance (baseline) to performance over the course of an intervention to evaluate the effectiveness of the intervention. Single-case designs have many advantages when used to evaluate psychoeducational services. Multiple samples of work may be represented over time helping to circumvent issues with one-shot measurement occasions, and they can be used at the individual, group, classroom, or systems level. In addition, these designs allow flexibility in assessing a variety of professional competencies. The primary disadvantage is that it is difficult to draw causal connections with the intervention and student growth (Riley-Tillman et al., 2013).

While it may be important to include some of the procedures described above in evaluating school psychological services, we advocate that the evaluation process must include student outcome data. According to the Personnel Evaluation Standards compiled by the Joint Committee on Standards for Educational Evaluation (Gullickson, 2009), a variety of data collection methods (observation checklists, interviews, products) and tools should be used to help evaluate outcomes. Waldron and Prus (2006) advocate that four components be included when evaluating the outcomes of a particular service area: (a) the use of multiple measures, including at least one measure of impact on student outcomes; (b) valid and reliable measures of student outcomes; (c) measures that are useful for distinguishing different levels of proficiency; and (d) systems that are linked to professional development and improvement. In addition, the National Alliance of Pupil Services Organizations (2011) recommends that evaluation methods be research based and include the primary role of the school psychologist in the creation of evaluation systems. Performance measures that are limited to high-stakes test scores or that only include activities performed by school psychologists are discouraged. Rather, services should be evaluated using multiple measures and include other measures such as student progress-monitoring data, permanent products, and stakeholder surveys. In many cases, services may be delivered collaboratively. In these instances, a team's assessment of student progress should be considered as a component of the multifaceted personnel performance evaluation.

This chapter addresses the domain of Research and Program Evaluation outlined by the NASP Practice

Model (NASP, 2010). The purpose of this chapter is to provide practitioners with viable methods of using student outcome data to improve psychoeducational services to students with and without disabilities. A step-by-step process is outlined to assist practitioners in evaluating the impact of their services on student outcomes. Case studies are provided to illustrate how this process can be applied to both academic and behavioral outcomes.

BASIC CONSIDERATIONS

More educational data are available now than ever before. The amount of data, as well as the various ways data can be analyzed, can be overwhelming. Guiding questions may help administrators consider how to use data to guide the work of the school psychologist with the goal of increasing student achievement. Examples of questions that may be used to aid in this evaluation are outlined in Table 27.1. These questions address not only student achievement, but also the ability of the school psychologist to have an impact on the school system. For instance, a school-level team may address the question: Is more time for interventions or extra daily doses of instruction available for students who are not meeting goals? If the school-level team indicated that additional time is not available for intervention, then the administrator may decide to use a portion of school psychological service to research various schedules used in other districts, as well as what materials and instructional strategies are used during that time and report back with a recommendation for finding intervention time in the building schedule. However, if it was determined time is available, then the administrator may allocate time to examine the implementation fidelity of current intervention materials being used. Exploring an answer to this question, as well as others, can help the building or district target the areas in which the school psychologist may have the greatest impact on student outcomes.

Formative Evaluation

Formative evaluation involves conducting assessment while instruction is occurring and then utilizing that information to plan modifications in instruction (Hosp, 2012). With a formative evaluation system, effective interventions identified during instruction are maintained, and ineffective interventions are modified. Formative evaluation can work on various levels within a system. Practitioners often think about formative evaluation in terms of individual students. For example, progress-monitoring data are collected and graphed regularly, and teams meet to discuss progress and any program modifications needed owing to lack of progress. In addition to informing decisions on an individual level, formative evaluation can have an impact on decisions on a systems level. For instance, a school may administer a brief screening tool to all students within the school. When compared to a benchmark, the administrator may observe that the third-grade class has the largest numbers of students below target proficiency. Based on these data, more resources may be directed toward that grade level to assist in analyzing the problem and developing a plan until a shift in the data is realized. School psychology and other educational services in the district can be targeted at providing instructional and behavioral consultation to third-grade teachers and students in need of assistance to improve outcomes. This systems perspective of progress monitoring can help make valuable decisions regarding the effectiveness of psychological services in order to make timely modifications.

Treatment Fidelity

Another type of information that is critical when making decisions regarding services in schools is fidelity information. Fidelity is the degree to which an intervention is implemented as planned (Sanetti & Kratochwill, 2009). Similar to formative evaluation

Table 27.1. Systems-Level Student Progress Questions

- What are the perceived barriers preventing progress?
- Are teachers and principals supportive of the school psychologist's change in roles and responsibilities?
- Are the resources of people, time, and materials flexibly assigned to meet student needs as they change over time?
- Is the percentage of time of psychological services allocated to instructional and behavioral consultation sufficient?
- Is more time for interventions or extra daily doses of instruction available for students who are not meeting goals?
- Are curricular programs in place that are empirically validated to produce positive outcomes for students?
- Is targeted professional learning available for regular and special education personnel to acquire skills needed to implement best practice instructional strategies?

information, fidelity information can be used at any time to make programming decisions on an individual or systems level. In fact, fidelity information can be viewed as formative assessment data. Information regarding the implementation of a program, either core or supplemental in nature, can aid in determining the reason a program may not be successful as well as provide information regarding what may need to be altered.

For example, upon discovery that screening data indicate that a particular grade level is not meeting identified targets, fidelity observations may be completed to ensure that the core instructional program is being delivered as intended. Once problems with student achievement are identified, many districts create intervention groups for students whose scores fall below target. The problem with this approach is that intervention groups may not be needed if the real problem lies with implementing the core program with fidelity. In this case, the focus of school psychological services may be directed toward increasing fidelity of implementation of those components of the core instructional program found to be implemented with unacceptable quality. Both implementation fidelity and formative evaluation information provide a mechanism to evaluate the contribution of the school psychologist in meeting the goals set by the education agency (Brown & Rahn-Blakeslee, 2009).

Summative Evaluation

While formative evaluation takes place during instruction, summative evaluation follows instruction. Summative evaluation typically occurs at the end of each academic year and is used to determine if individual students have met their goals or if systems-level goals have been met. If the goal has been met, it can be concluded that the service delivery model was effective and the focus can shift to maintaining the current model and level of school psychological services. If goals have not been met, information should be used to determine why this is the case and decisions made about the overall service delivery model and the allocation of resources, including psychological services.

Statistical Analysis Procedures

When formative and summative data are collected, they need to be analyzed to answer the questions outlined in Table 27.1. Previous research has examined the diagnostic accuracy of various statistical methods for setting systems-level goals for formative assessment tools, based

on their ability to predict success on high-stakes summative measures (Silberglitt & Hintze, 2005). This research has established logistic regression and receiver operating characteristic curve analysis as two especially useful procedures for this purpose. While either could be used effectively, this chapter will focus on the use of logistic regression, as we believe it to be a more widely accessible procedure, as well as for other technical reasons that are beyond the scope of this chapter.

BEST PRACTICES IN EVALUATING SYSTEMS-LEVEL PSYCHOEDUCATIONAL SERVICES

Best practices in evaluating psychoeducational services using outcome data include the following steps: (a) develop clearly defined goals, (b) identify performance indicators, (c) determine criteria for success, (d) describe the relationship between psychoeducational services and goals, (e) focus on collaboration and teamwork, and (f) evaluate progress toward goals. Each of these steps is described in detail in this section along with how evaluation of psychoeducational services may be conducted within a mulitiered service delivery framework.

Develop Clearly Defined Goals

The first step in evaluating psychoeducational services is to develop clearly defined goals that are linked to student outcome data. These goals are based on district and building-level initiatives. It is paramount that goals are identified in such a manner that the goals are clear and measurable. Goals must be clear enough that the collaborative teams can stay focused and pointed in the same direction each day. Goals must be measurable in order to allow for the building to monitor its ongoing progress. Specific goals provide focus and the best student outcomes are likely to occur when all staff are working toward the same goal in a targeted, focused manner.

Determine Performance Indicators

Once a goal is clearly defined, it is necessary to determine how student performance will be measured. When possible, measures should be selected than can be used when making both formative and summative decisions. Deno (1986) suggests that five criteria should be met when selecting a performance measure. First, the performance measure should be a reliable and valid indicator of student achievement or behavior. Second, it should be simple, efficient, and of short duration to facilitate frequent administration by teachers. Third, it should provide assessment information that helps teachers plan better instruction. Fourth, it should be sensitive to the improvement of the student's achievement and/or behavior over time. Fifth, teachers and parents should easily understand it. Using performance criteria that meet these criteria will ensure that goals can be evaluated in a formative manner and that resources can be reallocated when student progress is unsatisfactory. In basic skill areas, we suggest the use of curriculum-based measures (CBM) as performance indicators (Shinn, 2010). In the area of social behavior, we suggest using office disciplinary referral data or other social–emotional screeners to track outcomes.

Develop a Criterion for Success

When setting a criterion for success, a desired outcome needs to be established. As the use of CBM at the systems level grew, either local or national (Hasbrouck & Tindal, 2006) norms were suggested as tools to help determine desired outcomes on CBM assessments. However, with the advent of NCLB and high-stakes assessments, a criterion for success has been established in every state in the form of a specific score on the annual statewide assessment. These criteria scores on statewide assessments are dynamic rather than static, requiring districts to make progressive improvement over time.

Statewide assessment information is generally summative in nature and is not first measured until third grade. Alternatively, CBM allows practitioners the flexibility to continue to measure formatively within and across school years, to begin measurement as early as preschool, and to establish criteria for success along the way that will accurately predict whether a child is likely to be successful on the statewide assessment. CBM assessments can be linked to scores on statewide assessments such that a criterion for success is established at each grade level and time point. For instance, a target score for CBM math assessment at fall of Grade 2 can be set, such that students who reach that score are considered highly (e.g., 80%) likely to be successful on the statewide assessment of math in Grade 3 (Silberglitt & Hintze, 2005).

Logistic regression is a statistical procedure that allows the practitioner to create target scores relatively simply and flexibly. Logistic regression can be used to calculate the probability (0–100%) that a student will successfully reach the statewide assessment criterion

based on his or her current CBM score (Neter, Kutner, Nachtsheim, & Wasserman, 1996). Logistic regression can be conducted at the local level by gathering data on students who have taken both the statewide assessment and the CBM assessment. Target CBM scores can then be chosen locally based on the probability of proficiency at a later date.

There are areas of student performance for which criteria cannot be derived utilizing CBM and logistic regression. For instance, school-wide behavioral goals are often measured by school office referrals. These referrals can be monitored over time in various manners to aid in the setting of school-wide goals. For instance, a school may set a goal that 80% of students receive no more than one office referral per year. These goals should be based on an ambitious expectation for student behavior while also ensuring a meaningful outcome.

Describe the Relationship Between Psychoeducational Services and Goals

As practitioners well know, the trend in school psychology service delivery has moved away from assessment for diagnosis and classification of individual students toward a focus on assessment for the purposes of prevention and intervention to provide positive outcomes for all students. This change in service delivery provides a mechanism for school psychologists to assist in restructuring schools in positive ways. For example, school psychologists can have an indirect impact on student achievement by providing instructional and behavioral consultation, advocating for data-based practices, promoting research-based curricula, and assisting schools in setting up continuous and frequent measurement systems for all students.

However, successful functioning in any role requires a clear vision of the primary purpose of that role (Deno, 2002). As a result, if school psychologists take on the challenge of prevention and intervention, there must be a direct relationship between their roles and responsibilities and the goals identified by the system. To make this relationship clear, we recommend that school districts develop job descriptions that clearly state the district goals, roles and responsibilities of the school psychologists, percentage of time allocated for each responsibility, and outcome indicators of success, including student achievement outcomes when appropriate. As their role is modified to address more systems-level data-based decision-making activities, school psychologists should work with their supervisors to refine their job descriptions to reflect these changes.

If a school district is committed to reaching its goals by restructuring psychoeducational services, then it is crucial that school administrators support school psychologists in their new roles. Clearly, if school psychologists are to engage in assessment linked to intervention, then there has to be an awareness and understanding that they will not spend the majority of their time engaging in more traditional activities such as being gatekeepers to special education services. Once school psychology services have been clearly defined, we recommend that the school principal, along with the school psychologist, meet with teachers and support staff to outline the role and function of the school psychologist.

Collaboration and Teamwork

Obtaining results depends on the interdependency between collaboration and goals. Since it is nearly impossible for one teacher to possess all the knowledge, skills, time, and resources needed to ensure high levels of learning for all students, collaborative teams of teachers and related services staff have been recommended (Buffman, Mattos, & Weber, 2009). For example, suppose a school district sets a goal that all children will read at grade level by the end of the academic year. Many factors will influence whether this goal will be met. These factors include choice of curriculum, time allocated to instruction, instructional strategies, consultative support to teachers, data-based decision making, and administrative support. Teaching staff will need to examine the reading research and Common Core State Standards to determine the core knowledge and skills students need to learn at each grade level. The district's curriculum committee will need to select a well-designed curriculum that includes the core knowledge and skills students need to learn.

The school psychologist may assist teaching staff in administering screening assessments for the purpose of determining instructional groups. Teachers and support staff are responsible for teaching the curriculum using well-designed instructional strategies. Principals need to allocate common time for teachers to prepare and review student progress with other teachers from their grade level. The school psychologist may assist teachers in setting up a frequent and direct assessment system to monitor student progress. The school psychologist may meet with grade-level teams to review student progress and design individual or group interventions when progress is not satisfactory.

School psychology services play an important role in determining whether student goals are met, but the most important factor is collaboration and teamwork. Schools are encouraged to establish collaborative teams at each building and individual grade level for the sole purpose of reviewing data on system goals along with discussing how to make adjustments in instruction in response to student data. The key element in collaborative teams is a focus on the end result (i.e., student outcomes) and data-based decision making.

Evaluate Progress Toward Goals

Once goals have been identified and a plan for reaching the goals has been developed, evaluation of progress toward goals should be conducted using frequent and direct measures of student performance. Traditionally, goals are identified, a plan is developed, and progress toward goals is evaluated at the end of the school year. The problem with this type of evaluation is that ineffective programs are not identified until after the programs have been implemented for a significant amount of time. A combination of both formative and summative evaluation should be used to maximize effective decision making. School psychologists are in a unique position to aid with this evaluation and the subsequent modifications to resource allocation that may ensue. School psychologists often serve on teams that review these data on a regular basis (e.g., monthly) and have a picture of the overall performance of students within the building.

Evaluation of Psychoeducational Services Within a Multitier Model

In recent years, much emphasis is being placed on a multitiered model (Walker & Shinn, 2010) and a schoolwide model (Simmons et al., 2002). Each of the steps above may be used to evaluate psychoeducational services within a multitiered service delivery model. A summary of steps to evaluate psychoeducational services is provided in Table 27.2.

Tier 1: Core Instruction

Core instruction is the instruction provided to all students to ensure that they meet grade-level standards. First, at Tier 1, schools and districts will need to determine what percentage of students should be academically proficient based on the core curriculum alone. Many have argued that approximately 80% of students should reach proficiency based on the core curriculum alone. However, the 80% number is not a number set in stone, nor is it particularly empirically

Table 27.2. Sample Template of Evaluating Psychoeducational Outcomes Within a Three-Tiered Model

	Tier 1	Tier 2	Tier 3
Clearly defined goals	• 80% of students at or above proficiency levels	• 15% of students receiving supplemental instruction	• 5% of students receiving intensive instruction
Performance indicators	• Benchmark assessment using general outcome measures	• Strategic assessment using general outcome measures	• Intensive assessment using general outcome measures
Criterion for success	• Target scores established at each grade level	• Target scores established at each grade level	• Target scores established at each grade level
Relationship between psychoeducational services and goals	• Assist in benchmark assessment • Consultation with teachers regarding effective core instruction	• Assist in strategic monitoring procedures • Facilitate problem-solving teams • Assessment to identify effective supplemental interventions	• Assist in intensive monitoring procedures • Assessment to identify effective intensive interventions
Collaboration and teamwork	• Building-level grade-level teams • Consultation among staff	• Building-level grade-level teams • Building-level problem-solving teams	• Building-level grade-level teams • Building-level problem-solving teams • Special education decision-making teams • IEP teams
Evaluation of progress	• Monitor percentages at each tier, and movement of students between tiers	• Monitor percentages at each tier, and movement of students between tiers	• Monitor percentages at each tier, and movement of students between tiers

derived. Instead, it is based on a resource allocation model derived from public health. In the area of social behavior, schools will need to determine what threshold they will use for acceptable number of discipline incidents. Schools are encouraged to examine baseline data of student academic and behavior performance and use these data to set realistic yet ambitious goals for the school year.

Second, after setting goals, schools must determine the performance indicators to be used to measure student progress. We recommend conducting benchmark assessment (e.g., three times per year; Shinn, 2010) using general outcome measures in basic skills areas and a review of office disciplinary referral data in the area of social behavior. Students are identified from these assessments as being above or below pre-established targets. Students who meet or exceed grade-level expectations in assessment areas are rescreened at the next benchmarking period unless concerns emerge. All students who fall below grade-level expectations based on these screening assessments are considered for Tier 2 or Tier 3 interventions and should be placed on a schedule to be monitored in areas of concern more frequently. However, in buildings where large numbers

of students are below target, it is not feasible to provide Tier 2 and Tier 3 interventions to large numbers of students because of lack of resources. In these situations, many buildings target the bottom 20% of students for intervention services and, at the same time, work on improving core instruction in both academic and behavioral realms for all students.

Third, schools must determine a criterion for success. While the goal may be to have 80% of students proficient at each grade level, proficiency targets must be defined to determine what percentage of students are proficient. There are two primary methods used for determining proficiency levels: (a) norm-referenced approaches and (b) criterion-referenced approaches. Districts that use a norm-referenced approach set their proficiency targets using national, state, or district norms. Districts that use a criterion-referenced approach would use its own data and correlate those scores with state accountability test scores and build a regression formula from the results.

Fourth, the school psychologist and school administrators should discuss how psychoeducational services will be designed to support services at Tier 1. The NASP Practice Model (NASP, 2010) outlines overlapping areas of practice including both instructional design and mental health. There are a number of ways school psychologists can be involved at Tier 1. First, they can use their instructional and behavioral consultation skills along with their knowledge of research-based instructional practices to work with teachers on designing and implementing interventions for individual students and groups of students within the core instruction. Second, they could be responsible for facilitating the benchmark testing (e.g., logistical factors such as who, what, where, and when). Following the benchmark assessments, school psychologists could work with school administrators and grade-level teachers to review data. Third, the school psychologist can work with grade-level teams of teachers or professional learning communities (DuFour, DuFour, & Eaker, 2008) to use benchmark assessment data to make instructional decisions (e.g., assist in developing flexible instructional groups). Finally, they can apply a problem-solving model of decision making to evaluate core instruction in their buildings.

The fifth step is to determine if the school building is organized to support collaboration and teamwork. One way to support collaboration and teamwork is for the principal to establish grade-level teams that meet regularly to examine student achievement data. Through the grade-level team process, the goal is to have grade-level staff members collectively consider all students as one group to be supported together. School psychologists can assist grade-level teams in reviewing benchmark assessment results of students and in evaluating the percentage of students who are at or above target (Tier 1), somewhat below target (Tier 2), or significantly below target (Tier 3; Burns & Gibbons, 2012). They can assist grade-level teams in setting goals for improving core instruction, and they can assist in developing class-wide interventions within the core instructional time.

The sixth and final step is to evaluate progress toward goals set at Tier 1. Based on the criterion for proficiency described above, target scores can be set for each grade level and benchmark period. With the goal of 80% in mind, schools can look at the percentage of students at each grade level who reach these targets in the fall, winter, and spring. If the percentage reaching the target is decreasing, this indicates a concern with the Tier 1 curriculum, as the growth of students in this tier is not keeping pace with the growth necessary to remain on track for success. Conversely, if students who were in Tier 1 in the fall remain above target throughout the year, it indicates that growth for these students has been sufficient to remain on track for success.

Tier 2: Supplemental Instruction

Supplemental instruction is provided to some students who are in need of additional support, typically in addition to core instruction. Again, the first step in the process is to develop a clearly defined goal. At Tier 2, the goal will be to identify the acceptable percentage of students who will need supplemental instruction and intervention. The research literature provides some direction that no more than 15% of students should be in need of supplemental instruction. However, that number was not empirically derived. From a resource standpoint, schools often do not have the time, money, or expertise to provide supplemental instruction to large numbers of students. Thus, using 15% as a target goal makes logical sense. Furthermore, if large numbers of students are below target, school districts need to examine what is going on with the core instruction provided to all students. Again, schools are encouraged to utilize baseline data in assisting with goal setting.

Second, schools must determine student performance indicators. We suggest using the same performance indicators across all three tiers to ensure a common measure is used in decision making. Students can be monitored on either a monthly or biweekly basis depending on their needs. When establishing a criterion for success at Tier 2, the criterion is to accelerate student growth so they meet the Tier 1 target score in academic areas or reach an acceptable behavioral threshold similar to Tier 1. However, the bottom of the range of performance falling into Tier 2 should also be set. This will establish whether students are maintaining Tier 2 status and also provide a goal for Tier 3. Again, this goal can be flexibly determined based on the probability curve and the school's available resources and desired goals. As a starting point, if the Tier 1 target score was set at 70% probability of success, consider setting the Tier 2 target score at 30% probability. This establishes students across the range of Tier 2 as those who, roughly, have a 50/50 chance of success. Based on diagnostic accuracy of these target scores and on the individual schools performance and available resources, both of these targets can be adjusted upward when deemed appropriate.

Third, schools must determine how psychoeducational services can support the delivery of services at Tier 2. At this level, school psychologists can be responsible for facilitating progress-monitoring procedures and assisting in identifying research-based interventions. School psychologists can use their skills to help develop standard intervention scripts that can be used to train interventionists, assess treatment integrity, and provide needed support to interventionists.

When evaluating psychoeducational services at Tier 2, many sources of data may be used. Benchmark assessment data provide an opportunity for evaluation at the system level. Progress-monitoring data allow for evaluation of success at the individual level. Keeping the Tier 2 goal of 15% or less in mind, buildings can examine the percentage of students who fall into the Tier 2 range on the fall, winter, and spring benchmark assessments. However, remember that a rising percentage could be due to highly effective Tier 3 services (or ineffective Tier 1 services) rather than to inadequate services at Tier 2. Similarly, a falling percentage is not an indicator of strong Tier 2 services if the percentage of students at Tier 3 is growing. In addition to the percentages of students in each tier, examine the

number of students in Tier 2 who move up to Tier 1, down to Tier 3, and remain in Tier 2. A useful tool for organizing data is the summary of effectiveness chart (see Figure 27.1).

Tier 3: Intensive Instruction

Intensive instruction is provided to a few students who need an individually tailored intervention matched to their specific needs. Similar to Tiers 1 and 2, the first step is to develop a clearly defined goal of the percentage of students who will be in need of intensive instruction. If school districts use the 80% (core), 15% (supplemental) goals identified in research, then that leaves 5% of students who may be in need of the most intensive instruction and support. Again, similar to Tier 2, the goals that are set should be able to be accommodated with the existing resources within a school.

Figure 27.1. Summary of Effectiveness Chart

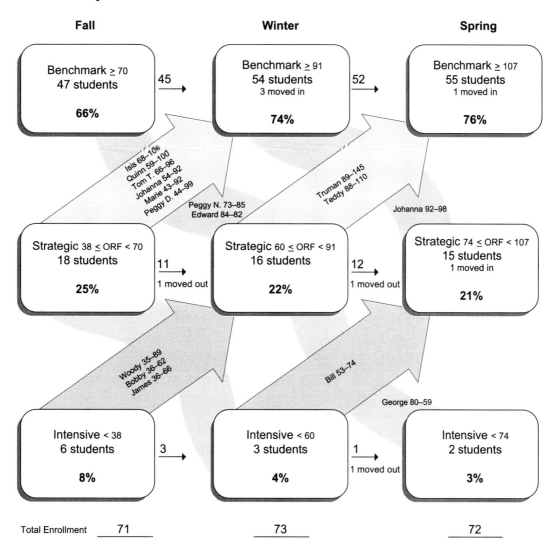

Once goals are set, the same set of performance indicators used in Tiers 1 and 2 should be used at Tier 3. We suggest using intensive monitoring procedures (Shinn, 2010), which involve monitoring student progress on at least a weekly basis using general outcome measures. For students who receive special education services and support, these measures can be used to write Individualized Education Program (IEP) goals and evaluate progress toward goals.

The criterion for success at Tier 3 is to close the gap between the expected level of achievement and the student's present level of performance in both academic and social behavior. The goal for most students is to reach the Tier 1 targets. Students who are extremely discrepant from grade-level expectations may require individually tailored goals. In this case, goals may be set for the students to reach the CBM score associated with the bottom of the Tier 2 range for the upcoming benchmark period (i.e., students in Tier 3 in the fall should aim for reaching Tier 2 in winter or spring, depending on the severity of the discrepancy). Once this intermediate goal is achieved, the ultimate goal of reaching grade-level proficiency can be reasonably set.

In restructuring school psychology services to align with school-level goals at Tier 3, numerous possibilities exist that incorporate collaboration and teamwork. To reinforce the link between assessment and intervention, school psychologists can collect assessment data that will assist teachers and teams in developing appropriate group and individual intensive intervention programs.

To support collaboration and teamwork at Tier 3, schools should consider establishing problem-solving teams. We suggest that problem-solving teams work in conjunction with grade-level teams to help identify appropriate interventions for students when the knowledge and resources of the grade-level teams have been exhausted and students have not made adequate progress in a Tier 2 intervention. In many districts, the school psychologist facilitates the problem-solving team. They ensure that a standard decision-making process and data collection activities are used to individually tailor interventions for students. They also assist the problem-solving team in regularly reviewing school benchmark data to identify which students are in need of Tier 3 interventions and supports. By regularly reviewing these data, the school psychologist is promoting a proactive system rather than a reactive system that is dependent on teacher referrals to the team.

For some students, problem-solving teams may determine that a special education evaluation is warranted.

With the 2004 reauthorization of the Individuals with Disabilities Education Act, districts may use a process that determines whether a child responds to scientifically based instruction as part of the evaluation criteria. This process, referred to as response to intervention (RTI), commonly is used within a problem-solving decision-making model. School psychologists can assist teams in identifying the problem, analyzing the problem, developing plans, implementing plans, and evaluating plans. In addition, if RTI is used as part of the evaluation process, then districts must have procedures in place to monitor treatment integrity. School psychologists can assist in conducting treatment integrity observations and follow-up training and support if necessary. Other students served at Tier 3 already qualify for special education services. School psychologists may be involved in assisting IEP teams set goals, design instructional programs, and evaluate progress toward goals.

Again, in evaluating progress, individual-level progress will be based on that student's graphed progress-monitoring data. However, the need for a systems-level evaluation of the effectiveness of Tier 3 services can be met through benchmark assessments. This provides the added benefit of measuring all students at their existing grade level expectations, rather than at their instructional level, as is often the case with individual progress monitoring. Keeping the goal of 5% in mind, examine the percentage of students in Tier 3 in the fall, winter, and spring. Also look for the number of students who move up into Tiers 2 and 1, as well as the number of students who fall into Tier 3 from the higher tiers.

Academic Case Study: Progress Monitoring

The following example demonstrates the process of evaluating the success of psychoeducational services to improve progress-monitoring practices for all students. The Lake Wobegon School District began implementing an RTI framework at the start of the 2010–2011 school year. They realigned their school psychology services to focus on assisting buildings in the district implement progress-monitoring practices with fidelity. Data from the fictional Sunnyside Elementary School are used in the case example.

Develop Clearly Defined Goals
The building-level leadership team set the three goals in the area of measurement of student outcomes. First, all students will be screened three times per year in grades

K–5 using general outcome measures. Second, all students (below target or receiving interventions) will have their progress monitored frequently (monthly, biweekly, or weekly depending on need). Third, all students who are on a progress-monitoring schedule will have goals set that are ambitious, meaningful, and measureable; and include the time frame, the conditions, the behavior, and the criterion for acceptable performance. In addition, a graph will be present for each goal, and there will be evidence of an instructional change when progress toward the goal is insufficient.

Determine Performance Indicators

The building chose to use the AIMSweb program as its tool to assist with benchmark assessment and progress monitoring. In the area of reading, students were given three reading passages from grade-level text and asked to read aloud for 1 minute. The district followed standard CBM administration and scoring methods. The score used was the number of words read correct in 1 minute. A rubric was developed to evaluate the quality of goals and data-based decision making (see Figure 27.2).

Develop a Criterion for Success

The district set a criterion for success for each of the goals. For the first goal, 100% of students will be screened three times per year in grades K–5 using general outcome measures. For the second goal, 100% of students receiving a Tier 2 or Tier 3 intervention will have their progress monitored using strategic or intensive procedures. For the third goal, graphs of students who are on a frequent progress-monitoring schedule will be reviewed once per year and evaluated using a 4-point rubric. The average scores in the area of goal setting and progress monitoring will increase from a score of 1.83 (2011–2012) to a 3.5 in 2012–2013.

Describe the Relationship Between Psychoeducational Services and Goals

School psychology services were realigned in Lake Wobegon District to assist buildings in implementing progress-monitoring practices with fidelity. The school psychologist assisted in each building to facilitate the benchmark assessment of all students, and the school psychologist attended grade-level team meetings, problem-solving meetings, and student support team meetings to help teams set goals for students receiving interventions and set up progress-monitoring procedures. Specifically, the school psychologist helped by (a) identifying students who would benefit from either strategic or intensive monitoring, (b) identifying goals and monitoring level material, and (c) organizing data collection procedures. In addition, the school psychologist, along with other education district staff, provided training to teachers and support staff on graphing student progress (i.e., setting up graphs, establishing baselines, setting goals, drawing trendlines). The school psychologist was responsible for meeting with grade-level staff on a regular basis to review student graphs. If individual students or groups of students were not making progress, then the team reorganized instructional resources and designed interventions. The school psychologist was available to these teams as an instructional consultant. Thus, the school psychologist observed in the classroom and made recommendations to teachers on how instruction could be modified for students.

Focus on Collaboration and Teamwork

Collaboration and teamwork was an integral factor in determining whether the building would meet its goals. The principal set the stage by obtaining consensus from staff on the building goal. The principal made sure that all building-level teams met regularly, and organized meeting schedules that would facilitate the school psychologist's involvement. In addition, the principal organized a team of staff from within the building, facilitated by the school psychologist, who would review student graphs midway through the school year to evaluate progress toward the goal.

Evaluate Progress Toward Goals

The district had collected data during the 2011–2012 school year on the first and second goals. The data indicated that only 72% of students receiving a Tier 2 or 3 intervention had their progress monitored on a strategic or intensive schedule. Student goals and graphs were evaluated using a rubric with a 4-point scale. The average score for goals was 3.4 and graphs was 2.1. To evaluate progress toward building goals, the same data were evaluated during the 2012–2013 school year. Significant progress was made in both goal areas. Data indicated that 100% of students receiving a Tier 2 or 3 intervention were on either a strategic or intensive monitoring schedule. When student goals and graphs were evaluated using the same rubric as the previous year, the average score for goals was 3.6 and graphs was 3.4.

Student outcome data are regularly incorporated as part of the evaluation process for school psychologists. The school psychologist shared building goal data

Figure 27.2. Rubrics for Evaluating Goals and Progress-Monitoring Graphs

	Quality Indicators			
Goal Setting	4	3	2	1
Goals are meaningful, measurable, and able to be monitored; whenever possible measures are fluency based.	Goals are meaningful, measurable, and able to be monitored. Fluency measures are used when appropriate.	Goals are meaningful and measurable but units of measurement should be changed.	Goals are measurable but not meaningful.	Goals are not meaningful, measurable, or able to be monitored.
Goals reflect high expectations but are realistic.	Goals are ambitious enough to drive interventions to allow the child to make meaningful progress.	Goals are somewhat ambitious to allow the child to make progress.	Goals are written such that the student would make progress regardless of the intervention.	Goals are not ambitious enough for the child to make meaningful progress.
The goal includes the time frame, the conditions, the behavior, and the criterion for acceptable performance.	The goal includes the time frame, the conditions, the behavior, and the criterion for acceptable performance.	A goal contains three of four elements.	A goal contains two of four elements.	Goals contain fewer than two elements.
The goal includes evaluation procedures, frequency of evaluation, and identifies the person responsible for monitoring.	The goal includes evaluation procedures, frequency of evaluation, and identifies the person responsible for monitoring progress.	The goal includes two of three elements.	The goal includes one of three elements.	The goal does not include evaluation procedures and frequency of evaluation.
Progress Monitoring				
A graph or checklist is developed for each goal. The graph must reflect what is written in the goal (i.e., a WPM graph for a WPM goal), including frequency of data collection.	Each goal has a graph or checklist and data are collected as per the goal.	Each goal has a graph or checklist and data are collected but less frequently than the goal indicates.	Each goal does not have a graph or checklist, but there is evidence of regular data collection, or each goal has a graph or checklist but there is no evidence of regular data collection.	There are not any graphs or checklists and little or no data are collected, or the graph does not accurately reflect the goal.
The graph or checklist has acceptable quality in the following elements: • Descriptive title (graph or checklist) • Labeled axes (graph) or columns/rows (checklist) • Consistent intervals on axes (graph) • Trendline (graph, when appropriate) • Able to identify progress or lack of progress (checklist) • Parent friendly (graph or checklist)	The graph or checklist has acceptable quality in all applicable elements.	The graph or checklist reflects acceptable quality in one item less than all applicable elements.	The graph or checklist reflects acceptable quality in two items less than all applicable elements.	The graph or checklist reflects acceptable quality in three items or less than all applicable elements.
There is evidence of an instructional change when progress toward the goal is insufficient.	• A decision-making rule is used to make decisions about instructional changes. • A line is drawn on the graph or checklist to indicate when a change occurs when progress is insufficient. • There is good evidence that interventions were documented and implemented when progress was insufficient. • Progress was sufficient; no instructional change was warranted.	Instructional change is documented; decision-making rule was used, but not in a timely manner (e.g., instructional change should have been implemented earlier).	No decision-making rules are used; interventions are implemented with students on an inconsistent basis.	There is insufficient evidence to determine whether any instructional change occurred when student progress is insufficient; there is evidence of insufficient student progress but no instructional change was documented.

with the supervisor on a regular basis. By using student outcome data as part of the evaluation process, the emphasis on accountability for student achievement was maintained. In addition, when the supervisor regularly examined this type of data, system-level issues could be identified and addressed.

Behavior Case Study: School-Wide Behavior Supports

The following case example will highlight a building's implementation of behavior support modeling process outlined in this chapter.

Develop Clearly Defined Goals

Miraculous Middle School's teachers had noticed that office discipline referral rates seemed to be rising each year. The behavior leadership team set four goals. First, the behavior leadership team will review building-wide office referral, failure rates, and attendance data every 6 weeks (twice per trimester). Second, the building will have interventions available for students with needs in the area of behavior that can be implemented with fidelity at any point in the school year. Third, all students who receive more than two office discipline referrals, or have any unexcused absences or failing grades during a data review, will be considered for a Tier 2 intervention in the area of behavior. Fourth, all students who are not successful in a Tier 2 behavioral intervention will be referred to the problem-solving team for potential referral to a Tier 3 intervention.

The school psychologist's role in this team is to bring the data to the team in a manner that can be easily analyzed by all team members. Additionally, the school psychologist brought recommendations regarding interventions and progress-monitoring measures.

Determine Performance Indicators

Miraculous Middle School identified office discipline referrals as a meaningful measure of student behavior. Referral information included time of day, class, and reason for referral.

Develop a Criterion of Success

Miraculous Middle School's team analyzed its data and found that 74% of the behavior referrals were obtained by the same 35 students. Because of this, the team believed that if it adequately met the needs of these 35 students, as well as clearly defined behavioral expectations for all students, the team could significantly decrease the number of office discipline referrals in a year. The team ambitiously set a goal of decreasing the number of referrals by 50% in one school year.

Describe the Relationship Between Psychoeducational Services and Goals

The services of the school psychologist were realigned to support the effort of the behavior leadership team and Miraculous Middle School. Specifically, the school psychologist stopped holding social skills groups for at-risk students and students with special education services as well as stopped processing with students when office discipline referrals were issued. Instead, the team determined the school psychologist should facilitate the behavior leadership team, bring building-wide data to each behavior team meeting, research and recommend Tier 2 interventions in the area of behavior, and support the fidelity of implementation of Tier 2 and Tier 3 behavior interventions.

Collaboration and Teamwork

Miraculous Middle School's behavior leadership team spent a significant amount of time collaborating in order to implement building-wide change. The change required all teachers to accurately document absences, consistently refer students to the office for misbehavior, and keep grades updated regularly on the district's information management system. Additionally, when deciding upon Tier 2 interventions, it was essential that team members had consensus regarding which interventions were chosen and why the interventions were thought to be appropriate for the students at Miraculous Middle School. Rather than simply design the intervention and present it to the team, the school psychologist brought several ideas to the team and the team developed its final recommended Tier 2 intervention together.

Evaluate Progress Toward Goals

At each behavior leadership team meeting, data are analyzed by the team regarding overall school-wide occurrence of office referrals, class failures, and unexcused absences, and these are compared to those at previous points in the year. Additionally, data regarding the success of the Tier 2 intervention are analyzed at the completion of each trimester. As long as the Tier 2 intervention continues to be successful, it will be implemented. If it is unsuccessful, then the intervention protocol and implementation will be revisited. The use of psychoeducational services on the team, as well as the larger impact of the change in the role as a result of this change, will also be examined across time.

SUMMARY

Schools are becoming increasingly more accountable for student outcomes. This accountability movement necessitates the use of student outcome data to evaluate the effectiveness of the services provided by school psychologists and other educational service providers. No longer is it just the teacher's responsibility to increase student achievement. All members of the educational team must work in concert to affect positive student outcomes. The educational research literature contains numerous references to results. However, results have rarely become operationalized. Using valid and reliable student outcome data is one way to operationalize educational results.

The NASP Practice Model (NASP, 2010) describes 10 domains of practice under which school psychologists practice. In each building, these services will need to be prioritized for maximum student benefit to be realized. In order to accomplish this, the role of the school psychologist must be clearly defined to support data-based decision making within a multitiered service delivery model. School psychologists must embrace a new skillset that includes instructional and behavioral consultation, assessment practices linked to intervention planning, and data-based evaluation practices at both an individual and systems level.

This chapter focused on how school psychoeducational services may be evaluated using student outcome data. Critical variables in this process include clearly defined goals, direct performance indicators, establishing a criterion for success, describing a relationship between psychoeducational services and goals, a focus on collaboration and teamwork, and formative and summative evaluation of progress toward goals. All of these variables operate interdependently to produce results. Concentrating on results does not negate the importance of process (i.e., a good service delivery model). Rather, results tell us whether the process is effective and to what extent the process needs to be reexamined and adjusted. Regular use of data, in tandem with adjustments to service based on the data, is the only way to expect long-term success.

AUTHOR NOTE

Disclosure. Kim Gibbons has a financial interest in books she authored or coauthored referenced in this chapter.

REFERENCES

Brown, S., & Rahn-Blakeslee, A. (2009). Training school-based practitioners to collect intervention integrity data: One agency's model. *School Mental Health, 1,* 143–153. doi:10.1007/s12310-009-9014-9

Buffman, A., Mattos, M., & Weber, C. (2009). *Pyramid response to intervention: RTI, professional learning communities, and how to respond when kids don't learn.* Bloomington, IN: Solution Tree Press.

Burns, M. K., & Gibbons, K. (2012). *Implementing response-to-intervention in elementary and secondary schools: Procedures to assure scientific-based practices* (2nd ed.). New York, NY: Routledge.

Deno, S. L. (1986). Formative evaluation of individual student programs: A new role for school psychologists. *School Psychology Review, 15,* 358–374.

Deno, S. L. (2002). Problem solving as "best practice." In A. Thomas & J. Grimes (Eds.), *Best practices in school psychology IV* (pp. 37–56). Bethesda, MD: National Association of School Psychologists.

DuFour, R., DuFour, R., & Eaker, R. (2008). *Revisiting professional learning communities at work: New insights for improving schools.* Bloomington, IN: Solution Tree Press.

Fairchild, T. N., & Zins, J. E. (1992). Accountability practices of school psychologists: 1991 national survey. *School Psychology Review, 21,* 617–627.

Gullickson, A. R. (2009). *The personnel evaluation standards: How to assess systems for evaluating educators* (2nd ed.). Thousand Oaks, CA: Corwin.

Harvey, V. S., & Pearrow, M. (2010). Identifying challenges in supervising school psychologists. *Psychology in the Schools, 47,* 567–581.

Hasbrouck, J. E., & Tindal, G. (2006). Oral reading fluency norms: A valuable assessment tool for reading teachers. *Reading Teacher, 59,* 636–644. doi:10.1598/RT.59.7.3

Hosp, J. L. (2012). Formative evaluation: Developing a framework for using assessment data to plan instruction. *Focus on Exceptional Children, 44*(9), 1–10.

Kane, T. J., Taylor, E. S., Tyler, J. H., & Wooten, A. L. (2011). Evaluating teacher effectiveness: Can classroom observations identify practices that raise achievement? *Education Next, 11,* 1–11.

Minke, K. M. (2011). Performance evaluation and accountability: Are you at the table? *Communiqué, 39*(6), 2.

Morrison, J. Q. (2013). Performance evaluation and accountability for school psychologists: Challenges and opportunities. *Psychology in the Schools, 50,* 314–324.

National Alliance of Pupil Services Organizations. (2011). *NAPSO policy statement: Utilizing multiple measures in determining professional performance of specialized instructional support personnel.* Retrieved from http://www.napso.org/personnel-systems.html

National Association of School Psychologists. (2010). *Model for comprehensive and integrated school psychological services.* Bethesda, MD: Author. Retrieved from http://www.nasponline.org/standards/2010standards/2_PracticeModel.pdf

National Association of School Psychologists. (2012). A framework for the personnel evaluation of school psychologists utilizing the NASP Practice Model. *Communiqué, 41*(3), 26–27.

Neter, J., Kutner, M. H., Nachtsheim, C. J., & Wasserman, W. (1996). *Applied linear statistical models.* New York, NY: McGraw-Hill.

Prus, J., & Waldron, N. (2008). Best practices in assessing performance in school psychology graduate programs. In A. Thomas & J. Grimes (Eds.), *Best practices in school psychology V* (pp. 1943–1956). Bethesda, MD: National Association of School Psychologists.

Riley-Tillman, C. T., Burns, M. K., & Gibbons, K. (2013). *RTI applications: Assessment, analysis, and decision making.* New York, NY: Guilford Press.

Sanetti, L. M. H., & Kratochwill, T. R. (2009). Toward developing a science of treatment integrity: Introduction to the special series. *School Psychology Review, 38,* 445–459.

Shinn, M. R. (2010). Building a scientifically based data system for progress monitoring and universal screening across three tiers, including RTI using curriculum-based measurement. In M. R. Shinn & H. M. Walker (Eds.), *Interventions for achievement and behavior problems in a three-tier model including RTI* (pp. 259–292). Bethesda, MD: National Association of School Psychologists.

Silberglitt, B., & Hintze, J. M. (2005). Formative assessment using CBM-R cut scores to track progress toward success on state-mandated achievement tests: A comparison of methods. *Journal of Psychoeducational Assessment, 23*, 304–325. doi:10.1177/073428290502300402

Simmons, D. C., Kame'enui, E. J., Good, R. H., Harn, B. A., Cole, C., & Braun, D. (2002). Building, implementing, and sustaining a beginning reading improvement model: Lessons learned school by school. In M. R. Shinn, H. M. Walker, & G. Stoner (Eds.), *Interventions for academic and behavior problems II: Preventative and remedial approaches* (pp. 537–569). Bethesda, MD: National Association of School Psychologists.

Steele, J. S., Hamilton, L. S., & Steecher, B. M. (2010). *Incorporating student performance measures into teacher evaluation systems*. Santa Monica, CA: RAND Corporation.

Waldron, N., & Prus, J. (2006). *A guide for performance-based assessment, accountability, and program development in school psychology training programs* (2nd ed.). Bethesda, MD: National Association of School Psychologists.

Walker, H. M., & Shinn, M. R. (2010). Systemic, evidence-based approaches for promoting positive student outcomes within a multitier framework: Moving from efficacy to effectiveness. In M. R. Shinn & H. M. Walker (Eds.), *Interventions for achievement and behavior problems in a three-tier model including RTI* (pp. 1–26). Bethesda, MD: National Association of School Psychologists.

28

Best Practices in Evaluating the Effectiveness of Interventions Using Single-Case Methods

Rachel Brown
Mark W. Steege
Rebekah Bickford
University of Southern Maine

OVERVIEW

This chapter will provide information about how to use single-case data for the purpose of evaluating individual students' school improvement. We will explain the specific attributes of single-case research designs and identify the ones best suited to use in schools. In addition the chapter will highlight how single-case methods fit into the National Association of School Psychologists (NASP) *Model for Comprehensive and Integrated School Psychological Services* (NASP, 2010), especially the domain of Research and Program Evaluation. Readers will learn the benefits of using several specific types of single-case methods, including the case study, alternating and multiple treatments, and multiple baseline methods to monitor students' progress. The chapter concludes with four examples showing the use of case study data to evaluate student progress.

Single-case methods are well aligned with the NASP Practice Model (NASP, 2010) because they show whether or not individual students are making progress. Of the 10 domains included in the NASP Practice Model, single-case methods are explicitly helpful for a number of domains: Data-Based Decision Making and Accountability, by providing a way to collect and understand individual student data; Consultation and Collaboration, by providing teachers with easy-to-understand graphs of student progress; Intervention and Instructional Support to Develop Academic Skills, by providing a way to see student progress over time and by providing ongoing progress data for students who need intervention; Preventive and Responsive Services, by documenting actual outcomes so that student response can be observed; and Research and Program Evaluation, by showing if specific methods have been helpful for multiple students. Using single-case methods requires knowledge of the specific steps necessary to capture and display the data.

The use of single-case methods to evaluate student progress has gained attention as a result of recent school policies that focus on the importance of measuring student progress. For example, the 2001 No Child Left Behind Act, the 2004 Individuals with Disabilities Improvement Act, and the 2009 American Recovery and Reinvestment Act (e.g., Race to the Top) all include language requiring schools that receive federal money to track student progress and identify whether students are meeting learning goals. A common theme across these three federal initiatives was the importance of identifying whether a student responds to intervention. A student's response can only be measured if the right kinds of data are collected while the student participates in an intervention. More recently, educators have begun to describe and use what are known as multitiered systems of support as a comprehensive framework for supporting all students (Brown-Chidsey & Steege, 2010). Importantly, such systems provide school- and district-wide methods for ensuring that all students who need help get it in a timely manner. Such supports include general education efforts to meet the needs of all students and include methods such as response to intervention (RTI) and positive behavioral interventions and supports.

BASIC CONSIDERATIONS

In order to know if a student is making progress in response to instructional supports, data must be reliably gathered on a regular basis. There are a number of methods for examining student progress, but the method that has been identified as the most effective and accurate for student progress monitoring is the single-case research design (Kazdin, 2010; Riley-Tillman & Burns, 2009). There are many types of single subject designs, and Table 28.1 provides a summary of them. Each type has uses for specific situations. A key component of single-case designs is the collection of preintervention baseline data. Gathering such data is essential because it provides a measure of the student's functioning preintervention, which can be compared to his or her functioning postintervention, to evaluate progress. Riley-Tillman and Burns (2009) described *baseline logic* and this description is helpful for understanding how to make sense of single-case data. Baseline logic means that only when the outcomes observed during intervention are significantly different from those at baseline can a treatment be considered truly effective. The extent to which the intervention implemented can be attributed to the observed change depends on the specific single-case design applied.

Case Studies

It is common for single-case designs to use a notation system involving letters to signify each condition. "A" always refers to the baseline condition, which is the student's behavior before any treatment is applied. The next letter is the first treatment condition. When the notation used is "AB" it refers to there being a baseline (A) phase and one treatment phase (B). Case study designs such as the "AB" model are the simplest of single-case methods and involve collecting only baseline and then treatment data. This design involves comparing the student's behavior or response during the baseline (e.g., no treatment) and treatment conditions. The benefits of a basic case study (AB) design are that the results of the treatment can be quickly known and the team does not have to wait a long time to evaluate results. The down side is that there is no true experimental control so the effect of the intervention is unknown. This is because there is no removal or comparison of the "B" condition after its application. The treatment results could be the result of a number of factors unrelated to the "B" intervention such as expectancy effects, maturation, or a change in some other variable.

Alternating and Multiple Treatments

Alternating and multiple treatments designs include multiple treatments for the purpose of comparing the effects of different treatments. Such designs are useful when it is important to find an effective treatment quickly. In such cases, the student receives multiple treatments in succession with or without a return to baseline (e.g., no treatment) conditions between each treatment change. The notation for a multiple treatment design is A-B-C with each letter after "A" representing a unique treatment. This design allows for a great deal of flexibility in terms of the order of interventions. However, a limitation of this design is a potential order effect. When time permits, there can be a return to the baseline condition after each treatment (e.g., ABACA). Returning to baseline after each treatment (multiple treatment with reversal design) provides more clarity about whether the behavior of interest was truly changed as a result of the intervention. However, it takes more time, and may not make sense if the intervention led to acquisition of skills that do not quickly regress (e.g., reading or math skills).

Another way to compare alternating treatments is to intersperse them such that conditions "B" and "C"

Table 28.1. Types of Single Case Designs and Conditions When They Are Appropriate

Type	Condition
Alternating treatments	Comparing two or more treatments in close alternating succession
Case study	Comparing no treatment to one specific treatment without a return to baseline
Changing criterion	When a student needs to make significant changes in a short period of time
Multiple baseline across conditions	Comparing effects of a treatment across settings
Multiple baseline across students	Comparing effects of a treatment across different subjects
Multiple treatments	Comparing the relative effectiveness of two or more treatments in succession with or without return to baseline
Reversal	Comparing the treatment with a previous condition
Withdrawal	Comparing whether the problem behavior recurs when the treatment is removed

happen near the same time in repeated fashion. For example, two interventions for improving reading fluency could be tried on alternating days. The "B" condition could be repeated reading and the "C" condition could be phrase drill correction. Each condition could be alternated to see which one leads to improved reading fluency. In concurrent alternating treatments, precise records of *what* treatment was applied *when* are needed so that it is clear which treatment methods contributed to each result. For example, repeated reading could be used on Mondays, Wednesdays, and Fridays, and phrase drills could be used on Tuesdays and Thursdays. Data showing the student's reading performance on those days would provide an indication if these two treatments yielded different results.

Multiple Baselines

Multiple baseline designs were introduced by Baer, Wolf, and Risley (1968). These designs involve comparing data between subjects, settings, or behaviors to determine if an intervention is effective. It is an important single-case design for use in schools because it can be used when removing a treatment is not possible or when obtained behaviors are not likely to regress, such as reading and math skills. There are several types of multiple baseline designs, including multiple baseline designs across subjects, settings, and behaviors. Multiple baseline designs across subjects involve having two or more students receive the same intervention at staggered times. Baseline data are collected for all the students and then the first student to show stable data is the first one to receive the intervention. Baseline data continue to be collected from the remaining students until the student who is receiving the intervention shows a stable and beneficial result from the intervention. This typically happens within 3–10 data points. Then another student begins intervention. The selection of which student goes next is based on which one has the most stable ongoing baseline. These steps are repeated until all target students are receiving the intervention.

When a multiple baseline design is implemented across settings, data are collected for the same student but in different settings. For example, data might be collected on a student's shouting out behavior in math, English, and science. The goal of the data collection is to see if an intervention designed to reduce the student's behavior of shouting out answers without being called on by the teacher worked. If the intervention were first applied in math, changes would be expected there first.

Once a change was observed in math, it would be applied in English. Finally, once stable improvements were seen in both math and English, it would be applied in science. Ideally, the data would show that the specific intervention for reducing shouted out answers was effective in all three settings.

Single-case data collection and display methods are useful in school settings because they allow teachers to collect and analyze data for individual students. With the rise of multitiered systems of support methods as a means of helping students, there is a need for easy-to-use data collection and interpretation methods. Single-case methods are easy to use and can be applied across a variety of classrooms and students. School psychologists are among the school personnel most likely to be able to use single-case methods. This is because school psychologists work with students individually and have the responsibility to evaluate students' school performance for the purpose of high-stakes decision making. In order for school psychologists to use single-case methods accuracy and effectively, it is essential that they are skilled in all of the specific steps involved in single-case methods.

BEST PRACTICES IN EVALUATING INTERVENTIONS

There are five steps necessary to use single subject design methods to gather data and review student progress. All of these steps are necessary for accurate use of single-case methods. These are (a) identify the behavior or skill that the student needs to change, (b) identify a measurement tool that can be used to measure changes in the student's behavior, (c) determine how frequently data will be collected, (d) gather the data, and (e) review the data and decide if the student's progress is adequate or if intervention change is needed. Skipping one or more steps could invalidate the process and make the obtained data useless.

Identify the Behavior

The first step is to decide what behavior will be targeted for change. Any observable behavior can be targeted for improvement, including overt classroom behaviors (e.g., getting out of a seat, calling out answers, pushing other students, running), academic skills (e.g., reading, writing, spelling, math skills), or other behaviors (e.g., work completion). Academic skills can be tracked through permanent products such as worksheets and tests. The identified behavior must be measureable and sensitive to change over time. It is ideal if the target behavior is something that happens often enough to generate regular data. Still, some less frequent problem behaviors are significant enough that tracking them over time is justified. For example, if a student has a history of severe but infrequent tantrums, these should also be monitored, particularly to measure progress when interventions are implemented.

Identify the Measurement Tool

Once the behavior is identified, the next step is to determine how it will be measured. There are a number of widely available measurement tools for academic behaviors. For example, curriculum-based measures are effective tools to measure students' reading, writing, spelling, and math skills over time. Available tools include the Dynamic Indicators of Basic Early Literacy Skills (https://dibels.org/next), AIMSweb (http://www.aimsweb.com), easyCBM (http://www.easycbm.com), and the Formative Assessment System for Teachers (http://www.faip.umn.edu/faip/login.do). Other behaviors such as time on task, time in seat, hand raising, and appropriate peer interactions can be measured with direct observation methods. The type of observation method used should match the behavior. For example, high-frequency behaviors can easily be recorded using rate measures (i.e., number of times out of seat per minute), but low-frequency behaviors are best measured using a frequency count (i.e., five tantrum episodes). Commonly used methods include recording the frequency, duration, latency, or intensity of the behavior. Frequency recording involves counting the number of instances of the behavior within a certain period of time. Duration refers to how long the behavior lasts from start to finish. Latency is how long after a specific start period a behavior happens. Intensity refers to how significant (or problematic) the behavior is. Table 28.2 lists these observation methods along with examples of their use. In some cases, multiple

observation recording methods may be used and shown in different graphs to display the different types of data.

Data Frequency

The next step is to decide how often data will be collected. Typically, this decision is based on the type of behavior observed and the urgency of change. The National Center on Response to Intervention (2013) recommends that students who receive Tier 2 interventions are progress monitored at least monthly and that students who receive Tier 3 interventions are progress monitored at least weekly. When a target behavior is problematic and causing significant disruption in the student's school progress, daily monitoring may be best. It is important to keep in mind that the frequency of data collection will drive how soon the data can be reviewed and interpreted. There must be at least three data points to identify a trend before single subject data can be interpreted (Kazdin, 2010; Riley-Tillman & Burns, 2009). Two data points cannot be interpreted because the direction of the trend is at chance levels. Three data points make it possible to consider if a trend is present. In some cases there will be a trend observed after three data points are collected. If there is no identifiable trend at this point, then additional data need to be collected. Usually, a trend in the data will be observable within 10 data points (Riley-Tillman & Burns, 2009). If there is no trend after 10 data points are collected, then there may be other factors influencing the stability of the data.

Data Collection

Planning for data collection procedures is important and increases the likelihood that the data will be gathered. Details to plan out include *who* will collect the data, *when* and *where* it will be collected, and *what* to do if the student is absent or school is cancelled for a day. The same person who is implementing the intervention might also conduct progress monitoring. This method

Table 28.2. Types of Behavior Recording and Examples of Use

Type	Description	Example
Frequency	The observer counts the number of the occurrences in a given period of time	Counting the number of words a student reads in 1 minute
Duration	The observer notes how long the behavior lasts from start to finish	Noting how long a student is on task during independent work
Latency	The observer records how long it takes for the behavior to begin after an indicated starting time	Noting how long it takes a student to begin an assignment after the teacher gives directions
Intensity	The observer records how intense the behavior is along a continuum	Noting the severity of an act of aggression on a predetermined scale

has the benefit of having data collection be aligned with the intervention. It is important that the person who collects the data be appropriately trained to use the data method chosen. Inadequate training can result in unreliable data that cannot be interpreted. Ideally, such training includes didactic instruction of the steps as well as practice in a classroom. The practice should include having two or more examiners gather or score the data so that interobserver agreement can be calculated. Interobserver agreement is typically calculated by counting how many agreements and disagreements two observers had for the same behavior sample. For example, the school psychologist and special education teacher could both observe the behavior during baseline and compare their measurements. If they agree at least 90% of the time, the special education teacher can continue to collect data independently. The number of agreements is then divided by agreements plus disagreements to yield the percentage of agreements. If interobserver agreement is less than 90%, the observer should be retrained to master the observation criteria.

In addition to the procedural planning for data collection, it is important to decide how data will be recorded. The simplest way to record the data is on a paper graph. Paper records have the benefit of being easy and accessible, especially for students. There are numerous computer-based data recording methods as well. The software program Microsoft Excel, as well as other spreadsheet programs, can be used to record and graph data. Cummings and Martinez (2012) have detailed instructions for how to use Excel to record and graph student data. Some of the measurement tools such

as AIMSweb and easyCBM have data recording features built into accompanying online programs. Many of these programs have browser-based (i.e., computer or touchpad device) scoring and data entry available and automatically graph the data as soon as it is entered into the database. A more generic online tool for data recording is Chart Dog (http://www.interventioncentral.org/teacher-resources/graph-maker-free-online). Chart Dog is free and allows users to enter a wide variety of data. The data are then graphed automatically to show student progress. Cummings and Martinez (2012) have detailed guidance for how to use Chart Dog.

Most of the above computer-based recording methods include the option to generate aimlines and trendlines on the graphs. An aimline is a line on the graph showing the trajectory that the data should take in order for the student to meet a learning goal. Aimlines are helpful because they remind students and teachers what level of performance is expected. Trendlines are indicators of the relative stability of the observed (e.g., actual) data. Trendlines are helpful in showing whether the student's performance is going in a certain direction or if it is scattered. In addition, a trendline can be compared to an aimline to show if the student is on track to meet a goal. This information is helpful during data review and subsequent intervention planning. Figure 28.1 (used in the example below) shows both an aimline and trendline.

Reviewing Data

After a series of three or more data points is collected, the data can be reviewed. The first consideration is

Figure 28.1. Casey's Multiplication Fact Accuracy

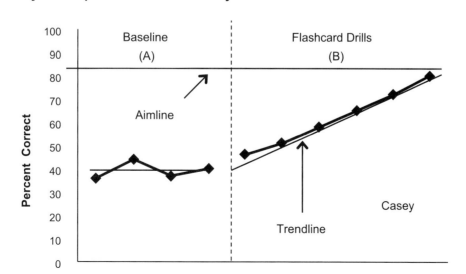

whether or not the data demonstrate a trend. A data trend is the extent to which the data demonstrate consistency over time (Johnston & Pennypacker, 2008). For example, if a student had oral reading fluency scores of 35, 33, and 36, there would be a stable trend because the scores are within expected variation for oral reading fluency. By contrast, if the same student's scores were 35, 67, and 105, there would not be a trend observed because the variation in these scores is far greater than expected over a week or a month's time. If the data do not demonstrate a trend, then additional data need to be collected and reviewed until a trend is observed. The computer tools mentioned above include the option to include a trendline on the graph. This can be helpful to teams when they review data.

Once a stable trendline is observed during baseline and intervention, the next task is to consider if the data show whether the student has made progress. There are two main ways to interpret single case data: visual inspection and percentage of nonoverlapping data points. Visual inspection involves looking at the data to see if meaningful changes in the target behavior have occurred. Questions to ask are: Did the score move in the direction expected? Has the student met the specified performance goal? Is the change sufficient or is more intervention needed? The other main way to interpret data is to calculate the percentage of nonoverlapping data points (Riley-Tillman & Burns, 2009; Scruggs, Matropieri, & Casto, 1987). This involves counting how many of the intervention data points do not overlap with any of the baseline data points. The bigger the percentage, the more effective the intervention is considered. This is because those intervention data points that are mutually exclusive from baseline are indicative of differences in observed behavior. By contrast, if there are few nonoverlapping data points, and thus many that are the same as baseline, then there is less change in the observed behavior. It may be that the intervention has not begun to work yet, or it may mean that a different intervention is needed.

Using Single-Case Methods

School psychologists are uniquely positioned to use single-case methods in their daily work. Most of the time, single-case methods are used with students for whom a specific intervention has been put into place. School psychologists can be instrumental in planning, implementing, and interpreting single-case methods. Starting at the planning stage, when school psychologists

serve on school problem-solving teams they are in a position to discuss with team members which students need intervention and progress monitoring. While all members of the problem-solving team are likely to identify which students need intervention, the school psychologist might be the only one who knows about a range of data collection tools and methods. When school psychologists understand the variety of data tools such as the range of curriculum-based measures and direct observation procedures, they are able to suggest specific tools matched to the intervention being planned.

School psychologists are also likely to be important in the process of implementing progress monitoring and data collection. For example, the school psychologist could model how to use specific data collection methods and train other personnel to use them for regular progress monitoring. Such training is essential so that the data will be accurate. Ideally, training should include direct instruction of the steps required for a specific measure as well as routine observation of data collection to verify accuracy and interobserver agreement. Data observations could be done monthly or quarterly to ensure the integrity of the data being collected. When an observation shows that there is inaccurate use of a measure or inadequate interobserver agreement, the school psychologist can provide additional training sessions and then observe data collection again.

An additional role relates to data interpretation. After the data are collected, it is important to review them regularly to determine if the intervention has resulted in desired effects. School psychologists can be in charge of checking with interventionists regularly to review student data. Such check-ins will help teams to know whether interventions are working or if changes are needed. If data are not reviewed regularly, then a student might end up receiving an ineffective intervention for a long period of time because no one reviewed the data. When students are responding well to interventions, the school psychologist can assist the team in determining when a student is ready to transition to less intensive support and eventually receive no intervention at all. But, when the data show that an intervention is not working, the school psychologist can assist with selection of alternate interventions.

In cases where a student's data indicate that the student has not responded to multiple interventions as hoped, a referral to special education is justified. The single-case data should be used as part of the comprehensive evaluation conducted during the special education referral process. The school psychologist can use the data for several purposes, depending on the state and district special education eligibility rules. In all cases, the single-case data should be reviewed to identify whether additional assessments are needed. In some cases, brief functional assessment of student behavior such as defined by Daly, Bonfiglio, Mattson, Persampieri, and Foreman-Yates (2006) could be used. This method can quickly show if a student's difficulties are specifically related to other variables, including current skills. In those states that require or allow the use of obtained data to show a student's response to intervention, the school psychologist should use these as part of the information collected to determine if the student has a specific learning disability. School psychologists have the training and skills to use single-case methods in strategic and important ways that document whether an intervention is working. The following examples illustrate how four specific types of single-case methods can be used by school psychologists to support individual student needs.

Example 1: Case Study

Casey is an eighth-grade student with math difficulties. On fall universal benchmark screening, Casey scored a 3 on the eighth-grade AIMSweb mathematics computation assessment. The eighth-grade fall benchmark goal is 10. Analysis of Casey's AIMSweb assessment and his homework assignments showed that he had inaccurate multiplication fact skills. Casey's score of 3 was consistent with his classroom performance, and his teacher began intervention. The intervention consisted of using flashcards to practice multiplication facts twice a week for 10 minutes each time. In order to monitor Casey's progress, once a week Casey completed a 4-minute timed multiplication fluency quiz. Casey's accuracy on each quiz was scored and graphed. Figure 28.1 shows Casey's data.

During the baseline (preintervention) phase, Casey's multiplication fact accuracy ranged from 36 to 44%. Once treatment began, his accuracy showed steady improvement, and after 6 weeks of intervention his accuracy was 80%. Despite this improvement, it is not possible to know for certain whether Casey's fact accuracy changed because of the intervention. It is possible that he began taking school more seriously, he enjoyed the individual attention from the teacher during the flashcard drills, or some other factor led to his improvement. A case study design such as Casey's is limited by the lack of a return to the baseline condition or evidence from other students that the same intervention worked for them. As noted, academic skills

such as multiplication facts are not likely to regress, so even if the flashcard drills were removed Casey's accuracy may not have returned to the preintervention level. Therefore, if we want to know for certain if a specific intervention was the reason for a student's behavior change, another single subject design might be better. In such cases, alternating treatments or multiple baseline designs could be a better choice. Nonetheless, it is important that Casey showed improvement, so knowing the source of the improvement may not have been essential.

Example 2: Case Study With Two Dependent Variables

Sometimes school psychologists are faced with the challenge of students who have both academic and other difficulties. For example, a student might have reading problems and problem behaviors in the classroom. In such cases it might be helpful to monitor the student's progress in both the academic and other concern (e.g., behavior). In such situations, it is often difficult to know if it is the behavior or the academic learning that is the primary problem. Thankfully, it is possible to monitor both types of behavior to learn whether one, or both, of the behaviors need changes. The school psychologist could arbitrarily decide which problem is most important or the school psychologist could test drive interventions and have data to inform later decisions. As described by Steege and Watson (2009), test driving an intervention that has multiple effects is a good way to see what type of intervention is most effective for addressing the student's educational needs. The following example shows how this can be done.

George is a student with autism who has trouble engaging in prolonged conversation with other students in the class. The school psychologist decides to take baseline (A) data on the kinds of conversation that George engages in to try and help with this problem. The school psychologist had the teacher code George's verbal communication with other students into two different types: verbal scripts and spontaneous conversation. Baseline data showed that when put in social situations, George engaged in verbal scripts (dependent variable 1) about 60% of the time and engaged in spontaneous conversation (dependent variable 2) about 5% of the time in the same social situations. Based on the graphed data (Figure 28.2), it was clear that George did not sustain conversation with classmates. Instead he depended on the use of verbal scripts in social situations.

Figure 28.2. George's Verbal Scripts and Spontaneous Conversations

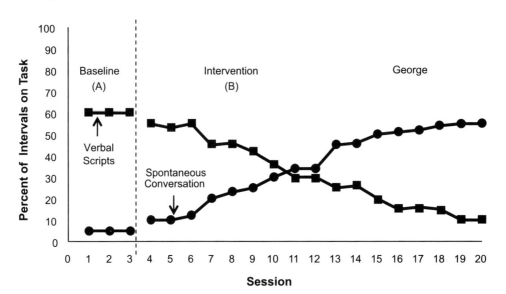

The school psychologist decided to try discrete trial teaching to help George learn how to engage in spontaneous conversation. The results from the intervention are shown in Figure 28.2. Once discrete trial teaching was implemented, the percentage of verbal scripts used in social situations decreased while the amount of spontaneous conversation in social situations increased. This is an example of a case study (AB) design with two dependent variables. Another way of defining the results of George's RTI is known as response covariance. This term refers to how George increased in his use of spontaneous conversation while simultaneously reducing his dependence on social scripts to engage in conversation. George's case shows how a student might show change in two dependent variables at the same time. When his spontaneous conversation skills improved, his dependence on social scripts was reduced.

Example 3: Alternating Treatments

Dale is a third-grade student who enjoys school but dislikes math class. He is often out of his seat and off task during math lessons. His teacher has noticed that Dale is more likely to be engaged in math lessons when they include hands-on projects rather than worksheets. After consulting with the school psychologist, Dale's teacher decided to intersperse didactic lessons with worksheets

Figure 28.3. Dale's On-Task Behavior During Hands-On and Worksheet Activities

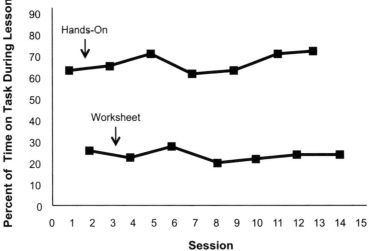

and practical applied lessons that require the students to solve everyday problems. To measure student response to these lessons, the school psychologist observed the math lessons each day for 2 weeks, with the even days being traditional lessons and the odd days being hands-on lessons. The results are graphed in Figure 28.3. Dale's response to the different lesson formats was very clear. He was on task far more often when the lessons consisted of hands-on activities than when the lessons were lectures followed by worksheets. For a student like Dale, hands-on activities appear to be more effective for maintaining student engagement.

In this case, the use of an alternating treatments design was important because it revealed that it was the nature of the instruction and not the subject matter that influenced Dale's classroom behavior. Had the school psychologist used a different single-case design such as AB, Dale's response to the hands-on instruction might not have been observed. Alternating treatments designs

are very helpful when specific details about a student's response to instruction need to be known.

Example 4: Multiple Baseline Designs Across Students

Gwen, Ryan, and Ben are three students in the seventh grade who frequently engage in attention-seeking behavior in the classroom. Specifically, all three students speak out of turn, say things that are inappropriate, and often delay responding to teacher requests. Their teachers requested assistance from the school psychologist, who agreed to collect baseline data, design an intervention, and provide consultation to the teachers to support implementation of the plan. Baseline data collected across students found that Gwen, Ryan, and Ben were engaged in attention-seeking behavior an average of 10 times per hour. In order to abate the students' motivation to seek attention, the school

Figure 28.4. Gwen's, Ryan's, and Ben's Attention-Seeking Behavior

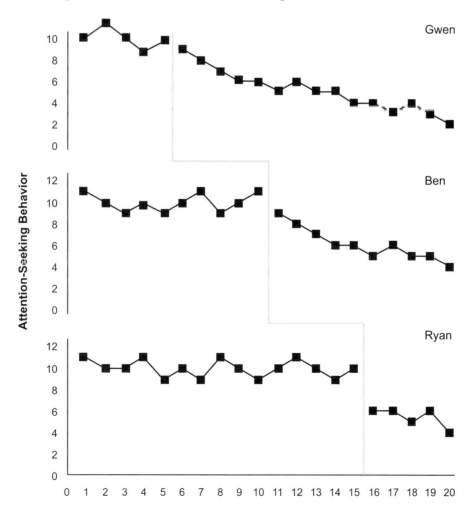

psychologist designed an intervention to provide the students with noncontingent attention at the initial rate of 15 times per hour. A multiple baseline across students design was used to assess the functional relationship between the noncontingent reinforcement intervention and any changes that might occur in the students' attention-seeking behavior.

The school psychologist collected baseline data across students using a 10-second partial interval recording procedure during 10-minute observations. The intervention was initiated first with Gwen after it was clear that her baseline rate of attention-seeking behavior was stable. The school psychologist continued to collect baseline data for Ben and Ryan. The intervention was put in place with Ben and then with Ryan after baseline stability was evident for each of those students.

Figure 28.4 depicts the result of the noncontingent reinforcement intervention in the context of a multiple baseline across students design. Visual inspection of the graphs for each student reveals that the rate of attention-seeking behavior declined for each student after the intervention was implemented with that student. The consistency across students of the relationship between intervention implementation and a reduction in attention-seeking behavior suggests that the decline in the students' attention-seeking behavior is the result of the noncontingent attention intervention. The positive response of all three students to this intervention indicates that noncontingent reinforcement was an effective intervention for reducing attention-seeking behavior in these students.

SUMMARY

School psychologists are often called upon to provide progress monitoring data that document whether an intervention is working for a student. Single-case designs are the best method for providing such data. The designs can be tailored to the needs of individual students, used with both academic and behavior interventions, and, when needed, incorporate features to document experimental control. In addition, the data generated from such methods are easy to interpret and can readily be understood by students, teachers, and parents. For these reasons, using single-case designs to evaluate the effects of interventions is best practice.

AUTHOR NOTE

Disclosure. Rachel Brown and Mark W. Steege have a financial interest in books they authored or coauthored that are referenced in this chapter.

REFERENCES

Baer, D. M., Wolf, M. M., & Risley, T. R. (1968). Some current dimensions of applied behavior analysis. *Journal of Applied Behavior Analysis, 1,* 91–97.

Brown-Chidsey, R., & Steege, M. W. (2010). *Response to intervention: Strategies and principles for effective practice* (2nd ed.). New York, NY: Guilford Press.

Cummings, J. A., & Martinez, R. S. (2012). Visual representation of progress monitoring and academic achievement data. In R. Brown-Chidsey & K. J. Andren (Eds.), *Assessment for intervention: A problem-solving approach* (2nd ed.; pp. 321–343). New York, NY: Guilford Press.

Daly, E. J., III, Bonfiglio, C. M., Mattson, T., Persampieri, M., & Foreman-Yates, K. (2006). Refining the experimental analysis of academic skills deficits: Part II. Use of brief experimental analysis to evaluate reading fluency treatments. *Journal of Applied Behavior Analysis, 39,* 323–331. doi:10.1901/jaba.2006.13-05

Johnston, J. M., & Pennypacker, J. S. (2008). *Strategies and tactics of behavioral research* (3rd ed.). New York, NY: Routledge.

Kazdin, A. (2010). *Single-case research designs: Methods for clinical and applied settings* (2nd ed.). New York, NY: Oxford University Press.

National Association of School Psychologists. (2010). *Model for comprehensive and integrated school psychological services.* Bethesda, MD: Author. Retrieved from http://www.nasponline.org/standards/2010standards/2_PracticeModel.pdf

National Center on Response to Intervention. (2013). *The essential components of RTI.* Washington, DC: Author. Retrieved from http://www.rti4success.org

Riley-Tillman, C., & Burns, M. K. (2009). *Evaluating educational interventions: Single-case design for measuring response to intervention.* New York, NY: Guilford Press.

Scruggs, T. E., Mastropieri, M., & Casto, G. (1987). The quantitative synthesis of single-subject research: Methodology and validation. *Remedial and Special Education, 8,* 24–33.

Steege, M. W., & Watson, T. S. (2009). *Conducting school-based functional behavioral assessment: A practitioner's guide* (2nd ed.). New York, NY: Guilford Press.

Section 3
Legal, Ethical, and Professional Practice

29

Trends in the History of School Psychology in the United States

Thomas K. Fagan
University of Memphis

OVERVIEW

Historical trends reveal the stability of some professional developments and the changeability of others and help us to understand our present by reflecting on our past. Thus, this chapter has relevance for the foundations of school psychology reflected in the National Association of School Psychologists (NASP) *Model for Comprehensive and Integrated School Psychological Services* (NASP, 2010), particularly the domain of Legal, Ethical, and Professional Practice. Broader histories of school psychology appear in D'Amato, Zafiris, McConnell, and Dean (2011); Fagan (2013); Fagan and Wise (2007), and Merrell, Ervin, and Gimpel (2012); and for professional psychology more broadly see Benjamin and Baker (2014).

NUMBER OF SCHOOL PSYCHOLOGISTS

The earliest survey of psychological practitioners serving school settings was conducted by Wallin (1914), who identified 115 persons. Growth in the number of school psychologists was gradual but persistent, and by 1950 there were about 1,000 (Cutts, 1955). The post-World War II baby boom, with its growth in school attendance, and the enactment of comprehensive special education laws, were dominant forces affecting the rapid growth of practitioners after 1950. By 1970 the field had about 5,000 practitioners. In recent decades, growth can also be attributed to the expansion of settings in which school psychological services are delivered and the impact of legislation (e.g., Family Educational Rights and Privacy Act, Individuals with Disabilities Education Act [IDEA], and the No Child Left Behind Act [NCLB]). In addition, broad social forces such as school crises and

violence have increased the emphasis on the school as a mental health setting for both intervention and prevention activities.

Estimates of the size of the workforce usually include trainers and state government employees as well as practitioners. Trainers constitute a small proportion of the workforce, perhaps 3–5%, and government personnel such as state consultants account for less than 1%. No definitive count of the number of school psychologists exists, and the term *school psychologist* has eluded consistent definition, adding to problems of whom to count and with whom past and future comparisons might be made. For example, Farling and Hoedt (1971) identified a range of preferred titles with "school psychologist" having only a 59% preference among respondents. With organizational developments, recent estimates are more accurate than early estimates, and a reasonable figure is 30,000–35,000 (see Figure 29.1).

School psychology has never suffered serious unemployment, and for most of the 20th century the demand exceeded the supply of practitioners (Fagan, 2004). Despite reports of job losses related to the economic recession of 2007–2012, job opportunities remained at satisfactory levels. The recession also corresponded to cutbacks in academic positions. The author's personal record of advertised (usually online) academic positions recorded the following annual totals from 2006–2007 to 2011–2012: 72, 80, 49, 26, 45, 21. By March 2013 there were already more than 40 academic positions posted, and it appears the academic marketplace is recovering. The shortage of doctoral graduates seeking academic school psychology positions continues to be a concern and could have a long-term impact on the stability of training programs and hence the supply of practitioners.

Figure 29.1. Estimated Numbers of School Psychologists

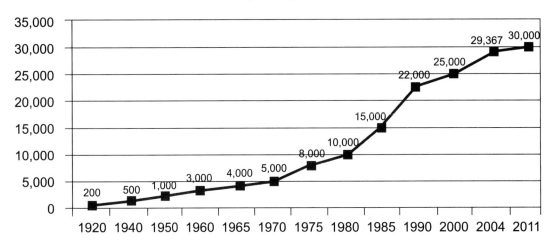

The personnel shortages of recent decades are expected to persist in academic and practitioner positions (see *Psychology in the Schools*, Vol. 41, No. 4). However, the trend in upward growth has been dramatic, and continued growth is expected in the future, but not of the magnitude witnessed since the 1960s. The production and retention of a strong practitioner workforce is important in maintaining service ratios that translate into broader practitioner roles and functions.

GENDER TRENDS

Throughout the 20th century school psychologists were drawn from the ranks of teachers, a field dominated by women. Even in recent years many school psychologists had teaching credentials and experience. It is known that many women were among the early practitioners of school psychology (e.g., Norma Cutts, Leta Hollingworth). Some held prominent district-level administrative positions (e.g., in Chicago, Cincinnati, Cleveland), state department of education positions (e.g., New York), and university positions (e.g., Columbia). Women composed one fourth of the members of the American Association of Clinical Psychologists (1917–1919) and one fourth of the Thayer Conference participants. Eminent women in applied psychology's history often entered the field at a young age, studied in and found employment in child-related fields, and often did not marry or have children. These women were highly dedicated to their work and made major contributions to the growth of school psychology despite discrimination in school and higher education settings. Clear instances of discrimination are seldom reported today in school psychology. Nevertheless, men and women in academic positions hold different opinions about the climate and opportunities in their departments (Little, Akin-Little, Palomares, & Eckert, 2012), and both are more likely to negotiate for salaries in comparison to practitioners (Crothers et al., 2012).

General Representation

The American Psychological Association's (APA) Division 16–School Psychology data indicated that women accounted for more than 60% of the membership and elected leadership in 1949, and 54% of its 600 members in 1956–1957. The figures appear to have declined to less than 50% by the 1960s (Hagin, 1993). A broader survey by Farling and Hoedt (1971) found an overall female representation of 40%, including 35% of the APA member respondents and 47% of the NASP member respondents. By 1982 a NASP survey found women composing 58% of the membership, and just 3 years later this had grown to 61%. NASP surveys in the early 1990s found representation of women at 70%, and a 74% figure was reported in 2006. The most recent NASP survey (2009–2010) found female representation at 76.6% of the entire field, and women represented 61.7% of university school psychology faculty (Curtis, Castillo, & Gelley, 2012).

Leadership Presence

Women's representation among the elected leadership of NASP improved from one third to two thirds of the positions during the period 1970–1993. In 2005–2006 women represented 63% of the NASP elected leadership, and 72% in 2012–2013. Across the history of NASP's elected national offices, men have served in 29 (67%)

of the 43 presidencies, only 3 (14%) of the 22 secretary positions, and 9 (47%) of the 19 treasurer positions.

Among Division 16's elected leadership, women held half or more of the elected positions on several occasions over its first several decades (Fagan, 1993) and no less than half since 1996. Women held 69% of Division 16's executive committee positions in 2005–2006, and 71% in 2012. There are probably few if any states where men are in the majority among school psychologist practitioners. Among state associations in NASP's 2012–2013 Leadership Directory (including Puerto Rico and the District of Columbia), women held 39 (75%) of the presidencies.

Editorial Presence

Despite their proportional advantage in recent decades, a woman did not serve as editor of a school psychology journal until 1996, when Patti Harrison was appointed to the *School Psychology Review* (Vol. 25, No. 1), followed in 1999 by LeAdelle Phelps to *Psychology in the Schools* (Vol. 36, No. 3), and in 2001 by Susan Sheridan to *School Psychology Review* (Vol. 30, No. 1). Of the four major journals in school psychology (*Journal of School Psychology*, *Psychology in the Schools*, *School Psychology Review*, *School Psychology Quarterly*), there were two female editors in 2005 but none in 2012. The *Journal of School Psychology*, *School Psychology Quarterly*, and *Journal of Applied School Psychology* have yet to select a female editor. However, women have served in associate editorship positions of these journals. For example, a 50th anniversary review of the *Journal of School Psychology* revealed that female representation on its editorial board had grown from about 7% in 1963 to 49% in 2012 (Fagan & Jack, 2012).

Gender Summary

The proportion of women in school psychology will rise above 80%. Although men have often held leadership positions since the 1970s, the trend has changed considerably at all levels, including state and national associations, academia, editorships, and state education agencies. The trend could be attenuated by recruiting more men into the field and/or by men continuing to be disproportionately successful in obtaining leadership roles. For example, over the 17 years 1996–1997 to 2012–2013, men have held 11 (65%) of the NASP presidencies and 4 (67%) of the treasurer positions, but women have held 7 (100%) of the secretarial positions. The overall gender balance of 30 elected officers was an even 50% during a period when males were less than 30% of the NASP membership.

The growth of female representation has occurred across several health services professions. The growing presence and contributions of women in school psychology is observed across psychology in general (Eagly, Eaton, Rose, Riger, & McHugh, 2012). It is difficult to demonstrate an effect, but the emphases on corporal punishment, bullying, women's issues, social justice concerns, and sexual orientation research and policies are associated with the increasing presence of women. Women's increasing presence continues to support Reschly's (2000) observation that shifts in gender representation are "the clearest changes in school psychology during the past two decades" (p. 508).

MINORITY REPRESENTATION

Minority participation in psychology has been a historical struggle with substantial accomplishments since the 1960s (Leong, Holliday, Trimble, Padilla, & McCubbin, 2013). Little has been written about the historical representation of minorities in school psychology and early information on their proportional representation is lacking, despite articles on the contributions of specific persons (Fagan & Flanagan, 2012; Graves, 2009). Nevertheless, efforts to increase minority representation have been promoted since the early years of NASP and in the APA's Division of School Psychology. The extent of minority representation in school psychology has been fairly consistent across several NASP surveys (Curtis et al., 2012). A comparison of the demographic survey data obtained by NASP in 1980–1981 and 2009–2010 indicate the following changes in representation:

- African American: 1.5–3.0%
- Caucasian: 96–90.7%
- Native American and Alaskan Native: <1.0–0.6%
- Asian Pacific Islander: <1.0–1.3%
- Hispanic: 1.5–3.4%
- Other: <1.0–1.0%

At least among the NASP membership, non-Caucasian representation increased just 5.3% over the period 1980–1981 to 2009–2010. A study by Loe and Miranda (2005) suggested that despite considerable disparity between the percentage of minority school psychologists and the schoolchildren served, there was no clear indication of bias in service delivery. The recruitment, training, and employment of minority school psychologists will continue to be significant issues (Lopez & Bursztyn, 2013).

SERVICE RATIOS

Figure 29.2 reveals that the ratio of school psychologists to children served (referred to as the service ratio) has improved dramatically over the past century. According to Reschly (2000), the national mean and median ratios were 1:1,930 and 1:1,750, respectively. Other reports estimated the ratio to be 1:1,621 and 1:1,483 for practitioners in 2004–2005. In the NASP demographic survey of 2009–2010, the ratio was reported as 1:1,383 (Curtis et al., 2012).

Smith (1984) is often cited for connecting improved (higher) ratios to broadened services, suggesting that a ratio of 1:1,500 was a reasonable break point at which less time was spent on assessment and more time was spent on intervention activities. Although this has been achieved as a national average, many school psychologists work in worse ratio conditions, perhaps because of personnel shortages and the continued emphasis on the assessment role of the school psychologist. Nevertheless, the trend throughout the century has been toward improved ratios, and gradual improvements are anticipated for the future, but the NASP Practice Model's (NASP, 2010) recommended general ratio of 1:1,000 remains an elusive goal for most school settings. For the delivery of comprehensive and preventive services, NASP recommends a ratio of 1:500–700. An international study of 48 countries reported 10 countries with better ratios than the United

States (Jimerson, Stewart, Skokut, Cardenas, & Malone, 2009). It is to be remembered that ratios are crude indications of service, and other factors must be considered in determining service quality.

PRACTICE SETTINGS

Historically, school psychologists have worked in several settings, although their primary identification has been consistently with public and private schools. In the early decades of practice they also worked in clinics and research bureaus affiliated with charitable agencies, juvenile courts, colleges and universities, and medical settings. Early data by settings do not exist, but it is possible that nonschool-setting practitioners outnumbered school-based practitioners in the early years. Prominent early "school psychologists" such as Lightner Witmer and Arnold Gesell worked in the schools but were from the University of Pennsylvania and Yale University, respectively. Another model provided school psychological services to several districts, often rural districts, on a regional basis emanating from university or mental health settings. As school psychologists increasingly became employees of individual school districts, they became enmeshed in the social, political, and professional system of education. The district employee model may be the most significant event in school psychology in the 20th century. Subsequently, the history of school psychology has been enmeshed in two worlds: that of professional education and that of professional psychology. This dilemma would gain some

Which countries?

Figure 29.2. Improvement of the School Psychologist-to-Student Ratio

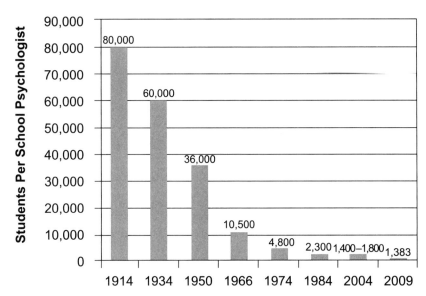

official recognition in the professional models for training, credentialing, and practice recommendations emanating from the Thayer Conference in 1954.

APA's Division 16–School Psychology was founded in 1945 and was originally intended only for school-based practitioners. A 1960 Division 16–School Psychology survey found that among 233 respondents, 12 (5%) were from private schools, 11 (5%) were from state school systems, 42 (18%) were from county school systems, and 168 (72%) were from city schools (APA, 1960). Setting expansion has been more noticeable since 1980, perhaps related to opportunities encouraged by federal legislation for the disabled (e.g., right to independent evaluations), the rapid growth of third-party insurance reimbursements for psychologists, the success of other psychologists in the private sector, increased numbers of school psychologists holding a doctoral degree, and a general maturing of the field. Some expansion also resulted from nondoctoral school-based practitioners achieving credentials for nonschool practice. Today, the field of school psychology is considered a respected adjunct to other agencies beyond the public and private schools.

Various sources have reported percentage distributions of employment settings for school psychologists, revealing in descending order the following settings: public schools, private practice, clinic/hospital/other, college or university, and institutional/residential. The 2009 2010 NASP demographic survey reported the primary employment settings as 83.7% in public schools, 6.4% in private schools, 2.6% in faith-based schools, 7.4% in universities, 3.5% in independent practice, 0.8% in hospital/medical settings, 0.6% in state department positions, and 3.7% in other settings (Castillo, Curtis, Chappel, & Cunningham, 2011). The same survey indicated that 26.5% of practitioners were in urban, 43.4% in suburban, 24% in rural, and 8.2% in combined practice settings (Curtis et al., 2012).

There will likely be a small increase in both the number of practice settings and the number of school psychologists serving nonschool settings, but the schools will continue to be the dominant employment setting, including a growing charter school movement. Postsecondary educational setting practice will be more available (e.g., campus Office of Student Disability Services), as will agency and private practice. The expansion of practice settings depends on the growth in the percentage of practitioners holding the doctoral degree, and on the influence of managed care on programs on private and clinic practice, and of course

on the productivity of specialist-level programs to meet the demand of school settings for new and replacement practitioners. The emphasis on school achievement gains (e.g., NCLB) and early literacy instruction may provide fertile opportunities for school psychologists with preschool education specializations.

CLIENTELE

Surveys of practice, research studies on assessment and intervention, and other descriptive reports reveal that school-age children have been the most common clients of the school psychologist. However, consultation increases the extent to which teachers and parents are service recipient clients. One impact of the NCLB has been the increased emphasis on academic achievement in the general education classroom and thus on direct services to children and their teachers. The academic emphasis is also observed in the learning disability eligibility shift toward response to intervention (RTI) models. Although the definition of *school-age* has expanded to include ages 3–21, some school psychologists provide services to persons outside this age range. With dominant practice settings being in public and private schools, the child and parents will continue to be the school psychologist's primary clients, with secondary clients to include teachers and school administrators. The question of who is the client has not been definitively addressed in school psychology ethics documents, and respecting the interests of several "clients" concurrently is a wise perspective (see, e.g., Fagan & Wise, 2007, pp. 98–101).

PRACTITIONER SALARIES

Although salary data are practically nonexistent for the first half of the 20th century, trends can be inferred from archival sources, from surveys conducted by state and national associations between 1940 and 1970, and from more recent surveys, especially those conducted by NASP. For example, when the Chicago Public School's Department of Scientific Pedagogy and Child Study was founded in 1899, its director was paid $2,000/year and the assistant was paid $100/month. Between 1915 and 1919, Arnold Gesell was paid $2,000 for his half-time, 9-month position with the state of Connecticut, and he was reimbursed for travel, meals, postage, and telephone expenses. Psychological examiners with lesser credentials no doubt commanded lower salaries. Gertrude Hildreth, with a master's degree, was paid $1,850 for her full-time, 9-month position in "mental testing" with the Okmulgee,

Figure 29.3. School Psychology Salary Growth

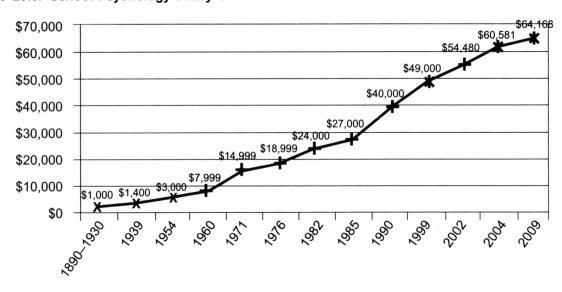

X Lowest Range ✚ Median ✳ Average

Oklahoma, public schools in 1921. The range of salaries in the period 1890–1930 probably was from $1,000 to $4,000 for full-time practitioners, and a typical figure was probably $2,000 or less. Figure 29.3 provides a historical summary of salary growth in school psychology based on several available sources. The 2004–2005 NASP member survey revealed an average salary of $60,581.

NASP's demographic survey of 2009–2010 indicated continued salary growth and reported salaries by degree as well as contract length for school-based practitioners. The mean salary for full-time, school-based practicing school psychologists who responded to the survey was $356.49 per day. When examining the data by degree the mean for those with nondoctoral degrees was $344.25, and for those with doctorates it was $409.42. The per diem salary can be used to calculate annual salaries based on contracts of different lengths. For example, for a contract of 180 days, the mean annual salary for full-time school-based school psychologists would be $64,168, for school psychologists with nondoctoral degrees the mean would be $61,965, and for those with doctoral degrees it would be $73,695.60 (Curtis et al., 2012, p. 30). Salaries for a 200-day contract were estimated at $71,298, $68,865, and $81,884, respectively.

The recessionary period from 2007 to 2012 does not appear to have seriously hindered the salary growth trend. With strong demand for employment and probable persistent personnel shortages, salary improvement appears likely for the future.

PREPARATION PROGRAMS

The earliest programs were designed to prepare clinical practitioners to provide services in the schools. The programs were not titled *school psychology* until the 1920s, when the first so-titled program was established at New York University. The second formal program appears to be the doctoral program founded at Pennsylvania State University in the late 1930s. By the time of the 1954 Thayer Conference there were 18 programs, including 5 at the doctoral level (Cutts, 1955). Figure 29.4 indicates the growth in the number of institutions offering training in school psychology.

The most recent compilation of programs and institutions appears in Miller (2008), who reported 244 institutions offering one or more degree programs, including 103 doctoral programs. In contrast to earlier reports, the list identifies several online and free-standing institutional programs. An online resource on program characteristics is available at the NASP website (http://www.nasponline.org/graduate-education/grad-edu.aspx). The NASP website list closely approximates that by Miller (2008) and provides updated program-by-program information. The total program enrollment reported was 8,908 (6,292 specialist and 2,616 doctoral; A. Thomas, personal communication, January 29, 2013). The data indicate about 39 students per program responding, which is close to the average per program reported in NASP's 1998 and 1977 program directories.

Figure 29.4. Growth in School Psychology Graduate Programs

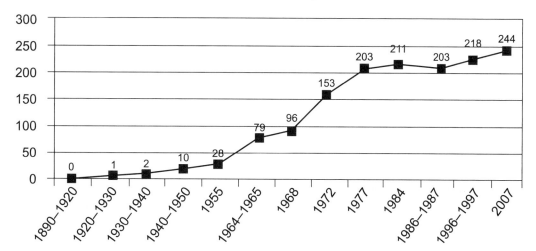

There has been growth in the number of programs offered by free-standing professional schools of psychology and by distance learning institutions offering online training (e.g., Argosy, Capella, Walden). The growth of these programs and their potential for accreditation by national and state agencies may present a challenge to the future of school psychology. Although the alternatives to traditional preparation appear to make up less than 10% of the extant programs, their increase seems inevitable as trainees seek more flexible avenues into school psychology practice. Many traditional training programs are increasingly using online courses to fulfill certain requirements.

CHARACTERISTICS OF PREPARATION

In the early part of the 20th century, school psychology programs were a mix of clinical and educational psychology appended to the experimental psychology curriculum. Under these circumstances, practitioner backgrounds varied greatly (Fagan, 1999). Perhaps the earliest unambiguous joint orientation of educational and clinical psychology was the University of Illinois doctoral program, founded in 1951 (see Cutts, 1955, pp. 168–170). Numerous doctoral and nondoctoral programs have been developed in both education and psychology administrative units, with few apparent differences (Fagan & Wise, 2007).

The content of training programs was largely unregulated until the 1960s in what might be called a long period of diversity of necessity, in which training emerged from programs designed for a variety of educational and psychological personnel. Many of those programs included traditional core psychology or

education courses with specialty training, including psychoeducational evaluation but with limited emphases on interventions. In the absence of national training standards, content was geared to meet whatever credentialing requirements the state used to approve school psychological personnel, or whatever requirements the program faculty deemed appropriate for school practice. Hence, programs were most influenced by the available courses in the department and by the training backgrounds of the faculty and the perceptions of the services needed by public education.

State departments of education, in the process of establishing regulations for special education, developed standards for the credentialing of those delivering psychological services linked to special education. As that relationship solidified, state departments of education regulations became more specific as to required degrees and coursework for credentialing psychological personnel. This gradually diminished the influence of academic programs over their own curricular judgments as to what was important for practitioner preparation.

With the reorganization of the APA, the founding of the National Council for Accreditation of Teacher Education (now the Council for the Accreditation of Educator Preparation) and the latter's recognition of NASP's program approvals, the profession entered a period of restriction for identity in which specific training standards were developed to provide a separate identity. In the past several decades, the training expectations of NASP and APA have all but forced a more consistent curriculum among doctoral and nondoctoral programs. In combination, accrediting and credentialing standards increased the expectations for entry-level training and broadened preparation to include various types of problem-solving assessment and intervention while pursuing related content in research, prevention, consultation, and basic psychological and educational foundations. A history of accreditation appears in Fagan and Wells (2000). The Miller (2008) listing updated the accreditation status of programs.

The current entry-level expectations of the specialist degree or its equivalent are more than twice the expectations published in the original NASP training guidelines of the early 1970s. In raising the expectations to meet job demands and establish a separate training identity, nondoctoral programs have been forced to become highly prescriptive in a pragmatic model geared to achieving state credentialing. Doctoral programs have tended to follow the scientist–practitioner or professional models of preparation, and program content is heavily influenced by national accreditation and state credentialing board expectations. Since the 1960s, state credentialing agencies' standards, closely tied to national accrediting standards, have all but dictated training program content.

Free-standing professional schools and online distance-learning training programs will need to adapt to the training and credentialing expectations, and those regulatory agencies can be expected as well to adapt to the nontraditional training formats. Such adaptation is observed in the number of nontraditional clinical psychology programs that have been APA approved and in their representation on the APA's Committee on Accreditation. The December 2012 *American Psychologist* identified 70 APA-accredited school psychology doctoral programs (including 8 combined programs) and 234 in clinical psychology. It remains to be seen if NASP and state departments of education will follow suit in making adaptations at the nondoctoral level.

The past several decades have seen an improved balance of psychology- and education-related content. Very noticeable changes have been the expansion of field experience requirements (practica and internships), and the hiring of faculty specifically prepared as school psychologists. While a sharp increase in training standards is not expected in the foreseeable future, an upward trend will occur, especially at the doctoral level where national forces are driving accrediting and credentialing toward the postdoctoral level. Many state psychology boards require 2 years of supervised experience, typically the predoctoral internship and one postdoctoral year. Nondoctoral standards are expected to remain similar in total length of preparation (e.g., 60–70 semester hours), though content shifts are anticipated to accommodate concerns in certain areas

(e.g., crisis intervention). Since specialist programs can hardly raise requirements without becoming the hourly equivalent of some doctoral programs, meeting increased content expectations necessitates the creative infusion of new content into existing content and a trading off of some contents for others. This is complicated by NASP's expectations that program content follow training standards that reflect its *Blueprint* documents. The field should encourage a future of diversity for maturity, where many forms of preparation will be available in order to better prepare persons for practice in a future of increasing diversity of settings and clients.

With the ongoing expansion of school psychology worldwide, an international perspective on school psychology is emerging in training. The University of Nebraska–Kearney, the first program fully accredited by the International School Psychology Association in May 2011, is now offering a course titled Globalization of School Psychology (McFarland, 2012). Another aspect of the international perspectives is growing interest in international field trips and immersion programs. The International School Psychology Association has done a great deal to foster an international perspective since its founding years in the late 1970s.

CREDENTIALING

Although the New York City Board of Education had provisions for examining and approving school psychological personnel in the 1920s, the earliest state education agency credentials for school psychologists were granted by New York and Pennsylvania in the mid-1930s. Licensing for nonschool practice by state boards of examiners in psychology was initiated in 1945 (Connecticut). By 1960, 15 states licensed psychologists, and all states did so by 1977. State board of education certification was available in at least 7 states by 1946, 20 states and the District of Columbia by the time of the Thayer Conference in 1954, 37 states by 1965, 42 states (including the District of Columbia) by 1973, and all states (including the District of Columbia) by 1977. In many states the terms *certification* and *licensure* are almost interchangeable and no longer reflect school- and nonschool-sector credentials, respectively. In contrast to the Boulder model for credentialing, the Thayer model (Cutts, 1955) recommended that school-based practitioners be credentialed by state departments of education.

A trend in credentialing now requires greater amounts of graduate education and supervised field experiences, and program approval or accreditation. For school-based practice most states require the specialist degree level (60 semester hours), including at least 1 school year of supervised experience. Teaching credentials and/or experience were not required in the original certification in New York and Pennsylvania, and such requirements have declined from 12 of the 20 states certifying school psychologists at the time of the Thayer Conference to only a few states at present. Currently, most states require the doctoral degree and 2 years of supervised experience for an independent practice license.

LITERATURE

The field has been served by many literary sources throughout its history (Fagan, 2013). Until the *Journal of School Psychology* in 1963, the field had no exclusive journal for its research and professional literature (Fagan & Jack, 2012) and instead relied upon an assortment of journals in psychology and education (e.g., *American Journal of Psychology*, *American Psychologist*, *Journal of Educational Psychology*, *Journal of Consulting Psychology*, and *The Psychological Clinic*).

After 1960, the growth of school psychology journals was rapid and included the founding of *Psychology in the Schools* in 1964, *School Psychology Digest* (now *School Psychology Review*) in 1972, *Professional School Psychology* (now *School Psychology Quarterly*) in 1986, and the *Journal of Applied School Psychology* (formerly *Special Services in the Schools*) in 2002. Related journals have continued to be important, including *Exceptional Children*, *Journal of Learning Disabilities*, *Journal of Psychoeducational Assessment*, *Professional Psychology: Research & Practice*, and *Educational and Psychological Consultation*, as well as a growing number of journals on specific techniques or disorders. North American school psychologists also subscribe to the *Canadian Journal of School Psychology* (founded in 1985), *School Psychology International* (founded in 1979), and the *International Journal of School and Educational Psychology* (founded in 2013). A few state school psychology associations have published a journal, including the *New Jersey Journal of School Psychology* in the 1980s and the *California School Psychologist* (now *Contemporary School Psychology*) in 1996. Several journals now offer online access exclusively or in addition to the hard-copy subscription, and *School Psychology Forum* is offered online to NASP members. The Student Affiliates of School Psychology (Division 16) publishes quarterly its *School Psychology: From Science to Practice*.

National school psychology newsletters date to 1947, with Division 16's newsletter (titled *The School Psychologist* since 1966) and 1969, with NASP's newsletter (titled *Communiqué* since 1972). An international newsletter, *World-Go-Round*, appearing since 1973, predated the founding of the International School Psychology Association in 1982. Newsletters for trainers of school psychologists include *The School Psych Scoop* in 1972 (titled *Trainers' Forum* since 1981) and the Council of Directors of School Psychology Programs' *CDSPP Newsletter* in 1982, retitled *CDSPP Press* in 1990–1991, but no longer published. State association newsletters are common and usually date to the earliest years of these groups. Lesser known newsletters include NASP special interest groups, and those of other organizations such as the Society for the Study of School Psychology.

The earliest book specifically about school psychological services was *Psychological Service for School Problems* (Hildreth, 1930). A period followed in which few books were published, and those few included the Thayer Conference proceedings, and then a surge of books appeared beginning in the 1960s. The number and diversity of books published follow the growth pattern for journals during the period 1960 to present. Content analyses have revealed emphasis on testing and assessment and role and function, and legal issues and future perspectives. A listing of journals and books specifically on school psychology appears in Appendix B of Fagan and Wise (2007). A comprehensive listing of literary sources up to 1985 appears in Fagan, Delugach, Mellon, and Schlitt (1985).

ORGANIZATIONS

Organizations exclusively serving school psychologists in the United States originated with APA's Division 16, established in 1944–1945, which evolved from the Educational and Clinical Sections of the American Association of Applied Psychologists (AAAP), established in 1937. Before these groups, school psychologists appear to have been members of various organizations, including the APA (founded in 1892) and its offshoot, the American Association of Clinical Psychologists (founded in 1917, which became the APA Section of Clinical Psychology in 1919), and the Association of Consulting Psychologists (founded in 1930), which evolved into the AAAP. Although some school psychologists were members of the National Education Association, throughout the first half of the 20th century most did not belong to any professional organization for psychologists (Fagan, 1993).

Figure 29.5. NASP Membership Growth

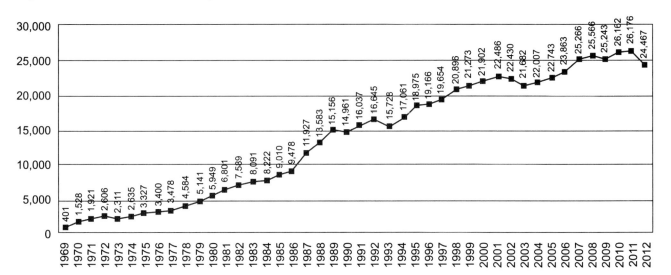

Division 16 was the only national-level organization for school psychologists until the founding of NASP in 1969. Since then both Division 16 and NASP have served as national representatives of school psychology. The extent of NASP representation can be seen in its membership growth (Figure 29.5). The founding of the American Psychological Society in 1988 and the American Association of Applied and Preventive Psychology in 1990 represent increasing organizational diversity. Their effect on school psychology appears to have been minimal, and school psychologists continue to hold their national memberships in Division 16 and/or NASP. Information about the history and activities of NASP and Division 16 can be obtained in Fagan (1993, 2013). A valuable historical perspective to the international school psychology movement is provided in a series of articles by Anders Poulsen in the International School Psychology Association *World-Go-Round* in 2004–2005 (Vol. 31, Nos. 2, 3, 4, 5; Vol. 32, Nos. 1, 2, 3).

Although some urban areas had local associations of psychologists, the earliest state association for school psychologists was founded in Ohio in 1943. The growth of such groups was gradual, and by 1969 there were only 17 state associations, several of which were sections of their respective state psychological associations and affiliates of APA. Growth in the number of states having separate school psychology associations that are affiliated with NASP was rapid in the 1970s and 1980s (Fagan, Hensley, & Delugach, 1986). At present, every state has an association for school psychologists, and in a few states there is both a division for school psychologists within the APA-affiliated state psychology association and a separate NASP-affiliated association. The situation

is similar, though more complicated, in Canada and its provinces (Saklofske et al., 2007; Jordan, Hindes, & Saklofske, 2009).

ROLES AND FUNCTIONS

U.S. education has been characterized by increased segmentation and sorting of children, presumably to intervene in their lives in more positive ways. This tradition dates to the acceptance of compulsory schooling and the employment of experts (e.g., school psychologists) to assist in the sorting process. The sorting for programmatic interventions has ranged from school lunch programs, vocational education, and honors classes, to several categories of special education, charter, and alternative schools. It is common for large school systems today to have numerous specialized programs operating concurrently and overlapping in general and special education settings.

As part of this growing bureaucratic process, school psychologists have served two primary roles. The first has been the assessment role in which the most visible function has been the psychoeducational assessment of children for placement in special education programs. That is, the school psychologists assisted in the schools' efforts to sort students into a variety of special educational programs. In earlier decades, the assessment role was predominantly psychometric. The conceptualization and practice of assessment has broadened, and school psychologists now work as members of service teams that take a more comprehensive approach to assessment. Since 2000, an increasing number of school psychologists have been called upon to assist in general education program assessments connected to district-wide achievement programs and the changing eligibility requirements of federal and state special education regulations (e.g., RTI). Thus, the assessment role for many school psychologists spans the entire school system, and school psychologists continue to be among the most qualified assessment specialists in the schools.

A second role as repairer has engaged school psychologists in individual and group interventions. In earlier decades, this often involved academic remediation and counseling. More intensive interventions such as psychotherapy were often restricted, prohibited, or considered too time consuming and costly to be done by district-based practitioners. This has changed since the 1970s as a result of broader training, supervised practica and internships, greater availability of school-based practitioners, and a gradual shifting of administrators' thinking in the direction of serving children's mental health as well as academic needs. School psychologists may assist in designing and executing academic and behavioral interventions in general educational settings as well. The most recent NASP demographic survey of activities revealed areas of the intervention role, although the special-education-related assessment continued to be dominant.

Consultation, a third role, could be considered a special case of the intervention role. There are many instances of consulting in the early literature of the field, but the in-depth, theory-based consultation characteristic of recent times was only occasionally practiced and seldom researched. All school psychologists occasionally consult with others, but to effectively function in the consultant role a practitioner now requires specialized preparation.

Engineer, a fourth role, is where the practitioner works with overall service delivery systems. This extension of the consultation role to systems analysis and development focuses its assessment, interventions, and preventive strategies at systemic needs, not the needs of individual children, parents, or educators, all of whom presumably benefit indirectly.

Entry-level specialist programs require preparation in all of these roles, and doctoral programs often provide greater specialization in one or more of them. Both training and practice are aligned with the NASP Practice Model (NASP, 2010) and the latest version of the *Blueprint* (Ysseldyke et al., 2006). Although school psychologists enjoy broader roles and functions than in earlier decades, most continue to practice the two traditional roles of sorter and repairer, with their attendant functions of psychoeducational assessment

and interventions with children. Curtis, Lopez, Batsche, and Smith (2006) compared NASP demographic results to previous studies. For example, compared to 1989–1990, school psychologists in 2004–2005 spent almost 28% more time in special education activities (52.3% versus 80.1%), and compared to 1999–2000 they were conducting fewer initial special education evaluations (39.9 versus 34.5) and reevaluations (37 versus 34), fewer 504 Plans (9.3 versus 5.9), fewer inservice programs (3.4 versus 2.6), and fewer student groups (3.2 versus 1.7), and in 2004–2005 they were on average counseling only 1–10 students per year and had 42 consultation cases. The demographic data (Castillo, Curtis, & Gelley, 2012) for the 2009–2010 school year continued to indicate a substantial traditional assessment role (47% of work time) despite conducting fewer initial evaluations, reevaluations, and 504 Plans. Although many other roles and functions were being reported, many practitioners reported little or no activity in such things as inservice programs and presentations for parents and student groups. Castillo et al. (2012) point to the continued call for role expansion beyond special education, especially in the realm of academic and behavioral interventions. Among their conclusions, they state:

> The data generated through the 2010 NASP national study suggest a field that engages in many of the practices reflected in the NASP Practice Model (2010) that are consistent with intervention-focused services. However, consistent with findings reported in several prior studies ... school psychologists continue to report spending the majority of their time in special education-related activities. (Castillo et al., 2012, p. 6)

It appeared that school psychologists were continuing to devote more time to fewer cases. Specific reasons for the persistence of traditional practices remain unclear, but may reflect personnel shortages, the time required for conducting alternative assessments (e.g., curriculum-based measures), the administrative duties attending special education services, and the general education employment context within which they work, including their own preferences and those of their administrative supervisors.

Although some aspects of role and function have persisted, the field has undergone considerable change. Perhaps the most striking changes have occurred in the context of practice regulations. In the early 1970s many school psychologists worked without requirements for parent/guardian permission, multidisciplinary teams, annual reviews, and least-restrictive environment placements with Individualized Education Programs. Federal laws related to the education of the handicapped (now known as IDEA) were nonexistent, and most special education services were provided in segregated settings. The category of learning disability was just gaining official recognition. The school psychologist typically held a master's degree, including a practicum, and had little or no internship experience. In some settings the school psychologist served in a dual capacity as psychoeducational assessment specialist and coordinator of special education. The school psychologist often was a one-person multidisciplinary team.

Contemporary school psychologists work within a team framework under much improved service ratios, serve both general and special education sectors of their districts, and are more likely to provide interventions. The technological adequacy of their instrumentation has improved, as has the multicultural sensitivity of the assessment–intervention process. The extent of internal and external regulation of practice is among the most salient changes since the 1970s.

REGULATION

The historical development of regulatory influences in school psychology is discussed in Fagan and Wise (2007) and the implications for school psychology practice in Jacob, Decker, and Hartshorne (2011). Until the post-World War II period, professional psychology had little federal-level regulation. Following the reorganization of APA and the Department of Veterans Affairs' need for assistance from psychology, the period 1945–1955 saw a substantial number of regulatory accomplishments that set professional psychology on a new course. In that decade, APA initiated professional psychology program accreditation, published its first code of ethics, created the American Board of Examiners in Professional Psychology (ABEPP), held the landmark Boulder Conference establishing the scientist–practitioner model, and worked with government agencies to establish a network of internships within the Veterans Department. State board of examiners licensure followed suit. The current level of internal and external regulation of professional psychology is a vast expansion of those early efforts. School psychology, though a later beneficiary of those efforts, would be recognized by APA with the ABEPP in 1968 and program accreditation in 1971. With the additional impetus from NASP, by 1990 the field established school psychology-specific training, provider, and credentialing standards; doctoral and

nondoctoral program accreditation; a specific code of ethics; and a national examination linked to a NASP certification program.

The regulations were matched by federal and state laws and regulations that govern the practice of school psychologists in the realm of special education, parental rights, disability services, and student progress in general education. The enforcement of the federal requirements in the context of the state's compliance rules drew additional attention to the two worlds within which school psychology needed to survive: the worlds of professional education and professional psychology. Changes in either world have implications for the field of school psychology. Training programs and practitioners alike are more regulated now than at any time in their history. The regulations, especially in special education, fostered unprecedented growth in the number of practitioners and training programs, while perhaps inhibiting role expansion beyond special education.

PROBLEM-SOLVING APPROACHES

This discussion of problem-solving approaches focuses only on the assessment (sorter) and intervention (repairer) roles and not on systems-level and preventive approaches.

Child-Centered Focus

Early descriptions of practice reveal a problem-solving strategy that focused almost exclusively on the individual child. The strategy sought solutions to children's school problems by studying their identifiable skills and the presumed underlying abilities, traits, or personality characteristics. Concerns for children's physical health and its relationship to school success were widespread. Problems were considered to rest with the skills and characteristics associated with the child, and the solutions primarily rested with their alteration. Diagnosis and intervention were child centered, in what some referred to as a medical model. Assessment methods included questionnaires; interviews of the child, parent, or teacher; informal tests (standardized and normed tests appeared later); inspection of the child's work; school and health histories; occasional classroom observations; and medical inspections. The rapid acceptance of the Binet-Simon intelligence scales and standardized norm-based achievement tests was attributable to the perceived objectivity they brought to an assessment process fraught with varying opinions about classification and symptoms. The new tests lent scientific respectability to child study by quantifying the extent of a problem and contributing to greater specificity in classifications and levels of severity (e.g., in intelligence or achievement). Interventions included counseling, remediation of academic skills, and an expanding array of instructional and community-based programs in special education. For some children, medical inspections resulted in medical interventions (see, e.g., Witmer, 1907).

Broadened Focus

In part as a result of debates over nature and nurture, as well as the increasing influence of behavioral psychology, the modal problem-solving strategy of school psychologists expanded to more often include the assessment and intervention of persons and factors beyond the individual child. The most obvious shift of focus was from the child to the parents and guardians and home conditions and to classroom variables, including teacher and teaching characteristics. As this strategy continued to expand, problem solving broadened to the concept of ecological assessment. The child continued to be the focus of study, but only in relation to the study of other variables in the child's home and school environment and especially the child's unique interaction with these environments. The etiology of children's problems expanded as well. Failure was no longer viewed in terms of child variables but also in terms of other factors, separately or in combination with child variables (e.g., ineffective teaching and/or parenting with children having specific learning deficits).

The methodology continued to include standardized and nonstandardized, normed and unnormed tests. Also included were an array of measures, formal and informal, of peer relationships and sociograms, attitude toward school, parenting, classroom climate and teaching, socioeconomic status, and formalized observations of child and peer behaviors (e.g., event and time sampling). Interventions continued to include the earlier forms, though with greater sophistication in special education programs and diversified therapeutic techniques applied to groups as well as to individuals (e.g., client-centered therapy, behavior modification). Problem solving was still focused on the child, although increasingly school psychologists relied upon indirect interventions such as teacher and parent consultation. Physical health concerns were alleviated for most children through vastly improved public health measures in homes and schools, and sophisticated medical and pharmacological interventions. Special education placements evolved from highly

segregated conditions to least-restrictive settings through mainstreaming and inclusion.

In recent years, the problem-solving approach has shifted some of its focus back to the child in the form of directly measured observable academic skills and behaviors and corresponding direct interventions. At least where the higher incidence problems of children are concerned (e.g., learning disability) the shift has been toward disavowing underpinning normative characteristics in favor of direct interventions for observable academic and social behaviors. A long-standing model of assessing skills through underlying supportive characteristics or traits (e.g., intelligence) is shifting to a model of direct assessment of skills and direct remedial instruction irrespective of underlying abilities or traits.

More recent conceptualizations are identified with an *outcome* orientation under various names, including authentic-, curriculum-, performance-, and portfolio-based assessment. These are variations on earlier themes of criterion-referenced assessments that have been popular at different times in the field's history and are often at odds with normative assessment. Other shifts in problem solving have focused on parent and teacher effectiveness and the child's family constellation. It is now common for school psychologists to consider family variables in both diagnostic and intervention efforts, and systems have been developed for family assessment, consultation, and therapy. Home–school collaboration has grown in popularity as an important case study and system-wide preventive approach. In addition, the field of genetics has offered increasing understanding of some conditions, and the contributions of neuropsychology and behavioral neuroscience offer additional explanations and potential interventions for child development and school success.

The shift toward greater involvement with interventions has been accompanied by changes in special education regulations requiring functional behavioral assessments and greater treatment accountability (e.g., empirically supported interventions). In the case of school psychology, this includes interventions applied to socioemotional as well as academic behaviors and skills (e.g., scientific, research-based instruction). These shifts complement requirements for validated assessment methods accompanying long-standing diagnostic regulations for eligibility.

Undergirding the shifting emphases in problem solving since the 1970s has been an intense effort to better understand the importance of multicultural influences on practice. Responding to federal and state initiatives, laws, and regulations, test publishers have included more representative content and norms, training programs have developed multicultural perspectives in many courses, and practitioners have been sensitized to the importance of considering cultural context in their services.

RTI or Multitiered Systems of Support

Since the 1970s, the ideology of school psychology has become increasingly identified with direct curricular assessment of academic skills linked to interventions, with a declining emphasis on normative assessments of traits, especially ability. The struggle involved an ongoing debate about the evaluation of children suspected of having specific learning disability. The debate influenced the revised management of learning disability referrals through an RTI/multitiered systems of support (MTSS) model bolstered by IDEA. The RTI/MTSS model draws together a number of best practices, including prereferral assessment, direct curricular approaches to assessment and intervention, criterion-referenced measurement, evidence-based interventions (especially behavioral approaches), and problem-solving consultation. The model is consistent with long-standing requirements for individual educational plans and least-restrictive environment placements.

The Iowa model has been in effect for many years (Grimes, Kurns, & Tilley, 2006). Even though RTI is not *required* in IDEA, the model appears to be replacing the traditional ability–achievement discrepancy model for learning disability identification in many states and school districts.

Although at first there was only a small percentage of school psychologists using RTI, most others were dissatisfied with the traditional discrepancy model. That viewpoint was aptly presented by Thomas (2006), who discussed RTI as a step in the overall evolution of services. His affirmative response to the question of whether it is time to try something else draws on the positions of various national panels and groups identifying concerns with the discrepancy model of the past. Still, caution has been advised by others and some state departments of education may take a wait-and-see attitude until more convincing evidence for the RTI approaches emerge. Sullivan and Long (2010) found more widespread involvement with implementing an RTI model than appeared to be true in the earlier findings of Dean and Tysinger (2006).

RTI/MTSS continues to pose a challenge to the school psychology leadership that for decades has called for less assessment and greater intervention involvement. Although resistance to long-established practice is to be expected, the strength of the IDEA regulations in promoting RTI is formidable. The most recent NASP member survey revealed a persistence of the school psychologist's connection to special education and the dominance of assessment activities (Castillo et al., 2011). The apparent lack of emphasis on some school psychologist services may be a reflection of the greater time commitment needed to implement RTI/MTSS models that blend assessment activities in both general and special education, the need to educate teachers and staff on its implementation, and the financial climate of the past several years.

School psychology publications and conferences have been fraught with RTI/MTSS research and opinion. For example, the 2011, 2012, and 2013 NASP annual meetings had 60, 50, and 51 RTI presentations, respectively, outnumbering those in the areas of behavioral and social–emotional intervention. Reviews of the model and its varied applications appeared in the *California School Psychologist* (Vol. 10) and *Psychology in the Schools* (Vol. 43, No. 7), and various publications have tied RTI to several other practice areas (e.g., neuropsychology, giftedness). *Psychology in the Schools* has published a special issue on RTI model implementation (see Vol. 49, No. 3).

The RTI/MTSS model will garner widespread acceptance if it can be successfully blended with existing school psychology practice and demonstrate a reduction in the number of formal evaluations for learning disability eligibility. Suggestions for this appear in *Psychology in the Schools* (Vol. 43, Nos. 7 and 8) on the topic of integration of cognitive assessment and RTI. For the masses of school psychologists trained in traditional normative assessment and special education eligibility models, considerable retraining and adaptation may be necessary. Unlike the earlier espousal of a normative assessment model (e.g., discrepancy) where the school psychologist made choices among competing tests to use in practice, applying intervention in an RTI/MTSS model requires the cooperation and follow-through of many others that may result in a decision for a formal eligibility assessment. Program preparation is not enough. Carryover into internships and practice will be important. If RTI/MTSS proves successful in its application to learning disability, it could spread to problem-solving models for other disability areas.

Nevertheless, the RTI/MTSS approach, like significant discrepancy, is not unitary. There are and will continue to be several versions of the approach based on the regulations adopted by state and local agencies. The RTI/MTSS approaches will draw review, research, and criticism as have the models of significant discrepancy.

These differences will be expressed in terms of the resulting rates of learning disability referrals and placements and the outcomes of interventions. It is this latter aspect on which the strength of RTI/MTSS could rest. Critics who cite the wait-to-fail problems of the significant discrepancy approach will need to contend with criticism of the RTI/MTSS model as delaying the most intense interventions and perhaps the specific learning disability eligibility evaluation (Reynolds & Shaywitz, 2009). Nevertheless, RTI/MTSS ought to result in fewer cases resulting in special education eligibility.

Perspectives on Problem-Solving Approaches

School psychologists have always been identified with one or more problem-solving approaches. Although it is easy to look back and be critical of the practices of earlier eras, those practices were influenced as much by broad societal ideologies of the period as by professionals' lofty aspirations. For example, the recent clamor of interest in the family has occurred after an era of governmental, societal, and professional alarm over family deterioration. There was less focus on the family in the 1950s, an era often viewed nostalgically as one of family strength. Another example can be seen in the current interest in risk assessment of children as a result of recent incidents of school violence perpetrated by students and other community members. The widespread use of functional behavioral analyses is reminiscent of the 1970s era of behavior modification in the classroom. Although the use of empirically supported behavioral and instructional interventions has a long history in education and psychology literature, the recent demand for such evidence may be a function of expectations on various fronts, including managed care insurers, outcome-based education, and NCLB. The RTI model is also reminiscent of an earlier time when school districts had more academic remedial personnel that buffered the onslaught of special education referrals. Prior to the official recognition of learning disability as a special education category in the late 1960s, it was popular for schools to have numerous remedial math and reading tutors available to children. The rapid growth of special education bisected U.S. education into general and special education sectors with fewer services in between and resulted in calls for seamless, integrated services.

In retrospect, we observe stages of development in problem-solving approaches associated with a broadening recognition and acceptance of the spheres of influence on children. The expansion generally has been from child, to parents and teachers, to home/family

and school, and to community and society. Even though the shifting approaches overlap and continue to be observed in the varied practices of professional psychologists, comprehensive assessment and intervention practices have expanded accordingly. Contemporary thinking is conceptualized in the systemic analyses of the late Urie Bronfenbrenner (microsystems, mesosystems, exosystems, and macrosystems) and their applications to children of disability (Seligman & Darling, 2007).

Critics of traditional school psychology contend that earlier practice was never based on a problem-solving model. However, all problem-solving models involve assessment and intervention. The traditional model identified the school psychologist primarily with assessment to determine eligibility for interventions most often provided by others via special classrooms and remedial programs. Most traditional school psychologists were, and many still are, not effectively linked to the intervention side of problem solving. However, that does not mean the overall process is outside the realm of problem solving. The shift from processing assessment to functional assessment does not mean that the former was outside the realm of a problem-solving model either. What have changed are the nature of the assessments and the involvement of school psychologists throughout the assessment and intervention process. Some advocates of the "new" problem-solving approaches have chosen to dissociate themselves from the earlier approaches to practice, preferring reform rather than transition in practice. However, even the current zeitgeist is historically linked to earlier approaches known as diagnostic teaching, precision teaching, directive teaching, and mastery learning. From a historical perspective, prior to the 1916 Binet and the rapid acceptance of normative ability and achievement tests, assessment was primarily criterion-referenced, and interventions were delivered from their results, an apparent precursor to contemporary models of direct assessment and intervention.

An additional concern is that approaches that successfully reduce formal referrals may be perceived as reducing state and federal categorical special education funds. Traditionally, these funds are tied to numbers of children found eligible for services and not those for whom interventions have been successful and who are either removed from special education or prevented from formal assessment for eligibility. The RTI/MTSS model, with its potential to reduce official placements by providing earlier interventions, could signal the necessity for funding connected to prevention and intervention instead of special education eligibility.

The recent shifts in problem-solving strategy could benefit services in the long run if the shifts successfully draw greater attention to the importance of interventions and recognize the complementary relationship between child-centered and ecological assessment approaches and normative-based and criterion-based measurement. The shift toward collaborative inclusion of parents and teachers as peers in the problem-solving process could also have positive implications. Finally, perhaps the school psychologist will earn a more balanced role than in the past as repairer instead of sorter of children's problems.

SUMMARY

In its first century, school psychology experienced unprecedented quantitative and qualitative growth, perhaps strongest since the mid-1970s. The rate of such quantitative growth is unlikely to be sustained in the foreseeable future. Nevertheless, school psychology continues to be an attractive area of training and employment. It has often been described as among the more promising employment areas in psychology. Although many school psychologists continue to practice in roles closely connected to special education, the legacy of school psychology is very strong in both assessment and intervention functions. As the field continues to expand in roles and settings, it will remain as psychology's most direct link to U.S. education. Its strong contributions to special education will continue, and more avenues into general education and the expansion into nonschool settings will emerge. For discussions of future trends in school psychology see Fagan and Wise (2007); Merrell et al. (2012); special issues of *Psychology in the Schools* (Vol. 37, No. 1, and Vol. 50, No. 3) and *School Psychology Review* (Vol. 29, No. 4); the journal issues covering the 2002 Multisite Conference on the Future of School Psychology, such as the *Journal of Educational and Psychological Consultation* (Vol. 15, Nos. 3 and 4); *Psychology in the Schools* (Vol. 41, No. 4); *School Psychology Quarterly* (Vol. 18, No. 4); and *School Psychology Review* (Vol. 33, No. 1). Publication of the papers and outcomes of the 2012 Futures Conference should be forthcoming in 2013. The historical trends in the development of school psychology reveal a persistent, favorable growth, with an attractive future.

AUTHOR NOTE

Appreciation is expressed to Isaac Woods, Research Assistant, Psychology Department, University of Memphis, for his assistance with the manuscript.

Disclosure. Thomas K. Fagan has a financial interest in books he authored or coauthored that are referenced in this chapter.

REFERENCES

American Psychological Association. (1960). Results of the questionnaire on working conditions of school psychologists. *Division 16 Newsletter, 14*(2), 4.

Benjamin, L. T., & Baker, D. B. (2014). *From séance to science: A history of the profession of psychology in America* (2nd ed.). Akron, OH: University of Akron Press.

Castillo, J. M., Curtis, M. J., Chappel, A., & Cunningham, J. (2011, February). *School psychology 2010: Results of the National Membership Study.* Paper presented at the annual meeting of the National Association of School Psychologists, San Francisco, CA.

Castillo, J. M., Curtis, M. J., & Gelley, C. (2012). School psychology 2010—Part 2: School psychologists' professional practices and implications for the field. *Communiqué, 40*(8), 4–6.

Crothers, L. M., Theodore, L. A., Ward, S. B., Schmitt, A. J., Hughes, T. L., Lipinski, J., & Radliff, K. (2012). Salary and negotiation practices in school psychology faculty and practitioners. *The School Psychologist, 66*(3), 17–22.

Curtis, M. J., Castillo, J. M., & Gelley, C. (2012). School psychology 2010—Part 1: Demographics, employment, and the context for professional practices. *Communiqué, 40*(7), *1*, 28–30.

Curtis, M. J., Lopez, A. D., Batsche, G. M., & Smith, J. C. (2006, March). *School psychology 2005: A national perspective.* Paper presented at the annual meeting of the National Association of School Psychologists, Anaheim, CA.

Cutts, N. E. (Ed.). (1955). *School psychologists at mid-century.* Washington, DC: American Psychological Association.

D'Amato, R. C., Zafiris, C., McConnell, E., & Dean, R. S. (2011). The history of school psychology: Understanding the past to not repeat it. In M. Bray & T. Kehle (Eds.), *Oxford handbook of school psychology* (pp. 9–60). New York, NY: Oxford University Press.

Dean, B., & Tysinger, J. (2006, March). *School psychologists' perceptions of the IQ–achievement discrepancy method.* Paper presented at the annual meeting of the National Association of School Psychologists, Anaheim, CA.

Eagly, A. H., Eaton, A., Rose, S. M., Riger, S., & McHugh, M. C. (2012). Feminism and psychology: Analysis of a half-century of research on women and gender. *American Psychologist, 67*, 211–230.

Fagan, T. K. (1993). Separate but equal: School psychology's search for organizational identity. *Journal of School Psychology, 31*, 3–90.

Fagan, T. K. (1999). Training school psychologists before there were school psychology training programs: A history 1890–1930. In C. R. Reynolds & T. B. Gutkin (Eds.), *The handbook of school psychology* (pp. 2–33). Hoboken, NJ: Wiley.

Fagan, T. K. (2004). School psychology's significant discrepancy: Historical perspectives on personnel shortages. *Psychology in the Schools, 41*, 419–430.

Fagan, T. K. (2013). School psychology. In D. K. Freedheim (Ed.), *History of psychology* (2nd ed., pp. 448–467). Hoboken, NJ: Wiley.

Fagan, T. K., Delugach, F. J., Mellon, M., & Schlitt, P. (1985). *A bibliographic guide to the literature of professional school psychology 1890–*

1985. Washington, DC: National Association of School Psychologists.

Fagan, T. K., & Flanagan, R. (2012). Remembering Laura Hines, 1922–2009. *The School Psychologist, 66*(1), 30–31.

Fagan, T. K., Hensley, L. T., & Delugach, F. J. (1986). The evolution of organizations for school psychologists in the United States. *School Psychology Review, 15,* 127–135.

Fagan, T. K., & Jack, S. (2012). A history of the founding and early development of the *Journal of School Psychology. Journal of School Psychology, 50,* 701–735.

Fagan, T. K., & Wells, P. D. (2000). History and status of school psychology accreditation in the United States. *School Psychology Review, 29,* 28–58.

Fagan, T. K., & Wise, P. S. (Eds.). (2007). *School psychology: Past, present, and future* (3rd ed.). Bethesda, MD: National Association of School Psychologists.

Farling, W. H., & Hoedt, K. C. (1971). *National survey of school psychologists.* Washington, DC: National Association of School Psychologists.

Graves, S. L. (2009). Albert Sidney Beckham: The first African American school psychologist. *School Psychology International, 30,* 5–23.

Grimes, J., Kurns, S., & Tilley, D. (2006). Sustainability: An enduring commitment to success. *School Psychology Review, 35,* 224–244.

Hagin, R. A. (1993). Contributions of women in school psychology: The Thayer Report and thereafter. *Journal of School Psychology, 31,* 123–141.

Hildreth, G. H. (1930). *Psychological service for school problems.* Yonkers-on-Hudson, NY: World Book.

Jacob, S., Decker, D. M., & Hartshorne, T. S. (2011). *Ethics and law for school psychologists* (6th ed.). Hoboken, NJ: Wiley.

Jimerson, S. R., Stewart, K., Skokut, M., Cardenas, S., & Malone, H. (2009). How many school psychologists are there in each country of the world? International estimates of school psychologists and school psychologist-to-student ratios. *School Psychology International, 30,* 555–567.

Jordan, J. J., Hindes, Y. L., & Saklofske, D. H. (2009). School psychology in Canada: A survey of roles and functions, challenges and aspirations. *Canadian Journal of School Psychology, 24,* 245–264.

Leong, F. T. L., Holliday, B. G., Trimble, J. E., Padilla, A. M., & McCubbin, L. D. (2013). Ethnic minority psychology. In D. K. Freedheim (Ed.), *History of psychology* (2nd ed., pp. 530–561). Hoboken, NJ: Wiley.

Little, S. G., Akin-Little, K. A., Palomares, R. S., & Eckert, T. L. (2012). Men in academic school psychology: A national survey. *Psychology in the Schools, 49,* 554–567.

Loe, S. A., & Miranda, A. H. (2005). An examination of ethnic incongruence in school-based psychological services and diversity training experiences among school psychologists. *Psychology in the Schools, 42,* 419–432.

Lopez, E. C., & Bursztyn, A. M. (2013). Future challenges and opportunities: Toward culturally responsive training in school psychology. *Psychology in the Schools, 50,* 212–228.

McFarland, M. (2012). A new international graduate course. *World-Go-Round, 39*(3), 11–12.

Merrell, K. W., Ervin, R. A., & Gimpel, G. A. (2012). *School psychology for the 21st century, foundations and practices* (2nd ed.). New York, NY: Guilford Press.

Miller, D. C. (2008). Appendix VII: School psychology training programs. In A. Thomas & J. Grimes (Eds.), *Best practices in school psychology V* (pp. clv–cxcviii). Bethesda, MD: National Association of School Psychologists.

National Association of School Psychologists. (2010). *Model for comprehensive and integrated school psychological services.* Bethesda, MD: Author. Retrieved from http://www.nasponline.org/standards/2010standards/2_PracticeModel.pdf

Reschly, D. J. (2000). The present and future status of school psychology in the United States. *School Psychology Review, 29,* 507–522.

Reynolds, C. R., & Shaywitz, S. E. (2009). Response to intervention: Ready or not? Or, from wait-to-fail to watch-them-fail. *School Psychology Quarterly, 24,* 130–145.

Saklofske, D. H., Schwean, V. L., Bartell, R., Mureika, J., Andrews, J., Derevensky, J., & Janzen, H. L. (2007). School psychology in Canada: Past, present, and future perspectives. In T. K. Fagan & P. S. Wise (Eds.), *School psychology: Past, present, and future* (3rd ed., pp. 297–338). Bethesda, MD: National Association of School Psychologists.

Seligman, M., & Darling, R. B. (2007). *Ordinary families, special children.* New York, NY: Guilford Press.

Smith, D. T. (1984). Practicing school psychologists: Their characteristics, activities, and populations served. *Professional Psychology: Research and Practice, 15,* 798–810.

Sullivan, A., & Long, L. (2010). Examining the changing landscape of school psychology practice: A survey of school-based practitioners regarding response to intervention. *Psychology in the Schools, 47,* 1059–1070.

Thomas, T. (2006). Is it time to try something else? *School Psychology in Illinois, 27*(3), 8–10.

Wallin, J. E. W. (1914). *The mental health of the school child.* New Haven, CT: Yale University Press.

Witmer, L. (1907). Clinical psychology. *The Psychological Clinic, 1*(1), 1–9.

Ysseldyke, J., Burns, M., Dawson, P., Kelley, B., Morrison, D., Ortiz, S., … Telzrow, C. (2006). *School psychology: A blueprint for training and practice III.* Bethesda, MD: National Association of School Psychologists. Retrieved from http://www.nasponline.org/resources/blueprint/FinalBluePrintInteriors.pdf

30 History and Current Status of International School Psychology

Thomas Oakland
University of Florida
Shane Jimerson
University of California, Santa Barbara

OVERVIEW

This chapter discusses the historic and contemporary infrastructure and practice of school psychology internationally. School psychologists engaged in this work potentially provide a wide range of services to children, their teachers, and parents. Services may include assessment of children who may display cognitive, emotional, social, behavioral, or mental health difficulties; development and implementation of primary and secondary intervention programs; consultation with parents, teachers, and other relevant professionals; crisis planning, prevention, and intervention; advocacy for and implementing of data-based decision making; engagement in program development and evaluation; research; and preparation and supervising of others (Jimerson, Oakland, & Farrell, 2007). School psychologists provide psychological services to children and youth, teachers, and parents, typically, yet not exclusively, within the context of education.

Terms used internationally to describe those who practice school psychology include psychologist, school psychologist, educational psychologist, psychologist in education, psychologist in the schools, counselor, and psychopedagogue. The National Association of School Psychologists (NASP) *Model for Comprehensive and Integrated School Psychological Services* (NASP, 2010) emphasizes the importance of the domain of Legal, Ethical, and Professional Practice, and the current chapter includes a discussion of school psychologists' legal, ethical, and professional practices internationally. An understanding of the international history and current status of school psychology requires some understanding of the history of the disciplines and professions of psychology and education. Readers are encouraged to see Saigh and Oakland (1989), Oakland (2000), and Jimerson et al. (2007) for additional information.

BRIEF HISTORY OF SCHOOL PSYCHOLOGY INTERNATIONALLY

The history of psychology is decidedly international. The foundation for the discipline of psychology was established in Greece, in part through the writings of Aristotle, Socrates, and Plato. Others trained in philosophy, biology, or medicine extended the discussion to describe and explain human behavior. For example, the Greek philosopher Galen (see *Galen on the Natural Faculties*, retranslated in 1963; Kagan, 1994) drew upon Hippocrates's writing and described four pathological temperaments (choleric, melancholic, phlegmatic, and sanguine) derived from four bodily fluids. This early work created considerable interest in the biological basis of temperament and personality, beliefs that continue to guide our work. Test development and use first was used in China approximately 3,000 years ago (Oakland, 2009).

Emergence of the Discipline of Psychology

The scientific basis for the discipline of psychology began to emerge in the late 1800s in Europe. For example, Jean-Marc Gaspard Itard (1775–1838) and Edouard Sequin (1812–1880) developed methods to help address the needs of children with mental retardation. In 1879, Wilhelm Wundt (1832–1920) established the first laboratory for the scientific study of psychology in Leipzig, Germany. Francis Galton (1822–1911) opened a research laboratory in London to study individual differences. William James (1842–1910) studied medicine, physiology, biology, and philosophy prior to joining the Harvard University faculty. His work focused on the scientific study of the human mind and led to the publication of *The Principles of Psychology* in 1890. Sigmund Freud's (1856–1939) work in Austria sparked considerable interest in clinical adult practices and focused attention on the importance of childhood. In 1904, in France, Alfred Binet (1857–1911) and Theodore Simon (1873–1961) developed the first practical test of children's intelligence. Thus, the emerging discipline of psychology began to be recognized as contributing to efforts that address important and chronic psychological and social issues, including those issues significant to children and their education.

Impact of the Industrial Revolution

During the 1800s in Europe and the United States, the population began to shift from rural areas to cities, lured by jobs that emerged during the industrial revolution. City life differed considerably and led to significant social and lifestyle changes. Families often were separated and lifestyles became more depersonalized. Children had to work under appalling conditions to help support their family financially. Difficulties exhibited by children (e.g., slow to learn, delayed sensory and motor development, inadequate social skills, emotional lability) that may have been accepted by families as being within the normal range while residing in rural areas often became more apparent once children became engaged in more competitive and less personalized urban environments. If children were in school, then their differences often became apparent to a level that warranted concern by educators. Children who were orphaned, homeless, or convicted of crimes also warranted concern.

These and other personal and social conditions required attention and social reforms from elected and appointed public servants. For example, labor laws to restrict child employment and to encourage school attendance were introduced and enforced over time. This led to the establishment of publicly supported elementary schools (often known then as grammar schools) and later middle and secondary high schools that often emphasized the preparation of skilled workers. The education of both boys and girls became more

common. Institutions were established to care for children who were orphaned as well as for juveniles with a chronic record of crime. The need for professional resources to help staff these institutions became apparent. Professional resources, including those from psychology, were needed in schools and the community to help address these and other personal and social conditions.

Emergence of Professional Services

In 1896, Lightner Witmer, at the University of Pennsylvania, established the first psychology clinic in the United States. This clinic is seen by some as the birthplace of child clinical and school psychology (Fagan & Wise, 2007). In 1899, in Antwerp, Belgium, the first school-based child study department was established. Later, in Europe and the United States, universities began to establish child study clinics, and large school districts established child study departments. Hugo Munsterberg first used the term *school psychologist* in print in English in 1898 (Fagan & Wise, 2007). Munsterberg suggested school psychologists could serve as a link between research psychologists and teachers. The term's second appearance occurred in 1910 when William Stern, a German psychologist, suggested the need for school psychologists to help address school-wide mental health needs. In 1918, Arnold Gessell was the first to hold the title of school psychologist in the United States and served in Connecticut between 1915 and 1919 (Fagan, 2002, 2005).

School psychology services worldwide grew slowly during the first half of the 20th century because the international economic depression restricted public funds, and the discipline of psychology was young and emerging and thus was viewed as not sufficiently mature to warrant the widespread provision of applied services. World War II and its aftermath changed psychology forever. Within the United States, psychologists involved in the war effort contributed importantly to establishing effective and efficient selection and training programs, thus helping to establish the utility of psychology theory and the use of tests. The practice of clinical psychology increased, in part, to help address the needs of returning combat personnel. The increase in clinical psychology helped spawn an interest in school psychology.

Within Europe, the war had a devastating impact on industrial, financial, educational, and human resources needed to rebuild an infrastructure for a modern and civilized society. The rebuilding of Europe's educational system was one key to its reemergence as a modern and civilized society. In 1948, the United Nations Educational, Scientific, and Cultural Organization (UNESCO) held a conference of representatives from 43 nations. Those members identified three ways their ministries of education could utilize psychological services to rebuild the educational infrastructure: establish research institutes to improve the quality of teaching and school achievement, establish guidance programs based on sound psychological practices, and improve the preparation of large numbers of school psychologists (UNESCO, 1948). Those attending a second UNESCO conference in 1956 underscored the importance of these three efforts (Wall, 1956). European countries that became leaders in school psychology (e.g., Denmark, France, Sweden, United Kingdom) were influenced by UNESCO's efforts.

Before World War II, school psychology was not particularly strong in any country. However, after World War II, and with the emergence of more progressive and sympathetic attitudes toward children and education, school officials and parents in many countries began expressing concern that some children seemed less able to learn in general education classes and thus needed special education and related (e.g., school psychology) services. This led to the employment of school psychologists to help distinguish those who could from those who were thought to be unable to succeed in regular education classes. These distinctions were made possible, in part, through measures of intelligence and other cognitive abilities developed and used by psychologists. Hence, the specialty of school psychology emerged in many countries due to the school psychologists' expertise in assessment (e.g., Australia, United Kingdom, United States).

In contrast, in the Soviet Union and in other communist and socialist countries, psychology, including test development and use, were disfavored and psychology departments were closed during the Cold War. The dismantling of the Soviet Union in 1991 prompted the independence of Eastern European countries, resulting in their desire to reestablish psychology as a discipline and profession after a 56-year hiatus. However, many of these countries did not have sufficient financial and professional resources needed to support quality education systems and to develop testing resources. Thus, the services of school psychologists in countries with strong socialist histories (e.g., Albania, Bulgaria, Czechoslovakia, Hungary, Latvia, Lithuania, Poland, Romania, Slovakia) typically did not offer assessment services because tests were not readily available. Those countries instead focused on children's social, emotional, behavioral, and mental health needs and promoted the country's values.

EMERGENCE OF AN INTERNATIONAL ASSOCIATION FOR SCHOOL PSYCHOLOGY

Professions are strong only to the extent they are represented by active and effective professional associations. Thus, the growth and legitimacy of school psychology internationally required, in part, the emergence of one or more professional associations dedicated to international interests. Calvin Catterall and Frances Mullen (Fagan & Wells, 1999) established international school psychology committees within the American Psychological Association's (APA) Division of School Psychology in 1972 and within NASP in 1973. In addition, Catterall led study tours of school psychology services to various countries, established a newsletter to link those interested in international school psychology, wrote books on international school psychology (Catterall, 1976, 1977, 1979), and developed wide-ranging correspondence with school psychologists internationally. Catterall and Anders Poulsen in Denmark were principally responsible for establishing the International School Psychology Association (ISPA) in 1982.

In 2012, ISPA membership was approximately 400 and came from individuals in approximately 38 countries. Membership was less than 5 in some countries and more than 150 in others. Thirteen national and state associations of school psychologists also are affiliated with ISPA. Members of the ISPA executive committee, as of 2013, are from Ireland, Malta, Switzerland, the United Kingdom, and the United States. Thus ISPA's membership and leadership are somewhat dispersed internationally. Its central office is in Amsterdam, the Netherlands (http://www.ispaweb.org).

ISPA has five overarching goals: (a) to promote the use of sound psychological principles within the context of education internationally, (b) to promote communication between professionals who are committed to the improvement of the mental health of children internationally, (c) to encourage the use of school psychologists in countries where school psychologists are not currently being used, (d) to promote the psychological rights of all children internationally, and (e) to initiate and promote cooperation with other organizations working for purposes similar to those of ISPA in order to help children and families. ISPA established a definition of school psychology (Oakland & Cunningham, 1997), preparation guidelines

(Cunningham & Oakland, 1998), and an ethics code (Oakland, Goldman, & Bischoff, 1997), given its belief that these institutional policies provide professional unity and assist the development of school psychology in emerging countries. These documents are based on findings from an international survey of school psychology in developed and developing countries (Oakland & Cunningham, 1992). These approved policies are discussed below.

ISPA's Definitions of School Psychology

Every profession is expected to define itself clearly through a definition that serves to establish the parameters of services, thus adding credibility to its services and informing other professions and the public as to the services they can expect. Professional associations typically assume leadership for preparing statements that define the nature and scope of services and their function. The term *school psychology* refers to professionals who are prepared in psychology and education and recognized as specialists in the provision of psychological services to children and youth within the contexts of schools, families, and other settings that affect growth and development of children and youth. School psychologists must have a degree from a university that provides an organized, sequential school psychology program. The school psychology program is accredited in those countries where accreditation is possible.

School psychology programs from which students graduate should embody the following characteristics:

- Offer an integrated and organized sequence of study, one that places primary emphasis on psychology, provides a strong emphasis on education, and has an identifiable program faculty
- Have a suitable administration for the program and an identifiable body of students
- Have academic and professional preparation in school psychology that is consistent with current research and literature; current and emerging roles to be performed; services to be provided; and preparation that enables practitioners to work with the ages, developmental characteristics, populations, problems, and issues found prominently in the schools and other settings in which school psychologists are employed
- Include a core curriculum that contains academic content in basic areas of psychology and education and information relevant to work in culturally diverse settings

- Include supervised field experiences in assessment, intervention, consultation, organizational and program development, supervision, and research
- Offer knowledge and experiences working in various settings in which school psychological services may be delivered

As discussed below, most domains of the NASP Practice Model (NASP, 2010) are included in the ISPA definition of school psychology. Practices may include individual, group, and organizational work in public and privately supported settings and utilize knowledge of various assessment models and methods, including psychological, behavioral (including task analysis), social systems, medical, and ecological models.

Assessment

Assessment refers to educational, social, psychological, neuropsychological, language, and vocational assessment, evaluation, and diagnosis of infants, children, youth, and adults. It may occur within various contexts and procedures, including but not limited to reviewing existing records, observing, screening, interviewing, and testing. A primary goal of assessment is to accurately describe intellectual, academic, affective, social, personality, temperament, adaptive, language, psychomotor, vocational, and neuropsychological functioning as well as values. Other important goals of assessment may be to assist in determining the etiology of disorders, in planning and evaluating interventions, and in preventing the onset of disabling conditions.

Interventions

School psychologists are involved in various forms of interventions in order to help promote development; to acquire and best utilize personal, school, family, and community resources; and to learn to compensate for individual weaknesses. Interventions often involve school psychologists working directly with individuals, groups, or systems or indirectly (e.g., through consultation) with teachers, principals, and other educational personnel; parents and other family members; as well as other professionals and paraprofessionals. Interventions may be directed toward promoting well-being and preventing the onset of problems (i.e., primary prevention), minimizing difficulties once they occur (i.e., secondary prevention), and stabilizing disabilities. School psychologists work to ensure that basic and needed services are provided to those who can be expected to manifest one or more disabling conditions over some years (i.e., tertiary prevention).

Consultation

Consultation generally refers to the provision of school psychological services using indirect methods to deliver services. Consultation services typically recognize and emphasize the importance of using cooperative and collaborative methods to address problems. Consultation services may be offered to teachers and other educational personnel, other professionals, religious and other community leaders, parents, and government officials at the local, regional, national, and international levels. Consultation often involves school psychologists participating with other professionals, parents, students, and others as members of a team.

Organizational and Program Development Services

Organizational and program development services are provided to schools, school districts, agencies, as well as other organizations and administrative units at local, regional, national, and international levels. Services may include assessment and evaluation, interventions, coordination, program planning, curriculum and instructional development, program evaluation, and consultation. Typical goals include promoting and strengthening the coordination, administration, planning, and evaluation of services within one unit or between two or more units responsible for serving infants, children, youth, or adults. Organizational and program development services provided by school psychologists typically focus on educational, psychological, and social issues.

Supervision

Supervision refers to professional services provided by those with advanced preparation and experience who are able to assume responsibility and accountability for the provision of school psychological services. A school psychologist should direct the administrative unit responsible for providing school psychological services.

Accountability

School psychologists, along with those responsible for financial, administrative, and programmatic influence on school psychological services, are accountable for the delivery of school psychological services in an effective and efficient manner. Accountability involves self-evaluations together with evaluations at the programmatic and institutional levels. Evaluations involve the providers and consumers of services, including professional, paraprofessional, and clerical staff; students;

parents; and persons within the community. A primary goal of the accountability process is to help ensure the effective and efficient delivery of school psychological services.

Commitment to Research and Theory

School psychologists are committed to a service delivery model in which research and theory form a primary basis for practice. They can be expected to be knowledgeable about research relevant to practice and guide their services accordingly. In addition, school psychologists are expected to contribute to research and theory by actively engaging in research, evaluation, professional writing, and other scholarly activities intended to advance knowledge and its applications relevant to school psychology.

Public Laws

School psychologists are knowledgeable about legislation, public policies, and administrative rulings that guide the delivery of psychological and educational services. They provide their services in ways consistent with these provisions. In addition, they work to ensure that suitable laws that promote school psychology services are enacted and enforced.

Professional Codes and Ethics

School psychologists are knowledgeable about professional codes of ethics that guide their profession, provide services in ways consistent with these ethics, and work to ensure the ethics have continued relevancy. School psychologists continue their professional development in ways that help ensure their practices are consistent with current knowledge, legislation, and codes of professional practice and conduct.

ISPA's Model School Psychology Preparation Program

The International School Psychology Association Guidelines for the Preparation of School Psychologists (Cunningham & Oakland, 1998) are consistent with the previously described behavioral definition of school psychology and describe a model curriculum for a school psychology program. Coursework includes core courses in psychology, including developmental, educational, social, and personality psychology; learning and cognition; and measurement, research design, and statistics. Courses in educational foundations promote knowledge of education. Specialization in school psychology is promoted through such courses as professional issues in school psychology, educational and psychological assessment, consultation, exceptional children, school-based interventions, and organizational and program development. The model program also includes provisions for research activities together with supervised practica and internships.

ISPA's accreditation program is a voluntary, nongovernmental, professionally developed and supervised process of self-study and external review intended to evaluate, enhance, and publicly recognize quality institutions and programs in higher education. Accreditation is intended to benefit the public, protect the interests of students, serve the interests of professional preparation programs, and improve professional practice. During 2005–2010, ISPA developed and approved a process leading to the accreditation of school psychology programs internationally. As of 2013, two programs have been accredited (i.e., University of Nebraska at Kearney, and Lewis and Clark College, Portland, Oregon). More are expected to apply for accreditation.

Accreditation offers various benefits to school psychology programs. The process of accreditation encourages self-study, leads to changes, assists program faculty in its effort to establish suitable preparation standards and to acquire additional needed resources, and unites school psychology programs in a common mission. Accredited programs that acquire international recognition are more attractive to qualified students, and they facilitate student and staff exchange, particularly between countries. The accreditation process is intended to promote consistent quality and excellence in education and professional preparation and thus to provide tangible benefits for consumers of school psychological services, students, the profession, and programs.

The accreditation process involves evaluating the degree to which a program has developed goals consistent with those of a profession as well as the degree to which a program's goals have been achieved. In order for a program to be accredited by ISPA, its goals and standards should match those that have been set out by ISPA. However, when viewed internationally, diversity in program goals and policies can be expected in light of differences between countries in their histories, cultures, political policies, university structures, professional entry levels, licensure requirements, educational needs and services, legal standards, and other important defining qualities. Thus, accreditation procedures would recognize and anticipate program differences.

ISPA's Ethical Standards for School Psychology

Ethics codes are developed with the firm belief that professional conduct is expected to exemplify a profession's values. Ethical principles typically stress doing no harm; helping others derive benefit from professional services; promoting a client's freedom to think; choosing and acting; displaying loyalty; and promoting justice. Most of these principles are supported universally, thus permitting the approval of an ethics code by an international professional community.

ISPA members approved an ethics code in 1990 (Oakland et al., 1997), thus affirming the belief that members of an international body, who come from more than 40 countries, can agree on a uniform ethics code, thereby testifying to professional similarities across national boundaries. The 1990 code was revised and then approved in 2011. This current ethics code addresses six principles that are discussed in some detail below, as well as the following seven professional standards: professional responsibility, confidentiality, professional growth, professional limitations, professional relationships, assessment, and research. The following information draws extensively from the revised code.

School psychologists are expected to exemplify the profession's principles. These include transcending narrow personal, social, and cultural values and attitudes; adopting positions that benefit professional–client relationships; as well as acting in ways that are consistent with the best interests of children and youth, educators, parents, institutions, the community, and the profession. Children's rights are to be respected. Should conflicts occur between the interests of these individuals or organizations, members should seek to resolve such differences by attempting to clarify the ethical principle or standard with a respective individual or the organization with which they are affiliated and work toward resolving the conflicts, recognizing the particular vulnerability that children present across cultures. As such, the following six principles constitute aspirational behaviors that underscore ISPA's standards.

Beneficence and Nonmalfeasance
School psychologists strive to enable others to derive help and benefit from their professional services. They strive to understand the nature of requested services and, personally or through referrals, attempt to provide or secure needed and desired services. They are aware of possible professional and personal conditions as well

as conflicts of interest that may limit their ability to help others. Minimally, they strive to do no harm.

Competence Services

Competence services provided by school psychologists reflect their areas of expertise established through their initial and continued academic and professional preparation. School psychologists strive to provide services at a high level of competence. When requested or needed to provide services for which they may be less qualified, school psychologists either refer to others or acquire needed training and work under consultation and/or supervision.

Fidelity and Responsibility

School psychologists acknowledge that trust provides a foundation for professional service. They work to establish and maintain a client's trust in them and their profession. They are knowledgeable about and uphold professional standards of conduct. When needed, they describe and clarify their professional roles, obligations, and professional limitations to clients. They accept appropriate responsibility for their behavior. They manage conflicts of interest.

Integrity

School psychologists strive to display integrity, including consistency in the expression of their thoughts, feelings, and behaviors. They are committed to the expression and promotion of accuracy, honesty, and truthfulness through their scholarship, teaching, and clinical practices as well as to the integrity of other professionals.

Respect for People's Rights and Dignity

School psychologists strive to promote and respect the dignity and worth of all people. They acknowledge an individual's rights to privacy, confidentiality, and self-determination. They acknowledge cultural, individual, and role differences associated with age, gender, gender identity, race, ethnicity, culture, national origin, religion, sexual orientation, disability, language, or socioeconomic status.

Social Justice

Consistent with the reciprocal commitment between their profession and society, school psychologists are committed to the principle that all people are entitled to have access to and to benefit from the contributions of school psychology. Thus, they strive to minimize biases; promote free access to educational, social, and psychological services; and promote changes in schools or other educational practice settings that are beneficial to children and youth as well as to educational staff.

CONTEMPORARY STATUS OF SCHOOL PSYCHOLOGY INTERNATIONALLY

The contemporary context and status of the specialty of school psychology varies considerably around the world. However, there are also numerous similarities. Since the 1970s several seminal publications compiled knowledge that has advanced understanding of psychology in the schools internationally, including *Psychology in the Schools in International Perspective* (Catterall, 1976, 1977, 1979), *International Perspectives on Psychology in the Schools* (Saigh & Oakland, 1989), and *The Handbook of International School Psychology* (Jimerson et al., 2007). Each of these books illustrates both similarities and differences in school psychology internationally. The Appendix provides a brief summary of 43 countries that have established or emerging school psychology services. The descriptions of school psychology in each of these countries appear in Jimerson et al. (2007).

Data from Jimerson et al. (2007) suggest there are between 80,000 and 100,000 school psychologists in 43 countries. As of 2007, the most contemporary study examining the number of school psychologists estimated 76,100 across 48 countries (Jimerson, Stewart, Skokut, Cardenas, & Malone, 2009). Most (60–90%) are female and tend to be in their 30s and 40s. The average age is youngest in countries in which school psychology is emerging (e.g., Albania, 23–25 years).

Ratios between school psychologists and students vary considerably between and within countries. Ratios tend to be smaller in countries with a history of providing school psychology services (e.g., 1:3,000 in England and Wales; 1:1,600 in the United States) and with a higher gross national product (i.e., are more wealthy). In contrast, ratios generally are larger in countries with emerging services (e.g., Romania, Russia, South Korea) and with lower gross national product. Exact estimates of the ratio between school psychologists and students often are not possible. Many countries, including the United States, do not keep records on the number of school psychologists. Some countries do not keep reliable records on the number of students. Thus, reliable data and meaningful ratios of school psychologist-to-pupils are difficult to calculate (Jimerson et al., 2007).

A study investigating 48 countries reported that only 12 countries had ratios of approximately 1:2,000 (Australia, Canada, Denmark, Estonia, Israel,

Lithuania, the Netherlands, Scotland, Spain, Switzerland, Turkey, and the United States; Jimerson et al., 2009). Moreover, the ratios increased fairly steadily, up to 1:10,000 (with Germany at 1:9,482) and higher in Namibia: 1:34,712. The very large ratios illustrate that there are many countries wherein few children have access to support services characteristic of those provided by school psychologists in the United States or the United Kingdom. Among the 1.89 billion school-age children in the world (considering 12 years of education as the basis for school age), an estimated 379 million children live in countries that do not have access to a school psychologist (Jimerson et al., 2009). Approximately 572 million children live in countries with a ratio less than 1:10,000, and an estimated 939 million children live in countries that have a ratio greater than 1:10,000. Comparisons between countries warrant careful consideration.

In addition, within-country ratios differ considerably between urban and rural areas. The quantity and quality of almost all professional services are stronger in urban than rural areas. In many countries, few if any school psychologists are employed in rural areas. For example, in Moscow, an urban area, the ratio is 1:700 (Malykh, Kutuzova, & Alyokhina, 2007). However, Russia's land mass is large and mostly rural. Few school psychologists work in its rural areas. Thus, the ratio between school psychologist and students is considerably larger throughout most of Russia. Similarly, in Estonia the ratios average between 1:700 and 1:800 in schools that employ school psychologists, almost all of which are private and in urban areas (Kikas, 2007). However, few if any school psychologists work in rural areas. Additionally, in developing countries school psychology often is stronger in private than public schools.

School psychology is stronger and more prominent in countries where school psychologists serve the broad needs of students, including those in regular and special education, and from preschool through secondary school and beyond. In contrast, school psychology is weaker when school psychologists serve a more restricted range of student needs.

For example, until the 1990s, school psychological services in Ireland were almost exclusively directed to secondary-level schools (i.e., ages 12–18) and focused more on guidance and vocational counseling. Few school psychologists were employed, resulting in high psychologist-to-pupil ratios, sometimes exceeding 1:20,000. In 1999, the National Educational Psychological Service advanced the model of comprehensive school psychological services to all students, one that

envisioned the employment of 200 school psychologists, a psychologist-to-student ratio of 1:5,000, and the provision of services to all primary schools in Ireland. Since 1990, two graduate programs in school psychology were established to meet newly established personnel needs. In 2005 the Psychological Society of Ireland established a Division of Educational Psychology. As of 2006 the service employed 128 school psychologists and provided services to half of the primary schools (Crowley, 2007).

The specialty of school psychology does not exist among the most populated countries in the world. Considering the data from Jimerson et al. (2007, 2009), it is evident that among the 20 countries with the largest populations, 16 do not have nationally established school psychology services (the numbers in parentheses reflect their ranking in population as of 2012): China (1), India (2), Indonesia (4), Pakistan (6), Bangladesh (7), Russia (8), Nigeria (9), Japan (10), Mexico (11), Philippines (12), Vietnam (13), Egypt (15), Ethiopia (16), Iran (18), Thailand (19), and the Democratic Republic of the Congo (20). Among the 20, two offer established services to most school-age children: the United States (3) and Turkey (17), and one, Germany (14), offers services in a few states. In Brazil, school psychology services generally are found only in some private schools.

School psychology services are woefully inadequate for the 1.9 billion children in emerging countries. Children under age 18 constitute the largest age group internationally, including 340 million in Sub-Saharan Africa, 153 million in the Middle East and North Africa, 585 million in South Asia, 594 million in East Asia and the Pacific, 197 million in Latin America and the Caribbean, and 108 million in Central and Eastern Europe and the Commonwealth of Independent States. Globally, the majority of the 2.2 billion children in the world do not have access to school psychology services. Nearly all future population growth will be in the world's less developed countries, with the poorest countries experiencing the largest percentage increase. Thus, school psychology is not well positioned to meet the needs of most children currently or in the foreseeable future (Farrell, Jimerson, & Oakland, 2007).

CONDITIONS THAT INFLUENCE SCHOOL PSYCHOLOGY INTERNATIONALLY

The emergence and development of a profession are influenced by centripetal and centrifugal forces.

Centripetal forces produce stability and regularity and thus have a unifying force. In contrast, centrifugal forces produce diversity and change. Both are needed. Centripetal forces are necessary for the establishment of a profession and its early life. However, professions must change to reflect changes in a country's social structure and values, its economic resources and allocations, as well as changes in professional knowledge and resources. Both centripetal and centrifugal forces have an impact on regulations. Additionally, professions also are influenced by two political forces: those that are internal to the profession and thus under its control as well as those external to the profession and thus not under its control (Cunningham, 2007).

A profession generally attempts to achieve professional autonomy; that is, to enjoy a high degree of independence to achieve its desired goals. School psychology displays two different levels of professional self-regulation and thus autonomy. Some countries have low levels of self-regulation as seen in the absence of a definition of school psychology service, training programs and standards, as well as credentialing and licensing processes. In contrast, other countries have high levels of self-regulation as seen in the presence of these aforementioned qualities.

The levels of self-regulation strongly affect the degree to which a profession is recognized by others, is thought worthy to be regulated by external sources, and is regulated by them. Thus, school psychology can be strong only after it has achieved high levels of self-regulation. Then, somewhat ironically, some degree of self-regulation is lost due to externally imposed requirements (e.g., restricting its services to specified areas, obtaining the desired professional title—for example, school psychologist—only after undergoing a credentialing process).

Thus, school psychology is strongest in those countries that have a well-defined specialty represented by a strong professional association whose practitioners are well prepared academically and professionally and who provide services needed by society. The profession balances the desire both to achieve unity and to diversify and strives to exert strong internal control of its members while working to maintain and strengthen its external support (e.g., to be seen by society as responding to important needs and social changes and thus worthy of society's support).

Among the more than 200 countries, school psychology is established in some, emerging in many, and not apparent in most. Two broad sets of conditions affect the development of school psychology: (a) conditions within a country or region that are not under the direct control of school psychology and (b) conditions within a country that are under school psychology's control (Russell, 1984). Issues related to each of these are discussed below.

Six Influences Beyond the Direct Control of School Psychology

Psychology, including school psychology, is highly influenced by conditions over which it has little control. These conditions include the status of public education, a country's economic vitality, a country's culture, the primary languages used, geography, and national needs and priorities.

Status of Public Education
School psychology is strong in those countries that have well-established public education systems that serve students from grades 1 to 12, including those students with various disabilities. In general, public schools first establish elementary education followed by secondary education. Services for students with medical or physical disorders (e.g., mental retardation, blind, deaf) then become well established, followed by services for students with learning, psychological, and behavioral disorders (e.g., learning disabilities, emotional and social disorders). School psychological services typically are established only after schools commit to serve students with psychological disorders. Thus, school psychology services often are meager in countries that lack a strong commitment or resources to serve students with psychological disorders through its public schools.

Country's Economic Vitality
School psychology is strong only in those countries with ample revenue to support both basic public education and additional school psychology services. Psychology is stronger in countries with a higher gross national product. In addition, in that a country's wealth typically is concentrated in urban areas, all professional services, including those from school psychologists, typically are more abundant and specialized in urban than in rural areas. Although a country's socioeconomic development has an impact on the development of school psychology, it alone does not fully explain its presence (Cook, Jimerson, & Begheny, 2010). Specifically, variables that reflect a country's modern mass cultural values as well as expenditures on social programs independently predict school psychology's presence.

Country's Culture

The strength and vitality of psychology, including school psychology, differ because of cultural differences. Professional services are most advanced and abundant in Australia, Canada, Israel, Europe (especially Western Europe), the United Kingdom, and the United States. People in these countries have shared cultural links for centuries. Moreover, these countries value and promote individual differences, a viewpoint that constitutes the keystone of psychology. Psychology generally is not as well advanced in countries that value and promote a more collective view of human behavior. The birth of and leadership for psychology in European countries and the United States were not accidental and instead attributable, in part, to the political value these countries place on understanding and valuing the individual.

Country's Primary Language

Historically, three languages were used predominantly to converse in the arts and sciences as well as in diplomacy: English, French, and German. Although all three remain important, English has become the most widely used second language internationally and the most prominent language used within the sciences. Many foreign-born psychologists who were educated in English-speaking countries returned to their home countries to establish academic and professional preparation programs in psychology, many of which require students also to be fluent in English. School psychologists who are not fluent in English are unlikely to have current world-class knowledge. Furthermore, countries in which English is not widely used as a second language are unlikely to have well-developed school psychological services at a national level.

Geographic Differences

Psychology, including school psychology, generally develops regionally. The availability and quality of school psychology services within a country tend to resemble the availability and quality in its neighboring countries. Countries that are close geographically are likely to have closer economic and cultural ties. For example, school psychology is strong throughout much of Western Europe. In contrast, school psychology is not strong in any of the 22 countries that are in the Arab League or in Asia, a region that contains approximately 67% of the world's population. School psychology is somewhat strong in only one African country, South Africa, a country with strong historic links to Western Europe.

National Needs and Priorities

National needs strongly influence the development, acceptance, and sustainability of school psychology services. These services emerge and are sustained only when local and national leaders believe the services are needed and of high quality. Public school systems in some countries are not sufficiently developed to accept or realize a need for school psychology services (Mpofu, Zindi, Oakland, & Peresuh, 1997; Jimerson et al., 2007).

Six Influences That Are Under Greater Direct Control of School Psychology

Psychology and school psychology also are highly influenced by conditions over which the profession and specialty have more control. These include promoting professionalism, expanding professional services, codifying the scope and practice of services, ensuring its strong interface with education, and promoting research and other forms of scholarship together with test development and use.

Promote Professionalism

School psychology is strong within a country to the extent it has one or more strong professional associations that represent its interests (Jimerson, Skokut, Cardenas, Malone, & Stewart 2008; Jimerson et al., 2009). Efforts must be directed toward forming and maintaining a strong professional association to represent the interests of school psychologists. One cannot assume that once-strong professional associations will remain strong. For example, Venezuela formed the first free-standing school psychology association (Oakland, Feldman, & Leon De Viloria, 1995). It now is inactive.

Expand Professional Services

School psychological services have tended to follow an evolutionary path. Services typically center initially on those who are mentally retarded, blind, and deaf. Later efforts may focus on students who display social, emotional, behavioral, and mental health needs. Still later efforts may focus on primary prevention, teacher–parent consultation, and other services that address school-wide needs, and not only those of individual students. The specialty of school psychology is most viable when its practitioners demonstrate a wide range of knowledge, skills, and abilities that enable these practitioners to provide direct and indirect services for students being served in regular and special education programs as well as to address school-wide needs (Cunningham, 2007).

Codify the Scope and Practice of Services

Professional associations must develop policies that define the specialty and establish standards for practice, including an ethics code, and certify preparation programs that maintain high standards. Armed with these policies, professional associations must lobby for the passage of legislation at national and regional levels that funds school psychology services and protects its title and practices (Jimerson et al., 2008).

Ensure School Psychology's Interface With Education

Most school psychologists work within education, settings in which they often have little power and authority. Leaders in special education often serve as gatekeepers of and strongly influence the nature of school psychology services. Thus, strong bridges between school psychology and education, including regular and special education, need to be built and maintained.

Promote Research and Other Forms of Scholarship

The birth of modern psychology occurred through research efforts that led to an empirical base for applied work. Psychology, including school psychology, generally is strongest in those countries that have active research agendas to address important national issues. Those who practice school psychology cannot expect other specialty areas of psychology to conduct research on issues relevant to their interests. School psychology must assume leadership for conducting and disseminating research. One or more quality peer-reviewed professional journals that feature research on issues important to school psychology are of primary importance.

Efforts to promote research and other forms of scholarship require doctoral preparation. Practitioners prepared at the subdoctoral level rarely conduct and publish research. Thus, the preparation of doctoral-level school psychologists who pursue careers as scholars is critical to the promotion of research and scholarship in all countries. Doctoral preparation is especially critical in those countries that have little or no scholarship that addresses issues important to school psychology. Nineteen countries reportedly had or currently offer doctoral-level preparation (Australia, Brazil, Canada, Cypress, England, Greece, Hong Kong, Iran, Jordan, Mexico, Nigeria, Philippines, Romania, Scotland, Slovakia, South Africa, South Korea, United States, and Wales; Jimerson et al., 2008).

Promote Test Development and Use

School psychologists often have ambivalent attitudes toward test use. Those working in countries that have few locally developed tests typically desire additional testing resources, in part to objectify and legitimize their work. They often are aware that school psychologists in other countries, including Australia and the United States, are employed initially to administer intelligence tests.

School psychology services in a number of countries developed because of the need for testing and the exclusive use of tests of intelligence by school psychologists. The use of tests opened the education door to the provision of other psychological services. School psychologists working in countries that have an abundance of tests often complain that their responsibilities focus too heavily on test use. Thus, knowledge of test development and use provides a window through which school psychology services can be viewed.

The use of tests in emerging countries that are developed elsewhere often first are merely translated from the host language to the target language, with little effort to establish local norms or to gather data on the translated measure's other psychometric qualities. Later, the tests may be adapted for use in the emerging country, at which time efforts are made to determine the relevance of the items, acquire norms, and examine the test's psychometric qualities (Oakland, 2009).

The International Test Commission is concerned about the widespread use of tests developed in one country and used in others. This use often leads to test misuse. Thus, the International Test Commission has developed guidelines to assist in the adaptation of tests, a process that promotes test changes intended to lead to valid measures (http://www.intestcom.org).

The levels of test development and use differ considerably between developed and emerging countries. In contrast to conditions in developed countries, school psychologists in emerging countries have fewer tests to use; the tests tend to be older; the tests are used for multiple purposes, often far beyond their intended use; and the tests rely more on theory than norms for interpretation.

School psychologists working in emerging countries generally face two challenges: few test resources and an absence of quality universal public school psychology services. Efforts to develop tests and to prepare practitioners in their ethical and standardized use are likely to add importantly to the services school psychologists can provide and thus strengthen and further legitimize their public school presence.

LAWS, ETHICS, AND PROFESSIONAL PREPARATION THAT GUIDE PRACTICE

The development of school psychology within a country often can be gauged by the presence of its efforts to define the parameters of its practices and inform the recipients of its services in part through its ethics code. Once established, the specialty of school psychology then is influenced by external controls, including laws that govern practices. These issues are summarized below.

Laws Governing School Psychology

School psychology generally is strong in countries that have laws requiring the provision of and financial support for its services. Examples from England and Finland illustrate this issue. In England, the 1944 Education Act required local education authorities to provide suitable education for subnormal, maladjusted, or physically handicapped children. This resulted in additional employment of school psychologists who were prepared to understand the needs of children with low academic ability. The 1981 Education Act mandated a major restructuring of all services for children with special educational needs and suggested school psychologists should be involved in the assessment of pupils who may have such needs (Squires & Farrell, 2007).

In Finland, prior to 1990, the municipalities established school psychologist positions without any support from the state. School psychologists numbered about 123 in 53 municipalities. Moreover, 90% served students in southern Finland. The 1990 revision of the Child Welfare Act (Child Protection Law) identified school psychologists as providers of support services to students who display learning or adaptation problems at school and created positions for 334 school psychologists, of which 47% are located in southern Finland (Laaksonen, Laitinen, & Salmi, 2007).

Laws that require school psychologists to be licensed or registered are important in advancing the profession. These laws involve establishing minimum initial professional preparation and minimum levels of continuing professional development to obtain and retain the use of a professional title (e.g., school psychologist) and typically require school psychologists to have defined the scope and functions of their practice.

For example, in New Zealand, all psychologists must be registered by the New Zealand Psychologists Board. The board assesses the suitability of applicants. Minimally, applicants must have a master's degree in psychology from a board-accredited institution and must have completed at least 1,500 hours of approved supervised practice. Qualified psychologists can apply for registration in specialist areas (e.g., school psychologist). Only those approved are entitled to use the professional title (Edwards, Annan, & Ryba, 2007).

Licensing may be controlled at the national (e.g., Russia, England, Wales) or regional, provincial, or state (e.g., Australia, Canada, Germany, United States) levels. Both national and regional, provincial, or state licensure laws may be influenced by policies established and promulgated by the national association. Thus, licensing requirements may be similar between regions, provinces, or states in some countries and differ considerably in others. For example, in Canada, some provinces grant school psychology credentials to school teachers who complete a few courses in school psychology, whereas other provinces require a degree in school psychology (Saklofske, Schwean, Harrison, & Mureika, 2007).

Variations in licensing requirements between countries are to be expected. Reciprocal arrangements in which one country recognizes the credentials of others are not common. However, efforts are under way in some areas to overcome these barriers and to promote professional mobility. For example, the European Union is engaged in the development of licensing requirements that will be the same for all member countries. Its full implementation may take years.

This initiative is part of the European Union's 1999 Bologna Plan, approved by the ministers of education of the member nations. This plan is intended to promote greater unity in higher education within the European Union member nations. Under this plan, academic and professional programs at the undergraduate and graduate levels, together with their courses, will be similar across universities in European Union countries, thus promoting greater unity and common standards as well as facilitating an exchange of teachers and students throughout European Union nations. In addition, a bachelor's degree can be attained in 3 years and a master's degree in a professional program in 1 or 2 years. Universities and professors are required to relinquish much of their autonomy to an overarching agency responsible for promoting this convergence. The implications for the preparation of school psychology could be immense.

In the United States and Canada, the Association of State and Provincial Psychology Boards has established the Certificate of Professional Qualifications in Psychology, a program designed to facilitate mobility of licensed psychologists between states in the United States and provinces in Canada (http://www.asppb.org). Similarly, in 1988, NASP established a Nationally Certified School Psychologist program that is recognized by 27 states.

Ranges in the Provision of School Psychology Services

To be viable, professions must provide services that reflect national needs. School psychological services can be expected to differ between countries. Nevertheless, school psychologists in most countries offer a range of services that often include direct (e.g., counseling, assistance with academic work) and indirect (e.g., assessment) services to children, indirect services to teachers and parents (e.g., consultation), and program services (e.g., planning, implementing, and evaluating interventions, including prevention programs) at a school or school system level to foster system change. The amount of time school psychologists devote to these services to meet critical country needs varies. For example, among school psychologists in Albania, counseling students is their most common activity, followed by teacher and parent consultation. In contrast, among school psychologists in Cyprus, attention to administrative responsibilities and psychoeducational evaluations are most common (Jimerson et al., 2004).

Professional practices should be based on solid theory and research communicated through journals, books, and other publications by scholars within the country in which the practices occur. These conditions generally are not found in most countries. More commonly, when viewed internationally, few school psychologists are scholars, and few scholarly journals are available to report research. These conditions severely limit the growth and viability of school psychology.

Various scholarly journals in Canada and the United States publish articles that have regional or international implications. However, two scholarly journals have a decided mission to feature regional and international articles central to school psychology: ISPA's *International Journal of School and Educational Psychology* and the independent *School Psychology International*. APA also has an internationally oriented journal, *International Perspectives in Psychology Research, Practice, Consultation*. The *Canadian Journal of School Psychology* also publishes articles that address international issues.

The development of school psychology nationally and internationally requires continued research efforts. Consistent with its ethical responsibilities to serve the public, the specialty of school psychology must accept responsibility for advancing knowledge and practices associated with its stated missions through scholarship that contributes empirical knowledge regarding assessment and intervention services that promote and in other ways address the cognitive, emotional, and social development of students. The negligence of school psychologists to engage in research, especially in emerging countries, will have an adverse impact on the future.

Academic and Professional Preparation of School Psychologists

Criteria for preparing school psychologists, including the length, nature, and duration of practica and internship, and the entry degree (e.g., bachelor's, master's, specialist, or doctoral degrees) vary somewhat between countries. Key considerations regarding program entrance, duration, and course content related to the preparation of school psychologists internationally are summarized below.

Program Entrance Criteria and Duration

All program applicants are required to obtain a high school education as a prerequisite to enter a university undergraduate program. Countries in which clinical services, including those of school psychologists, which are somewhat recent and are emerging, typically prepare professionals during a 4- to 5-year undergraduate program. Countries in which clinical services are well established and have a higher gross national product typically require graduate-level specialized professional development. In most countries, persons with a master's degree generally are eligible for university employment. Countries with higher gross national product are more likely to require graduate level specialized professional development.

Undergraduate programs in psychology that may lead to specializations in school psychology typically devote the first 2 years to foundation courses that are relevant to students seeking all applied psychology specializations (e.g., clinical, community, school, industrial, or organizational) and the last 2 years to courses that prepare students for professional practice in specific specialty areas. Some programs require a fifth year for an internship. Thus, undergraduate students generally complete a general course of study in psychology and then specialize in their area of interest (e.g., school psychology) during their third and fourth years and possibly their fifth year.

Countries with a longer history of providing a wide range of professional services and a higher gross national product generally require graduate-level specialized professional development to practice, often a master's degree that includes 1–2 years of full-time study, and possibly an internship. Entrance into these programs often requires the completion of an undergraduate degree in psychology or education.

As noted previously, doctoral degrees in school psychology (often 5–6 years of full-time study) presently are offered in fewer than 20 countries (Jimerson et al., 2008). The number of doctoral graduates varies greatly across these countries. The vast majority of doctoral degrees in school psychology are granted in the United States, along with some in England.

Some, but not most, countries require training and experience in teaching. For example, the German state of Bavaria requires school psychologists to receive their training as part of a professional preparation to become a teacher (Dunkel, 2007). Other countries (e.g., Australia, England, New Zealand, South Africa, Wales) once required school psychologists to have training and experience as a teacher. This requirement was dropped recently in England, New Zealand, and Wales and may be dropped in Australia.

Program Courses and Content

The academic and professional topics within school psychology programs are remarkably similar. The formation and approval of ISPA's previously described model school psychology preparation program underscores this similarity internationally.

SUMMARY

The specialty of school psychology is practiced in many, but not most, countries. In some, school psychology's origin occurred after World War II. In others, it occurred within the last few years. In most, it may occur in the future. Worldwide, school psychologists tend to be female and in their 30s. About half are prepared at the undergraduate level and half at the graduate level, typically with a master's degree. Extremely few are prepared at the doctoral level. In addition to differences in their degrees, their academic and professional preparation is somewhat diverse, displaying needed and varied emphases relevant to the local contextual considerations within a given country.

Worldwide, the nature of school psychology services has both similarities and differences. It includes providing direct and indirect services to children, teachers, and parents. The goals of their services generally are related to the application of psychology to enhance the mental health and educational well-being of children and youth, schools, families, and communities. The work of school psychologists is informed by core elements of academic psychology that are relevant to understanding learning and development, child psychopathology, and methods that encourage change.

The future of school psychology will be influenced by qualities both external and internal to the specialty. External qualities include the status of public education in a country and its economic status, culture, geography, language uses, and national needs and priorities. Qualities internal to school psychology and under its control include promoting professionalism, expanding professional services, codifying the scope and practice of services, ensuring its strong interface with education, and promoting research and other forms of scholarship together with test development and use. School psychologists in the United States and elsewhere are encouraged to become more engaged in international work as well as international efforts that promote the specialty of school psychology and its important missions (e.g., see Gerner, 1990; International Schools Services, 2006).

AUTHOR NOTE

Disclosure. Thomas Oakland and Shane Jimerson have a financial interest in books they authored or coauthored that are referenced in this chapter.

REFERENCES

Catterall, C. D. (Ed.). (1976). *Psychology in the schools in international perspective: Vol. 1.* Columbus, OH: International School Psychology Steering Committee.

Catterall, C. D. (Ed.). (1977). *Psychology in the schools in international perspective: Vol. 2.* Columbus, OH: International School Psychology Steering Committee.

Catterall, C. D. (Ed.). (1979). *Psychology in the schools in international perspective: Vol. 3.* Columbus, OH: International School Psychology Steering Committee.

Cook, C., Jimerson, S. R., & Begheny, J. (2010). Predicting the presence of school psychology: An international examination of sociocultural, sociopolitical, and socioeconomic influences. *School Psychology International, 31,* 438–461.

Crowley, P. P. (2007). School psychology in Ireland. In S. R. Jimerson, T. D. Oakland, & P. Farrell (Eds.), *The handbook of international school psychology* (pp. 177–188). Thousand Oaks, CA: SAGE.

Cunningham, J. L. (2007). Centripetal and centrifugal trends influencing school psychology's international development. In S. R. Jimerson, T. D. Oakland, & P. Farrell (Eds.), *The handbook of international school psychology* (pp. 463–474). Thousand Oaks, CA: SAGE.

Cunningham, J. L., & Oakland, T. (1998). International School Psychology Association guidelines for the preparation of school psychologists. *School Psychology International, 19*, 19–30.

Dunkel, L. (2007). School psychology in Germany. In S. R. Jimerson, T. D. Oakland, & P. Farrell (Eds.), *The handbook of international school psychology* (pp. 123–134). Thousand Oaks, CA: SAGE.

Edwards, T., Annan, J., & Ryba, K. (2007). Educational psychology in New Zealand. In S. R. Jimerson, T. D. Oakland, & P. Farrell (Eds.), *The handbook of international school psychology* (pp. 263–274). Thousand Oaks, CA: SAGE.

Fagan, T. K. (2002). Trends in the history of school psychology in the United States. In A. Thomas & J. Grimes (Eds.), *Best practices in school psychology IV* (pp. 209–221). Bethesda, MD: National Association of School Psychologists.

Fagan, T. K. (2005). Literary origins of the term, "school psychologist," revisited. *School Psychology Review, 34*, 432–434.

Fagan, T. K., & Wells, P. (1999). Frances Mullen: Her life and contributions to school psychology. *School Psychology International, 20*, 91–102.

Fagan, T. K., & Wise, P. (2007). *School psychology: Past, present, and future* (3rd ed.). Bethesda, MD: National Association of School Psychologists.

Farrell, P., Jimerson, S., & Oakland, T. (2007). School psychology internationally: A synthesis of findings. In S. Jimerson, T. Oakland, & P. Farrell (Eds.), *The handbook of international school psychology* (pp. 501–510). Thousand Oaks, CA: SAGE.

Galen. (1963). *Galen on the natural faculties* (A. J. Brock, Transl.). Cambridge, MA: Harvard University Press.

Gerner, M. (1990). Living and working overseas: School psychologists in American international schools. *School Psychology Quarterly, 5*, 21–32.

International Schools Services. (2006). *International Schools Services directory of international schools.* Princeton, NJ: Author.

Jimerson, S., Graydon, K., Farrell, P., Kikas, E., Hatzichristou, S., Boce, E., & Bashi, G. (2004). The International school psychology survey: Development and data from Albania, Cyprus, Estonia, Greece, and northern England. *School Psychology International, 25*, 259–286.

Jimerson, S. R., Oakland, T. D., & Farrell, P. T. (Eds.). (2007). *The handbook of international school psychology.* Thousand Oaks, CA: SAGE.

Jimerson, S., Skokut, M., Cardenas, S., Malone, H., & Stewart, K. (2008). Where in the world is school psychology? Examining evidence of school psychology around the globe. *School Psychology International, 29*, 131–144.

Jimerson, S. R., Stewart, K., Skokut, M., Cardenas, S., & Malone, H. (2009). How many school psychologists are there in each country of the world? International estimates of school psychologists and school psychologist-to-student ratios. *School Psychology International, 30*, 555–567.

Kagan, J. (1994). *Galen's prophecy: Temperament in human nature.* New York, NY: Basic Books.

Kikas, E. (2007). School psychology in Estonia. In S. R. Jimerson, T. D. Oakland, & P. Farrell (Eds.), *The handbook of international school psychology* (pp. 91–102). Thousand Oaks, CA: SAGE.

Laaksonen, P., Laitinen, K., & Salmi, M. (2007). School psychology in Finland. In S. R. Jimerson, T. D. Oakland, & P. Farrell (Eds.), *The handbook of international school psychology* (pp. 103–112). Thousand Oaks, CA: SAGE.

Malykh, S. B., Kutuzova, D. A., & Alyokhina, S. V. (2007). Psychology in education in the Russian Federation. In S. R. Jimerson, T. D. Oakland, & P. Farrell (Eds.), *The handbook of international school psychology* (pp. 329–338). Thousand Oaks, CA: SAGE.

Mpofu, E., Zindi, F., Oakland, T., & Peresuh, M. (1997). School psychology practices in east and southern Africa: Special educators' perspectives. *The Journal of Special Education, 31*, 387–402.

National Association of School Psychologists. (2010). *Model for comprehensive and integrated school psychological services.* Bethesda, MD: Author. Retrieved from http://www.nasponline.org/standards/2010standards/2_PracticeModel.pdf

Oakland, T. (2000). International school psychology. In T. Fagan & P. Wise (Eds.), *School psychology: Past, present, and future* (2nd ed.). Bethesda, MD: National Association of School Psychologists.

Oakland, T. (2009). How universal are test development and use? In E. Grigorenko (Ed.), *Assessment of abilities and competencies in an era of globalization* (pp. 1–40). New York, NY: Springer.

Oakland, T., & Cunningham, J. (1992). A survey of school psychology in developed and developing countries. *School Psychology International, 13*, 99–130.

Oakland, T., & Cunningham, J. (1997). International School Psychology Association definition of school psychology. *School Psychology International, 18*, 195–200.

Oakland, T., Feldman, N., & Leon De Viloria, C. (1995). School psychology in Venezuela: Three decades of progress and futures of great potential. *School Psychology International, 16*, 29–42.

Oakland, T., Goldman, S., & Bischoff, H. (1997). Code of ethics of the International School Psychology Association. *School Psychology International, 18*, 291–298.

Russell, R. (1984). Psychology in its world context. *American Psychologists, 39*, 1017–1025.

Saigh, P. A., & Oakland, T. D. (Eds.). (1989). *International perspectives on psychology in the schools.* Mahwah, NJ: Erlbaum.

Saklofske, D. H., Schwean, V. L., Harrison, G. L., & Mureika, J. (2007). School psychology in Canada. In S. R. Jimerson, T. D. Oakland, & P. Farrell (Eds.), *The handbook of international school psychology* (pp. 39–52). Thousand Oaks, CA: SAGE.

Squires, G., & Farrell, P. T. (2007). Educational psychology in England and Wales. In S. R. Jimerson, T. D. Oakland, & P. Farrell (Eds.), *The handbook of international school psychology* (pp. 81–90). Thousand Oaks, CA: SAGE.

United Nations Educational, Scientific, and Cultural Organization. (1948). *School psychologists* (Publication No. 105). Geneva, Switzerland: International Bureau of Education.

Wall, W. (1956). *Psychological services for schools.* New York, NY: New York University Press.

APPENDIX. COUNTRIES AND OTHER TERRITORIES WITH ESTABLISHED OR EMERGING SCHOOL PSYCHOLOGY SERVICES

Country	When Established or Emerging (Number of School Psychologists)	School Psychology Services
Albania	1990s (79)	1999: School psychology division established in Psychology Department at Tirana University
Australia	1920s (2,000)	1923: A psychological laboratory was established at Melbourne Teachers College, specially trained professionals employed as mental testers and educational advisors to both special and regular schools
Brazil	1960s	1964: Legislation defined professional areas of school psychology included school psychology
		1990: The Brazilian Association of Educational and School Psychology was founded
Canada	1920s (3,000–4,000)	1920s: Mental health specialists in Manitoba were employed to conduct educational measurements in the schools
		1980s: Provincial and national school psychology associations formed
China	1990s[a]	1999: Ministry of Education published documents indicating that all primary and secondary schools in China should include mental health education for students by 2002
Cyprus	1960s (185)	1960s: Psychology positions were established in the Ministry of Education and Ministry of Health
		1995: The School Psychology Services Section was established in the Ministry of Education and Culture
Denmark	1930s (880)	1930: A teacher with a degree in psychology assessed children to determine whether special education services were warranted; in 1934 this teacher was appointed as the first school psychologist in Denmark
England and Wales	1920s (2,647)	1920s: The London County Council employed Cyril Burt as a psychologist to help assess children's suitability for schooling; toward the end of the 1920s Burt helped to develop guidelines for the development of school psychology services
Estonia	1970s (150)	1975: Lia Hanso, a psychologist, was employed in a special school for children with mental diseases, and was noted as the Estonia's first school psychologist
		1992: Union of Estonian School Psychologists was established
Finland	1930s (300)	1938: First Finnish school psychologist was employed in Helsinki
		1974: Local authorities in Helsinki began to establish permanent posts for school psychologists
France	1890s (3,200)	1894: Alfred Binet created the Free Society for the Psychological Study of the Child and in 1897 wrote a paper describing psychology in primary schools; in 1899 Binet opened a psychological laboratory in a Parisian primary school; in 1905 Binet consulted with the Ministry of Public Instruction regarding children who could not follow the normal school curriculum
		1945: Bernard Andrey was appointed as the first French school psychologist by Professor Henri Wallon (founder of School Psychology) in France
Germany	1920s (982)	1922: Hans Lammermann began work as a school psychologist in Mannheim, employed until 1933
		West Germany, 1950s: School psychology positions were reestablished
		East Germany, 1975: School psychology reestablished
Greece	1980s (400)	1989: The first 50 psychologists were appointed in special education schools
Hong Kong	1960s (96)	1959: The Education Department established a special education section; during the 1960s school psychologists were employed in this section
Hungary	1960s (200)	1960s: Educational Child and Guidance Centers employed psychologists to serve the needs of school-age children, teachers, and families by providing psychological and educational services
		1986: Ministry of Education provided funding for 30 school psychologists to be employed in the schools for 2 years; all schools chose to keep their school psychologists at the end of the 2-year period

Continued

Country	When Established or Emerging (Number of School Psychologists)	School Psychology Services
India	1960s[a]	1960s: Vocational bureaus employing psychologists were established to facilitate educational and vocational guidance; as of 2006 there was no professional organization for school psychologists and the profession was not established in India
Ireland	1960s (128)	1960: City of Dublin Vocational Education Committee established first school psychological services, focused on secondary-level schools 1990: Pilot Project to Primary Schools was established by the Department of Education Psychological Services, which led to the development of the National Educational Psychological Service, which now provides services to about half of all primary schools and three quarters of postprimary schools
Israel	1930s (2,100)	1936: Center for Educational Psychology was established in Tel Aviv, primarily focusing on testing and placement of students 1962: Psychology and Counseling Service were established in the Ministry of Education
Italy	1970s[a]	1970s: Psychologists assisted in inclusionary efforts, and the Ministry of Public Instruction developed a psycho-socio-pedagogical model of service delivery 2004: Abruzzo was Italy's first region to legislate the service of school psychology; as of 2006, parliament was considering legislative proposals to introduce school psychology in all Italian schools; however, there were no nationally recognized regulations regarding licensure of school psychologists
Jamaica	2000s[a]	2000s: Some psychologists work in consultative roles with schools; as of 2006 there were no positions for school psychologists within the Ministry of Education
Japan	1990s (3,500)	1997: The Japanese Association of Educational Psychology started to certify "school psychologist" for teachers and counselors; though the certification is not official, school psychologists actively provide psychoeducational services to students 1999: A book entitled *School Psychology: Psychoeducational Services by a Team of Teachers, Counselors, and Parents* was published in Japanese
Lithuania	1980s (400)	1980s: Psychologists were employed to provide services to school children; Section of Pedagogical Psychology was established within the Lithuanian Psychologists' Society
Malta	1970s[a] (11)	1971: One school psychologist was employed in the School Psychological Service within the Department of Education until 1977; the position then remained vacant until 1990, when services were reestablished 1999: The University of Malta offered the first 2-year master's degree in psychology
The Netherlands	1920s (1,400)	1920s: Psychologists involved in testing students for possible placement in special education, both the University of Amsterdam and Amsterdam University had established psychotechnical (assessment) centers
New Zealand	1940s (200)	1948: Psychological services were established by the Department of Education; child guidance clinics were added in 1951 and school guidance counselors in 1959
Nigeria	1980s[a]	1980s: Psychologists employed to provide assessment and consultation for children with special needs; as of 2006, neither the title nor practice of school psychology was regulated
Norway	1930s (945)	1938: First private agency for school psychology services was established in Oslo by Charlotte Buhler 1939: First public agency was opened in Aker
Pakistan	2000s[a]	2006: There are very few opportunities for school psychologists and no university programs to prepare school psychologists

Continued

Country	When Established or Emerging (Number of School Psychologists)	School Psychology Services
Peru	1960s[a]	1967: Walter Blumenfeld, director of the Institute of Psychotechnics and Psychology at the Universidad Nacional de San Marcos published the first book in Peru on the psychology of learning 1970s: Definition of school psychology and discussion of its role and functions in psychology relative to other psychology specialties 2006: Only about 10% of state-supported schools employ psychologists; university programs provide preparation as general psychologists
Puerto Rico	1980s (100)	1980s: Several private schools started adding psychologists to their staff 1995: The Department of Education employed 10 full-time psychologists, 22 part-time psychologists, and 30 contract work psychologists to evaluate and intervene with special needs students; as of 2006, very few public schools employed full-time psychologists
Romania	1990s[a] (650)	1995: Ministry of Education established initiative to prepare and employ school psychologists/counselors 2004: Commission for Educational Psychology, School, and Vocational Counseling within the Romanian College of Psychologists regulates school psychology licenses
Russia	1980s[a]	1982: The Scientific Research Institute of General and Pedagogical Psychology within the Academy of Pedagogical Sciences initiated an experimental program employing school psychologists; broader implementation occurred in 1988; as of 2006, the number of school psychologists is small
Scotland	1920s (427)	1920s: Appointment of a child psychologist to Jordanhill College and Glasgow City who was a psychological advisor to the schools and prepared teachers to work with children with special needs
Slovak Republic	1970s (200)	1970s: School psychologists at universities in Bratislava and Kosice proposed core responsibilities and preparation of school psychologists; work ceased as a result of occupation of Czechoslovakia by Russia 1990s: Preparation of school psychologists commenced in the Department of Psychology at Comenius University and the School Psychology Association of Czechoslovakia was established
South Africa	1930s (1,178)	1937: A psychologist was appointed in the Western Cape Province, focused on testing and placement of students, subsequent emphasis on counseling and vocational guidance 1990s: There was one school psychologist for 5–10 schools in the Cape Province (white schools) and two school psychologists for more than 100 schools in Cape Town (black schools); redistribution of school psychologists following the dismantling of apartheid
South Korea	1980s[a] (40)	1987: First graduate-level school psychology program at Yonsei University in Seoul
Spain	1970s (3,600)	1970s: The General Law of Education established school and vocational guidance services; the Ministry of Education sanctioned psychological services in the schools in 1977; university programs were established to prepare psychologists to work in educational settings
Switzerland	1920s (800)	1920: First school psychologist service was established in Bern In 1927, another emerged in Basel
Turkey	1950s (11,327)	1953: Decree by the Ministry of National Education resulted in the establishment of the first center for psychological services in Ankara in 1955
United Arab Emirates	1980s[a] (64)	1980: The Ministry of Education established two offices of psychological services in which psychology specialists were hired; in 1980, the Ministry of Education and Youth established a research center to investigate issues related to the interests of the school community and to support the work of psychological specialists
United States	1910s (32,300)	1915: Arnold Gessell employed in Connecticut as a school psychologist and in 1918 given the title of school psychologist; in the 1920s, standards for preparing and credentialing school psychologists were established

Continued

Country	When Established or Emerging (Number of School Psychologists)	School Psychology Services
Venezuela	1950s (150)	1956: First school psychology program established at the Central University of Venezuela; no current national association
Zimbabwe	1970s (32)	1971: Psychology as a profession was regulated by statutes 1983: University of Zimbabwe offered for the first time a master of science degree program in school psychology

Note. Based on information from Jimerson et al. (2007). The decades indicated above loosely represent the beginning of the specialty of school psychology. *Established* refers to countries in which the available information reveals that professionals are employed as school psychologists. Many but not all of these countries have legislation related to the education of children with special learning needs and professional associations that represent the specialty of school psychology. *Emerging* refers to countries in which the available information reveals that there are initiatives and efforts to employ professionals to provide some services associated with the specialty of school psychology. However, there is no current recognition of the specialty of school psychology.

[a] Emerging.

Best Practices in Applying Legal Standards for Students With Disabilities

31

Guy M. McBride
Licensed Practicing Psychologist (NC)
John O. Willis
Rivier University (NH)
Ron Dumont
Fairleigh Dickinson University (NJ)

OVERVIEW

School psychologists are typically involved in all aspects of special education where decisions must be made with respect to a child's referral, evaluation, identification, and services. The purpose of this chapter is to assist practitioners in making defensible, ethical decisions within the context of applicable federal regulations and case law. The chapter is intended to provide information directly relevant to the Legal, Ethical, and Professional Practice domain of the National Association of School Psychologists (NASP) *Model for Comprehensive and Integrated School Psychological Services* (NASP, 2010a).

What we have written is not to be construed as offering legal advice. Also, the federal regulations give the states considerable discretion in implementation. Therefore, when confronted with a question about special education law, a school psychologist must consult his or her own state's special education regulations before giving a definitive response.

It is impossible in a chapter of this length to adequately summarize the content of the various federal regulations, much less interpret their applicability to the practice of school psychology in more than a representative fashion. The 2004 Individuals with Disabilities Education Improvement Act (IDEA) is implemented by the 2006 regulations (Assistance to States for the Education of Children With Disabilities and Preschool

Grants for Children With Disabilities) published at 34 Code of Federal Regulations (C.F.R.) Part 300.ff, the Section 504 Regulations at 34 C.F.R. Part 104.ff, and the regulations for the Family Educational Rights and Privacy Act at 34 C.F.R. Part 99.ff. The U.S. Department of Education provides a comprehensive and helpful IDEA website (http://idea.ed.gov). Additional essential references are listed in Tables 31.1 and 31.2.

BEST PRACTICES IN APPLYING LEGAL STANDARDS FOR STUDENTS WITH DISABILITIES

While not wishing to begin on a negative note, failure to understand and adhere to the legal standards imposed by the federal government, the state agencies, and the courts can have adverse consequences for school psychologists and their schools. For example, in the *Forest Grove v. T.A.* (2008, 2009, 2011) court cases, stringing out over 10 years, with one visit to the U.S. Supreme Court and two to the Circuit Court, a precipitating event was a school psychologist's unilateral decision not to test a child for attention deficit hyperactivity disorder because he decided it would not make any difference in the child's eligibility for services. Although the school eventually prevailed, legal costs ran into the millions (e.g., *Forest Grove v. T.A.*, 2011). In rare cases, unethical behavior can even lead to criminal

Table 31.1. Federal Agencies in the United States Department of Education Affecting Decision Making by Special Educators

- *Family Policy Compliance Office (FPCO):* Responsible for implementing and enforcing the Family Educational Rights and Privacy Act (FERPA) and the Protection of Pupil Rights Amendment.

  http://www2.ed.gov/policy/gen/guid/fpco/index.html

- *Office of Special Education and Rehabilitative Services (OSERS):* Has three main branches: special education, vocational rehabilitation, and research. Responsible for drafting and finalizing the regulations implementing IDEA.

  http://www2.ed.gov/about/offices/list/osers/index.html

- *Office of Special Education Programs (OSEP):* Enforcement arm of OSERS. Provides guidance both to individuals and the states and is responsible for monitoring state compliance with the IDEA regulations.

  http://www2.ed.gov/about/offices/list/osers/osep/index.html

- *Office for Civil Rights (OCR):* Separate office under the U.S. Department of Education responsible for implementing and enforcing (among others) Title VI of the Civil Rights Act prohibiting discrimination based on national origin, Title IX of the Education Amendments of 1972 prohibiting discrimination based on sex, and both the Americans with Disabilities Act and regulations implementing Section 504 of the Rehabilitation Act of 1964 prohibiting discrimination based on disability. Parents alleging violations of their child's civil rights may lodge their complaints directly with OCR.

  http://www2.ed.gov/policy/rights/reg/ocr/index.html

---

prosecution (see Rogers, 2006). In that case, a school psychologist allegedly forged special education documents in a vain effort to please her supervisors.

A Basic Principle

IDEA and Section 504 both give eligible children with disabilities the right to a free appropriate public education (FAPE) in the least restrictive environment. FAPE is not explicitly defined in the federal regulations, but since the U.S. Supreme Court ruled in the *Hendrick Hudson Central School District v. Rowley* (1982) case, it has been defined by the courts as an education reasonably calculated to provide nontrivial benefit in accordance with the procedural requirements of IDEA or an educational opportunity equal to that provided to a child who does not have a disability under 504. The application of these standards in any dispute is universally applicable. Even when a school system has complied with parental requests with respect to the provision of services, if it fails to offer those services within the procedural framework established by

Table 31.2. Regulatory and Nonregulatory Resources

Regulatory Resources
- *Family Educational Rights and Privacy Act (FERPA):* Carrying the force of law, these regulations explain the rights of parents of all school children with respect to their educational records. http://www2.ed.gov/policy/gen/reg/ferpa/index.html
- *The 2006 Final Regulations for the Individuals with Disabilities Act (IDEA) of 2004:* Regulations implementing IDEA apply to all public schools in the United States. http://idea.ed.gov/download/finalregulations.pdf
- *Section 504 Regulations:* Regulations explain the rights of all children with disabilities, including those identified under the IDEA. http://idea.ed.gov/download/finalregulations.pdf; http://www2.ed.gov/policy/gen/reg/ferpa/index.html
- *National Association of State Directors of Special Education (NASDSE):* Maintains an updated list of directors and contact links by state. http://www.nasdse.org/MeettheDirectors/tabid/60/Default.aspx

Nonregulatory Resources
- *Wrightslaw:* Parent-friendly website providing an extensive resource of court cases arranged by topic as well as interpretive materials. Offers an array of online references. http://www.wrightslaw.com
- *Equal Employment Opportunity Commission (EEOC):* Charged by Congress with the responsibility for writing rules in the workplace. Definitions and terms are the same as for Section 504 of the Rehabilitation Act.
- *Pennsylvania Training and Technical Assistance Network:* Comprehensive search engine of all Office of Special Education Programs letters from 2000 to present and is easier to use than the Office of Special Education Programs' own search engine. http://www.pattan.net/category/Legal/Osep/?page=1
- *LRP Institutes and Publications:* Extensive library of pamphlets, books, online courses, and conferences. Available for a fee. http://www.specialedconnection.com/LrpSecStoryTool/splash.jsp

---

Congress, it could find itself at a disadvantage in an adversarial dispute. (See *Goleta v. Ordway*, 2002.)

Frequently Asked Questions

School psychologists will in the course of their employment be asked many questions by colleagues. "I don't know, but I will find out" is a defensible response.

This chapter will deal with various topics in the relative order in which they might occur, covering some general topics first, including a parent's due process rights, a very brief review regarding the availability of damages, and when freedom of speech is and is not protected by the courts.

Due Process Rights

What legal remedies can parents invoke when they disagree with a district's decision?

Under both IDEA and 504, parents may appeal a decision on procedural grounds to the state education agency under IDEA or, if alleging a civil rights violation, appeal directly to the Office for Civil Rights under the 504 regulations. Before appealing to state or federal court, parents must exhaust available administrative remedies; for example, a hearing before a due process officer and, if unsatisfactory, then a state appeal of that decision (under IDEA). Optionally, they may avail themselves of state mediation (34 C.F.R. 300.506) if the school also agrees or, in the case of a disputed Individualized Education Program (IEP) and if the state offers it, a facilitated IEP meeting with state assistance. At the very least, parents with children identified under IDEA must agree to a resolution meeting before due process time lines begin to run (§300.510(b)(4)). Section 504 regulations also require schools to provide parents with a dispute resolution process. Those requirements can be met using the same procedures they would use for an IDEA dispute (34 C.F.R. 104.36).

Damages

Under what circumstances can a school psychologist be liable for damages?

Education laws in general would not hold any school employee liable unless his or her actions were so egregious as to offend the public sensibility. But, within the context of education laws affecting children with disabilities, things get a little more complex. School personnel cannot be held liable for an IDEA violation (Wright, 2008) or a Family Educational Rights and Privacy Act (FERPA) violation because neither law

allows for damages. The U.S. Supreme Court ruled that the only penalty available for violating FERPA would be the suspension of federal funds to a school system by the U.S. Department of Education (*Gonzaga Univ. v. Doe*, 2002). But once again, state laws may give parents additional rights not available under federal statute.

However, while still rare, there have been cases brought to the courts under 504 alleging a civil rights violation where parents are alleging that their child has suffered because of "deliberate indifference" on the part of school staff members to the adverse consequences of the school staff members' failure to meet their obligations under 504. The standard of proof is high (e.g., *Hill v. Bradley County School Board*, 2008). However, the number of lawsuits seeking damages from individuals (not just public entities), while still small, is increasing (e.g., *Mark H. v. Hamamoto*, 2010).

Additionally, Title VI of the Civil Rights Act of 1964 (42 U.S.C. § 2000d et seq.) prohibits discrimination against any student based on race, national origin, or sex. If a child is discriminated against based on any of the above, whether by staff or other students, and the administration fails to take prudent and effective action, then the administrators may be held personally liable. It is especially important to distinguish between "normal" bullying (which would be addressed presumably under board policy) and a civil rights violation (Office for Civil Rights, 2010b). If an investigation determines that the victim's civil rights were violated, then the school must take prompt and effective corrective action, documenting that action, to protect both the student from harm and itself from litigation seeking damages. State laws may permit a parent to seek damages alleging physical or mental cruelty (e.g., a case where, among other things, as punishment staff force fed oatmeal mixed with his own vomit to a student with a disability who had an oatmeal allergy; *Witte v. Clark County*, 1999).

Freedom of Speech

When can school psychologists exercise the right to free speech and expect court protection?

Freedom of speech does not end at the school house door, and speaking out on behalf of children's rights is protected by the courts. However, in an adversarial situation, school systems may vigorously assert one of two exceptions to free speech as a defense for dismissing an employee. The first defense would be that the school system would have dismissed the school employee for cause even if the school employee had not engaged in protected speech. The second defense would be that the speech was not protected because it was primarily about the conditions of the school employee's employment, not about the children's welfare or a matter of public interest (*Pickering v. Board of Ed.*, 1968). Even when a plaintiff prevails, the litigation can be lengthy and expensive. For example, Pamela Settlegoode said she was fired in in 2000 for speaking out on behalf of her students, but it took the courts 4 years and a major reversal for the Ninth Circuit to uphold her claim (*Settlegoode v. Portland*, 2004). An example where the second standard was applied to deny claims made by a special education teacher regarding free speech is *Lamb v. Booneville* (2010). In that case, involving a child with autism who had been paddled, the school produced e-mails showing that the teacher had told others that she was mostly upset that the school had not consulted her, not that they had paddled the child.

Screenings and Interventions

What are the school system's obligations under Child Find?

Generally speaking, a school system is responsible for finding, evaluating, and identifying children within its school district, whether they are enrolled in public school, enrolled in private school, or homeless, who are or who may have disabilities. Children with disabilities do not have to fail or be retained to be considered for special education and related services (34 C.F.R. 300.311).

Can a standardized test with national norms be administered for screening purposes, without parental consent, to a student prior to referral to assist in educational planning?

Generally, yes. Screening measures are typically brief, and if used for the purpose of developing educational interventions, parental consent is not required by the federal regulations (34 C.F.R. 300.302). For example, AIMSweb curriculum-based measurements are now nationally normed by grade but are typically used without parental consent to measure student progress in the general education student support team process (34 C.F.R. 300.302; AIMSweb, 2011; Office of Special Education Programs, 2009c). If a school does ask parents for consent, that would imply parents can withhold consent which would also limit general education in its ability to address specific areas of difficulty by providing effective research-based scientific instruction required by the Elementary and Secondary Education Act (ESEA; Pub.L. 89–10, 79 Stat. 27, 20 U.S.C. ch.70) as well as IDEA.

What is a scientific research-based intervention?

The definition of a scientific research-based intervention is taken from ESEA, was repeated in the Preface to

the 2006 Final Regulations, and can be summarized as instruction based on peer-reviewed research involving the "application of rigorous, systematic, and objective procedures to obtain reliable and valid knowledge relevant to education activities and programs" (Federal Register, 71, p. 46576).

Multitiered Interventions

What do the regulations and case law say about the use of response to intervention (RTI) in a problem-solving model?

There are four major points:

- IDEA 2004 and the 2006 Final Regulations permit but do not require the use of a problem-solving model (Section 300.307 of the 2006 Final Regulations). At least 14 states, however, have adopted problem-solving models as their only approved methodology for identifying children with specific learning disabilities for at least some age ranges or academic areas (e.g., reading; Zirkel, n.d.).

- There had been no significant ligation as of 2012 over the use of a problem-solving model whether implemented with professional integrity or not (Zirkel, 2012).

- Interventions are by law to be based wherever possible on scientific, research-based instruction (34 C.F.R. 300.307).

- Neither RTI nor an achievement/ability discrepancy model would in and of itself satisfy the requirements for a comprehensive evaluation (*Federal Register*, p. 46648).

Issues Regarding Parental Consent for an Evaluation

When is a consent considered a consent, and when is it not?

Before assessing a student, a school psychologist always needs to verify the student has a valid and current consent to test. The following are fairly typical scenarios. In each scenario, unless there was a court order terminating the biological parents' rights, the biological parents would have the right to assert their rights at any time.

- The parents of a child living in a group home cannot be located, and the group home parent has signed the initial testing consent. Group home parents may, if the child is a ward of the state, sign for initial evaluations only, but if a parent has not been found after the evaluations are completed, a surrogate parent must be appointed by the school system (Section 300.300, Assistance to States for the Education of Children With Disabilities and Preschool Grants for Children With Disabilities, 2006).

- A guardian ad litem appointed by a court has signed the consent for testing. In this instance, the consent is not valid unless (a) the guardian ad litem has provided the school with a court order giving the guardian the right to make educational decisions or (b) the guardian ad litem has been appointed by the school system as the child's surrogate parent (34 C.F.R. 300.30 (3)).

- The child is a ward of the state, is in a foster home, and a foster parent has signed the testing consent. The consent is valid until or unless the biological parents assert their rights. IDEA gives foster parents all the rights of a birth or adoptive parent unless the foster parents have a conflict of interest or are unwilling to assume those responsibilities, or unless it is otherwise prohibited by state law (34 C.F.R. 300.30).

- The child is a ward of the state and a social worker has signed the consent. The consent would not be valid because IDEA prohibits social workers and others working in any agencies serving the child from serving as surrogate parents, although they may be invited to the IEP team meetings by the school or parent (§ 300.519(d)(2)(i)).

- Consent is signed by a grandparent with whom the child lives. The consent would be valid without any additional documentation. Section 300.30 specifies that "parent" means (in part) "an individual acting in the place of a biological or adoptive parent (including a grandparent, stepparent, or other relative) with whom the child lives, or an individual who is legally responsible for the child's welfare."

May a school ask parental consent to use the parents' insurance to pay for a medical evaluation?

It is permissible to ask, but parents have no obligation to consent. The local education authority must obtain parental consent each time it seeks access to private insurance and must, each time, inform parents that the local education agency must still provide all necessary evaluations at no cost even if parents refuse access (34 C.F.R. 300.154(d)(iv)). Further, the school system must pay the deductible or copay even when the parent does consent to use of the insurance (34 C.F.R. 300.154(d)(ii)). If the parents are receiving public insurance (e.g., Medicaid), 2013 amendments to IDEA allow the school to obtain informed written consent only once; thereafter, the school would be able to use the public insurance as often as needed without getting additional parental consent. The federal amendment requires that the parents be given all their rights in writing before obtaining consent and before using their insurance and again at least once annually thereafter (Methods of Ensuring Services, 2013; Office of Special Education Programs, 2013).

Is consent required before evaluating a child under 504?

Section 504 regulations themselves (see Table 31.1 for the link) do not specifically require consent, but the Office for Civil Rights has always said that consent is required. Their advisory is also silent with respect to the form (written or oral) that consent should take (Office for Civil Rights, 2009). It is, however a well-known principle of general law that if something is not in writing, it did not happen.

If parents revoke consent for services under IDEA as permitted by the 2008 amendments, would the child still be entitled to services under 504?

No. At least since 1996, the Office for Civil Rights has opined that if a parent refuses consent for an IEP, the school has met its obligation to offer FAPE under 504 and is under no obligation to do anything more (Office for Civil Rights, 1996). However, there is nothing to prevent a school system from offering services under 504 to an otherwise qualified child under those circumstances, and in some cases (e.g., providing testing modifications to help meet No Child Left Behind benchmarks) that might also be in the school's best interests.

Under the amended IDEA, may parents withdraw consent for some services while continuing others?

No. The 2008 Amendments to the 2006 Regulations for IDEA (Assistance to States for the Education of Children With Disabilities and Preschool Grants for Children With Disabilities, 2008) do not provide a mechanism for partial withdrawal of consent (Office of Special Education Programs, 2009b). It is all or nothing. Parents may, of course, attempt to modify their child's IEP through mediation or due process.

Issues in Evaluations

A mother says she suspects her child has ADHD and requests a medical evaluation at district expense. Is the local education agency obliged to pay?

If the local education authority or public agency also suspects that a child has an educational disability, then it must provide an appropriate assessment at district expense. If the local education authority does not share in the parent's suspicion, then it must tell the parent, in writing, that it is declining his or her request and provide the parent with due process rights (Office of Special Education and Rehabilitative Services, 1991; Office for Civil Rights, 1992).

If the parents refuse to let the school evaluate their child, can they require the school to pay for an independent education evaluation?

No. Parents would only be entitled to an independent education evaluation at district expense if they disagree with the school's evaluation. The district can impose the same limitations it would set for hiring its own outside evaluators, unless there were no qualified evaluators in that region; in that case, the restrictions would not apply (34 C.F.R. 100.502). A school may defend itself by asserting through due process that its evaluation was appropriate and comprehensive, but the cost of complying is almost always far less than the cost of litigating the matter (34 C.F.R. 300.502).

May a school system use the same procedures it uses under IDEA to evaluate children under 504?

Yes, although it may also establish alternative procedures. One obvious disadvantage would be having to pay for the 504 evaluations out of general education funds. Also, the protections available to school systems under IDEA would not apply if parents had not been provided their IDEA due process rights. That could be problematic, especially if the district did not have clear and defensible guidelines for deciding which process to employ (e.g., making an a priori decision without giving parents their rights that special education was not a consideration could be regarded as a violation of the child's rights). Although not a 504 case per se, Hawaii was sued and received an adverse ruling from the Ninth Circuit because when parents referred their children, the schools sometimes provided an abbreviated evaluation without giving parents their IDEA rights (*Pasatiempo v. Aizawa*, 1996).

Since specific learning disabilities are defined in IDEA and the IDEA Regulations as a disorder in one or more of the basic psychological processes, does that mean a comprehensive evaluation for specific learning disabilities must include an assessment of psychological processes?

Unless your state requires it, an assessment for psychological processing disorders is not required by federal regulation, nor have there been any court cases of which we are aware that would support such assessments as being mandated. The Office of Special Education and Rehabilitative Services in the Preface to the Final Regulations (Assistance to States for the Education of Children With Disabilities and Preschool Grants for Children With Disabilities, 2006, 71 Fed.

Reg., p. 46,541) wrote, "The Department does not believe that an assessment of psychological or cognitive processing should be required in determining whether a child has [a specific learning disorder]. There is no current evidence that such assessments are necessary or sufficient for identifying [a specific learning disorder]. Further, in many cases, these assessments have not been used to make appropriate intervention decisions." If the IEP team determines that an assessment of processing skills is needed to help determine a student's special education needs, IDEA permits the team to request such assessments (Hale et al., 2010).

Evaluating Children With Limited English Proficiency

What legal principles govern the selection of an intellectual assessment when assessing a limited English proficient student?

The Office for Civil Rights investigates and prohibits discrimination based on race, color, or national origin in public schools (Office for Civil Rights, 2000a). IDEA, enforced and monitored by the Office of Special Education Programs, prohibits a child from being classified if the primary determinant of the "disability" is a lack of English proficiency (34 C.F.R. 300.309). Therefore, if a school psychologist used a test that was measuring a construct other than the one for which it was intended (e.g., English skills rather than general ability), that would not only be unethical but potentially a violation of the child's civil rights. In general, we recommend, with some caveats, that school psychologists use the results of a nonverbal measure of intelligence as the best estimate of the ability of a student with limited English proficiency, a recommendation endorsed by some courts (e.g., *Diana v. State Board of Education*, 1970).

Must a limited English proficient learner be tested in his or her native language?

Yes. However, while the language of a limited English proficient child's parents might be his or her native language, for the purpose of assessment, the term *native language* means "the language normally used by the child in the home *or* learning environment" (Assistance to States for the Education of Children With Disabilities and Preschool Grants for Children With Disabilities, 2006, 34 C.F.R. 300.29(a)(2); emphasis added). For a more thorough review of the civil rights held by children who speak English as a second language, we recommend reviewing the archived Office for Civil Rights document on high stakes testing (Office for Civil Rights, 2000b). Also consult state regulations. Some states require school psychologists to have a special certification before assessing children who speak English as a second language.

Eligibility Determinations

Can school psychologists classify students under IDEA?

School psychologists certainly can be part of the entitlement process, but only eligibility groups, composed of qualified professionals and the parent, are authorized to classify students under IDEA (34 C.F.R. 300.306).

May school psychologists diagnose students using the Diagnostic and Statistical Manual *(DSM) to meet 504 requirements?*

Appropriately trained school psychologists may diagnose children using, for example, the DSM (American Psychiatric Association, 2013) criteria. However, under federal regulations, a DSM diagnosis is not required for classification and a DSM diagnosis alone is never sufficient for classification. Classification (sometimes referred to as an eligibility determination or entitlement or identification) is not a diagnosis or an "educational diagnosis." Under the federal regulations, eligibility groups are empowered to classify children and determine if they need special education in order to receive FAPE. Check state regulations to see if the state requires additional members, such as a school psychologist, when a specific learning disorder is being considered. While districts may have a separate process for evaluating children under 504 from that employed under IDEA (Office for Civil Rights, 2009), if a child is evaluated under IDEA there is no reason, even in a district employing alternative processes, that a psychological evaluation completed to determine IDEA eligibility could not be used in determining 504 eligibility if the evaluator provided an appropriate diagnosis. (While federal regulations do not require a specific diagnosis under IDEA, some states may require a diagnosis for classification related to emotional disability or an Other Health Impairment.)

What diagnostic systems may be used in diagnosing a disability under 504?

Neither IDEA nor 504 limits practitioners to any single system. The Equal Employment Opportunity Commission (1997) and the courts have recognized DSM as one important tool (but not the only tool) for diagnosing a disability under the Americans with Disabilities Act/Section 504. We believe that a diagnosis from DSM should be within the competence of most school psychologists and that the level of training required to become proficient need not be as extensive as the level of training needed to prescribe appropriate treatments for those disabilities.

What are the standards to be applied in determining 504 eligibility?

While a much broader range of conditions may be considered a disability under 504 than under IDEA's 13 categories, not all conditions in DSM are disabling. Physicians would ordinarily use the International Classification of Diseases to record their diagnoses, and most diagnoses by physicians do not rise to the level of being substantially limiting over the long term, either (World Health Organization, 1990).

In addition to determining whether a child has a disability, the 504 committee would also have to determine that, as a result of the disability, the child had a substantial limitation in a major life function that could include one (and only one is required) of the following: caring for oneself, performing manual tasks, seeing, hearing, eating, sleeping, walking, standing, lifting, bending, speaking, breathing, learning, reading, concentrating, thinking, communicating, and working. The list is not intended to be exhaustive.

Following passage of the Amendments to the Americans with Disabilities Act in 2008, it is now not necessary to show that a major life function is *severely* limited by the disability to be *substantially* limiting. It is also not permissible to consider mitigating factors in determining whether a child is eligible for 504 protections (although they may be considered in determining what accommodations are needed). A disabling condition that is both transitory (expected to last for less than 6 months) and minor would not entitle a student to 504 protections, but an impairment that was transitory but major or an episodic condition expected to last for more than 6 months that was substantially limiting when not in remission could be entitling. Children who are only regarded as having a disability under the third prong of the definition of a disability (regarded as having a disability when the child does not) would not be eligible for services but would be eligible for civil rights protections. However, a child with a record of a disability (often referred to as the second prong, with the first prong being a current diagnosis) that continues to have effects substantially limiting the child in a major life function could be eligible for both civil rights protections and regular or special education and related aids and services (Office for Civil Rights, 2012a).

Is every child who is exited from special education automatically eligible for accommodations under 504?

Children who are exited from special education are not automatically eligible for services under 504. However, the Amendments to the Americans with Disabilities Act of 2008 made it a lot easier for a child exiting special educational services to establish eligibility for general education accommodations under 504.

Congress wrote in the Americans with Disabilities Act Amendment Act of 2008, "Congress finds that the current Equal Employment Opportunity Commission ADA regulations defining the term 'substantially limits' as 'significantly restricted' are inconsistent with congressional intent, by expressing too high a standard" (Sec. 2, (a)(8)).

The most common disability in schools, of course, is specific learning disability. In a footnote to House Report 110-730 on the Americans with Disabilities Act of 2008 (Final Equal Employment Opportunity Commission Regulations for the ADA, 2011) is the following:

> The Committee also seeks to clarify how the bill's concept of "materially restricts" should be applied for individuals with specific learning disabilities who are frequently substantially limited in the major life activities of learning, reading, writing, thinking, or speaking. In particular, some courts have found that students who have reached a high level of academic achievement are not to be considered individuals with disabilities under the [Americans with Disabilities Act], as such individuals may have difficulty demonstrating substantial limitation in the major life activities of learning or reading relative to "most people." When considering the condition, manner, or duration in which an individual with a specific learning disability performs a major life activity, it is critical to reject the assumption that an individual who performs well academically or otherwise cannot be substantially limited in activities such as learning, reading, writing, thinking, or speaking. As such, the Committee rejects the findings in *Price v. National Board of Medical Examiners*. (76 Fed. Reg., p. 16981)

The DSM-5 diagnostic criteria (pp. 66–74) for a specific learning disorder may trigger rights to services under 504 even when a child does not meet a state's criteria for having a specific learning disability. That would be especially true in schools still using an IQ/achievement discrepancy methodology because diagnosis under the DSM-5 is based primarily on substantial interindividual differences based on normed or criterion referenced tests and a comprehensive evaluation including documentation of a child's historical response to appropriate educational instruction. While the DSM-5 excludes children with intelligence in the intellectually disabled range (as well as children whose problems are better explained by a lack of instruction), it defines "normal" levels of intelligence as being above 70, plus or minus 5 points. "If there is an indication that another diagnosis could account for the difficulties learning keystone academic skills … specific learning disorder should not be diagnosed" (p. 74). A few states are also requiring documentation of deficits in psychological processing disorders for use in determining specific learning disorder eligibility under the IDEA, but the DSM-5 says explicitly that for a diagnosis of a specific learning disorder, testing for cognitive processing is not required. Nevertheless, a DSM-5 diagnosis would still require a comprehensive evaluation. Although the DSM-5 does provide guidelines for diagnosticians to rate the severity of the disability as moderate or severe (with differing recommendations for treatment intervention), it should always be remembered that only a 504 Committee composed of people knowledgeable about the student is authorized to determine if a diagnosed disability is substantially limiting that individual to such an extent that accommodations or other services are required.

If achievement test scores are used, the DSM-5 requires academic achievement "at least 1.5 standard deviations [SD] below the population mean for age" for the "greatest diagnostic certainty," but admits that thresholds are "to a large extent arbitrary" and allows for, "on the basis of clinical judgment, a more lenient threshold … (e.g., 1.0–2.5 SD below the population mean for age), when learning difficulties are supported by converging evidence" from other sources (p. 69).

Under 504, is a child with a disability entitled only to reasonable accommodations from the school, or is the child entitled to FAPE?

"Reasonable accommodations" are what must be provided in a work environment, but the Office for Civil rights has long held that children in public schools are entitled to FAPE irrespective of cost (34 C.F.R. 104.33). One significant difference between IDEA and 504 is that, in order to be eligible for IDEA protections, a child must demonstrate that he or she needs specially designed instruction (special education). Under 504, a child with a disability would be eligible for accommodations, related services, special education, or even a residential placement if needed to receive FAPE if he or she had a substantial limitation of a major life function (Conforming Amendments to the Regulations Governing Nondiscrimination on the Basis of Race, Color, National Origin, Disability, Sex, and Age Under the Civil Rights Restoration Act of 1987, 2000).

Should a child diagnosed with an oppositional disorder or conduct disorder (i.e., as socially maladjusted) be excluded from consideration in the category of serious emotional disturbance?

No. A diagnosis reflecting social maladjustment is not sufficient for classification, but neither is it exclusionary. If a child meets the criteria set forth in the federal definition, and if as a result needs special education, then the child can be classified even if he or she has been provided with a DSM diagnosis of a conduct disorder or oppositional disorder (34 C.F.R. 300.8; *Springer v. Fairfax*, 1998). If a child meets the other criteria in 34 C.F.R. 300.8 (4), whether he or she also has a social maladjustment would be irrelevant to the eligibility decision. Additionally, the Office for Civil Rights (1989) has said that social maladjustment could establish eligibility under 504 if a child established it was a mental condition that was substantially limiting him or her in a major life function such as learning. FAPE as defined by the 504 regulations is sometimes described in the literature as requiring schools to level the playing field, but more specifically FAPE requires the school to provide services that meet the educational needs of a child with a disability that are as adequate as services provided to children without disabilities (Office for Civil Rights, 2010c).

If a student is functioning at grade level academically, can he or she be excluded automatically from special education consideration?

No. IDEA regulations explicitly state that a child does not need to fail or be retained in order to qualify for services. "Each State must ensure that FAPE is available to any individual child with a disability who needs special education and related services, even though the child has not failed or been retained in a course or grade" (34 C.F.R. 100.101). Even if that child does not need specially designed instruction, he or she could still be eligible under 504 for other accommodations. (See Table 31.2 for a link to the 504 regulations.)

IEPs, 504 Plans, Related Services

Although parents may file a due process complaint over virtually any decision with which they disagree, the topic we have seen most frequently disputed is whether or not a school system has provided a student with FAPE in the least restrictive environment. Since the U.S. Supreme Court in 1982 (*Hendrick Hudson v. Rowley*) defined FAPE as an IEP developed in accordance with the regulatory procedural requirements that provided a child with a reasonable expectation of benefit, procedural errors in developing an IEP (e.g., changing a child's placement without parental participation or writing an IEP that has no measureable goals) may be regarded as fatal errors by

a judge. Other procedural errors (e.g., a time line violation) resulting in no harm to the child's education will usually be dismissed, but deficiencies in the IEP or its development, including procedural deficiencies, will be regarded with less tolerance by administrative hearing officers and judges.

Development of IEPs

If an IEP team determines that a child identified as having a speech learning impairment needs reading or written language services in a resource room from a specific language disability teacher, does the team have to reevaluate the child to identify the child as having a specific learning disability?

Not if the state regards a speech or language impairment as a disability, not just a related service. Services are not determined by the child's category of disability, but by the needs arising out of that child's disability (*Federal Register*, p. 46587).

If a child is initially identified as having a specific learning disability in reading, and 2 years later the IEP team wants to add another goal area (e.g., math), must the child be reevaluated and a severe discrepancy between intelligence and mathematics documented?

No. Once a child has been found eligible, if the team determines the need for additional special educational services, the team with parental participation need only modify the IEP to reflect that fact (Office of Special Education Programs, 2008). Once identified, a child's needs, not the label, always drive the IEP.

If one parent requests that a child be withdrawn from special education, and the other parent requests services be continued, whose request must the school honor?

The school must comply with the request from the parent who revokes consent for special educational services. The revocation must be in writing. Since it is not a violation of IDEA for a parent to revoke consent, due process procedures may not be invoked by the other parent or the school. However, the parent may use whatever other legal processes are available for dispute resolution between parents that their state allows. Either parent may subsequently re-refer the child for evaluation. The evaluation would be treated as an initial evaluation (not as a reevaluation), with all the initial evaluation requirements (Office of Special Education Programs, 2009a). Of course, the IEP team could choose to adopt previous screenings and/or evaluations if the screening or evaluations were sufficiently current before requesting new testing.

If a student with an IQ in the intellectual disability range has a severe discrepancy between ability and achievement, is he or she automatically excluded from consideration in the specific learning disability category?

Learning problems that are primarily the result of intellectual disability may not be classified as being a specific learning disability. However, not all children with intelligence scores in the range of intellectual disability qualify as having an intellectual disability based on adaptive behavior scores. Those children would not be excluded from consideration in schools using a discrepancy methodology unless state regulations imposed a higher burden (e.g., a minimum IQ score of 80). We want to emphasize that regardless of label, a child with an intellectual disability, for example, may have the same need for, and the same expectation of benefit from, a scientific research-based instructional intervention (e.g., a structured phonemics program) as a child classified as having a specific learning disability. Services and placements must not be predicated solely upon the category of disability (*Federal Register*, pp. 46540, 46549, 46588). Additionally, all evaluations must be sufficiently comprehensive to identify all of a child's special educational and related service needs, whether commonly linked to the category of disability or not (34 C.F.R. 300.304 (c) (6)). An evaluation composed solely of screenings and evaluations required by a state under a particular category will not always meet that standard.

Must a school psychologist attend IEP team meetings when a psychological evaluation has been administered?

Federal regulations do not impose such a burden. As the Office of Special Education and Rehabilitative Services explained in the Preface to the 2006 Final Regulations, "the person most qualified to interpret the instructional implications of the test results may not be the diagnostician who evaluated the child" (*Federal Register*, p. 46670). However, an eligibility group for a child suspected of having a specific learning disability must include someone qualified to conduct individual examinations, and the regulations specifically allow for that individual to be a school psychologist, speech pathologist, or reading teacher (34 C.F.R. 300.308).

When a child transfers from one school to another with an IEP but an incomplete folder, may the school provide the child with comparable services while updating the folder?

It must. School psychologists should be aware that even if they have been asked to update the folder with new evaluations, the school must provide the student with services comparable to those specified in the student's previous IEP until it has written a new one (34 C.F.R. 300.323). The requirement to provide comparative services applies equally to children transferring either within or from outside the state until the school has completed its evaluation and either

developed a new IEP or determined the child does not qualify (34 C.F.R. 300.323).

Who decides if a person or persons invited by the school or parent to an IEP team meeting has knowledge or expertise relevant to the child's education?

Regardless of who does the inviting, the party issuing the invitation determines whether or not those invited has relevant knowledge or expertise (34 C.F.R. 300.321).

A parent brings a lawyer to an IEP team meeting. As a result of the negotiations, the IEP team adopts most of the parent's recommendations. Is the parent entitled to reimbursement for the attorney fees?

No. Parents are entitled to attorney fees only as a result of a hearing officer or judge's enforceable decision. IDEA regulations (34 C.F.R. 300.502) allow for prevailing parties to obtain attorney fees, and the legal definition of a "prevailing party" is "the winner of a lawsuit." So when lawyers are present, IEP teams may consider parental requests without any fear that they might incur legal costs for the district by acceding to their requests (*Buckhannon Board and Care Home, Inc. v. West Virginia Dept. of Health and Human Resources*, 2001).

A child who was limited in English proficiency was identified as having a language impairment based on a recommendation by the speech/language pathologist. Can the IEP team provide the student with special education in reading and writing?

Yes. However, the team must still consider whether the reading and writing deficits were primarily the result of the identified disability and not the result of English being a second language. As we noted previously, the Office for Civil Rights investigates discrimination complaints based on national origin under Title VI of the Civil Rights Act of 1964. In writing the 2004 amendments to IDEA, Congress expressed concern that "Studies have documented apparent discrepancies in the levels of referral and placement of limited English proficient children in special education." And "such discrepancies pose a special challenge for special education in the referral of, assessment of, and provision of services for, our Nation's students from non-English language backgrounds" (20 U.S.C. 1400 (c)(11)). In response to that concern, Congress prohibited schools from classifying children as having a disability when the primary cause of their learning problems was that their native language was not English (34 C.F.R. 300.306). School psychologists should in their reports emphasize the legal responsibilities of the eligibility groups and IEP teams to protect those rights, including the right to have non-special education services sufficient to provide them with sufficient language skills to participate meaningfully in the school's programs (Office for Civil Rights, 1991).

Is parent participation required in determining eligibility or developing a plan under 504?

The 504 regulations and Office for Civil Rights frequently asked questions (Office for Civil Rights, 2009, 2012b) do not include such a requirement. However, it is recommended if only to ensure that the district can show it has provided the child with a comprehensive evaluation.

Is a medical diagnosis enough or required to classify a child as being eligible under 504?

No, students are entitled under 504 to a comprehensive evaluation provided by the school district (Office for Civil Rights, 2009). It would be up to the 504 committee composed of people knowledgeable about the child to determine if the disability caused a substantial limitation in a major life function triggering the right to services (34 C.F.R. 104.35(4)). A medical diagnosis could be helpful, but it is insufficient evidence for classification, nor is a medical always required, even for diagnoses of attention deficit hyperactive disorder. If the committee requires a medical evaluation, then that evaluation must be provided by the school district at no cost to the parents (34 C.F.R. 104.35(4)).

Related Services and / or Accommodations

If a child with a disability needs only a related service in order to receive FAPE, can he or she still be identified under IDEA?

Usually the answer is no. However, if the related services and other accommodations rise to the level of specially designed instruction, classification under IDEA could be considered. The definition of special education (specially designed instruction) in the IDEA regulations says: "*Specially designed instruction* means adapting, as appropriate to the needs of an eligible child under this part, the content, methodology, *or* delivery of instruction" (34 C.F.R. 300.39; emphasis added). Usually, however, a 504 team would be convened to determine the child's non-special educational need for services.

Is there any limitation on the costs a school system must incur if it is determined that a related service (e.g., hiring a full-time nurse) is needed in order to provide a child FAPE?

Not according to the U.S. Supreme Court. In *Cedar Rapids v. Garret* (1999), the U.S. Supreme Court ruled that cost was not an appropriate standard to be applied and ordered Cedar Rapids to provide the child in question with a full-time nurse during school hours.

What medically related services are a school system not required to provide?

A school system is not required to provide medical services that can only be provided by a physician, except of course for medical evaluations that are needed to establish eligibility and a child's need for special education or related services. One other area in which a school would not be responsible for providing medically related services would be the monitoring of surgically implanted devices, specifically cochlear implants (34 C.F.R. 300.34).

Reevaluations

May a special education administrator lawfully require a school system to retest children every 3 years and then bar services to those classified as having a specific learning disability when a severe achievement-ability discrepancy can no longer be documented?

No. An administrator may recommend that children be formally evaluated every 3 or 6 years, but only the IEP team is authorized to request additional testing if in its judgment additional testing is needed to determine eligibility or present levels of performance (34 C.F.R. 300.305). Even when an IEP team is following a supervisor's suggestion in recommending formal testing, written parental consent would be required. Of course, in a school system using an RTI methodology, the presence or absence of an ability-achievement discrepancy would be irrelevant. In any situation where district mandates are resulting in the diminution of parental or children's rights, those practices should be brought to the attention of one's supervisor (Standard IV, NASP, 2010b). Where conflicts between practice and law arise, we recommend documenting those perceived conflicts to a supervisor in writing, with a copy kept in one's personal file.

Is a reevaluation required every 3 years even if an IEP team and parents do not think it is needed?

Under federal regulations, if the parents and school agree in writing that it is unnecessary, then it need not be conducted; however, some states require the triennial evaluation regardless, so check the state's regulations. All reevaluations will not require new testing, of course, if the IEP team determines it has sufficient information, after reviewing previous evaluations, classroom observations, and current classroom performance, to determine the child's present levels of performance and that the child continues to have a disability and still needs special education (34 C.F.R. 300.305).

If a child was originally identified using a discrepancy methodology, but is reevaluated in a school using an RTI methodology, what factors should the IEP team consider in determining continuing eligibility?

The answer to this question does not hinge on what methodology was used or is currently being used by the school. The Office of Special Education and

Rehabilitative Services advised the states in the Preface to the 2006 Final Regulations:

> Obviously, the group should consider whether the child's instruction and overall special education program have been appropriate as part of this process. If the special education instruction has been appropriate and the child has not been able to exit special education, this would be strong evidence that the child's eligibility needs to be maintained. (Federal Register, p. 46648)

Do high school students identified as eligible for special education need to be reevaluated before graduating?

Not if they are graduating with a regular diploma or are aging out of the program (i.e., exceeding the maximum age for eligibility in the state regulations). However, if the student is receiving a certificate other than a regular diploma, then the school must reevaluate the student as the student retains the right to FAPE until he or she ages out of eligibility (34 C.F.R. 300.305). Sometimes parents ask the school to reevaluate their child in order for the child to qualify for 504 accommodations in a postsecondary institution. Schools are not prohibited from providing evaluations for postsecondary services, but neither are they required to do so (*Federal Register*, p. 46644). When a student graduates with a regular diploma, the school must provide the student with "a summary of the child's academic achievement and functional performance, which shall include recommendations on how to assist the child in meeting the child's postsecondary goals" (34 C.F.R. 300.305 (e)).

Is a reevaluation required before exiting a child from a special education program?

Yes. Both the 2006 IDEA regulations (34 C.F.R. 300.305) and the 504 regulations (34 C.F.R. 104.35) require a reevaluation before exiting a student, except, under IDEA, when graduating with a diploma or exceeding the maximum state age for eligibility (see above). We would usually recommend as best practice that the IEP team request some additional assessment be conducted, with informed written parental consent, to verify that the child's present levels of performance justify exiting the child. Even if standardized assessment and grade-level testing both confirm performance within the average range, the team should also consider whether the child would need to have special educational supports continued in order to maintain that progress or whether the student could still qualify for continued services under 504.

Special Case: Private School and Home Schooled Students

What are the rights of private school children to services?

The public schools have the same obligation to evaluate parentally placed private school children suspected of disabilities as they would to children who were enrolled in public school. Private school students do not, however, have a right to FAPE or an IEP. They do however have a right to a service plan if the services provided by the public school system using a proportion of federal funds would meet their needs. Parents do not have due process rights (34 C.F.R. 300.138), but they may appeal to the state education agency if they believe the school system did not meet its obligations during Child Find in collaboratively developing its plan for services (34 C.F.R. 300.140). We also recommend reviewing the Office of Special Education Programs (2006) topic brief regarding parentally placed private school students when FAPE is not an issue.

Educational Records: School Responsibilities

Are psychological test protocols (record forms) used by the school psychologist or other school-based assessors considered educational records?

Yes, and under FERPA they may be inspected and reviewed by parents. State statutes may add to those rights.

Can information regarding a child's disability be placed in the child's cumulative record?

Yes. Under FERPA, cumulative records enjoy the same confidentiality protections as special education records.

Do parents have to give written consent for special educational records to be transferred to another school system in which the student is enrolling?

No. Section 300.323 of the 2006 Final Regulations requires local educational agencies to request special education records and requires schools from which the student transferred to provide those records. FERPA (Section 99.31) allows schools to transmit educational records without written parental consent to any other school in which a child seeks to enroll, intends to enroll, or has already enrolled. Schools must publish an annual notice that includes, among other things, the fact that they forward school records to schools in which students intend to enroll. Schools must make reasonable efforts to notify (not ask permission from) parents when they forward records and must offer to provide copies of the records that were forwarded. Schools may not withhold special education records needed to determine a student's appropriate placement because the student has debts outstanding.

Does IDEA provide protections regarding the destruction of records in addition to what are provided by FERPA?

Yes. IDEA requires that special education records that are no longer needed for the provision of educational services must be destroyed at the parent's request. Also, schools must inform parents before destroying special educational records the school believes are no longer needed, a right not afforded parents under FERPA (34 C.F.R. 300.624). We would recommend as best practice retaining special education records for at least 3 years after a child exits from a special education program, as those records may be necessary for auditing purposes and also could be very important in any future legal proceeding. However, state laws and regulations would be controlling.

Do parents have a right to copies of a psychological or psychoeducational report?

IDEA gives parents the right to inspect and review any educational records relevant to their child before any IEP team meeting, including any existing educational reports (34 C.F.R. 300.316). IDEA (34 C.F.R. 300.306) also requires schools to provide parents with copies of the evaluation report and documentation regarding the determination of eligibility. Schools are not required to provide copies unless that would result in the parents being unable to access the information. The team's evaluation report is not the same as the individual psychological or psychoeducational evaluations (which in some states may be attached to the evaluation report). Refer to the state for guidance regarding what must be included.

Authority of School Personnel in Suspensions/Expulsions

How many days may a child with a disability be suspended without a manifestation hearing and without receiving services?

Ten consecutive days or 10 cumulative days when there is a pattern of suspensions because the behaviors causing the suspensions were substantially similar (Section 500.530 of 2006 Final Regulations).

What are the standards to be applied in determining whether or not behavior governed by the school's student code of conduct was a manifestation of the child's disability?

The child's behavior may be found to be a manifestation of the child's disability "(i) If the conduct in question was caused by, or had a direct and substantial relationship to, the child's disability; or (ii) If the conduct in question was the direct result of the [local educational agency's] failure to implement the IEP" (34 C.F.R. 300.530). While normally a manifestation hearing would not be required until a child had

been suspended for 10 consecutive days or, if resulting in a change of placement, 10 cumulative days, state rules may impose an additional burden.

If a student has a 504 plan and not an IEP, is a manifestation hearing still required before suspending the child long term?

Yes. The U.S. Supreme Court decision in *Honig v. Doe* (1988) requiring a manifestation hearing before a long-term suspension that was subsequently incorporated into the IDEA regulations applied to all children with disabilities. The Office for Civil Rights also reiterated that principle as recently as 2010, when it ruled that a principal in Springfield, IL, mistakenly believed a child being served under 504 did not merit a manifestation hearing because he had no IEP (Office for Civil Rights, 2010a). One difference between 504 and IDEA is that if the behavior was not a manifestation of the child's disability under 504, then the school system can suspend or expel with no services. Under IDEA, the school must still provide the child with services enabling the child to progress toward meeting the IEP objectives and to participate in the general curriculum while in another setting (34 C.F.R. 300.560, 2 (d)(i)).

When, if ever, would a bus suspension count toward the 10 days of suspension allowed by federal law?

Bus suspensions do not count unless bus transportation is written into the IEP as a related service or if as a result of the bus suspension the child was unable to participate in the general curriculum, receive services specified in the IEP, and/or participate in activities with general education students to the same extent as she or he had previously.

A child with a disability commits an unlawful act that is a manifestation of his or her disability while in school. May the principal notify law enforcement?

Yes. Section 300.535 of the 2006 IDEA regulations explicitly allows school administrators to report crimes to law enforcement.

What is "stay put"?

For a school-age child, "stay put" refers to the right of a child with a disability to stay put in his or her present placement when a parent is contesting his or her long term suspension or expulsion or a change in placement. If a child with an IDEA classification is suspended for weapons, drug, or incidents involving serious injury, school administrators can, through an IEP team meeting, place the child for up to 45 days in an alternative placement (34 C.F.R. 300.532). "Stay put" does not apply to children who transfer from a Part C program, early intervention services for infants and toddlers with disabilities (birth to 3 years of age), to a Part B program, services for school-age children (ages

3–22). The Office of Special Education and Rehabilitative Services has said that when a child ages out of a Part C program, that child no longer has a current educational placement (*Federal Register*, p. 46709).

SUMMARY

The conscientious application of legal standards for students with disabilities is a matter of best practice, ethics, and, of course, law. This chapter very briefly presents, along with helpful Internet links, some of the laws, regulations, and court cases most relevant to school psychology practice with children with disabilities and discusses the implications of those laws, regulations, and cases. However, best practice and prudence dictate that we download and save our own copies of ever-changing federal and state laws and regulations, update our copies whenever laws or regulations change, refer frequently to our copies, and never trust anyone else's interpretation (even those of our supervisors or of the authors of this chapter) without personally verifying the actual law or regulation. This chapter is not intended or able to offer legal advice.

This chapter provides as much information as possible about current federal laws and regulations, including IDEA, the Americans with Disabilities Act Amendment Act of 2008, Section 504 of the Rehabilitation Act of 1964, and FERPA. However, federal laws and regulations will change, state laws and regulations may expand rights of students and parents and obligations imposed on schools, and court cases may alter the legal interpretation of the laws. Also provided are links to key federal agencies, including the Office of Special Education and Rehabilitative Services, Office of Special Education Programs, Office for Civil Rights, and Family Policy Compliance Office. Those websites will help school psychologists stay up to date with regulations and official policies.

Professionals, including school psychologists, serving children through special education must continuously update their knowledge base to make defensible decisions as specific situations and questions arise in their practice. The basic references listed in this chapter are among the essential tools school psychologists can rely upon.

AUTHOR NOTE

This chapter is not intended to provide legal advice. Special education law is always changing. Decisions by one court may be overruled by another, and both state and federal regulations may be amended by publication in the *Federal Register* or by state departments of public instruction at any time. The states additionally have the burden of writing regulations to implement the federal law and may (and sometimes do) add additional rights to those provided parents by IDEA. It is the reader's responsibility to remain current with state regulations as well as with federal requirements.

REFERENCES

AIMSweb. (2011). *National norms technical information.* Retrieved from http://www.aimsweb.com/wp-content/uploads/AIMSweb-National-Norms-Technical-Documentation.pdf

American Psychiatric Association. (2013). *Diagnostic and statistical manual of mental disorders* (5th ed.). Washington, DC: Author.

Americans with Disabilities Act Amendment Act. (2008). 42 U.S.C. § 12101 *et seq.*, 47 U.S.C. § 225 and 611.

Assistance to States for the Education of Children With Disabilities and Preschool Grants for Children With Disabilities, 34 C.F.R. Parts 300 and 301. (2006). (IDEA Final Regulations). Retrieved from http://idea.ed.gov/download/finalregulations.pdf

Assistance to States for the Education of Children With Disabilities and Preschool Grants for Children With Disabilities. 73 Fed. Reg. 73,006-73,029 (proposed Dec. 1, 2008) (to be codified at 34 CFR pt. 300). Retrieved from http://www.gpo.gov/fdsys/pkg/FR-2008-12-01/pdf/E8-28175.pdf

Buckhannon Board & Care Home, Inc. v. West Virginia Dept. of Health and Human Resources 532 U.S. 598. (2001).

Cedar Rapids v. Garrett F., 526 U.S. 66. (1999). Retrieved from http://scholar.google.com/scholar_case?case=13901710157337917845&hl=en&as_sdt=2&as_vis=1&oi=scholarr

Conforming Amendments to the Regulations Governing Nondiscrimination on the Basis of Race, Color, National Origin, Disability, Sex, and Age Under the Civil Rights Restoration Act of 1987; Final Rule, 65 Fed. Reg. 68,049-68,057 (proposed Nov. 13, 2000) (to be codified at 34 CFR pts. 100, 104, 106, and 110). Retrieved from http://www2.ed.gov/legislation/FedRegister/finrule/2000-4/111300a.html

Diana v. State Board of Education, CA 70 RFT (N.D. Cal. 1970)

Equal Employment Opportunity Commission. (1997). *EEOC enforcement guidance: Americans with Disabilities Act and psychiatric disabilities.* Washington, DC: Author. Retrieved from http://www.eeoc.gov/policy/docs/psych.html

Equal Employment Opportunity Commission. (2011). *Title: PART 1630: Regulations to implement the equal employment provisions of the Americans with Disabilities Act context: Title 29: Labor. Subtitle B: Regulations relating to labor.* Washington, DC: Author. Retrieved from http://www.gpo.gov/fdsys/pkg/CFR-2011-title29-vol4/xml/CFR-2011-title29-vol4-part1630.xml

Family Educational Rights and Privacy Act. (2009). 20 U.S.C. § 1232g. Retrieved from http://www.law.cornell.edu/cfr/text/34/99

Family Education Rights and Privacy Act Regulations. 34 C.F.R. pt 99. (2009). Retrieved from http://www2.ed.gov/policy/gen/guid/fpco/pdf/ferparegs.pdf

Final Equal Employment Opportunity Commission Regulations for the ADA, 76 Fed. Reg. 16,977 (proposed Mar. 25, 2011) (to be codified at 29 C.F.R. 1630). Retrieved from http://federalregister.gov/a/2011-6056

Forest Grove v. T.A., 523 F.3d 1078 (9th Cir. 2008), aff'd, 129 S. Ct. 2484. (2009). aff'd No. 10-35022 D.C. No. 3:04-cv-00331-MO (9th Cir. 2011). Retrieved from http://www.wrightslaw.com/law/caselaw/11/9th.forest.grove.ta-2.pdf

Goleta v. Ordway, 248 F.Supp.2d 936 (C. D. Calif, 2002). Retrieved from http://www.wrightslaw.com/law/caselaw/2003/ca.goleta.ordway.damages.pdf

Gonzales v. National Board of Medical Examiners, 225 F.3d 620 (6th Cir. 2000)). Retrieved from http://law.justia.com/cases/federal/appellate-courts/F3/225/620/499816

Hale, J., Alfonso, V., Berninger, V., Bracken, B., Christo, C., Clark, E., ... Yalof, J. (2010). Critical issues in response-to-intervention, comprehensive evaluation, and specific learning disabilities identification and intervention: An expert white paper consensus. *Learning Disabilities Quarterly, 33,* 223–236.

Hendrick Hudson Central School District v. Rowley, 458 U.S. 176 (1982). Retrieved from http://www.law.cornell.edu/supremecourt/text/458/176

Hill v. Bradley County School Board, No. 07-6502 (6th Cir., Sept. 30, 2008). Retrieved from http://www.ca6.uscourts.gov/opinions.pdf/08a0585n-06.pdf

Honig v. Doe, 484 U.S. 305 (1988). Retrieved from http://supreme.justia.com/cases/federal/us/484/305/case.html

House Report 110-730-Part 1. Americans with Disabilities Act Amendments Act. (2008). Retrieved from http://thomas.loc.gov/cgi-bin/cpquery/?&r_n=hr730p1.110&dbname=cp110&sel=DOC&

Lamb v. Booneville School District, Civil Action No. 1:08CV254-SA-JAD (N.D. Mississippi, E. D., 2010). Retrieved from http://www.aaup.org/NR/rdonlyres/E13BCDC0-9A30-44D2-902B-B3F301C9A5F5/0/LambvBooneville.pdf

Mark H. v. Hamamoto, No. 09-15754 (9th Cir., Aug. 26, 2010). Retrieved from http://www.ca9.uscourts.gov/datastore/opinions/2010/08/26/09-15754.pdf

Methods of Ensuring Services, 78 Fed. Reg. 10,525-10,538 (proposed February 14, 2013) (to be codified at 34 C.F.R. pt. 300.154(d)(2)). Retrieved from http://www.bie.edu/cs/groups/xbie/documents/text/idc1-021885.pdf

National Association of School Psychologists. (2010a). *Model for comprehensive and integrated school psychological services.* Bethesda, MD: Author. Retrieved from http://www.nasponline.org/standards/2010standards/2_PracticeModel.pdf

National Association of School Psychologists. (2010b). *Principles for professional ethics.* Bethesda, MD: Author. Retrieved from http://www.nasponline.org/standards/2010standards/1_%20Ethical%20Principles.pdf

Office for Civil Rights. (1989). *Letter of finding to Irvine (CA) school district.* Washington, DC: Author.

Office for Civil Rights. (1991). *Policy update on schools' obligations toward national origin minority students with limited English proficiency.* Washington, DC: Author. Retrieved from http://www2.ed.gov/about/offices/list/ocr/docs/lau1991.html

Office for Civil Rights. (1992). *Letter from Lim. Clarification of school districts' responsibility to evaluate children with attention deficit disorders (ADD).* Washington, DC: Author. Retrieved from http://www.wrightslaw.com/info/add.eval.ocrmemo.htm

Office for Civil Rights. (1996). *Letter to McKethan,* 25 IDELR 295, 296.

Office for Civil Rights. (2000a). *The provision of an equal education opportunity to limited English proficient students.* Washington, DC: Author. Retrieved from http://www.ed.gov/about/offices/list/ocr/eeolep/index.html

Office for Civil Rights. (2000b). *The use of tests for high-stakes decision making for students. A resource guide for educators and policy makers.* Washington, DC: Author. Retrieved from http://www2.ed.gov/offices/OCR/archives/testing/index1.html

Office for Civil Rights. (2009). *Frequently asked questions about Section 504 and the education of children with disabilities.* Washington, DC: Author. Retrieved from http://www2.ed.gov/about/offices/list/ocr/504faq.html

Office for Civil Rights. (2010a). *Springfield School District #186,* 55 IDELR 206. Summary retrieved from http://randychapman.wordpress.com/2011/03/02/remember-that-504-requires-manifestation-determinations-for-students-not-eligible-under-the-idea

Office for Civil Rights. (2010b). *Dear colleague letter.* Retrieved from http://www2.ed.gov/about/offices/list/ocr/letters/colleague-201010.html

Office for Civil Rights. (2010c). *Free appropriate public education for students with disabilities: Requirements under Section 504 of the Rehabilitation Act of 1973.* Washington, DC: Author. Retrieved from http://www2.ed.gov/about/offices/list/ocr/docs/edlite-FAPE504.html

Office for Civil Rights. (2012a). *Dear colleague letter.* Washington, DC: Author. Retrieved from http://www2.ed.gov/about/offices/list/ocr/letters/colleague-201109.html

Office for Civil Rights. (2012b). *Frequently asked questions.* Washington, DC: Author. Retrieved from http://www2.ed.gov/about/offices/list/ocr/docs/dcl-504faq-201109.html

Office of Special Education and Rehabilitative Services. (1991). Joint policy memorandum (ADD). Washington, DC: Author. Retrieved from http://www.wrightslaw.com/law/code_regs/OSEP_Memorandum_ADD_1991.html

Office of Special Education Programs. (2006). *Topic brief: Children enrolled by their parents in private school.* Retrieved from http://idea.ed.gov/explore/view/p/%2Croot%2Cdynamic%2CTopicalBrief%2C5%2C

Office of Special Education Programs. (2008). *Letter to anonymous* Retrieved from http://pattan.net-website.s3.amazonaws.com/files/materials/osep/CY2008/Redactedb060308.pdf

Office of Special Education Programs. (2009a). *Letter to Cox.* Retrieved from http://www2.ed.gov/policy/speced/guid/idea/letters/2009-3/cox082109revocationofconsent3q2009.pdf

Office of Special Education Programs. (2009b). *Non-regulatory guidance on the IDEA Part B supplemental regulations.* Washington, DC: Author.

Office of Special Education Programs. (2009c). *Letter to Torres.* Retrieved from http://www2.ed.gov/policy/speced/guid/idea/letters/2009-2/torres040709eval2q2009.pdf

Office of Special Education Programs. (2011). *Questions and answers on serving children with disabilities placed by their parents in private schools.* Washington, DC: Author. Retrieved from http://idea.ed.gov/explore/view/p/%2Croot%2Cdynamic%2CTopicalArea%2C5%2C

Office of Special Education Programs. (2013). *IDEA Part B final regulations related to parental consent to access public benefits or insurance*. Washington, DC: Author. Retrieved from http://www2.ed.gov/policy/speced/reg/idea/part-b/idea-part-b-parental-consent--one-pager.doc

Pasatiempo v. Aizawa, No. 94-17092 (9th Cir., Dec. 9, 1996). Retrieved from http://caselaw.findlaw.com/us-9th-circuit/1279721.html

Pickering v. Board of Ed. of Township High School Dist. 205, Will Cty., 391 US 563 (1968). Retrieved from http://scholar.google.com/scholar_case?case=16997195768089298466&q=pickering+v.+the+board+of+education&hl=en&as_sdt=4000000002&as_vis=1

Rogers, C. (2006, August 31). D.A. will charge P.S. 276 psychologist for forgery, falsifying school records. *Canarsie Courier*. Retrieved from http://www.canarsiecourier.com/news/2006-08-31/TopStories/013.html

Section 504 of the Rehabilitation Act of 1973 29 U.S.C. § 794; 34 C.F.R. Part 104.

Settlegoode v. Portland School District, No. 02-35260 (9th Cir., April 5, 2004). Retrieved from http://www.wrightslaw.com/law/caselaw/04/9th.settlegoode.portland.htm

Springer v. Fairfax County School Board, 134 F.3d 659, 664, 27 IDELR 367 (4th Cir. 1998). Retrieved from http://scholar.google.com/scholar_case?case=5196716307127639252&hl=en&as_sdt=2&as_vis=1&oi=scholarr

Title VI of the Civil Rights Act of 1964 42 U.S.C. §§ 2000d - 2000d-7. Retrieved from http://www.justice.gov/crt/about/cor/coord/titlevistat.php

Witte v. Clark County, No. 98-16351 (9th Cir., Dec. 2, 1999). Retrieved from http://www.wrightslaw.com/law/caselaw/9th.witte.clarkco.nv.htm

World Health Organization. (1990). *International classification of diseases* (10th rev.). Geneva, Switzerland: Author. Retrieved from http://www.who.int/classifications/icd/en/

Wright, P. W. D. (2008). *Damages* Retrieved from http://www.wrightslaw.com/info/damag.index.htm

Zirkel, P. A. (n.d.). *The legal dimension of RTI: Part I. The basic building blocks*. Washington, DC: RTI Action Network. Retrieved from http://rtinetwork.org/learn/ld/the-legal-dimension-of-rti-part-i-the-basic-building-blocks

Zirkel, P. A. (2012). *A national update of caselaw 1998 to the present under the IDEA and Section 504/A.D.A.* Alexandria, VA: National Association of State Directors of Special Education. Retrieved from http://www.nasdse.org/LinkClick.aspx?fileticket=HVYx4RH8nOE%3D&tabid=36

32 Best Practices in Ethical School Psychological Practice

Susan Jacob
Central Michigan University

OVERVIEW

The decisions made by school psychologists in their professional roles have an impact on the lives of children and families. To build and maintain public trust in school psychologists, it is essential for every school psychologist to be sensitive to the ethical components of his or her work, knowledgeable of broad ethical principles and standards of professional conduct, and committed to a proactive stance in ethical thinking and conduct. (Portions of this chapter were adapted with permission from Armistead, Williams, & Jacob, 2011; Jacob, 2008; and Jacob, Decker, & Hartshorne, 2011.)

Two codes of ethics provide guidance to school psychologists in their ethical decision making. The American Psychological Association (APA) *Ethical Principles of Psychologists and Code of Conduct* (APA, 2010) was developed for psychologists with training in diverse specialty areas. The National Association of School Psychologists (NASP) *Principles for Professional Ethics* (NASP, 2010b) was developed to specifically address ethical issues associated with the provision of school psychological services. These codes of ethics serve to protect the public by educating professionals about the parameters of appropriate conduct and by providing a foundation for principled, ethically sound decision making. The codes also provide guidelines for adjudicating complaints (Bersoff & Koeppl, 1993; Koocher & Keith-Spiegel, 2008). In addition, because the codes of ethics of psychologists can now be accessed using the Internet, they increasingly serve to educate the public and recipients of services about the parameters of expected professional conduct by school psychologists (Bowser, 2009).

In joining NASP or APA, members agree to abide by these associations' codes of ethics. Additionally, school psychologists who are members of the National School Psychology Certification System are bound to abide by the NASP code of ethics. School psychologists are well advised to be familiar with both the NASP and APA codes of ethics, whether or not they are members of those associations. Trainees and practitioners may be expected to know and abide by both the NASP and APA codes of ethics in their work settings (Flanagan, Miller, & Jacob, 2005). Furthermore, professional ethics is identified as a foundational domain (Legal, Ethical, and Professional Practice) that permeates all aspects of the delivery of services in the NASP *Model for Comprehensive and Integrated School Psychological Services* (Practice Model; NASP, 2010a). Most important, a practitioner with a sound knowledge base of ethical principles may be better prepared to make good choices when challenging situations arise.

This chapter summarizes the development, organization, and content of the NASP *Principles for Professional Ethics* (NASP, 2010b) with the goal of assisting school psychologists in applying the code to their ethical decision making. It is not feasible to discuss all changes new to the 2010 code here. For that reason, special attention is given to issues raised in queries to the NASP Ethics and Professional Practices Committee and in commentaries on the code. (See Jacob, 2008, and Jacob et al., 2011, for general recommendations on developing ethical practices.)

NASP adopted its first code of ethics, *Principles for Professional Ethics*, in 1974 and revised the code in 1984, 1992, 1997, and 2000. In the years following the 2000 revision of the code (NASP, 2000), school psychology continued to emerge as a distinct discipline with specialized roles and unique ethical–legal challenges. The professional task force report titled *School Psychology:*

A Blueprint for Training and Practice III (Ysseldyke et al., 2006) both confirmed and guided the evolving professional identity and roles of school psychologists. At the same time, changes in federal education law supported new roles for school psychologists. For example, consistent with emerging multitiered service delivery models, the Individuals with Disabilities Education Improvement Act of 2004 (IDEA) provided enhanced opportunities for school psychologists to deliver instructional and behavioral support services within general education classrooms. In addition, the U.S. Department of Education's efforts to promote safe and welcoming schools expanded systems-level consultation opportunities for school psychologists. In 2007, the NASP Professional Standards Revision Committee began crafting a description of the contemporary roles of school psychologists to appear in the Introduction to its 2010 code of ethics and the companion documents, the *Standards for Graduate Preparation of School Psychologists* (NASP, 2010c), *Standards for the Credentialing of School Psychologists* (NASP, 2010d), and the Practice Model (NASP, 2010a).

The writing team responsible for drafting the 2010 NASP code of ethics was committed to developing a code appropriate for the contemporary identity and roles of school psychologists, with special attention to the ethical challenges of school-based practice. The multistage process of revising the code began by soliciting suggestions from NASP leadership and members and reviewing the professional literature on emerging ethical and legal issues in school psychology. Beginning fall 2009, drafts of a proposed new code were critiqued by targeted NASP and external stakeholder groups. After revisions based on this input, NASP members were invited to provide feedback via a Web-based call for comments. These critiques were extremely important to the revision process because of the challenges of identifying and taking into account—as much as feasible—the diverse expectations for professional practice across various states and job settings. The 2010 code was adopted by the NASP Delegate Assembly in March 2010.

BASIC CONSIDERATIONS

The 2010 revision of the NASP *Principles for Professional Ethics* (NASP-PPE), like its precursors, addresses the unique circumstances associated with providing school-based school psychological services and emphasizes protecting the rights and interests of schoolchildren and youth (NASP-PPE Introduction). For the purposes of the code, *school-based practice* is defined as "the provision of school psychological services under the authority of a state, regional, or local educational agency," whether the school psychologist "is an employee of the schools or contracted by the schools on a per case or consultative basis" (NASP-PPE Definition of Terms). *Private practice* occurs "when a school psychologist enters into an agreement with a client(s) rather than an educational agency to provide school psychological services and the school psychologist's fee for services is the responsibility of the client or his or her representative" (NASP-PPE Definition of Terms). The code takes into account the following aspects of school-based practice:

- School psychologists must "balance the authority of parents to make decisions about their children with the needs and rights of those children, and the purposes and authority of schools." Within this framework, school psychologists consider "the interests and rights of children and youth to be their highest priority in decision making, and act as advocates for all students" (NASP-PPE Introduction).

- The mission of schools is to maintain order, ensure pupil safety, and educate children (*Burnside v. Byars*, 1966). School-based school psychologists, like other school employees, "have a legal as well as an ethical obligation to take steps to protect all students from reasonably foreseeable risk of harm" (NASP-PPE Introduction).

- As school employees, school psychology practitioners are state actors; that is, their actions are seen to be an extension of the state's authority to educate children. This creates a special obligation for school psychologists to know and respect the rights of schoolchildren under federal and state law (NASP-PPE Introduction).

- Like other mental health practitioners, school psychologists often provide assessment and intervention services within the framework of an established psychologist–client relationship. However, at other times, as members of a school's instructional support team, school psychologists may provide consultative services to student assistance teams, classrooms, schools, or other recipients of service, that do not fall within the scope of an established psychologist–client relationship.

- Recent years have witnessed growing interest in better protection of the privacy of sensitive student information (Schwab & Gelfman, 2005). In addition, since 1996, many states have broadened the scope of their laws governing privilege to include confidential communications that occur within a school psychologist–client relationship (Jacob & Powers, 2009).

- School-based practitioners work in a setting that requires multidisciplinary problem solving and intervention (NASP-PPE Introduction).

The NASP 2010 code of ethics is organized around four broad aspirational ethical themes. These themes (described in the next section) were derived from the literature on ethical principles (e.g., Bersoff & Koeppl, 1993; Prilleltensky, 1997; Ross, 1930) and other ethical codes, especially that of the Canadian Psychological Association (2000). The Canadian code of ethics was particularly influential because of its emphasis on the profession's responsibility to the welfare of society; that is, the necessary commitment to promoting not only the well-being of schoolchildren but also healthy environments where children develop (Prilleltensky, 1991), and its explicit recognition of psychologists' special responsibilities to vulnerable persons such as children and individuals who have faced societal discrimination (Pettifor, 1998).

The four broad themes in the 2010 code of ethics subsume 17 ethical principles, and each principle is then further articulated by specific standards. The aspirational themes and corollary principles and standards are to be considered in ethical decision making. However, the statements of the broad themes are aspirational. The NASP Ethical and Professional Practices Committee will only seek to enforce the 17 ethical principles and associated standards of conduct (NASP-PPE Introduction).

The first broad aspirational theme (NASP-PPE I) in the NASP code is "Respecting the Dignity and Rights of All Persons." This theme states: "In their words and actions, school psychologists demonstrate respect for the autonomy of persons and their right to self-determination, respect for privacy, and a commitment to just and fair treatment of all persons." Under this theme, the code has specific principles and standards for respecting autonomy and self-determination (Principle I.1), privacy and confidentiality (Principle I.2), and fairness and justice (Principle I.3).

The code's second aspirational theme (NASP-PPE II) is "Professional Competence and Responsibility." *Beneficence*, or responsible caring, means that psychologists engage in actions that are likely to benefit others, or at least do no harm (APA, 2010; Canadian Psychological Association, 2000). "To do this, school psychologists must practice within the boundaries of their competence, use scientific knowledge from psychology and education to help clients and others make informed choices, and accept responsibility for their work" (NASP-PPE II). Under the second aspirational theme, the NASP code has specific principles and standards pertaining to professional competence and maintaining competence (Principle II.1) and accepting responsibility for actions (Principle II.2), including the obligation to monitor the effectiveness of services provided and to take steps to correct any ineffective recommendations. Responsible assessment and intervention practices (Principle II.3), school-based record keeping (Principle II.4), and ensuring the proper use of assessment and intervention materials (Principle II.5) also are addressed under the second broad theme.

The third aspirational theme (NASP-PPE III) is "Honesty and Integrity in Professional Relationships." The relationship between a school psychologist and recipients of his or her services is a fiduciary relationship, that is, one based on trust. The third theme encourages school psychologists to foster and maintain trust by being faithful to the truth and adhering to their professional promises. The principles and standards nested under this aspirational theme obligate school psychologists to be forthright about their qualifications and competencies (Principle III.1) and their roles and priorities (Principle III.2), work in full cooperation with other professional disciplines to meet the needs of students and families (Principle III.3), and avoid multiple relationships that diminish their professional effectiveness (Principle III.4).

The fourth broad theme (NASP-PPE IV) is "Responsibility to Schools, Families, Communities, the Profession, and Society." School psychologists have a responsibility to foster the well-being of individual students, but also to use their professional knowledge to help create healthy, safe, and caring environments for children and families (Prilleltensky, 1991; also APA, 2010; Canadian Psychological Association, 2000). The fourth section includes principles and standards for promoting healthy school, family, and community environments (Principle IV.1); respecting law and the relationship of law and ethics (Principle IV.2); maintaining public trust by self-monitoring and peer monitoring (Principle IV.3); contributing to the profession by mentoring, teaching, and supervision (Principle IV.4); and contributing to the school psychology knowledge base (Principle IV.5).

BEST PRACTICES IN ETHICAL SCHOOL PSYCHOLOGICAL PRACTICE

As noted in its Introduction, the NASP 2010 code, "like all codes of ethics, provides only limited guidance in making ethical choices. Individual judgment is necessary to apply the code to situations that arise in professional practice." The code goes on to encourage school psychologists to "use a systematic problem-solving process to identify the best course of action" when difficult situations arise and to reflect on the intent of the code in determining its application to a particular situation. The Introduction also encourages school psychologists to "strive for excellence rather than simply meeting minimum obligations" in their decision making.

The remaining portion of this chapter gives special attention to issues raised in queries to the NASP Ethical and Professional Practices Committee about the intent and meaning of language new to the 2010 code, particularly queries regarding the rationale for, and interpretation of, standards and definitions related to privacy, informed consent, confidentiality, and fairness and nondiscrimination. In response to questions raised in published commentaries on the code, the relationship of professional ethics, law, and best practices is also addressed. Only a portion of the principles new to the 2010 code are discussed here.

Privacy, Informed Consent, Confidentiality, and Fairness

In the years since publication of the NASP 2000 code of ethics, ethical and legal issues related to privacy rights, informed consent, confidentiality, and nondiscrimination have become increasingly complex and challenging for school-based practitioners.

Privacy

Siegel (1979) defined privacy as "the freedom of individuals to choose for themselves the time and the circumstances under which and the extent to which their beliefs, behaviors, and opinions are to be shared or withheld from others" (p. 251). Like its precursor, the NASP 2010 code of ethics requires school psychologists to minimize intrusions on privacy. Practitioners "do not seek or store private information about clients that is not needed in the provision of services" (Standard I.2.2). The code, as before, obligates school psychologists to adhere to the need-to-know rule: "School psychologists discuss and/or release confidential information only for professional purposes and only with persons who have a legitimate need to know. They do so within the strict boundaries of relevant privacy statutes" (Standard I.2.5). However, because of societal changes and the changing legal landscape, the 2010 code has additional and more specific language with regard to respecting privacy than the 2000 code. Three of those changes are described here:

Privileged communications. Following the *Jaffee v. Redmond* U.S. Supreme Court decision in 1996, the federal courts and many states extended privilege to include the confidential communications between a client and a school psychologist in the context of an established professional relationship (Jacob & Powers, 2009). The following language was added in the NASP 2010 ethics code to encourage practitioners to know and respect client rights under privilege laws in the jurisdiction where they provide services:

> School psychologists recognize that client–school psychologist communications are privileged in most jurisdictions and do not disclose information that would put the student or family at legal, social, or other risk if shared with third parties, except as permitted by the mental health provider–client privilege laws in their state. (Standard I.2.2)

Sexual orientation/gender identity. Standard I.2.6 expands privacy protections with regard to sexual orientation, gender identity, and transgender status:

> School psychologists respect the right of privacy of students, parents, and colleagues with regard to sexual orientation, gender identity, or transgender status. They do not share information about the sexual orientation, gender identity, or transgender status of a student (including minors), parent, or school employee with anyone without that individual's permission. (Standard I.2.6)

Consistent with their ethical obligations to respect autonomy, privacy, and do no harm, school psychologists allow individuals, including youth, to make their own choices about whether they feel safe and ready to disclose their sexual orientation and gender identity to others. Outing someone who is gay, lesbian, bisexual, or transgender may have an adverse impact on that individual. For example, in *Sterling v. Borough of Minersville* (2000), police officers told a young man, a senior in high school, of their intent to inform his family that he is gay. The teenager subsequently committed suicide. In his suicide note, the boy expressed fear that disclosure of his sexual orientation would damage the lives of his family. His mother subsequently filed a lawsuit against the police (state actors), alleging that their actions violated her son's constitutional right to privacy and caused harm. In his opinion, the federal judge wrote:

> We thus carefully guard one's right to privacy against unwarranted government intrusion. It is difficult to imagine a more private matter than one's sexuality and a less likely probability that the government would have a legitimate interest in disclosure of sexual identity. (*Sterling v. Borough of Minersville*, 2000, p. 196)

(As an aside, the police officers were not held liable for any wrongdoing in the initial trial but that verdict was set aside. To end the ordeal, the boy's mother settled for $100,000 in damages while a second trial was pending [Weinstein, 2005].)

Consonant with the ethical principles identified above, the legal opinion in this case suggests that school employees, as state actors, should not disclose the sexual orientation or gender identity of students, parents, or colleagues without their permission.

Sensitive physical and mental health information.

Partly as a result of changes that have occurred in healthcare settings, many parents now have a greater expectation of control of physical and mental health information about their children, even when information is to be shared internally in the school setting (Schwab & Gelfman, 2005). As Schwab and Gelfman noted:

> It is necessary to keep in mind that this personal information belongs to the student and family, not the school. Therefore, it is generally the student's (or parents') right to control who has access to that information, especially when disclosure might cause harm. (Schwab & Gelfman, 2005, p. 266)

Standard I.2.7 was added to explicitly address the privacy of sensitive health information:

> School psychologists respect the right of privacy of students, their parents and other family members, and colleagues with regard to sensitive health information (e.g., presence of a communicable disease). They do not share sensitive health information about a student, parent, or school employee with others without that individual's permission (or the permission of a parent or guardian in the case of a minor). School psychologists consult their state laws and department of

public health for guidance if they believe a client poses a health risk to others. (Standard I.2.7)

School practitioners should be aware that some states and school districts have adopted policies to ensure greater privacy protections for student education records that are maintained by school nurses and mental health professionals (see Schwab et al., 2005, for recommended school policies).

Informed Consent

As Bersoff (1983) observed, "It is now universally agreed, though not always honored in practice, that human beings must give their informed consent prior to any significant intrusion of their person or privacy" (p. 150). In ethics and law, the requirement for informed consent to psychological services grew out of deep-rooted beliefs about the importance of individual privacy. The NASP code of ethics definition of *client* is particularly important for school practitioners because the code's standards for informed consent are linked to whether services are provided within the context of a school psychologist–client relationship. For the purposes of the code of ethics, a client is defined as

> … the person or persons with whom the school psychologist establishes a professional relationship for the purpose of providing school psychological services. A school psychologist–client professional relationship is established by an informed agreement with client(s) about the school psychologist's ethical and other duties to each party. While not *clients* per se, classrooms, schools, and school systems also may be recipients of school psychological services and often are parties with an interest in the actions of school psychologists. (emphasis added, NASP-PPE Definition of Terms)

Academic and behavior support under the authority of the teacher.

As noted previously, school-based practitioners today often provide consultative services to teachers with the goal of assisting students who need academic or behavioral supports to succeed in school. In 2004, IDEA was amended to allow states to use up to 15% of their federal special education funds each year to develop and implement coordinated *early intervening services*. These services are targeted to those pupils who need additional support to succeed in the general education environment but who have not been identified as eligible for special education and related services (34 C.F.R. § 300.226[a]; C.F.R. is the Code of Federal Regulations; available from http://www.law.cornell.edu/cfr/text). Funds may be used for professional development to enable staff to deliver "scientifically based academic and behavioral interventions" and to provide "educational and behavioral evaluations, services, and supports" (34 C.F.R. § 300.226[b][1][2]). Under IDEA, parent consent is not required for the screening of a student by a teacher or specialist to determine appropriate instructional strategies for curriculum implementation (34 C.F.R. § 300.302) or for review of existing student data (34 C.F.R. § 300.300[d][1][i]).

Consistent with the evolving roles of school psychologists and IDEA, the NASP 2010 code of ethics states that it is ethically permissible for school-based practitioners

… to provide school-based consultation services regarding a child or adolescent to a student assistance team or teacher without informed parent consent as long as the resulting interventions are *under the authority of the teacher* and *within the scope of typical classroom interventions.* (emphasis added, Standard I.1.1)

It is the duty of the teacher to help students learn and to maintain discipline in the classroom. The NASP code of ethics and IDEA are consistent in indicating that parent consent is not needed when the school psychologist is involved in screenings to identify students who are struggling academically or behaviorally, planning and implementing commonly used classroom academic or behavioral interventions, or progress monitoring. Within-classroom instructional grouping (e.g., grouping children for Tier 2 intervention) also does not require parent consent. It is appropriate to advise parents (e.g., in the district's parent handbook) that school psychologists routinely assist teachers in planning classroom instruction and monitoring its effectiveness (NASP-PPE Footnote 1).

It is important, however, to make a distinction between collecting data on a student's visible classroom behaviors that interfere with learning or that are disruptive to others at school (i.e., there is no legitimate expectation of privacy) and soliciting information about a student's private behaviors, thoughts, and beliefs. If a student is instructed to complete a school- or classroom-wide screening for mental health problems that asks about certain types of personal information (e.g., potentially embarrassing psychological problems or

sexual or criminal behavior), then parent notice and the opportunity to have their child opt out of the survey is required by NASP's ethics code Standard I.1.1 and the 2001 amendments to the Protection of Pupil Rights Act. Furthermore, as soon as a disability is suspected, parent consent is required to collect data for the purpose of an eligibility evaluation (Musgrove, 2011).

Counseling services. In deciding whether parent consent is needed to provide school psychological services to a student, it is also important to distinguish between behavioral support provided under the authority of the teacher and counseling services. When a school psychologist provides counseling to a student, there is greater likelihood of intrusion on that student's private thoughts and behaviors and a greater likelihood that private family matters will be disclosed to the school psychologist than when classroom behavioral support services are provided. With regard to counseling services, the NASP code of ethics states:

It is ethically permissible to provide psychological assistance without parent notice or consent in emergency situations if there is reason to believe a student may pose a danger to others; is at risk for self-harm; or is in danger of injury, exploitation, or maltreatment. (Standard I.1.2)

This portion of the code attempts to balance the school's responsibility to monitor student well-being and safety with the authority of parents to make decisions about their children. It is recommended that school district parent handbooks advise parents that a minor student may be seen by school health or mental health professionals without parent notice or consent to ensure the student is safe or is not a danger to others. The code also includes the following language regarding minors who self-refer:

When a student who is a minor self-refers for assistance, it is ethically permissible to provide psychological assistance without parent notice or consent for one or several meetings to establish the nature and degree of the need for services and assure the child is safe and not in danger. It is ethically permissible to provide services to mature minors without parent consent where allowed by state law and school district policy. However, if the student is *not* old enough to receive school psychological assistance independent of parent consent, the school psychologist obtains parent consent to provide continuing assistance to the student beyond the preliminary meetings or refers the student to alternative sources of assistance that do not require parent notice or consent. (Standard I.1.2)

This second portion of Standard I.1.2. makes it ethically permissible to provide counseling services to mature minors who self-refer where allowed by law and district policy. There are numerous reasons why an adolescent (age 17 or younger) who is experiencing emotional distress might prefer to seek assistance from a caring adult who is not his or her parent. The student might be too embarrassed or uncomfortable to discuss a particular issue with his or her parents, the problems might be due to inappropriate parenting behaviors or an anticipated unfavorable parent reaction to the adolescent's problem, and some adolescents may be reluctant to talk with a parent for fear of overburdening an existing stressful family situation. For these reasons, some states (e.g., California) allow minors to receive general mental health outpatient services without parent notice or consent and grant minors control over who has access to their treatment records. A potential benefit of allowing minors access to psychological assistance without parent notice or consent is that it may encourage the minor to seek and receive the help needed to manage emotional or developmental challenges (Lehrer, Pantell, Tebb, & Schafer, 2007). A potential risk is that the parents may learn their child is receiving psychological assistance without their permission, possibly resulting in increased tensions within the family and the belief that the service provider interfered with their parental rights.

Confidentiality

Siegel (1979) described confidentiality as "an explicit promise or contract to reveal nothing about an individual except under conditions agreed to by the source or subject" (p. 251). The 2010 code provides greater detail than the 2000 code regarding interpretation of the principle of confidentiality as it relates to the delivery of school psychological services:

> School psychologists inform students and other clients of the boundaries of confidentiality at the outset of establishing a professional relationship. They seek a shared understanding with clients regarding the types of information that will and will not be shared with third parties. However, if a child or adolescent is in immediate need of

assistance, it is permissible to delay the discussion of confidentiality until the immediate crisis is resolved. School psychologists recognize that it may be necessary to discuss confidentiality at multiple points in a professional relationship to ensure client understanding and agreement regarding how sensitive disclosures will be handled. (Standard I.2.3)

Thus, with the exception of urgent situations, school psychologists define the parameters of confidentiality at the outset of establishing a school psychologist–client professional relationship. School psychologists must weigh a number of factors in deciding the boundaries of a promise of confidentiality such as the age and maturity of the student, self-referral or referral by others, and reason for referral. For example, when conducting an assessment of whether a student who made a verbal or written threat poses a danger to others, no confidentiality is promised. Whatever the parameters, the circumstances under which the school psychologist might disclose client confidences to others must be clear. Practitioners also recognize that it may be necessary to discuss the parameters of confidentiality at multiple points in a school psychologist–client relationship. The code also states:

> School psychologists respect the confidentiality of information obtained during their professional work. Information is not revealed to third parties without the agreement of a minor child's parent or legal guardian (or an adult student), except in those situations in which failure to release information would result in danger to the student or others, or where otherwise required by law. Whenever feasible, student assent is obtained prior to disclosure of his or her confidences to third parties, including disclosures to the student's parents. (Standard I.2.4)

In the provision of services to students, there are several situations in which the school psychologist may be obligated to share confidential disclosures with others. First, it is usually appropriate to disclose student confidences to others when the student requests it. Second, confidential information may be disclosed when there is a situation involving danger to the student or others. In every state, school psychologists are legally required to report suspected child abuse. Furthermore, in school-based practice, information shared in confidence must be disclosed when necessary to safeguard a student from *reasonably foreseeable risk of harm* to self or others. This standard emerged from civil lawsuits against school districts in cases involving foreseeable injury to a student. It is a less stringent standard for disclosure of confidential information than *clear* or *imminent danger*, terms often used in state laws regulating mental health providers. Consistent with the reasonably foreseeable risk of harm standard, court opinions indicate that schools are obligated to inform a parent if it is suspected that a student may be suicidal. Finally, it may be necessary for the psychologist to disclose confidential information when there is a legal obligation to testify in a court of law (Jacob et al., 2011).

If it becomes apparent when working with a student that confidentiality must be broken, the decision to disclose student confidences to others should be discussed with the student when feasible (Standard I.2.4). Also, as noted previously, if information learned within a school psychologist–client relationship is shared with third parties, such information is disclosed only on a need-to-know basis. Only information "essential to the understanding and resolution" of a student's difficulties is disclosed (Davis & Sandoval, 1982, p. 548; Standard I.2.5).

Fairness and Nondiscrimination

The broad theme of respect for the dignity of all persons encompasses the school psychologist's ethical responsibility to promote fairness, nondiscrimination, and justice. The 2010 NASP ethical principles and standards on fairness and nondiscrimination were foreshadowed by language in the APA and the Canadian Psychological Association codes of ethics and in a NASP position statement encouraging school psychologists "to ensure that all students have an opportunity for development and expression of their personal identity in an environment free from discrimination, harassment, violence, and abuse" (NASP, 2006, p. lxxxix). The code obligates school psychologists to

> … use their expertise to cultivate school climates that are safe and welcoming to all persons regardless of actual or perceived characteristics, including race, ethnicity, color, religion, ancestry, national origin, immigration status, socioeconomic status, primary language, gender, sexual orientation, gender identity, gender expression, disability, or any other distinguishing characteristics. (Principle I.3)

Furthermore, "school psychologists do not engage in or condone actions or policies that discriminate against

persons, including students and their families, other recipients of service, supervisees, and colleagues based on these or any other actual or perceived characteristics" (Standard I.3.1), and they "work to correct school practices that are unjustly discriminatory…" (Standard I.3.3). The growing emphasis on a systems-level approach to creating schools that are welcoming to all students is consistent with U.S. Department of Education initiatives to reduce harassment and bullying of students who are perceived to be "different" from their classmates (e.g., Ali, 2010).

The school psychologist's obligation to students from diverse cultural, linguistic, and experiential backgrounds goes beyond striving to be impartial and unprejudiced in the delivery of services. Practitioners have an ethical responsibility to

> … pursue awareness and knowledge of how diversity factors may influence child development, behavior, and school learning. In conducting psychological, educational, or behavioral evaluations or in providing interventions, therapy, counseling, or consultation services, the school psychologist takes into account the individual characteristics [enumerated in the code] so as to provide effective services. (Standard I.3.2)

Contrary to one interpretation (Myers, 2012), Standards I.3.2 and II.1.2 do not mandate participation in continued education workshops or classes on diversity. These standards obligate the school psychologist to be competent to provide effective services to his or her clients from diverse cultural, linguistic, and experiential backgrounds or to seek assistance to ensure the client receives services that are effective (Standard II.1.2.; also APA, 2010; Canadian Psychological Association, 2000).

Consistent with the broad ethical principle of justice, school psychologists also "strive to ensure that all children have equal opportunity to participate in and benefit from school programs, and that all students and families have access to and can benefit from school psychological services" (Standard I.3.4, also APA, 2010, Principle D).

Ethics, Law, and Best Practices

The purposes and typical practices of the NASP Ethical and Professional Practices Committee are described below. The remaining portions of the chapter address the following questions: What is the difference between ethical standards, law, and best practices? Is the NASP

2010 code of ethics too prescriptive or not prescriptive enough? As will be seen, there are no simple answers.

NASP Ethical and Professional Practices Committee.

The primary purposes of the NASP Ethical and Professional Practices Committee are as follows: " … to promote and maintain ethical conduct by school psychologists, … to educate school psychologists regarding NASP ethical standards, and … to protect the general well-being of consumers of school psychological services" (NASP, 2008, p. 1). The NASP ethics committee responds to questions regarding appropriate professional practices and is committed to resolving concerns informally, if possible. The NASP Ethics and Professional Practices Committee takes primarily an educative approach. However, the committee also investigates alleged ethical misconduct of NASP members or any psychologist who holds a Nationally Certified School Psychologist (NCSP) credential (NASP, 2008, p. 2). If, after investigation, the committee determines that a violation of the NASP code of ethics has occurred, the committee may require the respondent to engage in remedial activities such as education or training and to provide restitution or apology. The committee also may recommend probation, suspension, or termination of NASP membership and/or revocation of the NCSP. The imposition of probation is rare but may be deemed appropriate, particularly if there is a pattern of problematic conduct. Suspension or termination is also rare and typically only occurs in situations involving egregious conduct.

Professional ethics.

A number of broad ethical themes were identified in Ross's seminal description of the moral duties of the ethical person and in more contemporary scholarship in the area of applied professional ethics. These themes include beneficence, nonmaleficence, justice, respect for autonomy and privacy, and the duty to perform professional responsibilities competently (Bersoff, 1983; Ross, 1930). The NASP *Principles for Professional Ethics* "elucidate the proper conduct of a professional school psychologist" (NASP-PPE Introduction) by translating broad ethical themes into principles and standards to guide school psychologists in ethical decision making.

Law and law and law.

Law is a broad term encompassing constitutional, statutory, and case law. The NASP code of ethics obligates practitioners to know and respect the law (NASP-PPE Introduction, Standard IV.2.2). This is not an easy task, however, because there are multiple sources of legal regulation of school-based practice. Dilemmas arise because of conflicts between codes of ethics and law and inconsistencies between different sources of legal regulation. Furthermore, rules of practice and law vary across states and settings. The NASP code of ethics states that if the code establishes a higher standard of conduct than is required by law, school psychologists strive to meet that higher standard (NASP-PPE Introduction).

Historically, professional codes of ethics were viewed as requiring decisions that are "more correct or more stringent" than required by law (Ballantine, 1979, p. 636). However, with growing societal concerns about privacy rights, social justice issues, and ensuring that schools are safe and welcoming to all, case law and federal regulations have at times set higher and more explicit standards for promoting the well-being of students and respecting human rights than codes of ethics. The NASP 2010 code includes additional standards and language to ensure that school psychologists make decisions that meet or exceed obligations for respecting human rights and dignity that have been identified in case law and federal regulations.

If the ethical responsibilities of school psychologists conflict with law, regulations, or other governing legal authority, psychologists clarify the nature of the conflict, make known their commitment to their code of ethics, and "take steps to resolve the conflict through positive, respected, and legal channels. If not able to resolve the conflict in this manner, they may abide by the law, as long as the resulting actions do not violate basic human rights" (Standard IV.2.3). School administrators may not be familiar with the special ethical and legal responsibilities associated with the delivery of psychological services in the schools. When feasible, school psychologists are well advised to negotiate a job description that encompasses the freedom to adhere to the NASP code of ethics. The code can be a valuable tool to communicate the ethical obligations of school psychology practitioners to school administrators.

It is important to note that school psychologists are not expected to engage in insubordination as part of advocacy efforts. For the purposes of the code, *advocacy* is defined as follows:

> School psychologists have a special obligation to speak up for the rights and welfare of students and families, and to provide a voice to clients who cannot or do not wish to speak for themselves. Advocacy also occurs when school psychologists use their expertise in psychology and education to

promote changes in schools, systems, and laws that will benefit school children, other students, and families. Nothing in this code of ethics, however, should be construed as requiring school psychologists to engage in insubordination (willful disregard of an employer's lawful instructions) or to file a complaint about school district practices with a federal or state regulatory agency as part of their advocacy efforts. (NASP-PPE Definition of Terms)

The NASP Ethical and Professional Practices Committee must at times determine whether a complaint to the committee should be investigated as a possible ethics code violation or whether it is best addressed through legal channels. For example, parents may complain that a school psychologist engaged in unethical assessment practices after a school multidisciplinary team makes a decision that is not consistent with the parents' opinion about the eligibility, classification, or educational needs of their child under IDEA or Section 504 of the Rehabilitation Act of 1973. The Ethical and Professional Practices Committee typically does not accept and investigate complaints that are better addressed through special education due process procedures or other legal venues. However, a court record indicating that a school psychology practitioner was found guilty of, or pleaded no contest to, a crime against children will result in review of those court records and imposition of appropriate sanctions.

Best practices. *Best* or *model practices* refers to the highest ideals of professional practice. The NASP Practice Model (NASP, 2010a) identifies standards for excellence in the delivery of school psychological services. The four broad aspirational themes in the NASP 2010 code of ethics describe the highest ideals of ethical practice.

The NASP Ethical and Professional Practices Committee does not sanction practitioners for failure to meet the highest standards of practice. In fact, whether using the 2000 or 2010 code, Ethical and Professional Practices Committee members have at times engaged in lengthy discussion of whether the conduct of a practitioner is ethically acceptable "performance at a minimum standard" (McNamara, 2008, p. 1935) or a violation of enforceable code standards. The Ethical and Professional Practices Committee is not insensitive to dilemmas associated with school-based practice when deliberating whether an ethics code violation occurred. As noted in its Introduction, the NASP code acknowledges that practitioners often must balance the competing needs and

rights of multiple parties. Furthermore, two or more competing ethical principles may apply to a particular situation and sometimes no one course of action can be identified that is completely satisfactory.

Myers (2012) raised the question of whether the distinction between *best practices* and *ethical standards* is lost in the NASP 2010 code. For example, Standard II.2.2 of the 2010 code states: "School psychologists actively monitor the impact of their recommendations and intervention plans. They revise a recommendation, or modify or terminate an intervention plan, when data indicate the desired outcomes are not being attained." Myers asserted that "[n]ot monitoring one's recommendations went from 'poor judgment' to an unethical behavior in a very short period of time," particularly because the "standard implicitly requires that data be collected" (Myers, 2012, p. 8). However, the language of the 2010 standard is essentially the same as the language that appeared in the 2000 version of the code: "School psychologists develop interventions that are … consistent with *data* collected. They modify or terminate the treatment plan when the *data* indicate a plan is not achieving the desired goals" (emphasis added, NASP, 2000, Standard IV.C.6). Failure to follow up and remedy ineffective recommendations is inconsistent with the broad ethical principles of beneficence, nonmaleficence, and responsible caring. Unfortunately, this failure to monitor intervention outcomes appears to be one of the more commonly witnessed deficiencies in the delivery of school psychological services (Dailor & Jacob, 2011). It is important to note that both the 2000 and 2010 codes are silent regarding how follow-up is to be conducted. The term *data* is inclusive of qualitative (descriptive) and quantitative data. Thus, while "best practices" might indicate that collection of quantitative data is desirable, neither the 2000 nor the 2010 codes require a particular type of outcome monitoring. Ethically, this standard might be satisfied by a simple and brief communication with the teacher asking him or her to describe student progress toward meeting intervention goals.

Too prescriptive or not prescriptive enough? School psychology practitioners report that it is at times difficult to decide how ethics code statements apply to a particular situation (Dailor & Jacob, 2011). The NASP 2010 code is more detailed and prescriptive than its precursor. Is the NASP 2010 code too prescriptive (e.g., Myers, 2012) or not prescriptive enough (e.g., Pfohl, 2010)? This question will best be answered by monitoring feedback on the code from Ethical and Professional Practices Committee members, practitioners, and trainers and introducing modifications as needed in the years ahead. Because of frequent advances in technology, societal changes, emerging professional roles, and changes in law, the NASP code of ethics will likely always be a work in progress.

SUMMARY

This chapter summarizes the development, organization, content, and language of the NASP 2010 *Principles for Professional Ethics*. Unlike earlier versions of the code, the 2010 code identifies both aspirational ethical principles and specific standards to guide ethical decision making. One goal in revising the code was to improve its applicability to the contemporary identity and roles of school psychologists and the special considerations of school-based practice. In addition, the new code is more sensitive to societal concerns about privacy and social justice issues in schools and consonant with changes in federal law that have an impact on school psychology practices.

AUTHOR NOTE

The views expressed here do not reflect the official opinion of the National Association of School Psychologists Ethical and Professional Practices Committee. The author is not an attorney, and the information provided should not be construed as legal advice. A special thank you to Cody J. Bartow for his assistance.

Disclosure. Susan Jacob has a financial interest in books she authored or coauthored referenced in this chapter.

REFERENCES

Ali, R. (2010). *Dear colleague letter.* Washington, DC: U.S. Department of Education Office for Civil Rights. Retrieved from http://www2. ed.gov/about/offices/list/ocr/letters/colleague-201010.html

American Psychological Association. (2010). *Ethical principles of psychologists and code of conduct with the 2010 amendments.* Washington, DC: Author. Retrieved from http://www.apa.org/ethics/code/index.aspx

Armistead, L., Williams, B., & Jacob, S. (2011). *Professional ethics for school psychologists: A problem-solving model casebook* (2nd ed.). Bethesda, MD: National Association of School Psychologists.

Ballantine, H. T. (1979). The crisis in ethics, anno domini 1979. *New England Journal of Medicine, 301,* 634–638.

Bersoff, D. N. (1983). Children as participants in psychoeducational assessment. In G. B. Melton, G. P. Koocher, & M. J. Saks (Eds.), *Children's competence to consent* (pp. 149–177). New York, NY: Plenum Press.

Bersoff, D. N., & Koeppl, P. M. (1993). The relation between ethical codes and moral principles. *Ethics and Behavior, 3,* 345–357. doi:10.1207/s15327019eb0303&4_8

Bowser, P. B. (2009, March). *Comment in NASP ethics public comment responses, compiled and provided to members of the Principles for Professional Ethics 2010 revision team.* Bethesda, MD: National Association of School Psychologists.

Burnside v. Byars, 363 F.2d 744 (5th Cir. 1966).

Canadian Psychological Association. (2000). *Canadian Code of Ethics for Psychologists* (3rd ed.). Ottawa, Ontario, Canada: Author. Retrieved from http://www.cpa.ca

Dailor, A. N., & Jacob, S. (2011). Ethically challenging situations reported by school psychologists: Implications for training. *Psychology in the Schools, 48,* 619–631. doi:10.1002/pits.20574

Davis, J. M., & Sandoval, J. (1982). Applied ethics for school-based consultants. *Professional Psychology, 13,* 543–551. doi:10.1037/0735-7028.13.4.543

Flanagan, R., Miller, J. A., & Jacob, S. (2005). The 2002 revision of APA's ethics code: Implications for school psychologists. *Psychology in the Schools, 42,* 433–445. doi:10.1002/pits.20097

Jacob, S. (2008). Best practices in developing ethical school psychological practice. In A. Thomas & J. Grimes (Eds.), *Best practices in school psychology V* (pp. 1921–1932). Bethesda, MD: National Association of School Psychologists.

Jacob, S., Decker, D. M., & Hartshorne, T. S. (2011). *Ethics and law for school psychologists* (6th ed.). Hoboken, NJ: Wiley.

Jacob, S., & Powers, K. E. (2009). Privileged communication in the school psychologist–client relationship. *Psychology in the Schools, 46,* 307–318. doi:10.1002/pits.20377

Jaffee v. Redmond, 518 U.S. 1 (1996).

Koocher, G. P., & Keith-Spiegel, P. (2008). *Ethics in psychology and the mental health professions: Standards and cases.* New York, NY: Oxford University Press.

Lehrer, J. A., Pantell, R., Tebb, K., & Shafter, M. (2007). Forgone healthcare among U.S. adolescents: Associations between risk characteristics and confidentiality concerns. *Journal of Adolescent Health, 40,* 218–226. doi:10.1016/j.jadohealth.2006.09.015

McNamara, K. (2008). Best practices in the application of professional ethics. In A. Thomas & J. Grimes (Eds.), *Best practices in school psychology V* (pp. 1933–1941). Bethesda, MD: National Association of School Psychologists.

Musgrove, M. (2011). *Memorandum to: State directors of special education* Retrieved from http://www.rti4success.org/pdf/State%20Directors%20of%20Special%20Education_1-21-11.pdf

Myers, C. (2012). Lost: Distinctions between best practices in NASP's (2010) ethics code. *Communiqué, 40*(7), 8–9.

National Association of School Psychologists. (2000). *Principles for professional ethics.* In A. Thomas, & J. Grimes (Eds.), *Best practices in school psychology V* (pp. xxi–xxix). Bethesda, MD: Author.

National Association of School Psychologists. (2006). *Gay, lesbian, bisexual, transgender, and questioning (GLBTQ) youth* (Position statement). Bethesda, MD: Author.

National Association of School Psychologists. (2008). *Ethical and Professional Practices Committee procedures.* Bethesda, MD: Author. Retrieved from http://www.nasponline.org/standards/Adjudication2005.pdf

National Association of School Psychologists. (2010a). *Model for comprehensive and integrated school psychological services.* Bethesda, MD: Author. Retrieved from http://www.nasponline.org/standards/2010standards/2_PracticeModel.pdf

National Association of School Psychologists. (2010b). *Principles for professional ethics*. Bethesda, MD: Author. Retrieved from http://www.nasponline.org/standards/2010standards/1_%20Ethical%20Principles.pdf

National Association of School Psychologists. (2010c). *Standards for graduate preparation of school psychologists*. Bethesda, MD: Author. Retrieved from http://www.nasponline.org/standards/2010standards/1_Graduate_Preparation.pdf

National Association of School Psychologists. (2010d). *Standards for the credentialing of school psychologists*. Bethesda, MD: Author. Retrieved from http://www.nasponline.org/standards/2010standards/2_Credentialing_Standards.pdf

Pettifor, J. L. (1998). The Canadian Code of Ethics for Psychologists: A moral context for ethical decision making in emerging areas of practice. *Canadian Psychology*, *27*, 231–283.

Pfohl, B. (2010). Ethics and technology: Part 1. *Communiqué*, *39*(3), 32.

Prilleltensky, I. (1991). The social ethics of school psychology: A priority for the 1990s. *School Psychology Quarterly*, *6*, 200–222.

Prilleltensky, I. (1997). Values, assumptions, and practices: Assessing the moral implications of psychological discourse and action. *American Psychologist*, *52*, 517–535.

Ross, W. D. (1930). *The right and the good*. New York, NY: Clarendon Press.

Schwab, N. C., & Gelfman, M. H. B. (2005). Confidentiality: Principles and practice issues. In N. C. Schwab & M. H. B Gelfman (Eds.), *Legal issues in school health services: A resource for school administrators, school attorneys, school nurses* (pp. 261–295). New York, NY: Authors Choice Press.

Schwab, N. C., Rubin, M., Maire, J. A., Gelfman, M. H. B., Bergren, M. D., Mazyck, D., & Hine, B. (2005). *Protecting and disclosing student health information. How to develop school district policies and procedures*. Kent, OH: American School Health Association.

Siegel, M. (1979). Privacy, ethics, and confidentiality. *Professional Psychology*, *10*, 249–258. doi:10.1037/0735-7027.10.2.249

Sterling v. Borough of Minersville, 232 F.3d 190, 2000 U.S. App. LEXIS 27855 (3rd Cir. 2000).

Weinstein, B. S. (2005). A right with no remedy: Forced disclosure of sexual orientation and public "outing" under 42 U.S.C. 1983. *Cornell Law Review*, *90*, 811–838.

Ysseldyke, J., Burns, M., Dawson, P., Kelley, B., Morrison, D., Ortiz, S., … Telzrow, C. (2006). *School psychology: A blueprint for training and practice III*. Bethesda, MD: National Association of School Psychologists. Retrieved from http://www.nasponline.org/resources/blueprint/index.aspx

Best Practices in the Application of Professional Ethics

Laurie McGarry Klose
Jon Lasser
Texas State University-San Marcos

OVERVIEW

Ethical principles and standards in school psychology serve multiple purposes, including the articulation of the profession's values, the definition of roles and relationships, and the self-regulation of the profession. Moreover, ethical codes serve as an important resource for individuals seeking guidance when faced with ethical challenges. Although the philosophy of ethics and moral reasoning at times may seem esoteric and abstract, ethical principles were developed for the complex real world in which school psychologists interact with students, families, teachers, administrators, and other professionals. In this regard, school psychologists are engaged with applied professional ethics.

This chapter is most closely aligned with the Legal, Ethical, and Professional Practice domain of the National Association of School Psychologists (NASP) *Model for Comprehensive and Integrated School Psychological Services*:

> School psychologists have knowledge of the history and foundations of school psychology; multiple service models and methods; ethical, legal, and professional standards; and other factors related to professional identity and effective practice as school psychologists. (NASP, 2010a, p. 8)

The purpose of this chapter is to use ethical theory and models in an applied context to promote enhanced ethical thinking and decision making in school psychology. Recognizing that every ethical dilemma is situated in a unique contextual framework, the importance of gathering relevant information such that the application of ethical principles matches the particular circumstances of each concern is emphasized. This chapter provides examples of a process school psychologists can use to apply the ethical standards to real situations to successfully resolve challenging ethical dilemmas.

BASIC CONSIDERATIONS

Ethical decision making is a significant area of concern, as most school psychologists report that they do not feel fully prepared to handle ethical dilemmas (Dailor, 2007). The following concerns were rated highly by school psychologists surveyed by Dailor: (a) administrative pressure, (b) unsound educational practices, (c) assessment-related concerns, (d) confronting unethical colleagues, and (e) storage and disposal of records. Most respondents (66%) reported that they sought peer consultation to resolve ethical dilemmas, yet only 16% indicated that they used a systematic decision-making model.

School psychologists have a wide range of resources that provide considerable guidance when faced with ethical challenges (Lasser, Klose, & Robillard, 2013). These include the NASP's *Principles for Professional Ethics* (NASP, 2010b), the American Psychological Association's (APA) *Ethical Principles of Psychologists and Code of Conduct* (APA, 2010), the International School Psychology Association's (ISPA) *Code of Ethics* (ISPA, 2011), as well as valuable books and chapters (e.g., Armistead, Williams, & Jacob, 2011; Jacob, Decker, & Hartshorne, 2011). In spite of these tools, school psychologists are presented with complex cases and situations that require more than an ethical code or set of decision-making steps. In fact, the strict adherence to ethical rules without an appreciation of context can have adverse consequences.

Codes of ethics provide professionals with guidance with respect to the important principles and standards for practice, but these codes do not always inform school psychologists with regard to the subtleties involved in the decision-making process regarding difficult ethical situations. Without this type of guidance, practitioners must determine ways to apply these statements about what should and should not be done (e.g., school psychologists respect privacy, school psychologist do not engage in actions that discriminate). Such statements can be insufficient because the complex world of practice regularly presents practitioners with ethical challenges that are multifaceted and embedded in context. Ethical problem solving, decision analysis, and decision-making models emerged in response to the need for guidance in the application of ethical principles and standards (Armistead et al., 2011; Jacob et al., 2011; Koocher & Keith-Spiegel, 1998).

To enhance the use of decision making-models, school psychologists must consider and integrate context in their decision-making process and be aware of social psychological pressures that may interfere with the process. To underscore the importance of context for school psychologists facing ethical dilemmas, Table 33.1 provides an annotated version of the widely used ethical decision-making model with a step-by-step consideration of how context plays a role, the potential for harm if context is not considered, and a concise example.

Context has far-reaching implications for the way one perceives and reacts to the world. Consider the difference in perception and emotion for the following two situations that involve a person running toward another: (a) A person is standing at a finish line and sees his friend running toward him, about to complete her first 5K. (b) A person is standing in a dark alley at night and sees an unknown human figure running toward him. The context of each situation will likely have a powerful effect on feelings and actions. Instructions regarding the most appropriate response to a person running toward another will be of little help if one does not consider the context.

The field of psychology contains countless examples of ways in which context plays a pivotal role. Though personality traits may be stable over time, a powerful situational variable may better explain an individual's action. "One of the most important contributions of developmental psychology has been the discovery that patterns of behavior, and of process-behavior linkage, vary across contexts" (Dodge, 2008, p. 122). Ethical

decisions also occur in contexts that are considered when school psychologists attempt to resolve ethical dilemmas.

Cultural factors play a significant role in understanding the context of a challenging ethical situation. Pope and Vasquez (2011) note that "the same act can take on sharply different meanings in different societies, cultures, or religions" and that "what seems ethical in one context can violate fundamental values in another society, culture, or spiritual tradition" (p. 119). While ethical codes promote an understanding of and respect for diversity, the codes do not necessarily address the unique problem-solving skills and steps that may be required when individuals of different cultural backgrounds are enmeshed in an ethical quandary.

Another important aspect of the context of the ethical dilemma is an awareness of the influence of other pressures that have an impact on decision making. One of these factors is the social context of the process. Several social psychological phenomena have been identified as contributing to the process of decision making in school contexts (Lasser & Klose, 2007; Klose & Lasser, 2012; Klose, Lasser, & Reardon, 2012). In these theoretical and empirical works, several social psychology phenomena considered include the foot-in-the-door, obedience to authority, and conformity. For example, if all members of an Individualized Education Program (IEP) team express their support of a decision before the parent or caregiver has had an opportunity to speak, the parent or caregiver may feel social pressure to conform with the group. Considering the social psychological phenomenon that might be at play in a particular situation is an important part in evaluating the context of an ethical dilemma.

Ethical decision-making models and tools generally acknowledge context as an important variable and can be adapted to guide the process of addressing and resolving ethical dilemmas that are embedded in the contexts of culture and systems.

BEST PRACTICES IN APPLIED ETHICS

School psychologists make better ethical decisions when they recognize the unique circumstances of each case. Failure to consider contextual factors may result in inadvertently causing harm when one is actively trying to promote beneficence. A best practices approach to applied ethical decision making must always include knowledge of the NASP (2010b) *Principles for Professional Ethics*, and a process for applying the knowledge in the context of the specific situation. To promote better

Table 33.1. Application of Context-Sensitive Ethics to Koocher and Keith-Spiegel's (2008) Decision-Making Steps

Decision-Making Step	Considerations of Context at Each Step	Potential for Harm When Context Is Not Considered	Example
Determine whether or not the matter truly involves ethics	Context determines ethics. What are the ethical codes and guidelines of everyone involved and how are they similar/different?	If context is not considered, the school psychologist may fail to be aware of an ethical concern.	Failure to understand abusive spousal relationship results in an artificial informed consent process.
Consult existing guidelines that might apply as a possible mechanism for resolution	Standard guidelines such as ethical codes and decision-making models may be devoid of context; a context-sensitive approach expands a conceptualization of ethical dilemmas by considering, for example, how culture and family systems have an impact on the process of resolution.	In the absence of a context-sensitive approach, the professional may use such ethical codes as a simplistic "if/then" formula, which can result in harm (e.g., if there are significant cultural factors that may have an impact on the informed-consent process).	Strict adherence to confidentiality alienates extended family members who culturally regard themselves as equal in status to parents.
Pause to consider, as best as possible, all factors that might influence the decision that will be made	This step appears to address context ('all factors"), but may be too vague. Moreover, the context-sensitive approach directs the attention of the school psychologist to specific contextual factors for consideration.	A context-sensitive approach broadens the horizon of "all factors" by encouraging the professional to go beyond that which may be obvious. Harm results when important factors are not seen or considered.	Well-intentioned school psychologist fails to consider a parent's relationship with school staff outside of the school, which results in role confusion and bias.
Consult with a trusted colleague	Consider the colleague's professional context, as well as systems and cultural factors.	Without taking the colleague's context into consideration, one may misunderstand the colleague's advice in consultation, or may inadvertently fall into the trap of making a decision that is limited by the colleague's frame of reference.	A school psychologist's conceptualization of the case is narrowed after consulting with the colleague, largely because the colleague tends to see all problems as boundary issues.
Evaluate the rights, responsibilities, and vulnerability of all affected parties	A context-sensitive approach requires school psychologists to think about rights, responsibilities, and vulnerability not only from his or her perspective, but also from the perspectives of others.	Without a thoughtful assessment of the rights, responsibilities, and vulnerability of all affected parties from a context-sensitive framework, school psychologists may make faulty assumptions about others that results in harm (e.g., underestimating vulnerabilities).	A student has a history of arrests and detentions and has developed some vulnerability with respect to assent (e.g., perceives little agency). If this context is not considered, the student may assent against his better interests.

Continued

Table 33.1. Continued

Decision-Making Step	Considerations of Context at Each Step	Potential for Harm When Context Is Not Considered	Example
Generate alternative decisions	A context-sensitive approach may expand the range of alternatives by considering multiple perspectives, systems issues, and cultural factors that may otherwise be missed from a standard list of alternatives.	A list of alternatives that is generated without thinking in terms of contexts may be limited. Consequently, viable alternatives may be missed, leaving the school psychologist with inferior options.	A school psychologist engages in problem solving, but only within the context of what has typically been done in the district. Without considering the unique needs of the students, the interventions selected are inappropriate and result in wasted time and exacerbation of problems.
Enumerate the consequences of making each decision	Consequences in some contexts are more serious than others, and may affect individuals and systems differentially.	The identification of consequences without a contextual analysis may fall short of anticipating how the impact of each decision may differentially affect various individuals and systems. Harm can result for a failure to anticipate negative consequences.	With a focus that is exclusively on the child, the school psychologist fails to consider how a variety of options may have a negative impact on teachers and other students.
Make the decision	The school psychologist must take action, and context is considered not only in making the decision, but also in the ways in which the decision may be carried out, with sensitivity to culture, values, and other contextual variables.	Without recognizing context, the act of making a decision to resolve or address an ethical dilemma may backfire, potentially making matters worse.	Unable to reach consensus with divorced parents regarding the student's Individualized Education Program, the school psychologist fails to consider the impact on the family system when weighing alternatives and causes disruption.

Note. From "Context-Sensitive Ethics in School Psychology," by J. Lasser, L. M. Klose, and R. Robillard, 2013, *Contemporary School Psychology.* Copyright 2013 by the California Association of School Psychologists. Adapted with permission.

ethical decision making that is consistent with the NASP (2010a) Practice Model and sensitive to the unique contextual factors of each case, the following considerations for best practices for applied ethical decision-making are utilized in a decision-making process as illustrated by several case examples: (a) consider all relevant factors that make a case unique, including cultural, linguistic, developmental, and political; (b) try to see the concern through the eyes of all relevant parties (e.g., child, parent or caregiver, teachers, administrators); and (c) when applying the ethical principles, always ask what circumstances may complicate a simple use of the codes. The following fictional case studies underscore the importance of a best practices approach to applied ethical decision making. School psychologists can use these cases as examples of how to organize thinking about ethical dilemmas and strategies for ensuring the inclusion of contextual variables in each situation. While each case example includes discussion and examination of several specific standards and/or principles from NASP's *Principles for Professional Ethics*, ethical principles described for each case are not exhaustive. Given the interactive and connected nature of the ethical principles, it is possible that individual practitioners might identify additional standards that apply to the case examples.

Case 1

Ms. Gilbert, the school psychologist, has been working closely with the Park family. As the case manager for the son's special education placement, Ms. Gilbert has been consulting with the teachers who have not been following the student's IEP as it was developed. Ms. Gilbert has also experienced many challenges trying to be the mediator between the family and school personnel. Finally, after many meetings, the situation has been resolved. Ms. Park presented Ms. Gilbert a thank you card and a gift of a silk scarf from the Park's native country, South Korea. Ms. Gilbert is concerned that this gift may pose a dilemma for her.

Considering the context of the concern and remembering the social forces that may be at work, the scenario can be analyzed according to the steps of an ethical decision-making process.

Determine whether or not the matter truly involves ethics: If Ms. Gilbert accepts the gift, she may have created a situation where a relationship beyond case manager exists or is implied to exist. If so, her judgment in handling future situations with the mother could be clouded because Ms. Gilbert has developed a relationship with the mother

beyond simply being the case manager for her son. This could affect Ms. Gilbert's abilities in making sound and fair decisions regarding the child's educational program and could affect other staff members. On the other hand, sometimes a gift is just a gift with no strings attached or implied. Ms. Gilbert decides that, considering her uncertainty, she will approach the situation as an ethical dilemma.

Consult existing guidelines that might apply as a possible mechanism for resolution: NASP ethical principles provide several areas of guidance that apply to this situation. Ethical Principle III.4 deals with specific considerations regarding multiple relationships. In general, the principle states that multiple relationships should be avoided to ensure that effectiveness is not compromised. In addition, Ethical Standard II.1.2 addresses the need to have understanding of cultural considerations when working with families and systems. Ethical Standard III.2.4 relates to the reality that school psychologists work in situations where conflicted loyalties (teacher, parent, child, system) may come into play. Federal guidelines concerning gifts for government employees state that gifts should not exceed a dollar amount of $20 (U.S. Government Office of Ethics, 2013). In addition, some states and school districts have more stringent guidelines that disallow the acceptance of gifts at all.

Applying any or all of these ethical and legal principles as an "if/then" approach could result in negative outcomes. For example, if the gift creates the appearance of a multiple relationship or conflicted loyalties, it should not be accepted, given that school psychologists do not engage in multiple relationships that can affect their professional effectiveness. However, the cultural context of the giving of the gift must also be considered, complicating the application of the if/then application of the other ethical principles.

Pause to consider, as best as possible, all factors that might influence the decision to be made. Ms. Gilbert considers that if she accepts the gift, then the Park family may expect that she be more responsive to their requests in the future or other school personnel may assume that this is the case. However, if she declines the gift, she may offend the parent and risk the relationship that has been developed and has benefited the child.

Consult with a trusted colleague: Ms. Gilbert decides to poll her colleagues to see if they have received thank you gifts from families. Almost all report that they have received various forms of thank you gifts ranging from hand drawn art from children to blown glass flowers. Only one colleague had refused a thank you gift that involved attending a professional basketball game with the parent and child. Most colleagues reported that the thank you gift items remained in their school offices as a decorative object. Considering the context of the local norms related to thank you gifts gave Ms. Gilbert valuable information for resolving her ethical dilemma.

Evaluate the rights, responsibilities, and vulnerability of all affected parties: Ms. Gilbert considers the parties involved in this dilemma including herself, the child, the Park family, and the teachers. For herself, Ms. Gilbert evaluates her ability to maintain a professional relationship with the child and family after receiving a gift. Her responsibility is to ensure that the educational plan for the child is implemented with integrity and fidelity. The child's right is to receive a Free and Appropriate Public Education (FAPE) and to receive the services that are required to implement his educational plan. He is vulnerable to not receiving FAPE if the adults involved in his education experience have conflicts or competing interests. The Park family has the right to respect and dignity regarding their decisions for their child. In addition, the family has the right of an understanding and validation of their cultural heritage. The Park family is vulnerable to disenfranchisement if the school is viewed as dismissing their family's cultural mores.

Generate alternative decisions: Ms. Gilbert can accept the gift, decline the gift, or accept the gift and donate it to a cause that would benefit the school.

Enumerate the consequences of making each decision: Accepting the gift could result in the positive consequences of validating and respecting the Park family's culture and maintain a working relationship with the family. Negative consequences of accepting the gift include the appearance of a multiple relationship that goes beyond that of case manager and potential implications for meeting future demands of the family and/or teachers. Declining the gift risks the alienation of the family and this could have an impact on the willingness of the family to work together with school personnel in the future to ensure their child's educational progress. Accepting the gift and donating it may result in the acknowledging of the family's gesture but may imply a lack of respect as the gift would not be received for its intended purpose.

Make the decision: Ms. Gilbert determines that the receipt of the gift would not change her approach in working with the child with regard to the implementation of his educational plan. She further decides that she would not feel pressure to alter her approach to working with the family after receiving such a gift. She decides that the culture of the family includes the presentation of a small gift as a gesture of respect and she reasons that to

not accept the gift would be disrespectful to the family. To avoid any appearance of influence or pressure to take sides with the family against other school personnel, she determines the best approach is to acknowledge the gift to the child's teachers and maintain clear communication about her role as the case manager of the child's educational plan, not as a friend of the family or a family's advocate in an adversarial relationship with the teachers.

Case 2

Ms. Campos is a school psychologist in a rural school district and has lived her whole life in one of the small towns served by the district. Some of the teachers, administrators, and staff at the school where she works are the same as when she attended school. In addition to her job as a school psychologist, she is a Girl Scout troop leader and a Sunday school teacher at the church. Recently, Ms. Campos was asked to participate in a manifestation determination meeting for Liz, a sophomore who has violated the student code of conduct by possessing prescription medication with the intent to distribute on the school campus. Ms. Campos was the only school psychologist available to participate in the manifestation determination meeting. Liz's mother works as a secretary in the church where Ms. Campos teaches Sunday school and they have been friends since elementary school. In addition, Ms. Campos has known Liz since she was a child in Ms. Campos's Girl Scout troop. Liz's father is a teacher at the regional middle school, where Ms. Campos also serves as the school psychologist and she has worked closely with him on several cases. She is well aware of Liz's parents' strong opinions about teenage drug use as they have been quite active in lobbying the school board for a zero-tolerance policy.

Determine whether or not the matter truly involves ethics: Ms. Campos may have an ethical dilemma involving integrity in interpersonal relationships because of the multiple relationships of the parties involved. She could choose just to follow the procedures for a typical manifestation determination process. However, given her awareness of the NASP ethical standards related to multiple relationships, she determines that it is in the best interest of all parties to consider the ethical issues involved in this scenario.

Consult existing guidelines that might apply as a possible mechanism for resolution: At first glance, it may appear that related ethical principles involving honesty and integrity in professional relationships (specifically Ethical

Principle III.4 regarding avoiding multiple relationships) prohibit her from participating in this manifestation determination. However, when consulting NASP Ethical Principle III.2 related to forthright explanation of professional services, roles and priorities and more specific standards (NASP Ethical Standard III.2.4, regarding providing services to multiple groups and ensuring explanation of multiple clients, and NASP Ethical Standard III.4.2, involving resolving conflicts in a manner that provides the greatest benefit to the client) and considering the context of the immediate situation, Ms. Campos determines that this ethical dilemma requires further analysis.

Pause to consider, as best as possible, all factors that might influence the decision that will be made: A number of factors must be considered as Ms. Campos decides how to resolve her ethical dilemma. She considers the best interest of Liz as the primary concern. She has an ongoing professional relationship with Liz because it was she who conducted the initial evaluation that resulted in Liz's identification as a student with a specific learning disability. She also has a personal relationship with Liz because she has known Liz for many years outside of the school setting. In addition, she considers her relationship with Liz's father as a teacher with whom she must continue to work as a consultant in his role as a teacher at her other school and his role as a parent of a student to whom she provides services. She further considers the context of the situation by reflecting on her personal relationship with Liz's mother in the community and the probability of the future interactions with the entire family. A broader context that she considers is the community values that have received a great deal of attention that are related to school policies related to illegal drug use concerns.

Consult with a trusted colleague: Ms. Campos contacts other school psychologists in her area and leaders in her state school psychology association for consultation about the ethical dilemma. In addition, she reaches out to her former faculty supervisors at her graduate program. During this process, she has the opportunity to explain and describe the situation and is able to think through the contextual issues involved in her dilemma.

Evaluate the rights, responsibilities, and vulnerability of all affected parties: Several parties have vested interests in the outcome of Ms. Campos' resolution of this ethical dilemma. Liz and her parents have the right to effective and competent participation in the manifestation determination meeting to ensure that Liz receives due process under the law. In addition, school personnel have rights related to securing school policy is followed

and school safety is maintained. Ms. Campos has the right and responsibility to practice within the confines of ethical guidelines and her personal competence.

Generate alternative decisions: Ms. Campos essentially has two options: participate in the meeting or do not participate in the meeting.

Enumerate the consequences of making each decision: By participating in the meeting, Ms. Campos anticipates possible positive consequences of meaningful outcomes for Liz as a result of participation of a professional who is well informed regarding the specifics of the situation. Negative consequences include strained personal and professional relationships resulting from the appearance of lack of impartiality. By not participating in the meeting, she anticipates the consequences of due process not being received because of a lack of a qualified professional (other than herself) being available to participate in the meeting, participation of an outsider who lacks knowledge of the individuals and the system and the cost to the school district related to having to contract with an outside person to prepare for, and participate in, the meeting.

Make the decision: Ms. Campos decides to participate in the meeting. In order to maintain ethical standards for practice in the context of the situation, she meets with Liz and the parents prior to the meeting to discuss the ethical considerations that she has considered in deciding to participate in the meeting. She discusses the reality of the multiple relationships and her decision that Liz, the parents, and the school are best served through her participation. She offers Liz and the parents the opportunity to ask questions and they process the answers. In addition, she meets with the school principal to discuss the process that she has used to examine the ethical concerns of the context and allows the principal to ask for any clarification or raise any concerns. By engaging in this process, she feels secure that she has made an ethical decision based on principles that consider her unique context.

Case 3

Jessica's teacher expressed concerns about Jessica's reading skills. In spite of working closely with Jessica's teachers, her reading difficulties have persisted. Mr. Stein, the school psychologist, met with Jessica's parents and asked her parents for their consent to conduct a full individual evaluation, and assured the parents that he was seeking consent for evaluation only, and that this does not constitute consent for placement. In the process of obtaining the informed consent for evaluation, he explained to the parents their rights and responsibilities as parents of a student being evaluated under special education law. The parents gave their consent for the evaluation, and the results indicated that Jessica met the eligibility criteria for specific learning disability in basic reading. Jessica's parents were very reluctant to the idea of a placement in special education. Jessica's teacher asked Mr. Stein to speak to the parents and try to persuade them to consent to placement, since he had already obtained their consent for the evaluation.

Determine whether or not the matter truly involves ethics: Following a directive of an administrator is a frequent occurrence in school psychology and this usually does not create an ethical dilemma for a practitioners. However, in this situation, Mr. Stein feels this is an ethical dilemma in that he is being asked to potentially impede the parent's right to consent to placement.

Consult existing guidelines that might apply as a possible mechanism for resolution: Several standards provide guidance regarding this situation. Generally, NASP Ethical Standard II.2.3 relates to a school psychologist's responsibility for appropriateness for his or her own actions and taking affirmative actions to avoid harmful consequences. More specifically, NASP Ethical Standard II.3.10 relates to parental involvement in decisions for their children. Relating to the systems-level issues involved in this situation, NASP Ethical Standard III.2.4 relates to acknowledging competing loyalties and demands.

Pause to consider, as best as possible, all factors that might influence the decision that will be made: Mr. Stein considers Jessica's need for services as indicated by the evaluation and his respect for the parents' autonomy in their decision making regarding their child's services. In addition, he considers the impact of his exercising a foot-in-the-door–type social influence on the parents, given that they had consented to the evaluation and now might feel pressure to agree to his request that they consent to placement.

Consult with a trusted colleague: Mr. Stein consults with other school psychologists in his district and makes an e-mail inquiry to the authors of a *School Psychology Review* article examining the impact of social psychological phenomenon on ethical decision making. Through this process, he determines that, indeed, he would be exerting social influence should he ask the parents to consent to placement of their child in special education. In addition, he was concerned to learn that many of his colleagues did not see a problem with exercising this type of influence if the end result is the implementation of the school's plan.

Evaluate the rights, responsibilities, and vulnerability of all affected parties: Mr. Stein considers the rights of the parents to self-determination in the context of potential vulnerability because of a lack of understanding of the special education process and the nature of special education services. He also considers the right of Jessica to FAPE, and Jessica's vulnerability to impairment in her educational progress if she does not receive the specialized instructional services that are indicated by the initial evaluation. He also considers the teacher's expertise and contribution to the evaluation of the student's learning progress and needs.

Generate alternative decisions: Mr. Stein considers the alternatives of meeting with the parents and not meeting with the parents. He considers the context of the nature of the conversation that would occur in such a meeting.

Enumerate the consequences of making each decision: Mr. Stein realizes that if he is exercising a foot-in-the-door–type of influence with the parents, he might be able to get them to consent regretfully to placement in special education. However, he believes that he can meet with the parents and educate them regarding the special education process, the nature of special education services, and explain again their rights as parents regarding participation in all phases of the process, including the right to withdraw their consent at a later time thereby adhering to the ethical standard related to respecting the dignity of all persons. If he does not meet with the parents and apply influence, he risks alienating the school personnel with whom he must continue to work.

Make the decision: Mr. Stein decides to meet with the parents and the rest of the special education team at the same time. During that meeting, he carefully explains the nature of the special education services that are being suggested for Jessica and the parents' rights regarding giving and removing consent for such services. In addition, he explicitly states that the parents' agreement to the initial evaluation in no way obliges them to agree to the provision of services.

Case 4

An annual meeting has been scheduled to discuss sixth-grader Julian's educational program. The principal has scheduled a meeting of the members of the committee (without the parents) for a few days before the official meeting in order to make sure they are on the same page regarding Julian's behavior and recommendations for changing his level of services. When Ms. Green, the school psychologist, expresses concerns to the principal about this process, the principal indicated that the purpose of the meeting is to be sure that the school personnel are in agreement and work out any internal conflicts in advance of meeting with the parents. In the principal's experience, this eliminates potential sources of conflict among staff and results in a less problematic meeting with the parents. In Ms. Green's experience, these meetings of school staff without the parents present can result in situations where the principal's recommendations were usually followed, even if other school personnel were not initially inclined to agree.

Determine whether or not the matter truly involves ethics: Parents are encouraged to participate in all decisions that have an impact on the education of their child. However, having a meeting of school personnel involved in a child's educational program is a strategy that can result in more efficient and productive meetings with parents. However, having a meeting that may result in employing a groupthink-type social pressure on the parent to agree with the school's position may violate the parent's rights and create an ethical dilemma for a school psychologist.

Consult existing guidelines that might apply as a possible mechanism for resolution: Several ethical principles and standards relate to the resolution of this dilemma. At a broad level, NASP Ethical Principle I.1, Autonomy and Self-Determination (Consent and Assent), states that school psychologists respect the right of persons to participate in decisions affecting their own welfare. Specifically, NASP Ethical Standard II.3.10 relates to encouraging and promoting parental participation. NASP Ethical Standard III.3.1 discusses the need for school psychologists to cooperate with other professionals in relationships based on mutual respect.

Pause to consider, as best as possible, all factors that might influence the decision that will be made: Ms. Green is very concerned that she be able to maintain her relationship with the school staff that she has worked very hard to establish. In addition, she is concerned about her relationship with the family and is sensitive to the parents being able to participate in the meeting without feeling pressured to conform to the predetermined position of the rest of the group. In addition, she is sensitive to the cultural context of Julian's family's perceptions of the school as an authority and the need to comply with authority.

Consult with a trusted colleague: Ms. Green consults with other school psychologists in her city about the practice of conducting school staff-only meetings in their schools and learns that about half of her colleagues regularly engage in this process. Finding this not definitively

helpful, she contacted her regional representative of the NASP professional ethics committee for advice.

Evaluate the rights, responsibilities, and vulnerability of all affected parties: Ms. Green considers the parents' rights to participate in processes involving their child's education and have autonomy in making decisions. In addition, the school staff has responsibility in creating safe and effective educational environments, and has the right to engage in professional problem-solving processes that utilize effective and efficient strategies. She also considers her own vulnerability in conforming to group decisions and reflects on situations in the past where she may have been susceptible to pressures of conformity.

Generate alternative decisions: Ms. Green considers several possible resolutions to her ethical dilemma. She can encourage cancellation of the school staff-only meeting, participate or not participate, but not encourage cancellation.

Enumerate the consequences of making each decision: By encouraging cancellation, Ms. Green risks alienation of the staff or diminishing her relationship with the school staff. By not participating but not encouraging the cancellation, she risks her input being minimized or dismissed in the final recommendations for services and interventions for Julian. By participating, she may contribute to applying pressures of conformity and obedience to authority in the subsequent meeting with the parents.

Make the decision: Ms. Green decides to go ahead and participate in the meeting with school staff only. She decides that during the staffing, she will ensure that the school staff will focus on any issues that relate to possible outcomes or implications of more than one potential result of the "official" meeting with the parents. She insists that any paperwork completed or goals generated are clearly delineated as "drafts." In addition, she obtains permission from all the members of the group to inform the parents that the staffing has occurred and to summarize the process for the parents. During the meeting with the parents, she ensures that her role includes both participant and group process monitor. As group process monitor, Ms. Green will ensure that all parent input is considered and final decisions reflect this input, even if these are not the same as those decisions that resulted from the staffing.

SUMMARY

A best practices approach to ethical decision making uses ethical principles as a foundation, but then considers the unique contextual factors of each case before engaging in a decision-making process. Based on the belief that no two situations are identical, the context-sensitive approach assumes that a one-size-fits-all approach can limit the effectiveness of decision making. Therefore, the school psychologist must always gather relevant information to guide the decision-making process. Cultural, linguistic, developmental, and political variables must be assessed, and the school psychologist should try to take the perspective of all relevant parties to make effective decisions that are relevant to the lives of those affected. The case examples and associated discussions provided in this chapter illustrate the importance of context in ethical decision making and discourage the use of an overly simplistic application of ethical principles. Utilizing a stepwise process that considers the context of the ethical dilemma, school psychologists can be sure to make sound decisions for the students, families, and systems that they serve.

The process of ethical decision making from this perspective recognizes that the decisions made will vary from case to case, and that what may be appropriate under one set of circumstances may be inappropriate in another context. In the absence of a context-sensitive approach, practitioners run the risk of inadvertently causing harm as they strive to effectively resolve complex ethical challenges. Future directions of inquiry in this area need to focus on the outcomes of children, families, and systems when sound ethical decision-making processes are followed.

REFERENCES

American Psychological Association. (2010). *Ethical principles of psychologists and code of conduct with the 2010 amendments.* Washington, DC: Author. Retrieved from http://www.apa.org/ethics/code/index.aspx

Armistead, L., Williams, B., & Jacob, S. (2011). *Professional ethics for school psychologists: A problem-solving model casebook* (2nd ed.). Bethesda, MD: National Association of School Psychologists.

Dailor, A. N. (2007). *A national study of ethical transgressions and dilemmas reported by school psychology practitioners.* (Unpublished master's thesis). Central Michigan University, Mt. Pleasant, MI.

Dodge, K. A. (2008). Developmental psychology. In M. H. Ebert, P. T. Loosen, B. Nurcombe, & J. F. Leckman (Eds.), *Current diagnosis and treatment: Psychiatry.* (pp. 117–134). New York, NY: McGraw-Hill.

International School Psychology Association. (2011). *The ISPA code of ethics.* Amsterdam, The Netherlands: Author.

Jacob, S., Decker, D. M., & Hartshorne, T. S. (2011). *Ethics and law for school psychologists* (6th ed.). Hoboken, NJ: Wiley.

Klose, L. M., & Lasser, J. (2012). Selected social psychological phenomena's effect of educational team decision making. In G. Rossi (Ed.), *Psychology: Selected papers.* (pp. 295–306). Rijeka, Croatia: InTech.

Klose, L. M., Lasser, J., & Reardon, R. (2012). Effects of social psychological phenomena on school psychologists' ethical decision-making: A preliminary empirical analysis. *Educational Psychology in Practice, 28,* 411–424.

Koocher, G. P., & Keith-Spiegel, P. (1998). *Ethics in psychology: Professional standards and cases.* New York, NY: Oxford University Press.

Lasser, J., & Klose, L. M. (2007). The impact of social psychological phenomena on ethical decision making. *School Psychology Review, 36,* 484–500.

Lasser, J., Klose, L. M., & Robillard, R. (2013). Context-sensitive ethics in school psychology. *Contemporary School Psychology, 17,* 119–128.

National Association of School Psychologists. (2010a). *Model for comprehensive and integrated school psychological services.* Bethesda, MD: National Association of School Psychologists. Retrieved from http://www.nasponline.org/standards/2010standards/2_PracticeModel.pdf

National Association of School Psychologists. (2010b). *Principles for professional ethics.* Bethesda, MD: National Association of School Psychologists. Retrieved from http://www.nasponline.org/standards/2010standards/1_%20Ethical%20Principles.pdf

Pope, K. S., & Vasquez, M. J. T. (2011). *Ethics in psychotherapy and counseling: A practical guide.* Hoboken, NJ: Wiley.

U.S. Government Office of Ethics. (2013). *Gifts from outside sources.* Washington, DC: Author. Retrieved from http://www.oge.gov/Topics/Gifts-and-Payments/Gifts-from-Outside-Sources/

34 Ethical and Professional Best Practices in the Digital Age

Leigh D. Armistead
Winthrop University

OVERVIEW

In the digital age, rapidly accelerating changes in digital generation, storage, and communication of information have had an impact on how school psychologists work, how they interact with each other, and even how they think. It is essential that school psychologists understand the implications of contemporary digital technology for their profession and recognize the benefits of technology. They should, however, thoughtfully consider concerns and objections that have been raised about technology.

This chapter will introduce three ideas about the digital age, present a five-step decision-making model, and discuss best practices with four contemporary issues: digital communication with and about clients; digital record keeping; computerized testing, scoring, and report writing; and professional reputation and effectiveness.

The National Association of School Psychologists (NASP) *Model for Comprehensive and Integrated School Psychological Services* (NASP, 2010a) conceptualizes contemporary school psychological services as direct and indirect services delivered at both the student and systems level. The Practice Model identifies Legal, Ethical, and Professional Practice, the primary focus of this chapter, as a foundational knowledge and skill domain. The Practice Model recommends that school psychologists provide services consistent with ethical, legal, and professional standards and engage in ethical and professional decision making. Despite being relatively nonspecific about school psychology in the digital age, the Practice Model does encourage school psychologists to "access, evaluate, and utilize information sources and technology in ways that safeguard and enhance the quality of services and responsible record keeping" (NASP, 2010a, p. 51). This chapter is intended to help them do so.

BASIC CONSIDERATIONS

Research has not yet established a relationship between school psychologists' age and skepticism about digital technology. The author, however, when presenting workshops on digital technology, has observed such a relationship and has also noticed a paradox. Many school psychologists who embrace digital technology in their personal lives—who use smartphones, engage in online banking, and make purchases online—express serious concerns about the intrusion of digital technology into their professional lives. This paradox does not seem to be age related. Many novice practitioners also seem concerned about the rapid pace of change in school psychology. Discussions in those workshops have prompted consideration of the following ideas for digital coping.

Three Ideas About the Digital Age

Digital communication and information management has a long history and is well established. Although the pace of digital innovation—and especially Internet connectedness—seems to be increasing, many school psychologists have been using personal computers since the late 1970s. The Apple II was introduced in 1977, and the Macintosh in 1984. The Internet became available to the public in 1985, and the World Wide Web in 1990 (Polsson, 2012). In general, school psychologists have the knowledge and skills to use technology wisely.

Ethical concerns about digital technology are reasonable and also have a long history. Despite their knowledge and skills, school psychologists often express concern and confusion about the use of digital technology in their schools and practices. Some see digital communication and online data management systems as potential threats to client privacy. Many are concerned about complying with ethical and professional standards. Such concerns were expressed 30 years ago by Alex Thomas, who advised:

> [S]chool psychologists need to maintain a sense of curiosity and an active commitment to seek any assessment, intervention, theory, or technology that can enhance their effectiveness with children. Simultaneously, they must also be cautious, scientifically aware, and alert to the ethical considerations associated with any new approach to old problems. (Thomas, 1984, p. 469)

This was good advice in 1984, and it is still good advice for today's school psychologists.

Professional standards revisions are easily outpaced by technological change, so decision-making skills and professional judgment are required. Prediction of development of digital communication and data management for the next 5–10 years, the usual time between revisions of professional standards, is difficult if not impossible. Nevertheless, professional standards provide some guidance in the digital age, and school psychologists should be knowledgeable about relevant standards. Continual change, however, means that good decision-making skills and professional judgment are paramount for developing best practices in digital technology.

NASP Ethics Code

The most relevant ethics code for school psychologists concerned about digital issues is the 2010 revision of the NASP *Principles for Professional Ethics* (NASP, 2010b). This code was intended to be appropriate for the contemporary roles and functions of school psychologists and to address the unique ethical challenges of school-based practice. The Principles are organized around four aspirational themes that subsume 17 ethical principles. Each principle is then articulated with several standards that provide specific guidance for commonly encountered situations. Despite providing 90 specific standards, the Principles acknowledges the following limitations:

> The *Principles for Professional Ethics*, like all codes of ethics, provide only limited guidance in making ethical choices. Individual judgment is necessary to apply the code to situations that arise in professional practice. Ethical dilemmas may be created by situations involving competing ethical principles, conflicts between ethics and law, the

conflicting interests of multiple parties, the dual roles of employee and pupil advocate, or because it is difficult to decide how statements in the ethics code apply to a particular situation. Such situations are often complicated and may require a nuanced application of these Principles to effect a resolution that results in the greatest benefit for the student and concerned others. (NASP, 2010b, Introduction)

Another reason why ethics codes cannot prescribe some aspects of professional conduct is that the codes often fail to address new and emerging ethical and professional issues in a timely manner (Armistead, Williams, & Jacob, 2011). This limitation is especially apparent with ethical standards for the use of technology. Pfohl (2010a, 2010b) contends that NASP's current ethics code does not provide detailed standards for prohibited or permitted professional conduct with digital communication and record keeping or for the use of computers in assessment, intervention, or research. Jacob and Armistead (2011a, 2011b) agree with Pfohl's critique of the code but explain the lack of more detailed standards as intentional. Jacob and Armistead point out that ethics codes must be applicable to the various roles, functions, and work settings of school psychologists and must be broad enough to provide useful guidance after technological advances. With 10-year intervals between revisions of the Principles, specific advice about technology can quickly become dated. Today's graduate students, for example, may only vaguely recall what formatting a disk means, and some may not know what a tape cassette is. In a few years, the term flash drive may be similarly ambiguous and standards about their use may seem archaic.

Ethical Decision Making

Although the Principles provides guidance for ethical decision making, the code suggests that school psychologists may need to "use a systematic problem-solving process to identify the best course of action" (NASP, 2010b, Introduction). Jacob, Decker, and Hartshorne (2011) point out that ethical decision making may sometimes be almost automatic or may quickly lead to straightforward solutions. However, Jacob and colleagues also suggest that when situations are complex or no explicit standards exist, a decision-making model can be helpful. If a decision is challenged, then the use of a decision-making model also helps school psychologists explain how the decision was reached.

A five-step decision-making model is shown in Table 34.1. All five steps may apply to complex situations, but even with less complicated problems, utilization of the model may result in more confident decision making. The example below involves a situation that was best handled by applying all five steps.

Sharon's Flash Drive: A Step-by-Step Example

Sharon was employed as a school psychologist for 10 years by a small rural district. Recently her position was eliminated due to budget cuts; that is, the district will now contract for services. She left all of her paper files (reports, record forms) in a secure file cabinet. However, to safeguard digital files of psychological reports, she copied the files in her account on the district server to a flash drive and then deleted the files. A few weeks later, the superintendent called and asked about her digital files. She explained what she had done with them. The superintendent demanded that she return the flash drive. When she resisted and explained the need for security of these confidential files, the superintendent said he would need to take legal action. Now, Sharon has been contacted by the district's lawyer who says she can be charged with theft because the records belong to the district.

Step 1: Describe the situation. An objective description of the situation is that Sharon is being threatened with legal consequences for copying digital files from her former employer's computer system and deleting the originals.

Step 2: Define the potential ethical–legal issues involved. There are several legal and ethical issues apparent in this situation. The school district contends that Sharon has taken district property, so an issue is the ownership of the psychological reports that she created. Sharon found through an Internet search that, according to copyright law in the United States, and its "work made for hire" provision, her reports belong to her employer (U.S. Copyright Office, 2012). At first, Sharon believed she was acting responsibly because NASP (2010b) standards state that she should "take reasonable steps to ensure that school psychological records are not lost due to equipment failure" (Standard II.4.7). Furthermore, the district had no policies about access to or maintenance of digital records. Sharon had not noticed, however, that the complete standard she cited states:

> [To] the extent that school psychological records are under their control, school psychologists protect electronic files from unauthorized release or modification (e.g., by using passwords and encryption), and they take reasonable steps to ensure that school psychological records are not lost due to equipment failure. (Standard II.4.7)

Sharon found that the school district has the primary responsibility under the 2004 Individuals with

Table 34.1. A Five-Step Ethical and Legal Decision-Making Model

1. *Describe the situation.* Review available information in an attempt to understand and objectively state the issues. Breaking down complex, sometimes emotionally charged situations into clear, behavioral statements is helpful.

2. *Define the potential ethical–legal issues involved.* State these as clearly and accurately as possible, without bias or exaggeration. Research the issues in question using sources such as NASP's *Principles for Professional Ethics* (2010b); federal, state, and district guidelines governing special education; textbooks on ethics and legal issues in school psychology; and job descriptions and school district policies. Be sure to consider broad ethical themes as well as specific mandates. If necessary, talk with supervisors and trusted colleagues who are familiar with the legal and ethical guidelines that apply to school psychology. On a need-to-know basis, share information specifically about the issues that have been identified.

3. *Evaluate the rights, responsibilities, and welfare of all affected parties.* Look at the big picture rather than focusing on the details of the immediate controversy. Consider the implications for students, families, teachers, administrators, other school personnel, and oneself. Remember two basic tenets of NASP's Principles: (a) school psychologists act as advocates for their student-clients and (b) at the very least, school psychologists should do no harm.

4. *Consider alternative decisions for each issue and the potential consequences of each decision.* Brainstorming without evaluating possible solutions to the problem may be helpful. Carefully evaluate how each alternative decision could have an impact on the affected parties. Consider the immediate, ongoing, and long-term consequences. Think about psychological, social, financial, and other types of costs.

5. *Make the decision, take responsibility for it, and monitor the outcomes.* Make decisions that are consistent with ethical and legal principles guidelines and feel confident that the decisions are the best choices. Take responsibility for following through on decisions, attend to the details, and attempt to bring closure to the situation.

Note. Based on information from Koocher and Keith-Spiegel (2008) and Jacob et al. (2011).

Disabilities Education Improvement Act of 2004 (IDEA; Pub. L. No. 108–445) and the Family Educational Rights and Privacy Act (FERPA; 20 U.S.C. 1 1232) to maintain student records, permit appropriate access, and safeguard their confidentiality. Sharon decided that her responsibilities under these laws ended when she was no longer employed by the district. She also decided that she had no further responsibility to keep records under her control. However, she realized that school psychologists can and should advocate for district policies regarding student records that are consistent with the law and with ethical standards.

Step 3: Evaluate the rights, responsibilities, and welfare of all affected parties. Sharon recognized that the affected parties clearly included the school district and herself. The district had asserted its property rights. Sharon believed she had an ethical responsibility. However, after discussing this situation with some colleagues, Sharon realized that other affected parties might include other psychologists who need access to the digital files and ultimately the students and parents who had received psychological services.

Step 4: Consider alternative decisions for each issue and the potential consequences of each decision. Sharon thought through several actions that she could take. At first, she considered standing her ground and keeping the files. Sharon realized that she would be on shaky ground legally and could suffer legal consequences. Next, she considered simply returning the flash drive. This bothered Sharon because the district did not have any digital security policies and procedures. Then Sharon considered an attempt to compromise with the district and return the files under certain conditions.

Step 5: Make the decision, take responsibility for it, and monitor the outcomes. Sharon met with the superintendent and the district's attorney and expressed her concerns about the lack of district policies on digital record keeping. They agreed to consider adopting a FERPA-compliant policy that Sharon found on the Internet. She returned the flash drive.

BEST PRACTICES IN ETHICS IN THE DIGITAL AGE

As previously discussed, the pace of digital innovation, especially with Internet connectedness, seems to be increasing. In both our personal and professional lives, if something is not yet online, it soon will be. In this section we consider four aspects of school psychology practice that have been especially influenced by Internet connectedness: digital communication with and about clients; digital record keeping; computerized testing, scoring, and report writing; and professional reputation and effectiveness.

Digital Communication With and About Clients

Until recently, the most common technological methods of communicating with and about clients were the telephone and fax machine. Ethical considerations about these devices were basic: a private place to use the phone and a privacy cover sheet for faxes. Today, however, digital options for communicating with and about clients are proliferating and include the following:

- E-mail and e-mail file attachments
- Mobile phone audio and video calls
- Texts and instant messages
- E-mail lists, e-communities, e-mail discussion groups
- Web pages and blogs
- Social networking services such as Facebook, Twitter, and Google+
- School and classroom networking services such as http://www.edmodo.com and http://www.gaggle.com

A comprehensive discussion of these communication methods and their relevance to the practice of school psychology is beyond the scope of this chapter. For more information, see Cummings (2011) and Harvey and Struzziero (2008). Each of these communication methods, if used carelessly, has the potential to affect a school psychologist's professional reputation and effectiveness. This topic will be discussed in a later section of the chapter. This section discusses various aspects of communication with and about clients.

Ethical and Legal Guidelines

Regardless of the method used to communicate with and about clients, a primary consideration is respecting client privacy. NASP's *Principles for Professional Ethics* requires that "[s]chool psychologists respect the right of persons to choose for themselves whether to disclose their private thoughts, feelings, beliefs, and behaviors" (NASP, 2010b, Principle I.2). This principle is articulated further in the seven standards shown in Table 34.2. These privacy and confidentiality standards require that school psychologists minimize intrusions on privacy, respect parents' privileged communication rights, establish confidentiality agreements at the onset of providing psychological services, and discuss and release confidential information for professional pur-

Table 34.2. NASP Ethical Standards Regarding Privacy and Confidentiality

Standard I.2.1. School psychologists respect the right of persons to self-determine whether to disclose private information.

Standard I.2.2. School psychologists minimize intrusions on privacy. They do not seek or store private information about clients that is not needed in the provision of services. School psychologists recognize that client–school psychologist communications are privileged in most jurisdictions, and do not disclose information that would put the child or family at legal, social, or other risk if shared with third parties except as permitted by the mental health provider–client privilege laws in their state.

Standard I.2.3. School psychologists inform children and other clients of the boundaries of confidentiality at the outset of establishing a professional relationship. They seek a shared understanding with clients regarding the types of information that will and will not be shared with third parties. However, if a child is in immediate need of assistance, it is permissible to delay the discussion of confidentiality until the immediate crisis is resolved. School psychologists recognize that it may be necessary to discuss confidentiality at multiple points in a professional relationship to ensure client understanding and agreement regarding how sensitive disclosures will be handled.

Standard I.2.4. School psychologists respect the confidentiality of information obtained during their professional work. Information is not revealed to third parties without the agreement of a minor child's parent or legal guardian (or an adult student), except in those situations in which failure to release information would result in danger to the student or others, or where otherwise required by law. Whenever feasible, student assent is obtained prior to disclosure of his or her confidences to third parties, including disclosures to the student's parents.

Standard I.2.5. School psychologists discuss and/or release confidential information only for professional purposes and only with persons who have a legitimate need to know. They do so within the strict boundaries of relevant privacy statutes.

Standard I.2.6. School psychologists respect the right of privacy of students, parents, and colleagues with regard to sexual orientation, gender identity, or transgender status. They do not share information about the sexual orientation, gender identity, or transgender status of a student (including minors), parent, or school employee with anyone without that individual's permission.

Standard I.2.7. School psychologists respect the right of privacy of students, their parents and other family members, and colleagues with regard to sensitive health information (e.g., presence of a communicable disease). They do not share sensitive health information about a student, parent, or school employee with others without that individual's permission (or the permission of a parent or guardian in the case of a minor). School psychologists consult their state laws and department of public health for guidance if they believe a client poses a health risk to others

Note. From *Principles for Professional Ethics*, by National Association of School Psychologists, 2010, Bethesda, MD: National Association of School Psychologists. Copyright 2010 by National Association of School Psychologists. Reprinted with permission.

poses only (subject to certain restrictions). The privacy of all persons' sexual orientation, gender identity or transgender status, as well as any sensitive health information are highlighted as meriting special protection. When digital communication involves transmission of information in student records, the Principles' standards regarding record keeping shown in Table 34.3 should also be considered.

A unique aspect of school-based practice—in contrast with private practice—is a requirement to comply with FERPA and IDEA rather than the Health Insurance Portability and Accountability Act (HIPAA, Pub. L. 104–191) regarding privacy and confidentiality of client information and the transmission of client information by digital methods. As discussed in more detail by Jacob et al. (2011), school psychologists employed in schools receiving federal funds are typically required to comply with FERPA but not HIPAA.

Elementary and secondary schools are not usually considered HIPAA-covered entities (see U.S. Department of Health and Human Services & U.S. Department of Education, 2008).

FERPA does not prohibit the use of e-mail for transmitting student educational records. However, school psychologists should use e-mail sensibly and, before doing so, consider the sensitivity of information being sent as well as the consequences of any inadvertent disclosures. Even with sensitive information, however, FERPA does not mandate specific protective measures such as encryption. The U.S. Department of Education has advised schools that

reasonable and appropriate steps consistent with current technological developments should be used to control access to and safeguard the integrity of education records in electronic data storage and transmission, including the use of e-mail, websites, and other Internet protocols. (McDonald & Tribbensee, 2007)

FERPA provides little guidance regarding digital communication with clients, but HIPAA guidelines could be helpful in decision making. HIPAA's Security Rule, which covers storage and transmission of digital client health information, does not apply to video, fax, or telephone communication with clients. Practitioners may communicate with clients with digital methods if they take reasonable precautions such as checking e-mail addresses or limiting the types of client information conveyed (Baker & Bufka, 2011). Published guidelines about digital transmission of health information have been published by the U.S. Department of Commerce (Scarfone, Souppaya, & Sexton, 2007). Relatedly, Jacob and Armistead (2011a) suggest that, in the light of conflicting court opinions about whether e-mails may be educational records, school districts should develop their own guidelines for the use of digital technology in communication and data management.

Unlike FERPA, IDEA specifically permits parents to choose to receive prior written notices, procedural safeguards notices, and due process complaint notices by e-mail (IDEA, Sections 300.503, 300.504, 300.508). As a result, some districts seek consent to communicate by e-mail as part of the informed consent process prior to psychoeducational evaluations.

School psychologists should also be knowledgeable about any state laws or district policies about e-mailing, texting, and social networking with students. Some districts prohibit any digital communication with individual students, perhaps because of concerns about social relationships developing. In 2011, Missouri became the first state to enact legislation prohibiting educators from "friending" or having other direct communication with students over the Internet. Facebook Pages, to be discussed later in the chapter, were not prohibited. After pressure from educators, the law was repealed and replaced with legislation requiring districts to develop policies regarding employee–student digital communication (Protalinski, 2011).

Ethical and professional practices in online counseling have not yet received much attention in school psychology. In clinical psychology, however, Telehealth and Telemedicine have received considerable attention. For example, Fenichel et al. (2002) address what they term "myths and realities" (p. 481) of online therapy. Baker and Bufka (2011) discuss several relevant ethical and professional issues including informed consent, privacy,

e-mail, video conferencing, and reimbursement. The International Society for Mental Health Online (2000) has proposed its *Suggested Principles for the Online Provision of Mental Health Services*. The National Board of Certified Counselors (2012) has published the *NBCC Policy Regarding the Provision of Distance Professional Services*. School psychologists intending to provide online counseling services or use digital technology to augment face-to-face counseling should consult these sources and also reflect on how the NASP (2010b) *Principles for Professional Ethics* apply to such situations.

Best Practices: Mobile Phones

When communicating with and about clients, it is likely that most school psychologists use mobile phones and are aware of the lack of privacy when using their phones in public places. Some have questioned whether mobile phones are more susceptible to eavesdropping by electronic means. Such concerns apparently were valid in previous years when mobile phones used analog technology. Contemporary mobile phones are digital, and their signals are much more difficult to intercept. However, many of today's smartphones are able to create and store digital information about clients. As discussed in the following section, these digital records should be protected by passwords limiting access to the phone as well as to any sensitive documents stored on the phone.

Best Practices: E-Mail and Messaging Services

It is difficult to imagine practicing school psychology today without e-mail, file attachments, and text services. They enable rapid and frequent communication with parents, teachers, colleagues, and sometimes students at a low cost and often provide an almost instantaneous response. Harvey and Carlson (2003), however, have pointed out that it is easy to misinterpret the meaning of e-mails (and by extension, text messages). E-mail messages usually lack a social context and the nonverbal cues that we rely on when interpreting messages. Harvey and Carlson also note that the subjective experience of writing e-mails gives an illusion of privacy and of impermanence that is not realistic. It is ironic that e-mails and texts are more permanent than the paper messages that they replace. Even after e-mails are deleted, copies may remain on both the sender's and receiver's computers and backup systems as well as the service provider's servers.

Despite current concerns about e-mail, good advice about the ethics and etiquette of e-mail has been available for many years. It should also be noted that e-mails sent with an account provided by a public school district likely belong to—and can be accessed by—the school district. Although school psychologists would generally not be held accountable for the content of e-mail messages received (including spam), they should have little expectation of privacy regarding e-mails they send to others using an e-mail account provided by their employer (Jacob & Armistead, 2011b).

As illustrated in Vignette 1, personally identifiable information in e-mails and file attachments raises concerns for many school psychologists. The use of password protection and file encryption reassures some school psychologists as reasonable and appropriate measures consistent with the requirements of FERPA. Some are concerned, however, that e-mail communications with parents or about students are actually student records (as previously discussed) and seek to minimize the use of e-mail for communicating any type of student information.

Vignette 1: Your district's student support services department uses a district server-based system to compile multidisciplinary team reports for all student evaluations. School psychologists, speech pathologists, special education staff, and others have access only to their sections of the report shell, and only the writer can make changes to the draft. A departmental goal is to provide parents with a draft copy of the team report at least a week prior to multidisciplinary team meetings. In the past, reports have been mailed. Soon the online system will have the capability to e-mail draft and final reports to parents, clinicians, and other agencies. E-mail with parents is routinely used in your district. Parents are given notice in parent handbooks and in online postings that e-mail is routinely used for communication, that it may be less secure than conventional mail, and that parents may opt out if necessary. Your director has asked for your comments about the proposal to e-mail multidisciplinary team reports.

Best Practices: Social Media

Unlike e-mail, a consensus on recommended practices for using social media to communicate with students is still developing. Numerous social networking sites exist, with Facebook being the most widely used. The company recently reported having more than 1 billion user accounts. Users are required to be at least 13 years old to register, create a personal profile, add other users as friends, post photographs, and exchange messages.

To allay concerns about privacy, Facebook users may choose their own privacy settings and determine who may see various parts of their profile pages (Starks, 2011). Facebook is, of course, not just an online communication service. It is a cultural phenomenon that has affected the social life of users in many ways. It has also been the subject of criticism for issues such as violating users' privacy and threatening children's safety. The potential of social networking to enhance or diminish school psychologists' reputation and effectiveness will be discussed in a later section of this chapter.

Despite the controversy, social media have potential for school psychologists to communicate with students. Lehavot, Barnett, and Powers (2010) contend that social networking is now central to the lives of many young people and has become the primary way in which they communicate. In fact, they argue that young people who have grown up with social media could be considered almost bilingual; that is, they communicate fluently not just in their native language but also in a variety of digital media. So the question for school psychologists may be: How can we speak our students' so-called second language while doing so ethically and professionally? There are several ways.

School psychologists using Facebook should understand that they don't have to "friend" students in order to interact with them on Facebook. Instead, as Phillips, Baird, and Fogg (2011) suggest, educators should create Facebook Groups, which provide a private space for group members to interact. For example, a school psychologist who leads a counseling group for students with attention deficit hyperactivity disorder could create a closed Facebook Group for those particular students. If the school psychologist posted a link to an online video he or she wanted the group to view or sent a reminder about counseling homework, each member of the group would receive a message from Facebook to his or her phone, tablet, or computer.

Another Facebook tool that is potentially useful for school psychologists is Facebook Pages. These permit users to interact with a specified set of other Facebook members in a way that is transparent and secure. School psychologists using Facebook Pages to communicate with a counseling group, for example, may allow parents to have access to their pages. This negates concerns about inappropriate social contact with students. For an example of a public Facebook Page with useful content on this topic, see http://www.facebook.com/FBforEducators. Despite these efforts by Facebook to provide safe and transparent services for educators, some school districts restrict access to Facebook in their schools.

Many districts, however, permit access or subscribe to social networking sites developed specifically for schools. Two well-known services are http://www.gaggle.net and http://www.edmodo.com, both of which provide free accounts for individual educators. It is not clear, however, whether students accustomed to "checking Facebook" on the way home from school can be encouraged to "check Gaggle."

Best Practices: Web Pages and Blogs

A rewarding professional activity for many school psychologists is maintaining a website to provide information to both colleagues and clients. Sites are also maintained by NASP (http://www.nasponline.org), state school psychology associations, and district psychological services units. An example of a school psychologist's website that has grown into an invaluable resource is Jim Wright's http://www.interventioncentral.org. It provides information about both academic and behavioral interventions as well as curriculum-based assessment.

Cummings (2011) has suggested that school psychologists and their psychological services departments promote their services using Web pages and blogs to provide accurate information about mental health, disabilities, available services, district resources, and referral procedures. Very little has been published about how school psychologists should use websites professionally and ethically. An important consideration, of course, is providing clients with accurate information and links to authoritative and evidence-based resources.

Blogs are Internet personal publishing sites, some of which provide subscription and discussion features. They usually comprise discrete entries or posts by the author on a recurring basis. Popular free blogging services include http://www.wordpress.org, http://www.tumblr.com, and http://www.blogspot.com. NASP also provides a blogging service to its members. Several thousand school psychologists have created blogs and many post to them regularly. Some of these blogs are essentially personal narratives—online diaries. The relationship of such blogs to professional reputation and effectiveness will be discussed later in this chapter. Many blogs, however, feature regular informational posts on professional topics and are meant to communicate with colleagues, parents, teachers, and sometimes students. Informational blogs can be helpful to both colleagues and consumers of psychological services and may provide a way to keep in touch with current and former clients. As with Web pages, though, an important precaution is making sure that information published in online blogs is accurate and any provided links are to authoritative and evidence-based resources.

Digital Record Keeping

A topic that prompts many questions to the NASP Ethics Committee and to ethics workshop presenters is digital record keeping. As Nicholson (2011) discusses, record keeping has long been a problem for psychologists. As paper records have proliferated and file cabinets filled, psychologists and their employers have used various data storage methods, including microfilm, floppy disks, and then hard drives. Some school districts have outsourced their record keeping to data storage companies that scan records into digital files and destroy the originals. A current solution to this problem is online data storage on a district server or data in rented server space in "the cloud." Each of these methods has had benefits for practitioners and their employers, but each has resulted in new concerns.

Ethical and Legal Guidelines

The previous section of this chapter discussed ethical and legal standards regarding privacy and confidentiality of student records in the context of digital communication. All ethical standards and laws cited in that section also apply to digital record keeping. In addition, the NASP *Principles for Professional Ethics* (NASP, 2010b) requires that "[s]chool psychologists safeguard the privacy of school psychological records and ensure parent access to the records of their own children" (Principle II.4). This principle is articulated further by nine standards, several of which are shown in Table 34.3. These standards require that school psychologists personally discuss with parents how students' psychological records will be managed, ensure that parents can access those records, make sure that parents are notified of any digital storage and transmission of those records, and take steps to ensure that the confidentiality of records is appropriately maintained. These standards also acknowledge that record keeping is largely a responsibility of school districts. Nevertheless, the standards require that school psychologists work with their districts to ensure confidentiality of and appropriate access to school psychological records and, eventually, the proper disposal of those records.

It should be noted that the NASP *Principles for Professional Ethics* emphasizes the importance of maintaining access to records as well as maintaining confidentiality of records. This is consistent with the FERPA requirements that ensure that parents, and

Table 34.3. NASP Ethical Standards Regarding School Psychological Records (Selected)

Standard II.4.1. School psychologists discuss with parents and adult students their rights regarding creation, modification, storage, and disposal of psychological and educational records that result from the provision of services. Parents and adult students are notified of the electronic storage and transmission of personally identifiable school psychological records and the associated risks to privacy.

Standard II.4.4. School psychologists ensure that parents have appropriate access to the psychological and educational records of their child....

Standard II.4.5. School psychologists take steps to ensure that information in school psychological records is not released to persons or agencies outside of the school without the consent of the parent except as required and permitted by law.

Standard II.4.6. To the extent that school psychological records are under their control, school psychologists ensure that only those school personnel who have a legitimate educational interest in a student are given access to the student's school psychological records without prior parent permission or the permission of an adult student.

Standard II.4.7. To the extent that school psychological records are under their control, school psychologists protect electronic files from unauthorized release or modification (e.g., by using passwords and encryption), and they take reasonable steps to ensure that school psychological records are not lost due to equipment failure.

Standard II.4.9. School psychologists, in collaboration with administrators and other school staff, work to establish district policies regarding the storage and disposal of school psychological records that are consistent with law and sound professional practice....

Note. From *Principles for Professional Ethics*, by National Association of School Psychologists, 2010, Bethesda, MD: National Association of School Psychologists. Copyright 2010 by National Association of School Psychologists. Reprinted with permission.

adult students, have access to school records. In the case of digital records, the Principles suggests taking "reasonable steps to ensure that school psychological records are not lost due to equipment failure" (NASP, 2010b, Standard II.4.7).

As previously noted, FERPA, and not HIPAA, generally applies to school psychologists' records in elementary and secondary schools that receive federal funds. Special education laws and regulations provide somewhat greater protection for the education records of students with disabilities than does FERPA, and these laws and regulations should be consulted when developing guidelines for the sharing, storage, and disposal of digital student records (Daggett, 2008). School psychologists should also consult state and local policies regarding digital record keeping. At a minimum, FERPA requirements should be met. FERPA does not permit districts to leave education records unprotected or accessible by unauthorized individuals regardless of the format. This has been interpreted to mean that districts must use, for example, physical, technological, and administrative methods, including staff training, to protect records in ways that are reasonable and appropriate (McDonald & Tribbensee, 2007). Vignette 2 presents a situation in which FERPA requirements were likely not met.

Vignette 2: A professor wrote to say that an intern she supervises lost a computer flash drive containing a dozen or so psychological reports. Because

her district bills Medicaid for psychological services, her reports included students' Social Security numbers as well as the usual confidential student and family background information. Of course, prevention would have been the answer to this problem. Report templates can be set up to require a password for someone to open and read them and contents can even be encrypted. In this case, though, no password was set and no encryption used. The intern asked whether she should notify all of the families of the children she had evaluated of the loss (Armistead et al., 2011).

Best Practices. Databases

School districts use a variety of database systems for storing and accessing student information. Many of these systems run on district servers and are accessed over district intranets. In fact, school psychologists who log into user accounts with desktop computers are most likely storing data on a district server. Asking questions about the security of the system, about who has access, and whether the system is backed up would be sensible. It is likely that these local database systems, which are usually behind protective district firewalls, are safe and reliable. However, because local server storage can be expensive, some districts lease storage space on remote computers by using commercial services such as Google+, Amazon Cloud Drive, and Microsoft SkyDrive. The stored records are then accessed over the Internet. School psychologists should be cautious about the reliability and security of these systems and, if they must be used, be sure to use password protection and perhaps encrypt files.

Many school psychologists have found that free or inexpensive personal cloud storage systems such as iCloud or Dropbox are quite useful. With these systems, files are first saved on a laptop, tablet, or desktop computer and then automatically copied to the cloud server. Subsequent changes to the files are synchronized. School psychologists using multiple devices find these systems especially helpful as the files on the remote computer can be accessed from any device by logging into the account. Finally, groups of school psychologists collaborating on writing projects can use shared documents. Although some have questioned the security of these systems, Dropbox's security provisions (see https://www.dropbox.com/security) are quite impressive. Of course, users can, and perhaps should, use a password to protect sensitive files.

Best Practices: Case Management Systems

To efficiently manage response-to-intervention and special education systems and comply with increasingly complex regulations, many school districts and some states have invested in sophisticated Web-based case management systems. As described in more detail by Cummings (2011), these systems can provide an online referral-to-placement process, support the development of Individualized Education Programs, and help manage annual reviews and reevaluations. They permit secure storage of and access to special education records. Two examples of comprehensive solutions are *Exceed* (http://www.scantron.com/software/student-achievement/exceed-rti/overview) and netIEP (http://www.netchemia.com/products/netIEP).

School psychologists are often wary of submitting psychological and intervention reports to online management systems. They cite concerns about privacy and the possibility of reports being revised without their permission. Case management systems should have a hierarchical permission system to restrict access to certain categories of information to those with a need to know and prevent revisions by anyone but the creator of a document. School psychology departments should work with district administrators to ensure that such protections are included in any management systems that are purchased.

Best Practices: Laptop Computers and Mobile Devices

It is likely that the loss or theft of school psychologists' laptop, tablet, or smartphone presents a greater threat to data security than does a district database system. All such devices should be protected with an initial login password. Nicholson (2011) recommends that data on mobile computing devices (including flash drives) be encrypted as well as password protected and that only the minimum necessary information be stored on such devices. School psychologists should familiarize themselves with capabilities of their devices that can help safeguard their data. Apple computers, for example, feature a full hard drive encryption system called FileVault that is said to be very secure. To guard against loss, Apple computers, iPads, and iPhones include an application called *Find My iPhone*. If these devices are connected to the Internet, a user may locate them on a map, send a message to the home screen, lock the devices, and, as a last resort, erase them.

Best Practices: Disposal of Computers

When discarding or recycling computers, school psychologists have an ethical responsibility to be sure that all sensitive information is deleted from hard drives. Deleted files, however, remain on computer drives until new data are written over old data and can be recovered with simple undelete programs. Windows users should download a secure delete utility program. OS X users should use the Finder's *Secure Empty Trash* command or may reformat their drives with the *Secure Erase* option. Smartphone flash memory can also store sensitive information as well as allow unauthorized access to cloud storage. Before disposing of these devices, their memory should also be securely wiped using a factory reset command. Procedures for doing so depend on the phone's operating system. Instructions should be available online.

Computerized Testing, Scoring, and Report Writing

As summarized by Carlson and Harvey (2004), the use of computers in psychological assessment dates back at least to 1965 when a test interpretation system became available for a major personality inventory. Since then, computer-assisted test scoring has become routine, with some tests now being scorable only by computer software. Many school psychologists also use software for test interpretation and to assist their report writing. *Score and Report* (http://www.scoreandreport.com) is a popular online report writing tool that imports scores from scoring programs, generates tables and graphs, and suggests text to include in the report. The service also archives text that the school psychologist has previously written.

Computer-administered and online tests have not been prominent in school psychology, but this could be changing. Test developers have recently announced online versions of some assessment measures (e.g., http://www.pariconnect.com and http://www.aseba.com) and computer-assisted administration systems for others. An example of computer-assisted testing is the Q-interactive system, which uses Apple iPads and an online service to administer and score standardized aptitude and achievement tests.

As Jacob et al. (2011) suggest, school psychologists have a professional responsibility to consider the advantages of computerized and computer-assisted assessment. These advantages include improvements in accuracy, more sophisticated scoring algorithms (e.g., multiple regression), adaptations for students with disabilities, interpretative guidance, and, perhaps, less expensive instruments with more frequent revisions. There is also some evidence for increased client candor when responding to computer versions of behavior rating scales. Carlson and Harvey (2004) suggest that time saved due to computerized assessment could provide school psychologists with opportunities for other important responsibilities. Despite these advantages, a challenge has been to apply ethical and legal standards in this area of school psychology practice.

Ethical and Legal Guidelines

Although few specific guidelines exist regarding computerized assessment, scoring, and report writing, all NASP *Principles for Professional Ethics* assessment standards apply to computer-administered or -assisted assessment. Principle II.3, for example, requires that "[s]chool psychologists maintain the highest standard for responsible professional practices in educational and psychological assessment and direct and indirect interventions" (NASP, 2010b). A standard subsumed under this principle states:

> School psychologists use assessment techniques and practices that the profession considers to be responsible, research-based practice.

- School psychologists select assessment instruments and strategies that are reliable and valid for the child and the purpose of the assessment. When using standardized measures, school psychologists adhere to the procedures for administration of the instrument that are provided by the author or publisher or the instrument....

- When using computer-administered assessments, computer-assisted scoring, and/or interpretation programs, school psychologists choose programs that meet professional standards for accuracy and validity. School psychologists use professional judgment in evaluating the accuracy of computer-assisted assessment findings for the examinee. (NASP, 2010b, Standard II.3.2)

The 1999 revision of the *Standards for Educational and Psychological Testing* (American Educational Research Association, American Psychological Association, & National Council on Measurement in Education, 1999) includes recommendations that test manuals include data on comparability of traditional and computerized tests (Standard 6.11) and that publishers of test interpretation systems should provide more information about the basis for, and validity of, their systems (Standard 6.12). However, the standards also emphasize that professionals should not use test interpretations from digital systems unless they have the expertise to judge the appropriateness (Standard 11.21) and the quality of the interpretations (Standard 12.15).

Vignette 3: Two school psychologists attending a recent NASP convention heard about something new: tablet computer administration of some frequently used standardized tests. Concerned about the ethical implications of computerizing traditional tests, they met with a publisher's representative in the exhibit hall. They learned that the tablet was being used to record data usually entered on test record forms. They asked pointed questions about how personally identifiable information would be collected by the system and were relieved to find that a HIPAA-compliant digital system was used and that the data would be stored in Canada. Comparability studies were being performed to be sure that subtests administered with the tablet provided reliable and valid results. They were reassured that data temporarily stored on the tablet computer were secure. They concluded that the system would provide significant benefits to examiners with minimal risk.

Best Practices: Computerized Test Administration

Decisions to adopt computerized assessment methods are complex. Vignette 3 illustrates how two school psychologists began a decision-making process regarding computer-assisted testing. When school psychologists select assessment measures that have been adapted for computer administration, they need to be sure that the measures have been shown to have adequate reliability and validity for decision-making purposes. Schulenberg and Yutrzenka (2004) point out that computerized versions of tests should be empirically validated as equivalent to the traditional versions. Studies of equivalence between pencil-and-paper and computerized tests, however, have shown a range of results. School psychologists should carefully examine the evidence provided by test publishers regarding equivalence and consult expert reviews. They should also understand that equivalence studies provide group data, but for individual students, results may vary. If a student, for example, is not comfortable with computers, his or her results may not be equivalent to those from a traditional measure and may not be valid for decision-making purposes.

A second concern about computerized assessment methods is that they may encourage practitioners to go beyond their areas of competence in assessment (Carlson & Harvey, 2004). School psychologists should reflect on their training and experience both in the type of assessment and with the particular assessment measure. They should understand that they are professionally accountable for their assessment results regardless of any technological measures that are utilized.

Best Practices: Computerized Test Scoring

Computerized scoring saves time and reduces errors in scoring many assessment measures. Some tests are now sold with scoring software included, and the use of such software has become routine in school psychology. Pfohl (2010a) points out that school psychologists must be sure that they have the latest version of computer scoring programs and warns that not all publishers routinely notify users when updates are available. With computerized scoring, client information is usually stored on a school psychologist's computer. Issues regarding the security of such data were previously discussed. Online test scoring, however, as is evident in Vignette 3, raises concerns about privacy of client information as it is transmitted over the Internet and perhaps stored on a test publisher's server. School psychologists should review the publisher's precautions for maintaining privacy. In most cases, they should be using some form of HIPAA-compliant encryption during transmission and meet federal standards for data storage.

Best Practices: Computerized Test Interpretation and Report Writing

As Carlson and Harvey (2004) discuss in more detail, the use of computers to analyze and interpret test data provides benefits but presents risks of misuse. Interpretative software can quickly generate lists of intraindividual and normative strengths and weaknesses. Using an expert system approach, such software may also provide diagnostic hypotheses. More sophisticated systems may analyze multiple assessment measures (e.g., aptitude and achievement) when developing interpretations. Despite these benefits, school psychologists should proceed cautiously. Interpretative software output can provide an illusion of accuracy and certainty that may not be warranted. Carlson and Harvey (2004) suggest that school psychologists regard test interpretation programs and services as virtual consultants and consider their output as mere suggestions or hypotheses when analyzing and interpreting assessment data.

Test interpretation software is often embedded in computer software or online services that produce what may appear to be completed psychoeducational reports. As with test interpretation, Carlson and Harvey (2004) suggest that school psychologists be cautious when using these products and services. They should review the software's documentation for evidence of validity and consult expert reviews. They should be aware that computer-generated reports may appear comprehensive and authoritative but seldom take into account variables that influence test performance such as a student's language skills, prior history, test session behaviors, and ethnic or cultural background. Even with experts as authors, report-generation programs may suggest explanations that are not valid (e.g., a low processing speed score does not always indicate low processing speed). A final caution is that these programs may suggest interventions that are not valid, practical, or evidence based. School psychologists should remember that they are professionally responsible for the content of their reports regardless of any technological resources they utilize.

Professional Reputation and Effectiveness

School psychologists understand that they usually have little actual authority within their school districts but function with a blend of what French and Raven (1959) called expert and referent power. They may be able to quickly establish expert power by having good credentials and appearing knowledgeable, but they know that referent power takes longer to develop and requires that their clients perceive them as having goals and values similar to their own. For previous generations of school psychologists, maintaining their reputations in their schools and communities was an important part of establishing and maintaining referent power. Today, "whether we like it or not, we all live on the Internet—and our clients know where we live. It is impossible in our own current world to escape having an online identity" (Nicholson, 2011, p. 216). Having a positive online identity is essential to establishing and maintaining referent power and being effective school psychologists.

Ethical and Legal Standards

NASP's *Principles for Professional Ethics* was written to protect clients and other consumers of school psychologists' service and maintain the public's trust in the profession of school psychology. Therefore, in general, the code relates to professional conduct rather than private conduct. Standard III.4.1 states "… [s]chool psychologists, in their private lives, are free to pursue their own personal interests, except to the degree that those interests compromise professional effectiveness" (NASP, 2010b). Vignette 4 illustrates how private conduct can easily become public conduct in the digital age.

A second ethical standard that may be helpful with decision making in this area is Principle IV.3, which states that "[s]chool psychologists accept responsibility to monitor their own conduct and the conduct of other school psychologists to ensure it conforms to ethical standards" (NASP, 2010b).

Finally, ethical standards regarding multiple relationships may be applicable. Principle III.4 states that "[s]chool psychologists avoid multiple relationships and conflicts of interest that diminish their professional effectiveness" (NASP, 2010b). Jacob et al. (2011) point out that this reflects a contemporary understanding that not all social contacts between school psychologists and parents or other clients are likely to be harmful. In fact, some social contacts with parents may actually improve home–school relationships.

Vignette 4: Dr. Phelps is a school psychologist in a small town in a socially conservative part of the country. She keeps in touch with her graduate school cohort and other friends through Facebook but thinks she has adjusted her privacy settings to keep her private life out of the public eye. At a recent state conference social gathering, she upended an empty liquor bottle and pretended to drink from it. A colleague snapped a photo, uploaded it to Facebook, and tagged her in the photo. She was soon embarrassed to find that the photo could be viewed by both her friends and the friends of her colleague, some of whom were school administrators. After some time in the Facebook Help Center, she was able to untag the photo but found that it was still visible by her colleague's friends. At school on Monday morning, the assistant principal grinned at her and said "That must have been some party! Wish I'd been there."

Best Practices: E-Mail and E-Mail Lists

As previously discussed, e-mail is an invaluable communication tool, but the potential of e-mail to undermine a school psychologist's reputation and effectiveness should be considered. E-mail should always be used cautiously and used with no expectation of privacy. School district employees should assume that their employer can read their e-mails and so must avoid gossip, derogatory comments, or complaints in their e-mails. Because most e-mails cannot be recalled with certainty, hasty use of the Send button should be avoided. Users should save draft copies and consider revising potentially controversial e-mails before sending. School psychologists should avoid using "reply all" when responding to messages in e-mail lists.

Best Practices: Social Networking

As previously discussed, there are numerous ways to network online. Any social media, including Facebook, used by educators has become somewhat controversial. An online search using the search terms *Facebook* and *teacher* will yield hundreds, if not thousands, of accounts of educators' being disciplined by their school districts for posting inappropriate content on their pages. It is likely that many of these incidents resulted from users not adjusting privacy settings to prevent public disclosure of personal content. In response to these incidents, many districts have adopted policies about the use of social networking services by their employees. As Lehavot et al. (2010) discuss in more detail, social media is where the boundaries of personal and professional lives meet. As shown in Vignette 4 above, privacy settings are one key to keeping those boundaries intact.

If permitted by their employer, school psychologists should consider the use of social media to enhance their reputation and effectiveness. A social media page can present appropriate photographs of the school psychologist and his or her family, share some personal interests, and describe professional training, specializations, and services provided. This sort of online profile is likely to reassure parents who may be wary of psychologists and their services. School psychologists who are doubtful about having an online professional presence should reflect on their own tendency to immediately search online prior to their own appointments with other professionals. They should also periodically conduct an online search using their own name to protect their online reputation.

Best Practices: Web Pages and Blogs

As previously discussed, Web pages and blogs can be an excellent way for school psychologists to communicate with clients and colleagues. As with social networking, Web pages and blogs can present a personal/professional profile that can inform clients about a school psychologist's qualifications and services. School psychologists should be cautious about blending their professional and personal lives when blogging. As previously noted, some school psychologists' blogs appear to be autobiographical in nature and are, essentially, personal narratives or diaries. Lehavot (2009) notes that some bloggers have a false sense of privacy and seem unaware that their personal musings, although perhaps meant for a small group of subscribers, are actually public. School psychologists should, of course, avoid including any information about clients in their blogs and be cautious about other content as well. Public school employees who blog about their experiences with students, express frustrations with their work settings, or rant about their dissatisfaction with their careers can expect their employer's censure.

SUMMARY

This chapter has provided best practice guidelines regarding four contemporary issues: digital communication with and about clients; digital record keeping; computerized testing, scoring, and report writing; and professional reputation and effectiveness. The chapter encourages sensible but cautious use of technology to increase school psychologists' efficiency, enhance their practices, and safeguard their professional reputations. However, as Koocher and Keith-Spiegel (2008) have commented, "[n]ovel or emerging technologies will continually create new ethical issues. In making decisions about these issues, school psychologists should be aware of professional standards, laws, and regulations" (p. 144). Although the chapter has summarized those professional standards, laws, and regulations, it acknowledges that they may soon be out of date and may not provide clear-cut answers to professional

dilemmas. Therefore, the use of a decision-making model such as the one presented in this chapter is recommended, especially with complex situations. Most importantly, the chapter reminds school psychologists of their professional responsibilities when using technology in the digital age.

AUTHOR NOTE

The views expressed in this chapter do not reflect the official positions of the NASP Ethics and Professional Practices Committee. The author is not an attorney, so the information provided should not be regarded as legal advice.

Disclosure. Leigh D. Armistead has a financial interest in books he authored or coauthored that are referenced in this chapter.

REFERENCES

American Educational Research Association, American Psychological Association, & National Council on Measurement in Education. (1999). *Standards for educational and psychological testing.* Washington, DC: Author.

Armistead, L., Williams, B., & Jacob, S. (2011). *Professional ethics for school psychologists: A problem-solving model casebook* (2nd ed.). Bethesda, MD: National Association of School Psychologists.

Baker, D. C., & Bufka, L. F. (2011). Preparing for the Telehealth world: Navigating legal, regulatory, reimbursement, and ethical issues in an electronic age. *Professional Psychology: Research and Practice, 42,* 405–411. doi:10.1037/a0025037

Carlson, J. F., & Harvey, V. S. (2004). Using computer-related technology for assessment activities: Ethical and professional practice issues for school psychologists. *Computers in Human Behavior, 20,* 645–659.

Cummings, J. (2011). Technology in the practice of school psychology. In M. A. Bray & T. J. Kehle (Eds.), *The Oxford handbook of school psychology* (pp. 831–857). New York, NY: Oxford University Press.

Daggett, L. M. (2008). FERPA in the twenty-first century: Failure to effectively regulate privacy for all students. *Catholic University Law Review, 58,* 59–113.

Fenichel, M. S., Barak, J., Zelvin, A., Jones, E., Munro, G., Meunier, K., & Walker-Schmucker, W. (2002). Myths and realities of online clinical work. *Cyberpsychology & Behavior, 5,* 481–497.

French, J. P. R., Jr., & Raven, B. (1959). The bases of social power. In D. Cartwright & A. Zander (Eds.), *Group dynamics* (pp. 607–623). New York, NY: Harper and Row.

Harvey, V. S., & Carlson, J. F. (2003). Ethical and professional issues with computer-related technology. *School Psychology Review, 32,* 92–107.

Harvey, V. S., & Struzziero, J. A. (2008). *Professional development and supervision of school psychologists: From intern to expert* (2nd ed.). Bethesda, MD: National Association of School Psychologists.

International Society for Mental Health Online. (2000). *Suggested principles for the online provision of mental health services*. Retrieved from http://www.ismho.org/suggestions.asp

Jacob, S., & Armistead, L. (2011a). Ethics and technology: Response to Pfohl–Part I. *Communiqué, 39*(6), 24–25.

Jacob, S., & Armistead, L. (2011b). Ethics and technology: Response to Pfohl–Part II. *Communiqué, 39*(7), 26–27.

Jacob, S., Decker, S. M., & Hartshorne, T. S. (2011). *Ethics and law for school psychologists* (6th ed.). Hoboken, NJ: Wiley.

Lehavot, K. (2009). "MySpace" or yours? The ethical dilemma of graduate students' personal lives on the Internet. *Ethics and Behavior, 19*, 129–141. doi:10.1080/10508420902772728

Lehavot, K., Barnett, J. E., & Powers, D. (2010). Psychotherapy, professional relationships, and ethical considerations in the MySpace generation. *Professional Psychology: Research and Practice, 41*, 160–166.

Koocher, G. P., & Keith-Spiegel, P. (2008). *Ethics in psychology and the mental health professions: Standards and cases*. New York, NY: Oxford University Press.

McDonald, S. J., & Tribbensee. (2007). *A fresh look at FERPA*. Louisville, CO: EDUCAUSE. Retrieved from http://www.educause.edu

National Association of School Psychologists. (2010a). *Model for comprehensive and integrated school psychological services*. Bethesda, MD: Author. Retrieved from http://www.nasponline.org/standards/2010standards/2_PracticeModel.pdf

National Association of School Psychologists. (2010b). *Principles for professional ethics*. Bethesda, MD: Author. Retrieved from http://www.nasponline.org/standards/2010standards/1_%20Ethical%20Principles.pdf

National Board of Certified Counselors. (2012). *NBCC policy regarding the provision of distance professional services*. Greensboro, NC: Author. Retrieved from http://www.nbcc.org/DocumentLibrary

Nicholson, I. R. (2011). New technology, old issues: Demonstrating the relevance of the Canadian Code of Ethics for Psychologists to the ever-sharper cutting edge of technology. *Canadian Psychology, 42*, 215–224.

Pfohl, B. (2010a). Ethics and technology–Part I. *Communiqué, 39*(3), 32.

Pfohl, B. (2010b). Ethics and technology–Part II. *Communiqué, 39*(4), 34.

Phillips, L. F., Baird, D., & Fogg, B. J. (2011). *Facebook for educators*. San Francisco, CA: Scribd. Retrieved from http://www.scribd.com/collections/2978508/Facebook-for-Educators

Polsson, K. (2102). *A brief timeline of personal computers*. Retrieved from http://pctimeline.info/mini.htm

Protalinski, E. (2011). *Law repealed: Teachers can be Facebook friends with students*. New York, NY: ZD Net. Retrieved from http://www.zdnet.com/blog/facebook/law-repealed-teachers-can-be-facebook-friends-with-students/4846

Scarfone, K., Souppaya, M., & Secton, M. (2007). *Guide to storage encryption technologies for end user devices*. Washington, DC: National Institute of Standards and Technology, U.S. Department of Commerce. Retrieved from http://csrc.nist.gov/publications/nistpubs/800-111/SP800-111.pdf

Schulenberg, S. E., & Yutrzenka, B. A. (2004). Ethical issues in the use of computerized assessment. *Computers in Human Behavior, 20*, 477–490.

Starks, M. H. (2011). *Getting started with Facebook*. Retrieved from http://www.ccplonline.org/info/tutorials/facebook_starks.pdf

Thomas, A. (1984). Issues and concerns for microcomputer uses in school psychology. *School Psychology Review, 13*, 469–472.

U.S. Copyright Office. (2012). *Works made for hire*. Washington, DC: Author. Retrieved from http://www.copyright.gov/circs/circ09.pdf

U.S. Department of Health and Human Services & U.S. Department of Education. (2008). *Joint guidance on the application of the Family Educational Rights and Privacy Act (FERPA) and the Health Insurance Portability and Accountability Act of 1996 (HIPAA) to student health records*. Washington, DC: Author. Retrieved from http://www.hhs.gov/ocr/privacy/hipaa/understanding/coveredentities/hipaaferpajointguide.pdf

35 Best Practices in Using Technology

William Pfohl
Western Kentucky University
Susan Jarmuz-Smith
University of New England (ME)

OVERVIEW

Technology permeates many facets of the practice of school psychology. In assessment, it assists with gathering and analyzing data, scoring protocols, and writing reports. In consultation, it supports professional learning and presenting, online researching, and communication among colleagues. In intervention, it supports the development and delivery of instructional strategies and aids in evaluating education outcomes. For school psychologists, technology has become a critical tool in bettering student outcomes.

In 2010, the U.S. Department of Education's Office of Educational Technology released the National Education Technology Plan (Office of Educational Technology, 2010). This plan outlined five essential applications of technology for educators: learning, assessment, teaching, infrastructure, and productivity. The report called for the transformation of educational experiences to create engaging learning opportunities for students in and out of school; leverage assessment technologies to foster continuous improvement; and use the power of technology to connect teachers with each other, with data on student outcomes, and with resources to increase teaching effectiveness. The plan also addressed the need for all students and educators to have access to technology and the Internet and revolutionize how schools, districts, and states take advantage of the efficiencies technology can provide. In essence, the plan called for all educators to research and innovate in their use of technology to better prepare students academically, socially, and emotionally.

In the National Association of School Psychologists (NASP) *Model for Comprehensive and Integrated School Psychological Services* (NASP, 2010), the use of technological tools can be applied in each of the 10 domains of practice. The NASP Practice Model addresses the need for technology in data collection, in student- and systems-level services, evaluation of services, and record keeping. Notably, the NASP Practice Model stresses the importance of school psychologists gaining the needed technical skills to ensure competence in the Legal, Ethical, and Professional Practice domain. The overarching goal of this chapter is to provide school psychologists with the technological knowledge needed in the application of the 10 domains of practice.

A few years ago the idea of using tablets for assessment and scoring would have been a foreign, if not a radical, idea. Recently, this is now a reality, such as PsychCorp's introduction of tablets into administration and scoring of its standardized tests (WISC-IV). Hence, the first objective of this chapter is to describe the fundamental skills needed for school psychologists to keep themselves up-to-date on advancements. In the interest of teaching school psychologists to fish, the chapter will begin with an overview of basic hardware, software, operating systems, and connectivity.

The use of technology in the practice of school psychology has legal and ethical ramifications addressed in laws, regulations, and profession standards. A second objective in this chapter is to cover best practices in online security, data protection, and maintenance of confidentiality when communicating information with others. Consider that laws, regulations, and standards are changing quickly and that some perhaps required future practices do not exist at the time this chapter was written. School psychologists must consider it essential to their jobs to keep current with the newest technology developments in their assessment, consultation, and intervention practices. The third and final objective is to cover emerging technologies in the practice of school psychology. These technologies include mobile devices and applications, assessment, and the use of online resources for professional development.

As a side note, technology changes incredibly quickly and what is now commonplace in 2 years may become outdated. All of the material presented here was current as of 2013. Even as technology changes, the safeguards and safety issues remain.

BASIC CONSIDERATIONS

Technology has three fundamental components: hardware, software, and connectivity upon which all other tools operate, such as online professional development, scoring software, and data analysis programs. The three components are akin to fundamental behavioral principles from which everything else is derived, and require a brief review.

Hardware

Hardware options are exploding for school psychologists, evolving from a desktop computer to a laptop and now smartphones and tablets. Keyboards, disk drives, and large monitors are being replaced by touch screens, storage clouds, virtual keyboards, and voice commands. Presently there is no one unit that will do all school psychologists require, and so multiple devices will be needed. A small portable laptop plus a tablet or smartphone will serve most school psychologists in the field. A reliable all-in-one printer, with scanner, copier, fax, and wireless capability will be essential.

A first step is choosing hardware is to assess needs: portability, good battery life, reliability, compatibility with existing district platforms, and software requirements. Often scoring software or data analysis tools may be available for only one hardware platform (Windows or Apple). In addition, school psychologists must consider their school's selection criteria for maximum compatibility with colleagues. Many hardware platforms still favor either Apple or a PC (Windows)-based desktop or laptop computers, but Google's Android operating system is becoming more common. Smaller, mobile, and lighter seem to be where manufacturers are going (Google) and are beneficial for mobile school psychologists.

Before purchasing new hardware, take the time to read hardware reviews. An extensive and critical review of hardware and computers can be found at http://www.cnet.com. A second source is *Consumer Reports*, which does regular product reviews as well. In addition, consult major news sources (e.g., *USA Today*, *New York Times*, *Washington Post*), which usually provide technology-related articles, readable reviews, questions and answers, and updates to important hardware and software advances.

Testing companies may also play a role in which hardware is chosen. Each of the testing companies has introduced tablet-testing options with electronic scoring and digital manuals. This will change how school psychologists work and what devices they will carry with them. Therefore, screen size will be an influence in addition to durability and battery life. PAR has scoring options for its products for either iPad or Android-based tablets through its PAR Toolkit app. The app is free with useful software; the scoring and manuals are not free but low cost.

Software

Software, in general, is split into two categories: operating system (OS) software and application (also called apps) software. There have historically been three main players in the operating system software market: Microsoft Windows, Apple Mac OS, and Unix-based systems. This is changing however. Google has introduced Android and Chrome, and other companies will be sure to enter the market. The function of an operating system is to run application software (e.g., Mac Mail, Microsoft Outlook, Chrome) by organizing and facilitating access to different hardware components (e.g., hard drive, memory, mouse, monitor). In other words, the operating system is the middleman. The main decision criterion for school psychologists to consider when choosing an operating system is whether it runs the application software required.

The largest use of application software is productivity software, which includes mail access programs (e.g., Microsoft Outlook, Mac Mail), word processing programs (e.g., Microsoft Word, Apple Pages), spreadsheet programs (e.g., Microsoft Excel, Apple Numbers), and presentation software (e.g., Microsoft PowerPoint, Apple Keynote). The choice between Microsoft's productivity suite (Word, Excel, PowerPoint, Outlook, Access, One Note; MAC version is available) or Apple's (Pages, Numbers, Keynote, Mail) involves considering cost, ease of use, existing comfort with one or the other, and compatibility with peers and colleagues and the school district's technology infrastructure. Historically, educational settings have leaned more toward the use of Apple-based hardware and software.

However, this may not always be the case and may no longer be an important decision point for school psychologists. Platform-independent productivity suites (e.g., LibreOffice) function on several different types of operating systems; that is, they do not require a specific system for setup and allow school psychologists to share documents without the concern for compatibility issues. They are free, but not as feature rich as others. In addition, cloud-based productivity suites (e.g., Google Drive, Microsoft Office 365) operate completely within the realm of the Internet (the cloud) to enable collaboration without the need to download and install software. When school psychologists use cloud-based software, online security of confidential student data becomes a concern.

Connectivity and Cloud Computing

The Internet is essentially a collection of interconnected computers. What started out in the 1960s as a way to share information and resources has grown to more than 12.5 billion interconnected devices, nearly two devices per person on the Earth (Evans, 2011). There are two facets of Internet usage considered in this section, connectivity and cloud computing.

Connectivity to the Internet is measured in the amount of bandwidth (or throughput) available between a computing device and the Internet. Large amounts of available bandwidth allow for greater capabilities. According to Young (2013), only 66% of U.S. households have high-speed access. School psychologists planning to communicate with parents via electronic means need to consider there is a one in three chance the family may not have adequate access.

Cloud computing is the sharing of computing resources and data storage via the Internet. It is akin to borrowing someone else's computer and accessing it from a browser. Current examples of cloud storage include Google Drive, Microsoft's SkyDrive, and Dropbox. While it may appear that Google's word processor is running on your laptop or documents are stored in a folder called Dropbox on your personal system, these items are actually running and stored on a computer that may be hundreds or thousands of miles away. This has great implications in the ethical and legal practice of school psychology with respect to confidentiality.

Yet, simply accessing software or data via a browser does not necessarily mean information is stored in the cloud. PowerSchool and Infinite Campus generally provide a safe place for school psychologists to store confidential information, which usually resides within the school building or at a secure, remote district location. Other software or data storage applications may store information on local hardware servers. It is the responsibility of the school psychologist to clarify data storage and verify the confidentiality of electronic student data with local technology personnel. Also verification on who owns the data is becoming an issue with some cloud storage companies. Access to the cloud by multiple individuals can be a potential problem with data security. School psychologists are expected to keep their data confidential.

BEST PRACTICES IN USING TECHNOLOGY

After school psychologists acquire the necessary hardware, software, and Internet connectivity, they have the necessary foundation of any technology system. Layered on top of these basics are the issues of online security, data protection, communication, and other emerging technologies.

Online Security

School psychologists are required to protect personal and professional data from others. Not long ago, the Internet was used for checking e-mail, looking up a question, or viewing some news. Now, it is used for data storage (cloud), computer scoring of data, free software (Google Drive), and keeping up with friends, classmates, and others through social media (Facebook, Twitter). The Internet is the fastest growing resource in knowledge (e.g., Wikipedia), connecting others (e.g., Facebook, LinkedIn), research (e.g., PsychInfo), sharing photos (e.g., Flickr), and talking to others using Voice Over Internet Protocols or VOIP (e.g., Skype, Google Voice, VSee, Go-To-Meeting).

School psychologists deal with volumes of data every day and share it with others, such as teachers and parents, and need to be sensitive about and protective of data. Online access through networks and Internet makes sending and receiving data more troublesome, as others also may desire to gather or access these data. Data may also inadvertently fall into others' hands (e.g., lost laptop/smartphone/thumb drive). School psychologists are ethically and legally responsible for the protection of client data.

Connection Security

Typically, school psychologists will access the Internet through either a wired or wireless connection. Wired-connectivity networks usually do not use a broadcasted wireless network. Wireless networks pose a security threat that requires school psychologists to make sure the connection is secure. Ensure that the wireless network being used requires a password for connections and that only authorized users are connecting. It is imperative to ensure that the wireless network being connected to requires a password. Unsecured wireless networks (no password required), such as at many coffee houses and restaurants, allow anyone to log on and possibly monitor activity easily and access information. Consider this common scenario: A school psychologist who stops by a local coffee shop to catch up on reports or e-mail may be sharing information with everyone in the shop.

However, a wireless network requiring a password does not mean the proper level of security is available. Remember that anyone who was able to log on successfully to the network may have access to your device. There are school personnel who do not have the right to know the student information school psychologists maintain.

Firewall software will keep others from connecting to or remotely accessing the computer. Operating systems, security software, and antivirus software can ship with added firewall protection but many times must be enabled or purchased in a more deluxe package (Microsoft has Microsoft Security Essentials for free). The best firewalls are two-way because they block others from accessing the device and can block information from being sent from the device back to them. If a school psychologist accidently allows a website to access his or her device by clicking on an unsecure site or a link within an e-mail, then it is possible for that site to gather information from the school psychologist's laptop. A two-way firewall asks permission before sending data back.

An antivirus program guards against computer viruses, malware, and other computer infections. This is a critical component of protecting important student data from destruction by a virus. A comprehensive protection program (i.e., suite) can be purchased or downloaded for free (e.g., AVG, avast!). Malwarebytes is a free package that can guard against malware that can exist on the computer from Internet surfing or downloads. Many of these programs will run and check the system in the background, but detection programs should be run monthly if not weekly. Make sure the latest update is completed first. Until recently, Apple-based computers were relatively safe from viruses, but as more Apple computers, smartphones, and tablets are bought, they have become a new target for viruses and malware. This concern applies to Android-based phones and tablets as well and it will apply to Windows-based phones when they become more popular. Antivirus program apps are available for all platforms. (See the manufacture's app site, Mac App Store or Google Play.)

Browser Security

A browser, such as Internet Explorer, Safari, Chrome, or Opera, is the visual/graphic interface between the Internet and the device. Browsers have improved greatly in ease of use, but there are still security issues to consider. When accessing materials, a Web address is needed, and this is called the Uniform Resource Location or URL. If the URL is mistyped or not clear, then access may be denied or access to an unintended site may occur. Browsers can be set to identify unsafe websites before they are accessed. Each browser has the security option, but they differ on how they are turned on (see the browser's Help menu).

When looking at the URL in the address bar, "https://" is a sign that this site is secure and can be used for confidential or important information, such as passwords and student information. Without the *s* in "https://" the site is not secure. Newer browsers might light up in a color such as green to indicate the site is safe verses red to indicate it is not safe or spying.

There are many programs available to improve online security. Cookies (short pieces of computer code that store passwords and personal preferences) can be cleaned off the computer with cleaning software (e.g., SUPERAntiSpyware). CCleaner is free software that can clean up the computer's cookies, memory, registry, and Internet temporary files. ShieldsUp (free software) can monitor the Internet connection for possible security holes and potential malware. But to be really safe, school psychologists need to consider that there is no real anonymous way to use the Internet.

Social Media Security

School psychologists who use social media for updates and/or communication with teachers, parents, and colleagues open themselves up to a potential breach of confidentiality. If a school psychologist has a private or professional (or both) presence on the Internet, then clients, students, and parents may find him or her and may create an impression or formulate a prejudgment.

Students or clients may attempt to *friend* the school psychologist or *like* a particular post. Consider all the potential problems inherent in using social media and tread wisely. The recommendation for school psychologists is to avoid social media altogether.

A school psychologist may start a blog or webpage (on behalf of the district) to share information. Confidentiality must be protected, of course, if case samples are to be used for stories, research, or presentations. Graduate student and professional blog postings are held to the highest standards and include comments, pictures, and likes. Talking openly on social media about supervisors, parents, teachers, clients, or other personnel may be a source for program/professional sanction or dismissal from a program or organization. All social media events are currently discoverable under law. They are not confidential nor privileged.

Data Protection

Here we will discuss two methods to protect data: passwords and encryption.

Password

Security starts with passwords that protect devices so others cannot gain access to confidential data. Passwords are the first line of defense. Unfortunately, many use the same password for every device or simple passwords that are easily broken or guessed. (It has been reported that the most common passwords are 123456 or *password.*) Writing down a password on a Post-it note or paper near a computer is a security concern. Changing passwords is a must and should be done every few months. Keeping track of all the different and changing passwords can be troublesome but apps such as SplashID, Password Safe, or KeePass make it easier (be aware that some of the free password storage apps have been hacked). All devices that school psychologists use should be password protected at a minimum. A strong password, using all the characters allowed, a mix of capitals, numbers, and symbols, can make it stronger. Some sites will provide feedback on the strength of a password. Password Savvy (https://www. passwordsavvy.org) can help make strong and memorable passwords. New device protection options are also available that do not use passwords, such as fingerprint scanning in Apple's iPhone 5S.

Encryption

The next layer of security is encryption, or a scrambling of the data so that it is unreadable by others. Storing information/data on a device or sending it by e-mail

attachment needs some form of encryption protection. A password can keep others out—maybe—but in some cases the files behind the password are still readable. Encryption is the only method to ensure that no one can read a protected file. Encryption will include a cipher, which is similar to a password. So when a cipher is applied to a disk drive, folder, or file it locks the document and scrambles it so no one can read it without the cipher. Ciphers should be long, complicated, and hard to guess. Once the cipher has been set, no one can open the file without it. There is no recovery option, unlike password recovery options. With encryption, a file or folder can be stored or sent with little fear of an unintentional person reading it (a caution: do not include the cipher in the e-mail or instructions). TrueCrypt, Pretty Good Privacy, and Kruptos 2 Professional work as encryption software to encrypt entire drives, folders, or files. Also, any Word, Excel, and PowerPoint file can be encrypted with Microsoft Office software from 2003 to its current version (see the Help Menu). SanDisk's USB thumb drives have software called SecureAccess that encrypts the thumb drives, and the software can be downloaded free from SanDisk's website. Kanguru USB drive is an alternative. For the iPhone, there is the Symantec Mobile Encryption app for encrypting e-mails (special set up required). Additionally, the software packages mentioned above (TrueCrypt, Pretty Good Privacy, and Kruptos 2 Professional) can be used to locate or erase data from an external hard drive, USB thumb drive, or other external memory device if lost, stolen, or misplaced.

File sharing is another potential problem. Many apps and programs, such as Dropbox, allow others to be invited to share files or folders. Once the files are shared, the potential for breaching confidentiality increases. Cloud storage where others can access confidential data, unless encrypted, may become problematic if others also share access. The best solution is to have files encrypted by the original document creator. Viivo and Boxcryptor are free software that encrypt files before transmission to and storage in the cloud. For school psychology interns and supervisors who set up and use cloud storage encryption, note that supervisors are the only ones allowed to modify or change supervisee's reports under Health Insurance Portability and Accountability Act (HIPAA) guidelines but no one else is allowed to change files or reports.

There is a myth that a file saved as a PDF (portable document format) cannot be modified and can be considered encrypted. This is not true. Besides Adobe's own software, other software exists to open and change these files. In addition, simple search programs can access and decode PDF formatting, and thus PDFs are not secure. Word and most other word processors will allow saving in PDF format. However, its security against modification is not accurate.

Backup Data

Backing up data regularly is an essential task and ethical obligation of school psychological service. Practitioners have two main options for backing up data: (a) an external hard drive/server or (b) the cloud. Ideally, specific backup software will automatically and regularly capture backups of data while dating and organizing files and folders. Time Machine for Apple runs in the background of Mac devices at a frequency set by users and codes each backup with a time stamp. Then, users can figuratively step back in time through the backups to find the correct version of the stored file or data. School psychologists must weigh the cost of backup solutions with the need for space. Generally, reports, scoring data, and other documentation do not take up much space. However, if pictures and videos need to be stored as well then the space requirements increase rapidly. Again, knowing who owns the stored data is essential.

In a pinch, an encrypted USB thumb drive can be used to back up data, but be aware that USB thumb drives fail consistently. They are manufactured as cheap, low quality data transfer devices and not as long-term storage. If school psychologists use cloud storage, generally the data are automatically backed up by the cloud service (e.g., Dropbox, Google Drive). This is both a convenience and a security breach. Consider this fact: A school psychologist stores a file on Dropbox. That file is then backed up according to Dropbox's terms. While the school psychologist may delete the file from Dropbox, it still exists on Dropbox's server so it may be undeleted if it was deleted in accident or it may take a while to become overwritten by future backup processes.

School psychologists should read Dropbox's privacy terms (https://www.dropbox.com/privacy) or the privacy terms of other cloud storage before choosing to share files in this manner. It will become clear that storing unencrypted files in the cloud is not ethical or legal for the data school psychologists utilize in practice.

If a laptop or device is lost or stolen, software called LoJack will monitor its location for potential recovery. In addition to locating, the software will assist in locking the device, deleting sensitive data, and aiding in recovery. In urgent situations, deleting data may be the best way to protect the data. Adeona is a free version of the LoJack-type of software.

Electronic Records Security

Data and information that is generated professionally is considered to be restricted or confidential (HIPAA/Affordable Care Act [ACA]). However, how it is protected and who can access it is becoming more complex, as data are stored on more than one device and in more than one format. The American Psychological Association (APA) published *Record Keeping Guidelines* (APA, 2007), which is sadly out of date, in an effort to help field-based practitioners maintain data confidentiality. In addition, HIPAA outlined guidelines for keeping health records known as the Security Rule (http://www.hhs.gov/ocr/privacy/hipaa/understanding/srsummary.html). Be aware that state and federal regulations related to the protection of data and requirements for online security can change, particularly under the ACA. See http://www.HealthCare.gov for updates and further information on professional practice guidelines and regulations required to protect medical related information (note that school psychological related data are included under medical data according to HealthCare.gov). The file name on a stored record could reveal a name, which would be a security violation. See Table 35.1.

Table 35.1. Best Practices in the Ethical Use of Technology

Guidelines for Following HIPAA/ACA	Data Safeguards
• Covered entities (schools, private practitioners) are responsible for keeping records confidential • Covered entities must have a policy statement on the storage and retrieval of public health records (including psychological data) • Policy statements must also cover who has access, where data are stored, and data retrieval and recovery plans	• Know that data remain available even when deleted • Use software to delete data on hard drives and devices (e.g., Eraser) • Never leave the computer unprotected; lock it before walking away and do not let others use it • Supervisors are responsible for student's or supervisee's technology, ethical behaviors, and lost devices or data

Note. HIPAA = Health Insurance Portability and Accountability Act; ACA = Affordable Care Act.

School psychologists should be aware that data are seldom deleted by hitting the delete key. Deleting an e-mail, file, or folder leaves an electronic trail that can be recovered easily using available software. To ensure complete elimination of data from a hard drive, use software, such as Eraser, which can completely overwrite the hard drive or memory device, so data cannot be retrieved. Anything less will allow others to recapture the data or file.

Ethical violations can occur accidentally, such as a lost thumb drive. School psychologists need to define written policies about how data are kept and maintained, the school's or school psychologist's e-mail policy, the data storage and lost data recovery policy (discussed further in the next section), getting copies of materials, and how HIPAA-covered information will be protected. There are both HIPAA privacy and HIPAA security provisions. School psychologists need to be familiar with both, review each yearly, and have written plans to protect client/student data. As long as HIPAA policy is being followed, there is some protection for the school psychologist implied. Check with the school's information technology department and school attorney on the development of such policies.

One way that security leaks/breeches happen or data are lost is by installing a computer or device and its software and then never maintaining or updating it. Hence, the operating system software, application software (e.g., Microsoft Office), security software, and browser software become outdated. Under current ACA guidelines, this would be a violation if the computer and software are not maintained and updated. This process can be done automatically if enabled but it is safer if done manually.

Based on information detailed so far, a school psychologist's guidelines for ethical and legal practice would include:

- Use firewall software, and update it regularly
- Update all software regularly, including the operating system
- Encrypt professional data on computer and external devices, such as files and folders
- Password protect all devices; fingerprint recognition may work as well
- Secure work by logging out when not in front of the computer or at the desk
- Create policies to ensure confidentiality and appropriate storage of protected heath information, and give the policies to parents and teachers

- Backup all data regularly, preferably monthly, if not more often (for a sample data recovery plan, see http://security.arizona.edu/files/ISG901.pdf)
- Create a disaster data recovery plan (required by federal law; for more information see http://www.ready.gov/business/implementation/IT)
- Understand that the more individuals who have access to the data, the more likely a breach of that data will occur (i.e., using shared files can be risky)
- Encrypt e-mail attachments if sensitive data are involved, because e-mails are not confidential
- Be aware that using social media can potentially be a breach of confidentiality and ethics
- Erase all devices of data (e.g., phone, computer, tablets) before selling, recycling, or throwing them away
- Keep up to date on technology advances
- Use separate passwords if personal devices are used for professional work (this can be done through the Administrator settings); that is, do not comingle accounts and information
- Know the state laws regulating telemedicine, for example, or data storage
- Understand that ignorance is not an excuse concerning technology and its ethical use

The following toolkit would support the above guidelines:

- Firewall software (built in to the operating system or third party)
- Antivirus software
- Encryption software
- Backup software with external data storage
- Secure documentation of differing passwords (in a software package)
- Erasure software (to ensure deletion of data)
- Regularly scheduled software update plan (simply a list of software that needs updating)
- Regularly scheduled backup plan (simply a list of folders/files that need backing up)

See Table 35.2 for best practices in online security and ethical practices.

Communication

School psychologists typically use e-mail to contact parents, teachers, and colleagues as an integral part of their practice. However, e-mails are like sky writing or writing on a postcard. Anyone can read them. School psychologists need to be careful sending, replying to,

Table 35.2. Best Practices in Online Security and Ethical Practices

Password Protection	Wireless Security	Software	Encryption
• Do not write passwords on a Post-it note next to the screen • Create complex passwords that include a combination of letters, numbers, and other symbols • Change passwords frequently • Consider storing passwords on a locked Rolodex or a mobile application, such as SplashID	• Open networks are not secure (e.g., coffee houses, restaurants). • Check the URL for https:// (with the *s*) when a secure connection is needed	• Use a two-way firewall software to block others from connecting to the computer without permission • Use and regularly update antivirus software (e.g., McAfee, AVG) to avoid viruses, malware	• Do not send attachments with confidential information through public e-mail providers (e.g., Gmail, AOL) without encryption; Hushmail is an option for encrypted e-mail • Use software to encrypt confidential information (e.g., TrueCrypt, Pretty Good Privacy, Kruptos 2) before sending • Generally, PowerSchool and other internal e-mail systems do encrypt e-mails and attachments; check with the IT department first; Hushmail is an option

and receiving e-mails that have potentially confidential information. The current standard is to encrypt e-mails. It can be a challenge to encrypt them and keep them confidential.

Errant e-mails have been a source of embarrassment, reprimand, and even grounds for being fired. School psychologists have to be very careful of the confidential and identifying data in e-mails. The attached files have to be password protected, and the confidential materials need to be encrypted. Microsoft Office Outlook does have the ability to encrypt e-mails but the process is complicated (see http://office.microsoft.com/en-us/outlook-help/encrypt-e-mail-messages-HP001230536.aspx). Hushmail is an encrypted e-mail option for secure e-mail transfer (25 Mb for free or higher amounts for a cost) and it is HIPAA compliant (https://www.hushmail.com).

E-mails are best used for administrative purposes only, without identifying information, such as scheduling meetings and appointments (J. R. Younggren, personal communication, 2013). Legally, e-mails can be "discovered" with an appropriate court order (check the state's laws). It is important to know that information technology services at universities and schools keep each and every e-mail and the e-mail belongs to the organization, not the writer.

It cannot be emphasized enough that school psychologists should not send passwords/ciphers within an e-mail. It is suggested that the password/cipher be discussed with the person to be receiving the e-mail over a landline phone and not a cell phone. Also, school psychological supervisors and interns should not send file attachments to anyone, including himself or herself, without it being encrypted.

Communicating via Texting/SMS

Text/SMS messages have become a new area of concern, as they are not encrypted, secure forms of communication. Trainers, supervisors, and administrators will need to be responsible for monitoring this type of communication and data storage with their supervisees and clients. Supervisors are responsible for all the supervisee's actions under law. For example, it is not safe to use texting to set up appointments with parents or teachers because it may contain identifying information. Similarly, texting teachers about the status of a child or intervention that has identifying information should also be avoided. Texts are also legally discoverable so be extremely careful.

Communicating Resources to Teachers and Parents

School psychologists can use a variety of technologies to disseminate information to teachers, parents, administrators, and other related professionals. Generally, most school districts have websites, and school psychologists are allowed to add a page or two to describe their provided services. If this is not the case, then there are several software tools that can accomplish the creation of a Web presence. School psychologists can create free wikis or blogs that are linked to the school's or district's website. For wikis, free sites for educators include Wikispaces (http://www.wikispaces.com), Google Sites (http://sites.google.com), and Wikidot (http://www.wikidot.com). Wikis are easy to use and maintain. An example of a major, successful wiki is Wikipedia. For blogs, free sites for educators include Blogger (http://blogger.com), edublogs (http://edublogs.org), and WordPress (http://wordpress.com).

When sharing information with teachers and parents, school psychologists can provide useful links to multimedia sources on school psychology–related topics that have been referred and approved before dissemination. Examples could be podcasts, iTunes University presentations, TED Talks (http://www.ted.com), YouTube videos, Google Play videos, and other online media. NASP's website (http://www.nasponline.org), in particular, offers podcasts and webinars related specifically to the practice of school psychology and includes resources for teachers and parents.

Communication Etiquette

The requirement of online etiquette exists across all forms of communication: e-mail, tests, websites, blogs, and social networks. In 2007, Yale Library Services published guidelines for online etiquette that they coined *netiquette*. According to Yale, it is important to proofread messages before sending or posting, avoid offensive language, and avoid shouting (or using all capital letters). These are common sense suggestions, but a few others are good to note as well. When sending e-mail, never use the blind copy option (Bcc:) to copy someone on a message. Its use is considered to be unethical. Reserve the use of Bcc: when sending information to a large distribution list. Additionally, consider the audience when creating e-mails or posts. When reading posts/e-mails, readers more easily assume messages are negative. It is important to write carefully to avoid confusion. It is also important not to have a trigger finger when writing e-mails. Take time to consider the recipient. Disable the "reply to all" feature in the e-mail software to save embarrassing situations. Emoticons may seem cute but give the wrong professional impression. When using Listservs, try to avoid replying to all, and take the time to check that the correct recipient is in the To: box and not the address for the Listserv, unless replying to all members of the e-mail group. One suggestion is to keep the To: box blank until writing the e-mail is done, and thus no unwanted e-mails are sent accidentally.

Emerging Technologies

The assessment companies used most by school psychologists (Pearson, PAR Assessment, Riverside, and Multi-Health Systems) have made a commitment for using tablets/portable devices for testing/assessments and scoring. Each company has developed its own software and data storage platform: PAR uses iConnect, PsychCorp uses Q-interactive, and Multi-Health Systems uses Online Assessment Center. Most test publishers are expanding assessment instrument options using cloud-based scoring and offering HIPAA-compliant services on a per use basis. Online scoring ensures the latest software is used for scoring and also allows test publishers to collect a large amount of data for norming instruments. The collection of data almost guarantees norms are always current, but be aware that online scoring may add another layer of required permission.

PsychCorp has started offering testing instruments on tablets (iPads for administration and scoring). Tablet-based assessment kits come preloaded with the assessment battery (so the cost of two iPads and a stylus are in addition to the test kit itself). In addition, observations can be done with tablet devices with the appropriate software app (e.g., Behavior Lens, School Psychology Tool Kit). Video technology, within ethical limits, can be valuable to review intervention fidelity and progress monitoring. Emerging technology allows for assessing, scoring, observing, monitoring, and archiving student data quickly and efficiently.

Mobile Devices and Applications

Mobile devices and their apps are the fastest growth area of technology. Mobile devices a few years ago included only laptops or possibly the original PalmPilot. In 2008, laptops (Case, 2013) for the first time outsold desktop computers and the mobile race was on. New, smaller mobile devices are highly valued by school psychologists because of their portability (i.e., smartphone, tablets). Mobile school psychologists need to carry all their information, have Web access, and communicate with others. These mobile devices allow virtually nonstop connectivity and assessment/observation potential. Mobile devices are better at importing/viewing images and information than exporting or entering information to be sent to others. As of now, the ideal single all inclusive device has not been invented yet for all school psychologists to use, but the current pairing of either a laptop or tablet and a smartphone fits the bill.

Individuals choose mobile devices according to their features and operating systems. It is best to stay within an operating system—Apple iOS, Google Android—yet some choose one of each. Apple's mobile devices tend to be the more expensive choice. Another decision point is battery life. Being mobile requires a good battery or ability for frequent recharging. This mobile technology is constantly changing and there are many tips for saving battery life, but battery science is slow to develop. New processing chips conserve battery life. Go to the device or operating system's website for the latest battery saving suggestions.

Durability is an extremely important consideration. The devices are durable but prone to be instantly nonfunctional if dropped or exposed to water or extreme heat. A screen protector or protective case can keep the screen from becoming scratched or broken. A case can protect screens and body but add to the size and weight.

Devices have become smaller and mobile applications have increased. Mobile device capabilities have increased with more memory and longer battery life plus the ability to use more complex apps. Apps are software that may increase productivity, Internet access, picture taking and editing, and game playing. They can store in memory much information, such as books, medical records, and counseling apps. It appears that the options are becoming almost limitless. Apple has the lead in apps (more than 800,000 in 2013) and they control their app vetting closer than any other company. Samsung and many other smartphones are using Google's Android operating system. Google performs less vetting of apps for their devices (more than 700,000 apps). However, Apple has a very advanced operating system that is thought to be the easiest to use. Ironically, after years of shrinking size, mobile devices are currently growing in physical size to accommodate greater media requirements from videos, Internet, eBook reading, and social media. The choice will be based on individual factors for use. School psychologists can benefit from these devices for effective practice.

Tablets are now preferred by many over smartphones due to need for media-based access. Tablets are also excellent devices for movies, reading books, reading e-mail, and Internet surfing. As of 2013, only Microsoft's Surface Pro 2 has a real keyboard, as all the others use touch screens. Bluetooth-featured keyboards can be used on any Bluetooth-enabled device. Currently tablets are limited in ease of inputting data but excel in displaying most information.

Mobile devices continue to expand their features with connectivity for cell phone services, browsers for Web searches, entertainment viewing, and productivity, with an ever-expanding app library. Realistically, these devices integrate phone, calendar, Web searches, music player, game playing, and photo and movie storage. If the mobile device has both cell phone connectivity and Wi-Fi connectivity, then access to the Internet is nearly assured. Newer devices show improved features and capabilities, such as cameras and video recorders. Capabilities improve with each generation. Waiting for

the newest device or features seems fruitless as changes happen irregularly and sometimes without fanfare. Some new mobile devices have more incremental changes that offer little new. Reviews are readily available in magazines or online. Amazon's Kindle series seems to be more proprietary in limiting some Android-based apps from Google from working. eReaders (e.g., Kindle and Nook) are excellent for reading books, text, journal articles, and magazines. While the eReaders are useful, they are not as versatile as full-featured tablets and can cost almost the same.

Each software app store (Apple's App Store, Google's Play Store) offers free or paid apps for their devices. Amazon offers apps for their Kindle devices as well. An important issue is whether the app is proprietary and that may limit its use. A competing app for each device platform (Apple versus Google) may not be available. Books, particularly textbooks, are difficult to use across platforms. Publishers are struggling with myriad issues to find common ground. Movies, music, and visual and auditory media can all be played on the tablets and many smartphones with the appropriate app.

School psychologists will benefit from productivity apps, such as Evernote, which keeps track of files, to-do lists, photos, and links to social media apps like Skype and Facebook. These apps are improvements on the standard note app. Evernote syncs with all devices using cloud technology, so be sure to secure it with a password. In addition, Evernote materials can be shared with others but there is a fee for this upgrade. Couples, families, and fellow professionals can sync a great deal of their personal lives together. Make sure to keep personal and professional accounts separate.

School psychology–specific apps continue to evolve from suites (School Psychology Tool Kit) to individual observation apps, file tracking, scoring, and manuals. Recently, NASP's *Communiqué* began publishing app reviews by school psychologists, with reviews archived online (see http://www.nasponline.org/publications/ cq/archive/category-list.aspx?id=23).

Students

Mobile devices are not only for adults and school psychologists but also for the student (see http://www. appitic.com for a short list). Schools are buying tablets for their teachers and students to enhance education. Viewing a video on a foreign country for social studies, or conducting a complex experiment in virtual space for science, is exciting and helps students gain vast experiences that would otherwise be inaccessible. Music and art classes take on a different dimension with audio and visual apps. Knowledge bases, libraries, and even earning a college degree can be done online. The Khan Academy (https://www.khanacademy.org) was the first virtual website where students could learn math without a classroom teacher. The academy has expanded into many other academic areas. YouTube is popular with teachers and students to show how to do something or get more in-depth coverage of a topic.

Device Maintenance

With all these apps and mobile capabilities, maintenance is essential. Turning off the device periodically resets it and will likely increase its speed. Closing all the open apps regularly (using the Task Manager on Android apps or forcibly closing sleeping apps on an iPad) will increase battery life. Installing an antivirus program is recommended for all devices, even Apple. Accessing the Internet and viewing e-mail increases the security risk.

Assessment and Observation

Mobile technology will change how school psychologists schedule, assess, score, observe, consult, counsel, and monitor. Apps are emerging at a fast pace to help school psychologists be more productive. As mentioned earlier, *Communiqué* has a column devoted to app reviews that will help keep up with available apps. Testing companies will continue to evolve with assessment and scoring apps. Observation packages, such has Behavioral Lens or School Psychology Tool Kit, will continue to improve and new ones will appear. Since school psychologists work in such diverse settings, regularly search the Apple App Store or Google's Play Store for new app options. Calendars come on all devices but ones with more features are available (e.g., Evernote, Wunderlist). School psychologists are obligated to carefully review, select, and use apps as they have done previously with nontechnology instruments. Reliable, valid, and appropriate standardization should be evaluated for each app. Update apps regularly, if it is not done automatically. Check app stores for newer versions. See Table 35.3.

Online Resources for Professional Development

There are several informative and comprehensive websites covering information that would be helpful to school psychologists. The federal government website (http://www.usa.gov) aggregates information from federal and state websites for easy access. Entering school psychology into the main search box on the homepage provides a listing of many school psychology–related documents from federal, state, district, and local websites.

There are also several high-quality websites that cover specific topics. Examples include the National Center of Response to Intervention (http://www.rti4success.org/), which provides valuable resources on exploring, adopting, planning, implementing, and continuously improving response-to-intervention systems. Another example includes the Office of Special Education Programs' Technical Assistance Center on Positive Behavior Interventions and Supports (http://www.pbis.org), which includes information on implementation, evaluation, research, and training for schools, families, and communities.

Inarguably the largest storehouse of information about school psychology is NASP's website (http://www.nasponline.org). NASP's website contains position statements, fact sheets, information on PREPaRE training, the Online Learning Center, publications, and much more. NASP also supports the NASP Communities (http://www.nasponline.org/communities.aspx), which is a professional networking site where NASP members can share information and support each other by posting

Table 35.3. Best Practices in Mobile Devices and Applications

Purchasing Guidance	Application Types
• Research what is currently available using reputable sources (CNET, CNET download.com, *Consumer Reports*)	*Productivity* • Evernote • Quickoffice • Dropbox
• Research available software before deciding which platform (Apple, Google, Windows) to purchase (e.g., Apple's App Store, Google's Play Store)	*Communication* • Facebook • Mail • LinkedIn • Skype
• Choose one platform (Apple, Google, Windows) for all devices to ease maintenance and learning	*Learning* • Khan Academy • Wikipedia • WolframAlpha • Kindle *School Psychology Related* • PAR Assessment App • DBT Tools • Behavior Lens

questions and generating responses. The website is continuously updated to reflect the most important issues in the field of school psychology. In addition, the APA Division 16 website also contains resources for professionals and students. APA also supports a similar application as NASP Communities called the APA Communities (http://www.apa.org/apa-communities. aspx). These communities include psychologists from many different subfields of psychology. State associations have specific information about the practice of school psychology in their states on their association website (also linked through NASP's website).

The School Mental Health Project at UCLA has a treasure trove of information for school psychologists (http://smhp.psych.ucla.edu). Materials on bullying, school mental health, school mental health policy making, and school violence can be found here.

Beyond specific school psychology–related websites, valuable information can be found at the websites of related professions, such as behavior analysis and counseling. The Association for Behavior Analysis International (http://www.abainternational.org)

contains webinars, journal information, and access to special interest groups that may appeal to school psychologists. Association for Behavior Analysis International also supports regional, state, and local associations that would have more specific local information that may relate to school psychologists. The American Counseling Association (http://www. counseling.org) has webinars, podcasts, publications, public policy articles, and more that apply to the practice of school psychology.

There are an unlimited number of resources online for access to fast and abundant information. It is crucial to consider the source of the information and make sure quality resources are accessed that will better outcomes for students. Autism Speaks (http://www.autismspeaks. org), National Center on Student Progress Monitoring (http://www.studentprogress.org), and the IRIS Center (http://iris.peabody.vanderbilt.edu) are great examples of quality Internet resources. Doing a search can yield additional resources. Evaluate their scientific base before using the information. See Table 35.4 for an easy-to-see guide to websites.

Table 35.4. Best Practices in Using Online Resources

Website	Organization	Resources
http://www.usa.gov	Federal government	Federal and state educational information
http://www.rti4success.org	National Center of Response to Intervention	Assistance for exploring, adopting, planning, implementing, and improving response to intervention; webinars, training modules, live chats
http://www.pbis.org	Office of Special Education Programs' Technical Assistance Center on Positive Behavior Interventions and Supports	Assistance for planning, implementation, and evaluation of positive behavior interventions and support; print resources, videos, training information
http://www.nasponline.org	NASP	Online Learning Center, print resources, videos, training modules
http://www.nasponline.org/communities.aspx	NASP Communities	Members-only discussion groups on differing topics in school psychology. (The Graduate Educators Group is open to nonmembers.)
http://www.apa.org/apa-communities.aspx	APA Communities	Members-only discussion groups on differing topics in psychology
http://smhp.psych.ucla.edu	School Mental Health Project at UCLA	Practitioner toolbox, print resources, trainings, presentation, resource packets for technical assistance
http://www.abainternational.org	Association of Behavior Analysis International	Learning center, special interest groups
http://www.counseling.org	American Counseling Association	Webinars, podcasts, print resources, public policy articles

SUMMARY

NASP's Practice Model (NASP, 2010) addresses the need for technology at all levels of school psychology practice such as data collection, student- and systems-level services, evaluation of services, and record keeping. The use of technology opens up ethical and legal complications with respect to online security and data protection. Regardless of the level, type, or frequency of technology use, it is becoming critical that school psychologists begin or continue to use technology effectively, professionally, and safely. Technology continues to evolve in both hardware and software at an incredible pace. School psychologists need to keep current with what they use and explore and what new devices and software can be useful to be productive and ethical school psychologists.

REFERENCES

American Psychological Association. (2007). Record keeping guidelines *American Psychologist, 62*, 993–1004. doi:10.1037/0003-066X.62.9.993

Case, L. (2013, March). 30 years, 30 great tech events. *PC World, 31*, 81–84.

Evans, D. (2011). *The Internet of things: How the next evolution of the Internet is changing everything.* San Jose, CA: Cisco Internet Business Solutions Group. Retrieved from http://www.cisco.com/web/about/ac79/docs/innov/IoT_IBSG_0411FINAL.pdf

National Association of School Psychologists. (2010). *Model for comprehensive and integrated school psychological services.* Bethesda, MD: Author. Retrieved from http://www.nasponline.org/standards/2010standards/2_PracticeModel.pdf

Office of Educational Technology. (2010). *National education technology plan.* Washington, DC: Author. Retrieved from http://www.ed.gov/edblogs/technology/netp-2010/

Young, J. R. (2013, March 4). "Bandwidth divide" could bar some people from online learning. *Chronicle of Higher Education.* Retrieved from http://chronicle.com/article/The-Bandwith-Divide/137633

36

Best Practices in Using Technology for Data-Driven Decision Making

Benjamin Silberglitt
Technology and Information Education Services, St. Paul, MN
Daniel Hyson
University of Wisconsin–La Crosse

OVERVIEW

The use of information and communication technology in education has increased exponentially since the previous edition of *Best Practices*. Moore's law correctly predicted the exponential growth in computer processing speed (Moore, 1965), leading to similarly exponential growth in availability of technology. It appears this rate will only continue to accelerate, and the landscape of what technologies are available will continue to reinvent itself.

School psychologists continue to play a critical role in providing consultation and leadership to schools and districts in the effective use of technology to support the mission of schools, which is student learning. While technology is no longer called out as a foundational area in the National Association of School Psychologists (NASP) *Model for Comprehensive and Integrated School Psychological Services* (NASP, 2010), this may be because of the seeming ubiquity of technology. Without a doubt there is a need for NASP to continue to remind school psychologists not just of their role in helping schools grapple with the multitude of issues and questions that technology invariably brings in the area of student learning, but also of their role as leaders in bringing effective technologies to bear on many if not all of the domains of practice.

Certainly, data-driven decision making, as reflected in the NASP Practice Model (NASP, 2010) domain of Data-Based Decision Making and Accountability, is a major catalyst in the explosion of the use of technology in education (Johnson, Adams, & Cummins, 2012).

Concepts such as using technology for collecting, managing, and delivering data as information useful to the decision-making process; setting targets for performance and understanding expectations at both the individual and systems levels; understanding how technology is playing an increasing role in delivering instructional content; and even using technology for effective time management are all ways that technology plays a key role in effective data-driven decision making. As schools begin to realize the benefits of technology across all of these concepts, it is essential that school psychologists, whose breadth of training leaves them well prepared to lead in this arena, make certain that they are involved and even leaders in the decisions that are made around the use of technology.

Two specific ways that technology has an impact on data-driven decision making that are especially relevant to the practice of school psychology are in supporting the implementation of the problem-solving model and the implementation of multitiered systems of support. First, the problem-solving model serves as a guide to the process of using data for decision making and the process of communicating the results. Technology, and its capability to enforce consistency, is especially well suited to support the problem-solving model. Consistency is an essential feature of effective implementation of the problem-solving model. The questions asked in problem identification, for example, should not change from one teacher to another. Similarly, the problem-solving model is equally effective at the individual and the systems level, and consistency is needed to ensure that data-driven decision-making processes are aligned across the two. Technology can ensure this consistency by guiding the practitioner toward asking the right questions across individuals in the organization, across levels of the organization, and across time.

Second, the implementation of multitiered systems of support requires strong data management of both student academic and behavioral performance and tracking of the supports that are put into place. Technology has the capacity to organize all of these critical data, clearly communicate the information in real time to all stakeholders involved, and even gather metadata on the effectiveness of the various decisions that are being made about instruction. A shared software system across these tiers promotes the idea that special education is not a place we send students to because the special education software is not a place the student data get transferred into. The possibilities of technology to drive stronger practice via these models are practically limitless. School psychologists will play an essential role in guiding successful implementation.

BASIC CONSIDERATIONS

We will not be endorsing any specific product or tool. However, in many cases, examples are needed to help clarify the ideas and concepts being discussed, and these examples may be from a specific application or tool. In some cases, a specific technology may be the only one of its kind. Whenever possible, however, we will mention alternatives that provide parallel functionality to a given product being discussed.

BEST PRACTICES IN USING TECHNOLOGY FOR DATA-DRIVEN DECISION MAKING

This section will present key concepts and relevant examples of using technology for data-driven decision making. Specific topics include managing data, communicating student performance, setting expectations for performance, and other emerging technology considerations.

Using Technology to Manage Data

Quality data management is essential to having accurate data at the ready for presentation and communication. At numerous training seminars with school districts with which we work, we will often ask the district representatives whether the district has a technology plan in place (and nearly all respond that their district does).

Then we will ask if the district has a data management plan in place. It is the rare district that does. However, having a data management plan in place, regardless of the level of sophistication of the tools the district has at its disposal, can save the district a significant amount of time and energy spent in cleaning data files, in duplicating entry of data, or in having uncoordinated activities across departments despite common pursuits.

Using Spreadsheet Software

Spreadsheet software such as Microsoft Excel can be a powerful tool in data management. Most school psychologists are likely to be somewhat familiar with Excel or a similar tool. However, we encourage school psychologists to seek out training resources to become more aware of some of the features within Excel or any other spreadsheet software so they can use the software more efficiently.

For example, many school psychologists use spreadsheets to organize and synthesize summative and benchmark screening data to identify students at risk. They may then individually highlight the students in different colors to indicate their risk status. What they may not be aware of is that the software allows users to set conditional formatting rules that will automatically color code student data based on whether students scored above or below a target score on a particular academic or behavioral measure. Setting these rules not only saves the school psychologist the considerable time it takes to individually highlight rows of data for students at risk, but also can automatically color code additional records as the records are entered into the spreadsheet.

School psychologists using spreadsheets to synthesize data often want to create new variables that indicate the overall level of risk each student demonstrates across all of the data included in the spreadsheet. Hand counting risk points across several different columns in the spreadsheet to calculate a risk score for this summary column is a common, but highly inefficient, method used by many school psychologists and teams. Instead, spreadsheets provide simple formulas that can be used to automatically calculate these summary statistics by summing, averaging, or otherwise compositing data across multiple variables.

School psychologists should become familiar with pivot tables and charts. With pivot tables and charts, several parallel graphs can be generated from the same source data by simply dragging the needed variables in or out of and around the chart framework. For example, the second author found these tools critical in creating graphs comparing the percentage of students proficient in each of several districts within a special education cooperative. A click of a mouse was all that was needed to change which districts were displayed or to show data for only certain grades or only students receiving special education services. Each of the resultant graphs could then be copied and pasted into, for instance, Microsoft Word or PowerPoint.

Since Excel and the other spreadsheet software programs are updated frequently, and any navigation specifics shared here would therefore likely become outdated before *Best Practices* is revised again, we encourage school psychologists to consult training resources such as Excelcharts.com and the NASP online communities for the Computer and Technology Applications and Systems Level Data-Driven Decision-Making Interest Groups.

Using Relational Database Software

Spreadsheet software has built-in limitations when it comes to managing data. Each spreadsheet is essentially a file all to its own. While functions like Microsoft Excel's VLOOKUP can link together two separate spreadsheets by a common identifier, the capacity of VLOOKUP quickly gets overwhelmed when there are multiple spreadsheets of data where the common identifiers have different relationships with each other (one-to-one, one-to-many).

This is where relational database software comes in. Software such as Microsoft Access allows users to link multiple separate spreadsheets using common identification variables to update the data in one table to include data from another table and to generate new tables and graphs of data that cross-reference multiple tables. This can provide a great deal of flexibility in the data analysis process. For example, if there is one table with student assessment data, another table with the interventions attempted with those same students, and a third table that describes the characteristics of those interventions (i.e., group versus one on one, Tier 1 versus Tier 2), a query could be quickly created that examined the impact of different intervention characteristics on student performance.

The limitation of both relational database and spreadsheet software, however, is that each can only be accessed by a single person, and any data analyses produced using this software must then be manually distributed to all stakeholders, which is an extremely time-consuming and error-prone process. Enter Web-based software, such as the single function tools and data warehouses (described next) that allow a variety of users anytime–anywhere access to a common repository of data.

Using Single Function Software

Many software tools are available to help school psychologists in managing data around a specific function or type of data. These software tools are typically focused on a specific assessment system and are often sold along with the software designed to interpret data from that system. For example, websites for providers of academic or behavioral benchmark screening tools (i.e., AIMSweb, DIBELS, Northwest Evaluation Association, and School-Wide Information System) have data management and reporting capabilities within their sites. Typically these software capabilities are limited to the specific assessment they are designed to support but often have very strong analysis functions that are unique to that particular assessment.

These single function tools often include management functions that assist in governing the delivery of the assessment as well as the reporting. For example, school psychologists often take on roles such as managing benchmark windows when assessments can be delivered and results entered into the system, roster uploads that ensure all currently enrolled students are available to test in the system, and other management functions that ensure appropriate reports are available to different users of the system based on their role in the organization. In this way, single function tools are highly specific to the assessments that they are designed to manage, providing often valuable specificity to the idiosyncrasies of managing and reporting on that particular assessment.

However, appropriate management of these tools becomes essential to their effective use across the school or district, and the specific nature of the tools means that a broad and balanced assessment plan could well introduce multiple software tools to be managed. The school psychologist's contribution to this process can be invaluable in ensuring that these necessary management steps are well planned and are appropriate to the assessment. Unfortunately, without this planning, issues with poorly managed software can result in a school finding the underlying assessment itself to be not useful, sometimes leading to the assessment being discontinued simply because of software mismanagement.

Using Data Warehouse Technology

Multiple measures are often necessary to determine risk status or identify subskill strengths and weaknesses. The challenge with single function software is that these assessment data from multiple measures are housed within multiple software systems, requiring multiple logins and inconsistent displays of the data. Data warehouse technology is designed to address this problem, allowing one-stop shopping for all academic and behavioral assessment and other related data.

This is especially relevant in the implementation of a multitiered system of supports. Understanding what level of support is needed for a student requires ready access to a breadth of data. If an educator needs to log in to three different software tools to access all of the data needed to make an informed decision about a student, then that educator probably will not log in. That decision will end up being made based on a single assessment and often at a single point in time. Not only can data warehouse tools provide a single point of access to all relevant performance data about the student, but the tools can also track the specific instructional inputs or processes that occurred for that student. Which interventions the student has received in the past, what core curriculum and/or Tier 1 positive behavior support looks like for that student, and how much of each the student has received are all highly relevant to implementing a multitiered system of supports.

While data warehouses have this vast capacity to store and to serve a range of essential data to educators as needed, these warehouses also have the capacity to guide the process of navigating this forest of information. An example of this guided inquiry is in the problem-solving approach to systems-level decision making, where data warehouse technology can help to ensure that key steps are not skipped. Far too often in school-based problem solving it seems that schools are increasingly effective at problem identification and plan implementation, with less focus on problem analysis and plan evaluation. One likely reason for a failure to focus on problem analysis when problem solving at the group level is easy access to this information. Bernhardt (2006) provides an especially useful model for asking questions that cut across domains of information. Questions that disaggregate data by demographic subgroup, by other key performance data such as attendance and behavior, by information on the instructional environment such as classes and interventions, and by perceptions data allow an effective group-level problem analysis process to take place. Software systems such as data warehouses allow data from a range of sources to be used (student information systems, single function products focused on tracking a specific assessment or data source, human resource systems that track variables about staff, and financial systems that track funding). The business intelligence tools that often come with these warehouses allow the user to slice and dice the data by asking questions that cut across the domains of information described above.

School psychologists can play a key role in the proper use of these tools. Unlike single function tools, where the data analyses provided are often highly opinionated, and thus appropriate to the very specific assessment that the tool was designed to manage, data warehouses allow for any and all questions to be asked, both appropriate and misguided. School psychologists can call upon their training in data-driven decision making and assessment to ensure that the right questions are asked that do not lead to misleading information. Data warehouses also tend to provide an overwhelming amount of information. School psychologists can help ensure that a focused set of questions are asked in the problem analysis step, and ensure that the business intelligence tool is set up in a way that guides the user first to identify problems (i.e., via a data dashboard), then to analyze the problem (i.e., via a series of carefully considered analytic reports), and then to determine a plan. The use of a data dashboard can help bring the user back to the plan evaluation step by repeating the questions originally asked in the problem identification step to determine if the gap between expected and occurring has closed as a result of the plan.

The use of data warehouse and business intelligence tool sets in education is growing rapidly. The capacity to manage large volumes of diverse data and to answer a range of questions about these data makes them especially attractive to education leaders. With the power to analyze quickly also comes the power to make incorrect or misguided decisions quickly. One role that a school psychologist can play in the implementation of a data warehouse is to provide structure around the use of the data warehouse. The problem-solving model provides an excellent tool for establishing this structure around the types of systems-level decision making that a data warehouse invariably guides.

Future Directions in Managing Data

A key element in managing data is interoperability. Data are increasingly being stored in software systems and online databases, yet the nature of these software systems tends to be specific and focused. This leads schools to utilize multiple software systems to accommodate multiple initiatives. This can result in headaches for users who need to log in to multiple systems and for data management specialists who are responsible for keeping these systems in sync and up to date. This has an impact on daily use, for instance, in making sure the behavior software has up-to-date roster information from the student information system. It also has an impact on analysis, in being able to ask questions of the data that cut across these disparate systems.

Interoperability refers to the ability of these systems to effectively communicate. For instance, is the data warehouse being consistently updated with data coming from each of these systems and are changes to the student enrollment list in the student information system pushing out changes to the behavior and the curriculum-based measurement (CBM) software? Technologies are emerging, such as more efficient extract–transform–load tools for exchanging data across systems. However, these technologies require the allocation of resources for both setup and maintenance, which can be a tough sell to a school district. If a district wants access to effective charts and graphs to make well-informed decisions and present itself as a polished, tech-savvy institution, then the district needs to invest in data management.

Another option that schools can consider is to put pressure on the software vendors to improve interoperability. Application programming interfaces is an example of a tool that vendors can develop around their software application that allows other vendors to more easily exchange data. Another promising front is the continued improvement of standards of interoperability, which drive consistency in how vendors exchange school-related data. The Schools Interoperability Framework provides consistency in how education data are shared (SIF Association, 2013), so that any vendor who complies with these standards can easily make the data available to other vendors. These open approaches to software development encourage vendors to collaborate in helping schools achieve their mission. Since no software tool has everything, at least by being interoperable the tools help to break down the barriers that are created by having multiple siloed information systems. However, many vendors feel that taking these approaches is a bad business decision, because it opens them up to competition. Schools need to be reminding software vendors that not taking these approaches is a bad business decision because their software is less likely to be purchased by educators.

Another emerging trend in data management is the capability to analyze unstructured data. Data such as free responses to surveys, notes about specific conditions in a given assessment, or even data such as a student's sentiment posted about the school on social media are all examples of unstructured data in education. Unfortunately, while these data can have great value in understanding key concepts such as student performance (as in the assessment example) or student engagement (as in the social media example), these data are often looked at in isolation or ignored entirely. This is largely because of the difficulties in synthesizing these data with structured quantitative data such as attendance and test scores. New

tools are emerging to better analyze these unstructured data, and to capture them in a way that could help to provide a more complete picture of the student or the system when making decisions.

Using Technology to Report and Communicate Data

A well-managed data set is only the first step in the process of data-driven decision making. Technology is also crucial in guiding both to whom and how the data are displayed. Different audiences will be making different decisions. For example, some may require group-level data while others are focused strictly on individual-level data. The visual display of the data can also be crucial to ensuring that the decision is accurately informed. While data management ensures that all of these decisions are being made based upon a single accurate version of the truth, reporting and communication ensures that the way the data are presented is both valid and appropriate.

Considerations in the Visual Display of Information

Technology provides an increasing range of options to school psychologists either in developing their own custom display of information or in making decisions about selecting from existing displays generated by software tools. Before developing a graphical display of data, however, Tufte (2001) encourages the presenter to consider whether the graph is truly necessary and, if it is, then to use a graphical display that provides the greatest amount of information possible and uses the least amount of visual clutter. Some consider the visual display of information an art form. While the school psychologist may not need advanced coursework in data visualization to produce effective charts for a school data retreat, it is certainly useful to consider some of these key principles when designing displays of information. For example, a set of side-by-side pie charts showing the percentage of students at or above target in the fall, winter, and spring serves to visually disrupt information that should have a longitudinal flow to it. This makes it more difficult to quickly draw meaningful conclusions from the data than it would be if a series of stacked columns or perhaps even a line graph were used instead.

Telling Data Stories in Education

Another key consideration for the school psychologist charged with communicating data effectively is the concept that a story is being told with the data. Few

(2012) describes several characteristics of compelling stories told with numbers, emphasizing that, like all good stories, stories told with numbers must have a personal and emotional pull as well as clearly defined information. Use of techniques such as animated bubble charts can certainly aid the story, but the story itself must be a compelling one. Fortunately, education lends itself well to such stories, in part because of the natural longitudinal nature of the information and in part because of the strong emotional sentiment shared by most educators.

Like any story, a data story must have an introduction, a climax, and a resolution. There may be no better framework for data storytelling in education than the problem-solving model (Tilly, 2002). Problem identification serves as the introduction and allows us to measurably define the problem and visually present it by answering this question: What is the difference between what is expected and what is occurring? Problem analysis then serves as the rising action, providing additional background to the story, in the form of answers to those meaningful questions that logically stem from the identification of the problem: Why is this problem occurring? Plan development serves as the climax to the story. The results of the problem analysis step should make the answer to the next question obvious: What plan should be implemented? If it is not readily apparent what plan should be implemented, or at least what subissue of the problem needs to be directly addressed, then it is likely that the problem analysis step needs revisiting. Plan implementation acts as the falling action. Checking specifics such as treatment fidelity should be attended to in this step to answer this question: Was the plan implemented as intended? Plan evaluation provides the resolution to the story, and answers this question: To what degree did the plan reduce the gap between what is expected and occurring? As the question implies, this step can often be completed by simply asking the same data question that was asked in problem identification but presenting the answer in a way that allows for comparison across the time period before and after plan implementation.

In this way, the data stories told via the problem-solving model are cyclical. If the desired resolution was not achieved, then a mistake was made somewhere along the process; that is, perhaps a key variable contributing to the problem was overlooked, or the plan was not implemented as intended. In any case, the story begins again, either with revisiting the problem at hand or moving on to a new one.

One practical application of this storytelling approach to the display of data might be the use of guiding questions to help the consumer of data displays to interpret the tables or graphs within the context of the systems-level problem-solving model. The second author has found this approach successful in his design of yearly school district data book PowerPoints. (To access a sample data book PowerPoint, we suggest going to http://communities.nasponline.org, joining the NASP Systems-Level Data-Driven Decision Making Interest Group and visiting the library within that group's online community. A copy of this data book is available there as an example. Please note that at the time this chapter was written, these communities were only accessible to NASP members.) The summative, benchmark screening, and diagnostic subskill data drawn from state and local assessments are organized under a series of queries: (a) Are all of the students meeting standards or growing at a rate that will make them more likely to meet standards in the future? (b) Are all of the students in special population subgroups meeting standards or growing at a rate that will make them more likely to meet standards in the future? (c) What specific skill strengths or weaknesses do the students demonstrate based on standardized assessment results?

Many other district data books tend to be simply a series of graphs and tables, making it difficult for the consumer to see the story amidst all of the numbers. Alternatively, some data books include lengthy text interpretation of each table or graph created by the data expert (e.g., the school psychologist). We caution against this approach as well, since it encourages an expert consultation model in which district staff may come to believe that the only way the staff can successfully engage in systems-level data-driven decision making is by asking the school psychologist to create and interpret a data display. Instead, in addition to using guiding questions to encourage district staff to view data displays within the context of a systems-level problem-solving model, a good data book would also include direct links to directions and recorded webinar trainings explaining how consumers can on their own create similar tables and graphs in the future. To answer the inevitable "so what" question that often comes with data displays, a good data book would include information regarding how to access resources that can be used to translate the assessment results that are displayed into concrete intervention activities.

Communicating Data at the Group Level

Technology plays a key role in both communicating and helping users to understand and make good decisions about data. While clarity and elegance of display is essential, equally essential is that the presentation of the data helps to guide the user through an effective decision-making process while avoiding inaccurate assumptions. The problem-solving model is an effective example of this, and it can be applied to group- as well as individual-level decision making.

Consider a school where a larger percentage of students are below target in first grade than in second grade. An effective display of all grade levels in the school, along with the percentage of students above target, can provide instantly actionable information. It is a fairly simple data visualization, yet it is by nature guiding the decision-making process of the viewer by bringing attention to discrepancies across grade levels and using the underlying system of consistent target scores to do so. It is hard for a viewer of such a graph to argue that this cohort of students does not need additional help above and beyond the other cohorts.

An extension of this example would be to also include percentages of students above target across benchmark screening periods (i.e., fall, winter, and spring). This establishes not only the level of need, but also whether that level is changing in response to changes in resource allocation and/or programming. A further extension of this example would be to include percentages of students above target across years. This helps to identify whether the issue is more likely due to a cohort of students needing additional resources instead of a specific grade level where the instruction consistently does not appear to be leading to successful outcomes.

Technology can ensure that there is both specificity and consistency in the decision-making process across both the group and individual levels. Specificity comes from views of the data that are customized to the particular audience. One reason customized views are so valuable is that the more opportunities someone is given to click before he or she can access relevant information, the more likely he or she is to click in the wrong place or do the wrong thing. Customized views make sure everyone sees what is appropriate specifically to him or her, right when he or she first logs in.

An example of consistency would be that the same target scores that are used to establish how a cohort is performing, how that performance has changed over time, and how cohorts compare to each other are used to examine performance for individual students. This ensures that teachers, parents, and the students themselves are making decisions—about level of concern, strengths and weaknesses, and which students need additional support—that are in line with the decisions that building and district leadership are making about

the system. For example, if a teacher were making decisions about placing students in an intervention program based on percentile scores, and if the principal were making decisions about which grade levels will receive extra resources to support this intervention program based on target scores, then this could quickly lead to a conflicted and disorganized system. By limiting the scope of data and how those data are displayed, and by making sure the information is consistent regardless of who is viewing it, technology can contribute to improved system organization.

Communicating Data at the Individual Level

Increasingly, assessment systems are providing a component that explores student growth. While it might be argued that school psychologists who followed the work of Deno and Mirkin (1977) have understood the importance of growth for a long time, nevertheless four decades later it appears that assessments such as the Measures of Academic Progress (Northwest Evaluation Association, 2013), and even state-mandated assessments such as those being developed by PARCC and the Smarter Balanced Consortium (Educational Testing Service, 2012), are now paying attention to how their tools can help measure individual student growth over time.

Not surprisingly, when a problem-solving approach to the concept of growth is taken, the first question is how to define the "expected" in the question of the difference between what is expected and what is occurring. Technology comes into play here, in that the software systems typically come with their norm-referenced growth goals assigned as a default, often with no method to modify them. Certainly, any technology tool centered around the idea of tracking individual student growth must have the capacity to individualize growth targets. Allowing these growth targets to be customized, and allowing them to take into account factors such as how much growth is needed to catch back up to targets, what is a reasonable amount of time in which to catch up, and what growth goals should be for students already above target are questions that school psychologists who have studied the CBM literature are quite familiar with. An effective data-driven decision-making technology tool will provide ways to answer these questions flexibly, to automate the delivery of decisions about expectations for growth, and to standardize the ways that these expectations are presented and interpreted.

With the right technology tools, a flexible target-setting system can be developed that displays individual student accelerated (or catch-up) goals to teachers, such that almost all students who were below target would be above target if the students continued to hit their accelerated growth goals over a specified number of years (i.e., 3 years). This greatly simplifies the communication around what these accelerated goals mean. While some students would certainly catch up more quickly than in 3 years, explaining the complexity of which students would catch up sooner versus later is not necessary and would detract from the power of the message. Teachers simply look at their students' performance, and if a student's current status score is red or yellow, then the teacher will know the student needs to hit his or her accelerated growth goal for that year, which is also displayed. Technology in this example provides the ability to display the data efficiently and with a focus on actionable information, the ability to both simplify and automate the process of assigning goals for both status and growth, and the ability to drive consistency and large-scale implementation of a data-driven decision-making process that considers both status and growth.

Future Directions in Reporting and Communication of Data

As school psychologists well know, within an effective data-driven decision-making system, decisions about whether students are meeting status or growth goals need to be made more frequently than after each benchmark screening assessment. Waiting that long to know if students are responding to both good classroom instruction and any supplemental instruction being provided would be doing a disservice to the students and to the teachers. That is where more frequent progress monitoring data can come in handy.

But for progress monitoring data to be communicated and used most effectively, the data must be displayed and interpreted within the context of the aforementioned changes in instruction. This is the only way to use the data to truly judge student response to intervention. Many academic and behavioral progress monitoring technology tools (some, like Chart Dog, that are actually free; see Figure 36.1 for an example) offer easy ways for users to insert an indication of a change in intervention or phase. These tools also then typically recalculate the slope of the student's trendline following this change. This allows the team to examine whether the instructional adjustment appears to be related to an improvement in the student's growth.

When school psychologists share these progress monitoring graphs with others, however, they should be careful only to draw conclusions based on meaningful changes in student growth, taking into account what experts have found regarding the standard error of measurement (SEM) and standard error of slope (SEb) of progress monitoring probes (Christ, Zopluoglu, Monaghen, & Van Norman, 2013). The same, of course, is true when presenting diagnostic subskill strand

Figure 36.1. Example of a Progress Monitoring Technology Tool

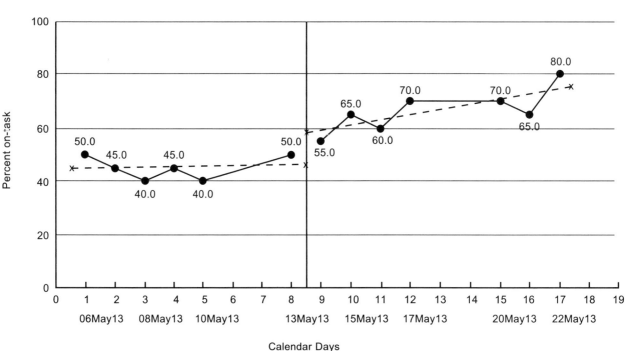

data. For example, Northwest Evaluation Association reports that the SEM for the standardized RIT scores is typically three to four points. RIT scores are the primary score derived from student performance on the Measures of Academic Progress test, a popular computer-adaptive test of reading and math (Northwest Evaluation Association, 2013). It is critical, then, that school psychologists either clearly indicate this SEM in any data displays involving RIT scores or only display differences that are meaningful given the SEM. Otherwise, small, insignificant subskill differences may be misinterpreted as meaningful and used to make high-stakes curricular planning decisions. It is our hope that software vendors take heed of these considerations (and this great responsibility) as well and incorporate concepts such as SEM and SEb into their visual displays of information. Technology certainly has the capacity to do so.

Using Technology to Set Expectations for Performance

Technology has the power to inform not only by managing and displaying data but also by analyzing these data. The capacity of technology to take existing sources of data and turn data into information is a rapidly growing area of interest. One aspect of this approach that is especially relevant to school psychology is predictive analytics. Predictive analytics is the process of leveraging statistical analysis to make predictions about future behavior based on past and current information. This approach allows us to not only make predictions, but also set expectations for current performance based on the statistical likelihood of a desired outcome. A specific example of predictive analytics that is now broadly used by school psychologists is that of setting targets on local assessments to predict success on high-stakes outcome assessments, such as state-mandated tests of reading and mathematics (Reschly, Busch, Betts, Deno, & Long, 2009). The goal of this approach is to set criterion-referenced benchmarks on local screening assessments, such as oral reading fluency, in such a way that achievement of these benchmarks for performance are highly predictive of success on the high-stakes outcome.

Why Use Target Setting

A target-setting approach provides context for performance on screening and progress monitoring assessments that is directly relevant to key outcomes. One distinct advantage of utilizing a target-setting framework

is that it raises awareness and the importance of the local assessment in the eyes of a broad range of stakeholders. Reports can be created for parents and students, teachers, building leaders, district leaders, and school boards that demonstrate the number and percentage of students who are likely to succeed on outcomes that are critical both to the success of the student and to the funding and public perception of the school, in some cases many years before those outcomes are assessed.

One key goal of the problem identification stage of the problem-solving process is to define the problem in observable and measureable terms by answering this question: What is the difference between what is expected and what is occurring? As leaders in the problem-solving approach, school psychologists have the opportunity to guide how this question is both asked and answered. However, the school psychologist may find that, in many schools, there are a range of perspectives on the definition of "what is expected." Often, these perspectives have much to do with the roles of the individual stakeholders; that is, how parents measure their expectations for their children may differ from how teachers measure expectations for all children in their classrooms, which may differ from how principals measure expectations for their buildings, and so on.

By using technology both to set the targets and to display data within the context of these targets, the school psychologist is providing a connection across these differing approaches to setting expectations. This provides a common understanding of how to measure "what is expected," as well as "what is occurring," and encourages consistency across both individual and systems-level decision-making frameworks. Anecdotally, the school psychologist may find that the problem-solving process often gets bogged down by this seemingly innocuous question of how expectations are defined. When this happens at the systems level, it can derail efforts to institute systematic approaches to decision making and leave individual-level decisions to be made in a haphazard and inconsistent manner. Using technology to set and communicate targets can resolve this.

Take the example of setting expectations for student growth, one that is especially relevant to a multitiered system of supports. With a target-setting approach, the expectation of "a year's growth in a year's time" is well defined. When universal screening data are collected systematically, a year's growth can simply be defined as the change in target scores from the fall to the spring benchmark data collection. Silberglitt (2008a, b) examined the norm-referenced growth targets generated by the Measures of Academic Progress and found that a student exactly at the fall benchmark target score typically has a norm-referenced growth goal that is not sufficient to reach the spring benchmark target. Using technology tools that are sufficiently flexible to set growth goals properly is critical to communicating these accurate criteria for success.

How to Set Targets

One of the most difficult steps in taking a target-setting approach to tracking student performance is the act of setting the targets themselves. Once these targets are established, the reporting and communication of data are greatly simplified and can be extremely powerful, both at the individual and group levels. For example, with targets and key performance indicators established, complex information can be communicated to stakeholders who may have a limited understanding of the underlying data. For instance, a county social worker collaborating with the school to support a student may not understand the meaning of a score on a particular assessment, but both the social worker and the school can easily visualize if the student has three red flags on his or her recent reading assessments and can thus provide supportive and coordinated services alongside the school.

A commonly used statistical approach to target setting is logistic regression, which can be especially valuable when the outcome being predicted is a categorical one, such as whether or not a student achieves grade-level standards on a high-stakes reading assessment (Neter, Kutner, Nachtsheim, & Wasserman, 1996). Applications of the logistic regression approach to target setting have been extended over time, across changes in the nature of the outcomes assessment being predicted (an Excel template for setting targets using logistic regression is available at the TIES Data-Driven Leadership page: http://ties.k12.mn.us/what-we-do/professional-development/data-driven-decision-making-resources). For example, state-mandated tests are changing over time, both in the version numbers of the assessments (due to periodic revisiting of and changes to the state standards) and in the vendors providing the assessments (due to periodic contract renewal) in consecutive years. In a series of studies examining the link between the Measures of Academic Progress mathematics test and a state's assessment, it was found that changes to both the version and the vendor significantly affected the target scores generated and warranted a reanalysis of the data and distribution of new targets (Silberglitt & Muyskens, 2012).

It is, of course, also important to be an educated consumer of targets promoted by other education agencies, test or intervention providers, or data management systems. Below is a list of some key questions to ask in evaluating the psychometric and practical utility of any set of targets:

- What method was used in setting the targets? Is this method consistent with what is understood to be best practice?
- What are the characteristics of the sample that was used (e.g., size, demographic characteristics, national or local origin)? Do these characteristics suggest that the targets are generalizable to the population to be served?
- How recently have the targets been calculated? Are the targets set to the most recent edition of the outcome test available? Have the sample characteristics changed significantly since the targets were set?
- Is the outcome used in calculating the targets the same as or at least consistent with the intended outcome (e.g., the same state accountability test or one of equal difficulty)? If the outcome is not similar to the outcome intended, then will the targets be artificially high or low, resulting in underidentification or overidentification of students at risk?

The target-setting approach, using predictive analytics to establish criteria on metrics that will effectively predict success on key outcomes, is certainly not limited to using local assessments to predict state test scores. Figure 36.2 shows an example of setting criteria across a variety of behavioral indicators of student performance in order to create a more comprehensive student profile. In the example shown, several metrics are defined within a domain of performance, with user-defined criteria on each metric. For example, four metrics are selected within the domain of attendance, and the school has established some meaningful criteria for how many absences in the last X number of days defines performance that exceeds expectations (diamond), meets expectations (circles), approaches expectations (triangles), and does not meet expectations (exclamation point). While this example is from a specific software tool, the concept of setting criteria on a range of student performance indicators is a critical one within which school psychologists can play a key role.

Future Directions in Using Technology for Target Setting

Additional technology tools are evolving that will significantly improve the quality of target setting across a wide range of student performance indicators. Many

Figure 36.2. Example of Setting Targets on a Comprehensive Student Profile

Personalized Learning

 Student: Balk, George **Grade:** 12 **School:** 0121 **School Year:** 2010

Personalized Learning provides detailed information about student performance and goals, as well as a comment log for discussion. Please click on the tabs below for more information.

☑ E-mail me about the changes to this student's comments or plan.

| Personal Profile | Personal Plan | Comment Log |

Personal Profile

This personal profile tracks student performance on measures within each domain. Icons update to reflect how performance compares to standards.

	Domain		Measure
	Overall		
▲	Attendance	●	Year-to-date percent attendance: 98.182%
		▲	Year-to-date number of absences: 4
		◆	Number of absences in most recent 30 days: 0
		●	Year-to-date percent tardy: 0.09%
		◆	Number of tardies in most recent 30 days: 0
▲	Behavior	●	Year-to-date number of Detention actions: 2
		◆	Number of Detention actions in most recent 14 days: 0
		◆	Year-to-date number of Suspension actions: 0
		◆	Number of Minor Incident behavior incidents in most recent 14 day: 0
		▲	Year-to-date number of Major Incident behavior incidents: 2
		●	Year-to-date number of Minor Incident behavior incidents: 2
◆	Grades -- Report Card Grades	◆	Year-to-date number of NC's: 0
		◆	Cumulative GPA: 3.518
		◆	Year-to-date number of F's: 0
❗	Grades -- Grade Book	◆	Number of grades less than or equal to D+: 0
		❗	Number of Missing and/or Absent Assignments: 3
		●	Number of grades greater than or equal to A: 0
●	Graduation on Track -- Graduation Tests	●	GRAD Math requirement: Passed
		◆	GRAD Reading requirement: Passed
		◆	GRAD Writing requirement: Passed
●	Graduation on Track -- Graduation Credits	◆	Credits required for Health in Grade 12: 0.5
		◆	Credits required for Math in Grade 12: 4
		◆	Credits required for Music in Grade 12: 1.5
		●	Credits required for Phy Ed in Grade 12: 0.5
		◆	Credits required for Science in Grade 12: 2
		◆	Total credits required in Grade 12: 30.5
❗	Tests	▲	Most recent MCA math achievement level: 2
		◆	Most recent MCA reading achievement level: 4
		◆	Most recent MCA science achievement level: 4
		▲	Most Recent MAP Test Mathematics Overall RIT Score: 233
		◆	Most Recent MAP Test Reading Overall RIT Score: 238
		●	Most Recent ACT/PLAN/EXPLORE English Scale: 22
		❗	Most Recent ACT/PLAN/EXPLORE Mathematics Scale: 18
		●	Most Recent ACT/PLAN/EXPLORE Reading Scale: 21
		●	Most Recent ACT/PLAN/EXPLORE Science Scale: 25

View Prior School Year Show Target Scores

Data current as of 6/28/2013 6:03:58 PM for school year 2009-2010

This student plan and comments are assigned to Dave Campen

Welcome Dave Campen
Monday, July 01, 2013
You are the plan manager for this student
You are a PLP Content Manager

Note. Copyright 2014 by TIES. Used with permission.

of these tools have already been established in other settings, such as the retail or healthcare industry. One tool that has broad use in retail and increasing use in healthcare today is the use of data mining. The use of

high-powered data mining tools to track customer behavior such as what purchases have been made, loyalty to a specific brand or store, and demographic information can all be accessed and synthesized in real time to help retailers make faster and more profitable decisions.

Using predictive analytics to synthesize a range of data, understand in real time which students may be headed for negative outcomes, and mine the vast quantities of education research to suggest an intervention represents a vision for education that is shared by many (U.S. Department of Education, 2010). In fact, the progress of such applications is likely only being restricted by a lack of sufficient funding or available research, and it is unlikely that an unscrupulous vendor would allow the latter to get in the way if the former is resolved.

With the rapidity of change in education technology, being a leader in making decisions about what technology to implement can be especially daunting.

Table 36.1 provides a series of questions that can help guide educators in making decisions about what technologies to implement. The table is organized by questions to ask and what to look for, with an attempt to provide questions that will remain relevant to decisions about data-driven decision-making technology, even as these technologies continue to advance.

Emerging Technology Considerations

Especially as school psychologists take on more technology and data-driven decision-making roles, they may need technology to help them with time management. The list of technology tools that can help with time management and productivity is nearly endless, but for the purposes of this chapter, we will briefly review

Table 36.1. Guide to Selecting Software to Support the Data-Driven Decision-Making Process

Questions to Ask	What to Look For
Are data displayed appropriately or can data be customized to prevent inappropriate display?	• No examples of misleading or inappropriate information (i.e., means calculated on percentile ranks, averages taken across grade levels when scores are not vertically equated) • Displays can be customized and controlled by educators with expertise in measurement before being displayed broadly to principals, teachers, and other stakeholders
Does the tool have or allow for customized views for different types of users?	• Users only see the information that is pertinent and appropriate to them (e.g., teachers only see students in their classroom or possibly grade level, coaches only see students on their team, the English language learner teacher only sees his or her students) • Unique data displays for a broad range of roles (i.e., school board members, principals, teachers, county service providers, parents)
If the tool customizes views for different types of users, does it maintain consistency in the decision-making process?	• Across levels of the organization (i.e., the same target scores apply to performance when viewed at the district level by the board member, the classroom level by the principal, and the student level by the teacher) • Across users in the organization (i.e., all elementary principals have a consistent dashboard and are asking the same types of questions about the data) • Across time (a consistent focus on established key performance indicators)
Does the software have flexibility as to the types of data being stored?	• One login to see all of the relevant data on a student or group of students • Data displays are appropriate and effective across the range of data
Does the software support a problem-solving approach?	• Data displays are relevant to problem identification • Guides the user so the user is less likely to skip problem analysis • Stores information about plans developed • Tracks fidelity to those plans (in some cases even delivers the relevant content) • Collects metadata to help the system understand when and why plans are particularly effective or ineffective
Does the software support tiered assessment and tiered intervention?	• Collects data and tracks interventions across the full range of tiers • Accessible to both general and special educators, so they are working as a team
Is the software tool interoperable?	• Supports the Schools Interoperability Framework and/or includes an application programming interface to make sure that data can move back and forth across relevant systems to prevent double-entry of data • Supports single sign-on integration to allow educators to easily jump back and forth between systems without needing to log in multiple times

tools serving three primary functions: (a) taking and keeping portable notes, (b) sharing and collaboratively creating or revising documents and resources, and (c) accessing or delivering virtual professional development.

A significant challenge for school psychologists, whether they are serving a primarily traditional or more comprehensive role, is to be able to document assessment and intervention decisions made during individual or group consultations in a manner that is easily accessible from the variety of locations where a school psychologist may find himself or herself during the course of the day. Evernote and other portable note-taking tools solve this problem by allowing school psychologists to record and access the same already-recorded notes, to sync files, and to save webpages with any device, such as smartphones, tablets, and laptop and desktop computers.

If school psychologists want to share or collaboratively create or revise more complete documents or resources, including items ranging from standardized test inventories to intervention plans and scripts, they may be tempted to use cloud computing software such as Google Drive or Dropbox. These tools can provide a much more efficient approach to document sharing than e-mailing successive updated versions of a document back and forth as attachments and avoid problems such as attachments being rejected by e-mail servers or collaborators losing track of which version of the document is the most current. However, recent reviews of cloud computing have cautioned users to seriously investigate potential issues with whichever cloud computing software they are choosing to use, including the ease of access to and security of information stored (Pfohl, 2011).

We advise readers to use cloud computing only to share nonsensitive documents and information unless they are able to obtain clear assurance that the software tool's privacy policy can protect the confidentiality of the material being shared. Of course, readers should also consult with administrators and technology coordinators within their school districts to determine whether their district has an official policy in place regarding the use of cloud computing software. Potential secure alternatives to cloud computing that could serve the same function might include school district password-protected Intranet or data warehouse systems.

Additionally, as school district professional development budgets are reduced and interstate travel becomes more limited, quality face-to-face options for continuing education opportunities for school psychologists become more difficult to find. This, along with improvements in the technology for delivering professional development, has led to a proliferation in recent years of virtual training opportunities, including live and recorded webinars and podcasts. School psychologists can earn continuing education credits for state or national recertification without leaving their school or home. For those serving a larger number of schools or serving a more systems-level consultation role, live or recorded webinars can also be useful vehicles for delivering professional development to others.

Another rapidly emerging technology arena is the use of technology tools that deliver instructional content and track student progress through the curriculum. Increasingly, schools are exploring classroom settings that offer a hybrid mix of in-person and online content delivery, or even completely online coursework. In these settings, teachers serve as more of a guide through the curriculum and less as the delivery mechanism for content. Technologies are increasingly available that deliver supplemental interventions (such as Study Island and Compass Learning) or supplemental content (such as Khan Academy). Technologies to manage the entire course content online (learning and content management systems such as Moodle) are also growing in popularity as teachers explore delivering more content online.

These tools have the potential to assist teachers in providing more opportunities for students to direct their own learning, more differentiation of content difficulty across the spectrum of students, and more personalized learning environments for students. However, the expansion of these technology tools and their capabilities in classroom settings has grown much faster than the rate of corresponding research and evaluation into their effectiveness and what best practices should be in place to ensure that these tools improve student learning (West, 2011). Many of these tools also come with assessment systems that track student progress through the content delivered by the software. School psychologists can be leaders in ensuring that data are gathered and evaluated that track individual student progress toward the outcome (rather than just within the specific content area) and that data are gathered and evaluated that track the effectiveness of these approaches at the systems level as well.

SUMMARY

Technology has tremendous capacity to facilitate and guide the data-driven decision-making process. As education grows increasingly data driven, the process of making data available to the right stakeholder, in the right format, at the right time becomes increasingly complex. Technology tools are absolutely necessary for data-driven decision making in education to continue to progress.

The potential of the data-driven decision-making approach to education is one of tremendous benefit to children. School psychologists have the ability to predict student outcomes years before they occur, can set performance benchmarks in ways that are clearly understood by stakeholders who may otherwise have a limited understanding of either statistics or assessment, and can provide powerful reporting that slices and dices these data in an infinite number of ways. With the right tools in place there is almost no question that cannot be answered.

However, these technology tools by themselves are by no means a panacea. Careful attention must be paid to ensure that best practices in using data are employed. Considerations include how data are presented, how data are managed, and whether the data and the technology are used within an appropriate decision-making framework.

School psychologists have the skills and training that can be essential in helping schools to make effective and appropriate use of technology for data-driven decision making. Whether this includes coordinating the use of technology to support a district data retreat, bringing technology into team meetings focused on individual students, assisting in the data management plan to ensure that all data are available when the data are needed, or all of the above, school psychologists can serve as leaders in helping the school to think carefully about how to make the most of its technology investments.

REFERENCES

Bernhardt, V. (2006). *Using data to improve student learning in school districts.* Larchmont, NY: Eye on Education.

Christ, T. J., Zopluoglu, C., Monaghen, B. D., & Van Norman, E. R. (2013). Curriculum-based measurement of oral reading: Multi-study evaluation of schedule, duration, and dataset quality on progress monitoring outcomes. *Journal of School Psychology, 51,* 19–57.

Deno, S. L., & Mirkin, P. K. (1977). *Data-based program modification: A manual.* Reston, VA: Council for Exceptional Children.

Educational Testing Service. (2012). *Coming together to raise achievement: New assessments for the common core standards.* Washington, DC: Author. Retrieved from http://www.k12center.org/rsc/pdf/Coming_Together_April_2012_Final.pdf

Few, S. (2012). *Show me the numbers: Designing tables and graphs to enlighten* (2nd ed.). Burlingame, CA: Analytics Press.

Johnson, L., Adams, S., & Cummins, M. (2012). *NMC horizon report: 2012 K–12 edition.* Austin, TX: New Media Consortium.

Moore, G. E. (1965). Cramming more components onto integrated circuits. *Electronics Magazine, 38*(8), 4.

National Association of School Psychologists. (2010). *Model for comprehensive and integrated school psychological services.* Bethesda, MD: Author. Retrieved from http://www.nasponline.org/standards/2010standards/2_PracticeModel.pdf

Neter, J., Kutner, M. H., Nachtsheim, C. J., & Wasserman, W. (1996). *Applied linear statistical models.* New York, NY: McGraw-Hill.

Northwest Evaluation Association. (2013). *Measures of Academic Progress.* Portland, OR: Author.

Pfohl, B. (2011). Tech corner: Working on a cloud. *Communiqué, 39*(6), 36.

Reschly, A. L., Busch, T. W., Betts, J., Deno, S. L., & Long, J. (2009). Curriculum-based measurement oral reading as an indicator of reading achievement: A meta-analysis of the correlational evidence. *Journal of School Psychology, 47,* 427–469.

SIF Association. (2013). *Understanding the basics of SIF.* Washington, DC: Author. Retrieved from http://www.sifassociation.org/Resources/Decision-Maker-Resources/Pages/default.aspx

Silberglitt, B. (2008a). Best practices in using technology for data-based decision making. In A. Thomas & J. Grimes (Eds.), *Best practices in school psychology V* (pp. 1869–1884). Bethesda, MD: National Association of School Psychologists.

Silberglitt, B. (2008b). *Target scores on Northwest Evaluation Association assessments that predict success on the Minnesota Comprehensive Assessments-II: Results from a TIES-wide study.* St. Paul, MN: Technology and Information Education Services.

Silberglitt, B., & Muyskens, P. (2012). *Predicting success on the Minnesota Comprehensive Assessments-III: Math using NWEA math assessments: Results from a TIES-wide study.* St. Paul, MN: Technology and Information Education Services.

Tilly, W. D., III. (2002). Best practices in school psychology as a problem-solving enterprise. In A. Thomas & J. Grimes (Eds.), *Best practices in school psychology III* (pp. 21–36). Bethesda, MD: National Association of School Psychologists.

Tufte, E. R. (2001). *The visual display of quantitative information.* Cheshire, CT: Graphics Press.

U.S. Department of Education. (2010). *National education technology plan.* Washington, DC: Author.

West, D. M. (2011). *Using technology to personalize learning and assess students in real-time.* Washington, DC: Brookings Institution. Retrieved from http://www.k12.wa.us/EdTech/pubdocs/TechInnovation-PersonalizeLearning.pdf

The Status of School Psychology Graduate Education in the United States

37

Eric Rossen
National Association of School Psychologists (MD)
Nathaniel von der Embse
Temple University (PA)

OVERVIEW

The profession of school psychology is continuously evolving. For this reason, graduate education must adapt to the changing needs of the field while concurrently helping shape future directions for practice and research. This chapter examines various trends in school psychology graduate education in the United States and discusses implications for school psychology faculty, current and prospective graduate students, and practitioners.

DIRECTORIES AND DATABASES OF SCHOOL PSYCHOLOGY GRADUATE PROGRAMS

Beginning in 1977, the National Association of School Psychologists (NASP) began compiling comprehensive directories of all available school psychology programs every 5 10 years with the intention of providing information to the field, prospective students, and potential employers. Data collection for the directories occurred in 1976 (Brown & Lindstrom, 1977), in 1982 (Brown & Minke, 1984), in 1988 (McMaster, Reschly, & Peters, 1989), in 1997 (Thomas, 1998), in 2006 (Miller, 2008), and annually from 2010 onward as part of the National School Psychology Program Database (NASP, 2013). Data from these directories are referenced throughout this chapter.

Caution should be exercised in the interpretation of the comparison data. As explained in the 1989 version of the directory (McMaster et al., 1989), the directories differed as to what data were collected and what constituted master's, specialist, and doctoral programs.

Response rates also differed, leading to some extrapolation within earlier versions. However, the 1998 directory, 2008 directory, and most recent program databases confidently report data from more than 99% of available programs. Notably, the 2008 data included both U.S. and Canadian programs. However, any reference to 2008 data refers only to programs based in the United States. Some data from the 2008 database were not included when U.S. and Canadian data could not be separated.

The annual data collection efforts beginning in 2010 were a product of the National Program Database Project, led by a subcommittee of the NASP Graduate Education Workgroup. The workgroup had representation from all constituent groups associated with graduate education in school psychology: NASP, Trainers of School Psychologists, Council for Directors of School Psychology Programs, American Psychological Association (APA) Division 16, Academy of School Psychology, School Psychology Specialty Council, and Society for the Study of School Psychology. Associated program data generated from this project can be accessed at http://www.nasponline.org/graduate-education/grad-edu.aspx.

AVAILABILITY OF SCHOOL PSYCHOLOGY GRADUATE EDUCATION IN THE UNITED STATES

The first graduate program to use the term "school psychology" was created in the 1920s at New York University. At the time of the Thayer Conference in

1954, 28 institutions were offering programs specifically in school psychology (Fagan, 2008). By 1976, 203 institutions were offering at least one graduate degree program in school psychology (Brown & Lindstrom, 1977), representing more than a sixfold increase across a 32-year span. This was followed by a leveling off in the growth of institutions offering graduate programs. The total number of institutions offering at least one program in school psychology has consistently remained within the range of 218–240 for the past 30 years (see Figure 37.1). As of 2013, 240 institutions were offering school psychology programs that minimally led to state school psychology certification or licensure within the United States.

Many institutions offer more than one graduate degree program (e.g., a specialist-level and a doctoral-level program). Therefore, the total number of programs available exceeds the number of institutions offering them. Table 37.1 provides a comparison of the total number of graduate preparation programs in school psychology in the United States since 1976. Similar to the number of institutions, the total number of school psychology degree programs offered has generally remained stable, marked by a relatively small 9% growth over the last 37 years (from 287 to 313).

The relative plateau in the number of programs or institutions offering programs does not necessarily reflect program or institutional longevity. Modifications to national-level and state-level graduate preparation and credentialing standards likely contributed to the closing of several programs that could not meet or keep up with

faculty and/or curriculum requirements while new programs emerged elsewhere (Thomas Fagan, personal communication, January 2, 2014). For example, programs that offered only master's-level preparation may have closed as a result of requirements from state departments of education and national standards focusing on specialist-level preparation as the entry level for credentialing.

Interestingly, the period with the highest number of total school psychology programs was recorded in 1981–1982 (Brown & Minke, 1984), with 333 identified programs. Nearly one-quarter of those programs consisted of master's-level degree programs. The brief drop and steady increase in total available programs since 1982 can largely be attributed to the steady decline of master's-level programs and the subsequent increase in specialist- and doctoral-level programs.

Growth in the number of school psychology graduate programs and institutions offering programs is expected to remain modest (Fagan, 2008). A stable availability of institutions and programs may indicate adequate supply and demand. However, with increasing attention given to the importance of mental health access in schools, coupled with NASP's modified recommended ratio for providing comprehensive and preventive school psychological services (1:500–700; NASP, 2010), an increase in national demand for school psychologists in the near future is plausible. The potential for future shifts in demand may prompt the establishment of more school psychology graduate preparation programs. However, such shifts may be geographically dependent. To

Figure 37.1. Number of U.S. Institutions Offering School Psychology Programs by Year

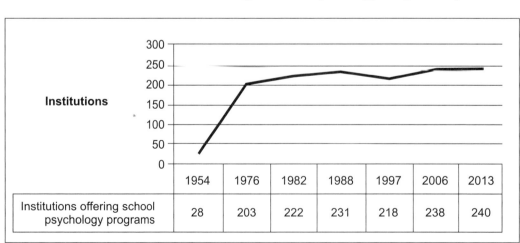

Note. Based on information from Brown and Lindstrom (1977), Brown and Minke (1984), Fagan (2008), McMaster et al. (1989), Miller (2008), NASP (2013), and Thomas (1998).

Table 37.1. Number of Graduate Education Training Programs in School Psychology

Total Institutions	1976 203		1982 211(222)[a]		1988 203(231)[b]		1997 218		2006 238		2013 240	
	#Prog.	%	#Prog.	%	#Prog.	%	#Prog.	%	#Prog.	%	#Prog.	%
Master's level	70	24.4	80	24.0	46	15.8	13	4.4	31	–	–	–
Specialist level	151	52.6	174	52.3	172	58.9	194	66.0	211	67.4	214	68.4
Doctoral level	66	23.0	79	23.7	74	25.3	87	29.6	99	31.6	99	31.6
All levels	287		333		292		294		313		313	

Note: # Prog. = the number of program levels responding; % = the percentages of programs responding at specified levels (master's level, specialist level, doctoral level). Currently, states without university school psychology training programs include Alaska, Hawaii, Vermont, and Wyoming. Based on information from Brown and Lindstrom (1977), Brown and Minke (1984), McMaster et al. (1989), Miller (2008), NASP (2013), and Thomas (1998). [a] Brown and Minke (1984) report that they knew of 11 additional institutions that possibly train school psychologists that did not respond to the survey. [b] 231 institutions were identified with 203 providing usable data.

illustrate, the number of institutions offering school psychology in New York increased by 47% from 1988 to 2013 (19–28). In contrast, Louisiana, Iowa, and Tennessee have a combined 33% fewer institutions offering programs in 2013 than in 1988, accounting for 12 current institutions across those states. Wyoming, Alaska, Hawaii, and Vermont have not had any institutions offering school psychology graduate programs during that same time span.

Degree and Preparation Levels

At present, graduate preparation programs are generally divided into either (a) specialist-level (i.e., at least 60 semester/90 quarter hour graduate hours) or (b) doctoral-level training (i.e., at least 90 graduate semester hours or the equivalent). Graduate preparation in school psychology has shifted away from terminal master's degree programs (i.e., programs requiring *fewer* than 60 graduate semester hours or 90 quarter hours). Several specialist-level programs offer a master's degree by title yet offer over 60 graduate semester hours, and such programs are considered specialist level.

This shift can be attributed to the majority of states requiring a minimum of a specialist-level program to obtain the school psychologist credential. Further, NASP standards approved in 1984 recognized only specialist- and doctoral-level programs (NASP, 1986), and as early as 1978 NASP recommended a gradual shift to the specialist level as the entry-level degree to the profession (Brown, 1989). This change is reflected in recent data collection efforts, as no terminal master's-level programs of fewer than 60 graduate semester hours were reported or identified. Meanwhile, the number of specialist-level and doctoral-level programs have both grown significantly since 1976 (42% and 50% growth, respectively; see Figure 37.2). At present, approximately one-third of all available school psychology programs in 2013–2014 offer the doctoral degree.

Since 1987–1988, both specialist- and doctoral-level programs on average have exceeded the minimum hours described above (see Table 37.2). Changes in NASP standards likely contributed to the more significant increase in average semester hours in doctoral programs since 1982. NASP's *Standards for Training and Field Placement Programs in School Psychology*, approved in 1984, identified a minimum of 60 graduate semester hours for specialist-level programs but only 84 semester hours for doctoral-level programs (NASP, 1986). Subsequent standards increased the minimum semester hours to 90 for doctoral-level programs.

Figure 37.2. Number of U.S. School Psychology Programs Offered by Degree Type

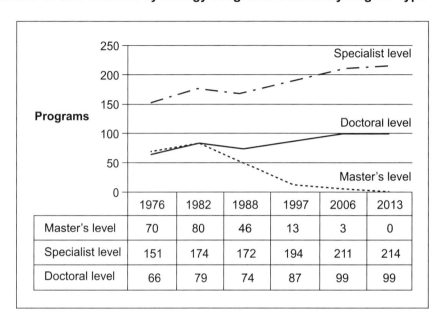

	1976	1982	1988	1997	2006	2013
Master's level	70	80	46	13	3	0
Specialist level	151	174	172	194	211	214
Doctoral level	66	79	74	87	99	99

Note. Based on information from Brown and Lindstrom (1977), Brown and Minke (1984), McMaster et al. (1989), Miller (2008), NASP (2013), and Thomas (1998).

Program Approval and Accreditation

NASP—as a specialized professional association (SPA) of the National Council for Accreditation of Teacher Education (NCATE)/Council for Accreditation of Educator Preparation (CAEP)—and APA are the primary professional organizations that approve, recognize, or accredit school psychology graduate programs in the United States. (July 1, 2013, marked the de facto consolidation of NCATE and the Teacher Education Accreditation Council to form CAEP.) Since 1988, NASP has conducted program reviews of both specialist-level and doctoral-level programs as part of the NCATE unit accreditation process. NCATE/CAEP accredits only units (e.g., colleges of education) rather than programs. However, as with other SPAs, NCATE recognizes NASP's standards and defers to NASP's

approval process to award "national recognition" to those programs housed in NCATE-accredited units. NASP also conducts reviews of programs not in NCATE units to provide all programs access to the review process. NASP currently approves programs, although it does not accredit them.

The APA's Commission on Accreditation accredits doctoral-level programs only. Most doctoral programs in school psychology pursue both NASP approval and APA accreditation, as each offers benefits associated with credentialing options for graduates, program status, and access to a programmatic peer-review process. Figure 37.3 reflects the general increase in the number of approved and accredited programs since 1988.

Importantly, the increase in approved/accredited programs has exceeded the growth of programs in general (see Figure 37.4). As a result, the majority of school psychology programs in the United States now maintain some form of program approval or accreditation. More programs have likely sought approval/ accreditation to maintain competitiveness while ensuring that their graduates can obtain the necessary credentials for employment, both in and out of state. Additionally, the NCATE State Partnership Program, which encourages states to meet national standards, led to many states requiring programs to seek and obtain approval from respective NCATE-affiliated specialized professional associations, including NASP. Regardless of

Table 37.2. Mean Graduate Semester Hours Required by U.S. School Psychology Programs

	1982	1988	1997
Master's	36	41	40
Specialist	63	66	68
Doctoral	91	101	106

Note. Data not collected in 2010–2013 directories. Based on information from Brown and Minke (1984), McMaster et al. (1989), and Thomas (1998).

Figure 37.3. Number of Approved/Accredited School Psychology Programs in the United States

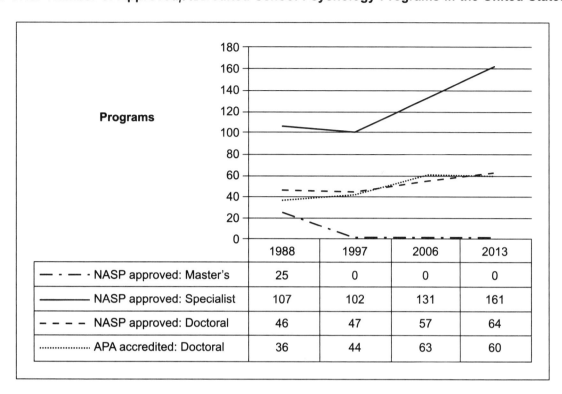

	1988	1997	2006	2013
— · — · NASP approved: Master's	25	0	0	0
—— NASP approved: Specialist	107	102	131	161
– – – NASP approved: Doctoral	46	47	57	64
·········· APA accredited: Doctoral	36	44	63	60

Note. Programs with either full approval/accreditation or with conditions/on probation were considered approved. Based on information from McMaster et al. (1989), Miller (2008), NASP (2013), and Thomas (1998).

Figure 37.4. Percentage of All Available Programs by Degree Type With NASP Program Approval/APA Accreditation

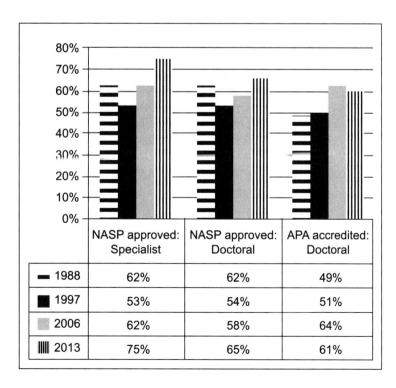

	NASP approved: Specialist	NASP approved: Doctoral	APA accredited: Doctoral
▬ 1988	62%	62%	49%
■ 1997	53%	54%	51%
▨ 2006	62%	58%	64%
⫴ 2013	75%	65%	61%

Note. Based on information from McMaster et al. (1989), Miller (2008), NASP (2013), and Thomas (1998).

the cause, this increase is largely positive for prospective students and the future of the profession, as the majority of all available programs have now been viewed as meeting a set of national standards based on peer review, which can help ensure the availability of high-quality practitioners.

Student Financial Support

The average percentage of students receiving some form of financial support (e.g., assistantships, fellowships, scholarships, and training grants) is provided in Table 37.3. The figures provided may overestimate the availability of financial support, however. Some programs did not answer this question across each of the data collection efforts (e.g., approximately 20% of institutions did not respond to this question in 2013), and those offering little to no support may be less likely to respond. These figures were generated by averaging the percentage of students supported within each program. However, data were not weighted based on program enrollment, thus adding to the potential for inaccuracy. Nevertheless, the percentage of doctoral students receiving support has continuously exceeded that of students in specialist-level programs, potentially contributing to the recent trend of increased doctoral enrollment compared to specialist-level enrollment.

Graduate Student Enrollment in U.S. School Psychology Programs

Table 37.4 provides a time-based comparison of graduate student enrollment across the previous directories and the most current program information. In the 2013–2014 academic year there were 9,663 graduate students enrolled across all U.S. school psychology graduate preparation programs (both specialist and doctoral level). Direct comparisons of enrollment data should be made with caution as response rates across previous directories range from 84% to 97%, with the

Table 37.3. Average Percentage of Students Receiving Financial Support by Degree Type and Year

	1988	1997	2013
Specialist	45	47	46
Doctoral	65	60	72

Note. Based on information from McMaster et al. (1989), NASP (2013), and Thomas (1998).

Table 37.4. Graduate Student Enrollment Data in U.S. School Psychology Programs by Degree Type and Year

	1976 N	1976 M	1976 %	1982 N	1982 M	1982 %	1988 N	1988 M	1988 %	1997 N	1997 M	1997 %	2013 N	2013 M	2013 %
Master's level	1774	28.2	28.2	1446	18.3	20.1	750	17.9	13.3	220	16.9	2.6	—		—
Specialist level	3936	27.5	27.5	3526	20.3	48.3	3180	19.4	56.4	5883	30.5	68.5	6502	30.4	67.5
Doctoral level	1740	27.2	27.2	2301	33.3	31.6	1704	25.4	30.2	2482	30.3	28.9	3161	31.9	32.7
All	7450			7293			5634	29.2		8587			9663		

Note. N = total reported graduate student enrollment; *M* = the average number of students per program, based on responding programs only; % = the percentages of all school psychology students at the specified program level, based on responding programs only. Each directory, aside from the most recent data collection efforts, had less than 100% response rate. 1977 had 96% response rate, 1984 had 95% response rate, 1989 had 84% response rate, and 1998 had more than 97% response rate. Based on information from Brown and Lindstrom (1977), Brown and Minke (1984), McMaster et al. (1989), NASP (2013), and Thomas (1998).

best response rates reported for the 1998 directory and data collection conducted between 2010 and 2013.

Noticeable trends include a sharp decline in master's-level students and a general increase in specialist-level students, doctoral-level students, and overall enrollment. Currently, one third of all identified U.S. school psychology students are enrolled in doctoral programs, with the remainder in specialist-level programs. The average number of students per specialist and doctoral programs remained relatively constant from 1997 to 2013 (specialist from 30.5 to 30.4, doctoral from 30.3 to 31.9). With the average time to graduation of 3–6 years for specialist- and doctoral-level programs, respectively, these data would translate into typical cohorts of approximately 10 students per specialist-level program and 5 students per doctoral-level program.

Aggregate data suggest significant variation across programs in the number of prospective students seeking to enroll, with some programs experiencing shortages of applicants while others experience relative abundance. To illustrate, in 2013–2014, reported program applicants for specialist-level programs ranged from 4 to 143, and 3 to 223 for doctoral programs. Acceptance rates for specialist-level programs ranged from 9% to 100% and 5% to 100% for doctoral-level programs in 2013–2014. This variation may be due to a number of factors, including reputation of the program, location, and financial support. Unfortunately, no data are currently available to provide a trend analysis or an accurate number of prospective students (i.e., the number of individuals each year hoping to enroll in a school psychology graduate preparation program).

Table 37.5 identifies more recent enrollment trends from 2010–2011 to 2013–2014. Trends suggest an increase in enrollment among doctoral programs and, conversely, a drop in enrollment among specialist-level programs. More specifically, from 2010–2011 to 2013–2014, specialist-level programs saw an 11% reduction in first-year enrolled students, a 5% drop in specialist-level interns, and a 10% drop in total enrollment. During that

same timespan, doctoral programs saw a 20% increase in first-year enrolled students, a 19% increase in interns, and a 13% increase in total enrollment. This increase occurred despite an evident difference in program acceptance rates. In 2013–2014, the average acceptance rate (i.e., number of students offered admission based on number of applicants) was 52% for specialist-level programs compared to 38% for doctoral-level programs.

Several reasons may explain this shift. First, the number of school psychologists holding a credential for independent practice (often at the doctoral level) has risen over the last 2 decades (Castillo, Curtis, Chappel, & Cunningham, 2011), with speculation of a continued increase in school psychologists seeking secondary forms of employment (Rossen, 2012). Thus, an increase in students seeking the doctoral-level degree may reflect a trend in students wanting to be eligible for practice both in and out of schools.

Second, from 2010–2011 to 2013–2014, the total number of specialist-level programs dropped from 215 to 214, whereas the number of doctoral programs increased from 91 to 99. Third, with discrepancies in the availability of financial aid between specialist-level and doctoral students, perhaps more students prefer a program that can help defray costs, even if the length of the program is longer.

Last, while unlikely to have had an impact from 2010–2011 to 2014, changes in Medicaid eligibility and definitions of eligible providers of services across states, which are associated with the Affordable Care Act (ACA), may contribute to this continuing trend. As more school-age students become eligible for Medicaid reimbursement as a result of the ACA, additional money may become available to schools for providing services to those students. However, this is dependent on practitioners being considered eligible providers under Medicaid within that state. Despite language in federal laws that include school psychologists in the definition of "mental health service professionals" and "qualified health professionals," some states have still excluded

Table 37.5. Graduate Student Enrollment Data in U.S. School Psychology Programs: 2010–2013

	2010–2011			2012–2013			2013–2014		
	First-Year Students	Interns	Total Enrolled	First-Year Students	Interns	Total Enrolled	First-Year Students	Interns	Total Enrolled
Specialist level	2,358	2,106	7,183	2,111	1,957	6,565	2,101	1,993	6,502
Doctoral level	515	498	2,804	590	566	2,792	617	593	3,161
All	2,873	2,604	9,987	2,701	2,523	9,357	2,718	2,586	9,663

Note. Based on information from NASP (2013).

school psychologists credentialed through the state education agency. Conversely, many of those states identify doctoral-level psychologists licensed by a state board of psychology (or equivalent licensing body) as eligible providers.

The shifts associated with ACA, along with APA's continuing position that the doctoral degree represents the minimum entry-level degree for professional psychology, may apply added pressure on specialist-level programs and their students. However, as the majority of practicing school psychologists and current programs are at the specialist level, an intentional shift to a doctoral-only profession in the foreseeable future is unlikely. State education agencies would experience great difficulty filling positions and maintaining compliance given that less than 17% of full-time practitioners in schools maintain a doctoral degree (Curtis, Castillo, & Gelley, 2012). Filling open positions in school districts would be particularly problematic in geographic areas experiencing shortages, including states or regions without graduate preparation programs. Further, state and local education agencies would experience financial constraints, as salaries in public schools are typically higher for those with a doctoral degree. The lack of evidence that doctoral-level preparation results in any significant improvement in service provision and outcomes for children makes these additional costs harder to justify.

Limited resources in higher education are another roadblock to moving the field to the doctoral level, given that doctoral psychology programs tend to be expensive. In most states, public universities would have to seek and attain state approval to offer doctoral programs. Such approval may not be possible for universities with missions that do not include doctoral-level training, and would certainly not be guaranteed for others, given increased state vigilance regarding costs.

The exemption for nondoctoral school psychologists within APA's Model Licensure Act (APA, 2010) provides additional substantiation for the specialist-level degree remaining the entry-level degree for school psychology. The Model Licensure Act offers recommendations to state agencies and psychology boards on the preparation, titling, and scope of practice for psychologists. While reinforcing APA's view of the doctorate as an entry-level degree for psychology, each version of the Model Licensure Act over the last 40-plus years has included an exemption for title and practice for specialist-level practitioners with a school psychologist credential from their state education agency.

Projected Shortages

There have been consistent projections of school psychologist shortages nearly every year since 1954 (Reschly, 2000). While numerous assumptions are taken into account when making workforce predictions (e.g., attrition and retirement), lack of accurate information about current graduate students and their career goals has rendered personnel predictions tentative at best (Reschly, 2000). The current directories provide meaningful data to assist in making much-needed projections about the potential for future shortages.

Although it is a complex topic, two basic factors must be considered when making projections about school psychology workforce shortages: (a) inadequate supply of school psychologists to meet the demand (i.e., vacant positions) and (b) inadequate number of positions available in states or districts (i.e., the need for school psychological services is not being met). In considering the concern about a shortage of school psychologists, analyses using recent data project a continued, albeit relatively small (2–4%), shortage that will continue through 2025 (Castillo, Curtis, & Yin Tan, in press).

Despite these findings, Table 37.5 demonstrates that the number of first-year students exceeds the number of interns for each degree level and each academic year from 2010 through 2014. These data suggest that the number of incoming students exceeds the number of students preparing to graduate, which may indicate that either the number of new practitioners is slowly trending upward or that programs experience student attrition. It should be noted that matriculation information presented in Table 37.5 is cross-sectional, and caution should be exercised when extrapolating numbers of future interns or graduates from current first-year student enrollment data.

Personnel shortages extend to the university, where many open faculty positions have remained unfilled, and retirements over the next 10–15 years are projected to significantly outpace the number of doctoral school psychologists entering academia (Castillo et al., in press; Curtis, Grier, & Hunley, 2004; Kratochwill, Shernoff, & Sanetti, 2004). A shortage of new school psychology faculty may hinder future program growth (Clopton & Haselhuhn, 2009) and the ability for current graduate programs to accept larger numbers of prospective students. Financial constraints facing higher education may also be a factor in limiting the growth of programs, especially given the relative expense of school psychology graduate preparation.

SUMMARY

The profession of school psychology is constantly changing and evolving to meet the unique and diverse needs of children, parents, teachers, and schools. It is the challenge and responsibility of graduate educators to be knowledgeable of these changes to inform the preparation of the next generation of school psychologists.

Several trends have emerged in reviewing the available data from current and previous program directories, including a relative plateau in the total number of school psychology preparation programs; a steady decline and end to master's-level programs consisting of fewer than 60 graduate semester hours, with a concurrent increase in both specialist-level and doctoral programs; a general increase in the number of programs obtaining NASP approval and/or APA accreditation; and more frequent opportunities for financial assistance among students in doctoral programs compared to those in specialist-level programs. More recently, data suggest a decrease in enrollment among specialist-level programs and an increase in both enrollment in and number of doctoral programs.

While there has been some change (both the creation of and phasing out of graduate preparation programs), the overall number of programs has remained relatively consistent. This trend is expected to continue into the foreseeable future (Fagan, 2008). The current availability of programs may be adequate to meet the needs in some areas (e.g., New York), whereas in others the scarcity of programs will present challenges in meeting regional demands for practitioners (e.g., Alaska, Wyoming). It should be noted that the increase in the number of programs seeking and/or obtaining NASP approval and APA accreditation bodes well for the provision of high-quality service delivery consistent with best practices and rigorous national standards. In addition, the continued availability of graduate student financial support is encouraging, albeit more readily available in doctoral training programs. This trend could be partially responsible for the increased enrollment in doctoral-level programs and the slight decrease in enrollment among specialist-level programs.

Since the 1980s, the specialist-level degree has been the agreed-upon entry-level degree within the school psychology profession. With that in mind, it bears watching if legislation, such as the ACA, spurs a gradual shift toward increased enrollment in doctoral-level programs. Additionally, as data suggest an increase in school psychologists pursuing the doctoral degree and credentials for independent practice, greater demand for the doctoral degree may prompt the establishment of more doctoral programs, and thus fewer specialist-level programs. Nevertheless, factors such as financial constraints among institutions, state education agencies maintaining the specialist level as the entry-level degree, and projected faculty shortages may significantly limit the number of sustainable doctoral programs. The specialist level will likely remain the recommended entry-level degree for school psychology by NASP for the foreseeable future.

Trends related to increases in the number of programs, the percentage of programs seeking and obtaining approval or accreditation, and total enrollment bode well for the profession, despite the relatively slow growth. It is possible that economic conditions in the United States, combined with inconsistent federal education funding, stalled more significant growth since 2009, and improvement in the economy would lead to an even greater outlook. Having regular, accurate data available such as those from the previous directories and now from the NASP National Program Database helps track the impact of such changes on the health of the profession. Developing an understanding of the current conditions of graduate education and gathering data to support workforce projections are critical to ensuring the security of the profession in the future, as they can help address gaps and identify important professional and legislative priorities.

REFERENCES

American Psychological Association. (2010). *Model Act for State Licensure of Psychologists*. Washington, DC: Author.

Brown, D. T. (1989). The evolution of entry-level training in school psychology: Are we now approaching the doctoral level? *School Psychology Review, 18*, 11–15.

Brown, D. T., & Lindstrom, J. P. (1977). *Directory of school psychology training programs in the United States and Canada*. Stratford, CT: National Association of School Psychologists.

Brown, D. T., & Minke, K. M. (1984). *Directory of school psychology training programs in the United States*. Stratford, CT: National Association of School Psychologists.

Castillo, J. M., Curtis, M. J., Chappel, A., & Cunningham, J. (2011, February). *School psychology 2010: Results of the National Membership Survey*. Poster presented at the annual meeting of the National Association of School Psychologists, San Francisco, CA. Retrieved from http://www.nasponline.org/advocacy/NASP_Mbr_Survey_2009-10_Conv_2011.pdf

Castillo, J. M., Curtis, M. J., & Yin Tan, S. (in press). Personnel needs in school psychology: A 10-year follow-up study on predicted personnel shortages. *Psychology in the Schools*.

Clopton, K. L., & Haselhuhn, C. W. (2009). School psychology trainer shortage in the USA: Current status and projections for the future. *School Psychology International, 30*(1), 24–42.

Curtis, M. J., Castillo, J. M., & Gelley, C. (2012). School psychology 2010: Demographics, employment, and the context for professional practices–Part 1. *Communiqué, 40*(7), 1, 28–30.

Curtis, M. J., Grier, J. P., & Hunley, S. F. (2004). The changing face of school psychology: Trends in data and projections for the future. *School Psychology Review, 33*, 49–66.

Fagan, T. K. (2008). Trends in the history of school psychology in the United States. In A. Thomas & J. Grimes (Eds.), *Best practices in school psychology V* (pp. 2069–2085). Bethesda, MD: National Association of School Psychologists.

Kratochwill, T. R., Shernoff, E. S., & Sanetti, L. (2004). Promotion of academic careers in school psychology: A conceptual framework of impact points, recommended strategies, and hopeful outcomes. *School Psychology Quarterly, 19*, 342–364.

McMaster, M. D., Reschly, D. J., & Peters, J. M. (1989). *Directory of school psychology graduate programs.* Washington, DC: National Association of School Psychologists.

Miller, D. C. (2008). Appendix VII: School psychology training programs. In A. Thomas & J. Grimes (Eds.), *Best practices in school psychology V* (pp. clv–cxcviii). Bethesda, MD: National Association of School Psychologists.

National Association of School Psychologists. (1986). *Standards for training and credentialing in school psychology.* Washington, DC: Author.

National Association of School Psychologists. (2010). *Model for comprehensive and integrated school psychological services.* Bethesda, MD: Author. Retrieved from http://www.nasponline.org/standards/2010standards/2_PracticeModel.pdf

National Association of School Psychologists. (2013). *National school psychology program database.* Bethesda, MD: Author.

Reschly, D. J. (2000). The present and future status of school psychology in the United States. *School Psychology Review, 29*, 507–522.

Rossen, E. (2012). Essential tools for prospective and early career school psychologists: Credentialing for school and independent practice. *Communiqué, 40*(2), 30.

Thomas, A. (1998). *Directory of school psychology graduate programs.* Bethesda, MD: National Association of School Psychologists.

38

Best Practices in Assessing Performance in School Psychology Graduate Programs

Joseph S. Prus
Winthrop University (SC)
Enedina Garcia-Vazquez
New Mexico State University

OVERVIEW

The National Association of School Psychologists (NASP) *Model for Comprehensive and Integrated School Psychological Services* (NASP, 2010a) provides a useful framework for school psychology in all settings, including higher education. This chapter addresses the domain of Legal, Ethical, and Professional Practice by providing an overview of best practice methods for performance assessment in school psychology graduate programs. The assessment of candidates in graduate programs and use of results for individual and program improvement are important to problem solving and accountability practices in higher education, are required by virtually all higher education accrediting organizations, and are critical to effectively preparing entry-level professionals to positively affect those they serve.

Assessment of postsecondary student learning has been cited as being part of a higher education paradigm shift from a teacher-centered to a learner-centered focus (Huba & Freed, 2000). A learner-centered institution or program is ultimately concerned with knowing what students have learned and how well they have learned it. Today, assessment is considered to be one of the distinguishing features of U.S. colleges and universities (Astin & Antonio, 2012).

School psychology faculty should be uniquely qualified to plan and implement performance assessment methods. An understanding of issues such as reliability and validity, familiarity with measurement options, and appreciation of the important implications of assessment

results should facilitate faculty and program decision making regarding assessment. Yet decisions regarding assessment methods often represent a compromise between the ideal and the reality. Such reality includes decreased resources for education exacerbated by what is usually an inverse relationship between the quality of measurement methods and their expediency. Additionally, many school psychology programs must respond to the demands of multiple internal, state, and/or national regulatory and accreditation authorities, each of which has its own set of expectations.

NASP and the American Psychological Association (APA) have established guidelines and standards relevant to assessment. Both the APA *Guidelines and Principles for Accreditation of Programs in Professional Psychology* (APA, 2009) and the NASP *Standards for Graduate Preparation of School Psychologists* (NASP, 2010b) require continuous assessment of candidate performance and evaluation of program outcomes. Table 38.1, adapted from Prus and Strein (2011), summarizes assessment requirements for NASP and APA accreditation.

School psychology programs must prepare graduates with the professional knowledge and skills needed to effectively address the increasingly diverse needs of those they will ultimately serve. A continual process of reflection, evaluation, and improvement is required to meet such goals. To assist program faculty in this effort, this chapter will present information on performance-based assessment that can be used for candidate and program development and improvement. The chapter will summarize key principles pertaining to program

Table 38.1. Summary of APA and NASP Assessment Requirements

Assessment Requirements	APA	NASP
Aggregated results of student performance	X	X
Aggregated distal data (e.g., job placements)	X	
Use of data for program improvement	X	X
Students' performance on the PRAXIS exam or state exam		X
Program- or course-embedded assessment of student knowledge	X	X
Assessment of students during practica	X	X
Intern evaluations by field supervisors		X
Summary of the results of a comprehensive, performance-based assessment of candidate abilities during internship		X
Assessment showing students' positive impact on clients		X

Note. From "Issues and Trends in the Accreditation of School Psychology Programs in the United States," by J. Prus and W. Strein, 2011, *Psychology in the Schools, 48,* pp. 887–900. Copyright 2011 by John Wiley & Sons. Adapted with permission.

assessment and accountability, and will cover a range of methods by which school psychology faculty can assess graduate student (often referred to as "candidate") competencies and professional work characteristics. Additionally, advantages and disadvantages of specific assessment methods, such as case studies, portfolios, examinations, surveys, and performance appraisals, will be presented, and ways in which the results of such methods can be documented and used to improve school psychology preparation programs will be discussed.

BASIC CONSIDERATIONS

School psychology programs should utilize performance assessment methods that are consistent with current knowledge and principles of effective assessment practices in general. For such methods to be effective, they should be planned and implemented as part of a system. An assessment system not only serves to inform the program of individual student performance, but also provides an opportunity for programs to consider assessment data across multiple candidates. This can be a powerful source of information for decision making and program evaluation that prompts development at both the individual and program levels. Given the high stakes of the many decisions about candidates to be made in school psychology programs, it is important that assessment be based on principles of best practice. Such principles may be found in higher education literature in general as well

as in literature specific to the preparation of professional educators and school psychologists.

The American Association for Higher Education (AAHE; 1992) set forth principles of good practice for assessing student learning that would appear to be as applicable to graduate programs as they are to K–12 or undergraduate student assessment. These principles emphasize that assessment is not an end in itself, but is a vehicle for educational improvement, and that assessment is most effective when it reflects an understanding of learning as being multidimensional, integrated, and accomplished over time. While it is recognized that assessment works best when it is based on clear, explicitly stated goals, there is also a need for assessment to attend not just to outcomes but to the educational experiences that lead to such outcomes. It is also important for assessment to be part of an ongoing, versus episodic, process that addresses questions important to educators and decision makers (AAHE, 1992).

The National Council for Accreditation of Teacher Education (NCATE) publication, *Assessing Education Candidate Performance: A Look at Changing Practices* (NCATE, 2003), suggests six criteria for evaluating the quality and uses of assessment in programs that prepare professional educators. These criteria emphasize that assessments should (a) be appropriate for the standards they are meant to address; (b) be accompanied by explicit statements of the proficiencies candidates are expected to demonstrate; (c) be constructed and scored so as to distinguish different levels of proficiency; (d) be used to reach meaningful decisions, including ones pertaining to individual candidates and the program in general; (e) include some authentic measures that include tasks similar to what candidates will face as practitioners, including assessment of their impact on clients they serve; and (f) be systematically evaluated to ensure fairness, accuracy, consistency, and avoidance of bias.

In discussing school psychology program assessment, Prus and Waldron (2005) indicate that measures need to be selected first and foremost on the basis of reliability, validity, and utility. They also stress the importance of gathering evidence that is credible to various stakeholders and constituencies. The following specific criteria are suggested to programs when selecting candidate assessment measures: (a) relevance to the profession and associated training standards, (b) appropriateness to program philosophy, (c) validity for assessing program goals and objectives, (d) relevance of both method and results to program faculty and candidates, (e) generalizability to performance external to the program, (f) utility of results for both assessing individual candidate performance and evaluating program effectiveness, (g) consistency with program pedagogy and with ongoing activities and requirements, (h) cost-effectiveness, (i) time demands in relation to program faculty resources, and (j) consistency with credentialing standards and requirements.

BEST PRACTICES IN GRADUATE PROGRAM ASSESSMENT

Higher education faculty have a range of performance assessment options to consider when selecting measures consistent with program goals and desired candidate and program outcomes. This chapter will present three general categories of performance-based assessments: examinations, competency-based methods, and self- and third-party reports. Within each category various assessment methods are presented, as well as advantages, disadvantages, and ideas for use within school psychology preparation programs.

Examinations

The examinations discussed include standardized credentialing examinations, faculty-developed comprehensive examinations, and oral examinations.

Standardized Credentialing Examinations

Standardized examinations are required for obtaining a credential in school psychology or psychology in most states and for obtaining national certification. Such exams include the School Psychologist Examination administered by the Educational Testing Service as part of the Praxis II series, the Examination for Professional Practice in Psychology administered by the Association of State and Provincial Psychology Boards, and licensing exams developed and administered by some states. These exams have the advantage of external validation and credibility, test development by measurement experts, objective scoring, and minimal faculty time and effort. However, multiple-choice tests can measure only a limited range of knowledge and few skills relevant to school psychology practice. Thus, it is not surprising that the validity of such tests for predicting actual professional performance is largely unproven. Additionally, tests designed primarily for credentialing may not reflect some important program objectives and may be of limited use in determining candidate and program strengths, weaknesses, and areas of needed improvement.

In today's era of increased external accountability, programs seeking state and national accreditation have little choice but to concern themselves with the performance of candidates and graduates on standardized credentialing exams. Thus, it is important that program faculty familiarize themselves with the content of such exams by requesting content specifications and technical characteristics from test publishers. Programs should have a systematic process in place for requiring that candidates submit full score reports (including category scores or subscores, if any) as part of program or internship requirements. Although faculty seeking NASP program approval must require that students take the Praxis exam in school psychology or a state exam, it is up to the program to determine whether to require a minimum score on such an exam for an institutional degree.

Faculty-Developed Comprehensive Examinations

Many school psychology programs require that candidates pass a written, comprehensive, objective, and/or subjective examination designed by program faculty. Such locally developed exams can be geared to the specific philosophy and goals of the program, and candidate performance can be judged in relation to the specific criteria established by program faculty. As a result, faculty have more control over interpretation of results and are perhaps more likely to see and accept the implications of results for program improvement. But locally developed comprehensive exams require extensive faculty time and effort in generating and grading questions, and they do not provide the same credibility as external measures linked to national standards. Additionally, such exams are seldom developed or evaluated in the same way as extensively as those developed by external parties. Further, there is the potential to consider candidates' cultural backgrounds more easily than with standardized national and state exams.

Programs that administer faculty developed comprehensive exams should provide candidates with content specifications and perhaps sample exam questions. If a subjective exam is administered, faculty are encouraged to develop and use rubrics for grading responses. Rubrics provide valuable opportunities for faculty to discuss expectations and to calibrate their grading of candidate responses. It is also recommended that more than one faculty member grade each response, which provides an opportunity to collect and analyze data on interrater reliability. As a means of reducing the time and effort associated with developing instruments and rubrics, programs should consider sharing questions and scoring criteria with other programs that have similar philosophies and objectives.

Oral Examinations

Oral examinations generally have the same basic advantages and disadvantages of other faculty-developed exams. They allow assessment of candidates' ability in considerably greater depth and breadth through follow-up questions and probes. The dialogue format decreases miscommunications and misunderstandings, in both questions and answers, increasing formative evaluation of learning through indications of how and why candidates reached their answers. Oral exams provide process evaluation of candidates' critical thinking, problem solving, application of knowledge, and speaking skills, which are all important to school psychology practice. Having candidates respond to oral questions designed to assess content knowledge and practice approaches is also part of many job interviews.

Oral exams do require considerably more faculty time, since such exams must be conducted individually with faculty present. The face-to-face inquisition by faculty can inhibit candidates' responsiveness as a result of anxiety and intimidation, and this approach might be more likely to benefit candidates with better oral language than written language skills. Inconsistencies in administration and probes across candidates, along with subjective evaluation, reduce standardization.

Programs that use oral examinations are encouraged to specify content areas to be covered and to predetermine standard questions and the most common follow-up probes. It is also recommended that programs establish and use specific criteria for evaluating performance. As with written comprehensive exams, candidates' cultural backgrounds can be more readily considered than with standardized national and state exams.

Competency-Based Methods

Competency-based methods include performance appraisals, simulations, portfolios and work samples, and course-embedded competency measures.

Performance Appraisals

Performance appraisals include systematic measurement of behavior in real-life situations by a faculty member or supervisor. Virtually all school psychology programs use performance appraisal methods in practica and internship. Such methods may consist of observations focused on specific skill areas (e.g., counseling, test administration, or consultation with a teacher or parent), practica or internship performance rating scales, or evaluation of professional work characteristics completed by faculty or field supervisors.

Performance appraisals provide a direct measure of skills and/or behaviors linked to both program goals and objectives and to national standards. They are preferable to most other methods in measuring the application and generalization of learning to specific settings and situations and are thus a critical assessment tool in professional preparation programs.

Although performance appraisals tend to have high credibility, they are quite subjective, especially if provided by a single person (e.g., one field supervisor). The actual basis for ratings will likely vary across content to be evaluated, and results across candidates will likely vary as a function of the setting (e.g., the internship site) and rater (e.g., the internship supervisor). Last, opportunities to demonstrate certain skills important to school psychologists (e.g., response to an ethical dilemma or crisis) may be limited.

It is important that performance appraisal instruments include specific, operational criteria for observing and appraising performance. Typically, such criteria are relative to a particular stage of practice. It is also helpful to work closely with intern supervisors to convey program expectations for candidates and interns, provide guidance on performance appraisals, and collaborate on responses to performance that do not meet minimum criteria. When possible it may be helpful to have candidates and interns evaluated by more than one source (e.g., an intern supervisor and a school administrator), although this may require having more than one instrument (or having some raters complete a limited number of sections of one instrument). On a practical level, performance appraisal instruments should be of a reasonable length.

Simulations

Simulations are approximations of real-life situations through which performance is appraised when more direct assessment of skills is impractical. Examples include in-basket exercises and structured responses to standardized case studies or videotaped professional situations. Simulations tend to be more valid for evaluating the depth and breadth of skills than tests or other non-performance-based measures. They are flexible enough to accommodate just about any target skill relevant to school psychology and can be incorporated into many forms of examinations. Simulations are particularly useful for more standardized assessment of responses to situations that may occur infrequently or may not be experienced by all candidates or interns (e.g., a crisis or ethical dilemma).

Simulations are not without disadvantages. They usually require considerable substantial frontloading effort (i.e., planning and preparation, especially if technology is required). They are more expensive and time consuming than traditional testing options. And, as with many other assessments in higher education, grading and rating tend to be subjective. Thus, it is important to establish and provide clear criteria for expected performance and to include multiple raters. Although the development of simulations may be time consuming, technology can be used to make material realistic and help standardize administration and grading.

Portfolios and Work Samples

This form of performance-based assessment represents collections of candidates' work samples, usually compiled longitudinally or as indicators of ability or work at a particular point in time. Portfolios can vary widely in purpose and content (Banta, 2003), with some containing substantial and varied artifacts of work accumulated over time and others containing more limited samples of professional cases completed by the candidate during field experiences such as practica and internship. Artifacts collected over time are more useful for assessing professional growth (i.e., the value added by professional preparation), and can be useful for determining the need for individual development or improvement. Samples of work submitted at or near the end of training are more useful for determining the attainment of abilities consistent with program goals. Thus, case studies completed by candidates during internship are invaluable culminating assessments in school psychology programs.

Portfolios of work samples or case studies are very flexible in assessing many program components and goals (e.g., writing, critical thinking, and problem solving). They are more likely than test results or responses to simulations to reflect candidates' ability to plan, to allow input from others, and to ensure that similar opportunities common to most work settings are available. The process of reviewing and grading portfolios provides an excellent opportunity for faculty exchange and development, discussion of curriculum goals and objectives, review of grading criteria, and program feedback. Portfolios of professional cases completed during internship, assuming appropriate protection for confidentiality of information, can be valuable to program graduates in the job search process (and applying for the Nationally Certified School Psychologist credential) and provide a useful basis by which prospective employers can evaluate job candidates.

Although portfolios of prior work or cases may be efficient in terms of candidate time (because the work has already been completed), they tend to be costly in terms of faculty evaluator time and effort, especially if evaluated on multiple occasions. The management of the collection and grading process, including the establishment of reliable and valid grading criteria, is also likely to be challenging. One reason why standardization of grading is likely to be challenging is that samples and cases will depend largely on opportunities candidates have had, which will vary from field site to field site. If samples to be included have been previously submitted for course grades or evaluation by intern supervisors, then there may be a concern that a hidden agenda of the process is to validate such grading or supervision. A negative evaluation of work that has been previously passed or even praised, for example, may highlight the subjectivity of the evaluation process but also prompt discussion among faculty or between faculty and field supervisors about program goals and associated evaluation criteria. Another concern with portfolios or case studies is that it is difficult to determine the extent to which the content represents the candidate's own work or input from or collaboration with others.

Given the variations of content for portfolios, it is important to establish and communicate clear expectations for content and evaluation. Such expectations should address the importance of eliminating all identifiable client information. When deciding on portfolio content, the program should limit volume to what can be thoroughly and effectively evaluated by faculty. Sample portfolios might help convey expectations. Evaluation criteria should be specific to the content to be submitted. For example, different criteria should be provided for counseling or behavioral intervention cases than for consultation or assessment cases. More than one professional should rate each portfolio, which will allow the program to establish interrater reliability. In rating portfolios in which the candidates select the artifacts, faculty need to recognize that such samples likely represent the best work of candidates.

Course-Embedded Competency Measures

Some of the competency methods described above, as well as papers, projects, and exams, are suitable for being embedded in courses throughout school psychology graduate programs. Course-embedded assessment measures are more familiar to and accepted by faculty and have the advantage of being integrated into the natural process of teaching and learning. Thus, the time and cost of such methods are already part of faculty and candidate accountability programs. Assessment conducted in courses also provides for more immediate feedback to candidates and thus more frequent and timely opportunities to use feedback to improve performance.

But course-embedded measures also have disadvantages as program assessment methods. Such measures tend to focus on specific content and skills related to particular courses rather than on integration and application across courses and experiences. Thus, they tend to be more useful for formative than for summative assessment. Another disadvantage of course-embedded measures, at least from the perspective of program assessment, is that these measures are typically designed and graded by the individual faculty members who teach the courses. As a result, these measures may not represent program values or provide the kind of objectivity or credibility that are desired (if not necessary) for performance assessment at the program level. Aggregating the results of course-embedded assessment may also prove challenging, and faculty may question whether such results will be used to evaluate them as individual instructors.

It is difficult to ignore the logistical and pedagogical advantages of course-embedded assessment by not making use of some assessments conducted in individual courses as part of a program assessment system. However, it is important that such assessments focus on key knowledge and skills addressed in program objectives and represent faculty agreement on both the abilities to be demonstrated and the basis on which they should be evaluated. One way to accomplish this is to establish, with input from all program faculty, rubrics for grading key course-embedded assessments. Such rubrics may have the added advantage of encouraging greater consistency in teaching across semesters and years. Last, it is important for documentation purposes that key performance assessment methods be reflected in course syllabi.

Self- and Third-Party Reports

What follows will be a discussion concerning student and candidate surveys; alumni surveys; employer surveys; and candidate, alumni, and employer interviews.

Student/Candidate Surveys

Candidates' perceptions of their own preparation can provide useful information for programs. In fact, exit surveys with graduates can be one of the more useful and efficient ways to obtain suggestions for program improvements. But unless the evaluations' focus is candidates' self-reflection (a useful goal for school psychology programs), candidates' perceptions are more likely to be useful for program evaluation purposes than for performance assessment and should be viewed cautiously.

One advantage of all surveys is that the survey can cover a broad range of content and program areas in a brief period of time and can address areas of learning and development that might be difficult or costly to assess via other means. Providing candidates with an opportunity to evaluate their own preparation is also likely to be beneficial to their professional development, especially if self-reflection is a program goal. It is also valuable for faculty and program administrators to hear the candidates' perspective and to consider this perspective when considering program changes.

Of course, survey results are dependent on what is asked and how it is asked and seldom shed light on why respondents gave the answers they did. Results reflect the perceptions that candidates are willing to share. Perceptions regarding one's own capabilities are particularly prone to bias (DeAngelis, 2003). Such self-reflections, while helpful if not critical to guiding professional development, are not likely to be an accurate measure of professional skills.

Alumni Surveys

Alumni can provide a unique perspective on their preparation for professional practice and thus should be considered to be important stakeholders in any program assessment and evaluation system. Alumni can reflect on the quality of their training in relation to the job expectations that they have encountered, although their responses might change over time as their experience increases (and memories of their preparation fade). Surveying alumni provides important benefits to the program that go beyond assessment. Good alumni relationships can lead to internship or job prospects for program candidates and can enhance program advocacy and fundraising.

The best way to involve alumni in program assessment is through surveys or possibly telephone or focus group interviews. But before that can occur, the program must have a system for tracking alumni. Once candidates graduate and move, finding them and getting them to respond to surveys will likely be challenging. This is why alumni surveys tend to have low response rates and potentially biased samples.

The university alumni association, or a program social media page like Facebook, can be helpful in tracking alumni. Qualitative research approaches such as the snowball sampling method can also be used to locate alumni. The use of e-mail addresses, text messages, and links to an electronic survey using Survey

Monkey (http://www.surveymonkey.com), Qualtrics (http://www.qualtrics.com), or a similar product or site are likely to be the most efficient means of transmitting alumni surveys and tracking results. Emphasizing the importance of the survey to the program, limiting the length of the survey, ensuring confidentiality, and conducting one or two follow-ups with nonrespondents will likely increase response rates. It is also advisable to include some open-ended items for more in-depth candidate responses and explanations.

Employer Surveys

Given that the professional employment and success of graduates are presumably important goals of every school psychology program, it is not unreasonable to think that surveys or interviews with employers of graduates should be considered as one possible assessment method. Some might suggest that such assessment is among the most credible of methods because of its strong external validity. Evaluations of graduates by work supervisors provide evidence of the generalization of knowledge and skills learned in the program and of practice independent of program supervision. Additionally, employer surveys and interviews can be very useful for obtaining input on professional work characteristics of alumni and ability to have a positive impact on K–12 students. Another potential benefit of such assessment is that it can help create links with important external stakeholders and prospective employers for future graduates.

Despite the belief by some that employer surveys are among the most objective forms of assessment, such third-party reports can be biased in directions more difficult to anticipate than self-reports and may reflect different values than those inherent in the program. But some of the greatest challenges in conducting employer surveys lie in the logistics and management of the process itself. Programs must track where alumni are employed and identify those persons most familiar with their performance. If individual identifying information is requested, then confidentiality becomes an important and problematic issue that must be addressed carefully. The fact that there may be less investment among some third parties (e.g., employers) in the assessment process may translate to low response rates to written surveys. As a result, employer surveys tend to be more problematic and time consuming than they first appear.

It is important to keep employer survey questions to a minimum and to base them clearly on the goals and objectives of the program. Although closed-response questions are likely to minimize time demands, including in the survey one or two open-ended questions about the preparation of the alumnus and suggestions for improvement is advisable. If personally identifiable information about an alumnus is sought, then the informed consent of that alumnus should be obtained and then conveyed to the respondent. An alternative is to have responses submitted anonymously with no references to the individuals being evaluated, although this may be difficult when one or a few graduates are employed at a particular site. To maximize response rates, it is important to make it as easy as possible for persons to respond (e.g., by including stamped, preaddressed envelopes in mail survey requests or using accessible Web-based instruments) and to follow up with nonrespondents by e-mail, telephone, and mail.

Candidate, Alumni, and Employer Interviews

Interviews have many of the attributes of written surveys, with the exception of requiring direct contact, which provides some specific additional advantages and disadvantages. Interviews can include a greater variety of items than is possible in written surveys and allow for follow-up probes based on the responses of interviewees. Interviews also can yield benefits beyond data collection, including opportunities to interact directly with stakeholders such as alumni and employers.

Of course, interviews usually require direct contact, which is time consuming for faculty and may be difficult to arrange with alumni or employers. That direct contact, whether face-to-face or by telephone, by Web-based teleconference, or by other methods, also means that responses cannot be anonymous. Thus, results may be dependent on the person conducting the interview and how much that person is able to encourage open, honest responses (providing assurance of confidentiality is also important to such responses). Interviews are also time intensive. One way to make interviews more efficient is to conduct focus group interviews, perhaps with employers or alumni in one region. But focus group interviews can be prone to influence by more assertive or outspoken individuals. Thus, it is important that those with effective interviewing skills conduct interviews of any kind. If interviews are to be done in groups, it may be worthwhile to have individuals complete a brief, prior written survey, which can both serve as documentation and help prompt interviewees' responses during group responses.

Multimethod Approaches

Combining elements of different assessment methods should be considered as a means of capitalizing on the advantages and reducing the disadvantages of individual methods. Examples of combinations include the following: (a) simulations, case studies, or vignettes embedded in comprehensive examinations; (b) oral examination or follow-up to a portfolio review to probe candidates' critical thinking and problem solving associated with presented cases; (c) in-class exercise or common case study in portfolios to standardize some content and assess candidates' ability to think and write spontaneously; (d) portfolio review as one component of a comprehensive examination, with exam questions to assess knowledge and skills that may not be addressed well in a portfolio (e.g., ethics); and (e) use of key external examiners, such as program advisory board members, local school psychology administrators, or intern supervisors, in designing and/or grading internally developed measures such as comprehensive examinations, simulations, or portfolios in order to add a greater element of externality to such measures.

Summary of Candidate Assessment Methods

Every available performance assessment option has advantages and disadvantages, and each method is more suitable to assessing certain types of abilities and program outcomes than others. There is also no single best method for all programs and situations, which makes it critical that school psychology programs use a combination of methods designed as part of a system.

Programs should implement new performance assessment measures with caution. Despite the measurement expertise that most school psychology faculty possess, the initial implementation of any locally developed method and associated criteria is best viewed as a pilot and as a learning opportunity for candidates and faculty. High-stakes decisions regarding candidates should be made only on the basis of methods with demonstrated reliability and validity and/or on the basis of convergent data from multiple methods and sources.

Assessing Impact on K–12 Student Learning

A key goal of most school psychology programs is to prepare candidates and graduates who can provide a range of services that positively affect children, youth, families, and other clients. The issue of positive effects on students has been addressed in NASP standards since 1994 (NASP, 1994) and has been required in NCATE unit accreditation standards since 2002 (NCATE, 2002). Beginning with the implementation of its 2010 graduate preparation standards (NASP, 2010b), NASP began requiring programs to submit data to show assessment of candidates' positive impact on K–12 students during internship for at least one academic/cognitive case and one behavioral/social case. Yet assessing positive impact remains a challenge for many programs.

Programs can assess and document the positive impact of their candidates and graduates in a variety of ways, including the following: (a) academic assessment or intervention case studies in which criterion-referenced or curriculum-based methods are used to assess the effectiveness of interventions; (b) single-case research measuring the impact of behavioral interventions; (c) behavioral/social intervention case studies in which observations, third-party reports, and/or self-report data are used to document the impact of interventions on student behavior; (d) internship psychoeducational assessment case follow-ups to determine whether recommendations were implemented and the extent to which they were effective; and (e) evaluations designed to measure the effectiveness of group or class-wide programs developed and implemented by interns in collaboration with teachers or others.

Intern evaluations by field supervisors, consumer follow-up surveys, and employer or supervisor evaluations of program graduates that contain questions addressing positive impact on clients can also be useful adjuncts to more objective assessments. But such subjective methods alone are not sufficient to satisfy accreditation requirements.

Goal attainment scaling (Kiresuk, Smith, & Cardillo, 1994) is an assessment methodology that can be adapted for virtually any type of intervention. A goal attainment score is used to indicate the level of attainment reached for each goal within a specified time period. Five levels are typically included and range from −2 (much less than expected outcome) to 0 (expected level of outcome or no change) to +2 (much more than expected outcome). The score is obtained using goal-specific, quantifiable indicators suitable for the particular type of intervention. An academic intervention might be assessed using a curriculum- or criterion-based measure, whereas a counseling intervention might be assessed through a self-report measure, pretest–posttest administration of an instrument, or behavioral observations. But regardless of the measure, goal attainment scaling requires that specific, quantifiable goals be established prior to the intervention and then be assessed after the intervention has been implemented and completed. Goal attainment scaling has been found to be useful in assessing the effectiveness of a variety of school psychology interventions, including consultation

(Kratochwill, Elliott, & Callan-Stoiber, 2002) and the monitoring of student progress (Roach & Elliott, 2005).

Other methodologies used to evaluate the outcomes of behavioral and academic interventions and single-case research may also be used to assess the positive impact of program candidates through cases completed during their field experiences. The percent of non-overlapping data and percent of all nonoverlapping data are two methods that can be converted into effect size statistics (Parker, Hagan-Burke, & Vannest, 2007). One promising methodology for evaluating positive impact is the improvement rate difference (Parker, Vannest, & Brown, 2009), which is a new effect size for summarizing single-case research data.

Bonner and Barnett (2004) used a combination of goal attainment scaling and effect size statistics to evaluate the outcomes of interventions implemented during school psychology practica. And in an impressive example of performance assessment and accountability in education, Morrison, Graden, and Barnett (2009) reported the use of goal attainment scaling, percent of nonoverlapping data, effect size, and other methods to evaluate a statewide school psychology internship.

School psychology programs can begin the process of assessing positive impact of candidates on those they serve by establishing data-based decision making as an important program value and teaching methods candidates can use for assessing the impact of their work. The extent to which faculty teach and model the importance of using systematic, valid assessment to make individual and programmatic decisions is likely to have an impact on the tendency of school psychology candidates to do the same with the K–12 students with whom they work. Additionally, impact on clients should be part of the criteria of all or most major performance assessments conducted in the program.

Conceptualizing Assessment as a System

A systematic, ongoing, comprehensive approach to assessment of candidate performance is likely to yield more valid and useful data for decision making than episodic or isolated measures. The need for a multi-method, multilevel approach in school psychology graduate programs suggests a corresponding need to view assessment more as a system by which information is gathered and decisions are made. This is exactly the approach advocated by both NCATE (2003) and NASP (Waldron & Prus, 2006). The Council for the Accreditation of Educator Preparation, which evolved from the merger of NCATE and the Teacher Education Accreditation Council, is also expected to emphasize the need for a strong assessment system in education programs.

The NASP *Guide for Performance-Based Assessment, Accountability, and Program Development in School Psychology Training Programs* (Waldron & Prus, 2006) provides suggestions for assessment systems in school psychology graduate programs. Such a system needs to include multiple methods and sources for gathering data on candidate knowledge, skills, and professional work characteristics. Methods should be tied to program goals and objectives as well as national standards for the profession, have specific operational criteria that are applied, and involve faculty and field supervisors or others in their implementation. More meaningful and effective assessment is integrated into the learning experiences and decision-making points of the program rather than constituting a series of course evaluation activities or unrelated add-on tasks implemented solely for accountability purposes.

In crafting an assessment system, faculty need to decide not just what methods to include but when they are to be administered. The results of individual performance assessment methods administered earlier in the program are more likely to be useful for making alterations in the instruction, program, or supervision of individual candidates, or for making decisions about the readiness of candidates for a subsequent stage of preparation. For example, a comprehensive exam or portfolio review administered prior to internship may provide information useful for determining whether candidates possess the knowledge and skills needed for internship. On the other hand, culminating assessments done at or near the end of training, or surveys of alumni or employers, are more likely to be useful for program evaluation and accountability. Table 38.2 shows a sample assessment system.

It is important that the program's assessment system be described in program materials so that prospective students, candidates, and others are aware of the means by which assessment of proficiencies will occur and how the information will be used. The system needs to ensure that all school psychology candidates, prior to program completion, have acquired and demonstrated the requisite knowledge and professional competencies identified by the program in accordance with standards of professional practice (Waldron & Prus, 2006). A checklist for evaluating program performance assessment and accountability can be found in Figure 38.1.

Table 38.2. Sample Assessment/Evaluation System

	Entry Level	Course Embedded	Preinternship	Internship	Culminating
Candidate performance assessment	Review of candidate: • GPA • GRE scores • References • Interviews • Essays	• Exams • Papers • Reports • Case studies/simulations • Video • Grades	• Comprehensive exam • Evaluation of candidate practica performance (including professional work characteristics) by faculty and field supervisors	Evaluation of intern performance (including professional work characteristics) by field supervisors	• Portfolio of select internship cases, including positive impact data • Praxis II exam
Program evaluation		Student evaluation of courses and instructors	Candidate evaluation of practica sites and supervision	Intern evaluation of internship sites and supervision	• Candidate exit survey • Alumni survey (periodic) • Employer survey (periodic)

Note. GRE = Graduate Record Examinations.

Aggregating Assessment Data

Information useful for decision making regarding individual applicants and candidates is obviously a critical goal of any assessment method or program. But assessment results should also lead to the identification of program strengths, weaknesses, and/or needs. If faculty or program administrators examine only individual candidate results, then the program is overlooking aggregate information that could be critical for program development. Accrediting bodies require the aggregation and use of performance assessment data for program evaluation and improvement.

As is the case for most higher education programs, school psychology graduate programs tend to have more experience aggregating input or process data than outcome or performance data. Historically, it was (and remains) quite common for graduate programs in psychology to gather and report such input data as the average Graduate Record Examinations scores of entering students, or the credentials of faculty, or such process data as the student-to-faculty ratio. But until recently, outcome measures such as candidate performance on licensing exams or field supervisor evaluations of interns tended to be less well documented. Increased educational accountability in general, and professional accreditation standards in particular, are bringing about greater attention to aggregating and reporting candidate performance assessment results in school psychology programs (Prus & Strein, 2011).

Aggregating assessment data is usually a relatively simple but fairly time-consuming process. Performance data can usually be summarized in simple electronic tables (e.g., Word) or spreadsheets (e.g., Excel). However, as the push for outcome data has become more important, various companies have developed software programs to assist disciplines, departments, and colleges in collecting and analyzing outcome data. While the range of services vary from collecting portfolio artifacts to other assessment data, the need for a more efficient system is obvious. Systems such as LiveText (http://www.livetext.com), Rcampus (http://www.rcampus.com), Digication (http://www.digication.com), and ChalkandWire (http://www.chalkandwire.com) have flourished in the last few years. Moodle and Sakai are course-management systems that have gained widespread popularity (e.g., epcop_learnspace).

Use of ePortfolios goes beyond the collection of paper artifacts compiled in binders. Love, McKean, and Gathercoal (2004) define ePortfolios differently than webfolios. In the former, artifacts are not available online as they are in the latter. Borrowing components from the American National Learning Infrastructure Initiative (Challis, 2005), these portfolios can be a collection of evidence gathered from a larger group of artifacts that represent a person's learning over time.

While this definition does not differ from paper portfolios, the big difference is the enhanced ability of students to represent their best self over time more easily because of the functionality of technology (Challis, 2005). The greater challenge, however, may be for the

Figure 38.1. Analyzing Program Documentation for Performance-Based Standards and Associated Expectations for Program Assessment and Accountability

This tool is intended to guide programs through the process of developing and/or evaluating an assessment and accountability system.

Documenting the Program's Assessment and Accountability System

I. **The program has clear goals/objectives for candidate knowledge, skills, and professional work characteristics or dispositions consistent with national standards that are conveyed in program materials:**
   ___ a. Clear goals/objectives are contained in program documents.
   ___ b. Goals/objectives describe candidate knowledge, skills, and/or professional work characteristics or dispositions.
   ___ c. Goals/objectives address critical competencies in relevant national standards.

II. **Program goals/objectives and associated national standards for the profession are addressed in the required curricula:**
   ___ a. Required coursework reflects program key goals/objectives and national standards relevant for the particular content area.
   ___ b. Course documentation (e.g., syllabi) reflects coverage of content related to cited program goals/objectives and relevant national standards.
   ___ c. Practica requirements and experiences are described in program documents.
   ___ d. Practica requirements reflect program goals/objectives and associated national standards.
   ___ e. Internship requirements and experiences are described in program documents.
   ___ f. Internship requirements reflect program goals/objectives and associated national standards.
   ___ g. Evidence (e.g., practica and internship documentation such as logs/summaries) exists that candidates complete required field experiences consistent with program goals/objectives and national standards.

III. **The program includes key assessments required by national accrediting bodies to show that candidates acquire knowledge, skills, and professional work characteristics consistent with program objectives and national standards, and are able to deliver a range of services that have a positive impact on children, youth, families, and other consumers. Such assessments may include:**
   ___ a. State and/or national credentialing examination for school psychology practice in schools
   ___ b. Other assessments of content knowledge including grades in courses containing content and assessments that clearly address national standards, comprehensive or qualifying examination, or other content measures reflecting program objectives and national standards.
   ___ c. Assessment of candidates during practica that shows they can effectively plan and carry out school psychological services.
   ___ d. Intern evaluations by field supervisors demonstrating that candidate knowledge, skills, and professional work characteristics are applied effectively in practice during internship.
   ___ e. A comprehensive, performance-based assessment of candidate abilities evaluated by faculty during internship (e.g., case studies, portfolio).
   ___ f. Assessment demonstrating that candidates are able to integrate and apply professional knowledge and skills in delivering a range of services that have a positive impact on children, youth, families, and other consumers.
   ___ g. Other assessments that address program objectives and national standards (e.g., exit surveys, alumni, and/or employer follow ups, theses).

Figure 38.1. Continued

IV. Processes and methods used to assess candidates in required courses and field experiences are described in program documents:

____ a. The program handbook describes candidate assessment methods and processes, as well as associated requirements and criteria for completion.

____ b. Course syllabi or similar documents address intended candidate outcomes and the processes, methods, and criteria of assessment used to determine if expectations are met in a specific enough manner to be linked to the content of national standards.

____ c. Practica syllabi or similar documents describe assessment processes, methods, and criteria that can be linked to program goals/objectives for candidates as well as to national standards.

____ d. Internship syllabi or similar documents describe assessment processes, methods, and criteria that can be linked to program goals/objectives for candidates as well as to national standards.

V. The program documents the attainment of candidate abilities consistent with program goals/objectives and national standards:

____ a. The program collects state or national credentialing exam score reports for all program completers.

____ b. The program documents candidate performance on key assessments in courses or documents how grades or other measures show attainment of knowledge consistent with national standards.

____ c. The program collects assessments of practica and intern performance.

____ d. The program aggregates/summarizes assessment data that show frequencies or percentages of candidates meeting minimum criteria for each assessment.

____ e. The program documents assessment results across cohorts.

VI. The program documents the use of assessment results for candidate and program development and improvement:

____ a. Processes for providing feedback to individual candidates are outlined in field experience manuals, program handbook, and/or similar materials.

____ b. Assessment results are regularly reviewed in relation to program goals and objectives as well as to relevant state and national standards and stimulate changes designed for the purpose of program development and improvement.

____ c. Documentation is maintained regarding specific program improvements/changes made in response to assessment data.

It is important that programs examine the validity or credibility of candidate assessment methods and use such information to make decisions about their ongoing use and/or revision.

Note. From *A Guide for Performance-Based Assessment, Accountability, and Program Development in School Psychology Training Programs* (2nd ed.), by N. Waldron and J. Prus, 2006, Bethesda, MD: National Association of School Psychologists. Copyright 2006 by National Association of School Psychologists. Adapted with permission.

institution or program to identify the system that will best fit their needs.

At a minimum, the institution may need to consider the following: program needs, system attributes to meet needs, number of users the system can accommodate, number of artifacts that can be uploaded, and cost. Another variable for consideration is the view that students (with whom these portfolios are used) may have regarding the utility of these electronic systems. For example, Ritzhaupt, Singh, and Seyferth (2008) sampled 204 students using the Electronic Portfolio Student Perspective Instrument. Interestingly, the system, which includes four domains (employment, visibility, assessment, and learning), was developed in response to the NCATE site visit scheduled at the authors' university.

The authors sought students' perspectives on the system's characteristics and whether it was easy to use and effective. The results showed that the technology was challenging and not easy to use. The students also felt negative about the lack of choice and control in creating their portfolios and about the technology support, and they believed faculty were not well versed in the program. Those making selections and implementing a system should keep in mind that whichever system they select should be user friendly and be implemented early in courses (Ritzhaupt, Singh, & Seyferth, 2008).

Another system, Tk 20 (http://www.tk20.com), describes itself as "integrated, enterprise class education, assessment and reporting systems." This standards-based system provides colleges and schools of education with an assessment system for use in providing outcome data to accrediting agencies. Rcampus, on the other hand, gives school psychology programs a way to organize portfolio artifacts, score them (done by various faculty), and aggregate data across faculty by candidate and cohorts.

Regardless of the approach, paper or electronic, data should include, at a minimum, the percentage of each cohort of candidates (typically, all graduate students within a given year in the program) attaining each rating, score, or grade on each required major assessment throughout the program. If subparts of assessments address key program objectives or national standards or domains, then ratings or scores on those subparts should also be reported (e.g., the subsections of intern evaluations, a program comprehensive examination, or the Praxis II exam). It is also important to report the score or rating considered to be passing for each assessment and the percentage of each cohort that passes that particular assessment. Measures of central tendency such as means or medians are of limited value when reporting performance assessment, as they do not show the range of student performance or the percentage of students who have met specific criteria or who have passed.

Using and Documenting Performance Assessment Results

A critical purpose of assessment in school psychology graduate programs is to acquire data for providing feedback to and making decisions about individual candidates. As depicted earlier in this chapter, there are key points in the program in which important decisions about candidates are made, beginning with the admissions process and continuing through practica, internship, and program completion. Some programs employ an annual candidate review process for this purpose, with results and decisions being documented in individual candidate records.

Another important goal of assessment is to obtain data with which to make programmatic decisions designed to improve the effectiveness of training. This requires a different level of using and documenting data that is a more recent addition to the role of many faculty and program directors. Documenting program changes and improvements made in response to assessment is also a requirement of higher education accrediting bodies. Thus, it is not enough to document that assessment has occurred or that data have been aggregated. Faculty and program directors need to

show that assessment is an ongoing process that includes consideration and use of results for program improvement.

A best practice assessment system closes the loop between assessment and decision making. That process can be facilitated and documented in a variety of ways. First of all, faculty can convey the value placed on assessment, and on using results for program self-evaluation, in such program documents as the program handbook. This has the added advantage of conveying to candidates the importance of data-based decision making at all levels of school psychology training and practice, including graduate preparation. The actual use of candidate assessment data for making program improvement can be facilitated through regular meetings of program faculty, perhaps with other program stakeholders, and documented through the following means: (a) minutes of regular program and/or department faculty meetings, (b) summaries of annual faculty retreats at which assessment results are discussed and ideas for program improvement are generated, (c) minutes of program advisory board meetings at which assessment results are presented and recommendations for program changes are made, (d) annual program reports that summarize assessment results and program changes made in response to such results, and (e) internal university program review documents.

Each program should select and use the method of using and documenting results best suited for its particular needs. For example, if the university requires an annual program review and resulting report from each department or program, then summarizing assessment data and program changes in such a holistic manner may be more advantageous than trying to do so in the minutes of department meetings. On the other hand, if the program has an active advisory board, then it may make sense to focus a portion of board meetings (and minutes) on discussing assessment findings and possible implications and actions.

SUMMARY

Performance-based assessment of school psychology program outcomes and use of results for individual and program evaluation and improvement is consistent with the NASP Practice Model (NASP, 2010a) and accountability expectations of higher education. Multiple methods and sources are needed to assess the knowledge, skills, and professional work characteristics school psychologists need to be effective. Each method has advantages and disadvantages, and thus more valid and useful information is likely to result when assessment is conceptualized and implemented as a system.

The development of a comprehensive assessment program is a dynamic process, even for faculty with considerable expertise in measurement and assessment. Ongoing evaluation of assessment methods themselves is an important part of that process. One challenge of assessment and accountability is the ongoing collection of data. However, software packages can help facilitate data collection. Although faculty are accustomed to aggregating and documenting results for making decisions at the individual level, they must now document the use of assessment data for program evaluation and improvement. All regional and national accrediting organizations require this type of accountability.

Given the importance associated with the outcomes of school psychology programs, it is worth investing the time to develop assessment methods that are as comprehensive, valid, and useful as possible. It is hoped that the increased attention paid to performance assessment in school psychology programs will also lead to more systematic research within and across programs on factors related to successful graduate preparation outcomes and to school psychology practice that positively affects children, youth, families, and other clients.

REFERENCES

American Association for Higher Education. (1992). *Nine principles of good practice for assessing student learning and development*. Washington, DC: Author.

American Psychological Association. (2009). *Guidelines and principles for accreditation of programs in professional psychology*. Washington, DC: Author. Retrieved from http://www.apa.org/ed/accreditation/about/policies/guiding-principles.pdf

Astin, A. W., & Antonio, A. L. (2012). *Assessment for excellence: The philosophy and practice of assessment and evaluation in higher education*. Lanham, MD: Rowan & Littlefield.

Banta, T. W. (2003). *Portfolio assessment: Uses, cases, scoring, and impact*. San Francisco, CA: Jossey-Bass.

Bonner, M., & Barnett, D. W. (2004). Intervention-based school psychology services: Training for child-level accountability: Preparing for program level accountability. *Journal of School Psychology, 42*, 23–43.

Challis, D. (2005). Towards the mature ePortfolio: Some implications for higher education. *Canadian Journal of Learning and Technology, 31*(3). Retrieved from http://www.cjlt.ca/index.php/cjlt/article/view/93/87

DeAngelis, T. (2003). Why we overestimate our competence. *Monitor on Psychology, 34*(2). Retrieved from http://www.apa.org/monitor/feb03/overestimate.aspx

Huba, M., & Freed, J. (2000). *Learner-centered assessment on college campuses*. Boston, MA: Allyn & Bacon.

Kiresuk, T. J., Smith, A., & Cardillo, J. E. (Eds.). (1994). *Goal attainment scaling: Applications, theory, and measurement*. Hillside, NJ: Erlbaum.

Kratochwill, T. R., Elliott, S. N., & Callan-Stoiber, K. (2002). Best practices in school-based problem-solving consultation. In A. Thomas & J. Grimes (Eds.), *Best practices in school psychology IV* (pp. 583–608). Bethesda, MD: National Association of School Psychologists.

Love, D., McKean, G., & Gathercoal, P. (2004). Portfolios to webfolios and beyond: Levels of maturation. *EDUCAUSE Quarterly, 27*(2), 24–37.

Morrison, J. Q., Graden, J. L., & Barnett, D. W. (2009). Steps to evaluating a statewide internship program: Model, trainee, and student outcomes. *Psychology in the Schools, 46*, 990–1005.

National Association of School Psychologists. (1994). *Standards for training and field placement programs in school psychology*. Bethesda, MD: Author.

National Association of School Psychologists. (2010a). *Model for comprehensive and integrated school psychological services*. Bethesda, MD: Author. Retrieved from http://www.nasponline.org/standards/2010standards/2_PracticeModel.pdf

National Association of School Psychologists. (2010b). *Standards for graduate preparation of school psychologists*. Bethesda, MD: Author. Retrieved from http://www.nasponline.org/standards/2010standards/1_Graduate_Preparation.pdf

National Council for Accreditation of Teacher Education. (2002). *Professional standards for the accreditation of schools, colleges, and departments of education*. Washington, DC: Author.

National Council for Accreditation of Teacher Education. (2003). *Assessing education candidate performance: A look at changing practices*. Washington, DC: Author.

Parker, R. I., Hagan-Burke, S., & Vannest, K. (2007). Percent of all non-overlapping data (PAND): An alternative to PND. *The Journal of Special Education, 40*, 194–204.

Parker, R. I., Vannest, K. J., & Brown, L. (2009). The improvement rate difference for single case research. *Exceptional Children, 75*, 135–150.

Prus, J., & Strein, W. (2011). Issues and trends in the accreditation of school psychology programs in the United States. *Psychology in the Schools, 48*, 887–900.

Prus, J., & Waldron, N. (2005, March). Performance assessment in school psychology graduate programs. Workshop presented at the annual meeting of the National Association of School Psychologists, Atlanta, GA.

Ritzhaupt, A. D., Singh, O., & Seyferth, T. (2008). Development of the electronic portfolio student perspective instrument: An ePortfolio integration initiative. *Journal of Computing in Higher Education, 19*(2).

Roach, A. T., & Elliott, S. N. (2005). Goal attainment scaling: An efficient and effective approach to monitoring student progress. *Teaching Exceptional Children, 37*(4), 8–17.

Waldron, N., & Prus, J. (2006). *A guide for performance-based assessment, accountability, and program development in school psychology training programs* (2nd ed.). Bethesda, MD: National Association of School Psychologists.

39

Best Practices in the Supervision of Interns

Jeremy R. Sullivan
Nicole Svenkerud
University of Texas at San Antonio
Jane Close Conoley
University of California, Santa Barbara

OVERVIEW

The purposes of this chapter are to describe school psychology internship supervision from a variety of perspectives, identify the basic considerations supervisors (or potential supervisors) should be thinking about, and make recommendations for best practices so that school psychologists who serve as internship supervisors will have some guidelines to shape their supervisory practices. While this chapter will likely be most useful for supervisors, it may provide helpful perspectives for interns as well. Further, while our specific focus is on supervision during internship, much of what we discuss could be applied to supervision of practicum students.

Our chapter is categorized within the Legal, Ethical, and Professional Practice domain in the National Association of School Psychologists (NASP) *Model for Comprehensive and Integrated Services by School Psychologists* (NASP, 2010a). Effective supervision during internship is foundational to the services provided by school psychologists; to the development of professional identity; and to behaviors consistent with the ethical, legal, and professional standards of the field. Like all other aspects of graduate preparation, the supervision that occurs during internship can have a lasting impact on the professional dispositions, behaviors, and decision making of school psychologists. Moreover, effective supervision is likely to result in better outcomes for students by enhancing the competencies of interns.

NASP defines supervision in school psychology as

> … an ongoing, positive, systematic, collaborative process between the school psychologist and the school psychology supervisor. This process focuses on promoting effective growth and exemplary professional practice leading to improved performance by all, including the school psychologist, supervisor, students, and the entire school community. (NASP, 2011, p. 1)

Further, NASP defines the term *school psychology internship* as

> … a supervised, culminating, comprehensive field experience that is completed prior to the awarding of the degree or other institutional documentation of completion of the specialist or doctoral level program. The internship ensures that school psychology candidates have the opportunity to integrate and apply professional knowledge and skills acquired in program coursework and practica, as well as to acquire enhanced competencies consistent with the school psychology program's goals and objectives. (NASP, 2010c, p. 7)

A common message across these definitions is that the central outcome of internship supervision is professional growth and increased competence.

Effective supervision of school psychology interns can accomplish several goals. The most important goals may be (a) developing autonomous knowledge and skills in services such as assessment, counseling, and consultation; (b) learning to translate knowledge into informed, competent practice; (c) learning to apply the most recent ethical guidelines and legal standards to professional practice; (d) enhancing interpersonal skills with clients and families; (e) developing a professional identity and sense of self-confidence; (f) learning to self-reflect on areas of professional strength and weakness; and (g) receiving opportunities to share personal and professional experiences with others on a regular basis (Crespi & Lopez, 1998; Kaslow, Falender, & Grus, 2012).

Both the American Psychological Association (APA, 2010) and NASP (2010b, 2010c) regard supervision as essential to the professional development and practice of school psychologists and, therefore, provide guidance about the provision of supervision. However, there continues to be a relative paucity of published literature and empirical research devoted to this area within the field of school psychology, especially when compared to the amount of supervision literature published in the fields of clinical psychology, counseling psychology, psychotherapy, school counseling, and general professional psychology (Goodyear, Bunch, & Claiborn, 2005). In addition, most supervisors report limited academic training in supervision or access to peer supervision, which is surprising given many school psychologists will serve as supervisors at some point in their careers (Harvey & Struzziero, 2008). This chapter will use the extant literature to inform best practices in the supervision of school psychology interns while also identifying areas where more research is needed.

BASIC CONSIDERATIONS

Frequent topics discussed in intern supervision include ethical and legal issues, intervention design, consultation with parents and teachers, classroom management, assessment and evaluation, diagnosis, preparation of psychological or psychoeducational reports, theories of psychotherapy, specific counseling techniques, crisis intervention, threat assessment, program evaluation, community resources, and larger administrative/system issues. Decisions based on assessment results are also common topics addressed in supervision, and these decisions include eligibility for special education services, change of placement, least restrictive environment, and appropriate interventions. These decisions have become even more complex with the advent of response to intervention (RTI) and resulting ambiguity related to eligibility criteria, amount of data necessary to

reach decisions, reliance upon treatment integrity, and variability with which RTI systems are implemented.

Supervision can be conducted either individually or in a group, both of which are widely practiced among internship sites. Advantages of group supervision include efficient use of time, as several interns can receive supervision simultaneously; peer feedback; support; group cohesion; access to multiple hypotheses and perspectives; and exposure to a wider variety of cases, assessment techniques, and diagnostic and treatment issues (Riva & Cornish, 2008). On the other hand, individual supervision may be more appropriate when the supervisee needs more personalized instruction, observation, evaluation, and support of self-care (Kaslow et al., 2012).

Partners in School Psychology Internship Supervision

Five partners in the school psychology graduate program and internship process that have a vested interest in interns' development and performance include (a) the internship site supervisor, (b) the intern as supervisee, (c) the intern's university graduate program and university supervisor, (d) the internship site, and (e) professional associations such as NASP and APA.

Internship Site Supervisors

Site supervisors have the responsibility to be available to interns; communicate the internship site's policies and expectations; assist with management of clinical cases and activities; collaborate with the intern to troubleshoot, encourage, challenge, and celebrate the intern's situations occurring throughout internship; model ethical and professional behavior; and share their own professional experiences, as this provides essential perspective to the developing intern. Site supervisors have a central role to play in the overall education, development, and evaluation of interns. They (along with the intern) are partially responsible for making sure interns learn the skills required by university programs and for monitoring the intern's experiences to ensure appropriate breadth and depth. Site supervisors typically complete formal evaluations at least once per semester, providing assurance to university programs the intern is functioning effectively and providing formative and summative feedback to the intern. University programs collect evaluations of interns' performance during internship to determine how well the students have been trained through their graduate coursework. This information helps university programs in school psychology assess whether the curriculum is working as intended and identify any skills or competencies that need to be emphasized more (or taught in a different way) during graduate study, or perhaps identify additional practicum experiences that would be beneficial not only for the interns themselves, but also for future interns and students in the program. Thus, internship site supervisors have important perspectives that are useful to university programs at both the individual and aggregate levels.

Interns

Interns are expected to arrive at their internship sites with the interpersonal skills, social awareness, enthusiasm, and problem-solving skills necessary to collaborate with others and the requisite knowledge base to perform school psychologist roles and functions. Clearly, these skills contribute to the intern's ability to help students achieve positive outcomes. Internship sites and university programs may want to have interns sign a document indicating their agreement to follow district policies, act according to NASP/APA ethical guidelines and state law, maintain appropriate professional liability insurance, and other requirements as appropriate. This communicates to the intern the importance of following these procedures while also providing documentation for the site (and site supervisor) should fitness-to-practice issues arise during internship. Interns also should create a formal professional development plan based on their training experiences and future goals. At the end of the internship, interns are encouraged to provide formal feedback about their experience to both the internship site and the university program.

University Programs and University Supervisors

An interdependent relationship exists between university programs and internship sites: Universities need internship sites to provide quality training experiences for their students, and internship sites rely on universities to provide them with highly qualified professionals in training. If the internship site exploits the intern and does not provide quality experiences and supervision, then the university may advise future interns to keep these experiences in mind when they consider their own placements. On the other hand, if an intern arrives without the knowledge base and professional dispositions necessary to be successful, the internship site may be hesitant to take on future interns from the same university program.

University supervisors should provide site supervisors with any information and materials necessary to support supervision (Prus, 2009). These materials may include the program handbook, university syllabus for the internship course with a thorough description of how interns will be evaluated, any documents that need to be signed, and a description of specific competencies interns are expected to demonstrate as a result of the internship experience (McCutcheon, 2009). University supervisors also need to maintain regular communication with the internship site. This allows university supervisors to quickly identify and remediate potential problems as well as monitor whether interns are getting a range of experiences (not just assessment for instance) and developing skills across the NASP domains. Generally speaking, university supervisors are mostly concerned with supervision at this more macro or administrative level, and site supervisors who are more familiar with district procedures and dynamics provide clinical supervision for specific cases.

Internship Sites

Aside from the site supervisor, the internship site also has a vested interest in interns' supervision and development because student outcomes are affected by interns' activities and skills. The internship site includes the school district, campuses, special education directors, teachers and other school staff, parents, and students served by the intern. The internship site should provide release time for university duties such as group supervision or graduation activities. These (and other) obligations should be clearly explicated on a Memorandum of Agreement or similar document signed by the intern, site supervisor, university supervisor, and others as appropriate. This agreement also may describe the nature of the supervision and supervisory relationship, characteristics of the internship site, credentials of the supervisor, goals of supervision, confidentiality, and how the intern will be evaluated (Jacob, Decker, & Hartshorne, 2011).

Professional Associations

Professional associations (e.g., NASP and APA, state licensing boards) play a role in supervision of school psychology interns by defining domains of professional competence, describing the amount of supervision interns should receive, and describing the types of experiences to which interns should be exposed. For example, Standard 3.4 of the NASP *Standards for Graduate Preparation of School Psychologists* (NASP, 2010c) speaks specifically to supervision during internship, requiring the site supervisor to hold the appropriate license to practice school psychology in their state; ensure an average of at least 2 hours spent on supervision per week; and provide supervision that is predominantly face-to-face, structured, consistently scheduled, and focused on skill development. There is emphasis on the importance of both formative and summative assessment by university and site supervisors. NASP also recommends that site supervisors have a minimum of 3 years of experience working as a school psychologist before providing supervision to interns and that supervisors participate in professional organizations in school psychology (NASP, 2010a). These recommendations are meant to provide a standardized supervision experience during internship with regard to a minimum amount of supervision, but specific internship sites and supervisors decide how to best implement these requirements. For example, supervision may include individual supervision every week to review specific cases, group supervision for general administrative or logistical issues, group case reviews with multiple supervisors and interns to facilitate suggestions for intervention, and colloquia or training seminars covering advanced assessment methods and intervention techniques. Some university programs also maintain some level of group supervision during internship, and this supervision may be conducted using face-to-face or virtual formats (or a combination of these) depending on logistical issues such as geographic location of interns and access to technology.

BEST PRACTICES IN SUPERVISION OF INTERNS

Supervision of school psychology interns represents a complex and ongoing series of interactions between the supervisor and intern. Thus, best practices related to supervision encompass a range of activities and processes. This section will consider best practices in evaluating interns' functioning, self-evaluation of supervisors' skills, engaging in ethical behaviors, considering interns' perspectives and expectations, and incorporating technology into supervision. Finally, we consider the application of the Eight-Step Problem-Solving Model (Jacob et al., 2011) to supervision.

Evaluating Intern Skills

A successful supervisor must develop a number of strategies for evaluating the level of intern skills so that appropriate teaching plans can be made and assessment activities accomplished. At the beginning of

the internship, the intern should prepare a professional development plan in which the intern describes specific goals and experiences he or she hopes to achieve during the internship year. This plan should be approved by both the site supervisor and university supervisor, and should be reviewed on a regular basis for purposes of formative and summative feedback to the intern (Jacob et al., 2011). These goals may address competency areas or specialized skills with which the intern would like to gain additional knowledge and experience and/or are unique to the internship site. These goals can then form the basis of the supervisor's evaluation of the intern's skill development throughout the internship.

In addition to goals identified by the intern's professional development plan, some of the most critical issues for the supervisor to investigate include the intern's level of competence (i.e., knowledge and skills), professionalism (i.e., maintaining a high standard with regard to professional behaviors such as organization, timeliness, preparation, self-direction, adherence to district procedures, and follow through), and acceptance of supervision (i.e., is the intern able to recognize situations where he or she needs to consult with a supervisor to successfully resolve a problem, and the intern actively seeks out and receives supervision in these situations). Additional characteristics, which may be more difficult to measure objectively, include professional identity, respect for individual differences, purpose and direction, autonomy, ethics, emotional awareness, and motivation. Making informed judgments along these dimensions will demand that the supervisor meet individually with the intern, observe the intern's professional functioning, and collect evaluations from others who are directly involved with the intern because the supervisor is not always in the same building as the intern. Supervisors working at internship sites are encouraged to develop objective evaluation instruments to monitor progress toward site-specific goals and competencies and to use these at the end of each semester to serve both formative and summative purposes. Sample evaluation forms are provided in the previous versions of this chapter and additional samples are available from the first author.

Common methods of assessing clinical skills during supervision include the use of audio, video (with parental consent as appropriate), role-plays, case presentations, portfolio reviews, record reviews, self-assessment, and rating scales from consultees such as teachers and principals, in addition to evaluating the accuracy and sophistication of case conceptualizations (see Kaslow et al., 2009). The use of audio and video to evaluate consultation or counseling sessions allows the supervisor to assess the intern's communication skills and also provides opportunities to identify process and relationship issues taking place within sessions that would not be apparent to the supervisor without the use of these devices or direct observation. When practical, supervision also often includes a live observation component (e.g., observing the intern report assessment results to parents at an Individualized Education Program (IEP) meeting, observing the intern administer a cognitive test, or observing the intern conduct a workshop for teachers or parents). An advantage of live observation is the opportunity for the supervisor to provide immediate and specific feedback on the intern's performance, which may not be possible with less direct methods of evaluation.

Interns should come to supervision sessions prepared to discuss specific cases and clinical issues and should bring questions to shape the discussion. Interns must be participants in the supervision process rather than relying on supervisors to direct the conversation. If the intern is struggling to identify topics or questions for supervision, then the intern can refer back to his or her professional development plan and use the supervision session as an opportunity to formatively assess progress with the supervisor.

Assessment of Supervisory Skills

In addition to meeting the requirements for being a supervisor from relevant professional organizations, internship supervisors should reflect upon their own supervisory skills and experience to prepare for the supervisory role. This might begin with supervisors describing or rating their skills along the dimensions listed in Table 39.1, as these have been identified as core competencies of supervision (Campbell, 2006; Kaslow et al., 2012; Sullivan & Conoley, 2008).

Table 39.1. Core Competencies of Internship Supervision

- Comfort in an authority role
- Appreciation for the importance of the supervisory relationship
- Ability to provide honest and constructive feedback
- Communication and rapport-building skills
- Ability to present information clearly
- Ability to model professional skills and behaviors
- Facilitation of self-reflection by the intern
- Awareness of cultural and other diversity factors that may have an impact on supervision
- Ability to provide multiple perspectives
- Knowledge of problem-solving models
- Knowledge of ethical and legal standards
- Skills in applying ethics to complex situations
- Knowledge of supervision methods and theoretical models
- Competence in all areas of service delivery provided by supervisees
- Ability to be flexible
- Ability to motivate and challenge interns to reach their goals

Completing this self-assessment may provide supervisors with some important learning goals and information about blind spots in their own behaviors. Additional questions supervisors might ask themselves in preparation for the supervisory role are provided in Table 39.2.

The field of school psychology is constantly changing. Supervisors need to stay current on advances such as new assessment methods, RTI procedures, curriculum-based measurement, evidence-based intervention, technology, and special education policy so they can effectively guide interns who are ready to show what they know in these areas (Harvey & Pearrow, 2010). Central to this commitment to professional development is self-reflection to assess areas of professional weakness and identify skills that need to be further developed. For many novice supervisors, supervision itself may be identified as an area of weakness, thereby prompting novice supervisors to seek so-called supervision of

Table 39.2. Critical Questions in the Self-Assessment of Supervisory Skills

- What is your preferred style or theoretical orientation of service delivery and supervision? How does your theoretical orientation inform and shape your supervision of school psychology interns specifically?
- What feedback have you received about your professional style in supervision of interns? For example, do you over explain, are you uninvolved, are you too verbose, are you able to give examples, are you challenging as well as facilitative?
- What strengths and limitations do you see in your supervision style when supervising interns? How might the strengths be used and the weaknesses be addressed?
- Can you remember an event of effective supervision you experienced during your practicum and/or internship? Do you remember an ineffective incident? Describe the critical dimensions of each.
- What did you look for in a supervisor when you were an intern? What worked best for you?
- What goals do you have for the intern? This may require the supervisor to reflect on the skill level expected of an intern so as to have an appropriate frame of reference for expectations of an intern compared to an accomplished practitioner. In addition, the internship site supervisor must mesh supervision goals, graduate program goals, and school district goals.

supervision from more experienced supervisors (Falender et al., 2004). Given the importance of supervision to interns' skill development, NASP (2011) has recommended all school psychologists who provide supervision receive some sort of training in this area, either through coursework, workshops, or consultation. Demonstrating an openness to further develop skills will foster similar attitudes within interns, and interns value supervisors who are open to the new research and ideas the interns bring from their graduate programs.

In addition to conducting a self-assessment in preparation for the supervisory role, it also is important for supervisors to engage in formative and summative assessment of their knowledge, skills, and positive outcomes for interns during their provision of supervision. One way to accomplish this is to seek feedback from interns about supervision skills. Interns can be asked to evaluate the supervisor's skills along the same dimensions listed in Table 39.1 (in addition to other relevant competencies identified by the supervisor) at planned times during the internship year, and the supervisor can then compare the ratings from the intern with the results of his or her own self-assessment. In this way, the internship becomes an opportunity for the supervisor to develop, not just the intern. These opportunities for the supervisor to refine his or her skills will increase the likelihood of positive outcomes and experiences for interns.

Ethical Standards

Internship supervisors must clearly understand the ethical standards guiding supervisory relationships and responsibilities. These standards are meant not only to ensure successful internship experiences and intern development but also to protect students and lead to positive student outcomes. Principle IV.4 of NASP's *Principles for Professional Ethics* (NASP, 2010b) addresses mentoring, teaching, and supervision. For example, Standard IV.4.2 states:

> School psychologists who supervise practicum students and interns are responsible for all professional practices of the supervisees. They ensure that practicum students and interns are adequately supervised as outlined in the NASP *Graduate Preparation Standards for School Psychologists.* Interns and graduate students are identified as such, and their work is cosigned by the supervising school psychologist. (NASP, 2010b, p. 13)

Standard II.2.4 also echoes that internship supervisors are responsible for the work of the interns under their supervision. NASP also makes it clear that all of the *Principles for Professional Ethics* (those related to, for instance, competence, assessment and intervention practices, record keeping) apply to supervisors' work with interns and practicum students, and supervisors should serve as role models for ethical behaviors and decision making.

Additional standards from the *Principles for Professional Ethics* address issues surrounding supervision. Standard I.1.3 states that parents need to know if services will be offered by an intern (as opposed to a credentialed school psychologist) to truly give informed consent. Along with Standard III.1.1, this also means that supervisors and interns need to correct any misperceptions of their qualifications. For example, if a principal introduces the intern as a school psychologist, then the intern/supervisor must clarify the distinction between intern and school psychologist so that everyone is aware of the intern's level of training. This may be confusing for schools and parents who sometimes have difficulty understanding the work of school psychologists and the rigorous training involved.

Standard I.3.1 warns against discrimination of supervisees based on characteristics such as race, ethnicity, gender, religion, language, socioeconomic status, sexual orientation, or similar distinguishing characteristics. Standard III.4.3 prevents school psychologists from exploiting their supervisees, including sexual harassment and sexual relationships with supervisees owing to the inherent power differential in these relationships. Note this standard includes both "participating in" and "condoning" these behaviors.

APA's *Ethical Principles of Psychologists and Code of Conduct* (APA, 2010) includes a general statement that the principles apply to all roles of the psychologist, including supervisor. Thus, all of the standards related to multiple relationships, competence, sexual harassment, exploitative relationships, and professional practices such as assessment and therapy also apply to supervisory relationships and the supervision of these services. As an example related to competence, just as school psychologists must practice within the boundaries of their own competence, they also provide supervision within these boundaries (Jacob et al., 2011). Thus, if the intern wants to gain experience in an area outside of the supervisor's competence, then the supervisor should recommend additional supervision from an individual with expertise in that particular area. This may be easy if the internship occurs in a large school district with many school psychologists who are willing to provide supervision for particular areas or skills (e.g., neuropsychological assessment, bilingual services), but it may be more difficult in smaller districts where the range of potential supervisors is narrower. Alternatively, supervisors may seek to broaden their own competence through professional development, thereby permitting them to provide supervision for a wider range of activities.

Similar to the NASP principles, the APA ethics code includes several standards that speak directly to supervision. Standard 2.05 states that when delegating work to supervisees, psychologists should avoid delegating work that will result in exploitation owing to multiple relationships, should only delegate work that the supervisee can be reasonably expected to perform competently given his or her level of education and training, and should monitor these services to make sure the services are provided effectively. This suggests supervisors should act as a filter between the referral mechanisms and the intern, to make sure the intern has a reasonable caseload and is not overwhelmed with overly complex cases that may have an impact on his or her ability to provide appropriate services.

Standard 7.06 requires supervisors to have a process for providing specific and timely feedback regarding supervisees' performance, and supervisees are informed of this process at the outset of the supervisory relationship. In other words, there are no surprises, and interns are aware of the criteria by which they will be evaluated. Further, these criteria are relevant to the standards and requirements of the graduate program. Standard 7.07 expressly forbids sexual relationships with supervisees who are in the supervisor's department or agency or with whom an evaluative relationship exists. Finally, and similar to the NASP principles, Standard 10.01 requires trainees to be identified as such when obtaining informed consent for therapy services so that clients understand the therapist is a trainee who is under the supervision of the supervisor.

Interns' Perspectives

In determining best practices in supervision, it is important to explore what interns think about the process of supervision, including their expectations and what they value most and least about supervision and supervisors. These perspectives are helpful in facilitating the generation of specific suggestions for supervisors. Satisfaction with supervision is one of the variables contributing to interns' overall satisfaction with the

internship experience. Ineffective supervision is likely to have a negative impact not only on interns' skill development but also on their self-efficacy and commitment to the field (O'Donovan, Halford, & Walters, 2011).

The themes and suggestions outlined below come from perspectives provided by practicum students and interns from several universities (i.e., the University of Nebraska, Texas A&M University, and the University of Texas at San Antonio; total $N = 138$; Sullivan, 2013) who had completed supervised field placements, in addition to our analysis of published empirical research and conceptual papers in the field of supervision. Unfortunately, the empirical research examining interns' perspectives of the supervision process is somewhat limited, especially within the specific context of training in school psychology. This represents an important area for future inquiry. Perhaps the most important message to be taken from the following discussion is that supervisors would be wise to elicit a careful consideration of these issues at the beginning of the supervisory relationship.

Supervisor Availability

Interns are sensitive to the accessibility of their supervisors. Even when they perceive the supervisor to be talented and competent, difficulties in contacting a supervisor during a critical period or in arranging for regular supervision result in poor evaluations and a diminished experience. Two hours each week of individual supervision must be given to the interns in addition to other group staffing and educational experiences, and supervisors should expect interns will sometimes need guidance outside of the regularly scheduled supervision times. Supervisors should be permitted to have only the number of interns who can be adequately served and must be well organized to have supervisory time available so as not to interfere with student outcomes at their own site. A typical week's worth of intern supervision might look something like this: 1 hour of individual supervision on Monday, opportunities to shadow the supervisor and check in on activities mid-week, group supervision with all district school psychologists and interns on Friday for case review and professional development, and opportunities to check in by e-mail or phone throughout the week as needed.

Dependence Versus Independence

Because they view themselves as independent and skillful, interns value direction with many options from which to choose and usually do not want to be told exactly what to do. They desire supervision that helps them get unstuck and that forces them to think for themselves about clients. Of course, the extent to which interns desire dependence or independence is variable and should be determined by the supervisor on a case-by-case basis. Therefore, supervisors should talk with supervisees about a format for supervision that seems acceptable to both parties and check in regularly to ensure the format is still working.

The developmental model of supervision suggests that supervision should change as interns continue to grow and learn new skills (Stoltenberg & Delworth, 1987). Beginning interns may lack confidence and are dependent on the supervisor for advice and direction. At this early stage, interns often are very cautious and concerned about how to do things the right way and may not have much insight into their own behavior or its potential impact. In most cases, supervision at this point should be direct; that is, the intern may observe the supervisor engage in an activity (e.g., conducting an IEP team meeting, leading a counseling group) several times before the supervisor directly observes the intern engage in the activity. With some experience, many interns begin to experience a conflict between dependence and autonomy, and as interns begin to gain confidence they may disagree with supervisors about the "correct" way to handle different situations. Eventually, a firmer sense of identity and self-confidence evolves. The intern becomes more tolerant of ambiguity and differences among professionals and is increasingly more flexible in choosing approaches to solve problems. In addition, the supervisee seeks help and advice without feeling overly dependent on the supervisor and develops a realization that there are often multiple ways to approach situations. At this point, supervision may focus more on problem solving and exploring options rather than on the direct supervision of microskills that often characterizes the early stages of internship supervision.

Excellent supervisors change their behaviors (from advice giving to support) according to the needs and developmental level of their supervisees. They do not overreact to predictable conflicts and are patient with interns' early feelings of helplessness and dependence. At the same time, they are comfortable with providing less specific direction as interns gain greater levels of competence and independence and eventually encourage the intern to take charge of cases. Ramos-Sanchez et al. (2002) suggest that early in the internship year, supervisors would be well advised to focus on building a strong and supportive relationship with interns, which can serve to create an environment of trust and a positive context for future supervisory interactions. This supportive relationship may be especially important as interns encounter challenging cases and frustrating situations throughout the internship year. Programs such as beginning-of-the-year orientations and ROPES activities that incorporate all of the interns and psychological services staff are conducive to relationship building. Supervisors can further build trust with interns by assessing their feelings about the relationship on a regular basis and remaining open to feedback from the intern (Ramos-Sanchez et al., 2002).

Intern Expectations

Briefly, interns generally expect that supervisors will be highly knowledgeable in both theory and practice, use a research-based framework to provide services, respect the intern's personal style of providing services, be supportive, and hold very high expectations for the interns. Supervisors are expected to help interns formulate hypotheses and construct case conceptualizations in addition to exploring all possibilities or competing scenarios regarding clients and their treatment. Some interns especially value a highly structured approach to supervision and cases and desire frequent feedback on competency and skill development. Further, interns expect supervisors to be positive and encouraging. Supervisors offer ongoing feedback, picking up on what the intern could have done differently in a case without being overly critical, judgmental, or negative (Heckman-Stone, 2003). Interns value supervisors who explain why they make particular suggestions (e.g., eligibility decisions, which tests to use for a certain purpose) rather than simply telling the intern what to do.

Communicating Internship Site Expectations

Several authors (e.g., Harvey & Struzziero, 2008; Jacob et al., 2011) note the importance of supervisors communicating their expectations, and those of the internship program, to interns as soon as possible. It makes sense that interns would desire transparency with regard to their roles and responsibilities within the internship program/school district, as these expectations will serve as the basis of supervisors' evaluations of interns' performance. Supervisors should make sure interns understand when they should contact their supervisors immediately (e.g., when a student expresses suicidal ideation, when the intern suspects child abuse or neglect), and should instruct interns on important rules or procedures of the site such as site-specific risk assessment procedures, how to pull students out of class, and campus check-in procedures (Jacob et al., 2011). These procedures are often second nature to the supervisor, so they may get overlooked. Making a specific point to communicate these procedures to the intern might lead to greater likelihood that the procedures are followed.

Creating a Safe Place

Because many interns are anxious and insecure about providing services and also about the ongoing evaluation that accompanies supervision, it is essential the supervisor create a safe place in supervision, wherein personal and professional growth is enhanced and fear is minimized (Emerson, 1996). This can be accomplished by creating an environment conducive to trust and open communication, encouraging brainstorming, never putting interns down, using humor, involving interns in decision making, treating interns fairly and with respect, and ensuring confidentiality. Both the supervision literature and student responses indicate that constant support and persistent encouragement are important to interns and can help to enhance their self-confidence, thereby facilitating skill improvement. Interns can be expected to make mistakes and obviously will not know everything, but should not let this get in the way of taking chances and learning (under close supervision). It may be helpful for supervisors to remember the one-for-two rule: for every one correction or criticism the supervisor offers the intern, the supervisor should provide two compliments or positive statements. This may help in keeping the overall climate of supervision positive and supportive, even when the supervisor must give constructive criticism. Offering harsh criticism or demonstrating overly critical attitudes in the absence of positive feedback can have a negative impact on the supervisory relationship and on the intern's confidence in his or her skills (Ramos-Sánchez et al., 2002).

Cultural Awareness

Estrada, Frame, and Williams (2004) provide useful guidelines for cross-cultural supervision, including the importance of demonstrating cultural awareness and helping interns from minority backgrounds feel safe to discuss cultural issues during supervision. Even beyond this openness to discussion is the recommendation that supervisors take the first step and initiate discussions about ethnicity and culture with their supervisees. This initiation communicates to supervisees that these issues are valid topics for discussion during supervision.

Burkard et al. (2006) examined differences between culturally responsive and unresponsive supervision within the context of cross-cultural supervision. The results suggest that when supervisors were responsive to exploring cultural issues during supervision, their doctoral student supervisees felt supported and validated for exploring cultural issues with clients and this support seemed to have a positive influence on the relationship between the supervisor and supervisee. On the other hand, under the culturally unresponsive condition supervisors ignored or dismissed the importance of cultural issues during supervision, which (as would be expected) had a negative influence on the cross-cultural supervisory relationship and on supervisees' satisfaction with supervision. Fortunately, recent research suggests that multicultural issues are quite frequently addressed in supervision sessions, at least within the context of group supervision (Riva & Cornish, 2008).

Time Management and Organization

Although all interns (we hope) expect to work hard, most are unprepared for the intensity of the internship experience. Interns commonly report feeling overwhelmed by the demands on their time and unaware that they should take some responsibility for controlling their assignments. They report feeling unwilling to refuse any assignment. This occurs sometimes because they (ambitiously) want to learn everything, and sometimes because they fear a negative reaction if they object or hesitate. Supervisors should be prepared to teach these professional management skills to interns by their own example and should help interns understand that because they are still learning how to write reports, analyze progress-monitoring data, prepare for counseling sessions, and so on, it will take them longer to complete these tasks than seasoned school psychologists.

Interns seem to appreciate supervisors who are highly organized and deliberate in monitoring the intern's experiences. This may be especially important during internship, as the intern often is learning how to juggle multiple campuses, responsibilities, paperwork, and deadlines. Having a supervisor who can model and teach organizational skills can provide the intern with a sense of structure and security. Similarly, supervisors are encouraged to establish a structured format for supervision sessions, which will help interns prepare for supervision because they know what to expect. Although specific activities during supervision may vary depending on the intern's needs at that particular time, a standard template for supervision sessions might include discussing questions from the intern; reviewing the intern's cases with input from the supervisor;

discussing upcoming tasks and the rationale/evidence-base, strategy, or troubleshooting related to them; and teaching the intern or leading a discussion on a specific topic (based on desired competencies/experiences from the intern's professional development plan). As appropriate, sessions also should include feedback from the supervisor gained from direct observation of the intern, review of the intern's psychoeducational reports, or information provided by principals, teachers, parents, and others. Harvey and Struzziero (2008) provide additional guidance on organizing supervision sessions, including strategies for structuring group supervision, eliciting success stories from interns, and maintaining supervision records.

Exploitation of Skills

Some sites may use interns for repetitive or unpopular tasks. The interns, who resent that their work for the organization is not met with a return of training opportunities, easily discern this attitude. Internships are organized training experiences, not mere on-the-job experiences. This basic fact about internships is sometimes not well understood at the internship site, especially sites that do not have a long history of training interns. Careful cooperation between university faculty and internship sites must be maintained to be sure that everyone stays invested in teaching the interns, not merely using them to ease the strain of overflowing caseloads. An advantage of using professional development plans (as previously described) is that these can hold internship sites accountable for helping the school psychology intern meet his or her training goals, which also can facilitate the alliance between intern and supervisor.

Negative Supervisor Attitudes

Interns are disillusioned by supervisors who are pessimistic or cynical about professional functioning. Often, under the guise of teaching the intern what the real world is like, supervisors fail to model enthusiasm and optimism in their work. Supervisors may act like victims in their systems rather than instructing interns on how to approach the long and difficult processes of organizational change. Indeed, this is an easy trap for supervisors to fall into when faced with their own frustrations and overwhelming workload. However, these negative attitudes are contrary to the supervisor's obligation to model professionalism and may result in interns learning more negative information than positive steps to create change. In short, effective supervisors want to supervise, express their enthusiasm

for supervision on a regular basis, and possess the awareness to detect when they are being perceived by the intern as negative or cynical.

Opportunities for Practice and Feedback

Although a complete discussion of different theoretical models of supervision is beyond the scope of this chapter, an important point made in the previous version was that most models of supervision include the components of instruction, modeling, practice, and feedback (Sullivan & Conoley, 2008). These may be the most important characteristics of the supervision process across theoretical models. Supervisors are encouraged to teach new competencies by modeling new skills, providing opportunities for supervised practice or role-play activities, and then giving feedback about performance (Falender et al., 2004). As one example, the intern can explain assessment results while the supervisor plays the role of parent or teacher, and the supervisor can then evaluate the intern's explanation and offer suggestions for improvement. As another example, the intern may shadow the supervisor during a crisis situation before responding to a crisis on his or her own. Supervisors also are encouraged to provide formative feedback throughout the internship year, rather than waiting until the end of the year to share concerns about the intern's development (O'Donovan et al., 2011). Further, feedback should be provided in clear, objective, and measurable terms, so interns know how to improve their skills. This practice is consistent with the educational nature of internship, as it affords interns the opportunity to respond to feedback, and supervisors can then reassess the intern's performance.

Personal Factors for Interns

The internship experience occurs within the context of family, financial, health, and academic concerns for many interns. Although problems in these areas can rarely be solved by supervisors, a mutual appreciation of what the internship site is offering the intern and what the intern is sacrificing to finish the demanding degree program can help both sides keep ultimate goals in view. This understanding would likely deepen the professional supervisor–intern relationship and open the door to discussions regarding time management and organization as the intern is balancing multiple roles. Supervisors can briefly ask a context question (e.g., are you feeling overwhelmed) as part of each supervision session, which can help interns discuss concerns such as time management or balancing activities with the supervisor.

Technology and Supervision

Internship supervision in school psychology typically has involved face-to-face contact between the supervisor and intern. However, with significant developments in technology and an increased demand to provide services in rural communities, face-to-face contact during supervision of interns may become less of a norm over the next decade. Supervision through technology may include the use of applications such as Skype, FaceTime, video conferencing, text messages, e-mail, online discussion boards, or blogging. Benefits to these approaches identified in the literature include collaborative learning among interns through the use of online discussion boards, providing a sense of belonging and support to the intern who may be completing internship in an isolated geographical area, serving rural areas that do not have services available, promoting professional identity, and facilitating professional development by accessing continuing education programs or advice from seasoned colleagues (Perry, 2012; Wilczenski & Coomey, 2006).

In addition to the issues that arise when technology is not working properly, possible negative consequences associated with providing supervision through technology include the time available for complex questions may be limited; lack of direct supervision in emergency situations; typing speed may influence participation; decrease in discussion, as interns may seem disconnected from their supervisors; and interns or supervisors who have disabilities may need additional accommodations to fully participate in this process. Perhaps most importantly, the use of technology presents new ethical issues surrounding confidentiality and data security (Wilczenski & Coomey, 2006). In addition, it is argued that the advanced skill development and intensive nature of support required during internship may require face-to-face interaction with supervisors (Wilczenski & Coomey, 2006), and supervisors need guidance regarding whether technology-based supervision meets supervision requirements from professional associations and state licensing boards. Perry (2012) elaborates that those who did not grow up with advanced technology may feel uncomfortable with establishing a working relationship through the use of digital media.

There is not currently enough research to fully understand all of the benefits and consequences of providing supervision through the use of technology, let alone provide guidelines for best practices. Further current research is limited to studies conducted in counseling, clinical, and medical education programs.

Our best recommendation is that before incorporating technology into the supervision of interns, supervisors should consult the literature and with colleagues (and perhaps with professional associations or local university programs) who have experience in this area, and develop a plan using the problem-solving model (discussed in the next section) with a special focus on the risk-benefits analysis and consideration of how to best meet the intern's supervision needs.

Problem-Solving Model Applied to Supervision

A major challenge often associated with supervision of school psychology interns is preparing the intern to analytically resolve the day-to-day issues that arise while working in the schools. As the recommended graduate preparation model put forth by NASP encompasses 10 domains that each requires developing a specific set of competencies, we argue an underlying component to each domain is the ability to effectively solve problems. Further, school psychology internship supervisors have a unique role that demands a higher degree of mentorship as the intern is presented with new challenges and various professional issues that cannot be fully learned from a textbook. As the responsibilities of a school psychologist are multifaceted in nature, it is essential to develop a consistent system for problem solving early during internship, with the opportunity to apply the skills during internship and supervision.

Currently there are several systematic problem-solving models in the literature, which extend beyond the scope of this chapter. However, we recommend using the Eight-Step Problem-Solving Model (Jacob et al., 2011) as it applies to supervision. The steps of the model, and how the steps might apply to internship supervision, are summarized in Table 39.3. It is important for the school psychology internship supervisor to understand that while systematic problem-solving models are typically designed for resolving ethical dilemmas, we argue for the model's utility in navigating challenging situations that arise throughout the supervision of school psychology interns. Some of the professional issues that would be appropriate for the application of a systematic problem-solving model during supervision include high-stakes eligibility decisions, manifestation determination decisions, resistance to implementing academic or behavioral interventions, choosing appropriate placements for students, being asked to provide services outside of competencies, working with culturally and linguistically diverse students, and/or dealing with limits of confidentiality.

Table 39.3. Summary of the Eight-Step Problem-Solving Model as Applied to Intern Supervision

1. Describe the parameters of the situation/problem/issue. As the internship experience is meant to move the intern toward more autonomous practice, the supervisor should allow opportunities for the intern to first define the presenting problem on his or her own before providing guidance.

2. Outline the potential ethical and legal issues involved. For some problems, this step may be fairly straightforward. For others, a greater level of knowledge and experience may be necessary for the novice practitioner to fully understand the ethical and legal implications.

3. Consult ethical and legal guidelines, relevant case law, and district policies that might apply to a well-supported resolution. Although interns should be familiar with general ethical and legal guidelines, they may need supervision on policies specific to the state/district.

4. Evaluate the rights, responsibilities, and welfare of all parties involved. The intern and supervisor should collaboratively consider all of the individual perspectives that may be involved with the presenting problem, with paramount focus on the intern's responsibilities to the student.

5. Create a comprehensive list of any and all possible decisions for each issue. Prior to approaching this step, the intern should have collected an abundance of material, information, and/or data that will help identify various resolutions. This step involves some careful planning in order to fully delineate all alternative decisions for the presenting problem. The supervisor should facilitate this process by guiding the intern to several different outcomes that may not be immediately apparent.

6. Critically analyze the short-term, long-term, and immediate consequences of making each possible decision and evaluate possible detrimental effects on all parties involved. The potential impact of each decision on positive student outcomes should be of primary importance. Consultation and collaboration between the intern and the supervisor, as well as with other colleagues, may be helpful during this step.

7. Conduct a risk-benefit analysis and focus on the degree to which any of the consequences and/or benefits (for the student) of the final decision will actually occur. As this step demands a great deal of personal and professional judgment to ensure that negative outcomes are kept to a minimum, the supervisor should examine all the data together with the intern to increase the likelihood of making the best decision for the situation. The supervisor should encourage the intern to complete detailed documentation of the problem-solving process as this may provide support and protection if litigation results from the actions taken.

8. Aligning with professional code of ethics, make a decision and accept responsibility for the final decision. It is also recommended to monitor and follow up with the consequences of the decision, which provides opportunities for supervisors to review data and reflect with the intern on the consequences of his or her decisions.

Note. Based on information from Jacob et al. (2011).

Despite the lack of research to support better outcomes for students as a result of using systematic problem-solving models, research demonstrates that school psychologists who are explicitly trained and supervised at the university level using such models are more likely to feel prepared to appropriately resolve various professional issues (Jacob et al., 2011). Thus, in the event that school psychology interns are supervised in applying this skill to practice, they are more likely to develop a greater sense of self-efficacy for their ability to appropriately solve problems early in their career, which (we hope) will result in positive outcomes for students by helping supervisors and interns think through different options before making a decision. During one-to-one sessions or direct supervision in the field, supervisors are presented with ideal opportunities to provide corrective and/or positive feedback for the intern's practical application of a problem-solving model.

One common example of applying the Eight-Step Problem-Solving Model to internship supervision is helping the intern work through the limits of student confidentiality. If the intern is presented with a student who reveals they have been engaging in risky behaviors (e.g., underage drinking, experimenting with drugs, unprotected sex), then the intern needs to make an ethically appropriate decision on how to professionally move forward with the client in a way that minimizes potential harm to the student and others. The intern would first identify all the parameters of the situation (Step 1) to his or her supervisor. Depending on the intern's knowledge of ethical codes, previous case law, and district policies, the supervisor may need to provide some additional support for Steps 2–5. This is especially true for mandatory reporting policies and procedures, which may vary widely by district and state. In evaluating the short- and long-term consequences (Step 6), the intern should be encouraged to consult with other professionals or colleagues to gain broader perspectives from those who are not directly involved with the situation. For example, if the intern breaks confidentiality to report dangerous risk-taking behaviors, what are the potential implications for the student, the student's parents and family, classmates, teachers, and psychological/academic functioning? As for the last two steps, it is recommended that the supervisor evaluate what the intern has concluded and offer suggestions as necessary, focusing on helping the intern navigate the risk-benefit analysis and monitoring the consequences of their decisions.

It may be beneficial for the intern supervisors to utilize a problem-solving approach for the resolution of issues associated with their own responsibilities and roles that surface during supervision. As a supervisor for school psychology interns, there is not only a professional liability involved with this process but also an ethical responsibility. By integrating the problem-solving model approach to supervision, it may be helpful for addressing and facilitating the development of interns' professional behaviors or competencies. A school psychology internship supervisor may also be presented with a wide range of problems that are a result of the intern's own behavioral challenges such as arriving late to meetings, lack of organization, or even poor report writing skills. A systematic problem-solving approach used to facilitate supervision sessions can provide the intern with alternative ways to overcome such challenges before more serious issues arise.

SUMMARY

The internship experience is often regarded as the pinnacle of preparation to become a school psychologist. Indeed, it represents the culmination of years of coursework, practicum experience, and research and offers interns the opportunity to integrate all they have learned with the ultimate purpose of refining clinical skills and promoting ethical practice. Supervisor competence and commitment, therefore, are critical. The central message is the parallel between internship supervision and teaching. That is, there is a clear distinction between supervision that focuses on simply ensuring that interns do not make mistakes and supervision that is thoughtful, deliberate, and truly emphasizes nurturance and the teaching of new skills in a safe environment. Clearly, this is a responsibility that supervisors must take seriously, as interns' performance and behaviors will reflect upon their university programs, internship programs, and supervisors.

All intern supervisors must be well versed both in current guidelines from their professional organizations that speak to basic expectations regarding state-of-the-art training of interns and in the research informing supervisory processes. Furthermore, they must be cognizant of their own competencies in assuming an educative and supervisory role with others. The exact sequence of activities offered to interns should be well articulated and responsive to the intern's strengths and weaknesses and academic program expectations, and internship supervision should be seen as an iterative process in which supervisors provide structure and formative assessment of the process over time and make adjustments as the skills of the intern evolve. Interns should be offered experiences in the best of professional functioning if the field is to progress in improving student outcomes. The vitality of school psychology depends on every supervisor who mentors an intern to high levels of skill, compassion, and the certainty that school psychologists can make a significant contribution to children, families, teachers, and the educational enterprise.

REFERENCES

American Psychological Association. (2010). *Ethical principles of psychologists and code of conduct with the 2010 amendments.* Washington, DC: Author. Retrieved from http://www.apa.org/ethics/code/index.aspx

Burkard, A. W., Johnson, A. J., Madson, M. B., Pruitt, N. T., Contreras-Tadych, D. A., Kozlowski, J. M., ... Knox, S. (2006). Supervisor cultural responsiveness and unresponsiveness in cross-cultural supervision. *Journal of Counseling Psychology, 53*, 288–301. doi:10.1037/0022-0167.53.3.288

Campbell, J. M. (2006). *Essentials of clinical supervision.* Hoboken, NJ: Wiley.

Crespi, T. D., & Lopez, P. G. (1998). Practicum and internship supervision in the schools: Standards and considerations for school psychology supervisors. *Clinical Supervisor, 17*, 113–126.

Emerson, S. (1996). Creating a safe place for growth in supervision. *Contemporary Family Therapy, 18*, 393–403. doi:10.1007/BF02197050

Estrada, D., Frame, M. W., & Williams, C. B. (2004). Cross-cultural supervision: Guiding the conversation toward race and ethnicity. *Journal of Multicultural Counseling and Development, 32*, 307–319.

Falender, C. A., Cornish, J. A. E., Goodyear, R., Hatcher, R., Kaslow, N. J., Leventhal, G., ... Grus, C. (2004). Defining competencies in psychology supervision: A consensus statement. *Journal of Clinical Psychology, 60*, 771–785. doi:10.1002/jclp.20013

Goodyear, R. K., Bunch, K., & Claiborn, C. D. (2005). Current supervision scholarship in psychology: A five year review. *The Clinical Supervisor, 24*, 137–147. doi:10.1300/J001v24n01_07

Harvey, V. S., & Pearrow, M. (2010). Identifying challenges in supervising school psychologists. *Psychology in the Schools, 47*, 567–581. doi:10.1002/pits.20491

Harvey, V. S., & Struzziero, J. A. (2008). *Professional development and supervision of school psychologists: From intern to expert* (2nd ed.; A joint publication with the National Association of School Psychologists). Thousand Oaks, CA: Corwin Press.

Heckman-Stone, C. (2003). Trainee preferences for feedback and evaluation in clinical supervision. *Clinical Supervisor, 22*, 21–33. http://dx.doi.org/10.1300/J001v22n01_03

Jacob, S., Decker, D. M., & Hartshorne, T. S. (2011). *Ethics and law for school psychologists* (6th ed.). Hoboken, NJ: Wiley.

Kaslow, N. J., Falender, C. A., & Grus, C. L. (2012). Valuing and practicing competency-based supervision: A transformational leadership perspective. *Training and Education in Professional Psychology, 6*, 47–54. doi:10.1037/a0026704

Kaslow, N. J., Grus, C. L., Campbell, L. F., Fouad, N. A., Hatcher, R. L., & Rodolfa, E. R. (2009). Competency assessment toolkit for professional psychology. *Training and Education in Professional Psychology, 3*, S27–S45. doi:10.1037/a0015833

McCutcheon, S. R. (2009). Competency benchmarks: Implications for internship training. *Training and Education in Professional Psychology, 3*, S50–S53. doi:10.1037/a0016966

McIntosh, D. E., & Phelps, L. (2000). Supervision in school psychology: Where will the future take us? *Psychology in the Schools, 37*, 33–38. doi:10.1002/(SICI)1520-6807(200001)37:1<33::AID-PITS4>3.0.CO;2-F

National Association of School Psychologists. (2010a). *Model for comprehensive and integrated school psychological services*. Bethesda, MD: Author. Retrieved from http://www.nasponline.org/standards/2010standards/2_PracticeModel.pdf

National Association of School Psychologists. (2010b). *Principles for professional ethics*. Bethesda, MD: Author. Retrieved from http://www.nasponline.org/standards/2010standards/1_%20Ethical%20Principles.pdf

National Association of School Psychologists. (2010c). *Standards for graduate preparation of school psychologists*. Bethesda, MD: Author. Retrieved from http://www.nasponline.org/standards/2010standards/1_Graduate_Preparation.pdf

National Association of School Psychologists. (2011). *Supervision in school psychology* [Position Statement]. Bethesda, MD: Author. Retrieved from http://www.nasponline.org/about_nasp/positionpapers/Supervision_in_School.pdf

O'Donovan, A., Halford, W. K., & Walters, B. (2011). Towards best practice supervision of clinical psychology trainees. *Australian Psychologist, 46*, 101–112. doi:10.1111/j.1742-9544.2011.00033.x

Perry, C. W. (2012). Constructing professional identity in an online graduate clinical training program: Possibilities for online supervision. *Journal of Systemic Therapies, 31*, 53–67. doi:10.1521/jsyt.2012.31.3.53

Prus, J. S. (2009). Best practice guidelines for school psychology internships. *Communiqué, 37*(8).

Ramos-Sanchez, L., Esnil, E., Goodwin, A., Riggs, S., Touster, L. O., Wright, L. K., … Rodolfa, E. (2002). Negative supervisory events: Effects on supervision satisfaction and supervisory alliance. *Professional Psychology: Research and Practice, 33*, 197–202. doi:10.1037//0735-7028.33.2.197

Riva, M. T., & Cornish, J. A. E. (2008). Group supervision practices at psychology predoctoral internship programs: 15 years later. *Training and Education in Professional Psychology, 2*, 18–25. doi:10.1037/1931-3918.2.1.18

Stoltenberg, C. D., & Delworth, U. (1987). *Supervising counselors and therapists: A developmental approach*. San Francisco, CA: Jossey-Bass.

Sullivan, J. R. (2013). *Interns' perspectives on supervision in school psychology*. Unpublished manuscript, Department of Educational Psychology, University of Texas at San Antonio

Sullivan, J. R., & Conoley, J. C. (2008). Best practices in the supervision of interns. In A. Thomas & J. Grimes (Eds.), *Best practices in school psychology V* (pp. 1957–1974). Bethesda, MD: National Association of School Psychologists.

Wilczenski, F., & Coomey, S. M. (2006). Cyber-communication: Finding its place in school counseling practice, education, and professional development. *Professional School Counseling, 9*, 327–331.

40

Best Practices in National Certification and Credentialing in School Psychology

Eric Rossen

National Association of School Psychologists (MD)

OVERVIEW

Credentialing is a generic term that refers to the establishment of qualifications and authorization of individuals for professional practice by a state agency. The general objective of credentialing is to protect the public by requiring professionals to meet specific qualifications before practicing (Jacob, Decker, & Hartshorne, 2011). Credentialing is not unique to school psychology. In fact, professionals in related professions (e.g., social work, speech–language pathology, and audiology) also must become credentialed; however, the specifics associated with credentialing practices for each of these specialty areas vary.

This chapter will review some of the basic trends in school psychology credentialing, the various credentials for which school psychologists may qualify, the impact of national credentials for school psychologists, and best practices for earning and maintaining credentials for school psychologists.

While many school psychologists consider *certification* as a school-based regulation and *licensure* as a process of qualifying for private practice outside of school settings, the terminology actually varies from state to state. Up until the 1980s, most states utilized the term *certification* to describe the process of earning a credential to allow for work in the public schools. During the 1980s and 1990s, some states began to change that terminology to include other terms such as *license* or *endorsement* (Merrell, Ervin, & Peacock, 2011). As such, using the term certification to imply school psychology practice in public schools may be misleading in some states. Therefore, for the purposes of this chapter, the term *credential* is an umbrella term that includes both certification and licensure.

Each state maintains its own individual laws and regulations around the qualifications, title, setting, and scope of practice for a credential. Despite a set of national credentialing standards in school psychology developed by the National Association of School Psychologists (NASP, 2010a), the credentialing practices across states vary substantially. Given that school psychology credentialing deals with the legal regulation of professional practice and identity, school psychologists should maintain this knowledge as a part of the Legal, Ethical, and Professional Practice domain of the NASP *Model for Comprehensive and Integrated School Psychological Services* (NASP, 2010b).

BASIC CONSIDERATIONS

The credentialing of school psychologists occurs at the state level. School psychologists working in public schools within the United States are required to hold a credential issued from the state education agency, which also is commonly known as a state department of education. Texas is the only exception. Therefore, the vast majority of school psychology practitioners in the United States hold a credential issued from the state education agency (Fagan & Wise, 2007). In Texas, school psychologists working in public schools are regulated by the Texas Board of Examiners of Psychologists, an organization that also credentials psychologists who provide services outside of schools.

School psychologists often have to meet core requirements and qualifications that must be met by other school-based professionals (e.g., teachers, special educators). Therefore, school psychology credentialing is often more influenced by education professional norms rather than professional psychology norms. In fact, in some states school psychologists technically hold a teaching credential with a specialty endorsement in school psychology. Thus, school psychologists often know the most about psychology within educational settings, and the most about education within mental health settings. This has led to a concerted effort among school psychologists to ensure parity and status in education and schools while maintaining an identity as psychologists and mental health professionals (Fagan & Wise, 2007).

The formal credentialing of educational professionals began in the 19th century, although these processes were often "irregular and diverse" (Ravitch, 2003). While the early part of the 20th century saw major improvements in teacher certification practices, official state-level certification and the title of school psychologist did not emerge until the mid-1930s in New York and Pennsylvania (Fagan & Wise, 2007).

In 1954, the Thayer Conference convened to clarify the role, function, and credentialing of school psychologists. The Thayer Conference marked an important rallying point for the profession. At the time, only 20 states and the District of Columbia had any credentialing regulations for school psychologists (Ysseldyke & Schakel, 1983). The proceedings of the conference generated recommendations about the definition, functions, training, and qualifications of school psychologists, including the need for two levels of training (doctoral and subdoctoral) and recommended that state education agencies maintain responsibility for certification. Although the recommendations of the Thayer Conference provided a major step forward in regulating the profession through credentialing, states continued to lack uniformity in the credentialing of school psychologists over the next several decades.

NASP developed and approved its first set of national standards in the late 1970s, including standards for school psychology credentialing. However, it was not until January 1989 that NASP officially adopted the Nationally Certified School Psychologist (NCSP) credential. The development of a national credential that followed a set of nationally approved standards, combined with efforts across states for uniformity and consistency, continues to influence state credentialing standards. For example, the current national standard requiring a specialist-level degree (i.e., 60 graduate semester hours) for entry-level practice has led the majority of states to follow suit, including states that had previously required a minimum of a master's-level degree. In addition, most state education agencies now explicitly require a degree in school psychology, rather than allowing individuals with degrees in related fields (e.g., clinical psychology, educational psychology) to become credentialed as school psychologists. Despite improvements in establishing consistency in credentialing across states, however, significant differences continue to exist and are highlighted throughout this chapter.

BEST PRACTICES IN NATIONAL CERTIFICATION AND CREDENTIALING IN SCHOOL PSYCHOLOGY

Credentialing for school psychologists requires knowledge of the requirements for entry into the field, availability for professional progression or advancement, appropriate use of title, settings in which one can practice, and the requirements for maintaining a credential. Table 40.1 offers a brief overview of the essential elements of school psychology credentialing and the various requirements to be considered. Knowledge of credentialing practices is relevant for graduate students, graduate educators, and practitioners who must maintain credentials or possibly transfer to another state. School psychology graduate preparation programs should prepare their students to become credentialed as school psychologists and/or psychologists to ensure smooth transition into professional practice. While most graduate students have every intention of earning credentials for practice, they likely need explicit guidance through the process. Among a sample of school psychology doctoral students ($n = 216$) who had planned to apply for various credentials, only 34% had actively researched the requirements to obtain them (Hall, Wexelbaum, & Boucher, 2007).

Requirements for Entry-Level School Psychologists

Most school psychologists referencing this chapter already have obtained a school psychology credential. However, all school psychologists should consider the possibility that they may at some point transfer to a state that has different credentialing procedures and requirements. As of 2013, no state education agency has an official two-way reciprocity agreement that would allow credentials to transfer directly from one state to another. However, many states offer a more streamlined process for individuals transferring from a state with similar credentialing standards or those with established experience as a school psychologist. In fact, some states

Table 40.1. Essential Elements of Credentialing in School Psychology

Stage	Common Elements and Requirements to Consider
Entry level	• Degree program and level (master's, specialist, doctoral) • Field experiences and practicum • Internship • National and/or state program approval or accreditation • Praxis II exam in school psychology or other school psychology exam • Additional exams required by the state • Additional state requirements (e.g., fingerprints, background checks) • Recognition of national credentials (e.g., NCSP) • Recognition of credentialing by another state • Title • Setting (e.g., public school, private school, nonschool settings) • Scope of practice
Maintenance or renewal	• CPD; types of approved or accepted CPD • Supervision or mentoring • Experience
Advancement or progression	• Availability of advancement or tiers • Whether required to maintain employment • Supervision or mentoring • Experience (in state or out of state)

Note. NCSP = Nationally Certified School Psychologist; CPD = continuing professional development.

may accept experience as a school psychologist in another state in lieu of meeting other requirements to earn a credential (e.g., Arizona; Arizona Department of Education, n.d.). Given the variability across states, though, even a highly regarded veteran school psychologist may have difficulty meeting the entry-level credentialing requirements in another state. Therefore, school psychologists interested in working in a different state should visit their state education agency's website and NASP's State School Psychology Credentialing Requirements webpage (http://www.nasponline.org/certification/state_info_list.aspx) to ensure that all requirements can be met.

Graduate Preparation

A significant component of state credentialing requirements in school psychology pertains to an individual's graduate preparation experience. In fact, school psychology credentials are most often provided at the completion of graduate preparation and prior to professional practice. Nevertheless, the general credentialing requirements for graduate preparation range substantially across states. For example, to earn a school psychology credential in Washington, DC, one must have a master's degree in school psychology or in educational psychology that includes a minimum of 42 graduate semester hours and 500 hours of supervised field experience (DC Municipal Regulations Register,

n.d.). In contrast, to earn the initial school psychology credential in Alaska, one must have completed a NASP-approved school psychology program or maintain the NCSP credential, both of which require a minimum of 60 graduate semester hours, 1,200 hours of field-based internship experience, and preinternship practicum experiences (Alaska Department of Education and Early Development, n.d.).

Degree Requirements

At present, no state requires a doctoral degree in order to practice as a school psychologist. The highest degree level required in any state, and within NASP's national credentialing standards, is the educational specialist-level degree (i.e., minimum of 60 graduate semester hours). An increasing trend has been to require a degree specifically in school psychology and to align with NASP's graduate preparation standards, although several states still remain an exception. For example, the entry-level credential for school psychology practice in Oregon requires a "master's or higher degree in the behavioral sciences or their derivative therapeutic professions from a regionally accredited institution in the United States, or the foreign equivalent of such degree approved by the commission" (Oregon Teacher Standards and Practices Commission, 2011, p. 1). Without any clear indication of movement toward state education agencies requiring a doctoral degree, the specialist-level degree in school psychology will likely position school psychologists for practice in any state in the United States for the foreseeable future.

Field Experience

Most states require some form of supervised field experience during graduate preparation prior to the issuance of a credential, and many follow NASP's standards (i.e., 1,200 internship hours, 600 of which must be within a school setting). However, here again variability in credentialing standards exists across states, in the amount of supervised experience required, in who can qualify as a supervisor, and in the type of supervision. As an example, school psychologists in New Mexico have various pathways to earn the school psychologist credential, and each pathway differs in the field experience hours required (ranging from 300 to 1,200 hours) and the nature and focus of those experiences (e.g., specifically requiring work with students with emotional disabilities; New Mexico Administrative Code, n.d.). In this regard, New Mexico is an exception, although this reinforces the need for those potentially considering work in any state to become familiar with the credentialing requirements.

Notably, few states explicitly require preinternship practicum experiences, whereas many have minimum internship hours required. The NCSP credential, however, requires the accrual of some practicum experience that was distinct from and occurred prior to the internship and designed to develop and evaluate mastery of professional skills. Typically, the expectation is for practicum experiences to supplement knowledge obtained in concurrent coursework (e.g., practicing giving assessments of cognitive ability during a course in cognitive assessment). No specific minimum practicum hour requirement or structure is stated in NASP's credentialing standards.

Program Approval or Accreditation

The approval or accreditation status of the program from which one has graduated may have an impact on the ability to earn a state education agency school psychology credential. Most states require applicants to have completed a program with some level of accreditation or approval; however, state education agencies often refer to regional accreditation by a university rather than approval or accreditation by the school psychology program itself. Having this broad institutional accreditation requirement, as opposed to requiring the individual program to have some level of distinct approval, is generally an artifact of systems-wide

state education agency credentialing requirements for all educators that do not differentiate among school psychologists and other educators. Nevertheless, some states have been more proactive in requiring or partially requiring school psychologists to graduate from a program that has NASP approval or American Psychological Association (APA) accreditation (e.g., Alaska, Georgia, Iowa, Minnesota; see http://www.nasponline.org/certification/statencsp.aspx and http://www.nasponline.org/certification/state_info_list.aspx for brief summaries of state requirements for school psychologist credentialing).

As of 2013, graduates of NASP-approved programs will have met the basic graduate preparation requirements in every state to earn the state school psychology credential, short of any additional exams that may be required (e.g., the Praxis II). Graduating from a NASP-approved program also qualifies individuals for the NCSP credential, which helps ensure smooth entry into professional practice as a school psychologist. NASP's program approval and credentialing processes offer an added level of accountability through peer review and compliance with national standards, allowing some states to defer to them in their credentialing language. Thus, by relying on NASP's graduate preparation and credentialing standards, states may reduce administrative time for reviewing applications from potential school psychologists.

Exams

The Praxis II school psychologist exam, administered by the Educational Testing Service, remains the standard exam required by many programs prior to graduation, by many states for school psychology certification or licensure, and by NASP for the NCSP credential. However, not all states require passing the exam. Taken further, not all states maintain the same passing score. NASP has set the passing score at 165, and many states have adopted this score as well. To date, no states require a higher passing score than 165. However, 15 states (as of 2013) have adopted a lower passing score (e.g., West Virginia's passing score is 148; Educational Testing Service, 2013). Thus, school psychologists who have achieved a state's passing score without meeting the national cut score of 165 may consider retaking the exam should the need arise to work in another state. Notably, the Educational Testing Service states that the Praxis II exam score expires after 10 years. Therefore, school psychologists who took the exam more than 10 years ago and plan to work in a new state may need to take the exam again. (For information on passing scores on the Praxis II for each state that has adopted the exam for certification or licensure, see http://www.ets.org/s/praxis/pdf/passing_scores.pdf.)

Some states may require individuals to pass additional exams beyond the Praxis II to become credentialed as a school psychologist. Florida and Alabama, for example, require all educators to pass basic skills examinations (Alabama State Department of Education, 2012; Florida Department of Education, 2010). Mississippi requires individuals to pass the Praxis I Pre-Professional Skills Test (Mississippi Department of Education, n.d.). Illinois requires individuals to pass an independently developed exam for school psychologists that closely aligns with state standards (Illinois Licensure Testing System, n.d.). Further, although generally rare, some states require individuals to complete additional coursework specific to practicing within that state. For example, North Dakota's state education agency requires a three-credit course in Native American and multicultural studies for all in-state and out-of-state applicants for a credential (North Dakota Education and Standards Board, n.d.). Nevada requires all educational personnel to show knowledge of the U.S. and Nevada constitutions either by examination, in normal school study, or through postsecondary transcripts (Nevada Legislature, n.d.; see NRS 391.021). No state education agency currently requires passing of the Examination for Professional Practice in Psychology, sponsored and administered by the Association of State and Provincial Psychology Boards, for a school psychology credential.

Methods for Obtaining State Education Agency Credential

Fagan and Wise (2007) describe two methods for applicants to obtain the state education agency school psychology credential: transcript review and program approval. During the transcript review process, applicants submit materials directly to the state education agency, including transcripts and other necessary forms of documentation (e.g., internship completion, official score reports for the Praxis II or other related exams, application processing fees). The state education agency then reviews the documents and either approves, defers, or denies the application. Most states follow this process. In contrast, only a few states (e.g., Alaska, California) employ a program-approval process, whereby the application must be submitted through the university or institution where the individual completed his or her graduate preparation. In this case, greater responsibility is placed on the program and institution to ensure that all credentialing requirements have been met before a letter of endorsement is issued to the state education agency. In some cases, out-of-state applicants may even need to work with an in-state program or institution to complete this process. Applicants should contact their state education agency to identify the appropriate application process to follow.

Progression or Advancement

Multiple levels of credentialing for school psychologists exist in several states that allow for natural progression and career advancement. Commonly, these levels will include some emergency or provisional credential, an initial or entry-level short-term credential, and then a longer-term professional credential. An emergency or provisional credential may allow a school psychologist to engage in temporary work while completing a final entry-level requirement, such as internship or coursework. The initial or entry-level credential may last anywhere from 2 to 5 years, at which time the school psychologist must apply for the next level by accruing experience or meeting some additional criteria such as holding the NCSP credential, participating in mentorship, or demonstrating positive personnel evaluations.

In some states, progression or advancement is not mandatory. For example, Mississippi's state education agency offers Class AAA and Class AAAA credentials. Both Class AAA and Class AAAA require completion of a NASP-approved program or its equivalent and renewal every 5 years. The only difference between the two levels is that Class AAAA requires a doctoral degree in psychology (not school psychology, specifically), whereas a specialist-level degree in school psychology qualifies for the Class AAA only (Mississippi Department of Education, n.d.). Certain districts may offer pay differentials among different levels.

Use of Title

Credentials also determine an individual's professional title and the jurisdiction in which that title can be used. The majority of states allow for the use of the title "school psychologist" in schools, particularly given that the term appears in federal law. However, a couple states have imposed restrictions on including "psychologist" anywhere within a title, limiting its use for those with a doctoral degree and licensed by a board of psychology for practice outside of schools. Currently, only Arkansas (Arkansas Department of Education, n.d.) and Texas (Texas State Board of Examiners of Psychologists, 2013; see Rule 465.38) legally restrict use of the title of school psychologist. Arkansas' state education agency school psychology credential requires use of the title "school psychology specialist," and Texas uses the title "licensed specialist in school psychology." Notice that both credentials do not include the term "psychologist" because of the view that the inclusion of this term could contribute to public confusion.

Perhaps antithetical to the goal of ensuring consistent credentialing practices across states, the Texas State Board of Examiners of Psychologists, which licenses school psychology practice in Texas, previously restricted use of the NCSP credential because it includes the word "psychologist." As a result, individuals in Texas who had rightfully earned and maintained the NCSP could have received sanctions and fines for including the credential on business cards, letterhead, and e-mails, or when signing reports and other official documents related to the professional practice of school psychology. However, following joint advocacy from NASP and the Texas Association of School Psychologists in 2012, the Texas State Board of Examiners of Psychologists acknowledged the NCSP as a credential—not a title— and has since allowed those holding the NCSP to include it on signature pages and other correspondence.

Model Licensure Act

For decades, APA maintained its position that psychological practice requires a doctoral-level degree, although it supported an exemption of this rule for those practicing in schools. In 2009 and 2010, however, APA proposed revisions to its Model Act for State Licensure of Psychologists that would have eliminated this exemption. Importantly, a proposed change from APA would not lead to a mandatory change in state credentialing statutes or regulations related to title. Rather, the proposed change would only offer recommendations that state credentialing bodies could follow, modify, or ignore. Nevertheless, the potential for widespread constraints on use of the title "school psychologist" for those without a doctoral-level degree caused NASP and other allied groups to strongly advocate against these changes. In February 2010, APA disseminated the final revisions of the Model Act after removing proposed language that might have restricted use of the "school psychologist" title. Instead, APA maintained the exemption for school psychologists who practice in the schools:

> The prior version of this Model Act included an exemption for the use of the terms "school

psychologist" or "certified school psychologist" for all individuals credentialed by the state agency regulating practice in public schools. This version acknowledges the authority of the relevant state education agency to credential individuals to provide school psychological services in settings under their purview.... Additionally, the title so conferred, which must include the word "school," is to be used solely while engaged in employment within those settings. (APA, 2010, p. 11)

Scope of Practice

State regulatory agencies have the authority to set rules and limits on the actual services provided by credentialed professionals. This may include the roles and range of services offered as well as the settings in which professionals can practice. Several states have adopted or aligned with NASP's practice standards (e.g., Kansas State Department of Education, 2009; Maine State Legislature, 2011), and in most cases the state education agency credential only allows for practice within school settings in that state, including work in schools on a contractual basis. As such, by providing psychological services outside of schools or school psychological services in a state outside the state education agency's jurisdiction, an individual may be operating outside the scope of practice of his or her existing credential. In those cases, the individual would require a credential from a licensing board that defines the scope of practice within that particular setting (e.g., a board of psychology).

Maintenance and Renewal

The majority of credentials require continued maintenance and regular renewal. However, like most aspects of the credentialing process, the specifics for renewal vary among states for school psychologists. To illustrate, entry-level school psychologists in New York first earn the provisional certificate. After 5 years of experience, they become eligible to earn the permanent certificate, which never expires and does not require renewal or any continuing professional development (New York State Education Department, 2012). Conversely, Pennsylvania requires 180 hours of continuing professional development (CPD) every 5 years from providers approved by Pennsylvania's state education agency.

Types of CPD

Many state education agencies and related licensing boards go beyond requiring a set number of CPD hours by prescribing certain types of CPD that must be obtained. As an example, beginning in July 2015, Connecticut's state education agency requires school psychologists seeking a professional certificate to have at least 20 CPD hours in "design, assessment and implementation of behavioral support and analysis services for students with behavioral disabilities or autism spectrum disorders" (Connecticut State Department of Education, n.d., p. 107). As another example, the NCSP credential requires 75 hours of CPD every 3 years, with three of those hours obtained on topics related to ethics or legal regulation in school psychology. The NCSP credential also requires that 10 of the 75 CPD hours be provided by NASP- or APA-approved sponsors of CPD. However, some CPD hours accepted by one state education agency may not be accepted by another, and school psychologists should be aware of the specific requirements for each credential they wish to maintain.

Compliance With Ethical and Legal Standards

Many credentialing boards also require adherence to ethical and legal standards in order to maintain a credential. Violations of legal and ethical conduct could sometimes result in sanctions, including probation, fines, or the removal of a credential. Following censure by a state board of psychology or state education agency, the nature of such violations, along with the name of the culpable individual, is often made available to the public. NASP maintains an Ethical and Professional Practices Committee (see http://www.nasponline.org/standards/ethics/index.aspx) that provides a mechanism for filing ethical complaints about NASP members or those holding the NCSP credential, as well as a public notice of previous NASP disciplinary actions against those individuals. The National Association of State Directors of Teacher Education and Certification also maintains a central database of individual state education agency reports on disciplinary actions taken against credentialed education personnel, known as the National Association of State Directors of Teacher Education and Certification Clearinghouse (http://www.nasdtec.net/?page=Resources). Inclusion in this database may preclude the renewal of a credential or the ability to earn a credential elsewhere. However, the National Association of State Directors of Teacher Education and Certification Clearinghouse does not allow public access or disclose disciplinary actions to the public.

Supervision or Experience

Some states require some degree of supervision and/or experience to maintain or advance a credential. As an example, Delaware requires school psychologists with the initial license to receive mentoring each year along with at least two out of three positive work evaluations (Delaware Office of the Registrar of Regulations, n.d.). Missouri requires mentoring during the first 2 years of employment, the first of which may be an internship, to advance from an initial to a continuous career state credential (Missouri Department of Elementary and Secondary Education, 2005). Nebraska, on the other hand, requires demonstration of work experience or preapproved graduate coursework within each renewal period (Nebraska Department of Education, 2011). Beginning in 2016, when NASP's 2010 Standards for the Credentialing of School Psychologists takes effect, first-time holders of the NCSP will also have to receive a minimum of one academic year of professional support from a mentor or supervisor, with a recommendation of 1 hour of supervision or mentoring per week.

NASP Standards for the Credentialing of School Psychologists

NASP introduced and approved its first set of national standards in the 1970s, including national credentialing standards that were officially adopted in 1978. Since then, NASP's standards have undergone several revisions, with the most recent revision occurring in 2010 following a 3-year process that involved analyzing the field, developing drafts by varied professionals, soliciting input and commentary from practitioners, and receiving final approval from the NASP leadership. The 2010 standards represent a unified set of national principles linking graduate preparation, professional practice, ethical behavior, and credentialing for school psychologists working primarily in schools. More specifically, the standards are designed to "provide guidance to state education agencies and other state and national agencies for credentialing school psychologists and regulating the practice of school psychology" (NASP, 2010a, p. 1).

NCSP Credential

The NCSP credential was introduced in 1989, and, as of 2013, 12,500 individuals hold an active NCSP credential. As noted above, NASP approved the first set of national credentialing standards in 1978. However, unlike other allied professional organizations that maintained a national credentialing system, NASP had no method of incentivizing or formally recognizing those who met those standards until the development of the NCSP credential (see Rossen & Williams, 2013, for a history of the NCSP credential).

The NCSP credential currently serves several purposes. First, the credential helps acknowledge and recognize individuals who have met NASP's national credentialing standards as determined by NASP's National School Psychology Certification Board. Second, standards that establish the NCSP credential act as a model of the implementation of the credentialing standards for state education agencies. Third, it promotes uniform credentialing standards across state agencies and facilitates streamlined credentialing of school psychologists across states.

Individuals earn the NCSP credential through two general pathways. One is for graduates of NASP-approved graduate preparation programs, and the second is for graduates of non-NASP-approved programs. Graduates of NASP-approved programs have a streamlined application process, given that the program itself has undergone peer review to ensure its alignment with national standards. The second pathway requires graduates of non-NASP-approved programs to apply through submission of a comprehensive portfolio and a case study to demonstrate their knowledge and skills across all domains of the national standards. Both pathways reflect identical eligibility requirements for the NCSP credential: (a) completion of 60 graduate semester hours or 90 quarter hours through an organized program of study that is officially titled "school psychology," of which at least 54 graduate semester hours or 81 quarter hours are exclusive of credit for the supervised internship experience; (b) successful completion of a 1,200-hour internship in school psychology, of which at least 600 hours must be in a school setting; and (c) achievement of a passing score (165) on the Praxis II examination. More information on the application process and requirements may be found on the NASP webpage (http://www.nasponline.org/certification/becomeNCSP.aspx).

The NCSP is a nonpractice credential. In other words, obtaining the NCSP does not certify or license an individual to provide services. Only state certification or licensing boards have that authority. Thus, a school psychologist with the NCSP credential must register with the appropriate state agency (e.g., state education agency). However, through ongoing advocacy efforts from NASP and state associations over the last 2 decades, 31 state credentialing agencies as of 2013 recognize the NCSP credential within state school psychologist credentialing laws or regulations. In these 31 states, an individual may need to simply provide documentation of his or her NCSP certificate to the state agency to be issued the appropriate state credential.

NASP recommends that states adopt the national credentialing standards to promote consistency across states, although NASP does not endorse the NCSP credential as the sole method of obtaining a state school psychology credential. See http://www.nasponline.org/certification/statencsp.aspx for a list of states that recognize the NCSP credential.

Credentialing for Practice Outside of Schools

Most school psychologists work in schools and approximately 87% of all working school psychologists maintain a credential through their state department of education (Curtis, Castillo, & Gelley, 2012). Nevertheless, more than 22% of school psychologists report engaging in some form of secondary employment (Curtis et al., 2008), with approximately 4% working in private practice as a source of primary employment and 6% as a source of secondary employment (Curtis et al., 2012). It might be anticipated that this figure may increase as the desire to supplement incomes rises (Rossen, 2011). In some states, such as Arizona (Arizona Department of Education, n.d.) and New Mexico (New Mexico Administrative Code, n.d.), the possession of a nonschool credential, such as a license issued by the board of psychology, supports an individual's eligibility for the state education agency school psychology credential.

Doctoral-Level Credentials

As previously mentioned, practicing psychology outside of schools typically requires a license from a state board of psychology or a related licensing board that governs the provision of mental health services. Further, the majority of states reserve the title "psychologist" for those with a doctoral degree, a passing score on the Examination for Professional Practice in Psychology (varies by state), and a prescribed number of hours of field supervision that in some cases must be completed after receipt of the doctoral degree (Association of State and Provincial Psychology Boards, n.d.). Some states also require individuals to pass an oral examination or state jurisprudence exam, to graduate from an APA-accredited program or its equivalent, and, in rare instances, to complete an Association of Psychology Postdoctoral Internship Center or APA-accredited doctoral internship (e.g., Mississippi; Mississippi Board of Psychology, n.d.). In most instances, the general psychology license typically offers a broad scope of practice, with the understanding that those professionals will work within their areas of competency. As noted earlier, APA supports the position that anyone providing psychological services should obtain a doctoral degree, with the included exemption of those providing services in schools.

The Association of State and Provincial Psychology Boards offers guidelines to states to help standardize the licensing requirements of psychologists across the United States and Canada. The Association of State and Provincial Psychology Boards also sponsors and administers the Examination for Professional Practice in Psychology and has developed several methods to improve the portability and mobility of licenses to practice psychology across states. First, the Association of State and Provincial Psychology Boards developed the Certificate of Professional Qualification in Psychology, which was designed to allow for improved reciprocity among psychology boards for doctoral-level psychologists. As of 2013, 42 jurisdictions within the United States and Canada recognize the Certificate of Professional Qualification in Psychology, and more jurisdictions are in the legislative processes for seeking acceptance. The Association of State and Provincial Psychology Boards also developed the Interjurisdictional Practice Certificate, which was designed to allow for temporary permission to practice in another jurisdiction. To illustrate, a psychologist licensed in Florida can apply for temporary permission to serve as an expert witness (i.e., practice psychology) on a case in Texas. Finally, the Association of State and Provincial Psychology Boards created the Agreement of Reciprocity, which contains a list of jurisdictions in a cooperative agreement to allow members with a license in one state to obtain a license in any of the others.

Nondoctoral-Level Credentials

Some states allow for practice outside of schools for school psychologists without a doctoral degree. These states vary significantly in the nature of the credentials they offer, the requirements to earn them, and the associated scope of practice. Therefore, school psychologists interested in potentially working outside of schools in some capacity should research their options thoroughly, including at the Association of State and Provincial Psychology Boards website (http://www.asppb.org) and NASP's State School Psychology Credentialing Requirements webpage (http://www.nasponline.org/certification/state_info_list.aspx). Some

examples of states that provide nondoctoral credentials for practice outside of schools include the following:

- *Massachusetts*: The Massachusetts Board of Registration of Allied Mental Health and Human Service Professionals (2013) grants licensure as an Educational Psychologist with 2 years of supervised experience as a school psychologist. This licensure allows for private practice and does not require a doctoral degree. The Board of Allied Mental Health and Human Service Professionals is distinct from the Massachusetts Board of Registration of Psychologists.
- *West Virginia:* The West Virginia Board of Examiners of Psychology (2010) has a two-level license. Level II allows for private practice of school psychology services as defined in the state statute. The Board of Examiners requires a passing score of 165 on the Praxis II.
- *South Carolina:* An individual who holds the state education agency school psychology credential may apply as a Licensed Psycho-Educational Specialist through the South Carolina Department of Labor, Licensing, and Regulation (n.d.) in order to practice in the private sector. To do so, the applicant must meet the following requirements: (a) have 2 years of experience as a school psychologist, with at least 1 of those years under the supervision of a Licensed Psycho-Educational Specialist; (b) maintain the state education agency credential as a Level II or III school psychologist in South Carolina; and (c) obtain a passing score of 165 on the Praxis II.
- *Wyoming:* The Wyoming State Board of Psychology (2012) offers a designation of Specialist in School Psychology that can be met by an individual who has the NCSP credential and maintains the state education agency credential. This designation requires supervision from a licensed psychologist.
- *California:* California offers the Licensed Educational Psychologist credential through the California Board of Behavioral Sciences (n.d.) to nondoctoral-level school psychologists. This board is distinct from the California Board of Psychology.

Some state psychology boards also offer a nondoctoral credential to work under the supervision of a licensed psychologist. Maryland, for example, offers a Psychology Associate credential that allows for the supervised practice of psychology (Maryland Board of Examiners of Psychologists, n.d.). This credential requires a master's degree in a program that has a primary emphasis on psychology, which qualifies all graduates of school psychology programs.

Other Potential Credentials

Aside from credentials as a psychologist, school psychologist, or the related credentials described above, school psychologists may have eligibility for other related credentials from various credentialing bodies, such as the following (not all-inclusive):

- Board Certified Behavior Analyst awarded by the Behavior Analyst Certification Board
- Diplomate in School Psychology awarded by the American Board of School Psychology, which is a member of the American Board of Professional Psychology
- Diplomate in School Neuropsychology awarded by the American Board of School Neuropsychology
- Licensed Professional Counselor, Licensed Clinical Professional Counselor, or Licensed Mental Health Counselor, which often varies by state
- Licensed Clinical Social Worker, Licensed Master Social Worker, or other variations by state
- Educational diagnostician or psychometrist
- Supervisory/administration credentials
- Marriage and family therapist

Note that some available credentials, such as the NCSP, are nonpractice credentials, meaning that holding the credential does not necessarily allow one to engage in practice.

Advocacy

School psychologists should consider themselves capable and proactive advocates, particularly on issues related to credentialing. Given the relatively low number of school psychologists in relation to other educators, the unique qualifications and national credentialing standards are often unknown or overlooked by state education agencies and other public policy makers. This fact is exacerbated by almost half of all state education agencies not having a credentialed school psychologist consultant on staff to provide assistance and guidance or a consistent voice for school psychology within the department. Thus, all school psychologists, with guidance from their states' school psychology associations, should actively work with the people responsible for overseeing credentialing in their state government to ensure that the national standards for school psychological practice are reflected in adopted state policies and laws.

Some aspects of educator credentialing reside in state laws and statutes, whereas the majority of credentialing components are incorporated within state regulation. State statutes and regulations are both legal avenues with which school psychologists must comply, although statutes have the force of law (i.e., mandate) and regulations are the interpretation of law (i.e., how to do it). Generally, state regulations provide more opportunity for change, whereas changes to state statutes require legislative action and therefore create more challenges and thus occur less frequently.

School psychologists who engage in advocacy efforts should consider the language used, particularly in state statutes, because any changes in the field may create difficulties in the future. As an example, if a state chooses to recognize NASP's national standards for practice and graduate preparation, the state might consider using the language such as "consistent with the National Association of School Psychologist's standards for the credentialing and graduate preparation of school psychologists, or the standards approved by its successor." This last phrase allows for the contingency of a change in name for NASP or revision of its standards without having to change the statute.

Acceptance of the NCSP credential as one path to state credentialing is also an important advocacy objective. Including language in state regulations or statutes that recognizes individuals who hold a current NCSP as being eligible for the state credential (in whole or in part) can help improve the recruitment of school psychologists to a state. It generally attracts a larger pool of applicants because the credentialing process is easier and less redundant. School psychologists interested in such advocacy should consider becoming active within their state school psychology association's legislative and advocacy work.

Many districts, and some states, offer stipends for educators holding a national credential. In many instances, schools provide stipends to nationally board certified teachers, although they do not provide such stipends to those holding the NCSP credential. NCSP parity refers to the equal treatment of school psychologists holding national certification as other educators with a national credential. Through local-level advocacy efforts, some districts and states have successfully incorporated NCSP parity into state legislation or district policy. For more information on this issue, school psychologists should visit NASP's webpage on advocating for NCSP parity (http://www.nasponline. org/advocacy/NCSPstateinitiatives.aspx), which includes advocacy tips, a table that compares national credentials across disciplines, recommended language for state statutes and school board policies, and an adaptable NCSP advocacy presentation that can be presented to a local school board.

SUMMARY

Credentialing refers to the establishment of qualifications for professional practice. School psychology credentialing, an umbrella term for certification and licensure, occurs at the state level. Marked improvements and increased consistency in state statutes and regulations that govern credentialing in school psychology have occurred across the United States since the offering of the first official school psychology credential in the 1930s. However, statutes and regulations for credentialing still vary considerably across states in relation to entry-level requirements for professional practice, titling, maintenance requirements, and the scope of practice. The development of NASP's national standards for credentialing, along with the NCSP credential, have helped set a benchmark model for states, with the NCSP credential having obtained official recognition from 31 states (as of 2013).

The overwhelming majority of practicing school psychologists work in public schools, suggesting that most school psychologists will need to abide by the credentialing guidelines provided by a state education agency. Nevertheless, an increasing number of school psychologists maintain other credentials for related practices outside of schools (e.g., psychology licensure from a state board of psychology), which can make the overall credentialing process difficult to navigate. In all cases, school psychologists should closely monitor the requirements for maintenance of their credentials and become cognizant of the credentialing requirements in states and settings that they may wish to seek future employment. Intern supervisors and graduate educators may support their school psychology graduate students by informing them of the various components of credentialing and may help position them to qualify for the credentials that align with their eventual career goals and ensure a smooth transition into professional practice.

REFERENCES

Alabama State Department of Education. (2012). *General information regarding Alabama certification.* Montgomery, AL: Author. Retrieved from http://public.alsde.edu/office/otl/tc/General%20 Information/General%20Information%20Regarding%20Alabama %20Certification.pdf

Alaska Department of Education and Early Development. (n.d.). *Type C special services certificate.* Juneau, AK: Author. Retrieved from http://www.eed.state.ak.us/teachercertification/typeC.html

American Psychological Association. (2010). *Model act for state licensure of psychologists.* Washington, DC: Author. Retrieved from http://www.apa.org/about/policy/model-act-2010.pdf

Arkansas Department of Education. (n.d.). *Levels and areas of licensure.* Little Rock, AR: Author. Retrieved from http://www.arkansased.org/public/userfiles/HR_and_Educator_Effectiveness/HR_Educator_Licensure/Levels_and_Areas_of_Licensure_1-2013.pdf

Arizona Department of Education. (n.d.). *Requirements for school psychologist, prekindergarten–12 certificate.* Phoenix, AZ: Author. Retrieved from http://www.azed.gov/educator-certification/files/2011/09/school-psychologist-certificate.pdf

Association of State and Provincial Psychology Boards. (n.d.). *Requirements for licensure or registration to practice psychology.* Peachtree, GA: Author. Retrieved from http://www.asppb.net/?page=reqpsych

California Board of Behavioral Sciences. (n.d.). *Licensed educational psychologist (LEP) requirements.* Sacramento, CA: Author. Retrieved from: http://www.bbs.ca.gov/app-reg/lep.shtml

Connecticut State Department of Education. (n.d.). *Regulations concerning state educator certificates, permits and authorizations.* Hartford, CT: Author. Retrieved from http://www.sde.ct.gov/sde/lib/sde/pdf/cert/regulations/Regulations_Adopted_on_12-1-2010.pdf

Curtis, M. J., Castillo, J. M., & Gelley, C. (2012). School psychology 2010: Demographics, employment, and the context for professional practices–Part 1. *Communiqué, 40*(7), 1, 28–30.

Curtis, M. J., Lopez, A. D., Castillo, J. M., Batsche, G. M., Minch, D., & Smith, J. C. (2008). The status of school psychology: Demographic characteristics, employment conditions, professional practices, and continuing professional development. *Communiqué, 36*(5), 27–29.

DC Municipal Regulations and Register. (n.d.). Rule: 5-E1659: School psychologist. Washington, DC: Author. Retrieved from http://www.dcregs.dc.gov/Gateway/RuleHome.aspx?RuleNumber =5-E1659

Delaware Office of the Registrar of Regulations. (n.d.). *Title 14 Education: Delaware administrative code.* Dover, DE: Author. Retrieved from http://regulations.delaware.gov/AdminCode/title14/1500/1510.pdf

Educational Testing Service. (2013). *The Praxis series passing scores by test and state.* Washington, DC: Author. Retrieved from http://www.ets.org/s/praxis/pdf/passing_scores.pdf

Fagan, T. K., & Wise, P. S. (2007). *School psychology: Past, present, and future* (3rd ed.). Bethesda, MD: National Association of School Psychologists.

Florida Department of Education. (2010). *Florida teacher certification examinations: Test information guide for school psychologist PK–12* (3rd ed.). Tallahassee, FL: Author. Retrieved from http://www.fl.nesinc.com/PDFs/School_Psych_TIG_3rdEdition_DOE061710.pdf

Hall, J. E., Wexelbaum, S. F., & Boucher, A. P. (2007). Doctoral student awareness of licensure, credentialing, and professional organizations in psychology: The 2005 National Register International Survey. *Training and Education in Professional Psychology, 1,* 38–48. doi:10.1037/1931-3918.1.1.38

Illinois Licensure Testing System. (n.d.). *Program Overview.* Amhearst, MA: Author. Retrieved from http://www.il.nesinc.com/1L17_overview.asp

Jacob, S., Decker, D. M., & Hartshorne, T. S. (2011). *Ethics and law for school psychologists* (6th ed.). Hoboken, NJ: Wiley.

Kansas State Department of Education. (2009). *Regulations and standards for Kansas educators.* Topeka, KS: Author. Retrieved from http://www.ksde.org/Portals/0/TLA/Licensure/Licensure%20Documents/CertHandbook8-2011%20FINAL.pdf

Maine State Legislature. (2011). *Maine revised statutes: Certification of educational personnel.* Augusta, ME: Author. Retrieved from http://www.mainelegislature.org/legis/statutes/20-A/title20-Ach502.pdf

Maryland Board of Examiners of Psychologists. (n.d.). *General information: Psychology associate.* Baltimore, MD: Author. Retrieved from http://dhmh.maryland.gov/psych/pdf/general_information_psychology_associate.pdf

Massachusetts Board of Registration of Allied Mental Health and Human Service Professionals. (2013). *262 CMR 5.00: Requirements for licensure as an educational psychologist.* Boston, MA: Author. http://www.mass.gov/ocabr/licensee/dpl-boards/mh/regulations/rules-and-regs/262-cmr-500.html

Merrell, K. W., Ervin, R. A., & Peacock, G. G. (2011). *School psychology for the 21st century: Foundations and practices* (2nd ed.). New York, NY: Guilford Press.

Mississippi Board of Psychology. (n.d.). *Rules and regulations of the Mississippi board of psychology.* Yazoo City, MS: Author. Retrieved from http://www.psychologyboard.state.ms.us/Psy%20Documents/Rules_Regulation_20130225.pdf

Mississippi Department of Education. (n.d.). *General guidelines: Mississippi educator licensure.* Jackson, MS: Author. Retrieved from http://www.mde.k12.ms.us/docs/educator-licensure/licensure-guidelines-revised-3-12.pdf?sfvrsn=0

Missouri Department of Elementary and Secondary Education. (2005). *Certification requirements for school psychologist.* Jefferson City, MO: Author. Retrieved from http://www.dese.mo.gov/schoollaw/rulesregs/EducCertManual/27%20School%20Psychologist%2004-final.pdf

National Association of School Psychologists. (2010a). *Standards for credentialing of school psychologists.* Bethesda, MD: National Association of School Psychologists. Retrieved from http://www.nasponline.org/standards/2010standards/2_Credentialing_Standards.pdf

National Association of School Psychologists. (2010b). *Model for comprehensive and integrated school psychological services.* Bethesda, MD: Author. Retrieved from http://www.nasponline.org/standards/2010standards/2_PracticeModel.pdf

Nebraska Education Department. (2011). *Rule 21: Regulations for the issuance of certificates and permits to teach, provide special services, and administer in Nebraska schools: Title 92, Nebraska administrative code, chapter 21.* Lincoln, NE: Author. Retrieved from http://www.education.ne.gov/legal/webrulespdf/clean_rule%2021_%202011.pdf

Nevada Legislature. (n.d.). *Chapter 391–Personnel.* Retrieved from http://www.leg.state.nv.us/NRS/NRS-391.html#NRS391Sec019

New Mexico Administrative Code. (n.d.). *Licensure for school psychologists, preK–12.* Retrieved from http://www.nmcpr.state.nm.us/nmac/parts/title06/06.063.0005.htm

New York State Education Department. (2012). *Types of certificates and licenses.* Albany, NY: Author. Retrieved from http://www.highered.nysed.gov/tcert/certificate/typesofcerts.html

North Dakota Education and Standards Board. (n.d.). *Licensure: How do I apply?* Bismarck, ND: Author. Retrieved from http://www.nd.gov/espb/licensure/apply3.html

Oregon Teacher Standards and Practices Commission. (2011). *Application instructions for an Oregon initial school psychologist license.* Salem, OR: Author. Retrieved from http://www.tspc.state.or.us/pdf/0016.pdf

Ravitch, D. (2003). *A brief history of teacher professionalism.* Washington, DC: U.S. Department of Education. Retrieved from http://www2.ed.gov/admins/tchrqual/learn/preparingteachersconference/ravitch.html

Rossen, E. (2011). Essential tools for prospective and early career school psychologists: Credentialing for school and independent practice. *Communiqué, 40*(1), 30.

Rossen, E., & Williams, B. B. (2013). The life and times of the National School Psychology Certification System. *Communiqué, 41*(7), *1,* 28–30.

South Carolina Department of Labor, Licensing, and Regulation. (n.d.). *Licensure requirements for applicants to be Licensed Psycho-Educational Specialists.* Columbia, SC: Author. Retrieved from http://www.llr.state.sc.us/pol/counselors/index.asp?file=LPES%20Req.HTM

Texas State Board of Examiners of Psychologists. (2013). *Act and rules.* Austin, TX: Author. Retrieved from http://www.tsbep.state.tx.us/files/agencydocs/TSBEPRuleBook.pdf

West Virginia Board of Examiners of Psychology. (2010). *Licensure requirements 2010.* Charleston, WV: Author. Retrieved from http://www.wvpsychbd.org/Licensure%20Info%202010.pdf

Wyoming State Board of Psychology. (2012). *Chapter 6: Certification requirements.* Cheyenne, WY: Author. Retrieved from http://soswy.state.wy.us/Rules/RULES/8710.pdf

Ysseldyke, J. E., & Schakel, J. A. (1983). Directions in school psychology. In G. W. Hynd (Ed.), *The school psychologist: An introduction* (pp. 3–26). Syracuse, NY: Syracuse University Press.

41

Best Practices in Early Career School Psychology Transitions

Arlene E. Silva
Massachusetts School of Professional Psychology
Daniel S. Newman
National Louis University (IL)
Meaghan C. Guiney
Fairleigh Dickinson University (NJ)

OVERVIEW

The early career of a school psychologist occupies a distinct place within the career trajectory, often marked by professional and personal transitions. The purpose of this chapter is to present a framework of essential tasks associated with the management of early career school psychology transitions, with the goal of facilitating a rewarding professional career. These tasks are relevant to interns seeking their first school psychology positions as well as early career school psychologists transitioning to subsequent professional roles.

The National Association of School Psychologists (NASP) Early Career Workgroup, created in 2009 to support what NASP recognized to be a unique cohort within the profession, defines the early career period as the first 5 years of working as a credentialed school psychologist (as either a practitioner or a faculty member). However, early career resources can also be relevant for school psychology interns applying for initial positions, post-internship doctoral candidates who hold masters/specialist-equivalent degrees, professionals transitioning to a career in school psychology from another field, early career school psychologists returning to the workforce after a leave of absence (e.g., due to parenting or illness), and experienced practitioners transitioning to new professional roles.

This topic area falls within the Legal, Ethical, and Professional Practice domain of the NASP *Model for Comprehensive and Integrated School Psychological Services* (NASP, 2010), as it involves lifelong learning and professional development as well as advocating for professional roles that enable the effective provision of learning and mental health services.

Early career school psychologists are entering into, and helping to shape, an evolving field of practice. First, well documented for a number of years is the expansion of school psychologists' roles and functions. Given their proximity to training and presumed exposure to a broader conceptualization of school psychology practice, early career school psychologists may be able to help bridge the domains of training and practice. Second, change is tied to the "graying" of the field: As of 2010, the mean age of respondents to a survey of NASP members was 47.4 years (up 1.2% in just 5 years) and more than one in six were age 60 or older (Curtis, Castillo, & Gelley, 2012). Many of these individuals are likely to retire in the coming years. Relatedly, graduate education programs report increasing difficulty filling a large number of open faculty positions (Clopton & Haselhuhn, 2009).

As a result of these issues, early career school psychologists may find themselves with a multitude of professional opportunities both immediately following graduate school and during the early career. Choices may exist regarding practice setting, areas of professional specialization, and role definition. Those who recognize and prepare for these opportunities are most likely to achieve their professional goals and find job satisfaction.

BASIC CONSIDERATIONS

In recent years, much attention in professional psychology has been focused on defining universal practice competencies for all specialties, including school psychology. Documents such as the NASP Practice Model (NASP, 2010) delineate foundational and functional competencies specific to school psychologists, and accordingly take into account the developmental nature of training.

Developmental Transitions in the Early Career

Though the NASP Practice Model highlights competence attainment as developmental during training, how levels of development are relevant for school psychologists following training is less readily apparent. Few would argue with the idea that early, middle, and late career school psychologists differ with regard to attributes such as breadth and depth of experience, confidence, autonomy, or flexibility in problem solving. Two important developmental transitions bookend early career school psychology practice: (a) graduate student to early career professional and (b) early career professional to experienced professional. Phases of development have research-based hallmarks that may be considered relevant for school psychologists.

Life-Span Development Model
Rønnestad and Skovholt (2012) provide a helpful framework to understand early career transitions for counselors and therapists that is also relevant for school psychologists. Their model posits that over the course of a professional life-span individuals move through the phases of lay helper (i.e., prior to beginning training), novice student (i.e., early training), advanced student (i.e., late training), novice professional (i.e., graduation to 5 years of practice), experienced professional (i.e., 5–25 years of practice), and senior professional (i.e., 25 years or more of practice). Most relevant for this chapter is the novice professional phase of development.

Novice Professional Phase
Four developmental tasks comprise the novice professional phase: (a) professionalization, or developing an identification with the profession/professional sector (i.e., school psychology); (b) transforming from dependence on supervisors to functioning independently as a professional; (c) overcoming the disillusionment that may surface postgraduation when reflecting on training, self, or the profession; and (d) exploring and defining one's professional role. In working through these developmental tasks, novice or early career professionals first confirm the validity of their training and identify

strongly with their profession (i.e., confirmation subphase). Next, they may struggle when faced with the complexities of practice, including limitations of training, self, and the profession (i.e., disillusionment subphase). Finally, in the exploration subphase, they explore (a) inwardly to better understand their own professional and personal self, including skills, limitations, attitudes, and interests; and (b) outwardly toward identifying a compatible work setting. Successful exploration results in the novice professional maintaining a reflective stance when faced with adversity in practice. Ideally, the novice professional will continue to grow from being challenged rather than become developmentally stagnant given the complexities of practice.

Developmental Considerations
Though developmental trends of novice professionals appear to have some universal characteristics, it is important to also remember that regardless of developmental stage, "all school psychologists are beginners when they enter situations in which they have no previous experience, either in terms of the population with which they are working, or with regard to the procedures and/or tools used" (Harvey & Struzziero, 2008, p. 41). In other words, both senior and early career school psychologists may be considered novices in some areas of practice. As such, some of the best practice considerations discussed here will apply at various times during a school psychologist's career.

Transitions During the Early Career Years

In addition to the developmental transitions experienced by all early career school psychologists (i.e., graduate student to early career professional and early career professional to experienced professional), there are a number of other transitions that often occur during the early career years. One of the most common transitions may be forced upon new practitioners during times of economic difficulty. When budgets must be cut, reduction in force affects all staff. By definition, early career school psychologists are relatively new to the field and unlikely to have accumulated sufficient seniority to survive deep cuts in staffing. This reality was reflected in a recent survey of NASP members: Of those who were not employed as school-based practitioners, 37% reported that they were unemployed or had been laid off (NASP Early Career Workgroup, 2009).

Some early career transitions occur by choice. Dissatisfaction with role, salary, opportunities for leadership advancement, or ability to maintain work–life balance may lead a new school psychologist to seek a change. Interests may also change. For example, a school-based practitioner may seek opportunities as an adjunct or full-time graduate school faculty member. Finally, changes in personal life can directly affect career plans. Events such as marriage or domestic partnership, starting or expanding a family, a need to care for aging family members, or job changes for a spouse or partner may necessitate relocating or transitioning out of full-time employment. What follows is an organizational framework and recommendations for best practices intended to support the transitions of early career school psychologists.

BEST PRACTICES IN EARLY CAREER TRANSITIONS FOR SCHOOL PSYCHOLOGISTS

In reviewing the literature relevant to transitions during the early career years, and by reflecting on their own personal experience with the topic, the authors propose the following framework as best practice for making transitions during the early career years as a school psychologist. Table 41.1 lists the relevant tasks for the initial transition from an intern to a first year school psychologist, as well as for practicing school psychologists who may be considering transitioning to a new position, and highlights steps school psychologists should take within each task of the framework. Each of these best practice tasks are explored in depth in the sections that follow.

Establish and Maintain a Network

Given the variety of reasons early career professionals are likely to face job changes, it is important to be prepared to initiate a job search relatively quickly. Maintaining connections with peers, faculty, supervisors, and colleagues can lead to a multitude of potential opportunities. The network of one early career school psychologist is illustrated in Figure 41.1.

Graduate School Connections
Graduate school classmates can forge bonds that last throughout lifelong careers. Peer consultation during and following graduate school can be a powerful means of support. Professors and supervisors also form an essential part of the professional network. In addition to providing essential knowledge and skills for school psychology practice, they also serve as references when applying for internships and initial positions in the field.

Table 41.1. Best Practices in Early Career School Psychology Transitions

Task	Examples of Steps to Take
Establish and maintain a network	• Maintain regular contact with colleagues and mentors from graduate school, internship, and prior positions. • Attend local and national professional conferences.
Maintain professional materials	• Keep an updated résumé and portfolio of exemplary work samples.
Consider various options and apply widely	• Determine priorities for new employment, such as a different work schedule, broader role, or alternative setting.
Negotiate an offer	• Consider factors such as salary, schedule, setting, caseload, and role.
Facilitate entry and understand organizational culture	• Assess workplace culture and climate. • Take the time to develop relationships with colleagues.
Define a professional role and do it well	• Send a written letter of introduction to school staff and families, describing the broad range of services offered. • Tackle role development and systems-change goals at a workable pace. • Engage in ongoing professional development, including self-study and peer consultation, to continuously develop clinical skills.
Ensure continued job satisfaction	• Reframe negative job attributes. • Seek opportunities for career enrichment, such as accessing supervision. • Meet with supervisors to problem solve negative aspects of the position. • Engage in self-care activities, such as getting appropriate amounts of sleep and exercise. • Develop supportive relationships with colleagues.
Periodically evaluate job satisfaction	• Maintain a pro and con list of job attributes. • Complete the Job Satisfaction Survey (Spector, 1994).
Adapt to challenges or consider new opportunities	• Complete the Maslach Burnout Inventory (Maslach & Jackson, 1981). • Ensure the decision to leave is appropriately justified.

Figure 41.1. Example Network of an Early Career School Psychologist

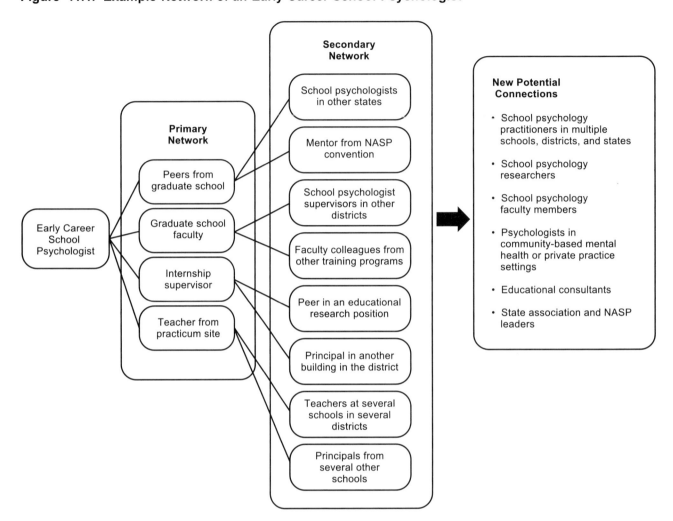

Thus, graduate students should seek out opportunities to show mentors their best work and to learn from the wealth of knowledge and experience that supervisors and professors have to share.

Internship Contacts

Internship and fieldwork supervisors have direct knowledge of a candidate's professional skills and personal attributes, making them essential references for and potential connectors to future professional opportunities. However, the professional network extends beyond direct supervisors to other school psychologists at a site or within a district, as well as to related-service providers and even teachers and parents who benefitted from the school psychologist's direct and indirect services. School psychology interns and early career professionals can broaden their understanding of the field and develop a more diverse set of skills by working across disciplines. By expanding professional networks at each stage of

graduate school training and throughout the early career years, school psychologists can deepen their knowledge base and increase the likelihood of learning about new opportunities.

Professional Organizations

Participation in professional organizations such as NASP and the American Psychological Association (APA), as well as state and regional organizations, are excellent ways to sustain and extend a professional network. At the international, national, and local levels, organizations bring together professionals with common interests and vast knowledge of school psychology practices. This networking is accomplished face-to-face at conventions and conferences and in the virtual realm through tools such as the NASP Communities (including one specifically developed for early career school psychologists: http://communities. nasponline.org/Home). Both NASP (http://www. nasponline.org/earlycareer/earlycareer_resources.aspx) and APA (http://www.apa.org/careers/early-career/index.aspx) maintain a variety of resources designed specifically for early career professionals, including handouts on topics from ethics to advocacy to managing stress. The NASP Career Center (http://www.jobtarget.com/home/index.cfm?site_id=15381) lists job openings across the country, allows members to share their résumés with potential employers, and lists salary information.

Professional organizations also provide opportunities for practitioners and school psychology faculty members to meet and share information on current research and practices. Local and national conferences can be valuable opportunities to meet leaders in the field as well as regional or local professionals who might serve as resources during times of professional transition. Similarly, participation in online networks such as LinkedIn, and resources such as the NASP Early Career Professionals Communities and NASP Facebook group, provide access to school psychology professionals and resources. Early career school psychologists should work to develop skills and routines for deliberately networking with colleagues, including leaders in the field, who are doing work that is of interest and value to the individual's professional development and practice.

Maintain Professional Materials

In addition to maintaining a broad professional network, early career school psychologists should engage in the frequent updating of materials such as résumés or curriculum vitae (CV), portfolios, and references. Periodically, perhaps at the end of each marking period or semester, a résumé review can be helpful. Any additional training, leadership experience, or newly acquired skills should be added, along with any inservice trainings provided, presentations delivered, or research presented at a local, regional, or national levels. It is also important to consider which experiences may have become dated and should be deleted from the résumé. Periodic updates of the résumé or CV will ensure it is the strongest and most up-to-date representation of current skills and experience, and will allow for quick dissemination as needed.

All professionals, including early career school psychologists, are well served to maintain a portfolio that reflects the quality of their work. Often graduate students are required to develop strategies for capturing and retaining permanent products that reflect their skills and accomplishments (e.g., a summative internship portfolio). A portfolio may include copies of exemplary evaluation reports (with all identifying information completely removed), group counseling plans, functional behavioral assessments and behavior intervention plans, problem-solving consultation write ups, examples of innovative or successful interventions and the data used to monitor effectiveness, and supporting materials such as copies of certifications, earned continuing education credits, and letters of recommendation. For school-based practitioners yet to achieve tenured status, such a portfolio may be required by a school district for documenting progress during the early career years. As with the résumé or CV, quarterly or semiannual reviews of the portfolio will keep it current and ensure that it includes a wide range of strong work.

Consider Various Options and Apply Widely

Whether transitioning to a first school psychology position or moving from an existing position to a new school district or work setting, school psychologists are encouraged to consider all career opportunities and apply widely. As is well known, application materials and professional record may result in an invitation to interview, but personality and interview performance is what ultimately closes the deal.

Job Interviews

NASP has developed a number of resources dedicated to preparing interns and early career school psychologists for job interviews. These are available on the NASP website (http://www.nasponline.org). What follows are some of the most important recommendations to consider when interviewing:

- Schedule lower-priority interviews first if possible, so the interviews can be used as practice opportunities.
- Research the district and school beforehand and come prepared with thoughtful questions.
- Prepare in advance for commonly asked questions (e.g., Tell us about yourself. Why are you interested in working here? What are your biggest professional strengths and weaknesses?).
- Be prepared to elaborate on examples of work with students, families, and staff from your practica, internship, or prior school psychology positions.
- Dress professionally and conservatively.
- Be punctual.
- Be explicit about why the position is a good match.
- Bring hard copies of the résumé and application materials and be able to speak intelligently about every experience listed on the résumé.

- Act kindly and professionally to everyone encountered.
- Send a note to thank the interviewer for his or her time and to reiterate your interest in the position.

In general, the chances of being hired are stronger if the interviewee is able to show that if hired he or she will be able to make the interviewer's professional life easier. School psychologists should be likeable and positive during their interviews, demonstrating their many professional competencies and interpersonal skills, as they apply and interview widely.

In addition to preparing thoroughly for interviews, interns and early career school psychologists should approach job interviews as opportunities to determine whether the particular setting will be a match for their interests and skills. For instance, itinerant positions that typically involve a heavy testing load across many schools may not be a good fit for school psychologists looking for building-based positions in which they can emphasize their counseling and consultation skills. Research suggests the following specific work characteristics are associated with increased job satisfaction among school psychologists: (a) working in schools implementing a response-to-intervention (RTI) model (McKellar & Unruh, 2011), (b) serving one school compared to serving more than one school (Proctor & Steadman, 2003), and (c) having a direct supervisor who is a credentialed school psychologist (Worrell, Skaggs, & Brown, 2006). Early career school psychologists should consider these factors when job searching and interviewing.

School psychologists should try to get a sense of the climate and culture of the schools and organizations they are considering working for. Do adult staff members smile and greet each other when they pass in the halls? In school settings, do children seem engaged and happy? Is there a culture of collaboration or of suspicion when an administrator speaks with a teacher or enters the classroom? School psychologists should pay attention to their impressions as they walk through interview settings and speak with potential colleagues and supervisors.

Alternative Careers

The authors of this chapter all know colleagues who are currently satisfied in positions they might not have considered when they were graduate students. When faced with a transition, it is important to consider all available options. In addition, school psychologists early in their career would do well to make deliberate choices to foster diverse experiences and skill sets

that will create additional opportunities later in their career. NASP (2011) describes the following examples of alternative careers for school psychologists, some of which may require additional training and/or licensure: (a) university faculty, (b) private practitioner providing mental health services, (c) educational consultant, (d) test publishing professional, (e) educational researcher, (f) behavioral specialist, and (g) school neuropsychologist.

In addition to considering alternative career options, it may be useful to explore logistical possibilities. Full- or part-time work in one school district or alternative setting is just the beginning, as positions can often be creatively combined. Benefits of such arrangements can include a wide range of interesting job activities and experiences, access to additional supervision opportunities, and increased salary. An example of one doctoral-level early career school psychologist's multiple professional roles is shown in Figure 41.2.

New parents and parents-to-be may wish to consider scaling back from a full-time schedule or taking a break from working outside the home altogether while their children are young. These decisions are personal and often difficult to make because there is no right answer. Parents can take comfort in international research suggesting that factors such as parental education levels and quality of interaction with their children have greater influences on child development than early maternal employment (Huerta et al., 2011).

A final option is for early career school psychologists to consider returning to graduate school to pursue (a) a doctorate in school psychology or a related field, (b) an area of specialization (e.g., school neuropsychology), or (c) a credential in educational administration (e.g., in order to become a principal or director of special education). Advancing training may lead to additional career opportunities, increased pay, and, ideally, enhanced job satisfaction.

Negotiate an Offer

As one transitions to a new position, it is important to be aware of hiring processes, including negotiating and signing a contract. Regarding salary, a 2012 survey of school psychologists by Curtis et al. (2012) found that mean salaries (adjusted based on days worked per contract year) for full-time school-based practitioners were $64,168, with doctoral-level school psychologists earning an average of approximately $12,000 more in salary annually ($73,695) than those without doctorates ($61,965). A number of additional factors may influence

Figure 41.2. Example of an Early Career School Psychologist's Multiple Professional Roles and Supervisory Experiences

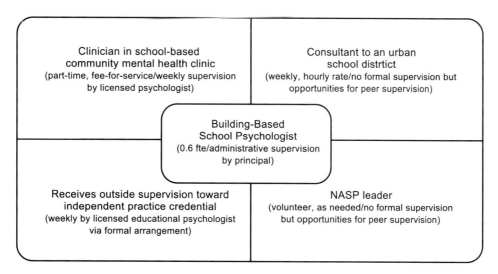

school psychology salaries, including the geographic location of the position, the length of the contract (e.g., 10 month versus 12 month), the inclusion of administrative duties, and the applicant's level of education and experience. Some districts give bonuses or higher salaries to school psychologists who possess certain value-added factors, such as the NASP Nationally Certified School Psychologist (NCSP) credential.

In school districts it is unlikely employees have leeway in negotiating a starting salary, given unions or other associations that may be present in the public education system. Instead, schools may have a ladder scale that increases based on benchmarks such as number of years experience, graduate credits accumulated, or highest degree earned. However, other items to be negotiated can include building-based versus itinerant positions, access to supervision, caseload and number of schools assigned, and breadth of practice. Faculty members may engage in negotiations around number and content of courses taught, number of advisees and/or institutional committees, time onsite, office space and equipment, administrative support, professional development funds, and startup research funds.

Unfortunately, discrimination based on demographic characteristics such as gender and race also may play a role in compensation determination as well as contract negotiation practices (see, e.g., Crothers et al., 2010). Enhancing training regarding contract negotiation tactics (e.g., composing a strong rationale for the proposed salary or raise, researching local and national salaries for comparable positions, consulting with

colleagues, and interviewing elsewhere for leverage) may help mitigate this seemingly antiquated problem (Crothers et al., 2010).

Facilitate Entry and Understand Organizational Culture

Many models of consultation devote careful consideration to the process of entry into a system. Such concepts can be applied broadly by a school psychologist transitioning into any new role, including transitioning back to a position held prior to a leave of absence. For example, part of the entry process involves assessing the alignment of skills and the needs of the new organization. In a school setting, conversations with the school principal, special services providers, teachers, and other key members of the faculty and staff could provide valuable information about goals for the school or upcoming initiatives through which a school psychologist could help facilitate change. In a university setting, conversations with department heads, deans, colleagues, and students could provide important insight into the type of pedagogy, scholarship, and service that is valued within the university.

The entry process should also involve an assessment of workplace culture and climate. As Deal and Peterson (2009) note, school culture consists of "unwritten rules and traditions, norms, and expectations ... the way people act, how they dress, what they talk about or consider taboo, whether they seek out colleagues or isolate themselves, and how teachers feel about their work and their students" (p. 8). While new school psychology practitioners and faculty may arrive full of enthusiasm and ideas about how to improve an organization's performance, taking time to observe and learn "the ways in which things actually get done versus the ways in which things are supposed to get done" (Erchul & Martens, 2001, p. 54) is essential before attempting to facilitate change. This observation process includes assessing the expectations for the role played by the school psychologist, as it can vary widely from district to district, or even building to building in the same school system.

Other aspects of school culture to consider include (a) documentation of items such as the school mission statement, handbooks, discipline policies, and special education referral procedures; (b) communication patterns between students, teachers, and administration; (c) closeness of relationships between faculty members; (d) opportunities for and acceptability of collaboration; and (e) existing teams and their operations.

Although some opportunities for cultural assessment and relationship building occur during formally scheduled meetings, new members of the staff can also begin building relationships with colleagues by attending or assisting with back-to-school events, school committees, or extracurricular activities. Branstetter (2012) provides additional information on the importance of building relationships with key staff, including the secretary, principal, school social worker, and school counselor.

In addition to assessing the culture of a new school, district, or university setting, it is important for a school psychologist to consider the impact of his or her own background and readiness to provide culturally responsive services within the new setting. It can be helpful to begin with a self-assessment of cultural competency, such as the Promoting Cultural Diversity and Cultural Competency checklist provided through the NASP website (Goode, 2002). School psychologists should carefully consider how multicultural factors affect all domains of their work. Esquivel, Lopez, and Nahari (2007) address multicultural competencies across a variety of school-based practice domains, from assessment to therapeutic interventions to working with special populations.

Newman (2013) highlights several additional actions that may promote entry to a school including (a) being proactive (e.g., self-reflective, prepared, and aware of one's own goals), (b) stepping outside one's comfort zone (e.g., seeking out new opportunities), (c) walking around to introduce oneself to other staff, and (d) asking questions about the system. Connecting with a building or district mentor who can provide the school psychologist information on the written and unwritten rules of the setting will also be helpful. Schools or districts sometimes have formal mentoring programs, but, if not, the school psychologist can seek out someone who may be willing to fill this role.

Define a Professional Role and Do It Well

If school psychologists have done their due diligence in terms of finding and negotiating a match for their professional skills and interests, and have taken the time to learn about the organizational culture, a new position brings the opportunity to define a professional role, along with the responsibility to do it well. School psychologists need to recognize the strengths (and limitations) in their training and professional skills and be prepared to advocate for the opportunity to use these skills in order to effectively meet the needs of the children, school professionals, and parents they serve. School psychologists also need to be able to deliver what they promise by setting appropriate boundaries in order to realistically fulfill obligations, working within their limits of competence, seeking additional supervision and professional development, and consulting with peers and supervisors whenever they are unsure.

During the first few weeks in a new building, in conjunction with facilitating entry, school psychologists should actively engage in public relations efforts in order to become someone that teachers, administrators, parents, and staff seek out as a resource and problem solver for a wide variety of concerns. School psychologists should use e-mail, letters, and professional websites to introduce themselves and describe the services they can offer to teachers and families (Branstetter, 2012, offers sample letters that can be adapted for this purpose). School psychologists should distribute informational brochures at back-to-school nights and decorate their workspace with items that advocate for the profession (e.g., the posters distributed annually in NASP's *Communiqué* for School Psychology Awareness Week work well for this purpose). If they are fortunate enough to have an office with a door, school psychologists should put their name and title on it and then leave it open whenever possible so that others feel comfortable approaching them for assistance.

In addition, as school psychologists begin to work within their systems, how they respond to requests for help will shape their professional roles. A predecessor may have quietly but resentfully accepted an overwhelming number of assessment referrals for students who were ultimately not found to have an educational disability. However, an early career school psychologist with knowledge of effective instruction, social–emotional and behavioral supports, and consultation may have the opportunity to approach the concerns from a systemic perspective by working with administrators and staff to improve the general education academic and behavioral curriculum, and offering collaborative consultation to teachers in order to help them better meet the needs of their students.

Early career school psychologists should also remember that it takes time to develop a professional role. School psychologists should prioritize goals for their role development and systems change efforts, and tackle these goals at a workable pace.

A note on change efforts: School psychologists are often change agents and leaders in their settings, which can at times feel frustrating and isolating. The authors have encountered many early career school psychologists who have found it challenging to implement evidence-based practice or systems change efforts in the real world. School psychology graduate students and faculty have reported that graduate students may lack the skills needed to implement such change in the field, and may have difficulty coping when their ideas are not immediately accepted in a practice setting (Forman et al., 2013). Unless change and implementation skills have been adequately addressed during their previous training and professional experience, it will be important for early career school psychologists to seek supervision and professional development, engage in self-study, and participate in online networks as they attempt to bridge this research-to-practice divide.

A wise mentor advised, "Look for the open doors to change" (S. Rosenfield, personal communication, n.d.). In every setting, no matter how bleak the situation, it is always possible to find someone who is open to doing things differently. Meaningful change can begin with one individual, but it takes time to work through a thoughtful problem-solving process with key stakeholders. School psychologists are advised to work within their spheres of influence, set reasonable goals, and nurture relationships with others who have similar views in their work settings. Although change does not happen overnight and sometimes occurs in the smallest increments, having the opportunity to participate in change efforts during the early career can lead to satisfying personal and professional growth, regardless of the ultimate outcome of those initial efforts.

Ensure Continued Job Satisfaction

Once acclimated to a new position, school psychologists should take steps toward maintaining job satisfaction after the honeymoon phase has ended. Periodic reflection on the specific positive and negative attributes of the job will help to identify whether any of the negative attributes can be improved, either by taking proactive steps toward problem solving or by reframing the way the negative attributes are viewed. Miller, Nickerson, Chafouleas, and Osborne (2008) provide suggestions for school psychologists to incorporate research on subjective well-being toward increasing their job satisfaction, including:

- Frequently remembering and focusing on the positive aspects of the job
- Developing close relationships with colleagues
- Understanding and accepting that negative experiences at work can and do feel better over time (i.e., the concept of adaptation in positive psychology)
- Remembering that more money does not necessarily lead to greater happiness
- Promoting a positive work environment for themselves and the rest of the school staff, particularly in the areas of relatedness, autonomy, and competence (for specific suggestions in these areas, please refer to Table 1 in Miller et al., 2008, p. 688).

Accessing resources can also help school psychologists prepare for a new position and setting. The NASP Student Development and Early Career Workgroups maintain handouts on the NASP website geared toward the professional concerns of early career school psychologists. In addition, Branstetter (2012) provides a helpful survival guide for novice school psychologists employed in public school settings, and Keeley, Afful, Stiegler-Balfour, Good, and Leder (2013) provide a similar resource for early career faculty members.

Career Enrichment

Armistead and Smallwood (2011) use the term *career enrichment* to describe the myriad activities in which school psychologists can engage in to enhance job satisfaction in the absence of traditional career advancement opportunities. These include (a) seeking continuing professional development; (b) pursuing additional credentials (e.g., NCSP, doctoral degree, state licensure in psychology or other independent practice credential, or the American Board of Professional Psychology's Diplomate in School Psychology); (c) accessing supervision, mentoring, and peer support; (d) developing a specialty; (e) supervising interns (typically after three years of practice); (f) developing and evaluating programs; (g) presenting at local and national conferences; (h) supplementing positions in schools with part-time private practice, consulting, or teaching; and (i) maintaining membership and involvement in state and national professional associations. Toward the last point, school psychologists should be aware that NASP currently offers a reduced-dues structure for early career members in their first 2 years of practice, as well as publication opportunities through the NASP Early Career Workgroup.

According to Armistead and Smallwood (2011), novice professionals should focus on exploring the job market, developing a professional identity, and decision making around future goals. Specific professional development and involvement tasks include (a) developing a continuing professional development plan, (b) acquiring practice management and organizational skills, (c) refining and mastering practice skills, (d) maintaining membership in professional associations, (e) becoming actively involved in state associations, (f) attending state and national conferences, (g) initiating self-study, (h) participating in peer support groups and online professional communities, and (i) receiving mentoring and supervision (Armistead & Smallwood, 2011).

Supervision

Given the increasingly broad role of school psychologists, early career professionals are likely to be faced with situations they have not previously encountered. For example, imagine a school psychologist who is hired to fill a need at an elementary school even though his or her school-based internship was at the secondary level. Or, consider an early career school psychologist who must respond to a crisis during the first year on the job, having never received formal education in crisis intervention.

It is simply not possible for graduate students to engage in every activity a school psychologist might encounter in practice. Therefore, just as during graduate education programs, professional supervision maintains an important role during one's early career and beyond (Harvey & Struzziero, 2008). Supervisors help normalize feelings of disillusionment or doubt that early career professionals will likely encounter in their first few years of practice, encourage ongoing reflection and professional development, and help novice professionals move toward finding an integrated and fulfilling work role.

As novice school psychologists ideally have reached levels of competence to practice by the end of their school psychology internships or entry into the field, professional supervision may help them transition beyond competence toward proficiency and eventually expertise (Harvey & Struzziero, 2008). Advanced developmental stages are characterized by practitioners' decreased levels of anxiety, increased levels of independent functioning and self-confidence, and flexibility in practice composed of high levels of both innovation and efficiency. Yet, despite the presumed importance of supervision beyond graduate-level training, descriptive data suggest limited availability and perceived insufficiency of professional supervision for practicing school psychologists (Chafouleas, Clonan, & Vanauken, 2002). If a school district or other practice setting does not offer professional supervision, then novice professionals may benefit from seeking out professional mentors or accessing peer supports.

Self-Care

"Self-care is a personal challenge and ethical imperative that every psychologist—literally every one—must consciously confront" (Norcross & Barnett, 2008, "In Closing," para. 1). School psychologists, like all helping professionals, are likely to be emotionally affected by their work, whether positively (e.g., pride about a student's progress) or negatively (e.g., inability to control difficult situations in the lives of others). Examples of challenges early career school psychologists may face include working independently in a new role and new setting, feeling disheartened about their own skills or daily work stressors, and establishing clear boundaries between their personal and professional lives. For instance, an early career faculty member in a school psychology program realized he needed to stop reading and replying to e-mails after 8:00 p.m. so as to stop thinking about work when it came time to fall asleep.

Newman (2013) reviews the literature on stress and burnout and suggests individual self-care behaviors that are especially relevant for interns and early career school psychologists, such as designing a stress management plan and seeking peer consultation. Norcross and Barnett (2008) suggest 12 self-care strategies for novice and expert psychologists, summarized in Table 41.2. The key is to choose an individualized combination from the wide range of activities that constitute self-care, and perform them on an ongoing basis in order to prevent burnout and ineffectiveness. Ideally, in conjunction with effective preservice-level training and ongoing organizational supports (e.g., supervision, peer support, reasonable workload, role clarity), early career psychologists will be able to prevent and cope with stress

Table 41.2. Strategies for Self-Care

Strategy	Explanation
Valuing the person of the school psychologist	• Prioritize self-care; assess and track your own self-care as would be done for a client, including vulnerabilities and strengths
Refocusing on the rewards	• Attend to job and career satisfaction
Recognizing the hazards	• Acknowledge the demanding, challenging nature of the work and share with colleagues; accept that some stressors are inevitable
Minding the body	• Get sufficient rest and sleep, nutrition, and exercise
Nurturing relationships	• Cultivate a support network at the work setting (e.g., a supervision group) as well as outside of work (e.g., family, friends, spiritual advisors)
Setting boundaries	• Maintain boundaries between yourself and others and personal life and professional life • Schedule breaks, and be okay with saying "no"
Restructuring cognitions	• Monitor internal dialogues that are harmful (e.g., "I should not have problems. I am a school psychologist.") and replace with realistic mantras
Sustaining healthy escapes	• Restore yourself with breaks, days off, and vacations • Beware of and avoid unhealthy escapes such as substance abuse and isolation
Creating a flourishing environment	• Evaluate the work environment in terms of its contribution to your stress and satisfaction and enhance your environment accordingly
Undergoing personal therapy	• Seek out therapy and also integrate self-development activities such as meditation, yoga, or creative arts
Cultivating spirituality and mission	• Focus on why you entered the profession and spiritual sources of hope and optimism regarding making a difference
Fostering creativity and growth	• Strive to be adaptive and open to challenges, become involved in diverse professional activities, and engage in ongoing professional development

Note. Based on information from Norcross and Barnett (2008).

before it snowballs into distress or burnout, or interferes with one's professional competence.

Social Support in the Workplace

Actively developing social support in the workplace is also an important task in maintaining job satisfaction. Bjorkman (2010) encourages school psychologists to apply the RTI triangle heuristic toward building a three-tier model of workplace social support. Tier 1 includes the adults encountered in the halls on a daily basis. Being friendly toward these individuals can deepen a sense of community, and has the added benefit of helping build rapport should they seek consultation from the school psychologist. Tier 2 involves developing relationships with those who can answer questions and provide information about the ins and outs of the school and district, such as policies and procedures, scheduling, and how to procure supplies. Tier 3, the smallest and most intense level of social support, involves developing close and honest relationships with trustworthy colleagues. These individuals are typically fellow school psychologists, administrators, and other mental health professionals to whom school psychologists can vent on difficult days and from whom to seek best practices advice as issues arise. School psychologists should seek out any built-in mentoring, supervision, or peer-support arrangements provided by the district to help build

connections in this tier. In smaller districts, school psychologists may also wish to include past supervisors and former graduate school classmates at this level.

Periodically Evaluate Job Satisfaction

As part of the framework for making transitions during their early career years, school psychologists should routinely reflect on their positions and assess their levels of job satisfaction. To provide context for this exercise, *U.S. News & World Report* (2013) named school psychology as the top social service job and the fourteenth best job overall in its ranking of best jobs, noting above-average levels of upward mobility and flexibility as well as projected employment growth. School psychologists report high levels of job satisfaction. Survey and meta-analytic techniques indicate approximately 90% of school psychologists are "satisfied" or "very satisfied" with their jobs (Worrell et al., 2006). General aspects of job satisfaction in school psychology include independence, responsibility, social service, values, job activities, and colleagues (Worrell et al., 2006).

Although these research findings may provide reassurance about having chosen the profession of school psychology, they do not guarantee job satisfaction for any individual school psychologist. Armistead and

Smallwood (2011) note several areas in which school psychologists have indicated job dissatisfaction, including compensation, opportunities for promotion and advancement, and school district policies and practices, particularly those relating to school psychology roles and functions. In any given job there are also a number of individual factors that may decrease job satisfaction, such as poor relationships with colleagues or over whelming quantities of assigned work.

Early career school psychologists should set aside time to identify the negative aspects associated with their work so that they can be proactively mitigated or eliminated. As a starting point, early career school psychologists can take the Job Satisfaction Survey (http://shell.cas.usf.edu/~pspector/scales/jsspag.html; Spector, 1994), which assesses an individual's job satisfaction in nine facets: pay, promotion, supervision, fringe benefits, contingent rewards, operating procedures, coworkers, nature of work, and communication. Job Satisfaction Survey norms are reported for jobs in both education and social services and can help respondents interpret their results. Early career school psychologists can also keep a running log of events or circumstances that make them feel satisfied and unsatisfied at work. Reviewing this periodically may help identify broader issues and themes for further consideration.

It seems apparent the transition from graduate school to the first years of practice would result in some amount of stress for most individuals. For some, typical levels of stress may elevate to levels of distress or even burnout, a prolonged response to work-related stress including exhaustion, cynicism, and inefficacy (Maslach, 2003). Stress and burnout can be conceptualized for school psychologists in terms of (a) personal risk and resiliency factors, (b) organizational context, and (c) professional roles and functions (Huebner, Gilligan, & Cobb, 2002).

Younger, less-experienced school psychologists, such as early career professionals, may be more likely to experience symptoms of professional burnout. Contextual factors with which early career school psychologists may struggle include developing professional relationships (e.g., Who are my collaborators at this school?), work efficiency (e.g., How will I get all of these evaluations completed?), time management (e.g., I have arrived early and stayed late every day this week.), role conflict (e.g., Should I really be spending an hour a day doing bus duty?), role ambiguity (e.g., My role at this problem-solving team meeting is not clear.), and role overload (e.g., There is too much to do and not enough time; Huebner, Gilligan, & Cobb, 2002).

In terms of professional roles and functions, novice professionals must find a good match between personal interests and professional roles, the level of challenge faced, and responses to the job's adversities (Rønnestad & Skovholt, 2012). It is important to seek supervision and support from other school psychologists and to advocate for one's professional needs. In addition, the self-care strategies described in Table 41.2 are pivotal in terms of helping school psychologists mitigate stress, distress, and burnout and in so doing may help prevent problems of professional competence.

Adapt to Challenges or Consider New Opportunities

Well before deciding to leave a position, school psychologists should meet with their supervisors and/or administrators in an attempt to problem solve areas of concern. For example, if workload concerns are a significant source of dissatisfaction, school psychologists are advised to arrange an in-person meeting with their supervisor to seek assistance and support in accomplishing their to-do lists and meeting their deadlines (Branstetter, 2012). Even if additional resources are not available, collaboratively prioritizing tasks can provide a sense of direction and renewed energy.

Sometimes, despite the best intentions and efforts, it becomes clear the time has come to move on. To summarize, some of the common reasons for transitioning to a new job during the early career years include (a) organizational budget cuts, (b) system changes having a negative impact on the school psychologist, (c) poor job satisfaction in aspects beyond a school psychologist's control, (d) an organizational environment or job role linked with professional burnout, (e) interest in a new role, (f) being prematurely promoted into a role for which a school psychologist does not have the prerequisite skills and experiences, and (g) family-related needs.

Though deciding (or being forced) to make a transition can be anxiety provoking, it can be helpful to remember it is a common occurrence during the early career years and, it is hoped, will be a positive one. Sharing one's experience with peers, and online in the NASP Early Career Professionals Community, can be a valuable source of ideas and support during this time. With a little networking, maintenance of professional materials, and interview preparation, savvy early career school psychologists will likely find a number of interesting new career opportunities to pursue. If possible, school psychologists should try to take time off to reflect and recharge before starting a new position. It is worth remembering that along with challenges, transitions also bring new beginnings and a renewed sense of optimism.

SUMMARY

The first 5 years working as a credentialed school psychologist are typically marked by a number of professional transitions, bookended by the transition from graduate student to early career professional, and early career professional to experienced professional. This chapter has presented a framework (Table 41.1) for how to effectively manage such transitions, with the goal of facilitating a rewarding professional career. Specifically, recommendations are given for how school psychologists should establish and maintain a network, maintain professional materials, consider various options and apply widely, negotiate an offer, facilitate entry and understand organizational culture, define a professional role and do it well, periodically evaluate job satisfaction, ensure continued job satisfaction, and adapt to challenges or consider new opportunities.

While many of the tasks described in this framework are relevant for all school psychologists experiencing career transitions, early career school psychologists are particularly concerned with developing an identification with the profession of school psychology, functioning independently as a school psychologist for the first time, overcoming any disillusionment that may surface post-graduation, and exploring and defining a professional role (Rønnestad & Skovholt, 2012).

REFERENCES

Armistead, L. D., & Smallwood, D. (2011). Making a career of school psychology. In T. M. Lionetti, E. P. Snyder, & R. W. Christner (Eds.), *A practical guide to building professional competencies in school psychology*. (pp. 245–261). New York, NY: Springer. doi:10.1007/978-1-4419-6257-7_15

Bjorkman, S. (2010, February). *Developing professional relationships, a social support system, and managing stress*. In NASP Early Career Workgroup (Chair), *Essential tools for early career school psychologists*. Symposium conducted at the annual meeting of the National Association of School Psychologists, Chicago, IL.

Branstetter, R. (2012). *The school psychologist's survival guide*. San Francisco, CA: Jossey-Bass.

Chafoleaus, S. M., Clonan, S. M., & Vanauken, T. L. (2002). A national survey of current supervision and evaluation practices of school psychologists. *Psychology in the Schools, 39*, 317–325. doi:10.1002/pits.10021

Clopton, K. L., & Haselhuhn, C. W. (2009). School psychology trainer shortage in the USA: Current status and projections for the future. *School Psychology International, 30*, 24–42. doi:10.1177/0143034308101848

Crothers, L. M., Hughes, T. L., Schmitt, A. J., Theodore, L. A., Lipinski, J., Bloomquist, A. J., & Altman, C. L. (2010). Has equity been achieved? Salary and promotion negotiation practices of a national sample of school psychology university faculty. *The Psychologist-Manager Journal, 13*, 40–59. doi:10.1080/10887150903553790

Curtis, M. J., Castillo, J. M., & Gelley, C. (2012, May). School psychology 2010: Demographics, employment, and the context for professional practices–Part 1. *Communiqué, 40*(7), 1, 28–30.

Deal, T. E., & Peterson, K. D. (2009). Shaping school culture: Pitfalls, paradoxes, and promises (2nd ed.). San Francisco, CA: Jossey-Bass.

Erchul, W. P., & Martens, B. (2001). *School consultation: Conceptual and empirical bases of practice* (2nd ed.). Hingham, MA: Kluwer.

Esquivel, G. B., Lopez, E. C., & Nahari, S. (2007). *Handbook of multicultural school psychology: An interdisciplinary perspective*. Mahwah, NJ: Erlbaum.

Forman, S. G., Shapiro, E. S., Codding, R. S., Gonzales, J. E., Reddy, L. A., Rosenfield, S., … Stoiber, K. C. (2013). Implementation science and school psychology. *School Psychology Quarterly, 28*, 77–100. doi:10.1037/spq0000019

Goode, T. D. (2002). *Promoting cultural diversity and cultural competency: Self-assessment checklist for personnel providing services and supports to children and their families*. Washington, DC: Georgetown University Center for Child and Human Development. Retrieved from http://www.nasponline.org/resources/culturalcompetence/checklist.aspx

Harvey, V. S., & Struzziero, J. A. (2008). *Professional development and supervision of school psychologists: From intern to expert*. (2nd ed.; A joint publication with the National Association of School Psychologists). Thousand Oaks, CA: Corwin Press.

Huebner, E. S., Gilligan, T. D., & Cobb, H. (2002). Best practices in managing stress and burnout. In A. Thomas & J. Grimes (Eds.), *Best practices in school psychology IV*. (pp. 173–182). Bethesda, MD: National Association of School Psychologists.

Huerta, M., Adema, W., Baxter, J., Corak, M., Deding, M., Gray, M. C., … Waldfogel, J. (2011). *Early maternal employment and child development in five OECD countries (Report No. 118)*. Paris, France: The Organisation for Economic Co-operation and Development. doi:10.1787/5kg5dlmtxhvh-en

Keeley, J., Afful, S. E., Stiegler-Balfour, J. J., Good, J. J., & Leder, S. (Eds.). (2013). *So you landed a job: What's next? Advice for early career psychologists from early career psychologists*. Washington, DC: Society for the Teaching of Psychology. Retrieved from http://teachpsych.org/ebooks/ecp2013/index.php

Maslach, C. (2003). Job burnout: New directions in research and intervention. *Current Directions in Psychological Science, 12*, 189–192. doi:10.1111/1467-8721.01258

Maslach, C., & Jackson, S. E. (1981). *Maslach Burnout Inventory: Human services survey*. Menlo Park, CA: Mind Garden. Retrieved from http://www.mindgarden.com/products/mbi.htm

McKellar, N. A., & Unruh, S. (2011, August). *School psychologists' job satisfaction and challenge in RTI and traditional model schools*. Paper presented at the annual convention of the American Psychological Association, Washington, DC.

Miller, D. N., Nickerson, A. B., Chafouleas, S. M., & Osborne, K. M. (2008). Authentically happy school psychologists: Applications of positive psychology for enhancing professional satisfaction and fulfillment. *Psychology in the Schools, 45*, 679–692. doi:10.1002/pits.20334

National Association of School Psychologists. (2010). *Model for comprehensive and integrated school psychological services*. Bethesda, MD: Author. Retrieved from http://www.nasponline.org/standards/2010standards/2_PracticeModel.pdf

National Association of School Psychologists. (2011). *Alternative careers and additional training for school psychologists*. Bethesda, MD: Author. Retrieved from http://www.nasponline.org/students/documents/ Alternative_Careers_and_Additional_Training_for_School_ Psychologists.pdf

National Association of School Psychologists Early Career Workgroup. (2009) [Survey of early career members]. Unpublished raw data.

Newman, D. S. (2013). *Demystifying the school psychology internship*. New York, NY: Routledge.

Norcross, J. C., & Barnett, J. E. (2008, Spring). *Self-care as ethical imperative. National Register of Health Service Psychologists The Register Report*. Adapted from Norcross, J. C., & Guy, J. D. (2007). *Leaving it at the office: A guide to psychotherapist self-care*. New York, NY: Guilford. Retrieved from http://www.nationalregister.org/trr_spring08_ norcross.html

Proctor, B. E., & Steadman, T. (2003). Job satisfaction, burnout, and perceived effectiveness of "in-house" versus traditional school psychologists. *Psychology in the Schools, 40*, 237–243. doi:10.1002/ pits.10082

Rønnestad, M. H., & Skovholt, T. M. (2012). *The developing practitioner: Growth and stagnation of therapists and counselors*. New York, NY: Routledge.

Spector, P. E. (1994). *Job satisfaction survey*. Retrieved from http:// shell.cas.usf.edu/~pspector/scales/jsspag.html

U.S. News & World Report. (2013). *Best jobs 2013: Best social services jobs*. Washington, DC: Author. Retrieved from http://money. usnews.com/careers/best-jobs/school-psychologist

Worrell, T. G., Skaggs, G. E., & Brown, M. B. (2006). School psychologists' job satisfaction: A 22-year perspective in the USA. *School Psychology International, 27*, 131–145. doi:10.1177/ 0143034306064540

42

Best Practices in Supervision and Mentoring of School Psychologists

Virginia Smith Harvey
Joan A. Struzziero
Sheila Desai
University of Massachusetts Boston

OVERVIEW

The increasing demands and complexities of contemporary school psychology practice necessitate ongoing skill development and knowledge acquisition. Effective supervision and mentoring can enable constant skill development and thereby foster optimal service delivery. The purpose of this chapter is to provide an introduction to supervision and mentoring of practicum students, interns, and credentialed school psychologists. After reading the chapter, school psychologists will have learned and be able to apply in their daily work (a) an understanding of mentoring and supervision processes; (b) knowledge of best practices and practical strategies to use while serving in a mentoring or supervisory role; (c) knowledge regarding critical variables in mentor–mentee and supervisee–supervisor relationships; (d) understanding of the requisite knowledge, skills, and training needed in providing supervision and mentoring; and (e) an understanding of the benefits of supervision and mentoring such that they are better enabled to advocate for such services in their schools.

Supervision and Mentoring Components

In both psychology and education, supervision is typically divided into administrative and clinical/professional supervision. Administrative supervision is defined as providing leadership, recruiting, hiring, delegating assignments, conducting formal personnel evaluations, designing corrective actions, and ensuring that the service unit functions well. In contrast, mentoring and clinical/professional supervision require discipline-specific training and knowledge in order to meet the ultimate goal of enabling the mentee or supervisee to acquire sufficient competency to practice independently. There is considerable overlap between the roles of clinical supervisors and mentors as they both focus on fostering professional growth. Whereas mentors generally do not evaluate mentees, clinical/professional supervisors do not have a primarily evaluative role but assume one whenever they indicate that a supervisee is fit to be licensed or certified. Nevertheless, both supervisors and mentors are ethically obliged to ensure that mentees are practicing skillfully and ethically, and to address substandard performance that negatively affects clients (Johnson, Barnett, Elman, Forrest, & Kaslow, 2012).

A third type of supervision, systemic supervision, has been identified as relevant to school psychology (Harvey & Pearrow, 2010). Systemic supervision involves addressing problems at the larger, systems level such that practitioners are enabled to work effectively and function to their fullest potential. Concrete examples include ensuring that each school psychologist has a mailbox and adequate workspace in every assigned school or serving on a state-level committee to operationally define state special education eligibility guidelines. While tasks assumed in systemic supervision range widely, they center on having the time, ability, and motivation to make systemic changes within the school setting (Dixon & Burns, 2012).

The format of mentoring is highly variable. Mentoring can be highly informal or formal, can be local or long distance, and can focus on a wide variety of issues. Many advanced practitioners identify multiple individuals who served as mentors sequentially throughout their careers. For example, they might have received mentoring from (a) more advanced graduate students during their graduate training that helped them successfully negotiate courses and other program requirements, (b) graduate program faculty regarding conducting and publishing research, (c) district-based senior colleagues during years as early practitioners regarding professional practice and successful negotiation of school district politics, (d) officers in a state or national association as they became active in a professional organization, and (e) junior colleagues with greater knowledge of response to intervention (RTI) as they implement new RTI programs in their district.

Supervision and mentoring are most obviously related to the domain of Legal, Ethical, and Professional Practice in the National Association of School Psychologists (NASP) *Model for Comprehensive and Integrated School Psychological Services* (NASP, 2010a). However, because they are required to help their supervisees and mentees apply knowledge and skills across all domains of practice, effective supervisors and mentors must possess current knowledge and skills across all domains.

BASIC CONSIDERATIONS

Both NASP and the American Psychological Association (APA) support supervising and mentoring school psychologists. The *Standards for Graduate Preparation of School Psychologists* (NASP, 2010b) reviews the supervision required in training programs. Practicum students are described as requiring close supervision, provided by both program faculty and field-based supervisors, which includes performance-based evaluations. Interns are described as requiring supervision from a credentialed school psychologist, for an average of at least 2 hours per week, primarily on a weekly, individual, and face-to-face basis. The NASP Practice Model (2010a) goes on to address the importance of supervision and mentoring for practicing school psychologists, and recommends that all school psychologists receive sufficient supervision or mentoring to ensure effective and accountable services. NASP recommends that supervisors have a valid state school psychologist credential, a minimum of 3 years of experience as a practicing school psychologist, and

education or experience in providing supervision. NASP also recommends that novice school psychologists receive intensive individualized supervision beyond the internship year as needed. For more experienced school psychologists who do not have access to or the need for intensive individual supervision, NASP suggests the use of alternative strategies such as mentoring, peer support, and supervision groups to foster continual professional growth and obtain support in dealing with difficult cases.

In contrast, APA standards (APA, 2009) indicate that nondoctoral school psychologists should receive face-to-face supervision throughout their careers. At the internship level, APA mandates at least 4 hours of supervision per week, 2 hours of which must be face-to-face and individual. APA also recommends that each intern should have at least two supervisors who are appropriately skilled, hold doctoral degrees, are integral members of the organization, and participate actively in internship development and evaluation. Further, APA recognizes supervision as a distinct professional competency requiring development through both graduate coursework and applied training.

Availability in School Psychology

Often school psychologists receive administrative supervision from school administrators rather than school psychologists; that is, more than half (56.2%) of school psychologists receive their administrative supervision from administrators and unit heads (Curtis, Castillo, & Gelley, 2012). Historically, school psychologists have received clinical supervision as practicum students and interns, but rarely received such supervision as practitioners. Only 28.5% of school psychologists receive systematic professional support, mentoring, and/or peer supervision for the professional practice of school psychology through an organized, district-provided program (Curtis et al., 2012).

Just as school psychologists do not always have access to clinical/professional supervision or systemic supervision, they also do not always have access to mentoring. While mentoring relationships are predominantly informal and developed individually by the participants, more formal mentoring programs are becoming increasingly common. NASP encourages conference attendees to become mentors or mentees (see http://www.nasponline.org/conventions/2013/students/mentoring.aspx). APA and some of its divisions have developed semistructured mentoring programs for early career practitioners who are interested in being mentored by senior psychologists with common interests such as multicultural practice. Formal mentoring assignments and programs have also been developed by several states in order to increase school personnel retention and effectiveness (e.g., see the North Carolina Department of Education mentoring program for novice teachers at http://www.ncpublicschools.org/educatoreffectiveness/beginning).

Owing to the administrative structures of schools, practicing school psychologists tend to receive simultaneous supervision and mentoring from a number of sources and in a number of settings. Often school psychologists receive direct administrative supervision from both special education administrators and general education administrators such as principals. The lack of formal clinical/professional supervisory structures in school psychology tends to result in experienced practitioners turning to peers, both other school psychologists and other mental health practitioners, for consultation and informal supervision (Annan & Ryba, 2013).

Case example 1: Ann, who has 10 years of experience as a school psychologist, also maintains her license as a mental health counselor, a credential she earned prior to returning to graduate school for her doctorate in school psychology. As one of two school psychologists assigned to a large high school, she participates in a variety of activities as a mentor, supervisor, and supervisee. Ann regularly participates in three different types of administrative supervision meetings as a supervisee. During the mandatory weekly, hour-long session run by the building principal, the school psychologists, school social workers, guidance counselors, and adjustment counselors discuss ongoing cases and issues. During another weekly session, building-based administrators meet with the staff at large to address various school-related concerns. While it is not atypical for the material covered to have little to no relative meaning for the day-to-day activities of the school psychologist, the meetings are considered supervisory in nature and are mandatory. On a monthly basis Ann meets with other school psychologists across the district to discuss nuts and bolts issues such as what kinds of tests to adopt/explore, how many protocols need to be ordered, and what clinical issues are arising that suggest common concerns. These meetings are overseen by the special education director (a non-school psychologist) and tend to focus on issues of law and policy rather than professional practice.

Ann also regularly participates in several clinical/professional supervision sessions. On a monthly basis she participates in a voluntary meeting with other district

mental health personnel for the provision of peer supervision focusing on issues that traverse mental health positions and responsibilities across the district. These meetings are partially held outside school hours and are supported by various administrators who agree to release any practitioner who expressed an interest (as long as it did not interfere with bus duty). Also on a monthly basis, she meets with local area school psychologists as they gather for informal peer supervision and to discuss topics ranging from presentation of specific cases to state initiatives. Finally, on a weekly basis Ann participates in small group peer supervision sessions with three other school psychologists who also hold (or who are seeking) licensure as mental health counselors. Because this license is not required by the state department of education, these sessions are considered outside of the scope of school duties and thus are held prior to school opening. All participants hold egalitarian positions in the district and none has a formal supervisory responsibility for others in the group.

In addition, Ann serves as a formal supervisor herself. She provides 2 hours of individual supervision for each of the interns (one doctoral and one specialist level) who are working in her school and also runs a group supervision session at least once per week. She relies on members of her informal school psychology peer-support group to provide her with mentoring/supervision of supervisors, since her district does not provide support for supervisors.

Positive Outcomes

Good supervision and mentoring can play a pivotal role in fostering professional growth and strengthening practice for several reasons. First, graduate training alone cannot provide all the requisite skills necessary for optimal professional functioning. Because the job of a school psychologist is complex and multifaceted, and because it takes several years to develop expertise in each facet of practice, it is likely that only after several years of supervised or mentored practice will school psychologists demonstrate expertise across all 10 domains of practice in the NASP Practice Model (NASP, 2010a) and in the three tiers of service delivery. Second, without corrective feedback in practice, skills acquired in graduate coursework may not transfer to actual practice. Furthermore, acquired skills can actually deteriorate over time without feedback. For example, targeted supervision makes it much more likely that practitioners will adhere to treatment guidelines (Milne,

2009). Third, skilled supervision can mitigate the emotional exhaustion stemming from working in the complex and emotionally challenging situations encountered frequently by school psychologists. School psychologists are called upon to help students deal with trauma such as the loss of a friend or family member, they serve as members of school crisis teams, they work with students expressing suicidal ideation, and they can be employed in schools or communities in which there are persistent threats to personal safety and well-being. Appropriate supervision and peer support can enable school psychologists to function effectively in the face of these challenges. It can thus reduce the likelihood of school psychologists' experiencing professional burnout (Dixon & Burns, 2012). Fourth, practitioners who receive mentoring and supervision are more likely to self-reflect, determine whether practice is effective, and subsequently take steps to improve their practice. Isolated professionals tend to neglect these activities (Falender & Shafranske, 2008). Fifth, although yet to be identified in the practice of school psychology, a considerable body of literature in a wide variety of fields, including business, education, and medicine, speaks to the positive effects of mentoring. Mentoring programs for beginning teachers have a positive impact on variables such as teacher retention, and when well structured in terms of careful selection of mentors and weekly contact between mentors and mentees, have been found to have a positive impact on student achievement as well (Fletcher, Strong, & Villar, 2008).

Challenges

Although there is increasing acknowledgment regarding the positive contributions that effective clinical/ professional supervision can make in the practice of school psychology, substantive literature regarding supervision in clinical and counseling psychology, and mounting support and commentary regarding the need for mentoring across all applied psychology disciplines, there are a number of variables that render effective supervision and mentoring of school psychologists difficult. These include insufficient high-quality research; insufficient support for supervision and mentoring in the schools; inadequate training of supervisors and mentors; and a lack of consensus regarding methods, definitions, and measurement of competency in supervision and mentoring. In short, the field is greatly challenged to meet the current professional standards for outcomes- and competency-based practice regarding supervision and mentoring.

BEST PRACTICES IN SUPERVISION AND MENTORING

Essential values, knowledge, and skills necessary for effective supervision and mentoring have been identified. Effective supervisors develop strong working alliances and positive relationships with their supervisees, uphold the ethical principles mandated by the profession, assume vicarious responsibility for their supervisees' practice, and are committed to maintaining a high level of expertise for both their own practice and that of their supervisees (Falender & Shafranske, 2008). Characteristics of successful mentors have also been identified and have much in common with those of successful supervisors. Successful mentors are technically advanced and proficient in the skills and information that the mentee hopes to attain and are equally adept in interpersonal skills that facilitate and support a positive mentor–mentee relationship. They model expert professional practice and life skills. They provide career support by having high expectations for their mentees and taking the time to provide them with relevant materials, resources, learning activities, and collaborative work opportunities. They establish clear goals and expectations and provide structured means to help their mentees meet these goals. They also provide psychosocial support that includes developing a human connection, providing encouragement, being interested in their mentees' ideas and situations, and supporting their mentees' increasing independence (Véronneau, Cance, & Ridenour, 2012). School psychology supervisors and mentors also need to acquire and maintain considerable knowledge regarding the school, district, community, and sociopolitical contexts (including organizational structures, policies, and delegation of duties) in their employing school systems.

Effective supervisors and mentors are skillful teachers in that they identify learning needs, write learning goals, devise instructional strategies, present material didactically and/or experientially, assess learning, give constructive comments, and promote professional growth and self-assessment. They continuously attend to the developmental level of their mentees and supervisees and address multicultural issues effectively. They accurately assess their own skills, solicit and respond to supervisees' and mentees' feedback, and seek consultation when they encounter issues beyond their competence. They are honest about their experiences, including challenges that they face in their own practice, and welcome supervisees and mentees who help them move beyond their own knowledge and skills.

Attending to three overarching variables is critical in the supervision process: (a) building a strong working alliance (Bernard & Goodyear, 2008); (b) using a goal-directed, problem-solving model for supervision itself and for the professional development of the supervisee/mentee that involves setting high yet attainable goals (Carless, Robertson, Willy, Hart, & Chea, 2012); and (c) creating and using effective formative and summative evaluations and progress monitoring (Ladany, Mori, & Mehr, 2013).

Building a Strong and Positive Working Alliance

Strong supervisee–supervisor working alliances result in positive outcomes for supervision, services provided, and student functioning. Supervisory alliances are fostered by collaboration, focusing on competencies, addressing the perspectives of both the supervisor and supervisee, creating an optimal learning environment, considering developmental factors, and attending to diversity. Fostering positive working alliances also increases the likelihood that supervisees will adhere to appropriate recommendations made by the supervisor. A working alliance that supports honest disclosure by supervisees is essential because otherwise they might hide their difficulties and the supervisor will not be able to adjust supervision accordingly. Mehr, Ladany, and Caskie (2010) found that a distressingly high proportion of supervisees (83%) admitted to nondisclosure with their supervisors.

In building effective working alliances, supervisors and mentors employ the same basic communication strategies (attending, reflecting, responding, and following up) used when effectively consulting with teachers, parents, and administrators. Supervisors and mentors should schedule supervision/mentoring sessions at mutually convenient times; prevent interruptions by ignoring e-mails, texts, and phone calls during the sessions; listen with focused attention; and reinforce oral communications and recommendations with written notes at each session's end.

Addressing Developmental Levels

As described in Harvey and Struzziero (2008), several authors have developed models describing characteristics of professionals as they acquire skills (Rønnestad & Skovholt, 2013; Stoltenberg & McNeill, 2010). Across these models, beginners are characterized as shifting from rule-based to intuitive behavior, from an analytical to a holistic perspective, and from being highly anxious

to having increased self-confidence. Lifelong professional growth is described as being propelled by an intense commitment to learn and continuous reflection. In turn, these stages of professional development have been linked to changing supervision requirements (Stoltenberg & McNeill, 2010). Effective supervisors provide more structure and support for novices and a more reflective, collaborative, conceptual, and systemic approach for advanced practitioners. Table 42.1 summarizes the characteristics of supervisees and appropriate strategies for supervision at each developmental level.

It should be noted that school psychologist practitioners' developmental stages are task specific, and whenever individuals learn a new skill, they are novices regarding that skill. For example, the same school psychologist may be an experienced counselor yet a beginner in monitoring the effectiveness of academic interventions. Furthermore, learning and implementing new approaches can be very stressful, and practitioners can be tempted to continue ineffective or outdated practice because it is familiar and feels safe (Harvey & Pearrow, 2010). Thus, whenever they are learning a new skill, practitioners are likely to need close supervision or mentoring until they gain expertise. Similarly, individuals who begin supervising and mentoring may be highly skilled practitioners but novice supervisors. They will need concrete supervision and support as they take on this role.

Addressing Anxiety

Novices are inevitably and appropriately anxious. Even highly expert practitioners are often anxious when someone else is examining their practice, or when they are being evaluated. Although moderate anxiety is helpful in that it raises motivation, excessive anxiety diminishes the ability to learn, has a detrimental effect on performance, and can cause supervisees to hide areas of weakness. Strategies supervisors and mentors can use to help reduce anxiety are (a) acknowledge that anxiety is normal; (b) provide support and positive feedback; (c) assign challenging but manageable assignments; (d) provide greater guidance in areas that are novel or are universally challenging such as crisis response; (e) clarify expectations through modeling and work samples; and (f) share one's own imperfect case conceptualizations, diagnoses, treatments, and intervention implementations.

Addressing Interpersonal Conflicts

Interpersonal difficulties with supervisors are among the most frequently mentioned factors contributing to

Table 42.1. Supervisee Developmental Stage, Characteristics, and Supervisor's Role

Developmental Stage and Authors' Categorization	Supervisees' Characteristics	Supervisor's Roles
• Novice (Harvey & Struzziero, 2008) • Beginning student (Rønnestad & Skovholt, 2013) • Level 1 (Stoltenberg & McNeill, 2010) • Practicum student and intern (Harvey & Struzziero, 2008)	• Rulebound • Simplistic, partial understanding • Difficulty with context • Anxious • Integrate poorly • Motivated • Dependent	• Supervise closely • Provide structure • Assign mild/simple problems and cases • Obtain raw data of supervisee practice such as video and audio recordings, live observation • Provide opportunities for role-playing, interpretation of dynamics, readings, group supervision, shadowing of advanced practitioners, and collaborative work • Focus on strengths and mention positive qualities before criticizing • Monitor clients closely to ensure appropriate care is being provided • Facilitate, prescribe
• Advanced beginner (Harvey & Struzziero, 2008) • Advanced students and Novice professionals (Rønnestad & Skovholt, 2013) • Level 2 (Stoltenberg & McNeill, 2010) • Internship and first few years of professional practice (Harvey & Struzziero, 2008)	• Demonstrate marginally acceptable performance • Focus on mastery of technical aspects • Begin to perceive recurring situations • Start considering context but have difficulty setting priorities and determining relative importance • Demonstrate excessive thoroughness • Continue to feel vulnerable, insecure, and in need of supervision	• Provide less structure and more autonomy • Provide guidelines for recognizing patterns • Continue to obtain raw data • Expose to complex issues • Be less prescriptive and instead facilitate and help conceptualize • Continue to monitor client functioning to ensure quality of services • Employ recordings, live observation, role-playing, interpretation of dynamics and parallel process, and group supervision
• Competent (Harvey & Struzziero, 2008) • Novice professionals (Rønnestad & Skovholt, 2013). • Level 3 (Stoltenberg & McNeill, 2010) • 2 or 3 years of professional practice (Harvey & Struzziero, 2008)	• Better able to see relationships and match patterns • Balance skills and empathy • Plan and think ahead • Analyze self well • Intensely engage in practice and feel responsible for client outcome • Recognize deficiency in training	• Encourage the supervisee to structure supervision sessions themselves • Continue using direct observation when possible • Focus on challenging cases, the development of specialized knowledge, and integration of the supervisee in a complex organization • Use peer and group supervision • Ensure that supervision is available • Support acquiring additional models, methods, and techniques needed to work effectively • Encourage systemic thinking
• Proficient (Harvey & Struzziero, 2008) • Experienced professionals (Rønnestad & Skovholt, 2013) • Can be reached after 3–5 years of practice but does not come from practice alone; requires reflective and integrative practice and usually requires ongoing supervision and/or participation in communities of learning (Harvey & Struzziero, 2008)	• Recognize patterns and see what is of primary importance ("throw out the clutter") • Be attuned to and engaged in the situation • Move from analysis to pattern recognition • Use context and focus on systemic issues • May feel that professional development programs do not meet their needs	• Require inductive reasoning via complex case studies • Review both cases with which supervisees feel success and those with which they do not • Encourage participation in appropriate professional development activities, peer supervision groups, and reading of professional journals so that supervisees are less likely to rely solely on personal experience to guide practice • Help supervisee with challenges such as dealing with client resistance and child advocacy • Continually upgrade skills

Continued

Table 42.1. Continued

Developmental Stage and Authors' Categorization	Supervisees' Characteristics	Supervisor's Roles
• Expert (Harvey & Struzziero, 2008) • Senior professionals (Rønnestad & Skovholt, 2013)	• Rely on experiences to create paradigms • Feel at home in complex and rapidly changing situations • Not rely on guidelines • Integrate across domains of practice • Tend to seek collaboration and teamwork • Often actively seek peer supervision • Enjoy mentoring or supervising	• Evaluate qualitatively • Employ self-case analysis • Use context in evaluation strategies • Encourage supervising the next generation and/or participating in research and other high-level professional development activities to reduce likelihood of apathy or burnout • Provide supervision of supervision when relevant • Encourage to actively participate in, and take leadership positions in, local, state, and national professional associations • Focus on continuing professional development activities that address students' needs and improve outcomes • Encourage to participate in peer support activities (online discussion groups, peer supervision groups), as well as to mentor junior practitioners

supervisees' stress and are manifested in personality conflicts, overly critical supervision, and conflicts regarding supervision session activities, content, and goals (Bernard & Goodyear, 2008). Additional sources of interpersonal difficulties are supervisors who devalue best practices and evidence-based practice; conflicting expectations from multiple supervisors, either within the district or between the university and the field supervisor; and ethical conflicts (Harvey & Struzzierro, 2008). Effectively resolving interpersonal conflict and communication barriers involves seeing differences as natural and appropriate, honestly addressing differences, using objective problem solving, and integrating both views into a common good. Such conflict resolution requires adopting a problem-solving perspective that progressively steps back until common goals are evident.

Addressing Multicultural Issues

Culturally responsive supervision and mentoring, during which supervisees and mentees feel support for exploring cultural issues, can lead to improved supervision and client outcomes (Bernard & Goodyear, 2008). A critical first step in acquiring multicultural competence both for supervisors and supervisees is increasing self-awareness regarding cultural issues. Supervisors can also appraise their own multicultural competencies using a self-report scale, and encourage their supervisees to, with the understanding that they will be subject to the biases inherent in any self-report instrument. An example of a

self-report scale is found in Bernard and Goodyear (2008, pp. 336–339).

Supervisors should ensure that they themselves and their supervisees are familiar with the cultures of the students, parents, teachers, and administrators with whom they work. Both can become better informed about cultural similarities and differences and increase their understanding of the complexity of cultural questions by attending relevant professional workshops, reading targeted professional literature, conducting interviews with members of the cultural group, reading pertinent first-person accounts, and visiting pertinent websites such as the Society for the Psychological Study of Ethnic Minority Issues (http://www.apa.org/divisions/div45). During individual and group sessions, supervisors and mentors can encourage supervisees and mentees to relinquish stereotypes through increased knowledge of pertinent research findings, to increase empathy for the psychological energy required by members of nondominant cultures to cope with diversity issues, and to understand that every person's culture arises from a broad spectrum of characteristics, such as age, ethnicity, race, socioeconomic status, gender, sexual identity, religion, and acculturation.

Both early- and later-career school psychologists may experience diversity issues relative to age. Because of the cohort effect, a supervisor or mentor who is close to retirement is likely to be from a different culture, regardless of ethnicity, than a junior colleague 40 years younger. In this situation—and in all relationships with parents, teachers, and administrators with whom supervisees and mentees have considerable age differences—they will need to be encouraged to employ appropriate empathy and understanding in order to be effective.

Although a pivotal source of identity, issues of ethnicity, race, and class are often marginalized, denied, ignored, and inappropriately left unspoken. This is problematic in that initiating open and supportive discussions regarding race facilitates both supervisory and therapeutic alliances. Such discussions can be critical in creating a trusting relationship and providing both effective interventions and supervision.

Similarly, religion is another area of diversity that affects supervision of school psychologists, but is often ignored. Supervisors and mentors, particularly in diverse settings, may find that their supervisees and mentees have extremely limited knowledge regarding the students' religious lives, which can be a significant factor in student, family, and community life.

Supervisors and mentors of school psychologists often need to address sexual orientation for several reasons. First, young practitioners need help understanding how to create a safe environment for self-disclosure and support for students, since they are very likely to encounter students of diverse sexual orientations. Supervisors and mentors can help develop an understanding of what it is like for nonheterosexuals to maintain invisible relationships, of the coming out process in both the personal and professional spheres, of the gay rights movement and current social battles, and of the effects of homophobia, including threats of physical harm or death. Additionally, supervisees may be of a different sexual orientation than their supervisors, and it is important that supervisors create a safe environment for self-disclosure within the supervisory relationship. Supervisees and mentees who are lesbian, gay, bisexual, or transgender may need help understanding the implications and repercussions, if any, of self-disclosure to administrators and to others within the school district.

Supervisors and mentors should regularly and consciously recommend multicultural case studies and readings, and they should ask supervisees and mentees to review role-plays and recordings for lack of sensitivity and language biases. Supervisors can support multicultural assessment methods by ensuring that the district has and uses assessment tools that address multiple facets of ability and that respect cultural and linguistic diversity.

In turn, supervisors and mentors can assess the impact of multicultural skill development on their own practice by reviewing recordings of their sessions for evidence of multicultural awareness, sensitivity, and responsivity. It can be particularly helpful to ask a colleague or supervisor from a different culture (e.g., age, class, ethnicity, race, gender, sexual orientation, religion) for feedback regarding recorded sessions. Biases can be subtle, so even veterans should appraise their multicultural skills on an ongoing basis.

Addressing Cross-Cultural and Cross-Racial Supervision

When working with supervisees from nonmainstream races or cultures, school psychology supervisors should determine the supervisees' levels of acculturation, skills in managing language barriers, and abilities to manage differences between their cultures and the mainstream culture. To develop a safe supervisory environment, it is also important for supervisors to adapt their communication style to the supervisees' needs. Many cultural variables result in differences in communication style that can, in turn, result in misunderstanding and miscommunication. Differences can include body language, rate of speech, volume of speech, tone of voice, hand gestures, reliance on context, and the use of subtle and indirect communication versus the expectation of direct communication (Ng & Smith, 2012).

It is very important for the supervisors of school psychologists to "make the invisible visible" and raise issues of power differences and initiate conversations regarding race, class, gender, social status, disabilities, sexual orientation, theoretical orientation, and religion. Because of the power differential inherent in the supervisory relationship, supervisees are not positioned to open these discussions themselves. Yet if they are not raised, "unspoken social processes—such as power differentials between supervisor and intern, supervisors who do not attend to racial dynamics and issues, interns who feel a lack of trust and psychological safety—all may inhibit the development of the intern's professional voice, skills, and sense of confidence" (Proctor & Rogers, 2013, p. 2). These discussions can be opened by initiating conversations that candidly discuss power differences in the supervisory relationship as well as differences and similarities among the cultures of the supervisor and the supervisees in terms of communication styles, educational expectations, the meaning of mental health and mental illness, and the role of schools and education.

Adopting a Goal-Directed Problem-Solving Model of Supervision and Mentoring

As does effective work with children, effective supervision and mentoring require the development of mutually agreed upon SMART goals (specific, measurable, attainable, realistic, and time oriented). Goals need to address both the mentee/supervisee's knowledge and skills and the process of mentoring/supervision itself.

Goals regarding knowledge and skills should be collaboratively developed with the mentee or supervisee, should be both long and short term, and should be both high and attainable. In setting long-term goals, the authors have found it to be extremely helpful to use job descriptions or evaluation tools, similar to those provided by Bernard and Goodyear (2008, pp. 313–335) or Harvey and Struzziero (2008, pp. 451–456, 458–459, and 460–470). Such tools provide a framework for discussion and help generate ideas for long-term learning needs and goals. Determining meaningful long-term goals leads to the generation of specific short-term goals, learning activities, and timelines, and these should be written down to ensure a common understanding.

Long-term goals regarding the supervisory or mentoring process can be written in a formal agreement that clarifies expectations, outlines the responsibilities of each person, provides direction for occasions when difficulties arise, and provides a concrete method to measure the performance of all concerned. Short-term goals for each session help focus them appropriately. For example, "continuous feedback," or completing evaluation forms regarding the effectiveness of each supervision and therapy session, improves the outcomes of the therapy (Reese et al., 2009).

Creating and Using Effective Evaluations and Progress Monitoring

Whether the performance evaluation addresses the work of a practicum student, intern, experienced school psychologist, supervisor, or entire department, the same principles apply. Effective appraisals determine whether school psychologists use critical thinking, exercise professional judgment, respond to context, and use self-reflection to evaluate and modify practice as appropriate. Evaluations should determine whether practice, knowledge, skills, behavior, and outcomes (a) meet professional standards; (b) adhere to local, state, and federal guidelines; and (c) result in services that have a positive impact on the functioning of students, school staff, and the school district.

Performance appraisals can be summative or formative. Evaluations that occur at the end of a specified time period and emphasize conclusions and gatekeeping are summative, while those that occur on an ongoing basis and emphasize corrective feedback are formative. The evaluation process is most effective when it integrates formative and summative information. Unfortunately, many school psychologists with a few years of experience are evaluated only with summative evaluations, and only every year or so. Formal and meaningful evaluations by mentors are even more infrequent, and when they occur, mentors are likely to rate every mentee as "excellent" on every scale item, due to discomfort with assigning a negative "grade" (Johnson et al., 2008). Furthermore, summative evaluations used in school districts are often conducted by administrators using inappropriate teacher evaluation forms that do not address school psychologists' critical skills, knowledge, and behaviors. Hence, it will be important for professional organizations at the state and national levels, unions, and individual school districts to ensure that the job requirements of school psychologists are adequately represented and assessed in emerging, new evaluation processes.

The desired frequency of performance appraisals depends on the supervisee's developmental level. Beginners should be evaluated continuously regarding their plans, procedures, alternatives, and implications. Areas of strength and weakness should be determined, and a plan generated for learning activities within the next time frame. Continuous evaluations are formative, but they are also valuable contributors to future summative evaluations.

As much as possible, evaluation methods must be reliable and consistent across raters and time. Reliability is often reduced when supervisors fail to use the full range of rating scales and restrict responses to either the high or low ends of a scale. Thus, supervisors should take care to use the full ranges of the rating scale. Another reliability threat occurs when evaluators do not consider each category independently, resulting in "halo effects" wherein those who are superior (or inferior) in one area are presumed to be superior (or inferior) in others. Again, supervisors need to consciously avoid such response sets.

Evaluation methods also must be valid and measure relevant aspects of performance, and should not discriminate on the basis of personal characteristics that are not job related. Evaluation methods must impart clear information to supervisees regarding expectations and the manner in which to achieve them. Further, appraisals should have minimal contamination by elements outside the individual's control. Strengths should be addressed as much as deficiencies, by using a "fair pair" approach, minimizing criticism, collaboratively developing specific goals for improvement, and focusing discussions on behaviors and outcomes rather than personal attributes. Evaluations have increased meaning when they are incorporated into both personal and organizational professional development plans. It helps to involve supervisees in setting goals and time lines for progress review over the coming year.

Evaluating practicum students and interns is further complicated because it is cooperatively conducted with training programs. Collaboration is seriously compromised if the university and site supervisors do not have the same expectations. Thus, in addition to ensuring that the practicum student or intern's job description or prospectus is aligned with school district goals, supervisors must ensure that their expectations (and those of the school and district) are aligned with training program requirements. Such alignment can be especially demanding when training program requirements exceed the expectations for the practicing school psychologist.

Supervisors should base individual performance evaluations on behaviors or outcomes rather than solely on attributes. Behaviorally anchored rating scales require raters to rate supervisees on operationally defined attributes of excellent, satisfactory, and unsatisfactory performance. The process of constructing these operational definitions can be enlightening because it forces the clear definition of behavioral requirements for the job as well as corresponding data points. Other benefits of behaviorally anchored scales are that they link performance to strategic goals and provide clear and specific guidelines for performance improvement. Examples of behaviorally anchored scales regarding foundational competencies in psychology can be found in Fouad et al. (2009).

Another effective evaluation approach is an outcomes evaluation that focuses on the improvement of students' behavior and learning. Most often, school psychologists will employ single-case study methodology for this process. At least three data points are required during the baseline, and data should be collected at least weekly throughout the intervention.

Finally, the portfolio method involves collecting multiple work samples over time that demonstrate competence. This method is widely used in university training programs to attain national certification, but developing and evaluating portfolios can be too time consuming—for both supervisees and supervisors—to be practical for use outside those settings.

Communicating Evaluation Feedback

Communication with supervisees both before and after the performance appraisal is critical. Insufficient communication results in supervisees' perceiving the process as arbitrary, feeling disconnected from the evaluation process, misunderstanding or being surprised by the feedback, and ignoring the results. In addition, evaluations sometimes become problematic when the supervisor and supervisee have built such a strong supervisory alliance that it becomes difficult for the supervisor to conduct a fair and honest evaluation (Johnson et al., 2008).

It is very helpful to encourage self-assessment by asking the supervisee to complete a written self-appraisal prior to the feedback session. The supervisor can also draft a written appraisal ahead of time. After appraisal information is gathered, the supervisor meets with the supervisee to review the appraisal and make plans. The feedback session should be conducted privately and without interruptions. The supervisor should begin the feedback session with a detailed discussion of strengths, then address weaknesses simply, clearly, and explicitly. It is important to make positive and specific suggestions for improvement, emphasize performance and activities rather than the person, state suggestions for improvement positively, convey specific criticisms clearly, and provide specific examples regarding areas in need of change. The supervisor should encourage supervisees to express their feelings regarding the evaluation and empower them to provide honest reactions. It is also helpful to ask supervisees what can be changed to help them do their jobs better. To determine an appropriate course of action when difficulties have been previously identified yet little progress has been made, the supervisor should explore whether the difficulties stem from a skill deficit or whether an underlying problem exists that requires referral to outside services. Throughout the feedback session, the supervisor should be honest, straightforward, and kind. At the conclusion of the feedback session, the supervisor should link the supervisee's individual learning needs to organizational objectives, develop a plan of action, and summarize the session.

The evaluation process must protect the due process rights of supervisees. Supervisees should never be surprised by an evaluation outcome. To avoid surprises, supervisors should give frequent and honest feedback over time so that the supervisee already knows the forthcoming results prior to the formal evaluation. Supervisors should always voice concerns immediately upon becoming aware of them, discuss them along a continuum, and communicate using a variety of modalities to respect varied learning styles. Supervisors should follow verbal statements with written feedback that includes timelines and specific criteria for the measurement of improvement. If there are serious concerns, the supervisor should give multiple written warnings before finalizing a formal negative review, indicating that, "The review will say [this] if [the following] does not change." By the time a negative evaluation occurs, the supervisee should have received multiple verbal and written communications about any concern, and (if relevant) the training program faculty should have been involved in developing the remediation plans. Supervisees should never be given a negative evaluation that leads to dismissal unless they have first been given adequate notice of inadequate performance, specific criteria for improvement, and time to improve their performance (Bernard & Goodyear, 2008).

Addressing Substandard Performance

Unfortunately, performance evaluations sometimes reveal that a supervisee exhibits chronic substandard performance to the extent that he or she is unable to meet the demands of being a school psychologist. A disconcerting percentage of psychologists exhibit such compromised practice, most commonly due to significant substance abuse, ongoing psychiatric disorders such as severe depression, or violations of ethical codes of conduct such as dual relationships with clients (Mahoney & Morris, 2012). If school psychologists continue to provide substandard services over time, they and their supervisors violate both professional standards and ethical principles. As much as possible, supervisors must protect clients from the ill effects of being subject to such professionals while still protecting the due process rights of supervisees. To ensure that due process rights are not ignored, supervisors can provide regular, ongoing, and goal-directed supervision to supervisees so that they have adequate opportunity to improve skills before dismissal. They can also encourage supervisees to monitor their own functioning by using the self-report instrument published in Mahoney and Morris (2012). Identifying and dealing with substandard performance is one reason that it is very important for job descriptions and specifications and appraisal materials to reflect all critical aspects of job performance. If the supervisee does

not correct the problems, the supervisor consults with administrators to determine and implement a course of action. Supervisors also should address repercussions from the supervisee's actions with school personnel, clients, and training program if applicable.

Supervisor and Mentor Training and Support

Although doctoral-level programs supply coursework in supervision, most school psychology practicum students and interns are supervised by specialist-level school psychologists who may not have completed supervision training. Even when training in supervision is required in a graduate program, it tends to be limited to the development of discrete microskills such as supervision of consultation, assessment, and counseling. Because most graduate students have not yet acquired substantive experience in schools, they are not likely to be able to provide adequate supervision regarding complex services such as systems change.

It seems that opportunities for training in the mentoring of school psychologists have yet to be developed. Although the authors of this chapter are aware of limited professional development programs and support groups provided for mentors by individual school districts, they are not aware of formal coursework regarding mentoring skills being offered to school psychologists. This is in contrast to programs and courses that have been developed for mentoring teachers, typically run by school administrators.

According to a demographic survey by Flanagan and Grehan (2011), few supervising school psychologists have completed formal supervision training. They found 20% had completed graduate coursework in supervision; 20% had completed postgraduate coursework, workshops, or inservice presentations; 63% read articles on supervision; and 73% developed their supervisory knowledge by discussing supervision with other supervisors. Cochrane, Salyers, and Ding (2010) similarly found that supervisors of school psychology interns seldom have been trained in supervision, 15% had taken a course in supervision in graduate school, and 9% took a postgraduate course in supervision. While approximately 40% received postgraduate training in supervision via workshops, the majority of intern supervisors employed reading articles (64%) and having discussions with other supervisors (71%) as strategies to learn about supervision.

There is some evidence that participating in even short-term training increases supervisor effectiveness, particularly when it includes critical feedback, educational role-playing, and modeling via live or video demonstrations (Milne, Sheikh, Pattison, & Wilkinson, 2011). Novice school psychology supervisors and mentors can obtain training in a number of ways. They can attend professional workshops; participate in peer supervision networks; attend university-run training for field supervisors; or complete formal coursework that includes didactic instruction, role-playing, and applied practice. A number of state professional organizations and training programs have collaborated to provide supervision institutes. These provide support and training for supervisors and also foster increased networking and peer support (Harvey et al., 2010). Attending workshops, taking courses, and participating in supervision institutes are good introductions to critical issues but must be supplemented by deliberate self-study and participation and ongoing supervision support to make a lasting impact. All supervisors should seek consultation and collegial supervision from other supervisors or expert school psychologists, particularly when supervising in relatively unfamiliar areas.

Case example 2: In her first 3 years of practice, Rupa has worked with diverse students, families, school staff, and administrators. She has gained invaluable experiences in assessment, prevention, intervention, and consultation in her early career and now feels ready to assume the responsibility of supervising a practicum student. Rupa's supervisor, Dr. Murphy, is responsible for overseeing the placement of practicum students and interns across the district. Dr. Murphy conducts interviews with school psychology students to select practicum and internship candidates, and then matches them with appropriate supervisors. With Rupa's input, Dr. Murphy pairs Rupa with a student Dr. Murphy believes will be a good match for both Rupa and the school district. To provide support for practitioners providing supervision of practicum students and interns, Dr. Murphy leads mandatory supervision meetings every month. Through these meetings, Rupa is able to receive both peer and administrative support to navigate her first year as a practicum supervisor.

Evaluating Supervisor Effectiveness

Effective supervisor evaluations can improve performance, focus professional development activities, identify and improve programs and procedures, provide professional recognition, and document effectiveness. Like supervisee evaluations, supervisor evaluations should address critical skills such as ethical practice, communication and interpersonal skills, multicultural skills,

data-based decision making, clinical planning and provision, and evaluative expertise. Improved functioning of supervisees and of students is perhaps the most valid assessment of supervision effectiveness. To this end, direct observations of the supervisor's method, style, and content of communication with supervisees are recommended (Bernard & Goodyear, 2008; Falender & Shafranske, 2008).

Cochrane et al. (2010) investigated the extent to which school psychology intern supervisors are evaluated, and found that 60% were not evaluated as an intern supervisor. Of those who were evaluated, 18% were evaluated by the intern, 12% by the intern and university coordinator, and 11% by the university coordinator alone. Rating scales and interviews were the most frequently used methods. Such supervisor evaluation tools are available from a variety of sources, including Bernard and Goodyear (2008), Falender and Shafranske (2008), and Harvey and Struzziero (2008).

In a comprehensive approach to supervisor evaluation, the supervisor's professional behaviors, leadership, program management, and professional development are assessed by tapping information from a variety of sources. The role description is used to help develop rating scales that address professional behaviors, leadership behaviors, and program management. Those rating scales are then completed by the supervisor, administrators, peers, parents, and supervisees. The rating scale responses are augmented by a supervision portfolio that provides evidence of technical skills, including personnel management, program leadership, program development, training and consultation, public relations, and program evaluation. The supervisor meets with his or her administrator to review the gathered information and develop goals, objectives, and activities for the coming year (Harvey & Struzziero, 2008).

SUMMARY

Good professional practice supervision and mentoring play a pivotal role in fostering professional growth, reducing stress and burnout, and strengthening practice in school psychology. Both APA and NASP support ongoing professional practice supervision beyond the internship level. Supervisors and mentors work to help others maintain current competencies, develop new ones, and provide effective services. Supervisors also assess professional competencies of supervisees, and while mentors do not formally evaluate, they do ensure that students with whom their mentee works receive appropriate services. Evidence-based supervision and mentoring strategies can be grouped into three categories: building a strong working alliance; using a goal-directed problem-solving model; and using effective monitoring. Building a strong and successful working alliance depends on effective communication, attending to the development level of the supervisee or mentee, addressing anxiety, resolving conflict, and addressing multicultural issues. Goal-directed problem-solving supervision and mentoring requires the development of mutually agreed upon goals regarding the development of professional knowledge and skills, the delivery of services to students, and the content and process of supervision and mentoring itself. Effective monitoring includes evaluations that determine whether school psychological practice, knowledge, skills, and behavior meet professional standards and local, state, and federal guidelines. Novice supervisors and mentors can obtain training by attending professional workshops, participating in peer support groups, attending university-run training, or completing formal coursework. All of these are good introductions to critical issues, but ongoing self-study and/or support is necessary to make a lasting impact.

AUTHOR NOTE

Disclosure. Virginia Smith Harvey and Joan A. Struzziero have a financial interest in books they authored or coauthored referenced in this chapter.

REFERENCES

American Psychological Association. (2009). *Guidelines and principles for accreditation of programs in professional psychology*. Washington, DC: Author. Retrieved from http://www.apa.org/ed/accreditation/about/policies/guiding-principles.pdf

Annan, J., & Ryba, K. (2013). Networks of professional supervision. *School Psychology Quarterly, 28*, 170–182. doi:10.1037/spq0000015

Bernard, J. M., & Goodyear, R. K. (2008). *Fundamentals of clinical supervision* (4th ed.). Boston, MA: Allyn & Bacon.

Carless, S. A., Robertson, K., Willy, J., Hart, M., & Chea, S. (2012). Successful postgraduate placement experiences: What is the influence of job and supervisor characteristics? *Australian Psychologist, 47*, 156–164. doi:10.1111/j.1742-9544.2012.00085.x

Cochrane, W. S., Salyers, K., & Ding, Y. (2010). An examination of the preparation, supervisor's theoretical model, and university support for supervisors of school psychology interns. *Trainer's Forum: Journal of the Trainers of School Psychologists, 29*(1), 6–22.

Curtis, M. J., Castillo, J. M., & Gelley, C. (2012). School psychology 2010: Demographics, employment, and the context for professional practices–Part 1. *Communiqué, 40*(7), 1, 28–30.

Dixon, R. J., & Burns, B. R. (2012). The relationship of supervision to burnout for school psychologists. *Trainer's Forum: Journal of the Trainers of School Psychologists, 31*(1), 58–70.

Falender, C. A., & Shafranske, E. P. (2008). *Casebook for clinical supervision: A competency-based approach*. Washington, DC: American Psychological Association. doi:10.1037/11792-000

Flanagan, R., & Grehan, P. (2011). Assessing school psychology supervisor characteristics: Questionnaire development and findings. *Journal of Applied School Psychology, 27*, 21–41. doi:10.1080/15377903.2011.540504

Fletcher, S., Strong, M., & Villar, A. (2008). An investigation of the effects of variations in mentor-based induction on the performance of students in California. *Teachers College Record, 110*, 2271–2289.

Fouad, N. A., Grus, C. L., Hatcher, R. L., Kaslow, N. J., Hutchings, P. S., Madson, M. B., … Crossman, R. E. (2009). Competency benchmarks: A model for understanding and measuring competence in professional psychology across training levels. *Training and Education in Professional Psychology, 3*(4, Suppl.), S5–S26. doi:10.1037/a0015832

Harvey, V. S., Amador, A., Finer, D., Gotthelf, D., Hintze, J., Kruger, L., … Wandle, C. (2010). Improving field supervision through collaborative supervision institutes. *Communiqué, 38*(7), 22–24.

Harvey, V. S., & Pearrow, M. (2010). Identifying challenges in supervising school psychologists. *Psychology in the Schools, 47*, 567–581. doi:10.1002/pits.20491

Harvey, V. S., & Struzziero, J. A. (2008). *Professional development and supervision of school psychologists: From intern to expert* (A joint publication with the National Association of School Psychologists). Thousand Oaks, CA: Corwin Press.

Johnson, W. B., Barnett, J. E., Elman, N. S., Forrest, L., & Kaslow, N. J. (2012). The competent community: Toward a vital reformulation of professional ethics. *American Psychologist, 67*, 557–569. doi:10.1037/a0027206

Johnson, W. B., Elman, N. S., Forrest, L., Robiner, W., Rodolfa, E., & Schaffer, J. B. (2008). Addressing professional competence problems in trainees: Some ethical considerations. *Professional Psychology: Research and Practice, 39*, 589–599. doi:10.1037/a0014264

Ladany, N., Mori, Y., & Mehr, K. E. (2013). Effective and ineffective supervision. *The Counseling Psychologist, 41*, 28–47. doi:10.1177/0011000012442648

Mahoney, E. B., & Morris, R. J. (2012). Practicing school psychology while impaired: Ethical, professional, and legal issues. *Journal of Applied School Psychology, 28*, 338–353. doi:10.1080/15377903.2012.722100

Mehr, K., Ladany, N., & Caskie, G. I. L. (2010). Trainee nondisclosure in supervision: What are they not telling you? *Counselling and Psychotherapy Research, 10*, 103–112. doi:10.1080/14733141003712301

Milne, D. L. (2009). *Evidence-based clinical supervision: Principles and practice*. Leicester, England: British Psychological Society.

Milne, D. L., Sheikh, A. I., Pattison, S., & Wilkinson, A. (2011). Evidence-based training for clinical supervisors: A systematic review of 11 controlled studies. *The Clinical Supervisor, 30*, 53–71. doi:10.1090/07325223.2011.564955

National Association of School Psychologists. (2010a). *Model for comprehensive and integrated school psychological services*. Bethesda, MD: Author. Retrieved from http://www.nasponline.org/standards/2010standards/2_PracticeModel.pdf

National Association of School Psychologists. (2010b). *Standards for graduate preparation of school psychologists*. Bethesda, MD: Author.

Retrieved from http://www.nasponline.org/standards/2010standards/1_Graduate_Preparation.pdf

Ng, K.-M., & Smith, S. D. (2012). Training level, acculturation, role ambiguity, and multicultural discussions in training and supervising international counseling students in the United States. *International Journal of Advanced Counselling, 34*, 72–86. doi:10.1007/s10447-011-9130-8

Proctor, S. L., & Rogers, M. R. (2013). Making the invisible visible: Understanding social processes within internship supervision. *School Psychology Forum: Research in Practice, 7*(1), 1–12.

Reese, R. J., Usher, E. L., Bowman, D. C., Norsworthy, L. A., Halstead, J. L., Rowlands, S. R., & Chisholm, R. R. (2009). Using client feedback in psychotherapy training: An analysis of its influence on supervision and counselor self-efficacy. *Training and Education in Professional Psychology, 3*, 157–168. doi:10.1037/a0015673

Rønnestad, M. H., & Skovholt, T. M. (2013). *The developing practitioner: Growth and stagnation of therapists and counselors.* New York, NY: Routledge.

Stoltenberg, C. D., & McNeill, B. (2010). *IDM supervision: An integrated developmental model for counselors and therapists* (3rd ed.). San Francisco, CA: Jossey-Bass.

Véronneau, M.-H., Cance, J. D., & Ridenour, T. A. (2012). Mentoring early-career preventionists: Current views from mentors and protégés. *Prevention Science, 13*, 493–503. doi:10.1007/s11121-012-0276-3

43

Best Practices in School Psychologists' Self-Evaluation and Documenting Effectiveness

Barbara Bole Williams
Rowan University
Laura Williams Monahon
Philadelphia College of Osteopathic Medicine

OVERVIEW

Evaluation of school psychologists' professional performance refers to methods of appraising or assessing the effectiveness of their knowledge, skills, and professional work characteristics in the field of school psychology. Consistent with the domain Legal, Ethical, and Professional Practices in the National Association of School Psychologists (NASP) *Model for Comprehensive and Integrated School Psychological Services* (NASP, 2010a), school psychologists are responsible not only for adhering to ethical, legal, and professional standards, but also for addressing factors related to professional identity and effective practice.

The rationale for engaging in self-evaluation is to encourage school psychologist practitioners to become involved in a multimethod process to examine their own professional practices. Simply stated, the primary reasons for undertaking the process of self-evaluation are for school psychologists to understand and improve their performance with the ultimate goal of practicing more effectively so they can contribute to improving student outcomes. Through self-evaluation, school psychologists can judge the effectiveness of their knowledge, skills, and beliefs to help make decisions about the strengths and weaknesses of their practices with the intent of self-improvement. Armed with this information, school psychologists can collaborate with students, teachers, administrators, and parents to ensure that school psychological services have a positive impact on student outcomes.

School psychologists can also use self-evaluation techniques and strategies as methods for documenting their effectiveness in response to feedback from supervisors. Documentation of performance improvement through self-evaluation can be incorporated into a larger picture of personnel evaluations and accountability measures (e.g., supervisory job performance ratings and evaluations of how well school psychologist practitioners are fulfilling their job descriptions and responsibilities). Ultimately, improved and enhanced job performance by school psychologists leads to improved student outcomes.

School psychologist practitioners who engage in self-evaluation by using the strategies and techniques outlined in this chapter will learn how to (a) better assess their own knowledge, skills, and professional work characteristics; (b) be better able to incorporate feedback from supervisors and other stakeholders to improve their job performance; (c) use student outcome data to determine their effectiveness and to document the value of their contributions to improved student outcomes; and (d) become familiar with and learn to implement several methods of self-evaluation, including NASP's Self-Assessment Checklist for School Psychologists (http://www.nasponline.org/standards/survey/survey_launch.aspx) and the Framework for School Psychologists' Self-Evaluation tool included in the Appendix. This chapter provides a framework by which school psychologists can engage in a standards-based self-evaluation of their knowledge, skills, and professional work characteristics and measure the effectiveness of their services for students.

These tools offer school psychologists practical, user-friendly methods of self-evaluation.

The information contained within this chapter is a resource for school psychologists who are seeking ways to (a) address the need for measures of professional competencies using self-evaluation methods, (b) identify methods to incorporate sources of student outcome data to demonstrate the effective impact of their work, and (c) learn how to use the documented positive impact of their services to advocate for maintaining or increasing school psychology positions.

BASIC CONSIDERATIONS

Historically, the focus of educational reform initiatives has moved away from focusing on process and content (e.g., what is taught to students of all ages) and moved toward issues related to measurable student outcomes (Waldron & Prus, 2006). In other words, it is not just the knowledge or *what* has been taught that is the measure of students' abilities; rather it is the degree to which the students are able to demonstrate the knowledge and skills via their performance. According to Waldron and Prus (2006), "standards, outcomes, and accountability are now seen as the foundation of education" (p. 2).

Skalski and Cowan (2010) state that "everything in educational policy reform today in some way connects to student outcomes" (p. 1). These authors espouse that school psychologists should become advocates for action in order to demonstrate how their services are essential and connected to priority student outcomes, so they are more likely to survive school district budget cuts during economic hard times.

Similarly, school psychologists in professional practice are also being asked to engage in continuous self-assessment of their knowledge and skills as they plan for areas of continuing professional development and improvement. For example, those school psychologists who hold the credential of Nationally Certified School Psychologist (NASP, 2010c) not only must meet the entry-level requirements to earn that credential but also are required to engage in self-determined, ongoing professional development through the acquisition of continued professional development to maintain their credential and to demonstrate their commitment to lifelong learning. Most state departments of education have requirements for professionals to engage in continuing professional development to renew state credentials (e.g., certificates of license) for work in schools.

Performance-based assessment in school psychology focuses on evidence that school psychologists' services

contribute to positive, measurable changes in the education, learning, and mental health of children (i.e., student outcomes). In terms of performance-based assessment, emphasis is now on encouraging a broader array of, or multiple methods for assessing and documenting student outcomes. Thus multiple sources of data across multiple domains of knowledge and skills are required to measure whether or not school psychologists are achieving their intended outcomes. Waldron and Prus (2006) cite a variety of assessment methods used within graduate education programs in school psychology, including "examinations, performance appraisals, case studies, simulations, portfolios, candidate and graduate questionnaires, exit interviews and survey of supervisors, employers, and other external constituents" (p. 7). Practicing school psychologists can examine a variety of student outcomes (e.g., students' progress in academic, behavioral, and mental health areas) and seek feedback from teachers and parents to gauge the effectiveness of their direct and indirect interventions.

To assess how school psychology practitioners improve student outcomes, Skalski and Cowan (2010) recommend that every school psychologist reflect upon his or her own practices and answer the following questions:

How do I improve student outcomes? How can I demonstrate that what I do is of critical importance to children? Who knows about the breadth of my training and value of my services to student success and who else do I need to tell? How do my services support the priorities of my school district? (Skalski & Cowan, 2010, p. 18)

Self-Evaluation as a Method of Assessing Educator Effectiveness

Other educators are using self-evaluation as one method among many of assessing competencies within their professions. The work of Danielson (Danielson & McGreal, 2000) has been used by educators to identify methods for enhancing professional practice with the goal of improved student outcomes. Danielson's comprehensive framework incorporates tools to assist teachers in reflecting upon, understanding, and enhancing their practice. Danielson's work describes four factors that contribute to professional learning by educators: reflective practice, collaboration, self-assessment, and self-directed inquiry. Supporting self-assessment and self-directed inquiry with evaluator input, Danielson states that teachers not only tend to know their areas of strength and weakness, but also desire to bring areas of practice to a higher level. Advocating for the use of self-assessment to determine areas in need of improvement, Danielson believes that teachers are able to assess their own practice accurately. She differentiates between experienced teachers' abilities to engage in accurate self-assessment and the type of guided self-assessment required of novice teachers. According to Danielson, self-assessment requires reflection on the quality of an individual's teaching and is based on evaluative criteria or teaching standards. Central to Danielson's model is the necessity of identifying a coherent, clear set of principles or standards that define effective teaching.

Marzano (Marzano, Norford, Paynter, Pickering, & Gaddy, 2001) is another educator who specializes in assessing teacher effectiveness and has synthesized 30 years of accumulated research on types of instructional strategies that work best to improve student achievement. Marzano has identified nine such categories of instructional strategies. Among his methods of assessment are systematic monitoring of teaching goals and the process of self-examination. Teachers are required to examine their own instructional strategies within these nine categories, test the effectiveness of their current practice, and consider new practices. Marzano et al. (2001) note, "Ultimately, this process of self-examination, testing the effectiveness of what we do, and considering new ways of doing things is the key to success in the classroom" (p. 347).

As in the contemporary work of Danielson and Marzano, school psychologists can advocate for the use of self-evaluation in a manner parallel to that being used to contribute to assessment of teacher effectiveness. The coherent set of principles represented by the NASP standards in general, and the NASP Practice Model (NASP, 2010a) specifically, serves as the criteria by which school psychologists can judge their own effectiveness in professional practice. Furthermore, self-assessment becomes a tool for self-study, and perhaps a vehicle to form self-study groups to provide social support as school psychologists acquire knowledge and build skills through discussion, analysis, and self-reflection.

Determining Effectiveness Through Improved Student Outcomes

In addition to using methods of self-evaluation, school psychologists can engage in other methods of data collection to demonstrate the effectiveness of their services. School psychologists are in a unique position to collaborate with students, educators, and parents to address the issues of improving student outcomes. *Student outcomes* refers to indices of academic achievement, positive behavior, and mental wellness of all students. Student outcome data in the areas of academic achievement include, for example, (a) district-wide and state tests, (b) benchmark assessments (e.g., end-of-unit and grade-level tests), (c) formative assessments (e.g., writing samples, student science journals, math problems, and other student work), and (d) classroom performance-based assessments utilizing rubrics to assess student work products. In the behavioral and mental health areas, methods of collecting student outcomes include, for example, teacher narratives, information shared during parent–teacher conferences, and direct observations of the student in natural settings.

School psychologists also work with educators and school administrators to develop systems to monitor student progress in behavioral and mental health areas. For example, positive behavior support systems teach, model, and reinforce appropriate student behavior at the classroom and school-wide level. Another example is the use of population-based assessment of mental health issues that help school psychologists and other educators identify those students who may be at risk for mental health problems that create barriers to learning and succeeding in school. The result of identifying potentially at-risk students is to naturally develop interventions to address their needs (Baker, 2008).

Adelman and Taylor (2006) described a set of six characteristics of a school environment, termed *learning supports*, that enhance students' mental health and thereby increase students' abilities to benefit from good-quality instruction. These learning supports are (a) classroom and curricular adaptations and modifications, (b) prevention orientation that promotes healthy development and early intervention in crisis situations, (c) a welcoming and caring school community that provides continuity and support for students and families across school transitions, (d) family involvement, (e) community outreach and engagement, and (f) systems to provide specific interventions to students and families. Knowing these six characteristics allows school psychologists to document their involvement in establishing and maintaining these learning supports and in so doing contribute to positive student outcomes.

Given access to these types of student outcome data, school psychologists can analyze and interpret the data to demonstrate improved student outcomes following their direct or indirect school psychological service delivery (i.e., through consultation, counseling, or other methods) with students, teachers, administrators, and parents. Methods of data analysis might involve comparison of pre- and post-treatment data, progress monitoring data, individual or group data, and narrative or anecdotal data, or testing hypotheses to determine the effectiveness of interventions via single-subject design.

Dreyfus and Dreyfus Developmental Model

Dreyfus and Dreyfus (1991) developed a five-stage phenomenological model to describe how individuals gain expertise and improve their skills. Because the model was developed using a phenomenological rather than a contextualized approach, it can be applied to the development of professional competencies in a variety of areas. Indeed, Dreyfus and Dreyfus (1991) demonstrated the universality of the model by providing the examples of driving a car and playing a game of chess in their seminal description of the five-stage model.

The five-stage model outlines a process whereby individuals progress through five levels: novice, advanced beginner, competence, proficiency, and expertise (Dreyfus & Dreyfus, 1991). While the model was conceived to describe the development of expertise specifically in the area of ethics, the phenomenological nature of the model invites application of its principles to a variety of areas within professional school psychology. Further investigation of the five-stage model suggests that the initial stage (novice) could be applied most meaningfully to those school psychology students whose exposure to ethical principles and issues is limited to didactic classroom instruction. The second stage (advanced beginner) is characterized by the novice "gain[ing] experience actually coping with real situations" (Dreyfus & Dreyfus, 1991, p. 232). As such, the advanced beginner stage naturally aligns with school psychology interns, or those students who have completed foundational coursework and are participating in supervised field experiences. The remaining three stages—competence, proficiency, and expertise—describe levels of experience that can be gained as practicing school psychologists build their careers in the field (Dreyfus & Dreyfus, 1991).

As with any professional practice, graduate students in school psychology programs and school psychologist practitioners demonstrate varied levels of knowledge, skills, and professional work characteristics as they progress along the developmental continuum. For example, applying the five-stage model to acquisition of ethical skills, Dreyfus and Dreyfus (1991) describe a

process whereby "beginners" make decisions based on "strict rules and features" until they gain sufficient experience to allow them to "[see] intuitively what to do without applying rules and making judgments at all" (p. 235). In terms of skill acquisition, the same five stages (novice, advanced beginner, competence, proficiency, and expertise) can be applied to school psychologist practitioners as they move through their professional career.

Variability also is apparent across the multiple roles school psychologists assume within their job, including assessment, counseling, consultation with teachers and parents, and planning and development of educational programs. For example, a beginning school psychologist may feel he or she is competent in administering a specific cognitive assessment (based on training and experience), and yet may feel less competent in another area of the practice of school psychology, such as consultation with teachers and parents.

Assessing Competence

The American Psychological Association formed a Task Force on Assessment of Competence in Professional Psychology to delineate the guiding principles for the assessment of competence (Rubin et al., 2007). The task force concluded that competency-based education and assessment for professional psychologists requires reflective practice and self-assessment. Professional competencies are viewed as clusters of integrated knowledge, skills, and abilities that should be evaluated continuously and redefined in relation to standards throughout one's career. The task force further recommended establishing benchmarks for professional practice for measuring performance. Key components for assessing progress toward achieving these benchmarks include self-awareness, self-reflection, self-understanding, and self-evaluation. To accomplish this process, the task force recommended establishing a culture that supports self-evaluation beginning in graduate school, wherein students practice incorporating feedback from others, integrating input from multiple sources, and experiencing opportunities for peer, professor, and supervisor review.

Kaslow et al. (2007b) state that assessment of competence should be a multitrait, multimethod, and multi-informant process. Self-assessment is defined as "the ability to validly ascertain one's strengths and areas in need of improvement and have an awareness of one's own limits of expertise" (p. 445). Further, Rubin et al. (2007) conclude that central to maintaining professional competence is for psychologists to use data for assessing their own performance, with an increased focus on ongoing self-assessment that incorporates learning, practice, feedback, and standards-based comparisons.

Validity of Self-Evaluation

Inherent in the use of various methods of self-evaluation is the issue of establishing the validity of the data collected. Self-evaluation of professional practices and performance may be subject to questions of validity as a reliable source of assessment data. However, the more precise and specific the criteria upon which an individual school psychologist is evaluating himself or herself, the more valid and precise the assessment will become. To enhance validity, multiple methods of sampling behavior (e.g., rating scales, portfolios) by multiple evaluators (e.g., self, supervisor, peer) over time will bolster validity and reliability and reduce sources of potential bias. Kaslow et al. (2007a) conclude that the face validity of self-assessment methods is strong, but acknowledge that there are few self-assessment measures that have been standardized with reported reliability and validity. Self-assessment measures are most effective when used in conjunction with ratings from other informants. However, Kaslow et al. (2007a) state that self-assessment requires accurate self-appraisal, which is often difficult to teach, and therefore recommends that self-assessment be used in conjunction with other assessments.

Model of Evaluation

Alkin (2011) recommends that personnel evaluations need to be conducted in a systematic way. Employing a model of evaluation that incorporates both formative and summative assessments will enhance the value of self-assessment. Formative assessment that takes place on an ongoing basis offers feedback on performance and can be defined operationally as assessing baseline knowledge, skills, and professional work characteristics; identifying areas of strengths and weaknesses; developing learning objectives; and progress monitoring growth. Summative evaluation, according to Alkin (2011), is designed to inform decisions by focusing on the measurement of outcomes relative to the anticipated objective. Thus, in terms of self-assessment of school psychologists' knowledge, skills, and professional work characteristics, using formative self-assessment will assist school psychologists in monitoring ongoing progress and encouraging self-awareness and self-reflection. In turn, summative evaluation focuses on measurement of outcomes.

Diversity

Issues related to diversity also need to be considered when using self-evaluation as a means of determining the effectiveness of school psychological services. As with all types of assessment, self-evaluation needs to be sensitive to both individual and cultural differences by considering the impact of one's beliefs, values, and attitudes relative to the evaluative decisions that an individual uses when assessing his or her own strengths and weaknesses.

Moreover, school psychologists are ethically responsible for developing multicultural awareness, sensitivity, and responsiveness. The term *multicultural* refers to issues of age, socioeconomic status, disability, ethnicity and race, gender, sexual orientation, and religion. Harvey and Struzziero (2008) recommend that supervisors of school psychologist practitioners self-evaluate their multicultural skills on an ongoing basis and include improvement of multicultural skills as on ongoing goal.

BEST PRACTICES IN SCHOOL PSYCHOLOGISTS' SELF-EVALUATION TO DOCUMENT EFFECTIVENESS

The process of school psychologists' self-evaluation to document effectiveness occurs in stages involving (a) assessing baseline knowledge, skills, and professional work characteristics to determine levels of competency in relationship to criterion-based outcomes; (b) identifying areas of strengths and weaknesses; (c) engaging in self-reflection and decision making to determine learning objectives and action needed; and (d) monitoring progress and evaluating growth. Woven into these above steps is the critical examination of student outcomes as measures for documenting effectiveness. Each of these stages will be discussed briefly below.

Assessing and Determining Effectiveness by Examining Student Outcomes

Best practice recommends school psychologist practitioners engage in self-evaluation. Practical guidelines suggest that first school psychologists need to become knowledgeable about the expectations, objectives, or requirements of their role. Sources of this information include, but are not limited to, the NASP Practice Model (NASP, 2010a), state department of education models, and/or standards and local school board policies. Furthermore, school psychologists should become familiar with their school district's priorities, as well as how state- and federal-level regulations support certain programs and target specific student outcomes. Once they identify the criteria or domains of school psychology practice relevant for the school psychologists' roles and functions in their particular employment settings, school psychologist can assess how well they are meeting the criteria in these targeted areas. Using a rubric format is an effective method to self-assess where individuals are in relationship to their desired goals and stated criteria.

During the assessment stage, school psychologists can utilize external feedback regarding their performance (supervisor ratings, direct observation of their performance, interviews with stakeholders) to begin to gather data on the effectiveness of their professional practice. These sources of feedback may already exist or could be readily secured.

Self-evaluation of knowledge and skills can also be a valuable method to assess self-efficacy and to contribute to personnel evaluations of school psychologists. NASP (2012) endorses "accurate, high quality and reliable personnel evaluation" for two purposes: to enhance professional school psychological practice and to improve student outcomes in the areas of achievement, behavior, and social–emotional functioning. NASP recommends the use of the NASP Practice Model (NASP, 2010a) as the framework for personnel evaluations and the involvement of affected professionals in creating a relevant feedback system. Individual state departments of education also may develop state standards for school psychologists that include tools for self- and personnel evaluation. For example, the Louisiana Department of Education and Louisiana School Psychological Association (2010) have proposed the use of value-added portfolios to evaluate the effectiveness of school psychologists by requiring each school psychologist in the state to complete and submit case studies that include evidence of improved student outcomes. Whether referencing national or state models, NASP advocates for the use of valid, reliable, and meaningful methods of personnel performance evaluation. Among the multiple methods for evaluation of professional performance is self-evaluation.

It is at the assessment stage that school psychologists should begin to consider student outcome data in academic, behavioral, and mental health areas. State department of education and individual school district websites typically house school report cards that supply student outcome data that can be directly related in part to the impact of services school psychologists provide to students, parents, teachers, and administrators. School psychologists can analyze these data to determine how effectively fulfilling their job responsibilities contributes to improving student outcomes. Certainly, school psychologists do not work single-handedly to have an impact on all of these outcome measures directly, but through their collaboration with students, parents, teachers, and administrators, school psychologists contribute in many ways. Self-assessment activities at this stage will seek to determine the areas in which school psychological services have a positive impact on student learning, behavior, and mental health. Once these areas are isolated, the data can be used to document the effectiveness of school psychologist practitioners.

NASP's *Ready to Learn, Empowered to Teach: Excellence in Education for the 21st Century* (NASP, 2008) outlines five guiding principles for effective educational policies and practices calling for schools to provide the following: (a) comprehensive curricula matched with individualized instruction, (b) sufficient student support services to address barriers to learning for all students on a continuum of care that engages families and community providers, (c) comprehensive accountability and progress-monitoring measures that provide a valid picture of student and school functioning, (d) professional development and supports for teachers and other educators necessary for instructional excellence, and (e) federal leadership and school-based research to promote effective services that support the whole child in the learning context.

Examining the five guiding principles for effective educational policies and practices outlined above, a parallel clearly exists between these identified needs and school psychological services. NASP's *School Psychologists: Improving Student and School Outcomes* (NASP, 2010b) outlines numerous examples of how school psychologists' roles and responsibilities support the *Ready to Learn, Empowered to Teach* (NASP, 2008) five guiding principles and how these services directly link to improved outcomes for students. For example, the *Ready to Learn, Empowered to Teach* Guiding Principle 3 calls for comprehensive accountability in the form of progress-monitoring measures that provide a valid picture of student and school functioning. Such measures are ideal methods by which school psychologists can demonstrate their skills and effectiveness as measurement experts within the school district. The following methods of determining school psychological services' effectiveness are organized within a three-tiered model of universal, indicated, and selected levels.

Universal Level

School psychologists who collaborate with administrators and school leadership teams can collect, analyze, and examine data related to student outcomes on district-adopted and/or state-mandated tests that are included in the No Child Left Behind (NCLB) school accountability systems. Has the school achieved annual yearly progress goals as established by NCLB? At the school- and district-wide level, these data can contribute to determining if the school psychologist has been effective in assisting in meeting the school accountability mandates. Furthermore, at the district level, school psychologists often play key roles in the implementation of a positive behavioral support (PBS) system. School psychologists can examine student outcome data within the PBS system to document their role in promoting positive outcomes and reducing behavior problems that represent barriers to learning.

Selected Level

School psychologists who help to design, implement, and analyze population-based screening assessments in behavioral and mental health areas (e.g., bullying surveys and depression screenings) should examine theses data to help determine their effectiveness.

Moreover, participating as a catalyst to extend the scope of school psychological services to all students through population-based services is an important contribution and worthy of examining.

Indicated Level

School psychologists who consult with teachers and parents to design and implement academic and behavioral progress-monitoring systems at the classroom or building level can investigate individual student outcome measures to help determine if their collaboration has contributed to student growth. Through progress monitoring, student's academic and behavioral growth is readily apparent.

Taken together, each of these methods, as well as others, can be used to examine student outcomes to determine the effectiveness of school psychological services. Table 43.1 offers additional examples of academic and behavioral student outcomes at the universal, selected, and indicated levels.

Identifying Strengths and Weaknesses

As school psychologists review and reflect upon the feedback from various sources (i.e., supervisor rating,

Table 43.1. Examples of Academic and Behavioral Student Outcomes at the Universal, Selected, and Indicated Levels

Level	Academic	Behavioral/Mental Health
Universal	• Scores on state-mandated and district-adopted tests • Attendance rates • Dropout rates • Graduation rates	• Positive behavioral support data • Attendance rates • Dropout rates • Graduation rates • Student suspension rates • Student expulsion rates • Population-based screening results (e.g., depression screening)
Selected	• Progress monitoring through classroom assessments, curriculum-based measurement, and other teacher-collected data; review of building-based intervention team's progress notes	• Positive impact of school psychologist-led communication and social skills groups (e.g., anger management, self-regulation, and positive psychology practices) • Progress monitoring through ongoing tracking of student data (e.g., behavioral incidences, such as detentions, suspensions); review of building-based intervention team's progress notes
Indicated	• Progress monitoring of the individual student's academic progress through classroom assessments, conferences with teachers and parents, report cards, observation of the student. • Completion of single-subject case studies to monitor impact of intervention on the student's academic growth in the targeted area	• Progress monitoring of the individual student's behavioral/mental health status through discipline referrals; counseling progress notes (by the school psychologist); conferences with teachers, parents, and students; report cards; observation of the student • Completion of single case studies to monitor the impact of the intervention of the student's behavioral/mental health growth in the targeted area

interviews with stakeholders, surveys) and consider their impact on improving student outcomes, the capacity for self-evaluation becomes increasingly important. Using the data gathered from multiple sources, school psychologists can reflect upon their identified areas of competence (strengths) in knowledge, skills, and professional work characteristics as well as areas needing enhancement (weaknesses). Through this process of self-reflection utilizing the feedback from others and considering student outcomes, school psychologists can improve their capacity for effective practice in their work with students, parents, families, teachers, administrators, and other school personnel. These methods of self-evaluation can provide evidence of how effectively school psychologists are having an impact on student learning and, in general, helping children and adolescents achieve academically, behaviorally, emotionally, and socially. In addition to reflecting upon the feedback of other stakeholders, school psychologists can directly self-evaluate their knowledge and skills in the field of school psychology.

During the second phase of the self-evaluation process, school psychologists should reflect upon the information obtained during the assessment phase. Based upon where they fall within the Dreyfus and Dreyfus (1991) model (novice, advanced beginner, competence, proficiency, and expertise), school psychologists can identify areas of strength and weakness in terms of expectations as outlined in the national and/or state standards and local policies. In which areas is the school psychologist excelling? In what areas or situations is the individual school psychologist not performing to a desired level? Once the data are analyzed, the school psychologist practitioner should reflect upon the information and consider how best to address any deficiencies in order to improve.

Developing Learning Objectives

Based upon an analysis of strengths and weaknesses and student outcome data, the school psychologist should develop learning objectives to identify areas for development and opportunities for professional growth. The school psychologist may benefit from conferring with a trusted colleague to reflect upon opportunities for professional growth. Is there an area where professional development would help address a knowledge or skill deficit? The school psychologist might consider reading contemporary journal articles or books on the field of school psychology, writing about practice issues by journaling or researching and writing an article for the

state or local school psychologist newsletter, or engaging in self-study.

Progress Monitoring and Evaluating Growth

The fourth and final stage is to engage in the selected intervention (e.g., enroll in a workshop or online professional development experience, join a peer supervision group, or join a district-level committee whose purpose is to examine specific student outcomes) and begin to consider and implement the new knowledge and skills acquired. Once these are implemented, school psychologist practitioners should seek feedback from teachers, administrators, students, and parents as to the effectiveness of the innovation. In general, practitioners should reassess levels of targeted knowledge and skills to determine levels of competency.

Before examining other methods of self-evaluation, it is important to consider the roles and responsibilities of the supervisors of school psychologist practitioners. In their discussion of effective clinical supervision for school psychologists, Harvey and Struzziero (2008) describe the importance of supervisors helping school psychologists engage in self-appraisal to encourage reflective practice and to increase self-sufficiency. The authors suggest that effective supervision techniques include fostering supervisee self-appraisal and encouraging supervisees to repeatedly consider three questions: "What did I do? How well did it work? How should I modify my practice in the future?" (p. 248). Through the supervision process, supervisors help supervisees assess their own strengths and weaknesses, identify areas of weakness to target, and develop learning goals to address the areas of weakness. Harvey and Struzziero (2008) encourage school psychologists to use executive skills and metacognition as they engage in self-appraisal and develop goals to improve their practice.

Lazarus (2000) recommends psychologists use weekly or biweekly self-assessments to ameliorate stress. Recognizing the stress inherent in the school psychologist's professional role as problem solver for students, teachers, parents, and administrators, Harvey and Struzziero (2008), based on Lazarus' work, propose a series of self-assessment questions for school psychologists to consider. For example, "What behaviors do I want to increase? What behaviors do I want to decrease? What do I want to stop doing? What do I want to start doing?" (p. 248).

Central to the implementation of effective self-evaluation and a process to document effectiveness is the need for methods for authentically and accurately assessing knowledge, skills, and professional work characteristics in school psychology. These methods can be used at the baseline level and during the progress-monitoring phase. The next two sections below describe two valuable tools for school psychologists to use during the self-evaluation process.

Self-Assessment Checklist for School Psychologists

Self-assessment of school psychologists' knowledge and skills to determine strengths and areas needing development can be accomplished using the NASP (n.d.) Self-Assessment Checklist for School Psychologists (http://www.nasponline.org/standards/survey/survey_launch.aspx). The checklist was developed using the NASP Practice Model (NASP, 2010a) as its organizational structure. When completing the checklist, the school psychologist is asked to respond to a variety of statements describing school-based services that might reasonably be expected to be available from a school psychologist. The survey respondent is asked to identify how the statement describes the work he or she is currently engaged in and to indicate how important the activity is to his or her overall effectiveness. Once the survey is complete, the respondent is provided with a ranking of those areas in which he or she is currently engaged in school psychological services and a separate ranking of the perceived importance of each of those activities. By analyzing and comparing the results, the school psychologist can establish goals for expanding his or her current role. As a logical outgrowth, the next step would be to use the survey results to determine his or her professional development needs.

Thus, by using the checklist, individual school psychologists can engage in self-evaluation by examining what activities he or she is currently engaged in, determining how important those activities are to his or her overall effectiveness, and using the survey results to develop goals for the purpose of self-improvement. In addition, if graduate educators desire to use the checklist to self-examine how well each area is covered in their graduate education program and to determine how important each of those areas is to the program graduates' effectiveness, the survey results will serve as a needs assessment to determine the self-perceived judgment of how well the program's curriculum is addressing each area.

Framework for for School Psychologists' Self-Evaluation

Below is a step-by-step approach to utilizing the Framework for School Psychologists' Self-Evaluation (see the Appendix) to document professional effectiveness across the 10 NASP domains. School psychologists will engage in performance-based assessment to determine their level of functioning within each domain. Combined in part with the degree of longevity of the school psychologist's career, the data can be used to assist school psychologists in determining where they fall within the Dreyfus and Dreyfus (1991) five-stage model for each skill or set of skills. Moreover, use of the framework will allow school psychologists to evaluate their knowledge, skills, and professional work characteristics relative to the standards or benchmarks sent by the NASP Practice Model. Examining the results of the framework will enable school psychologists to note the variability among their knowledge, skills, and professional work characteristics within various domains. Using the instrument as both a formative and summative method of self-evaluation will allow school psychologists to follow the recommended progress-monitoring process toward achieving their intended goals. Finally, by incorporating these self-evaluation results with appraisals from other sources, (e.g., supervisors, peers, and stakeholders), the validity of the evaluation of the school psychologists' professional performance will be enhanced.

The five-step self-evaluation process follows: (a) Complete the framework to establish a self-evaluation baseline of knowledge, skills, and professional work characteristics across the 10 domains in the NASP Practice Model (NASP, 2010a). Review the data and engage in self-reflection. (b) Review and reflect upon other sources of feedback (supervisors and peer evaluations, student outcome data). Incorporate the data gathered via these multiple methods of assessment of the skills, knowledge, and professional work characteristics with the self-evaluation results. (c) Establish measurable objectives to identify goals for improving performance. (d) Participate in professional development (e.g., attend a workshop, complete an online training, engage in self-study, join a committee) to address differences between current and desired levels of practice. (e) Readminister the framework as a summative method to measure progress across the 10 NASP domains.

Case Example

According to the Dreyfus and Dreyfus (1991) taxonomy, Ms. Brown considers herself a competent school psychologist with 3 years of professional experience working in her position at Middletown Elementary

School. Her supervisor ratings during her first 3 years have highlighted her strengths, as well as areas where she could improve. During her first 2 years of personnel evaluations by her supervisor, Ms. Brown received high ratings in her ability to deliver consultative services to parents, teachers, and administrators, with exemplary comments regarding her ability to collaborate effectively with others. However, her self-evaluation identified behavioral interventions in the planning and decision process at an individual, group, and systems level as areas that she would benefit from additional knowledge and skills through professional development and self-study.

At the end of each of her 3 years, she routinely completed a self-evaluation of her knowledge, skills, and professional work characteristics and has developed professional goals for self-improvement based upon the results. When she completed her first self-evaluation at the end of her first year using the Framework for School Psychologists' Self-Evaluation, she had identified her knowledge and skills in the NASP Practice Model (NASP, 2010a) domain of Interventions and Mental Health Services to Develop Social and Life Skills as a general area for improvement. Specifically, she had acknowledged section 4.4, "I utilize ecological and behavioral approaches when developing behavior change programs and other evidence-based interventions," as an area that she desired to improve and included this area in her professional improvement plan, a document she is required to complete each year to outline areas for professional growth. She completed this document in collaboration with her direct supervisor.

During her second and third years, Ms. Brown volunteered to participate in training in PBS provided to her district through a grant-funded program and delivered by a state-level team of experts in PBS. Ms. Brown was aware that improving student behavioral and academic outcomes is a priority goal for her district. She was particularly interested in the training on behavior intervention planning that included functional behavioral assessment to learn more about behavioral reduction strategies, methods of teaching replacement behaviors to students, and monitoring of individual progress.

As part of the PBS leadership team at her school, Ms. Brown participates in biweekly meetings both to review building-level program development issues and to consider individual student issues referred to the PBS team by parents, teachers, or other school personnel. In October of this year, a third-grade student named Jack was referred to the PBS team by his teacher because Jack was displaying disruptive behaviors that were interfering with the classroom routine and thus other students' learning. The referring third-grade teacher, Mr. Jones, provided information regarding the student's behavioral difficulties to the PBS team. As a result of the PBS team meeting, Ms. Brown agreed to consult with Mr. Jones to further address the behavior problems Jack was exhibiting in the classroom.

Based upon Ms. Brown's PBS training, Ms. Brown and Mr. Jones followed the steps to complete both a functional behavioral assessment and the positive interventions process to address Jack's behavior problems. These steps are (a) identify goals for intervention, (b) gather relevant information, (c) develop summary statements, (d) generate a behavioral support plan, and (e) implement the strategies and monitor the outcomes.

In summary, Ms. Brown and Mr. Jones collaboratively identified the goals of intervention by determining what Jack was saying or doing that was problematic (observable behaviors), considered to what extent these behaviors were occurring, and agreed on what goals they hoped to achieve through the intervention. Jack's parents were invited and agreed to participate in this process to maximize home–school collaboration. Through this process, Ms. Brown, Mr. Jones, and Jack's mother identified that Jack's disruptive classroom behaviors included slamming materials, making noises, and arguing with peers. Teacher data collection indicated that these behaviors occurred 10–15 times per day. They agreed that their goals were to decrease Jack's disruptive behaviors, increase his time on task to complete assignments, and improve his peer relationships. Ms. Brown assumed the responsibility of gathering additional relevant information by reviewing Jack's existing records and conducting interviews with his family members, his teachers, and Jack. Mr. Jones continued to tally incidents of Jack's disruptive behaviors in the classroom and Ms. Brown completed additional classroom observations to collect antecedent, behavior, and consequence (ABC) data to identify events and circumstances that may have affected Jack's behavior. Together, they reviewed the information gathered to discern any patterns in Jack's behavior. During the next step in the process, they developed a summary statement detailing when, where, and with whom Jack's behavior was least and most likely to occur; what happens following the behavior; and other variables that appeared to affect his behavior.

Based on this information, they generated a behavioral support plan for Jack that addressed adjustments to the environment that would reduce the likelihood of the problems occurring, teach Jack replacement skills and build his competencies, and determine appropriate consequences to promote positive behaviors and to deter problem behaviors. Together, they determined each of their roles in ensuring that the plan is implemented consistently, progress monitoring the interventions, evaluating the outcomes, and making adjustments to the plan, as needed. Six weeks later, upon review of the collected progress monitoring data, all three met to evaluate the outcomes and were delighted to confirm that there had been positive changes in Jack's behavior.

Now as Ms. Brown begins to prepare for her end-of-year personnel evaluation meeting with her supervisor, she reflects upon the goals she established for her professional growth over the past 2 years. She readministers the Framework for School Psychologists' Self-Evaluation and rates herself as much improved in the area of behavioral interventions, noting all she learned through participation in the PBS training and in her work with parents and teachers. In order to collect additional information for her self-evaluation and in light of what she knows are priority school outcome goals, she decides to examine student outcome data in the areas of behavioral interventions for Middletown Elementary School. She recognizes that student outcome data are important sources of information to consider when determining the effectiveness of her work.

Analysis of student outcome data with regard to teacher office referrals at the third-grade level due to disruptive student behaviors (e.g., calling out, out of seat behaviors) revealed a high rate of referrals from third-grade teachers. Specifically, one of the third-grade teachers completed an average of two office referrals per day for a total average of 10.5 referrals per week. These data were collected from Mr. Jones' class over 2 consecutive years *prior* to Ms. Brown's consulting with Mr. Jones and his involvement in developing an intervention plan to address Jack's disruptive behaviors. Interestingly, in analyzing this year's office referrals for disruptive behaviors completed by Mr. Jones, there has been a distinct downward trend of fewer office referrals. In fact, comments by the building principal suggest that Mr. Jones rarely refers students to the office for consequences, except when crisis intervention is needed. Ms. Brown subsequently meets with Mr. Jones to share the data she uncovered and the two discuss the implications. Through this interview, Ms. Brown finds that Mr. Jones has been approaching behavior problems from a different perspective and is working to better understand the function of the students' behaviors and attempting to implement positive interventions to help teach replacement behaviors to the students. Ms. Brown explains that she would like to use the decline in office referrals data from

Mr. Jones as evidence of the effectiveness of their consultative work together and he readily agrees.

Ms. Brown organizes her information, including her yearly self-evaluations and the student outcome data she has collected. She feels rather confident going into her conference that her supervisor will acknowledge the evidence of her growth in the area of her abilities to link assessment data to development of behavioral interventions and to use ecological and behavioral approaches when developing behavior change programs as evidence of her effectiveness in her role as a behavioral consultant. She plans to emphasize that these goals are consistent with district priority goals of improving student academic and behavioral outcome for all children.

SUMMARY

School psychologists have multiple methods for evaluating their effectiveness, including, for example, supervisor ratings, interviews and surveys completed by stakeholders, and examining student outcome data in academic, behavioral, and mental health areas. Self-evaluation is another method to document school psychologists' knowledge, skills, and professional work characteristics. By utilizing self-evaluation measures, school psychologists can gain insight into how effectively they can change the students' ability to function academically, behaviorally, emotionally, and socially. Within the context of this chapter, self-evaluation refers to school psychologists reflecting upon the feedback from others and school psychologists directly rating their own knowledge, skills, and professional work characteristics.

Determining the effectiveness of school psychological services by examining student outcomes is another powerful tool for school psychologists to use to demonstrate their value and positive contributions to school improvement. School psychologists, through collaboration with students, parents, teachers, and administrators, can have a positive impact on student outcomes.

REFERENCES

Adelman, H. S., & Taylor, L. (2006). *Student learning supports: New directions for addressing barriers to learning*. Thousand Oaks, CA: Corwin.

Alkin, M. C. (2011). *Evaluation essentials*. New York, NY: Guilford Press.

Baker, J. (2008). Assessing school risk and protective factors. In B. Doll & J. A. Cummings (Eds.), *Transforming school mental health services* (A joint publication with the National Association of School Psychologists; pp. 43–65). Thousand Oaks, CA: Corwin.

Danielson, C., & McGreal, T. L. (2000). *Teacher evaluation to enhance professional practice.* Alexandria, VA: Association for Supervision and Curriculum Development.

Dreyfus, H. L., & Dreyfus, S. E. (1991). Towards a phenomenology of ethical expertise. *Human Studies, 44*, 229–250.

Harvey, V. S., & Struzziero, J. A. (2008). *Professional development and supervision of school psychologists* (2nd ed.; A joint publication with the National Association of School Psychologists). Thousand Oaks, CA: Corwin.

Kaslow, N. J., Grus, C. L., Campbell, L. F., Fouad, N. A., Hatcher, R. L., & Rodola, E. R. (2007a). Competency assessment toolkit for professional psychology. *Professional Psychology: Research and Practice, 38*(Suppl.), S27–S45.

Kaslow, N. J., Rubin, N. J., Bebeau, M. J., Leigh, I. W., Lichtenberg, J. W., Nelson, P. D., … Smith, I. L. (2007b). Guiding principles and recommendations for the assessment of competence. *Professional Psychology: Research and Practice, 38*, 441–451.

Lazarus, A. A. (2000). Multimodal replenishment. *Professional Psychology: Research and Practice, 31*, 93–94.

Louisiana Department of Education & Louisiana School Psychological Association. (2010). *Assessment of "value added" by school psychologist: Task force recommendations.* Baton Rouge, LA: Author.

Marzano, R. J., Norford, J. S., Paynter, D. E., Pickering, D. J., & Gaddy, B. B. (2001). *A handbook for classroom instruction that works.* Alexandria, VA: Association for Supervision and Curriculum Development.

National Association of School Psychologists. (n.d.). *Self-assessment checklist for school psychologists.* Bethesda, MD: Author. Retrieved from http://www.nasponline.org/standards/survey/self-assessment-intro.aspx

National Association of School Psychologists. (2008). *Ready to learn, empowered to teach: Excellence in education for the 21st century.* Bethesda, MD: Author. Retrieved from http://www.nasponline.org/advocacy/2008educationpolicydocument.pdf

National Association of School Psychologists. (2010a). *Model for comprehensive and integrated school psychological services.* Bethesda, MD: Author. Retrieved from http://www.nasponline.org/standards/2010standards/2_PracticeModel.pdf

National Association of School Psychologists. (2010b). *School psychologists: Improving student and school outcomes.* Bethesda, MD: Author. Retrieved from http://www.nasponline.org/advocacy/SP_Improving_Student_School_Outcomes_Final.pdf

National Association of School Psychologists. (2010c). *Standards for the credentialing of school psychologists.* Bethesda, MD: Author. Retrieved from http://www.nasponline.org/standards/2010standards/2_Credentialing_Standards.pdf

National Association of School Psychologists. (2012). *A framework for the personnel evaluation of school psychologists utilizing the NASP Practice Model.* Bethesda, MD: Author. Retrieved from http://www.nasponline.org/standards/survey/survey_launch.aspx

Rubin, N. R., Bebeau, M., Leigh, I. W., Lichtenberg, J. W., Nelson, P. D., Portney, S., … Kaslow, N. J. (2007). The competency movement within psychology: An historical perspective. *Professional Psychology: Research and Practice, 38*, 452–462.

Skalski, A., & Cowan, K. C. (2010, September). Demonstrating how school psychologists improve student outcomes. *Communiqué, 39*(1), 1, 18. Retrieved from http://www.nasponline.org/publications/cq/39/1/DemonstratingImprovedOutcomes.aspx

Waldron, N., & Prus, J. (2006). *A guide for performance-based assessment, accountability, and program development in school psychology training programs* (2nd ed.). Bethesda, MD: National Association of School Psychologists. Retrieved from http://www.nasponline.org/standards/approvedtraining/perfassess.pdf

APPENDIX. FRAMEWORK FOR SCHOOL PSYCHOLOGISTS' SELF-EVALUATION

Practices That Permeate All Aspects of Service Delivery

Data-Based Decision Making and Accountability

1.1 I demonstrate knowledge of varied methods of assessment that yield information useful in identifying strengths and needs, in understanding problems, and in measuring progress.	Needs Improvement 0	Effective 1	Very Effective 2
1.2 I demonstrate effective development and implementation of academic and behavioral interventions that are based on data gathered from the team problem-solving and assessment processes and are linked to goals and outcomes.	Needs Improvement 0	Effective 1	Very Effective 2
1.3 I demonstrate effective problem-solving (decision-making) process skills and procedures at the individual, group, and systems levels.	Needs Improvement 0	Effective 1	Very Effective 2
1.4 I demonstrate effective skills in selecting appropriate measures to monitor and evaluate the success of individual, group, and systems interventions that compare outcome(s) to desired goals.	Needs Improvement 0	Effective 1	Very Effective 2
1.5 I demonstrate a knowledge base of problem-solving (decision-making) processes that are related to educational research and systems-level and/or building-level concerns.	Needs Improvement 0	Effective 1	Very Effective 2

Consultation and Collaboration

2.1 I demonstrate knowledge of behavioral, mental health, collaborative, and/or other consultation models and methods.	Needs Improvement 0	Effective 1	Very Effective 2
2.2 I collaborate effectively with others in planning and decision-making processes at the individual, group, and systems levels.	Needs Improvement 0	Effective 1	Very Effective 2
2.3 I communicate and collaborate effectively with school personnel.	Needs Improvement 0	Effective 1	Very Effective 2
2.4 I communicate and collaborate effectively with families.	Needs Improvement 0	Effective 1	Very Effective 2
2.5 I communicate and collaborate effectively with students.	Needs Improvement 0	Effective 1	Very Effective 2
2.6 I communicate and collaborate effectively with community professionals.	Needs Improvement 0	Effective 1	Very Effective 2
2.7 I collaborate effectively with others throughout the problem-solving and assessment process.	Needs Improvement 0	Effective 1	Very Effective 2
2.8 I collaborate with others at a universal systems level to develop prevention and intervention programs that help to create healthy learning environments.	Needs Improvement 0	Effective 1	Very Effective 2

Direct and Indirect Services for Children, Families, and Schools
Student-Level Services

Interventions and Instructional Support to Develop Academic Skills

3.1 I demonstrate knowledge of human learning processes, techniques to assess these processes, and direct and indirect services applicable to the development of cognitive and academic skills.	Needs Improvement 0	Effective 1	Very Effective 2
3.2 I demonstrate knowledge of and skills in developing effective instructional strategies/interventions to promote learning of students at individual, group, or systems levels.	Needs Improvement 0	Effective 1	Very Effective 2
3.3 I demonstrate skills in adhering to procedures for administering standardized assessments of intelligence.	Needs Improvement 0	Effective 1	Very Effective 2
3.4 I demonstrate skills in adhering to procedures for administering standardized assessments of academic achievement.	Needs Improvement 0	Effective 1	Very Effective 2
3.5 I demonstrate skills in conducting curriculum-based, progress monitoring, or other authentic methods of assessments of academic skills.	Needs Improvement 0	Effective 1	Very Effective 2
3.6 I demonstrate skills in appropriately administering and interpreting assessment data.	Needs Improvement 0	Effective 1	Very Effective 2
3.7 I demonstrate skills in linking assessment data to development of instructional interventions.	Needs Improvement 0	Effective 1	Very Effective 2
3.8 I assess treatment integrity of intervention implementation.	Needs Improvement 0	Effective 1	Very Effective 2

Interventions and Mental Health Services to Develop Social and Life Skills

4.1 I demonstrate knowledge of human developmental processes, techniques to assess these processes, and direct and indirect services applicable to development of behavioral, affective, adaptive, and social skills.	Needs Improvement 0	Effective 1	Very Effective 2
4.2 I properly administer, analyze, and interpret assessment strategies to measure behavioral, affective, adaptive, and social domains.	Needs Improvement 0	Effective 1	Very Effective 2
4.3 I demonstrate skills in linking assessment data to development of behavioral interventions, including functional behavioral assessment under IDEA.	Needs Improvement 0	Effective 1	Very Effective 2
4.4 I utilize ecological and behavioral approaches when developing behavior change programs and other evidence-based interventions.	Needs Improvement 0	Effective 1	Very Effective 2
4.5 I appropriately evaluate outcomes of interventions and assess treatment integrity of intervention implementation.	Needs Improvement 0	Effective 1	Very Effective 2
4.6 I utilize intervention and progress-monitoring data to guide instructional decisions.	Needs Improvement 0	Effective 1	Very Effective 2
4.7 I demonstrate skill In providing direct interventions (i.e., individual counseling, group counseling, applied behavior analysis, social problem solving skills). Indicate those that apply.	Needs Improvement 0	Effective 1	Very Effective 2
4.8 I demonstrate skills in providing indirect intervention (i.e., collaborative consultation with teachers, support staff, and parents).	Needs Improvement 0	Effective 1	Very Effective 2

**Direct and Indirect Services for Children, Families, and Schools
Systems-Level Services**

School-Wide Practices to Promote Learning

5.1 I demonstrate knowledge of general education, special education, and other educational and related services.	Needs Improvement 0	Effective 1	Very Effective 2
5.2 I work with individuals and groups to facilitate policies and practices that create and maintain safe, supportive, and effective learning environments.	Needs Improvement 0	Effective 1	Very Effective 2
5.3 I apply principles of systems theory to promote learning, to prevent problems, and to create effective learning environments (e.g., participating in building-level intervention assistance teams and understand its procedures).	Needs Improvement 0	Effective 1	Very Effective 2
5.4 I participate in the development, implementation, and/or evaluation of programs that promote safe schools.	Needs Improvement 0	Effective 1	Very Effective 2
5.5 I review roles and responsibilities of school personnel.	Needs Improvement 0	Effective 1	Very Effective 2
5.6 I review district/school policies and procedures (e.g., prevention, crisis intervention, suicide intervention, discipline).	Needs Improvement 0	Effective 1	Very Effective 2
5.7 I review school curricula.	Needs Improvement 0	Effective 1	Very Effective 2

Preventive and Responsive Services

6.1 I demonstrate knowledge of human development and psychopathology, and associated biological, cultural, and social influences on human beings. I am aware of current theory and research in these areas.	Needs Improvement 0	Effective 1	Very Effective 2
6.2 I work collaboratively with others at the systems level to implement prevention and intervention programs that promote mental health and physical well-being of students.	Needs Improvement 0	Effective 1	Very Effective 2
6.3 I demonstrate knowledge of crisis policies and procedures including collaboration with school personnel, parents, and the community in the aftermath of a crisis.	Needs Improvement 0	Effective 1	Very Effective 2
6.4 I demonstrate skills in providing direct preventive and responsive interventions (i.e., individual counseling, group counseling, social problem-solving skills). Indicate those that apply.	Needs Improvement 0	Effective 1	Very Effective 2
6.5 I demonstrate skills in providing indirect preventive and responsive intervention (i.e., collaborative consultation with teachers, support staff, and parents).	Needs Improvement 0	Effective 1	Very Effective 2

Family–School Collaboration Services

7.1 I demonstrate knowledge of family systems, including family strengths and influences on student development, learning, and behavior.	Needs Improvement 0	Effective 1	Very Effective 2
7.2 I demonstrate knowledge of methods and strategies to involve families in education and service delivery.	Needs Improvement 0	Effective 1	Very Effective 2
7.3 I establish and maintain collaborative relationships with families, educators, and others in the community to promote and provide comprehensive services to children and families.	Needs Improvement 0	Effective 1	Very Effective 2
7.4 I demonstrate skills to facilitate home–school communication and collaboration.	Needs Improvement 0	Effective 1	Very Effective 2
7.5 I collaborate effectively with families, teachers, school personnel, and others throughout the assessment process and during interventions.	Needs Improvement 0	Effective 1	Very Effective 2
7.6 I demonstrate knowledge of school-based and community services and resources for children with diverse needs, and help to create links between schools, families, and community resources.	Needs Improvement 0	Effective 1	Very Effective 2

Foundations of School Psychological Service Delivery

Diversity in Development and Learning

8.1 I demonstrate knowledge of individual differences, abilities, and disabilities and of the potential influence of biological, social, cultural, ethnic, experiential, socioeconomic, gender-related, and linguistic factors in development and learning.	Needs Improvement 0	Effective 1	Very Effective 2
8.2 I demonstrate the sensitivity and skills needed to work with individuals of diverse characteristics and implement strategies selected or adapted based on individual characteristics, strengths, and needs.	Needs Improvement 0	Effective 1	Very Effective 2
8.3 I demonstrate an awareness of school-based and community services for students with diverse needs.	Needs Improvement 0	Effective 1	Very Effective 2
8.4 I demonstrate an understanding and appreciation for human diversity, including knowledge of the importance of differences in families, cultural backgrounds, and individual learning characteristics of students.	Needs Improvement 0	Effective 1	Very Effective 2
8.5 I demonstrate an awareness of and work to eliminate biological, social, cultural, ethnic, experiential, socioeconomic, gender-related, and linguistic biases to ensure equal outcomes.	Needs Improvement 0	Effective 1	Very Effective 2

Research and Program Evaluation

9.1 I demonstrate knowledge of and am able to translate evidence-based research, statistics, and evaluation methods into practice.	Needs Improvement 0	Effective 1	Very Effective 2
9.2 I understand research design and statistics to plan and conduct investigations and program evaluations for improvement of services.	Needs Improvement 0	Effective 1	Very Effective 2
9.3 I am able to apply principles of research design (quantitative and qualitative techniques) and single-case design.	Needs Improvement 0	Effective 1	Very Effective 2
9.4 I select and implement evidence-based assessment and intervention strategies.	Needs Improvement 0	Effective 1	Very Effective 2
9.5 I collect and analyze data to evaluate the effectiveness of interventions at an individual, program, or systems level.	Needs Improvement 0	Effective 1	Very Effective 2
9.6 I demonstrate knowledge of research and program evaluation.	Needs Improvement 0	Effective 1	Very Effective 2

Legal, Ethical, and Professional Practice

10.1 I demonstrate and adhere to professional, ethical, and legal standards in school psychology and education.	Needs Improvement 0	Effective 1	Very Effective 2
10.2 I have knowledge of the history and foundations of school psychology, education, special education, healthcare, and related fields and use this understanding in working with children, parents, and school personnel.	Needs Improvement 0	Effective 1	Very Effective 2
10.3 I demonstrate reliable, responsible, and dependable behaviors.	Needs Improvement 0	Effective 1	Very Effective 2
10.4 I interact with others in a professional manner.	Needs Improvement 0	Effective 1	Very Effective 2
10.5 I present information in writing and orally in a clear and professional manner.	Needs Improvement 0	Effective 1	Very Effective 2
10.6 I respond appropriately to feedback from others and am flexible and open to suggestions.	Needs Improvement 0	Effective 1	Very Effective 2
10.7 I appropriately prepare and utilize supervision, including making effective use of feedback.	Needs Improvement 0	Effective 1	Very Effective 2
10.8 I demonstrate a commitment to continued professional development and learning, self-improvement, and self-evaluation.	Needs Improvement 0	Effective 1	Very Effective 2

Professional Work Characteristics

Demonstrate respect for human diversity: I respect racial, cultural, socioeconomic, religious, gender-related, sexual-orientation, and other human differences. I demonstrate the sensitivity and skills needed to work with diverse populations.	Needs Improvement 0	Effective 1	Very Effective 2
Demonstrate effective oral communication skills: I speak in an organized and clear manner.	Needs Improvement 0	Effective 1	Very Effective 2
Demonstrate effective written communication skills: I write in an organized and clear manner.	Needs Improvement 0	Effective 1	Very Effective 2
Demonstrate professional identity and ethical responsibility: I identify with the profession of school psychology and conduct myself in an ethically responsible manner.	Needs Improvement 0	Effective 1	Very Effective 2
Demonstrate attending/listening skills: I attend to important communications and listen effectively.	Needs Improvement 0	Effective 1	Very Effective 2
Demonstrate adaptability and flexibility: I adapt effectively to the demands of a situation, and I am sufficiently flexible in dealing with change.	Needs Improvement 0	Effective 1	Very Effective 2
Demonstrate initiative and dependability: I initiate activities when appropriate and can be counted on to follow through on a task in a timely manner once a commitment to it has been made.	Needs Improvement 0	Effective 1	Very Effective 2
Demonstrate time management and organization: I organize my work and manage my time effectively.	Needs Improvement 0	Effective 1	Very Effective 2
Demonstrate effective interpersonal relations: I relate effectively with colleagues, faculty, supervisors, and clients.	Needs Improvement 0	Effective 1	Very Effective 2
Responsiveness to supervision/feedback: I am open to supervision/feedback and respond to such appropriately.	Needs Improvement 0	Effective 1	Very Effective 2
Demonstrate skills in data-based case conceptualization: I am able to use data/information to conceptualize cases and generate hypotheses and possible solutions. I use evidence to evaluate outcomes.	Needs Improvement 0	Effective 1	Very Effective 2
Demonstrate systems orientation: I understand that schools, families, and organizations are systems. I recognize and effectively utilize rules, policies, and other characteristics of the system.	Needs Improvement 0	Effective 1	Very Effective 2
Demonstrate problem solving/critical thinking: I think critically and effectively analyze problem situations and conceptualize alternative approaches and solutions.	Needs Improvement 0	Effective 1	Very Effective 2

44

Best Practices in the Professional Evaluation of School Psychologists Utilizing the NASP Practice Model

Anastasia Kalamaros Skalski
National Association of School Psychologists (MD)
Mary Alice Myers
Volusia County (FL) School District

OVERVIEW

The reauthorization of the Elementary and Secondary Education Act (ESEA) in 2001 paved the way for a new federal role in education that moved beyond funding and compliance to an emphasis on accountability for all student learning. The reforms attached to this law focus on the need for higher standards; highly effective teachers, principals, and schools; increased parental choice and flexibility; and improved student achievement. In 2009, the passage of the American Recovery and Reinvestment Act gave $100 billon to the U.S. Department of Education, much of which was dedicated to existing programs (like Title I) which focused on implementing improved outcomes linked to these ESEA reforms. Additionally, new programs like the Race to the Top Fund and the Teacher Incentive Fund also made available large sums of money to states willing to reform their policies and practices to align with federal priorities.

The most sought after of these new programs was Race to the Top, which set aside $4.35 billion in grant funds for states that implemented these federal priorities. The highest scoring component of Race to the Top is called Great Teachers and Leaders, which includes Improving Teacher and Principal Effectiveness Based on Performance. The Race to the Top grant priorities, combined with the existing emphasis on high quality teaching and student achievement testing within ESEA, triggered sweeping reforms across the country to teacher

and principal evaluation systems. State educational agencies and local educational agencies are adjusting professional policies and practices to emphasize these federal priorities so that states can be eligible to compete for these funds.

One of the eligibility requirements in Race to the Top declares that states must

> … design and implement rigorous, transparent, and fair evaluation systems for teachers and principals that (a) differentiate effectiveness using multiple rating categories that take into account data on student growth as a significant factor, and (b) are designed and developed with teacher and principal involvement…. Student growth means the change in student achievement for an individual student between two or more points in time. A State may also include other measures that are rigorous and comparable across classrooms. (U.S. Department of Education, 2009, p. 59753)

The Race to the Top requirement reflects a new emphasis in educator evaluation and compensation that moves from measuring inputs (such as training, education, and professional development) as evidence for performance, to measuring outputs that are linked directly to student achievement. The Race to the Top language has prompted several states to adopt or consider adopting statewide personnel evaluation systems that utilize value-added models to capture the effects of teacher instruction, and assign a weight (i.e., a percentage) of a teacher's evaluation based upon specific student test score gains or other performance outcomes as determined by the state.

In general, school psychologists typically benefit from being treated similarly to teachers and other educators within a school system. However, the current trends in professional evaluation have led school psychology to a crossroads. How should school psychologists respond to this personnel evaluation movement that may at times be at odds with research and best practices? How can the National Association of School Psychologists' (NASP) standards help school psychologists navigate this difficult terrain and address the challenges presented by emerging educator evaluation practices?

This chapter, which addresses critical elements of the NASP *Model for Comprehensive and Integrated School Psychological Services* (NASP, 2010), domain of Legal, Ethical, and Professional Practice, will review basic issues involved in contemporary professional personnel evaluation of educators, discuss best practices for incorporating the NASP Practice Model (NASP, 2010) into personnel evaluation, and offer suggestions for the development of personnel evaluation tools for school psychologists.

BASIC CONSIDERATIONS

NASP has long advocated for the delivery of comprehensive and integrated school psychological services. Along with this advocacy has been an emphasis in research, policy, and practice on the importance of fair and reliable personnel evaluations. The Joint Committee on Standards for Educational Evaluation defines personnel evaluation as "the systematic assessment of a person's performance and/or qualifications in relation to a professional role and some specified and defensible institutional purpose" (Gullickson, 2009, p. 3). Inherent in this definition is an emphasis on the importance of strengthening the professional competence of the educator practitioner within his or her stated role and the mission and purpose of the system. For schools, it is not enough to simply focus the evaluation process on the growth of the practitioner, but schools must also consider how an educator practitioner's delivered services address the school district's defined scope of practice as well as the outcomes achieved by students receiving services. Given that, ultimately, the mission and purpose of schools is student learning, it should not surprise anyone that greater attention would be paid to how the services delivered by

educators help facilitate or deter that learning. Thus, the purposes of professional evaluations of educators include (a) assessing the professional competence of the practitioner; (b) guiding the growth and development of the practitioner; (c) reviewing the breadth, scope, worth, and adequacy of the services delivered by the practitioner; and (d) providing evidence for accountability, employment, staffing, and program decisions.

Assessment of Student Outcomes Using Value-Added Models

The Race to the Top requirements reflect a growing trend in teacher evaluation that emphasizes the concept that student outputs can be measured utilizing student standardized assessments within a value-added model. The basic process in value-added modeling involves determining how students are expected to score on assessments (based upon previous performance) against how students actually score. Value-added modeling seeks to identify the effect that a teacher actually has on student achievement through the use of complex statistical formulas that measure instructional gains while isolating noninstructional effects (like student and school characteristics) on student performance. Examples of value-added models include the Tennessee Value-Added Assessment System (Sanders & Horn, 1994) and the Dallas Value-Added Accountability System (Webster & Mendro, 1997). Although value-added models are generally thought to be fairer comparisons of teacher performance than evaluations that are based solely on student test scores or cohort comparisons, prominent researchers caution against their use in high-stakes decision making about teacher retention and promotion (Baker et al., 2010.) Baker et al. (2010) states that

> there is broad agreement among statisticians, psychometricians, and economists that student test scores alone are not sufficiently reliable and valid indicators of teacher effectiveness to be used in high-stakes personnel decisions, even when the most sophisticated statistical applications such as value-added modeling are employed. (p. 2)

Student Performance Weighting in Personnel Evaluations

Despite the cautions of researchers, there is a growing interest by some policy makers to utilize value-added models within a personnel evaluation framework for teachers and principals. For example, in Florida the Student Success Act requires 50% of the evaluation to be based on student growth. For classroom teachers, this means that 50% percent of the evaluation must be based on value-added data (e.g., test scores) from annual student assessments. This weight can be adjusted for nonclassroom instructional personnel like school psychologists, such that annual student assessments account for a minimum of 30% of the evaluation, while other student outcomes (like graduation rates, truancy rates, and other behavioral measures) account for up to 20% of the evaluation. The concept of weighting various aspects of evaluations is not new and can be a beneficial practice as districts seek to emphasize roles or services associated with weights. However, the challenge is determining how much weight should be given to different factors and for which personnel. Baker et al. (2010) cautioned states eager to link student test scores to performance evaluations:

> [S]ome states are now considering plans that would give as much as 50% of the weight in teacher evaluation and compensation decisions to scores on existing poor quality tests of basic skills in math and reading. Based on the evidence we have reviewed ..., we consider this unwise. (p. 20)

Models of Teacher Evaluation

Although there are a variety of researchers that have studied personnel evaluation, inarguably, two of the most popular educator personnel evaluation frameworks that are currently used in schools for teachers are the Danielson Framework for Teaching (Danielson, 2013) and the Marzano Causal Teacher Evaluation Model (Marzano, 2011). Given the focus on accountability and alignment of systems within districts, it is not surprising that rubrics for school psychology evaluation may also be required to be aligned with one of these two models.

Danielson Framework for Teaching
The Danielson Framework for Teaching was first published in 1996. The system's use among teachers and administrators grew as a result of the research indicating that the 22 components that are currently used in the Danielson system have evidence of improving academic outcomes. An evaluation tool was constructed that incorporated these components into four broad domains: Planning and Preparation, Classroom Environment, Instruction, and Professional Responsibilities. The tool also rates four levels of professional performance (i.e., unsatisfactory, basic, proficient, and distinguished). Danielson indicates that the value of the tool is maximized when the framework is linked to mentoring, coaching, professional development, and teacher evaluation.

Marzano Causal Teacher Evaluation Model
The Marzano Causal Teacher Evaluation model is based on Marzano's *Effective Supervision: Supporting the Art and Science of Teaching* (Marzano, 2011) and is substantiated by meta-analytic research. The model focuses on student achievement, and at the center of the model is a correlation between instructional strategies and student achievement. The model contains four broad domains with 60 supporting elements: Classroom Strategies and Behaviors (with 41 elements), Planning and Preparing (with 8 elements), Reflecting on Teaching (with 5 elements), and Collegiality and Professionalism (with 6 elements).

Marzano recommends that evaluators consider multiple data sources when constructing a teacher's final evaluation (i.e., summative) score. Sources of data may include reflection and collaboration, value-added student data, student surveys, walkthroughs/observations, and professional growth plans.

Utilizing the NASP Practice Model in Personnel Evaluations

The NASP Practice Model (NASP, 2010) affords an ideal foundation for the construction of evaluation systems and tools to address the specific skills, services, and needs of school psychologists. The model is composed of two major sets of principles that describe the responsibilities of individual school psychologists in the delivery of school psychological services and the responsibilities of school systems in supporting these services.

The professional practice principles of the NASP Practice Model are organized around three broad areas that serve to support the overall structure for the model: (a) foundations of service delivery, (b) practices that permeate all aspects of service delivery, and (c) direct and indirect services for children, families, and schools. Within each of these areas are domains of practice that provide a general frame of reference for the services delivered by school psychologists. Within each domain the standards articulate specific examples of school psychologists' professional practices that are commonly associated with that domain. For example, within the Systems-Level Services: School-Wide Practice to Promote Learning domain, school psychologists participate "in the design and implementation of universal screening programs to identify students in need of additional instructional or behavioral support services...." (NASP, 2010, p. 45). This professional practice as articulated in the NASP Practice Model could be included as part of the school psychologist's personnel evaluation.

The organizational principles guide the responsibilities of the school systems in supporting the delivery of school psychological services, and these principles focus on a school systems responsibility for (a) delineating how these services should be organized and delivered; (b) promoting a positive work climate; (c) providing adequate physical, personnel, and fiscal support for the services needed; (d) ensuring professional communication; (e) providing supervision and mentoring; and (f) offering professional development and recognition systems (NASP, 2010). These principles can form the foundation for evaluating a system's capacity to support the delivery of school psychological services. The organizational principles help a district look at issues like the level and quality of supervision, whether the school psychologist has the proper technological support to perform his or her duties, and if there are adequate numbers of school psychologists to meet the needs of students. These organizational principles should also be considered when evaluating individual school psychologists. For example, in settings where a school psychologist's staff-to-student ratio is well above the maximum recommended ratio detailed in Organizational Principle 3.2, the scope of services that the school psychologist can feasibly deliver is likely to narrow significantly and, thus, the evaluation should also.

A professional evaluation model for school psychologists should assess the quality and effectiveness of the services delivered to individual students to remediate academic and/or mental health needs including the specific interventions (i.e., counseling, behavior remediation, skill instruction) and the evaluation process utilized to determine what services are appropriate and to what extent these services should be delivered. Additionally, a professional evaluation should also look at the contributions of school psychologists to the whole system. It is important that evaluators conceptualize the NASP Practice Model as a synthesized framework that supports the interaction between the domains rather than as 10 separate silos. Additionally, the ability of a school psychologist to perform a comprehensive set of activities that includes all of the domains is contingent on his or her workload, assignment, setting, and job description and should be considered in the development and implementation of any evaluation system. Crucial to this work then is the need to understand the components of any model considered and then constructing personnel evaluation tools that reflect an integration of the theoretical evaluation model adopted by the district and the NASP Practice Model.

BEST PRACTICES IN THE PROFESSIONAL EVALUATION OF SCHOOL PSYCHOLOGISTS UTILIZING THE NASP PRACTICE MODEL

In the early 2000s, an increasing number of states and local school districts began significant reforms to their school psychologists' personnel evaluation processes. Subsequently, NASP formed a task force to study this issue and offer recommendations to the field.

NASP Personnel Assessment Task Force

The primary responsibility of the task force was to develop a framework for school psychologists' evaluations that could help guide state and local education agencies in establishing fair, reliable, and instructive personnel evaluation policies and practices for school psychologists. In 2012, NASP adopted *A Framework for the Personnel Evaluation of School Psychologists Utilizing the NASP Practice Model* (NASP, 2012) as a set of guiding principles for personnel evaluation in schools. The framework suggests four overarching principles for the development of personnel evaluation processes.

Principle 1: Use the NASP Practice Model as the Overarching Framework for Personnel Evaluations

NASP standards for professional practice have existed for more than 30 years. These standards articulate the breadth and scope of services to be delivered by school psychologists. Research has demonstrated that when school psychologists are engaged in the delivery of a broad array of services and supports for students, improved student outcomes are realized (NASP, 2010). It is only natural that the NASP Practice Model, which articulates the standards for school psychologists' practice, be the cornerstone for any personnel evaluation process.

When applying Principle 1, it is first and foremost critical that the policy documents that guide practice within a state or local education agency reflect national standards. Consequently, school districts and state governments seeking to adopt evaluation tools based on the NASP Practice Model should also align the NASP Practice Model with regulatory, statutory, and/or board policies (e.g., job descriptions, scope of practice descriptions) that describe the role and scope of practice of school psychologists. Policy and practice alignment is essential, as it will help school psychologists know what they are expected to do and will establish a clear connection between expectations, the performance evaluation, and the associated NASP standards.

As an example, in June 2011, Maine passed into law LD 1094, which defined the scope of services of a school psychologist as follows:

> A school psychologist delivers services to children from birth to Grade 12 who are eligible to be enrolled in educational and intermediate educational units, special education programs, and approved private schools. The services delivered are the services articulated under the domains of practice in the current *Model for Comprehensive and Integrated School Psychological Services* developed and published by the National Association of School Psychologists. (Sec. 2. 20-A Maine Rev. Stat. Ann. §13022, as enacted by P.L. 1993, c. 207, §3)

Recognizing the challenge of aligning national and state policies with existing practices, policy makers also included in the law the creation of an Advisory Committee on School Psychologists within the Maine Department of Education. The advisory committee was charged with the development of rules to guide appropriate state-level practice and ethical standards for school psychologists. By including this advisory committee requirement, policy makers built in a structure that assured that the alignment of policy and practice would be intentionally addressed.

It is also often helpful to visually illustrate how the NASP Practice Model standards are aligned with the performance standards of a state or local school district and also how these standards align with the theoretical frameworks upon which the evaluation systems are based. The Florida Student Services Personnel Evaluation Model and Guide (Student Support Services Project, 2012) provides excellent examples of tables that illustrate these alignments. Table 44.1 provides a summary of the tables in the Florida Guide

for the school psychology domain of Data-Based Decision Making and Evaluation of Practices and represents the alignment of a state's professional practice standards, NASP's standards, and the critical components of two theoretical models (Marzano and Danielson) driving educator evaluation.

It is also important to consider how the NASP Practice Model can be infused into evaluation tools and systems. Although there is no one recommended process, there are some reflection questions that can help school psychologists:

- Should all 10 NASP Practice Model domains be examined separately or within the three broad areas upon which the model is framed?
- Should each domain be considered equally or should certain domains count more than others?
- If some of the domains are naturally interacting with other domains (like the domains that permeate all aspects of service delivery), then should these domains be evaluated across all services or treated separately?

To answer these questions, it is critical to understand how the NASP Practice Model was conceived and reflect that design in the questions asked as part of the evaluation. The NASP Practice Model was not designed to be evaluated as 10 separate domains that have no interaction with each other. Instead, the NASP Practice Model is built upon three foundational domains: (a) Diversity in Development and Learning; (b) Research and Program Evaluation; and (c) Legal, Ethical, and Professional Practice. It also considers two practices as permeating all service delivery: (a) Consultation and Collaboration and (b) Data-Based Decision Making and Accountability. Five types of direct and indirect services to children, families, and schools are then delivered: (a) Mental Health Interventions, (b) Academic Interventions, (c) School-Wide Practices That Promote Learning, (d) Prevention and Response Services, and (e) Family–School Collaboration Services. The foundational domains and the practices that permeate all aspects of service delivery should be considered when evaluating each type of service that is delivered. To illustrate this point, the five questions below could be asked as part of an evaluation of the domain representing a school psychologist's delivery of interventions and instructional support to develop academic skills:

- In what ways did the school psychologist consider the child's development, language, and culture in select-

Table 44.1. An Example of the Alignment of Professional Practices, NASP Standards, and Educator Evaluation Frameworks for School Psychologists' Data-Based Decision Making in the Florida Student Services Personnel Evaluation Model and Guide

Professional Practice	NASP Standards	Marzano	Danielson
Collects and uses data to develop and implement interventions within a problem-solving framework	Domains 1 and 2; Standard II.3.9	Domain 2.3	Domain 4
Analyzes multiple sources of qualitative and quantitative data to inform decision making	Domains 1 and 9; Standard II.3.2	Domain 2.2	Domain 3
Uses data to monitor student progress (academic, social/emotional/behavioral) and health and evaluate the effectiveness of services on student achievement	Domain 1 and 9; Standard II.2.2	Domain 2.3	Domain 1f

Note. Based on information from Student Support Service Project (2012).

ing and delivering interventions? (Domain: Diversity in Development and Learning)

- How were the interventions that were selected supported by research and implemented with fidelity? (Domain: Research and Program Evaluation)
- Were the interventions implemented consistent with legal and professional expectations? (Domain: Legal, Ethical, and Professional Practice)
- In what ways did the school psychologist consult and collaborate with the student's teacher, parents, and/or other professionals when implementing the interventions? (Domain: Consultation and Collaboration)
- What sources of data did the school psychologist collect to show the present performance level of the student prior to treatment and the student's progress as a result of the implementation of the interventions? (Domain: Data-Based Decision Making and Accountability)

Each evaluation tool will reflect the unique factors influencing personnel evaluation in that state or district. Applying Principle 1 is largely about keeping the focus of personnel evaluation on school psychologists by firmly grounding evaluation systems on the standards that guide professional practice and conduct. Furthermore, to be most effective, a seamless alignment must exist between job descriptions, self-assessment tools, the evaluation system, and professional development.

Principle 2: Recognize the Critical Importance of Personnel Evaluations

As previously stated, personnel evaluation is the assessment of performance and/or qualifications in relation to the assigned role and the mission and purpose of schools, which is student learning. Effective personnel evaluations include as their primary function the completion of a fair and reliable evaluation that results in objective, instructive feedback to the prac-

titioner that is designed to strengthen and improve professional practice and subsequent student outcomes.

A critical aspect of personnel evaluation is the involvement of the practitioner in the creation and implementation of these systems. For personnel evaluations to have positive effects, the practitioner must buy in and contribute to the process. Given our knowledge of assessment, evaluation, and measurement methodology, school psychologists are good candidates to be engaged in the design of their own personnel evaluation systems. For example, if the school district uses performance rubrics as an evaluation tool, then school psychologists can help district administrators design rubrics based on the NASP Practice Model domains. Many school psychologists have expertise in operationalizing behavior, an essential skill for rubric construction, and this can be applied to the professional behaviors associated with their services as well.

Additionally, school psychologists should contribute data about the effectiveness of their work to their personnel evaluations. Many school psychologists regularly gather student progress data while monitoring student response to interventions. School psychologists working with individual students to reduce classroom outbursts will typically keep counts of the frequency, duration, and intensity of outbursts in different settings. A school psychologist will continue to monitor and record measures of the student's outbursts following the delivery of interventions designed to reduce them. These measurement data reflect the student's response to the interventions and can contribute to the body of evidence representing whether the services delivered by a school psychologist were effective at improving student outcomes.

Participating in the creation of these evaluation tools also helps ensure that these tools can be practically implemented by the evaluators and that school psychologists have a clear understanding of the criteria upon which they are being judged. Some other questions important to Principle 2 relate to the practical application of personnel evaluation: (a) How should the domains be evaluated during each evaluation cycle? (b) How should the domains be weighted? (c) What domains should require student outcome measures as evidence of effectiveness? (d) What sources of evidence best reflect competence in each domain?

These practical questions must be considered by each evaluation developer, and how these questions are answered will largely depend on the individual state or district policies, practices, and traditions. In some cases, these questions will be answered by law or board policy and, in other cases, school psychologists will have opportunities for input.

For example, the Washington, DC, personnel evaluation system, IMPACT, requires that all educator evaluations are weighted based on three variables: commitment to school community, value-added school data, and group specific standards. The requirement that these three variables are consistent across all educator evaluations is set in district policy. However, the content of the group-specific standards was determined with input from the district school psychologists and is generally based on the NASP standards.

In Washoe County School District, Nevada, the NASP Practice Model is used as the basis for the school psychologists' evaluation. The school psychologists provided input into the design of the evaluation rubric and procedures. For each evaluation cycle, the school psychologist is evaluated on three domains: Data-Based Decision Making and Accountability, Consultation and Collaboration, and Legal, Ethical, and Professional Practice, and one additional domain of his or her choosing. Additionally, the school psychologist completes an annual professional development plan including professional goals. By allowing school psychologists to help design the rubric and a process that takes into account their unique professional development needs, the buy in of the school psychologists in the evaluation system has proven to contribute positively to their performance (Coordinator of School Psychological Services, Washoe County School District, Nevada, personal communication, February 8, 2012).

Finally, a review of the collective evaluations of all of the school psychologists working in a school district can also help administrators gather information about the adequacy of the school psychological programs and services being offered. Although personnel evaluations are generally not designed specifically as program evaluation tools, they can contribute information that can be helpful as part of program review efforts. For example, by looking at the collective evaluations of all of the school psychologists, an administrator can see what services are most often needed by students, what services are typically offered or seldom offered by school psychologists, and also what general student outcomes are commonly associated with the services that are delivered. Additionally, these data, taken in consideration with other system's data, can provide a glimpse at growing trends in services, increasing needs of students, or additional supports that may benefit teachers, administrators, or parents.

Principle 3: Use Measurements That Are Valid, Reliable, and Meaningful

Policies that require the use of value-added models or prescribe certain weights for components of personnel evaluations for educators pose a particular challenge for school psychologists as many contractually fall under the classification of "instructional personnel" and are thereby subject to the same evaluation systems as teachers. Because legislatures are adopting language requiring educator evaluation policies, state and local education agencies are finding themselves in the situation where they are required to apply these requirements to school psychologists and other related services personnel. Despite the theoretical support for value-added modeling, many of the policies and practices that have been adopted have preceded quality research about the validity and reliability of applying value-added models to the performance evaluations of school psychologists. Additionally, in some cases, the emphasis on value-added modeling has moved the focus of personnel evaluation discussions away from how to best improve professional performance to how to get rid of ineffective practitioners.

School psychologists are all keenly aware of the importance of utilizing statistically valid and reliable assessment tools and methodologies. There is no point engaging in practices that have invalid meaning or contribute negatively to decision making. The growing use of value-added models and many of the accompanying reforms to personnel evaluation policies and practices currently being embraced generally reflect good intentions but may also result in unintended negative outcomes. For example, the theoretical rationale for value-added modeling is promising and potentially could result in fairer evaluations of professional performance. However, the research supporting the use of these models in teacher evaluation is in its infancy and the application to other professional educators, like school psychologists, is nonexistent. Thus, it is critical that school psychologists actively advocate that state and district administrators who are responsible for creating evaluation tools heed the cautions of experts discouraging the widespread use of value-added modeling and its application to high-stakes decision making until the research demonstrates that this can be done validly and reliably.

In addition to utilizing tools that are valid and reliable, it is also critical that school psychologist evaluations be based upon multiple measures. The Joint Committee on Standards for Educational Evaluation (Gullickson, 2009) recommend that a variety of data-gathering methods and instruments (observation checklists, interviews, products) be used in personnel evaluation in order to ensure comprehensive performance markers are measured. Personnel evaluations that rely exclusively or heavily on the standardized test scores of students are discouraged. Conversely, personnel evaluations that do not include any measure of student outcomes are also discouraged. These evaluations will fail to measure the impact of services delivered. Student outcome measures utilized need to be sensitive to the growth of students in all areas that have an impact on student success (academic, social–emotional, and behavioral) while also measuring the tangible effects of services delivered.

Another consideration in this area pertains to the breadth of services evaluated in the personnel appraisal process. Some districts may choose to develop evaluation processes that reflect only a narrow set of services articulated in the NASP Practice Model, even though school psychologists are engaged in much broader practice. If an evaluation tool only assesses a portion of what a practitioner is providing, then there is a good chance that the quality of some services will go unchecked. Thus, we encourage the use of evaluation tools and methods that examine the broad services of the school psychologist while also factoring into the evaluation ratings the extent in which services can and need to be delivered given the student and school needs, caseloads, administrative responsibilities, and environmental considerations of the work setting.

As evaluation systems develop as a result of policy and practice, state and local education agencies would be wise to assess the effectiveness of their evaluation systems on improving performance and outcomes. Universities and professional organizations should be active participants in these discussions as research-based evidence of efficacy should drive future policy considerations, training, and practice.

Principle 4: Evaluation Should Be Embedded Within an Administrative Structure That Ensures Meaningful Feedback and Offers Resources in Support of Continuous Improvement

The NASP organizational principles within the Practice Model recommend that supervision and/or mentoring be provided by a credentialed and experienced school psychologist (see Organizational Principle 5.1; NASP, 2010). Having the input of a trained school psychologist in the professional evaluation of school psychologists is essential so that the technical and esoteric nature of services can be reviewed and accurately evaluated. When supervising school psychologists are not available to contribute to a personnel evaluation, school districts should consider utilizing peer models of supervision as a component of the evaluation process. These models might include input from peers following reviews of assessment protocols, intervention delivery protocols, consultation records, and data collection and analysis practices and procedures. Additionally, input provided by other school administrators is also valuable as they can provide meaningful feedback about professional conduct, interactions with school systems, and educational practices.

Another priority for consideration within administrative structures is the capacity in which the evaluation process is able to inform the professional development needs of school psychologists. An effective evaluation system will help school psychologists evaluate their individual needs and seek out professional development specifically designed to improve their skills and practice. Evaluators need to also consider that the proficient delivery of school psychological services evolves over time and that the professional development and mentoring needed by early career professionals may be very different than that which is needed by the seasoned professional.

A final benefit of infusing the professional evaluation process within administrative structures is the capacity for the findings of evaluations to inform program needs and resource allocation. At the end of the annual evaluation cycle, school administrators may benefit from collectively reviewing the professional evaluations of school psychologists to see if the trends across these evaluations suggest the need for specific professional development or supervision and mentoring. When a common standard, like the NASP Practice Model, is used as the basis for articulating practice expectations and evaluating performance, inconsistencies in practice can reflect both individual needs as well as systemic needs.

Considerations for Developing Evaluation Tools for School Psychologists

Given that no one framework for personnel evaluation has been adopted nationally or emerged in the research as the single method worthy of discussion, it is reasonable to expect that the trend where state and local education agencies develop their own systems is likely to continue. Therefore, in designing a system it is important to consider the guiding principles that have already been discussed as well as some of the features of personnel evaluation tools that enhance their usefulness.

Rating Systems
Ideally, evaluation tools that are built on a multilevel assessment of functioning that also operationally measure indicators of performance are the most instructive and fair. At a minimum, evaluation tools should be sensitive enough to measure performance at three basic levels: below expectations, within expectations, and above expectations. The degree to which the evaluation tool is sensitive to changes in performance over time is also important. A tool that is multileveled but does not also contain clear descriptions about what movement between the levels represents often has a degree of subjectivity that is less helpful in discerning competence levels. The most informative design that accomplishes

this is typically a rubric rating system where descriptors accompany a set of criteria at each level allowing for more objectivity in rating and differentiation in performance.

The Johnson County School District 1 in Buffalo, Wyoming, uses a multilevel rating evaluation rubric based on the NASP Practice model (Johnson County School District, 2012). Table 44.2 is an excerpt from Johnson County's personnel evaluation rubric and illustrates how one level of proficiency builds off of the previous level in the evaluation of school psychologist's data-based decision-making practices.

Evidence of Performance
For school psychologists, the use of formative or summative student assessments may serve as a piece of the evidence for personnel evaluations of school psychologists if they have been involved in delivering services that could have a direct impact on the student performance being measured. For example, if a school psychologist is involved in providing reading interventions to students, then it is reasonable to assume that student performance on progress-monitoring assessments—such as curriculum-based measurement probes or standardized measures of reading—could provide evidence of student growth in response to the reading interventions. School psychologists need to regularly ask themselves, "What is the evidence of my effectiveness in working with students?" By considering this question as part of the evaluation process,

Table 44.2. Sample Evaluation Rubric for Data-Based Decision Making and Accountability

Developing	Proficient	Accomplished	Distinguished
Conduct assessments to identify eligibility for SPED	... and • Data collected systematically from multiple sources • Use of valid and reliable assessment techniques • Conduct assessments to identify eligibility for SPED as part of the interdisciplinary team	... and • Problem-solving framework as basis for all data-based decision making • Data collected and used to recommend appropriate and research-based instructional and mental health services • Use of systematic and valid data collection procedures	... and • Data collected systematically from multiple sources and considers ecological factors (e.g., classroom, family, community characteristics) • Understand and help facilitate design/ implementation of treatment fidelity • Use of systematic and valid system to evaluate effectiveness of own service and school systems • Use of information and technology resources to enhance data collection and decision making

Note. Excerpt from Johnson County School District 1, Buffalo, WY, School Psychologist Evaluation System.

school psychologists begin to move beyond simply measuring their performance based on what they did to a level of whether it mattered.

Practical Implementation of the Evaluation Process

An important consideration for the development of a professional evaluation process is the degree to which the process is practical and manageable. Systems need to reflect the breadth of the domains articulated in the NASP Practice Model, but also need to be manageable for supervisors to implement. In many school systems a supervising school psychologist will have dozens of supervisees. It is unreasonable to think that a supervisor can observe every activity within every domain for every supervisee. It is also impractical to think that every activity will have the same level of measureable evidence of student performance effect. Thus, those involved in the design of school psychologist's evaluations need to consider it a priority to develop systems that are fair, reliable, informative, instructive, and manageable.

In summary, school psychologists' evaluations need to be built utilizing appropriate comprehensive design methodologies while maintaining their focus on the purpose of professional evaluation; that is, practitioner growth. By engaging the school psychologist in the design of these evaluation systems, districts increase the buy in of the professional and tap his or her professional knowledge of school psychology ensuring that evaluation systems will be meaningful and beneficial for all involved.

Case Example of a Personnel Evaluation System That Utilizes the NASP Practice Model

NASP has not developed a specific structure or tool for the personnel evaluation of school psychologists. However, state and local education agencies are developing these tools and processes. Below is a case example of the development of a school psychology evaluation system that reflects many of the NASP principles discussed in this chapter.

In 2011, Volusia County Florida School District adopted the Danielson framework for their evaluation model for instructional personnel, and the school district's union required that any evaluation instrument developed for nonclassroom teachers would also have to be aligned with the Danielson framework. Upon review, the district school psychologists found that the model typically used for classroom teachers was not aligned with the school psychologists' training and practice. As a result, the district school psychologists in collaboration with their supervisor reviewed the NASP Practice Model professional practices listed for all domains and identified the practices that most closely aligned with

Table 44.3. Volusia County Rubric Cross-Walking NASP Practice Model and Danielson Framework Model

Component	Unsatisfactory	Basic	Proficient	Distinguished
2b: Establishing a Culture for Goal Achievement The school psychologist promotes the development and maintenance of learning environments that support resilience and academic growth, promote high rates of academic engaged time, and reduce negative influences on learning and behavior.	The school psychologist rarely promotes the development and maintenance of learning environments that support resilience and academic growth, promote high rates of academic engaged time, and reduce negative influences on learning and behavior.	The school psychologist regularly promotes the development and maintenance of learning environments that support resilience and academic growth, promote high rates of academic engaged time, and reduce negative influences on learning and behavior.	Through data analysis and systematic observations of classroom and school settings, the school psychologist consistently provides educators with research-based interventions and strategies to promote academic engaged time and reduce negative influences on learning and behavior.	In addition to meeting proficiency in this component, the school psychologist evaluates the outcomes of the research-based interventions and strategies on academic engaged time and behavior and modifies the interventions accordingly through the continuous use of the problem-solving framework.

Note. Column 1 information is from the NASP Practice Model (NASP, 2010, p. 45). Columns 2–4 information is from Volusia County Florida School District (2013).

the Danielson components. Once these key practices were identified, a smaller group of school psychologists then worked to build a multilevel rubric that descriptively identified specific performance indicators for each level. Once the rubric was constructed, it was then further reviewed by the other district school psychologists, a union representative, and district-level administrators. Table 44.3 shows how one Danielson framework model component, 2b: Establishing a Culture for Goal Achievement, was linked to one of the NASP Practice Model professional practices identified under the domain of School-Wide Practices to Promote Learning.

Similarly, the remaining 21 NASP Practice Model components that were selected and cross-walked with the Danielson framework were used as the foundational expectation, with rubric language developed to delineate ratings from unsatisfactory through distinguished. A comprehensive evaluation system based on the Dainelson framework and the NASP Practice Model was subsequently developed (Voulsia County Florida School District, 2013.)

SUMMARY

Given the current focus on the evaluation of education personnel, school psychologists have a unique opportunity to revisit their existing evaluation systems and create meaningful evaluation tools based on best practices in the delivery of school psychological services. Since the NASP Practice Model is the standard for practice in the provision of school psychological services, it serves as an ideal foundation for personnel evaluation models.

School psychologists must advocate for the opportunity to be involved in educational reforms, like the current personnel evaluation efforts, to ensure their voices are represented. By being involved in these reforms, school psychologists not only have an opportunity to improve their craft but, as importantly, they have the capacity to help advance the profession and enhance student outcomes.

REFERENCES

Baker, E. L., Barton, P. E., Darling-Hammond, L., Haertel, E., Ladd, H. F., Linn, R. L., … Shepard, L. A. (2010). *Problems with the use of student test scores to evaluate teachers.* (Briefing Paper #278). Washington, DC: Economic Policy Institute.

Danielson, C. (2013). *The Framework for Teaching Evaluation Instrument.* Princeton, NJ: The Danielson Group.

Gullickson, A. R. (2009). *The Personnel Evaluation Standards: How to assess systems for evaluating educators.* (2nd ed.). Thousand Oaks, CA: Corwin Press.

Johnson County School District #1. (2012). *School Psychologist Evaluation System.* Buffalo, WY: Author. Retrieved from http://www.jcsd1.us/files/1692715/jcsd1%20school%20psychologist%20evaluation%20system.pdf

Marzano, R. J. (2011). *Effective supervision: Supporting the art and science of teaching.* Alexandria, VA: ASCD.

National Association of School Psychologists. (2010). *Model for comprehensive and integrated school psychological services.* Bethesda, MD: Author. Retrieved from http://www.nasponline.org/standards/2010standards/2_PracticeModel.pdf

National Association of School Psychologists. (2012). *A framework for the personnel evaluation of school psychologists utilizing the NASP Practice Model.* Bethesda, MD: National Association of School Psychologists. Retrieved from http://www.nasponline.org/publications/cq/41/3/pdf/V41N3_AframeworkforthepersonnelEvaluation.pdf

Sanders, W. L., & Horn, S. P. (1994). The Tennessee Value-Added Assessment System (TVAAS): Mixed model methodology in educational assessment. *Journal of Personnel Evaluation in Education, 8,* 299–311.

Student Support Services Project. (2012). *Florida's Student Services Personnel Evaluation Model and guide.* Tallahassee, FL: Florida Department of Education. Retrieved from http://sss.usf.edu/resources/format/memos/2012/dps_2012_98a.pdf

U.S. Department of Education. (2009). *Race to the Top Fund: Notice of final priorities.* Washington, DC: Author.

Volusia County Florida School District. (2013). *VSET handbook: Volusia system for empowering teachers.* DeLand, FL: Author. Retrieved from http://myvolusiaschools.org/rttt/Documents/Teacher/VSET_Manual%20as%20of%207%2031%20%202012%20FINAL.pdf

Webster, W., & Mendro, R. (1997). The Dallas Value-Added Accountability System. In J. Millman (Ed.), *Grading teachers, grading schools: Is student achievement a valid evaluation measure?* (pp. 81–99). Thousand Oaks, CA: Corwin Press.

45

Best Practices in Continuing Professional Development for School Psychologists

Leigh D. Armistead
Winthrop University

OVERVIEW

It is widely accepted that completion of a graduate preparation program, although certainly an initial career milestone, is just the beginning of a school psychologist's professional development. Novice practitioners understand that they have acquired just the basics of their profession and will need to learn much more on their own through continuing professional development. The National Association of School Psychologists (NASP) professional development standards as presented in the Nationally Certified School Psychologist (NCSP) Renewal Guidelines and NASP Continuing Professional Development Program (NASP, 2010b) and the *Model for Comprehensive and Integrated School Psychological Services* (NASP, 2010a) recognize that practitioners' competence develops over time and that development requires supervision and continuing professional development.

Experienced school psychologist practitioners engage in continuing professional development for a variety of reasons. They understand that continuing professional development is necessary to ward off professional obsolescence as school psychology changes and evolves. Practitioners who were traditionally trained, for example, must contend with the challenges of new approaches to practice, including, most recently, response to intervention, problem solving, and multi-tiered service delivery systems. School psychologists also engage in professional development to maintain credentials, including the Nationally Certified School Psychologist (NCSP), certification/licensure by state departments of education, and licensure for private practice by state psychology boards. Finally, school

psychologists believe that lifelong learning is a professional and ethical obligation, one that is required by the NASP Practice Model's (NASP, 2010a) Legal, Ethical, and Professional Practice domain.

For some school psychologists, continuing professional development implies a process of attending workshops, conference presentations, and inservice sessions to accrue a certain number of hours of credit necessary for renewing credentials. Within most professions, such mandatory continuing education has a long history. As early as 1879, physicians in several states were required to update their skills before relicensure. Even in medicine, though, continuing education was mostly voluntary and relatively informal until the 1960s. In 1967, Oregon became the first state to propose a mandatory system, and it was enacted in 1970 (Garganta, 1989).

During the 1970s and 1980s, most professions began developing, and many state legislatures began requiring, mandatory continuing professional development programs. Edwards and Green (1983) propose three reasons for this trend. First, in medicine, an increase in malpractice lawsuits prompted mandatory programs. Often, the basis for such litigation was the physician's failure to have or use up-to-date skills. Physicians who could document continuing medical education were regarded as at lesser risk for litigation. Second, the *Report on Licensure and Related Health Personnel Credentialing* by the Department of Health, Education, and Welfare (HEW) was presented to Congress in 1971. This report encouraged professional organizations to ensure the competence of healthcare practitioners when they were recredentialed. The report was immediately interpreted to mean that HEW endorsed mandatory continuing professional development. HEW attempted to clarify its recommendations in later years, but by then there was a widespread misunderstanding that HEW regarded mandatory continuing professional development as equivalent to continued competence. Third, and possibly as a result of the HEW report, professional organizations began promoting mandatory continuing professional development as a way to preempt demands by regulatory bodies for periodic reexamination or peer review as requirements for recredentialing.

Of course, the healthcare professions were not the only ones influenced to develop what were at first voluntary, and later mandatory, professional development requirements. Accounting, law, pharmacy, real estate, and others followed suit (Garganta, 1989). By 1980, at least half of the members of several different professions studied by Houle (1980) favored mandatory continuing professional development. In this context, the American Psychological Association (APA) and NASP began developing continuing professional development programs in the 1970s.

In 1975, APA established its continuing education program (Hynd, Pielstick, & Schakel, 1981). APA's initial focus was on developing a system of approved sponsors of continuing education programs, a focus the association continues today with what is now known as the Sponsor Approval System (APA, 2012). APA-approved sponsors of professional development activities for psychologists must comply with guidelines intended to ensure high-quality training.

In 1975, NASP also established its professional development program, a voluntary system that encouraged and recognized completion of various types of professional development activities in specified areas of professional competence (Batsche, 1990). Participants could earn a certificate for completion of 150 professional development contact hours, 50 in each of three broad competency areas (assessment and evaluation; intervention and remediation; and program planning, development, and research). Perhaps because few states at the time required continuing professional development for certification/license renewal, few school psychologists participated in the certification program, and it was discontinued in 1984. In 1987, however, NASP began developing its National School Psychology Certification System. One purpose of this system was to promote continuing professional development for school psychologists. NASP's professional development guidelines were revised in 1989 (NASP, 1996).

NASP continues to promote continuing professional development as a planned and intentional learning process intended to maintain as well as advance professional

capabilities. The NASP Practice Model (NASP, 2010a) states that "school psychologists engage in lifelong learning and formulate personal plans for ongoing professional growth" (p. 9) and recommends that school psychologists should "have sufficient access to continuing professional development at a level necessary to remain current regarding developments in professional practices that benefit children, families, and schools" (p. 12).

BASIC CONSIDERATIONS

Continuing professional development has long been regarded as a hallmark of a profession and a lifelong responsibility of a professional (Houle, 1980), and because continuing professional development is so important for delivering effective professional services to clients, both NASP and APA regard it as an ethical and professional responsibility. The APA ethics code (APA, 2010) requires that psychologists "undertake ongoing efforts to develop and maintain their competence" (p. 5). The NASP ethics code (NASP, 2010c) contends that "[s]chool psychologists engage in continuing professional development. They remain current regarding developments in research, training, and professional practices that benefit children, families, and schools" (p. 6). Both professional associations have included these provisions in their enforceable codes of professional conduct, emphasizing the importance of continuing professional development for practitioners, and those practitioners apparently agree. In a national survey of continuing professional development preferences and practices, Armistead, Castillo, Curtis, Chappel, and Cunningham (2013) found that 78.9% of practitioners agree with the importance of continuing professional development and regard engaging in it as an ethical and professional responsibility.

Need for Continuing Professional Development

Effective school psychologists participate in continuing professional development for several reasons: (a) to develop initial professional competence, (b) to maintain professional competencies, (c) to respond to role changes and professional transitions, (d) to develop specialties, and (e) to maintain their credentials.

Becoming Professionally Competent

Hynd et al. (1981) observed that no graduate education program can produce practitioners who will not need immediate professional development. This is still true today. The role of professional development in helping novice practitioners become fully competent is as important as the usual rationale of helping practitioners keep current. Ysseldyke et al. (2006) asserted that

> the job of training programs is to ensure that students are at a "novice" level in all domains by the time they complete the coursework phase of their training, and are at a "competent" level by the conclusion of internships, with the expectation that "expert" practice will be achieved only after some postgraduate experience and likely only in some domains. (p. 11)

They also suggested that such expertise could take 5–10 years of practice to achieve.

Dreyfus and Dreyfus (1991) proposed that professionals progress through five stages of growth: novice, advanced beginner, competent, proficient, and expert. Although most graduate students function at the novice level, Harvey and Struzziero (2010) pointed out that the level at which a practitioner functions is really "context dependent." That is, one may be proficient in a certain area of practice but a complete novice in another area. After several years of practice, most school psychologists function at the competent level. Moving beyond the competent level requires effective supervision as well as other types of continuing professional development.

A challenge faced by novice practitioners trying to become more competent is that they often "know about" practices that they do not yet "know how to" perform well (Benner, 1984). Guest (2000) interviewed school psychologists regarding their professional development. Respondents recalled that, as novices, they had how-to difficulties in five areas of their practice: (a) organization, time management, and special education procedures (48%); (b) feelings of inadequacy and uncertainty and fears about making mistakes (40%); (c) inadequate consultation skills (25%); (d) inadequate preservice training for specific job requirements of their initial employment setting (24%); and (e) feeling overwhelmed with the needs of clients and the lack of resources to meet those needs (20%). When asked what resources they drew upon to meet these challenges, school psychologists reported receiving help from other psychologists, supervisors, and former professors, and through what was usually informal rather than formal mentoring. A number of Guest's respondents, however, described themselves as essentially on their own, with little support from others. Besides support from colleagues, continuing professional development experiences were said to have been very helpful in overcoming these challenges.

Continuing to Be Professionally Competent

School psychologists traditionally have been advised that an important reason for engaging in continuing professional development is to avoid professional obsolescence. Dubin (1972) borrowed the concept of half-life from nuclear physics to suggest that, without continuing professional development, psychologists lose about half of their competence in 10–12 years. Others have suggested that, with the rapid increase in school psychology's knowledge base, the half-life is now shorter, perhaps as short as 3–5 years (Hynd et al., 1981). Dubin (1972) also suggested that school psychologists may be particularly susceptible to the half-life phenomenon because they often practice in isolation from colleagues and seldom have adequate supervision.

Some practice areas may be more vulnerable to the half-life effect than others. For example, Guskey (1991) pointed out that competence with technology can erode in a matter of months. Keeping up with technological advances is a continual responsibility for school psychologists today. In a quest for efficiency, school districts are rapidly adopting online systems for service delivery documentation, test inventories, individual education plan management, and even psychological report writing and archiving. E-mail has become the predominant communication method among practitioners, allied professionals, and parents. Practitioners are encouraged to master the use of hand-held computers for behavior observation, test scoring, and personal information management. An increasing number of students with disabilities use assistive technology to learn and communicate. School psychologists are also expected to be knowledgeable about technology-related student issues including social media, cyberbullying, and helping students be good technological citizens.

The Internet is rapidly displacing professional libraries for many school psychologists. It has brought online professional discussion groups, intervention resources, digital journals, and online test scoring. Along with these potential benefits of the Internet comes the availability to both school psychologists and their clients of an overwhelming amount of information about, for example, disabilities, diagnoses, interventions, and curricula. Some of this information has questionable empirical support, and school psychologists are often in the position of being asked to help their clients determine its validity.

So being adept in the use of technology is rapidly becoming a major focus of continuing professional development (Kruger, Maital, Macklem, Weksel, & Caldwell, 2002; Macklem, Kalinsky, & Corcoran, 2000).

Being knowledgeable about the challenges to practicing ethically in our digital age is paramount.

Coping With Changing Roles and Functions

It is possible that because school psychologists have such varied roles and experience frequent shifts in their schools' expectations, they go through a series of mini-careers for which they need retraining (Guest, 2000). The NASP Practice Model (NASP, 2010a) certainly reflects contemporary shifts in expected roles and functions. The model's emphasis on problem solving and intervention-focused, multitiered service delivery presents a professional development challenge to traditionally trained practitioners. Armistead et al. (2013) asked survey respondents about continuing professional development topics engaged in during the previous year. As shown in Table 45.1, of 13 topical areas, the one most frequently engaged in was response to intervention (61%). Of the five topical areas endorsed by more than a quarter of respondents, all addressed some aspect of intervention-focused service delivery. Standardized psychoeducational assessment, a role traditionally associated with school psychology, was ranked in sixth place. The five intervention-focused topic areas were also strongly endorsed as projected needs during the following school year.

Table 45.1. Topical Focus of Continuing Professional Development Activities Engaged in by School Psychologists

Topic	N	Percent
Response to intervention	309	61.0
Behavioral intervention	225	44.1
Academic intervention	149	29.2
Academic screening and progress monitoring	136	26.7
Social–emotional intervention	135	26.5
Standardized psychoeducational assessment	109	21.4
Consultation and problem solving	103	20.2
Behavioral assessment	96	18.8
Ethical and legal issues	93	18.2
Crisis prevention and intervention	84	16.5
Social–emotional assessment	65	12.8
Neuropsychology	61	12.0
Diversity in development and learning	57	11.2

Note. From "School Psychologists' Continuing Professional Development Preferences and Practices," by L. D. Armistead, J. M. Castillo, M. J. Curtis, A. Chappel, and J. Cunningham, 2013, *Psychology in the Schools*, *50*, 415–432. Copyright 2013 by John Wiley & Sons. Adapted with permission.

Managing Professional Transitions

Many school psychologists experience transitions from one type of position to another over the course of their careers (Armistead & Smallwood, 2011). Some take on additional responsibility as mentors, lead psychologists, or supervisors of psychological services units. Others transition to administrative positions. Some move to new states with different practice expectations. A few become faculty members in school psychology graduate education programs. Any of these transitions would likely require a well-planned program of professional development to be successful.

Although this chapter emphasizes the benefits of continuing professional development for practitioners, the professional development needs of those who become university faculty should not be overlooked. School psychology professors should have a personal plan of research and study that enhances their professional development and informs both their practice and their teaching (Knoff & Curtis, 1997). Hettich and Lema-Stern (1989) suggest that at small colleges, faculty teaching loads may preclude traditional professional development activities. They surveyed academic psychologists and found four activity areas that could contribute to professional development: involvement in training and staff development programs, research outside of the graduate specialty area, clinical or consulting work within the college, and other areas, including committee work.

Developing Specializations

School psychologists completing a NASP-approved graduate program in school psychology receive a comprehensive preservice training experience. Graduates of specialist-level programs are expected to have knowledge and skills in all 10 domains of the NASP Practice Model (NASP, 2010a); be able to provide a comprehensive range of services; and have a positive impact on children, families, and schools. Graduates of doctoral-level programs may also study one or more of the domains in greater depth. Regardless of graduate preparation, however, many school psychologists develop one or more specialty areas. They are often motivated to do so by personal interest, current work assignments, or efforts to improve services to clients.

Armistead et al. (2013) found that about 33% of survey respondents reported having a professional specialty. Even more—38.6%—said that learning about a specialty topic was an important reason for their engaging in professional development. Frequently reported specialty areas included autism, positive behavior support, bilingual practice, crisis prevention and intervention, and preschool services. Although perhaps more informal than the specialization in training and practice advocated by Reynolds (2011), such specialty areas seem to provide an important motivation for engagement in continuing professional development and likely increase school psychologists' positive impact.

Maintaining Credentials

The NASP National School Psychology Certification Board requires 75 hours of continuing professional development every 3 years for those renewing the NCSP credential. Three of the 75 hours must address ethical practice and/or the legal regulation of school psychology, and 10 of the 75 hours must come from NASP- or APA-approved providers of continuing professional development. In addition, almost all state departments of education require continuing professional development for periodic license renewal. Most school psychologists credentialed for private practice must meet the continuing professional development renewal credit requirements of a state licensing board (e.g., board of psychology). Of the 50 states, 42 psychology licensing boards require continuing professional development for relicensure (Association of State and Provincial Psychology Boards, 2012). The number of mandated hours ranges from 6 to 30 per year with a median of 20 hours per year. Thirty state licensing boards require continuing professional development in ethical and professional practices, with a median requirement of 1.5 hours per year.

Mandated continuing professional development requirements such as these have been advocated as a necessary incentive for what Phillips (1987) described as continuing education "laggards"; that is, the minority of licensed psychologists who would not otherwise engage in appropriate amounts of continuing professional development. A study suggests this may be the case. Neimeyer, Taylor, and Wear (2009) surveyed 6,095 professional psychologists and found that those without a mandated continuing education renewal requirement completed one third fewer hours than those with a mandate. Of those without a mandate, 25% completed fewer than 5 hours per year. In contrast, among the school psychologists responding to the national continuing professional development survey (Armistead et al., 2013), there was no significant difference in continuing professional development engagement among those holding the NCSP or those with an independent practice credential. Nevertheless, 71% of these school psychologists reported that renewal of some type of credential was a reason for their engagement in continuing professional development.

Given the varied purposes of continuing professional development outlined in this section—developing and maintaining competencies, managing role changes and transitions, developing specialties, and maintaining credentials—the extent of practitioner involvement in it may be relevant. Fowler and Harrison (2001), in one of the first empirical studies of the topic, found that most school psychologists regard continuing professional development as important and actively engage in it. Seventy-six percent of their sample reported continuing professional development involvement at least quarterly. About 60% of school psychologists reported 26 or more hours of continuing professional development in the previous year, and 28% reported more than 41 hours per year. A survey by Armistead et al. (2013) indicated even higher levels of engagement, with about 80% of the respondents reporting more than 25 hours per year. Because NASP standards recommend a minimum of 75 hours of continuing professional development every 3 years, the Armistead et al. data suggest that most school psychologists meet or exceed the NASP standard for professional development.

So, school psychologists devote considerable time (and money) to continuing professional development and regard it as an important professional obligation that results in better outcomes for their clients. It could be assumed that school psychologists carefully plan their continuing professional development activities. The following section will examine that assumption.

Planning a Continuing Professional Development Program

The NASP Practice Model (NASP, 2010a) encourages school psychologists and their school districts to develop formal professional development plans and revise them each year. Three consecutive editions of *Best Practices in School Psychology* included chapters on continuing professional development that encouraged school psychologists to plan their own professional development programs, taking into account their specific skill development needs and the needs of their employment settings (Armistead, 2008; Brown, 2002; Fowler & Harrison, 1995). Whether school psychologists develop plans in this way has not been adequately investigated. Armistead et al. (2013) suggest that perceived need as well as availability of topical offerings are factors in continuing professional development decisions. Armistead et al.'s (2013) results suggest that school psychologists often participate in professional development activities at conferences and other venues that are not especially high on their list of needs but are what is available. Thus, we recommend that conference planners conduct needs assessments to align programs more closely with professional development needs that participants are likely to have.

Another consideration is that few school psychologists receive preservice training in any aspect of planning or management of their own professional development (Fowler & Harrison, 2001). Therefore, several models for self-management of continuing professional development have been proposed (e.g., Brown, 2002; Fowler & Harrison, 1995; Rosenfield, 1981). These models generally suggest a three-step planning process: (a) considering contextual factors, (b) assessing competencies, and (c) prioritizing continuing professional development needs.

Considering Contextual Factors

School psychologists practice in various settings and assume diverse roles, including those of instructional consultant, mental health practitioner, program evaluator, and systems consultant. Thus, their continuing professional development planning must consider their current roles and functions; impending changes in roles and functions; employer expectations; as well as individual career plans, specialty areas, and interests. As a framework for this consideration, the NASP Practice Model is recommended (NASP, 2010a).

As shown in Figure 45.1, the NASP Practice Model (NASP, 2010a), at the student level, envisions two broad outcomes: (a) providing interventions and instructional supports to develop children's academic and social–emotional competencies and (b) providing interventions and mental health services to develop children's social and life skills. At the systems level, the model envisions school psychologists helping schools, communities, and families improve their capacity to develop these competencies. The model includes two important skill sets—data-based decision making and accountability as well as consultation and collaboration—that are required for school psychologists to provide these

Figure 45.1. Relationships Among School Psychology Professional Practice Domains, a Multilevel Delivery System, and Outcomes for Varied Clients

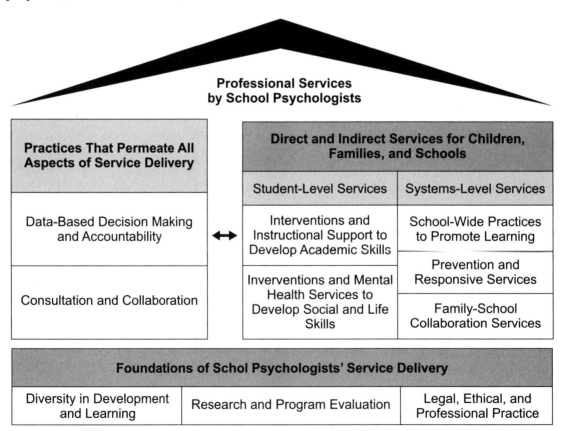

Note. From *Principles for Professional Ethics*, by National Association of School Psychologists, 2010, Bethesda, MD: National Association of School Psychologists. Copyright 2010 by National Association of School Psychologists. Adapted with permission.

services. Finally, the model recognizes school psychologists' foundational knowledge base regarding student diversity in development and learning, practitioners' competencies in research and program evaluation, and a commitment to ethical and professional practice. Although the NASP Practice Model reflects a contemporary view of school psychological services, it includes skills and services traditionally associated with school psychology.

Using the model as a framework for planning their continuing professional development can help practitioners examine their current roles and functions and contemplate future expansion or changes in them. For example, practitioners whose districts are considering school-wide positive behavior programs might assess their knowledge and skills in such systems-level service delivery.

Assessing Competencies

Once contextual factors are considered, a school psychology practitioner's consideration of skill level is necessary. This, however, may not be an easy task. The NASP Practice Model (NASP, 2010a) acknowledges that school psychologists function at various levels along a continuum of skill development and, through work experience or advanced graduate education, may develop specialty areas. Brown (2002) has developed a listing of knowledge and skills items, the Professional Development Needs Checklist, which can be useful in identifying strengths and needs relative to current as well as anticipated practice demands. However, using such a checklist can be difficult due to the interrelatedness of various skills. Additional information from such sources as supervisors and mentors may be helpful. When appropriate, the results of program evaluation measures and client needs assessments should be considered. Presland (1993) also suggests conducting a "critical incident analysis." To do so, the practitioner reviews recent situations that were difficult to handle and reflects on any improvements in knowledge, skills, or dispositions necessary to handle such situations in the future.

NASP has created the online Self-Assessment for School Psychologists (available at http://www.nasponline.org) to help school psychologists examine activities inherent in their current roles and evaluate their own perception of the importance of those activities. Organized by the 10 domains of the NASP Practice Model (NASP, 2010a), this assessment tool can help practitioners determine skill areas in which they need additional professional development and establish goals for expanding their present roles. It is noteworthy that NASP reported using anonymous aggregated data from this online tool in planning its continuing professional development programs.

Prioritizing Continuing Professional Development Needs

Armistead and Smallwood (2011) suggested that once professional development needs are identified, several factors should be considered when prioritizing those needs. Practitioners' continuing professional development goals, objectives, and activities should be determined first—and foremost—by the needs of their clients. Of secondary consideration are the needs of school districts or other employers. After those first two priorities are met, practitioners should consider individual interest areas, specializations, and career enrichment needs. Brown (2002) suggested that another factor to consider is the immediacy of identified needs. Needs related to current job demands should be a higher priority than those related to future career development. Finally, competence in the NASP Practice Model (NASP, 2010a) domains should be considered when setting priorities. The three foundational competencies of Diversity in Development and Learning; Research and Program Evaluation; and Legal, Ethical, and Professional Practice are regarded as supportive of the other domains. Relatedly, the practice domain of Data-Based Decision Making and Accountability and of Consultation and Collaboration permeate all aspects of delivering of school psychological services. Practitioners—especially novices—should give high priority to developing these basic skills when planning a professional development program.

Selecting Continuing Professional Development Activities

Once continuing professional development needs have been identified and prioritized, a variety of both traditional and nontraditional learning activities are available to school psychologists. Many are provided or sponsored by professional associations. For example, NASP professional development guidelines recognize the following activities as appropriate for continuing professional development: workshops, conferences, and inservice training; college and university coursework; teaching and training activities; research and publication; supervision of graduate students; postgraduate supervised experience; program planning and evaluation; self-study (including online activities); and leadership in professional organizations (NASP, 2010b). Before selecting such activities, however, school psychologists should be familiar with the professional associations' continuing professional development guidelines.

APA Professional Development Guidelines

APA asserts the need for psychologists to engage in professional development yet does not recommend a minimum number of hours or specify required content areas. Instead, APA recommends that these requirements be determined by state psychology licensing boards. To ensure quality, APA's Sponsor Approval System regulates providers of continuing professional development for psychologists, and most state licensing boards require that a portion of a psychologist's mandated continuing professional development hours be from an APA-approved sponsor. (An online directory of APA-approved providers is available at http://www.apa.org/education/ce/sponsors.aspx.) APA and its divisions also directly provide continuing professional development activities. Many of its annual convention sessions and home-study offerings are relevant to school psychology.

NASP Continuing Professional Development Program

NASP's continuing professional development program and guidelines are innovative in that they are related to a comprehensive and integrated system of standards for graduate education, credentialing, service delivery, and ethical and professional practices. The guidelines were established in 1989 and have been revised several times. The *Nationally Certified School Psychologist (NCSP) Renewal Guidelines and NASP Continuing Professional Development Program* (NASP, 2010b) emphasizes the necessity of professional development for NCSPs and includes guidelines and forms for the triennial renewal of their credential. However, NASP professional development guidelines apply to all school psychologists regardless of their NCSP status.

National School Psychology Certification System

The National School Psychology Certification System recognizes school psychologists whose training is consistent with NASP standards and provides a national credential that is recognized by 31 states as a standard for licensure or certification. It also recognizes school psychologists who meet NASP's guidelines for continuing professional development. The NCSP system is administered by the National School Psychology Certification Board, which determines renewal requirements for the NCSP credential. School psychologists who hold the NCSP must participate in a minimum of 75 hours of professional development activities every 3 years to renew their national certification. Ten hours of the 75 hours of professional development must come from NASP- or APA-approved providers of continuing professional development (see below), and 3 hours of the 75 hours must address legal and ethical issues in school psychology. Beyond these requirements, NCSPs may select their professional development activities according to personally developed professional growth plans. To determine an activity's suitability, however, NCSPs must answer "yes" to the following four questions: (a) Did the activity enhance or upgrade my professional skills or add to my knowledge base? (b) Was the activity relevant to the professional practice of school psychology? (c) Did the activity fit into my personal plan for continuing professional development? (d) Did the activity go beyond the ordinary aspects of my employment?

For workshops, conferences, or inservice training activities, either a letter of attendance or an Activity Documentation Form is acceptable. This form may also be used by NCSPs to self-document their involvement in other categories of professional development except university courses for which a transcript is required. For many activities, including workshops, conferences, teaching, research, and self-study, participants may claim one continuing professional development credit for each hour of engagement. Maximum allowable credit varies among the different types of activities. For example, although there is a 25-hour limit for self-study, there is no limit for workshops, conferences, or university courses. The *NCSP Renewal Guidelines* (NASP, 2010b) contains further details regarding approved activities and other aspects of the NCSP renewal process and is available at http://www.nasponline.org.

NASP-Approved Provider System

In 2005, NASP's professional development program was enhanced with the establishment of the NASP-Approved Provider System (NASP, 2011b). This system assists school psychologists in accessing high-quality continuing education activities that will enhance their professional growth. NASP and its approved graduate education programs are regarded as de facto approved providers of continuing professional development. Other organizations may apply to become approved providers. Examples include state associations of school psychologists, school psychology training programs that are not NASP approved, related national professional organizations, other organizations and individuals offering professional development for school psychologists (e.g., school districts, colleges and universities, public agencies, private and other national organizations), commercial organizations, and qualified individuals. An application and biennial renewal process ensures that approved provider professional development programs will provide an appropriate level of training, content appropriate for school psychologists, adequate documentation and infrastructure, and sound organizational policies. An online directory of approved providers is available at http://www.nasponline.org/profdevel/approvedprovider/apdirectory.aspx.

The NASP-Approved Provider System guidelines (NASP, 2011b) include quality indicators for certain professional development activities offered by it and its approved providers. The following quality indicators primarily apply to more formal activities such as workshops, conferences, and online webinars and self-study modules—activities for which participants receive documentation of attendance or completion—and are often described as Documented Continuing Professional Development by approved providers. Such programs must meet all of the following requirements:

- The activity must fall within approved content areas, that is, one or more of the NASP Practice Model domains.
- The activity's instructional level must be appropriate for credentialed school psychologists.
- The activity must enhance school psychologists' professional knowledge, competencies, or skills.
- The activity must have stated instructional objectives related to one or more approved content areas.
- The activity must be 1 hour or more in duration.
- Instructors must have training or experience that qualifies them to be considered experts in the subject matter being taught.
- The provider and instructors must comply with guidelines regarding financial conflict-of-interest disclosure.
- The provider must verify attendance and provide documentation of completion.
- The provider must require participants to complete evaluations of the activity, including the extent to which learning objectives are met.
- The activity may not be a business meeting, professional committee meeting, or administrative meeting, or a presentation intended primarily for a lay audience.
- The activity must be conducted in compliance with NASP *Principles for Professional Ethics* (NASP, 2010b).

NASP's Continuing Professional Development Offerings

Providing continuing professional development opportunities for school psychologists is one of NASP's major functions. As previously discussed, NASP's more formal offerings provide Documented Continuing Professional Development credit. These include selected professional growth workshops offered during its annual convention. In addition, NASP provides summer conferences, each providing 3 days of high-quality, documented professional development credit. Since 2011, NASP has also developed an Online Learning Center, which offers NASP- and APA-approved continuing professional development for live and archived webinars, as well as recorded sessions from previous conventions or summer conferences. Figure 45.2 depicts continuing professional development activities offered by NASP as of 2014. Many do not provide Documented Continuing Professional Development credit but may be appropriate for self-documentation as described in the preceding section.

Other Professional Development Opportunities

Although NASP provides a comprehensive array of continuing professional development opportunities, survey results suggest that only about 20% of NASP members are able to attend its more formal offerings such as its annual convention and summer conferences in any given year (Armistead et al., 2013). Because it is estimated there are more than 38,000 credentialed school psychologists in the United States (Charvatt, 2005), additional resources are required. In this section, a variety of traditional as well as nontraditional options for continuing professional development are discussed.

NASP-Affiliated State Associations
NASP's 52 affiliated associations (50 states plus the District of Columbia and Puerto Rico) are also important providers of continuing professional development. Almost all provide at least one conference each year, and many provide more than one. Some provide summer institutes, regional workshops, and a variety of other activities, including self-study programs. State conferences can be more accessible and less expensive to attend, especially for practitioners whose employers do not reimburse for continuing professional development expenses. Survey results suggest that 42% of school psychologists attend a state association conference each year (Armistead et al., 2013). Links to state association websites are available at http://www.nasponline.org.

Figure 45.2. NASP Professional Development Programs

NASP Professional Development Programs		
CPD Provided Directly to Practitioners	**CPD Provided to Practitioner Indirectly**	**CPD Through Leadership Development**
Convention workshops, papers, seminars, posters, keynotes, special strands, and documented sessions / Online webinars and self-sturdy modules / Publications including books, *School Psychology Review*, *School Psychology Forum*, *Communiqué*, "tool kits," and convention CDs / NASP-sponsored sessions at state conferences (i.e., presidential keynotes and workshops) / PREP<u>a</u>RE / Government/ professional relations training / Summer Conferences	Speakers bureau / NASP-approved provider programs / Train-the-trainer initiatives including PREP<u>a</u>RE	New leader orientation / Regional leadership meetings / Delegate Assembly activities and presentations

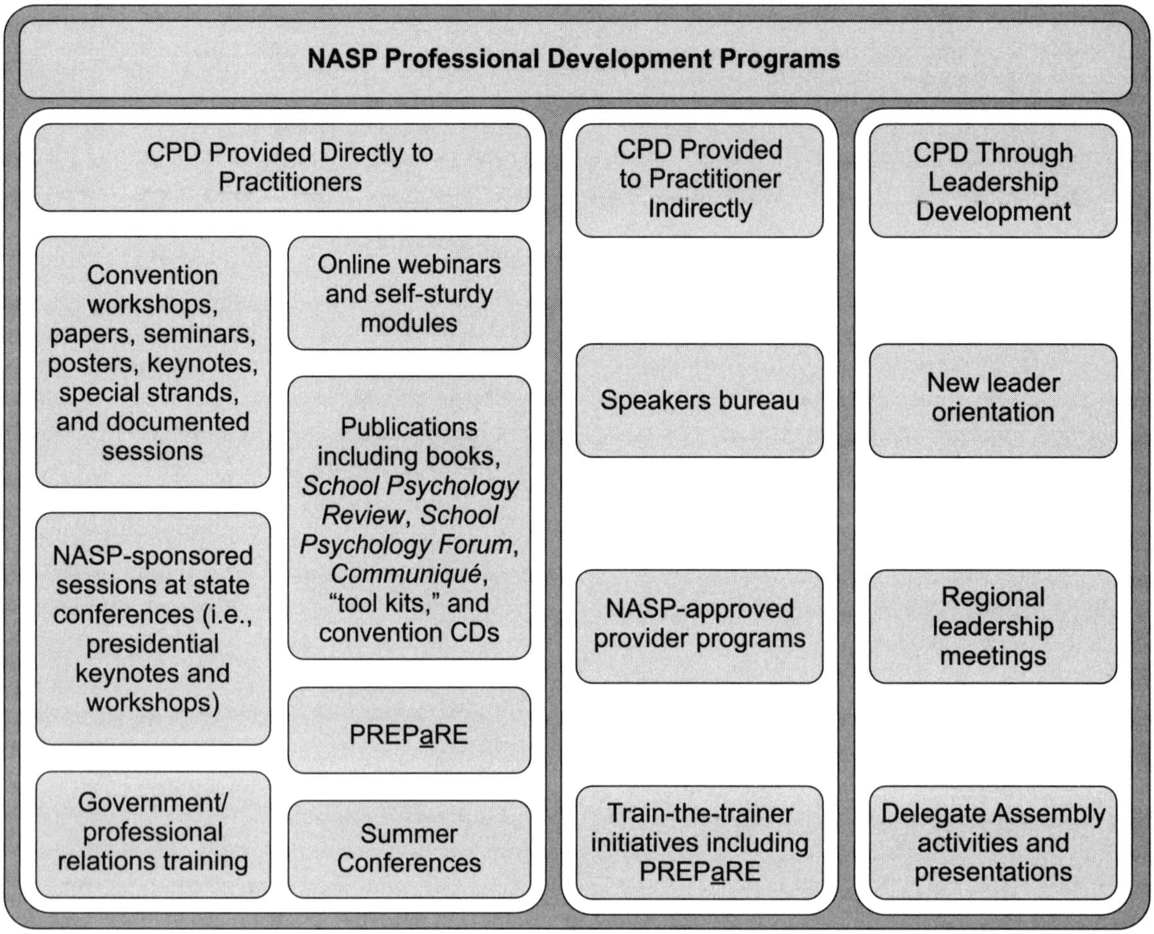

Note. From "Best Practices in Continuing Professional Development for School Psychologists," by L. D. Armistead, 2008, in A. Thomas and J. Grimes (Eds.), *Best Practices in School Psychology V*, 2008, Bethesda, MD: National Association of School Psychologists. Copyright 2008 by National Association of School Psychologists. Adapted with permission.

The International School Psychology Association provides continuing professional development. It comprises national associations in 12 countries, publishes a newsletter and journal, and holds an international colloquium in a different country each year. Practitioners might consider the possibility of combining overseas travel with a continuing professional development opportunity (see http://www.ispaweb.org).

NASP-Approved Graduate Education Programs

NASP standards require that its approved graduate programs provide or collaborate in the provision of continuing professional development for practitioners (NASP, 2010d). Programs meet this criterion in several ways. Some sponsor or cosponsor workshops or summer institutes. Some open their coursework to alumni or

other practitioners. Some assess the needs of local practitioners and attempt to meet their needs by sponsoring or cosponsoring continuing professional development programs. Many collaborate with their state school psychology association in providing professional development opportunities.

School Psychological Services Units

The NASP Practice Model's Organizational Principle 6 (NASP, 2010a) provides this standard for the professional development responsibilities of school districts:

> Individual school psychologists and school systems develop professional development plans annually. The school system ensures that continuing professional development of its personnel is both adequate for and relevant to the service delivery

priorities of the school system. School systems recognize the need for a variety of professional development activities. These activities could include those provided by the school system, NASP-approved providers, other educational entities, or other activities such as online training, formal self-study, and professional learning communities. (p. 57)

Related NASP (2010a) standards encourage school districts to provide support to ensure that school psychologists have access to continuing professional development at a level necessary for their skills to remain current and to provide the resources necessary to systematically document the continuing professional development activities of their employees.

If a school psychological services unit is to have an effective professional development program, then it should take into account the needs of individual school psychologists as determined by a planning process similar to the one previously discussed. Programs should also take into account institutional needs and long-term goals. Large school districts with many school psychologists are more likely to be able to provide effective staff development than smaller districts. They are also more likely to provide supervision and mentoring.

School District Staff Development
Staff development or inservice programs provided by school districts are available to most school psychologists. Such programs are often generic in nature and offered to diverse groups of educators. Although these programs may meet state requirements for certification renewal, they may not be especially relevant to the continuing professional development needs of school psychologists. A national continuing professional development survey (Armistead et al., 2013) found that 68% of school psychologists had attended a generic staff development program in the previous year and 42% of the respondents had attended a school district staff development program intended specifically for school psychologists. Staff development programs have been criticized as generally ineffective because they may not be planned with specific district or employee needs in mind. Nevertheless, school psychologists could benefit from inservice programs if they evaluate the extent to which the content is relevant, whether the training is skill based, and whether there will be school district support for the utilization of new skills.

Regardless of quality and relevance, school psychologists are not satisfied that district-provided professional development programs are adequate. Armistead et al. (2013) report that 77% disagreed with the following statement: "My school district provides enough [continuing professional development] activities that I don't really need to attend state conferences or national conventions."

Presenting a Professional Development Activity
Most school psychologists will be asked to present a professional development session at some point in their careers, often a training session for colleagues at a district, state, or national meeting. Armistead et al. (2013) found that about 50% of their survey respondents had conducted workshops or inservice training activities in the previous year. As previously noted, preparing and presenting a training program is an effective form of continuing professional development that practitioners may use for NCSP renewal purposes.

A brief summary of Guskey's (2000) advice about effective training might be helpful. Training sessions are, of course, the most common type of continuing professional development activity and are familiar to practitioners. There are many types of training sessions: the large group lecture/discussion format, workshops, seminars, panel discussions, and breakout sessions. Training sessions should have clear objectives. Presenters should be clear about whether their participants are expected to acquire awareness, knowledge, skills, or all three. Confusion about this is common in school district inservice programs. Workshops that merely convey awareness and knowledge are expected to result in practitioners acquiring skills but seldom do. Guskey points out that if skill acquisition is intended, then effective training programs should include presentation of a knowledge base, modeling of skills, practice in simulations and role playing, feedback, and then follow-up coaching in the school setting.

Supervision, Mentoring, and Peer Support
Professional supervision has long been regarded as essential for continuing professional development, and NASP standards emphasize the value of supervision. The NASP Practice Model's Organizational Principle 5 (NASP, 2010a) recommends "all personnel have levels and types of supervision and/or mentoring adequate to ensure the provision of effective and accountable services" (p. 56). The NASP (2010e) credentialing standards encourage at least 1 hour per week of mentoring or supervision for beginning school psychologists. NASP's (2011a) position statement on supervision further emphasizes the need for high-quality supervision. However, few

school psychologists receive supervision that is consistent with these guidelines. Ross and Goh (1993) reported that fewer than a third of survey respondents who had less than 3 years of experience reported at least an hour of supervision each month. These authors also raised questions about the effectiveness of professional supervision. Few supervisors in their study reported having training in supervision and often reported having degrees in specialties other than school psychology.

Some have attempted to redefine supervision in a way that deemphasizes the hierarchical and administrative qualities often associated with it. One such definition is "an interpersonal interaction between two or more individuals for sharing knowledge, assessing professional competencies, and providing objective feedback with the terminal goals of developing new competencies, facilitating effective delivery of psychological services, and maintaining professional competencies" (McIntosh & Phelps, 2000, p. 33–34). This type of supervision could be regarded as occurring within mentoring or peer support relationships. Many school districts assign new school psychologists to a mentor. If not so assigned, it seems sensible for new school psychologists to attempt to find a mentor. Little is known about how often this occurs or the effectiveness of the mentoring relationships.

Peer consultation or peer-mediated support groups, however, can be helpful to school psychologists. Zins and Murphy (1996) found that 64% of the school psychologists they surveyed had participated in a peer support group. Benefits reported by a majority included improved skills, expanded range of services, increased professional enthusiasm, more involvement in professional associations, and a better professional knowledge base. Effective groups comprise enthusiastic participants, structure meetings, and arrange for convenient meeting locations and times. Administrative support for these meetings is helpful. Peer support groups apparently are more successful if they develop goals and plans and strive for open communication and a supportive atmosphere. It seems apparent that such groups are also an important source of social support for coping with the stress of a challenging occupation.

Online Communities

A contemporary version of the peer support group is the e-mail Listserv or online discussion group. A prominent provider of e-mail discussion groups, Yahoo Groups (http://www.yahoogroups.com), hosts many groups that are specific to school psychology and many more that are relevant to psychology and education in general.

These groups regularly include prominent researchers and test authors sharing their viewpoints, and lengthy discussions with multiple participants are frequent. An advantage of advertising-supported providers such as Yahoo is that there is no cost to an individual or group to set up a discussion group or to its participants. Listserv discussion groups can be developed by and for large groups with varied interests or small groups with narrow specialty interests.

NASP created its Communities system in early 2011 and offers it as a member service (http://communities. nasponline.org/Home/). There are communities for NASP leadership groups and its general membership and special interest groups. Each community features member blogs and a library for downloadable files. The general membership area is the largest—about 7,000 members—and the most active. For interest groups, NASP Communities feature interests as diverse as adoption and foster care, reading, positive psychology, social justice, traumatic brain injury, and urban school psychology.

The potential of such online communities to enhance continuing professional development has had little study. An early attempt to create an online professional development community was the Global School Psychology Network developed by Louis Kruger and colleagues at Northeastern University (Macklem et al., 2000). A survey of its members showed that it is possible to develop a sense of community among school psychologists who frequently participate in online discussions even if they never meet face to face. Given that school psychologists describe talking with their colleagues as an important factor in their professional development, their enthusiastic adoption of online communities can be expected to continue (Kruger et al., 2002).

Study Groups

Somewhat more formal and structured than peer support groups and online communities, professional study groups are not well documented in school psychology. Armistead et al. (2013) report that 13.7% of their respondents had engaged in a study group, but no details of their participation were elicited by that survey. Study groups, however, have been reported by school counselors to be an effective professional development alternative. Robertson (1998), for example, described a program for counselors that used a guided book discussion approach. Groups of counselors read a common book on a particular topic relevant to their practices. Meeting periodically, they took turns leading the group's discussion of the book. A key factor in the success of this project was relating the book to their own current work problems. Wilcoxon and Archer (1997) have described a group of counselors in private practice who formed the Consortium for Education and Training. Meeting monthly in a member's office, they participated in presentations and discussions relevant to their practices. The primary presenter (a university faculty member and an approved provider with the National Board of Certified Counselors) was able to facilitate formal evaluation and documentation for license renewal purposes. Three aspects of the consortium seem to account for its success: formal but local and low-cost activities, ongoing participant contact, and active selection of topics by participants.

Self-Study and Online Professional Development

Self-study using professional books, journals, and audio or video recordings has long been associated with continuing professional development in school psychology. As previously noted, the National School Psychology Certification System permits up to 25 of the 75 hours of continuing professional development activities required every 3 years to be self-study, which may include sequenced programs (self-study programs developed and published to provide training in specific knowledge and skill areas) or informal self-study of an interest area using books, journals, and manuals.

A recent development is the availability of continuing professional development credit for online self-study. Armistead et al. (2013) reported that about half of their survey respondents had participated in a live webinar or completed an online training module and 48% said they would prefer to get more of their continuing professional development online. To facilitate this, NASP has developed the Online Learning Center, which provides a range of prerecorded sessions that meet the approved provider guidelines for documented continuing professional development. Many of these sessions were developed from NASP convention presentations and range from 1 to 9 hours in length. Most of the sessions feature video recording of the original convention session synchronized with the speaker's slides and provide downloadable handouts. Users who view the session in its entirety, complete an evaluation, and pass an online multiple-choice test are able to print documentation of completion. More information is available at http://www.nasponline.org/profdevel/index.aspx. APA offers a similar service called Online Courses (more information is available at http://www.apa.org/education/ce/).

NASP also offers live webinars that feature prominent speakers and provide documented continuing professional development credit. Numerous commercial providers also provide online continuing professional development programs to school psychologists. A review of their offerings suggests that, while a few online courses feature multimedia content, most involve reading text online or reading books offline and then taking an online test.

BEST PRACTICES IN CONTINUING PROFESSIONAL DEVELOPMENT

To become, and continue to be, competent and effective—and to make a positive impact on children, families, schools, and communities—school psychologists must commit to be lifelong learners. This commitment is an ethical and professional obligation that can be achieved through the following best practices.

School psychologists should join and actively participate in their local, state, and national professional associations. Membership in these associations provides a context in which school psychologists and their colleagues reinforce each other's professionalism and provides access to high-quality continuing professional development activities. School psychologists should also seek leadership positions in their professional associations. This is in itself a professional development activity and facilitates the professional development of others.

School psychologists should participate in continuing professional development activities provided by their school districts. They should recognize, however, that generic inservice activities, although perhaps inexpensive and convenient, seldom address their professional needs. So school psychologists should work within their psychological services units to plan and deliver continuing professional development activities for those units. Ideally, practitioners should be able, at various times, to take on the roles of teacher, leader, mentor, and coach, as well as be participants in such activities (Brody & Davidson, 1998).

Adults learn best from continuing professional development when they examine their own strengths and weaknesses and then choose activities that are relevant to their own personal and professional needs (Rosenfield, 1981), and they should engage in a variety of activities. This chapter has emphasized the many types of activities that are available to school psychologists. For example, combining a convention workshop on a particular topic with a planned program of self-study of journal articles and ongoing discussions with a peer support group on the topic will be more likely to result in enhanced benefits to clients than any of the individual options alone. One should remember that continuing professional development, when successful, is more of a process than an event (Guskey, 1991). For optimal benefit, school psychologists' professional development should be a sustained, long-term effort within a context of frequent dialog with a network of colleagues with similar interests.

School psychologists should be critical consumers of continuing professional development, examining presenters' affiliations, apparent conflicts of interest, learning objectives, and instructional approaches before deciding on whether to participate. When possible, school psychologists should engage in activities that provide Documented Continuing Professional Development credit. NASP professional development standards (NASP, 2011b) ensure a level of quality, presenter credentials, and appropriate content for school psychologists. Participants should carefully consider the nature of prospective activities, especially if they are intended to improve skills. If an activity includes active learning strategies such as modeling, simulation, role playing, discussion, case studies, and problem solving, it is more likely that skills will be acquired and transfer to the work setting. If an activity is part of a sustained effort to assist practitioners in translating new knowledge into practice, rather than a one-time event, then it is more likely to be effective, especially if ongoing coaching is available (Joyce & Showers, 1980).

Effective continuing professional development activities have appropriate learning objectives. Presenters often plan in terms of what they are going to do or what material they will present rather than what they want participants to know, how they want to influence attitudes, and what they want participants to be able to do. Learning objectives may provide insight into whether an activity was planned with the end in mind as recommended by Guskey (1991). At the end of a continuing professional development activity, participants should help evaluate whether the activity met its own stated objectives. Participants should also assess whether changes in knowledge, skills, and attitudes resulted from an activity.

Variety in continuing professional development is good. School psychologists are encouraged to participate in both traditional and nontraditional continuing professional development activities. They should be aware, however, of the advantages as well as the limitations of some nontraditional forms of continuing professional development. For example, optimal benefit

from continuing professional development activities requires active engagement. Passively listening to an online presenter may result in some awareness but in little acquisition of knowledge or skills and may not result in transfer of training to the work setting.

Engaging with colleagues should be part of every school psychologist's professional development program, and there are several important ways to do so. Engagement is certainly an advantage of traditional continuing professional development activities such as conferences and conventions. Online discussion groups, however, are also a way to conveniently engage with colleagues and have conversations about issues of mutual interest. Peer support groups are the only way that many school psychologists are able to engage in professional supervision, and such groups are also an important source of social support in dealing with stress and burnout. Finally, every new school psychologist should have a mentor, and every experienced and qualified school psychologist can be a mentor. Both will benefit from enhanced professional development.

It is important for school psychologists to evaluate their continuing professional development program regularly. When a plan is developed using the guidelines in this chapter, an appropriate measure of the worth of an activity is not a certificate of completion but whether the activity improves a practitioner's knowledge, skills, and competence and enhances career development (Fowler, 1996).

School psychologists should actively address any apparent constraints on their engaging in continuing professional development. These include the need for time away from work, expense, family commitments, and attitudinal factors such as uncertainty and lack of motivation (Fowler & Harrison, 1995). Most school psychologists, about 84%, cite the cost of travel and registration fees as burdensome; about 80% regard a heavy workload as a constraint; and about 46% find family obligations constraining (Armistead et al., 2013). Some constraints, such as availability of continuing professional development activities, can be managed by taking advantage of nontraditional forms of continuing professional development. In any case, it is recommended that practitioners try to recognize these constraints and weigh them against the benefits of continuing professional development as documented in this chapter. Making a commitment may be the key. We usually make time for things to which we are committed.

Organizers and presenters of continuing professional development in school psychology are encouraged to become more aware of key principles of adult learning and continuing professional development and should use those principles when designing and delivering continuing professional development programs.

School psychologists should maintain a certain level of professional skepticism when participating in professional development programs. This was perhaps best expressed by Alex Thomas (1984), who advised that

[s]chool psychologists need to maintain a sense of curiosity and an active commitment to seek any assessment, intervention, theory, or technology that can enhance their effectiveness with children. Simultaneously, they must also be cautious, scientifically aware, and alert to the ethical considerations associated with any new approach to old problems. (p. 469)

SUMMARY

Continuing professional development has long been regarded as one of the hallmarks of a profession. NASP has provided leadership in this regard, and the importance of continuing professional development is reflected in its ethical and professional standards. School psychologists understand its role in their own careers: acquiring and maintaining professional expertise, adapting to changing roles and functions, and enabling professional transitions.

This chapter emphasizes the importance of the NASP Continuing Professional Development Program (NASP, 2010b) in providing guidelines for both practitioners and providers of continuing professional development. It highlights the role of the National School Psychology Certification System in encouraging and recognizing practitioners' engagement in continuing professional development. It challenges individual school psychologists, regardless of NCSP or professional membership status, to take responsibility for assessing their continuing professional development needs, to plan personal programs, to implement the plans, to evaluate results, and to reassess needs on an ongoing basis. Finally, the chapter advocates continuing professional development programs that are client centered and make a difference in outcomes of children, families, schools, and communities.

REFERENCES

American Psychological Association. (2010). *Ethical principles of psychologists and code of conduct.* Washington, DC: Author. Retrieved from http://www.apa.org/ethics/code/index.aspx

American Psychological Association. (2012). *Approval of sponsors of continuing education: Policies and procedures manual.* Washington, DC: Author. Retrieved from http://www.apa.org/ed/sponsor/about/policies/policy-manual.pdf

Armistead, L. D. (2008). Best practices in continuing professional development for school psychologists. In A. Thomas & J. Grimes (Eds.), *Best practices in school psychology V* (pp. 1975–1990). Bethesda, MD: National Association of School Psychologists.

Armistead, L. D., Castillo, J. M., Curtis, M. J., Chappel, A., & Cunningham, J. (2013). School psychologists' continuing professional development preferences and practices. *Psychology in the Schools, 50,* 415–432.

Armistead, L. D., & Smallwood, D. (2011). Making a career of school psychology. In T. M. Lionetti, E. Snyder, & R. W. Christner (Eds.), *A practical guide to developing competencies in school psychology.* New York, NY: Springer.

Association of State and Provincial Psychology Boards. (2012). *Handbook on licensing and certification.* Peachtree City, GA: Author. Retrieved from http://www.asppb.org/HandbookPublic/before.aspx

Batsche, G. (1990). Best practices in credentialing and continuing professional development. In A. Thomas & J. Grimes (Eds.), *Best practices in school psychology II* (pp. 887–898). Bethesda, MD: National Association of School Psychologists.

Benner, P. (1984). *From novice to expert: Excellence and power in clinical nursing practice.* Menlo Park, CA: Addison-Wesley.

Brody, C., & Davidson, N. (1998). Introduction: Professional development and cooperative learning. In C. M. Brody & N. Davidson (Eds.), *Professional development for cooperative learning: Issues and approaches* (pp. 3–21). Albany, NY: State University of New York Press.

Brown, M. (2002). Best practices in professional development. In A. Thomas & J. Grimes (Eds.), *Best practices in school psychology IV* (pp. 183–194). Bethesda, MD: National Association of School Psychologists.

Charvat, J. L. (2005). NASP study: How many school psychologists are there? *Communiqué, 33*(6). Retrieved from http://www.nasponline.org/publications/cq/cq336numsp.aspx

Dreyfus, H. L., & Dreyfus, S. E. (1991). Towards a phenomenology of ethnical expertise. *Human Studies, 44,* 229–250.

Dubin, S. S. (1972). Obsolescence or lifelong education: A choice for the professional. *American Psychologist, 27,* 486–498.

Edwards, R. L., & Green, R. K. (1983). Mandatory continuing education: Time for reevaluation. *Social Work, 28,* 43–48.

Fowler, A. (1996). How to manage your own CPD. *People Management, 2,* 54–57.

Fowler, E., & Harrison, P. L. (1995). Best practices in continuing professional development for school psychologists. In A. Thomas & J. Grimes (Eds.), *Best practices in school psychology III* (pp. 81–89). Bethesda, MD: National Association of School Psychologists.

Fowler, E., & Harrison, P. L. (2001). Continuing professional development needs and activities of school psychologists. *Psychology in the Schools, 38,* 75–88.

Garganta, K. J. (1989). *The question of mandatory continuing education for professionals* (Unpublished doctoral dissertation), Harvard University, Cambridge, MA.

Guest, K. E. (2000). Career development of school psychologists. *Journal of School Psychology, 38,* 237–257.

Guskey, T. R. (1991). Enhancing the effectiveness of professional development programs. *Journal of Educational and Psychological Consultation, 2,* 239–247. doi:10.1207/s1532768xjepc0203_3

Guskey, T. R. (2000). *Evaluating professional development.* Thousand Oaks, CA: Corwin.

Harvey, V. S., & Struzziero, J. A. (2010). *Professional development and supervision of school psychologists: From intern to expert.* Bethesda, MD: National Association of School Psychologists.

Hettich, P., & Lema-Stern, S. (1989). Professional development opportunities in small colleges. *Teaching of Psychology, 16,* 12–16.

Houle, C. O. (1980). *Continuing learning in the professions.* San Francisco, CA: Jossey-Bass.

Hynd, G. W., Pielstick, N. L., & Schakel, J. A. (1981). Continuing professional development in school psychology: Current status. *School Psychology Review, 10,* 480–486.

Joyce, B., & Showers, B. (1980). Improving inservice education: The messages of research. *Educational Leadership, 37,* 379–385.

Knoff, H. M., & Curtis, M. J. (1997). The future of school psychology: Perspectives on effective training. *School Psychology Review, 26,* 93–104.

Kruger, L. J., Maital, S., Macklem, G., Weksel, T., & Caldwell, R. (2002). The Internet and school psychology practice. *Journal of Applied School Psychology, 19,* 95–111.

Macklem, G. L., Kalinsky, R., & Corcoran, K. (2000, July). *International consultation, professional development, and the Internet: School psychology practice and the future* (ERIC No. ED 452 476). Paper presented at the Colloquium of the International School Psychology Association, Durham, NH.

McIntosh, D. E., & Phelps, L. (2000). Supervision in school psychology: Where will the future take us? *Psychology in the Schools, 37,* 33–38.

National Association of School Psychologists. (1996). *Continuing professional development program.* Bethesda, MD: Author.

National Association of School Psychologists. (2010a). *Model for comprehensive and integrated school psychological services.* Bethesda, MD: Author. Retrieved from http://www.nasponline.org/standards/2010standards/2_PracticeModel.pdf

National Association of School Psychologists. (2010b). *Nationally certified school psychologist (NCSP) renewal guidelines and NASP continuing professional development program.* Bethesda, MD: Author. Retrieved from http://www.nasponline.org/certification/New%20NCSP%20booklet.pdf

National Association of School Psychologists. (2010c). *Principles for professional ethics.* Bethesda, MD: Author. Retrieved from http://www.nasponline.org/standards/2010standards/1_%20Ethical%20Principles.pdf

National Association of School Psychologists. (2010d). *Standards for graduate preparation of school psychologists.* Bethesda, MD: Author.

Retrieved from http://www.nasponline.org/standards/2010standards/1_Graduate_Preparation.pdf

National Association of School Psychologists. (2010e). *Standards for the credentialing of school psychologists.* Bethesda, MD: Author. Retrieved from http://www.nasponline.org/standards/2010standards/2_Credentialing_Standards.pdf

National Association of School Psychologists. (2011a). *Position statement: Supervision in school psychology.* Bethesda, MD: Author. Retrieved from http://www.nasponline.org/about_nasp/positionpapers/Supervision_in_School.pdf

National Association of School Psychologists. (2011b). *Procedures and implementation guidelines for the NASP-Approved Provider System.* Bethesda, MD: Author. Retrieved from http://www.nasponline.org/profdev/approvedprovider/documents/APS_Procedural_Guidelines.pdf

Neimeyer, G. J., Taylor, J. M., & Wear, D. M. (2009). Continuing education in psychology: Outcomes, evaluations, and mandates. *Professional Psychology: Research and Practice, 40,* 617–624. doi:10.1037/a0016655

Phillips, L. E. (1987). Is mandatory continuing education working? *Mobius, 7,* 57–64.

Presland, J. (1993). Planning for continuing professional development. *AEP: Association of Educational Psychologists Journal, 8,* 225–233.

Reynolds, C. R. (2011). Perspectives on specialization in school psychology training and practice. *Psychology in the Schools, 49,* 922–930.

Robertson, J. R. (1998). Study groups for counselor professional development. *Professional School Counseling, 1*(4), 59–62.

Rosenfield, S. (1981). Self-managed professional development. *School Psychology Review, 10,* 487–493.

Ross, R. P., & Goh, D. S. (1993). Participating in supervision in school psychology: A national survey of practices and training. *School Psychology Review, 22,* 63–81.

Thomas, A. (1984). Issues and concerns for microcomputer uses in school psychology. *School Psychology Review, 13,* 469–472.

U.S. Department of Health, Education, and Welfare. (1971). *Report on licensure and related health personnel credentialing.* Washington, DC: Author.

Wilcoxon, S. A., & Archer, G. D. (1997). Professional development and training: A consortium model. *Journal of Mental Health Counseling, 19,* 191–199.

Ysseldyke, J., Burns, M., Dawson, P., Kelley, B., Morrison, D., Ortiz, S., … Telzrow, C. (2006). *School psychology: A blueprint for training and practice III.* Bethesda, MD: National Association of School Psychologists.

Zins, J. E., & Murphy, J. J. (1996). Consultation with professional peers: A national survey of the practices of school psychologists. *Journal of Educational and Psychological Consultation, 7,* 61–70. doi:10.1207/s1532768xjepc0701_5

Best Practices in Using Technology for Continuous Professional Development and Distance Education

46

Jack A. Cummings
Indiana University
Susan Jarmuz-Smith
University of New England (ME)

OVERVIEW

The digital revolution has transformed opportunities for learning. A short time ago it took imagination to believe that whole libraries of books, journals, and newsletters could be accessed from a computer and a connection to the Internet. We now have access via mobile phones, tablets, notebooks, and desktop computers. The number of locations on the planet where the Internet cannot be accessed dwindles as advances in technology march forward at a mind-boggling pace. As Bonk (2009) suggested, the world of learning is open 24/7. Access to knowledge and skills is no longer place based. Learning is now anywhere, anytime. Opportunities for learning can come to learners, assuming, that is, they know where to look.

This chapter provides a roadmap to the many continuing education options for school psychologists. We take an expanded view of continuing education that is more than, for example, the yearly accumulation of 25 hours of continuing professional development (CPD) credits. The advent of Internet search engines along with professional journal databases allows access to resources in seconds as opposed to the time to search through a book's table of contents or to make a trip to the library. In the context of all the instantly accessible resources, the title of the chapter includes the term *continuous*, rather than continued professional development. The notion that a school psychologist is in a continuous state of learning, through the use of technology, is a theme promoted throughout the chapter.

This chapter relates specifically to the Legal, Ethical, and Professional Practice domain of the National Association of School Psychologists (NASP) *Model for Comprehensive and Integrated School Psychological Services* (NASP, 2010a), as it is critical for school psychologists to maintain their competences and learn new skills to engage in legal, ethical, and professional practice. Hebb (1975) wrote that "the obsolescence of knowledge is far more rapid in psychology today than at any time in the past..." (p. 7). If Hebb's observation was true in 1975, we only need to reflect on the past few years in the field of school psychology to realize the importance of being a lifelong learner.

Thus, continuous professional development is a necessary and ongoing process. Rather than limit the focus of this chapter to how an individual school psychologist may plan and carry out professional development, it will expand the conception of an individual's professional development to recognize the mission of the school psychological unit as well as the expertise that colleagues contribute to the mission. An individual's professional development plan should be developed in the context of the mental health goals of the team of mental health professionals. In the case of a school district, this plan would include all the school psychologists as well as the school counselors and school social workers.

BASIC CONSIDERATIONS

The mid-1990s was a time when the professional development of teachers was seen as a key ingredient in school reform. Professional development was conceptualized not as the simple transfer of knowledge, but rather as contextualized and ongoing (Borko, 2004; Lieberman, 1995). Little (1993) stated, "professional development offers meaningful intellectual, social, and emotional engagement with ideas, with materials, and with colleagues..." (p. 138). Although Little focused on teachers' professional development, the principles she articulated apply to the professional development of school psychologists. She suggested that professional development be grounded in the big picture perspective, meaning the mission/goals of the school district. For school psychologists, this means the mission/goals of the school psychology service unit and the profession. Professional development should be built on local context and practiced within the profession's model for comprehensive and integrated services. For school psychologists this means that the strengths and weaknesses of individuals within the school psychology service unit must be taken into account. Rather than the delivery of standardized content, Little (1993) encouraged individuals to think about the match between old and new practices. The professional development needs of a district with a 10-year history of implementing response to intervention (RTI) would be quite different than one where the school psychologists are in the initial stages of changing from a traditional referral approach to an RTI approach.

Accepting Little's (1993) definition of professional development as meaningful intellectual and social engagement with ideas and colleagues, the challenge is to situate an individual professional development plan within a broader professional development plan of the local school psychology service unit. School psychologists' individual professional development plans are interwoven with opportunities for interaction with school psychology colleagues and other mental health providers within the school.

Gaible and Burns (2005) noted that professional development includes workshops, reflection, follow-up supervision, and assessment in the learner's natural setting. This repaints individuals as active learners in their own ongoing professional milieu rather than passive participants in a one-shot workshop. To make professional development effective, several factors have been found to be best practice: timely access, context based learning, ongoing and cumulative skill development, and interactive learning.

Timely access to professional development and distance education means that instructional content relevant to what school psychologists need to know is available at the moment they need to know it. Effective professional development is based on data-driven objectives for skills needed to achieve successful student outcomes (L'Allier & Elish-Piper, 2006). The promise of online, 24/7 access to professional development resources potentially fulfills this requirement.

As Little (1993) discussed, contextual learning is critical to connect learning to practical experience. In addition, effective professional development is ideally ongoing and cumulative so that skills are shaped through continuous support (Gaible & Burns, 2005). L'Allier and Elish-Piper (2006) described this as a gradual unfolding of needed skill development toward the goal of skill building within the practitioner. Contextual learning and ongoing cumulative skill development can be supported through learner-to-learner and trainer-to-learner interactions. Ideally, these interactions are supported during learning (through discussions) and generalize to practice (through professional learning communities). Both discussions and communities of learning may translate to online delivery during online professional development and distance education.

An interesting way to view these practices may be through what *not* to do. Varela (2012) wrote about three major sins of professional development: (a) a one-size-fits-all mentality, (b) workshops provided separate from classroom practice, and (c) a lack of follow-up or supervision of learned skills in the learner's natural work environment. Clearly, the one-size-fits-all mentality violates the need for timely, contextual, and data-driven objectives. Workshops offered separate from practice violate the need for contextual learning. The third sin is arguably the worst because the lack of supervision violates the need to build competency (and create actual behavior change in the practitioner) through ongoing, supported, and interactive practice of skills.

Learner Readiness

Hung, Chow, Chen, and Own (2010) identified factors that contribute to readiness for online learning. These included motivation for learning, self-directed learning and computer/Internet self-efficacy, and online communication self-efficacy. Having the desire to obtain knowledge or skills is a prerequisite to developing expertise in the 10 domains of the NASP Practice Model (NASP, 2010a). Relative to face-to-face workshops, online learning often requires more self-direction. A useful tool for assessing readiness to pursue online instruction is the University of Georgia's Student Online Readiness Tool (http://www.occc.edu/OnlineResources/sort/html/tool.html). It taps into technology experience, access to tools, study habits, goals, and learning preferences.

Foundation of Online and Distance Education: Technology

Computer hardware and software are required to connect to online professional development and distance education. Hence, this section of the chapter begins with a brief overview of the technological components needed to get connected.

The advancement of technological devices roars on at an exponential pace. If this chapter included specific recommendations, it would be out of date before being published. For this reason, the goal is to describe skills needed for practitioners to access the latest information in hardware and software for themselves. This section begins with a brief overview of available hardware and software and then delves into the online world of connectivity and cloud computing.

Hardware Considerations

Smartphones and tablet computers have changed how people interact with information. Gone are the days of desktops that sat in one spot in your office. Now we are using mobile devices and taking computers with us wherever we go. Traxler (2010) aptly stated, "when we say we can ignore desktop technologies but not mobile technologies it means that desktop technologies operate in their own little world, mobile technologies operate in *the* world" (p. 3). Professional development and distance education can happen anywhere, not just at a desk.

The following considerations warrant review when purchasing new hardware: (a) ease of use, (b) support for the mobile application that is to be run, (c) quality of the product, and (d) price. Quality and price fluctuate significantly among manufacturers and across time. It would be wise to connect with district technical support, ask questions of tech-savvy school psychologists who have experience with distance education as a consumer or instructor, and consult online magazines for updated information. The following websites aggregate data on

existing technologies and may assist in research on hardware: Mobile Tech Review (http://www.mobiletechreview.com), c|net (http://www.cnet.com), and Engadget (http://www.engadget.com). Browsing hardware manufacturers' websites will yield critical information for deciding which hardware to choose.

Before moving on to software, it is essential to cover the critical need for a quality headset to be an active participant in a Web conference. Participants connecting to online educational offerings may need a good-quality headset to avoid experiencing or causing audio issues. Relying on a tablet's or computer's microphone and speakers may cause a disruptive echo or buzzing, or will transmit the participant's voice too softly. Participants without headsets will cause other participants' voices to be fed back from their speakers to their microphone, causing a loop, which is difficult to overcome. A headset is a must for a successful learning experience.

Software Considerations

Software is also constantly changing and evolving based on market demand and ongoing innovation. There are three main types of software applications utilized for connecting to online educational offerings: (a) website links where the software application runs completely within your browser (e.g., learning management systems such as Blackboard and Moodle), (b) website links that require the user to download a small piece of software known as a plug-in or add-on (e.g., Adobe Connect), and (c) software applications that have to be downloaded (e.g., Skype, GoToMeeting). Outside of this three-tiered structure, which is largely laptop and netbook based, online providers will generally have their own mobile application for specific mobile devices. For instance, Adobe Connect has a mobile application for devices that run iOS and Android called Adobe Connect Mobile. GoToMeeting has applications for iOS and Android devices as well. These applications should be installed on the mobile device to access educational offerings through these providers.

Connectivity Considerations

Connecting to online professional development and distance education requires a range of connectivity needs. Connectivity is described as the amount of bandwidth (or throughput) available between the computing device and the Internet. Large amounts of available bandwidth allow for greater capabilities and the use of more online components. Also, there are two modes through which users can connect to online education: synchronous and asynchronous. Synchronous means that many users are connecting and interacting with each other and/or the trainer at the same time. Asynchronous means that learners and trainers are connecting at different times throughout a learning period and are not required to be online at the same time.

Asynchronous connectivity bandwidth needs are relatively low. These usually involve reviewing online materials (such as articles and presentation slides), watching a video, uploading files, and/or responding to discussion board posts. These types of online interactions require relatively low bandwidth needs because there is no requirement for learners to sync with each other for real-time conversations.

Synchronous connectivity, however, requires greater bandwidth. When several users are connecting to the same educational offering at the same time, much information in the form of data must be shared back and forth across the Internet to keep each participant's system in sync. In addition, synchronous sessions usually add audio, video, and document sharing that maximize connectivity needs.

Not too long ago, educators were concerned about the digital divide: the separation between students who had computers at home and students who did not. Now, the concern turns to the bandwidth divide: the separation between people with high-speed access to the Internet and those with slow-speed dial-up access. According to Young (2013), 66% of U.S. households have high-speed access. Yet, access to a high-speed connection does not guarantee that the Internet provider is optimizing the connection or avoiding connecting too many homes through the same pipeline. Despite the reality of the bandwidth divide, online providers frequently use the full capabilities of software that supports online professional development, such as synchronous video, chat, animation, and graphics. To engage in online learning from home, it would be wise to have a broadband connection.

If the online education session is going well, then the level of connectivity is appropriate. If, however, there are audio issues, video issues (such as starts and stops), or document-sharing issues (such as blank lines across the screen or too many skips), then it will be necessary to upgrade the level of connectivity to the Internet to increase the bandwidth. If a wireless connection is not working, then a network jack is needed to physically connect to the network through a wired connection. This will likely reduce the connection issues. If being wired does not work either, then the connection is not fast enough. Options include completing the session at work, at a library, or at a friend's.

BEST PRACTICES IN CONTINUOUS PROFESSIONAL DEVELOPMENT AND DISTANCE EDUCATION

Best practice in continuous professional development means that a school psychologist is in a constant state of seeking knowledge and learning. The ability to efficiently locate current research and resources serves as a foundation for providing state-of-the-art school psychological services. Best practice in continuous professional development is about making connections with the research literature and with other school psychologists addressing similar issues. Before addressing the myriad ways a school psychologist can connect with colleagues via technology, this chapter highlights best practices in the use of efficient search strategies.

Finding Information Online

When school psychologists consider online professional development, webinars and online courses come to mind. However, the first place practitioners may look for an answer is from peers. If face-to-face communication is not possible, this peer assistance may occur in the form of an Internet search, through online communities, or through social networking. These forms of support are covered in this section, along with more traditional forms of online instruction, such as webinars and online courses.

Online Searching

When school psychologists need the latest information about a disorder or need to refresh their previous learning about topics, they turn first to an online search engine. For instance, a child presents with a relatively rare neurological condition (e.g., Charcot-Marie-Tooth disease). A quick search of the Medline database reveals, "distal motor weakness and muscle atrophy, foot deformities, gait disturbances and sensory impairment are the clinical hallmarks of CMT" (Boentert et al., 2010). More clicks would reveal information about the prevalence of depression and psychosocial issues with this population. The challenge is to find pertinent information without having to sort through many irrelevant items. To achieve this goal, it is best practice to know and understand the *language* of searching online databases.

The Massachusetts Institute of Technology's (MIT) Library Services offers a set of guidelines for searching databases (Database Search Tips: Research Guides at MIT Libraries, http://libguides.mit.edu/database-search). One of the first points made by MIT Library Services is that searching professional databases is different from completing a Google search. For instance, databases have predefined (controlled vocabulary) subject headings and keywords. These headings and keywords can be used to avoid irrelevant articles and to increase the likelihood of pertinent ones.

EBSCO offers informative tutorials on the use of EBSCO Online Databases to locate professional literature (http://support.epnet.com/training/tutorials. php) including user-friendly YouTube videos, flash videos, and PowerPoint presentations. Table 46.1 offers a summary of the most pertinent guidelines for school psychologists.

NASP Communities

NASP implemented a secure system of online communities to support interaction among members (see http://communities.nasponline.org). NASP communities offer a vehicle for practitioners to continuously monitor conversations about professional topics as well as to contribute to the dialogue. NASP communities offer a venue to network with other school psychologists. These online communities are especially valuable for rural and other school psychologists who have limited opportunities to regularly interact with peer school psychologists. Thus, using communities to interact with peers represents a best practice to stay connected with timely questions and answers posted by school psychologists.

Table 46.2 provides a selective listing of NASP Communities. A complete listing of NASP Communities may be found on the *Communities* tab of the NASP homepage (http://www.nasponline.org).

To join one or more of the NASP Communities, the first step is to create a profile. Add as much or as little professional information as desired, such as a title, work address, work history, a biographical statement, awards, professional associations, contact information, and a picture. The intent of this first step is to let other community members know something about the new individual who is joining the community.

The NASP Communities are password protected. This means that access to the communities is restricted to members only. In contrast, the public can view interactions among school psychologists that take place in open social networks like Facebook or Twitter. While

Table 46.1. Guidelines for Searching Online Databases

1. Use an online thesaurus to determine synonyms for the keywords that are being used in the search. Once a few relevant articles are found, review the *subject* or *descriptor* field of the results to see if other keywords warrant searches as well.

2. Use Boolean operators (**AND**, **OR**, and **NOT**) in the search string. (Note: The operators do not need to be bold or capitalized; we add it here for emphasis and clarity.)
   - Enter "Positive psychology **AND** life satisfaction **AND** Huebner" (to locate articles that E. Scott Huebner has written that address both topics).
   - Enter "Positive psychology **OR** life satisfaction **AND** Huebner" (to locate articles that E. Scott Huebner has written on either topic).
   - Enter "Positive psychology **AND** life satisfaction **NOT** Huebner" (to locate articles that address both topics but do not include Huebner as an author).

3. Search phrasing: Putting quotation marks around a phrase will narrow the search by requiring that the words appear to together, rather than separated. The advantage of phrase searching is that the search is narrowed considerably, returning fewer irrelevant items.

4. EBSCO simplifies the search process by providing multiple ways of searching (basic search, advanced search, and visual search). Each search type provides a *search options* link below the search text box where the following modes can be utilized:
   - Boolean/phrase
   - Find all my search terms
   - Find any of my search terms

   Also, search dates may be limited to a starting month/year and ending month/year. Other checkboxes allow the results to include only peer-reviewed journals, apply related words, and search the full text of articles.

6. When performing Google searches, be aware that **AND** is assumed between the search terms. All the words in the search box must be present on a webpage for listing in the search results. If one of the words is missing on a webpage, a link to that page will not be received.

Table 46.2. Selected Listing of NASP Online Communities

- Autism and Pervasive Developmental Disorders
- Behavioral School Psychology
- Bilingual School Psychology
- Crisis Management in the Schools
- Gay, Lesbian, Bisexual, Transgender, and Questioning
- Gifted/Talented
- Graduate Educators
- Military Families
- NASP Early Career Professionals
- NASP Graduate Students
- Pediatric School Psychology
- Positive Psychology
- Prevention and Promotion of Psychological Wellness
- Response to Intervention
- Social Justice
- Supervision

NASP communities are open only to NASP members, an exception is the Graduate Educators community, which is open only to those listed as faculty members of graduate programs in school psychology. Unlike other communities, the Graduate Educators community is open to school psychology faculty who are not members of NASP.

APA Communities

The American Psychological Association (APA) also has a secure professional network for engaging in peer professional dialogue. It is designed to be a collaborative platform and allows documents to be uploaded, including version controls. Through this network, APA members can discuss ongoing professional development needs, provide peer support, and announce upcoming training opportunities. Additional uses include the sharing of agenda books, polling, and voting. Similar to the NASP communities, the first step to participate in the APA communities is to create a personal profile (a complete listing of APA communities may be found at http://www.apacommunities.org).

Other Social Media

As mentioned above, Facebook and Twitter are open social networking sites. On both of these sites, information about upcoming continuing professional events and various announcements are posted in addition to regular updates about NASP initiatives and postings on position openings and internships. Users of Facebook and Twitter should recognize that the best

practice for these digital tools is creating awareness of events, rather than professional dialogue about cases or professional topics.

NASP Online Learning Center

The NASP website provides an excellent portal to continuing education options. In the Online Learning Center, there are live and archived webinars. Even for experienced users of online live webinars, it is wise to join sessions 15 minutes prior to the start of a live presentation. This allows time to install or update an add-in if it is required to view the webinar. Additionally, there are often resources that are available for downloading. The PowerPoint slides or articles may then be perused while waiting for the session to start.

A valuable asset of the Online Learning Center is access to archived presentations. Most of the CPD sessions must be purchased, but a limited number are free to NASP members. A selective listing of NASP categories of on-demand CPDs is included in Table 46.3. A complete listing of NASP archived webinars may be accessed from the NASP website.

APA Online Continuing Education

Finding continuing education options from the APA homepage (http://www.apa.org) is similar to NASP's. There are multiple options to earn APA continuing education credits. In addition to accessing online archived presentations, there are articles, books, DVDs, and newsletters that will yield APA continuing education credits after passing an exam on the content.

Online Conferences

Another avenue for continuing professional development comes from online conferences. Anderson and Anderson (2009) advocated the use of online conferences as an alternative to face-to-face meetings by outlining their economic and environmental benefits. They listed the economic benefits as decreased time away from work and home and decreased travel costs. Anderson and Anderson also wrote about the decreased environmental impact of online conferences, such as reductions in carbon emissions due to eliminating the need for travel. With these benefits, it appears the time for online conventions has arrived.

In the fall of 2012, the School Psychology Roundtable hosted an online school psychology conference titled, "School Psychology: Creating Our Future(s)." More

Table 46.3. Selected Listing of Opportunities for Distance Learning From Multiple Online Providers

NASP categories of on-demand CPD (http://www.nasponline.org/profdevel/index.aspx):
- ADHD and Executive Functioning
- Assessment
- Bullying
- Discipline and Behavior
- Early Childhood
- ELL/Diversity/Multicultural Issues
- Health and Wellness
- Instruction and Learning
- Intervention
- Legal, Ethical, and Professional Issues
- Mental Health
- Response to Intervention
- School Safety/Crisis
- Schools and Systems

APA categories of continuing education most likely to be of interest to school psychologists (http://www.apa.org/education/ce/index.aspx):
- Addiction
- Anxiety and Depression
- Death, Grief, and Suicidology
- Eating and Eating Disorders
- Ethics in Psychology
- Gender and Sexuality
- Positive Psychology
- Race, Culture, and Identity
- Supervision
- Violence, Families, and Children at Risk

National Center on Response to Intervention webinars and training modules (http://www.rti4success.org):
- Train the Trainer Materials: Response to Intervention Implementer Series
- Developing an RTI Professional Development Plan: Things to Consider
- Culturally Responsive Response to Intervention
- Implementing Effective Literacy Practices for Instructing English Language Learners Within the Response to Intervention (RTI) Framework

Council for Exceptional Children's prerecorded webinars (http://www.cec.sped.org/Professional-Development/Webinars/Recorded-Webinars):
- Behavior and Positive Behavior Interventions and Supports
- Common Core State Standards
- Cultural and Linguistic Diversity
- Response to Intervention/Tiered Intervention
- Transition

Association for Behavior Analysis International's learning center with webinars (http://www.abainternational.org/index.asp):
- Autism
- Community Interventions
- Social and Ethical Issues
- Developmental Disabilities
- Human Development
- Experimental Analysis of Behavior
- Theoretical, Philosophical, and Conceptual Issues

American Counseling Association webinars (http://www.counseling.org/):
- Ethics and Legal Issues
- Assessment, Testing, and Evaluation
- Child and Adolescent Counseling, Counseling Theory
- LGBTQ Issues
- School Counseling
- Human Development

than 4,000 school psychologists, students, and related professionals from around the world registered to engage in the 3-day conference on the future of school psychology. The conference demonstrated how the use of technology could gather professionals and students from across the globe. A major benefit of the conference was the recording and archival of the presentations on the conference website. CPD credits are available to users who view the archived webinars and complete written paperwork. More information about the conference can be found at its website (http://www.indiana.edu/~futures/).

Other Online Providers

Of the 75 hours of CPD credits required every 3 years to renew the Nationally Certified School Psychologist (NCSP) credential, up to 25 hours may be counted in the category of self-study. The last 5 years have seen rapid growth of online learning opportunities available beyond NASP and APA. All signs point to these opportunities continuing to grow exponentially. The goal of the next section is to provide sources of online learning from professional associations delivering content aligned with knowledge and skills reflected in NASP's 10 practice domains.

From the National Center on Response to Intervention (http://www.rti4success.org) webpage, webinars and training modules can be assessed. The webinars may be viewed using a streaming connection or downloaded and viewed later when an Internet connection is not available. The lengths of the videos vary from 10–90 minutes (see Table 46.3).

The Council for Exceptional Children webpage (http://www.cec.sped.org) serves as the gateway to a rich set of live and recorded webinars. Prerecorded webinars available fall under the categories of Behavior and Positive Behavior Interventions and Supports, Common Core State Standards, Cultural and Linguistic Diversity, Response to Intervention/Tiered Intervention, and Transition (see Table 46.3).

The home page of the Association for Behavior Analysis International (http://www.abainternational.org/index.asp) offers links to presentations from recent conferences. The available sessions are categorized by topic and include Autism; Community Interventions; Social and Ethical Issues; Developmental Disabilities; Human Development; Experimental Analysis of Behavior; and Theoretical, Philosophical, and Conceptual Issues. The webinars count as Type 2 continuing education credits accepted by the Behavior

Analyst Certification Board (http://www.bacb.com). In addition, the site lists upcoming continuing education events, many of which require attendance at the physical site of the session. However, providers may allow learners to attend the session as a live webinar (see Table 46.3).

The American Counseling Association (ACA; http://www.counseling.org) features podcasts, online courses, and conference sessions. A free continuing education credit is available to members each month. Although selected ACA sessions qualified for APA continuing education, a relationship has not been established with NASP to allow credits to count as CPDs for NCSP certification. Inquiries may also be made to the NASP Continuing Professional Development Committee.

State school psychology associations and other psychological associations are also a valuable source for online learning opportunities. As an association member, watch for e-mail announcements for scheduled live webinars and the subsequent availability of archived sessions. There are also webinars and home-study courses that are available to school psychologists via the home pages of state associations.

The California Association of School Psychologists is a state association that provides access to webinars. Nonmembers may view webinars and receive NASP CPD credits for an additional fee. The following webinars are available in archived form: Collecting and Using RTI Data at Each Tier; Educators and Self-Injury: Focus on Intervention; SLD Eligibility Decisions: Differences Among Models; and A MODEL Approach to Conducting Assessment of Bilingual (English and Spanish) Students: A Psychoeducational Assessment Approach Grounded in CHC Theory.

The Ohio Psychological Association has identified some of its webinars as open to nonmembers. Among their webinars are ADHD: Update on Medication Management, and Obesity, Willpower, and Psychology.

Publishers also provide live and archived online webinars. For example, Pearson sponsors free live and archived presentations on a variety of topics ranging from executive functioning and working memory to sessions that focus on specific measures. (See http://www.pearsonassessments.com/pai/ca/training/webinars/Webinars.htm for examples.) A feature of the archived presentations is the ability to move to different parts of the presentation.

Publishers have a monetary stake in the promotion of their products. Thus, it should be recognized that the content of publisher-sponsored webinars may highlight the positive attributes of their products. It is not incumbent on the publisher to provide a neutral evaluation of the competition. Potential bias is not a reason to avoid such webinars. However, viewers of a publisher-sponsored presentation put the content of presentations in the context of refereed publications and reviews of the merits of competing tools. Some of the webinars are designed to support current customers who have already made the decision to purchase the product. While such webinars may be highly beneficial, they must also be viewed as a tool of the publisher to keep the user engaged with the product.

This section would be incomplete without mentioning two gateways to open courses, Coursera and iTunes-U, as well as introducing the concept of massive open online courses. Coursera was founded by two Stanford faculty members and started at Stanford University, the University of Michigan, Princeton, and the University of Pennsylvania. The founders had a vision of a future where the top universities educate students beyond their campus walls. They wanted to reach students who are not enrolled in their respective universities, without cost being a factor. Access to the courses comes free of charge. Coursera may be accessed from https://www.coursera.org.

The iTunes-U may be accessed through the iTunes app. There is a wide range of topics of interest to school psychologists in the category of Teaching and Learning, such as Creative Problem Solving, Apps for the Classroom, Classroom Management Tutorial for Teachers, and the 2013–14 Common Core Implementation Plan.

Massive open online courses bring together individuals with interests in learning about a topic. The courses are open in that there is no fee to participate. They also are open in the sense that all the lectures, notes, and materials of the instructor are available for all to see. The dialogue and work products generated by participants are likewise open to all. Unlike most online courses there are no assignments that are turned in to the instructor. A massive open online course is a series of events that provide a stimulus for individuals to participate and discuss a topic. The goal of the courses is to promote dialogue among the course participants who share ideas, materials, and links to resources. In the process of sharing, networks of people with similar interests develop. Unlike reading a text-based chapter (like this one), there is no linear path through the content. Rather, there are multiple pathways a participant may take, thus taking advantage of one of the unique features of the Web.

Participation in Distance Education

There are many advantages of online courses as compared with conventional face-to-face courses. For learners, those advantages are accessibility without the need to travel to a classroom and flexibility to engage asynchronously (as opposed to all participants meeting at the same time). Another advantage is the ability to control the pace by hitting rewind to review something that was not clear the first time, fast forward to skip material, and pause to stop the presentation and return later. To get the most out of an online course, school psychologists need to be informed consumers of differing options for online learning. This section will cover best practices in online delivery of instruction so that practitioners can make informed decisions and choose courses that will be effective at building skills to improve practice.

The staff of the Office of Instructional Consulting at the Indiana University School of Education developed a comprehensive set of best practices in course planning, content delivery, course activities, student assessment, and course evaluation (http://www.indiana.edu/~icy/resources/tutorial/). Additionally, California State University–Chico developed a specific evaluation matrix aligned with six domains of best practices in online instruction (http://www.csuchico.edu/roi/the_rubric.shtml). Both of these tools address best practices such as promoting interaction among course participants (icebreakers, reflections, collaborative writing, and debate), timely access to information, contextual learning, ongoing and cumulative supervision, and interaction of learners and providers across these areas. This section will describe these best practices and how practitioners can get the best from their online learning.

Structure and Organization

Online learning is most effective when delivered and received in a structured and organized way (MarylandOnline, 2011; Miller & Hutchins, 2009; Signer, 2008). Structure means lessons are broken out into a framework that aligns with individual and contextual learning objectives so that lessons are not too content rich or too content thin. Organization means learning objectives are aligned with instructional materials and assessment methods.

When searching for providers of online learning, it is critical to ensure that objectives, materials, and assessments are structured and organized to increase instructional effectiveness. In addition, practitioners can set clear objectives for themselves, access materials relevant to their objectives, and find or create a self-assessment to gauge success in skill building, even before training begins.

California State University–Chico's rubric covers structure and organization in their second domain: Online Organization and Design. This domain includes four criteria: organization and navigation, aesthetic and user-friendly design, functional consistency throughout the course, and consideration of accessibility issues. In addition, the California State University–Chico rubric details the importance of assessment and evaluation in their third domain: Assessment and Evaluation of Student Learning. This domain includes five criteria: assessment of student readiness, explicit alignment of objectives with assessments, the use of multiple assessment strategies, regular feedback to students about performance, and the opportunity for students to provide self-assessment and peer assessments. Practitioners looking for more detailed information about these specific guidelines would be well served by reviewing these domains (http://www.csuchico.edu/roi/).

Technological Support

Technological support means getting the assistance needed to use the technology involved in online learning. School psychologists may need to partner with tech-savvy colleagues and professionals to understand fully the capabilities of the tools being used. This means spending the time to become competent in using technology needed to access online learning. The goal is to ensure the tools used are not a barrier to learning, but a facilitator and enhancer of achieving learning outcomes.

First and foremost, software should always be kept updated. As hardware and operating systems continue to evolve, software developers continue to update their applications and encourage end users to install updates to fix problems. Technical glitches and hiccups may occur because end-user software is not up to date.

Further, practitioners should always use the most recent software programs. It will be a challenge at first for users to learn new software, but outdated programs are not able to provide the required access to online learning materials. In fact, they now act as significant barriers to interacting with others, either within a district or across the world.

California State University–Chico's rubric covers technology support in their first domain: Learner Support and Resources. This domain includes three criteria: access to resources for online learning support, course-specific support, and course content support.

Access to Information

Access to information encompasses the many different ways to get information online, such as search engines, online providers of learning, and distance education. It is important to support practitioners' abilities to access course information and resources outside of the course. Quality online education providers will supplement their materials with online resources that practitioners can access long after the completion of the course or webinar. It is critical for practitioners to understand how to access information independently and what sources are available.

California State University–Chico's rubric covers access to information in their fifth domain: Innovative Teaching with Technology. This domain includes four criteria: use of a variety of technology tools to access information, use of a variety of tools to increase access to fellow students, use of a variety of multimedia learning tools and strategies, and efficient use of tools to optimize bandwidth.

Supporting Interaction During Training

Inarguably most important is that online providers of professional development support or deliver opportunities for interaction among participants. California State University–Chico's rubric delves into online interaction in their third domain: Instructional Design and Delivery. This domain includes five criteria, with one specifically focused on interaction and communication. According to the rubric, exemplary online instruction offers plenty of student-to-student, student-to-instructor, and student-to-content interaction opportunities. Domains discussed earlier also listed the importance of peer feedback and peer support.

MarylandOnline's (2011) Quality Matters rubric emphasizes the importance of learner interaction and engagement to support active learning. As described earlier, learner interaction can be student-to-student, teacher-to-student, and student-to-content. In addition, when learners interact with each other, one becomes the teacher and the other the learner, with dynamic switching between roles as the students interact with the course content. Online professional development best practices require the inclusion of opportunities for students to collaborate and share their work. This interaction could be in the form of online discussions, peer review of projects, and online learning communities.

L'Allier and Elish-Piper (2006) wrote about the importance of instructor-led discussions in online professional development. They described a synchronous model where the first 10 minutes of an online learning session would include instructor-led class discussions. The second author of this chapter has experienced an asynchronous model where discussion questions were posted weekly and students were required to respond to the questions in addition to two or more peers. The requirement to respond to peers encouraged analysis of and reflection on other students' responses and facilitated lively online discussion.

Chen (2011) described a model of project-based online learning where students created a rough draft of a project and then received peer feedback. Then students would revise and resubmit for further review. This form of review occurred multiple times, setting up a situation where students were creating, reviewing, and revising several projects at once, including their own.

Last is the importance of setting up and encouraging the use of online learning communities. These communities can exist through multiple different formats: a forum, an e-mail group, NASP communities, and APA communities, to name just a few. The goal of online learning communities is to not only foster learning during the training phase, but also to provide support after training and when students attempt to apply what they have learned. In this way, online learning communities bridge the gap between interactions during the learning phase of the course and interaction afterward.

If a school psychologist finds himself or herself in an online learning course that does not support participant interactions, it would be beneficial to find and set up participant interactions independently to increase understanding of course content.

Supporting Interaction After Training

School psychologists have two main pathways to continue receiving support after training: online learning communities (discussed earlier) and professional learning communities. While the terms are often interchangeable, there is general agreement that online learning communities occur completely online while professional learning communities exist through face-to-face meetings.

It would be ideal for school psychologists to be able to connect with other school psychologists face-to-face to support peer learning. However, Beach (2012) described this as the biggest challenge of professional learning communities. Owing to time constraints, geographical constraints, and the fact that many school psychologists are the only school psychologist in the building, professional learning communities may be impractical.

Beach (2012) offered a model for effective online communities. He stated that a successful online learning community requires the following components: (a) a long-term, sustained commitment by all involved to be active in and maintain the online learning community; (b) a detailed plan that considers the potential interaction options (discussion forums, social networking, video conferencing) and the technology platform that can implement the chosen tools; (c) a detailed plan to maintain member motivation and to explicitly communicate the value of the online learning community; and (d) a selection of a team that will be the change agents for using the online learning community and implementing new tools and strategies learned through the community.

Through the development and use of online learning communities, learning does not end when the online education ends. It would be beneficial for practitioners to find or create an online community that would support ongoing professional development.

Ethical Considerations in Online Professional Development

In online professional development and distance education, providers and participants need to consider the ethical issues of competency. The issues of competency are the same as with face-to-face training but have a different perspective in the online world. According to NASP's *Principles for Professional Ethics*, school psychologists "understand that professional skill development … requires well-planned continuing professional development and professional supervision" (NASP, 2010b, p. 6). This means that competence is built through a combination of knowledge acquisition and supervision of skills in the learner's practical setting. Online professional development and distance education may come with a barrier to accessing follow-up support and supervision.

It is critical that school psychologists do not consider themselves competent and then practice outside of their boundaries of competency based on online professional development experiences alone. Competency comes from a combination of instruction and supervision.

Technology has been used in the performance of supervision since the 1950s and 1960s when bug-in-the-ear devices allowed a supervisor to be in a different room from the supervisee. This evolved into telecommunication applications in the 1970s and 1980s and eventually into supervision via the Internet in the 1990s. Currently, there are two main models of online supervision (Woods, Miller, & Hargrove, 2005). First is live, real-time, synchronous viewing of a supervisee, usually through the use of videoconferencing software (e.g., Adobe Connect, Skype) that allows in-the-moment supervisee feedback. Second is video recording of supervisee–client sessions and uploading the video for the supervisor to review at a different time. This latter, asynchronous form of supervision may use technology such as shared folders to store videos and e-mail to communicate feedback and follow up (Woods et al., 2005). School psychologists could use either of these methods of supervision to practice newly learned skills.

According to Woods et al. (2005), online supervision breaks down geographical barriers to accessing ongoing professional development. It also provides the opportunity for supervisees to gain access to expertise not available to them. There are also challenges to consider when engaging in online supervision. The online nature of the communication spurs concerns about confidentiality and compliance with federal regulations, such as the Family Educational Rights and Privacy Act and the Health Insurance Portability and Accountability Act. Also, the cost of technology can be quite high for practitioners who reside in more rural areas without ready access to broadband Internet connectivity. Last, there are the concerns of overall quality and user acceptability.

In an attempt to determine the balance point in the cost–benefit analysis, researchers have begun to explore the effectiveness and efficiency of online supervision. Wilsie and Brestan-Knight (2012) used a video analysis software tool to capture supervisees' application of Parent–Child Interaction Therapy skills. The supervisees had previously engaged in a 40-hour face-to-face workshop and were to use asynchronous video supervision for skill building. In the study, the supervisors rated highly the ability to watch and provide targeted, specific feedback to trainees while the trainees rated highly the feedback and its links to specific video sections. Challenges included difficulties with uploading videos and cost of the technology. A drawback of the study is that Wilsie and Brestan-Knight did not collect data on measurable, observable behavior change among the supervisees.

Online supervision can be offered by an individual practitioner, a university faculty member, or a private company. Two private organizations that currently provide online supervision are Rethink First (http:// www.rethinkfirst.com) and Butterfly Effects (http:// www.butterflyeffects.com). More information about the types of supervision offered can be found at their websites.

The take-away message for this section is that competency does not come just from participation in an online course. Supervision of newly learned skills is required for the ethical and legal practice of school psychology. This supervision may occur through practitioners local to the learner or may be required remotely. Research in online supervision is a hot topic at the moment, and any practitioner interested in seeking online supervision would benefit from a library search of recent findings.

An Illustration of Best Practices in Continuous Professional Development

Jean Jones is a school psychologist working for a school district serving 5,000 students. She completed her internship 5 years ago. Her primary role is serving two medium-sized elementary schools.

There are four other school psychologists, six counselors, and four social workers in her schools. In August, the week prior to the start of school, the psychologists, counselors, and social workers spent a day collectively reviewing feedback from the survey of teachers and parents that was collected at the end of the previous school year.

Several themes emerged from the survey. Teachers reported that students with autism were having limited success with their social development. The social skills program they were using was not having the intended consequences. Both teachers and parents noted that a significant number of students were exhibiting emotional struggles due to one of their parents having been deployed to a military zone. The third issue that emerged was teachers' readiness for a crisis.

The school psychologists, counselors, and social workers considered their existing resources to address each of the three issues. Because Jean had a minor in special education and specialized coursework in autism spectrum disorders, she was designated to lead the effort to investigate options for improving social skills instruction. The team of school psychologists, counselors, and social workers recognized that the local community behavioral health center had a psychologist who recently spent a postdoctoral year at the Center for Autism and Related Disorders of the Kennedy-Krieger Institute.

Before school started, Jean's first step was to use EBSCO host to conduct a search to locate research on social skills programs for students with autism. Her goal was to find studies that would provide insights and nuances. The default view of search results presented the most cited sources first. Since she was especially interested in recent publications, she used an advanced search function to limit the results to those that were published in the last 5 years.

In her second step before school started, she reached out to the behavioral health psychologist who had worked at Kennedy-Krieger. Jean learned several details about the existing after-school program at the behavioral health center and about two model school-based programs within a 2-hour drive. (While this chapter is focused on the use of technology for continued professional development, it is important to note that the use of technology does not replace conventional personal interactions and visits to exemplary sites.)

In September, Jean joined the online NASP Community, Autism and Pervasive Developmental Disorders. While visiting the NASP Community she noticed a question that was posted about structuring classrooms to accommodate children with autism. One of the responses provided a link to the National Professional Development Center on Autism Spectrum Disorders. The center is a federally funded, multiple-university effort with the goal of promoting evidence-based practices for children with autism spectrum disorders. Jean spent several hours using three modules: Social Skills Group, Peer-Mediated Instruction and Intervention, and Response Interruption/Redirection.

Also in September, Jean visited the home pages of NASP, APA, Council for Exceptional Children, and Association for Behavior Analysis International to find archived and upcoming webinars on autism and social skills. She learned that a live webinar would be offered by NASP in the following month. She was excited to participate in the live format and prepared a list of questions to pose to the presenter during the live session. While waiting 3 weeks for the live webinar, she took advantage of two of the archived webinars.

On October 1, Jean shared a detailed summary of her research efforts with the team of school psychologists, counselors, and social workers who met 6 weeks earlier. The team leader compiled a brief summary of Jean's efforts and initial findings, along with reports from those who were working on the two other issues, military deployment and crisis preparedness. The team leader sent a note to teachers and parents letting them know that their concerns had been heard and were being acted upon.

At midyear, Jean received an announcement that a professor was to offer an online course of the social skills instruction for children with autism. From her EBSCO search, she knew he had published several meta-analyses on social skills instruction for children with autism. Prior to the course, she contacted him to obtain the syllabus and to review the organization of the course and the requirements and manner in which students in the course will interact. Since the course involves video, she checked to determine whether the video would be blocked by the school district network.

Jean's professional development during the year illustrated several best practices that merit highlighting. First, the focus was both data driven by the teacher and parent survey. Her focus was contextualized based on the goals of the team of school psychologists, counselors, and social workers. Jean's individual professional development was further contextualized by the fact the team recognized that Jean had more previous preparation in autism than others on the team. Throughout the year she made continual use of professional literature searches and joined and helped contribute to the NASP autism community.

From the interactions in the NASP autism community, she met school psychologists she made plans to meet at the February NASP conference. Prior to the conference, she had several Skype meetings with a school psychologist who shared data on the effectiveness of her social–emotional intervention program. Thus, during the year Jean was able to accumulate webinar-based CPD credits, self-study hours, and hours associated with taking an online course.

SUMMARY

High-quality professional development is characterized by meaningful intellectual and social engagement with ideas and colleagues. The evolution of the digital world has revolutionized professional development. Continuous learning is possible through connectivity to online search engines, professional databases, professional communities, and webinars. NASP and APA offer a diverse set of webinars that may be used for continuing education credit. The Council for Exceptional Children, American Counseling Association, Association for Behavior Analysis International, and National Center on Response to Intervention also have many webinars with content relevant to school psychologists. Although these webinars do not come with NASP or APA credits, renewal of the NCSP credential allows for up to 25 hours of self-study.

Online courses allow instructors to reach individuals for whom travel or scheduling would make attendance at a face-to-face course impossible. Thus school psychologists living on one coast can take a course with an instructor on the opposite coast. Similar to conventional face-to-face courses, online courses are best when delivered in a carefully planned and structured manner. Provision of technical support facilitates learners' ability to access online resources. Electronic forms of interaction allow learners to connect with colleagues and achieve meaningful engagement with the knowledge-based content. If skill development is the goal of a course, provisions for either face-to-face or online supervision are necessary.

REFERENCES

Anderson, L., & Anderson, T. (2009). Online professional development conferences: An effective, economical and eco-friendly option. *Canadian Journal of Learning and Technology, 35*(2), 1–15.

Beach, R. (2012). Can online learning communities foster professional development? *Language Arts, 89*, 256–262.

Boentert, M., Dziewas, R., Heidbreder, A., Happe, S., Kleffner, I., Evers, S., & Young, P. (2010). Fatigue, reduced sleep quality and restless legs syndrome in Charcot-Marie-Tooth disease: A Web-based survey. *Journal of Neurology, 257*, 646–652. doi:10.1007/s00415-009-5390-1

Bonk, C. J. (2009). *The world is open: How Web technology is revolutionizing education.* San Francisco, CA: Jossey-Bass.

Borko, H. (2004). Professional development and teacher learning: Mapping the terrain. *Educational Researcher, 33*(8), 3–15.

Chen, C. (2011). Transforming online professional development: The design and implementation of the project-based learning management system (PBLMs) for in-service teachers. *British Journal of Educational Technology, 42*, E5–E8.

Gaible, E., & Burns, M. (2005). *Using technology to train teachers: Appropriate uses of ICT for teacher professional development in developing countries.* Washington, DC: infoDev/World Bank. Retrieved from http://www.infodev.org/en/Publication.13.html

Hebb, D. O. (1975). Science and the world of imagination. *Canadian Psychology, 16*, 4–11. doi:10.1037/h0081788

Hung, M., Chou, C., Chen, C., & Own, Z. (2010). Learner readiness for online learning: Scale development and student perceptions. *Computers & Education, 55*, 1080–1090.

L'Allier, S. K., & Elish-Piper, L. (2006). Ten best practices for professional development in reading. *Illinois Reading Council Journal, 35*, 22–27.

Lieberman, A. (1995). Practices that support teacher development: Transforming conceptions of professional learning. *Phi Delta Kappan, 76*, 591–596.

Little, J. W. (1993). Teachers' professional development in a climate of educational reform. *Educational Evaluation and Policy Analysis, 15*, 129–151.

MarylandOnline. (2011). *Quality Matters rubric standards 2011–2013 edition with assigned point values.* Annapolis, MD: Author. Retrieved from http://www.qmprogram.org

Miller, T. W., & Hutchens, S. A. (2009). 21st century teaching technology: Best practices and effectiveness in teaching psychology. *International Journal of Instructional Media, 36*, 254–262.

National Association of School Psychologists. (2010a). *Model for comprehensive and integrated school psychological services.* Bethesda, MD: Author. Retrieved from http://www.nasponline.org/standards/2010standards/2_PracticeModel.pdf

National Association of School Psychologists. (2010b). *Principles for professional ethics.* Bethesda, MD: Author. Retrieved from http://www.nasponline.org/standards/2010standards/1_%20Ethical%20Principles.pdf

Signer, B. (2008). Online professional development: Combining best practices from teacher, technology and distance education. *Journal of In-Service Education, 34*, 205–218.

Traxler, J. (2010). Students and mobile devices. *Research in Learning Technology, 18*, 149–160.

Varela, A. M. (2012). Three major sins of professional development: How can we make it better? *Education Digest, 78*, 17–20.

Wilsie, C. C., & Brestan-Knight, E. (2012). Using an online viewing system for parent-child interaction therapy consulting with professionals. *Psychological Services, 9*, 224–226.

Woods, J. A. V., Miller, T. W., & Hargove, D. S. (2005). Clinical supervision in rural settings: A telehealth model. *Professional Psychology: Research and Practice, 36*, 173–179.

Young, J. R. (2013, March 4). "Bandwidth divide" could bar some people from online learning. *Chronicle of Higher Education.* Retrieved from http://chronicle.com/article/The-Bandwith-Divide/137633

47

Best Practices in Maintaining Professional Effectiveness, Enthusiasm, and Confidence

Brian P. Leung
Jay Jackson
Loyola Marymount University

OVERVIEW

School psychology is an incredible profession. It has been ranked as one of the best careers by *U.S. News and World Report* for the past several years and again ranks as the "Best" in social service jobs in 2013 (*U.S. News and World Report*, 2013). Beyond those benefits cited by *U.S. News and World Report*, which include strong job opportunities, quality of life, salaries, and potential for job growth, the Bureau of Labor Statistics (2013) indicated "employment of psychologists is expected to grow 22 percent from 2010 to 2020, faster than the average for all occupations. Job prospects should be best for those ... with a specialist or doctoral degree in school psychology." Despite recent years of difficult economic conditions in educational funding, school psychology as a career is still highly regarded by both private and government estimates. A. Thomas (personal communication, June 10, 2013) describes school psychology as the "most widespread, multifaceted, and available mental health service delivery system for this nation's youth."

Yet, there exist multiple factors that cause stress and burnout that contribute to diminished professional effectiveness, dampened enthusiasm, and lowered confidence throughout the course of a school psychologist's career. When candidates in school psychology graduate programs are asked why they have chosen the field, invariably their answer is because they want to make a difference in the lives of children, and envision themselves influencing decisions that will result in discernible changes in the positive trajectory of students' development. Research indicates that new school psychologists enter the field with high levels of enthusiasm, optimism, and self-efficacy (Huebner, Gilligan, & Cobb, 2002). While there is no documentation of large numbers of school psychologists leaving the profession, as evident with significant teacher turnover, in our work with new school psychologists, anecdotes from the field, and review of published articles, there is an alarming rate of burnout, particularly those assigned to certain urban settings. Whether these school psychologists leave or remain, the stressors affect job satisfaction and self-efficacy, and diminish their original idealism of having life-altering influences on the lives of children.

The purpose of this chapter is to describe factors that can have an impact on the effectiveness, enthusiasm, and confidence of school psychologists and to summarize strategies that school psychologists can use to promote their own resiliency when faced with obstacles and challenges. The chapter relates to the domain of Legal, Ethical, and Professional Practice within the National Association of School Psychologists (NASP) *Model for Comprehensive and Integrated School Psychological Services* (NASP, 2010) by highlighting practical resources and techniques for use by school psychologists to enhance professional practice, job satisfaction, and positive experiences in their work.

BASIC CONSIDERATIONS

The construct of burnout, which represents the effects of stress on one's ability to perform on the job with satisfaction and enthusiasm (Reiner & Hartshorne, 1982), has been extensively studied in the general population of mental health practitioners (e.g., Jenero, Flores, & Arias, 2007). Specific to school psychology, Reiner and Hartshorne (1982) completed one of the earlier empirical studies to explore the unique conditions and factors inherent in the role of school psychologists that Maslach (as cited in Reiner & Hartshorne, 1982) called the *emotional exhaustion syndrome*. Reiner and Hartshorne's sample of school psychologists identified excessive caseloads as the primary source of stress, followed by the feeling of not having enough time to deal with job responsibilities, role definition confusion/overload, unclear expectations, and excessive demands.

In a study of burnout factors with 600 school psychologists as participants, Huberty and Huebner (1988) found that four significant factors affected the school psychologist's perceived ability to provide effective services: job and role definitions, time pressure, external pressure, and internal pressures. Indeed, school psychology remains as one of the most demanding jobs in the schools, often placing its practitioners in high-stake situations (e.g., assigning educational labels to students, placing students in restrictive environments), requiring them to make decisions that have significant ramifications in the lives of children.

Huebner et al. (2002) and Thomas (1995) have addressed aspects of this topic. The impact of organizational stress is also discussed in the work of Huebner et al. (2002), who cite several additional factors, including interpersonal conflict, high risk to self and others, obstacles to efficient job performance, and required public speaking as stressors. Four broad but identifiable categories of short-term stressors that can evolve into long-term debilitating effects on school psychologists' satisfaction and efficacy are described in Table 47.1: inadequate administrative support, resistance from the consumer, having limited impact on students, and intensity of workload.

To remain a viable resource for others and to maintain mental health, physical well-being, and job vitality, it is critical that school psychologists are active and thoughtful managers of their professional practice. Indeed, failure to effectively manage their practice diminishes their potential contribution in all domains of the NASP Practice Model (NASP, 2010). While acknowledging what can be referred to as the deficit model, focusing on a model of resiliency, which is consistent with the more current positive psychology framework, will be more fruitful for school psychologists managing their professional practice.

Positive psychology is the scientific study that focuses on what goes right in life. It shifts the attention from focusing on the deficits that impede an individual's ability to assets that maximize effectiveness and satisfaction in all aspects of life. Moreover, positive psychology also stresses the concept of resiliency, which has been defined in various ways. Wolin and Wolin (1993, 1995, 1998) have written extensively describing resiliency as individuals' capacity to bounce back, to withstand hardship, and to repair themselves. Higgins (1994) considers resiliency as the "process of self-righting and growth" (p. 1). In essence, the positive psychology framework speaks to the inherent ability of individuals to manage, and in fact grow from, stressful events. Most importantly, resiliency researchers emphasize that characteristics associated with resiliency are not only a collection of traits that are inborn, but they can be learned and developed (Higgins, 1994; Werner & Smith, 1992). Resilience is a characteristic that can be nurtured and actively managed, and can be preventive in nature, as well as serving as a buffer during hardship, resulting in positive outcomes.

Assets that serve to strengthen, nurture, and sustain resilience are often referred to as protective factors. The concept of protective factors is becoming more recognizable and is consistent with the positive psychology framework (Peterson, 2006). The role of protective factors in resilience building has been thoughtfully and extensively researched and discussed in the literature (Garmezy, 1996; Henderson, 2002; Werner & Smith, 1992). Internal factors (individual personality traits, strengths) and external factors (support systems) serve to buffer or inoculate an individual against stress. Protective factors serve to encourage resiliency traits such as autonomy, initiative, competence, and strong self-efficacy (Jackson, 2003). The benefits of bolstering the school psychologist's resilience, nurtured through protective factors, promote the potential for greater experiences of professional effectiveness, enthusiasm, and confidence.

Covey's (1989) seminal work presents seven habits that elevate one's life. His work instructs on the enduring principles that support individuals' ability to be "guided by their own missions and manage their lives according to principles" (Covey, 2003, p. 13). Habit 7, "sharpen the saw" represents an additional resiliency builder. In keeping with Covey's concept of the seven habits as paradigms or ways of thinking, sharpen the saw is the paradigm that addresses "continuous improvement of the whole person; it stands for education, learning, and recommitment—what the Japanese call kaizen" (Covey, 2004, p. 156). A school psychologist's investment in continuous improvement benefits both

Table 47.1. Four Common Categories of Stressors Affecting School Psychologists

Stressor	Examples	Potential Impact on School Psychologists
Inadequate administrative support	• A lack of visionary leadership from administration that has a limited view of school psychological practice (i.e., testing) leading to role restriction and/or performance evaluation on a narrow range of activities (e.g., how many cases written), resulting in school psychological work that is repetitive and nonstimulating • Weak leadership that is unwilling or unable to manage inappropriate special education placement decisions from local IEP teams or is unable to stand up to advocates or lawyer challenges • Inadequate leadership, which can occur at the school level or at the district level	These stressors are demoralizing and reduce the desire for taking on risks and challenges, which diminishes enthusiasm.
Resistance from consumer	• Teachers' active or passive resistance to school psychologists' recommendations (e.g., classroom modification to support diverse learners) • Administrators' reluctance to support new ideas or approaches (e.g., RTI) • Parents' or families' lack of follow-through with strategies to support their children beyond school	These stressors limit opportunities for meaningful collaboration and exploration of innovative practices, which has an impact on effectiveness in problem solving to benefit students.

Having limited impact on students	• Not seeing discernible improvement in students due to:
	  • Entrenched policy/practice barriers in school or government agencies
	  • Apathetic parents or caregivers
	  • Dealing with decreasing school and community services from budget cuts, poor resource management, inappropriate priorities, and wasteful spending
	  • Witnessing institutional racism that limits appropriate services for culturally and linguistically diverse learners
		These stressors promote helplessness and undermine confidence.

Intensity of workload	• Unrelenting amount of work from various stakeholders and needs throughout the school year
	• Emotionally intense work
	  • Defending one's work (e.g., standing up to an advocate, fair hearing)
	  • Nature of crisis work (e.g., dealing with a suicidal student, death of a student/staff, managing school-wide crisis)
	  • Personal safety concerns (e.g., working with law enforcement in gang-related situations)
	  • Pressure to regularly make high-stake decisions affecting students' lives
		These stressors lead to both physical and mental exhaustion and affect effectiveness, enthusiasm, and confidence.

personal and professional self-awareness and growth, ultimately serving as a resilience builder.

This chapter uses the positive psychology/resiliency framework to inform strategies that sustain school psychologists' professional effectiveness, enthusiasm, and confidence over the course of a career. Predictable stressors (see Table 47.1) have differential effects on school psychologists' effectiveness, enthusiasm, and confidence depending on the phase of their career. Therefore, this chapter is organized around three global developmental phases of the career of a school psychologist: early

practitioners, midcareer practitioners, and veteran practitioners. There is no research on the relationship between career phase and approaches to enhancing professional effectiveness, enthusiasm, and confidence, and the present chapter identifies these phases based roughly on those cited in teacher burnout literature (Thompson, 1994) and from our experiences with hundreds of school psychologists employed in school districts across a wide geographical area. Although their schools differed in district size and student demographics, observations, and interactions, the interview data that we collected revealed certain key characteristics and experiences unique to career time lines.

There are obvious limitations in the generalizability of recommended best practices to all school psychologists across the country. State education code as well as district policies and procedures dictate the way school psychological services are governed and administered. The type of professional role (e.g., site-based practitioner or office-based specialist) further structures the school psychologist's role and responsibilities. Moreover, the school psychologist's academic preparation provides opportunities for a variety of specialized experiences, such as due process specialist. While an advanced degree often enhances professional effectiveness, enthusiasm, and confidence, competence as perceived by administrators and supervisors often dictates the scope and breadth of school- and district-based assignments.

BEST PRACTICES IN MAINTAINING PROFESSIONAL EFFECTIVENESS, ENTHUSIASM, AND CONFIDENCE

While the growing resiliency literature offers many possible approaches, three resiliency builders (also referred to as protective factors) will be highlighted that will frame the discussion of best practices to empower school psychologists in managing their careers. The three resiliency builders are summarized first, followed by how they can be used within each phase of a school psychologist's career (see Table 47.2 for additional resiliency builders).

Inner Direction (Know Yourself)

Perhaps no other internal protective factor supports satisfaction and effectiveness of a school psychologist than that of strong self-awareness. According to Covey (1989), self-awareness is fundamental to human development, enabling people to stand apart and examine even the way they see themselves, the most fundamental paradigm of effectiveness. The level of self-awareness fosters resiliency in school psychologists' professional role. Inner direction includes behaviors such as reflection and reframing aligned with one's vision, as well as recognizing one's strengths and limitations. Ultimately, self-exploration that results in knowing what one needs so as to experience professional effectiveness, enthusiasm, and confidence in work activities is crucial to recognizing and actively seeking those activities that meet these needs.

Sharpen the Saw (Need for a Balanced Life)

Covey (1989) exalts the virtues of maintaining balance in every aspect of life to achieve satisfaction and continued professional effectiveness. To the typical idea of developing interests and hobbies outside school psychology and maintaining a framework of self-care, the need to seek balance of the type of work within school psychology practice is added (e.g., administrative work versus direct service, following mandates versus leadership roles). Sharpening the saw draws on both internal and external protective factors. The commitment to maintaining an attitude of self-empowerment through

Table 47.2. Resiliency Builders for School Psychologists

Relationships	Social ability; ability to be a friend; ability to form positive relationships
Service	Gives of self in service to others and/or a cause
Life skills	Includes good decision making, assertiveness, and impulse control
Humor	Has a good sense of humor
Inner direction	Bases choices/decisions on internal evaluation (internal locus of control)
Perceptiveness	Insightful understanding of people and situations
Independence	"Adaptive" distancing from unhealthy people and situations; autonomy
Positive view of personal future	Expects a positive future
Flexibility	Can adjust to change; can bend as necessary to positively cope with situations
Love of learning	Capacity for and connection to learning
Self-motivation	Internal initiative and positive motivation from within
Competence	Is good at something; personal competence
Self-worth	Feelings of self-worth and self-confidence
Spirituality	Personal faith in something greater
Perseverance	Keeps on despite difficulty; does not give up
Creativity	Expresses self through artistic endeavors

Note. Based on information from Henderson (2002).

balance is the internal source of resilience. Activities and responsibilities that provide diversity in a practitioner's role act as external protective factors that buffer the exposure to stressors as well as provide potentially rewarding opportunities for job satisfaction.

Love of Learning (Lifelong Learner)

Curiosity that fuels the desire for new learning experiences is another basic human characteristic, and when practiced routinely, it is a powerful internal protective factor able to mitigate stressors. Reframing challenges as opportunities for learning defuses stress, and indeed, each new learning experience contributes to a renewal process that buffers against future stress. New learning often provides novel solutions to existing problems, which validates one's competence and builds confidence. Learning can occur in formal professional development opportunities at the local level or at professional conferences, as well as through interactions with peers and other colleagues. Self-learning through online learning opportunities abounds. Additional opportunities to expand knowledge in the field are available through certification (e.g., neuropsychology) and doctoral programs.

Developmental Phases and Resiliency in School Psychology Careers

The following sections describe how resiliency builders might look and be utilized in each of the developmental phases of the career of a school psychologist.

Early Practitioners (1–8 Years)

Novice school psychologists, especially those entering the workforce for the first time, are decidedly idealistic. As noted earlier, they envision themselves as highly capable and expect to make a significant impact on the lives of those they serve. In many ways, they are driven by this idealism and desire to do everything for everyone. Early practitioners are often overwhelmed as they have difficulty saying "no," both as a desire to serve and to prove their competence. Those school psychologists at this early stage of their career who were interviewed often talked about working as hard and as fast as possible to get it all done. While they may not arrive at the classic burnout, they are susceptible to what Farber (2000) termed as practitioners who "wear out."

The resiliency framework can offer useful strategies for early practitioners to set the foundation for a vibrant career, and not just to offset stressors. Indeed, the first

resiliency builder of know yourself should be considered as early as graduate school. Recognizing how the profession of school psychology matches up with ideals of a career (e.g., maximizes strengths and passion, appropriate compensation), and refining these ideals into a vision, is invaluable to nurturing a long and rewarding career in school psychology. A clear personal vision that includes knowing all aspects of the profession (e.g., NASP Practice Model, 2010) as well as oneself (preferences, interests, life stage) is integral in searching for the first job. To ensure the best beginning, it is desirable to find a setting with a good match between characteristics of the district (e.g., the size: small, medium, large; the setting: urban, suburban, rural; the population: ethnic, cultural, language diversity) and the early practitioner's interests, desires, and strengths. Next, understanding the consumers (principal, teacher, community) and their expectations leads to tailoring practice for a credible performance in the early years. It is important for early practitioners to take time to learn the formal and informal leaders of the school, leadership style of the principal, as well as the culture and politics that guide decision making. Equally important is for the early practitioners to know themselves enough to articulate their strengths and passions to their consumers. Early career school psychologists who were interviewed reported feeling much more confident and effective when there are opportunities to align their skills and passion with the gaps and needs of their consumers.

Inner direction. At the early phase of a school psychologist's career, school psychologists who were interviewed confirmed the literature on burnout, pointing to all four categories of stressors (see Table 47.1) as being highly salient. Thus, it is not uncommon for these stressors to overcome early practitioners' coping skills despite foundational development of the above protective factors. It is recommended that school psychologists enhance these three resiliency builders: knowing yourself, maintaining balance, and nurturing a love of learning. Some sample strategies follow:

- Instead of feeling discouraged with inadequate administrative support, simply reset expectations and sometimes stretch a policy so work can be continued.
- Take a longer term view; that is, recognize that it may take a few years before an impact is observable in students.
- Instead of being frustrated with resistance from some teachers, nurture relationships with teachers who are willing to try new ideas, even if it is just one teacher.

- Instead of focusing on those students where there was a failure, refocus sights on those students with whom a positive impact was made and learn to internalize successes more than failures.

- Instead of working faster, devise ways to work smarter (e.g., schedule appointments to talk with teachers instead of numerous chit-chat sessions in the hallway that kill time); shorten test battery; use no-test triennials; attend only selected Individualized Education Program (IEP) meetings; do more group- and class-wide counseling instead of individual counseling; conduct staff development to teach new skills to teachers and parents; develop peer helper programs; enhance Tier 1 programs; seek out community partners; reconnect with university professors and former peers for advice; hold pre-IEP meetings; and always seek collaborators to share responsibility, lighten the load, and generate creativity.

Sharpen the saw. This internal protective factor should also be considered as early as graduate school. A rigorous school psychology graduate program can easily monopolize a person's life. While many graduate students expect to spend much of their time in school-related assignments, nurturing this protective factor early can lead to a lifelong habit. Huebner et al. (2002) suggest that early career practitioners report feeling overwhelmed with their job demands, and developing off-work routines early, if not started in graduate school, will set a healthy foundation to manage expected stressors. Some sample strategies follow:

- Set time aside every week for personal interests, hobbies, friends, and family. Engage in at least one such activity every week and/or rotate these activities every week. Ask friends and family for help in engaging in these activities, even if the duration of some activities is not long.

- Maintain regular physical exercise/activity for physiological stress relief. Alter the type, frequency, or duration of activity if needed, but always do something every week.

Some sample strategies to support within-work balance include the following:

- Alternate between office work with outside activities (e.g., visiting the kindergarten class to "play," having lunch with students, visiting the community).

- Get involved with school committees to help set new directions for the school. Leadership opportunities, especially if they fit with the school psychologist's interests, have a secondary benefit of potentially changing the workload. For example, educating and persuading the school advisory committee or PTA to adopt response to intervention (RTI) can alter the testing load.

- Get involved with special projects at the school or district level (e.g., a district-wide planning committee for school-wide positive behavioral interventions and supports). Time management and credibility issues may more likely limit opportunities for district-level involvement to later-phase early practitioners.

Love of learning. As a practitioner, a school psychologist has the freedom to choose the topic of learning, and when coupled with personal interest and needs at the school, such learning can result in gaining additional skills and knowledge to solve long-standing problems at the school. Solving such problems can bolster the school psychologist's feelings of professional effectiveness and confidence. Some sample strategies include the following:

- Seek professional development activities that reinforce what has been learned in graduate school as validation of practice, as well as learn new skills.

- Supervise an intern or practicum student. Not only do students bring new knowledge, but interacting with school psychology students also solidifies the school psychologist's knowledge base.

Midcareer Practitioners (10–18 Years)

Midcareer school psychologists have gone through many changes throughout the first phase of their career. At this point, many of these school psychologists have matured personally, have attained typical life stages such as family and children, and have gained considerable comfort and credibility with their colleagues and consumers. (Many early practitioners, especially those who have chosen school psychology as a second career, may also have attained these typical life stages.) Depending on interests and passions, it is not uncommon for this group of school psychologists to have gained leadership positions within the school district, as some may not even practice school psychology at school sites (e.g., as lead or supervisory school psychologist in his or her district). Not surprisingly, this group of school psychologists is more likely to present a much calmer demeanor and appear less frantic compared to the early practitioners.

Inner direction. Midcareer school psychologists who were interviewed all spoke of having a clearer understanding of the nature of their work, given the policies, politics, and people they work with. Those interviewed readily acknowledge the constraints in their school system but are not perturbed by them so much because they have devised ways to adapt or circumvent these limiting factors. They realize that their impact is invariably tied to their assignment, as well as to procedures and policies of their school or district. Moreover, they have selectively focused on those aspects of their work that they find satisfaction with and derive their feeling of professional effectiveness from this work. This focus can be on a narrow aspect of the work (e.g., completing a well-structured case study) to a broad aspect (e.g., networking with outside contacts to bring more services to a school). A greater sense of self-efficacy is evident due to acknowledgment of personal strengths and acceptance of systemic limitations. Some sample strategies follow:

- Reflect on work, recognize areas of fulfillment, and make time to actively seek more of them. This can be daily (e.g., read to kindergartners), weekly, or monthly (e.g., eat lunch with students).
- Set manageable and realistic goals (short term or longer term) based on strengths and passions.
- Focus on immediate successes and remember the teachers who changed their long-held beliefs about certain students and have modified their expectations.
- Acknowledge that there may have been a positive long-term impact on some students' lives and on their parents' lives.

Sharpen the saw. Typically, after at least 10 years in the field, midcareer school psychologists have streamlined and refined their practice (e.g., report writing, meeting participation) to a large extent. The willingness to set limits to maintain role integrity also contributes to a stronger ability to manage workload. For those who work in districts where schools have the latitude and resources to purchase additional school psychologist time, the opportunity to be an in-house school psychologist greatly enhances the diversity of his or her role and feeling of professional effectiveness. This role expansion is consistent with Proctor and Steadman's (2003) finding for increased job satisfaction and decreased burnout. Moreover, life-stage demands related to family and children often require some separation of work and life. Nonetheless, an intentional separation is still needed to take time from work for family events (e.g., attend children's school performances, visit elderly parents, spend time with aging siblings). Some sample strategies include the following:

- Take time to eat lunch every day. It was amazing to hear how this simple, but often neglected act by early practitioners can bring a sense of balance to a hectic day.
- Make time to complete paperwork at school and take as little work home as possible. Invest time in health and fitness and other personal interests.
- Build deeper relationships, beyond work, with coworkers.
- Reach out to develop new professional networks locally or nationally through professional organizations.
- Seek out different kinds of work (e.g., at the district central office), which offers leadership opportunities to offset predictable work at the school level.
- For bilingual school psychologists, ask to work on nonbilingual cases.
- Strategize and advocate to gain additional days at an assigned school. More time at one site allows for a greater role expansion that increases feelings of effectiveness, enthusiasm, and confidence.

Love of learning. The enthusiasm and participation in professional development activities were evident in this group of school psychologists interviewed. They seem to sense a plateau of their skill sets, and driven by seeing their work from a big-picture perspective, midcareer school psychologists are energized by the possibility of new learning. While life events (e.g., caring for young children or aging parents) precluded traveling to conferences, it is common for many to find opportunities in more accessible places, such as their own districts, regional gatherings, or cyberspace, such as webinars and other online resources. For some, gaining additional formal education to enhance their knowledge base (as well as reputation) was highly desirable. Some sample strategies follow:

- Return to school to gain additional certification, degrees, or specialization to build knowledge base and expand professional effectiveness and confidence. This could also open new avenues for professional work (e.g., private practice).
- Supervise an intern and/or practicum student. Not only do interns bring new knowledge, but interacting with an intern also solidifies the school psychologist's knowledge base. At the same time, a well-trained intern allows the school psychologist time to perform other duties.

- Reconnect with university graduate programs to support activities that prepare future school psychologists (e.g., teach a class, review a portfolio, present guest lectures during school psychology awareness week).

Veteran Practitioners (19+ Years)

If the early practitioner strives to do everything for everyone, experiencing an in-basket that is never empty yet feeling compelled to check off everything on his or her to-do list, the veteran school psychologist has cultivated a mind-set that Carlson (2007) describes as an in-basket that is designed to have to-do items in it but does not need to be constantly emptied. Or as Carlson (2007) quips, "Remind yourself that when you die, your in-basket won't be empty" (2007, p. 8).

Seasoned school psychologists with years of experience are more likely to demonstrate a strong belief in their ability to successfully manage the demands of their role while experiencing a high sense of personal accomplishment. Our research reveals that those at this developmental stage experience a strong sense of mastery and personal achievement while experiencing little sustained emotional exhaustion, defined as continual loss of energy, physical exhaustion, and tiredness. These dimensions established in the work of Maslach and Jackson (1986) in the Maslach Burnout Inventory express a relationship between levels of burnout and coping strategies. Phenomenological data from our interviews of these school psychologists reveal a high sense of personal accomplishment and a low level of emotional exhaustion lead to successful management of the stressors inherently affecting the role of the school psychologist. A sense of self-efficacy pervades the behavior and motivation of the veteran as noted in the way veterans approach the challenges and tasks of their work, their belief in their capabilities, and a heightened sense of commitment to those things that bring them feelings of personal accomplishment (Bandura, 1995). The self-efficacy that is experienced is directly related to the impact of the resiliency builders.

Inner direction. Veteran school psychologists identified inadequate administrative support and a lack of role diversity as significant stressors. A lack of understanding of the complexity of case development and the measuring of product (quantity of cases) over quality are cited as deterrents to professional effectiveness. However, veteran school psychologists are prone to intentionally engage in self-reflection and reframing, where their understanding of decisions that are forged from policy and the presence of stressors do not have to

serve as barometers for feelings of effectiveness, enthusiasm, and confidence. Veteran school psychologists tend to look beyond obstacles and seek possibilities. As one school psychologist said, "A sense of (professional) mission overrides negativity." Another school psychologist spoke to the experience of professional effectiveness, enthusiasm, and confidence as being engaged in a collaborative experience with others on a mission of helping students. Perhaps this emotional satisfaction of effectiveness, enthusiasm, and confidence is consistent with what Erikson (1963) refers to in his description of the developmental stages that adults with healthy psychosocial development experience in middle adulthood and maturity. In middle adulthood adults seek successes that nurture feelings of accomplishment. This sense of completion is heightened in the mature adult as a deeper sense of fulfillment.

One school psychologist expressed effectiveness, enthusiasm, and confidence as the integration of professional and personal behaviors and beliefs, with the importance of the work peaking to an "emotional roundedness," and this poignantly sums up the relationship between self-efficacy and self-actualization. For this 38-year veteran, the satisfaction derived from work is in large part due to the contentment of a balanced personal life and the certainty that his professional career represents significant contributions to the well-being of children and families. The sense of control, an element of self-efficacy, encourages a sense of optimism. Boy and Pine (1980) encourage a sense of hopefulness in counselors as an antidote to burnout. Some sample strategies include the following:

- Proactively seek opportunities that align with professional interests.
- Accept the limitations of the role while accentuating its influence.
- Recognize indicators of both short-term and long-term successes.

Sharpen the saw. The deleterious effects of prolonged exposure to stressors have been well established in the literature. Burnout in school psychologists, while not as widely studied, is recognized as harmful to the experience of effectiveness, enthusiasm, and confidence across the span of a career. Increasing job satisfaction and lessening the impact of stressors increase a sense of efficacy and pride in work (Smith & Miller, 2013). As school psychologists wear many relationship hats in their personal as well as professional lives, maintaining vitality in one's life is necessary, yet it can be elusive. The veteran school psychologists interviewed identified six themes that support their balance and therefore professional effectiveness, enthusiasm, and confidence:

- Connect personally and professionally through meaningful relationships.
- Invest in health and fitness.
- Invest in personal and professional interests.
- Set limits to maintain role integrity.
- Compartmentalize professional and personal roles.
- Specialize in professional skills.

Similarly described priorities and activities were identified within these themes:

- Proactively schedule quality time (during the week and on weekends) with family and friends regularly, and extend one's network of relationships beyond work.
- Collaborate with colleagues and share ideas.
- Focus on particular personal interests and hobbies and exercise curiosity to generate new and novel opportunities.
- Invest in health and fitness with others but find time for solitude.

Compartmentalization is a useful method when managing multiple demands. As one school psychologist stated, "Younger school psychologists are frazzled because they spend too much time thinking about the work." One veteran actually schedules lunch in her planner to ensure its priority. Some sample strategies include the following:

- Avoid the temptation of taking work home. If work is done at home, schedule a beginning and end of the work session.
- Allow time to participate in general education activities during the workday.

Understanding how one's body and mind react to stress and identifying a personal plan for self-care highlight the veteran school psychologist's ability to maintain balance by sharpening the saw and sustaining professional effectiveness, enthusiasm, and confidence.

Love of learning. NASP provides nationally recognized guidelines for credentialing school psychologists (NASP, 2010). The advanced degree required for earning a credential as a school psychologist requires a graduate-level degree. The rigorous academic preparation and multiple hours of field experiences (practicum and internship) require an investment and commitment to the learning process sustained over several years. Whether the school psychologist candidate is starting out in a first career or, as with many other candidates, is building from a career as a teacher, the high regard for learning is a common attribute across candidates. Henderson (2002) defines this love of learning as the capacity for and connection to learning. Rath (2007) describes the talent theme of learner as someone who loves to learn and is drawn to the process more than the product. Some sample strategies follow:

- Serving as an intern field supervisor remains a strong resiliency builder. Veteran school psychologists, like those in other phases, are eager to share their knowledge and experience. Their qualifications render them ideal to serve as field mentor, guiding and modeling the development of the intern in the 10 domains of the NASP Practice Model (NASP, 2010).
- Seeking an advanced degree/certificate/credential is useful. Many veteran school psychologists seek a doctoral degree in school psychology or in a related field. Additional options for advancement include specializations (e.g., neuropsychology, behavior specialist) and state licensing as a psychologist.
- School psychologists' training and experience in assessment, intervention, and consultation can be applied to other professional roles on a campus or at the district level. In one large urban district, veteran school psychologists have assumed the role of due process specialist, intervention coordinator, and school administrator.
- Many school psychology graduate programs consider veteran school psychologists as ideal adjunct faculty members to teach in their programs
- Many veteran school psychologists, including most of those interviewed, are very active in professional development activities at their schools, as well as in their local, state, and professional organizations.

Other approaches that successfully cultivate the love of learning also include actively pursuing collaborative relationships with school-based and community-based professionals that expand problem-solving networks and increase the breadth of resources. Intentionally streamlining practices (e.g., assessment) capitalizes on prior knowledge, freeing up time to pursue other activities in the typical daily and weekly routines. Becoming familiar with or learning about district policy and procedures, beyond the implementation level, encourages feelings of confidence and professional effectiveness in the veteran school psychologist. Serving on district-level committees where policy and procedures are developed is another approach to nurturing and sustaining effectiveness, enthusiasm, and confidence.

SUMMARY

There are predictable categories of stressors that decrease professional effectiveness, enthusiasm, and confidence during all phases of the career of a school psychologist. Positive psychology, including resiliency concepts, has much to offer and can support school psychologists over the long haul of a career. There are many protective factors that can be employed. For example, Henderson (2002) provides a list of 16 personal resiliency builders that are gleaned from seminal research (see Table 47.2). Differential effects of stressors based on differences (e.g., type of graduate preparation, school district location) among all practicing school psychologists is impossible to pinpoint, but being proactive and seeking opportunities to increase resilience will lead to greater levels of professional effectiveness, enthusiasm, and confidence throughout careers. Potentially, these resiliency builders not only will have an impact on professional life (e.g., improve positive student outcomes, increase longevity of professional practice, serve as role models for newer practitioners), but also will have an impact on personal lives as a benefit from living a more balanced life overall.

REFERENCES

Bandura, A. (1995). *Self-efficacy in changing societies.* Cambridge, MA: Cambridge University Press.

Boy, A. V., & Pine, G. J. (1980). Avoiding counselor burnout through role renewal. *The Personal and Guidance Journal, 59*, 161–163.

Bureau of Labor Statistics. (2013). *Occupational outlook handbook: Psychologists.* Washington, DC: Author. Retrieved from http://www.bls.gov/ooh/life-physical-and-social-science/psychologists.htm

Carlson, R. (2007). *The big book of small stuff.* New York, NY: Hyperion.

Covey, S. R. (1989). *The 7 habits of highly effective people.* New York, NY: Simon & Schuster.

Covey, S. R. (2003). *The 7 habits of highly effective people: Personal workbook.* New York, NY: Simon & Schuster.

Covey, S. R. (2004). *The 8th habit. From effectiveness to greatness.* New York, NY: Free Press.

Erikson, E. (1963). *Childhood and society* (2nd ed.). New York, NY: Norton.

Farber, B. (2000). Treatment strategies for different types of teacher burnout. *Psychotherapy in Practice, 56*, 675–689.

Garmezy, N. (1996). Reflections and commentary on risk, resilience, and development. In R. J. Haggerty, L. R. Sherrod, N. Garmezy, & M. Rutter (Eds.), *Stress, risk and resilience in children and adolescents: Processes, mechanisms and interventions* (pp. 1–18). New York, NY: Cambridge University Press.

Henderson, N. (2002). *The resiliency training program.* San Diego, CA: Resiliency in Action.

Higgins, G. (1994). *Resilient adults: Overcoming a cruel past.* San Francisco, CA: Jossey-Bass.

Huberty, T. J., & Huebner, E. S. (1988). A national survey of burnout among school psychologists. *Psychology in the Schools, 25*, 54–61.

Huebner, E. S., Gilligan, T. D., & Cobb, H. (2002). Best practices in preventing and managing stress and burnout. In A. Thomas & J. Grimes (Eds.), *Best practices in school psychology IV* (pp. 173–182). Bethesda, MD: National Association of School Psychologists.

Jackson, J. (2003). *Effective teacher traits that foster the development of social competence as a factor of resilience in elementary-school-age foster children* (Doctoral dissertation). Pepperdine University, Los Angeles, CA.

Jenero, C., Flores, N., & Arias, B. (2007). Burnout and coping in human services practitioners. *Professional Psychology, 38*, 80–87.

Maslach, C., & Jackson, S. E. (1986). *Maslach Burnout Inventory.* Palo Alto, CA: Consulting Psychologists Press.

National Association of School Psychologists. (2010). *Model for comprehensive and integrated school psychological services.* Bethesda, MD: Author. Retrieved from http://www.nasponline.org/standards/2010standards/2_PracticeModel.pdf

Peterson, C. (2006). *A primer in positive psychology.* New York, NY: Oxford University Press.

Proctor, B., & Steadman, T. (2003). Job satisfaction, burnout, and perceived effectiveness of "in-house" versus traditional school psychologists. *Psychology in the Schools, 40*, 237–243.

Rath, T. (2007). *Strengths Finder 2.0.* New York, NY: Gallup Press.

Reiner, H., & Hartshorne, T. (1982). Job burnout and the school psychologist. *Psychology in the Schools, 19*, 508–512.

Smith, H. J., & Miller, L. G. (2013). Keep the fires burning. *ASCA School Counselor, 50*(14), 32–34.

Thomas, A. (1995). Best practices in facilitating professional effectiveness and avoiding professional burnout. In A. Thomas & J. Grimes (Eds.), *Best practices in school psychology III.* Bethesda, MD: National Association of School Psychologists.

Thompson, M. W. (1994, October 17). Putting commitment to the test: Novice teachers are "at risk" in stressful profession. *The Washington Post*, A1, A8.

U.S. News and World Report. (2013, May). *Money careers.* Retrieved from http://money.usnews.com/careers/best-jobs/rankings

Werner, E., & Smith, R. (1992). *Overcoming the odds: High-risk children from birth to adulthood.* New York, NY: Cornell University Press.

Wolin, S., & Wolin, S. J. (1995). Resilience among youth growing up in substance abusing families. *Pediatric Clinics of North America, 42*, 415–429.

Wolin, S. J., & Wolin, S. (1993). *The resilient self: How survivors of troubled families rise above adversity.* New York, NY: Villard Books.

Wolin, S., & Wolin, S. J. (1998). Shaping a brighter future by uncovering "survivor's pride." *Reaching Today's Youth, 2*, 61–64.

Index

Best Practices in School Psychology: Series List

Best Practices in School Psychology: Data-Based and Collaborative Decision Making

INTRODUCTION AND FRAMEWORK

DATA-BASED DECISION MAKING AND ACCOUNTABILITY

CONSULTATION AND COLLABORATION

Best Practices in School Psychology: Student-Level Services

INTERVENTIONS AND INSTRUCTIONAL SUPPORT TO DEVELOP ACADEMIC SKILLS

Best Practices in School Psychology: Systems-Level Services

SCHOOL-WIDE PRACTICES TO PROMOTE LEARNING

Best Practices in School Psychology: Foundations

DIVERSITY IN DEVELOPMENT AND LEARNING

RESEARCH AND PROGRAM EVALUATION

LEGAL, ETHICAL, AND PROFESSIONAL PRACTICE